Business Ethics
Case Studies and Selected Readings

Tenth Edition

Business Ethics
Case Studies and Selected Readings

Marianne M. Jennings
Arizona State University

Tenth Edition

 Cengage

Australia • Brazil • Canada • Mexico • Singapore • United Kingdom • United States

Business Ethics: Case Studies and Selected Readings, Tenth Edition
Marianne M. Jennings

SVP, Product: Erin Joyner

VP, Product: Thais Alencar

Portfolio Product Director: Jason Fremder

Portfolio Product Manager: Effie Tsakmaklis

Product Assistant: Adam Graber

Learning Designer: Jason Fremder

Content Manager: Flora Emanuel, Lumina Datamatics Ltd.

Digital Project Manager: Mark Hopkinson

VP, Product Marketing: Jason Sakos

Director, Product Marketing: Neena Bali

Content Acquisition Analyst: Nichole Nalenz

Production Service: Lumina Datamatics Ltd.

Designer: Gaby McCracken

Cover Image Source: 317929406/Rawpixel.com/ ShutterStock

> For product information and technology assistance, contact us at
> **Cengage Customer & Sales Support, 1-800-354-9706
> or support.cengage.com**.
>
> For permission to use material from this text or product,
> submit all requests online at **www.copyright.com**.

Library of Congress Control Number: 2022949775

SE ISBN: 978-0-357-71777-6
LLF ISBN: 978-0-357-71778-3

Cengage
200 Pier 4 Boulevard
Boston, MA 02210
USA

Cengage is a leading provider of customized learning solutions. Our employees reside in nearly 40 different countries and serve digital learners in 165 countries around the world. Find your local representative at **www.cengage.com**.

To learn more about Cengage platforms and services, register or access your online learning solution, or purchase materials for your course, visit **www.cengage.com**.

Notice to the Reader

Printed in the United States of America
Print Number: 01   Print Year: 2022

Brief Contents

Contents

Unit 2   Solving Ethical Dilemmas in Business

Section A

Section B

Unit 3   Business, Stakeholders, Social Responsibility, and Sustainability

Contents

Unit 4   Ethics and Company Culture

Unit 7   **Ethics, Business Operations, and Rights**

Unit 8   Ethics and Products

Unit 9	**Ethics and Competition**

Preface

For many years, the Josephson Institute conducted a nationwide survey of high school students and found that 51% to 65% admitted to some form of academic dishonesty, whether turning in downloaded or unsourced papers or copying a classmate's answers during an exam. Interestingly, the figure could be somewhat higher because the work in surveying the students found that the definition of cheating was not always clear. When the Josephson researchers asked the high school students if they had copied another's homework, 76% said that they had but did not consider it cheating. "Teamwork" was their label for this practice. The International Center for Academic Integrity (ICAI) is dedicated to the work of educating college students about the importance of academic integrity and how to prevent cheating. Scholars at ICAI meetings have found that while the number of students who self-report cheating is going down, the number of cheating incidents reported by faculty is increasing. The late professor Donald McCabe of Rutgers spent his academic career researching cheating by college students and found that it grew from 11% in 1963 to 49% in 1993 to 75% in 2006.[1] Another study puts the level at 85%.[2] Professor McCabe also found that MBAs have the highest rate of self-reported academic dishonesty (57%) of all graduate disciplines. During the COVID pandemic, cheating became pandemic. As one expert phrased it, "Cheating became habitual."[3] This headline on another cheating scandal is ironic and not particularly encouraging, "Dartmouth Suspends 64 Students for Cheating in 'Sports, Ethics, and Religion' Course."[4]

All the studies and data indicate that there remains a disconnect between conduct and an understanding of what ethics is. The Josephson Institute also found that the high school students who report that they cheat feel very comfortable about their behavior, with 95% saying they are satisfied with their character and ethics. Perhaps we have begun to believe that cheating is not an ethical issue.

Research indicates that if students cheat in high school, they will bring the practices into college. And if they cheat in college, they will bring those practices into the workplace. A look at some of the events in business since the publication of the ninth edition of this book tells us that we are not quite there yet in terms of helping businesspeople understand when they are in the midst of an ethical dilemma and how those dilemmas should be resolved. Following the collapses of Enron and WorldCom, and the ethical lapses at Tyco and Adelphia, we entered the Sarbanes–Oxley era, with fundamental changes in the way we were doing business and audits. However, we did not make it even five years before we found ourselves

> Never trust the people you cheat with. They will throw you under the bus.
>
> **—Marianne M. Jennings**

> Maybe if you did ethics, you would not have to do so much compliance.
>
> **—Marianne M. Jennings**

> I diverted the auditor while the others created the ledger the auditor wanted to back up the trades for securities we said we owned. When it came hot off the office printer, they cooled it in the refrigerator and the tossed it around the office like a medicine ball to give it a well-worn look that an ordinary ledger would have.
>
> **—Former Madoff Securities employee on how they fooled the auditors**

---

[1] The International Center for Academic Integrity (ICAI) study was conducted by the late professor Donald McCabe on a regular basis over the years. This survey had 4,500 student respondents. For more information on Professor McCabe and his work on academic integrity and ICAI, go to https://academicintegrity.org.

[2] Corey Ciochetti, "The Uncheatable Class," Proceedings, Academy of Legal Studies in Business, August 2013 (unpublished paper).

[3] Julie Norgon, "Cheating Is the Norm in Some Virtual Classes," *Wall Street Journal*, December 23, 2020, p. A12.

[4] *National Review*, February 9, 2015, p. 12.

in the midst of the collapse of the housing market and revelations about shoddy, undisclosed lending practices for home mortgages. When mortgagors defaulted on those risky loans, the derivative securities based on mortgage pools crashed in value. The end result was a dramatic drop in the stock market and a recession. As the reforms enacted by the Dodd–Frank bill (Wall Street Reform and Consumer Protection Act) were being implemented, we learned that British banks were fixing the LIBOR interest rate, and Bernie Madoff pulled off an 18-year, $50 billion Ponzi scheme. From 2015 through 2017, we witnessed the auto industry's ethical lapses. GM paid a billion-dollar fine for its failure to disclose the problems with its engine switch, a defect that caused the cars to stop suddenly and resulted in fatalities when those sudden stops came on freeways. Volkswagen had installed software in its diesel cars that allowed the company to cheat on emissions levels, a scandal that cost the company $35 billion in fines, penalties, and damages. Employees at Wells Fargo created 3.5 million fake accounts so that they could meet their quarterly goals for new business. WeWork (We) tried to go public, but when its financial statements were scrutinized, the company nearly collapsed instead of issuing a public stock offering. When Hollywood producer Harvey Weinstein's sexual harassment behavior became public, CEOs, television anchors, actors, and Olympic trainers and physicians faced litigation from "Me Too" victims. Not a news day passes without some story about a business and its ethical lapses.

Beyond the business events that result in new regulations, fines, and prison time, there are the day-to-day ethical breaches that capture media headlines and cause continuing concerns about the ethical culture of business. There are the questions about television reality shows: Was the storage locker a setup, or were those things really in there? Why were graduates not told about the cheaper options available for repaying their student loans? Did Subway really cut us short with an 11-inch sub sandwich when we thought we were buying a footlong? The world of sports brought us such questions as: Is it really cheating if everyone does the same thing? Horse racing saw the 2021 Kentucky Derby winner, Medina Spirit, lose his title because postrace drug tests found a prohibited substance. Even parents were caught paying large amounts to coaches, proctors, and fake nonprofits to get their children admitted into Ivy League schools.

From analysts not offering their true feelings about a company's stock to the factory workers not safely producing a peanut base for cookies and crackers, pressure often got in the way of ethical clarity in business decisions. Those pressures then translated into ethical lapses that involved everything from emissions falsification to earnings management that crosses over into cooking the books and fraud. Weak product designs and product defects often emerge as deliberate actions documented by a chain of memos or emails that reflect employee concerns about product safety. College sports, baseball, and politics all have had their ethical issues. The cycles between major ethical and financial collapses seem to be growing shorter. Businesses do exist to make a profit, but business ethics exists to set parameters for earning that profit. Business ethics is also a key element of business decision processes and strategies. The cases in this book teach us that the long-term perspective, not ethical shortcuts, serves businesses better in that profit role.

This book of readings and cases explores ethical parameters and their importance. This book teaches, through detailed study of the people and companies, that business conducted without ethics is a nonsustainable competitive model. Ethical shortcuts translate into a short-term existence. Initially, these shortcuts produce a phenomenon such as those seen with banks crypto currency, mortgage lenders, auto manufacturers, and even nutritional supplement producers. In some cases, the companies' conduct was self-destructive. For a time, they were at the top of their games—flummoxing their competitors on how they were able to do what they were doing, and so profitably. But then that magnificent force of truth finds its way to the surface, and the company that does not factor in the ethics of its decisions and conduct finds itself falling to the earth like a meteor's flash. Long-term personal and business success demand ethics. This edition takes a look at everything from horse racing, to the world of college sports, to cheating to get good grades, to the downfall of so many. This book connects the moral sentiments of markets with the wealth of nations. Business without ethics is self-destructive.

New to This Edition

A Slightly New Structure and Approach to Address the Chronic Repetition of the Ethical Lapses

We've been down this road before, and the historic patterns are now emerging for study and insight. In 1986, before Ivan Boesky was a household name and Michael Douglas was Gordon Gekko in *Wall Street*, I began teaching a business ethics course in the MBA program in the College of Business at Arizona State University. The course was an elective. I had trouble making the minimum enrollments. However, two things changed my enrollments and my fate. First, the American Association of Collegiate Schools of Business (AACSB) changed the curriculum for graduate and undergraduate business degree programs and required coverage of ethics. The other event was a series of events. Indictments, convictions, and guilty pleas by major companies and their officers—from E. F. Hutton to Union Carbide, to Beech-Nut, to Exxon—brought national attention to the need to incorporate values in American businesses and instill them in business leaders.

Whether out of fear, curiosity, or the need for reaccreditation, business schools and students began to embrace the concept of studying business ethics. My course went from a little-known elective to the final required course in the MBA program. In the years since, the interest in business ethics has only increased. Following junk bonds and insider trading, we rolled into the savings and loan collapses. Once we had that straightened out, we rolled into Enron, WorldCom, HealthSouth, Tyco, and Adelphia. We even lost Martha Stewart along the way. We were quite sure—what with all the Sarbanes–Oxley changes and demands on boards, CEO, CFOs, and auditors—that we were through with that level of misconduct. We were, however, wrong. New Century Financial, one of the first of the subprime lenders to collapse, found one angry bankruptcy trustee. The trustee's report concluded that he found astonishing the acquiescence of the auditor to the client's refusal to write down the bad loans in what he called "the post-Enron era." The Lehman Brothers bankruptcy trustee found a letter from a risk officer at the investment banker who tried to warn the CEO and CFO that the firm's financial reports violated its code of ethics. The trustee also found that the risk officer had been fired.

Three decades plus after Boesky, we have the GM engine-switch case, which reads very much like the Pinto exploding case tank of the 1970s, and wonder, "Do they not see the ethical and legal issues? Do they just not know that they are crossing these lines? Do they see the patterns from business history?" The good thing about repetitive patterns is that we gain insight into the paths, the reasoning, and the pressures of those involved. The key is to bring out those patterns and train our new business leaders to recognize them and, most importantly, to stop the train of self-destruction those patterns set off. This edition is reorganized to offer greater insights, knowledge, and perspective on these patterns for a new generation of leaders. Today, nearly 100% of the *Fortune* 500 companies have a code of ethics. We are up to over 75% of companies having some form of ethics training. But we are not quite there until our business leaders grasp the perspective of ethics and its relationship to economics, organizational behavior, company culture, reputation, and financial performance. This edition is structured to walk us through all aspects and types of ethical dilemmas and how we can cope with the pressures that often deprive us of good ethical analysis.

Unit 1: Ethical Theory, Philosophical Foundations, Our Reasoning Flaws, Types of Ethical Dilemmas, and You

Unit 1 addresses the following questions: What is this ethics thing? How do I manage to work philosophy into my decision processes? How do I find solutions to ethical dilemmas? How do I know when I am really analyzing as opposed to rationalizing or succumbing to pressure? This unit begins with introspection, a right-out-of-the-blocks focus on developing a credo—a way of helping us think about ethical issues in advance and decide what we would and would not do in a situation. If we think about issues in advance, then when the pressure hits, we at least have the cognitive dissonance for realizing that we did see the issues differently when we were not under so much pressure.

The cases and readings in Units 1 and 2 have been realigned to place personal ethics in Unit 1 along with all of the topics and skills needed for analysis. The students have a solid foundation before heading into Unit 2 and its transition to the business cases.

Unit 2: Solving Ethical Dilemmas in Business

Once we have focused on our ethical standards and ourselves, we move into analysis of ethical issues in business. This unit offers the introspection of this question: Are my personal ethical standards different when I am at work? Should they be? Why are they different? Further, the magnitude of the mistakes that businesspeople continue to make, despite all the warnings from ongoing debacles, did not indicate that these were close calls. Something had gone awry in their ethics training in business school for them to drift so far from virtue. I continue to emphasize in teaching, consulting, and writing that helping students and businesspeople see that personal ethics and business ethics are one and the same and that principle is critical to making ethics a part of business culture. Virtue is the goal for most of us in all aspects of our lives. Whether we commit to fidelity in a personal relationship or honesty in going back into the store to pay for the laundry detergent that we forgot was on the bottom of our grocery cart, we show virtue. Ethics in business is no different, and we need not behave differently at work than we do in that grocery store parking lot as we make the decision to be honest and fair with the store owner. Substitute a shareholder and the disclosure of option dates and true costs, and we have our laundry detergent example with a stock market twist.

This unit also focuses on the patterns that interfere with good ethical analysis in business, such as pressure, hubris, and a singular focus on moral relativism, as opposed to a deeper look at the consequences of reliance on that model. This unit allows us to switch back and forth from personal dilemmas to business dilemmas so that we are able to see that the ethical issues are the same in our personal lives as they are in business—only the fact patterns change. We can see that honesty is important, whether studying the complexities of an offshore oil rig construction or the redesign of a commercial jet or answering the simple questions about how we are reporting and recording what our daily fitness trackers say. Instructors and students gain the ability to reduce the most complex of financial cases to the common denominators found in returning that laundry detergent to the store—Is this honest? Is this fair? With this understanding of the common denominators, we are free to focus on the psychology of our decision processes rather than on the details of the underlying transactions. The obligation of good faith in dealing with each other does not change simply because we are buying a CDO rather than Tide. This unit also includes the overarching theme of the book over all of its editions: plenty of real-life examples from newspapers, business journals, and my experiences as a consultant and board member. Knowing that other instructors and students needed examples, I have turned my experiences into cases and coupled them with the most memorable readings in the field to provide a training and thought-provoking experience on business ethics.

Unit 3: Business, Stakeholders, Social Responsibility, and Sustainability

Unit 3 offers us the bigger perspective—once we slog through the decision processes of fraud, embezzlement, puffing résumés, and cheating on our travel expenses, we move to discussion and understanding of the role of business in society. The cases in this unit are broken into an introduction that covers economics, social responsibility, and business, including the historical perspectives on corporate social responsibility. A second section focuses on applying social responsibility and stakeholder theory with cases on Fannie Mae's collapse and pharmaceutical pricing. A third section of this unit focuses on leadership, stakeholders, and the regulatory cycle. Cases in this unit focus on the role of business in pharmaceutical pricing, Fannie Mae and moral hazards, wages, cancel culture, and environmental and sustainability issues. A final section focuses on the government as a stakeholder.

Unit 4: Ethics and Company Culture

Unit 4 is the psychology section that tackles companies' ethical lapses, with the realization that beyond individual ethical lapses (as with one bad apple), there are barrel factors that must be addressed to prevent future ethical lapses. This unit, through the finance cases and the weaving in of corporate governance, explores those barrel factors with the recognition that beyond individual lapses, there are company, industry, and societal norms that do cause companies and individuals to move that line away from ethical standards to "everybody does it" here at the company, in our industry, and in society. The cases here explore how incentives, organizational behavior practices and processes, reporting mechanisms, industry practices, and societal norms contribute to poor ethical analysis, decisions, and self-destructive behavior. Recognizing and addressing those barrel issues is the theme of Unit 4.

Culture is universal, and in this unit you will find cases involving the government's launch of the Space Shuttle despite warnings about the effects of freezing temperatures on the rocket boosters, publicly traded companies, and the ethical lapses of nonprofit organizations. The Wells Fargo case is now included as an example of how a culture can drive employees to just "make stuff up" to meet their sales quotas. The psychology of organizations and employee decision making in organizations does not change because they work in a nonprofit or government agency. Nonprofit employees have the pressures of raising funds.

Pressure, compensation systems, cultural factors, and governance issues all play a role in culture and ethical lapses. Government employees experience the pressure of dealing with the powerful as wel as the prospect of losing their jobs. The Atlanta Public School system experienced nearly a decade of administrators and teachers falsifying children's test scores. The issues these employees and organizations face are the same as those in for-profit businesses. The principles of ethics are universally applicable to all organizations.

Unit 5: Ethics and Contracts

This unit has a special focus on the ethics of contracts, from advertising through negotiations to performance. Issues related to Johnny Depp's battles with his lawyers, Kardashian tweets, pension promises, and Scarlett Johansson's revenue disputes with Disney illustrate the battles over legal vs. ethical. The ethical challenges in contract formation and performance, again, cross all sectors, so this unit has nonprofit and government examples integrated as well.

Unit 6: Ethics in International Business

This unit helps students understand the need for better and deeper ethical analysis of the issues in international business and the importance of analyzing the countries and their ethical standards prior to doing business there. The section addresses the risks and costs of ethical lapses and succumbing to local standards as opposed to establishing company standards prior to those pressure points that occur in international competition. Case studies in international business are rich with the actions taken and the sheer extent of corruption, including a look at the bribery involving FIFA and the Foreign Corrupt Practices Act and GlaxoSmithKline's bribery of physicians in China. New to this edition are cases on the effects of COVID on supply chains and the NBA's relationship with China.

Unit 7: Ethics, Business Operations, and Rights

This revised unit draws together all the cases on workplace issues that affect employees and managers: from safety to conflicts, to privacy, to diversity, to the lost art of confrontation about employee conduct. This section on confrontation is the one for understanding how ethics bumps into production demands, technology, profits, and privacy, including a new case about Theranos and its collapse due to fraud. Also new is a case on Carlos Ghosn, the former CEO of Nissan, and his use of company resources. From honesty in letters of recommendations to felony convictions to office romances, all matters that affect employers and employees are now in one unit.

Unit 8: Ethics and Products

Unit 8 includes all the issues related to product development, sales, safety, and advertising. From Elon Musk "puffing" about going private to the tricky language on fuel in rental contracts, this section focuses on the ethical issues that involve the how, what, and where of sales of products. The issues of social responsibility and products are found here in cases that address everything from Johnson & Johnson's COVID-19 vaccine to the PG&E transmission lines and resulting fires. There are issues of risk in trying to be safe and necessarily deep analysis when human life is at stake.

Unit 9: Ethics and Competition

Unit 9 has the luxury of focusing entirely on competition. This unit has expanded coverage of the ever-growing concerns about covenants not to compete and employee breaches of those covenants. The nooks and crannies in Thomas' English muffins are a competitive edge. Even the Hallmark Channel had to deal with the issue of talent poaching when it faced competition from another channel with Christmas movies. The saga of the competitors selling guardrails to governmental highway builders is updated and expanded because the litigation revealed the fierceness of competition in this industry. The societal issues of possible infringement at Costco of Tiffany engagement rings are emphasized as students analyze cases that illustrate the costs of not honoring intellectual property rights.

What's New and What's Back

The tenth edition continues the features students and instructors embraced in the first nine editions, including both short and long cases, discussion questions, hypothetical situations, and up-to-the-moment current, ongoing, and real ethical dilemmas. Some of the long-standing favorites remain by popular demand—such as the Enron case and Union Carbide in Bhopal—with their timeless lessons in doing the right thing.

Compare & Contrast

The tenth edition continues the new training tool introduced in the previous edition to help businesspeople who are working their way through an ethical dilemma. Following the discussion questions for many of the cases, the "Compare & Contrast" questions continue. These questions provide an example of a company making a decision different from the one made by management in the case at hand. For example, in the Tylenol case (Case 8.6—an "oldie but goodie" that has been updated for this edition to include the company's problems with metal flecks in its infant products and the issues with COVID-19 vaccines), students find a question that highlights this company's past conduct in comparison with its conduct in a current situation in which the FDA has accused the company of surreptitiously buying up tainted product in order to avoid a recall. There is a contrast between its recall of a product in the 1980s, which was so rapid and received so much acclaim, and its behavior in this event. Why do some companies choose one path, whereas others succumb to pressure? What was different about their decision-making processes? What did they see that the other companies and their leaders did not take into account?

This feature is a response to those who worry that students are not given examples of "good companies." The problem with touting goodness is that it is impossible to know everything a company is or is not doing. For example, Fannie Mae was named the most ethical company in America for two years running. Yet, it had to do a $7 billion restatement of earnings and is struggling as a shored-up government entity. BP was an environmental darling for nearly a decade for its responsible environmental programs. However, the explosions at its Deepwater Horizon well and Texas City refinery along with the Alaska pipeline failure illustrate cultural problems within the company. There is a risk in learning of goodness if that goodness is superficial or limited. Studying individual scenarios of contrasting behavior is the learning tool, not the touting of a single company that can always have a lapse. There are no saints in this journey, and keeping the text credible requires a recognition of that limitation but uses it to emphasize the vigilance we all need, as individuals and in business, to avoid lapses and progress in moral development.

Ethics in Action

This new feature provides a shorter follow-up hypothetical or a deeper thought question about the case to further develop analytical skills. For example, in Unit 1, students can tackle a situation in which a mother "boundary hops" to get her children into a better public school system and ends up with a criminal charge. In Unit 2, we have a situation in which employees are manipulating the numbers on their fitness trackers to reach the goals that will give them lower health insurance payments. Unit 3 discusses the boycott of Major League Baseball's All-Star Game in Atlanta because of its new voting laws. Unit 4 asks students to determine whether they would give up their paychecks by quitting their job at a company when the company's practices are troubling to them.

This feature is found in each unit and provides a brief, thought-provoking example for reflection and analysis.

Why Didn't They Say Something?

This new feature provides a question about a case or example that asks students to explore how they would feel if the same circumstances if they were an employee who saw an ethical or legal issue and said nothing. Exploration of their feelings, reactions, and concerns helps them understand how easy it can be to "just let it go" when you are in the midst of an ethical issue. This feature provides training for spotting ethical issues and learning how they can grow into organizational problems.

History Repeats: Ethical Lessons Not Learned

This feature weaves in another example or refers back to an earlier case in a different unit to show the repeating patterns in organizations that get into ethical difficulty. This tool helps develop application skills, as students use what they have learned from examples and case studies to recognize signs, symptoms, and patterns when they are living in an unfolding ethical dilemma as opposed to studying one in which they know the outcome. For example, since the time of the Penn State case that involved sexual molestation of children on campus, two others major institutions (Michigan State and Ohio State) have had eerily similar conduct on their campuses. Sometimes simply studying history of ethical and legal lapses provides as way to self-correct.

Famous Lines from Art & Literature

There are so many quotes, lines from movies and literature that apply to ethics or to a particular case. Those quotes and lines are tools in learning because they help us to remember the concepts you are studying. This new feature provides short, pithy thoughts, quotes, or a few lines of dialogue to show the presence of ethical dilemmas all around us. In addition, we see how many times characters see the ethical issues or offer bottom-line assessments in difficult situations but hesitate to act or simply ignore the issue.

COVID-19 Cases and Discussion

The issues of the pandemic, vaccines, and masks are sprinkled throughout this edition. There is the nursing home death rate manipulation issue in New York and the issues with vaccines. In Unit 1, there is the example of how people cut in line to get classified for the first group to obtain vaccines. In Unit 5, there is the issue of not paying your rent because of COVID-19 when you were not affected economically but rather benefited from eviction protections. The pandemic brought out our true character, as we grappled with personal risk and learned that we could game the system.

Key Terms

New to this edition is a list of key terms from the cases and readings. The list is found at the end of each unit and the terms are defined in the glossary.

Learning Objectives

New to this edition is a summary overview of the key learning points of each unit. Provided at the beginning of each unit, the objectives summarize the skills and knowledge students should acquire in studying the unit.

Finding and Studying the Cases and Readings

The tenth edition continues the classic readings in business ethics that provide insight into the importance of ethics in business and how to resolve ethical dilemmas. The tenth edition also continues to include integrated readings throughout the book to provide substantive thoughts on the particular areas covered in each section. The organizational structure and indexes, continued from the ninth edition, make topics, companies, people, and products easy to locate. A case can be located using the table of contents, the alphabetical index, the topical index, the people index, or the product index, which lists both products and companies by name. There is also an index for business disciplines grouping the cases and readings by accounting, management, and the other disciplines in colleges of business. A case can also be located using the "Ethical Common Denominator Chart," which is explained below.

How to Use the "Ethical Common Denominators across Business Topics Chart"

The Ethical Common Denominators across Business Topics chart, or simply the ECD chart, is a tool that appears along with the book's indexes and can be used to help students understand the point that facts change, but ethical dilemmas remain the same. This chart provides some ease for that slight discomfort some instructors have with the financial cases and helps students understand that underlying every ethical dilemma are common patterns. The topic area could be finance or marketing, but the categories of ethical issues, the psychological forces, and organizational pressures remain the same. And the ECD shows the common thread in all topic areas of the need for solid ethical analysis.

The ECD chart provides instructors with the opportunity to structure their courses in a way that is comfortable for them. All an instructor needs to know is a general business term; that term can then be referenced in the ECD chart in various ways for instruction, according to instructor preference, needs, and time constraints. The chart groups the cases by the usual business and ethics topics. If, for example, you wanted to cover the environmental cases all in one fell swoop, simply go to "environmentalism" or "sustainability" to find the cases and readings listed there. However, if you were looking for a variety of fact patterns to teach, for example, the role of pressure in ethical decision making, you could look under that topic and find the BP case (also an environmental case) as well as the financial factors in the Enron case. If you wanted students to see what pressure can do in the area of contracts, you can use the Wells Fargo case to show how employees make "sales" when incentivized to do so. Students will learn that pressure affects all aspects of business operations. Adam Smith and his theories on markets appear in Section 9, but there is no reason this reading could not be shifted back to the coverage of the philosophical foundations.

An instructor can mix in cases from all the units in covering ethical analysis. The ECD includes a case from each unit under "Ethical Analysis," because you can pick and choose what topics to cover as you teach how to analyze ethical issues. The ECD chart allows you to introduce that broad exposure to the pervasiveness of ethical issues early in your course, or you can simply use the cases in that unit and go on to topical areas. The chart also allows you to break up the finance cases into areas of discussion on psychology, culture, organizational behavior, hubris, and pressure. You need not focus on the structure of CDOs and secondary instruments markets to understand the culture at Lehman and how its culture led its sales force and managers down a path that proved to be self-destructive. Likewise, you can mix in a Ponzi scheme in a nonprofit to help students understand how similar the cases are in the issues missed as those running the organizations pursued a business model that could not be sustained over time. The case on the gifts to the governor of Virginia teaches students about conflicts, but it would fit well in Unit 1 as you ask students to analyze the subtle missteps that lead to larger ethical issues. The ECD chart allows a mix-and-match approach or a straight topical approach—both of which allow us to see that the facts change, but good ethical analysis applies, always.

Supplements

Additional instructor resources for this product are available online. Instructor assets include an Instructor's Manual, PowerPoint® slides, and a test bank powered by Cognero®. Sign up or sign in at **www.cengage.com** to search for and access this product and its online resources.

Acknowledgments

This book is not mine. It is the result of the efforts and sacrifices of many. I am grateful for my many colleagues around the world who continue to provide me with insights, input, and improvements.

I am grateful for the students and professors who continue to help me with ideas for new cases, corrections (those typos!), and insights that help me as I work on each edition.

I am fortunate to have Jennifer Ziegler onboard as my project manager. Jenny has worked with me on several books with great patience and professionalism all while being most pleasant. I continue to love editors. Where I see only deadlines, they see both the big picture of the book and its details: they have vision. I am grateful for all the editors over the years who had a vision in supporting this book at a time when ethics was not a hot topic. They trusted me and understood the role of ethics in business and supported a project that was novel and risky. From the headlines, we now know that ethics instruction in business and business schools is a growth industry.

Kris Tabor and I have been working together since 1986. This 36-year partnership has been delightful and critical to all my work. There is no better eye for detail when it comes to manuscripts and page proofs. She knows how valuable a role she plays each time I send this email response to one of her corrections, "How on earth did you catch that?"

I am grateful to my late parents for the values they inculcated in me. Their ethical perspective was an inspiration; a comfort; and, in many cases, the final say in my decision-making processes. I am especially grateful to my father for the continual research on and quest for examples of ethical and not-so-ethical behavior in action that he provided throughout his life. I am grateful for my family's understanding and support. I am most grateful for the reminder their very presence gives me of what is truly important. In a world that measures success by "stuff" acquired, they have given me the peace that comes from devotion, decisions, and actions grounded in a personal credo of "others first." This road less taken offers so many rich intangibles that we can, with that treasure trove, take or leave "the stuff." My hope is that those who use this book gain and use the same perspective on "stuff."

Marianne M. Jennings
Professor Emeritus of Legal and Ethical Studies in Business
W. P. Carey School of Business
Arizona State University
marianne.jennings@asu.edu

Ethical Theory, Philosophical Foundations, Our Reasoning Flaws, Types of Ethical Dilemmas, and You

In the 21st century will occur something worse than the great wars, namely, the total eclipse of all values. The pain the human beast will feel when he realizes he can believe in … nothing … will be worse than any he has felt before.

—Nietzsche

I would disguise myself in my nice white-girl clothes and go to the salad bar and ask for a new plate as if I had already paid. I'm not proud of it, but I'm desperate. It's survival of the fittest.

Erin Gilmer, attorney and advocate for those with disabilities, on how she got food when she was broke.[1]

Cheating can become habitual. With kids, you're trying to develop good habits so they can apply them to later situations in life.[2]

Professor Steven Mintz
California Polytechnic University

Learning Objectives

- Explain what we mean by "ethics."

- List the categories of ethical dilemmas and give examples of each.

- Discuss the sequential process for analyzing ethical dilemmas.

- Describe the psychological tools we use to justify unethical conduct.

- Discuss the philosophical schools of thought on ethics and give examples of the application of their theories to ethical dilemmas.

- Provide examples of questions to apply in resolving ethical dilemmas.

- Apply the ethical schools of thought and questions to the cases and questions in the chapter to develop answers to the ethical dilemmas presented.

Before we begin the study of business ethics, we should do some introspection: What does ethics mean to you personally? The purpose of this unit is to provide you with an introspective look at yourself and your views on ethics before we bring the business component to you and ethics.

This unit explains four things: What ethics are, the types of ethical dilemmas, our ethical reasoning flaws, and how to resolve ethical dilemmas. The materials in this unit serve as the foundation for the study of issues in business ethics.

---

[1]Clay Risen, "Erin Gilmer, 38, Lawyer and Disability Rights Activist," *New York Times*, July 19, 2021, p. B6.

[2]Julie Jargon, "Cheating Is the Norm in Some Virtual Classes," *Wall Street Journal*, December 23, 2020, A12.

Understanding Ourselves and Ethical Lapses

Reading 1.1

You, That First Step, the Slippery Slope, and a Credo

Watch That First Step Because You Are Starting a Slippery Slope Descent!

We tend to look at folks who get into ethical and legal trouble and say, "I know I would never behave like that." For example, you would look at an executive who embezzled almost $280,000 from an employer and conclude, "I know I could not steal that much money from anyone." You probably would not, but you are making your evaluation based on the final total—the full $280,000. You did. Not see the tiny steps that led to that amount and the eventual downfall. In all likelihood, the executive began the years-long embezzlements by accidentally using a company American Express card to pay for the airline tickets for a family ski trip. We do not notice the mistake until the last minute when leaving for the trip and conclude, "I will just take care of it when I return from vacation." Upon return, work re-entry was difficult and the error continued to go unnoticed. Then began of use the card for more personal charges, charges that increased in number and size.

There are neurological studies that indicate brain activity changes when ethical lapses become a way of life. Dr. Tali Sharot of the University College of London found that the more comfortable we get with unethical choices, the easier it is for our brain to accept what we are doing. "At first, even a little lie provokes a big response in brain regions associated with emotion, such as the amygdala and insula. The tenth time you lie, even if you lie the same amount, the response is not that high. So while lying goes up over time, the response in your brain goes down."[3] Dr. Sharot is describing the infamous "**slippery slope**." Once we begin unethical behavior, the unscientific concept of the slippery slope, which is moving downward at an increasing pace with our unethical choices, is now known in science through studies of brain activity. We keep going, and even grow our deceptions because our brains get comfortable with our actions.

The proverbial slope does become more slippery. Professor Dan Ariely of Duke University found that folks who knowingly wore fake designer sunglasses were more than twice as likely to cheat on an unrelated task given to them as those

---

[3]Neil Garrett, Stephanie C Lazzaro, Dan Ariely, Tali Sharot, "The Brain Adapts to Dishonesty," *Nature Neuroscience* (2016), https://www.sciencedaily.com/releases/2016/10/161024134012.htm.

Famous Lines from Art and Literature

"It's a simple plan."

In Scott Smith's book *A Simple Plan*, the lead character, Hank; his brother, Jacob; and a friend, Lou come upon a small plane buried in the rural snowdrifts of Ohio. Upon opening the plane's door, they find the decomposing body of the pilot and a duffel bag full of $100 bills in $10,000-dollar packets—$3 million total. Initially, Hank tells his brother and Lou not to touch the money so that the police can conduct a proper investigation, but then a plan is hatched. Lou and Jacob want to keep one packet of the money and ask Hank what's wrong with doing that. Hank scolds them and says, "For starters, it's stealing." Hank reminds them that with so much money involved, someone would be looking for it and would know that they had taken a packet. Hank also reminds them that even if he didn't take a packet, he would be an accomplice if Jacob and Lou did.

Lou then proposes a solution: take it all. Hank wisely warns the two that they could not spend it because everyone in their small town would know. So, Lou proposes a "simple plan." They will sit on the money for a while, and when the investigation is over and things have cooled down, they can move away and live on their shares of the money. Again, Hank reminds them that it is stealing. But Jacob calls it by a different name: lost treasure. Hank succumbs. Such an easy thing, a simple plan.

But the initial decision was flawed. Whatever its soft label, their decision to walk away with the duffel bag was indeed taking something that did not belong to them. From there, the characters begin a game of whack-a-mole. With each twist and turn, they have to cross another line to cover up their seizure of the duffel bag. There is a lie to the sheriff and the problem of a neighbor seeing them near the plane, and more problems come at them each day. Each new problem requires a resolution that involves more dastardly choices. The characters keep slipping, eventually committing murder.

who were not wearing the fake sunglasses.[4] Once we have made peace with trademark infringement, we are willing to cross other lines. We just get comfortable with each step.

Ethical Reasoning Lost in the Pressure of Doing Our Jobs

Perhaps the most important part of studying ethics is studying how and why very smart and capable people made the poor ethical choices that they did. As you study, try to avoid judgment or feeling superior to those who have made mistakes; real learning about ethics and ethical lapses comes with understanding how easily those ethical missteps can happen. They happen through flaws in our analyses and gradual declines in disciplined reasoning processes. Sometimes those processes are lost in the pressures we feel to meet our goals, numbers, or performance metrics. Doing what we do to meet our job assignments can allow us to feel justified in our actions. For example, reasonable minds can differ on depreciation formulas. And you may make a change in your company's depreciation formula that makes your financial performance for the quarter more favorable. But just like the executive's

---

[4]Dan Ariely home page, http://web.mit.edu/ariely/www/MIT. Accessed July 20, 2010.

Why Didn't They Say Something? 1.1

The Travel Expense That Got Away

The executive's assistant was responsible for submitting the receipts for the executive's company travel and reconciling what was on the card statement vs. what was on the receipts. The paperwork and verification then went to Accounts Payable. The receipts submitted for the air tickets were for a destination different from all the other trips the executive took that month for business. There were no hotel bills at the resort even though they had flown there. There was no documentation about who the executive met with, any meetings attended, or receipts for meals. At that moment, there were questions the assistant could have raised.

1. Why did they not raise those questions?
2. What goes through your mind when you see someone at work or in your classes do something unethical?

credit-card use, once we cross a line, it becomes easier to keep going. Changing the depreciation formulas becomes a way of life and rises to such a level that you touch down in accounting fraud. "I would never commit accounting fraud" is easy to say. Could you be persuaded to change depreciation formulas "just this one time"? That initial small question, with reasonable minds differing, is the point at which we need to understand the implications of what we are doing. That focus on that first step is a critical part of ethical analysis.

Famous Lines from Art and Literature

"Watch that first step. It's a doozy." Ned Ryerson to Phil Connors (Bill Murray) in the film, *Ground Hog Day.*

Framing Ethical Issues Carefully and Using Business History

When facing an ethical dilemma, you need a process for analysis and reasoning, one that finds you looking at ethical issues more deeply instead of through the prism of emotions, desires, and financial and time pressures. To understand how to think more deeply about all your ethical choices you will study not just ethics; you will be studying business history. And you will also be studying you. Try to relate your vulnerabilities to those involved in the cases, questions, and "What would you do?" problems. Remember as you read these cases that you are reading about bright, capable, and educated individuals who made mistakes. The mistakes often seem clear when you study them in hindsight. But the ethical analyses of those who made those mistakes were flawed at the initial decision point because of the way they framed the issue. They framed their ethical analysis within the pressures they felt, a lack of complete and accurate information (that they may or may not have wanted) or, sometimes, the stuff of Greek tragedies, hubris. You will collect examples, stories of companies and their ethical collapses, and the realities of the consequences ethical missteps bring. That knowledge will help you spot those decision points and flaws in framing and reasoning.

As you study the cases in this unit and the others that follow, try not to be too hard on the human subjects. Learn from them and try to discover the flaws in their ethical analyses. Where were their decision points? What did they miss? What flaws were there in their analyses?

Ethics in Action 1.1

Boundary-Hopping for a Better Education

Kelley Williams-Bolar was a single mother in 2011, living in Akron, and trying to earn her degree at the University of Akron. Her two daughters were attending Akron School District public schools where the test scores were low, and the facilities were crumbling. Ms. Williams-Bolar's father lived in the Copley-Fairlawn School District. The Copley-Fairlawn School District met all 26 of Ohio's educational standards. The Akron School District met only four of those standards.

Ms. Williams-Bolar's girls spent time with their grandfather, Edward Williams. Ms. Williams-Bolar decided to list her father's address as her and her girls' address and got them into the Copley-Fairlawn District. Ms. Williams-Bolar's father took them to school each day.

Copley-Fairlawn hired a private investigator to follow Ms. Williams-Bolar and her girls and found that she was "boundary-hopping" or "district-hopping," a felony in Ohio. She and her father were both charged. They went to trial because they did not believe they were guilty. They did not believe that they had done anything wrong and did not know that what they were doing was a crime. The jury in Edward Williams's trial could not reach a verdict. Ms. Williams-Bolar was convicted of several charges and received two five-year sentences. Her sentence was suspended to 10 days. The judge said that the sentence was necessary to stop others thinking of defrauding the system.[5] Governor John Kasich did grant her partial clemency, reducing her felony convictions to misdemeanors.

1. How do you react emotionally to the decision Ms. Williams-Bolar faced?
2. What pressures was Ms. Williams-Bolar facing?
3. What did she miss in making her decision to use her father's address?
4. What factors would make her believe that what she did was necessary?
5. What questions did she fail to ask herself before filling in those addresses?
6. Does it matter that the Akron schools were not delivering on their promises about improving the schools?
7. Was there another way to solve the school-quality issue?

---

[5]Annie Lowry, "Her Only Crime Was Helping Her Kids," *The Atlantic*, September 13, 2019, https://www.theatlantic.com/ideas/archive/2019/09/her-only-crime-was-helping-her-kid/597979/.

An Initial Step Toward Ethical Clarity

One step that can give us greater clarity when we face ethical dilemmas is a **credo**. A credo is different from a code of ethics and does not consist of the virtues that companies usually list in a code of ethics, for example, "We are always honest; we follow the laws." The credo demands more because it sets the parameters for those virtues. A credo is virtue in action. A credo defines you and your ethical boundaries.

You get your personal credo through introspection using two questions:

1. Who are you? Many people define themselves by their titles, the size of their offices, or the number of people who report to them. Some define themselves through the trappings of success, such as how much money they have or make, the type of cars they drive, their clothes, and all things tangible and material. A credo requires you to find a way to describe yourself in terms or qualities that are part of you, no matter what happens to you financially, professionally, or in your career. For example, one good answer to "Who are you?" might be that you are kind and fair, showing Solomon-like virtues (see p. 20) to others around you. List the qualities you value and have and could keep regardless of all the outer and tangible trappings.

    Jimmy Dunne III was the only partner who survived the near destruction of his financial firm, Sandler O'Neill, when the World Trade Center collapsed on September 11, 2001. Only 17 of Sandler O'Neill's 83 employees survived the tower's collapse. Mr. Dunne has been tireless in raising money for the families of the employees who lost their lives that day. When asked by *Fortune* magazine why he works so hard to provide for the families of those employees, Mr. Dunne responded, "Fifteen years from now, my son will meet the son or daughter of one of our people who died that day, and I will be judged on what that kid tells my son about what Sandler O'Neill did for his family."[6] As of 2021, Sandler O'Neill had paid the college tuitions of 54 children (there were 71 total) of the employees who died on September 11, 2001.[7] When asked in 2021 why he made the decision to help the children of the firm's employees (in addition to providing health insurance for their families for five years), Mr. Dunne said, "Because we believed that what we did would echo for a hundred years in the families of our people, their kids and their grandkids. Because how we conducted ourselves in those first few hours and days would define who we really were and what we were about."[8]

    Mr. Dunne's personal credo focuses on both the long-term reputation of his firm and the impact his choices can have on his children's reputations.[9]

---

[6]Katrina Booker, "After September 11: Starting Over," *Fortune*, September 11, 2015, http://fortune.com/2015/09/11/september-11-sandler-oneill/.

[7]"Bank That Lost Dozens of Employees on 9/11 Has Sent 54 of Their Kids to College," http://www.huffingtonpost.com/entry/bank-pays-tuition-children-employees-september-11_us_55f97f83e4b0e333e54bfe95. *Huffington Post*, September 17, 2015.

[8]Aaron Lee, "Bank That Lost 66 Workers on 9/11 has Paid for All Their Kids to Go to College," *Good News Network*, September 11, 2021, at Lost 66 Workers on 9/11 has Paid for All Their Kids too, https://www.goodnewsnetwork.org/bank-that-lost-66-workers-on-911-has-paid-for-kids-college/.

[9]In 2020, Sandler O'Neill merged with Piper Jaffray and became Piper, Sandler, O'Neill.

2. The second part of your credo consists of answering these questions: What are the things that you would never do to get a job? To keep a job? To earn a bonus? To win a contract or gain a client? The answers to these questions result in a list, one that you should be keeping as you read the cases and study the individual businesspeople who made mistakes. Perhaps the title of your list could be "Things I Would Never Do to Be Successful," "Things I Would Never Do to Be Promoted," or even "Things I Would Never Do to Make Money." One scientist reflected on the most important line that he would never cross, and after you have studied a few of the product liability cases, you will come to understand why this boundary was important to him, "I would never change the results of a study to get funding or promise anyone favorable results from my work in exchange for funding." A worker at a refinery wrote this as his credo: "I would never compromise safety to stay on schedule or get my bonus." An auditor in a state auditor general's office wrote, "I would never sign a document that I know contains false information." The credo is a list, gleaned from reading about the experiences of others, that gives us perpetual guidance even before specific ethical dilemmas arise.

Using the Credo in Decisions About Ethics

A woman who had been a lawyer for 30 years reflected on her career and realized that she had conducted her professional life in line with two admonitions a senior partner had given to her on her first day as a young associate and new hire in a law firm. The senior partner came into her office and said, "I want you to remember two things: Don't ever lie to a client. Don't ever lie to the FBI." She recalled wondering most of that first day, "What kind of firm am I working for that these are the only two rules? I would never lie to a client. I would never lie to the FBI." Within the first month of her career, she came to understand the senior partner's wisdom, as well as the fact that she had a credo. During that first month, a client called and wondered how far along she was on his project that she had been assigned. She had not even begun the project; the file was still on her credenza, not having even made it to her desk for review. Human tendency and business practice when you are asked about a longer term project that remains a nonstarter is to want to say, "Fine. Making progress. Coming along. I have it right here. Under control." However, because of the credo parameters, she did not want to lie to the client. She told the truth, "I have not started the project yet, but I have two clear days next week that I will set aside to really get at it—could I call you then?" The client stayed with her and the firm.

Famous Lines from Art and Literature

Polonius's immortal advice to his son, Laertes, in Shakespeare's *Hamlet:*

"To thine own self be true" (*Hamlet,* Act I, Scene III).

Many of us quote Polonius without really asking, "What does that mean?" A credo puts the meat on the lofty philosophy. A credo takes us from eloquent Shakespearean advice to daily action. The credo is a personal application of the lessons in the cases. You will spot the lack of definitive lines in these case studies and begin to understand how the decision processes of those involved were flawed because the thinking was short sighted. The goal of developing your credo is to help you think more carefully, deeply, and fully about ethical issues.

She also noted that she came up short on her billable hours that first month, a problem for a new associate in a law firm who is expected to meet billable hour goals. She considered adding a few minutes here and there to clients' bills, but then reasoned, "That would be lying to a client!" She stopped herself over what might have been rationalized away as, "Oh, it's such a little thing!" She then had a government agent (not FBI) visit her to ask questions because the agent was doing a background check on a classmate who had applied for a government job. She was not a reference for the classmate. However, during the course of a national security background check, investigators ask references for names of others who may know the individual as a way of getting unscreened sources. She recalled thinking that she should paint the best picture possible about the classmate, even though she referred to him and his behavior as "sketchy" during their law school years. "Instead," she explained, "I just told the truth."

As she reflected on her decades-long career she noted, "I can't tell you how many times those two simple rules given to me that first day have saved me from mistakes." That's what a credo does for you. You no longer shift with the winds as you make ethical choices. You have set general parameters for what you will and will not do. The lawyer will not have to worry about whether she should exaggerate her experience to a new client. That would be lying to a client, and she has already made the decision not to do that. The lawyer would never withhold a settlement offer from a client because that would be lying to the client. So many decisions we cannot anticipate are made through a thoughtful credo that predefined our ethical lines.

Discussion Questions

Explain the role that "How do I want to be remembered?" plays in developing your credo. Discuss the difference between these two attempts at developing a credo:

1. I will always try to do the right thing.

2. I will never be dishonest with my spouse.

Ethics in Action 1.2

Customs Doesn't Need to Know

Granite Parts had a sales incentive program for its wholesalers located around the world. Those wholesalers who sold more than 10,000 units would win Apple's most expensive iPad. Jeremy's supervisor asked him to handle shipping out the iPads to the wholesalers who qualified, a large number that Granite had not anticipated. His supervisor instructed Jeremy, "Just describe what we're sending as the cheapest iPad Apple makes on the shipping form. That will save us import tariffs and fees." Jeremy will be required to sign the shipment form for the international carrier. The customs form has the following warning above the signature line, "You must truthfully declare the value of all goods being shipped. Undervaluation and other *Customs Act* offenses may lead to seizure and/or prosecution in a court of law and/or penalties that usually exceed the amount of duties and taxes payable for accurate declarations." Jeremy has just started his job with the company and is anxious to please his supervisor.

1. Provide Jeremy with some advice using examples of a credo.

2. What would you have done in Jeremy's circumstances?

Reading 1.2

What Did You Do in the Past Year That Bothered You? How That Question Can Change Lives and Cultures[10]

It began as a simple exercise to gauge what was on the minds of my students and training and seminar participants. On the first day of the seminar or class, I gave them two index cards and asked them to do the following:

- Describe one thing you did at work during the past year that really bothers you.
- Describe one thing you did in your personal life during the past year that really bothers you.

Note two important things about the exercise. First, participants were asked to do a work and a personal card. For nearly five decades now, one of my greatest challenges has been getting organizations and individuals to see that there is no difference between ethical standards in their personal lives and those at work. If you would not be dishonest with a neighbor in selling her your freezer, you should not be dishonest with a customer, vendor, or regulator at work. Second, the operative word is "bothers," meaning that they have not remedied what happened or made peace with it.

In the short time given for this challenge, the results were stunning. Just two souls in the thousands who have participated in this exercise since 2010 wrote on a card, "I haven't done anything that bothers me." For the remaining students, 60% of whom are executives with a minimum of 10 years' business experience, there were cathartic experiences as they used the index-card exercise as an outlet for letting go of their ethical demons. Herewith, some examples, and, in the words of the great Dave Barry, "I am not making this up":

- I used a previous salary number for a loan application even though we had just been assessed a 25% across-the-board salary reduction.
- I followed the advice of my tax accountant who "recommended" that I expense the luxury vehicle as a work vehicle versus the vehicle I really used for business because it had more tax benefits.
- I was asked to alter a head count so that we billed more to a customer.
- When I took over a global customer, I discovered that one of the local branches had received an overpayment of $50,000 (due to a supplier cost reduction/time issue). The branch had kept the overpayment and was using it as a "piggy bank" to offset pricing discrepancies. They told me they wanted to continue this practice and keep the money.
- I misstated my brokerage account value to my wife, as she doesn't know that I lost twice as much due to aggressive investment.
- I lied on budget reports at work.
- I let someone else take the blame for a mistake I made at work.
- I held profits for a following quarter to balance earnings.
- I contested a contract agreement because the terms no longer favored us even though we had agreed to the terms when the contract was signed.

---

[10]Adapted from "Ethics at Work: What Did You Do in the Past Year That Bothered You? How That Question Can Change Lives and Cultures," 29 *AHIA New Perspective* 40 (2010).

- I walked out of Costco knowing that the register did not catch an item in my basket.
- I sold a bike to a friend and it was later stolen. He asked me to inflate the sales price (on the claim form) so he could get a larger sum from the insurance company.
- I borrowed a garbage can from a neighbor's house that is abandoned. I plan on returning the can if/when someone moves in.
- Every once in a while I will drink pretty heavy with the guys. Not a big deal, but the fact that I have three kids. These are times I feel guilty because as a dad and parent, it's important to lead by example and be a role model.

There is one more question asked of the students, which was "Do you consider yourself to be an ethical person?" Some answers:

- Absolutely.
- Better than most people.
- I work hard at being ethical.
- I have really good ethical judgment.
- I am not as tempted as most people.

Hailing from the academic world, I am quite accustomed to the "in theory" rejections of my work. The irony is that most of those surveyed believe themselves to be ethical in theory. They are, however, having some difficulty in application. "Lost in translation" is an apt description, and an example is in order. In one of my textbooks is a short case study in which two friends who have just seen a movie realize, as they are leaving the theater, that the other theater doors in the multiplex are wide open and that no theater employee is present to monitor patrons. So, the two friends duck in and see two movies for the price of one. The case study, when presented early in the course, nets the usual, "It's no big deal," "Everybody does that," and "It doesn't really hurt anyone." On occasion I hear, "Hollywood can afford to spring for another movie for me." However, there will also be a student or two who will pipe up and exclaim, "It's not right. You didn't pay." Interestingly, the student who chimed in with the moral high ground this past semester came to class one day with a bootleg copy of *The Hurt Locker* to share with another student. I reminded her of her moralizing on the twofer. "This is different!" she sniffed back.

That "this is different" is where we lose employees in our training and cultures. To bring *The Hurt Locker* student around, I had to have her return to the methodical tools we use to analyze ethical issues, the tools that force us to go beyond the emotional reactions and relatively shallow opinions we all bring initially to resolving ethical dilemmas. Who's affected by your decision to use a bootleg copy? What would happen if everyone participated in movie bootlegging? Why, the producers of *The Hurt Locker* would make even less money than they did. However, when quality movies do not reflect their real draw and economic power, we are all affected in that producers no longer undertake those projects. When we bootleg or duck in for free, we are not just seeing a movie for free; we are fooling around with the delicate balances in market forces that are dependent on real demand, transparency, and accurate pricing.

In every example participants gave on their cards, they had engaged in the behavior that ultimately bothered them because they had neglected to do the hard analysis initially: What are the real costs here? What if everyone does what I am doing? Who else is affected by my decision? For example, mortgage applications misrepresentation of income is not "fudging" income. That application is the basis for a loan that the lender and subsequent purchasers of that loan are relying on in investing and assessing risk. We have affected others up and down the economic chain.

Ethics in Action 1.3

Those Little White Lies

Wall Street Journal editorial writer, Andy Kessler, wrote a column that appeared on August 9, 2021 entitled, "To Lie Is Human."[11] He began the column by confessing that as he and his family visited Lake Louise, Alberta, he did the following:

> He told his son to lie about his age when they were going to go horseback riding. His son was 6 and turning 7 that day (his birthday). The minimum age was 9. His son lied about his age, saying he was 8 and turning 9 that day, and got his birthday horseback ride.

> Later that day the Kessler family went to ride the ski lift. The fare was $35 unless you are five or under. Then the ride is free. Mr. Kessler told his son to tell the lift operator that he was 5—the son did so and the ride was free.

For those of you following closely, Mr. Kessler's son was ages 5, 6, 7, 8, and 9 all in one day for various activities controlled by age and price. Mr. Kessler said that he felt "awful" about telling his son to lie. However, he ended the column happily with the assurance that everyone else (particularly in politics) lies all the time.

1. List all those affected by the Kessler lies.
2. What were the motivations for the lies?
3. Why did he encourage the lies at the time and then feel guilty later?
4. What would you have done in those age/cost situations if you were Mr. Kessler?

---

[11]Andy Kessler, "To Lie Is Human," *Wall Street Journal*, August 9, 2021, p. A13.

There is a translation from theory over to the health care field, with an example from Omnicare, a pharmacy services company that dominates the nursing home care market. Physicians follow Omnicare pharmacists' recommendations 80% of the time. McNeil offered rebates to Omnicare that increased with more Omnicare purchases of McNeil drugs. Omnicare pharmacists also received other perks from McNeil. As a result, Omnicare increased its Johnson & Johnson drug purchases (McNeil is a subsidiary of J & J) from $100 million to $280 million per year. The other result was that McNeil paid a $98-million civil settlement for getting too close to that Medicare kickback line with rebates and perks. That line is a fine one, one that requires introspection and a daily dose of, "Have I gone too far with this sales program?"

Yet another translation from theory comes from Pfizer and its $2.3-billion fine to settle charges that its sales reps crossed another fine line between selling a drug for its approved purpose and touting it for non-FDA-approved uses. This situation involves an even tougher close call because how does a sales rep respond when a doctor asks about a study and a use? The translation of the law, that you cannot promote your company's drug for a purpose not approved by the FDA, is lost somewhere in those sales calls because those who are in the trenches each day are not asking the following: What happens if everyone does what I am doing? What do I gain for the company through this action? What does the company lose if I have crossed that line?

If bells and whistles went off each time a toe went over the line, we would self-monitor. There's that doozy of a first step again. Sometimes the bells and whistles are delayed because we are at a place that is too close to call or no one is monitoring enough to catch the slip. Internalizing those moments and translating them from "in theory" to "in practice" require a bit more attention to that question, "What did you do in the past year that still bothers you?" If it bothered you, determine why. If it bothered you, determine whether you need to make amends, return an item, pay for something that you did not pay for, and apologize for the falsehood you told another.

This exercise is one of reflection, on both our conduct and then who we really are. That is, when we determine something has bothered us, how do we react? Cover up more and hide from those affected, or do we face the issues head-on and acknowledge our mistakes. Introspection comes from answering "both" question and then by fixing the "bother."

Discussion Questions

1. Try doing the exercise yourself. Ask friends and family members for examples and discuss with them whether they "fixed" the bother, how, and why.

2. What kinds of things could this exercise reveal about an office or workplace?

Ethical Theory and Philosophical Foundations

Reading 1.3

What Are Ethics? From Line-Cutting to Kant

What Do We Mean When We Say "Ethics"?

The temptation is remarkable. The run is long. The body screams, "No more!" So, when some runners in the New York City Marathon hit the Queensboro Bridge, temptation sets in, and rather than finishing the last 10 miles through Harlem and the Bronx, they hop a ride on the subway and head toward the finish line at Central Park. A total of 46 runners used the subway solution to finish the race in the 2008 New York City Marathon. We look at this conduct and react, "That is *really* unfair." Others, particularly the 46, respond, "So I skipped a few boroughs. I didn't do anything illegal." That's where **ethics** come in; ethics apply where there are no laws, but our universal reaction is, "It just doesn't seem right."

We all don't run marathons (or claim to have run partial marathons), but we do see ethical issues and lapses each day. A high school student was required to memorize the Preamble to the U.S. Constitution for an in-class quiz. When he reported to class, one of his classmates, not known for his sartorial splendor, was wearing a suit and tie. When asked why he was so dressed up, the student lifted his tie to show the inside, where he had taped a copy of the Preamble. We call it cheating on a quiz, but there is no criminal act involved in cheating. However, the other students, who have taken the time to memorize the Preamble, look at this conduct and exclaim, "That's not fair!"

In college, some students use apps to print out labels for their soda cans and chip bags that seem to be normal but have exam information embedded in everything from the bar code to the trademark. Students who study and rely on memory watch others use these unauthorized materials and think, "That's cheating!" No one will be arrested, but it is not fair. And the grading system will not reflect accurately who really knows the material and who has skated through, although their GPAs will be virtually the same. That idea of self-policing, of stopping ourselves when we take advantage of others, even though our conduct does not violate a law is the self-restraint that ethics brings.

We are probably unanimous in our conclusion that those in the examples cited all behaved unethically. We may not be able to zero in on what bothers us about their conduct, but we know an ethics violation, or an ethical breach, when we see one.

But what is ethics? What do we mean when we say that someone has acted unethically? Ethical standards are not the standards of the law. In fact, they are a higher standard.

The Schools of Ethical Thought: From Philosophers to Economists

A great many philosophers have gone round and round trying to define *ethics* and debated the great ethical dilemmas of their time and ours. They have debated everything from the sources of authority on what is right and what is wrong to finding the answers to ethical dilemmas. An understanding of their language and views might help you to explain what exactly you are studying and can also provide you with insights as you study the cases about personal and business ethics. Ethical theories have been described and evolved as a means for applying logic and analysis to ethical dilemmas. The theories provide us with ways of looking at issues so that we are not limited to concluding, "I think …" The theories provide different perspectives to provide you with the means for you to approach an ethical dilemma. The theories help you to determine why you think as you do, whether you have missed some issues and facts in reaching your conclusion, and if there are others with different views who have points that require further analysis.

Normative Standards as Ethics

Sometimes referred to as **normative standards** in philosophy, ethical standards are the generally accepted rules of conduct that govern society. Ethical rules are both standards and expectations for behavior, and we have developed them for nearly all aspects of life. For example, with the exception of laws covering lines for boarding the vehicle ferries in Washington, no statute makes it a crime for someone to cut in line in order to save the waiting time involved by going to the end of the line. But we all view those who "take cuts in line" with disdain. We sneer at those cars that sneak along the side of the road to get around a line of traffic as we sit and wait our turn. We resent those who tromp up to the cash register in front of us, ignoring the fact that we were there first and that our time is valuable too.

If you have ever resented a line-cutter, then you understand ethics and have applied ethical standards in life. Waiting your turn in line is an expectation society has. Waiting your turn is not an ordinance, a statute, or even a federal regulation. Waiting your turn is an age-old principle developed because it was fair to proceed with the first person in line being the first to be served. Waiting your turn exists because when there are large groups waiting for the same road, theater tickets, or fast food at noon in a busy downtown area, we found that lines ensured order and that waiting your turn was a just way of allocating the limited space and time allotted for the movie tickets, the traffic, or the food. Waiting your turn is an expected but unwritten behavior that plays a critical role in an orderly society.

So it is with ethics. Ethics consists of those unwritten rules we have developed for our interactions with each other. These unwritten rules govern us when we are sharing resources or honoring contracts. Waiting your turn is a higher standard than the laws that are passed to maintain order. Those laws apply when physical force or threats are used to push to the front of the line. Assault, battery, and threats are forms of criminal conduct for which the offender can be prosecuted. But these laws do not address the high school taunters who make life miserable for the less popular. In fact, trying to make a crime out of these too-cruel interactions in the teen years often finds the courts holding that such a statute is too vague. But ethical standards do come in to fill that gap. The stealthy line-cutter who simply sneaks to the front, perhaps using a friend and a conversation as a decoy for edging into the front, breaks no laws but does offend our notions of fairness and justice. Individuals put themselves above others and took advantage of their time and too-good natures.

Because line-cutters violate the basic procedures and unwritten rules for line formation and order, they have committed an ethical breach. Ethics consists of standards and norms for behavior that are beyond laws and legal rights. We don't put line-cutters in jail, but we do refer to them as unethical. There are other examples of unethical behavior that carry no legal penalty. If a married person commits adultery, no one has committed a crime, but adulterers have broken a trust with their spouses. We do not put adulterers in jail, but we do label their conduct with adjectives such as *unfaithful* and even use a lay term to describe adultery: *cheating.*

Speaking of cheating, looking at someone else's paper during an exam is not a criminal violation. You may be sanctioned by your professor, and there may be penalties imposed by your college, but you will not be prosecuted by the county attorney for cheating. Your conduct was unethical because you did not earn your standing and grade under the same set of rules applied to the other students. Just like the line-cutter, your conduct is not fair to those who spent their time studying. Your cheating is unjust because you are getting ahead using someone else's work.

In these examples of line-cutters, adulterers, and exam cheaters, there are certain common adjectives that come to our minds: "That's *unfair!*" "That was *dishonest!*" and "That was *unjust!*" You have just defined *ethics* for yourself. Ethics is more than just common, or normative, standards of behavior. Ethics is honesty, fairness, and justice. The principles of ethics, when honored, ensure that the playing field is level, that we win by using our own work and ideas, and that we are honest and fair in our interactions with each other, whether personally or in business. However, there are other ways of defining ethical standards beyond just the normative tests of what most people "feel" is the right thing to do.

Divine Command Theory

The **Divine Command Theory** is one in which the resolution of dilemmas is based upon religious beliefs. Ethical dilemmas are resolved according to tenets of a faith, such as the Ten Commandments for the Jewish and Christian faiths. Central to this theory is that decisions in ethical dilemmas are made up of the guidance provided by a divine being. In some countries, the Divine Command Theory has influenced the law, as in some Muslim nations in which adultery is not only unethical but also illegal and sometimes punishable by death. In other countries, the concept of natural law runs in parallel with the Divine Command Theory.

Natural Law

Natural law proposes that there are certain rights and conduct controlled by God, and that no matter what a society does, it should not drift from those tenets. For example, in the United States, the Declaration of Independence relied on the notion of natural law, stating that we had rights because they were given to us by our Creator.

Ethical Egoism Theory: Ayn Rand and *Atlas*

Ethical egoism holds that we all act in our own self-interest and that all of us should limit our judgment to our own ethical egos and not interfere with the exercise of ethical egoism by others. This view holds that everything is determined by self-interest. We act as we do and decide to behave as we do because we have determined that it is in our own self-interest.

One philosopher who believed in ethical egoism was the novelist Ayn Rand, who wrote books such as *The Fountainhead* and *Atlas Shrugged* about business and business leaders' decisions in ethical dilemmas. These two famous books made Ms. Rand's point about ethical dilemmas: The world would be better if we did not feel so guilty about the choices we make in ethical dilemmas and just acknowledged that it is all self-interest. Ms. Rand, as an ethical egoist, would maintain order by putting in place the necessary legal protections so that we did not harm each other.

"Hobbesian" Self-Interest and Government

Philosopher Thomas Hobbes also believed that ethical egoism was the central factor in human decisions, that self-interest was part of human nature. However, Hobbes warned that there would be chaos because of ethical egoism if we did not have laws in place to control that terrible drive of self-interest. Hobbes felt we needed great power in government to control ethical egoism and that we all subscribe to that control through a social contract as outlined in his work *Leviathan,* a book that describes the chaos and confusion that would result without government.

Adam Smith, Self-Interest, and Moral Sentiments

Although he too believed that humans act in their own self-interest, and so was a bit of an ethical egoist, Adam Smith, a philosopher and an economist, also maintained that humans define self-interest differently from the selfishness theory that Hobbes and Rand feared would consume the world if not checked by legal safeguards. Adam Smith wrote, in *The Theory of the Moral Sentiments,* that humans are rational and understand that, for example, fraud is in no one's self-interest—not even that of the perpetrator, who does benefit temporarily until, as in the case of so many executives today, federal and state officials come calling with subpoenas and indictments. (For an excerpt from Adam Smith's *Moral Sentiments,* See Reading 9.6).That is, many believe that they can lie in business transactions and get ahead. Adam Smith argues that although many can and do lie to close a deal or get ahead, they cannot continue that pattern of selfish behavior because just one or two times of treating others this way results in a business community spreading the word: Don't do business with them because they cannot be trusted. The result is that they are shunned from doing business at least for a time, if not forever. In other words, Smith believed that there was some force of long-term self-interest that keeps businesses running ethically and that chaos only results in limited markets for limited periods as one or two rotten apples use their ethical egoism in a selfish, rather than self-interest, sense, to their own temporary advantage.

The Utilitarian Theory: Bentham and Mill

Philosophers Jeremy Bentham and John Stuart Mill moved to the opposite end of ethical egoism and argued that resolution of ethical dilemmas requires a balancing effort in which we minimize the harms that result from a decision even as we maximize the benefits. Mill is known for his *greatest happiness principle,* which provides that we should resolve ethical dilemmas by bringing the greatest good to the greatest number of people. There will always be a few disgruntled souls in every ethical dilemma solution, so we just do the most good that we can.

Some of the issues to which we have applied utilitarianism include those that involve some form of rationing of resources to provide for all, such as with providing universal health care, even though some individuals may not be able to obtain advanced treatments, in the interest of providing some health care for all. There is a constant balancing of the interests of the most good for the greatest number when the interests of protecting the environment are weighed against the need for electricity, cars, and factories. **Utilitarianism** is a theory of balancing that requires us to look at the impact of our proposed solutions to ethical dilemmas, from the viewpoints of all those who are affected, and try to do the greatest good for the greatest number.

The Categorical Imperative and Immanuel Kant

Philosopher Immanuel Kant's theories are complex, but he is a respecter of persons. That is, Kant does not allow any resolution of an ethical dilemma in which human beings are used as a means by which others obtain benefits. That might sound confusing, so Kant's theory reduced to simplest terms is that you cannot use others in a way that gives you a one-sided benefit. Everyone must operate under the same usage rules. In Kant's words, "One ought only to act such that the principle of one's act could become a universal law of human action in a world in which one would hope to live." Ask yourself this question: If you hit a car in a parking lot and damaged it, but you could be guaranteed that no one saw you do it, would you leave a note on the other car with contact information? If you answered, "No, because that's happened to me twelve times before, and no one left me a note," then you are unhappy with universal behaviors but are unwilling to commit to universal standards of honesty and disclosure to remedy those behaviors.

There is one more part to Kant's **Categorical imperative**: You not only have to be fair but also have to want to do it for all the right reasons. Self-interest was not a big seller with Kant, and he wants universal principles adopted with all goodwill and pureness of heart. So, not to engage in fraud in business because you don't want to get caught is not a sufficient basis for a rule against fraud. Kant wants you to adopt and accept these ethical standards because you don't want to use other people as a means to your enrichment at their expense.

Philosophers are not the easiest folks to reason along with, so an illustration can help with application of their deep thoughts. For example, there are those who find it unethical to have workers in developing nations labor in garment sweatshops for pennies per hour. The pennies-per-hour wage seems unjust to them. However, suppose the company were operating under one of its universal principles: Always pay a fair wage to those who work for it. A "fair wage" in that country might be pennies, and the company owner could argue, "I would work for that wage if I lived in that country." The company owner could also argue, "But if I lived in the United States, I would not work for that wage, would require a much higher wage, and would want benefits, and we do provide that to all of our U.S. workers." The employer applies the same standard, but the wages are different.

The company has developed its own ethical standard that is universally applicable, and those who own the company could live with it if it were applied to them, but context is everything under the categorical imperative. The basic Kant question is, are you comfortable living in a world operating under the standards you have established, or would you deem them unfair or unjust?

The Contractarians and Justice

Blame philosophers John Locke and John Rawls for this theory, sometimes called the **theory of justice** and sometimes referred to as the **social contract**. Kant's flaw, according to this one modern and one not-so-modern philosopher (Rawls is from the twentieth century and Locke is from the seventeenth), is that he assumed we could all have a meeting of the minds on what were the good rules for society. Locke and Rawls preferred just putting the rules into place via a social contract that is created through reflecting and imagining what it would be like if we had no rules or law at all. If we started with a blank slate, or *tabula rasa* as these philosophers would say, rational people would agree—perhaps in their own self-interest or perhaps to be fair—that certain universal rules must apply. Rational people, thinking through the results and consequences if there were no rules, would develop rules such as "Don't take my property without my permission" and "I would like the same type of court proceeding that rich people have, even if I am not so rich."

Locke and Rawls have their grounding in other schools of thought, such as natural law and utilitarianism, but their solution is provided by having those in the midst of a dilemma work to imagine not only that there are no existing rules but also that they don't know how they will be affected by the outcome of the decision, that is, which side they are on in the dilemma. With those constraints, Locke and Rawls argue that we would always choose the fairest and most equitable resolution of the dilemma. The idea of Locke and Rawls is to have us step back from the emotion of the moment and make universal principles that will survive the test of time.

Rights Theory

The **Rights Theory** is also known as *Entitlement Theory* and is one of the more modern theories of ethics, as philosophical theories go. Robert Nozick was the key modern-day philosopher on this theory, which has two big elements: (1) Everyone has a set of rights and (2) it's up to the governments to protect those rights. Under this big umbrella of ethical theory, we have the protection of human rights that covers issues such as sweatshops, abortion, slavery, property ownership and use, justice (as in court processes), animal rights, privacy, and euthanasia. Nozick's school of thought faces head-on all the controversial and emotional issues of ethics including everything from human dignity in suffering to third-trimester abortions. Nozick hits the issues head-on, but not always with resolutions because governments protecting those rights are put into place by Egoists, Kantians, and Divine Command Theory followers.

A utilitarian would resolve an ethical dilemma differently from a Nozick follower. Think about the following example. The FBI has just arrested a terrorist who is clearly a leader in a movement that plans to plant bombs in the nation's trains, subways, and airports. This individual has significant information about upcoming planned attacks but refuses to speak. There may be clues on his iPhone. However, the FBI has not been able to gain access to the phone; it is locked. The FBI files a petition in federal court for a judge to order Apple to assist the FBI with obtaining access. Apple's CEO refuses on the grounds of privacy and that providing such access would violate the promises and trust the company has with its customers in preserving their privacy. A utilitarian would want the greatest good for the greatest number and would feel that a court order forcing Apple to assist with access is justified to save thousands of lives. However, Nozick might balk at such a proposal because the captured terrorist's human right of privacy is violated. As different as they are, ideological views enhance our ability to see issues from a 360-degree perspective as we analyze them.

Moral Relativists

Moral relativists believe in time-and-place ethics. Arson is not always wrong in their book. If you live in a neighborhood in which drug dealers are operating a crystal meth lab or crack house, committing arson to drive away the drug dealers is ethically justified. If you are a parent and your child is starving, stealing a loaf of bread is ethically correct. The proper resolution to ethical dilemmas is based upon weighing the competing factors at the moment and then making a determination to take the lesser of the evils as the resolution. Moral relativists do not believe in absolute rules, virtue ethics, or even the social contract. Their beliefs center on the pressure of the moment and whether the pressure justifies the action taken. Enron's former chief financial officer Andrew Fastow, in his testimony against his former bosses at their criminal trial for fraud, said, "I thought I was being a hero for Enron. At the time, I thought I was helping myself and helping Enron to make its numbers" (Andrew Fastow, trial testimony, March 7, 2006). In classic moral relativist mode, a little fraud to help the company survive was not ethically problematic at the time for Mr. Fastow. In hindsight, Mr. Fastow would also comment, "I lost my moral compass."[12]

---

[12]John R. Emshwiller and Gary McWilliams, "Fastow Is Grilled at Enron Trial," *Wall Street Journal*, March 9, 2016, p. C1.

Back to Plato and Aristotle: Virtue Ethics

Although it seems odd that Aristotle and Plato are last in the list of theorists, there is reason to this ethical madness. Aristotle and Plato taught that solving ethical dilemmas requires training, that individuals solve ethical dilemmas when they develop and nurture a set of virtues. Aristotle cultivated virtue in his students and encouraged them to solve ethical dilemmas using those virtues that he had integrated into their thoughts. One of the purposes of this book is to help you develop a set of virtues that can serve as a guide in making both personal and business decisions. Think of your credo as something that comes from your desire to have certain universally recognized virtues at all times in your personal and professional life.

Solomon's Virtues

Some modern philosophers have embraced this notion of **virtue ethics** and have developed lists of what constitutes a virtuous businessperson. The following list in Figure 1.1 of virtue ethics was developed by the late professor Robert Solomon:

Figure 1.1	
Virtue Standard	**Definition**
Ability	Being dependable and competent
Acceptance	Making the best of a bad situation
Amiability	Fostering agreeable social contexts
Articulateness	Ability to make and defend one's case
Attentiveness	Listening and understanding
Autonomy	Having a personal identity
Caring	Worrying about the well-being of others despite power
Charisma	Inspiring others
Compassion	Sympathetic
Coolheadedness	Retaining control and reasonableness in heated situations
Courage	Doing the right thing despite the cost
Determination	Seeing a task through to completion
Fairness	Giving others their due; creating harmony
Generosity	Sharing; enhancing others' well-being
Graciousness	Establishing a congenial environment
Gratitude	Giving proper credit
Heroism	Doing the right thing despite the consequences
Honesty	Telling the truth; not lying
Humility	Giving proper credit
Humor	Bringing relief; making the world better
Independence	Getting things done despite bureaucracy

Integrity	Being a model of trustworthiness
Justice	Treating others fairly
Loyalty	Working for the well-being of an organization
Pride	Being admired by others
Prudence	Minimizing company and personal losses
Responsibility	Doing what it takes to do the right thing
Saintliness	Approaching the ideal in behavior
Shame (capable of)	Regaining acceptance after wrong behavior
Spirit	Appreciating a larger picture in situations
Toughness	Maintaining one's position
Trust	Dependable
Trustworthiness	Fulfilling one's responsibilities
Wittiness	Lightening the conversation when warranted
Zeal	Getting the job done right; enthusiasm

Source: From *A Better Way to Think about Business* by Robert Solomon, copyright © 1999 by Robert Solomon, p. 18. Used by permission of Oxford University Press. See also Kevin J. Shanahan and Michael R. Hyman, "The Development of a Virtue Ethics Scale," 42 *Journal of Business Ethics,* 2002, pp. 197, 200.

The list offers a tall order because these are difficult traits to develop and keep. But as you study the companies, issues, and cases, you will begin to understand the mighty role that these virtues play in seeing the ethical issues, discussing them from all viewpoints, and finding a resolution that enables businesses to survive over the long term.

Discussion Questions

1. Review each of the Solomon virtues and evaluate which virtues you already live by and those virtues with which you struggle. Explain why some virtues are a part of your credo and others are not. Are there experiences you have had that have taught you about the importance of those virtues? Are there virtues that you were taught were not important? Why were they discounted?

2. Your friend, spouse, child, or parent needs a specialized medical treatment. Without the specialized treatment, your friend, your spouse, or your child cannot survive. You are able to get that treatment for them, but the cost is $6,800. You don't have $6,800, but you hold a job in the Department of Motor Vehicles. As part of your duties there, you process the checks, money orders, and other forms of payment sent in for vehicle registration. You could endorse these items, cash them, and have those funds. You feel that because you open the mail with the checks and money orders, no one will be able to discover the true amounts of funds coming in, and you can credit the vehicle owners' accounts so that their registrations are renewed. Under the various schools of thought on ethics, evaluate whether the embezzlement would be justified.

Ethics in Action 1.4

Applying Theory in Reality

a. Three employees of a department store were conversing about their futures. One employee was sharing that when the new year arrived, in just a few days, most of them would be going to part-time status because of slow sales, the economy, and health care costs. The remaining two employees seemed crestfallen. But the knowledgeable employee explained that there was something that they could do. "Get yourself fired because the money you make on unemployment will be better than part-time work here, and you can get ninety-nine weeks of unemployment. Plus, you are eligible for medical care through the government because you are unemployed. It's a better deal. It is so not worth it to keep working." When they asked how they could get fired, he had a solution: "Just don't meet your numbers. You'll be gone in no time." Classify the suggestion of getting yourself fired and collecting unemployment under the appropriate ethical school of thought.

b. In the movie *Changing Lanes,* Ben Affleck plays a young lawyer who is anxious to become a senior partner in a law firm in which one of the senior partners is his father-in-law, played by the late Sidney Pollack. Affleck discovers that his father-in-law has embezzled from clients, forged documents, and committed perjury, all felonies and all certainly grounds for disbarment. Affleck finally confronts Pollack and asks, "How do you live with yourself?" Pollack responds that he did indeed forge signatures and embezzle from clients. He also perjured himself and even aided and abetted others with perjury, but with the money that he made he became one of the city's greatest philanthropists. "I can live with myself because at the end of the day I think I do more good than harm. What other standard have I got to judge myself by?" Under which ethical theories would you place the characters' ethical postures? Could you develop a different standard for Mr. Pollack to use for judging his actions? What ethical theory is he currently following?

c. Could businesses use moral relativism to justify false financial reports? For example, suppose that the CFO says, "I did fudge on some of the numbers in our financial reports, but that kept 11,000 employees from losing their jobs." What problems do you see with moral relativism in this situation?

The Types of Ethical Dilemmas

Reading 1.4

The Types of Ethical Dilemmas: From Truth to Honesty to Conflicts

The following 12 categories were developed and listed in *Exchange,* the magazine of the Brigham Young University School of Business. Ethical analysis begins with identification of the ethical issue or issues involved. Regardless of your final decision as to what you should do in the midst of an ethical dilemma, the critical first step is recognizing when you are in the midst of an ethical dilemma.

Taking Things That Don't Belong to You

In the book, *How to Become a Grown-Up in 468 East (ish) Steps,* author Kelly Williams Brown lists step number 176 as "Do not steal more than $3 worth of office supplies per quarter." In today's age of casual, moral relativism, the issue is often framed not as whether it is wrong to steal office supplies but where the line is for how much you can take without giving rise to an ethical dilemma. Regardless of size or motivation, unauthorized use of someone else's property or taking property is still taking something that does not belong to you. That you feel you demonstrate ethical behavior by having a self-imposed limit does not change the fact that you took property belonging to someone else for a purpose they did not intend. We experience these seemingly small ethical dilemmas daily. The amount involved is not the ethical issue. Recognizing that we have taken something that does not belong to us is the critical first step in your analysis and framing of your ethical dilemma. For example, a chief financial officer of a large electric utility reported that after taking a cab from LaGuardia International Airport to his midtown Manhattan hotel, he asked for a receipt. The cab driver handed him a full book of blank receipts and drove away. The ability to use those receipts and submit them as an expense for business travel does not eliminate the ethical issue of taking money from your company for expenses that you did not really have.

Saying Things You Know Are Not True

This category of ethical dilemmas focuses on the virtue of honesty. Assume you are trying to sell your car, one in which you had an accident and that damage has been repaired. If the potential buyer asks whether the car has been in an accident and you reply, "No," then you have given false information. If you take credit for someone else's idea or work, then you have, by your conduct, said something that is not true. If you do not give credit to others who have given you ideas or helped with a project, then you have not been forthright. If, in evaluating your team members on a school project, you certify that all of them carried their workload when, in fact, one of your team members was a real slacker, you have said something that was not true. If you do not disclose a health condition that you had in the last year on a life insurance application, you have not told the truth. If you state that you have a college degree on your résumé but have not yet graduated, you have committed an ethical breach under this category. If, in filling out a credit application, you put the salary you have now when your employer has announced a 25% pay cut beginning next quarter, you have not told the truth.

Giving or Allowing False Impressions

This category of ethical breach is the legal technicality category. What you have said is technically the truth, but it does mislead the other side. For example, if your professor asks you, "Did you have a chance to read the assigned ethics cases?" even if you had not read the cases, you could answer, "Yes!" and be technically correct. You had "a chance" to read the cases, but you did not read them. The answer is not a falsehood because you may have had plenty of chances to read the cases, but you didn't read the cases.

If you were to stand by silently while a coworker was blamed for something you did, you would leave a false impression. You haven't lied, but you allowed an impression of false blame to continue. Many offers that you receive in the mail have envelopes that make them seem as if they came from the Social Security Administration or another federal agency. The desired effect is to mislead those who receive the envelopes into trusting the company or providing information. That effect works, as attorneys general verify through their cases of fraud brought on behalf of senior citizens who have been misled by this false impression method.

Buying Influence or Engaging in Conflict of Interest

This category finds someone in the position of conflicting loyalties. An officer of a corporation should not be entering into contracts between his company and a company that he has created as part of a sideline of work. The officer is conflicted

---

Ethics in Action 1.5

The Ozy Media Funding Meeting

Ozy Media has been on the Internet since 2013. Ozy had the usual podcasts, interviews, and some YouTube documentaries. The story was that an Ozy Media executive, Samir Rao (co-founder and COO), posed as a YouTube executive during a conference call with Goldman Sachs. Goldman was considering a $40 million investment in the company. The role of the YouTube executive, fake though he may have been, was to verify Ozy's presence and hits on social media.

Goldman thought the executive's voice sounded digitally altered and, showing surprisingly good judgment, opted not to go with an investment in the company. Discuss whether this type of action fits under the false impression category. Does it make a difference that Goldman Sachs should have checked on identities or perhaps used a Zoom call with screens turned on to show participants? A mantra in Silicon Valley for entrepreneurs is "Fake it until you make it." Are there any categories in following this mantra?

Why Didn't They Say Something? 1.2

The Silent Ozy Media Executives and Employees

Think about the other Ozy Media executives and employees in the room when the Goldman Sachs call was taking place. Think about the employees who knew about the planned impression prior to the call. List everyone who was affected or will be affected by the conduct on the phone call. List some examples of who is affected. Why didn't those involved raise questions about this plan for securing investors in the company? What kinds of things were they thinking about that allowed them to remain silent as the scheme was carried out over the phone? Were they thinking of the present only instead of anticipating future consequences? Would the pressures of keeping their jobs be part of their thinking at the time? Is allowing this conduct to proceed without objection a "doozy" of a first step?

between his duty to negotiate the best contract and price for his corporation and his interest as a business owner in maximizing his profits. In his role as an officer, he wants the most he can get at the lowest price. Bribery is a legal issue but is grounded in conflicts of interest. For example, when nine Fédération Internationale de Football Association (FIFA) executives of the NGO's marketing affiliates were indicted and arrested, they were accused of accepting bribes from cities and countries in exchange for the award of World Cup locations and other events cities and countries sought for economic purposes. When executives for FIFA accept payments from those who seek to win contracts with FIFA, they compromise their judgment and loyalty to FIFA, that is, what is best for soccer, to which country pays the most.

A county administrator has a conflict of interest by accepting paid travel from contractors who are interested in bidding on the stadium project. Certainly, it is a good idea for the administrator to see the stadiums around the country and get an idea of the contractors' quality of work. But the county should pay for those site visits, not the contractors. The administrator's job as a county employee is to hire the most qualified contractor at the best price. However, the benefits of paid travel would and could vary, and contractors could use those site visits and travel perks to influence the decision on the award of the county contract for the stadium. Their interests in obtaining the contract are at odds with the county's interest in seeking the best stadium, not the best travel perks for the administrator. The administrator's loyalties to the county and the accommodating contractors are in conflict.

In 2014, a Texas legislator discovered that lawmakers were writing to the chancellor of University of Texas at Austin (UT), requesting special consideration for friends and family members who had applied for admissions. The general admissions rate for UT applicants is 15.8%. The admission rate for those who had letters from legislators was 58.7%. Public outrage resulted because of the perception of political favoritism—that the chancellor's duty to the university conflicted with his need to have good relationships with legislators for budget and tuition rate purposes. The issue was whether the admissions process was compromised as a result of deference to the legislators writing letters.

Those who are involved in these conflict-of-interest situations often protest, "But I would never allow that to influence me." The ethical violation is the conflict.

Whether the conflict can or will influence those it touches is not the issue, for neither party can prove conclusively that a *quid pro quo* was not intended. The possibility exists, and it creates suspicion. Conflicts of interest are not difficult. They are managed in one of two ways: Don't do it, or disclose it. Sometimes the conflict is so great that the person involved must give up one of the roles. For example, a lawyer cannot represent a client when their firm is litigating against that client on another matter. There is no way to manage the conflict. When an executive in Corporation A owns a company, Corporation B, that wishes to do business with Corporation A, there is a conflict of interest. However, the board or an outside attorney could monitor the contracts, costs, and expenses to determine whether the executive has entered into contracts that do not cost the company more for lesser services or goods.

Hiding or Divulging Information

This category involves hiding what others should be told or divulging what others should not have revealed to them, i.e., privacy protections. For example, the late basketball great, Kobe Bryant, was killed in a helicopter crash. His wife won a privacy suit against the police department that investigated that crash that also

---

Ethics in Action 1.6

McKinsey's Bankruptcy Conflicts

a. McKinsey & Company, a 100-year-old international consulting firm, has a division known as McKinsey RTC that works with companies on restructuring when those companies have declared Chapter 11 bankruptcy. That division of McKinsey & Co. advised United Airlines, American Airlines, Edison Mission Energy, NII Holdings, Inc., Alpha Natural Resources, Inc., GenOn Energy, and SunEdison, Inc. during their restructurings.

McKinsey RTC did not disclose to the bankruptcy court that McKinsey & Co.'s retirement fund, MIO Partners, through its hedge fund investors, held a stake in the debt or other obligations of those six companies. How a company is restructured controls what creditors and investors receive as the company emerges from bankruptcy to start anew. For example, in the GenOn bankruptcy, the bondholders received large recoveries in the bankruptcy. MIO Partners held GenOn bonds.

The disclosure form to the bankruptcy court is a sworn statement that the consultant/adviser is a "disinterested party." McKinsey released a statement saying that it met all legal requirements and that it had been approved for participation by the bankruptcy courts handling the Chapter 11 proceedings for the companies. McKinsey believes that the retirement fund is run separately and therefore disclosure about the retirement fund's investments was not required under the regulations.[13] Discuss whether there is a conflict with McKinsey's work in the bankruptcy restructuring and its ownership interests through its retirement fund and why or why not the conflict can be managed.

---

[13]Gretchen Morgenson and Rebecca Davis O'Brien, "McKinsey Probed on Bankruptcy Disclosures," *Wall Street Journal*, November 12, 2021, p. B3.

killed their daughter. Police officers who were first on the scene took photos and shared those photos with others at police headquarters. Any photos beyond official investigative photos should not have been taken and should not have been shared with anyone. Taking your firm's product development or trade secrets to a new place of employment is the ethical breach of divulging proprietary information (See the Boeing case (2.2) in Unit 2).

Using information that no one else is aware of to profit from their lack of knowledge is hiding information. Dayakar Mallu, a former Mylan vice president of global operations information technology, received some very valuable, nonpublic information from Mylan's former chief information officer, Ramkumar Rayapureddy. The VP used the information (advance notice of drug approvals) to trade in stock options in Mylan. Mr. Mallu tried to conceal the transactions by making them overseas in Indian rupees. However, the Securities Exchange Commission is into analytics. By watching trading patterns and then matching those patterns with releases of information, finding the culprits is not difficult. Mr. Mallu entered a guilty plea and agreed to pay back the $4.27 million in profits on the sales as restitution.[14]

Medtronic was investigated by the federal government for its failure to adequately disclose the side effects of its bone growth products. Eventually, Medtronic agreed to release the data it had collected on patients using the product so that independent researchers could provide adequate disclosure of this pertinent information.

Taking Unfair Advantage

Many consumer protection laws exist because so many businesses took unfair advantage of those who were not educated or were unable to discern the nuances of complex contracts. Credit disclosure requirements, truth-in-lending provisions, and new regulations on soliciting students for credit cards all resulted because businesses misled consumers who could not easily follow the jargon of long and complex agreements. *USA Today* illustrated the fairness issues with a riddle. Suppose you have no cash and need to buy $100 worth of groceries. Which would cost you more?

a. Taking out a payday loan with a 450% APR

b. Overdrawing your debit card and paying the $27 fee

The answer is b because the $27 fee on your debit card would be equal to a 704% interest rate (assuming a 14-day repayment period and an average $17.25 fee per $100 for a payday loan).[15] In 2016, Uber paid a $25 million penalty to the cities of Los Angeles and San Francisco for unfair business practices. As part of the settlement, Uber promised to no longer use the phrase "safest ride on the road" in its ads as well as no longer use "the gold standard" to describe its background checks. San Francisco's district attorney said of Uber, "in the quest to quickly obtain market share, laws designed to protect consumers cannot be ignored."[16]

Committing Acts of Personal Decadence

Although many argue about the ethical notion of an employee's right to privacy, it has become increasingly clear that personal conduct outside the job can influence performance and company reputation. Conduct in our personal lives does have

---

[14]Jonathan Stempel, "Former Mylan Executive Pleads Guilty to Insider Trading," *Reuters*, September 20, 2021, https://www.reuters.com/business/former-mylan-executive-pleads-guilty-insider-trading-2021-09-17/

[15]Kathy Chu, "Anger at Overdraft Fees Gets Hotter, Bigger and Louder," *USA Today*, September 29, 2009, p. 1B.

[16]Elizabeth Weise, "Uber Hit with Hefty $25M Penalty for Unfair Practices," *USA Today*, April 8, 2016, p. 1B.

Ethics in Action 1.7

Real Portland vs. Ad Portland

Sparked by large, lengthy, and often unruly political protests combined with cutbacks in police department funding, the city of Portland, Oregon recently experienced a significant increase in crime rates. Security fencing was raised around the Hatfield Federal Court Building, and looters attacked the downtown district on multiple occasions. There were 56 homicides in Portland in 2020, the highest number in 26 years. Through April 6 of 2021, there were 25 homicides. For 2020, Portland finished the year with 5,436 burglaries, up from 4,190 in 2019.

The amount of property damage during 2020-2021 was somewhere between $2.3 million and $23 million. As one commentator noted, the amount depends on the actual number of Louis Vuitton bags looters took from the downtown mall.

Portland, its tourist trade suffering, ran the following in a full-page ad in national newspapers:

"Some of what you've heard about Portland is true. Some is not. What matters most is that we're true to ourselves."

"Anything can happen. We like it this way."

"We have some of the loudest voices on the West Coast. And, yes, passion pushes the volume all the way up. We've always been like this. We wouldn't have it any other way."

Evaluate whether the ad is misleading to potential tourists. Is the ad effective?

---

an impact on how well we perform our jobs, including whether we can perform our jobs safely. For example, a company driver must abstain from substance abuse because with alcohol or drugs in his blood, he creates both safety and liability issues for his employer. Even the traditional company Christmas party and picnic have come under scrutiny, as the behavior of employees at and following these events has brought harm to others in the form of alcohol-related accidents.

When Elon Musk appeared online in an interview while smoking marijuana his conduct affected his company, SpaceX, a federal contractor. While states have legalized marijuana use, the federal government has not. Federal contractors agree to abide by the federal standard and are tested for drug use, including marijuana. Personal conduct in this situation can cost the company its federal contracting status.

Even affiliations of executives can affect a company. In 2020, Scotland Yard concluded that Jess Staley, then-CEO of Barclay's Bank, had not been truthful in response to questions about his relationship with Jeffrey Epstein. The late Jeffrey Epstein (he hung himself while in prison) hosted Mr. Staley on the Epstein island where Mr. Epstein allegedly flew in underage young women who then were allegedly forced into sexual relations with the rich and powerful who stayed on the island. Mr. Staley assured the board and Scotland Yard that his wife was with him and he knew nothing about the underage girls brought to the island by Mr. Epstein. However, Mr. Epstein was well known in criminal law circles. He had previously worked out a plea deal with Florida authorities in 2008 on charges of sex trafficking. That level of criminal activity did not stop Mr. Staley, though he assured the board that he had stopped that Epstein affiliation. The board, upon learning about the Scotland Yard findings, terminated Mr. Staley for alleged lack of candor. Mr. Staley's personal conduct was affecting the bank's regulatory relationships as well as its credibility with law enforcement.

Perpetrating Interpersonal Abuse

Managers can be demanding, but they cross ethical lines when their conduct steps on employee rights. For example, a Forever 21 sales clerk brought suit against that company for on-call scheduling, a practice that requires employees to keep the time for a shift clear so that they can be called in if they are needed. However, there is no compensation for keeping the time clear. There have been several class-action suits by interns who felt they were being used as employees for "grunt" work instead of being given educational and experience opportunities. Long hours and no pay without the rewards of knowledge and experience have resulted in numerous lawsuits for what amounts to workplace abuse. Interpersonal abuse consists of conduct that is demeaning, unfair, or hostile or involves others so that privacy issues arise. A manager who is verbally abusive to an employee falls into this category. The former CEO of HealthSouth, Richard Scrushy, held what his employees called the "Monday morning beatings." These were meetings during which managers who had not met their numbers goals were upbraided in front of others and subjected to humiliating criticism. A Merrill Lynch executive who dreaded the chastisement when Merrill did not match Goldman Sachs' earnings complained, "It got to the point where you didn't want to be in the office on Goldman earnings days."[17] A manager correcting an employee's conduct in front of a customer has not violated any laws but has humiliated the employee and involved outsiders who have no reason to know of any employee issues. In some cases in this category, there are laws to protect employees from this type of conduct, but when there are no laws, we are able to look at this conduct and see the ethical issue as we sum up with, "That's not fair" or "That's not right."

Permitting Organizational Abuse

This category covers the way companies treat employees. This ethical category is one that is a focus of companies with their production facilities outside the United States because the issues of child labor, sweatshop conditions, and low wages emerge. Nike, the NBA, and other companies have experienced backlash for their use of production facilities in the Chinese Xinjiang Uyghur labor/re-education camps. (See cases 6.1 and 6.8 in Unit 6.)

There are ongoing battles in the United States because of the structure of the gig economy. Companies such as Uber, Lyft, and other service companies do not use the traditional employee model; they are relying on independent contractors, a model that allows the companies to escape the expenses of benefits and wage taxes. However, those who work for the start-ups have no stability and find health insurance expensive and the lack of unemployment coverage risky. States and the U.S. Department of Labor have begun regulating the independent contractor status of so many working in the gig economy with the goal of obtaining for them better wages and hours along with benefits.

Violating Rules

Rules can be organizational rules or the laws and regulations that govern certain business activities. Breaking those rules is an ethical lapse. Natalie Mayflower Sours Edwards was once a senior advisor in the Department of Treasury's Financial

---

[17]Randall Smith, "O'Neal Out as Merrill Reels from Loss," *Wall Street Journal*, October 29, 2007, pp. A1, A16.

Crimes Enforcement Network. During the Trump administration, from October 2017 until her arrest in October 2018, Ms. Mayflower Sours Edwards leaked SARs (suspicious activity reports) to BuzzFeed. The SARs included information about former Trump campaign aides, Paul Manafort and Richard Gates. Ms. Mayflower Sours Edwards entered a guilty plea in January 2021 to conspiring to unlawfully disclose confidential financial reports. Ms. Mayflower Sours Edwards was sentenced to six months in prison on June 3, 2021.

Ms. Mayflower Sours Edwards violated a clear rule but felt justified because she disagreed politically. Her defense was moral relativism—her belief was that she was justified in breaking the rules because her cause was noble. Her reasoning resulted from her failure to recognize one of the categories of ethical dilemmas. That self-perceived virtue is at the heart of actions does not eliminate the ethical breach. Rules are put into place for reasons that reach beyond our individual view that a rule is not important because we have something more important. How federal employees feel politically about their commanders-in-chief or their aides does not control whether that employee should follow the rules for all federal employees. All laws, rules, and regulations have a "Why?" underlying them. They were put into place for a reason, generally a reason of protection. SARs are confidential for a very valid reason. SARs are just that: Suspicious. It is a fundamental deprivation of due process to leak such reports before an investigation, and perhaps most importantly, before those named have an opportunity to explain. For example, if you have ever wired money in excess of $10,000 for your deposit for buying a home, you had a SAR. You would want the chance to explain before there was a criminal charge and certainly before there was a public disclosure of your financial transaction.

Rationalizing (See Reading 1.5 "On Rationalizing") your personal determination to make an exception to laws, regulations, and rules creates an atmosphere of uncertainty and political corruption of governmental processes. Just understanding what category applies to your actions provides you with some critical information in avoiding ethical missteps.

Condoning Unethical Actions

In this category, the wrong is the failure to report an ethical breach in any of the other categories. For example, a state employee who was attending a business conference paid for by the state, and who was allowed to attend as part of her workweek, won an iPad in a vendor raffle. A fellow employee who also attended the conference knows that state law requires employees who win more than nominal prizes (T-shirts, pens, baseball caps) to report those prizes to and turn them over to the state. The winner of the iPad tells his coworker, "If anyone asks you about the iPad, you don't know anything, and this conversation never happened." The employee who says nothing becomes part of the problem. Suppose that questions about the vendor who sponsored the raffle arose. The public disclosure of the iPad giveaway would appear nefarious as the public looks back from the perspective of problems with the vendor. Allowing ethical breaches that you know about to occur often brings greater harm to everyone involved. The employee who won the iPad, the employee who knew, and the agency would all be affected in terms of employment and reputation.

Recent studies indicate that over 80% of students who see a fellow student cheating would not report the cheating. Yet there are harms to those students who actually study. The value of their degree is discounted when the cheating students enter the work force without the knowledge they should have gained and the skills they should have developed.

Why Didn't They Say Something? 1.3

Kitty Genovese and the Mute Bystanders

On the night of March 13, 1964, Kitty Genovese died at the hands of an assailant as 38 "respectable, law-abiding citizens" of Kew Gardens in Queens, NY that heard her cries did nothing. The story became one of "egocentrism in the urban jungle."[18] No one called the police, no one went to help Kitty, and even after the assailant left, only one person went to check on Kitty. A neighbor, a friend of Miss Genovese, found her friend slumped inside the rear building door. The then-30-year-old mother of a new baby held Kitty as they waited for help. Miss Genovese died in the ambulance en route to the hospital.

It was Miss Genovese's brother who restored some semblance of hope in society as he featured that neighbor, Sophia Farrar, in his documentary about the night his sister was murdered. Mrs. Farrar explained what she did with one hope: That Kitty knew she was there with her and for her. Mrs. Farrar took a risk that 37 others would not. Why did no one step in to help? Why did the only help come after the assailant had left? Why do we hesitate to get involved? List reasons you hesitate to get involved when you see actions that fall into the previous 10 categories.

[18]Sam Roberts, "Sophia Farrar Dies at 92; Belied Indifference to Kitty Genovese," *New York Times,* September 3, 2020, p. B11.

Balancing Ethical Dilemmas

In these types of situations, there are no right or wrong answers; rather, there are dilemmas to be resolved. Regardless of the resolution, it is likely that someone will be adversely affected. PGA golfer Phil Mickelson was scheduled to play in the 2009 Masters Tournament when he learned that his wife Amy had cancer. Mr. Mickelson had sponsors for his participation but felt that he needed to be with his wife and children. He withdrew from the tournament. This is a true balancing dilemma. If Mr. Mickelson played, his wife and children would be without his emotional support. If he did not play, his commitment to his sponsors would be breached. Think about the consequences for others affected when Mr. Mickelson did not play.

Mr. Mickelson did play in the 2010 Masters, where his wife Amy made her first public appearance following her cancer treatments on the 13th hole of the last round. Mr. Mickelson described his win that year as being "for Amy." Think about the lessons you can glean for your own credo from this example.

Discussion Questions

1. Consider the following situations and determine which of the 12 categories each issue fits into.

   a. Vilma Kari, a 65-year-old woman who had come to the United States from the Philippines, was on the streets of New York near Times Square. In the cold, cruel light of day, and unprovoked, a man kicked her in the stomach. She fell to the ground and her assailant then kicked her three times in the head.

He walked away with this parting shot, "You don't belong here." Ms. Kari is so tiny that her attacker seemed to be twice her size.

Three staff members in the lobby of a highfalutin Manhattan apartment complex stood inside and watched the attack but did nothing to help. As Ms. Kari struggled to stand, one of them did take action: He closed the lobby door.

One resident of the building commented after seeing the security camera video of the attack, "I'm not asking them to fight. But when you see someone on the ground who clearly needs help, as a human, our instinct isn't to close the door."[19]

b. A manager at a bank branch requires those employees who arrive late for work to clean the restrooms at the bank. The branch does have a janitorial service, but the manager's motto is "If you're late, the bathrooms must look great." An employee finds the work of cleaning the bathrooms in professional clothes demeaning. Which category/categories apply?

c. Jack Walls is the purchasing manager for a small manufacturer. He has decided to award a contract for office supplies to Office Mart. No one knows of Jack's decision yet, but Office Mart is anxious for the business and offers Jack a three-day ski vacation in Telluride, Colorado. Jack would love to take the trip but can't decide if there is an ethical question. Help Jack decide whether there is and describe the category.

2. In November 2008, golfer J. P. Hayes was participating in the PGA Tour's Qualifying Tournament, often called Q-School. Mr. Hayes, then 42, discovered after the second round of play that he had used a Titleist prototype ball for play that day, a ball not approved for PGA play. After his discovery, Mr. Hayes called a PGA official to let him know what had happened. As he suspected, Mr. Hayes was disqualified from Q-School. Achievement at Q-School results in a type of automatic right to participate in the PGA's top tournaments for the year. Without Q-School status, golfers do not qualify automatically for tournament play and have to take a different path to get into tournaments. The difference in earnings for the year for the golfer who does not qualify at Q-School versus the golfer who does is millions. Mr. Hayes said, "I'm kind of at a point in my career where if I have a light year, it might be a good thing. I'm looking forward to playing less and spending more time with my family. It's not the end of the world. It will be fine. It is fine."[20] What ethical category/categories are involved here? Classify Mr. Hayes under the ethical schools of thought. Describe his credo.

3. Ivan Fernandez Anaya is a world-class runner who stopped short of crossing the finish line in a cross-country race in Burlada, Spain, because he realized that Abel Mutai, who had held a comfortable lead throughout the race, thought he had crossed the finish line but had stopped short (10 yards). His Kenyan not being as good as his Spanish, Ivan motioned and gestured to Abel to cross the finish line ahead of him. Abel caught on, finished first, and Ivan took second place. Ivan's coach said he "wasted an opportunity." Ivan responded, "I did what I had to do. I didn't deserve to win it." Into which categories would you place the ethical issues involved here?

---

[19]Nicole Hong, Juliana Kim, Ali Watkins, and Ashley Southall, "Asian Woman Attacked in City as Others Watch," *New York Times*, March 31, 2021, p. A1.

[20]"Hayes Turns Himself in for Using Wrong Ball, DQ'd from PGA Qualifier," espn.com news, November 23, 2008, http://sports.espn.go.com/golf/news/story?id=3712372. Accessed April 28, 2010.

Our Reasoning Flaws

Reading 1.5

On Rationalizing and Labeling: The Things We Do That Make Us Uncomfortable, but We Do Them Anyway

We see ethical issues around us, and we understand ethics are important. But we are often reluctant to raise ethical issues, or sometimes we use strategies to avoid facing ethical issues. These strategies help salve our consciences. This section covers the conscience strategies: **rationalizations** and avoidance techniques we use to avoid facing ethical issues.

Call It by a Different Name: "Way Harsh" Labels versus Soft Labels/Warm Language

If we can attach a lovely label, often called a **soft label** or **warm language** to what we are doing, we won't have to face the ethical issue. For example, some people, including U.S. Justice Department lawyers, refer to the downloading of music from the Internet as **copyright infringement.** However, many who download music assure us that it is really just the lovely practice of **peer-to-peer file sharing**. How can something that sounds so generous be an ethical issue? Yet there is an ethical issue because copying copyrighted music without permission is taking something that does not belong to you or taking unfair advantage.

To get around a company rule that prohibited salespeople from being reimbursed for entertaining customers at strip clubs, a salesperson referred to the activity as seeking reimbursement for an "adult entertainment venue." The teachers and administrators who were gathering at their homes on the weekends to change student standardized test answers to improve test scores referred to their actions as "having test clean-up parties." Employees charged with stealing company inventory called their actions "making allocation adjustments."

When baseball star Roger Clemens was confronted with lying about steroid use, he denied it, and the language his spokesperson used to explain the statements was that Mr. Clemens "misremembered." When Connecticut Attorney General Richard Blumenthal was confronted with the fact that he had overstated his military service as being in Vietnam when he served in the Marine Reserves only in the United States, he said, "I misspoke." When National Director of Intelligence, James Clapper, was confronted by journalist Andrea Mitchell on what appeared to be a false statement in a hearing before congress he explained, "I responded in what I thought was the most truthful, or least untruthful manner, by saying no."[21] Other euphemisms for lying include "I short-circuited," "I told you versions of the truth," "I was just managing the optics," or "I used incremental escalations of half-truths."

The financial practice of juggling numbers in financial statements, sometimes referred to as **smoothing earnings, financing engineering,** or sometimes just **aggressive accounting** is less eloquently known as **cooking the books**. The latter description helps us see that we have an ethical issue in the category of telling the truth or not leaving a false impression. But if we call what we are doing **earnings management,** then we never have to face the ethical issue because we are doing something that is finance strategy, not an ethics issue. One investor, when asked what he thought about earnings management, said, "I don't call it earnings management. I call it lying." Referring back to the categories helps us to be sure we are facing the issue and not skirting it with a different name.

Rationalizing Dilemmas Away: "Everybody Else Does It"

We can feel very comfortable and not have to face an ethical issue if we simply assure ourselves, "Everybody else does it." We use majority vote as our standard for ethics. Following Maria Sharapova's failed drug test and her admission of taking meldonium, reports emerged that indicated 150 other players were taking the drug as well, thus building the defense of "Everybody does it."

A day-to-day example is "Everybody speeds, and so I speed." There remains the problem that speeding is still a breach of one of the ethical categories: following the rules. Although you may feel the speed limit is too low or unnecessary, your ethical obligation is to follow those speed limits unless and until you successfully persuade others to change the laws because of your valid points about speed limits. One tool that helps us overcome the easy slip into this rationalization is to define the set of *everybody*. Sometimes if we just ask for a list of "everybody," our reasoning flaw becomes obvious. "There's no list," we might hear as a response; "We just know everyone does it." With the speeding example, defining the set finds you in a group with some of the FBI's most wanted criminals, such as Timothy McVeigh, the executed Oklahoma City bomber; Ted Bundy, the executed serial murderer; and Warren Jeffs, the polygamist convicted of being an accessory to rape, all of whom ran afoul of traffic laws while they were at large and were caught because they were stopped for what we do as well: minor traffic offenses.

When "everybody" is doing something, we say that the norm has shifted. Acceptable behavior has moved in a direction upward, in terms of the speed limit. Known as a shifting norm, behavior outside the rules becomes the standard for proper behavior, not the rule itself. However, it is important to understand that if something goes wrong while we are operating in our shifted norm, we may be surprised to learn that the shifted norm will not protect us. For example, if we have an accident while speeding within the accepted, shifted norm for the speed limit, that norm is not what standard we are held to. The rule, the actual speed limit, is applied to our conduct, and one of the causes of the accident can be listed as "excessive speed." When something goes wrong in the shifted norm, hindsight allows the attribution of cause to our falling into the "everybody does it" trap.

---

[21]Glenn Kessler, "Clapper's 'Least Untruthful' Statement to the Senate," *Washington Post,* June 13, 2013, https://www.washingtonpost.com/blogs/fact-checker/post/james-clappers-least-untruthful-statement-to-the-senate/2013/06/11/e50677a8-d2d8-11e2-a73e-826d299ff459_blog.html.

Ethics in Action 1.8

Speeding: Hows, Whys, and Whats

The shifted norm referred to in the readings means that we have an acceptable level of conduct beyond what laws and regulations require. For example, the North Carolina State Troopers have a motto or speeding ticket philosophy that goes, "Nine you're fine; ten you're mine."

On the television show *Speeders*, the camera follows the reaction of drivers who are pulled over for speeding. One woman who was caught speeding on "Alligator Alley," aka I-75, in Florida, asked the officer who had pulled her over what the speed limit was. When he explained that it was 70 mph, she then asked how fast she was going, and the officer responded, "Eighty-five." The woman then exclaimed, "That's not speeding. Look at all these cars going by. They are going faster than that!" She was relying on the **shifted norm** as a defense to exceeding the speed limit.

There are other reasons that we give for speeding:

- I am in a hurry and can get there faster.
- The speed limit is arbitrary and has nothing to do with safety.
- If I don't go with the flow and exceed the speed limit, I present a danger to other drivers.
- It is much easier to just keep up with traffic.
- I like the feeling of speeding.

Think of a response to each of the reasons drivers give for speeding. What are the risks in speeding? Consider who is affected by your speeding.

Ethics in Action 1.9

The Speed Limit Issues and Police Officers

Two police officers were caught on photo radar traveling (in their police cars, but not with sirens on) at 72 and 76 mph. The two officers were issued tickets. The policy of the police department was to require the officers to pay their own tickets when caught speeding on the job (when the sirens are not on, obviously) and to disclose the citations and officers' names to the public. When the media confronted the officers about speeding on the job, one responded, "We thought the speed limit was 65 mph." The speed limit was 65 mph normally in the photo-radar segment of the freeway, but construction work had it reduced to a 55 mph rate.

1. What does the observation of the police officers illustrate about speed limits?
2. What does the officers' behavior do to behavioral norms?

Ethics in Action 1.10

COVID-Shifting Norms

As you think about the example of speeding as part of the officers' work, ask yourself whether in your business or personal life there might be other areas where you are speeding and feel comfortable because the normative standards have shifted. For example, the *Wall Street Journal* had a headline, "Kids Are Cheating in Their Online Work" in 2021 that perhaps reflected the shifted norms of COVID lockdowns.[22]

1. Has working from home or taking courses from home caused you to be more casual about using outside resources when taking exams?
2. Have you been doing what is assigned as individual work with others in your class to make things easier?
3. Would a credo for your academic work or how you work when you are working from home help?

[22]*Wall Street Journal,* December 23, 2020, p. A12

Ethics in Action 1.11

What if I Stopped Speeding?

The following is an e-mail sent to the author at the end of a semester course in business ethics.

> You briefly cited an example of following the traffic laws, and the members of the class took it quite out of proportion, and indeed the general reaction turned out to be one of rationalizing. But something about what you said really caused me to consider that subject and, within those five minutes of discussion, form a resolve. You see, I had always been an exceedingly excessive speeder, to the point where, if caught, I could get in big trouble. This always surprised people to find out about me, but I think it developed in my first year at ASU, when I had an hour commute to campus. Regardless, I terrified everyone but myself. But when you said of speeding, "Is it ethical?" it really took me aback. I looked at the fact of it itself: It is a law to follow the speed regulations, which are in place for safety and order. I looked at myself: someone who wants to be able to be ethical in all things and for all of her life. I realized that if I give room for allowances on what I know is wrong, then how can I know that those allowances won't grow? I could not allow it. And in those five minutes, when the class was going on about photo radar, I grasped an understanding of my speeding that had previously escaped me: It's just not ethical.
>
> It has now been five months from that day, and I can report that for five months I have not exceeded the posted speed limit. It is something of which I am constantly aware, and though I often rely on my cruise control, I have seen that choosing to be ethical has given me strength to overcome other questions and situations. There have also been moments, as simple as that of peacefully coming to a stop at a red light, where I have

been impressed with the thoughts, "That could have been a dangerous situation, but because you chose to follow the standards you are safe." I also notice that, though I may be running late or excited to get somewhere, I just have no desire to speed, and things, occurrences on the road, or actions by other drivers that may have previously upset me have no effect on me, maybe aside from chuckling at a reaction I may have seen myself having before. So I say thank you for your words and lessons, for I have seen a change in myself and a change in my life.

What message does this student have for you? Is she living by a new credo?

Rationalizing Dilemmas Away: "If We Don't Do It, Someone Else Will"

This rationalization is one businesspeople use as they face tough competition. They are saying, "Someone will do it anyway and make money, so why shouldn't it be us?" For Halloween 1994, there were O. J. Simpson masks and plastic knives, and Nicole Brown Simpson masks and costumes complete with slashes and bloodstains. When Nicole Simpson's family objected to this violation of the basic standard of decency, a costume shop owner commented that if he didn't sell the items, someone down the street would. Nothing about the marketing of the costumes was illegal, but the ethical issues surrounding profiting from the brutal murder of a young mother abound.

In the Phoenix, Arizona, area, summer storms can cause significant damage to roofs. Contractors who go to customer homes to give repair estimates are often asked by homeowners to add in other repairs in their insurance claim as "storm-caused damages" even though they were pre-existing. The contractors often explain, "If I don't agree to do that for them, they will just hire another contractor who will put it in as an insurance claim." Although that may be true, it still does not allow the contractor to participate in insurance fraud.

Rationalizing Dilemmas Away: "That's the Way It Has Always Been Done"

When we hear, "That's the way it's always been done," our innovation feelers as well as our ethical radar should be up. We should be asking, "Is there a better way to do this?" Just as "Everybody does it" is not an ethical analysis, neither is relying on the past and its standards a process of ethical reasoning. Business practices are not always sound. For example, the field of corporate governance within business ethics has taught for years that a good board for a company has independent directors, that is, directors who are not employed by the company, under consulting contracts with the company, or related to officers of the company. Independent boards were good ethical practice, but many companies resisted because their boards had always been structured a certain way that they wanted to continue; they'd say, "This is the way our board has always looked." With the collapses of Enron, Adelphia, WorldCom, and HealthSouth and the scandal of substantial officer loans at Tyco, both Congress, through the Sarbanes-Oxley (SOX) Act of 2002 and the Dodd-Frank Act of 2009 and the Securities and Exchange Commission (SEC), through follow-up regulations, now mandate an independent corporate board (See Reading 4.18 "A Primer on Sarbanes-Oxley and Dodd-Frank). When board members performed consulting services for their companies, there was a conflict of interest. But everybody was doing it, and it was the way corporations had always been governed. This typical and prevailing practice resulted in lax corporate boards and company collapses. Unquestioning adherence to a pattern or practice of behavior often indicates an underlying ethical dilemma.

Rationalizing Dilemmas Away: "We'll Wait until the Lawyers Tell Us It's Wrong"

Many people rely only on the law as their ethical standard, but that reliance means that they have resolved only the legal issue, not the ethical one. Lawyers are trained to provide only the parameters of the law. In many situations, they offer an opinion that is correct in that a company's conduct does not violate the law. Whether the conduct

Ethics in Action 1.12

"Colloquial" vs. "Legal"

Actor Jussie Smollett made a report to police that he was attacked in Chicago's Streeterville area by two white men wearing the red caps associated with the Donald Trump campaign. His report alleged that the men had yelled racial and homophobic slurs, poured bleach on him, and wrapped a rope around his neck. The Chicago police investigation concluded that there was no such attack, and Mr. Smollett was charged with allegedly making a false police report.

Cook County State's Attorney, Kim Foxx dismissed the case and Mr. Smollett agreed to do community service. Following that settlement, public outrage resulted in disclosure of Ms. Foxx's contacts with Mr. Smollett's "people."

Ms. Foxx indicated that her office had made the decision and that she had recused herself from the Smollett case because she had communicated with outsiders (representatives for Smollett). When text messages emerged that indicated her continued involvement in the case, including concerns about the number and level of charges, her office explained that when Ms. Foxx said recusal she did not mean it in the "legal" sense, she meant it in the "colloquial" sense.

"Colloquial" means not formal or literary. "Recusal" is a legal term, not a colloquial one. "Recusal" is used by lawyers, judges, and board members, and it means that you step out of the matter: No more participating in discussions, decisions, or voting.

The legal opinion on the issue came from April Perry, the chief ethics officer for Ms. Foxx's office, and Mark Rotert, the chief of the office's Conviction Integrity Unit. Ms. Foxx received the legal opinion but handled the case anyway with Mr. Smollett originally ending the matter with community service. Both Ms. Perry and Mr. Rotert submitted their resignations. The Cook County Inspector General's investigation concluded that the office's sudden dismissal of all charges against Mr. Smollett was improper, and the case was refiled by a special prosecutor outside Foxx's office. Mr. Smollett was later convicted on the refiled charges of making a false police report.[23] He was sentenced to 150 days in Cook County Jail and required to pay $120,106 in restitution for the costs to the city of Chicago for the investigation as well as a $25,000 fine.

1. Apply the appropriate category of ethical dilemma.

2. Without the legal opinion from the ethics, Integrity, and Inspector General officers, was there an ethical lapse?

---

[23]Julia Jacobs and Mark Guarino, "Smollett Guilty In Fake Report Of Hate Crime," *New York Times*, December 10, 2021, p. A1.

they have passed judgment on as legal is ethical is a different question. For example, a team of White House lawyers concluded in a memo in March 2003 that international law did not ban torture of prisoners in Iraq because they were technically not prisoners of war. However, when pictures of prisoner abuse at the Abu Ghraib prison in Iraq emerged, the reaction of the public and the world was very different. The ethical analysis, which went beyond interpretation of the law, was that the torture and abuse were wrong, regardless of their compliance with treaty standards. Following the abuse scandal, the U.S. government adopted new standards for interrogation of prisoners. Although the lawyers were perfectly correct in their legal analysis, that legal analysis did not cover the ethical breaches of interpersonal and organizational abuse.

Rationalizing Dilemmas Away: "It Doesn't Really Hurt Anyone"

We often think that our ethical missteps are just small ones that don't really affect anyone else. We are not thinking through the consequences of our actions when we rationalize rather than analyze ethical issues in this manner. The ethical mind is able to analyze dilemmas by thinking about the effect of their conduct on others; for example, going back to the rule of not taking more than $3.00 of office supplies per quarter. What would happen if every employee took $3.00 of office supplies per quarter? What would be the impact on their companies? What would be the impact on the economy? In ethical analysis, we are turning to Kant and other schools of thought and asking, "What if everyone behaved this way? What would the world be like?"

When we are the sole rubberneckers on the freeway, traffic remains unaffected. But if everyone rubbernecks, we have a traffic jam. All of us making poor ethical choices would cause significant harm. A man interviewed after he was arrested for defrauding insurance companies through staged auto accidents remarked, "It didn't really hurt anyone. Insurance companies can afford it." The second part of his statement is accurate. The insurance companies can afford it—but not without cost to someone else. Such fraud harms all of us because we must pay higher premiums to allow insurers to absorb the costs of investigating and paying for fraudulent claims.

Rationalizing Dilemmas Away: "The System Is Unfair"

Somehow an ethical breach doesn't seem as bad if we feel we are doing it because we have been given an unfair hand. The Ozy Media example (Ethics in Action 1.5) involved young entrepreneurs trying to get noticed and unable to find a financial break-through. So, one of their executives pretended to be someone else in order to break through the system. However, what they did was a false impression—a breach of one of the ethical categories, no matter how unfair the capital markets can be.

Rationalizing Dilemmas Away: "It's a Gray Area"

One of the most popular rationalizations of recent years has been to claim, "Well, business isn't all black and white. There's a great deal of gray." Sometimes the extent of ethical analysis in a business situation is to merely state, "It's a **gray area**," and the response from the group holding the discussion is "Fine! So long as we're in the gray area, we're moving on." In an interview with *Sports Illustrated*, race car driver Danica Patrick was asked, "If you could take a performance-enhancing drug and not get caught, would you do it if it allowed you to win Indy?" She responded, "Yeah, it would be like finding a gray area. In motorsports we work in the gray areas a lot. You're trying to find where the holes are in the rule book."[24]

---

[24]Dan Patrick, "Just My Type," *Sports Illustrated*, June 2, 2009, from http://sportsillustrated. cnn.com/2009/racing/06/02/Danica_PED/index.html. Accessed July 10, 2010. Ms. Patrick has subsequently said she was only kidding in her response.

Famous Lines from Art and Literature

The Working Girl Pretending to Be a Highfalutin Deal-Maker

In the Mike Nichols film, *Working Girl,* Tess McGill plays an administrative assistant trying to break into a financial career. She has gone to night school, graduated with honors, and been denied admission into the company's leadership training program each time she has applied. She then pretends to be her boss while her boss is gone and pulls together a merger deal with a mergers and acquisitions specialist in another firm. Just before the mega-deal is made, her true identity and position in her company are discovered and she explains, "You can bend the rules plenty once you get to the top, but not while you're trying to get there. And if you're someone like me, you can't get there without bending the rules."

However, would those involved in their gray areas change their actions and decisions with the benefit of hindsight or even just more analysis of the issue? There will always be a gray area, but it may be a short-lived strategy. The sophisticated securities that were based on pools of mortgages were easily created, sold, and resold in an unregulated area of the market. But when the mortgages went south, so also did these investments and the companies that had based their strategies for growth on these gray areas (Lehman Brothers and Bear Stearns). Others, such as Goldman Sachs and Citigroup, struggled to recover. Ethical analysis demands more than being satisfied with, "It's a gray area." The following questions help test assumptions about the gray area and help to assess the risk of acting in gray areas:

- Why is it important that it be gray to you?
- Is it legally gray?
- Is it ethically gray?
- Is it a good-faith disagreement?
- What if it's not a gray area?
- What if the gray area ends?
- Does everyone believe it's a gray area?
- Is this my interpretation?
- Am I taking advantage of an unintended loophole?
- Am I avoiding disclosure of relevant information?

Ethics in Action 1.13

COVID-19 Vaccine Line-Cutting by a SoulCycle Instructor

Because pandemics come along once a century, handling the logistics of vaccines can be challenging. When the vaccines for the COVID-19 virus became available, production was just ramping up and the demand in the United States for the vaccine was great. Each state developed its own priorities and distribution plans for the vaccine. In most states, Group 1A included those over the age of 65, first responders, health-care workers, and educators. The terms used to define the priority groups were very general and did leave room for interpretation. Stacey Griffith, a SoulCycle instructor, did some interpretation to fit into that first high priority group. She put on her form for vaccine clearance in Group 1A that she was an "educator."

Ms. Griffith then boasted about her clever ploy and vaccination status on social media. She was promptly lambasted online with one comment being, "If I'm in a line trying to get my fried clam sandwich and some idiot jumps in front of me, I don't like it. It's just the same thing."[25]

The result of line-cutting in many states was that there were vaccine shortages for those intended to be in Group 1A, defined as those most at risk for getting the virus and those whose work was critical in health care and teachers so that the schools could be reopened with them being protected.

Use the questions in the discussion of the gray area to evaluate the ethics of Ms. Griffith in her obtaining the vaccine. Be sure to discuss who was affected by her decision. Apply the schools of ethical thought to reach conclusions on which philosophers would see the action as unethical and those who would see her obtaining the vaccine as just and/or ethical.

Think about the following additional examples of the methods others used to jump ahead of their assigned categories and get the vaccine early.

- Canada had a rugged roll-out of its vaccines. So, Mark Machin, the now former CEO of Canada's government pension plan, one of the world's largest pension funds, flew to the UAE and got his vaccine there. As Canadians struggled and waited in line, a CEO of their pension plan found the time for a round trip to UAE and a shot. When the *Wall Street Journal* reported on the trip, Mr. Machin resigned. Comments from Canadians were filled with the word "trust." If someone will leap-frog ahead of distribution guidelines, just think of the risk involved in having that person in charge of the pension fraud.

- Judges being permitted to step ahead of others and be vaccinated sooner than their category.

- Board members of a medical system getting the vaccine before the system's employees and ahead of their turns by their classification.

- Top executives in corporations traveling to Saudi Arabia to obtain the vaccines as under that country's policies for protecting those who could receive the vaccine included business travelers.

- Hospital systems defining "hospital employees" as all of their employees, even those who did not work in their hospitals.

- Some members of Group 1A shared their 1A vaccine codes with friends and relatives so that they could jump ahead to the 1A vaccination group.

---

[25]Scott Calvert and Cameron McWhirter, "Vaccine Line-Cutters Scrutinized," *Wall Street Journal*, February 8, 2021, p. A6.

Rationalizing Dilemmas Away: "I Was Just Following Orders"

In many criminal trials and disputes over responsibility and liability, many managers will disclaim their responsibility by stating, "I was just following orders." Often called the **"superior orders"** or **"Nuremberg" defense**, the rationalization is "I had no choice," which is a way of transferring conscience and responsibility. While that defense was prominent in the post–World War II war criminal trials, it has emerged in business ethical collapses. When Lehman Brothers collapsed in 2008 because of its substantial holdings in high-risk mortgage pool instruments, many of its fund managers, who were aware of the risks, said, "I have blood on my hands." But they then explained the reason they kept selling the toxic securities even though they were aware of the problems: "They made me do it; I don't have to examine what I did."[26] Following orders does not excuse us from responsibility, both legally and ethically, for the financial harm to those who purchased those toxic securities. Judges who preside over the criminal trials of businesspeople who did what their managers and supervisors asked often remind defendants that an order is not necessarily legal or ethical. Good ethical analysis requires us to question or depart from orders by analyzing the harm or wrong our actions are creating.

Rationalizing Dilemmas Away: "We All Don't Share the Same Ethics"

This rationalization is used quite frequently in companies with international operations. We often hear, "Well, this is culturally acceptable in other countries." We need a bit more depth and a great deal more analysis if this rationalization creeps into our discussions. This statement limits our analysis to the one thing we want to do in a culture. That limit means we do not look at the common values all cultures share. Name one culture where individuals are known to claim, "There is nothing I like better than having a good old-fashioned fraud perpetrated against me," or "I really enjoy being physically abused at work." This rationalization is a failure to acknowledge that there are some common values that demand universal application and consideration as we grapple with our decisions and behaviors around the world. You will never hear anyone, regardless of cultural differences, who says, "Well, we here in [location] readily accept being swindled." This rationalization does not take a hard look at the conduct and whether there are indeed some universal values.

Discussion Questions

1. A recent *USA Today* survey found that 64% of patients in hospitals took towels, linens, and other items home with them.[27] Give a list of rationalizations these patients and their families might use that give them comfort in taking the items.

2. Commercial truckers keep track of their hours on the road through paper logs. The logs were mandated to track the federal maximums for commercial truck drivers. The law places a limit of 70 hours of driving in any eight-day period, followed by a mandated 34-hour rest period. The American Trucking Association indicates that the paper logs allow truckers to drive illegally, that is, beyond the limits, something that creates a safety hazard. What rationalizations would the drivers be using for their violations of the safety standards?

3. A man has developed a license plate that cannot be photographed by the red light and speeding cameras. When asked how he felt about facilitating drivers in breaking the law, he replied, "I am not the one with my foot to the gas pedal. They are. I make a product they can use." What rationalization(s) is he using?

---

[26]Louise Story and Thomas Landon, Jr., "Life after Lehman: Workers Move On," *New York Times*, September 14, 2009, p. BU1.

[27]"Theft a Problem at Hospitals," *USA Today*, March 5, 2010, p. 1A.

4. A parent has instructed his young son to not mention his Uncle Ted's odd shoes and clothing: "If Uncle Ted asks you how you like his clothes or shoes, just tell him they are very nice." His son said, "But that's not the truth, Dad." The father's response was, "It's a white lie, and it doesn't really hurt anyone." Evaluate the father's ethical posture.

Famous Lines from Art and Literature

"You Chose to Get Ahead"

The movie, *The Devil Wears Prada,* follows the story of Andrea (Andy) in her first job as an assistant to the demanding, diabolical, and powerful editor-in-chief of a fashion magazine, Miranda Priestly. When Miranda asks Andy to undermine her colleague, Emily, to get ahead in her job, she does what Miranda asks. Andy later tells Miranda that undercutting one of her loyal editors in his opportunity for a new job was wrong for Miranda to do. Miranda tells Andy that she did the same thing to Emily, and they have the following exchange,

Andy: "That's not what I... no, that was different. I didn't have a choice."

Miranda: "No, no, you chose. You chose to get ahead. You want this life. Those choices are necessary."

This simple exchange is a reminder to step back and analyze each time we are saying, "I was following orders," or "I had no choice." That the choice is difficult (i.e., losing a job) does not change the presence of ethical dilemmas and the impacts our decisions have on others.

Case 1.6

"They Made Me Do It": Following Orders and Legalities: Volkswagen and the Fake Emissions Tests

The EPA issued a complaint against Volkswagen AG (VW) for using a "defeat device" in 482,000 of its cars since 2008 in order to make the cars test clean during emissions testing. The EPA alleged that the company used software that activated the full emissions controls only during testing, but that the rest of the time the cars were running without the emissions controls required under the Clean Air Acted. The effect of the defeat devices was that the cars emitted 40 times the amount of nitrogen oxide permitted under the Clean Air Act. Several research organizations uncovered the alleged devices in their testing and referred the information to the EPA.

Volkswagen admitted that 11 million cars had software installed that allowed emissions control systems to work only during emissions tests and in 2017 paid a $4.3 billion criminal fine to the United States.[28] When the vehicles were being driven on the highways and byways, they were emitting the pollutants of diesel-fueled cars. Volkswagen's CEO resigned, and there were numerous new appointments and realignments that continued into 2016. The head of Volkswagen North America, only in his position for three weeks, resigned.[29] Initially, Volkswagen attributed the emissions issues to "a couple of software engineers" who had been fired with this description, "[Deception] was not a corporate decision; this was something individuals did."[30]

(continued)

[28]William Boston, "Volkswagen Goes After Former CEO," *Wall Street Journal*, March 27-28, 2021, p. B3.

[29]Nathan Bomey, "New Volkswagen North America Chief Winfried Vahland Out after Three Weeks," *USA Today*, October 14, 2015, http://www.usatoday.com/story/money/

cars/2015/10/14/new-volkswagen-north-america-chief-winfried-vahland-out-after-three-weeks/73916418/.

[30]Mike Spector and Amy Harder, "VW's U.S. Chief Apologizes, Says Engineers at Fault," *Wall Street Journal*, October 9, 2015, p. B1.

Case 1.6

(continued)

However, as more details emerged, the story of the emissions software changed substantially. Volkswagen's goal of developing a fuel-efficient diesel engine proved to be elusive. Following years of research, the engineers concluded in 2008 that the two goals were incompatible and began installing the illegal software.[31] In addition, the oft-recited VW goal was to become the #1 car manufacturer in the world by 2018. For example, in 2013, VW's then-CEO Martin Winterkorn told a group of journalists listening to the goal of becoming the #1 car company in the world, "VW won't cut back. We will stay in the fast lane."[32] Another VW officer acknowledged in his testimony before Congress that the cheating may have been triggered by "pressure in the system to get resolutions and also in conjunction with cost pressure as well."[33] A former car company engineer observed, "[A] declared market penetration goal several times the current status can cloud judgments."[34] As a result, the fear of failure found engineers and other employees willing to do things that were dishonest and deceptive in order to meet the goals.[35] One employee wrote in an e-mail, "We won't make it without a few dirty tricks."[36] German prosecutors have alleged that the former CEO may have known about the emissions issue in 2014, earlier than his public statements have disclosed.[37]

Volkswagen's internal investigation revealed that it had "yes-men" who lacked the courage to speak up about issues and problems because of the driven culture. Herbert Diess, Volkswagen's CEO who took over after Mr. Winterkorn left, said that the company had the emissions fraud because of "a combination of too much pressure and lack of a speak-up culture."[38] Though the deception was wrong, the employees were responding to management demands that left them with the impossible task of meeting emission goals and deadlines with no legal way to do so.[39] In conducting an internal investigation of how the "defeat devices" came to be installed, Volkswagen offered amnesty to any employees who came forward with information.[40] Employees who came forward were told they have "nothing to fear from the company in the way of repercussions on the job as being fired or held liable for damages."[41]

Volkswagen entered a guilty plea to criminal charges on the emissions falsification and agreed to pay a $4.3 billion fine.[42] Volkswagen operated under a federal monitor from 2017 through 2020 that required it to reform its ethics and compliance structure and corporate culture to ensure that such wrongdoing would not occur again. (For more information about federal monitors of businesses, see Unit 4.) Volkswagen agreed to a $28 billion civil settlement for those who purchased the emissions-deceptive cars. The U.S. government indicted seven Volkswagen executives, several of whom reported directly to Mr. Winterkorn.[43] German prosecutors charged Mr. Winterkorn and four other executives with defrauding customers.[44]

Discussion Questions

1. What evidence do you see of the "following orders defense"?

2. Explain why employees believed that they had to follow orders and achieve the emissions results by doing whatever it took.

3. What rationalizations were used by those involved and what consequences did they not anticipate?

4. What did Volkswagen not make clear about following orders?

---

[31]Jack Ewing, "VW Engine-Rigging Scheme Said to Have Begun in 2008," *New York Times*, October 5, 2015, p. B1.

[32]Nicola Clark and Melissa Eddy, "Volkswagen's Chief in the Vortex of the Storm," New York Times, Sept. 22, 2015, https://www.nytimes.com/2015/09/23/business/international/volkswagens-chief-in-the-vortex-of-the-storm.html.

[33]*Id.*

[34]Jayne O'Donnell, "Cheating Devices Not Likely Used by Other Carmakers," *USA Today*, September 22, 2015, p. 1B.

[35]Jack Ewing and Graham Bowley, "Volkswagen Sowed Seeds of Forceful Ambition," *New York Times*, December 14, 2015, p. B1.

[36]Jack Ewing, "First Court Case in VW Scandal Is Set to Begin," *New York Times*, September 30, 2020, p. B1.

[37]William Boston, "Former CEO Named in VW Probe," *Wall Street Journal*, January 28–29, 2017, p. B3.

[38]Jack Ewing, "VW Completes Reforms Agreed to in Plea Bargain," *New York Times*, September 15, 2020, p. B3.

[39]William Boston, Hendrik Varnholt, and Sarah Sloat, "VW Says 'Culture' Flaw Led to Crisis," *Wall Street Journal*, December 11, 2015, p. B1.

[40]Jack Ewing and Julie Creswell, "Seeking Information, VW Offers Amnesty to Employees," *New York Times*, November 13, 2015, p. B1.

[41]William Boston, "VW Seeks Whistleblowers," *Wall Street Journal*, November 13, 2015, p. B3.

[42]Jack Ewing and Hiroko Tabuchi, "Volkswagen Set to Plead Guilty and to Pay $4.3 Billion in Deal," *New York Times*, January 11, 2017, p. B1.

[43]William Boston, "Former CEO Named in VW Probe," *Wall Street Journal*, January 28–29, 2017, p. B3.

[44]William Boston, "VW's Ex-CEO Must Stand Trial Over Emissions Scandal," *Wall Street Journal*, September 10, 2020, p. B3.

Reading 1.7

The University of North Carolina: How Do I Know When an Ethical Lapse Begins?

In a profile of the cheating scandal involving bogus courses at the University of North Carolina, also known as UNC, a *Sports Illustrated* writer provided information about UNC's special admits committee, a process used by many universities to admit students with talent in art or music but who did not have the academic credentials. Of the 32 special admits allotted each year, only a dozen were for the artistically gifted with the remainder of the admits being athletes. A vice chancellor explained how the special admits committee process deteriorated, "Every time you thought you had seen a too-marginal case, they'd give you a new excuse: This guy can make it."[45] A professor who sat on the committee and voted in the "no" minority on many of the athletes expressed, "To this day I regret that I didn't blow the whistle right then and there."[46] Once the committee made those decisions, they had athletes they felt their teams needed to be successful who could not perform academically.

With those initial decisions to admit athletes with academic deficiencies, UNC was then faced with this issue: How can we keep them academically qualified to participate in NCAA sports? While many strategies were used, the university eventually devolved into creating nonexistent courses in which the student-athletes earned passing grades for courses that never met and had no content. No one woke up one day at UNC and said, "Fake courses! That's the way to get and keep talented athletes!" There was a slow progression of moving lines and increasing tolerance until the NCAA investigation revealed a culture in which staff, faculty, and the athletic department found ways to help the student-athletes obtain passing grades in their courses. There were examples of the student-athletes going to residences to pick up papers that were required for their classes. One professor "taught" a summer-school course known as a "paper class" that never met but for which grades were awarded, mostly to student-athletes for turning in a paper, a paper done by someone else.

In 2014, the NCAA issued its report on the student-athlete academic advantages noting that their GPAs in paper-only classes were 3.61 whereas their GPAs in classes that required attendance and testing averaged 1.917.[47] In 2009, UNC learned that Deborah Crowder, who was the administrator of the Afro-American Studies Department (AFAM-AFRI) (home of the "paper classes"), was grading the papers because the professor was traveling so much. In addition, Ms. Crowder admitted that although the courses were open to all students she gave student-athletes preferential treatment for enrollment in the courses because of their demanding schedules. The so-called "paper classes" were eventually halted. Ms. Crowder said that the courses were created to provide students with demanding schedules the right to obtain the education they had been promised by UNC.

The academic counselling staff for the football department then held a meeting to discuss the end of their long-term reliance on that department. The content of a PowerPoint slide for that meeting is revealing:

What was part of the solution in the past?

---

[45]S. L. Price, "How North Carolina Lost Its Way," *Sports Illustrated*, March 18, 2015, pp. 66, 67.

[46]*Id.*

[47]Peter Jacobs, "UNC Used an Insane Slide to Defend Fake Classes for Athletes," *Business Insider*, October 13, 2017, https://www.businessinsider.com/ncaa-unc-athletics-slide-fake-classes-sanctions-decision-2017-10.

- We put them in classes that had degree requirements in which
  - They didn't go to class
  - They didn't take notes, have to stay awake
  - They didn't have to meet with professors
  - They didn't pay attention or necessarily engage with the material

- AFAM/AFRI SEMINAR COURSES
  - 20-25 page papers on course topic
  - THESE NO LONGER EXIST!

During its investigation the NCAA found the following paper earned an A- in the course:

> "On the evening of December Rosa Parks decided that she was going to sit in the white people section on the bus in Montgomery, Alabama. During this time blacks had to give up there seats to whites when more whites got on the bus. Rosa parks refused to give up her seat. Her and the bus driver began to talk and the conversation went like this. 'Let me have those front seats' said the driver. She didn't get up and told the driver that she was tired of giving her seat to white people. 'I'm going to have you arrested,' said the driver. 'You may do that,' Rosa Parks responded. Two white policemen came in and Rosa Parks asked them 'why do you all push us around?' The police officer replied and said 'I don't know, but the law is the law and you're under arrest.'"[48]

The solution those at the meeting developed was to ask the AFAM Department to bring back the "paper classes."

After a 3.5-year investigation, the NCAA did not impose sanctions on UNC because "academic fraud" is not within the NCAA's jurisdiction. The only sanctions imposed were related to two employees in the AFAM Department who refused to cooperate in the investigation. Ms. Crowder did cooperate with the NCAA. UNC spent $18 million in legal fees fighting the right of the NCAA to sanction it for failure to monitor academic integrity at UNC. The NCAA rules provide that the individual institutional members have exclusive jurisdiction over monitoring academic fraud. The NCAA has jurisdiction over situations in which the institution offers extra benefits to student-athletes above and beyond the scholarship, housing, and tutoring support permitted under the rules, There was no evidence that student-athletes received academic free-rides that were not also available to other students who registered for the courses.[49]

Discussion Questions

1. Was this a gray area? Was there cheating but the NCAA rules did not fit?

2. Who is affected by this decision by the NCAA?

3. Did the members of the NCAA structure a loophole for themselves in the set-up of the rules and academic fraud?

---

[48]Peter Jacobs and Tony Manfred, "The NCAA Will Not Sanction UNC After an Academic Scandal," *Business Insider*, October 13, 2017, https://www.businessinsider.com/ncaa-unc-athlete-essay-decision-sanctions-2017-10. All errors were in the original paper.

[49]Jeremy Bauer-Wolf, "NCAA: No Academic Violations at UNC," *Inside Higher Ed*, October 16, 2017, https://www.insidehighered.com/news/2017/10/16/breaking-ncaa-finds-no-academic-fraud-unc.

4. UNC's vice chancellor said that the classes were not fraudulent but rather were "lacking professorial oversight with easy grading—akin to an independent study model."[50] What rationalization tactic is the vice chancellor using?

5. Explain the content and significance of the PowerPoint slide.

6. Was there an initial decision that was flawed in this situation? Describe it and why professors allowed it to continue. Why did the professor not blow the whistle?

7. If there had been academic fraud, the NCAA could have imposed the "death penalty" on UNC. Since the NCAA is a trade association paid for by its members, is there a conflict when the NCAA investigates because of its financial support from the success of the schools' sports teams?

Ethics in Action 1.14

The Dean with No College Degree

Marilee Jones, the former dean of admissions of the Massachusetts Institute of Technology (MIT), resigned after 28 years as an administrator in the admissions office. The dean for undergraduate education had received information questioning Ms. Jones's academic credentials. Her résumé, used when she was hired by MIT, indicated that she had degrees from Albany Medical College, Union College, and Rensselaer Polytechnic Institute. In fact, she had no degrees from any of these schools or from anywhere else. She had attended Rensselaer Polytechnic as a part-time nonmatriculated student during the 1974–1975 school year, but the other institutions had no record of any attendance at their schools.

When Ms. Jones arrived at MIT for her entry-level position in 1979, a degree was probably not required. She progress through the ranks of the admissions office, and in 1997, she was appointed dean of admissions. She later explained that she'd wanted to disclose her lack of degrees at that point but that she had gone on for so long that she did not know how to come clean with the truth.

1. Point to the initial decision, why it was flawed, why Ms. Jones made that decision, and what we learn about the importance of truth.

As you think about those questions, there is another piece of important information. MIT was notified about the degree problem by Rensselaer Polytech. The press release on Ms. Jones's appointment as dean of admissions included her inflated academic credentials. Rensselaer was about to capitalize on one of its graduate's achievements. Claiming alums who fare well professionally is a marketing tool for academic institutions. To Rensselaer's dismay, they had no record of Ms. Jones as an admitted student. In ethical analysis, add the risk of public exposure as one of the consequences of false or misleading information.

2. Why did Ms. Jones make that initial decision?

3. Can you list some lines for your credo that you can glean from Ms. Jones's experience?

---

[50] Id.

Analyzing and Resolving Ethical Dilemmas

Reading 1.8

Some Simple Tests for Resolving Ethical Dilemmas

Nearly every business professor and philosopher have weighed in with models and tests that can be used for resolving ethical issues. The following sections offer summaries of the thoughts and models of others in the field of ethics.

Management Guru: Dr. Peter Drucker

An internationally known management expert, Dr. Peter Drucker offers the following as an overview for all ethical dilemmas: **primum non nocere**, which translated means "Above all do no harm." Adapted from the motto of the medical profession, Dr. Drucker's simple ethical test is a short phrase encouraging us to make decisions that do not harm others. This test would keep us from releasing a product that had a defect that could cause injury. This test would have us be fair and decent in the working conditions we provide for workers in other countries. This test would also encourage us to disclose relevant information during contract negotiations. At one time, Johnson & Johnson followed Dr. Drucker's simple approach as the core of its business credo (see Case 8.6).

Laura Nash: Harvard Divinity School Meets Business

Ethicist Laura Nash of the Harvard Divinity School has one of the more detailed decision-making models, with 12 questions to be asked in evaluating an ethical dilemma:

1. **Have you defined the problem accurately?** For example, philosophical questions are often phrased as follows: Would you steal a loaf of bread if you were starving? The problem might be better defined by asking, "Is there a way other than stealing to take care of my hunger?" The rephrasing of the question helps us think in terms of honoring our values rather than approaching the issue from rationalizations to justify taking property from another.

2. **How would you define the problem if you stood on the other side of the fence?** This question asks us to live by the same rules that we apply to others. For example, Donald Trump, during his days as a contractor, once explained that when his employees develop a construction proposal for a customer for a price of $75 million, he simply adds on $50 to $60 million to the price and tells the customer the price is $125 million. Mr. Trump's firm then builds it for $100 million and is praised by the

client for bringing the project under price. Mr. Trump explains that the customer thinks he did a great job when he really did not. If Mr. Trump were on the other side, would he feel the same way about this method he uses for "managing customer expectations"? And note the use of the soft label here. This question forces us to look at our standards in a more universal way.

3. **How did this situation occur in the first place?** This question helps us in the future. We use it to avoid being placed in the same predicament again. For example, suppose that an employee has asked a supervisor for a letter of recommendation for a new job the employee might get if the references are good. The supervisor has always had difficulty with the employee, but has found the employee to be tolerable, has kept the employee on at the company, and has never really discussed any performance issues or even put those concerns in an annual evaluation. Should the supervisor make things up for the letter? Refuse to write the letter? Say innocuous things in the letter such as "X was always on time for work"? This reluctant supervisor is in this situation because the supervisor has never been honest and candid with the employee. The employee is not aware that the supervisor has had any problems or issues; the fact that the employee has asked for the reference shows that there has not been forthright communication.

   This question is a way to look back as we face a dilemma to see those decision points that we missed. By not having the difficult conversation with the employee about improvement in performance, the employee came to believe that a recommendation could be expected. At the heart of this issue was a supervisor giving an employee a false impression about that employee's performance.

4. **To whom and what do you give your loyalties as a person?** Suppose that you discover that your friend's husband is having an affair because you saw him at a hotel with his paramour while you were on vacation in Napa Valley. He saw you and asked that you not tell his wife. You have been a friend to her husband as well. If you tell, you break a promise to that friend. But if you do not tell, you have left your other friend unaware of a painful problem in her marriage. Because you feel loyalty to both perhaps there is a solution that removes you from the painful choice and an either/or conundrum. For example, rather than withholding information, one of the ethical categories, perhaps talking candidly with your friend's husband and encouraging him to be forthright is the best solution for these three friends.

   When you are working in an organization, there are times when your loyalty is torn between that of an employee and your personal ethical standards. For example, a bank manager did not believe that her bank was being forthcoming about the overdraft fees it charged and when they were charged. There were disclosures made to customers but they were lengthy and not clear. The manager felt that the bank was taking unfair advantage of the bank's customers because it would have been easy to show the customers a simple diagram to explain the costs of an overdraft. The manager was torn between personal standards and loyalty to the bank's customers, and yet another competing loyalty to the bank.

   In situations of conflicting loyalties, the bank manager has two choices: (1) Find other employment; or (2) use interpersonal skills

and experience to persuade the bank to change its disclosures.
One of the ironies in this example is that it was a reality in all banks. Because the banks did not voluntarily fix their disclosures, there was litigation and regulation that imposed requirements, including diagrams and examples, on all banks for overdraft disclosures. In 2010, Congress passed the Overdraft Protection Law, and the Federal Reserve and the Comptroller of the Currency promulgated extensive federal regulation that required banks to have customers actually agree to overdraft fees and overdraft fee protection plans following full disclosure of the fees and how they work, complete with diagrams.[52] Silent loyalty sometimes harms the party to whom the silenced employee professes loyalty even as that silence harms the customer relationship. The end result is a sort of lose, lose, lose proposition.

History Repeats

When Ethical Lessons Are Not Learned: Overdrafts, Again

Following new disclosure requirements on overdraft fees, banks followed the rules carefully. However, there were costs associated with compliance with the rules. In addition, banks again saw overdraft fees as a stable, indeed, increasing source of revenues. The result was that overdraft fees steadily increased. In addition, bank customers had disputes over how banks were computing their available balances at the time of their "alleged" overdrafts. Consumers became aware of fairness issues because they were uncertain how banks were computing their balances and even when those balances were being computed. Even with statutory full disclosure, there were still gray areas and with gray areas come litigation. As of 2021, the class-action and individual lawsuits involving overdraft fees were climbing into the ranks of largest class-action suits. Settlements are reaching over $100 million and individual recoveries on theories of balance computation are in the million-dollar range.[51]

[51]*Sallis v. Digital Credit Union*, 349 F. Supp.3d 81; *Liggio v. Apple Federal Credit Union*, (D. Mass. 2018; 835 F.3d 1228 (11th Cir. 2019); Bank of America Summary of Overdraft Litigation, October 21, 2016, https://www.bankofamericaoverdraftsettlement.com/en; Dan Ennis, "Bank of America, TD to Pay a Combined $116.5M to Settle Overdraft Fee Suits," *BankingDive*, May 17, 2021, https://www.bankingdive.com/news/bank-of-america-td-to-pay-a-combined-1165m-to-settle-overdraft-fee-suits/600278/

5. **What is your intention in making this decision?** Often we offer a different public reason for what we are doing as a means of avoiding examination of the real issue. An officer of a company may say that "liberal" accounting interpretations help the company, smooth earnings, and keep the share price stable. But her real intention may be to reach the financial and numbers goals that allow her to earn her bonus. Our motivation for a decision is often a form of clarification for our true motives and insight into the ethical issue. For example, Lordstown Motors released information that it had 100,000 pre-orders for its Endurance, an electric truck.[53] At the time of the release the company needed cash to begin production. As a later board and SEC investigation revealed, the 100,000 pre-orders were not pre-orders but only "pretty binding" and did "not commit counterparties to purchase vehicles." Rather, the company explained they were released to show "a significant

[52]12 C.F.R. §1030 *et seq.*

[53]Ben Foldy and Micha Maindenberg, "Lordstown Executives Exit After Preorders Turmoil," *Wall Street Journal*, June 15, 2021, p. A1.

indicator of demand for the Endurance."[54] There were two different intents and only the demand intent was used to justify the pre-order false impression. The real intention was to raise cash through a securities offering.

6. **How does this intention compare with the likely results?** Continuing with the Lordstown example, the stated intention of trying to raise capital may work for a time, but eventually Lordstown had to face the truth about the company's actual potential for sales. Ironically, not only does the truth emerge but raising capital becomes more difficult because market trust has been dissipated through the false impression of the preorders.

7. **Whom could your decision or action injure?** This is a question for facing facts: Whom could I hurt with what I am about to do? For example, perhaps trying to mimic the art of *Breaking Bad*, two chemistry professors, Terry David Bateman and Bradley Rowland, at Henderson State University in Arkansas, were arrested for allegedly trying to produce methamphetamine in the Reynold's Science Center at Henderson. The building had to be closed because of an odor that turned out to be benzyl chloride. Benzyl chloride can be used to make meth.[55] Professor Bateman went to trial and was found not guilty despite the process for making meth being found on his desk and a safe in his office containing vials of meth. He testified at his trial that those documents with the process were in response to student questions related to *Breaking Bad*. He testified that the safe belonged to Professor Rowland and that he had no idea what was in it. Professor Rowland entered a guilty plea to manufacturing meth and will be paying restitution to Henderson State. Just thinking through the harm can stop the most creative minds consumed with a potential cash cow. The campus, its buildings, the students, and their careers were all potential victims of their sideline careers.

8. **Can you engage the affected parties in a discussion of the problem before you make your decision?** You are selling your home because your neighbors are loud, rude, and relentless partiers. You know that disclosing that information will affect your ability to sell your home and its price. However, making the decision to just explain that you are selling in order to live closer to family is an ethical issue. That reason is not your real motivation. You would not be able to discuss what you are about to say and do with those buyers because you are withholding the truth about your neighbors. If you don't want your boss to know that you are having your nails done during the time that you are working from home, then you have to answer the ethical question of whether you should be having your nails done during working hours. You are giving a false impression about your work hours, withholding information from your boss, and taking pay for hours not worked (something that does not belong to you). These questions also help you return to those basic ethical categories.

---

[54]Dave Sebastian, "Lordstown Clarifies Nonbinding Orders, *Wall Street Journal*, June 18, 2021, p. B3.

[55]Shelby Rose, "Former Henderson State Professor Found Not Guilty to Making Meth on Campus," KATV News, October 27, 2021, https://katv.com/news/local/former-henderson-state-professor-found-not-guilty-to-making-meth-on-campus.

9. **Are you confident that your position will be as valid over a long period of time as it seems now?** Sometimes cheating on an exam or purchasing a paper on the Internet seems to be an expedient way of solving time pressures, financial worries about going to school, or even just the concerns about finishing a semester or a degree. However, this question asks you to think about this small decision over the time frame of your life. When you look back, how will you feel about this decision? For example, Joseph Jett, a Wall Street investment banker was at the heart of a trading scandal at Kidder Peabody that falsified the level of earnings from bond trades. When his credentials, a Harvard MBA, were reported, the fact-checkers in the media seized upon an opportunity. Upon checking with Harvard, the sleuths discovered that although Mr. Jett had finished his coursework at Harvard, he did not have his degree because he had not paid some fees. The fees may have been unpaid parking tickets or perhaps library fines, the types of charges from universities that will travel to your graves with you. What seemed like an expedient budget decision at the time he was a graduate student turned out to be something that harmed Mr. Jett's credibility when he was most in need of a good reputation.[56] Over the long term, your decision might not seem as practical as it did during the pressure crunch of college.

10. **Could you disclose without qualms your decision or action to your boss, your CEO, the board of directors, your family, or society as a whole?** This question asks you to evaluate your conduct as if it were being reviewed by those who run your company. This question also has a second part to it: Could you tell your family? Sometimes we rationalize our way through business conduct or personal conduct but know that if we had to face our families, we would realize we had landed on the wrong side of the ethical decision.

11. **What is the symbolic potential of your action if understood? If misunderstood?** A good illustration for application of this question is in conflict-of-interest questions. For example, during 2021, Andrew Cuomo was the governor of New York and his younger brother, Chris Cuomo, had a news and opinion show on CNN. Chris had engaged in strategy discussions with his brother about handling sexual harassment allegations from 12 women. He did so while he was covering his brother's activities as governor and also had his brother on the show for interviews, even as he was helping with strategy for dealing with the accusations, report, and looming impeachment. Chris Cuomo then made a decision to no longer cover any stories about his brother despite his brother's impeachment being the biggest story in the country for several weeks.

    There was no way to prevent how the public perceived the conflicting activities, even though both men said nothing about them working together on how Andrew Cuomo should manage the media crisis he was facing. There was a perceived conflict just with a journalist interviewing his brother, a controversial political figure. Both the symbolism and actual optics of their being together on television was a problem for their credibility long before their strategy meetings were disclosed.

---

[56]Mr. Jett did pay those fees and was officially awarded his MBA degree by Harvard.

Famous Lines from Art and Literature

In the movie *While You Were Sleeping,* Peter is a wealthy lawyer who has fallen away from his parents' simple values. When his mother learns that Peter is engaged to marry an already married woman, she exclaims, "You proposed to a married woman?" Peter looks very sheepish. What seemed to be a fine decision in the confines of his peers and social life suddenly looked different when his family knew.

12. **Under what conditions would you allow exceptions to your stand?**
   Sometimes as we balance ethical dilemmas we find circumstances that require refinement of strict stands. For example, at a recent open-to-the-public event there was a strictly enforced rule that no bags, backpacks, or purses were permitted unless made of clear plastic. At the entrance a tiny, young girl arrived in a lovely dress carrying a tiny toy purse that she was proud and oh-so-grown-up to have. She also suffered from scoliosis and struggled to walk because she was missing part of her right leg and had a prosthetic device to allow her to walk. If the security guard stopped her and her family because of the purse, their only choice was to walk back to their car, located five blocks away, and put the purse in their car. The security guard said to his partner at the entrance, "I will take full responsibility for this but I am going to let her take in her purse."

   The security guard made an on-the-spot exception because the size of the purse meant there could not be a weapon. His experience had trained him to make assessments and he concluded that this was a family attending a family event. His exception was compassionate, reasonable, and based on his experience. The event experienced no safety problems and was a success.

Ethics in Action 1.15

The Little Girl's Purse and Either/Or

Can you develop an alternative solution that would have allowed the security guard to uphold his standards on honoring the rules but permit his values of compassion and understanding to be given some weight?

A Minister and a One-Minute Manager Do Ethics: Blanchard and Peale

The late Dr. Norman Vincent Peale, an internationally known minister, and management expert Kenneth Blanchard, author of *The One Minute Manager,* offer three questions that managers should ponder in resolving ethical dilemmas: Is it legal? Is it balanced? How does it make me feel?

If the answer to the first question, "Is it legal?" is no, you might want to stop there. Although conscientious objectors are certainly needed in the world, trying out those philosophical battles with the SEC and Internal Revenue Service (IRS) might not be as effective as the results achieved by Dr. Martin Luther King Jr. or Mahatma Gandhi. There is a place for these moral battles, but your role as an agent of a business might not be an optimum place to exercise the Divine Command Theory.

In early 2010, four individuals from the company Wise Guys, Inc., were indicted for wire fraud as well as gaining unauthorized access to computers for their cornering of the ticket markets for the 2006 Rose Bowl, the 2007 MLB playoffs, the play *Wicked*, and concerts for Bruce Springsteen and Hannah Montana.[57] The four had hired Bulgarian programmers to circumvent the controls placed on ticket sites to require entry of data prior to being able to purchase tickets. The result was that the four cornered the primary and, consequently, secondary ticket markets for the events noted. Regardless of how strongly we may feel about having access to tickets, the four were accused of circumventing computer access controls.

Answering the second Blanchard and Peale question, "Is it balanced?" requires a manager to step back and view a problem from other perspectives—those of other parties, owners, shareholders, or the community. For example, an M&M/Mars cacao buyer was able to secure a very low price on cacao for his company because of pending government takeovers and political disruption. M&M/Mars officers decided to pay more for the cacao than the negotiated figure. Their reason was that one day their company would not have the upper hand, and then they would want to be treated fairly when the price became the seller's choice.

Answering "How does it make me feel?" requires a manager to do a self-examination of his or her comfort level with a decision. Some decisions, though they may be legal and may appear balanced, can still make a manager uncomfortable. Although they've done nothing illegal, managers who engage in such practices often suffer such physical effects as insomnia and appetite problems. For example, from 2016-2019, Under Armour, the famed underwear and athletic-wear company, had two CFOs leave the company, with two citing personal reasons. The SEC began investigating the company in 2019 and in 2021 charged the company with inaccurate disclosures in its financial statements by using a tactic of pulling forward future sales to book them before the time customers had asked for goods to be shipped. The former executives have indicated that they departed because of the pressures to meet sales goals. "It was all in the name of hitting the number. They didn't think there was anything improper about it."[58] Sudden executive departures in publicly traded companies are a signal for the SEC. Individuals in the C-suite do not leave their compensation and perks behind unless they are troubled about conduct within the company. Under Armour paid a $9 million fine to settle the issues with the SEC surrounding its accounting and financial statements for the years if 2016-2019.

The Oracle of Omaha: Warren Buffett's Front-Page-of-the-Newspaper Test

This very simple ethical model resulted when Warren Buffett had to step in and manage Salomon Brothers following its illegal cornering of the U.S. government's bond market. During the aftermath of the bond market scandal, as interim chairman of Salomon, Mr. Buffett, told employees, "Contemplating any business act, an employee should ask himself whether he would be willing to see it immediately described by an informed and critical reporter on the front page of his local paper, there to be read by his spouse, children, and friends. At Salomon we simply want no part of any activities that pass legal tests but that we, as citizens, would find offensive."

This simple test requires only that a decision maker envision how a reporter would describe a decision or action on the front page of a local or national

---

[57]Joel Stonington, "Four Charged in Bid to Buy, Resell Tickets," *Wall Street Journal*, March 2, 2010, http://online.wsj.com/article/SB10001424052748703943504575095622582020594.html.

[58]Khadeeja Safdar and Aruna Viswanatha, "Under Armour Pushed To Meet Sales Goals," *Wall Street Journal*, November 15, 2019, p. A1.

newspaper. For example, with regard to the NBC News report on the alleged fires resulting from sidesaddle gas tanks in GM pickup trucks, the *USA Today* headline read, "GM Suit Attacks NBC Report: Says Show Faked Fiery Truck Crash." Would NBC have made the same decisions about its staging of the truck crash if that headline had been foreseen?

A manager of a company came up with a slight variation of the newspaper test by having all of his employees begin every meeting and discussion by asking, "What if the cameras were running? Would we be proud of this discussion or would we be worried?" The purpose of the "What if the cameras were rolling?" test is to have you step back from the business setting in which decisions are made and view the issue and choices from the perspective of an objective outsider.

The Jennings *National Enquirer* Test

Named for its author, the *National Enquirer* test is: "Make up the worst possible headline you can think of and then re-evaluate your decision." In late 2007, when several large investment banking firms had to take multibillion-dollar losses for their excesses in the subprime lending market, the cover of *Fortune* magazine read, "What Were They Smoking?" Such a candid headline turns our heads a bit and forces us to see issues differently because of its metaphorical punch to the gut. Their views and perceptions can be quite different because they are not subject to the same pressures and biases. The purpose of this test is to help managers envision how their actions and decisions look to the outside world. Here are some sample headlines from the past few years that illustrate how to use this test:

"Overstock Chief Resigns a Week After Disclosing His Romance With a Russian Agent," *New York Times,* August 23, 2019, B1.

"Prosecutors Say Two Men Posing as Federal Agents Duped Secret Service," *New York Times,* April 9, 2022.

"Some Cry Foul After de Blasio's Security Detail Helped Daughter Move," *New York Times,* August 23, 2019, A26.

"Novartis Defends Decision to Keep False Data From FDA," *New York Times,* August 8, 2019, p. B6.

"SEC Investigates Ex-Head of Auditing Industry Regulator," *Wall Street Journal,* June 18, 2021, p. B14.

As these headlines illustrate, this simple test requires thinking about the reactions and perceptions of others before engaging in conduct that crosses ethical lines.

The *Wall Street Journal* Model

The *Wall Street Journal* model for resolution of ethical dilemmas consists of three components: (1) Am I in compliance with the law? (2) what contribution does this choice of action make to the company, the shareholders, the community, and others? and (3) what are the short- and long-term consequences of this decision? Like the Blanchard-Peale model, any proposed conduct must first comply with the law. The next step requires an evaluation of a decision's contributions to the shareholders, the employees, the community, and the customers. For example, furniture manufacturer Herman Miller decided both to invest in equipment that would exceed the requirements for compliance with the 1990 Clean Air Act and to refrain from using rain forest woods in producing its signature Eames chair. The decision was costly to the shareholders at first, but ultimately they, the community, and customers enjoyed the benefits of a reputation for environmental responsibility as well as good working relationships with regulators, who found the company to be forthright and credible in its management of environmental regulatory compliance.

The initial consequences for Herman Miller's decisions were a reduction in profits because of the costs of the sustainability changes it made in its products and operations. However, the long-term consequences were the respect of environmental regulators, a responsive public committed to rain forest preservation, and Miller's recognition by *BusinessWeek* as an outstanding firm for 1992.

The impact of Delta CEO Gerald Grinstein's decision not to accept his bonus for bringing the airline through a massive and successful Chapter 11 restructuring had profound effects on both the stock price and the morale of company employees. A decision to accept the perfectly legal bonus could have had adverse consequences that he avoided with his thoughtful decision to forgo a $10 million payment.

Other Models

Of course, there are much simpler models for making ethical business decisions. One stems from Immanuel Kant's categorical imperative (see pp.17–19), loosely similar to the Golden Rule of the Bible: "Do unto others as you would have them do unto you." Treating others as we would want to be treated is a powerful evaluation technique in ethical dilemmas. Another way of looking at issues is to apply your standards in all situations and think about whether you would be comfortable. In other words, if the world lived by your personal ethical standards, would you be comfortable or would you be nervous? This test has proven universal as we compare it in Figure 1.2 with other religions and the views of philosophers:

Figure 1.2

A Possible Uniform Standard for Ethical Choices

Categorical imperative: How would you want to be treated?

Would you be comfortable with a world with your standards?

Christian principle: The Golden Rule

> And as ye would that men should do to you, do ye also to them likewise. (Luke 6:31) Thou shalt love . . . thy neighbor as thyself. (Luke 10:27)

Confucius: What you do not want done to yourself, do not do to others.

Aristotle: We should behave to our friends as we wish our friends to behave to us.

Judaism: What you hate, do not do to anyone.

Buddhism: Hurt not others with that which pains thyself.

Islam: No one of you is a believer until he loves for his brother what he loves for himself.

Hinduism: Do nothing to thy neighbor which thou wouldst not have him do to thee.

Sikhism: Treat others as you would be treated yourself.

Plato: May I do to others as I would that they should do unto me.

Discussion Questions

1. Take the various models and offer a chart or diagram to show the common elements in each.

2. After viewing the chart, make a list of the kinds of things all those who have developed the models want us to think about as we resolve ethical dilemmas. Remember, you are working to develop a 360-degree perspective on issues. Stopping at legality is not enough if you are going to think through all the consequences of decisions. Just because something is legal does not mean it is ethical.

Ethics in Action 1.16

The Ethically Challenged Former Mayor of Baltimore

The now former mayor of Baltimore, Catherine Pugh, streamlined the process authors generally go through for selling books. She has written children's books, known as the Healthy Holly series, that help children learn about healthy living. The books are self-published and Ms. Pugh was able to find bulk purchasers for her books. The former state senator had served on a number of nonprofit boards, and those organizations would purchase large numbers of Healthy Holly books. The University of Maryland Medical System was one of the book purchasers ($500,000 for 100,000 books), and then-Senator Pugh went on to sponsor legislation that would have benefited the System (had it passed). In fairness to Ms. Pugh, there were 9 board members of the System who themselves had contracts with the System. Contracts with the city were awarded closely timed to book sales. Kaiser Permanente purchased $100,000 in books, and then received a $48 million contract from the city. When the information on her book sales emerged, then-Mayor Pugh took an extended leave of absence (for pneumonia).

The entire city council wrote to then-Mayor Pugh asking that she resign because of the book deals. Then-Mayor Pugh issued this bizarre apology: "I sincerely want to say that I apologize that I have done something to upset the people of Baltimore. I never intended to do anything that could not stand up to scrutiny."

During her tenure as mayor, crime rates climbed in Baltimore, along with police resignations. When Ms. Pugh took office, she replaced the former Baltimore mayor who was convicted of embezzlement in 2010. The federal government then began its investigation into Ms. Pugh's conduct.

Catherine Pugh resigned on May 2, 2019. To her credit she said, "I am sorry for the harm that I have caused to the image of Baltimore and the credibility of the office of Mayor. Baltimore deserves a mayor who can move our great city forward."

Catherine Pugh made $800,000 selling her self-published children's health books to those Maryland and Baltimore nonprofits and foundations that could benefit from the mayor's *noblesse oblige* in spreading around city grants and funding to those purchasing the books. Eventually, she was charged with and entered a guilty plea to charges of conspiracy to commit wire fraud, conspiracy to defraud the United States, and two counts of tax evasion. She was sentenced to three years in prison and ordered to pay $411,948 in

(continued)

restitution and to forfeit $669,688 including property in Baltimore and $17,800 from the Committee to Re-elect Catherine Pugh.[59] The government charges painted a picture of a single checking account receiving payments, being used for personal expenses, and financing her campaigns.

At her sentencing Ms. Pugh said, "I apologize for all that has led me here."

1. What did lead her to the point of being sentenced to federal prison? Use what you have studied to pinpoint the decision points that she missed as well as some questions that might have helped her visualize the consequences of her choices.

2. What are the ethical issues in her conduct?

3. Provide the ethical analysis for the nonprofits and foundations in whether they should have purchased the books in exchange for government contracts and grant. Be sure to walk through rationalizations and an analysis of who was affected by her conduct.

---

[59]"Former Baltimore Mayor Catherine Pugh Sentenced to Three Years in Federal Prison for Fraud Conspiracy and Tax Charges," U.S. Department of Justice Press Release, February 20, 2020, https://www.justice.gov/usao-md/pr/former-baltimore-mayor-catherine-pugh-sentenced-three-years-federal-prison-fraud

Reading 1.9

Some Steps for Analyzing Ethical Dilemmas

Although you now have a list of the categories of ethical breaches and many different models for resolution, you may still be apprehensive about bringing it all together in an analysis. Here are some steps to help you get at the cases, issues, and dilemmas from all perspectives.

Steps for Analyzing Ethical Dilemmas and Case Studies in Business

1. Make sure you have a grasp of all of the facts available.

2. List any information you would like to have, but don't, and what assumptions you would have to make, if any, in resolving the dilemma.

3. Take each person involved in the dilemma and list the concerns they face or might have. Be sure to consider the impact on those not specifically mentioned in the case. For example, product safety issues don't involve just engineers' careers and company profits; shareholders, customers, customers' families, and even communities supported by the business are affected by a business decision on what to do about a product and its safety issue.

4. Develop a list of resolutions for the problem. Apply the various models for reaching this resolution. You may also find that as you apply the various models to the dilemma, you see additional insights for questions 1, 2, and 3. If the breach has already occurred, consider the possible remedies, and develop systemic changes so that such breaches do not occur in the future.

5. Evaluate the resolutions of the dilemma for costs, legalities, and impact. Try to determine how each of the parties will react to and be affected by each of the resolutions you have proposed.

6. Make a recommendation on the actions that should be taken.

In some of the cases, you will be evaluating the ethics of conduct after the fact. In those situations, your recommendations and resolutions will center on reforms and perhaps recompense for the parties affected.

Each case in this book requires you to examine different perspectives and analyze the impact that the resolution of a dilemma has on the parties involved. Return to these models to question the propriety of the actions taken in each case. Examine the origins of the ethical dilemmas and explore possible solutions. As you work through the cases, you will find yourself developing a new awareness of values and their importance in making business decisions. Try your hand at a few dilemmas before proceeding to the following sections. The following diverse cases offer an opportunity for application of the materials from this section and give you the chance to hone your skills for ethical resolutions.

Reading 1.10

A State of the Union on Cheating: Recognizing the Types and Scope of Cheating — Plagiarism

Plagiarism is easier than ever now with materials just a cut-and-paste away on the Internet. With the presence of Facebook, YouTube, Instagram, and other similar sites, we have become accustomed to posting, sharing, copying, and passing along. In a way, information has become a shared commodity. Norms for use of others' materials have shifted. (See Reading 1.5). However, the use of others' materials from the Internet without attribution in our academic work is taking what does not belong to us and gives a false impression about our skills and knowledge being tested through our writing and research. It is important to understand where the line is in doing writing for academic purposes.

Consider the following source and three ways that a student might be tempted to make use of it:

Source: "The joker in the European pack was Italy. For a time hopes were entertained of her as a force against Germany, but these disappeared under Mussolini. In 1935, Italy made a belated attempt to participate in the scramble for Africa by invading Ethiopia. It was clearly a breach of the covenant of the League of Nations for one of its members to attack another. France and Great Britain, as great powers, Mediterranean powers, and African colonial powers, were bound to take the lead against Italy at the league. But they did so feebly and half-heartedly because they did not want to alienate a possible ally against Germany. The result was the worst possible: the league failed to check aggression, Ethiopia lost her independence, and Italy was alienated after all."[60]

Version A: Italy, one might say, was the joker in the European deck. When she invaded Ethiopia, it was clearly a breach of the covenant of the League of Nations; yet the efforts of England and France to take the lead against her were feeble and half-hearted. It appears that those great powers had no wish to alienate a possible ally against Hitler's rearmed Germany.

Comment: Clearly plagiarism. Though the facts cited are public knowledge, the stolen phrases aren't. Note that the writer's interweaving of his own words with the source's does not render them innocent of plagiarism.

Version B: Italy was the joker in the European deck. Under Mussolini in 1935, she made a belated attempt to participate in the scramble for Africa by invading

---

[60]J. M. Roberts, *History of the World* (New York: Knopf, 1976), p. 845.

Ethiopia. As J. M. Roberts points out, this violated the covenant of the League of Nations (J. M. Roberts, *History of the World* [New York: Knopf, 1976], p. 845). But France and Britain, not wanting to alienate a possible ally against Germany, put up only feeble and half-hearted opposition to the Ethiopian adventure. The outcome, as Roberts observes, was "the worst possible: the league failed to check aggression, Ethiopia lost her independence, and Italy was alienated after all" (Roberts, p. 845).

Comment: Still plagiarism. The two correct citations of Roberts serve as a kind of alibi for the appropriating of other, unacknowledged phrases. But the alibi has no force: Some of Roberts's words are again being presented as the writer's.

Version C: Much has been written about German rearmament and militarism in the period 1933–1939. But Germany's dominance in Europe was by no means a foregone conclusion. The fact is that the balance of power might have been tipped against Hitler if one or two things had turned out differently. Take Italy's gravitation toward an alliance with Germany, for example. That alliance seemed so very far from inevitable that Britain and France actually muted their criticism of the Ethiopian invasion in the hope of remaining friends with Italy. They opposed the Italians in the League of Nations, as J. M. Roberts observes, "feebly and half-heartedly because they did not want to alienate a possible ally against Germany" (J. M. Roberts, *History of the World* [New York: Knopf, 1976], p. 845). Suppose Italy, France, and Britain had retained a certain common interest. Would Hitler have been able to get away with his remarkable bluffing and bullying in the later 1930s?

Comment: No plagiarism. The writer has been influenced by the public facts mentioned by Roberts, but he hasn't tried to pass off Roberts's conclusions as his own. The one clear borrowing is properly acknowledged.[61]

Discussion Questions

1. List the important tools you have learned from this reading that will help you during your education.

2. List those affected by plagiarism.

3. Are there some additions you could make to your credo based on this instruction?

4. Make a list of what students gain through plagiarism. Make a list of the risks. Make a list of what students forgo when they engage in plagiarism.

Case 1.11

The Little Teacher Who Could: Piper, Kansas, and Term Papers

Piper High School is in Piper, Kansas, a town located about 20 miles west of Kansas City, Missouri. Christine Pelton was a high school science teacher there. Ms. Pelton, age 26, had a degree in education from the University of Kansas and had been at Piper for two years. She was teaching a botany class for sophomores, a course that included an extensive project as part of the course requirements. The project, which included a lengthy paper and creative exhibits and illustrations, had been part of the curriculum and Piper High School tradition for 10 years. Students were required to collect 20 different leaves, write one or two paragraphs about the leaves, and then do an oral presentation on their projects.

(continued)

---

[61]Quoted from Frederick Crews, *The Random House Handbook*, 6th ed. (New York: McGraw-Hill, 1992), pp. 181–183.

Case 1.11

(continued)

When Ms. Pelton was describing the writing portion of the project and its requirements to her students, she warned them not to use papers posted on the Internet for their projects. She had her students sign contracts that indicated they would receive a "0" grade if they turned in others' work as their own. The paper counted for 50% of their grade in the course.

When the projects were turned in, Ms. Pelton noticed that some of the students' writing in portions of their papers was well above their usual quality and ability. Using an online service called Turn It In (http://www.turnitin.com), she found that 28 of her 118 students had taken substantial portions of their papers from the Internet.[62] She gave the students a "0" grade on their term paper projects. The result was that many of the students would fail the semester in the course.

The students' parents protested. Several of the parents noted that there was no explanation in the Piper High School handbook on plagiarism. They also said that the students were unclear on what could be used, when they had to reword, and when quotations marks were necessary. Other parents complained about Ms. Pelton's inexperience. One teacher said, "I would have given them a chance to rewrite the paper."

In response, both her principal, Michael Adams, and the school district superintendent, Michael Rooney, supported her decision. However, the parents appealed to the school board, and the board ordered Ms. Pelton to raise the grades. Mr. Rooney, acting at the board's direction, told Ms. Pelton that the board's decision was that the leaf project's weight should be changed from 50% to 30% of the course's total semester grade, and that the 28 students should have only 600 points deducted from their grade rather than the full 1,800 points the project was originally worth.

Ms. Pelton said, "I was really shocked at what their decision was. They didn't even talk to me or ask my side."[63] The result was that 27 of the 28 students

avoided receiving an "F" grade in the course, but the changed weight also meant that 20 of the students who had not plagiarized their papers got a lower grade as a result. She resigned in protest on the day following the board's decision. She received 24 job offers from around the country following her resignation. Mr. Adams, the principal, and one teacher resigned at the end of the year to protest the lack of support for Ms. Pelton. Mr. Adams cited personal reasons for his resignation, but he added, "You can read between the lines."[64] At the time of Ms. Pelton's experience, 50% of the teachers had indicated they would resign. The superintendent, Michael Rooney, remained and said he stood by the teacher but did not think that the school board was wrong: "I take orders as does everyone else, and the Board of Education is empowered with making the final decisions in the school district."[65]

The board had debated the case in executive session and refused to release information, citing the privacy rights of the students. The local district attorney for Wyandotte County, Nick A. Tomasik, filed suit against the board for violating open meetings laws. Citizens of Piper began a recall action against several of the school board members. The local chapter of the National Education Association, representing the 85 teachers in the district, was brought into settlement negotiations on the suit because of its concerns that action that affects teachers can be taken without input and without understanding the nature of the issues and concerns.

The fallout for Piper has been national. *Education Week* reported the following as results of the actions of the students and the school board:

All 12 deans of Kansas State University signed a letter to the Piper school board that included the statement, "We will expect Piper students ... to buy into [the university's honor code] as a part of our culture."

Angered, Piper school board member James Swanson—who is one of the targets of the recall drive—

(continued)

---

[62]Another program that can be used is http://www.mydropbox.com.

[63]"School Board Undoes Teacher's F's," *Wichita Eagle*, January 31, 2002, http://www.kansas.com/mld. The original site for the article is no longer available. However, similar quotes from Ms. Pelton can be found at http://www.mskennedysclass.com/Plagiarism_Controversy_Engulfs_Kansas_School.pdf. Accessed August 23, 2013.

[64]Andrew Trotter, "Plagiarism Controversy Engulfs Kansas School," *Education Week*, April 3, 2003, http://www.edweek.org/ew/articles/2002/04/03/29piper.h21.html.
[65]Id.

Case 1.11

(continued)

wrote to the university to note that the implication that Piper students might be subject to greater scrutiny because of one controversial incident involving only 28 students was unfair. He received an apology from university officials.

More troubling to the community, Piper students have also been mocked. At an interscholastic sporting event involving Piper, signs appeared among the spectators that read "Plagiarists."

Students have reported that their academic awards, such as scholarships, have been derided by others. And one girl, wearing a Piper High sweatshirt while taking a college entrance exam, was told pointedly by the proctor, "There will be no cheating."[66]

Both the school board and the principal asked Ms. Pelton to stay, but she explained, "I just couldn't. I went to my class and tried to teach the kids, but they were whooping and hollering and saying, 'We don't have to listen to you any more.'"[67] Ms. Pelton began operating a day care center out of her home.

A senior from the Piper, Kansas, school told CBS News, "It probably sounds twisted, but I would say that in this day and age, cheating is almost not wrong."[68]

Almost one year later the school board adopted guidelines on plagiarism for use in the district's school as policy. The Center for Academic Integrity gave its Champion of Integrity Award for 2002 to Ms. Pelton and

Mr. Adams.

The center's criteria for this award are that the teacher or administrator took:

1. An action, speech, or demonstration that draws attention to a violation of academic integrity.

2. An action that, in an attempt to promote or uphold academic integrity, may subject the nominee to reprisal or ridicule.

3. An action motivated by commitment to and conviction about the importance of academic integrity and not by public acclaim or monetary gains.[69]

Discussion Questions

1. Do you believe the students understood that what they did was wrong? Why is this information important in your analysis?

2. Was the penalty appropriate?

3. What do you think of the grading modifications the board required? Be sure to list those who were affected by their decision when you answer this question.

4. What did the parents miss in their decisions to intervene?

5. Evaluate the statement of the senior that cheating is no longer wrong.

6. What were the consequences for Piper and the students?

Source: Jodi Wilgoren, "School Cheating Scandal Test a Town's Values," *New York Times,* February 14, 2002, pp. A1, A28.

---

[66]Trotter *Id.*

[67]*Id.*

[68]Leonard Pitts, Jr., "Your Kid's Going to Pay for Cheating—Eventually," June 21, 2002, http://www.jewishworldreview.com/0602/pitts062102.asp. Accessed July 20, 2010.

[69]This statement no longer appears on the Center for Academic Integrity's website. However, the late Professor McCabe's decades of work can be reviewed at http://www.business.rutgers.edu/tags/332. Accessed November 1, 2013. There is still similar information available at the Center for Academic Integrity's website: http://www.academicintegrity.org/icai/home.php.

Reading 1.12

A State of the Union on Cheating: Academic Data and Examples

A 2017 Kessler International Survey revealed the following data on college cheating:

- 86% of students say they have cheated in some way
- 54% of students said cheating is okay because it is necessary to compete

- 97% of cheaters say they have never been caught
- 76% have copied word-for-word someone else's assignment
- 12% said they would never cheat because of their ethics
- 42% purchased papers, theses, etc.
- 28% paid to have someone take their online courses
- 72% have used phones, tablets, and/or computers to teach.[70]

The annual Rutgers University survey on academic cheating reveals that 15% of college papers turned in for grades are completely copied from the Internet. In a look at Internet papers, the New Jersey Bar Foundation found the following:

> A Rutgers University survey of nearly 4,500 high school students revealed that only 46 percent of the students surveyed thought that cutting and pasting text directly from a Web site without attributing the information was cheating, while only 74 percent of those surveyed thought that copying an entire paper was cheating. Donald McCabe, the Rutgers University researcher that conducted the survey told USA Today, "In the students' minds what is on the Internet is public knowledge."[71]

> From 2019-2021, the anecdotal evidence of academic cheating seemed to ripen into statistical evidence as the following examples illustrate.

The U.S. Naval Academy Cheating Scandals

The U.S. Naval Academy expelled 18 midshipmen for cheating on an online physics exam. Another 82 entered a five-month remediation program for violation of the academy's "Honor Concept." Four were found not guilty of any violations and one is awaiting final determination. That's 105 midshipmen out of a class of 653.[72] The investigation checked their browsing histories and found that they had visited websites with lovely physics problems solutions during the time of their exam. The most interesting part of the story is that it was not a coordinated effort. The midshipmen all acted as sole operators.

This cheating scandal was the largest since 1974 when 125 midshipmen were disciplined for cheating by obtaining advance information and answers for an engineering exam.

West Point – The U.S. Military Academy

At the U.S. Military Academy (West Point), 73 "plebes" (cadets in their first year) were accused of cheating on their calculus exam. The scandal was uncovered as faculty graded the exams and found that all of the cadets charged had uncannily used the same steps in their work for arriving at their answers. The exam was held online during the pandemic lockdowns. When questioned, 59 of the 73 admitted that they had cheated. Six resigned and left West Point, four were acquitted by their peers, eight were expelled, two had the charges dropped because of insufficient evidence. And the remainder entered the wilful-admissions process. Under that

---

[70]Susan Portman, "Addressing Cheating in Online Testing," *Moving Forward Together,* June 15, 2020, https://collaborativemomentum.com/2020/06/15/addressing-cheating-in-online-testing/.

[71]New Jersey State Bar Foundation, http://www.njsbf.com/njsbf/student/eagle/winter03-2.cfm. Accessed July 20, 2010.

[72]Talal Assari, "Midshipmen Are Expelled Over Cheating," *Wall Street Journal,* August 8, 2021, p. A3.

process the greatest penalty is graduating a year later but by agreeing to complete a supervised program they cannot be dismissed from the academy.

The scandal was the largest one since 1976 when 153 upperclassmen cheated on an electrical engineering exam. Of the 153 that were caught, 90 were re-admitted and permitted to finish their degrees.[73] West Point had an informal "second chance" program that was codified in 2015. The program permitted cadets to return to West Point after violating the honor code and, after repeating a year, could graduate and become officers. The program ended in 2020 after the Internet cheating scandal because of heavy criticism for its leniency.[74]

All of the cheating scandals at the military academies have involved student athletes.

Discussion Questions

1. Are the data and anecdotal evidence consistent?
2. Do you think there is a correlation between the subject matter and cheating?
3. What correlations do you see among the discussion of cheating and cheating scandals?
4. What is the effect of the Internet on cheating?

Case 1.13

Dad, the Actuary, and the Stats Class

Joe, a student taking a statistics course, was injured by a hit-and-run driver. The injuries were serious, and Joe was on a ventilator. Although Joe did recover, he required therapy for restoring his cognitive skills. He asked for more time to complete his course work, but the professor denied the request. Joe would have to reimburse his employer for the tuition for the course if he did not complete the course with a passing grade. Joe's father works with stats a great deal. Joe's father took the course final for Joe, and Joe earned an "A" in the course.

Discussion Questions

1. What category(ies) of ethical dilemma is involved in this scenario?
2. What school of ethical thought does Joe's father follow?

3. Was Joe's father justified in helping Joe, an innocent victim in an accident? Does your answer change if you learn that Joe's father is an actuary?
4. List those who are affected by Joe's father's actions.
5. Can you think of alternatives to Joe's father's solution that would get him out of the either/or conundrum?
6. Evaluate the systemic effects if everyone behaved as Joe's father did.
7. What effects do emotions and feeling have on ethical analysis?

---

[73]Michael Hill, "51 West Point Cadets Caught Cheating Must Repeat a Year," *ArmyTimes*, April 18, 2021, https://www.armytimes.com/news/your-army/2021/04/18/51-west-point-cadets-caught-cheating-must-repeat-a-year/.

[74]Ed Shanahan, "West Point Scraps Second-Chance Program After Major Cheating Scandal, *New York Times*, April 16, 2021, https://www.nytimes.com/2021/04/16/nyregion/west-point-cheating-scandal.html.

Case 1.14

Cheating: Culture of Excellence

High School Cheating: A Case Study at a First-Rate High School

Stuyvesant High School is an elite New York City high school that the "best of the best" high school students attend. Stuyvesant is ranked as the best of nine free public schools in New York City that admit students on the basis of their scores in the Specialized High Schools Admissions Test (SHSAT). The students are counseled and groomed for admission into elite colleges and universities. They also know that their grades are key determinants in getting into those schools. Stuyvesant's website posts scores of students who got into certain schools, along with their SAT scores and averages. As a result, one student described it as follows: "It became a numbers game. It was kind of addictive in a bad way, in a sick way. People will assume, well, I have a 92, most kids who got into that school got a 94, so there's no way I can get in."[75]

As a result, 80% of the students at the high school indicated that they had cheated in some way while at the school, including copying homework from a Facebook site, tipping off classmates who were taking an exam in the same class later in the day, hiding formulas in sleeves or bathroom stalls and then using a restroom break to get that information, Googling questions and getting information on an iPhone (such as facts for history or a formula they had forgotten for math), and taking photos of test questions for their friends.[76]

In a bizarre way, the competitive students developed a sort of cheating cooperative in which they shared answers, workload, and talents in order to get the GPA numbers that they needed for elite colleges and universities. For example, they had tapping systems worked out for signaling each other answers on exam questions during the test.

Copying homework did not carry any disciplinary actions and that's why the students felt free to post the assignments on Facebook. Students also noted that they cheated because it was a way to get into the college or university they wanted and that they could then return to ethical behavior once they reached that goal. *New York Magazine* referred to this attitude as the practice of "cheating upwards."[77]

As a result of the cheating culture, the students at Stuyvesant also cheated on their Regents exams, something that was picked up by test administrators. Those who were strong in math and physics helped their friends on those subjects on the New York State Regents Exams, whereas those weak in math and physics helped out their friends who were weak in English and foreign languages. One student said, "The lines did get a little blurry."[78] Another student said, "It's seen as helping your friend out. If you ask people, they'd say it's not cheating. I have your back, you have mine."[79]

Seventy-one Stuyvesant students were accused of cheating on their Regents exams, but many of the students had already been admitted to elite colleges and universities, and there would be no penalty for them. The Regents exam cheating took place by the simple act of one student, Nayeem Ahsan, typing the questions into his iPhone and sending them along to other students. Other students used their iPhones to send messages asking for verification of answers while they were taking the tests. Nayeem sent exam questions he had typed in via text message to 140 students. When he was caught, the penalty was his expulsion from Stuyvesant. He commented, "I didn't know I could have gotten kicked out of Stuy if I pulled this off. That was never made clear to me."[80] There was an online petition from his fellow Stuy students in support of keeping him at Stuy, part of which included this comment: "There's a lot of people that do a lot worse in Stuy. There's people that smoke weed, people that do drugs. True, it's unethical, it's an extreme breach of academic integrity, and

(continued)

---

[75]Vivian Yee, "Stuyvesant Students Describe the How and Why of Cheating," *New York Times*, September 26, 2012, p. A1.

[76]James Marshall Crotty, "Stuyvesant High School Has a Cheating Problem. Here's How to Fix It," *Forbes*, September 29, 2012, http://www.forbes.com/sites/jamesmarshallcrotty/2012/09/29/new-yorks-elite-stuyvesant-high-school-has-acheating-problem-heres-how-to-solve-it/.

[77]Robert Kolker, "Cheating Upwards," *New York Magazine*, September 16, 2012, http://nymag.com/news/features/cheating-2012-9/.

[78]Yee, *supra* note 79.

[79]Id.

[80]Robert Kolker, "Cheating Upwards," *New York Magazine*, September 16, 2012, http://nymag.com/news/features/cheating-2012-9/.

Case 1.14

(continued)

it's at an elite school. It is bad, but I don't get how kicking you out would help anything."[81]

Discussion Questions

1. One student said that the lines got "blurry" and that's why they cheated. What did the student mean, and what have you read in Unit 1 that might help this student with his take on the situation at the school?

2. Is it possible to act unethically to reach a goal and then change behaviors once the goal is reached?

3. Find the flaws in the students' comments. That is, point out using the structured approach you have been given the flaws in their analysis that minimize the effects of cheating.

4. What advice would you give to the administrators of the school in order to help them curb cheating?

---

[81]*Id.*

Reading 1.15

A State of the Union on Cheating: Puffing on Your Résumé and Job Application and in Your Job Interviews

The résumé is a door opener for a job seeker. In theory, what's on it can get you in the door or cause the door to be slammed in your face. A 2012 survey by the American Institute of Certified Public Accountants (AICPA) found that 54% of résumés contain false information and that 70% of college graduates' résumés contain false information.[82] Those numbers seemed quite high at the time. However, it seems that a new type of rationalization has crept into the whole job application/ résumé process. While there may be lying going on, both job applicants and HR directors have created the standard of "white lies." That is, the line for what is acceptable as "puffing" your résumé has moved considerably.

A 2020 study conducted by Checkster surprised even the data gatherers because they were not sure whether respondents would be candid about lying on their résumés. However, their study showed that 78% of job applicants say that they "fudge" in their résumés, applications, and job interviews.[83] Investopedia puts the number at 50%, but that 50% number appears to be the floor among all the recent surveys.[84] The most likely to lie on their résumés? College students—at 92%.[85] The types of "fudges" include:

- 60% listed mastery of a skill while actually having only basic knowledge (second language, Excel)

- 42% fabricated relevant experience

---

[82]"Skeletons in Closet Need Not Apply," http://www.cpai.com/risk-management/employergard/resume-fraud.jsp.

[83]Maura C. Ciccarelli, Résumés, Lies, and Repercussions, *Human Resource Executive*, March 6, 2020. https://hrexecutive.com/resumes-lies-and-repercussions/

[84]Janet Fowler, "How Lying On Your Résumé Will Get You in Trouble," *Investopedia*, August 8, 2021, https://www.investopedia.com/financial-edge/0912/how-lying-on-your-resume-will-get-you-in-trouble.aspx.

[85]Rebecca Lake, "Beware: 23 Résumé Falsification Statistics," *CreditDonkey*, May 26, 2015, https://www.creditdonkey.com/resume-falsification-statistics.html

- 45% lied about their reasons for leaving a previous job
- 39% lied about where their degrees were from (using the name of a prestigious university or college instead of their own)
- 41% lied about their level or title at their previous job, e.g., claimed "director" status when they had only reached "manager" level

Is the line moving because perhaps employers receiving the false information do not see "white lies" and larger lies as grounds for rejecting a candidate. If a manager discovered that an applicant had "inflated résumé claims", the following percentages show the effects on decisions about the inflating candidate:

- 3% would always hire the candidate despite the inflated information
- 15% would hire if those in HR approved
- 14% would hire if they cannot find other candidates
- 36% would never hire
- 31% would hire if there is a good explanation for the inflation

Without consequences, norms do shift (See Reading 1.5), and the norms in hiring appear to have shifted away from falsification being a deal killer to maybe, sometimes, and always hire. In a different survey, 79% of those who admitted to putting false information on their résumés said nothing happened. Just 14% said they were caught and nothing happened. Only 7% were caught and experienced consequences.[86] The lack of enforcement of standards does cause standards to slip and norms to shift. Perhaps companies are not placing a high priority on ethics and that attitude is reflected in the hiring process.

What We Don't Like to Put in Our Résumés

Ed Andler, an expert in credential verification, says that one-third of all résumés contain some level of "creative writing." Mr. Andler notes that assembly-line workers don't mention misdemeanor convictions, and middle managers embellish their educational background. One reference-checking firm looked into the background of a security guard applicant and found he was wanted for manslaughter in another state. Executives also manage to remove bad management experiences from their credentials. Al Dunlap, the former CEO of Sunbeam who was forced to resign his position there when questions were raised about the company's accounting practices, omitted from his résumé his employment as president at Nitec Paper, where he resigned after the owner accused Mr. Dunlap of inflating the company's inventory.

How Easy Is It to Find out False Information in Résumés?

Vericon Resources, Inc., a background check firm, has found that 2% of the applicants they investigate are hiding a criminal past. Vericon also notes, however, that potential employers can easily discover whether job candidates are lying about previous employment by requesting W-2s from previous employers.

In one "résumé-puffing" case, according to Michael Oliver, a former executive recruiter and one-time director of staffing for Dial Corporation, there was a strong candidate for a senior marketing management position who said he had an MBA from Harvard and four years' experience at a previous company where he had been a vice president of marketing. Actually, a few quick phone calls uncovered that Harvard had never heard of him; he had worked for the firm for only two years; and he had been a senior product manager, not a vice president.

---

[86]Maria Vultaggio, "Everyone Lies on Their Résumés, Right?" *statista.com*, March 3, 2020, https://www.statista.com/chart/21014/resume-lie-work-jobs/.

Ethics in Action 1.17

His Daughter in the Hospital? That Crosses a Line

Grayson, Inc. had been looking for an analyst to fill a critical void in its strategy team. They had hired one analyst who was hired away by a competitor just two weeks after he had started his employment. Finally, the strategy team had found a qualified analyst who interviewed well and was able to tackle the sample analytical projects given to him during the interview. However, his background check revealed that he had been to prison for a felony following a guilty plea and that he had tested positive for marijuana at his previous job. When the strategy team followed up with the candidate about these issues, he explained that he had been to rehab, that he was now married, and working hard daily to turn his life around. The team and HR approved his being hired. After the new analyst had been on the job for eight days, he called in and said that his daughter had been hospitalized and that he would have to be gone for two weeks. The head of the strategy team had his assistant call the hospital to check. The story checked out—there was a child in the hospital with the new employee's last name. The head of the strategy team told his team, "Give him a week. If he is not back, he's gone."

1. Discuss whether the hiring decision was a good one. Is there a risk in hiring someone who fails to disclose this type of material information?

2. Does a tight job market and necessary skill set trump concerns about background and ethics?

3. Was calling the hospital to verify the story about the daughter ethical?

4. Was there another way to handle verification of the story?

5. Was the one-week deadline an appropriate resolution of the situation?

6. List all of the categories of ethical dilemmas in the scenario, the decision points, the responses of the parties, and the consequences for others.

Executives and False Résumés

A *Wall Street Journal* analysis of the credentials of 358 executive and board members at 53 publicly traded companies found discrepancies between their background/experience and reality in seven of the executives'/board members' claims, most dealing with them claiming to hold MBAs when they did not.[87]

The problems with résumés in the executive suite have been steady. *Business publications* documents the following examples:

Company	Executive	Title	Problem
Bausch & Lomb	Ronald Zarrella	CEO	No claimed MBA
RadioShack	David Edmondson	CEO	Inflated degrees
MGM Mirage	J. Terrence Lani	CEO	Questions about degrees

[87]Keith J. Winstein, "Inflated Credentials Surface in Executive Suite," *Wall Street Journal*, November 13, 2008, p. B1.

Herbalife	Gregory Probert	COO	Embellished degree
Veritas	Kenneth Lonchar	CFO	Claimed having an MBA but had no MBA
A. T. Kearney	Gene Shen	CEO	Exaggerated academic credentials and work experience
CSX	Clarence Gooden	CCO	Misrepresented academic credentials[88]
Abbott	Richard A. Gonzalez	Almost CEO—AbbVie	Claimed BS from University of Houston and master's from University of Miami; had no degrees[89]
Notre Dame	George O'Leary	Head football coach	Exaggerated accomplishments as football player at University of New Hampshire; claimed master's degree
Mylan	Heather Bresch	CEO	Falsely claimed MBA[90]
Veteran's Administration	Robert A. McDonald	Secretary of the VA	Claimed to have served in Special Forces[91]
U.S. Senate	Richard Blumenthal	Senator, Connecticut	Lied and/or misrepresented serving in Vietnam when he took military deferments from 1965-1970 to avoid going to war and served in 1970 in the Marines Reserves—his unit fixed a campground and organized Toys for Tots drives
U.S. Senate	Elizabeth Warren	Senator, Massachusetts	Claimed Cherokee indigenous status in her job and bar applications since 1986; DNA testing revealed the same level of Native American DNA as most Americans (from 6 to 10 generations ago); the claim gave her minority status and she was claimed as such by Harvard
Walmart	David Tovar	VP for corporate communications	Claimed art degree from University of Delaware—two credit hours short and never received his diploma[92]
Yahoo	Scott Thompson	CEO	Claimed degree in computer science; had a degree in accounting[93]

[88]Id.

[89]Christopher Weaver, "Abbott Executive's Credentials Misstated," *Wall Street Journal*, September 29–30, 2012, p. B3.

[90]Jen Wieczner, "Why Wall Street Loves to Hate Mylan's CEO," *Fortune*, September 15, 2015, p. 132.

[91]Julie Hirschfield Davis, "Head of the V.A. Receives Support after Apologizing," *New York Times*, February 25, 2015, p. A16.

[92]Rachel Abrams, "Walmart Vice President Forced Out for Lying about Degree," *New York Times*, September 18, 2014, p. B3.

[93]Amir Efrati and Joann S. Lublin, "Yahoo CEO's Downfall," *Wall Street Journal*, May 15, 2012, p. B5.

Some Troubling, Very Public, and Very Consequential Résumé Debacles

Yahoo! A Computer Science Degree

Scott Thompson, made CEO of Yahoo in March 2012, had the following information on his résumé, from the beginning of his career with VISA, PayPal, and other tech companies: B.S. in Accounting and Computer Science, Stonehill College, 1979. However, Stonehill College did not offer a degree in computer science until 1983. The discrepancy was uncovered by one of Yahoo's investors, the hedge fund Third Point, an investor who was not happy with Mr. Thompson's work as CEO or with the direction of the company.[94]

The then 54-year-old Thompson opted not to address the issue, either publicly or with Yahoo employees who were with him at a series of strategic meetings for

[94]Amir Efrati and Joann S. Lublin, "Résumé Trips up Yahoo's Chief," *Wall Street Journal*, May 5–6, 2012, p. A1. http://online.wsj.com/article/SB10001424052702304749904577384221920051 852.html. See also, "Yahoo's CEO among Many Notable Résumé Flaps," http://blogs.wsj.com/ digits/2012/05/07/yahoos-ceo-among-many-notableresume-flaps/?mod=google_news_blog.

the company after the public revelations about the résumé issue. Some board members and employees did not want Mr. Thompson to resign because he was a relatively new CEO and Yahoo needed stability at that time. Other board members and employees believed Mr. Thompson's credibility was damaged and that morale among employees was driven to an all-time low by the revelation. Yahoo's stock had been hovering at $10 to $20 per share for the last four years prior to the Thompson résumé issue. Microsoft was trying to acquire the company for $33 per share using the shareholder dissatisfaction. Citing health reasons related to cancer, Mr. Thompson left Yahoo, but two months later, healthy and recovered, he was named as the CEO of ShopRunner, Inc. ShopRunner executives and board members were aware of the Yahoo and résumé issues and concluded that regardless of what had happened before, Mr. Thompson was "the right person for the job."[95]

The Shakespearean Tragedy in a Résumé Falsification

In 1997, Dianna Green, a senior vice president at Duquesne Light, left her position at that utility. The memo from the CEO described her departure as one that would allow Ms. Green to pursue "other career interests she has had for many years." Despite the memo's expression of sadness at her departure, Ms. Green was fired for lying on her résumé by stating that she had an MBA when, in fact, she did not.[96]

Ms. Green had worked her way up through the company and had been responsible for handling the human resources issues in Duquesne's nine years of downsizing. At the time of her termination, she was a director at Pennsylvania's largest bank and known widely for her community service.

On the day following her termination, Ms. Green was found dead of a self-inflicted gunshot wound.[97]

Discussion Questions

1. List all the warm language terms (See Reading 1.5 for the explanation of soft labels/warm language) you found in the discussions of résumés.

2. Explain what motivates individuals to include false information in their résumés. Think about the risks and give some examples of puffing versus falsehoods versus false impressions that you have heard of or seen in résumés.

3. Does the fact that Scott Thompson landed on his feet so quickly bother you? Does his experience teach you that dishonesty pays?

4. What do you learn from the tragedy of Ms. Green? Peter Crist, a background check expert, said, "You can't live in my world and cover stuff up. At some point in time, you will be found out if you don't come clean. It doesn't matter if it was 2 days ago or 20 years ago." As you think through these examples, can you develop some important principles that could be important for your credo?[98] Was the tragedy of Ms. Green avoidable? Was Duquesne Light justified in terminating her?

5. George O'Leary was hired by Notre Dame University as its head football coach in December 2001. However, just five days after Notre Dame announced

---

[95]Amir Efrati and Greg Bensinger, "Ousted Yahoo Chief Lands New CEO Role," *Wall Street Journal*, July 24, 2012, p. B3.

[96]The information was revealed after Ms. Green was deposed in a suit by a former subordinate for termination. Because Ms. Green hesitated in giving a year for her degree, the plaintiff's lawyer checked and found no degree and notified Duquesne officials. Duquesne officials then negotiated a severance package.

[97]Ms. Green was suffering from diabetes to such an extent that she could no longer see well enough to drive. Also, during the year before her termination, her mother had died of a stroke and her youngest brother also had died. Carol Hymowitz and Raju Narisetti, "A Promising Career Comes to a Tragic End, and a City Asks Why," *Wall Street Journal*, May 9, 1997, pp. A1, A8.

[98]Joann S. Lublin, "No Easy Solution for Lies on a Résumé," *Wall Street Journal*, April 27, 2007, p. B2.

Mr. O'Leary's appointment, Mr. O'Leary resigned. Mr. O'Leary's résumé indicated that he had a master's degree in education from New York University (NYU) and that he had played college football for three years. O'Leary had been a student at NYU, but he never received a degree from the institution. O'Leary went to college in New Hampshire but never played in a football game at his college and never received a letter as he claimed. When Notre Dame announced the resignation, Mr. O'Leary issued the following statement: "Due to a selfish and thoughtless act many years ago, I have personally embarrassed Notre Dame, its alumni and fans." Why did the misrepresentations, which had been part of his résumé for many years, go undetected? Evaluate the risk associated with the passage of time and a résumé inaccuracy. Would it be wrong to engage in résumé puffing and then disclose the actual facts in an interview? Be sure to apply the models in doing your analysis.

6. Is there something for your credo that you learn from all the résumé experiences?

Ethics in Action 1.18

When Is the Past Forgiven?

James Joseph Minder was appointed to the board of gun manufacturer Smith & Wesson, headquartered in Scottsdale, Arizona, in 2001. In early 2004, he assumed the position of chairman of the board. One month later, he resigned as chair of the board because the local newspaper, the *Arizona Republic*, reported that Mr. Minder had completed a three-and-a-half- to ten-year prison sentence for a series of armed robberies and an escape from prison. He had carried a sawed-off shotgun during the string of robberies, committed while he was a student at the University of Michigan. Mr. Minder indicated that he had never tried to hide his past. In 1969, when he was released from prison, he finished his degree and earned a master's degree from the University of Michigan. He spent 20 years running a successful nonprofit center for inner-city youth until his retirement in 1997, when he moved to Arizona. Mr. Minder's position is that the subject of his troubled youth and criminal past never came up, so he never disclosed it.[99]

1. Evaluate Mr. Minder's position and his silence. What do you think of Smith & Wesson's press release indicating that Mr. Minder "had led an exemplary life for 35 years"?
2. Mr. Minder remains on the board. Why did the public react so negatively to his past and position?
3. Is there redemption for past deeds?
4. Is there selective redemption, that is, are some deeds forgiven and others not?
5. Is there an ethical standard for redemption?

[99]"Smith & Wesson Chief Quits over Crime," CNN Money.com, February 27, 2004, http://money.cnn.com/2004/02/27/news/smith_wesson/?cnn=yes. Accessed July 20, 2010.

Reading 1.16

Résumés and the Ethics of Using Analytics

The résumé reading and cases have focused on cheating by those applying for jobs. However, a new tool has resulted in some ethical issues that have not yet been addressed in the field of ethics and are often unknown to those applying for jobs. Analytics (AI) have become a central piece in recruiting.

According to a Harvard study, 90% of all companies are using some form of analytics, from the simplest screening for certain words and phrases to more sophisticated models that eliminate candidates on what is missing from their résumés.[100] Smaller companies use software programs or contract with job posting companies to do first-level screening. Multinational companies use consulting firms and third-party vendors for screening but may also have in-house screening. All these forms of screening became possible when online applications began.

The Legal and Ethical Problems with Recruiting Analytics

Because the employee-screening models are so new and still evolving, both employers and applicants may not realize that the elimination of a discerning and thinking eye in reviewing applicants has resulted in legal and ethical issues. The somewhat mechanical review finds many qualified candidates passed over for jobs due to errors in the design of the analytics used or in the types of screens developed.[101] Ironically, in this era of alleged complete information and uniform and detailed analysis, companies are finding it more difficult to find the candidates they need. Companies such as Amazon and IBM are starting to study the filters being used to understand why the talent pool seems so shallow. For example, IBM found that the college degree requirement eliminated many qualified candidates for their cybersecurity and software development areas. A college degree requirement eliminated many candidates whose skills were developed in a wide variety of ways. Screening for applicants with degrees in programming or specialization in analytics eliminates candidates with criminal justice degrees who have developed their skills through hobbies.

A 2021 Harvard study found that 90% of executives believe that highly qualified job candidates are being excluded because they did not meet all of the criteria listed in the job description.[102] What was intended to streamline hiring processes may in fact result in the most qualified candidates being rejected in the first-pass screening. The effects of rigid requirements on the hiring processes and applicants are now under review in both academic literature and many of the Fortune 500 companies.

Unintended Illegality

Companies are not always fully aware of the sources of information that are used by screening firms. AI presents a pool of qualified candidates. Many of the candidates presented to companies and some companies themselves have used information from social media that is then considered by employers. A 2020 study found that the following illegal information was available to employees from AI reports on candidates: gender, race, and ethnicity (evident in 100% of profiles), disabilities (7%), pregnancy status (3%), sexual orientation (59%), political views (21%), and religious affiliation (41%). Many other categories were included such as: 51% of

---

[100]Joseph B. Fuller, Manjari Raman, Eva Sage-Gavin, and Kristen Hines, "Hidden Workers: Untapped Talent," *Harvard Business School: Managing the Future of Work,* (2021), https://www.hbs.edu/managing-the-future-of-work/Documents/research/hiddenworkers09032021.pdf.

[101]Kathryn Dill, "The Millions of Résumés Employers May Never See," *Wall Street Journal,* September 4-5, 2021, p. B1.

[102]Joseph B. Fuller, Manjari Raman, Eva Sage-Gavin, and Kristen Hines, "Hidden Workers: Untapped Talent," *Harvard Business School: Managing the Future of Work,* (2021), https://www.hbs.edu/managing-the-future-of-work/Documents/research/hiddenworkers09032021.pdf. P. 2.

the candidates' information contained profanity, 11% gave indications of gambling, 26% showed or referenced alcohol consumption, and 7% referenced drug use.[103]

The conclusion of that study was that the use of such information, largely found in social media sources, "did not appear to improve the prediction rate for successful job performance or withdrawal intentions."[104]

Less Diversity

The online era has brought about unintentional discrimination. The use of computers and online screening is based on the assumption of access to technology. That assumption screens out qualified candidates from those groups. For example, minority applicants are less likely to own a personal computer. Having them participate in a Zoom interview process online is problematic because 58% of Blacks and 57% of Hispanics do not have the resources to participate.[105] The set-up for the job process is an unintended filter for minorities.

The mechanical scheduling of interviews only during business hours excludes candidates who are going to school and working because they lack the flexibility to come for interviews between 8 and 5 Monday through Friday. That assumption means that many of the candidates with time management skills, strong work ethics, and the ability to prioritize their time are removed from the hiring process.

The minimum GPA, a common analytics screen, is not a predictor of job success. Again, minority candidates are screened out because their GPAs are lower due to lower incomes and the need to work more hours during college. Data show "GPA is rarely correlated to performance."[106] GPA screens, like so many screens in analytics, are not based on correct correlations but are easy to program.

In hiring analytics, the sourcing for the talent pool is as important as the screens. School sourcing limits the pool of diverse applicants. Too many employers assume that minority applicants are all in certain sources. One company's diversity officer noted that recruiting from Historically Black Colleges and Universities (HBCUs) limits employer searches. For example, Spielman College is an HBCU with 2,000 students, but Rutgers University has 3,000 Black students.[107] In effect, employers have made assumptions that group minorities in ways that limit their opportunities to even enter the pool of candidates.

Skills Requirements and Job Descriptions

Analytics can only screen for the input given by employers or according to the AI screens used for all employers. For example, some jobs require the ability to enter data, but if the analytics include "computer programming experience" as the rote screen for that skill, the screening will eliminate qualified candidates. With that type of description, a health-care company will miss hiring qualified registered

---

[103]Liwen Zhang, *et al.,* "What's on Job Seekers' Social Media Sites? A Content Analysis and Effects of Structure on Recruiter Judgments and Predictive Validity,"105 *Journal of Applied Psychology* 1530 (2020)

[104]*Id.,* at p. 1530.

[105]Roy Maurer, "8 Diversity Recruiting Mistakes and How to Avoid Them," *SHRM,* September 28, 2020, https://www.shrm.org/resourcesandtools/hr-topics/talent-acquisition/pages/8-diversity-recruiting-mistakes-how-to-avoid-them.aspx.

[106]*Id.*

[107]*Id.*

nurses because they cannot check that analytics box.[108] What most health-care companies need is the ability to enter patient data. The ability to enter patient data in the computer is not found by screening for computer programming nor is programming skill necessary for entering data.

Analytics screens tend to be literally and figuratively mechanical and are used across too many categories. Some of the screens used by screening firms require "floor-buffing experience" for retail clerks and customer service experience for transmission line workers for a power company.[109] As one frustrated job seeker put it, "You're racing against everyone applying for the job and an algorithm you don't understand."[110]

Employer Reforms

Because of these shortcomings in analytics, some employers are beginning to introduce reforms into their recruiting processes. Beyond changing job descriptions and eliminating some of the screens, some employers are contacting rejected applicants after having used an actual pair of eyes to examine the applications.

Employers are also blocking some of the traditional analytics screening tools. For example, blocking applicants who have gaps in their résumés is one easily triggered through analytics. However, that screen may eliminate many highly qualified women who often have gaps due to family demands. Again, analytics assumptions unwittingly discriminate on the basis of a mechanical screen when the complexities of individuals paint a different picture. It is that complete picture that employers need for recruiting and contacting applicants who can do the job. Analytics were adopted by most employers with differing levels of sophistication. The promise of saving time now requires a re-evaluation of the use of those analytics and when, where, and how the human element is needed.

Discussion Questions

1. Is there an ethical category that continuing use of analytics fits into? That is, after understanding what analytics do in terms of unwitting discrimination, do companies fall into one of the ethical categories in continuing their use?

2. What should employees do when applying for jobs given what they know about analytics?

3. Could analytics be driving false impressions and lack of truth in résumés?

4. If you were in HR, what changes would you make in a company's hiring processes based on what you have learned about using AI in screening?

A State of the Union on Cheating: Cheating in Real Life

To close out this introductory unit on ethics in our personal lives, we now move into cheating in general. Just as we have cheating in school and in finding jobs, we have cheating in our other activities. This final portion of the unit requires introspection on our personal conduct.

---

[108]Kathryn Dill, "The Millions of Résumés Employers May Never See," *Wall Street Journal*, September 4-5, 2021, p. B1.

[109]*Id.*

[110]*Id.*, at B2.

Case 1.17

Moving from School to Life: Do Cheaters Prosper?

In a book entitled *Cheaters Always Prosper: 50 Ways to Beat the System without Being Caught*[111] James Brazil (a pen name), a college student from the University of California, Santa Barbara, has provided 50 ways to obtain a "free lunch." One suggestion is to place shards of glass in your dessert at a fancy restaurant and then "raise hell." The manager or owner will then come running with certificates for free meals and probably waive your bill.

---

[111]James Brazil, *Cheaters Always Prosper: 50 Ways to Beat the System without Being Caught* (1996).

Another suggestion is, rather than spend $400 on new tires for your car, rent a car for a day for $35 and switch the rental car tires with your tires. So long as your car tires are not bald, the rental car company employees will not notice, and you will have your new tires for a mere $35.

Discussion Questions

1. Are these suggestions ethical?
2. Was publishing the book with the suggestions ethical?
3. Do any of these suggestions cost anyone any money?

Case 1.18

Cheating in Real Life: Wi-Fi Piggybacking and the Tragedy of the Commons

An issue that involves technology is developing and might require legal steps. Internet users are piggybacking onto their neighbors' wireless service providers. The original subscriber pays a monthly fee for the service, but without security, those located in the area can tap into the wireless network. They bog down the speed of the service. *Piggybacking* is the term applied to the unauthorized tapping into someone else's wireless Internet connection. Once limited to geeks and hackers, the practice is now common among the ordinary folk who just want free Internet service.

One college student said, "I don't think it's stealing. I always find people out there who aren't protecting their connection, so I just feel free to go ahead and use it." According to a recent survey, only about 30% of the 4,500 wireless networks onto which the surveyors logged were encrypted.

Another apartment dweller said she leaves her connection wide open because "I'm sticking it to the man. I open up my network, leave it wide open for anyone to jump on." One of the users of another's wireless network said, "I feel sort of bad about it, but I do it anyway. It just seems harmless." She said that if she gets caught, "I'm a

grandmother. They're not going to yell at an old lady. I'll just play the dumb card."

Some neighbors ask those with wireless service if they can pay them in exchange for their occasional use rather than paying a wireless company for full-blown service. But the original subscribers do not really want to run their own Internet service.

Discussion Questions

1. What do you think of the statements of the users?
2. Apply Kant's theory to this situation to determine what his rule would be.
3. What will happen if enough neighbors piggyback on their neighbors' wireless access?
4. In 1833, Victorian economist William Forster Lloyd used a hypothetical example in an essay on the effects of unregulated grazing on what was called "the commons" in England—areas available for public use. Although it was in everyone's best interest to keep the commons green and going, overuse caused its destruction. Does this theory apply to Wi-Fi piggybacking? Can you explain your answer?

Compare & Contrast

Compare this conduct to cuts in line. What's different about piggybacking from cutting in line? What similarities are there between the explanations the piggybackers give and those offered by the employees who pad their expense accounts? What role does "sticking it to the man" play in ethical analysis? What does that phrase do for piggybackers and expense account padders?

Case 1.19

Cheating in the Carpool Lane: Define Car Pool

Often called the HOV (High Occupancy Vehicle) lane or carpool lane, we see them around the country. Those who have a passenger can scoot into that lane at any time and sail along as the rest of the world inches forward on congested freeways. But, there are issues. What about the parent who has a toddler in a car seat in the back seat of the car? Wasn't the carpool lane intended to encourage people to double and triple-up in getting to and from work? And what about a woman who is pregnant? Do we have an interpretation of whether her unborn child constitutes a passenger? And if there is no one in the carpool lane, even in high-traffic travel times, should we let it go to waste or are we justified in slipping over and moving traffic along?

Discussion Questions

1. Have you ever used the carpool lane as a driver-only car? Why?
2. What are the intentions of having a carpool lane? Does that answer provide answers for the dilemmas presented above?
3. Apply any of the models in analyzing the car pool lane questions.

Case 1.20

Cheating in Real Life: The Pack of Gum

You have just purchased $130 of groceries. Upon returning home you discover that you did not pay for a pack of gum you picked up from the assortment of gums and mints at the checkout belt at the grocery store. You have the gum, but it is not on your receipt.

Discussion Questions

1. Would you take the gum back?
2. Should you take the gum back?

Case 1.21

Mylan and Its CEO's Ethical Standards: Does Academic Cheating Matter in Real Life?

Mylan had an interesting marketing strategy for its treatment for severe allergies. Mylan purchased the EpiPen, a device-with-a-drug-built-in that the company purchased from Dey Laboratories. The EpiPen was an auto-injector device. Mylan put its generic drug, epinephrine, into the EpiPen and marketed it as a convenient tool for administering the drug, particularly in schools where food allergy attacks among children are common causes for visits to the nurse's office. Mylan created a new exclusive right by offering a generic drug with a patented delivery method.

(continued)

Case 1.21

(continued)

For purposes of Medicaid billing, if the device-with-a-drug was classified as generic, Mylan was required to offer the government a 13% discount. If, however, the device-with-a-drug was a brand-name drug, Mylan had to offer the government a 23% discount. So, for purposes of Medicaid sales, EpiPen was generic. However, for everyone else, EpiPen was a brand-name drug. Over a six-year period after MyLan's acquisition, the price went from $100 to $600, that's 500%, which lands us near Martin Shkreli and Turing territory.[112]

During a Senate investigation into drug-price increases, EpiPen popped up because of the price increase. The prices popped up in a survey by the National Association of Medicaid Directors on EpiPen price increases. Then *Political Pro* figured out the "having it both ways" strategy.

Epinephrine had been a cheap generic for some time. While the drug itself was generic, the drug in the EpiPen was not. There was a legitimate debate about how to classify the EpiPen.

The Amoral Technician Approach

A lawyer could support a sort of "Who knows?" theory and go along with the dual price structure. However, this approach touches on the Laura Nash question about perception of conduct and into the ethical categories of rule breaking and taking unfair advantage. There is that line-cutting sense of fairness that arises when interpreting and applying rules.

But, beyond legal and ethical difficulties with dual pricing, there was the accompanying price increase with the strategic pairing. The EpiPen pricing and discount issues emerged in 2016. Mylan settled over-billing charges with the federal government for $465 million. Mylan, without admitting or denying the allegations, also settled SEC charges that related to its failure to disclose to investors the possible loss that could come from the classification debate. That fine was another $30 million. Mylan did not share the possible losses with its shareholders, which were clearly going to be imposed, before settling with the SEC in October 2016.

Additional Background: Ms. Bresch, and Her Family

There is more information that adds to an ethical theorem that often brings up past lives of academic cheating: Until caught, those who have ethical lapses never do just one thing.

In 2014, the board of directors approved a compensation plan that would require 16% growth in annual earnings. That goal was a challenge because Mylan, at that time, was operating with a product buffet that was 90% generic. By the time the dual classification was uncovered EpiPen was generating 10% of Mylan's revenue and 20% of its profits.

Mylan was, however, operating profitably and many affiliated with the company were benefiting from its profitable operations. Mylan moved to new headquarters outside Pittsburgh to a building that was partially owned by the board's leading outside director and chairman of its compensation committee. That director transferred his interest in the building to his partner before Mylan made the purchase.

Heather Bresch, the CEO of Mylan, is the daughter of Joe and Gayle Manchin, the former governor (current senator) and first lady of West Virginia, respectively. Gayle Manchin was appointed in 2007 to the West Virginia State School Board for a nine-year term by then Governor Joe Manchin. Mrs. Manchin then became a director of the National Association of State Boards of Education (NASBE) in 2010. Ms. Bresch became CEO of Mylan in 2012, the same year in which Mrs. Manchin became president of the NASBE. When she became CEO, Ms. Bresch announced the Mylan marketing program known as "EpiPen4Schools."[113] Later that year, NASBE held its annual meeting with sessions on student health initiatives, sponsored by Mylan following a $25,000 donation. Mrs. Manchin, through NASBE, headed an initiative to require schools to purchase medical devices for life-threatening allergic reactions.

The White House in 2013 gave funding preference to the EpiPen (known as "the EpiPen Law") and 11 states passed laws requiring auto-injector epinephrine devices in the school. At that time, Mylan had the only such device.

(continued)

---

[112]Jonathan D. Rockoff, "Behind the Push for High-Price EpiPen," *Wall Street Journal*, August 7, 2017, p. B3.

[113]Jayne O'Donnell, "CEO's Mother Used Post to Push EpiPen into Schools," *USA Today*, September 21, 2016, p. 1A.

Case 1.21

(continued)

The FDA had denied Teva approval for its similar device. Teva received approval in 2018—Mylan had a monopoly because of the regulation until the time of the Teva approval. By 2016, the EpiPen had been adopted by one-half of the schools in the country.[114]

Additional Background: Heather Bresch and Her Claimed MBA Degree

a. The Press Release

When Ms. Bresch was named to the position of COO at Mylan, the press release indicated that she had received her MBA from West Virginia University. A reporter for the *Pittsburgh Post-Gazette* discovered when he called to verify Ms. Bresch's credentials that she had completed only 22 credit hours of the 48 credit hours required for the MBA degree. As the reporters made inquiries to the university, they were given multiple explanations for the discrepancy between Ms. Bresch's claim of earning the degree and the university's records not reflecting the award of the MBA degree. The explanations were evolving and conflicting:

- "She completed all the course work necessary to graduate, but we discovered that wasn't put on the record because the fee [graduation fee of $50] was not paid."[115]

- The university had failed to transfer some of Ms. Bresch's grades to the admissions and records office because of the $50 clerical mix-up.

- There were other students (70) who experienced the same mix-up.

While the explanations were flowing, university officials added courses to Ms. Bresch's transcript along with grades for those courses.[116] The *Gazette* uncovered the document alterations, and the university appointed an independent panel consisting of two West Virginia University professors and three outside academicians to review what had happened given the different and inconsistent explanations.

The report found that Ms. Bresch had not earned an MBA degree, that there were no problems in the university's recordkeeping, and that the changes to Ms. Bresch's record should not have been made. The allegations about 70 other students being treated differently were found to be without merit. Provost Gerald E. Lang and business school dean R. Stephen Sears had awarded Ms. Bresch the degree retroactively and signed the forms required for the grade assignments in the courses. To get this result, there had been considerable pulling by those within the university and those at Mylan. Those doing the pulling from the university's end were facing various personal pressures. Michael Garrison was a long-time Manchin family friend and former business co-worker of Ms. Bresch. Ms. Bresch had been instrumental in his appointment as president. There were the financial pressures for the dean and provost of losing Mylan's generous support for the university.

There was also some pulling from Mylan's end. Then Mylan chairman of the board, Milan Parker, was West Virginia University's largest donor. Before findings of the independent report were published in the newspaper, the editor of the *Gazette* received a threatening letter from David M. Shribman, a Mylan attorney, that the degree had not been granted because necessary paperwork was not processed and threatened the newspaper that a story based on anything other than those facts would result in litigation. Mylan had removed the "MBA degree" from Ms. Bresch's credentials from its website from the time the panel was appointed.

The independent panel concluded that the courses and grades awarded were "simply pulled from thin air" after the questions about the degree were raised by the media.[117] The panel also concluded:

- That the pressure perceived by those within the university to not "rock the boat" and to award the degree was "palpable."[118]

---

[114]Interestingly, Teva staged an unsuccessful hostile takeover of Mylan in 2018. "Profiles of CEOs," "Heather Bresch," *Fortune*, September 15, 2018, p. 94.

[115]Barbara Sabatini and Len Boselovic, "The Story of a Coverup," *Pittsburgh Post-Gazette*, May 4, 2008, https://www.post-gazette.com/local/2008/05/04/The-story-of-a-cover-up/stories/200805040203.

[116]Id.

[117]Id.

[118]Id.

Case 1.21

(continued)

- That the decision to award the degree despite the lack of coursework was "seriously flawed" and "reflected poor judgment."[119] *Business Insider* had a satirical take on the series of events:

- Bresch lied about earning an MBA from West Virginia University

- When a fact-checker from the *Pittsburgh Post-Gazette* called WVU about biographical detail, the university was all "Um, no, she doesn't have an MBA"

- After Bresch leaned on the president's chief of staff, suddenly she did have an MBA

- WVU called the *Pittsburgh Post-Gazette* back to maintain as much, claiming "record-keeping" errors

- The *Pittsburgh Post-Gazette* called BS and tried to get to the bottom of the BS

- WVU kept being all "No, really, she's got an MBA"

- The *Pittsburgh Post-Gazette* was like, "You sure about that?"

- WVU, for the price of what could probably buy a handful of EpiPens, launched "a special panel" (!!) to see if Bresch really did have an MBA

- Was like, "Just kidding, she doesn't have one"

- Three people involved in the scandal resigned[120]

Shortly after the MBA controversy, Ms. Bresch was promoted to Mylan's CEO slot, where she began the drive for the EpiPen. It took five years, but West Virginia University eventually closed the record on this whole series of events by rescinding the degree that had been awarded from "thin air." University misconduct charges brought against Mr. Lang and Mr. Sears were ended because the university had not followed due process in handling the complaint. Mr. Lang filed suit against the university and the professors involved in the alleged misconduct investigation seeking relief on due process grounds. The university settled the suit because the judge agreed that there were conflicts of interest in those participating in the misconduct hearing. Some of the professors who had participated in the misconduct hearings were present during original discussions of awarding Ms. Bresch the degree. The judge halted the proceedings because of significant delays as well as the due process issues that resulted from the conflicts.[121]

Discussion Questions

1. Make a list of the categories of ethical issues you see in the case.

2. Refer to the titles of the articles used as source for the case. How do the titles help in the ethical analysis of this case?

3. What was the initial ethical breach that started the series of events?

4. What ethical lapses resulted from the initial ethical lapse?

5. What advice would you have for universities in preventing the retroactive award of degrees and alteration of records to justify those degrees?

6. Is there a pattern in the ethical choices Ms. Bresch makes?

7. What observations do you have about financial conflicts of interest?

[119]Bess Levin, "CEO Who Jacked Up the Price of EpiPens 500% Has Long History of Being a Total Nightmare: Lying About Having an MBA Edition," *Business Insider,* August 25, 2016, https://dealbreaker.com/2016/08/heather-bresch-epipen
[120]*Id.*

[121]Len Boselovic and Patricia Sabatini, "WVU Closes Book on Fraudulent Awarding of MBA," *Pittsburgh Post-Gazette,* August 20, 2012. https://www.post-gazette.com/local/region/2012/08/22/WVU-closes-book-on-fraudulent-awarding-of-MBA/stories/201208220175

Unit 1 Summary

We have ethical categories so that we can recognize and anticipate issues and dilemmas. This list helps as you study the cases throughout the book. Always ask yourself first– What type of ethical dilemma is this? The list provides a way for organized thinking to spot ethical dilemmas and shows you that there really are some absolutes to follow. Think about all cases in a way that begins with classification of the conduct under one or more of the categories.

Rationalization is a type of mental gymnastics used to avoid analysis of an ethical dilemma. If we rationalize we can feel comfortable about ignoring an ethical issue. Rationalization gives us comfort with decisions that allow us to continue conduct that is one of the categories of ethical dilemmas.

There are many small decisions that we make without considering the consequences of those decisions and what they mean for our ethical fiber. The incremental steps that we take permit us to feel comfortable, along with the tools of rationalization, as the categories of ethical lapses increase in number and scope. Small decisions control future opportunities and present risks that we fail to consider by simply asking who is harmed by our seemingly small ethical choices.

Ethical lapses (cheating) follow us through school, job-seeking, and into real life. The types of dilemmas in all three areas still fit under the same classifications and are resolved using the same analysis and asking the same questions as we reason through a lifetime of ethical dilemmas.

Unit 1 Key Terms

Categorical imperative   p. 18
Contractarians   p. 18
Copyright infringement   p. 33
Credo   p. 7
Divine command theory   p. 16
Earnings management   p. 34
Ethical egoism   p. 16
Ethics   p. 14
Gray area   p. 39
Hobbesian ethics   p. 17
Moral relativists   p. 19
Natural law   p. 16
Normative standards   p. 15
Nuremberg defense   p. 42

Peer-to-peer file sharing   p. 33
Quid pro quo   p. 26
Rationalization   p. 33
Rights theory   p. 19
Shifted norms   p. 35
Slippery slope   p. 3
Smoothing earnings   p. 34
Social contract or theory of justice   p. 18
Soft label (or warm language)   p. 33
Superior orders defense   p. 42
Tabula rasa   p. 18
Utilitarianism   p. 17
Virtue ethics   p. 20

Solving Ethical Dilemmas in Business

Learning Objectives

- Explain how individual ethical standards and business ethics intersect.

- Discuss the obstacles that prevent businesses from creating a credo as a means of integrating ethics into decisions.

- Describe the effects business pressures have on individual decisions in a company.

- Outline the characteristics of hubris that affect ethical decision analysis by organizational leaders.

- List the components of structured ethical analysis in business.

The study of business ethics is not the study of what is legal but of the application of ethics to business decisions. For example, regardless of legislative and regulatory requirements, most of us are committed to safety and fairness for employees in the workplace. But what happens when you have met legal and regulatory standards, yet employees are still experiencing injuries?

Employees also have certain ethical standards, such as following instructions, doing an honest day's work for a day's pay, and being loyal to their employers. But what happens when their employers are producing products that, because of inadequate testing, will be harmful to users? When does their loyalty end if there is a safety issue? To whom do employees turn if employers reject them and their concerns about the products?

Businesses, consumers, and employees too often subscribe to the "what's good for GM is good for the country" theory of business ethics. Jeff Dachis, the founder and former CEO of Razorfish, once said when he was questioned about the lack of independence on his board, "My partner and I control 10% of the company. What's good for me is good for all shareholders. Management isn't screwing up. We've created enormous shareholder value."[1] He spoke when his stock was worth $56 in June 1999. In May 2001, when he added three independent directors to his board and resigned as CEO, Razorfish stock was trading at $1.11 per share. No one at Razorfish did anything illegal, but it is the presence of perspective in a company through its board and through the analytical framework of ethics that may save a company from its hubris. Businesses have now begun to realize that even though Sir Alfred Coke alleges that a corporation has no conscience, the corporation must develop one. That conscience develops as firms and the individuals within them develop the perspectives on ethics discussed in Unit 1 and then develop guidelines, a credo, for their conduct as an ethical business.

---

[1]Erick Schonfeld, "Doing Business the Dot-Com Way," *Fortune*, March 20, 2000, p. 116.

How does a business behave when the law does not dictate its conduct or the law permits conduct that might benefit shareholders but is harmful to others? And what do businesspeople do when their personal values conflict with what's in the best interest of their companies? This unit deals with the overlapping ethical issues—those that affect us personally *and* in our business lives. From Carr to Drucker, you have the opportunity to explore what some of the best minds in the field of business and society have offered in thinking about ethics and business.

This unit has three parts. Section A defines business ethics and offers some insights into how business and personal ethics work together. Section B delves into the psychological factors that affect us as we work in a business setting: What gets in the way of effective ethical analysis in business? Section B also provides an important discussion of the reality of pressure at work and continues to explore: What gets in the way of ethics in business? Section C gives you the chance to understand a structured approach for analyzing ethical dilemmas and includes cases to help you apply all that you have learned about analysis, categories, rationalizations, and the reality of pressures in business.

Business, Ethics, and Individuals: How Do They Work Together?

Reading 2.1

The Layers of Ethical Issues and the Ethical Mind

As we transition from individual ethics to business ethics, we need to understand what types of ethical issues exist in businesses. There are layers of ethical issues in businesses that require different tools, checks and balances, and analyses. Recognizing which layer we are in is important as businesses work to be ethical. Figure 2.1 diagrams the layers.

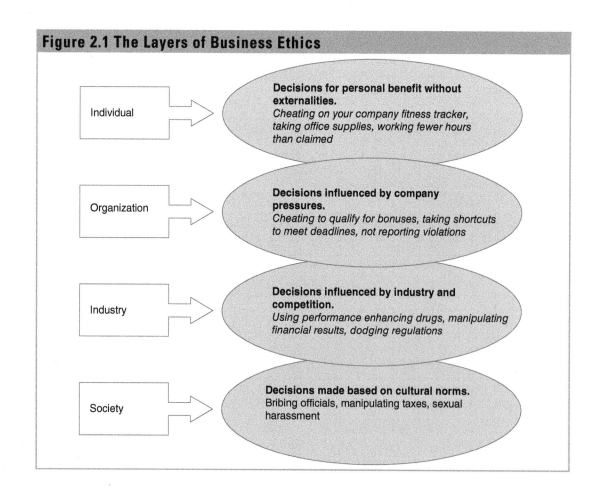

Figure 2.1 The Layers of Business Ethics

Individual → **Decisions for personal benefit without externalities.** *Cheating on your company fitness tracker, taking office supplies, working fewer hours than claimed*

Organization → **Decisions influenced by company pressures.** *Cheating to qualify for bonuses, taking shortcuts to meet deadlines, not reporting violations*

Industry → **Decisions influenced by industry and competition.** *Using performance enhancing drugs, manipulating financial results, dodging regulations*

Society → **Decisions made based on cultural norms.** Bribing officials, manipulating taxes, sexual harassment

The four layers of ethical issues reveal the complexity of ethics in business.

Layer 1: Individual Choices

Layer 1 consists of decisions by individual employees working within an organization. In these types of issues, the individuals have brought into the organization their ethical standards. For example, employees make their own decisions about claiming more hours than they worked or taking office supplies home. Their ethical standards exist inside and outside of work. Companies root out those individuals through pre-screening or through enforcement if they have begun work. Many companies provide a reduction in health insurance premiums for employees if they are willing to wear a fitness tracker and clock at least 10,000 steps per day and stand at least 2 minutes per hour. Companies know that additional activity, as measured by steps, improves health and companies' insurers often provide price reductions for such programs. Employees who cheat on their steps or standing to get the reduced rate have made an individual decision that affects the business.

Ethics in Action 2.1

Those Fitness Trackers

Employee imagination knows no limits when it comes to getting fitness trackers to register even when there is no activity. Employees have strapped their fitness trackers to table saws so that the motion registers steps. Others have strapped their fitness trackers to their hamsters that register steps as they run in their wheels. Some employees simply lift their arms overhead to meet their standing number for the day. Using the models in Unit 1 analyze the ethics of employees' actions to meet their health goals. Apply the categories and use the models to ask questions that provide your analysis. Be sure to focus on who is affected by their conduct.

Layer 2: Organizational Choices Carried Out by Employees

Layer 2 involves decisions that are made by individuals but they are decisions that involve the organization or are motivated by the organization's decisions and policies. For example, executives have manipulated the earnings of their companies to qualify for their bonuses. Employees are aware of the earnings manipulation but they are doing what someone else has directed them to do. The decisions management is making are not the choices they would make personally.

A phenomenon known as "pandemic accounting" developed during the COVID-19 lockdowns. All companies were affected economically but some came up with ways to keep their earnings at a decent level so that their stock prices did not drop dramatically. Ulta Beauty, a retailer that had been growing had to temporarily close its stores during the lockdowns. Ulta's earnings fell from $613 million in October 2019 to $13 million in October 2020. Ulta opted to take out a $40 million one-time impairment charge for the loss of value of their stores but then used a one-time $51 million in tax credits to raise its operating income to a respectable $98 million.[2] The definition of "one-time" varied on costs versus credits. Some companies have continued to use the pandemic as justification for changing

---

[2]Jean Eaglesham and Nina Trentman, "Pandemic Accounting Scrutinized," *Wall Street Journal*, February 24, 2021, B5.

their accounting numbers in ways that are inconsistent but feel justified in doing so because of the extraordinary nature of the pandemic. For example, many businesses were completely closed or disrupted so that their purchases declined and their suppliers had to extend out the recognition of revenue. However, there came a time when the businesses were back but wanted to continue with the deferred charges because it helped them with recovery. Allocating revenues and expenses on long-term contracts necessarily changed during the pandemic but with recovery, it was important to go back to the normal billing processes and booking of revenue.

Decisions about accounting are made at the executive level. Employees simply enter the numbers and print out the financial statements. Employees may question the consistency and honesty of the accounting treatments but do what they are told to do. They follow orders but do not make the decisions. These types of ethical issues cannot be fixed by providing employees with ethics training or encouraging anonymous reporting. Those at the executive-decision level make these decisions over which employees have no control unless they use external disclosure through whistleblowing. (See Units 4 and 7.)

Layer 3: Industry Pressures "Force" Decisions

In Layer 3, the executives in an organization are making the choices and decisions but have put themselves in the position of employees in Layer 2. "The industry made me do it!" For example, subprime mortgages spread like wildfire during the real estate boom that ended in 2007 and caused the financial market collapse in 2008. There mortgages had no underlying appraisals or verified income from the borrowers. Many of the mortgages were destined for default. That risk and those financial consequences were ignored as banks and other lenders reasoned that if they did not get involved in subprime mortgages, that they could not compete. While executives make these kinds of decisions, analysis of the issues are no different from the process covered in Unit 1. The rationalizations are also the same: "Everybody does this."

Layer 4: Society Has Changed

Layer 4 affects businesses and individuals as they process ethical issues. Their ability to use the analysis covered in Unit 1 is affected by a general view that there is just more cheating going on in society. The comfort level with dishonesty and harming others is decreasing and decisions focus on a series of rationalization, including "society has shifted," "we all do these kinds of things," "these are tough times," and "there really aren't consequences."

Desensitization to the categories and the need for analysis results as norms shift. Enforcement becomes more difficult and tolerance for behaviors in the categories grows. During the pandemic, the traditionally genteel competitions in the world of bridge fell victim to cheating. The competitions had to be held online and officials could not watch the players to stop secret signals between players. With little enforcement by the American Contract Bridge League, cheating became rampant. COVID cheating crosses all fields. A complex disciplinary code of 29,000 words did not help in bringing successful cases against players. As one player noted, "If we don't do something for the survival of the game, it's going to die with us."[3] There are slippery slopes in business ethics, too. We have more difficulty distinguishing between truth and error, right and wrong, fairness and injustice—regardless of where we are in the layers.

---

[3]Alan Yuhas, "'Rampant' Cheating Roils Genteel Bridge World," *New York Times*, October 27, 2021, p. A1.

Famous Lines from Art and Literature

Sly and the Family Stone, *Stand* (1969)

Stand
You've been sitting much too long
There's a permanent crease in your right and wrong

The Common Thread: The Ethical Mind

There is a common thread in all the layers: the ability to analyze is lost in a maze of rationalizations and emotion. The **ethical mind** is missing. Professor Howard Gardner of Harvard University has developed a simple test for business ethics that provides an overall view for all layers, A person with an ethical mind asks, "If all workers in my profession . . . did what I do, what would the world be like?"[4] An analytical mind deals in probabilities. An ethical mind counters with, "But we are talking about risk to human life when we have safety compromises." Creative minds have ideas and want to develop a hydrogen truck. The ethical mind says, "But we cannot raise money based on a fake video of a truck with no motor being shoved down a hill to raise money for your idea." In the pandemic, public health officials and experts wanted to stop the virus. Their expert minds saw lockdowns as the solution. The ethical mind saw the risks of postponing necessary medical care, depression and suicides, and long-term economic harm with a health crisis that would last beyond the virus itself. The key to ethics in business is bringing the various types of minds together, including the ethical mind, to walk through issues from all perspectives.

Discussion Questions

1. The Cadet Honor Code among U.S. military academies is as follows: "A cadet will not lie, cheat, steal, or tolerate those who do." Following the discovery of a cheating scandal at West Point during an online calculus exam in 2020 (refer to Reading 1.12 in Unit 1), many of the institution's alumni were critical because those who admitted to having cheated avoided expulsion and most penalties. A professor was disappointed in the reaction of the alumni and offered, "I'm not making excuses for it, but the environment they lived in, none of us has ever dealt with that."[5] Is the professor offering a "pandemic pass" for cheating? Is the professor saying that Layer 4 made it impossible not to cheat?

2. Todd Anderson, the owner of a bar in Clements, California, was arrested on charges of identity theft, forging government documents, falsifying medical documents, and, for good measure, having a loaded, unregistered handgun.[6] Mr. Anderson allegedly sold four fraudulent vaccine cards to undercover agents from the California Department of Alcoholic Beverages. The transactions—$20 per card—went down at Anderson's Old Corner Saloon. The agents obtained a

---

[4]Bronwyn Fryer, "The Ethical Mind," *Harvard Business Review*, March 2007, https://hbr.org/2007/03/the-ethical-mind.

[5]Tawnell D. Hobbs, "West Point to End Policy of Leniency for Cadets After Covid-19 Pandemic Cheating Scandal," *Wall Street Journal*, April 16, 2021, https://www.wsj.com/articles/west-point-to-end-policy-of-leniency-for-cadets-after-covid-19-pandemic-cheating-scandal-11618581602.

[6]Johnny Diaz, "California Bar Owner Accused of Selling Fake Covid-19 Vaccination Cards," *New York Times*, August 31, 2021, https://www.nytimes.com/2021/05/07/us/fake-covid-vaccination-card-california.html.

warrant and found 30 blank vaccine cards and a laminating machine. Is this an example of COVID-19 ethics? Using your Unit 1 knowledge, make a list of who was affected by Mr. Anderson's conduct? What if Mr. Anderson held a sincere belief that vaccines are harmful or should not be required? What tests from Unit 1 can you apply to analyze his conduct? Does it make a difference that the cards are ubiquitous on social media sites, commerce platforms, and blogs?

3. Classify the Unit 1 cases according to their layer of ethical issues.

Reading 2.2

What's Different About Business Ethics?

No Business Is an Island

The cases in Unit 1 focused on individual conduct. Figure 2.1 and the discussion explain that business decisions are not always made by individual employees. Businesses are groups of individuals, and those individuals' ethical standards may not translate well into a group setting. Culture and financial pressures influence decisions and decision processes. While individual ethical analysis requires thinking through who would be affected by your decisions, businesses face that issue in a different way. Those who will be affected by a company's resolution of an ethical dilemma are also those to whom the company is financially accountable. Businesses are accountable to shareholders and creditors whose economic well-being is affected by business success or failure. Businesses are financially accountable to customers for legal liability for products that injure. Some communities cannot survive economically without the presence of a major profitable business. When the auto industry experiences a downturn, hundreds of suppliers of parts and dealerships feel the effects. No business is an island when it comes to the impact of business decisions.

If It's Legal, We're Good?

Businesses and managers also need a framework and process for ethical analysis that can be applied consistently in an organizational structure. Developing an ethical mind for an organization is a tall order. Some businesses simply adopt an "If it's legal, then it's ethical" standard. However, many actions well within the law still raise ethical issues. For example, the federal standard for slaughtering cows is that they must be "standers," that is, able to stand up as they enter the pens. If they are "downers," they cannot be put into the meat supply and must be euthanized. However, because they were motivated not to lose those sunk costs in lost cattle, in 2008, the employees at Hallmark/Westland Meat Packing Co. used water hoses, electric prods, and forklifts to get the cattle to their feet so that they could be slaughtered for meat. A Humane Society undercover video documented this interpretation of the "stander" regulation. The result was the largest recall of beef in the United States. The company was following a legal standard, but by not considering the intent of the regulation or looking beyond the immediate cost savings of getting more cattle into the meat supply, its analysis did not weigh the risk of diseased meat making its way into the meat supply. Just the discovery of Hallmark/Westland's production processes resulted in a shutdown of the company's operations. The plant reopened under new ownership but the company was forced to change its name to American Beef Packers because its brand had been so negatively affected by its actions.

The defense of compliance with the law ignores the underlying ethical issues and the resulting risk. The company was not walking through the categories, rationalizations, and analytical steps that you studied in Unit 1. Nor was the company seeing the potential long-term harm.

Ethical decisions require businesses to look beyond compliance. There will always be a loophole, as evidenced in the discussion "It's a Gray Area" in Unit 1. But as you will come to learn throughout the remainder of this unit and the book, those loopholes are temporary and risky. A standard of legal compliance is akin to a pilot shaving the treetops. A pilot who flies well above the treetops has room for correction when there are wind gusts or sudden weather fronts, while a pilot who flies right at the treetops has no margin for correction. For a business, those treetops represent legal boundaries. When you are as close as you can be to those boundaries any misstep or sudden change finds the business in violation of the law. As military pilots advise, "You can only tie the record for low-altitude flying." Asking whether conduct is legal is but one part of an ethical analysis.

Group Decisions vs. Individual Autonomy

Businesses have other factors at play in ethical dilemmas beyond the personal introspection that you studied in Unit 1. There are organizational behavior factors, such as performance and incentive plans, and the power of group think (See Case 1.6) takes hold.

For example, at Hallmark/Westland, the manager of the cattle pens told police that he had to meet a quota of 500 cattle per day for slaughter.[7] Those performance pressures have to be factored in as you make business decisions. In fact, setting up those performance incentives without considering their impact on employees as they make decisions is an ethical issue unique to business. The issue of "standers" would be clear to us in the laboratory setting of the classroom because our job, bonus, retention, or promotion is not on the line. But business decisions are made in the midst of economic pressures that must be studied and understood in order to analyze an ethical issue completely. This Unit covers those pressures and organizational factors and stopping them from countermanding objective ethical analysis.

Discussion Questions

1. As you did in Unit 1, think of something that you did at work in the past year that may have been motivated by economic pressures but that still bothers you. For example, one manager wrote, "I knew that we had consistently overcharged a customer on his insurance premiums for almost five years. I did not fix it or tell anyone about it." Fit these actions and your own example into the categories of ethical dilemmas in Unit 1. Then think through the reasons that the manager in this example and you in your example did something that resulted in that nagging feeling. Would you have fixed the premium if it were just you in charge? What factors influence your decisions at work that are different from what we would do personally?

2. Now think of something that you did in your personal life in the past year that still bothers you. For example, one student wrote, "I lied to relatives on the phone so that they wouldn't come and visit." Another wrote, "I accepted cable [TV] I had not paid for," or "I didn't tell my wife about a bonus I received." Again, think through the categories that apply as well as the reasons for doing these things. Are there different motivations?

---

[7]David Kesmodel, "Oversight Flaw Led to Meat Recall," *Wall Street Journal*, March 11, 2008, p. B1.

Reading 2.3

The Ethics of Responsibility[8]

Peter Drucker

Countless sermons have been preached and printed on the ethics of business or the ethics of the businessman. Most have nothing to do with business and little to do with ethics.

One main topic is plain, everyday honesty. Businessmen, we are told solemnly, should not cheat, steal, lie, bribe, or take bribes. But nor should anyone else. Men and women do not acquire exemption from ordinary rules of personal behavior because of their work or job. Nor, however, do they cease to be human beings when appointed vice-president, city manager, or college dean. And there has always been a number of people who cheat, steal, lie, bribe, or take bribes. The problem is one of moral values and moral education, of the individual, of the family, of the school. But there neither is a separate ethics of business, nor is one needed.

All that is needed is to mete out stiff punishments to those—whether business executives or others—who yield to temptation. In England a magistrate still tends to hand down a harsher punishment in a drunken-driving case if the accused has gone to one of the well-known public schools or to Oxford or Cambridge. And the conviction still rates a headline in the evening paper: "Eton graduate convicted of drunken driving." No one expects an Eton education to produce temperance leaders. But it is still a badge of distinction, if not privilege. And not to treat a wearer of such a badge more harshly than an ordinary workingman who has had one too many would offend the community's sense of justice. But no one considers this a problem of the "ethics of the Eton graduate."

The other common theme in the discussion of ethics in business has nothing to do with ethics.

Such things as the employment of call girls to entertain customers are not matters of ethics but matters of esthetics. "Do I want to see a pimp when I look at myself in the mirror while shaving?" is the real question.

The first responsibility of a professional was spelled out clearly 2,500 years ago, in the Hippocratic oath of the Greek physician: *Primum non nocere:* "Above all, not knowingly to do harm."

No professional, be he doctor, lawyer, or manager, can promise that he will indeed do good for his client. All he can do is try. But he can promise that he will not knowingly do harm.

Discussion Questions

1. Does Dr. Drucker believe that personal ethics and business ethics can be separated?

2. What is the Drucker test for ethics for business managers?

3. What role does knowledge of harm play in the Drucker approach to business ethics?

Reading 2.4

Is Business Bluffing Ethical?[9]

Albert Z. Carr

In the following classic reading, Albert Carr compares business to poker and offers a justification for business bluffing. Mr. Carr provides a different perspective from the previous discussion with its various models and categories geared more toward absolutes.

A respected businessman with whom I discussed the theme of this article remarked with some heat, "You mean to say you're going to encourage men to bluff? Why, bluffing is nothing more than a form of lying! You're advising them to lie!"

I agreed that the basis of private morality is a respect for truth and that the closer a businessman comes to the truth, the more he deserves respect. At the same time, I suggested that most bluffing in business might be regarded simply as game strategy—much like bluffing in poker, which does not reflect on the morality of the bluffer.

I quoted Henry Taylor, the British statesman who pointed out that "falsehood ceases to be falsehood when it is understood on all sides that the truth is not expected to be spoken"—an exact description of bluffing in poker, diplomacy, and business. I cited the analogy of the criminal court, where the criminal is not expected to tell the truth when he pleads "not guilty." Everyone from the judge down takes it for granted that the job of the defendant's attorney is to get his client off, not to reveal the truth; and this is considered ethical practice. I mentioned Representative Omar Burleson, the Democrat from Texas, who was quoted as saying, in regard to the ethics of Congress, "Ethics is a barrel of worms"[10]—a pungent summing up of the problem of deciding who is ethical in politics.

I reminded my friend that millions of businessmen feel constrained every day to say *yes* to their bosses when they secretly believe *no* and that this is generally accepted as permissible strategy when the alternative might be the loss of a job. The essential point, I said, is that the ethics of business are games ethics, different from the ethics of religion. He remained unconvinced. Referring to the company of which he is president, he declared:

> "Maybe that's good enough for some businessmen, but I can tell you that we pride ourselves on our ethics. In thirty years not one customer has ever questioned my word or asked to check our figures. We're loyal to our customers and fair to our suppliers. I regard my handshake on a deal as a contract. I've never entered into price-fixing schemes with my competitors. I've never allowed my salesmen to spread injurious rumors about other companies. Our union contract is the best in our industry. And, if I do say so myself, our ethical standards are of the highest!"

He really was saying, without realizing it, that he was living up to the ethical standards of the business game—which are a far cry from those of private life. Like a gentlemanly poker player, he did not play in cahoots with others at the table, try to smear their reputations, or hold back chips he owed them.

But this same fine man, at that very time, was allowing one of his products to be advertised in a way that made it sound a great deal better than it actually was. Another item in his product line was notorious among dealers for its "built-in-obsolescence." He was holding back from the market a much-improved product because he did not want it to interfere with sales of the inferior item it would have replaced. He had joined with certain of his competitors in hiring a lobbyist to push a state legislature, by methods that he preferred not to know too much about, into amending a bill then being enacted.

In his view these things had nothing to do with ethics; they were merely normal business practice. He himself undoubtedly avoided outright falsehoods—never lied in so many words. But the entire organization that he ruled was deeply involved in numerous strategies of deception.

Pressure to Deceive

Most executives from time to time are almost compelled, in the interest of their companies or themselves, to practice some form of deception when negotiating with customers, dealers, labor unions, government officials, or even other departments of their companies. By conscious misstatements, concealment of pertinent facts, or exaggeration—in short, by bluffing—they seek to persuade others to agree with them. I think it is fair to say that if the individual executive refuses to bluff from time to time—if he feels obligated to tell the truth, the whole truth, and nothing but the truth—he is ignoring opportunities permitted under the rules and is at a heavy disadvantage in his business dealings.

But here and there a businessman is unable to reconcile himself to the bluff in which he plays a part. His conscience, perhaps spurred by religious idealism, troubles him. He feels guilty; he may develop an ulcer or a nervous tic. Before any executive can make profitable use of the strategy of the bluff, he needs to make sure that in bluffing he will not lose self-respect or become emotionally disturbed. If he is to reconcile personal integrity and high standards of honesty with the practical requirements of business, he must feel that his bluffs are ethically justified. The justification rests on the fact that business, as practiced by individuals as well as by corporations, has the impersonal character of a game—a game that demands both special strategy and an understanding of its special ethics.

The game is played at all levels of corporate life, from the highest to the lowest. At the very instant that a man decides to enter business, he may be forced into a game situation, as is shown by the recent experience of a Cornell honor graduate who applied for a job with a large company.

This applicant was given a psychological test which included the statement, "Of the following magazines, check any that you have read either regularly or from time to time, and double-check those which interest you most. *Reader's Digest, Time, Fortune, Saturday Evening Post, The New Republic, Life, Look, Ramparts, Newsweek, Business Week, U.S. News & World Report, The Nation, Playboy, Esquire, Harper's, Sports Illustrated.*"

His tastes in reading were broad, and at one time or another he had read almost all of these magazines. He was a subscriber to *The New Republic*, an enthusiast for *Ramparts*, and an avid student of the pictures in *Playboy*. He was not sure whether his interest in *Playboy* would be held against him, but he had a shrewd suspicion that if he confessed to an interest in *Ramparts* and *The New Republic*, he would be thought a liberal, a radical, or at least an intellectual, and his chances of getting the job, which he needed, would greatly diminish. He therefore checked five of the more conservative magazines. Apparently it was a sound decision, for he got the job.

He had made a game player's decision, consistent with business ethics.

A similar case is that of a magazine space salesman who, owing to a merger, suddenly found himself out of a job:

This man was 58, and, in spite of a good record, his chance of getting a job elsewhere in a business where youth is favored in hiring practice was not good. He was a vigorous, healthy man, and only a considerable amount of gray in his hair suggested his age. Before beginning his job search he touched up his hair with a black dye to confine the gray to his temples. He knew that the truth about his age might well come out in time, but he calculated that he could deal with that situation when it arose. He and his wife decided that he could easily pass for 45, and he so stated his age on his résumé.

This was a lie, yet within the accepted rules of the business game, no moral culpability attaches to it.

The Poker Analogy

We can learn a good deal about the nature of business by comparing it with poker. Although both have a large element of chance, in the long run the winner is the person who plays with steady skill. In both games ultimate victory requires intimate knowledge of the rules, insight into the psychology of the other players, a bold front, a considerable amount of self-discipline, and the ability to respond swiftly and effectively to opportunities provided by chance.

No one expects poker to be played on the ethical principles preached in churches. In poker it is right and proper to bluff a friend out of the rewards of being dealt a good hand. A player feels no more than a slight twinge of sympathy, if that, when—with nothing better than a single ace in his hand—he strips a heavy loser, who holds a pair, of the rest of his chips. It was up to the other fellow to protect himself. In the words of an excellent poker player, former President Harry Truman, "If you can't stand the heat, stay out of the kitchen." If one shows mercy to a loser in poker, it is a personal gesture, divorced from the rules of the game.

Poker has its special ethics, and here I am not referring to rules against cheating. The man who keeps an ace up his sleeve or who marks the cards is more than unethical; he is a crook, and can be punished as such—kicked out of the game or, in the Old West, shot.

In contrast to the cheat, the unethical poker player is one who, while abiding by the letter of the rules, finds ways to put the other players at an unfair disadvantage. Perhaps he unnerves them with loud talk. Or he tries to get them drunk. Or he plays in cahoots with someone else at the table. Ethical poker players frown on such tactics.

Poker's own brand of ethics is different from the ethical ideals of civilized human relationships. The game calls for distrust of the other fellow. It ignores the claim of friendship. Cunning deception and concealment of one's strength and intentions, not kindness and openheartedness, are vital in poker. No one thinks any the worse of poker on that account. And no one should think any the worse of the game of business because its standards of right and wrong differ from the prevailing traditions of morality in our society.

Discard the Golden Rule

This view of business is especially worrisome to people without much business experience. A minister of my acquaintance once protested that business cannot possibly function in our society unless it is based on the Judeo-Christian system of ethics. He told me:

> I know some businessmen have supplied call girls to customers, but there are always a few rotten apples in every barrel. That doesn't mean the rest of the fruit

isn't sound. Surely the vast majority of businessmen are ethical. I myself am acquainted with many who adhere to strict codes of ethics based fundamentally on religious teachings. They contribute to good causes. They participate in community activities. They cooperate with other companies to improve working conditions in their industries. Certainly they are not indifferent to ethics.

That most businessmen are not indifferent to ethics in their private lives, everyone will agree. My point is that in their office lives they cease to be private citizens; they become game players who must be guided by a somewhat different set of ethical standards.

The point was forcefully made to me by a Midwestern executive who has given a good deal of thought to the question:

> So long as a businessman complies with the laws of the land and avoids telling malicious lies, he's ethical. If the law as written gives a man a wide-open chance to make a killing, he'd be a fool not to take advantage of it. If he doesn't, somebody else will. There's no obligation on him to stop and consider who is going to get hurt. If the law says he can do it, that's all the justification he needs. There's nothing unethical about that. It's just plain business sense.

This executive (call him Robbins) took the stand that even industrial espionage, which is frowned on by some businessmen, ought not to be considered unethical. He recalled a recent meeting of the National Industrial Conference Board where an authority on marketing made a speech in which he deplored the employment of spies by business organizations. More and more companies, he pointed out, find it cheaper to penetrate the secrets of competitors with concealed cameras and microphones or by bribing employees than to set up costly research and design departments of their own. A whole branch of the electronics industry has grown up with this trend, he continued, providing equipment to make industrial espionage easier.

Disturbing? The marketing expert found it so. But when it came to a remedy, he could only appeal to "respect for the golden rule." Robbins thought this a confession of defeat, believing that the golden rule, for all its value as an ideal for society, is simply not feasible as a guide for business. A good part of the time the businessman is trying to do unto others as he hopes others will not do unto him.[11] Robbins continued:

> Espionage of one kind or another has become so common in business that it's like taking a drink during Prohibition—it's not considered sinful. And we don't even have Prohibition where espionage is concerned; the law is very tolerant in this area. There's no more shame for a business that uses a secret agent than there is for a nation. Bear in mind that there already is at least one large corporation—you can buy its stock over the counter—that makes millions by providing counterespionage service to industrial firms. Espionage in business is not an ethical problem; it's an established technique of business competition.

"We Don't Make the Laws."

Wherever we turn in business, we can perceive the sharp distinction between its ethical standards and those of the churches. Newspapers abound with sensational stories growing out of this distinction:

1. We read one day that Senator Philip A. Hart of Michigan has attacked food processors for deceptive packaging of numerous products.[12]

---

[11]See Bruce D. Henderson, "Brinkmanship in Business," *Harvard Business Review*, March–April 1967, p. 49.

[12]*The New York Times*, November 21, 1966.

2. The next day there is a congressional to-do over Ralph Nader's book *Unsafe At Any Speed*, which demonstrates that automobile companies for years have neglected the safety of car-owning families.[13]

3. Then another Senator, Lee Metcalf of Montana, and journalist Vic Reinemer show in their book, *Overcharge*, the methods by which utility companies elude regulating government bodies to extract unduly large payments from users of electricity.[14]

These are merely dramatic instances of a prevailing condition; there is hardly a major industry at which a similar attack could not be aimed. Critics of business regard such behavior as unethical, but the companies concerned know that they are merely playing the business game.

Among the most respected of our business institutions are the insurance companies. A group of insurance executives meeting recently in New England was startled when their guest speaker, social critic Daniel Patrick Moynihan, roundly berated them for "unethical" practices. They had been guilty, Moynihan alleged, of using outdated actuarial tables to obtain unfairly high premiums. They habitually delayed the hearings of lawsuits against them in order to tire out the plaintiffs and win cheap settlements. In their employment policies they used ingenious devices to discriminate against certain minority groups.[15]

It was difficult for the audience to deny the validity of these charges. But these men were business game players. Their reaction to Moynihan's attack was much the same as that of the automobile manufacturers to Nader, of the utilities to Senator Metcalf, and of the food processors to Senator Hart. If the laws governing their businesses change, or if public opinion becomes clamorous, they will make the necessary adjustments. But morally they have, in their view, done nothing wrong. As long as they comply with the letter of the law, they are within their rights to operate their businesses as they see fit.

The small business is in the same position as the great corporation in this respect. For example:

> In 1967 a key manufacturer was accused of providing master keys for automobiles to mail-order customers, although it was obvious that some of the purchasers might be automobile thieves. His defense was plain and straightforward. If there was nothing in the law to prevent him from selling his keys to anyone who ordered them, it was not up to him to inquire as to his customers' motives. Why was it any worse, he insisted, for him to sell car keys by mail than for mail-order houses to sell guns that might be used for murder? Until the law was changed, the key manufacturer could regard himself as being just as ethical as any other businessman by the rules of the business game.[16]

Violations of the ethical ideals of society are common in business, but they are not necessarily violations of business principles. Each year the Federal Trade Commission orders hundreds of companies, many of them of the first magnitude, to "cease and desist" from practices which, judged by ordinary standards, are of questionable morality but which are stoutly defended by the companies concerned.

In one case, a firm manufacturing a well-known mouth-wash was accused of using a cheap form of alcohol possibly deleterious to health. The company's chief executive, after testifying in Washington, made this comment privately:

---

[13]Ralph Nader, *Unsafe at Any Speed: The Designed-in Dangers of the American Automobile* (1965).

[14]U.S. Senator Lee Metcalf and Vic Reinemer, *Overcharge: How Electric Utilities Exploit and Mislead the Public, and What You Can Do About It* (1967).

[15]*The New York Times*, January 17, 1967.

[16]Cited by Ralph Nader in "Business Crime," *The New Republic*, July 1, 1967, p. 7.

> We broke no law. We're in a highly competitive industry. If we're going to stay in business, we have to look for profit wherever the law permits. We don't make the laws. We obey them. Then why do we have to put up with this "holier than thou" talk about ethics? It's sheer hypocrisy. We're not in business to promote ethics. Look at the cigarette companies, for God's sake! If the ethics aren't embodied in the laws by the men who made them, you can't expect businessmen to fill the lack. Why, a sudden submission to Christian ethics by businessmen would bring about the greatest economic upheaval in history!

It may be noted that the government failed to prove its case against him.

Cast Illusions Aside

Talk about ethics by businessmen is often a thin decorative coating over the hard realities of the game:

> Once I listened to a speech by a young executive who pointed to a new industry code as proof that his company and its competitors were deeply aware of their responsibilities to society. It was a code of ethics, he said. The industry was going to police itself, to dissuade constituent companies from wrongdoing. His eyes shone with conviction and enthusiasm.
>
> The same day there was a meeting in a hotel room where the industry's top executives met with the "czar" who was to administer the new code, a man of high repute. No one who was present could doubt their common attitude. In their eyes the code was designed primarily to forestall a move by the federal government to impose stern restrictions on the industry. They felt that the code would hamper them a good deal less than new federal laws would. It was, in other words, conceived as a protection for the industry, not for the public.
>
> The young executive accepted the surface explanation of the code; these leaders, all experienced game players, did not deceive themselves for a moment about its purpose.

The illusion that business can afford to be guided by ethics as conceived in private life is often fostered by speeches and articles containing such phrases as, "It pays to be ethical," or, "Sound ethics is good business." Actually this is not an ethical position at all; it is a self-serving calculation in disguise. The speaker is really saying that in the long run a company can make more money if it does not antagonize competitors, suppliers, employees, and customers by squeezing them too hard. He is saying that oversharp policies reduce ultimate gains. That is true, but it has nothing to do with ethics. The underlying attitude is much like that in the familiar story of the shopkeeper who finds an extra twenty-dollar bill in the cash register, debates with himself the ethical problem—should he tell his partner?—and finally decides to share the money because the gesture will give him an edge over the s.o.b. the next time they quarrel.

I think it is fair to sum up the prevailing attitude of businessmen on ethics as follows:

> We live in what is probably the most competitive of the world's civilized societies. Our customs encourage a high degree of aggression in the individuals striving for success. Business is our main area of competition, and it has been ritualized into a game of strategy. The basic rules of the game have been set by the government, which attempts to detect and punish business frauds. But as long as a company does not transgress the rules of the game set by law, it has the legal right to shape its strategy without reference to anything but its profits. If it takes a long-term view of its profits, it will preserve amicable relations, so far as possible, with those with whom it deals. A wise businessman will not seek advantage to the point where he generates dangerous hostility among employees, competitors, customers, government, or the public at large. But decisions in this area are, in the final test, decisions of strategy, not of ethics.

The Individual and the Game

An individual within a company often finds it difficult to adjust to the requirements of the business game. He tries to preserve his private ethical standards in situations that call for game strategy. When he is obliged to carry out company policies that challenge his conception of himself as an ethical man, he suffers.

It disturbs him when he is ordered, for instance, to deny a raise to a man who deserves it, to fire an employee of long standing, to prepare advertising that he believes to be misleading, to conceal facts that he feels customers are entitled to know, to cheapen the quality of materials used in the manufacture of an established product, to sell as new a product that he knows to be rebuilt, to exaggerate the curative powers of a medicinal preparation, or to coerce dealers.

There are some fortunate executives who, by the nature of their work and circumstances, never have to face problems of this kind. But in one form or another the ethical dilemma is felt sooner or later by most businessmen. Possibly the dilemma is most painful not when the company forces the action on the executive but when he originates it himself—that is, when he has taken or is contemplating a step which is in his own interest but which runs counter to his early moral conditioning. To illustrate:

- The manager of an export department, eager to show rising sales, is pressed by a big customer to provide invoices which, while containing no overt falsehood that would violate a U.S. law, are so worded that the customer may be able to evade certain taxes in his homeland.

- A company president finds that an aging executive, within a few years of retirement and his pension, is not as productive as formerly. Should he be kept on?

- The produce manager of a supermarket debates with himself whether to get rid of a lot of half-rotten tomatoes by including one, with its good side exposed, in every tomato six-pack.

- An accountant discovers that he has taken an improper deduction on his company's tax return and fears the consequences if he calls the matter to the president's attention, though he himself has done nothing illegal. Perhaps if he says nothing, no one will notice the error.

- A chief executive officer is asked by his directors to comment on a rumor that he owns stock in another company with which he has placed large orders. He could deny it, for the stock is in the name of his son-in-law and he has earlier formally instructed his son-in-law to sell the holding.

Temptations of this kind constantly arise in business. If an executive allows himself to be torn between a decision based on business considerations and one based on his private ethical code, he exposes himself to a grave psychological strain.

This is not to say that sound business strategy necessarily runs counter to ethical ideals. They may frequently coincide; and when they do, everyone is gratified. But the major tests of every move in business, as in all games of strategy, are legality and profit. A man who intends to be a winner in the business game must have a game player's attitude.

The business strategist's decisions must be as impersonal as those of a surgeon performing an operation—concentrating on objective and technique, and subordinating personal feelings. If the chief executive admits that his son-in-law owns the stock, it is because he stands to lose more if the fact comes out later than if he states it boldly and at once. If the supermarket manager orders the rotten tomatoes to be discarded, he does so to avoid an increase in consumer complaints and a loss of goodwill. The company president decides not to fire the elderly executive in the belief that the negative reaction of other employees would in the long run cost the company more than it would lose in keeping him and paying his pension.

All sensible businessmen prefer to be truthful, but they seldom feel inclined to tell the *whole* truth. In the business game truth-telling usually has to be kept within narrow limits if trouble is to be avoided. The point was neatly made a long time ago (in 1888) by one of John D. Rockefeller's associates, Paul Babcock, to Standard Oil Company executives who were about to testify before a government investigating committee: "Parry every question with answers which, while perfectly truthful, are evasive of bottom facts."[17]

This was, is, and probably always will be regarded as wise and permissible business strategy.

For Office Use Only

An executive's family life can easily be dislocated if he fails to make a sharp distinction between the ethical systems of the home and the office—or if his wife does not grasp that distinction. Many a businessman who has remarked to his wife, "I had to let Jones go today" or "I had to admit to the boss that Jim has been goofing off lately," has been met with an indignant protest. "How could you do a thing like that? You know Jones is over 50 and will have a lot of trouble getting another job." Or "You did that to Jim? With his wife ill and all the worry she's been having with the kids?"

If the executive insists that he had no choice because the profits of the company and his own security were involved, he may see a certain cool and ominous reappraisal in his wife's eyes. Many wives are not prepared to accept the fact that business operates with a special code of ethics. An illuminating illustration of this comes from a Southern sales executive who related a conversation he had had with his wife at a time when a hotly contested political campaign was being waged in their state:

> I made the mistake of telling her that I had had lunch with Colby, who gives me about half my business. Colby mentioned that his company had a stake in the election. Then he said, 'By the way, I'm treasurer of the citizens' committee for Lang. I'm collecting contributions. Can I count on you for a hundred dollars?'
>
> Well, there I was. I was opposed to Lang, but I knew Colby. If he withdrew his business, I could be in a bad spot. So I just smiled and wrote out a check then and there. He thanked me, and we started to talk about his next order. Maybe he thought I shared his political views. If so, I wasn't going to lose any sleep over it.
>
> I should have had sense enough not to tell Mary about it. She hit the ceiling. She said she was disappointed in me. She said I hadn't acted like a man, that I should have stood up to Colby.
>
> I said, 'Look, it was an either–or situation. I had to do it or risk losing the business.'
>
> She came back at me with, 'I don't believe it. You could have been honest with him. You could have said that you didn't feel you ought to contribute to a campaign for a man you weren't going to vote for. I'm sure he would have understood.'
>
> I said, 'Mary, you're a wonderful woman, but you're way off the track. Do you know what would have happened if I had said that? Colby would have smiled and said, Oh, 'I didn't realize. Forget it.' But in his eyes from that moment I would be

---

[17]Babcock in a memorandum to Rockefeller (Rockefeller Archives).

an oddball, maybe a bit of a radical. He would have listened to me talk about his order and would have promised to give it consideration. After that I wouldn't hear from him for a week. Then I would telephone and learn from his secretary that he wasn't yet ready to place the order. And in about a month I would hear through the grapevine that he was giving his business to another company. A month after that I'd be out of a job.'

She was silent for a while. Then she said, 'Tom, something is wrong with business when a man is forced to choose between his family's security and his moral obligation to himself. It's easy for me to say you should have stood up to him—but if you had, you might have felt you were betraying me and the kids. I'm sorry that you did it, Tom, but I can't blame you. Something is wrong with business!'

This wife saw the problem in terms of moral obligation as conceived in private life; her husband saw it as a matter of game strategy. As a player in a weak position, he felt that he could not afford to indulge an ethical sentiment that might have cost him his seat at the table.

Playing to Win

Some men might challenge the Colbys of business—might accept serious setbacks to their business careers rather than risk a feeling of moral cowardice. They merit our respect—but as private individuals, not businessmen. When the skillful player of the business game is compelled to submit to unfair pressure, he does not castigate himself for moral weakness. Instead, he strives to put himself into a strong position where he can defend himself against such pressures in the future without loss.

If a man plans to take a seat in the business game, he owes it to himself to master the principles by which the game is played, including its special ethical outlook. He can then hardly fail to recognize that an occasional bluff may well be justified in terms of the game's ethics and warranted in terms of economic necessity. Once he clears his mind on this point, he is in a good position to match his strategy against that of the other players. He can then determine objectively whether a bluff in a given situation has a good chance of succeeding and can decide when and how to bluff, without a feeling of ethical transgression.

To be a winner, a man must play to win. This does not mean that he must be ruthless, cruel, harsh, or treacherous. On the contrary, the better his reputation for integrity, honesty, and decency, the better his chances of victory will be in the long run. But from time to time every businessman, like every poker player, is offered a choice between certain loss and bluffing within the legal rules of the game. If he is not resigned to losing, if he wants to rise in his company and industry, then in such a crisis he will bluff—and bluff hard.

Every now and then one meets a successful businessman who has conveniently forgotten the small or large deceptions that he practiced on his way to fortune. "God gave me my money," old John D. Rockefeller once piously told a Sunday school class. It would be a rare tycoon in our time who would risk the horse laugh with which such a remark would be greeted.

In the last third of the twentieth century even children are aware that if a man has become prosperous in business, he has sometimes departed from the strict truth in order to overcome obstacles or has practiced the more subtle deceptions of the half-truth or the misleading omission. Whatever the form of the bluff, it is an integral part of the game, and the executive who does not master its techniques is not likely to accumulate much money or power.

Discussion Questions

1. Do you agree or disagree with Carr's premise?

2. What components of ethical analysis from Unit 1 does Carr overlook? What component of the ethical mind is missing in his analysis?

3. Does everyone operate at the same level of bluffing?

4. How is the phrase "Sound ethics is good business" characterized?

Compare & Contrast

Carr notes that espionage has become so common that it is no longer considered an ethical issue but an effective means of competition. Compare this comment with the list of rationalizations and apply them to the statement. What are the key differences in the two scholars' views on ethics in business? Then compare Dr. Drucker's simple means of analysis with Carr's views. Can Dr. Drucker's views help in Carr's complex situations?

Ethics in Action 2.2

Baseball's Sticky Wicket

Pitchers' use of sticky substances on baseballs is a longstanding tradition of the game. Stickiness is not legal under the rules of the game, but teams and the commissioner of Major League Baseball (MLB) look the other way. The teams assert "Everyone does it." Sometimes players are disciplined. For example, in 2014, Yankees pitcher Michael Pineda went to the mound with pine tar on his neck. When the fans can see the violation, the violation is called.[18]

There are laws of physics in the use of pine tar on baseballs. Trevor Bauer (currently with the Los Angeles Dodgers) had revolutions per minute (RPM) of 2,776 in 2020. In 2019, his RPM was 2,412. In 2018, he was at 2,322. Appearing on HBO's *Real Sports*, Mr. Bauer said that he could add 400 RPM with pine tar. He also said that pine tar has a greater effect on baseball games than steroids.

The real skinny on pine tar use came out in 2021 following the Los Angeles Angels firing of a clubhouse attendant for allegedly giving pine tar and rosin to players. The attendant filed suit and lawsuits do bring out sordid details. Hell hath no fury like locker-room staff sacked for helping players do what they would do anyway.

Where does this example fit in the readings in Section A? Did the attendant have any choice on the pine tar distribution? Does the inconsistency in MLB rules enforcement create issues for the game?

---

[18]Jared Diamond, "MLB Plans to Crack Down on Ball Doctoring." *Wall Street Journal*, March 29, 2021, A14.

What Gets in the Way of Ethical Decisions in Business?

Reading 2.5

How Leaders Lose Their Way: The Bathsheba Syndrome and What Price Hubris?[19]

Companies such as Enron, WorldCom, Adelphia, Lehman, New Century Financial, Fannie Mae, MF Global, UBS, Chase, Valeant, Volkswagen, Theranos, WeWork (WE), Nissan, Nikola, and GM (many companies that you will study) engaged in outrageous behaviors, but their journey into the hinterlands of huckstering and other forms of conduct that showed poor judgment was one of a gradual sort. They descended gradually to their ethical and, eventually, financial collapses.

No one in these companies sat together in the initial stages of either their success or the beginning of their declines, numbers difficulties, or inability to meet the quarterlies and plotted, "You know what would be great! A gigantic fraud that we perpetuate on the shareholders, the creditors, and analysts. It will make us more money than we ever dreamed of. Fraud—that's the answer."

There is a tendency to create the comforting image in our minds that somehow those who engaged in these outrageous behaviors were misled, duped victims, or were so corrupt that they are part of only a limited number of souls who would dare tread in areas where the landmines of lies explode and the traps of fraud ensnare. We want to believe that they are so ethically different from the rest of us, cut from a different ethical fabric altogether and hence more susceptible to the temptations of fraud. A piece in the *Wall Street Journal*, following the collapses of Enron and WorldCom was entitled, "How Could They Have Done It?," the essence of which was the exploration of the two questions all observers posed as they watched, mouths agape, when these $9 billion frauds dribbled out: Where were their minds when they made these decisions? What on earth were they thinking?[20]

Following Martha Stewart's indictment, a reporter called to inquire, "What is the difference between us and a Martha Stewart? Or us and a Dennis Kozlowski?" My response was very simple, "Not much." They begin as entrepreneurs with novel ideas, willing to work hard to enjoy success. They end with much of their success lost and tarnished reputations from criminal trials. How do intelligent and capable people find themselves reduced to the behaviors that find them in felony trials?

---

[19]Adapted from Marianne M. Jennings, "The Disconnect Between and Among Legal Ethics, Business Ethics, Law, and Virtue: Learning Not to Make Ethics So Complex," 1 *University of St. Thomas Law Journal* 995 (2004).

[20]Holman W. Jenkins Jr., "How Could They Have Done It?" *Wall Street Journal*, August 28, 2001, p. A15.

Arthur Andersen, the accounting firm that met its demise because of its certification of the fraudulent financial statements of Enron, had a history peppered with examples of the firm's absolute ethical standards that went well beyond the accounting rules. In 1915, Andersen was certifying the financial statements for a steamship company, one of its biggest clients. The financial statements were for the period through December 31, 1914. However, in February 1915, as the statements were being finalized, the company lost one of its ships in a storm. Arthur Andersen refused to certify the 1914 statements without disclosing the loss of the ship, a loss that would have a fundamental impact on income, despite the fact that it was in the next year.[21] In the 1980s, when the savings and loan industry collapsed, all of the then–Big 8 accounting firms, except for Andersen, experienced heavy losses because of their liability for audit work on the collapsed financial institutions. Andersen professionals did not think that the S&L accounting practice of including the value of deferred taxes in earnings was sound. When its S&L clients refused to change their accounting, under the guise of "everybody does it," Andersen resigned all of its S&L accounts rather than put its imprimatur to financial statements it believed contained improper accounting.[22] Yet, just a little over a decade later, Andersen, through David Duncan, was authorizing thousands of off-the-book-entities at Enron in order to hang on to a valuable audit and consulting client.

Apart from the organizational incentive systems and culture shifts that can affect reliance on absolute standards, there are individual lapses. The literature in ethical decision making indicates that the decline in ethical standards begins gradually and can consume those with tremendous ability and track records of success precisely because they have enjoyed so much success to that point.[23] These are the individuals to whom everyone turns for problem resolution, outstanding work effort, and results. Success has been the reward for their ability. They are the "go-to" people in an organization who have always been able to find resolutions for problems and ways to remove obstacles that stand in the way of achievement and success. Hubris consumes them when they find that eventual setback or obstacle they cannot conquer. Unwilling to admit that there may not always be a legal or ethical fix, they seek ways to avoid disclosure of a downturn or that they have hit a wall. They cannot get the product out on time and still guarantee its safety. They cannot complete the job on time and still meet quality standards. They are faced with the harsh reality of their human limitations. Releasing financial statements that are something less than projections when you have been on an earnings roll is difficult because you have been on a pedestal for so long.

Yet, like the figures in Greek tragedies, we all have our walls that we hit that require an admission that the fix will take a while and we may need a little help. Every successful lawyer must face that trial when no one can pull a win from the hat. Every athlete has that game or race when victory is not theirs. How do they face this setback? Too often with steroids, falsified financials, and withheld evidence. It is not always greed that drives ruthless ambition; both fiction and biography teach that hubris spawns deceit. Pride, that inability to face the wall, as the saying teaches, goeth before a fall. Even if no money were involved, it is difficult for them to step down, even if just for a time, while at the top of their go-to game.

---

[21]Susan E. Squires, Cynthia J. Smith, Lorna McDougall, and William R. Yeack, *Inside Arthur Andersen: Shifting Values, Unexpected Consequences* (2003), p. 32.

[22]Barbara Ley Toffler, *Final Accounting: Ambition, Greed and the Fall of Arthur Andersen* (2004), p. 19.

[23]David M. Messick and Max H. Bazerman, "Ethical Leadership and the Psychology of Decision Making," 37 *Sloan Management Review* 9 (1996).

From the Greek tragedies to Shakespeare's nobles, literature teaches us what newspapers bear out: the rise, fall, and costs of hubris. Erroneous confidence and an exaggerated sense of control emerge, in fiction and nonfiction alike, in Greek mythology and in the Napoleonic wars, do drive poor ethical choices in high-pressure situations.

How do leaders know when they are losing their ways? What do the classics teach us? What have we learned from the case studies in business ethics? In an article in the *Journal of Business Ethics*, Professors Ludwig and Longnecker analyzed how leaders lose their way through a look at the rise and fall of King David in the Old Testament of the Bible.[24] David, a young shepherd boy, caught King Saul's attention when he felled the giant Goliath with a stone and a sling. David joined his king to fight for Israel and became beloved of the people, who sang his praises more so than they did for Saul, "Saul hath slain his thousands, and David his ten thousands."[25] Still, David was loyal to King Saul and refused to try a takeover of the throne. In fact, David had such integrity that he allowed Saul's jealousy to drive him into the wilderness rather than harm the king. After Saul's death in battle, David was anointed king. With all the trappings of being king, David stayed at the palace more, away from work and the battlefield. One evening, he took note of Bathsheba, a neighbor and wife of Uriah, one of King David's commanders, who was away on the battlefield. King David sent messengers to bring Bathsheba, and these messengers, being unwilling to dissent from the king's will, brought Bathsheba to David. Bathsheba conceived as a result of their liaison. David then brought Uriah home immediately to have him be with his wife for a night so that the child Bathsheba was carrying will appear to be Uriah's. However, Uriah the Hittite had the integrity David once had and refused to partake in the comforts of home while his men were still in battle. He slept with the servants in the palace rather than partake of the pleasures of home. Frustrated in the attempted cover-up, David sent Uriah to the worst part of the battle and ordered his commanders to put Uriah at the frontline. Uriah was killed. King David believed he had successfully ended the story, but the child conceived died shortly after birth and David was condemned by his church leaders for his conduct. King David, rising from the humblest of circumstances through his merits to a position of leadership, lost his way.[26]

From this Biblical story that puts Shakespeare to shame, we see the common characteristics of business people who lose their ways, what Professors Ludwig and Longnecker call "the **Bathsheba Syndrome**," a concept our military academies still teach in their leadership training for cadets and officers:

a. They become increasingly isolated because they are unwilling to tolerate dissent. They have but one perspective, a trait that is antithetical to good ethical analysis, something that requires a 360-degree perspective to remedy.

b. They fancy themselves as being above the rules, different from the "average person," who must follow the mundane rules of the world. Like a teenager, they believe the rules do not apply to them.

c. They have defined themselves by the trappings of their success: their salaries, bonuses, cars, houses, and material possessions. The possibility of losing their material possessions and social status becomes the driving force of their decisions and leadership. They are no longer pursuing leadership for the sake of helping society with their products or services

---

[24]Dean C. Ludwig and Clinton O. Longnecker, "The Bathsheba Syndrome: The Ethical Failure of Successful Leaders," 12 *Journal of Business Ethics* 265 (1993).

[25]1 Samuel 18:7. Holy Bible, King James Version.

[26]To read the details in the story of King David, see 2 Samuel 11 in the Bible, King James Version.

or employees by helping them advance. Their leadership is for their personal status.

d. They have a sense of invincibility—that they can solve any problem because they have been so successful for so long. That invincibility finds them taking larger risks with the hope of staying on top.

e. They have lost a good purpose in being a leader in business. Initially, their leadership role sprang from their desire to help others or improve the world. They had a good new product or they had a way of working with people that propelled them to success. When they switch from that purpose of their leadership to one of more, more, more, they lose the self-confidence and inner purpose that gave them perspective on their decisions, including the perspective of their ethical values.

Discussion Questions

1. What would the role of adherence to your credo play in preventing you from losing your way?

2. Looking at the list of how leaders lose their way, develop a list of actions that would stop these problems from taking hold.

3. Give examples of how leaders lose their way. David's weakness was using his power to commit adultery. Has this been a downfall for any leaders of this era? Do some leaders have too much focus on material things and amassing a fortune or "stuff"? Be sure to look for examples as you study the cases in the remaining units of the book.

Compare & Contrast

William Wilberforce was a member of the British Parliament who is credited with obtaining passage of the Slavery Abolition Act of 1833 in England. Mr. Wilberforce has been identified by historians for his persistent leadership in seeing the act to passage. Mr. Wilberforce was also a philanthropist and a founder of the Society for the Prevention of Cruelty to Animals.

Mr. Wilberforce died just three days after the Abolition Act was passed. What distinguishing characteristics do you see in Mr. Wilberforce that are different from the characteristics that indicate a leader is losing his or her way?

Reading 2.6

Moral Relativism and the Either/or Conundrum

A typical form of flawed reasoning that businesses fall into is the **either/or conundrum**. This flawed analysis finds us reaching a decision, because the pressure is great, the consequences even greater, and the justification compelling. Defining dilemmas in the either/or conundrum commit the ultimate flaw in logic by assuming the outcome. Defining the dilemma in this way also produces artificial choices that somehow ignore the ethics and values we brought with us before we run into the pressure of the moment.

Many company CFOs fall into this trap—either I inflate the financials this quarter or 3,000 people will lose their jobs, including me. Sales employees often engage in practices such as shipping goods customers have not ordered so that they can meet their quarterly sales numbers. They box themselves into an either/ or situation without realizing the dilemma will now never go away, "What will you do next quarter to make up the shortage?" In defining the issue by achievement of a predetermined goal, we fall victim to the either/or conundrum. Sometimes we reach the goal, but other times we find a wealth of experience that we use in reaching the summit or goal the next time or in understanding that we need to pursue a different summit or goal.

However, analyzing a decision by values rephrases the question from "Does our present need justify my departure from my values?" to "Is there a way to solve this problem that is consistent with my values?" For example, in 2000, the Swedish retailer Ikea was on the eve of the grand opening of its flagship store in Moscow. Government officials who run the public electric utility came requesting their personal payoffs for providing the retail store with electricity. One part of Ikea's code of ethics—indeed, its credo—is that it does not pay bribes anywhere it does business. On the other hand, Ikea did have commitments to vendors, creditors, and employees for the opening of the store. If Ikea phrases the ethical issue as "To bribe or not to bribe, that is the question," it will fall into the either/or conundrum. If, however, it phrases the question as "Is there a way to get the store open without compromising our values?" it will begin exploring alternatives rather than accepting the compromise of its ethics as the only solution. Ikea did come up with a solution; it rented generators to provide power for the store. Indeed, that approach to electricity has become its business model in Russia. Avoiding the either/or trap removes the blinders that moral relativism often imposes as we try to analyze an issue.

Discussion Questions

1. Describe a time when you have fallen into an either/or trap.

2. In 2009, Ikea discovered that the Russian executive it had hired to manage its generator contracts was accepting kickbacks from the companies that wanted to do business with Ikea.[27] What lessons should Ikea and other companies learn from this experience?

Reading 2.7

P = f(x) The Probability of an Ethical Outcome Is a Function of the Amount of Money Involved: Pressure

The CFA (Chartered Financial Analyst) Institute has a saying, $P = f(x)$. For you non-mathematicians out there, the translation is that the probability of an ethical outcome is a direct function of the amount of money involved. The more money involved, the less likely an ethical outcome. So, the slope of the line is negative.

There is the hubris, the pedestal effect, the inability to accept a setback, and the failure to understand that we all hit a wall once in a while. Sometimes we have to take a loss. Sometimes we need to step off the pedestal. When managers at high-performing companies succumb to these pressures, they do go ethically nuts.

An article in the *Academy of Management Journal* presents research that high-performing companies are more likely to break the law.[28] Professor Yuri Mishina

---

[27]Ikea terminated the executive. Andrew E. Kramer, "Ikea Tries to Build Public Case against Corruption," *New York Times*, September 12, 2009, p. B1.

[28]Yuri Mishna, Bernadine J. Dykes, Emily S. Block, and Timothy G. Pollock, "Why Good Firms Do Bad Things: The Effects of High Aspirations, High Expectations, and Prominence on the Incidence of Corporation Illegality," 53 *Academy of Management Journal* 701 (2010).

from Michigan State and his coauthor colleagues, Professors Dykes, Block, and Pollock, in "Why 'Good' Firms Do Bad Things: The Effects of High Aspirations, High Expectations, and Prominence on the Incidence of Corporate Illegality," conclude that there is something about being on an earnings roll that clouds judgment. In addition to the cyclone of hubris, managers are trying to grapple with the pressures of sunk-cost avoidance, investor relations, and the sandbox mentality of just "making those numbers," even when they are not real.

But again, business managers face pressures similar to those we encounter in our personal lives. A friend rented a truck to help his aunt move from the large home she had enjoyed with her recently deceased husband of many years to a more easily managed apartment. He did not take the insurance coverage for the truck because, as he said, "I know how to drive!" Safety tip for renting moving trucks: Your auto insurance probably doesn't cover you! And the coverage charge by the truck rental business is expensive! The large truck proved to be a challenge, and my friend scraped the back top of the truck on some eaves as he turned a corner rather inartfully. There were two thoughts that came to his mind: (1) That's gonna be expensive and (2) Should I try and hide this from the rental guy? Oh, that second thought! There is that little part in all of us that doesn't want to ante up, and another little part that believes we can actually dupe the other guy so that we need not pay for something that really is our responsibility. But my friend drove into the U-Haul rental center and pointed out the hole, the scratch, and the damage in all of its uninsured glory. The initial response from the rental guy was, "Wow! That's bad!" Then he paused and said, "I'm not going to worry about it."

My friend wonders how different the ending might have been had he not 'fessed up. How different this generous soul of a rental manager might have been had he discovered the damage if my friend skedaddled or skulked out of there. There is that simple but powerful and decisive model from Unit I: "If I were the U-Haul manager, how would I feel if someone tried to hide damage from me?" The fog and pressures that interfere with good ethical decisions can be managed with the simple recall of those questions.

Discussion Questions

1. Think of an example of a situation in which you resisted pressure to act unethically.

2. Make a list of the pressures described in the reading so far.

3. How could your credo help in resisting pressure?

Case 2.8

BP and the Deepwater Horizon Explosion: Safety First

Background and Nature of Market

BP PLC is a holding company with three operating segments: Exploration and Production; Refining and Marketing; and Gas, Power, and Renewables. Exploration and Production's activities include oil and natural gas exploration and field development and production, together with pipeline transportation and natural gas processing. Refining and Marketing's activities include oil supply and trading, as well as refining; manufacturing and marketing of petrochemicals; and the marketing and trading of natural gas. BP is also involved in low-carbon power development, including solar and wholesale marketing and trading (BP Alternative Energy). At the time of the events in this case study, BP had a presence in 100 countries and employed 96,000 people in these countries.

(continued)

Case 2.8

(continued)

It had nearly 24,000 retail service stations around the world, and, at the time of the events discussed here, BP was the second largest oil company in the world and one of the world's 10 largest corporations.

Until 2007, BP had been a perennial favorite of nongovernmental organizations (NGOs) and environmental groups. For example, *Business Ethics* named BP the world's most admired company and one of its top corporate citizens. Green Investors named BP its top company because of BP's continuing commitment to investment in alternative energy sources. BP was so socially responsible, that all of its stations sold coffee made from fair-trade beans. BP social and community policy appears below:

Objectives

- To earn and build our reputation as a responsible corporate citizen
- To promote and help the company achieve its business objectives
- To encourage and promote employee involvement in community upliftment
- To contribute to social and economic development

BP has been recognized for its work in helping AIDS victims in Africa. BP Alternative Energy was launched in 2005 and anticipated investing some $8 billion in BP Alternative Energy over the next decade, reinforcing its determination to grow its businesses "beyond petroleum."

In July 2006, BP and GE announced their intention to jointly develop and deploy hydrogen power projects that dramatically reduce emissions of the greenhouse gas carbon dioxide from electricity generation. Vivienne Cox, BP's chief executive of Gas, Power, and Renewables, said, on announcing the joint venture, "The combination of our two companies' skills and resources in this area is formidable, and is the latest example of our intent to make a real difference in the face of the challenge of climate change."[29]

There were issues that belied BP's good-citizen status. In 2001, BP admitted that it had hired private investigators

to collect information on Greenpeace and The Body Shop. Also in 2001, its annual meeting created a stir when a shareholder proposal to stop the erection of a pipeline in mainline China was defeated when the board of directors opposed the proposal.

BP's political donations were also a controversial and newsworthy subject until it abandoned the practice with the following statement:

In early 2002 the company Chairman, Lord Browne, announced that it will no longer make donations to political parties anywhere in the world. In a speech to the Royal Institute of International Affairs, Browne, [sic] said "we have to remember that however large our turnover might be, we still have no democratic legitimacy anywhere in the world. . . . We've decided, as a global policy, that from now on we will make no political contributions from corporate funds anywhere in the world." However, BP will continue to participate in industry lobbying campaigns and the funding of think-tanks. "We will engage in the policy debate, stating our views and encouraging the development of ideas—but we won't fund any political activity or any political party," he said. In response to a question, Browne said that over the long term donations to political parties were not effective.[30]

BP was facing market pressure. The energy market was volatile during 2006. Crude oil futures slid below $60 in mid-September 2006, when the government report on winter heating fuel was released. The El Niño weather patterns resulted in a warm winter and very little demand for home heating oil, and a resulting glut in supply with the accompanying dip in price.

Natural gas prices declined during the same period because of mild temperatures. With no hurricane activity and resulting disruption in production or damage to pipelines, the natural gas inventory remained high. Also, the warmer temperatures meant that the utilities' peaker plants, or plants used in periods of high demand, were not fired up, as it were. With peaker plants run by natural gas,

(continued)

---

[29]"BP and GE to Jointly Develop Hydrogen Technologies," sustainablebusiness.com, July 18, 2006, http://www.sustainable-business.com/index.cfm/go/news.display/id/10466. Accessed September 2, 2013.

[30]Adapted from BP political donation press release, http://www.bp.com/centres/press_detail.asp7icM47 (as accessed in original research).

Case 2.8

(continued)

the lower demand crossed into commercial contracts. Amaranth Advisors, the internationally known hedge fund that is based in Connecticut, lost $3 billion in September 2006 because of its position in natural gas.

An Unfortunate Series of Events

From January 2005 through May 2010, BP experienced some production, legal, and operations setbacks. These events resulted in company sanctions through 2016 and changed BP's public image even further.[31]

The Texas City Refinery Explosion

In 2005, BP had a deadly explosion at one of its refineries, located in Texas City, Texas. Fifteen employees were killed, and 500 other employees were injured. OSHA levied the largest fine in its history against BP for its failure to correct safety violations at the refinery, a violation that resulted in a fine of $87 million—four times larger than any fine OSHA had ever before issued against a company.

BP had entered into a 2005 agreement with OSHA to fix the safety violations, but it had failed to do so. At that time, OSHA had found 271 violations at the refinery. After completing its investigation following the explosion, OSHA found 439 "willful and egregious" violations, a finding that resulted in the large fine.

OSHA attributed many of the violations at the plant to overzealous cost cutting on maintenance and safety, undue production pressures, antiquated equipment, and fatigued employees. The OSHA report concluded "BP often ignored or severely delayed fixing known hazards in its refineries."[32] Jordan Barab, a deputy assistant secretary of labor, stated the following OSHA findings, "The only thing you can conclude is that BP has a serious, systemic safety problem in their company."[33] The Chemical Safety Board (CSB) Report concluded that cost cutting played a role in BP's failure to address the ongoing OSHA violations:

> Beginning in 2002, BP commissioned a series of audits and studies that revealed serious safety problems at the Texas City refinery, including a lack of necessary

preventative maintenance and training. These audits and studies were shared with BP executives in London, and were provided to at least one member of the executive board. BP's response was too little and too late. Some additional investments were made, but they did not address the core problems in Texas City. Rather, BP executives in 2004 challenged their refineries to cut yet another 25 percent from their budgets for the following year.[34]

Carolyn Merritt, the chair of the CSB, said, "As the investigation unfolded, we were absolutely terrified that such a culture could exist at BP."[35] CSB ordered that the company launch its own investigation by an independent panel. The panel, headed by former Secretary of State James A. Baker, found "instances of a lack of operating discipline, toleration of serious deviations from safe operating practices and apparent complacency toward serious process safety risks at each refinery."[36]

The CSB report noted that cost cutting at the refinery had "drastic effects," with "maintenance and infrastructure deteriorating over time, setting the stage for the disaster."[37]

The following chart shows workplace deaths in the oil and gas industry.

Company	2003	2004	2005	2006
Exxon-Mobil	23	6	8	10
Royal Dutch Shell	45	37	36	37
BP	20	11	27	7
Total Coil Co.	23	16	22	NA
Chevron	12	17	6	NA[38]

(continued)

---

[31]Justin Scheck and Selina Williams, "BP: The Makeover," *Wall Street Journal*, October 25, 2013, p. B1.
[32]Guy Chazan, "BP Faces Fine over Safety at Ohio Refinery," *Wall Street Journal*, March 9, 2010, p. A4.
[33]Accessed May 19, 2010, http://www.publicintegrity.org/articles/entry/2085.

[34]The report recommended that BP comply with 29 CFR § 1910.119. Process Safety Management of Highly Hazardous Chemicals and implement an effective means of process safety management.
[35]Sheila McNulty, "BP Safety Culture under Attack," *Financial Times*, March 20, 2007, p. 15.
[36]Id.
[37]Id.
[38]Ed Crooks, "BP's Record on Safety Pinned Down," *Financial Times*, March 20, 2007, p. 17.

Case 2.8

(continued)

The International Association of Oil and Gas Producers pointed to progress, with fatalities at a rate of 3.5 per 100 man-hours worked in 2005 versus 5.2 in 2004. The companies also noted the extraordinary danger of the industry. For example, all 37 of Royal Dutch's fatalities in 2006 were from kidnappings of workers.

BP had already entered into an agreement with the EPA for a guilty plea to Clean Air Act violations and paid a $50 million fine. BP settled civil suits (4,000 in total) and paid the claimants from a fund of $2.1 billion that the company set aside for the litigation.

Prudhoe Bay

Prudhoe Bay is one of BP's refineries located on the 478,000 acres of land BP owns in Alaska.[39] In March 2006, a pipeline at BP's Prudhoe Bay, Alaska, facility burst and spilled 267,000 gallons of oil. The 22-mile pipeline carries oil from BP's facility to the Trans-Alaska Pipeline. State and federal investigators onsite following the spill indicated that the pipeline was severely corroded. As a result of the spill, both internal and government investigations of Prudhoe Bay and BP began. BP would eventually pay a $12 million criminal fine for the leaking pipes at Prudhoe Bay.[40]

The Inspecting and Cleaning of Pipes

BP used a coupon method of pipe inspection that sends pieces of metal into the pipeline to run with the flow. The "coupons" are then inspected to detect for corrosion. Of the 1,495 locations that BP monitored using the coupon method, only five were located in the area of the spill. BP did not use "smart pig" technology, the industry standard, as other companies do. The *smart pig* is a detection device that runs along the inside of a pipeline to detect corrosion. Larry Tatum, an engineer with corrosion expertise and an officer of the National Association of Corrosion Engineers, said of smart pigging, "If you want to find this type of random, spotty

corrosion, you've got to do 100% ultrasonic scanning, or the smart pig approach."[41] Industry standards require smart pigging every five years. BP had not done smart pigging on the Prudhoe Bay line since 1998. The pipes had not been cleaned since 1992.[42] BP had increased its pipeline maintenance budget to $71 million for 2006, an increase of 80% since 2001. The speed of the oil through the pipes had declined over the years, and the flow in 2006 was at a speed one-fourth of the flow rate that existed when the pipes first opened. The BP field manager at Prudhoe Bay said, following the spill, "If we had it to do over again, we would have been pigging those lines."[43]

During the 1990s, when oil was at $20 per barrel, all companies cut down on pipeline maintenance. More pipeline accidents and spills occurred during the 1990s but did not receive the attention that Prudhoe Bay did, because gas prices were low. A family of 12 was killed in 2000 when a BP pipeline near its New Mexico campground exploded. The only coverage of the explosion was a small paragraph in the *New York Times*. BP's 2000 spill and pipeline issues occurred at a time when gasoline prices were at an all-time high, and the talk of oil company profits was pervasive and across all forms of the media. The number of accidents in 1995 was 250; by 2005, that number had dropped to 50, after a steady decline. However, as the price of oil increased, the incentives for not shutting the pipes down increased. BP employees described Lord John Browne, the former head of BP (refer to the earlier discussion on the company background), as the industry's best cost cutter, who created "a ruthless culture."[44]

The economic life of the pipes was estimated at 25 years when the pipes were first installed in 1977. At the time, no one believed that the oil production in the

(continued)

---

[39]For complete information about BP's presence in Alaska and its contribution to the economic base there, go to http://www.alaska.bp.com (as accessed in original research).

[40]Department of Justice, "British Petroleum to Pay More than $370 Million in Environmental Crimes, Fraud," October 27, 2007, https://www.justice. gov/archive/opa/pr/2007/October/07_ag_850.html. (Accessed April 11, 2016).

[41]Matthew Dalton and John M. Biers, "Consultant Warned BP of Pipe-Network Corrosion," *Wall Street Journal*, August 24, 2006, p. A3.

[42]Jon Birger, "What Pipeline Problem?" *Fortune*, September 4, 2006, pp. 23–24.

[43]Chris Woodward, Paul Davidson, and Brad Heath, "BP Spill Highlights Aging Oil Field's Increasing Problems," *USA Today*, August 14, 2006, pp. 1B, 2B.

[44]Birger, "What Pipeline Problem?" pp. 23–24.

Case 2.8

(continued)

area would last longer than 25 years. One expert likened anticorrosion sensing and repairs to maintenance on a car: They have to be done regularly in order to keep the car running.

The External Pressure on the Pipes

In 2004, Walter Massey, the chair of BP's board's environmental committee, wrote a memo to fellow board members expressing concerns about the corrosion problems. Mr. Massey's memo described "[c]ost cutting, causing serious corrosion damage" to the pipes and creating the possibility of a catastrophic event that would put the Prudhoe Bay employees at risk. Internal documents uncovered in the government investigation show that a corrosion consultant who BP hired in 2004 issued a report that described the 22-mile pipeline as experiencing "accelerated corrosion."

Environmental groups called for additional government investigations into BP's environmental record and oil pipeline, refinery, and drilling activities: "The North Slope corrosion problem is simply the latest example of a pattern of neglect and less-than-adequate maintenance over the years."[45] The groups released information about BP's environmental record. The groups' releases were printed in newspapers around the world, including lengthy stories in the newspapers of London, where BP headquarters were located. A 2003 leak from the BP pipeline had harmed caribou in the area. BP officials promised government officials that it would conduct inspections of the pipeline to determine whether corrosion was causing the leaks. In 1999, BP paid a $6.5 million penalty for dumping hazardous waste at the Prudhoe Bay site. BP did report the hazardous waste spill voluntarily.

BP had been operating on borrowed goodwill when it came to regulatory relations. In 1999, the State of Alaska agreed to approve the proposed Arco–BP merger provided BP would agree to semiannual meetings with state officials to discuss progress on the "serious" corrosion problems for the Prudhoe Bay pipelines. The meetings did not take place as promised.

In the same year as the merger and the promises to Alaska, Chuck Hamel, a union advocate, corporate gadfly, and close friend of actress Sissy Spacek, filed a report with BP management about worker safety concerns based on the corrosion problems with Prudhoe Bay pipes. The memo indicated that workers were asked to skimp on the use of anticorrosion chemicals in the pipe because of expense. Prudhoe Bay BP employees were paid very well and were loyal. They earned $100,000 to $150,000 per year. They worked for two weeks and then had two weeks off because of the remote location of the facility and the near-total darkness, 24 hours per day during the winter months.

Hamel took his complaints and information to the U.S. Environmental Protection Agency (EPA) that year, based on the lack of response from BP management.[46] Mr. Hamel at one point owned an oil field in Prudhoe Bay, but subsequently sold it to Exxon. Exxon would later hit a gusher on the field, and Hamel sued for Exxon's failure to disclose to him the potential for oil discovery on his field. Ms. Spacek said Hamel was like an uncle to her: kind, generous, and trustworthy, and someone who spoke for those who cannot speak for themselves.

One executive at BP described the Prudhoe Bay spill and pipeline problems as follows: "Sometimes bad things happen to good companies."[47] An executive from Kinder Morgan (a pipeline company) said that Prudhoe Bay has been blown out of proportion: "That pipeline is still the safest part of the journey, including safer than when you put gas in your tank.[48]

One environmentalist wondered how BP could call itself a "green company" when its environmental record was so poor. The BP response was that "[w]e are investing in alternative energy sources. We are putting our money where our mouth is."[49] Environmental groups took the position that the conduct of BP should be the "nail in the coffin" for any plans to allow drilling in the north refuge area of Alaska (the Arctic National Wildlife Refuge, or ANWR, one of the world's greatest,

(continued)

---

[45]Woodward, Davidson, and Heath, "BP Spill Highlights Aging Oil Field's Increasing Problems," p. 1B.

[46]Jim Carlton, "BP's Alaska Woes Are No Surprise for One Gadfly," *Wall Street Journal*, August 12–13, 2006, pp. B1, B5.

[47]Id.

[48]Birger, "What Pipeline Problem?" pp. 23–24.

[49]Id.

Case 2.8

(continued)

yet untapped, sources of oil). "These companies simply cannot behave responsibly," stated one environmentalist leader in reaction to BP's conduct at Prudhoe Bay.

In September 2006, the executives of BP were summoned to appear at congressional hearings on oil pipelines. The executives found few friends during their hearings. The chair of the House Energy and Commerce Committee told BP's CEO, "Years of neglecting to inspect the most vital oil-gathering pipeline in this country is not acceptable."[50]

The committee heard testimony from an employee who raised concerns about Prudhoe Bay corrosion in 2004 and was then transferred from the facility. Richard Woolham, BP's chief inspector for the Alaska pipelines, was subpoenaed to testify but took the Fifth Amendment.[51] Another BP executive testified that BP had fallen short of the high standards the public had come to expect of it.

The Trading Markets

In June 2006, the Commodities Futures Trading Commission filed a civil complaint against BP, alleging that its brokers had tried to manipulate the price of propane by manipulating the supply, or at least access to information about the real supply levels. One broker wrote in an email that if they "squeezed" the pipeline, they could drive up the price of propane, "and then we could control the market at will," and "we would own them."[52] The brokers commented to each other about how easily they could control the supply and therefore the market price for propane.

Following the Prudhoe Bay pipeline incident, government investigators also began looking into BP's trading practices. On August 29, 2006, the Justice Department announced investigations into BP's energy trading and stock sales by executives and others. BP officials said it gets such requests regularly.

One of the investigations focused on alleged insider trading by BP brokers. BP ran one of the world's largest energy-trading firms, dealing not only in the sale of oil and gas but also in energy futures. BP also provided risk-management services for other companies. One regulator referred to the BP operation as one large commodities trading desk. Based on information about BP's storage, refinery, and pipeline facilities, as well as a wide expanse of information about other companies and their risk and exposure, the brokers were indicted for trading in commodities prior to announcements about BP's production quantity and transport systems, information that affects market prices and hence stock prices of companies affected by energy prices. BP had warned its brokers about the inability to use information gained from their positions to profit personally in the markets, commodities or stock, but there are no guarantees that such an artificial wall between information gained, but not used in a personal context, would be effective. For example, when the Texas City refinery explosion occurred, BP traders were warned not to trade on that information prior to its dissemination to the public. The shutdown of a major refinery can impact market prices for oil.

Following the indictments, one BP trader entered a guilty plea. BP also entered into a deferred prosecution agreement and paid a $303-million fine, $53 million of which was used to repay investors for the losses they experienced as a result of BP's advance trading. However, in September 2009, a federal judge tossed the indictments of the BP traders because he concluded that the law used for the basis of the indictments was not violated.[53]

The series of events resulted in negative press coverage. One London newspaper carried the headline "BP = Big Problems for Oil Giant."[54] From this headline,

(continued)

[50]Paul Davidson, "Congressmen Slam BP Executive at Oil Leak Hearings," *USA Today*, September 8, 2006, p. 2B.
[51]John J. Fialka, "BP's Top U.S. Pipeline Inspector Refuses to Testify," *Wall Street Journal*, September 8, 2006, p. A3.
[52]Tom Fowler, "How the Case against BP Traders Went Wrong," *Houston Chronicle*, September 18, 2009, http://www.chron.com/disp/story.mpl/business/energy/6626251.html.

[53]*U.S. v. Radley* et al., CA H-08-411 at https://www.justice.gov/sites/default/files/criminal-vns/legacy/2010/04/26/09-17-09radley-dismiss.pdf. Accessed April 11, 2016. *See also,* Fowler, "How the Case against BP Traders Went Wrong," http://www.chron.com/disp/story.mpl/business/energy/6626251.html.
[54]"BP: Big Problems for Oil Giant," *Red Independent*, August 30, 2006, http://news.independent.co.uk/business/analysis_and_features/article1222607.ece (as used in original research).

Case 2.8

(continued)

the public began developing its own translations for the BP acronym, such as "Beyond Pitiful" and "Big Putzes." The BP brand was damaged significantly by the unfortunate series of events.

BP Responses

In August 2006, when BP shut down the Prudhoe Bay pipeline for repair and replacement, it announced that it would replace 16 of the 22 miles of pipe from Prudhoe Bay.

On Tuesday, September 19, 2006, BP was downgraded by several agencies when it announced further delay in bringing Project Thunder Horse up and on line. Thunder Horse is a subsea drill in the Gulf of Mexico that suffered a severe setback the previous year when Hurricane Dennis hit the area and caused substantial damage to the work to date on the project. BP had anticipated having the site on line by early 2007.

The following is an excerpt from a lengthy announcement that BP issued in August 2006:

BP today announced an acceleration of actions to improve the operational integrity and monitoring of its US businesses. BP announced the addition of smart-pigging technology to the monitoring of all of its pipelines, worldwide.

The company said it would add a further $1 billion to the $6 billion already earmarked over the next four years to upgrade all aspects of safety at its US refineries and to repair and replace infield pipelines in Alaska.

Speaking in London, BP chief executive Lord Browne said: "These events in our US businesses have all caused great shock within the BP Group. They have prompted us to look very critically at what we can learn from ourselves and others and at what more we can do in certain key areas to assure ourselves and the outside world that our US businesses are consistently operating safely, and with honesty and integrity."

"We are, of course, continuing to co-operate to the fullest possible extent with the US regulatory bodies investigating these events. But we do not believe we can simply await the outcome of those

investigations. In addition to the significant steps we have already taken we have decided we must do more now." Browne said it is intended to appoint an advisory board to assist and advise the Group's wholly owned US subsidiary, BP America Inc. and its newly appointed chairman, Robert A. Malone, in monitoring the operations of BP's US businesses with particular focus on compliance, safety and regulatory affairs.

The measures Browne announced today include a step-up in the scale and pace of spending at BP's five US refineries on maintenance, turnarounds, inspections and staff training. Spending will now rise to $1.5 billion this year from $1.2 billion in 2005 and will jump further to an average [of] $1.7 billion each year from 2007 to 2010.

Systems to manage process safety at the refineries will undergo a major upgrade, with some $200 million earmarked to pay for 300 external experts who will conduct comprehensive audits, and redesigns where necessary, of all safety process systems. The new systems are targeted to be installed and working by the end of 2007, a year ahead of the original schedule.

BP today also pledged more rapid action to restore the integrity of its infield pipelines in Alaska. With corrosion monitoring already upgraded, it now plans to remove pipeline residues—through a process known as "pigging"—by November, six months ahead of the original schedule.

The pipeline which leaked in the recent oil spill has been taken out of service and will be replaced by a new line which has already been ordered. If other transit lines are found to be faulty, they will also be replaced.

Browne said a major review by independent external auditors had also been set in motion to review BP's compliance systems in its US trading business. In the wake of allegations of market manipulation in US propane trading, the auditors had examined the design of the trading organisation, delegations of authority, standards and guidelines, resources and the effectiveness of control and compliance. The results of the review were then shared with

(continued)

Case 2.8

(continued)

relevant US regulatory authorities and the auditors' recommendations were implemented by BP.[55]

BP also hired former federal judge Stanley Sporkin to investigate what happened at Prudhoe Bay and why. Judge Sporkin was famous for one line in his work in handling the criminal and civil cases resulting from the savings and loans frauds of the 1990s: "Where were the lawyers? Where were the auditors and the other professionals when this fraud was occurring?" Upon his appointment to the BP position, Judge Sporkin said, "I'll call them as I see them."[56]

On September 20, 2006, BP announced that it would spend $3 billion to upgrade its oil refinery in northwest Indiana, so it could process significantly more heavy crude from Canada, while also boosting its production of motor fuels at the site by up to 15%. The heavy crude from Canada was taken from Canada's vast oil sands resources, a source that had been left untapped and was seen as an alternative to the switch to ethanol. BP PLC's U.S. division said the upgrade would create up to 80 new, permanent, full-time jobs and 2,500 jobs during the three-year construction phase. The Whiting refinery, about 10 miles from Gary, Indiana, originally produced about 290,000 barrels a day of transportation fuels such as gasoline and diesel. Mike Hoffman, BP's group vice president for refining, said the project would modernize the equipment at the refinery, include environmental precautions beyond regulatory requirements, "and competitively reposition it as a top tier refinery well into the future." BP indicated that it would deliver the oil to the refinery by an existing pipeline but that the pipeline would be upgraded. The Indiana Economic Development Corporation provided $450,000 in training grants and $1.2 million in tax credits in order to attract the BP refinery.

BP stepped up both its safety programs as well as training for those operating refineries and other facilities in the company.[57] By 2010, Judge Sporkin's

contract as an external ombudsperson (one of the former terms for the functions of ethics and compliance in corporations; another former term was *employee concerns officers*) had ended. While the end of Judge Sporkin's assignment was seen as a negative action, BP explained that it was always its intention to internalize the function when "the internal processes were sufficiently robust."[58]

Offshore Oil Rigs and Safety

As BP was working to recover from its unfortunate series of events, another area was evolving that BP would need to address: its offshore oil production. Almost two years after Texas City and Prudhoe and nearly two years before the April 2010 Deepwater Horizon rig explosion and spill in the Gulf of Mexico, BP had a 193-barrel oil spill on June 5, 2008, at its Atlantis rig (also in the Gulf of Mexico). The internal report included the following information:

[Managers] put off repairing the pump in the context of a tight cost budget.

Leadership did not clearly question the safety impact of the delay in repair.

A BP safety officer told company investigators, "You only ever got questioned on why you couldn't spend less."[59]

The same problems that dogged refinery and pipeline operations had carried over into offshore production. Nonetheless, during this period of ongoing safety lapses and resulting casualties, BP continued its stellar financial performance. In 2007, BP's shares were at $77. Its debt/equity ratio was .31, its dividend rate was 15%, and it had a 20% return on equity (ROE), with gross margins of 27% and net margins of 7.47%. EPS growth in 2008 was at 64%. Managers were rewarded for their performance at the well for trimming 4% off costs.

(continued)

---

[55]From Securities and Exchange Commission, BP 6-K, http://www.sec.gov, August 6, 2006.

[56]Jim Carlton, "BP Hires Former Judge to Be U.S. Ombudsman," *Wall Street Journal*, September 5, 2006, p. A3.

[57]Daniel Gilbert, "Oil Rigs' Biggest Risk: Human Error," *Wall Street Journal*, April 20, 2015, p. B1.

[58]"Is This the Time to Be Closing BP's Ombuds Office?" 24 *Ethikos 1*, November/December 2010, http://compliancestrategists.com/csblog/wp-content/uploads/2014/01/December-2010-Ethikos-PDF-Download.pdf.

[59]Guy Chazan, Benoit Faucon, and Ben Casselman, "Safety and Cost Drives Clashed as CEO Hayward Remade BP," *Wall Street Journal*, June 30, 2010, p. A1.

Case 2.8

(continued)

However, that financial performance suffered a blow when one of BP's oil-drilling platforms, located about 50 miles off the coast of Louisiana in the Gulf of Mexico, experienced an explosion followed by an oil spill. The Deepwater Horizon rig, one that drilled at levels down to 18,000 feet, also experienced a fire on that fateful date of April 20, 2010. Eleven workers were killed. Oil began leaking from the rig in three places and had drifted ashore in Alabama by May 14 and in Louisiana by May 19. By July 7, 2010, the oil had reached Houston and Lake Ponchartrain in New Orleans.

Following the spill, BP lost $30 billion, or 16%, of its market value.[60] From the time of the explosion until the well was capped, BP spent $7 million per day trying to contain the spill, not much of which worked. Since that time, BP has continued working to restore the Gulf, efforts that cost the company billions. Tony Hayward, then CEO who took over following Browne's tenure, was onsite in Louisiana, overseeing the work to stop the leak. He pledged to pay for all damages and summarized his experience with the tragedy by quoting Winston Churchill: "When you are going through hell, keep going."[61] BP struggled, trying to contain the spill. Several engineering fixes did not work, and the relief wells took months to complete. As BP worked to stop the spill, oil drifted ashore. In total, 200 million gallons of oil spilled. On August 2, 2010, engineers were able to contain the spill.

A whistleblower allegation that had emerged early in 2010 resurfaced, as it were, following the explosion with the release of emails related to government investigations of BP, the rig, the well, the explosion, and the deaths and injuries. The emails express concern about whether other companies had completed crucial engineering drawings and paperwork necessary prior to operation of offshore rigs. Other information emerged related to BP's focus on costs versus best practices. Emails indicated that engineers who asked for an additional 10 hours in the critical path to address their concerns about the well, by installing 21 centralizers instead of just 6, were dismissed by the lead engineer

with an "I do not like this."[62] At hearings before the House of Representatives, other oil company CEOs testified that BP did not follow appropriate design standards in drilling the well.[63] A study by the EPA's special commission on the spill found that BP managers made 11 critical decisions that led to the explosion. A *Wall Street Journal* analysis found that BP used a risky design for one out of three of its deepwater wells that was cheaper than the preferred type of design.[64] The so-called long string design uses a single pipe for bringing the oil to the surface. Experts indicate that the result of using one long pipe is that natural gas accumulates around the pipe and can rise unchecked. Most experts recommend its use only in low-pressure wells, not in wells such as Deepwater Horizon. They also note that long string drilling would not be appropriate when a company does not know the area, something that was true about this well for BP.

In addition, evidence emerged that Halliburton officials knew that the cement mixture used to seal the bottom of the well was unstable; three laboratory tests indicated that the cement mixture did not meet industry standards.[65]

Deepwater Horizon is the largest oil spill in history and has been called the largest environmental disaster in history. BP agreed to a $20-billion fund that would be used to compensate businesses, workers, and others who were damaged as a result of the spill. The costs, in terms of cash outlays, have continued for BP. BP was given an ultimatum by the Obama administration and, shortly after a White House meeting, placed $20 billion in an escrow account for the U.S. government to distribute to those in the Gulf-area states who were harmed by the spill. BP sold off $7 billion in assets to cover the expenses and the $20 billion. BP took a

(continued)

[60]Peter Coy and Stanley Reed, "Lessons of the Spill," *BusinessWeek*, May 10–16, 2010, p. 48.
[61]*Id.*, at 61.

[62]Neil King Jr. and Russell Gold, "BP Crew Focused on Costs: Congress," *Wall Street Journal*, June 15, 2010, pp. A1, A5.
[63]Julie Schmit, "Oil Execs: BP Didn't Meet Standards," *USA Today*, June 16, 2010, p. 1B; and Siobahn Hughes and Stephen Power, "BP Spill-Panel Staff Cites Management Failings," *Wall Street Journal*, December 3, 2010, p. A6.
[64]Russell Gold and Tom McGinty, "BP Relied on Cheaper Wells," *Wall Street Journal*, June 19–20, 2010, p. A1.
[65]John M. Broder, "Companies Knew of Cement Flaws before Rig Blast," *New York Times*, October 29, 2010, p. A1.

Case 2.8

(continued)

$32 billion charge in July 2010 for the Gulf Oil spill costs and added the following about its losses in its July 27, 2010, SEC filing:

> The costs and charges involved in meeting our commitments in responding to the Gulf of Mexico oil spill are very significant and this $17 billion reported loss reflects that. However, outside the Gulf it is very encouraging that BP's global business has delivered another strong underlying performance, which means that the company is in robust shape to meet its responsibilities in dealing with the human tragedy and oil spill in the Gulf of Mexico.[66]

The Oil Industry Post–Deepwater Horizon

The federal government placed a moratorium on all new offshore drilling following the Deepwater Horizon explosion and spill. However, a federal court issued an injunction against the moratorium taking effect on the grounds that the federal government had acted arbitrarily and capriciously.[67] The Secretary of the Interior redrafted the moratorium, which stayed in effect until the Obama administration lifted it in October 2010. In the initial decision, Federal District Judge Martin Feldman concluded that the failure of one well, even with safety issues, was not grounds for prohibiting all offshore drilling.

> After reviewing the Secretary's Report, the Moratorium Memorandum, and the Notice to Lessees, the Court is unable to divine or fathom a relationship between the findings and the immense scope of the moratorium. The Report, invoked by the Secretary, describes the offshore oil industry in the Gulf and offers many compelling recommendations to improve safety. But it offers no timeline for implementation, though many of the proposed changes are represented to be implemented immediately. The Report patently lacks any analysis of the asserted fear of threat of irreparable injury or safety hazards posed by the thirty-three permitted rigs also reached

by the moratorium. It is incident-specific and driven: Deepwater Horizon and BP only. None others. While the Report notes the increase in deepwater drilling over the past ten years and the increased safety risk associated with deepwater drilling, the parameters of "deepwater" remain confused. And drilling elsewhere simply seems driven by political or social agendas on all sides. The Report seems to define "deepwater" as drilling beyond a depth of 1000 feet by referencing the increased difficulty of drilling beyond this depth; similarly, the shallowest depth referenced in the maps and facts included in the Report is "less than 1000 feet." But while there is no mention of the 500 feet depth anywhere in the Report itself, the Notice to Lessees suddenly defines "deepwater" as more than 500 feet.

The Deepwater Horizon oil spill is an unprecedented, sad, ugly and inhuman disaster. What seems clear is that the federal government has been pressed by what happened on the Deepwater Horizon into an otherwise sweeping confirmation that all Gulf deepwater drilling activities put us all in a universal threat of irreparable harm. While the implementation of regulations and a new culture of safety are supportable by the Report and the documents presented, the blanket moratorium, with no parameters, seems to assume that because one rig failed and although no one yet fully knows why, all companies and rigs drilling new wells over 500 feet also universally present an imminent danger.[68]

Tony Hayward was replaced as CEO of BP on July 27, 2010, by Robert Dudley, a U.S. citizen and native of Mississippi. Mr. Hayward issued a statement upon his forced retirement: "The Gulf of Mexico explosion was a terrible tragedy for which—as the man in charge of BP when it happened—I will always feel a deep responsibility, regardless of where blame is ultimately found to lie."[69] The Deepwater Horizon well was plugged permanently in September 2010.

(continued)

---

[66]BP's 6-K filing, July 27, 2010, https://www.sec.gov/Archives/edgar/data/313807/000119163810000878/bp201007276k3.htm. Accessed April 11, 2016.
[67]*Hornbeck Offshore Services, LLC v. Salazar*, 696 F.Supp.2d 627 (E.D. La. 2010).

[68]*Id.*
[69]www.bp.com. Click Press Releases. July 27, 2010. Accessed August 6, 2010.

Case 2.8

(continued)

Following BP's guilty plea on charges related to the explosion at its Deepwater Horizon oil rig, the EPA announced that BP could not hold any federal contracts (which would include drilling on federal lands) until it was able to demonstrate that its operations meet federal standards.

BP agreed, as part of its plea, to have a safety monitor on its deepwater operations and to retain an ethics monitor to ensure that employees do not violate federal laws and standards in BP operations.[70] Until the ban was lifted, BP could not bid on federal oil leases that become available.

The ban proved costly because 25% of BP's oil production is in the United States. BP has spent $52 billion on operations in the United States over the past few years.[71] BP has also been selling assets in other places throughout the world in order to meet the costs of the settlement and other issues related to the Deepwater explosion and spill. BP has paid the following fines and settlements:

$50 million fine to EPA

$58 million fine to OSHA (largest in U.S. history) for pre–Deepwater Horizon explosion

$4 billion for crimes related to Deepwater Horizon explosion

$20 billion civil penalty

Including cleanup costs, BP released the total cost of the Deepwater explosion as $61.6 billion.[72]

Other Costs to BP and Its Future

The costs to BP's business operations were documented in a series of graphs done by the *Wall Street Journal*.[73] The graphs tell the story of the impact ethical and legal lapses can have on a company.

As the graphs show, since the time of Deepwater Horizon, BP has been digging its way out of holes in drilling, capitalization, production, and earnings.

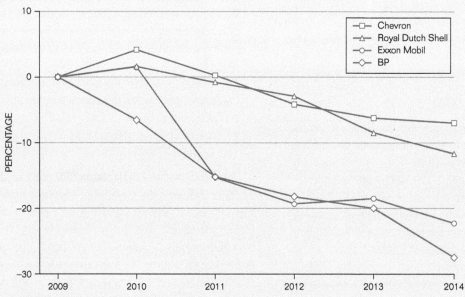

Annual Oil Production, change since 2009

(continued)

---

[70]John M. Broder and Stanley Reed, "BP Is Barred from Taking Government Contracts," *New York Times*, November 29, 2012, p. B1.
[71]Ann Davis, "Probes of BP Point to Hurdles U.S. Case Faces," *Wall Street Journal*, August 30, 2006, p. C1.

[72]Michael Amon and Tapan Panchal, "BP's Gulf-Spill Tab Hits $62 Billion," *Wall Street Journal*, July 15, 2016, p. B3.
[73]Justin Scheck and Saurabh Chaturvedi, "After Settlement, BP Faces Rocky Landscape," *Wall Street Journal*, July 22, 2015, pp. A1, A12.

Case 2.8

(continued)

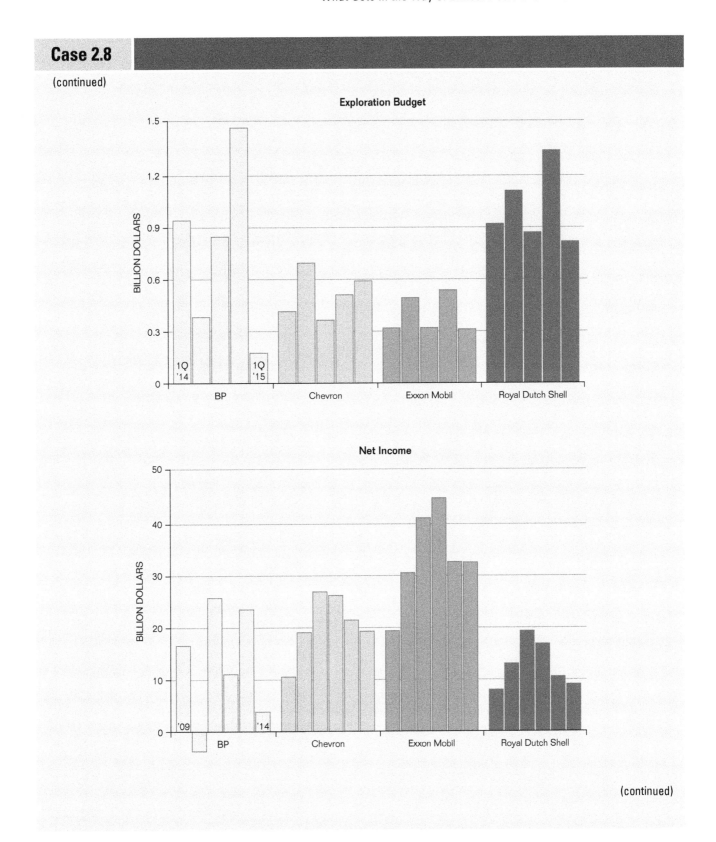

(continued)

Case 2.8

(continued)

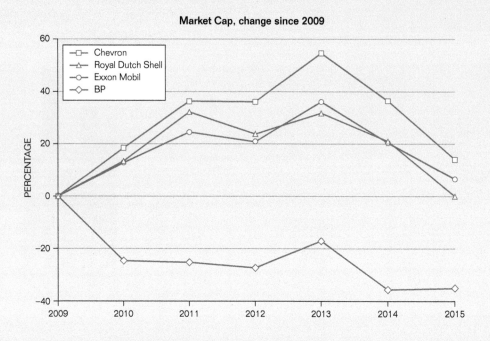

Market Cap, change since 2009

The size of this industry giant has shrunk. Today BP has 60,000 employees and 18,700 stations in 78 countries. By 2021, BP reduced its debt to $35 billion and was planning to buy back shares.[74] BP's strategic plan calls for reducing its dependence on oil for income and for increasing its investment in wind and solar power. The effects of the decisions about Deepwater Horizon's type of drilling, cuts in maintenance budgets, and silencing employees who had questions resulted in a lost decade for BP.

Discussion Questions

1. Discuss the ethical, negligence, and environmental issues that you see in this case.

2. Make a list of the questions from Unit 1 that might have helped BP do a better analysis for their decisions on these key issues that resulted in significant harm to employees, communities, and the environment.

3. BP rented the rig from Transocean for $500,000 per day. Transocean had been recognized by the U.S. government for its safety record.[75] Can companies

distance themselves from liability and responsibility through the use of contractors? What are the risks of using third-party contractors?

4. Discuss how BP got into the position in which it found itself in late 2006, and what might have prevented the spill, financial fallout, and loss of reputation. Be sure to factor in the financial implications of any decision made during the period from 2001 to 2006.

5. What was the impact of the emphasis on cost cutting on BP's culture? What was the impact on the company's performance? List the key decision points that you saw in the case.

6. Evaluate the social responsibility positions of BP in light of the refinery explosion and the pipeline issue. What can companies learn from the BP experience?

7. OSHA assessed criminal penalties in this case. What might have helped internal BP discussions about refinery conditions and the safety of their deep-water drilling program?

8. Apply the layers of ethics to this scenario. Who was making the decisions? The employees were concerned about those decisions. Did their views carry any weight within the company?

---

[74]Sarah McFarlane, "Recovery in Energy Industry, *Wall Street Journal*, April 7, 2021, p. B3.

[75]Ben Casselman, Russell Gold, and Angel Gonzalez, "Workers Missing after Gulf Rig Explodes," *Wall Street Journal*, April 22, 2010, pp. A1, A4.

(continued)

Case 2.8

(continued)

9. The judge's opinion on the moratorium contained this discussion of the government's use of a report by experts on offshore drilling:

> Much to the government's discomfort and this Court's uneasiness, the Summary also states that "the recommendations contained in this report have been peer-reviewed by seven experts identified by the National Academy of Engineering." As the plaintiffs, and the experts themselves, pointedly observe, this statement was misleading. The experts charge it was a "misrepresentation." It was factually incorrect. Although the experts agreed with the safety recommendations contained in the body of the main Report, five of the National Academy experts and three of the other experts have publicly stated that they "do not agree with the six month blanket moratorium" on floating drilling. They envisioned a more limited kind of moratorium, but a blanket moratorium was added after their final review, they complain, and was never agreed to by them. A factor that might cause some apprehension about the probity of the process that led to the Report.

The draft reviewed by the experts, for example, recommended a six-month moratorium on exploratory wells deeper than 1000 feet (not 500 feet) to allow for implementation of suggested safety measures.

The Report makes no effort to explicitly justify the moratorium: it does not discuss any irreparable harm that would warrant a suspension of operations, it does not explain how long it would take to implement the recommended safety measures. The Report does generalize that "[w]hile technological progress has enabled the pursuit of deeper oil and gas deposits in deeper water, the risks associated with operating in water depths in excess of 1,000 feet are significantly more complex than in shallow water."[76]

Evaluate the ethics of the Secretary of Interior regarding the representations of what the experts concluded.

10. Evaluate Mr. Hayward's parting statement and his views on accountability.

---

[76]*Hornbeck Offshore Services, LLC v. Salazar*, 696 F. Supp. 2d 627 (E.D. La. 2010).

Resolving Ethical Dilemmas in Business

Reading 2.9

Framing Issues Carefully: A Structured Approach for Solving Ethical Dilemmas and Trying Out Your Ethical Skills on an Example

The issues in ethics cases may range from driving solo in the carpool lane to Wi-Fi piggybacking, to issues of bribery, insider trading, and capitalization of ordinary expenses, but they still hark back to the same questions and considerations (after the fact versus in the midst of) that you learned in Unit 1.

However, because you will be a businessperson evaluating ethical issues, adding some considerations to those given in Reading 1.8 provides the business perspective for ethical analysis.

1. Do your numbers. Think about the costs of your decision, both long and short term. For example, not disclosing information about the company's financial performance buys you time and prevents a drop in the company's share price. But if things do not improve, you will be grappling with two problems: the drop in the share price and the company's loss of trust and credibility for not disclosing the information sooner. Just as ethical analysis requires you to gain a 360-degree perspective, a look at the numbers considers all costs. Will we lose customers? Will our cost of capital increase if we do have a major accident or an unsafe product? What happens if we cut the maintenance budget too much? We save money temporarily, but will the lack of maintenance affect safety?

2. Recall the categories of ethical dilemmas from Reading 1.4 and be sure that you have considered all the ethical issues.

3. Make sure that you have applied all the questions that are used under the various models in Reading 1.8 to verify that you have really thought through the issue, such as whether what you want to do is even legal.

4. Check for those warm language labels and rationalizations that may find you overlooking an issue as you find comfort in avoiding real analysis.

5. Be sure to consider other cases that you have studied and whether there are historical precedents that might be of help in analyzing your present situation and dilemma.

6. Bring in other areas of business to be sure that you are looking at the ethical issue fully. For example, consider any strategic advantages in your decision. Be sure to apply economic principles to proposed actions.

Think through the organizational behavior implications of your decision. In other words, integrate what you know about business as you analyze from an ethical perspective.

7. Watch the framing of the issue. If you look at an issue within the framework of "This could really hurt us if it went public," you are destined to make ethical mistakes and risk reputational capital. Instead, frame the issue as, "What are the consequences of what we know?" "What will happen if we do nothing to fix it and what we know becomes public?" "Am I overlooking the harm that we are doing to someone through our actions?"

Discussion Question

Review these examples side by side. Make a list of your answers to the components of analysis in Reading 2.9. What is different about the two scenarios? What is the same?

Example 1—The Bakery	Example 2—The Real Estate Financing Deal
"When working at a bakery, I was asked to repackage the old bread/cake and make it look nice and sell that first to the customers."	"I was asked to 'fudge' information and a bid value for a private equity firm that I interned for. When creating the investment teaser and memoranda for the investors, I listed the analyst's experience in real estate that was as longer than what they actually had. And I worked backwards from a final bid value of £90 M rather than reach an intrinsic value from assumptions because 'that's the number we need to get past the first round.'"

Case 2.10

Penn State: Framing Ethical Issues

The Penn State Nittany Lions football team, begun in 1887, has been a powerhouse. The team has had seven undefeated seasons, two national titles, two Big Ten conference titles, and five other national championships. In addition, the team has tied with Stanford University for the number 10 slot on player graduation percentages, with 87% in 2011. The team has been referred to as a "grand experiment" for its devotion to performance both on and off the field. From 1966 through 2011, the late Joseph "Joe" Paterno, fondly known as JoePa, coached the Nittany Lions. He was recognized, prior to the events covered here, as the "winningest coach" in college football, accumulating 409 wins to 164 losses and three ties.

The National Collegiate Athletic Association (NCAA) stripped Mr. Paterno of 112 of his wins (from 1998 through 2012), required Penn State to pay a fine of $60,000,000, banned the team from bowl games, cut 10 scholarships

for the 2011–2012 season and 20 scholarships from 2012 to 2016. These levels of sanctions, just shy of the rare death penalty in college athletics in which a sports program is shut down, are generally the result of recruiting violations, payments to student-athletes, or falsification of academic records. However, these sanctions were not the result of violations in any of those areas. Penn State suffered from a near death penalty from inaction related to the criminal activity of one of its assistant coaches, Jerry Sandusky, and the failure of Mr. Paterno, the athletic director, and other university officials to take action to stop Mr. Sandusky at any time during his long history of child abuse, from 1998 to 2011. Those events resulted in a forever-changed atmosphere in State College, Pennsylvania, the home of Penn State that once carried the nickname, "Happy Valley."

However, in 2014, the NCAA lifted the postseason ban. In 2015, the NCAA restored the 112 wins to Penn State,

(continued)

Case 2.10

(continued)

111 of which belonged to Paterno. This case has strong emotions on both sides, but its purpose in being included in a textbook is to teach you the skills of evaluating ethical issues in real time. No matter your opinion about the Penn State events and outcome, there are two important concepts to keep in mind: (1) lives and an organization were forever changed by these events and (2) opinion is not ethical analysis—feeling something as right or wrong does not help you see the issues in situations. As you read the case, think about the decision points that each of the individuals faced as events unfolded. Think about their reasoning processes, list any issues or perspectives that they missed, and think about who was affected by their decisions. Regardless of hindsight, your ethical education involves learning to spot ethical issues and apply reasoning to determine choices that help the organization, not bring sanctions. To help you as you read the case, the following chart identifies the individuals involved in the case.

Name	Title/Role
Joe Paterno	Head football coach at Penn State from 1966–2011
Gerry Sandusky	Assistant football coach at Penn State from 1969–1999
Wendall Courtney	Attorney for Sandusky charity and outside counsel for Penn State for twenty-eight years
Alycia Chambers	Psychologist in State College, PA—first contacted about Sandusky abuse
Ron Schreffler	Detective at Penn State University Police Department
Jerry Lauro	Case worker who handled the first Sandusky complaint
Graham Spanier	Penn State president during Sandusky years until 2011
Tim Curley	Penn State athletic director during Sandusky years
Gary Schultz	Penn State senior VP for finance and business
Thomas Harmon	Penn State police chief
Jim Calhoun	Penn State janitor in football facilities who witnessed a Sandusky incident in 2000
Michael McQueary	Grad student and assistant football coach under Paterno
Cynthia Baldwin	Penn State general counsel
Vicky Triponey	Penn State standards and conduct officer who left the university

The First Investigation of Jerry Sandusky's Conduct

Gerald A. Sandusky (Jerry) was a Penn State University alum, having attended the university from 1962 to 1966. Following his graduation, Mr. Sandusky became a graduate assistant in the Penn State football program for one year.[77] He then left to take a position as a physical education instructor and coach at Juanita College from 1967 to 1968. He was also a physical education instructor and coach at Boston University

(continued)

released publicly, there were objections and proposals to have another investigation. Eventually, Penn State students opposed another investigation in the interest of moving on. http://www.collegian.psu.edu/news/campus/article_c8de970e-4d07-11e4-aa5a-001a4bcf6878.html. For a perspective on the Freeh Report, see Rodney Hughes, "Reflections of a Former Trustee: Putting the Freeh Report into Perspective, One year Later," *Onward State*, November 26, 2012, http://onwardstate.com/2012/11/26/reflections-of-a-former-trustee-putting-the-freeh-report-into-perspective-one-year-later/.

---

[77]Freeh Sporkin & Sullivan, LLP, *Report of the Special Investigative Counsel Regarding the Actions of the Pennsylvania State University Related to the Child Sexual Abuse Committed* by Gerald A. Sandusky (2012), p. 39. This report will hereafter be abbreviated as "Freeh Report." When the Freeh report was

Case 2.10

(continued)

from 1968 to 1969. Penn State hired Mr. Sandusky in 1969 as an assistant football coach and assistant professor of physical education, a position he held until his retirement in 1999.[78]

In 1977, with the help of attorney Wendall Courtney, Mr. Sandusky founded the "Second Mile," a nonprofit organization dedicated to providing recreational and sports experiences for disadvantaged Pennsylvania children.[79] Second Mile has a board of trustees, and many Penn State employees or members of their families served as trustees. In addition, Penn State employees and their families supported Second Mile with donations and through their service at events sponsored by Second Mile. Second Mile was permitted very open access to Penn State facilities for its events. Because of this access and sporting events held on campus for Second Mile children, Mr. Sandusky was seen frequently (prior to 1998) in the showers of the Lasch Building (showers used by the Penn State football team) with those children.

Sandusky's Sexual Abuse of Second Mile Boys and University and Law Enforcement Responses

It was in 1998 that activities by Mr. Sandusky resulted in third-party involvement. On May 3, 1998, Mr. Sandusky picked up an 11-year-old boy at his home based on a prior invitation to the boy and his mother to have the child use the exercise facilities at the Lasch Building. The young boy showered with Mr. Sandusky after exercising and was upset by Mr. Sandusky's touching and holding. Mr. Sandusky told the boy that he loved him and that they had a special relationship. When he returned home, the boy's mother was concerned because he was behaving in a way that she knew indicated he was upset about something.

He explained to his mother that he had showered with Mr. Sandusky.

On May 4, 1998, the boy's mother called Alycia Chambers, a psychologist in State College, Pennsylvania, who had been working with the young boy, seeking her advice on whether she was right to be concerned about what had happened between her son and Mr. Sandusky. Ms. Chambers told the boy's mother to report the incident to authorities.

The boy's mother reported the incident that same morning (the morning after the shower events with her son) to Detective Ron Schreffler of the University Police Department. Detective Schreffler interviewed the boy one-half hour later and was given all the details, including the additional information that one of the boy's 10-year-old friends had experienced the same type of treatment by Mr. Sandusky in the Lasch showers.

After Ms. Chambers met with the boy, she called the Pennsylvania child abuse hotline and made a report. Her subsequent consultation with colleagues convinced her that what was occurring was a classic pattern in which the pedophile builds a relationship with a child through activities. Affection and trust build and then the pedophile begins touching the child gradually.[80] The child permits the touching because of the close relationship that has been built. Many of the victims of pedophiles have not experienced having so much attention or enjoying so many different activities.

Detective Schreffler notified the Centre County Children and Youth Services (CYS) about the investigation but was referred to the Department of Public Welfare because of connections between CYS and the Second Mile, and Mr. Sandusky. Caseworker Jerry Lauro handled the case for the Department of Public Welfare. Detective Schreffler also contacted the Centre County prosecutor but did not notify officials at Penn State. When asked why he did not talk with university officials, he said that he did not want to have to "worry about Old Main sticking their nose in the investigation," something he had experienced in the past.[81]

(continued)

---

[78]Mr. Sandusky received tenure in 1980.

[79]Mr. Sandusky's book, *Touched: The Jerry Sandusky Story*, is an autobiographical tome that focuses on Mr. Sandusky's supposed dedication to helping youth as described in Second Mile's website. Second Mile was there described as a "nonprofit organization for children who need additional support . . . . to promote self-confidence as well as physical, academic, and personal success." John W. Miller, Darren Everson, and Dionne Searcey, "Abuse Case Rocks Penn State," *Wall Street Journal*, November 7, 2011.

---

[80]Freeh Report, p. 43.
[81]Freeh Report, p. 43.

Case 2.10

(continued)

As the investigation progressed, Mr. Sandusky continued to telephone the boy, and those involved worked to develop reports and information. Ms. Chambers turned over her report to Detective Schreffler, a report that emphasized the gravity of the events. However, for some reason, Mr. Lauro did not receive the Chambers report and only received a report from John Seasock, a counselor who had a contract with CYS. Mr. Seasock's report ruled out that there was a situation in which boys were being groomed for sexual victimization and recommended only that someone visit with Mr. Sandusky about acceptable behavior with children.[82] Mr. Seacock wrote that he did not want to "cast dispersion [sic]" on Mr. Sandusky but did want to warn him about gray areas in his conduct.[83] Mr. Seacock believed that there was no risk because he had never heard of a 55-year-old man becoming a pedophile.[84] There were also no records indicating any similar conduct by Mr. Sandusky prior to this filing.

About a week after the shower incident, Mr. Sandusky returned to the boy's home and met with the boy's mother as Detective Schreffler and a local police officer hid and listened. Mr. Sandusky, when confronted by the mother about her son's acting odd, explained that he might have just worked him out too hard. The mother suggested that Mr. Sandusky should leave her son alone. Mr. Sandusky apologized.

One week after the apology, Mr. Sandusky again met at the home of the boy with his mother (with Detective Schreffler and a local police officer listening) and was asked about the bear hug in the shower. Mr. Sandusky said that "maybe" his private parts touched those of the boy. He denied having sexual feelings and explained that he showered with other boys. The mother asked Mr. Sandusky to stay away from her son, and he responded, "I understand. I was wrong. I wish I could get forgiveness. I know I won't get it from you. I wish I were dead."[85]

One week later, Detective Schreffler and Mr. Lauro talked with Mr. Sandusky in the Lasch building, and Mr. Sandusky assured them that "honest to God nothing happened."[86] After that discussion, the investigation ended without anyone discussing what had happened with the district attorney.

Between May 4 and May 30, 1998, there were notes and emails among and between Penn State University President Graham Spanier; Gary Schultz, the senior vice president for finance and business at Penn State; and Tim Curley, the Penn State athletic director. It is not clear how Mr. Schultz first learned of the events of May 4, 1998, but his notes reflect that he knew almost immediately and instructed University Police Department Chief Thomas Harmon to let him know everything as the investigation proceeded. His notes concluded that Mr. Sandusky's behavior was "at best—inappropriate @ worst sexual improprieties."[87] After he received more information about the second boy's experience and the hotline report, his notes ask, "Is this opening of pandora's box? Other children?"[88]

The correspondence and notes also indicate that Mr. Curley had notified Mr. Schultz and Coach Paterno, and both had asked to be kept informed about the investigation. Other documents indicate that Dr. Spanier was also notified, but he denied being aware of the issue and noted that he received many emails each day that keep him informed about an array of evolving concerns.

At some point, Mr. Harmon made the decision not to make a crime log entry related to the Sandusky allegations. Mr. Harmon wrote to Mr. Schultz that he felt justified in not entering the case in the university crime log, as was required by law and procedurally under university regulations. Mr. Harmon said that he had concluded that he had not found clear evidence of a crime.[89] All the investigation paperwork was then labeled "Administrative Information" and never recorded as a criminal investigation.

Also, at some point the administrators and University Police made the decision not to notify the Penn State

(continued)

---

[82](Freeh Report, p. 44).

[83]Freeh Report, p. 44.

[84]Mr. Seasock did have a contract with Penn State from 2000 through 2006, receiving payments of $11,448.86 for counseling services. No one has made any connection between his relationship to Penn State and his decisions in the 1998 case.

[85]Freeh Report, p. 45.

[86]Freeh Report, p. 46.

[87]Freeh Report, p. 47.

[88]*Id.*

[89]Freeh Report, p. 48.

Case 2.10

(continued)

Office of Human Resources (OHR), a practice that was typical in other cases in which staff or faculty were under investigation.

As the investigation continued, inquiries came from the athletic department. On May 13, 1998, Mr. Curley sent an email with the subject line "Jerry" to Mr. Schultz, asking, "Anything new in this department? Coach is anxious to know where it stands."[90] Mr. Curley also requested updates on May 18 and May 30, 1998.[91]

When the investigation was concluded, and after the investigators' meeting with Mr. Sandusky, Mr. Schultz sent the following email to Dr. Spanier and Mr. Curley:

> [Investigators] met with Jerry on Monday and concluded that there was no criminal behavior and the matter was closed as an investigation. He was a little emotional and expressed concern as to how this might have adversely affected the child. I think the matter has been appropriately investigated and I hope it is now behind us.[92]

None of the documents or correspondence indicates that Mr. Sandusky was warned not to shower with children. There was no discussion of whether Penn State should continue to allow its facilities to be used by Second Mile and no advice given to Mr. Sandusky to seek counseling. In addition, no one in risk management was notified about the incident or the investigation. In 1999, when Mr. Sandusky retired, there was considerable correspondence regarding Mr. Sandusky's request to continue to use Penn State facilities, particularly the Lasch Building, for Second Mile programs and events. When

Mr. Sandusky wrote to request "access to training and workout facilities" in his retirement, risk management officials hand wrote their response on the request, "Is this for personal use or 2nd Mile kids. No to 2nd Mile. Liability problems."[93]

The Impact of Inaction—1998–2001

The 2012 convictions of Mr. Sandusky for child sexual assault involved the following incidents:

- Victim 2—assaulted in the Lasch Building in February 2001
- Victim 3—assaulted in the Lasch Building on dates between July 1999 and December 2001
- Victim 4—assaulted in Old Lasch and the Lasch Building between 1999 and 2000, as well as during a Penn State bowl game trip to Texas in December 1999
- Victim 5—assaulted in the Lasch Building in August 2001
- Victim 8—assaulted in the Lasch Building in November 2000

In fall 2000, Jim Calhoun, a janitor in the Lasch Building, told a coworker that he had witnessed Mr. Sandusky in the Lasch Building showers pinning a boy against the wall and sexually assaulting him. Mr. Calhoun told his coworker that he had "fought in the [Korean] War . . . seen people with their guts blowed out, arms dismembered . . . I just witnessed something in there I'll never forget."[94] Later that night, the janitor who listened to Mr. Calhoun's report saw two pairs of feet in the same shower in the Lasch Building. He waited for the two to finish and then saw Mr. Sandusky and a young boy (about 12) leave the locker room holding hands. The supervisor for Mr. Calhoun and the other janitor who witnessed the Sandusky conduct advised them to report the incidents. Mr. Calhoun responded, "No, they'll get rid of all of us."[95] The second janitor responded that reporting the incidents "would have been like going against the President of the United States in my eyes. I know Paterno has so much power, if he wanted to get rid

(continued)

---

[90]Freeh Report, p. 49. When Mr. Paterno testified before the Sandusky grand jury in 2011, he testified that he knew of no other incidents involving Jerry other than the Mike McQueary report on the incident that he witnessed (see *infra* for more information on this incident). Freeh Report, p. 53.

[91]Freeh Report, 52. When the investigation of Mr. Sandusky was before the grand jury, Mr. Curley testified that he could not recall that any incident involving Mr. Sandusky and children in the showers was ever brought to his attention. Freeh Report, p. 52.

[92]Freeh Report, p. 50. When Mr. Schultz testified before the grand jury he said that he was never aware that there had been a 1998 investigation of Mr. Sandusky's conduct in the showers. Dr. Spanier told investigators in the later Sandusky grand jury case that the first he knew of the 1998 incident was in 2011, when he appeared before the grand jury.

[93]Freeh Report, p. 51.
[94]Freeh Report, p. 65.
[95]Freeh Report, p. 65.

Case 2.10

(continued)

of someone, I would have been gone [because] football runs this University."[96] No report was made, there was no investigation, and university officials were unaware of the incidents witnessed by the janitors.

Mr. Sandusky retired from Penn State with a lump-sum payment of $168,000. During the negotiations for his retirement, Dr. Spanier and Mr. Curley considered the possibility of giving Mr. Sandusky a position as assistant athletic director, but that possibility was abandoned. Mr. Sandusky had hoped to become head coach following Mr. Paterno's retirement but was told by Mr. Paterno in February 1998 that there was no way he would become head coach. There was some discussion of making Mr. Sandusky the head coach at the university's Altoona campus for a possible Division III football program there, but it proved financially unfeasible after Mr. Sandusky was given time to pull together a plan and resources for such a program. Mr. Sandusky was given emeritus rank, a retirement privilege awarded in colleges and universities on the basis of merit and career achievement. The Freeh Report concluded that Mr. Sandusky did not meet the eligibility requirements for emeritus status but also concluded that the retirement package awarded was not related to the 1998 investigation. The emeritus rank entitled Mr. Sandusky to access to university facilities, including Penn State's East Area locker room and its showers.

The 2001 Allegations Against Jerry Sandusky

In February 2001, a graduate assistant with the football program, Michael McQueary, heard what he called "rhythmic slapping sounds" coming from the Lasch Hall showers at about 9:30 p.m. on a Friday evening. Using a mirror, Mr. McQueary looked into the showers and saw Mr. Sandusky with a "prepubescent" boy.[97] Mr. Sandusky was directly behind the young boy and had his arms around the boy's waist. Mr. McQueary said that he believed Mr. Sandusky was sexually molesting the boy. Mr. McQueary slammed his locker, the conduct stopped, and Mr. Sandusky and the boy saw Mr. McQueary.

Mr. McQueary left the locker room and went to his office, where he called his father, seeking advice. His father advised him to tell Mr. Paterno. Mr. McQueary called Mr. Paterno the next morning and requested a meeting. Mr. Paterno was somewhat gruff and told Mr. McQueary that he did not have a job for him and if that were the subject of the meeting, "don't bother coming over."[98] Upon Mr. McQueary's assurance that the matter was serious, the two met on the Saturday morning following the shower incident, and Mr. McQueary told Mr. Paterno that he had witnessed Mr. Sandusky involved in conduct with a young boy that was "extremely sexual in nature." Mr. Paterno told Mr. McQueary that he would figure out what needed to be done.

Mr. Paterno then had a meeting on Sunday in his home with Mr. Curley and Mr. Schultz, where he discussed what Mr. McQueary had seen. Mr. Schultz then called Penn State's outside legal counsel, Wendell Courtney, about reporting child abuse. Mr. Courtney had been Penn State's outside legal counsel for 28 years, and his law firm had represented the university for almost 50 years.

The next day, February 12, 2001, Mr. Curley, Mr. Schultz, and Dr. Spanier met.[99] The three agreed to meet with Mr. Paterno later in the week to discuss their obligations to report the conduct to the state's Department of Public Welfare. Dr. Spanier asked Mr. Curley to meet with Mr. Sandusky and tell him that Second Mile boys could no longer use the showers. Prior to the meeting, Mr. Schultz had used the Internet to research the names of the Second Mile board members. Mr. Schultz also sent an email to Mr. Harmon to inquire whether there were university records related to the 1998 event involving Mr. Sandusky. Mr. Harmon's email response indicated that there were records and that they were in the university's "imaged archives."[100]

(continued)

---

[96]Freeh Report, p. 65.

[97]Bill Pennington & Nate Schweber, "Aspiring Coach, in Middle of College Scandal," *New York Times*, November 10, 2011, p. A1.

[98]Freeh Report, p. 67.

[99]The notes of this meeting and other documents related to Mr. Sandusky were removed from Mr. Schultz's office in November 2011 by Mr. Schultz's assistant after the grand jury returned an indictment of Mr. Sandusky on criminal charges of child sexual assault. The existence of those files was not known until May 2012, as Mr. Freeh conducted his investigation of the university's actions involving Mr. Sandusky's conduct (Freeh Report, pp. 69–70). No one at the university made any attempt to find out who the boy in the showers was and inquire after his well-being.

[100]Freeh Report, p. 71.

Case 2.10

(continued)

About 10 days after he met with Mr. Paterno, Mr. McQueary met with Messrs. Schultz and Curley and discussed the incident. Messrs. Schultz, Curley, and Spanier then met again. Notes from the meeting reflect a three-step action plan of telling Mr. Sandusky that he was banished from the facilities, informing Second Mile about the incident, and notifying the Department of Public Welfare about the incident.[101]

One day later, on February 27, 2001, Mr. Curley proposed to Dr. Spanier and Mr. Schultz a different plan of simply talking to Mr. Sandusky first before involving third parties, explaining that he was uncomfortable revealing the information to others until they had Mr. Sandusky's response.[102] He then proposed that Mr. Sandusky go with him to talk to Second Mile board members, after he was able to get Mr. Sandusky to agree to disclosure to Second Mile's board. He also proposed that Mr. Sandusky be required to obtain counseling. Dr. Spanier's response was as follows:

> Tim: This approach is acceptable to me. It requires you to go a step further and means that your conversation will be all the more difficult, but I admire your willingness to do that and I am supportive. The only downside for us is if the message isn't "heard" and acted upon, and we then become vulnerable for not having reported it. But that can be assessed down the road. The approach you outline is humane and a reasonable way to proceed.[103]

Mr. Schultz also responded favorably:

> Tim and Graham, this is a more humane and upfront way to handle this. I can support this approach, with the understanding that we will inform his organization, with or without his cooperation (I think that's what Tim

proposed). We can play it by ear to decide about the other organization.[104]

Mr. Curley and Mr. Sandusky both agreed that the meeting was held, that he agreed to the proposed course of action, and that Dr. Spanier and Mr. Schultz were informed about the discussion and considered the matter closed.[105] During his grand jury testimony in 2011, Mr. Paterno reflected, "I didn't know exactly how to handle it and I was afraid to do something that might jeopardize what the University procedure was. So I backed away and turned it over to some other people, people I thought would have a little more expertise than I did. It didn't work out that way. In hindsight, I wish I had done more."[106]

Neither the 2001 nor the 1998 incidents and follow-ups were disclosed to the Penn State board of trustees. However, the board of trustees was asked to approve the sale of a parcel of land to Second Mile for $168,500. Penn State had purchased the land in 1999 and approved the sale to Second Mile in September 2001. At the time of the approval, Mr. Schultz, who handled the transaction as the vice president of finance and operations, issued a press release on the sale and lauded Mr. Sandusky for his efforts with Second Mile.

The 2011 Grand Jury Indictment and Penn State's Response

In early 2010, the Pennsylvania attorney general issued a subpoena to Penn State for documents and subpoenaed Messrs. Spanier, Schultz, Paterno, Curley, and other members of the athletic department. On March 31, 2011, the first news report emerged about the Sandusky investigation as well as the Penn State subpoenas and the appearances before the grand jury of Penn State administrators. Prior to the news report,

(continued)

---

[101]In 1999 emails and pre-February 26, 2001, emails (those following the February 26th meeting involving Messrs. Spanier, Curley, and Schultz that resulted in the three-part action plan) referred to Mr. Sandusky by name, but the 2001 emails referred to him as "the subject" or "person," Second Mile as "the organization," and the Department of Public Welfare as "the other organization." Jo Becker, "E-Mails Suggest Paterno Role in Silence on Sandusky," *New York Times*, July 1, 2012, p. SS1

[102]Jo Becker, "E-Mails Suggest Paterno Role in Silence on Sandusky," *New York Times*, July 1, 2012, p. SS1

[103]Freeh Report, p. 75.

[104]Freeh Report, p. 76.

[105]Records reflect that Mr. Curley did meet with the executive director of Second Mile and informed him that Penn State would no longer permit Second Mile children on the campus "to avoid publicity issues." When the executive director talked with Mr. Sandusky, Mr. Sandusky indicated that he felt the restriction only applied to use of the locker rooms on the campus (Freeh Report, p. 78). Two trustees of Second Mile were told about the Curley meeting and outcome and concluded that it was a "non-incident" for Second Mile.

[106]Freeh Report, pp. 77–78.

Case 2.10

(continued)

neither Dr. Spanier nor the university's general counsel informed the board of trustees about the incidents, the investigation that had begun, the subpoenas, or the testimony of university officials before the grand jury. At the May 2011 meeting, Dr. Spanier disclosed that there was an investigation after a trustee had inquired about the press reports. Dr. Spanier's tone was dismissive regarding the events and the university's involvement. One trustee referred to Dr. Spanier's report on the matter as an "oh, by the way" report given at the end of the day. Several trustees noted that Dr. Spanier did not explain why university officials had been subpoenaed in the case if the issues were, as Dr. Spanier explained, involving Second Mile. The board took no action and there were no additional reports until the Sandusky indictment became public in November 2011. The initial article on the investigation was not circulated to the board members.

Prior to the indictment on November 4, 2011, on October 27, 2011, the university's general counsel, Cynthia Baldwin, was informed by the state attorney general's office that Mr. Curley and Mr. Schultz would also be indicted. This news started a series of meetings among the parties as well as interaction with the Penn State Communications Office. One draft, objected to by communications staff members but not actually voiced because of the "sheep" atmosphere at the university was as follows:

> I have known and worked daily with Tim and Gary for more than 16 years. I have complete confidence in how they have handled the allegations about a former University employee. Tim Curley and Gary Schultz operate at the highest levels of honesty, integrity, and compassion. I am confident the record will show that these charges are groundless and that they conducted themselves professionally and appropriately.[107]

The above press release was issued on November 5, 2011. A board conference call resulted in several board members being concerned about the university's response. For example, despite the knowledge of the pending indictment, several board members noted that Mr. Sandusky was in the Nittany Lion Club at the

university's October 29, 2011 football game. In addition, several board members called for an independent investigation of what had happened but were opposed by both Dr. Spanier and Ms. Baldwin, who opined in an email to Dr. Spanier, "If we do this, we will never get rid of this group in some shape or form. The Board will then think that they should have such a group."[108]

Following a board meeting on Sunday, November 6, 2011, the university announced that Mr. Curley would be placed on administrative leave and that Mr. Schultz would retire. The announcements also included the fact that there would be a special task force appointed to determine how to create appropriate policies and procedures for the protection of children on the campus. The press release with the information was, as the Freeh Report notes, a turning point for the board. Because its authority and decisions were not reflected in the language of the press release, several trustees began demanding additional meetings, a new chair, and other actions so that the board could know exactly what had happened and could control actions going forward. By November 8, 2011, the board issued its own statements expressing its outrage over the "horrifying details" in the Sandusky case and creating a task force to handle issues of university leadership going forward.[109]

Prior to the next board meeting, on November 9, 2011, Mr. Paterno announced his retirement following the end of the team's season. When the board met, it quickly acted to terminate Dr. Spanier for cause. The board's debate over Mr. Paterno was a lengthier and more contentious one, with some board members urging that the "worst mistake of his life" be weighed against the good that Mr. Paterno had done for Penn State. Some trustees urged administrative leave for Mr. Paterno; others felt the board was getting ahead of the facts; and others felt that the board needed to take charge and that the retirement usurped the board's authority. The final decision was to terminate Mr. Paterno. There was no plan for communication to Mr. Paterno of his termination, and as a result Mr. Paterno learned of his fate via a hand-delivered note from the board. Mrs. Paterno then called the board to

(continued)

---

[107]John W. Miller, Darren Everson, and Dionne Searcey, "Abuse Case Rocks Penn State," *Wall Street Journal,* November 7, 2011.

[108]Freeh Report, p. 92.
[109]Freeh Report, p. 94.

Case 2.10

(continued)

protest the treatment of her husband. The result of this ill-managed situation was a series of student protests, some violence, and some destruction of property.

The Interrelationships

Following the public disclosure of the indictment of Mr. Sandusky and Messrs. Curley and Schultz, additional information about the parties' activities became public. Mr. Schultz had contacted a bank for Mr. Sandusky to encourage the bank to meet with Mr. Sandusky about a loan for Second Mile. Mr. Schultz wrote that Second Mile "are really good people and this is a great cause related to kids."[110] The bank did meet with Mr. Sandusky.

Penn State worked with Second Mile on many events, including the Second Mile Golf Tournaments that were held at the Penn State Golf Course. Second Mile had the distribution rights on cards that had pictures of the Penn State Football players along with the Second Mile and Penn State logos on the other sides of the cards. The sale of the cards raised money for both the university and Second Mile. Football players and other student-athletes worked routinely as volunteers for Second Mile and its events. Following his retirement from Penn State, Mr. Sandusky was paid $57,000 per year plus travel expenses to serve as a consultant to Second Mile. From 1999 through 2008, Mr. Sandusky handled the six one-week-long camps that Second Mile held in university facilities. The camps involved the use of athletic fields, the outdoor swimming pools, and the football facilities on the campus.

The Sandusky Guilty Verdict

A total of eight young men testified about Mr. Sandusky molesting them. There were a total of 10 boys who were molested over a 15-year period. One juror noted that the young men were very credible witnesses, and there was nothing to indicate that they were not telling the truth. Mr. Sandusky was convicted on all 45 counts of child sexual abuse. Mr. Sandusky has appealed his conviction a number of times on several different grounds, including that his lawyers were "rushed to trial."[111] Another appeal, in 2022, on a claim of newly discovered evidence, was denied in

January 2022. Mr. Sandusky appealed to challenge his sentence as well and a different judge was given the case for resentencing. The new judge resentenced Mr. Sandusky to the original maximum sentence of 442 years. When he was taken into prison, the other inmates sang some of the lyrics from Pink Floyd's "Brick in the Wall," to wit, "Hey, teacher! Leave them kids alone."

Mr. Sandusky was placed in isolation because of the attitudes of general prisoner populations toward child molesters. One expert calls the fates of child molesters in prison, "a special circle of hell." Sadly, one of Mr. Sandusky's six adopted sons, Jeffrey, entered a guilty plea in 2017 to child sexual abuse charges.[112] Matthew Sandusky, another adopted son, has detailed sexual abuse by Mr. Sandusky from the age of eight until he was 17. Matthew is the founder and executive director of Peaceful Hearts Foundation, a nonprofit that assists victims of child sexual abuse in their recoveries.[113]

The Conclusions of the Freeh Report

The special report, commissioned by the board of trustees, concluded that Mr. Paterno, Mr. McQueary, and Mr. Curley were all required, under the provisions of Pennsylvania reporting statutes, to report what they had seen or been told to the proper law enforcement authorities. Penn State was fined $2.4 million by the U.S. Department of Education for its failure to report the sexual assault allegations against Mr. Sandusky.[114] Reporting the information to Mr. Schultz did not satisfy the statutes, because they were required to report the information to a law enforcement official. The special report also concluded that the university had not done enough to establish policies and procedures related to the presence of children on the campus and had not trained employees on their reporting duties with regard to child sexual abuse. Indeed, even the administrators of these programs had not been given training on their responsibilities toward children in the

(continued)

---

[110]Freeh Report, p. 108.

[111]Kris Maher, "Penn State Faces Years in Court," *Wall Street Journal*, June 25, 2012, p. A3.

[112]Mitch Smith, "Sandusky Son Faces Sexual Abuse Charges," *New York Times*, February 4, 2017, p. B10.

[113]Matthew Sandusky, *Undaunted* (2017).

[114]Melissa Korn, "Penn State Fined for Crime Reporting Lapses," *New York Times*, November 4, 2016, p. A2.

Case 2.10

(continued)

campus programs. The report noted that the processes for background checks were not known or understood. The investigation revealed several occasions in which university employees expressed concerns about these policies, the failure to follow them, and the resulting risk to the university. Employees who raised concerns were dismissed because their concerns were not seen as consequential.

Board Governance

The special report was scathing in its indictment of the inaction and inappropriate actions of the board of trustees in their responses to an evolving situation. The report also noted that strengthening the governance processes and procedures of the board would help it to be more effective in its role as a checks-and-balance mechanism for management actions and inactions.

The "Penn State Way" and Culture

The report recommended changes in the culture of the university, noting that the "Penn State Way" philosophy had permeated the organization to such an extent that other perspectives or outside advice were seen as unnecessary. The report recommended creation of a values- and ethics-centered community as a substitute for the somewhat arrogant approach of the "Penn State Way." In addition to establishing values, the report also recommended ethics training for faculty, staff, and students so that values and rules are clear and that all who are on the campus have mechanisms for ethical decision making. Details in the report include the creation of an ethics council as well as the appointment of an ethics officer. The report also recommended additional efforts on transparency, communication, and reporting requirements.

In addition, the report recommended that decision processes and the interaction of departments and colleges, as well as the athletic department, be transparent and that the processes not be overridden through deference to the football program or collegiate athletics. Dissenting opinions were not a part of the "Penn State Way." One incident that was troubling in this area of culture involved a clash between Penn State's standards and conduct officer and Mr. Paterno over

the level of discipline that was appropriate for student-athletes who violated the university's code of conduct (and worse). At one point, the then standards and conduct officer, Dr. Vicky Triponey, wrote to Dr. Spanier about her concerns following assaults by football players on other students. "I would respectfully ask that you do something to stop this atrocious behavior before this team and an entire generation of Penn State students leave here believing that this is appropriate and acceptable behavior within a civil university community."[115] Dr. Triponey would soon resign her position, citing "philosophical differences."[116]

The Aftermath: Disputes and Conclusions

The university accepted the Freeh Report without taking exception and, as of November 2012, had implemented one-half of the 199 changes Mr. Freeh had recommended.

There have been other reports done on the Sandusky scandal.[117] Those reports conclude that the Freeh Report is based on speculation and conclusion and is an embarrassment to law enforcement. The major flaw the reports found was that the principals involved were not interviewed. Those principals (the administrators criminally charged) were not available for interviews because of those criminal charges. However, the Freeh investigation did rely on emails and other documents produced by those principals. In addition, the Freeh investigation did interview university employees who

(continued)

---

[115]Reed Albergotti, "A Discipline Problem," *Wall Street Journal*, November 22, 2011, p. A3.

[116]There are two views on Dr. Triponey and her time at Penn State. Some saw her actions as courageous, while others feel that her tenure was marked by clashes with student groups over consolidation of budgets and power as well as the student appeal process. Reed Albergotti and Rachel Bachman, "Two Views on Administrator," *Wall Street Journal*, November 23, 2011, http://www.wsj.com/articles/SB100014240529702044434045770546320 30945696. Accessed April 13, 2016.

[117]"Report to the Board of Trustees of the Pennsylvania State University on the Freeh Report's Flawed Methodology and Conclusions," June 29, 2018. The report was sponsored by former and current members of the Penn State Board of Trustees. https://www.scribd.com/document/399416472/Report-to-the-Board-of-Trustees-of-the-Pennsylvania-State-University-on-the-Freeh-Report-s-flawed-methodology-and-conclusions#from_embed

Case 2.10

(continued)

had knowledge of events surrounding the university's handling of Mr. Sandusky's conduct.

A second report, commissioned by Mr. Paterno's family, and done by former Pennsylvania Governor Dick Thornburgh, concluded that the Freeh Report was "a rush to injustice" with "inaccurate and unfounded findings related to Mr. Paterno."[118]

A careful reading of the three reports provides some insight into the core of the battles between the commissioned reports. The reports challenging the Freeh Report disagree with the conclusions Mr. Freeh reached about Penn State officials and the need for culture change. The reports do not provide challenges to the Freeh Report. In addition, the conclusions in the trials (during which all evidence was available) are consistent with the information in the Freeh Report.

The Trials and Convictions

In 2013, Penn State's board of trustees authorized payment of $60,000,000 to settle 25 of 30 claims made against the university in relation to the Sandusky issues.[119] Ironically, Penn State received its second largest amount of donations ($208 million) in 2011 and its Nittany Lions booster club collected $82.4 million in the same year.[120]

Mr. Sandusky gave his first interview to filmmaker John Ziegler, who had made the documentary, *The Framing of Joe Paterno*. Mr. Sandusky said that the witnesses, including Mike McQueary, were confused about what they saw.[121] Mr. Ziegler said that his goal was to "get Joe Paterno's day in court."[122] Mr. Paterno, suffering from lung cancer that was revealed following the Sandusky indictment, died on January 22, 2012. His family still maintains that he did not know about the 1998 incident and felt that he did the right thing in reporting

Mr. McQueary's eyewitness report to university officials. Mr. Paterno's son, Jay, has tried to clear his father's name, particularly after the release of the Freeh Report. The defamation suit that he brought against the university was dismissed for the failure to establish that the university had made stigmatizing statements about Coach Paterno.[123] In September 2016, Mr. Paterno was honored at Penn State in celebration of the 50th anniversary of his first game as head coach.[124]

Mr. McQueary filed a whistleblower lawsuit against Penn State, alleging that the university's response has made it impossible for him to find employment as a coach and that the atmosphere at Penn State is hostile. Mr. McQueary was a key witness for many of the plaintiffs in the civil actions filed against the university. His lawsuit was contentious, but the jury awarded Mr. McQueary $7.3 million.[125]

Mr. Curley and Mr. Schultz entered "not guilty" pleas to their felony charges of perjury and failure to report. Dr. Spanier was fired as president when the indictments were announced but was given a $2.5 million severance package in addition to his salary of $700,000 that he had earned for 2011. The university said that it was bound to honor the terms of its contract with Dr. Spanier and that because he was "terminated without cause," the severance package applied.[126] Dr. Spanier remained a tenured, faculty member at Penn State on paid leave during this time. One year later, Dr. Spanier was indicted on eight counts of conspiracy, endangering child welfare, and perjury.[127] The charges were related to what the state attorney general called "a conspiracy

(continued)

---

[118]Genaro C. Armas, "Penn State Scandal," *Savannah Morning News*, February 10, 2013, https://www.savannahnow.com/story/sports/2013/02/10/paternos-challenge-freeh-report-penn-state-scandal/13647234007/.

[119]Kris Maher, "Penn State Settlement Pegged at $60 Million," *Wall Street Journal*, July 18, 2013, p. A3.

[120]Pablo S. Torre, "Cost of Doing Nothing," *Sports Illustrated*, August 6, 2012, p. 31.

[121]Kevin Johnson, "Sandusky Speaks Out for First Time since Sentencing," *USA Today*, March 26, 2013, p. 3A.

[122]*Id.*

[123]*Paterno v. Pennsylvania State University*, 149 F. Supp. 3d 530 (E.D. Pa. 2016). An appeal has been filed.

[124]Christine Brennan, "Penn State Still Doesn't Get It," *USA Today*, September 15, 2016, p. 1C.

[125]*McQueary v. Pennsylvania State University*, Trial order, 2012 WL 12337381 (Pa. Comm. Pleas. 2012); and Marc Tracy, "Mike McQueary Is Awarded $7.3 Million in Penn State Defamation Case," *New York Times*, October 26, 2016, p. B12.

[126]Jack Stripling, "Penn State Paid Spanier $3.3 Million in 2011," *The Chronicle of Higher Education*, November 28, 2012, http://chronicle.com/article/Penn-State-Paid-Spanier/135970/.

[127]Kris Maher, "Penn State's Ex-president Charged," *Wall Street Journal*, November 2, 2012, p. A2.

Case 2.10

(continued)

of silence."[128] Dr. Spanier entered a not guilty plea and undertook a defense related to the substances of the charges and the exclusion of testimony.

In January 2016, the Pennsylvania Superior Court reversed a trial judge's ruling upholding the obstruction of justice, conspiracy, and perjury charges in the case. The charges remaining against Dr. Spanier and the others were third-degree felony child endangerment and the failure to report suspected child abuse. The other charges had to be dropped because the testimony of Cynthia Baldwin, former chief counsel for Penn State, was quashed.[129] In her testimony, Ms. Baldwin, now Judge Baldwin of the Pennsylvania Supreme Court, testified that the information Dr. Spanier gave to reporters about his knowledge regarding Sandusky and his conduct was false. She testified, "He is not a person of integrity. He lied to me."[130] Without that testimony, the conspiracy and perjury charges could not be established.

Messrs. Schultz and Curley entered guilty pleas to one misdemeanor charge each in exchange for their testimony against Dr. Spanier. Dr. Spanier was convicted in 2017 of one charge of child endangerment for the failure to report the Sandusky abuse. At the heart of the Freeh report was this same conclusion: the failure of administrators to act when told of allegations. Even if those making the reports were mistaken, the obligation to report transcends doubt and leaves that determination to properly conducted criminal investigations. Dr. Spanier was found not guilty of two felony charges. The following email that Dr. Spanier wrote was a critical part of the prosecution's case: "The only downside for us is if the message isn't heard and acted upon, and we then become vulnerable for not having reported it".[131]

Following several appeals of his conviction, Dr. Spanier reported to prison in June 2021 and served two months followed by two months of house arrest with electronic monitoring.[132] Messrs. Schultz and Curley served similar sentences.

The state attorney general elected in November 2012, Kathleen Kane, began an investigation of Governor Tom Corbett's handling of the Penn State situation. Mr. Corbett was the Pennsylvania attorney general at the time of the emerging Penn State issues, and Ms. Kane's investigation focused on why three years had lapsed before criminal charges were brought in the case.[133] The investigation concluded in 2014 with findings that the case was riddled with "lousy investigation" but that there was no "political influence" or "slow-walking."[134] One year later, Ms. Kane's office was under investigation, and she was indicted in 2015 for leaking grand jury information. The Pennsylvania Supreme Court suspended her law license, but she remained ensconced as the state's top lawyer until her conviction for perjury and official oppression. At that point, she announced her resignation, which had been preceded by a pretrial announcement that she would not run for reelection in 2016. Her resignation halted the impeachment proceedings that were in process following an unsuccessful senate vote to have her removed from office.[135] She was

(continued)

[132]Associated Press, "Former Penn State President Graham Spanier Reports to Jail in Sandusky Scandal," *Philadelphia Inquirer*, June 10, 2021, https://www.inquirer.com/news/pennsylvania/graham-spanier-reports-prison-penn-state-20210610.html.

[133]Trip Gabriel, "Investigation to Focus on Governor's Handling of Penn State Abuse Case," *New York Times*, January 31, 2013, http://www.nytimes.com/2013/02/01/us/investigation-to-focus-on-governors-handling-of-penn-state-abuse-case.html?_r=0. Accessed April 13, 2016.

[134]Michael Wines, "Scandal's Web Trips Prosecutor," *New York Times*, December 19, 2015, p. A1. See also the AP story at http://www.aol.com/article/2015/11/05/porn-scandal-top-prosecutor-keeps-releasing-raunchy-emails/21259529/?icid=maing-grid7%7Cmain5%7C-dl3%7Csec1_lnk3%26pLid%3D-136288842.

[135]Karen Langley, "Embattled Attorney General Kane Says She Won't Seek a Second Term," *Pittsburgh Post-Gazette*, February 16, 2016, http://www.post-gazette.com/news/politics-state/2016/02/16/Kane-scheduled-to-speak-today-about-the-future-of-AG-s-office/stories/201602160142.

[128]Steve Eder, "Former Penn State President Is Charged in Sandusky Case," *New York Times*, November 2, 2012, p. B9.

[129]*Commonwealth v. Spanier*, 132 A.3d 481 (Pa. Sup. 2016).

[130]Susan Snyder and Craig R. McCoy, "Ruling Reverses Charges against Spanier, Others in Sandusky Case," January 24, 2016, philly.com, http://articles.philly.com/2016-01-24/news/70015302_1_elizabeth-ainslie-spanier-lawyer-graham-b. Accessed April 13, 2014.

[131]Jess Bidgood & Richard Perez Pena, "Former Penn State President Is Found Guilty of Child Endangerment," New York Times, March 25, 2017, p. A17.

Case 2.10

(continued)

sentenced to 10 to 23 months and served 8 months before being released in 2019. On April 27, 2022, a judge issued a warrant for her arrest for DUI charges filed against her following a crash into another vehicle.[136] Those charges placed her in violation of her terms of probation. Her probation was revoked and she was ordered into rehab for 45 days.

Penn State initially accepted the NCAA sanctions on the university's football program without protest or a hearing. The NCAA executive committee chair at that time, Oregon State President Ed Ray, in announcing the sanctions, indicated, "I was so appalled at just the thought of those children and what was being done, and that nobody made a phone call, for God's sake."[137] When the NCAA sanctions were accepted, the University removed the statue of Coach Paterno from in front of the stadium during the wee hours of the morning. However, Pennsylvania Senator Jake Corman and Pennsylvania treasurer Robert McCord filed suit against the NCAA and Penn State itself challenging the sanctions.[138] At the time of the suit, the NCAA was in the process of lifting the bulk of the sanctions, as noted earlier. Fans have pressed thus far unsuccessfully to have Mr. Paterno's statue restored to its original place on campus.[139] The statue remains a subject of folklore, speculation, bloggers, April Fool's day pranks, and rumors.[140] After the first season following the trial and conviction and the revelations of the Freeh Report, Penn State disclosed that its operating revenue was

down $7.9 million, although its donations had increased by 350%.[141] The series of events at Penn State tell a powerful story about both the consequences of harmful behaviors and decisions of leaders about those behaviors. The case brings to mind the poignant line of the prince in *Romeo and Juliet* as he mourns with the city over the loss of two young lives and those of so many of their family and friends: "All are punished."[142]

Discussion Questions

1. "Penn State is an honorable institution that is trying desperately to defend it's [sic] ethics and all of the individuals who had nothing to do with this horrific scandal, which have been destroyed by the actions/inactions of a few individuals. . . ."

   This quote comes from a blog about the Penn State scandal. Evaluate the accuracy of the blogger's thoughts. Why does it happen that many are punished for the actions of a few? Or is that an accurate assessment—is it the actions of a few?

2. Oregon State President Ed Ray, who announced the Penn State sanctions, said that what happened occurred because of the Penn State culture, that the football program had consumed the values of the university. What does he mean? What can you point to in the case that illustrates his point?

3. List all of the categories of ethical issues that occurred over the course of the events.

4. Make a list of all the stakeholders in this case.

5. Are there layers of ethical issues in this case?

6. What does the case teach us about the importance of speaking up? Of raising objections? Give examples of why people did not speak up in this case.

[136]Avery Van Etten, "Bench Warrant Issued for Former Pa. AG Kathleen Kane," *ABC News 27*, April 27, 2022, https://www.abc27.com/news/pennsylvania/bench-warrant-issued-for-former-pa-ag-kathleen-kane/.

[137]NCAA Chair Ray, "I Was So Appalled," *USA Today*, July 30, 2012, p. 2c.

[138]Rachel Axon and Erik Brady, "Did Penn State Really Face Shutdown?" *USA Today*, January 16, 2015, p. 1C.

[139]Kris Maher, "Fans Press Penn State to Restore a Coach's Legacy," *Wall Street Journal*, September 20, 2015, p. A3.

[140]Michael T. Mondak, "New Paterno Statue Awaited," *The Herald*, March 5, 2015. https://www.sharonherald.com/opinion/letters_to_the_editor/letter-new-paterno-statue-awaited/article_4b3a55f5-465b-5d60-8d3d-f56c683bc569.html.

[141]Steve Berkowitz and Jodi Upton, "Athletic Revenue Falls at Penn State," *USA Today*, April 9, 2013, p. 1c.

[142]William Shakespeare, *Romeo and Juliet*, Act V, Scene III, l. 295.

Compare & Contrast

After his release from prison, Dr. Spanier told a reporter in an interview that he was the victim of a false narrative about his actions:

> Well, if you go back to 2001 or late 2000, I never knew then that Mike McQueary was the member of the athletic department staff who was being referenced when I heard a brief report about an unnamed staff member witnessing horseplay. I only learned from a news story on Monday night, November 7, 2011, that Mike McQueary was that person. There was nothing in the initial report I heard about anything abusive or sexual. I wasn't told which facility it was, or the time of the day, or anything about the circumstances other than that a member of the athletic department staff was uncomfortable when he saw, indirectly and around the corner, that Jerry Sandusky was "horsing around" with a youth in a locker room facility. That was about all I heard in a 10-minute conversation.
>
> Had I been told anything more than that or suspected child abuse or sexual abuse, of course I would have sprung into action much more aggressively. As a victim myself of child abuse, I have always been very sensitive to such issues, and I would have been greatly disturbed had I ever heard anything along those lines.[143]

Compare what appears in the case you have read with these statements and choose which version is correct.

---

[143]"Graham Spanier, on the Record," statecollege.com, January 9, 2022, https://www.statecollege.com/town-and-gown/graham-spanier-on-the-record-a-decade-after-the-sandusky-scandal-penn-states-former-president-shares-his-views-on-a-false-narrative-prison-reform-following-his-jail-stin/.

History Repeats

Ethical Lessons Not Learned: Two More Universities, Two More Abuse Scandals

The tragedy of the Penn State case is studied with the hope that other organizations can learn from the mistakes that were made in not thoroughly investigating a raised matter and in trying to protect friends and employees even as others are being harmed. The chart below shows that Michigan State and Ohio State had allegations of sexual abuse by staff members and they too went for years before newspaper reports made it necessary to investigate and take action. At Michigan State, another university president resigned amidst allegations for the failure to act. At all three, the problem at the root of it all was the unwillingness or inability of those who knew to report issues and receive a response.

Figure 2.2 A Tale of Three Universities

	Penn State	**Michigan State**	**Ohio State**
Type of conduct	Child molestation by assistant coach Sandusky	Physician (Nassar) molestation of female gymnasts	Physician (Strauss) molestation of male student athletes
Public disclosure	2011	2016	2019
Initial report	1998	1997	1978
Number of reports	11	32	177
First date for action	2001 (talk with Sandusky) 2011 Paterno fired	2014 — Title IX Complaint — no external expert	1996 — physician permitted to leave
Est. # of people who knew	31	205 + *Indianapolis Star*	>1,000
Criminal actions	4	3; 4 loss of licenses	Statute of limitations
Litigation	Victims (11) and grad student	55 lawsuits; 500 victims	17
Costs	$67.3 million	$500 million	????

Case 2.11

How About Those Astros?

On November 12, 2019, an article appeared in *The Athletic* in which player Mike Fiers, once a member of the Houston Astros Major League Baseball (MLB) team stated that in 2017, the Astros had violated the MLB rules on sign-stealing methods. Based on the article, the league Commissioner, Robert D. Manfred, Jr., ordered an investigation of the allegations for the period from 2016 through the World Series games in 2020. Based on the investigation's findings. Commissioner Manfred issued a report and imposed sanctions on the Astros and some team members.[144]

---

[144]"Statement of the Commissioner," January 13, 2020, https://www.crawfishboxes.com/2020/1/13/21064270/mlb-commissioner-rob-manfreds-full-statement-on-the-houston-astros-sign-stealing-investigation (hereinafter referred to as "Statement").

The Astros' Sign-Stealing Methodology: A Gradual Expansion

In 2017, employees in the video replay room of the Astros used the live-feed cameras to try to decode the sign sequences of the opposing team. Once they had determined the coding, a "runner" would go to the dugout and provide that information. A person in the dugout then passed the information to the player on second base. The second base player would watch the catcher's sign and signal to the batter from second base.

The strategy evolved so that Alex Cora (bench coach for the Astros) would just call the replay room and get the information over the phone, thus eliminating the middleman runner. However, on occasion, the employees in the video room would just text the information. Texts would go to coaches' smart watches or to a special cell phone in the dugout.

(continued)

Case 2.11

(continued)

The strategy continued to evolve when a group of players asked that the technical folks install a monitor outside the dugout that displayed the center field camera. Players would then just watch the monitor (thus eliminating the video room altogether except for their responsibility of keeping the electronics running) and decode the signs themselves. To communicate to the batter, the players experimented with clapping, whistling, and yelling but eventually settled on banging on the trash can. The trash can code was "no bang" for a fast ball, and "two bangs" for an "off-speed" pitch.[145]

Houston won the World Series in 2017. In the 2018 season, there was no evidence that the players used electronic equipment for decoding. However, the video room did resume its role of running information on the codes to the dugout.

Who Knew?

Alex Cora, the bench coach, often watched the monitor. The players all benefited from the banging signals. Many assumed that what they were doing was acceptable and told investigators that if they had been told to stop that they would have stopped. However, some players had the sense that what they were doing violated the rules. The Commissioner described the intent from the following:

> "Several players told my investigators that there was a sense of "panic" in the Astros' dugout after White Sox pitcher Danny Farquhar appeared to notice the trash can bangs. Before the game ended, a group of Astros players removed the monitor from the wall in the tunnel and hid it in an office. For the Postseason, a portable monitor was set up on a table to replace the monitor that had been affixed to the wall near the dugout."[146]

However, as it turned out, Mr. Farquhar just asked the umpire to ask the Astros to quit banging on the garbage can. Nothing had been uncovered.

The Consequences

The Commissioner did not offer conclusions on whether the decoding and banging helped the Astros.

However, some analytics might provide some insight. In postseason play, the Astros were 2–6 in their road games and 8–1 at home. Ah, the power of those Hometown cheers.

The Commissioner found that the team owner was not aware of the decoding and banging. However, the Commissioner did conclude that the General Manager had some knowledge but did not give it supervisory attention. The Commissioner noted that the General Manager's operational approach contributed to the decoding and banging:

> . . . the baseball operations department's insular culture—one that valued and rewarded results over other considerations, combined with a *staff of individuals who often lacked direction or sufficient oversight.*[147]

As for the field manager, he twice damaged the monitor to signal his disapproval and believed that the monitor was both "wrong and distracting." However, he did nothing further to stop the decoding and banging. He also did not stop the runners from leaving the video review room with their real-time information.

Alex Cora's sanctions were not part of the statement because he had moved on to the Boston Red Sox, who won the 2018 World Series. By the time the Commissioner made that statement, the Sox were under investigation for sign stealing. The Commissioner was awaiting the outcome of that investigation. However, sanctions may be moot, because the Red Sox fired Mr. Cora.

No players were sanctioned because of a promise that the Commissioner had made to sanction management for rules violations as a means of stopping behaviors of players. The video room employees are still there. Management was sanctioned with a $5 million fine and had to forfeit the Astros' regular first- and second-round selections in the 2020 and 2021 First-Year Player Drafts. The General Manager and Field Manager were suspended without pay for the 2020 season. If the two have any further violations, they will

(continued)

---

[145]Statement, p. 2.
[146]Statement, p. 5.

[147]Statement, pp. 6–7.

Case 2.11

(continued)

be permanently ineligible for MLB team positions. Jim Crane, owner of the Astros, had already fired both of them.

The Players Follow Up

After the statement was issued, the players held a sort of meeting/press conference. What they offered was, "Who knew?" and "It didn't make a difference." There was a follow-up question for the it-made-no difference comment: "Then why did you do it?" There was a great deal of hedging, hemming, hawing, hesitation, and hubris

in the meeting. The meeting in a nutshell: "It was bad. We are done with this. We still won."[148]

Discussion Questions

1. What layers are involved in sign stealing?

2. Will the penalties imposed be effective in curbing cheating? Why were the players not sanctioned?

---

[148]Jarod Diamond, "Astros Offer Few Apologies," *Wall Street Journal*, February 14, 2020, p. A12 and Tyler Kepner, "Astros Apologize But Say 2017 Rings Have Not Lost Luster," *New York Times*, February 14, 2020, B7.

Why Didn't They Say Something? 2.1

The Baseball Player with Regrets

Some of the Astros blamed Carlos Beltrán as the sign-stealing ringleader. However, Carlos Correa responded that the sign stealing helped them all and, referring to Mr. Beltrán, "Whatever he said and whatever we were doing, we had the chance to stop it as a team—everybody. Everybody had the chance to say something, and we didn't."

1. Give a list of rationalizations that the players made that would have comforted them and stopped them from speaking up.

2. Based on the Commissioner's statement, one sportswriter remarked, "Are we still trying to say that illegal sign-stealing isn't a league issue?"[149]

3. What rationalizations do you find in the case?

4. Why can't the problem of sign stealing be solved?

---

[149]Jason Gay, "A Trashy Scandal for Baseball," *Wall Street Journal*, January 16, 2020, p. A12.

Case 2.12

Boeing: Decades of Major Ethical Setbacks from Lockheed Document Heists to the 737 MAX

Boeing, founded in 1916, has long been an admired and successful company. Cited by management books for its excellence, the experts praised Boeing's ability to "stick to its knitting,"[150] with "knitting" being (originally)

---

[150]Thomas J. Peters and Robert H. Waterman, *In Search of Excellence* (1982); Tom Peters, *The Pursuit of WOW!* (1987); and James C. Collins and Jerry I. Porras, *Built to Last: Successful Habits of Visionary Companies* (1994).

the commercial airline market which was responsible for 90% of its revenue. In the 1940s, Boeing expanded by entering the military aircraft market. However, government contracting does carry its share of minefields. Those ethical minefields in defense contracts were the focus of the 1985 Packard Commission report on government waste that famously included the $600 toilet seats and $400 hammers. Public outrage not only fueled additional oversight and regulation but also provided the impetus

(continued)

Case 2.12

(continued)

for the Defense Industry Initiative (DII), a voluntary group that was the beginning of the focus on ethics and compliance beyond just the 1977 focus on bribery and foreign corruption. Boeing was one of the original 32 signatories to the initiative and became one of the original 25 paying members.[151] The DII developed a code of ethics for defense contractors and has continually worked with companies to develop and maintain ethical cultures.

The Boeing–Lockheed Competition for the U.S. Satellite (EELV) Project

However, ironically, it was in the pursuit of military contracts just 10 years following the DII that Boeing had its first major legal and ethical missteps in its history. In 1996, Boeing and Lockheed Martin were in a head-to-head competition for a multibillion-dollar government contract for furnishing the rockets that are used for launching satellites into space (a project referred to in the industry as the Evolved Expendable Launch Vehicle, or EELV). The satellites perform various functions and could be communication or spy satellites.

It was during this competitive time frame for the rocket launcher project that Kenneth Branch, a space engineer and manager at Lockheed facilities in Florida, traveled to McDonnell Douglas facilities at Huntington Beach, California, for a job interview.[152] McDonnell Douglas was working on the EELV bid at the same time that it was being acquired by Boeing. Boeing's acquisition of McDonnell Douglas had been finalized by the time of the Branch interview, but the logistics of acquisition had not yet been completed (it would be completed in August 1997). Boeing's acquisition of McDonnell Douglas and the combination of Lockheed with Martin Marietta meant that the federal government would be dealing with only two large contractors.

Near the end of his interview at McDonnell Douglas, Mr. Branch showed the participants in the interview process a copy of Lockheed's proposed presentation for the government project. Six months after his interview, in January 1997, Branch began work at Boeing on the $5 billion EELV project. The pressure for Boeing to win the contract became intense, and Boeing executive Frank Slazer, the director of business development, encouraged Boeing employees working on EELV to develop "an improved Lockheed Martin EELV competitive assessment."[153] He also encouraged the employees to find former Lockheed employees to get their thoughts and impressions about the project.

Sometime during the first quarter of 1997, Lockheed sent Mr. Branch a letter reminding him of his confidentiality agreement with Lockheed and his duty to not disclose any proprietary information at Boeing. During this same period, Kimberly Tran, a Boeing software engineer, filed a report that she had seen Mr. Branch in the hallway with a notebook that had the Lockheed logo on the outside. She was reprimanded by Tom Alexiou, Branch's supervisor, for not going first to her own supervisor.[154] Although Boeing claimed to have begun an investigation as a result of Tran report, it admitted that there was no record of that investigation.[155]

Shortly after, Boeing was awarded 19 of the planned 28 rocket launches in the EELV, a total contract value of $1.88 billion. After the Boeing contract award, rumblings began in both the industry and government agencies about Boeing's possible possession of Lockheed proprietary documents during the time of the bids. In June 1999, Steve Griffin, a Boeing engineer, heard William Erskine, an EELV project engineer, boast that he had offered Branch the Boeing job in exchange for the Lockheed EELV proposal. The following was an exchange between the two:

Griffin: We just took a Procurement Integrity Law class. I can't believe you did that.

Erskine: I was hired to win . . . and I was going to do whatever it took to do it.[156]

(continued)

---

[151]Edmund Boyle, Mark M. Higgins, and S. Ghon Rhee, "Stock market Reaction to Ethical Initiatives of Defense Contractors: Theory and Evidence," 8 *Critical Perspectives on Accounting* 541 (1997).

[152]*Lockheed Martin Corp. v. Boeing Co.*, 314 F. Supp. 2d 1198 (M.D. Fla. 2004).

[153]Anne Marie Squeo and Andy Pasztor, "U.S. Probes Whether Boeing Misused a Rival's Documents," *Wall Street Journal*, May 5, 2003, pp. A1, A7.

[154]*Lockheed Martin Corp. v. Boeing Co.*, 314 F. Supp. 2d 1198, 1203.

[155]*Id.*

[156]*Lockheed Martin Corp. v. Boeing Co.*, 314 F. Supp. 2d 1198, 1205.

Case 2.12

(continued)

Mr. Griffin reported these remarks to the Boeing Human Resources Representative. Coincidentally, Mr. Griffin's wife, Bridget Griffin, who was an engineer with Lockheed at this time, made a similar report outlining Mr. Erskine's remarks to a Lockheed ethics officer.

The issues were then reported to Boeing attorney, Mark Rabe, who interviewed both Messrs. Branch and Erskine with Mr. Branch disclosing a stack of Lockheed documents that he had in his office. Boeing notified Lockheed that it had found Lockheed documents and returned them to Lockheed. Mr. Rabe assured Lockheed that Boeing did not use any of the information in the EELV proposal. Mr. Branch was then suspended. However, six months later, Boeing attorneys found another 15 Lockheed documents; they returned them to Lockheed but did not disclose that their internal investigation found that Messrs. Branch and Erskine had used proprietary information. Boeing then terminated Messrs. Branch and Erskine, who then filed suit against Boeing for wrongful termination.

The Litigation and Discovery of Additional Documents

During discovery in the case, Lockheed asked to receive copies of what turned out to be boxes of Lockheed documents that Boeing had but had not previously disclosed or return to Lockheed. The judge refused to grant the request. However, in April 2002, Boeing's assistant general counsel and vice president wrote to Lockheed to return the documents and offer that she had no explanation as to why the documents were not returned to Lockheed in 1997. She added:

> "At any rate, all documents have now been transmitted to you and I would like to apologize for the series of errors that have occurred in handling this case."[157]

Just days later, Boeing sent an additional 11 boxes of documents to Lockheed. The documents in the boxes had the Lockheed Martin logo and were stamped "Proprietary." In June 2003, Boeing turned over another 1,850 pages of proprietary documents.[158]

The judge terminated the wrongful discharge suit brought by Messrs. Erskine and Branch and required them to pay Boeing's legal fees. However, the two men signed agreements promising not to disclose details about the case or discuss it with the media in exchange for Boeing waiving its rights to collect its legal fees.

The Fallout from the Document Disclosures

When the boxes of documents arrived at Lockheed, the entire sordid Erskine–Branch history emerged in the press.[159] Boeing failed to make any disclosures about the documents or litigation in its SEC documents until May 2003, after a *Wall Street Journal* report on the investigations and litigation appeared. Jim Albaugh, CEO of the Defense Systems Division, indicated that management had not really focused on the inquiries and investigations until that public disclosure.[160]

Following the news reports, Congress began investigating the government contracts with Boeing.[161] Boeing had a bid pending at the time of the erupting document scandal for an $18 billion contract with the U.S. Air Force for the delivery of Boeing 767 tankers, aircraft used to refuel fighter jets in midair. Congress held hearings on the tanker contract and found that CEO Albaugh had called Air Force Assistant Secretary Marvin Sambur for help in closing the deal. Mr. Sambur stepped in to help Boeing. The late U.S. Senator John McCain (R-Ariz.) noted, "It's astonishing. Even in light of serious allegations, they [Boeing] continued to push to railroad the [tanker] deal through, and they still are."[162]

The Penalties, Sanctions, Consequences, and Losses

On July 24, 2003, the United States Air Force (USAF) suspended the space launch services business and

(continued)

---

[157]*Lockheed Martin Corp. v. Boeing Co.*, 314 F. Supp. 2d 1198, 1206.
[158]*Id.*

[159]Anne Marie Squeo and Andy Pasztor, "U.S. Probes Whether Boeing Misused a Rival's Documents," *Wall Street Journal*, May 5, 2003, pp. A1, A7.
[160]Anne Marie Squeo, J. Lynn Lunsford, and Andy Pasztor, "Boeing's Plan to Smooth Bumps of Jet Market Hits Turbulence," *Wall Street Journal*, August 25, 2003, pp. A1, A6.
[161]Stanley Holmes, "Boeing: Caught in Its Own Turbulence," *BusinessWeek*, December 8, 2003, p. 37.
[162]Byron Acohido, "Boeing's Call for Help from Air Force Raise More Questions," *USA Today*, December 8, 2003, p. 3B.

Case 2.12

(continued)

the former Boeing employees involved from receiving government contracts for an indefinite period because of Boeing's possession of the Lockheed Martin information during the EELV source selection in 1998. The USAF also terminated 7 out of 21 Boeing contracts as a penalty for its conduct with the Lockheed documents.[163] USAF Undersecretary Peter Teets released the following statement in making the announcement:

> We do not tolerate breaches of procurement integrity, and we hold industry accountable for the actions of their employees.[164]

Boeing took a $1.1 billion charge to reflect overstated revenues from the earlier booking of those canceled contracts.[165] Messrs. Erskine and Branch were indicted for their role in the documents scandal.[166] Larry Satchell, another Boeing employee, was also charged a year later.[167] Mr. Erskine entered into a pretrial diversion agreement that allowed his charges to be dismissed if he remained free of any additional legal charges for one year. Mr. Branch pleaded guilty to obstruction of justice and received six months of home detention, one year of probation, and a $6,000 fine.[168] The fallout from the problems at Boeing caused the contract for the tankers to go back and forth several times, with the USAF ultimately, in 2009, suspending the bidding and ordering a new process of bidding for those planes.

Following the actions of the Air Force, CEO Philip Condit provided a statement that included, "Boeing must and will live by the highest standards of ethical conduct."[169] However, Condit departed abruptly on December 1, 2003.[170] Mr. Condit's departure followed disclosure of personal conduct that involved his four marriages, two to Boeing employees, one of whom was pink-slipped during her relationship with Condit. In addition, a board investigation found that Mr. Condit had moved into the Four Seasons Olympic Hotel in Seattle and had the suite remodeled at company expense. At the time, the board members were saying among themselves that they had "another Clinton" on their hands.[171]

New Commercial Jet Competition

As these events continued, the culture of the company deteriorated, the public and governmental oversight were demoralizing, and Boeing missed strategic opportunities. Doubting the ability of Airbus to bring the A380 555-passenger jet to market, Boeing opted out of that jumbo-jet market. Airbus forged ahead, winning 120 orders for its super jumbo jet thereby seizing market share from Boeing. Boeing did develop the Dreamliner 777 jetliner, but its commercial production was delayed several times for both design flaws and supplier issues. Boeing was scheduled to deliver 50 of the new aircraft to All Nippon Airways, for a total contract price of $6 billion in 2008, but the jet was not unveiled in Everett, Washington, until July 8, 2007. The jet's first public flight did not happen until 2009.

The Rocky Road Following the Document Issues

After the management shake-up and all the fallout from the documents and the defense employee recruitment, Boeing worked toward a culture change.[172] However, issues continued to arise. In April 2004, the U.S. Attorney's Office in Los Angeles expanded its investigation of the Lockheed Martin document case into Boeing's work for

(continued)

[163]J. Lynn Lunsford and Anne Marie Squeo, "Boeing CEO Condit Resigns in Shake-Up at Aerospace Titan," *Wall Street Journal*, December 2, 2003, pp. A1, A12.

[164]Edward Iwata, "Air Force Punishes Boeing by Taking 7 Contracts," *USA Today*, July 25, 2003, p. 1B.

[165]Squeo, Lunsford, and Pasztor, "Boeing's Plan to Smooth Bumps of Jet Market Hits Turbulence," *Wall Street Journal*, pp. A1, A6.

[166]https://www.justice.gov/archive/criminal/cybercrime/press-releases/2003/branchCharge.htm.

[167]Leslie Wayne, "More Charges in Theft of Lockheed Files," *New York Times*, May 12, 2004, https://www.nytimes.com/2004/05/12/business/more-charges-in-theft-of-lockheed-files.html.

[168]Douglas E. Oliver, "Engineers and White-Collar Crime," *ASCE Library*, https://ascelibrary.org/doi/10.1061/%28ASCE%291943-4162%282009%291%3A1%2832%29. Originally published in 1 *Journal of Legal Affairs and Dispute Resolution* 1(2009).

[169]Gary Strauss, Byron Acohido, Elliot Blaire Smith, and Marilyn Adams, "Boeing CEO Abruptly Quits after Controversy," *USA Today*, December 2, 2003, p. 1B.

[170]Stanley Holmes, "Boeing: What Really Happened," *Business-Week*, December 15, 2003. p. 33.

[171]*Id.*

[172]For full disclosure purposes, the author worked with Boeing during the time that it was recovering from the EELV project ethical issues.

Case 2.12

(continued)

NASA to determine whether Lockheed documents were used on NASA projects.[173]

Former CEO Harry Stonecipher was tapped to return from retirement to reassume the CEO role following Mr. Condit's resignation. Mr. Stonecipher's initial remarks in assuming the role included a pledge, "We're cleaning up our own house."[174] When asked if he could provide assurance to investors and customers that the scandals were behind Boeing, Mr. Stonecipher said, "Well, as in definitely behind us, they'll never be definitely behind us until all the lawsuits are finished. Rather than trying to convince people that it's all behind us, I have convinced them that we have a process and a will to deal with it, vigorously and summarily."[175]

In 2005, Mr. Stonecipher was removed as CEO after an internal investigation revealed that he had had an affair with one of the company executives. The affair was uncovered by an employee responsible for monitoring emails. Mr. Stonecipher's emails to the female executive revealed not only an affair between the two but also reflected poor judgment in the use of company email. The employee reported anonymously the content of the emails, including "graphic content," to an ethics officer.[176] The ethics officer investigated the concern and turned the findings over to general counsel, who took the information to the Boeing board. When confronted with the issue, even Mr. Stonecipher agreed that he was no longer the right person to lead the company in its recommitment to ethics, "We set—hell, I set—a higher standard here. I violated my own standards. I used poor judgment."[177] Mr. Stonecipher's departure was announced within 10 days following the employee's anonymous tip. The board found that he had

violated the following provisions of Boeing's code of ethics:

> In conducting its business, integrity must underlie all company relationships, including those with customers, suppliers, communities, and other employees.

> Employees will not engage in conduct or activity that may raise questions about the company's honesty, impartiality, [or] reputation or otherwise cause embarrassment to the company.[178]

Lou Platt, former Hewlett-Packard CEO, and chairman of Boeing's board, said that Mr. Stonecipher's "poor judgment . . . impaired his ability to lead."[179]

The Simultaneous Procurement Problems

As Boeing struggled with the EELV proprietary documents issues and its CEOs, there was another ethical lapse percolating that involved a government official who held the power to award contracts to Boeing. Darlene Druyun was a lifetime government employee, working her way up through the system to a position of USAF acquisition officer. There were some precursors to her eventual newspaper-headline actions with Boeing. In the early 1990s, she was mentioned in an inspector general's report for speeding up payments to McDonnell Douglas through the backdating of some records. She was the only one of five defense department employees involved who was not disciplined for her actions.[180]

Despite this dust-up and investigation, she rose to the level of principal deputy assistant secretary in the USAF. Known as the "Dragon Lady," Ms. Druyun was knowledgeable and had developed tough negotiating skills. Former Secretary of Defense Donald Rumsfeld said that Ms. Druyun acquired a great deal of authority and made a lot of decisions, and that "there was very little adult

(continued)

---

[173]Andy Pasztor and Jonathan Karp, "Federal Officials Widen Probe into Boeing's Use of Rival's Data," *Wall Street Journal*, April 27, 2004, pp. A7, A10.

[174]Ron Insana, "We're Cleaning Up Our Own House," *USA Today*, January 5, 2004, p. 4B.

[175]Laura Rich, "A Boeing Stalwart, War or Peace," *New York Times*, July 18, 2004, p. BU4.

[176]J. Lynn Lunsford, Andy Pasztor, and JoAnn S. Lublin, "Boeing CEO Forced to Resign over His Affair with an Employee," *Wall Street Journal*, March 8, 2005, pp. A1, A8.

[177]Id.

[178]Id.

[179]Bryan Acohido and Jayne O'Donnell, "Extramarital Affair Topples Boeing CEO," *USA Today*, March 8, 2005, p. B1.

[180]Geroge Caglink, "Fallen Star," *Government Executive*, February 1, 2004, http://www.govexec.com/magazine/2004 /02/fallen-star/15929/.

Case 2.12

(continued)

supervision."[181] In the last quarter of 2002, Ms. Druyun, nearing her retirement, indicated that she was interested in job opportunities after leaving government service.

Ms. Druyun's daughter, Heather McKee, was an employee at Boeing's St. Louis facilities. In court documents, Ms. Druyun indicated that Michael Sears, who was then Boeing's chief financial officer (CFO) helped place her daughter in her job at Boeing.[182] Ms. McKee's husband also worked for Boeing and was hired along with Ms. McKee when he was her fiancé.[183] In her plea agreement, Ms. Druyun admitted that she was influenced in her decisions about awarding contracts to Boeing due to Boeing's hiring of her daughter and son-in-law.[184] Ms. Druyun also admitted that she asked for Mr. Sears's help when her daughter expressed concern that she was about to be fired for poor performance at Boeing.[185] Mr. Sears also kept Ms. Druyun posted on a transfer for her daughter in addition to a pay raise.[186]

In September 2002, Ms. McKee sent an email to Mr. Sears to let him know that her mother was planning to retire.[187] Ms. McKee mentioned to Mr. Sears that her mother would probably end up working for Lockheed following her retirement from her government position, but that Ms. Druyun really wanted to work for Boeing. Their email exchanges were obtained through an external law firm investigation by Boeing. Mr. Sears wrote to Heather:

> I met with your mom last week. She informed me of her plans, and I suggested that she and I chat. She said she needed to wait until she got some of our work completed before she could chat with me. Did I miss a signal or have the wrong picture? I'm with you . . . we need to be on her menu.

Heather responded:

> Oh! I think she is referring to the tanker deal—might be too much of a conflict right now. She hopes to have the tanker deal made or scrapped by early Dec seems like a long time off, maybe she has to wait that long before approaching us. It still makes me very worried that she is talking to Lockheed! She is visiting me tomorrow for a couple days. . . . I hope that I can get a better understanding then. She is also talking to Raytheon and L3 (formerly E-systems, I think?) Anyway, we need to talk to her. . . .[188]

As a result of this contact, Mr. Sears met with Ms. Druyun in October 2002, one month before Ms. Druyun recused herself from working on any contract decisions involving Boeing as a bidder. At the end of the meeting, Ms. Druyun testified that they discussed the F-22 contract and, that Mr. Sears said, "This meeting never took place."[189] When he returned to the offices, however, Mr. Sears sent out emails indicating that Ms. Druyun was receptive to employment. In a note sent to the chairman's office, Mr. Sears wrote:

> Howdy. Had a "non-meeting" yesterday re: hiring Jim Evatt's deputy. Good reception to job, location, salary, longer-term outlook. Recommend we put together a formal offer:
>
> *Job as we discussed *Location as we discussed *Salary $250K (assuming that fits) *Recruitment bonus $50K (important dimension of offer~could get by with $40K) *Start date 3 Jan 03 (and immediately travel to Desert meeting) FedEx offer to home for 14 Nov arrival. . . .

In October 2002, the two reached an employment arrangement. In January 2003, Ms. Druyun went to work for Boeing in its Chicago offices as a vice president for Boeing's missile defense business, at a salary of $250,000 per year plus benefits.[190] Pending before the Air Force at the time

(continued)

[181]Thomas E. Ricks, "Rumsfeld: Druyon Had Little Supervision," *Washington Post*, November 24, 2004, http://www.washington-post.com/wp-dyn/articles/A8689-2004Nov23.html.

[182]*U.S. v. Druyun*, Supplemental Statement of Facts, (D. Va. 2004) CR 04-150-A.

[183]Letter from Kenneth F. Boehm, Chairman, National Legal and Policy Center, to Joseph E. Schmitz, Inspector General, U.S. Department of Defense (Oct.6, 2003), http://www.nlpc.org/view.asp?action=viewArticle&aid=46.

[184]Renae Merle, "Long Fall for Pentagon Star: Druyun Doled Out Favors by the Millions," *Washington Post*, Nov. 14, 2004, at A1.

[185]Statement of Facts at 7, United States v. Druyun (E.D. Va. 2004) (No. 04-150-A).

[186]*Id.*

[187]Statement of Facts at 8, Druyun (No. 04-150-A).

[188]Statement of Facts at 4, Sears (No. 04-310-A).

[189]Statement of Facts at 7, United States v. Druyun (E.D. Va. 2004) (No. 04-150-A).

[190]Press Release, Boeing, Druyun Joins Boeing As Deputy General Manager for Missile Defense Systems, Jan. 3, 2003, http://www.boeing.com/news/releases/2003/ql/nr 030103m.html.

Case 2.12

(continued)

of the employment agreement was the tanker deal. During this same time period, John Judy, a Boeing lawyer who was moving from Boeing offices in St. Louis to the Washington, D.C., area, purchased Ms. Druyun's home in D.C.[191]

In the summer of 2003, Boeing began an internal investigation of the circumstances surrounding Ms. Druyun's hiring. Based on the investigation, Boeing concluded that there was "compelling evidence" that the two had conspired to employ Ms. Druyun while she still had contracting authority, and that they had engaged in subsequent attempts to cover up their conduct. Ms. Druyon amended her plea agreement twice to reflect corrections in her original statements to investigators. Boeing dismissed both Ms. Druyun and Mr. Sears. Their dismissal by Boeing for cause cost them any severance benefits.[192]

Ms.Druyun was charged by the federal government with violations of procurement statutes and conspiracy. She entered a guilty plea to conspiracy in April 2004 and told the court, "I deeply regret my actions and I want to apologize."[193] Ms. Druyun was originally scheduled to be sentenced to six months in prison because she had agreed to cooperate with federal investigators. However, she was ultimately sentenced to nine months because federal investigators established that she had lied when asked whether she had ever showed favoritism to Boeing in awarding defense contracts.[194] She initially stated that she had not shown such favoritism but, after failing a lie detector test, admitted, as noted earlier that she had given Boeing several contracts and pricing breaks in exchange for Boeing hiring her daughter and son-in-law. The supplemental factual statement for her second plea agreement also indicated that Ms. Druyun altered her notebook and the collection of contemporaneous notes that she had given to prosecutors. After failing the lie

detector test, she acknowledged changing entries and adding materials.

In addition, Ms. Druyun had attempted to cover up her first meeting with Mr. Sears when she heard about the investigations into their employment negotiations. On July 4, 2003, she sent the following email to Mr. Sears:

> I have an appointment on Monday with Judy . . . , a lawyer hired by the company to review the process used by the company to ensure that the rules were properly followed and to help offset anymore negative comments I wanted to reverify my recollection of our first discussion of potential employment. You came in to see me on 5 Nov, the day before I went on leave. I had signed a recusal letter and given it to my AF lawyer since I thought that your meeting with me would probably go into the area of potential employment since my announcement had been publicly made of my retirement in mid October. I believe it was not until 16 Dec that I officially made up my mind and called you and then faxed the paperwork to the company. I see Judy (Boeing attorney) at 0900 Monday AM and wanted to verify with you that this was also as you remember it. I expect that she might call you. Hope you are enjoying Great Britain and get some aircraft sales![195]

Mr. Sears responded, "Precisely as I recall. You obviously take good notes/have good memory . . . much better than mine. And we're all thrilled that things have worked out this way re: your employment choice!!!"[196]

Ms. Druyun also disclosed that she had approved a settlement with Boeing that was too high. Boeing and the Department of Defense eventually renegotiated that settlement. Then Boeing CEO Harry Stonecipher pledged that the company would address "any inadequacies that need to be corrected."

Ms. Druyun's daughter no longer works for Boeing. Mr. Sears served a four-month sentence. Along with serving her nine-month sentence, Ms. Druyon was ordered to pay restitution and contribute hours of

(continued)

[191]Supplemental Statement of Facts at 8, Druyun (No. 04-150-A).
[192]George Cahlink, Fallen Star: The Cautionary Tale of a Celebrated Federal Executive's Corporate Flameout, GOVEXEC, Feb. 15, 2004, at 5, http://www.govexec.com/story.page.cfm?articleid=27660. Leslie Wayne, "Boeing Dismisses 2 In Hiring of Official Who Left Pentagon," *New York Times*, November 25, 2003, p. A1.
[193]J. Lynn Lunsford and Andy Pasztor, "Former Boeing Official Pleads Guilty," *Wall Street Journal,* April 21, 2004, p. A1.
[194]Supplemental Statement of Facts at 2, Druyun (No. 04-150-A).

[195]Statement of Facts at 11, Sears (No. 04-310-A).
[196]*Id.*

Case 2.12

(continued)

community service.[197] Ms. Druyun was released from prison in October 2005.

The final result was a federal and congressional investigation, criminal charges, and banishment from government projects for a five-year period while Boeing lived under a corporate integrity agreement that required it to change its ethical culture.[198] Boeing also lost the $23 billion airborne-tanker deal and a 2002 NATO airborne warning system restructuring to Airbus. Boeing's CFO, Michael Sears, entered a guilty plea to aiding and abetting illegal job discussions with Druyun and subsequent attempts to cover up his contacts with her.[199] Mr. Sears had a book released just as he was terminated by Boeing. The title was "Soaring," and Wiley canceled its publication. However, a quote did escape: "Either you are ethical or you are not. You have to make that decision; all of us do. And there is no in between."[200]

On May 15, 2006, Boeing announced that it had settled the charges with the federal government that were related to the federal contracts and the Darlene Druyun matter. Boeing agreed to pay a $615 million fine, but the government did not require the company to admit any wrongdoing and acknowledged that employees had acted without "authority and against company policy."[201]

The 737 MAX

Once again, within a little over a decade following the Lockheed, CEO, and government procurement officer issues, Boeing was struggling with a different type of ethical lapse. Boeing was facing competitive pressures because it did not have a plane that could hold the

number of passengers and tackle the longer distances that the Airbus 321 planes offered. Rather than design such a model from scratch, Boeing decided in 2011 to redesign its existing 737 plane, and add bigger engines for lift of a wider and heavier plane that could carry more passengers. The result of these changes was an impact on what is known as the plane's "angle of attack." Boeing made the decision to not install an extra sensor as part of the alert system for tracking the plane's angle of attack. Pilots had only 10 seconds to respond to alerts that the systems were pushing the plane downward because of the altered angle of attack on the heavier plane. In addition, Boeing had promised customers that no additional training would be necessary for pilots of the new plane. That training is expensive for Boeing to provide and expensive for airlines because of the time investment of their pilots. However, without training, pilots would be taken by surprise by the problems with the angle of attack and most likely could not correct it within the 10 seconds.

The 737 MAX had its first flight in 2016. What was theorized about the effects of the lack of training and only limited reaction time materialized when a Lion Air 737 MAX flight crashed in October 2018, killing everyone on the plane. The analysis of the crash concluded that there was a sensor malfunction that caused the plane to keep the nose of the plane down even as pilots were working to get the planes to climb. The FAA made the decision to inform pilots about the hazards of an onboard sensor malfunction that led to the flight-control system pushing down the plane's nose. The analysis concluded that Boeing should "Get something out immediately and then mandate something more permanent."[202] Boeing was given 10 months to implement the new design and make the necessary changes, with a deadline of April 2019. However, another 737 MAX crash occurred on a takeoff by Ethiopian Airlines on March 10, 2019. A total of 346 lives were lost in the two crashes. The crashes were identical in physics and were eventually tied to the sensors, the angle of attack, and the lack of training.

(continued)

---

[197]William Matthews, Ex-Boeing Exec Going to Jail, *Federal Times*, Oct. 5, 2004, at http://federaltimes.com/index.php?S=388578.

[198]Anne Marie Squeo and Andy Pasztor, "U.S. Probes Whether Boeing Misused a Rival's Documents," *Wall Street Journal*, May 5, 2003, p. A1.

[199]Andy Pasztor and Rebecca Christie, "Boeing Ex-CFO Pleads Guilty In Hiring Case," *Wall Street Journal*, November 16, 2004, p. A2.

[200]James P. Miller, "Boeing CFO's New Book in Need of Timely Footnote on His Ouster,"
Chicago Tribune, November 26, 2003, https://www.chicagotribune.com/news/ct-xpm-2003-11-26-0311260162-story.html.

[201]"Boeing Pays a Biggie," *BusinessWeek*, May 29, 2006, p. 30.

[202]Natalie Kitroeff and David Gelles, "F.A.A. Loath to Rush Test to Clear Max," *New York Times*, November 16, 2019, p. B1.

Case 2.12

(continued)

The eventual finding was that it would be difficult for pilots to manage the downward angle triggered by the faulty sensors, even with the warning. As internal and governmental investigations continued, both emails and instant messages of Boeing employees emerged that indicated in-house concerns about the plane's safety. In 2016, instant messages between Mark Forkner, then Boeing's chief technical pilot for the Boeing 737 MAX, and Patrik Gustavsson, another Boeing employee working on the development of the 737 MAX, discuss the problems with the plane's MCAS (flight control) system. Mr. Forkner had some problems in the simulator with the MCAS performance: "Granted, I suck at flying, but even this was egregious." Mr. Forkner added that the MCAS was acting unpredictably, "It's running rampant." Boeing had data indicating that it took test pilots more than 10 seconds to respond to the MCAS faulty signal, and employee emails confirmed that: "I still think we need a bulletin to let [the pilot's] (*sic*) know what they are missing."[203]

During the time of the plane's design and initial production, later-revealed emails and other electronic communication showed the reality of the plane's problems as well as the fears of Boeing employees about what they were doing about the training and design changes. Federal prosecutors began investigating whether Boeing employees misled the Federal Aviation Administration (FAA) during the approval process for the 737 MAX.[204]

Mr. Forkner sent another email to his colleagues in reference to the simulator and pilot training issues that read, "So, I basically lied to the regulators (unknowingly)."[205] A colleague defended his actions, "Mark was under an enormous amount of pressure . . . He was clearly stressed."[206] Mr. Forkner feared that he would lose his Boeing job if regulators rejected Boeing's proposal to minimize pilot training for the new plane. There are worse emails, such as one employee who described the 737 MAX plane to his colleagues, "This airplane is designed by clowns, who are in turn supervised by monkeys."[207] One of the issues that emerged as a result of the email content was whether the relationship between Boeing and the FAA had become too close and perhaps too casual.[208]

Another employee working on the 737 MAX added, "I still haven't been forgiven by god [*sic*] for the covering up I did last year," in reference to his responses to FAA questions.[209] Another employee wrote, "Would you put your family on a Max simulator trained aircraft? I wouldn't."[210]

While these concerns were woven throughout Boeing employee communications during the development of and approval for the 737 MAX, managers were unaware of the issues and the emails until the House Transportation Committee report on the crashes was released in September 2020.

Fallout for Boeing

The problems with the 737 MAX and Boeing's responses affected its stock price. In March, just three days prior to the second crash, Boeing's share price was $422.56.

One year later, that price was down to $262.30. Boeing's reputation for excellence and quality has been damaged. Trust in the company by its airline customers and their passengers has been dissipated. As of January 2020, Boeing had no new orders for planes. By contrast, Airbus, its competitor, had a record 274 orders for its planes in January. Today, 40% of air travelers say that they would be unwilling to board a 737 MAX once it is permitted to fly

(continued)

[203]Final Committee Report House Transportation Committee, September 20, 2020, p. 100, https://transportation.house.gov/imo/media/doc/2020.09.15%20FINAL%20737%20MAX%20Report%20for%20Public%20Release.pdf.
[204]Natalie Kitroef and Michael S. Schmidt, "Prosecutors Are Eyeing Boeing Pilot," *New York Times*, February 22, 2020, p. B1.
[205]Andy Pasztor and Andrew Tangel, "Ex-Boeing Pilot Cited MAX Pressure," *Wall Street Journal*, October 24, 2019, p. B4.
[206]*Id.*
[207]Natalie Kitroeff, "Boeing Employees Mocked F.A.A. and 'Clowns' Who Designed the 737 MAX," *New York Times*, January 20, 2020, p. B1.
[208]David Gelles and Natalie Kitroff, "F.A.A. Admits Mistakes in How It Handled Boeing Disasters," *New York Times*, December 12, 2019, p.B1; Andy Pasztor, Andrew Tangel, and Alison Sider, "FAA Left 737 MAX Review to Boeing," *Wall Street Journal*, May 15, 2019, p. A1.
[209]*Id.*
[210]*Id.*

Case 2.12

(continued)

again.[211] The costs to Boeing have been staggering. It has undertaken $13 billion in debt to fund compensation to 737 MAX customers for its failure to deliver planes and to cover costs during its shutdown.[212] In May 2020, Boeing announced its plan for laying off 13,000 employees as it cut back its 737 MAX production.[213]

The costs to Boeing and the financial markets have been staggering. As of January 2020, Boeing had undertaken $13 billion in debt to fund compensation to 737 MAX customers for its failure to deliver planes and cancelations resulting from those delays and to cover costs during its shutdown.[214]

The 737 MAX planes remained grounded as Boeing developed fixes that were acceptable to the FAA.[215] Because of the trust issue, the FAA proceeded slowly and with great caution.[216] Boeing made its first sale of a 737 MAX in December 2020.[217] However, because of the production slow-down, analysts predicted a difficult 2021 with the struggles faced in making deliveries if and when the orders arrive.[218]

The dissipation of trust impacted other areas of Boeing as the federal government launched a criminal investigation into contacts between a Boeing official and NASA over contracts on a lunar-lander contract.[219] By September 7, 2020, the FAA was examining quality issues on Boeing's 787 jets at its South Carolina facilities.[220]

In November 2020, the FAA notified Boeing of possible penalties and enforcement actions related to quality control issues.[221]

Boeing Management Role

Boeing struggled throughout the period following the crash with what came across in the media as Boeing's difficulty in releasing full information about the plane, the crashes, causation, design issues, and the approvals from the FAA. Some of the headlines included, "U.S. Faults Disclosures by Boeing On 737 Max,"[222] "Boeing Snubs Dutch Inquiry of '09 Crash,"[223] and "House Democrats Slam Boeing, FAA For 737 Max Failures."[224] The dribs-and-drabs releases of information on what Boeing knew and when it knew seemed to create more questions. The two crashes appeared to be identical in identical in their physics, and experts were raising questions about defective designs and failed sensors early on as the public tried to understand the unusual nature of the back-to-back crashes. The tin ear of Boeing's CEO at the time, Dennis A. Muilenburg, to the issues and scope of the crisis was troubling to investors, employees, and the media.[225] In November 2019, Boeing's board made a change in leadership with a vow by new CEO David Calhoun to be more "transparent."[226]

During the House Transportation Committee hearings, Boeing executives offered complex statements with the same conclusion of "I did not know." For example, Michael Teal, former Boeing vice president and Chief Project Engineer and Deputy Program Manager for the 737 MAX program, was asked whether he was responsible for the

(continued)

[211]David Gelles and Natalie Kitroeff, "The Many Steps to Return Boeing's 737 MAX to the Sky," *New York Times*, February 10, 2020, p. B1.

[212]Doug Cameron, "Boeing's Orders Dried Up in January," *Wall Street Journal*, February 12, 2020, p. B7.

[213]Doug Cameron, "Boeing Details Plans for Mass Job Cuts," *Wall Street Journal*, May 28, 2020, p. B1.

[214]Cameron, "Boeing's Orders Dried Up in January."

[215]John Bacon and Jane Onyanga-Omara, "CEO Accepts Fault in Two Boeing Max Jet Crashes," *Wall Street Journal*, April 5–7, 2019, p. 1A.

[216]Niraj Chokshi, "Boeing 737 Max Is Deemed Safe to Fly by F.A.A.," *Wall Street Journal*, November 19, 2020, p. A1.

[217]Andrew Tangel, "Boeing Makes First Delivery of 737 Max Since End of FAA Ban," *Wall Street Journal*, December 9, 2020, p. B1.

[218]Jon Sindeu, "Boeing's 2021 Looks Troubling," *Wall Street Journal*, October 29, 2020, p. B12.

[219]Andy Pasztor, Andrew Tangel, and Aruna Viswanatha, "U.S. Probes Boeing-NASA Contacts," *Wall Street Journal*, August 15–16, 2020, p. A1.

[220]Andrew Tangel and Andy Pasztor, "Flaws in Boeings 787 Jets Prompt Review," *Wall Street Journal*, September 8, 2020, p. A1.

[221]Andy Pasztor and Andrew Tangel, "Boeing Faces Possible FAA Action," *Wall Street Journal*, November 11, 2020, p. B1.

[222]Niraj Chokshi, U.S. Faults Disclosures by Boeing On 737 Max," *New York Times*, July 3, 2020, p. B4.

[223]Chris Hamby and Claire Moses, "Boeing Snubs Dutch Inquiry of '09 Crash," *New York Times*, February 7, 2020, p. B1.

[224]Andy Pasztor and Andrew Tangel, "House Democrats Slam Boeing, FAA For 737 Max Failures," *Wall Street Journal*, September 17, 2020, p. A1.

[225]Natalie Kitroeff, "Boeing's C.E.O. Expresses Regret," *New York Times*, November 12, 2019, p. F18.

[226]Andrew Tangel, "For CEO of Boeing a Crisis Deepens," *Wall Street Journal*, April 11–12, 2020, p. B1.

Case 2.12

(continued)

requirements, configuration, design, testing, certification, and oversight of the 737 MAX explained, "No employees actually report [ed] to me . . . no engineers directly report[ed] to me. They are functionally aligned to the engineering leaders of the company. . . . But from a daily direction and overseeing of the program, you know, you could say that none of them worked for me but all of them worked for me."[227]

When Boeing was asked to respond to internal Boeing emails that the House Committee on Transportation had received about the problems in the simulators, Boeing responded, "These communications contain provocative language, and in certain instances, raise questions about Boeing's interaction with the FAA in connection with the simulator qualification process. Having carefully reviewed the issue, we are confident that all of Boeing's MAX simulators are functioning effectively."[228] The response was not confidence-inspiring for members of congress. CEO David Calhoun said that he found the emails "appalling."[229]

The pressure to get the 737 MAX built and out on the market quickly and the technical issues and concerns expressed in employee emails during that rush-to-market, turned out to be the problems that the regulators have focused on in their fix mandates for Boeing to get the 737 MAX airborne. The report of the House Transportation Committee on the 737 MAX reveals the tragic concerns that employees had about both the design and production of the 737 MAX. Their concerns, never raised and/or never addressed, were the root cause of the fatal accidents.

Boeing has issued several admissions of problems as it works through the FAA fixes.[230] Boeing did finally issue an admission of the design and software issues with the 737 MAX airplanes.[231] The FAA-mandated fixes including hardware, software, crew training, and maintenance changes, meant a longer runway, as it were, for Boeing's return of the 737 MAX to the air.[232] But getting the planes back in the air was perhaps one-third of Boeing's climb back, as it were. Boeing has a damaged brand and a plane that will remain scary in the hearts and minds of passengers. Savvy travelers (think business travelers who play the percentages on everything from on-time arrivals to the odds for survival) will be checking the type of aircraft in the flight details section of their online reservations. If they see a 737 MAX, they seem to be leaning toward taking another flight. The damage to the brand is significant. Boeing sold 4 commercial planes in July 2020, compared with two years ago earlier, when it was selling 61 per month. Granted, some of the decline in orders and sales was due to the effects of the COVID-19 pandemic on air travel. But even without the pandemic, Boeing would have had a tough slog on its flight to recovery. Now add in the general airline industry decline that beset the industry, with fewer routes, fewer passengers on planes, and sparse cash, and this blue-chip company has had rough air.

The Problems Continue

Boeing finished 2020 with an $11.84 billion loss and burned through a total of $18.4 billion in cash.[233] Boeing did get the 737 MAX back in the air on December 29, 2020–just months shy of two years after its grounding.[234] Southwest Airlines then placed an order for 100 737 MAX airplanes.[235] By April 2021, the 737 MAX had additional

(continued)

[227]Final Committee Report House Transportation Committee, September 2020, p. 117, quoting transcribed interview of Michael Teal, May 11, 2020, p. 692.

[228]Final Committee Report House Transportation Committee, September 2020, pp. 160–161.

[229]Andrew Tangel and Andy Pasztor, "Boeing Fires Executive After Emails," *Wall Street Journal*, February 13, 2020, p. B1.

[230]John Bacon and Jane Onyanga-Omara, "CEO Accepts Fault in Two Boeing Max Jet Crashes," *Wall Street Journal*, April 5–7, 2019, p. 1A.

[231]John Bacon and Jane Onyanga-Omara, "CEO Accepts Fault in Two Boeing Max Jet Crashes," *Wall Street Journal*, April 5–7, 2019, p. 1A; "FAA Gives Boeing MAX Fix List," *Wall Street Journal*, August 4, 2020, B1. "FAA Chief Pilots 737 MAX to Test Boeing's Latest Fixes," *Wall Street Journal*, October 2, 2020, p. B3.

[232]Andy Pasztor and Andrew Tangel, "FAA Gives Boeing MAX Fix List," *Wall Street Journal*, August 4, 2020, p. B2.

[233]Doug Cameron and Andrew Tangel, "Boeing's Biggest Loss Reflects Pandemic's Toll," *Wall Street Journal*, January 28, 2021, p. A1.

[234]"Boeing MAX Soars Again in U.S. After 20-Month Grounding," *Wall Street Journal*, December 30, 2020, p. A1.

[235]Alison Sider, "Southwest 737 MAX Order Boosts Boeing," *Wall Street Journal*, March 30, 2021, p. B1.

Case 2.12

(continued)

problems when Boeing discovered quality issues in its manufacturing processes.[236] Boeing notified several carriers about 90 of the jets that would require inspection and possible repairs because of manufacturing defects. Boeing has agreed to pay the FAA a $17 million penalty for the production lapses.[237] Boeing was charged with one count of conspiracy to defraud the FAA. The company is under a deferred prosecution agreement and will pay a $244 million fine and set aside $500 million for the families of the crash victims. Boeing will also pay $1.77 billion to the purchasers of the 737 MAX.[238] Boeing will not be criminally prosecuted if it avoids any felonies for a period of three years. Boeing has reached a stipulation with many of the families by accepting responsibility for the crashes. The amount that the families will receive will be determined in mediation and the families retained the right to proceed with full litigation if they remain unsatisfied with the mediation conclusions.[239]

In late February 2021, an engine on a United Airlines 777 flight taking off from Denver fell off into a residential neighborhood.[240] The planes were grounded until inspections could be done on the Pratt & Whitney engines. United had placed an order with Boeing for new planes but the engine issue is now a big one for Boeing (despite the issue being the engines themselves and not Boeing). Correcting the news stories after the bizarre Denver accident has been difficult for Boeing. Because of Boeing's already damaged reputation, any type of incident that involves a Boeing aircraft reinforces the concerns of potential passengers.

In June 2021, Boeing suspended Dreamliner deliveries because of, again, quality issues in production.[241] The delivery delay was extended one month in September to October 2021 because of safety issues raised by the FAA.[242] By November 2021, Boeing announced further delays in the Dreamliner production, delays that could last weeks.[243] And early in 2022 Boeing pushed back delivery dates yet again, due to titanium shortages and defects in certain aluminum parts of the planes such as windows and doors.

Boeing's quality reputation suffered yet another blow when the Pentagon decided against awarding Boeing a contract for a new antimissile defense system. Boeing had led the U.S. military's domestic program for two decades, but the Department of Defense decided to allow Lockheed Martin and Northrup Grumman to compete for the project.[244] The loss of the contract was also a setback to Boeing's strategic focus to rely more on military contract income than its earnings from the commercial airline business, a business that is years away from recovery.

Despite shareholder rumblings, David Calhoun, Boeing's current CEO, a director, and former chairman of the Boeing board, was retained and given a five-year contract with the company to continue as CEO.[245] The shareholders also reelected the full board. However, a judge has permitted a lawsuit by a group of shareholders against the Boeing board for its failure to supervise the safety of the 737 MAX to move forward. If successful, the directors could be held personally liable for the company's losses following the 737 MAX accidents and recall.[246]

(continued)

[236]Alison Sider, "Boeing's MAX Jet Electrical Problem Expanded," *Wall Street Journal*, April 12, 2021, p. B3.
[237]Andrew Tangel, "FAA Fines Boeing for 737 Lapses," *Wall Street Journal*, May 28, 2021, p. B1.
[238]Doug Cameron, "Boeing Is in Crisis Three Years After Fatal Crashes," *Wall Street Journal*, October 18, 2021, p. A3.
[239]Alison Sider, "Boeing, Families of Victims in Pact," *Wall Street Journal*, November 11, 2021, p. B3.
[240]Niraj Chokshi, "F.A.A. Orders Inspections of Boeing 777 Pratt & Whitney Engines," *New York Times*, February 25, 2021, p. B4.

[241]Andrew Tangel, "Boeing Dreamliner Deliveries Suspended," *Wall Street Journal*, May 29–30, 2021, p. B1.
[242]Andrew Tangel, "Boeing Faces Dreamliner Setback," *Wall Street Journal*, September 7, 2021, p. B3.
[243]Andrew Tangel, "Boeing Dreamliner Defects Further Bog Down Production," *Wall Street Journal*, November 20–21, 2021, p. A1.
[244]Doug Cameron, "Pentagon Deals Boeing a Setback," *Wall Street Journal*, March 26, 2021, p. B1.
[245]Andrew Tangel, "Boeing Extends Tenure for CEO," *Wall Street Journal*, April 21, 2021, p. B1.
[246]Andrew Tanegl, "Boeing Board Must Face MAX Suit," *Wall Street Journal*, September 9, 2021, p. B1.

Case 2.12

(continued)

Boeing currently has two new Air Force One planes under construction in San Antonio. In late September 2021, inspectors found two empty tequila bottles on one of the Air Force one planes.[247] This most recent finding of debris (as opposed to the previous discoveries in commercial airliners in production in which inspectors found tools, rags, and other garbage) is additionally sensitive because it involves alcohol use by employees on a high-security classified jet. A Boeing spokesperson indicated that the presence of the tequila bottles is under investigation, that it is a personnel matter, and that Boeing is working to improve quality and manufacturing operations. The spokesperson also added that alcohol is not allowed at any of Boeing's manufacturing facilities. Boeing is about one year behind on the production of the Air Force one planes due to the pandemic and shortages in materials and expects cost overruns of $500 million.

It is now four years since the two 737 MAX crashes, and the issue has emerged again with the indictment of Boeing's former chief pilot, Mark Forkner. Forkner was charged with six counts of fraud related to his representations to the FAA on pilot training. Mr. Forkner entered a not guilty plea and a jury acquitted him on all charges after only two hours of deliberation.[248] Following the trial, a juror commented that while Mr. Forkner should not have done what he did the management was responsible for the pressures and drivers of employee choices and actions.

Discussion Questions

1. What factors are there in common with the four ethical lapses described in the Boeing case:

   a.   The Lockheed documents

   b.   The Druyon hiring

   c.   The Condit and Stonecipher issues

   d.   The 737 MAX

[247]Andrew Tangel, "Bottles Found on Presidential Jet Boeing Is Building," *Wall Street Journal*, September 20, 2021, p. B1.
[248]Doug Cameron, "Boeing Is in Crisis Three Years After Fatal Crashes," *Wall Street Journal*, October 18, 2021, p. A3; Andrew Tangel, "Boeing Verdict Sends Key Message," *Wall Street Journal*, March 26–27, 2022, p. B1.

2. List the decision points for each of the four events. How were the issues framed at those times?

3. List the questions that Boeing employees and executives did not address as they faced decisions in these four areas.

4. Was the Bathsheba factor present in this case?

5. The time frames indicate that the issues came in nearly even spacing between the beginning of one ethical lapse and the start of another. Were there issues that went unaddressed that prevented reforms in the culture?

6. Evaluate Boeing's response to the crashes and the delay in admissions.

7. Can regulatory oversight be too weak? Is a weak regulator a temptation for a business?

8. Why were Boeing employees not as candid in meetings about their feelings and opinions on risk and safety as they were in emails?

9. What can leaders do to encourage candor from employees on evolving projects?

10. What types of behaviors by leaders discourage candid employee feedback?

11. Evaluate the testimony of the Boeing project manager for the 737 MAX. Is there a better approach to accountability?

12. Going back to the Lockheed document issue, what was management's position when the story of the documents appeared in the *Wall Street Journal*? Does management set a tone for ethics through its public actions?

13. Ms. Druyon had to issue two supplemental filings to her guilty plea to correct what she had told investigators. She had also written the email confirmation of their series of events to Mr. Sears. What lessons could ethics and compliance officers use from this experience to train employees?

14. What layers of ethics were present in these Boeing events? For example, was it Mark Forkner's decision to convince the FAA that the pilot training was not necessary?

Famous Lines from Art and Literature

The Gang That Couldn't Shoot Straight (1969)

The novel and subsequent movie tell the story of a crime family described by one of its members as follows, "He couldn't run a gas station for profit even if he stole the customers' cars."

Why Didn't They Say Something? 2.2

Boeing Employees Knew But Were Mute

From the emails and the actions of employees in each of the scenarios, it is clear that many Boeing employees were aware of the significant ethical and safety issues. List examples of when the personal ethics of Boeing employees differed from those of their company. From what you read in the case, list the reasons that the employees did not speak up.

Unit 2 Summary

There are layers of ethical dilemmas. Unit 1 dealt with our individual ethical choices. Unit 2 focuses on ethical dilemmas in business and industry and the additional factors that are involved in doing ethical analysis for these types of dilemmas.

There are different views on the standards for business ethics. Albert Car discusses his view that business ethics are part of a poker game in business. We are all bluffing in our actions in business, from dying our hair to look younger to compromising our principles to donate to a customer's political candidate, a candidate we personally oppose. Mr. Carr believes you have to do what is necessary to survive. The Drucker philosophy is that businesspeople should not harm others in taking action and making decisions. Many businesses follow a type of Carr philosophy by following moral relativism, which is, if the goal we are trying to achieve is noble, how we get to that goal does not give rise to ethical issues. In this view, businesspeople frame issues as an either/or conundrum in which they set up the issue as if they have no choice except to harm some stakeholders in the interest of preserving the business.

The culture of a business can cloud ethical analysis as employees and managers frame decisions according to the current pressures they are facing. They are not looking to examine underlying values and principles or even follow a credo. They simply do what is required to survive. Both the BP and Penn State cases illustrate how businesses miss longer term impact on their organizations by analyzing only for the present. They discount impact on reputation, the value of the business, and the additional costs when there are regulatory actions taken against their company for decisions that harmed stakeholders. The Boeing case walks through three ethical dilemmas in the same company to show how the same mistakes are repeated when pressure puts employees and managers into a corner of either I violated the law or the business survives.

The cases and problems help develop the necessary skills and insight for evaluating an
ethical dilemma in a business by framing the issue according to the impact on the business
and not the pressures of the moment.

Unit 2 Key Terms

Bathsheba syndrome   p.103   either/or conundrum   p.104
Ethical mind   p.87

Business, Stakeholders, Social Responsibility, and Sustainability

The people that build Porsches, you don't want your gasoline taken away from you. You're trying to work at the top of your field.

—**Chef Casey Lane on *foie gras* being banned in California because of the producers' practices of stuffing the geese in order to produce more foie gras**

Why don't you tell those chefs to have a duck cram a lot of food down their gullets and see how they like it?

—**John Burton, the California legislator who wrote the legislation banning *foie gras*[1]**

There will be a time for them to make profits, and there will be a time for them to get bonuses. Now's not that time.

—**President Barack Obama in a speech to Wall Street on January 29, 2009**

I am running a business. I am a for-profit business.

—**Heather Bresch, then CEO of Mylan Pharmaceutical, a company that raised its price for its allergy product, the EpiPen, 17 times, for a total increase of 548% to $600.[2]**

Learning Objectives

- Discuss the history of social responsibility and how it evolved.

- Explain what the regulatory cycle is and how it relates to social responsibility.

- Define stakeholders and discuss why they are important in ethical analysis for businesses.

- Describe the types of factors used in rating the social responsibility of businesses.

- Compare and contrast the various views on social responsibility of Berle, Dodd, Friedman, Drucker, Bowen, Entine and Jennings, Robert Halfon, John Mackey, and Marjorie Kelly.

Still another level of ethics is the responsibility of the corporation to its community—what contributions and efforts should corporations make to others beyond their shareholders? A company produces high-yield goose liver but does so through cruelty to the geese. A company has its cell phones produced in China through the use of Uyghur slave labor camps. Many companies pay the minimum wage in Vietnam for shoes produced in factories there, but those shoes bring millions of dollars in profit. Call centers in India have young people working round-the-clock on shifts that result in the loss of their personal and family time. Factory conditions for clothes production in other countries meet those nations' standards but violate nearly all U.S. minimum standards. Without cheap labor, manufacturers believe they can't compete. Without jobs, nations can't develop, but children are working 50-hour weeks in these countries. Fair and just treatment in the workplace is an issue discussed in Unit 1 as the ethical category of organizational abuse that companies face in making a decision on foreign outsourcing of labor. But even the workers in those countries and the parents of the children make compelling points about the use of cheap labor as a benefit to them and their countries' economic development.

And how do corporations best contribute to communities and societies? Some business practices may be legal, but are they ethical? And how do companies respond to these societal concerns? Is it best to boycott certain countries, or can businesses help the citizens of these countries through economic development? These are difficult questions that have brought some of the past century's greatest minds in search of answers. This unit provides you with the depth of their thoughts on the social responsibility of corporations. Following the discussion are two sections on the application of the theories of social responsibility by businesses, investment firms, and government entities.

---

[1] Jesse McKinley, "Waddling into the Sunset," *New York Times*, June 6, 2012, p. D1.

[2] The Chatter, *New York Times*, August 28, 2016, p. BU2.

Business and Society: The Tough Issues of Economics, Social Responsibility, Stakeholders, and Business

In the following readings, you will find various views on social responsibility, or **corporate social responsibility (CSR)**. The views of the late Dr. Milton Friedman, a Nobel Laureate, and stakeholder theory present different takes on the role of ethics in business as well as the role of business in society as an economic-based analysis. The views of other philosophers and practitioners differ, and their divergent views will help you understand the scope of the difficult questions that businesses face in assessing their social responsibility.

Reading 3.1

The History and Components of Social Responsibility[3]

There have been four phases of the corporate social responsibility (CSR) movement.[4] Those phases provide a foundation for understanding the various schools of thought on social responsibility and provide a framework for analyzing CSR issues.

Phase 1: 1900–1930: Labor's Voluntary and Legislative Movements

CSR issues arise in different ways that reveal differences in how CSR issues are resolved. There are voluntary changes by businesses, there are legislative and regulatory changes brought about because of needs on both sides of CSR issues, and there are changes that come through public demand that carries CSR issues through to litigation and/or regulation for their resolution. The CSR issues in the early labor movements were resolved differently but involved all three change methods.

Voluntary Changes by Business

There are times when, sensing the impact of CSR issues and forces on profits and individuals, businesses make changes unilaterally. For example, in the early 1900s, General Electric (GE) plants became what were referred to as "fertile grounds" for union organizers.[5] With turnover rates of 100% because of the increasing

---

[3]Adapted with permission from Marianne M. Jennings, "The Social Responsibility of Business Is Not Social Responsibility: Assume That There Are No Angels and Allow the Free Market's Touch of Heaven," 16 *Berkeley Business Law Journal* 325 (2019).

[4]In early research in the field, the term *corporate social performance (CSP)* was used. However, after 2009, CSR became the preferred term. Samuel B. Graves and Sandra A. Waddock, "Institutional Owner and Corporate Social Performance," 37 *The Academy of Management Journal* 1034 (1994).

[5]Douglas M. Eichar, *The Rise and Fall of Corporate Social Responsibility* (2015).

speed demands on production lines, GE experienced a strike in 1917 at its Lynn, Massachusetts facility, a plant that was organized by the International Workers of the World.[6] GE's general counsel, Owen Young, commissioned a report on the origins, purposes, and demands of the strikers. The report characterized the strikers as "Socialists, the Russian Labor Union, the IWW, the anarchists, the Bolsheviks, and the more radical men of the established labor unions."[7] Despite the findings, the report for Mr. Young still concluded that GE needed a new approach to its personnel policies.

When Young became GE's chairman of the board, GE began experimenting with its personnel policies to develop employee loyalty. The policy changes included health care, grievance boards, mortgage assistance, and life insurance. GE led a different approach in its treatment of employees, treatment that was designed to address the high cost of turnover as well as the social issues at that time, such as job security and safety. Those voluntary changes came in 1922 following the strikes.[8]

Tandem Changes: Business and Labor Obtain Mutually Beneficial Regulatory Changes

This GE era of voluntary corporate personnel changes followed a stream of state-level legislation that had resulted in the worker compensation system. However, those changes came about in a different way. The initial push on worker compensation regulations initially came from the business side because of the costs of litigation and the desire to limit employer liability for workplace injuries.[9] The industrial age had brought levels of injuries, in both numbers and type, which far exceeded those in what had been an agrarian society.[10] The interests of employees in being covered (medically and for missed income) and the employers in limiting liability walked on the same side of the street. Legislatures passed various forms of injury compensation systems.

The interests of employers and employees may have walked on the same side of the street, but their motivations were different. Neither side could solve the overarching issues and concerns without some form of governmental action. Employers could not be assured of limited liability, and employees could not be guaranteed financial compensation without legislative mandates because individually executed agreements or company programs were not guaranteed. There was a compromise between the business and its stakeholders. The legislation established an *ex ante* "contract" between workers and employers, who promised to pay a specified set of benefits for all accidents arising out of or in the course of employment. Further, the legislation raised the expected post accident payments that workers received. However, workers forfeited their rights to common-law negligence suits.[11] Not all CSR issues can be solved through voluntary actions because some issues require legal protections to blend and address the concerns and interests of all the parties (stakeholders – see Reading 3.2).[12] Those legal protections came following input from all stakeholders. For example, insurance companies were included in the development of legislation because their payouts were affected by the resolution of liability and coverage issues. Today, worker compensation systems continue to evolve as stakeholders raise concerns. For example, new workplace injuries, such as carpal tunnel syndrome and stress-related maladies, have been added as compensable.

---

[6]*Id.*, at p. 1.

[7]*Id.*

[8]Daren Fonda, "GE's Green Awakening," *Time – Inside Business*, August 2005, A10, at A11.

[9]*See* generally, Price V. Fishback & Shawn Everett Kantor, "The Adoption of Workers' Compensation in the United States," 41 *Journal of Law & Economics* 305 (1998).

[10]Chrystal Eastman, *Work Accidents and the Law* (1910).

[11]Price V. Fishback & Shawn Everett Kantor, "The Adoption of Workers' Compensation in the United States, 1900–1930," *Journal of Law & Economics* 305 (1998).

[12]Fishback & Kantor, *Id.*, at 312–313.

Compulsory Change: Resolution of CSR Issues by Regulation
Opposed by Business

In contrast to these two initial forms of CSR in the labor law movement, there was a follow-up movement of compulsory changes. When employees initially organized against their employers to increase wages, for example, their efforts were met with charges and criminal convictions because strikes had been criminalized. The first recorded labor case in the United States (1806) involved a demand for wage increases by shoemakers that ranged from 25 cents to 75 cents per pair of boots. Those participating in the organized demand and strike were charged and convicted of criminal conspiracy (*Commonwealth v. Pullis*).[13] The social issues involved in the labor disputes that led to federal regulation included poverty, housing, and the societal impact of low wages. Because of the disparity in bargaining power between employers and employees and employer resistance to employee strength derived from their organized effort, a series of federal laws governing the right to and processes for worker unionization emerged despite business efforts to stop it.

In *NLRB v. Jones & Laughlin*, the U.S. Supreme Court noted, "Long ago we stated the reason for labor organizations. We said that they were organized out of the necessities of the situation; that a single employee was helpless in dealing with an employer; that he was dependent ordinarily on his daily wage for the maintenance of himself and family; that if the employer refused to pay him the wages that he thought fair, he was nevertheless unable to leave the employ and resist arbitrary and unfair treatment; that union was essential to give laborers the opportunity to deal on an equality with their employer."[14]

The employer resistance to employee organization that ripened into violence and deaths was an example of an issue that resulted in governmental mandates for business. The passage of the National Labor Relations Act (the Wagner Act) was the beginning of a series of federal labor laws that resulted in a complete regulatory framework for employer and employee contracting when employees exercised their statutory rights to organization.[15] From oversight of the processes for organization to the subject matters in collective bargaining agreements, the relationship between employers and employees who choose to organize is highly structured and heavily regulated. On unionization and underlying wage and work conditions, there was no voluntary reform, nor did stakeholder interests coalesce to develop acceptable protections and solutions.

The U.S. Supreme Court noted that Congress had stepped in to eliminate the strife and violence that resulted from the suppression of employee organizational efforts, noting that "'instead of being an invasion of the constitutional right of either, was based on the recognition of the rights of both.'"[16]

Phase 2: The 1930s and 1940s: The Berle and Dodd Theories and Debates and the Early Regulatory Cycle

Amidst the evolving employer–employee issues of the 1930s, legal scholars first trotted into CSR on a theoretical basis. The legal debate was not directed at specific issues (as with the labor movement). Rather, the legal debate set up the resolution of CSR issues as an either/or conundrum based on the notion that businesses faced a false choice of profits vs. goodness.

---

[13](Phila. Mayor's Court), as discussed in John Commons & Eugene Gilmore, *A Documentary History of American Industrial Society*, 59–248 (1910).

[14]*N.L.R.B. v. Jones & Laughlin Steel Corp.*, 301 U.S. 1, at 33 (1937).

[15]29 U.S.C. §151 *et seq.* (2018).

[16]301 U.S. 1, at 34. The violence that led to the eventual labor legislation is beyond the scope of this discussion but is well documented. Kenneth Casebeer, "Aliquippa: The Company Town and Contested Power in the Construction of Law," 43 *Buffalo Law Review* 617 (1995). (Documents the efforts of Jones & Laughlin to cut off outside contact with its company town north of Pittsburgh (Aliquippa) and the resulting violence.)

In 1932, the Berle and Dodd debates emerged. Dodd maintained that businesses owed a responsibility to community, whereas Berle rejected that duty. Professor Berle opened the debate with his view that managers are trustees operating the corporation and using its assets for the stockholders as sole beneficiaries.[17] Dodd's response recognized a practical reality of social demands:

> [P]ublic opinion, which ultimately makes law, has made and is today making substantial strides in the direction of a view of the business corporation as an economic institution which has a social service as well as a profit-making function. [This] view has already had some effect upon legal theory, and that it is likely to have a greatly increased effect upon the latter in the near future.[18]

Dodd's point was accurate. Public opinion and activism do drive laws and regulations. There is a **regulatory cycle** based on public activism, a cycle that follows a consistent pattern from the issue's emergence to regulatory action or litigation. Berle & Dodd were debating in the aftermath of the 1929 stock market crash, a painful economic period that found many questioning corporate conduct and responsibility. The reforms put into place in the national securities markets, in response to public outcry, reined in conduct related to the sales and resales of corporate securities. Berle and Dodd were debating who moves that cycle of reform, and how and when it moves.

The power of public opinion drives CSR measures and behavior. The distinction of Dodd's underlying public opinion theory of CSR is that Dodd put CSR issue resolution under the constraint of legal process. Legal process was the means for achieving CSR. Dodd's legal process is a consistent process, a system of guardrails, required prior to CSR tenets' becoming *mandatory*, i.e., law. For example, environmental laws and regulations followed a slow and steady flow of information from the public, research, and businesses.[19] Similarly, the Consumer Product Safety Commission does not ban products based on the number of online posts the agency sees. Should the agency become aware of online posts, the agency could commission research, hold hearings, release reports, and take responses from the public through the comment periods afforded by administrative law.[20]

Famous Lines from Art and Literature

From *Heaven Can Wait* (1978)

Newspaper reporter question to the chairman and CEO of a multinational energy company:

> *Isn't it true that an accident in your West coast nuclear plant could stimulate seismic activity in the San Andreas Fault, which could destroy most of Ssouthern California?*

Response of energy company executive:

> *I think you'd have to define "destroy."*

---

[17]Adolf A. Berle, Jr., "Corporate Powers as Powers in Trust," 44 *Harvard Law Review* 1049 (1931).
[18]E. Merrick Dodd, Jr., "For Whom Are Corporate Managers Trustees," 45 *Harvard Law Review* 1145, 1148. (1932).
[19]*See* Jedediah Purdy, "The Long Environmental Justice Movement," for a discussion, details, and resources on the environmental movement. 44 *Ecology Law Quarterly* 809 (2018).
[20]Jill Wieber Lens, "Product Recalls: Why Is Tort Law Deferring to Agency Inaction?" 90 *St. John's Law Review* 329 (2016).

However, there is a considerable time lag in relying on legal process. During that lag period, from realization of harmful consequences of corporate behavior, the dangers, risks, and harm continue. For example, in the General Motors (GM) defective ignition switch litigation, evidence emerged that GM was aware of the defect in its cars for 13 years prior to issuing a recall (see Case 8.7 in Unit 8).[21]

Berle wanted some clear and definitive lists of responsibilities, how those would be determined, and who would determine them. Ironically, Berle conceded Dodd's point after 20 years of debate.[22] His limited embrace, however, related to the role of lawyers in working with corporations:

> Unchecked by present legal balances, a social–economic absolutism of corporate administrators, even if benevolent, might be unsafe; and in any case it hardly affords the soundest base on which to construct the economic commonwealth which industrialism seems to require. Meanwhile, as lawyers, we had best be protecting the interests we know, being no less swift to provide for the new interests as they successively appear.[23]

In other words, lawyers had a duty to protect the interests of clients as public policy issues arose. Berle inserted a means of voluntary action into the debate, actions that lawyers might spur in pointing out to their clients the evolving interests of the public and their communities on particular issues that could affect those clients.

Phase 3: The 1950s–1970s and Bowen, Drucker, and Friedman

By the 1950s, the Berle and Dodd debate had moved from a legal scholar/law review focus into the areas of management and economics. The legal process, and its start and finish, were no longer the focus of the debate. The debate migrated to an either/or proposition on one side and economic analysis on the other. Either business has a social responsibility, or it does not, but, in some cases, it will not know the answer unless and until there is an economic analysis of any benefits of being socially responsible.

The Bowen Proposition of Cost and Benefit Analysis

This movement is sometimes marked by the publication of economist and professor Howard Bowen's book, *Social Responsibilities of the Businessman*.[24] Professor Bowen did not see the CSR debate as an either/or conundrum. Rather, he saw the CSR

---

[21]Marianne M. Jennings & Lawrence J. Trautman, "Ethical Culture and Legal Liability: The GM Switch Crisis and Lessons in Governance," 22 *Boston University Journal of Science & Technology Law* 187 (2016).

[22]For a full look at the Berle–Dodd debate, see Adolf A. Berle, Jr., "Corporate Powers as Powers in Trust," 44 *Harvard Law Review* 1049 (1931); Adolf. A. Berle, Jr., "For Whom Corporate Managers Are Trustees," 45 *Harvard Law Review* 1365 (1932); E. Merrick Dodd, Jr., "For Whom Are Corporate Managers Trustees," 45 *Harvard Law Review* 1145 (1932).

[23]Adolf A. Berle, *The 20th-Capitalist Revolution* 169 (1954); 16 *Delaware Journal of Corporate Law* 33, 37 (1991).

[24]Howard Bowen, *Social Responsibilities of the Businessman* (1953). The book was republished in 2013 by Professor Bowen's son, Peter Geoffrey Bowen, at the suggestion of a number of colleagues who had used the book in their teaching. At p. vii.

decisions through the eyes of an economist, recommending that decisions be made on the basis of economic costs and benefits.

> [S]ome of the many socially desirable improvements in business practice have been found to "pay" in the sense of cutting costs or increasing revenues of the individual firm. There has never been any doubt, of course, that if a given change in business practice reduces costs or increases revenue, self-interest will lead to adoption of the practice. Thus, when it was discovered that shorter hours or better light or cleaner washrooms increased the efficiency of workers and reduced unit labor costs, there was little hesitation in adopting these measures which were good from both commercial and social viewpoints.[25]

Bowen recognized that gains are not measured solely by increases in production. However, Bowen's concern was whether the accepted standards of society would influence business decisions even though there might be minimal economic benefit. For example, if a culture accepts a 12-hour workday as being "reasonable and proper," then shortening the workday may reduce production. But, in a culture in which a 12-hour workday is perceived to be too long, reduction of that workday may increase production.[26] In one cultural milieu, a business may find gains in reducing work hours, but in another, experience a reduction.[27] Bowen believed cost reduction is a rational basis for adopting CSR proposals. His warning was that cultures vary and universal CSR principles will not yield the same cost-savings results based on cultural norms.

The Drucker Management Perspective on CSR (with a Touch of Philosophy)

During this period, Peter Drucker, the management guru, weighed in with his overarching principle of *primum non nocere,* a motto that is part of the Hippocratic oath, meaning to above all not knowingly do harm (see Reading 1.8).[28] Drucker viewed business as an "organ of society" which owes an obligation to society.[29] That obligation was to not knowingly lie, cheat, or steal, and also to not knowingly harm society. In addition, Drucker believed that where much has been given—success, education, and opportunity—there is an expectation of a higher standard of behavior.

The Drucker theory has been embellished and remains part of the CSR debate today. During her ultimately successful U.S. Senate campaign in Massachusetts, Elizabeth Warren made what would become known as the "You Didn't Build That" speech:

> There is nobody in this country who got rich on his own. Nobody.
>
> You built a factory out there? Good for you. But I want to be clear: you moved your goods to market on the roads the rest of us paid for; you hired workers the rest of us paid to educate; you were safe in your factory because of police forces and fire forces that the rest of us paid for. You didn't have to worry that marauding bands would come and seize everything at your factory, and hire someone to protect against this, because of the work the rest of us did.

---

[25]Bowen, at p. 111.
[26]Bowen, at p. 111.
[27]*Id.*
[28]Peter F. Drucker, *Management Tasks, Responsibilities, Practices* (1974), at 367.
[29]Peter F. Drucker, *The Practice of Management* (1954), at 37.

Now look, you built a factory and it turned into something terrific, or a great idea? God bless. Keep a big hunk of it. But part of the underlying social contract is you take a hunk of that and pay forward for the next kid who comes along.[30]

Senator Warren, and subsequently President Obama, advanced a Drucker-like theory that would involve greater government control over businesses, including reimbursement via taxes for the use of roads and other community resources in operating a business.[31]

The Friedman View: Agents of Corporations and Their Responsibilities

However oddly, **Milton Friedman's** clearest statement on his views on CSR appeared in a *Playboy* interview. That interview would bring about the never-ending either/ or debate that pitted social responsibility against free markets.[32] The interview was a pithy summary of Friedman's long article in the *New York Times Magazine* that referred to social responsibility as a form of socialism, with decisions being made for businesses by those not involved in those businesses, or even in general economic development.[33] Dr. Friedman's theme was along the lines of Bowen's view that decisions for businesses on issues of CSR are best made by the business on economic grounds: "[A] corporate executive's responsibility is to make as much money for the shareholders as is possible, as long as he operates within the rules of the game."[34] Friedman added the Berle component in noting that it is possible that voluntary action by a business, beyond compliance, may be an economically sound thing for a business to do, regardless of that decision's contribution to CSR. However, Friedman did not believe that simply succumbing to cultural forces should be the grounds for business decisions:

> I wouldn't buy stock in a company that hired that kind of leadership. A corporate executive's responsibility is to make as much money for the shareholders as possible, as long as he operates within the rules of the game. When an executive decides to take actions for reasons of social responsibility, he is taking money from someone else—from the stockholders, in the form of lower dividends, from the employees, in the form of lower wages, or from the consumer, in the form of higher prices.[35]

Friedman's discussion in *Playboy* provided an example of how his views on CSR should be applied. An example was the pollution from the steel mills in Gary, Indiana. At the time of the interview, there were no environmental regulations that controlled the emissions from the U.S. Steel plants located there. Reducing the emissions would be voluntary and costly for U.S. Steel. However, Friedman

---

[30]https://elizabethwarrenwiki.org/factory-owner-speech/ (accessed October 11, 2018). For the video of the speech, *see* https://www.youtube.com/watch?v=0AMoBU7lFUA. Aaron Blake, "Obama's 'You Didn't Build That' Problem," *Washington Post*, July 18, 2012, https://www. washingtonpost.com/blogs/the-fix/post/obamas-you-didnt-build-that-problem/2012/07/18 /gJQAJxyotW_blog.html?noredirect=on&utm_term=.f188b630ae05.

[31]The speech was actually a restatement of the views of Berkeley professor George Lakoff, a cognitive linguist and philosopher and architect of the "Occupy Wall Street" movement. George Lakoff, "How to Frame Yourself: A Framing Memo for Occupy Wall Street," *Huffington Post*, October 9, 2011; updated Dec. 19, 2011, https://www.huffingtonpost.com /george-lakoff/occupy-wall-street_b_1019448.html. *See also*, George Lakoff & Elisabeth Wheling, "The Public: Obama's and Romney's Opposite Visions for a Free America," September 16, 2012, https://georgelakoff.com/2012/09/ (accessed October 11, 2018).

[32]Geoffrey Norman, "Interview: Milton Friedman," *Playboy*, February 1973, 59.

[33]Milton Friedman, "The Social Responsibility of Business Is to Increase Profits," *New York Times*, September 13, 1970, at 22–26.

[34]Milton Friedman, "*The Social Responsibility of Business Is to Increase Profits*," *New York Times*, September 13, 1970, at 32, 33.

[35]Geoffrey Norman, *Playboy* Interview: Milton Friedman, *Playboy*, February 1973, at 59.

added, "It's to the company's advantage to do something about it. Why? Because if it doesn't, workers will prefer to go where there is less pollution, and U.S. Steel will have to pay them more to live in Gary, Indiana."[36]

Since the time of that interview, the debate has been vibrant, controversial, emotional, and, as will be discussed, often conducted in a vacuum. Friedman's view was definitive but still misunderstood. His concerns centered on the "lack of rigor" and loosely analytical qualities of social responsibility. Some of those concerns about business exercise of CSR initiatives are summarized in the following question format:

- What is the scope of social responsibility?
- Who makes the decisions about what is and is not socially responsible behavior?
- How far does social responsibility take the company? Are companies, for example, required to refrain from price increases because of inflation in the name of its good for society? And are they required to hire the hard-core unemployed over hiring based on qualifications?

Friedman saw the actions of companies responding to social good as really being the imposition of a tax on the company's owners—its shareholders—because they were being required to pay for decisions that spent their investment in the company. The imposition of a tax for social programs was, in Dr. Friedman's view, the province of government, not private entities or citizens acting unilaterally.

> The businessmen believe that they are defending free enterprise when they declaim that business is not concerned "merely" with profit but also with promoting desirable "social" ends; that business has a "social conscience" and takes seriously its responsibilities for providing employment, eliminating discrimination, avoiding pollution, and whatever else may be the catchwords of the contemporary crop of reformers. In fact, they are—or would be if they or anyone else took them seriously—preaching pure and unadulterated socialism. Businessmen who talk this way are unwitting puppets of the intellectual forces that have been undermining the basis of a free society these past decades.[37]

Phase 4: The Regulatory Cycle's Evolution and Update[38]

While the regulatory cycle was introduced in Phase 2 of CSR, it largely disappeared until the 1980s, when it was resurrected in political science. When he was serving as the CEO for Motorola, before going on to become Kodak's CEO, George Fisher spoke to a group of our master's students from both engineering and business. One of the questions the students asked was, "How do you become a leader in business?" Mr. Fisher's response was that those in business should take an evolving problem in their business unit, their company, their industry, or their community and fix it before the problem is regulated or litigated. He assured the students that businesspeople who voluntarily undertake self-correction are always ahead of the game.

---

[36]*Id.*
[37]Geoffrey Norman, *Playboy* Interview: Milton Friedman, *Playboy*, February 1973, at 59.
[38]Adapted and updated from Marianne M. Jennings, "How Ethics Trump Market Inefficiencies and Thwart the Need for Regulation," 10 *Corporate Finance Review* 36 (2006).

There is a diagram used to illustrate this Fisher principle of leadership that shows how its best execution is found in focusing on ethics. That diagram, based on the political science model developed by Professor James Frierson, is presented in Figure 3.1.

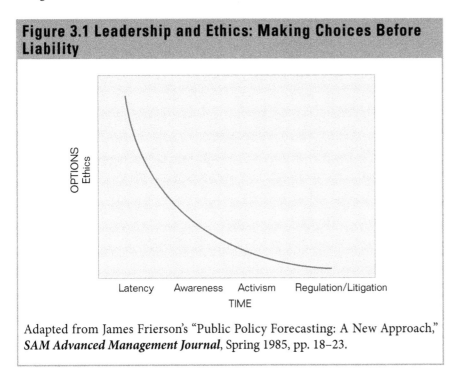

Figure 3.1 Leadership and Ethics: Making Choices Before Liability

Adapted from James Frierson's "Public Policy Forecasting: A New Approach," *SAM Advanced Management Journal*, Spring 1985, pp. 18–23.

Understanding this cycle, what it represents, what moves it, and how companies and industries should respond is a critical part of the study of business and social responsibility. The phenomenon of a rapidly moving regulatory force drives home the reality that businesses and industries are always better off self-regulating than waiting for government regulations. A historical study of the cycle phenomenon reveals that regulators, as bureaucratic as they are, can move far more quickly than market forces to solve market frauds, abuses, and other perversions that occur when the moral sentiments of markets do not prevail as Adam Smith intended in his assumptions about economic efficiencies.

Every market, consumer, or industry issue that is subject to regulation or litigation began as an ethical issue. Because the law and regulations afforded businesses wide latitude in a particular area, some seized the moment a bit too aggressively. That aggressive seizure of a loophole, without the checks and balances of ethics, puts companies, industries, and individuals at a disadvantage when the inevitable regulation arrives because their practices have been so foreign to the now-mandated morality. The *x*-axis of the diagram represents time, and the *y*-axis represents options for self-regulation. The longer companies and industries wait before taking self-corrective action, the less likely their self-correction will be allowed and the more likely regulators will impose regulation with often unintended consequences, including additional costs, as illustrated in Figure 3.2 (with the addition of a second curve that depicts costs). This diagram depicts the regulatory cycle, with an additional line to illustrate the fact that the firm's costs increase the longer it takes to address the evolving issues.

Examining ethical issues through the cycle provides firms with the opportunity for self-regulation, an opportunity that is often a cheaper and more efficient means

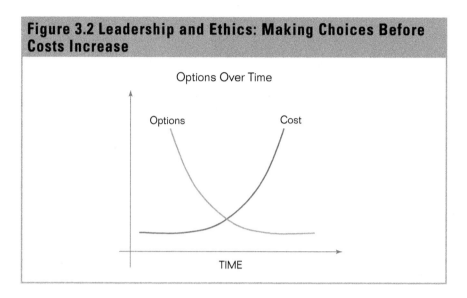

Figure 3.2 Leadership and Ethics: Making Choices Before Costs Increase

Options Over Time

Options

Cost

TIME

of curbing the misdeeds that too often occupy loophole areas of markets and industries. The voluntary changes described earlier involving GE were examples of a company taking advantage of the time frames in the regulatory cycle.

The Stages and Activities of the Regulatory Cycle

Every area that is now the subject of regulation or litigation began at the left side of the regulatory cycle, in the **latency stage**, with plenty of options for how to handle a gray area. During this phase of the cycle, only those in the industry and perhaps academics and researchers are aware of the evolving issue. For example, the issue of underfunding pensions has been an evolving concern for the past 25 years. Companies, researchers, and corporate governance experts expressed concerns about the funding, investments, and reporting on pension plans. But the issue remained of interest only to those in the financial field. It failed to gain traction in daily newspapers such as *USA Today* or in weekly news magazine publications. However, the bankruptcy of United Airlines (UA) and its bankruptcy court ruling excusing it from its pension obligations moved the issue from the latency stage to the **public awareness stage**. Suddenly, the issue of pensions and sudden losses was the cover story for *Time* and *Newsweek*. Consumers and employees were demanding to know "How safe is my pension?"[39] Once the public was aware of the pension underfunding, they demanded a response, moving the cycle to activism, or the demand for reform. Shortly thereafter, the pension funding issue moved into the **regulation/litigation stage**, with new statutory mandates for companies on pension funding.

The Pension Funding Cycle

Regulatory cycles bring new regulations in unregulated areas and close loopholes discovered by amoral technicians (see Reading 2.1 on the layers of ethical issues). Companies had been able to capitalize on a rather large loophole in pension reporting requirements. Through the UA bankruptcy, the Federal Pension Benefit Guaranty Corporation discovered that UA's pension was underfunded by 50%. The shortage that the federal agency needed to supply in order to provide

[39]Marilyn Adams, "Fundamentally 'Broken' Pension System in 'Need of a Fix,'" *USA Today*, November 15, 2005, pp. 1B, 2B.

UA employees with their pension benefits was estimated at $8.4 to $10 billion. UA did nothing that violated the law in its pension funding and reporting.[40] However, bankruptcy of one airline brought a percolating latency issue to regulation that closed the loophole.

Under a federal pension law enacted in 1974, companies found and were using a loophole that enabled them to report better financial results: they were not required to report any pension shortfalls to the Federal Pension Benefit Guaranty Corporation unless their pension funding fell below 50% of requirements. The 50% figure was, however, a guide for reporting a "state of emergency" in the pension plan and its funding. Under the interpretations of the law, most companies declared their plans fully funded as long as they did not dip below 50%. UA reported a shortfall in 2004 of about $74 million.

However, the Securities and Exchange Commission (SEC) requires companies to report pension funding shortfalls in their annual reports when pension funding falls below 90%. Of the 100 largest pension funds examined by a U.S. Department of Labor study in 2003, only six of the plans were truly at the 90% funding level, and the SEC reports of those six companies were consistent with their Federal Pension Benefit Guaranty Corporation requirements. The audit estimated the shortfall in total private pension plan funding at $450 billion. The Federal Pension Benefit Guarantee Corporation's deficit from paying pensions is now $23.5 billion. With that level of shortfall and media attention, massive reforms came about with the passage of the Pension Protection Act – the end of this particular regulatory cycle.

Other Cycle Examples

The pattern in the regulatory cycle is always the same. Someone finds a loophole in the law, and those in the industry take advantage of that loophole as a strategy for maximizing their returns. History repeats itself when it comes to the regulatory cycle. For example, prior to the savings and loan crisis and collapse of the late 1980s and early 1990s, appraisers were not regulated. The qualifications for an appraiser were limited, and issues such as conflicts of interest (where the appraisers stood to benefit in a transaction if the land value came in at an appropriate level) were not controlled. In an area in which there are few legal guidelines, leeway translates into licentiousness and then abuses that often graduate into fraud. The firms begin by crossing those ethical lines of conflicts of interest or by only asking whether something *can* be done (such as the pension funding and reporting issues) and not whether it *should* be done. (Refer to Unit 2 and Figure 2.1 for the layers of legal compliance vs. "could vs. should" analysis.)

Those ethical violations, centering on basic values such as fairness in real estate transactions or honoring the pension commitment made to employees, cause emotional reactions and outrage. Courts and/or legislatures step in to legislate ethics.

What is perhaps difficult for executives to grasp about the regulatory cycle is that it moves not by data or logic but by emotion and public perception. Public perception changes laws and regulations through examples and anecdotes.

The tax deductibility limits on CEO pay in the United States, as ill defined and designed as they were, resulted from public emotion and outcry over executive compensation. There are continuing demands for reforms. Stock option grants were a gently percolating issue to watch as continuing attention and outrage build at

---

[40]Mary Williams Walsh, "Pension Loopholes Helped United Hide Its Troubles," *New York Times*, June 7, 2005, pp. C1, C3.

the time of this article's publication.[41] The granting, disclosure, and accounting for stock options has been fully regulated since 2002.

When the Sarbanes–Oxley (SOX) regulations took effect after the market collapses that followed the collapses of Enron, WorldCom, and most of the dot-com companies, most companies were grappling with the expensive and intense mandates of the regulations. The statutorily imposed mandates on board structure, conflicts, financial reporting, and certification of processes and reports found many firms with delayed filings and restatements. But some companies already had most of the requirements in place and had based their governance structure on concerns about issues in the ethical categories, such as conflicts of interests, withholding information, and taking unfair advantage. These companies changed their governance processes and exercised transparency in disclosures to shareholders. They were operating under ethical standards ahead of the regulatory cycle curve. One of the benefits of anticipating issues in the latency stage is that a company is then prepared for implementation and may enjoy a period of competitive advantage because it is not distracted by complex regulations and their implementation.

How to Seize the Moment and Manage the Cycle

There are businesses that do seize the latency moment. There is little question that the electric utility industry would look a great deal differently today if it had not handled the issue of EMF (electromagnetic fields) as effectively and openly as it did.

As we look back over the art of financial reporting, we see a host of ethical issues that went on unmanaged until SOX was passed and mandated. The audit firms themselves are now fully regulated for their complicity in the frauds at WorldCom, Enron, Adelphia, and others. The federal government must authorize them to conduct audits, and the role of the accounting profession in setting ethical standards has been usurped by the government—federal laws now determine what constitutes a conflict of interest on the part of an auditor because the profession had not defined a conflict broadly enough to cover the clearly conflicting interests that auditors had with their clients. Officers are now required to pay back bonuses earned because of inflated earnings reports. That the company should be repaid bonuses earned on fraudulent earnings was not a debatable issue. However, too few executives saw the issue. SOX now requires that the officers restore their bonus payments to the company if the financial statements were inflated.

How can a director who is not independent be an effective member of the board audit or compensation committee? The conflict is overwhelming and is not remedied by the disclosure of a director's dual role. The result of too many abuses of conflicting relationships by too many directors is that federal law now permits only independent directors on the audit and compensation committees of the board. How could the issue have evolved to the point of federal mandates? There was a wild ride in both compensation levels and inaccurate financial reports. When the degree of abuses unfolded, the public became emotional and demanded action. That action came in the form of strict oversight through the reforms noted here.

Public concern emerges when research becomes known or business inaction, despite awareness, continues. If business inaction continues or a business remains intransigent toward reforms, as it did with the labor organization movement, the public becomes activated. The public's issue proceeds to regulation and litigation, as it did with labor. Indeed, the fear of litigation and liability brought about the compromise reforms in worker compensation regulation. Business has a choice, as the cycle progresses, to

---

[41]The result was an SEC investigation of over 250 companies for backdating their options grants.

voluntarily change or to wait and be forced to change through legislative and judicial mandates, the results of which come without their input and because of their resistance.[42]

The regulatory cycle begins when an issue of public concern emerges, which is preceded by significant awareness in the academic and business worlds.[43] There are ethical issues that are now in the latency stage. The following questions help anticipate the cycle:

- What is the topic of discussion in the industry?
- What concerns are academics and others expressing about the product, its production, and the future?
- Is the company capitalizing on a loophole in the law?
- Has it disclosed what loophole it is using?
- If it has not disclosed the loophole, what are the company's reasons for keeping it close to the vest?
- Are the company's actions fair or do they put someone at risk?
- Are others in the industry doing the same thing?

Discussion Questions

1. What issues were being addressed by businesses in the Phase 1 stage of CSR, and how were they resolved?

2. What were the views of Berle and Dodd and how did they differ in their approach to CSR?

3. Suppose that the federal government proposed a tax on businesses for the number of miles driven by the vehicles used in their business. Which of the scholars whose work is explained in the reading would favor such a tax? Why would they favor it? Who would be opposed, and why?

4. In thinking about the pension funding issue, explain the ethical analysis that the companies did in offering two sets of numbers on funding: one for purposes of SEC disclosure and one based on the funding required to meet pension promises for retirees. Draw on Unit 1 to offer insights on rationalizations and questions not addressed as businesses determined their pension-funding levels.

5. During the COVID-19 pandemic, some businesses discovered that their employees were far more productive when working from home. Other businesses discovered that their employees were less productive when working from home. When lockdown restrictions were lifted, some employers required that employees return to work, some required that employees come to the office for two days each week and work from home the remaining days, and some employers had employees work from home full time. Using what you have learned in this reading about various approaches to CSR, provide a list of all the factors for employers and employees to consider in making decisions about work-from-home and work-at-the-office employment.

---

[42]*See*, e.g., Marianne M. Jennings & Sally Gunz, "A Proactive Proposal for Self-Regulation of the Actuarial Profession: A 'Means' of Avoiding the Audit Profession's Post-Enron Regulatory Fate," 48 *American Business Law Journal* 641 (2011); and Marianne M. Jennings, "The Cycle of Litigation Crises: Foreseeable But Not Foreseen: How Ethics Trumps Market Inefficiencies and Thwarts the Need for Regulation," 10 *Corporate Finance Review* 36 (2006).

[43]For information on the stages of the regulatory cycle, *see* Marianne M. Jennings, "The Cycle of Litigation Crises: Foreseeable But Not Foreseen, "11 *Preventive Law Reporter* 7 (1992), and James Frierson, "Public Policy Forecasting: A New Approach," Spring 1985, *SAM Advanced Management Journal* 18 (1985).

6. Name some issues that you have seen or are seeing moving through the regulatory cycle. As a starting point, think about an issue that you face that is annoying or the practices of businesses when you are a customer. For example, we were once inundated with telemarketing calls. Consumer protests and activism led to the federal do-not-call registry that permits you to opt out of those calls.

7. Based on your CSR readings so far, what are some strategies that businesses can use in shaping their regulatory frameworks?

Case 3.2

Uber and Its Regulatory Cycles

In 2010, when Travis Kalanick founded Uber, an international ride service, he was operating a business that was outside of all regulatory radar. Uber was not a cab service, so no licensing was required. Uber was not a limousine service because the drivers used their own cars and worked as independent contractors, not employees. Even the Uber pricing model was different. Cabs and limousine services had fixed pricing and had not changed that model or its regulation in 100 years. Uber pricing was like airline pricing: traveling closer to holidays costs more because of demand. Uber had surge pricing: rides cost more on Friday nights because demand surges that night.[44] By 2014, Uber was operating in 65 cities using a business model that blew up the old model of waiting for a car or a taxi, often in the rain.[45] If you had a smartphone, you could schedule a ride when and where you needed one.

Once Uber took off, local regulators began their imposition of licensing, fee structures, and other laws on this transportation niche that Uber had found. State and local officials struggled with this new form of transportation: Was it a form of transportation or just a ride-sharing app? Would licensing laws apply? Competitors (taxi and limo drivers) were putting pressure on state and local officials to "do something" about Uber. Residents were complaining about the resulting additional traffic: Anyone who had a car could be an Uber driver, and traffic

congestion at airports and in the cities was overwhelming. Safety became an issue when a six-year-old child was killed by an Uber driver in San Francisco as she crossed the street in a crosswalk with her family.[46] Because the Uber driver did not have a passenger in his car at the time of the accident, was he an "Uber driver"? Did Uber have to provide insurance? Did the policies of the drivers on their own cars cover their commercial activity when they were transporting Uber passengers? Would Uber be liable for the accidents of its drivers? What if Uber drivers had been drinking? When Uber drivers assaulted and robbed passengers, the issue of whether background checks and drug testing regulations for public transportation drivers applied to Uber drivers came to light.

Cab drivers lobbied for regulation: they staged protests in cities around the country and their moving blockades jammed traffic. Uber customer complaints and safety issues began to arise. Uber drivers were complaining about Uber taking 20% of their charges and keeping their tips. More questions came about because of these objections: Were Uber drivers independent contractors? Employees? Partners? Were they covered under workers' compensation? Would wage laws apply? Driver discontent was building for Uber. Former cab drivers who were driving for Uber began to realize that while they had flexibility, they had no union, no health insurance, and no other benefits. Furthermore, while Uber executives were being paid well, the drivers were not. They had to subtract a 20% Uber commission, gas, and extra maintenance from their take.

(continued)

---

[44]Douglas MacMillan, "CEO of Uber Car Service Drives Pricing," *Wall Street Journal*, January 8, 2014, p. B7.

[45]David Streitfield, "Rough Patch for Uber Services Challenge to Taxis," *New York Times*, January 27, 2014, p. A1.

[46]Id.

Case 3.2

(continued)

Uber was a fierce competitor. Soliciting drivers from other start-ups was a problem. In New York City, Uber technology employees ordered and then canceled 100 cars from a New York competitor. The goal of the technology employees for the company was to get the phone numbers of the competitors' drivers and then recruit them to Uber. When confronted with this conduct, Uber apologized and conceded that its scheme was "too aggressive."[47] Was it aggressive, or should Uber and/or its drivers be subject to antitrust laws on monopolization and unfair practices?

When Uber went public in June 2014, it was valued at $18.2 billion, a value higher than that of United Airlines. Uber received a cash infusion of $1.2 billion, and a good portion of that money was used to hire lobbyists to help the company address its regulatory issues.[48] Uber also faced public backlash as a result of ballot propositions in several cities that would ban ride-sharing services. Where there were no ballot propositions, there were regulations being put into place on ride-sharing services that limited where drivers could wait at airports for [icking up their passengers.

---

[47]Id.
[48]Holam W. Jenkins, Jr., "What the Taxi Wars Teach," *Wall Street Journal*, August 20, 2014, p. A11.

1. List the areas of regulation that you see percolating in Uber's development.

2. How should Uber have handled the cycles that it was experiencing on these issues?

3. How should a business respond when the public is emotionally charged about its practices, products, or operations?

4. In the United States and other countries, Uber has been losing the regulatory battles over whether Uber drivers are employees and thus are entitled to all the statutory protections and benefits of employees. For example, Uber lost its court challenge to the United Kingdom's determination that drivers were entitled to a minimum wage and other benefits while working for the company.[49] In California, the voters put into place similar statutory protections for Uber drivers.[50] Discuss what Uber missed in its regulatory cycle and what different approaches it might have taken.

---

[49]Sam Schechner, "Ubers Loses Drivers' Challenge in U.K.," *Wall Street Journal*, February 20, 2021, p. A1.
[50]Kate Conger & Daisuke Wakabayashi, "2nd State Sues to Force Uber and Lyft to Treat Drivers as Employees," *New York Times*, July 15, 202, p. B3.

Case 3.3

The NFL, Colin Kaepernick, and Taking a Knee

In 2016, former San Francisco 49ers quarterback Colin Kaepernick "took a knee" during the national anthem prior to the start of his team's final National Football League (NFL) preseason game.[51] According to Mr. Kaepernick, "Taking a knee," was his right. "I am not going to stand up to show pride in a flag for a country

that oppresses black people and people of color. To me, this is bigger than football and it would be selfish on my part to look the other way. There are bodies in the street and people getting paid leave and getting away with murder."[52] The symbolic action spread throughout the

(continued)

---

[51]Tom Krasovic, *Colin Kaepernick Takes a Knee During National Anthem in San Diego and Is Booed,"* *L.A. Times*, September 1, 2016. http://www.latimes.com/sports/nfl/la-sp-chargers-kaepernick-20160901-snap-story.html.

[52]Steve Wyche, "Colin Kaepernick Explains Why He Sat During National Anthem," *NFL Media*, August 27, 2016, https://www.nfl.com/news/colin-kaepernick-explains-why-he-sat-during-national-anthem-0ap3000000691077.

(continued)

NFL, with various team owners struggling to determine the appropriate response to Mr. Kaepernick, to the social justice movement, and to the fans (customers)—many of whom were offended by what they perceived to be Mr. Kaepernick's disrespect for the national anthem and the U.S. flag.[53] Kaepernick was booed by San Diego Chargers fans when he was playing in that city.[54]

The NFL flailed about, and team owners made different decisions on what to do with their players following Mr. Kaepernick's symbolic action, ranging from joining the players to implementing bans on "taking a knee."[55]

The effect of the controversy was a reduction in the value of NFL franchises because of declining popularity, along with a reduction in ad revenues for NFL networks because of reduced ratings.[56] Because of low ratings, the NFL TV networks had to give back free ad time to companies that had purchased ad times during the game. "When advertisers and ad agencies buy commercial time on NFL partner TV networks, they're promised certain numbers in terms of ratings and audiences. If the game fails to reach those numbers, the networks have to "make good" for the audience shortfall by providing the equivalent of free commercial time."[57]

After losing fans, viewers, and ad revenues, the NFL made it league policy that players could no longer kneel during the national anthem. However, players were free to stay in the locker room during the anthem. NFL commissioner Roger Goodell joined with the players in their social justice efforts.[58]

Mr. Kaepernick drifted for several years after opting out of his $126 million contract with the 49ers in 2017. While he was hoping for a better contract with another team, none of the 32 teams in the NFL stepped up to sign him. He would spend the next three years litigating a grievance against the NFL, accusing the teams of colluding to keep him out of the league.[59] While his grievance was pending, Nike made Mr. Kaepernick a successful face and voice of its 2018 ad campaign.

The NFL and Mr. Kaepernick eventually settled for an undisclosed amount, and he was given a tryout with various NFL teams at the Atlanta Falcons' training facility. Because of media issues, Mr. Kaepernick moved the workout to a local high school with eight NFL scouts on hand. None of the teams made him an offer. Joe Lockhart, the former vice president of communications for the NFL, said, "No teams wanted to sign a player—even one as talented as Mr. Kaepernick—whom they saw as controversial, and, therefore, bad for business."[60]

The NFL experienced a drop in television ratings through 2019 because of fans' concerns about political statements. As the Kaepernick effect waned, the COVID-19 pandemic took hold. There were no 2020 pre-season games, and a lack of fans once live games resumed affected viewership. However, in 2021, NFL ratings jumped 17%.[61] Although still down from the three previous years, the league's games are now the most watched television programs.

(continued)

[53]Galin Clavio, "For NFL Players, Social Media Is the Key for Winning PR Battles over Anthem Protests," *The Conversation*, May 23, 2018, http://theconversation.com/for-nfl-players-social-media-is-key-to-winning-pr-battle-over-anthem-protests-97292.
[54]Victor Mather, "A Timeline in Kaepernick vs. the N.F.L.," *New York Times*, February 19, 2019, https://www.nytimes.com/2019/02/15/sports/nfl-colin-kaepernick-protests-timeline.html.
[55]Andrew Beaton, "NFL Declines to Change Anthem Policy," *Wall Street Journal*, October 19, 2017, at A14.
[56]Mike Ozanian, "NFL Sale Prices Being Hurt by League's Declining Popularity," *Forbes*, June 2, 2018, https://www.forbes.com/sites/mikeozanian/2018/06/02/nfl-sale-prices-being-hurt-by-leagues-declining-popularity/#355282407e94. Richard Dietsch, "The Colin Kaepernick Effect: CBS Study Says Protests Were a Factor in NFL Ratings," *Sports Illustrated*, August 31, 2017, https://www.si.com/tech-media/2017/08/31/colin-kaepernick-nfl-ratings-cbs-study-sean-mcmanus.
[57]Michael McCarthy, "Kaepernick Effect: Falling Ratings Force NFL TV Networks to Give Back Free Ads," *Sporting News*, October 7, 2016, http://www.sportingnews.com/us/nfl/news/nfl-tv-ratings-dropping-colin-kaepernick-49ers-boycottnfl-twitter-social-media-fans-politics-player-protests/1qtrec7b21cf11u70nodc10j0q.

[58]Nancy Armour, "Goodell Joins NFL Players in Fight Over Issues," *USA Today*, September 14, 2018, at 1D.
[59]Ken Belson, "The NFL's Tug of War With Kaepernick Didn't Resolve Anything," *New York Times*, November 19, 2019, https://www.nytimes.com/2019/11/17/sports/football/colin-kaepernick-workout.html.
[60]Charles Robinson, "In Light of George Floyd's Death, Ex-NFL Executive Admits What We Knew All Along: Protests Ended Colin Kaepernick's Career," *Yahoo! Sports*, May 31, 2020, https://www.yahoo.com/now/in-light-of-george-floyds-death-ex-nfl-exec-admits-what-we-knew-all-along-protests-ended-colin-kaepernicks-career-17561637.
[61]Frank Pallotta, "The NFL's Ratings Are Up. Here's Why," *CNN Business*, October 7, 2021, https://www.cnn.com/2021/10/07/media/nfl-ratings-2021/index.html.

Case 3.3

(continued)

1. Milton Friedman once noted that there are some social issues that affect businesses where no one wins when those issues take hold. He noted that no matter what position businesses take on social issues, they lose customers. Was the NFL facing such an issue in handling the Kaepernick protests during the national anthem?

2. Was there a regulatory cycle issue underlying Mr. Kaepernick's actions? What was it? Who was affected? Could the NFL have taken a position on the regulatory cycle issue?

Ethics in Action 3.1

BP: Learning to Factor in Future Costs in Ethical Decisions

Return to the BP case in Unit 2 (Case 2.8). List all the costs BP did not anticipate or did not estimate accurately in making its decisions on the Prudhoe Bay pipeline and the single-thread design for its deep-water drilling. How does working on these questions help move an organization from compliance with the law to integrating ethical issues into all decision processes? Refer back to Figure 2.1 in Unit 2 to help you visualize the layers of ethical issues and how they are analyzed in organizations, including what may be missing with social responsibility factors.

Reading 3.4

Components of Social Responsibility: Stakeholder Theory

In this phase of the history of CSR, which runs from the 1980s to 2010, stakeholder theory emerged and there was a transition to topical CSR: a focus on individual issues.

Stakeholder Theory Origins

Following the either/or debates and decades of Dodd, Berle, Bowen, Friedman, Drucker, and Coase, CSR moved into a different era. CSR transferred fully from the fields of economics and law into the management arena, even as it added the component of philosophical grounding. In 1996, and in a reflective mode, Friedman noted that CSR "was a very fashionable topic some 20 years ago, and then it sort of died down. I think it is all rhetoric."[62]

---

[62]John F. Dickerson, Adam Zagorin, Stacy Perman, & Jane Van Jessel, "The New World of Giving," *Time*, May 20, 1996, at 40–41.

However, if it had died down, it was perhaps only in economics; it was resurrected among the philosophers in 1984 when R. Edward Freeman's work on stakeholders appeared.[63] Freeman borrowed the term, which was originally coined in a 1963 internal research memorandum of the Stanford Research Institute. The original definition of stakeholder was "a member of the groups without whose support the organization would cease to exist."[64] Freeman's work, which he has modified over the years, was grounded in a utilitarian approach, which was that corporations should function for the good of the whole.[65] Indeed, Freeman engaged in debate with himself. He went from a utilitarian "good of the whole view" to a Kantian view. The definition of "good of the whole" was dependent upon a definition of stakeholder, and there was considerable debate in the literature following Freeman's initial work on who and what constituted a stakeholder.[66]

Stakeholder Definitions

Freeman's definition in his initial work was "any group or individual who is affected by or can affect the achievement of an organization's objectives." The definitions by other scholars have been broad and varied:

> "an individual or group that asserts to have one or more stakes in a business," [67]

> "any individual or group who feel that they have a stake in the consequences of management's decisions and who have the power to influence current or future decisions,"[68]

> "an individual, a coalition of people, or an organization whose support is essential or whose opposition must be negated if major strategic change is to be successfully implemented," [69]

> "persons that have, or claim, ownership, rights, or interests in a corporation and its activities, past, present, or future," [70]

> "stakeholders are persons or groups with legitimate interests in procedural and/or substantive aspects of corporate activity." [71]

---

[63]R. Edward Freeman & David L. Reed, "Stockholders and Stakeholders: A New Perspective on Corporate Governance," 25 *California Management Review* 88 (1983). For a summary of the expansion of stakeholder theory, see Robert A. Phillips, "Stakeholder Theory and a Principle of Fairness," 7 *Business Ethics Quarterly* 51 (1997). See also, "Stakeholder Capitalism," *The Economist*, February 10, 1996, 23.
[64]Freeman and Reed, p. 89.
[65]It is difficult to obtain permission to reproduce Professor Freeman's works such as William R. Evan & R. Edward Freeman, *A Stakeholder Theory of the Modern Corporation: Kantian Capitalism,"* and R. Edward Freeman, "The Politics of Stakeholder Theory," 4 *Business Ethics Quarterly* 409 (1994). His work appeared in three editions of the author's *Business Ethics: Cases and Selected Readings,* but Professor Freeman refused to grant permission for the 9th edition because he felt that his views had changed.
[66]Evan & Freeman, p. 409.
[67]Archie B. Carroll, *Business and Society: Ethics and Stakeholder Management,* 2nd ed. (1993), 60.
[68]Frederick D. Sturdivant & Heidi Vernon-Wortzel, *Business and Society: A Managerial Approach,* 4th ed. (1990), 64.
[69]Ian C. Macmillan and Patricia E. Jones, Strategy Formulation: Power and Politics, 2nd ed. (1986), 60.
[70]M.E. Clarkson and M. Deck, "The Stakeholder Theory of the Corporation," *Proceedings of a Workshop on the Stakeholder Theory of the Firm and the Management of Ethics in the Workplace* (University of Toronto), The Toronto Conference, May 20–21, 1993, p. 9.
[71]Thomas Donaldson and Lee E. Preston, also at the Toronto Conference, note 10 Paper #37.

Based on these definitions, there appeared to be several large groups of stakeholders, such as employees, vendors, employees of vendors, vendors of employees, community where the corporation is located, customers, communities where the customers are located, and next generations. Figure 3.3 provides a web diagram of the foundation of stakeholder theory.

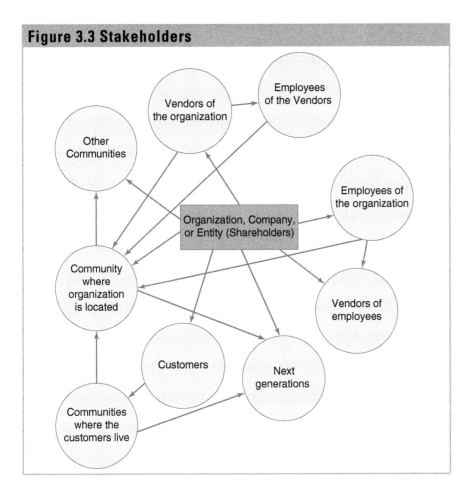

Figure 3.3 Stakeholders

Some academics believe that competitors should be considered stakeholders.[72] Another view is that the inclusion of competitors and other extraneous groups as "stakeholders" indicates a confusion between "stakeholder management" and "ethical business behavior."[73] Others keep expanding the stakeholder set, including even the flora and fauna as stand-alone stakeholders.[74] Philosopher Peter Singer has argued that the interests of animals are no less than the interests of humans and should not be discounted simply because they cannot speak.[75]

With the broad expansion of stakeholder theory from its initial use in strategic planning to protection of both human and nonhuman interests, there was a

---

[72]Elaine Sternberg, "The Defense of Stakeholder Theory," 5 *Corporate Governance International Review* 3 (1997).

[73]Lee E. Preston & James E. Post, "Author Response," 35 *Business & Society* 479 (1996).

[74]Mark Starik, "Should Trees Have Moral Standing? Toward Stakeholder Status for Non-Human Nature,"14 *Journal of Business Ethics* 207, 210 (1995). *See*, generally, Peter Singer, *In Defense of Animals* (1985).

[75]*See*, generally, Singer, 1985.

significant shift in the application of stakeholder theory. Its application was on an issue basis. For example, stakeholder theory during this time was used for analysis of downsizing, with a full exploration of the effect on employees, communities, and vendors. However, stakeholder theory was not used in discussions of unionization, i.e., corporations were not stakeholders in consideration of the unionization votes.[76]

The underlying assumption of this shift toward broad protections under stakeholder theory was that businesses, by taking advantage of all the resources in a community (water, roads, employees, educational facilities, transportation, and waste management), entered into an implied contract to give back to that community and involve that community in their decisions. Referred to as "fairness" or "social contract" theory, it seeks to avoid the "free-rider problem."[77] This approach of applying the philosophical view of a normative contract between businesses and society for the use of roads, community resources, and capital was the management version of the Warren/Obama/Lakoff theorem **"You didn't build that,"** which entitled the government to collect compensation from companies in the form of taxes (see Reading 3.1, Phase 3, and the Drucker Management Perspective for more detail).

In other words, during this phase, stakeholder theory traveled from utilitarianism through Kant and into normative principles, and perhaps over to "You didn't build this," as enforced by informal sanctions and mechanisms.[78]

Which Stakeholders and What Priority?

If the definitional hurdle of "stakeholder" could be clarified, and the nature of a corporation's responsibilities to those stakeholders could also be carefully outlined, there remained the issue of the hierarchy of stakeholders. Which of the stakeholders would or should have the ultimate say when the interests of the various stakeholders were conflicting? Who would set the controlling factors? Who would be the stakeholder with the final say on the social contract? The inherent assumption in stakeholder theory is that there would be clarity in assessing the differing interests and the impact on each group of stakeholders as well as on the business itself. The experience of Smith & Wesson provides insights into the confusing application of stakeholder theory to a social issue.

In 1992, Smith & Wesson, a gun manufacturer in the United States, was struggling to survive. There were class-action product liability suits against gun manufacturers seeking recovery for the injuries and damages experienced by victims of crimes committed while perpetrators were guns. Smith & Wesson was owned by Tomkins, P.L.C., a British manufacturer of plumbing supplies and lawn mowers, and its survival hung in the balance because of the litigation. To find its way out of its financial crunch, Tomkins decided to have Smith & Wesson break rank with its fellow gun manufacturers who were fighting the suits.[79] Tomkins

---

[76]Marianne M. Jennings, "Teaching Stakeholder Theory: It's for Strategy, Not Business Ethics," 16 *Journal of Legal Studies Education* 203 (1998), at 206.

[77]Robert A. Phillips, "Stakeholder Theory and a Principle of Fairness," 7 *Business Ethics Quarterly* 51 (1997).

[78]Thomas Donaldson & Thomas Dunfee, "Toward a Unified Conception of Business Ethics: Integrative Social Contract Theory," 19 *Academy of Management Review* 252 (1994).

[79]Christine W. Westphal & Susan M. Wheeler, *When Ethical Decisions Alienate Stakeholders: Smith & Wesson as a Case Study*, Paper Presented at the Academy of Legal Studies, August 8, 2001, Albuquerque, New Mexico.

settled the suits with agreements to make donations; put safety locks on all pistols; and, among other things, stop selling guns that could accept large-capacity ammunition magazines.

Financially, Smith & Wesson had saved itself from bankruptcy. Business ethicists and the British heralded the decision as an example of corporate social responsibility.[80] However, because of the decision, Smith & Wesson experienced a boycott by outraged consumers and was forced to shut down two facilities and lay off a substantial portion of its workforce. Its sales dropped by one-third in less than a year. Tomkins was forced to sell Smith & Wesson to a U.S. firm for $15 million (Smith & Wesson had $97 million in assets at the time).[81]

The stakeholder praise came because the CSR screen of "guns" and "weapons" has been a mainstay in socially responsible investing. If a company is subject to a screen, then stakeholder analysis is applied selectively. If a company is involved in the production and/or sale of products that are screened out by CSR investment screens and consumer purchasers, then stakeholder analysis dismisses the vendors, employees, and communities of the screen-banished companies.

If stakeholder analysis were applied uniformly, we would ask: Whose interests were served by the actions of Tomkins? A large number of Smith & Wesson employees lost their jobs, and the communities with the two factories lost a portion of their economic base. Yet, the actions were responsive to a critical CSR issue, that of high-capacity magazines. The appeasement of one group of stakeholders harmed the remaining stakeholders.[82] The downward spiral was exacerbated by the stakeholder decision to change the company's products in response to public pressure through litigation and the general attitude about handguns. With the limited application of the stakeholder model a company was nearly destroyed. Smith & Wesson was eventually released from the settlement agreements, but the company had lost $57 million in income by then.[83]

Apart from the lack of clarity on who stakeholders are and how the stakeholder model is applied, there remains the question of which issues (and, *ergo*, also which stakeholders) are those for which corporations are held accountable. In the case of Smith & Wesson, their product was the issue. During this phase of CSR, certain CSR issues were nonstarters for purposes of stakeholder analysis. That is, employees of companies that make guns are not considered stakeholders for purposes of making decisions about the future success of their companies. Investment screens became the measures for determining both stakeholder standing and priority.[84]

Discussion Questions

1. Explain the categories of stakeholders and why there is disagreement among scholars about who should be included as stakeholders.

---

[80]*See The Guardian* (London), Aug. 5, 2000, p. 24; Gary Fields, "For Smith & Wesson, Blanks Instead of a Magic Bullet," *Wall Street Journal*, August 24, 2000, A24; and Paul M. Barrett, Joe Mathews, & Vanessa O'Connell, "Arms Deal," *Wall Street Journal*, March 21, 2000, p. A1.
[81]Tish Durkin, "Goods Deeds Can Misfire: Consider a Gunmaker's Tumble," *National Law Journal*, April 28, 2001, p.12.
[82]E. Judson Jennings, "Saturday Night. Ten P.M.: Do You Know Where Your Handgun Is?" 21 *Seton Hall Legislation Journal* 31 (1997); Randy E. Barnett & Don B. Kates, "Under Fire: The New Consensus on the Second Amendment," 45 *Emory Law Journal* 1139 (1996); and Susan DeFrancesco, "*Children and Guns*," 19 Pace Law Review 275 (1999).
[83]Westphal & Wheeler, *supra* note 70.
[84]Marianne M. Jennings & Jon Entine, *Business with a Soul: A Reexamination of What Counts in Business Ethics*, 20 Hamline J. L. & Public Policy 1 (1998).

Ethics in Action 3.2

Disney Battles Florida Legislation

In 2022, the Disney Corporation announced that it would remain neutral on legislation passed in Florida that involved limitations on teaching issues of sexuality to children in kindergarten through third grade. The legislation became known as the "Don't Say Gay" bill. Disney's reticence resulted in pushback from Disney employees who were disappointed that their company did not take a position so they staged a walkout.

Disney CEO Bob Chapek apologized for not speaking out sooner and told employees that he had called Governor Ron DeSantis to express his concerns about the bill. Mr. Chapek said that he had made a "mistake."[85] He also said that Disney would reassess its political contributions and embark on a listening tour among employees to discuss their concerns.

After reversing its silence on the bill, Disney executives received a letter from employees urging the company to remain "politically neutral":

"The Walt Disney Company has come to be an increasingly uncomfortable place to work for those of us whose political and religious views are not explicitly progressive. . . . We watch quietly as our beliefs come under attack from our own employer, and we frequently see those who share our opinions condemned as villains by our own leadership."

1. Analyze the type of issue Disney was facing. Who were the stakeholders?
2. Is there any way to address the issue without risking the alienation of some stakeholders?
3. At this time, Disney is also now facing boycotts for its position on the bill. What would Friedman's view be on this issue?

---

[85]Adam Manno, "Enraged Disney Employees Say Their Beliefs 'Are Coming Under Attack' in Their Calling for Company to be 'Politically Neutral," *The Daily Mail*, March 24, 2022, https://www.dailymail.co.uk/news/article-10648001/Conservative -workers-call-Disney-politically-neutral-Dont-Say-Gay-bill.html.

Reading 3.5

Measuring Social Responsibility

The lack of clarity on aspects of stakeholder theory and different schools of thought on what is socially responsible behavior necessitated third-party creation of some measurement mechanism for what were and were not socially responsible companies.[86] There was a movement from analysis of organizations' ethical decisions and processes to more of a checklist approach that made it easier to classify companies as socially responsible and/or ethical. In addition, there was market power in being rated and ranked as a socially responsible company by third-party services. High social responsibility ratings and rankings bring customers and investors to companies. CSR began using the forces of the free markets as a means of exercising decision and behavioral control over businesses' ethical and social responsibility decisions.

---

[86]Peter Kok, Tom Van der Weile, Richard McKenna, & Alan Brown, "A Corporate Social Responsibility Audit Within a Quality Management Framework," 31 *Journal of Business Ethics* 285 (2001), at 288. The authors developed a process for CSR audits, different from the CSR screens.

There are three prongs to CSR ratings and rankings: the screens for investment, the screens for consumer products, and the screens for corporate philanthropy. Investors, both individual and institutional, respond to CSR screens developed by third-party groups in these three areas.

Initial Topics and Screens for CSR Investment

The initial screens for socially responsible investment focused on two criteria: no weapons and no vices (e.g., alcohol, gambling, tobacco, and pornography).[87] Initial screens, such as the Kinder, Domini, and Lydenberg (KDL) index, were used by publications like *Business Ethics* to determine their ratings and rankings of CSR In companies.[88] Today, these basic bans and screens, however unwittingly, continue as measures of CSR. For example, faced with an employee rebellion in 2018, Google announced that it would end its contracts with the U.S. military for the development of artificial intelligence (AI) tools.[89] Google initially made the decision to be accountable to its employee stakeholders and forego revenue opportunities in work with the U.S. military because Google's code of ethics prohibited Google from providing AI services if those services would be used for the development of "weapons or other technologies whose principal purpose or implementation is to cause or directly facilitate injury to people."[90]

However, in 2021, Google announced that it would pursue a cloud computing contract with the U.S. Department of Defense (DoD) worth $10 billion over 10 years.[91] The head of Google's cloud unit said, "We understand that not every Googler will agree with this decision, but we believe Google Cloud should seek to serve the government where it is capable of doing so and where the work meets Google's A.I. principles and our company values."[92] Google's CEO, Sundar Pichai, added, "I think we are strongly committed to working with the government in a way that's consistent with our A.I. principles."[93] Microsoft and Amazon are both involved in seeking AI projects with the DoD. Microsoft was awarded a $10 billion contract in the original bidding, from which Google withdrew. However, litigation by Amazon against Microsoft caused the DoD to withdraw the contract and have it rebid. Upon that announcement, Google announced its willingness to participate in the process.

Ethics in Action 3.3

Googlers and the War and Weapons Screen

Discuss whether this issue of working for defense contractors is one that finds employees and customers on both sides. Consider this question: AI is used in ways to prevent having to resort to the force of weapons or sending in troops.

1. Does a powerful military deter war?

2. Should these factors be part of the Google and CSR debates on the weapons screens?

---

[87]Bill Shaw, "Sources of Virtue: The Market and the Community," 7 *Business Ethics Quarterly* 33 (1997).

[88]Founded in 1989, Kinder, Domini, and Lydenberg (KDL) was one of the first firms to develop social screens for investment and was used by *Business Ethics* to develop its list of CSR organizations.

[89]Daisuke Wakabayashi & Scott Shane, "Google to Quit Pentagon Work That Riled Staff," *New York Times*, June 2, 2018, p. A1.

[90]Alexia Fernández Campbell, "How Tech Employees Are Pushing Silicon Valley to Put Ethics Before Profit," *VOX*, October 18, 2018, https://www.vox.com/technology/2018/10/18/17989482/google-amazon-employee-ethics-contracts.

[91]Kate Conger & Daisuke Wakabayashi, "Google Pursues Pentagon Contract Despite Revolt," *New York Times*, November 17, 2021, p. B7.

[92]Id.

[93]Id.

Adding New Screens

The CSR investment screens developed by various organizations began adding more automatic disqualifiers from the CSR label, such as product safety, excessive compensation of executives, diversity, and nuclear power. The effect of the screens was the power to dictate the resolution of ethical dilemmas by companies in predefined social responsibility areas. Other screens that focused on products and practices followed: greenhouse gases, mining, ozone layer depletion, climate change, pesticides, road builders, tropical hardwood, water polluters, animal testing, fur, and meat/dairy production.[94] The screens have now evolved into rankings that include whether company products have earned labeling rights for certain screens such as "certified animal-free testing." These product labels are often focused on the newer **environmental, social, and governance (ESG)** screens.[95]

The Regulatory Cycle and SEC Screens in Required Company Disclosures: New Regulation

The topical area of CSR screens has moved along a regulatory cycle for the past five years to a point of the promulgation of the Securities Exchange Commission's (SEC) Regulation S-K that took effect in 2020.[96] What was once voluntary conduct on the part of companies has been codified through disclosure mandates. Publicly registered companies must make certain types of ESG disclosures in their mandatory SEC filings. Those areas are what the SEC views as risk areas that require disclosure because of their material effect on company earnings. Required disclosures include workplace diversity (including demographic measures), employee engagement, turnover, workplace safety, workplace training and development, succession planning for executive positions, career development, talent recruiting, relationships with unions, safety training, and risk disclosure for all levels of risk (including financial, strategic, safety, product liability).[97]

In 2021, the SEC requested public comment on proposed climate-related disclosures. The final disclosure rule was adopted in 2022, yet another category of CSR and ESG disclosure regulation.[98] In addition, the SEC also regulates investment advisers on their CSR and ESG ratings for companies to clients.[99] The SEC has begun reviewing the now-mandated CSR and ESG disclosures for accuracy in the same way as the agency reviews the accuracy of company financial disclosures.

The Flaws in the Investment Screens and Rankings

So Many Rankings, So Many Differences

There are hundreds of CSR and ESG rankings and ratings. Some are rankings by investment companies and advisors. Some are rankings by nonprofits and research organizations. Some are marketing surveys conducted by companies and

---

[94]*See generally,* Archie B. Carroll, *A History of Corporate Social Responsibility: Concepts and Practices* (2008), 32–42.

[95]Christopher P. Skroupa, "Define Metrics For ESG, CSR and the Like, And You'll Grab Wall Street's Attention," *Forbes,* February 6, 2018, https://www.forbes.com/sites/christopherskroupa /2018/02/06/define-metrics-for-esg-csr-and-the-like-and-youll-grab-wall-streets -attention/#79f119995444.

[96]17 C.F.R. §§ 229.10 *et seq.*

[97]Margaret Engle, "New Human Capital Disclosures," *Harvard Law School Forum on Corporate Governance,* February 6, 2021, https://corpgov.law.harvard.edu/2021/02/06 /new-human-capital-disclosure-requirements/.

[98]Matthew Goldstein & Peter Eavis, "S.E.C. Rule Would Make Firms Reveal Climate Toll," *New York Times,* March 22, 2022, p. B1.

[99]17 C.F.R. §§270 and 275 (2004).

businesses trying to tap into what consumers value and respect. Some are surveys of consumers and their perceptions of companies. Some are surveys of businesses and their leaders' perceptions of companies. No matter what the survey, the results are based on checklist evaluations of companies: Do the companies hit the pre-defined CSR/ESG screens? With so many CSR and ESG measurements and their checklist natures, there are some counterintuitive and inconsistent results among and between the surveys and analyses. Tesla, because of its electric cars but also because of its ownership of SolarCity, would seem to be a CSR company. Yet, Tesla's overall ESG ranking by CSR/ESG investment firms is in the red at 24 (with 80–100 being the highest level).[100] The two checklist issues that hurt Tesla's ratings were (1) military contractor (its SpaceX efforts); and (2) gay and lesbian rights sensitivity. These CSR/ESG investment screen evaluations are very different from consumer perceptions of Tesla. Tesla ranks in the top 10 companies that consumers perceive to be socially responsible. The Harris Poll's top 10 consumer-ranked companies for CSR/ESG are listed in Figure 3.4.[101] The Harris Poll's lowest consumer-ranked companies for CSR/ESG are listed in Figure 3.5.[102]

Figure 3.4 The Top 10 Consumer-Ranked CSR/ESG Companies for 2021

Rank	Company	Rating	Change in rank
1	Patagonia	82.7	Up 31
2	Honda	81.6	Up 14
3	Moderna	81.3	Same
4	Chick-fil-A	81.1	Up 7
5	SpaceX	81.1	Same
6	Chewy	80.9	Same
7	Pfizer	80.2	Up 54
8	Tesla	80.2	Up 18
9	Costco	80.1	Down 2
10	Amazon.com	80.0	Down 7

These consumer rankings are different from the rankings that are provided by investment firms and various nonprofits that rank companies for their commitments to CSR/ESG by their varying measurements. Figure 3.6 provides a comparison of six rankings of the top CSR/ESG companies CSR/ESG by these third parties.

---

[100]Skroupa, *Forbes*, February 6, 2018.
[101]https://theharrispoll.com/axios-harrispoll-100/.
[102]https://theharrispoll.com/axios-harrispoll-100/.

Figure 3.5 The Bottom 10 Consumer-Ranked CSR/ESG Companies for 2021

Rank	Company	Rating	Change
91	My Pillow	66.0	Same
92	Comcast	65.8	Up one
93	Twitter	63.4	Up two
94	TikTok	63.0	Same
95	Wells Fargo & Company	63.0	Up one
96	Sears Holding Corporation	61.2	Same
97	Wish.com	60.7	Same
98	Facebook	60.0	Down 5
99	Fox Corporation	59.2	Down 5
100	Trump Organization	56.9	Down 1

Figure 3.6 Investment and Nonprofit Rankings of CSR and ESG

Company	Investors.com	Just Capital	Motley Fool	Alpha-Sense	Refinitiv.com	Investis
Microsoft	1	3	2	4	4	3
Salesforce.com	7	4	6	9	NR[103]	4
Nvidia	12	8	1	2	NR	8
Alphabet	54	1	NR	NR	NR	1
Apple	51	7	NR	NR	NR	7
GlaxoSmithKline	NR	NR	NR	10	6	7
PayPal	NR	6	NR	15	NR	6
Accenture	3	17	NR	NR	NR	NR
Qualcomm	16	63	NR	NR	NR	NR
HP	19	75	NR	NR	NR	NR
Intel	NR	2	NR	NR	NR	2
Lam Research	47	NR	10	NR	NR	NR
IBM	NR	19	NR	NR	1	NR
Danaher	81	NR	NR	13	NR	NR
Bank of America	NR	5	NR	NR	NR	5
Johnson & Johnson	MR	49	NR		5	NR
Merck	NR	26	NR	NR	14	NR
Verizon	NR	9	NR	NR	NR	9
Cisco	NR	10	NR	NR	NR	10
Best Buy	NR	95	3	NR	NR	NR

[103]NR means not ranked in the Topp 20, 25, or 100 of this study.

The following companies were mentioned in only one of the rankings and their ranking number in their solo appearances appears following their names: Linde (2), JB Hunt (4), Xylem (5), Texas Instruments (6), Gildan Achiever (8), Metropolitan Bank (9), HIS Markit (10), STMicroelectronics (11), Rogers (12), Oracle (14), Motorola (15), Sherwin-Williams (17), TE Connectivity (18), Exponent (20), Exelon (11), PepsiCo (12), Mastercard (13), Hartford (13), Citigroup (15), Anthem (16), AT&T (18), Ford (20), Adobe (4), Pool (5), Cadence (7), Intuit (8), Indexx (9), NextEra (1), CR Hansen (3), Home Depot (5), Prologis (6), Emcor (7), West Pharma (8), Republic Services (11), Flower Foods (12), Honeywell (14), SAP (14), Tata Consulting (2), Nestlé (Malaysia) (6), BTS Group (7), Stockland Corp. (8), Roche (9), SEB SA (10), Gilead Services (11), Dexus (12), Bayer AG (13), Nestlé (SA) (15), Rallye (SA) (16), Fleury SA (18), Greek Organization of Football Prognostics (19), and Telefonica (20).

Ethics in Action 3.4

Why the CSR/ESG Rankings and Ratings for Companies?

Compare the companies at the top and bottom in the consumer rankings (3.4 and 3.5) lists. Think about the following questions:

1. Why are the lists so different? What explains the completely different results? Are there any companies that cross the lists? Think about this question to help you: What is being measured that makes the companies good or bad?

2. Pick two companies from the top and the bottom of each list as well as from the third-party rankings. Research those companies that give a list of reasons for their rankings as well as the wide variations in their rankings.

Reading 3.6

The Lack of Virtue/Aristotelian Standards in CSR/ESG Evaluations and Surveys

A recent editorial in the *Wall Street Journal* titled "How Did Activision Pass the ESG Test?"[104] revealed some irony in ESG ratings for another company. Activision is the maker of "Call of Duty," "World of Warcraft," and "Candy Crush Saga" and has been included in prominent ESG funds. BlackRock, Vanguard, and Fidelity ESG all list Activision in their ESG and sustainability funds.[105] Activision was very vocal about its ESG activities, citing its characters of color and of the LGBTQ communities in its games as well as its decisions to stand with "all Black Americans and with all those fighting against systemic inequality and violence." Activision has been a darling of the ESG community.

Yet the California Department of Fair Employment (CDFE) has filed suit against the company for its discrimination against women due to sexual harassment. The following description of the atmosphere is from the CDFE complaint in the suit:

---

[104]Allysia Finley, "How Did Activision Pass the ESG Test?" *Wall Street Journal*, November 26, 2021, p. A15.
[105]*Id.*

Defendants (Activision/Blizzard) have also fostered a pervasive "frat boy" workplace culture that continues to thrive. In the office, women are subjected to "cube crawls" in which male employees drink copious amounts of alcohol as they "crawl" their way through various cubicles in the office. and often engage in inappropriate behavior toward female employees. Male employees proudly come into work hungover, play video games for long periods of time during work while delegating their responsibilities to female employees, engage in banter about their sexual encounters, talk openly about female bodies, and joke about rape.[106]

The missing components in the rankings and in consumer perceptions are the ethical and legal issues. Activision has a tough slog ahead in resolving its legal issues. Tesla's conflicts of interest among board members in their close connections on multiple boards and controls is not covered in the governance screens. Tesla has been given high corporate governance ratings despite its directors' conflicts, such as Elon Musk's brother running SolarCity even as he served on the Tesla and SolarCity boards and even as the Tesla board approved the purchase of SolarCity.[107]

There is also the possibility with the checklists of measures for rankings that companies can game the rating and ranking systems. Some researchers have noted that CSR and ESG rankings fail to capture the essence of ethics and social responsibility. BP was named #1 on *Fortune* and AccountAbility's annual rankings of the world's most responsible companies in 2007. BP's record fine for OSHA violations at the refinery did not affect its ranking much because BP remained in *Fortune's* Top Ten (#9) in 2008. In 2010, BP was a 2010 runner-up for the "Open and Honesty" public reporting award given to a corporation with the most transparent financial and shareholder reports.[108] The awards and rankings, in BP's case, were public relations tools for a company that was operating in a manner that ran directly against CSR and ESG standards. The recognition that BP received perhaps prevented the scrutiny needed during the time of the events that spanned a decade (see Case 2.8).

Beyond the rankings and ratings, companies should still be examined for the basic ethical categories studied in Units 1 and 2: Are they in compliance with the law? Are they harming stakeholders through interpersonal and organizational abuse? Are they allowing false impressions? The tools of ethical analysis are still necessary for evaluating a company commitment to social responsibility.

Discussion Questions

1. Most companies now disclose their carbon emissions each year. These disclosures include Scope 3 emissions, or greenhouse gases that are made by a company's vendors but are not under the company's control. For example, Microsoft, Apple, P&G, and McDonald's all report their Scope 3 emissions but rely on data furnished to them by their vendors. That data are not verified. However, as noted in the tables on rankings, Microsoft has high ratings because of its reduction in greenhouse emissions, 97% of which come from vendors.[109] Evaluate whether the rankings could be subject to gaming. What ethical categories are at issue in this reporting?

---

[106]https://www.documentcloud.org/documents/21014638-activision_lawsuit.

[107]Ziati Meyer, "This Musk Brings Farms to the City with Square Roots," *USA Today*, February 19, 2018, 2b.

[108]Natalya Sverjensky, "Beyond Petroleum: Why the CSR Community Collaborated in Creating the BP Oil Disaster," *Ethical Corporation*, August 2, 2010, http://www.ethicalcorp.com/stakeholder -engagement/beyond-petroleum-why-csr-community-collaborated-creating-bp-oil-disaster.http: //www.ethicalcorp.com/stakeholder-engagement/beyond-petroleum-why-csr-community -collaborated-creating-bp-oil-disaster.

[109]Jean Eaglesham, "Firms Tally Carbon Emissions, But the Data Can Be Squishy," *Wall Street Journal*, September 4–5, 2021, B3.

2. McKinsey and Company, the century-old international consulting firm, was a consultant to Purdue Pharma, the company that produced the opioid OxyContin. Increasing addiction and death rates caused by overprescribing of the drug resulted in a national crisis. Purdue declared bankruptcy and currently owes $8.3 billion under a settlement approved by the court. Pharmacy chains have had multibillion jury verdicts handed down for their role in filling the prescriptions.

During a trial in Oklahoma that was part of litigation by state attorneys general to recover health care costs incurred because of opioid addiction treatments, evidence emerged about McKinsey's role as a consultant to Purdue. McKinsey had advised Purdue on how to "turbocharge" sales of OxyContin through a structured rebate program. McKinsey's PowerPoint slides showed Purdue how to use higher rebates for higher strength prescriptions. The soft language of "innovative contracts" was used to describe these pay-to-prescribe program.[110] It's as if the two parties had been weighing the benefits of consumer coupons for Uncrustables.

A McKinsey spokesperson emphasized that the rebates were not intended to boost sales. However, the slides appear to contradict that statement.[111] One McKinsey executive noted, "While we can't change the past, we can learn from it." Referring to Reading 3.3 and Units 1 and 2, make a list of the lessons that McKinsey could learn about ethical analysis when choosing its clients as well as when developing recommendations for those clients.

Reading 3.7

Business with a Soul: A Reexamination of What Counts in Business Ethics[112]

Jon Entine and Marianne M. Jennings

Business and business ethics are much more complex than the breeziness of social responsibility. Understanding the corporate soul requires far more than the shallow categories of the CSR. The soul of a company is more complex than that of an individual.

The notions built into the continuum about business ethics present a Hobbesian choice between a faddish concept of social responsibility, such as an opposition to animal testing, and classic stakeholder concepts, such as responsiveness to investors, customers, and employees. For instance, helping the homeless is a noble cause, and certainly one that would place a company at the top of the social responsibility continuum. Few would suggest that a small grocery store with thin profit margins should be judged by whether it feeds the homeless in the town in which it operates. The owners and employees of that store depend upon profit for their livelihood, its customers depend on the store being open, and the community prospers if the store becomes more profitable and expands. By devoting its resources to feeding the homeless, such a grocery store would possibly exacerbate the homeless problem: its employees would no longer be employed because the business had become extinct.

[110]Walt Bogdanich & Michael Forsythe, "Rare Apology by McKinsey for OxyContin Work," *New York Times*, December 9, 2020, p. B9.

[111]https://beta.documentcloud.org/documents/20421781-mckinsey-docs.

[112]Jon Entine & Marianne M. Jennings, "Business with a Soul: A Reexamination of What Counts in Business Ethics," 20 *Hamline Journal of Law & Public Policy* 1 (1998).

For years after its introduction in 1990, "Rainforest Crunch" ice cream, the flagship product of Ben & Jerry's, was touted as a successful experiment in the partnering of American business with Amazon preservationists. According to company materials, the Rainforest Crunch flavor was created in part to help indigenous peoples find an alternative to selling their timber rights to mining and forestry industrialists. (It was a noble impulse but turned out to be little more than a brilliant marketing gimmick. For years, Ben & Jerry's purchased no nuts for its ice cream from rainforest aboriginals; more than 95% of the Brazil nuts it sourced were purchased off commercial exchanges supplied by businesses, not indigenous peoples, in Latin America that now dominate the Brazil nut market.)

Moreover, many anthropologists maintain that the harvest has actually contributed to falling nut prices and an increase in the selling off of land rights to industrialists to compensate for the economic shortfall. The Ben & Jerry's program actually exacerbated the very problem it was purported to address. In early 1995, Ben & Jerry's pulled the claims on its Rainforest Crunch label. Although the disastrous details of the harvest are widely known in the activist media and SR business community, Ben & Jerry's has been given a relative pass on the disastrous consequences.

Body Shop International (BSI) has long been touted as the premier socially responsible business. By its own estimates, BSI was averaging 10,000 positive media mentions a year—until 1994. In September 1994, investigative work by Jon Entine, coauthor of this article, and numerous journalists and social researchers, revealed a huge ethical gap between BSI's marketing image and its actual practices. This deception—conscious or not—is pervasive: [Anita] Roddick [founder of the Body Shop] stole The Body Shop name and marketing concept, fabricated key elements of the company myth, misrepresented its charitable contributions and fair trade programs, and has been beset by employee morale and franchise problems. Moreover, its "natural" products are filled with petrochemical colorings, fragrances, preservatives, and base ingredients such as mineral oil and petrolatum. Its cosmetics are considered "low-end products at a premium price," according to a recent article in *Women's Wear Daily* and numerous reviews by cosmetic product experts.

Can a shareholder or customer trust a firm simply because it has adopted a posture of social responsibility? Can a shareholder or customer assume that a firm is less honorable if it states that it is accountable first and foremost to its shareholders? The answer to both questions is "no."

No company is ethically perfect. No company, just as no individual, is without sin or exempt from mistakes. Consequently, the obsession to anoint icons of CSR only interferes with candid evaluations of the soul of a company.

Determining the soul of a company requires looking beyond ever-changing political issues. CSR has come to promote narrow and contradictory social agendas as opposed to universal measures of integrity. For example, honesty in business dealings is a universal measure of a company's soul. Looking beyond facile symbolism opens up an examination of ethics. The following eight questions should be asked about a company in order to determine the character of its soul.

1. Does the company comply with the law?
2. Does the company have a sense of propriety?
3. How honestly do product claims match with reality?
4. How forthcoming is the company with information?
5. How does the company treat its employees?
6. How does the company handle third-party ethics issues?
7. How charitable is the company?
8. How does the company react when faced with negative disclosures?

This modest proposal provides the basis for an objective look at companies.

Discussion Questions

1. Contrast the authors' views with those of Friedman and stakeholder theory.

2. What is the difference between the authors' eight questions and traditional measures of social responsibility?

3. Would the model mean that a tobacco company could be labeled an "honest" company?

Reading 3.8

Appeasing Stakeholders with Public Relations[113]

Robert Halfon

The problem in today's era of corporate pseudo-ethics is that the pendulum has shifted too far. From genuine philanthropy "corporate responsibility" has mutated into a dangerous form of political correctness. The enlightened, entrepreneurial philanthropy of old has, through activist agitation, become the burden of today's so-called corporate responsibility. At least four distinct trends are in evidence here: the rise of single-issue activist groups; the targeting of companies with dealings in specific countries or specific industries; a rise in public sympathy for such actions; and a seal of approval guaranteed by many Western governments today.

Corporations have an obligation to anticipate and deal with these threats. This can be done in a number of ways. First, every important commercial activity should be rigorously assessed for its political risk, meaning the risks or threats that a business may face (from pressure groups, governments, *et al.*) in undertaking a particular activity. Business needs to inform itself at the highest level of the political environment in which it operates. As one commentator on these matters argues without hesitation:

> The lessons that need to be understood are simple. It does not matter where you are, or how big you are, if you are not prepared, pressure groups have the ability to make your company a member of the endangered species. You cannot respond effectively in six minutes to a campaign that has probably taken six months to organize. . . . Our first option is to ignore the increasing threat of pressure groups and lose everything. Our second option is to fight back, challenge, and probably win. We have the opportunity to deliver results by promoting morality; challenging credibility; setting policy and practices; offering solutions and advice.[114]

Once the political risks have been evaluated, then two actions are required: first, businesses must mount an efficient public relations campaign, arguing the case for corporate capitalism and stressing how their activities are benefiting the national—or global—economy in which they operate. All businesses, forewarned, should be proactive, not reactive. They must be prepared to fight fire with fire and, if necessary, be prepared to take their case all the way to the courts. Secondly, companies across the spectrum must band together and act in unison to limit the unaccountable, undemocratic, and often extra-legal activities of the activist groups they are up against.

---

[113]From Robert Halfon, *Corporate Irresponsibility: Is Business Appeasing Anti-business Activists?* (1998), p. 7.
[114]Tony Meehan, "The Art of Media Manipulation," *The Herald*, May 10, 1997.

Discussion Questions

1. What does Halfon see as the proper tools for handling stakeholder objections?

2. Can you describe a situation in which his tools may not be effective? What are the costs to the company if his tools fail to halt the opposition of stakeholders to a proposed corporate action?

Ethics in Action 3.5

Voting Laws, Baseball Boycotts, and Cancel Culture

Robert Halfon perhaps did not anticipate that businesses would sometimes face social responsibility issues and public backlash on issues for which they had not taken a position. In 2020, many states had passed election law reforms that permitted early voting, expanded mail-in voting, and increased flexibility on times for voting. Some questions arose following the 2020 presidential election about irregularities in the voting process and in counting the ballots. In some states, there were recounts, but audits could not always be completed. Ballots with envelope signature verification could not be authenticated, for example, because the envelopes had been destroyed. In 2021, state legislatures began to tighten up voting laws to prevent fraud. The motto for the reforms was "Making it easy to vote and harder to commit fraud."

Georgia was one of the first states to reform its election laws with identification requirements, limitations on absentee voting, signature requirements, and time periods for voting. As the legislation became law, the hue and cry about the Georgia reforms were that they were racist and that Georgia was returning to the Jim Crow era. Voting rights activists urged Major League Baseball (MLB) Commissioner Rob Manfred to punish Georgia by moving baseball's All-Star Game out of Atlanta. Manfred quelled the rebellion by immediately agreeing to move the All-Star Game. Manfred did not provide a critique of the Georgia law, only that the law "required drastic intervention."[115]

The MLB boycott of Atlanta for the All-Star Game had no effect on the players. They are paid regardless of which city hosts the game. The effect was to punish the local vendors and stadium workers who could sell their wares and earn extra pay only if the game came to Atlanta. Economists disagreed on the scope of the economic impact, but Job Creators Network filed suit against the MLB, seeking $100 million in lost revenues for the small businesses affected by the move. Commissioner Manfred made no other changes to the schedule: the Atlanta Braves played a normal season of home and travel games, eventually winning the World Series title in October 2021.

Fay Vincent, MLB Commissioner from 1989–1992, wrote that MLB "can't become a weapon in the culture wars."[116] Once the dust had settled and the

---

[115]Fay Vincent, "Rob Manfred's All-Star Error," *Wall Street Journal*, April 7, 2021, p. A13.
[116]Fay Vincent, "Rob Manfred's All-Star Error," *Wall Street Journal*, April 7, 2021, p. A13.

content of the new legislation was examined, most realized that the abrupt withdrawal of the game from Atlanta was done without sufficient analysis of the issue or the underlying law. The much-maligned Georgia law was not very different from the voting laws of other states, including those in Colorado, where the All-Star game was played eventually.

- Georgia is one of 2/3 of the states that permits absentee ballots without offering an excuse.
- Like 11 other states, Georgia permits a request for an absentee ballot at least 11 days prior to the election (most other states allow 7 days).
- Like four other states, Georgia requires a valid driver's license to register to vote.
- Like 11 other states, Georgia permits absentee ballots to be dropped in the mail or at an open early voting facility. Georgia allows drop boxes to be placed for ballots but requires that the boxes be located at a government building where there is video surveillance.
- Georgia allows food and water to be distributed to those in line as long as those distributing are not wearing campaign garb.[117]

There was nothing that Georgia was doing with its new voting structure except setting up procedures for processing ballots that are handed in when buildings with ballot boxes are closed that restricted the voting processes more than in other states.

1. Would you, if you were the MLB Commissioner, have taken the same action? List all the stakeholders and impacts before you decide.
2. What is distinctive about the MLB experience in this situation? Was their product being boycotted?
3. Could this issue have been anticipated?
4. The CEO of Atlanta-based Coca-Cola issued a statement following the promulgation of the new Georgia voting laws:

> We want to be crystal clear and state unambiguously that we are disappointed in the outcome of the Georgia voting legislation. Throughout Georgia's legislative session we provided feedback to members of both legislative chambers and political parties, opposing measures in the bills that would diminish or deter access to voting.
>
> Our approach has always been to work with stakeholders to advocate for positive change, and we will continue to engage with legislators, advocacy groups, business leaders, and others to work towards ensuring broad access to voting is available to every eligible voter in our home state.
>
> Additionally, our focus is now on supporting federal legislation that protects voting access and addresses voter suppression across the country. We all have a duty to protect everyone's right to vote, and we

---

[117]David Wickert, "Voting Laws: How Georgia Compares to Other States," *The Atlanta Journal Constitution*, April 3, 2021, https://www.ajc.com/politics/georgia-state-legislature/election-laws-how-georgia-stacks-up/KYO7CBZFVFAC5HFUT4XHZURKWI/.

will continue to stand up for what is right in Georgia and across the United States.

James Quincey, Chairman and CEO, The Coca-Cola Company

Identify Coca-Cola's stakeholders on this issue. Is this an issue raised against Coca-Cola? Is this an issue that Friedman pointed to as one that requires you to lose customers no matter which position you take?

5. When an issue blindsides a company because the so-called cancel culture takes hold and uses boycotts until a company supports its position, how should the company analyze its position, risk, and eventual response?

Reading 3.9

Conscious Capitalism: Creating a New Paradigm for Business[118]

John Mackey, the founder and CEO of Whole Foods, has taken a sort of blended position on the role of business in society. He begins his analysis by asking the purpose of hospitals and schools and concludes that they exist to benefit society. Those who work in hospitals and schools—doctors and teachers—undertake their work for the purposes of benefiting others. Mackey then concludes with this thought: Why should business be any different from other institutions and those who work in them?

Mackey believes that those who found businesses rarely go into business for the purpose of maximizing profits and that the goal of maximizing profits is a myth. Rather, he believes that most entrepreneurs create businesses for reasons other than maximizing profits. Their reasons could be as simple as not wanting to work for someone else. Some businesspeople simply enjoy the challenge of creating and growing a business; some are referred to as "serial entrepreneurs." Sometimes the act of creating helps business founders increase their self-esteem or gives them an outlet for their creativity. Often, businesses are formed because the founder wanted to prove something to a parent, teacher, or friend—the business is a way of showing determination or gratitude. Quite often, a business is formed because founders believe that they have a product or service that could make the world a better place. In other words, many begin their businesses with a goal of improving society. Maximizing profits may be, in Mackey's mind, a by-product of the other reasons businesses are created.

Mackey does understand that companies can do more good by being profitable; the profitability of business contributes to a healthy economy, something that helps those within a community. In fact, he regards profitability as one constituency of a business, a type of stakeholder. He also realizes that businesses cannot grow without capital, and obtaining capital requires that the business operate profitably. However, he believes that great businesses, and businesses that last, are dedicated to "Service to Others." He believes that JetBlue, Southwest Airlines, Wegmans, Nordstrom, REI, The Container Store, and Whole Foods are all examples of successful businesses that live the mantra of "Service to Others."

Mackey believes that profits follow when managers optimize the health and well-being of employees, customers, and vendors. Focusing on the health and value of the entire interdependent system (like the web of stakeholders in Figure 3.1) ensures that the company will be a dynamic, evolving entity that allows all within that web to grow and develop.

---

[118]http://www.wholeplanetfoundation.org/files/uploaded/John_Mackey-Conscious _Capitalism.pdf (accessed October 2015).

Discussion Questions

1. Explain Mackey's theory about entrepreneurs and why they go into business.

2. What is Mackey's concept of interdependent constituencies?

Compare & Contrast

In 2017, Mackey changed Whole Foods's pricing model because its stock had lost one-half of its value since 2013. One of its investors wanted a stronger board and recognition that its prices were too high to compete. In 2017, Amazon purchased Whole Foods for $13 billion. In 2020, John Mackey said, "We've told a bad narrative and we've let the enemies of business and the enemies of capitalism put out a narrative on us that's wrong. . . . from an ethical standpoint, we need to change the narrative of capitalism, to show that it's about creating shared value, not for the few, but for everyone." *Wall Street Journal*, December 2, 2020, p. A16. How have Mr. Mackey's views changed?

Reading 3.10

Marjorie Kelly and the Divine Right of Capital[119]

Marjorie Kelly challenges the notion that stockholders fund a corporation by pointing out that only the initial shareholders actually do this. When shares subsequently change hands, the company does not actually receive that money from the shareholder. Only when companies sell new shares of stock do they receive money from shareholders. The secondary sales of stock benefit investment houses, brokerage firms, and the stockholders who choose to sell those shares, but companies receive no money from these secondary sales transactions.

In Kelly's view, shareholders contribute very little to justify what she calls companies' extraordinary allegiance to them in their decisions and loyalties. Her view is that the employees are the ones who create value for the corporation. Employees shoulder the burdens and yet are given very little consideration in return for their efforts. Employees' incomes are not determined according to the success of the corporation, but shareholders' returns and dividends are determined by the success of the corporation. Kelly does not see this system as a function of markets but a system of governance that could be changed very easily without affecting the role of the corporation in economic systems. Kelly often quotes Lycophron, the ancient Greek philosopher who said, as he was observing an Athenian slave uprising, "The splendor of noble birth is imaginary and its [prerogatives] are based upon mere word."

Because shareholder primacy is a mere structural and superficial system, Kelly believes that it can be changed quite easily. She also sees shareholder primacy as an entitlement and concludes that economists agree that entitlements have no place in a free market economy. Her proposal is to eliminate shareholder primacy and revise the primary responsibility of corporations to one of wider economic distribution

---

[119]From Marjorie Kelly, *The Divine Right of Capital: Dethroning the Corporate Aristocracy* (2001).

of wealth. She notes that of the marketable wealth gain achieved between 1983 through 1998, more than half went to the richest 1%.

Kelly would like to place employees as the top priority in corporate responsibility. Employee stakeholders would be the primary responsibility of corporations, with shareholders classified as stakeholders along with others in the web of connections. Employees would not earn wages but would rather share in the profits of the corporation, taking their share before any distributions to shareholders. The current business financial model is:

Profits = Revenues − Cost

Kelly would change that model to:

Profits = Revenues − Employee Income + Cost of Materials

Under her model, employee income would be a percentage of the profits from the first model. Shareholders' profits would be reduced by a primary distribution of those profits to employees as a cost of doing business. Kelly believes that this system will benefit not only the employees but also provide them with the incentives to do what is best to maximize those profits because of the interest they would hold in maximization. Kelly also notes that her model would solve the stakeholder issue of employee compensation because employees would be entitled to a percentage of the profits that they work to earn for the corporation.

Discussion Questions

1. List the differences in perceptions between Friedman and Kelly about corporations.

2. What distinction does Kelly make about shareholder ownership?

Applying Social Responsibility and Stakeholder Theory

Issues of social responsibility can dominate the press coverage of a corporation and infiltrate its annual meeting through shareholder proposals on social responsibility issues. Now that you have both the decision models for ethical analysis, ethical theory, and the schools of thought on social responsibility, you are ready for analysis. This section provides you with practice in the analysis of ethical issues.

Case 3.11

Fannie, Freddie, Wall Street, Main Street, and the Subprime Mortgage Market: of Moral Hazards

Background on Fannie Mae

Fannie Mae was created as a different sort of business entity, a shareholder-owned corporation with a federal charter. The federal government created Fannie Mae in 1938 during the Roosevelt administration to increase affordable housing availability and to attract investment into the housing market. The charge to Fannie Mae was to be sure that there was a stable mortgage market with consistent availability of mortgage funds for consumers to purchase homes. Initially, Fannie Mae was federally funded, but in 1968 it was rechartered as a shareholder-owned corporation with the responsibility of obtaining all its capital from the private market, not the federal government. On its website, Fannie Mae describes its commitment and mission as follows:

- Expand access to homeownership for first-time home buyers and help raise the minority home-ownership rate with the ultimate goal of closing the homeownership gap entirely;

- Make homeownership and rental housing a success for families at risk of losing their homes;

- Expand the supply of affordable housing where it is needed most, which includes initiatives for workforce housing and supportive housing for the chronically homeless; and

- Transform targeted communities, including urban, rural, and Native American, by channeling all the company's tools and resources and aligning efforts with partners in these areas.

A Model Corporate Citizen

In 2004, *Business Ethics* magazine named Fannie Mae the most ethical company in the United States. It had been in the top 10 of corporate citizens for several years (number nine in 2000 and number three in 2001 and 2002).[120] Marjorie Kelly, the editor-in-chief of the magazine (see Reading 3.7), described the standards for the award, which was created in 1996, as follows:

> Just what does it mean to be a good corporate citizen today? To our minds, it means simply this: treating a mix of stakeholders well. And by stakeholders, we mean those who have a "stake" in the firm—because they have risked financial, social, human, and knowledge capital in the corporation, or because they are impacted by its activities. While lists of stakeholders can be long, we focus on four groups: employees, customers, stockholders, and the community. Being a good citizen means attending to the company's impact on all these groups.[121]

(continued)

---

[120]In 2003, Fannie Mae was number 12, *Business Ethics*, March/April 2003.
[121]*Business Ethics*, May/June 2000.

Case 3.11

(continued)

In 2001, the magazine explained why Fannie Mae was one of the country's top corporate citizens:

Fannie Mae scores high in the areas of community and diversity and has been ranked near the top of everyone's "best" list, including *Fortune*'s "Best Companies for Minorities," *Working Mother*'s "Best Companies for Working Mothers," and *The American Benefactor*'s "America's Most Generous Companies." Franklin D. Raines, an African American, is CEO, and there are two women and two minorities among the company's eight senior line executives.[122]

In 2002, *Business Ethics* described third-ranked Fannie Mae as follows:

The purpose of Fannie Mae, a private company with an unusual federal charter, is to spread home ownership among Americans. Its ten-year, $2 trillion program—the American Dream Commitment—aims to increase home ownership rates for minorities, new immigrants, young families, and those in low-income communities.

In 2001, over 51% of Fannie Mae's financing went to low- and moderate-income households. "A great deal of our work serves populations that are under-served, typically, and we've shown that it's an imminently bankable proposition," said Barry Zigas, senior vice president in Fannie Mae's National Community Lending Center. "It is our goal to keep expanding our reach to impaired borrowers and to help lower their costs."

"That represents a striking contrast to other financial firms, many of which prey upon rather than help low-income borrowers. To aid the victims of predatory lenders, Fannie Mae allows additional flexibility in underwriting new loans for people trapped in abusive loans, if they could have initially qualified for conventional financing. In January the company committed $31 million to purchasing these types of loans."[123]

The Community Reinvestment Act (CRA) is a federal statute that established a government program to get people who would otherwise not qualify (i.e., no credit history and no down payment) into homes with the goals of helping them and thereby revitalizing blighted areas. Banks and lenders were evaluated for their commitment to these loans, and no bank or lender wanted a bad rating.

Simultaneously, the federal government anticipated pushback from lenders who would point out that these were high-risk loans and required greater returns. However, lenders were evaluated for their CRA commitment, which included their creativity in granting the loans. In addition, lenders faced prosecution by the Justice Department for discrimination in lending if their loan portfolios did not include a sufficient number of CRA loans. All the while, Fannie Mae served as the purchaser of these loans, eventually packaging them and selling them as securitized mortgage pools. The CRA loans had borrowers with less equity, higher default rates, and more foreclosures. There was also an exacerbating effect of this false sense of security on the part of the high-risk borrowers about their mortgages. Because these risky borrowers were not really anteing up the actual cost of their homes (and remember, these were people who had never had a mortgage before, had bad credit histories, and may not have had much in the way of financial literacy), they overextended and overspent in other areas. In short, they were maxed out in all areas because they were lulled into a false sense of financial security with such a low mortgage payment.

Because Fannie Mae owned or guaranteed half of the $12 trillion mortgage debt in the United States, any problems with those mortgages could and did lead to a financial crisis for Fannie, the U.S. stock market, and the economy.[124] Then Federal Reserve Chairman Alan Greenspan warned of the looming problems at Fannie Mae in 2005. He testified before Congress, "The Federal Reserve Board has been unable to find any credible purpose for the huge balance sheets built by Fannie and Freddie other than profit."[125] Others, including St. Louis Federal Reserve

(continued)

---

[122]*Business Ethics*, May/June 2001.
[123]*Business Ethics*, May/June 2002.

[124]Julie Creswell, "Long Protected by Washington, Fannie and Freddie Ballooned," *New York Times*, July 13, 2008, p. A7.
[125]*Id.*, at A18.

Case 3.11

(continued)

Chairman William Poole, warned that the huge debt load rendered Fannie and Freddie insolvent.

The Darker Side of Corporate Citizen Fannie

Even as the mortgage issues were evolving under the radar and Fannie was being recognized for its corporate citizenship, there were issues in Fannie's operations that went undetected for nearly a decade.

Fannie Mae: The Super-Achiever with an EPS Goal

Fannie Mae was a company driven to earnings targets through a compensation system tied to those results. And Fannie Mae had a phenomenal run based on those incentives in terms of its financial performance:

- For more than a decade, Fannie Mae achieved consistent, double-digit growth in earnings.[126]

- In that same decade, Fannie Mae's mortgage portfolio grew by five times, to $895 billion.[127]

- From 2001 to 2004, its profits totaled $24 billion.[128]

- Through 2004, Fannie Mae's shares were trading at over $80.[129]

- Fannie Mae was able to smooth earnings through decisions on the recording of interest costs and used questionable discretion in determining the accounting treatment for buying and selling its mortgage assets. Those decisions allowed executives at the company to smooth earnings growth, with a resulting guaranteed payout to them under the incentive plans.[130]

Those incentive plans were based on earnings per share (EPS) targets that had to be reached for the officers to earn

their annual bonuses. The incentive plans began in 1995, with a kick-up in 1998 as Franklin Raines, then chairman and CEO, set a goal of doubling the company's EPS from $3.23 to $6.46 in five years.[131] Raines, the former budget director for the Clinton administration, was able to make the EPS goal a part of Fannie Mae's culture. Raines said, "The future is so bright that I am willing to set a goal that our EPS will double over the next five years."[132] Sampath Rajappa, Fannie Mae's senior vice president of operations risk (akin to the Office of Auditing), gave the following pep talk to his team in 2000, as the EPS goals continued:

> By now every one of you must have a 6.46 branded in your brains. You must be able to say it in your sleep, you must be able to recite it forwards and backwards, you must have a raging fire in your belly that burns away all doubts, you must live, breathe and dream 6.46, you must be obsessed on 6.46. . . . After all thanks to Frank, we all have a lot of money riding on it. . . . We must do this with a fiery determination, not on some days, not on most days but day in and day out, give it your best, not 50%, not 75%, not 100%, but 150%. Remember Frank has given us an opportunity to earn not just our salaries, benefits, raises . . . but substantially over and above if we make 6.46.

> So it is our moral obligation to give well above our 100% and if we do this, we would have made tangible contributions toward Frank's goals.[133]

For 1998, the size of the annual bonus payout pool was linked to specific EPS targets:

- Earnings per share (EPS) range for 1998 annual incentive plan (AIP) corporate goals;

- $3.13, minimum payout; $3.18, target payout; $3.23, maximum payout.[134]

(continued)

---

[126]James R. Hagerty & John D. McKinnon, "Fannie Mae Board Agrees to Changes It Long Resisted," *Wall Street Journal*, July 28, 2004, p. A1.

[127]Id.

[128]Alex Berenson, "Assessing What Will Happen to Fannie Mae," *New York Times*, December 17, 2004, p. C1.

[129]Paul Dwyer, Amy Borrus, & Mara Hovanesian, "Fannie Mae: What's the Damage?" *Fortune*, October 11, 2004, p. 45.

[130]"Report of the Special Examination of Fannie Mae," Office of Federal Housing Enterprise Oversight (OFHEO), report, November 15, 2005, http://www.fhfa.gov/Default.aspx?Page-4 (accessed July 20, 2010). The OFHEO was merged into the federal Finance Housing Agency in 2009 following Fannie Mae's collapse.

[131]Bethany McLean, "The Fall of Fannie Mae," *Fortune*, January 25, 2005, pp. 123, 128.

[132]Id.

[133]Office of Federal Housing Enterprise Oversight (OFHEO), "Final Report of the Special Examination of Fannie Mae," May 2006 (Washington, DC: OFHEO), p. 50 (hereinafter referred to as OFHEO Final Report).

[134]OFHEO, Office of Compliance, "Report of Findings to Date: Special Examination of Fannie Mae," September 17, 2004 (Washington, D.C.: OFHEO), pp. vii, 149 (hereinafter referred to as OFHEO Interim Report).

Case 3.11

(continued)

For Fannie Mae to pay out the maximum amount in incentives in 1998, EPS would have to come in at $3.23. If EPS were below the $3.13 minimum, there would be no incentive payout. The 1998 EPS was $3.2309. The maximum payout goal was met, as the OFHEO report noted "right down to the penny." The final OFHEO report concluded that the executive team at Fannie Mae determined what number it needed to get to the maximum EPS level and then worked backward to achieve that result. One series of emails finds the executives agreeing on what number they were comfortable with using for the "volatility adjustment."[135]

The following table shows the difference between salary (what would have been paid if the minimum target were not met) and the award under the annual incentive plan (AIP).

1998 Salary and Bonus of Senior Fannie Mae Executives			
Officer	**Title**	**Salary**	**AIP Award/Bonus**
James A. Johnson	Chairman and CEO	$966,000	$1,932,000
Franklin D. Raines	Chairman and CEO designate	$526,154	$1,109,589
Lawrence M. Small	President and COO	$783,839	$1,108,259
Jamie Gorelick	Vice chairman	$395,000	$493,750
J. Timothy Howard	Executive vice president (EVP) and CFO	$567,000	$779,625
Robert J. Levin	EVP, housing and community development	$395,000	$493,750

"Right down to the penny" was not a serendipitous achievement. For example, Fannie Mae's gains and losses on risky derivatives were kept off the books by treating them as hedges, a decision that was made without determining whether such treatment qualified under the accounting rules for exemptions from earnings statements. These losses were eventually brought back into earnings with a multibillion impact when these types of improprieties were uncovered in 2005.[136]

Fannie Mae and Volatility

Fannie Mae's policies on amortization, a critical accounting area for a company buying and holding mortgage loans, were developed by the chief financial officer (CFO) with no input from the company's controller. Fannie Mae's amortization policies were not in compliance with GAAP (generally accepted accounting principles).[137] The amortization policies relied on a computer model that would shorten the amortization of the life of a loan to peak earnings performance with higher yields. Fascinatingly, the amortization policies were developed because of a mantra within the company of "no more surprises."[138] The philosophy was that to attract funding for the mortgage market, there needed to be stability that would attract investors. The officers at the company reasoned that "volatility" was a barrier to accomplishing its goals of a stable and available source of mortgage funds for homes. When the computer model was developed, the officers reasoned that they were simply adjusting for what was "arbitrary volatility." However, "arbitrary volatility" turned out to

(continued)

---

[135]OFHEO Final Report, p. 51.
[136]*Id.*, p. 45.

[137]Fannie Mae's "Purchase Premium and Discount Amortization Policy," its internal policies on accounting and financial reporting on its loan portfolio, did not comply with GAAP. OFHEO Interim Report, pp. vii, 149. The final report was issued in February 2006, with no new surprises or altered conclusions beyond what appeared in this interim report Greg Farrell, "No New Problems in Report on Fannie," *USA Today*, February 24, 2006, p. 1B.
[138]OFHEO Interim Report, p. v.

Case 3.11

(continued)

be a difficult-to-grasp concept for those outside Fannie Mae.[139] Further, the volatility measures and adjustments appeared to have a direct correlation with the EPS goals that resulted in the awards to the officers. Even those within Fannie Mae struggled to explain to investigators what was really happening with their adjustments.

In the OFHEO report, an investigator asked Janet Pennewell, Fannie Mae's vice president of resource and planning, "What is arbitrary volatility in earnings?" Ms. Pennewell responded,

Arbitrary volatility, in our view, was introduced when—I can give you an example of what would cause, in our view, arbitrary volatility. If your constant effective yield was dramatically different between one quarter and the next quarter because of an arbitrary decision you had or view—changing your view of long-term interest rates that caused a dramatic change in the constant effective yield that you were reporting, you could therefore be in a position where you might be booking 300 million of income in one quarter and 200 million of expense in the next quarter, introduced merely by what your assumption about future interest rates was. And to us that was arbitrary volatility because it really just literally because of your view, your expectation of interest rate and the way that you were modeling your premium and discount constant effective yield, you would introduce something into your financial statements that, again, wasn't very reflective of how you really expect that mortgage to perform over its entire expected life, and was not very representative of the fundamental financial performance of the company.[140]

The operative words "to us" appeared to have fueled accounting decisions. But there was an overriding problem with Fannie Mae's reliance on arbitrary volatility. Fannie Mae had fixed-rate mortgages in its portfolio. Market fluctuations on interest rates were irrelevant for most of its portfolio.[141]

Fannie Mae's Accounting

The accounting practices of Fannie Mae were so aggressive that when Raines, lawyers, and others met with the SEC to discuss the SEC's demand for a restatement in 2005, the SEC told Raines that Fannie Mae's financial reports were inaccurate in "material respects." When pressed for specifics, Donald Nicolaisen, head of the SEC's accounting division, held up a piece of paper that represented the four corners of what was permissible under GAAP and told Raines, "You weren't even on the page."[142] The OFHEO report on Fannie Mae's accounting practices "paints an ugly picture of a company tottering under the weight of baleful misdeeds that have marked the corporate scandals of the past three years: dishonest accounting, lax internal controls, insufficient capital, and me-first managers who only care that earnings are high enough to get fat bonuses and stock options."[143]

When Franklin Raines and Fannie Mae CFO J. Timothy Howard were removed by the board at the end of 2005, Daniel H. Mudd, the former COO during the time frame in which the accounting issues arose, was appointed CEO.[144] When congressional hearings were held following the OFHEO report, Mudd testified that he was "as shocked as anyone" about the accounting scandals at the company at which he had served as a senior officer.[145] He added, "I was shocked and stunned," when Senator Chuck Hagel confronted Mudd with "I'm astounded that you would stay with this institution."[146]

There were other issues that exacerbated the accounting decisions at Fannie Mae. Howard, as CFO, had two functions: to set the targets for Fannie's financial performance and make the calls on the financial reports that determined whether those targets (and hence his incentive pay and bonuses) would be met.[147] In effect, the

(continued)

---

[139]*Id.*

[140]OFHEO Final Report, p. 6.

[141]This portion of the discussion was adapted from Marianne M. Jennings, "Fraud Is the Moving Target, Not Corporate Securities Attorneys: The Market Relevance of Firing Before Being Fired upon and Not Being 'Shocked, Shocked' That Fraud Is Going On," 46 *Washburn Law Journal* 27 (2006).

[142]McLean, "The Fall of Fannie Mae," pp. 123, 138.

[143]*Id.*, p. 45.

[144]Stephen Labaton, "Chief Is Ousted at Fannie Mae under Pressure," *New York Times*, December 22, 2004, p. A1.

[145]David S. Hilzenrath & Annys Shin, "Senators Grill Fannie Mae Chief," *Washington Post*, June 16, 2006, p. D2.

[146]Marcie Gordon, "Fannie Mae Execs Face Intense Questioning from Senators," *USA Today*, June 16, 2006, p. 4B.

[147]*Id.*

(continued)

function of targets and determination of how to meet those targets rested with one officer in the company. The internal control structure at Fannie Mae was weak even by the most lax internal control standards.[148]

In 1998, when Fannie Mae CEO Raines set the EPS goals, the charge spread throughout the company, and the OFHEO report concluded that the result was a culture that "improperly stressed stable earnings growth."[149] Also in 1998, Armando Falcone of the OFHEO issued a warning report that challenged Fannie Mae's accounting and stunning lack of internal controls. The report was buried until the 2004 report, readily dismissed by Fannie Mae executives and members of Congress who were enamored of Fannie's financial performance, as the work of "pencil brains" who did not understand a model that was working.[150]

The Unraveling of the Fannie Mae Mystique

Employees within Fannie Mae did begin to raise questions. In November 2003, a full year before Fannie Mae's issues would become public, Roger Barnes, then an employee in the Controller's Office at the company, left Fannie Mae because of his frustration with the lack of response from the Office of Auditing at Fannie Mae. He had provided a detailed concern about the company's accounting policy that internal audit did not investigate in an appropriate manner.[151] No one at Fannie Mae took any steps to investigate Barnes's warnings about the flaws in the computer models for amortization. Worse, in one instance, Barnes notified the head of the Office of Auditing that at least one on-top adjustment had been made in order to make Fannie Mae's results meet those that had been forecasted.[152] At the time Barnes raised his concern, Fannie Mae had an Ethics and Compliance Office, but it was housed within the company's litigation division and was headed by a lawyer whose primary responsibility was defending the company against allegations and suits by employees.

When those in charge of the Office of Auditing (Rajappa, of EPS 6.46 pep talk fame, was the person who handled the allegations and investigation) investigated Barnes's allegations, they were not given access to the necessary information and the investigation was dropped.[153] Many of the officers at Fannie Mae disclosed in interviews that they were aware of the Barnes allegation of an intentional act related to financial reporting, but none of them followed up on the issue or required an investigation.[154]

Barnes was correct but ignored, and he left Fannie Mae. He would later be vindicated by the OFHEO report, but the report was not issued until after he had left Fannie Mae.[155] Fannie Mae settled with Barnes before any suit for wrongful termination was filed. In 2002, at about the same time Barnes was raising his concerns internally, the *Wall Street Journal* began raising questions about Fannie Mae's accounting practices.[156] Those concerns were reported and editorialized in that newspaper for two years. No action was taken, however, until the OFEHO interim report was released.

The final OFHEO report noted that Fannie Mae's then-CEO Mr. Daniel Mudd listened in 2003 as employees expressed concerns about the company's accounting policies. However, Mudd took no steps to follow up on either the questions or concerns that the employees had raised in the meeting that also subsequently turned out to accurately reflect the financial reporting missteps and misdeeds at Fannie Mae.[157] The special report written for Fannie Mae's board indicated that the Legal Department at Fannie Mae was aware of the Barnes allegations but deferred to internal audit for making any decisions about the merits of the allegations.[158]

(continued)

---

[148]*Id.*
[149]Stephen Labaton & Rick Dash, "New Report Criticizes Big Lender," *New York Times*, February 24, 2006, pp. C1, C6.
[150]*Id.*, p. 128.
[151]OFHEO Interim Report, p. iv.
[152]OFHEO Interim Report, p. 75.
[153]*Id.*, p. 78.
[154]*Id.*, p. 76. However, the OFHEO investigation reveals inconsistencies in the Office of Auditing's take on the Barnes allegations.
[155]Paul, Weiss, Rifkind, et al., "A Report to the Special Review Committee of the Board of Directors of Fannie Mae," February 23, 2006, p. 25 (hereinafter referred to as Board Report).
[156]"Systemic Political Risk," *Wall Street Journal*, September 30, 2005, p. A10.
[157]Eric Dash, "Regulators Denounce Fannie Mae," *New York Times*, May 24, 2006, p. C1. Mudd said, "I absolutely wish I had handled it differently."
[158]Board Report, p. 28.

Case 3.11

(continued)

The investigation of then New York Attorney General Eliot Spitzer (Mr. Spitzer became governor in 2007 and resigned in 2008 because of a sex scandal) into insurance companies added an aside to the Fannie Mae scandal and revealed yet another red flag from a Fannie Mae employee. In 2002, Fannie Mae bought a finite-risk policy from Radian Insurance to shift $40 million in income from 2003 to 2004. Radian booked the transaction as a loan, but Fannie Mae called it an insurance policy on its books. In a January 9, 2002, email, Louis Hoyes, Fannie Mae's chief for residential mortgages, wrote about the Radian deal, "I would like to express an extremely strong no vote. . . . Should we be exposing Fannie Mae to this type of political risk to 'move' $40 million of income? I believe not."[159] No further action was taken on the question raised; the deal went through as planned, and the income was shifted to another year.

The Fallout at Fannie Mae

Fannie Mae paid a $125 million fine to OFHEO for its accounting improprieties.[160] As part of that settlement, Fannie Mae's board agreed to new officers, new systems of internal control, and the presence of outside consultants to monitor the company's progress. The agency concluded that it would take years for Fannie Mae to work through all of the accounting issues and corrective actions needed to prevent similar accounting missteps in the future.[161] Fannie Mae settled charges of accounting issues with the SEC for $400 million.[162] Investigations into the role of third parties and their relationships to Fannie Mae and "actions and inactions" continued.[163] Former head of the SEC Harvey Pitt commented, "When a company has engaged in wrongful conduct, the inquiry [inevitably turns to]

who knew about it, who could have prevented it, who facilitated it."[164]

The head of the OFHEO, upon release of the Fannie Mae report, said of the company's operations, "More than any other case I've seen, it's all there."[165]

When he was serving as the CEO of Fannie Mae as well as the chair of the Business Roundtable, Franklin Raines testified before Congress in March 2002 in favor of the passage of Sarbanes–Oxley. The following are excerpts from his testimony, which began with a reference to the tone at the top:

> The success of the American free enterprise system obtains from the merger of corporate responsibility with individual responsibility, and The Business Roundtable believes that responsibility starts at the top.
>
> We understand why the American people are stunned and outraged by the failure of corporate leadership and governance at Enron. It is wholly irresponsible and unacceptable for corporate leaders to say they did not know—or suggest it was not their duty to know—about the operations and activities of their company, particularly when it comes to risks that threaten the fundamental viability of their company.
>
> First, the paramount duty of the board of directors of a public corporation is to select and oversee competent and ethical management to run the company on a day-to-day basis.
>
> Second, it is the responsibility of management to operate the company in a competent and ethical manner. Senior management is expected to know how the company earns its income and what risks the company is undertaking in the course of carrying out its business. Management should never put personal interests ahead of or in conflict with the interests of the company.[166]
>
> The final Fannie Mae report was issued in May 2006 with no new surprises or altered conclusions beyond what appeared in the interim report.[167]

(continued)

[159]Dawn Kopecki, "It Looks Like Fannie Had Some Help," *BusinessWeek*, June 12, 2006, pp. 36, 38. *Id.* Radian's general counsel had this comment on the deal: "We have not done anything improper or illegal in this particular case or in any other case"; odd to get that kind of a wide swath from general counsel.
[160]Edward Iwata, "Celebrated CEO Faces Critics," *USA Today*, October 6, 2004, pp. 1B, 2B.
[161]"Fannie Mae Overhaul May Take Years," *New York Times*, June 16, 2006, p. C3.
[162]Elliott Blair Smith, "Fannie Mae to Pay $400 Million Fine," *USA Today*, May 24, 2006, p. 1B.
[163]Kopecki, "It Looks Like Fannie Had Some Help," p. 36.

[164]*Id.*
[165]Dwyer, Borrus, & Hovanesian, "Fannie Mae: What's the Damage?" pp. 45, 48.
[166]Statement by Franklin D. Raines, Chairman, Corporate Governance Task Force of the Business Roundtable, Before the U.S. House Committee on Financial Services, Washington, D.C., March 20, 2002.
[167]Farrell, "No New Problems in Report on Fannie," p. 1B.

Case 3.11

(continued)

Fannie Mae concluded the financial statement questions and issues with, among other things, a $6.3 billion restatement of revenue for the period from 1998 through 2004. Raines earned $90 million in bonuses for this period. The report also concluded that management had created an "unethical and arrogant culture" with bonus targets that were achieved through the use of cookie jar reserves that "manipulated earnings."[168] OFHEO filed 101 civil charges against Raines, former Fannie Mae CFO Mr. J. Timothy Howard, and former controller Ms. Leanne G. Spencer. The suits asked for the return of $115 million in incentive plan payouts to the three.[169] The suit also asked for $100 million in penalties. The three settled the case by agreeing to pay $31.4 million. Raines issued the following statement when the case was settled: "While I long ago accepted managerial accountability for any errors committed by subordinates while I was CEO, it is a very different matter to suggest that I was legally culpable in any way. I was not. This settlement is not an acknowledgment of wrongdoing on my part, because I did not break any laws or rules while leading Fannie Mae. At most, this is an agreement to disagree."[170]

The Evolving Financial Meltdown and the Conflicts

Once the restatement was completed, Fannie Mae returned to increasing its mortgage portfolio. But Fannie Mae also built relationships. Through its Fannie Mae Foundation, Fannie Mae (subsequently investigated by the IRS for violating the use of a charitable foundation for political purposes) made donations to charities on the basis of the political contacts they were able to list on their applications for funding.[171] Bruce Marks, the CEO of Neighborhood Assistance Corporation, a recipient of Fannie Foundation funds explained, "Many institutions rely on Fannie Mae and understand that those funds are contingent on public support for its policies. Fannie Mae has intimidated virtually all of them into remaining silent."[172]

Donations went to those groups that supported CRA loans, including the annual fundraisers for several congressional groups. In exchange, when regulatory or legislative action was pending that was unfavorable to Fannie Mae, those members of Congress would come out in support of Fannie Mae, what one member of Congress called, "a gorilla that has outgrown its cage."[173] When the SEC wanted to push to have Fannie Mae register its securities as other companies did, at least six members of Congress wrote letters of support for Fannie Mae, and the SEC backed down from its demand.

Fannie Mae's board members also stood to benefit from continuing the company's growth and mortgage policies. Lenders, seeking to curry favor with Fannie in having it purchase their mortgages, offered special loan terms to Fannie executives and board members as well as to members of Congress. The following chart lists those loans that were given by Countrywide under a special program that was nicknamed, "FOA," for "Friends of Angelo."[174] Angelo Mozilo was the CEO of Countrywide, a company that collapsed under the weight of its subprime mortgages, nearly all of which were purchased by Fannie Mae.

FOAs at Countrywide			
Name/Title	**Amount**	**Rate**	**Years**
Franklin Haines Former CEO Fannie Mae	$982,253 $986,340	5.125% 4.125%	10 10
Jamie Gorelick Vice Chair Fannie Mae	$960,149	5.00%	10
James Johnson Former CEO Fannie Mae	$971,650	3.875%	3
Daniel Mudd COO/CEO Fannie Mae	$2,965,000	4.250%	7

(continued)

---

[168]OFHEO, Report of Findings to Date, Special Examination of Fannie Mae, September 17, 2004, http://www.ofheo.gov (accessed June 19, 2010).

[169]Eric Dash, "Fannie Mae Ex-Officers Sued by U.S.," *New York Times*, December 19, 2006, pp. C1, C9.

[170]James R. Hagerty, "Fannie Mae Settlement Proves Anticlimactic," *Wall Street Journal*, April 21, 2008, p. A3.

[171]Dawn Kopecki, "Philanthropy, Fannie Mae Style," *Business-Week*, April 2, 2007, p. 36.

[172]Id.

[173]Creswell, "Long Protected by Washington, Fannie and Freddie Ballooned," p. A7.

[174]Paul Gigot, "The Fannie Mae Gang," *Wall Street Journal*, July 23, 2008, p. A17.

Case 3.11

(continued)

Between 2005 and 2008, Fannie Mae guaranteed $270 billion in risky loans, an amount that was three times the amount of risky loans it had guaranteed in all of its existence (since 1938, when it was created during the Roosevelt administration). The mortgage loans were risky because the income of the borrowers had not been verified; the borrowers had little or no equity in the property; the real level of payments that would be due under the loans did not take effect until three to five years after; and most of the borrowers had little or poor credit history.

When employees expressed concerns that there were too many mortgages being evaluated, that the computer system was not effective in determining risk, and that Fannie Mae's exposure was too great, Mr. Mudd, then CEO, instructed them, "Get aggressive on risk-taking or get out of the company."[175] During the years from 2004 to 2006, the company operated without a permanent chief risk officer. When a permanent risk officer was hired in 2006, he advised Mudd to scale back on risk. Mr. Mudd rebuffed the suggestion because he explained that Congress and shareholders wanted him to take more risks.

In the fall of 2008, following the collapse of the real estate market, major Wall Street banks and investment firms collapsed because their loan portfolios dropped significantly in value and, as a result, the derivatives investments they held in those portfolios became worthless. Mortgage defaults around the country were so numerous that there is still litigation pending in 2022 on many of those loans.

In September 2008, the federal government had to pay $200 billion to restore Fannie Mae to solvency and prevent the quake that would have shaken other firms if Fannie Mae had defaulted on its guarantees. Fannie Mae is currently, along with Freddie Mac, under the control of a conservatorship created by the federal government for purposes of supervising the quasi-public entities' activities with the hope of recouping some of the bail-out money. Both Fannie and Freddie are once again selling mortgage-backed instruments with the claim that there is no risk for taxpayers in their activities.[176]

At the end of 2015, an effort was underway in Washington, D.C., to displace Fannie Mae from the U.S. mortgage market.[177] The plan has its opponents and their fear is of putting too much under the control of banks who have a history of toxic mortgages.[178]

The Fannie Mae Mortgages—The Ripple Effect and Stakeholder Analysis

Even with the $200 billion bailout, Fannie Mae was still left as the guarantor on all the subprime mortgages that were now in default. Defaults on those mortgages carried ripple effects. The issues of the subprime market provide a structure for understanding stakeholder analysis. Suppose Bob is a subprime borrower or suppose that Bob misrepresents his qualifications for a mortgage on a loan application. Either way, Bob represents a riskier type of mortgage than those borrowers who have a minimum income, down-payment, and verification requirements. Suppose further that Bob defaults—and there is a greater likelihood that Bob will default if he is a subprime borrower or a borrower who has misrepresented his status. Because Bob has defaulted, the lender has to go through foreclosure and take a write-down for a loan gone bad. Those who have purchased bundled mortgages or securities based on bundles of mortgages also have devalued assets, particularly if, in addition to subprime Bob, there are other subprime borrowers such as Betty, Bill, Brent, and others all through the alphabet.

(continued)

[175]Charles Duhigg, "Pressured to Take More Risks, Fannie Reached Tipping Point," *New York Times*, October 5, 2008, p. A1.

[176]"Fannie and Freddie Forever," *Wall Street Journal*, December 31, 2015, p. A12.
[177]Gretchen Morgenson, "Insiders Aid Big Banks in Effort to Displace Fannie and Freddie," *New York Times*, December 7, 2015, p. A1.
[178]*Id.*

Case 3.11

(continued)

But there is a far more local impact. Bob's home and others are in foreclosure, with the resulting effect of an ill-maintained or unoccupied property in a neighborhood. Other homeowners in the neighborhood are affected by the loss in value generally, as well as by the sale of the homes at foreclosure for what is inevitably a much lower price. All those who live in the area have the value of their homes affected. Lower property values mean taxes are lower, with a resulting effect on government services.

In addition, Bob's original lender tightens credit and lending standards, even for those who would have been good credit risks under original standards. There are more homes on the market, which also means lower prices. With more existing homes on the market, construction firms scale back on building, which results in reduced labor forces, which could mean more defaults because of loss of income. Decorators, landscapers, lawn services, and companies that provide services to real estate and construction firms are all affected by these events. There is a ripple through the economy that produces more foreclosures, tighter credit standards, a smaller funds pool, little opportunity for business expansion, and credit markets frozen because of the fear of increased risk.

Walking Away, Refinancing, and Moral Hazards

Ethical analysis looks at this question: How did you get in to this situation in the first place? In the words of the not-so-great Bob Dylan, "When you ain't got nothin', you got nothin' to lose." In the words of the great University of Texas–Dallas economics professor Stan Liebowitz, "skin in the game" is the single most important factor in determining default on mortgage and—too often after the market collapse—the walk-away. If you have a little down payment and no equity to speak of, you walk when your mortgage is more than your property value—in other words, underwater. Some walked away with arms full—taking everything that moved (or didn't) from their homes, including copper plumbing.

Of the foreclosures in the second half of 2008, only 183,447 resulted from the loss of employment. Other foreclosures?

Negative net equity: 283,305
A down payment of 3% or less: 130,014
Low initial interest rate going higher: 60,942
Poor FICO score: 148, 697

So, in 2008, there were 624,958 foreclosures for financial folly as compared to 183,447 for loss of employment. The 12% of the homes with negative equity are responsible for 47% of the foreclosures. Pick-a-Pay re-default rates were at 55%. That is, lenders who refinanced mortgages faced a 55% chance of default on the refinance.

The drop in home values after the market collapse was about 50% in Phoenix, Atlanta, and Las Vegas. Detroit had homes for sale for $7,000. Short sales reduced the value of all homes in their neighborhoods. The presence of so many abandoned properties became a blight and city workers, paid by tax dollars, were mowing lawns and doing upkeep on abandoned properties. Vandalized vacant properties attracted so much criminal activity that Baltimore and Detroit began bulldozing areas with high concentrations of walk-away properties.

The Fannie Mae shareholders were harmed by their losses in the value of their shares and have filed suit claiming that the federal government took their property without just compensation. The federal government's defense in the suit has been that Fannie Mae was in a death spiral and had to be rescued. Proof of that defense has been elusive as documents have emerged in the litigation that indicate officials believed Fannie Mae could make a profit.[179] As the litigation proceeds in Federal Claims Court, Fannie Mae's real role in the crisis will become clearer and its future may hinge on what the litigation reveals.

Fannie Mae's future remains uncertain as a plan to have it raise capital and convert the secondary shareholders (secondary to the federal government) to common shareholders who could be paid dividends has been pulled off the table.[180] And Fannie Mae is currently facing another mortgage crisis. By May 2020, because of the pandemic,

(continued)

[179]Gretchen Morgenson, "Fannie Mae Documents Case Doubt on U.S. Acts," *New York Times*, April 13, 2016, p. B1.
[180]Juliet Chung and Andrew Ackerman, "Fannie, Freddie Bets Torment Hedge Funds," *Wall Street Journal*, January 22, 2021, p. A1.

Case 3.11

(continued)

Fannie Mae had to set aside money for projected loan losses, as 7% of all mortgage holders had already missed payments.[181] The level of this housing slump is expected to be the deepest since 1940. Fannie Mae's income dropped 81% for the first quarter of 2020, and it is expecting loan losses of $4.1 billion from the pandemic.[182] It appears that a third financial crisis is pending for Fannie Mae. However, Fannie Mae did announce that it will begin providing mortgage guarantees for up to $1,000,000.[183] Some say the change is in response to increasing home prices. However, regardless of the reason, Fannie Mae's debt level will be increasing substantially despite the economic crunch it faces with defaults.

Discussion Questions

1. Consider the ethics recognition that Fannie Mae received and the reasons given for those awards. Then consider that Fannie Mae was rated by Standard & Poor's on its corporate governance scoring (CGS) system as a 9, with 10 being the maximum CGS score. Fannie Mae received a 9.3 for its board structure and process.[184] What issues do you see with regard to these outside evaluations of companies that relate to governance and ethics? Is there a difference between social responsibility and ethics? Is there a connection between good governance practices and ethics?

2. List the signals that were missed in Fannie Mae's devolution. Were they missed or ignored? Evaluate the actions of Barnes and Fannie Mae's response to him.[185]

3. What observations can you make about incentive plans and earnings management? Incentive plans and internal controls?

4. Why was dealing with the volatility not the issue? Why were the changes in the numbers necessary?

5. Evaluate the pep talk of the vice president of risk operations and its effect on Fannie Mae's culture. Are there some ideas for your credo that stem from the conduct and responses of various executives at Fannie Mae? Did Mr. Mudd carry that culture forward in his positions on risk?

6. The theory of moral hazard holds that failure is a necessary part of an economic system. Where would this theory have applied in preventing the demise of Fannie Mae? Be sure to look at all aspects of the case in providing your answer. Now apply the theory of moral hazard to those who walk away from their mortgages. Angelo Mozilo is the former CEO of Countrywide Mortgage, a company that sold all of its mortgages to Fannie Mae and, as noted, was a major lender to Fannie Mae officers and board members. At his deposition in a lawsuit brought against him by a mortgage insurer, he was asked, "After all the foreclosures and ruined lives and lawsuits, do you have any regrets about the way you ran Countrywide?" Mr. Mozilo's response about the role of his company in the market collapse was as follows:

> This is a matter of record. The cause of the problems of foreclosures is not created by Countrywide. This is all about an unprecedented, cataclysmic situation, unprecedented in the history of this country. Values in this country dropped 50%. This is not caused by any act of Countrywide. It was caused by an event that was unforeseen by anyone, because if anybody foresaw it, you would never have insured it, we would never have originated the loan. And it spread across the world. Any judgment made on a foreclosure—on a loan being made is because values deteriorated.
>
> And for the first time in the history of this country, people decided that they were going to leave their homes because the value of their homes was below the mortgage amount. Never in the history of this country did that ever happen, and that could never have been assessed in the risk profile. These people didn't lose their jobs. They didn't lose their health. They didn't lose their marriage. Those are the three factors that cause foreclosure. They left their homes because the values went below the mortgage. That's what caused the problem.

(continued)

---

[181]Andrew Ackerman, "Fannie Mae's Earnings Slide on Skipped Mortgage Payments," *Wall Street Journal*, May 2–3, 202, p. B12.
[182]Id.
[183]Andrew Ackerman, "Fannie, Freddie Set to Back Mortgages Near $1 Million," *Wall Street Journal*, November 17, 2021, p. A1.
[184]Standard & Poor's, "Setting the Standard," January 30, 2003, http://www.standardandpoors.com (accessed April 28, 2010).
[185]Mr. Barnes now travels and addresses ethics, audit, accounting, financial reporting, and internal control issues. Mr. Barnes has been particularly active in working with college students in helping them to sort through the ethical issues in these areas.

Case 3.11

(continued)

So, I have no regrets about how I—how Countrywide was run. It was a world-class company. So your tirade about foreclosures and lawsuits is nonsensical and insulting. Countrywide did not cause this problem. We made no loans in Greece. We made no loans in Ireland. We made no loans in Portugal. This is a worldwide financial crisis that was totally a shock to the system.[186]

What is Mr. Mozilo's view on walking away? Does he take responsibility for the loans?

7. In 2001, Jim Collins included Fannie Mae in his book *Good to Great*. His praise for Fannie Mae and its financial performance was glowing. In addition, he characterized Fannie Mae as a model corporate citizen.

Fannie Mae was indeed philanthropic, part of *American Benefactor*'s list of "America's Most Generous Companies." The Fannie Mae causes were noble. It

---

[186]Deposition of Angelo Mozilo in *MBIA Insurance Corporation v. Countrywide Home Loans, Inc.*, No. 602825/08, Supreme Court of the State of New York, http://www.mbia.com/investor/publications/073011_AppellateDivision RulingReMotionto Dismiss.pdf.

was the accounting that was bad. If you are measuring with these metrics, Fannie Mae has so many accolades that you could say that it was gaming the system for recognition for measurements that counted for social responsibility.

The ability of companies to game metrics is also limitless when it comes to the human imagination. What you have witnessed in studying Fannie Mae's incentives also serves to illustrate why so many of the management gurus got duped and were so wrong in their analyses of high-performance companies. Their rankings were only as good as the companies' numbers. If the numbers were incorrect, their models and rankings fall apart. The gurus did not dig deep enough into the companies, and those at the top of the companies whom they interviewed were not going to lean in and offer, "You know, we cook the books here. That's really the secret of our success." In short, the gurus got rolled by Fannie Mae because they relied on incorrect or falsified numbers.

Which reading(s) in Section A address the relationship between social responsibility and ethics in a company? What ethical categories are involved in gaming the CSR rankings?

History Repeats

Ethical Lessons Not Learned: Fannie Is Pursuing More Lending Assistance Programs

Fannie Mae has been under federal conservatorship since its rescue by the U.S. Treasury Department in 2009 with a $190 billion bailout. Ironically, in 2022, President Biden announced that he needed a three-year plan to implement "Equitable Housing Finance Plans." Fannie must find ways to boost the number of minority homeowners. The plans being discussed were to provide minority purchasers with their down payments and reduced interest rates for minority borrowers. Other proposed programs would include reimbursements for appraisal fees for minority applicants and subsidy programs to help purchasers avoid foreclosure.[187] The programs are similar to those that began in 2003. Those programs, like the ones proposed yet again, gave so much assistance and so much in subsidies that purchasers bought and financed more homes than they could afford. Even with the subsidies, there were high levels of default among minority-subsidized borrowers. What followed the defaults were the real estate and financial market collapses that began in 2007 and ended with Fannie's bailout. History does repeat in every way.

---

[187]Fannie's New Racial Bias, *Wall Street Journal*, June 14, 2022, p. A18.

Why Didn't They Say Something? 3.1

Fear at Fannie

Make a list of all those mentioned in the case who were aware of the accounting issues and did not make disclosures in a way that led to the issues being addressed. Why did they give up or leave? What do we learn about how managers treat those who raise questions about company practices? Given the political environment, was there any hope of having the issues addressed?

Case 3.12

Pharmaceuticals: A Tale of 4,834% Price Increases and Regulatory Cycles

The pharmaceutical industry has been living in the awareness stage of the regulatory cycle since 2016 elections. The case involving Turing Pharmaceutical and its colorful CEO, Martin Shkreli, was the marking point for moving the issue to the **activism stage**.

Turing and Its Acquisition of Daraprim

The prescription drug Daraprim is used to treat toxoplasmosis, a parasitic disease that generally occurs in patients with weakened immune systems, such as pregnant women or people suffering from AIDS. In 2015, Turing Pharmaceutical acquired the patent rights to Daraprim for $55 million.[188] The drug, developed in 1957, costs about $1 to produce and had been selling for $13.50 per pill. Upon acquisition of the patent rights, Turing raised the price to $750 per pill: an increase of 4,834%. The Infectious Diseases Society of America and the HIV Medicine Association raised objections to the price increase, explaining that hospitals and pharmacies were no longer able to stock the medication. The two societies offered the following calculations for a year-long treatment: the cost would be $336,000 for those who

weigh less than 132 pounds and $634,500 for those who weigh more than that.

According to the *Wall Street Journal*, Martin Shkreli, 32, Turing's then CEO, had developed a strategy of buying lifesaving one-of-a-kind drugs from companies that he knew would not raise prices on the drugs because of the potential backlash.[189] The *Wall Street Journal* cited the Food and Drug Administration's (FDA) longstanding overregulation as the cause for the lack of development of new drugs and competition for these unique drugs. Mr. Shkreli had discovered this niche for profit and created a company for purchasing drugs and increasing prices.

The Turing and Shkreli Strategy

Following the price increase, the backdrop behind the Turing acquisition of Daraprim emerged. Later investigations revealed emails in which Mr. Shkreli described his plans for Daraprim upon acquiring the drug: "So 5,000 paying bottles at the new price is $375,000,000—almost all of it is profit and I think we will get three years of that or more. Should be a very handsome investment for all of us. Let's all cross our fingers that the estimates are accurate."[190] Another internal email at Turing from the

(continued)

---

[188]Chris Spargo & Kelly McLaughlin, "Martin Shkreli Again Defends Massive Price Hike," *The Daily Mail*, September 22, 2016, http://www.dailymail.co.uk/news/article-3245006 /Martin-Shkreli-defends-massive-price-hike-AIDS-drug-claiming -HELPING-need-life-saving-medication-funds-research -necessary-case-disease-evolves.html.

[189]"The People vs. Martin Shkreli," *Wall Street Journal*, December 19, 2015, p. A14 (editorial).
[190]Andrew Pollack & Matthew Goldstein, "Email Shows Profit Drove Drug Pricing," *New York Times*, February 3, 2016, p. B1.

Case 3.12

(continued)

senior director of business analytics and customer insights attached a copy of a purchase order for 96 bottles of Daraprim at the full price, and this comment, "Another $7.2 million. Pow!"[191] At a panel discussion on the pharmaceutical industry, Mr. Shkreli indicated that he owed a duty to his investors to maximize profits and that he acquires pharmaceutical firms for the purposes of owning the patents for the drugs and then raising the prices of those drugs.

The Backlash to the Price Increase and Public Policy

The public appeared to be astonished at the level of the price increase, and Mr. Shkreli became in the public's eye what the *Wall Street Journal* called "a jerk" and "obnoxious."[192] Shkreli took to social media to defend the price increase. He explained that the drug had been unprofitable, so any company selling it would be losing money. He also noted that there were "altruistic properties" to selling the drug at that price, because there had not been any new research or development focused on the treatment or cure for toxoplasmosis in 70 years.[193]

However, the public outcry was so great that Turing announced that it would reduce the price.[194] Turing also indicated that it would also create a program that would help patients obtain the drug.

The Pricing Dynamics of Daraprim and Other Prescription Drugs

About 2,000 Americans take Daraprim, making it one of the most expensive drugs for any company to produce because of the lack of volume sales. The costs for prescription drugs include the costs of the research, development, and approval of the drugs, generally a 7- to 10-year process. When the drug is used widely the price is lower because the sales volume is higher. However, Daraprim is one of those very valuable drugs needed by only a small group of patients.

The practice of raising prescription drug prices on drugs that are not widely used is not new but always results in emotional public reaction. The laws on price gouging generally apply in situations where the price of ordinary goods is increased because of demand that arises through circumstances not controlled by either buyer or seller. Hurricanes, earthquakes, fires, and other large tragic events often result in the shutdown of supply lines and shortages of basic goods such as food, water, and fuel. Many states prohibit price gouging, as defined by percentage increases, in their statutes so as to prevent panic and violence when goods are in short supply.

The situation with prescription drug prices is different from the situations covered by price-gouging statutes because there is no unforeseen change in the market or demand: there is simply a change of ownership or an inability to produce the drug without increased profit margins.

Governmental Reaction to Daraprim

The public reaction continued, and Congress held hearings on the pricing of pharmaceuticals. In his appearance before the House Committee on Oversight and Government Reform, Mr. Shkreli took the Fifth Amendment.[195] The *Wall Street Journal* reported that "Mr. Shkreli appeared to smirk, look away, and otherwise goad lawmakers."[196] Mr. Shkreli's lawyer explained that any movements or expressions his client made during the hearing were the results of nervous energy and that his client meant no disrespect. Following the congressional hearings, Mr. Shkreli tweeted, "Hard to accept that these imbeciles represent the people in our government."[197]

(continued)

[191]*Id.*, p. 8.
[192]"The People vs. Martin Shkreli," *Wall Street Journal*, December 19, 2015, p. A14 (editorial).
[193]Spago & McLaughlin, *supra* note 17.
[194]Hadley Malcolm & Liz Szabo, "After Outrage, Turing Pharma CEO Lying Low," *USA Today*, September 24, 2015, p. 1B.

[195]Stephanie Armour & Jonathan D. Rockoff, "Shkreli Takes Fifth before Congress," *Wall Street Journal*, February 5, 2016, p. B1.
[196]*Id.*
[197]Laura Lorenzetti, "Martin Shkreli Calls U.S. Lawmakers 'Imbeciles,'" *Fortune*, February 4, 2016, http://fortune.com/2016/02/04/martin-shkreli-calls-u-s-lawmakers-imbeciles/ (accessed April 18, 2016).

Case 3.12

(continued)

Turing's and Mr. Shkreli's conduct continued to infiltrate the political world. When presidential candidate Hillary Clinton asked that he lower prices on drugs, he tweeted, "lol." Presidential candidate Bernie Sanders returned Mr. Shkreli's $2,700 campaign contribution.

Scrutiny of Shkreli

Between the time of the price increase and the congressional hearings, Mr. Shkreli was arrested on securities fraud charges. He was freed on a $5 million bail bond. He was arrested on December 16, 2016, at 6:30 A.M. in his apartment and entered a not guilty plea to charges that he was running a Ponzi scheme at his former company.

The charges were based on Shkreli's MSMB Capital, a hedge fund that he had founded with investments from others of $3 million. The indictment alleged that he spent the money and, that at one point, the fund had only $310. When MSMB Capital collapsed, he founded MSMB Healthcare with $5 million from 13 total investors. According to the indictment, in addition to the 1% management fee that he had promised investors, he took a 20% profit incentive for compensation. MSMB Healthcare then invested in Retrophin, another pharmaceutical company that had no products or assets. Retrophin was founded for the purpose of acquiring older pharmaceuticals that would then be sold for higher prices, which was the same as the Turing/Daraprim strategy.

There is litigation by investors in MSMB over the Retrophin investment. Mr. Shkreli indicated that he was innocent and that what should be a civil litigation matter had turned into a government action. He insisted that investors made money and that he would prevail in both the civil litigation and the government criminal case. Lawyer Evan Greebel was also charged in the indictment. Shkreli offered statements in response to the civil action on a pharma blog:

Hi Guys,

This is Martin Shkreli. The 8-k is completely false, untrue at best and defamatory at worst. I am evaluating my options to respond. Every transaction I've ever made at Retrophin was done with outside counsel's blessing (I have the bills to prove it), board approval and made good corporate sense. I took Retrophin from an idea to a $500 million public company in 3 years—and I had a lot of help along the way.

I am happy to explain any transaction. I am confident that anyone who looked into the transactions would find them perfectly legal, reasonable and quite intelligent (the results of the company speak for themselves). I welcome any scrutiny by any party and have faith any investigation will be resolved without issue—it would not be the first time and it won't be the last that my moves have been looked at—this is not my first rodeo and I have too many scars to do something stupid.

By the way, it is nice to see the rational community here, and I will enjoy joining some of the discourse here on various companies and drugs.

Best,
Martin Shkreli

(continued)

Case 3.12

(continued)

Part of his defense was to throw his indicted lawyer, Evan Greebel, under the bus. Mr. Greebel was convicted of conspiracy to commit wire fraud and conspiracy to commit securities fraud following an 11-week trial. He was sentenced to 18 months in prison.[198]

The indictment also alleged that Mr. Shkreli used his company as a piggy bank, recruiting new investors to cover his spending and falsifying returns statements to keep the investors believing. One example given in the indictment is that in early December 2015, Mr. Shkreli purchased the only copy of Wu-Tang Chan's album, "Once Upon a Time in Shaolin," for $2.2 million.[199]

The Shkreli Trial and Conviction

Following his arrest, Mr. Shkreli was removed and/or resigned as CEO of two of the pharmaceutical companies he had acquired, Turing and KaloBios.[200] Meanwhile, ex-CEO Shkreli entered a not guilty plea to charges of securities fraud. Mr. Shkreli, an active Tweeter, rebutted the negative attention he was receiving with a reminder that he received no salary as CEO of Turing.

The jury selection process was unique and a function of Mr. Shkreli's personality and antics. One potential juror who was being screened said, "I looked right at him, and in my head I said, 'That's a snake'—not knowing who he was."[201] Even after the judge reminded the potential jurors that the trial was not related to Mr. Shkreli's role as CEO of Turing Pharmaceuticals, the comments continued:

"He is the face of corporate greed in America."

"You'd have to convince me he is innocent."

"Who does that? A person who puts profit above everything else."

"The most hated man in America."

"I honestly don't think I can be impartial."[202]

The judge reminded the panel of potential jurors about the presumption of innocence. But jurors were not buying this justice stuff. One responded, "I understand that, but everything I've seen. . . ."[203]

The judge interrupted him mid-sentence and had to hold a side bar because the defense raised the legitimate point that the jurors who were being excused for cause were tainting the remainder of the pool with their comments. The questioning proceeded with potential jurors waiting outside so as to avoid the commentary. Sixty-nine jurors were dismissed—dozens for cause. The judge had to ask for 100 more for the panel. Shkreli proved to be a defendant so notorious that the court struggled mightily to bring together an unbiased panel. You may have crossed a few ethical lines when you can't find a juror with an open mind about you.

As the trial proceeded, there were new insights into Mr. Shkreli's conduct as CEO. When Mr. Shkreli proposed increasing the price of Daraprim by 5,000%, Turing's now former vice president and general counsel joined with other managers to tell Shkreli that the move "would have a severely negative impact on Turing's business and reputation." Taking the price from $13.50 to $750 per pill was too much for Howard Dorfman, and he spoke up. The price went up anyway, and Mr. Dorfman was fired a few weeks later. Mr. Dorfman also testified before a Senate committee about his experience and job loss.

Mr. Shkreli was convicted of three of eight counts, including securities fraud, conspiracy to commit securities fraud, and fraud through false consulting agreements at Retrophin to pay MSMB investors.[204] His attorney, Ben Brafman, offered this thought at his

(continued)

---

[198]Rebecca Davis O'Brien, "Shkreli's Former Lawyer Sentenced to 18 Months in Prison," *Wall Street Journal*, August 18–19, 2018, p. A3.

[199]Corinne Ramey, "Unique Album Owned by Shkreli Is Sold," *Wall Street Journal*, July 28, 2021, p. A3.

[200]Andrew Pollack, "Shkreli Is Removed from C.E.O. Post of a 2nd Drug Makers," *New York Times*, December 22, 2015, p. B1.

[201]Stephanie Clifford, "Presumed Innocent? Shkreli Is Target of Name Calling at Jury Selection," *New York Times*, June 27, 2017, p. B5.

[202]Id.

[203]Id.

[204]Stephanie Clifford and Colin Moynihan, "Guilty of Fraud, Shkreli Grins and Shrugs It Off," *New York Times*, August 5, 2017, p. A1.

Case 3.12

(continued)

sentencing hearing, "There are times when I want to hug him and hold him. There are times when I want to punch him in the face."[205] With defense lawyers like this, who needs prosecutors? The maximum sentence for Mr. Shkreli was 21 years. He was sentenced to seven. His conviction was upheld by the Second Circuit Court of Appeals, and his appeal to the U.S. Supreme Court was denied *certiorari*.[206]

Shkreli Prison Activities

Mr. Shkreli managed to have an in-prison romance. An *Elle* magazine article revealed that a former Bloomberg reporter covering the Shkreli case had confessed to being in love with Mr. Shkreli. Christie Smythe, the reporter who broke the story of Mr. Shekreli's arrest, confessed to a federal judge in April 2020 that she had found both love and joy in Mr. Shkreli.[207]

The confession of the reporter, soulmate to "Pharma Boy," as he became known during the trial, was part of a federal district court filing that sought compassionate release of Mr. Shkreli from his seven-year fraud sentence. Ms. Smythe was offering to have Mr. Shkreli live with her in her Manhattan apartment.

Ms. Smythe divorced her husband, left Bloomberg, and remains confused about her ethical obligations of continuing to report on Mr. Shkreli, despite her feelings. That last issue is not a tough call. She was warned by her Bloomberg editors about her social media posts that included personal correspondence with Mr. Shkreli. However, she could not give him up, so she resigned. She explained to the federal judge, "In journalism school, they don't really tell you what to do when this comes up. . . . I hadn't had a romantic relationship with him at the time.

I hadn't slept with him. I cared about him. So it's messy. How do you deal with that?"[208]

Unfortunately, Mr. Shkreli stopped replying to her emails in the summer of 2020. Never trust hedge-fund traders who end up in jail for fraud. Dumping the reporters who cover them is not a big step. Ms. Smythe has not been able to sell a book about her romance but has sold the movie rights. She said, "I love him. I am here for him."[209] Not the stuff of a Hallmark movie, but enough for a good draw on a Netflix or HBO series.

When Mr. Shkreli's lawyer was asked about the romance he said, "Nothing about Martin or this case surprises me."

During his time in prison, Mr. Shkreli has been popular with the inmates. He is known as "Pharma Bro" or "A-hole" and has been helping fellow prisoners, including "D-Block" and "Krispy," with investment strategies.[210] Not eligible for parole until 2023, Mr. Shkreli has been able to maintain control of Phoenixus, the parent company for Turing, now renamed as Vyera.[211] His former confidant at Turing, Kevin Mulleady, along with other investors, staged a proxy battle to wrest control of Vyera from Mr. Shkreli. However, Mr. Shkreli is still able to vote his shares from prison, and his shares amount to 44% ownership in the company. And vote he did, winning a proxy battle from his jail cell in July 2021.[212] CEO and chairman Averill Powers was ousted by Mr. Shkreli, operating from jail via collect phone calls. Mr. Shkreli promised another shareholder the CEO position in exchange for his votes to oust Powers.

Technically, Mr. Shkreli forfeited his shares along with his other property, but the court has failed to sign over the shares, leaving Mr. Shkreli to vote them as he sees fit. The court did take care of the $2 million Wu-Tang Chan's

(continued)

[205]Jane Ridley, "Even 'Pharma Bro' Martin Shkreli's Lawyer Wanted to 'Punch Him in the Face," *New York Post*, September 29, 2021, https://nypost.com/2021/09/29/insiders-explain -why-pharma-bro-martin-shkreli-is-a-jerk/.
[206]*U.S. v. Shkreli*, 779 Fed. Appx. 38 (2nd Cir. 2019); *Shkreli v. U.S.*, 140 S.Ct. 538 (2019).
[207]Katie Robertson, "Reporter Who Covered 'Pharma Bro' Says She Fell for Him," *New York Times*, December 22, 2020, p. B3.

[208]*Id.*
[209]*Id.*
[210]Rob Copeland and Bradley Hope, "Shkreli, from Cell, Plots Comeback," *Wall Street Journal*, March 8, 2019, p. A1.
[211]Michael J. de la Merced, "A Move to Push 'Pharma Bro' Out of His Own Company," *New York Times*, July 10, 2021, p. B4.
[212]Lydia Moynihan, "'Pharma Bro' Martin Shkreli Wins Proxy Battle from Prison," *New York Post*, July 14, 2021, https://nypost. com/2021/07/14/pharma-bro-martin-shkreli-wins-proxy-battle -from-prison/.

Case 3.12

(continued)

album, "Once Upon a Time in Shaolin." It was sold for a sufficient markup to cover the remainder of the $7.7 million that Mr. Shkreli had to pay as part of his sentence.[213] Price increases appear to have helped Mr. Shkreli repay his debt to society. When asked if he could do anything over—for example, the Turing price increase—Mr. Shkreli replied, "I probably would have raised prices higher." [214]

Mr. Shkreli takes care of the prison cats and has arguments with his cellmates about grammar. Until the account was deleted, he was tweeting away, chastising Jack Dorsey, the now former CEO of Twitter, for apologizing for making billions. Mr. Shkreli calculates that Phoenixus could be worth $3.7 billion by the time he leaves prison. He read pharmaceutical research and now planned to acquire more drugs and develop new ones. Those plans are now in effect because on May 21, 2022, Mr. Shkreli was released from prison after serving nearly all of his sentence.[215]

The Pharma Industry Post-Shkreli

In 2021, there were 1,283 prescription drug price increases just through August.[216] Figure 3.8 provides a summary of the price increases that have fueled the public outcry on the costs of life-saving prescription drugs. In 2021, price increases ranged from $0.12 to $1,785.00 per dose.[217]

Figure 3.8 Price Increases in the Pharmaceutical Industry

Company	Drug	Date created	Original price	New price	% increase	Date of increase	Purpose of drug
Turing	Daraprim	1957	$13.50	$750.00	4,834%	2016	Treats toxoplasmosisv, a parasitic disease in patients with weakened immune systems (AIDS patients)
Mylan	EpiPen	2008	$57.00	$700.00	550%	2008–2016	Asthma treatment
Jaguar Health	Mytesi	2020	$688.52	$2,206.52	230%	2021	Anti-diarrhea treatment
Horizon Pharma	Duexis	2011	$18,287.00	$29,342,00	60%	2020	Pain relief
Pfizer	Lyrica	2004	$5,827.00	$8,562.00	47%	2020	Fibromyalgia treatment
Novo Nordisk	Victoza	2015	$7,936.00	$11,300.00	42%	2020	Diabetes medication
Bristol-Myers Squibb	Eliquis	2012	$4,109.00	$5,473.00	39%	2020	Atrial fibrillation

(continued)

[213]Jonah E. Bromwich, "U.S. Sells a Prized Album to Pay Off Shkreli's Debt," *New York Times*, July 28, 2021, p. B3.
[214]Jane Ridley, "Even 'Pharma Bro' Martin Shkreli's Lawyer Wanted to 'Punch Him in the Face," *New York Post*, September 29, 2021, https://nypost.com/2021/09/29/insiders-explain -why-pharma-bro-martin-shkreli-is-a-jerk/.

[215]Joseph De Avila, "'Pharma Bro' Shkreli Released From Prison," *Wall Street Journal*, May 19, 2022, p. B5.
[216]"Report: Prescription Drug Prices Continue to Rise Throughout 2021," *The Checkup*, August 5, 2021, https://www.singlecare. com/blog/prescription-drug-price-increases-july-2021/.
[217]Id.

Case 3.12

(continued)

Drug prices have risen in numbers but decreased in percentage amounts since the time of the Daraprim and Mylan increases. For example, in January 2020, pharmaceutical firms announced price increases in 639 drugs by an average of 6%. In January 2021, there were 722 drug price increases that ranged on an average of 4.5% for brand-name drugs and $2.7% for generic drugs.[218]

Controls on drug prices remained elusive for several years following the Shkreli/Turing outrage and events. But the activism kept the increases at much lower levels than when Turing began a trend. In 2022, congress passed and the president signed into law the Inflation Reduction Act. The law included several provisions related to prescription drugs. Medicare can now negotiate the prices of high-cost prescription drugs directly with pharmaceutical firms.

Those firms will pay tax penalties if the increase their drug prices by more than the government-determined rate of inflation. Those covered under Part D Medicare prescription drug plans now have a $2,000 cap on their out-of-pocket costs for their prescription drugs. The regulatory cycle on prescription drug pricing ended with price controls on the pharmaceutical industry.

Discussion Questions

1. Explain Mr. Shkreli's business model and approach to returns for investors.
2. Explain the economics of drug production and pricing.
3. Make a list of the costs to the business of Mr. Shkreli's approach to business profits.
4. Apply the Bathsheba Syndrome (Reading 2.5) to this case. List the factors you can find in Shkreli that are part of that syndrome. Is it possible to curb the behaviors of someone like Shkreli? Why can't proxy takeovers work in these situations?

---

[218]Marilyn Lewis, "Prepare to Pay More for These 31 Drugs in 2021," *MoneyTalksNews*, January 14, 2021, https://www.moneytalksnews.com/brace-to-pay-more-for-these-26-prescriptions-in-2020/.

Why Didn't They Say Something? 3.2

The Wild Boss

List the people who tried to stop Mr. Shkreli with his pricing and other behaviors. List the expressed frustrations of those closest to him. Are there some organizations in which speaking up is not possible? In those situations what are the options for those who are witnessing conduct that will hurt the organization?

Case 3.13

The Social, Political, Economic, and Emotional Issue of the Minimum Wage

The issue of a "living wage" or "minimum wage" is a topic that brings out strong feelings and is another example of a regulatory cycle issue. Presently, there are statutorily mandated minimum wages, voluntary increases by employers of their wage levels, and some employers caught in between. As Unit 2 provided, looking at the issue with full economic, social, and political information is critical for a business in processing its response to the emotional demands that fuel activism in the regulatory cycle.

A Historical and Current Study in Contrasting Approaches to Employee Compensation[219]

Amazon and Sears are a study in contrasts in terms of how business decisions, policies, and behaviors on compensation affect the lives of employees. Fifty years ago, a Sears salesman could retire from Sears with a retirement nest egg of over a million dollars.[220] The reason for the large retirement savings was that Sears gave employees an interest in the company. The company had an egalitarian approach to compensation. Sears matched employee contributions to their retirement plans. At the beginning, the match was dollar for dollar, but the longer an employee stayed with Sears, the greater the company's contribution.

For long-term employees, Sears was putting in $3 for every $1 the employee contributed.[221] The people who produced or sold Sears products were given top priority in terms of retention and compensation. Vacations were generous, and the pension plan held a diverse group of stocks that cushioned employees from the all-in-one-bucket risk of single-stock plans. One employee described his experience as a Sears appliance salesman, "It was like working in heaven."[222] The program began its curtailment in the 1970s, and the Sears story went downhill from there to its October 2018 bankruptcy.

Since the time of that share-the-wealth philosophy that distributed company gains to employees, a "winner take all" approach has landed. On October 2, 2018, Amazon announced its minimum wage increase to $15, a move that was lauded as a CSR thing to do.[223] The announcement was met with cheers and Amazon's YouTube video was viewed over 400,000 times. However, with that wage hike, Amazon stopped giving stock to employees. For longer-term employees, the result was a net loss.[224] The company also ended monthly attendance and productivity bonuses. The stock share bonuses (generally two per year) would be worth about $3,725 at today's prices. Amazon matches employee retirement contributions up to $680 per year. Sears' match figure was, in today's dollars, $2,744 per year.[225]

Once Amazon was alerted to the impact on employees of halting stock distributions, it appeared to have been caught flat-footed. The head of public policy at Amazon did not know how to respond to concerned employees and had not yet received information from Amazon. In a general statement, Amazon indicated that hourly wages were more "immediate and predictable." Amazon also pledged to adjust for employees who were negatively affected.

One company—Sears—developed a loyal and productive workforce. The other—Amazon—was not even aware of the impact of its decision on the compensation of its most valued and loyal employees. Which compensation practices benefited the business most and which benefited society the most?

The Data on Minimum Wage Mandates

Perhaps the lesson from the two contrasting studies of major companies and their treatment of employees is that one had a longer-term plan grounded in the strategic goals of retention of quality of employees. The other was responding to the CSR pressures of a societal movement for much higher minimum wages. The minimum wage is a CSR measurement put into place without considering the consequences, an issue that continues today beyond Sears and Amazon. When Seattle mandated a minimum wage of $13 per hour, inexperienced workers suffered. They spent less time on the clock because their

(continued)

[219]Adapted with permission from Marianne M. Jennings, "The Social Responsibility of Business Is Not Social Responsibility: Assume That There Are No Angels and Allow the Free Market's Touch of Heaven," 16 *Berkeley Business Law Journal* 325 (2019).

[220]The 1 million is reflected in today's dollars. Nelson D. Schwartz and Michael Corkery, "In Its Heyday, Sears Spread the Wealth. Companies Today Don't," *New York Times*, October 24, 2018, p. A1.

[221]*Id.*

[222]*Id.* at A17.

[223]Karen Weise, "Amazon Lauded for Raises, But Workers Are at a Loss," *New York Times*, October 10, 2018, p. B1.

[224]*Id.*, at B3. Employees shared their pay stubs with the *New York Times* reporter to prove their decline in compensation but refused to be identified for fear of retaliation.

[225]Schwartz and Corkery, *supra* note 439 at A17.

Case 3.13

(continued)

employers could not afford to pay them; many resorted to two jobs.[226] In response to the Seattle study, a University of California, Berkeley, study reached the opposite conclusion: minimum wage hikes do not cost jobs.[227]

The studies on minimum wage are all over the map, literally and figuratively. The differences are complex, but there are clearly issues among the studies that explain the different conclusions researchers have reached about positive versus negative effects of mandatory minimum wages—"living wage" in CSR lingo. Explanations include that no two labor markets are alike, franchise operations are different from mom-and-pop stores, there are differing labor markets, and there are various theories about equilibrium on wage pricing.[228] Additionally, the rapid implementation of statutory increases wreaks havoc on local economies (as opposed to the gradual increases over time).[229]

Anecdotal evidence abounds. Bank of America proudly ran a full-page ad in the national newspapers on May 18, 2021, announcing that it would require all of its vendors to pay their employees $15 per hour minimum wage and would increase its minimum wage for employees to $25 per hour by 2025.[230] However, at the same time, Bank of America was closing branches: during 2021, 10 of its 18 branches in the Buffalo area were closed. In many cases, branches are closed in poorer areas; residents there have only online banking options if they have

computer access.[231] With fewer branches and fewer employees, it is possible to pay remaining employees more, but customer service is more limited. Closures have resulted in what NPR referred to as "banking deserts," areas where residents have no access to a physical bank facility.[232] The stakeholders in the minimum wage debate are significant.

In making decisions about employee compensation, those running the business will respond to market forces, including both the forces of competition for qualified employees and the costs of turnover and training versus the costs of compensation that builds loyalty. One size does not fit all businesses, but all businesses can be held ultimately accountable to the market forces that set equilibrium.

The Walmart Wage Experience

Walmart obtained approval after a long regulatory battle to build five stores in the Washington, D.C., area. After the company had obtained the approvals, Washington, D.C., approved a ballot measure and a city council proposal to increase the minimum wage from $11.50 to $15 per hour. Walmart told the city council it could not make two of the stores profitable with that wage level, and the plans for the stores were nixed.[233]

Walmart had already announced a plan for increasing the wages of its employees. In late 2015, the company announced that it would increase its minimum wage to $10 per hour. On December 31, the company boosted wages 2% for its 1.2 million employees at both its Walmart and Sam's Club stores.[234] The total cost of the wage boost was $2.7 billion over 2016 to 2017. When Walmart announced its minimum wage increase, there were objections from current employees who had begun their employment at $9 per hour and would be making the

(continued)

[226]University of Washington, The Minimum Wage Study, https://evans.uw.edu/sites/default/files/MWS%20overview_final.pdf.
[227]Jacqueline Sullivan, "New Study: High Minimum Wages in Six Cities, Big Impact on Pay, No Employment Losses" *Institute for Research on Labor and Employment*, September 6, 2018, http://irle.berkeley.edu/high-minimum-wages-in-six-cities/. Accessed December 4, 2018.
[228]Dee Gill, "Why It's So Hard to Study the Impact of Minimum Wage Increases," *Quartz at Work*, October 5, 2018, https://www.washingtonpost.com/news/wonk/wp/2018/02/05/raising-the-minimum-wage-doesnt-cost-jobs-multiple-studies-suggest/?utm_term=.b44b21a9c63d.
[229]Christopher Ingraham, "The Effects of 137 Minimum Wage Hikes in One Chart," *Washington Post*, February 5, 2018, https://www.washingtonpost.com/news/wonk/wp/2018/02/05/raising-the-minimum-wage-doesnt-cost-jobs-multiple-studies-suggest/.
[230]"Bank of America Increases US Minimum Hourly Wage to $25 by 2025," *Bank of America Newsroom*, May 18, 2021, https://newsroom.bankofamerica.com/content/newsroom/press-releases/2021/05/bank-of-america-increases-us-minimum-hourly-wage-to-25-by-2025.html.

[231]Hugo Dante, Veronica Carrion, and Tyler Mondres, "The Real Story on Bank Closures," *ABA Banking Journal*, April 6, 2021, https://bankingjournal.aba.com/2021/04/the-real-story-on-bank-branch-closures/.
[232]Scott Horsley, "'What Are We Going to Do?'" *NPR*, March 26, 2021, https://www.npr.org/2021/03/26/979284513/what-are-we-going-to-do-towns-reel-as-banks-close-branches-at-record-pace.
[233]Holman Jenkins, "Bad Days for Wal-Mart Americans," *Wall Street Journal*, January 20, 2016, p. A11.
[234]Sarah Nassauer, "Wal-Mart Broadens Pay Increase," *Wall Street Journal*, January 21, 2016, p. B1.

Case 3.13

(continued)

same amount as new hires. The result was the decision to raise the wages of those already working by 2%. Walmart usually gives employees a 2% raise on the anniversary of their hiring date. Awarding the 2% on December 31 expedited the raise for most employees.

When announcing the wage increases, Walmart also revealed that it would be closing 154 stores in the United States and 115 internationally. Walmart shares experienced the biggest drop in price in a single day in 17 years. Because of investor skittishness, Douglas McMillon, Walmart's then CEO, issued the following statement: "The reaction by the market—while not what we'd hoped—was not entirely surprising. Those investments [wage increases] are critical to our current and future success as a company. Simply put, it's the right thing to do."[235] Walmart indicated that growth in sales was slowing and that these stores were not profitable. In addition, Walmart had several quarters of reduced profits and reduced its sales forecasts for 2016.[236] The company's share price fell 3% during this time.

Walmart's competitors were slightly behind on pay increases. For example, Target's minimum wage was below $10 per hour when Walmart made its increase announcement. According to government data, the average national wage at that time was $14.95 per hour.[237]

Cities and states, such as California and New York, during this time, began passing state minimum wage laws that have brought the minimum wage to $15 per hour. When Seattle raised its minimum wage, it experienced a wave of restaurant closures. With California's passage of its new minimum wage, fast-food retailers announced their expansion into automated service technology, something that would reduce the number of employees needed at fast-food sites.

Subsequent Wages Increases

In 2018, Walmart raised its wages to $11 per hour but also announced that it would be cutting 10,000 jobs by closing 10% of its U.S. Sam's Club stores.[238] At that time, Costco was paying its employees $14.11 per hour and Target's hourly wage was $9.89.

2018 ushered in new forms of employee compensation. Following changes in U.S. tax law that reduced corporate income taxes, many companies announced bonuses for employees. Walmart added a $1,000 bonus to its wage increase for 2018. Fiat Chrysler paid its 60,000 U.S. salaried employees a $2,000 bonus.[239]

In 2019, Walmart began a program to help its employees attend college. An employee survey had indicated that most Walmart employees wanted to pursue some form of additional education. Walmart worked with three universities to set up degree programs in computer science and cybersecurity as well as other fields that associates could enter for the cost of $1 per day. Employees in high school were given the opportunity to set up their work schedules up to 13 weeks in advance so they could finish their high-school coursework; Walmart also offered to pay for the time demands and costs for ACT and SAT prep courses.[240]

As of January 2022, Walmart's minimum starting wage is $12, a hike of $1 for 550,000 employees. Its average wage has increased to $16.40 per hour. However, Walmart has ended its quarterly bonus program, explaining that employees indicated that known, regular pay was most important to them.[241]

Discussion Questions

1. Explain which stakeholders are involved in minimum wage decisions.

2. Discuss the effects of an increase in the minimum wage.

3. What is the purpose of the minimum wage law?

4. Discuss government's role in structuring wage markets. What effect do government unemployment benefits have on wages?

5. Review Walmart's pay structure issue and determine what its goals are with its workforce. Describe the trade-offs being made as wages increase. Do all employers make economic trade-offs as they increase wages?

[235]Julie Creswell and Hiroko Tabuchi, "Walmart Chief Defends Investments in Labor, Stores and the Web," *New York Times*, October 19, 2015, p. B1.
[236]Sarah Nassauer and Chelsey Delaney, "Wal-Mart Comeback Slips," *Wall Street Journal*, February 19, 2016, p. B1.
[237]Associated Press, "Walmart to Give Pay Raises Next Month," *New York Times*, January 21, 2016, p. B9.
[238]Sarah Nassauer, "Wal-Mart Boosts Wages After Tax Overhaul," *Wall Street Journal*, January 12, 2018, p. A1.

[239]Id.
[240]Charisse Jones, "Walmart Helps More Workers Attend College," *USA Today*, June 5, 2019, p. 2B.
[241]Sarah Nassauer, "Walmart to End Quarterly Bonuses," *Wall Street Journal*, September 9, 2021, https://www.wsj.com/articles/walmart-to-end-quarterly-bonuses-for-store-workers-11631190896?st=ws872k4zzeakbbi&reflink=desktopwebshare_twitter.

Case 3.14

Ice-T, the *Body Count* Album, and Shareholder Uprisings

Ice-T (Tracy Morrow), a Black rap artist signed under the Time Warner label, released an album called *Body Count* in 1992 that contained a controversial song, "Cop Killer." The lyrics included, "I've got my twelve-gauge sawed-off. . . . I'm 'bout to dust some cops off. . . . Die, pig, die."

The song set off a storm of protest from law enforcement groups. At the annual meeting of Time Warner at the Beverly Wilshire Hotel, 1,100 shareholders as well as police representatives and their spokesman, Charlton Heston, denounced Time Warner executives in a five-hour session on the album and its content. Heston noted that the compact disc had been shipped to radio stations in small replicas of body bags. One police officer said the company had "lost its moral compass, or never had it." Others said that Time Warner seemed to cultivate these types of artists. One shareholder claimed that Time Warner was always "pushing the envelope" with its artists, such as Madonna with her *Sex* book and its products, and such as the film *The Last Temptation of Christ,* which drew large protests from religious groups. Another shareholder pointed out that Gerald Levin, then–Time Warner president, promised a stuttering-awareness group that cartoon character Porky Pig would be changed after that group made far fewer vocal protests than the number of protests from religious groups.

Levin responded that the album would not be pulled. He defended it as "depicting the despair and anger that hang in the air of every American inner city, not advocating attacks on police." Levin announced that Time Warner would sponsor a TV forum for artists, law enforcement officials, and others to discuss such topics as racism and free speech. At the meeting, Levin also announced a four-for-one stock split and a 12% increase in Time Warner's dividend.

The protests continued after the annual meeting. Philadelphia's municipal pension fund decided to sell $1.6 million in Time Warner holdings to protest the Ice-T song. Said Louis J. Campione, a police officer and member of the city's Board of Pensions and Retirement, "It's fine that somebody would express their opinions, but we don't have to support it."

Several CEOs responded to Levin's and Time Warner's support of the song.[242] Roger Salquist, then-

CEO of Calgene, Inc., who went on to be a controversial technology liaison at UC Davis, noted,

> I'm outraged. I think the concept of free speech has been perverted. It's anti-American, it's anti-humanity, and there is no excuse for it.

> I hope it kills them. It's certainly not something I tolerate, and I find their behavior offensive as a corporation.

> If you can increase sales with controversy without harming people, that's one thing. [But Time Warner's decision to support Ice-T] is outside the bounds of what I consider acceptable behavior and decency in this country.

David Geffen, chairman of Geffen Records (who was a founding co-owner with Steven Spielberg and Jeffrey Katzenberg of film production company DreamWorks), who had refused to release Geto Boys records because of their lyrics, said,

> The question is not about business, it is about responsibility. Should someone make money by advocating the murder of policemen? To say that this whole issue is not about profit is silly. It certainly is not about artistic freedom.

> If the album were about language, sex, or drugs, there are people on both sides of these issues. But when it comes down to murder, I don't think there is any part of society that approves of it. . . . I wish [Time Warner] would show some sensitivity by donating the profits to a fund for wounded policemen.

Jerry Greenfield, cofounder of Ben & Jerry's Homemade, Inc., responded that "songs like 'Cop Killer' aren't constructive, but we as a society need to look at what we've created. I don't condone cop killing. [But] to reach a more just and equitable society everyone's voice must be heard."

Neal Fox, then-CEO of A. Sulka & Company (an apparel retailer owned by Luxco Investments), said,

> As a businessperson, my inclination is to say that Time Warner management has to be consistent. Once you've decided to get behind this product and support it, you can't express feelings of censorship. They didn't have recourse.

> Also, they are defending flag and country for the industry. If they bend to pressures regarding the material, it opens a Pandora's box for all creative work being done in the entertainment industry.

(continued)

[242]*Wall Street Journal,* Eastern ed. (Staff-Produced Copy Only) by Wall Street Journal News Round Up. Copyright 1992 by Dow Jones & Co. Inc. Reproduced with permission of Dow Jones & Co. Inc. in the format textbook via Copyright Clearance Center.

Case 3.14

(continued)

On a personal basis, I abhor the concept, but on a corporate basis, I understand their reasoning.

John W. Hatsopoulos, then–executive vice president of Thermo Electron Corporation (who then became president and CEO), had this to say:

I think the fact that a major U.S. corporation would almost encourage kids to attack the police force is horrible. Time Warner is a huge corporation. That they would encourage something like this for a few bucks.... You know about yelling fire in a crowded theater.

I was so upset I was looking at [Thermo Electron's] pension plan to see if we owned any Time Warner stock [in order to sell it]. But we don't own any.

Bud Konheim, longstanding CEO of Nicole Miller, Ltd., weighed in with the following:

I don't think that people in the media can say that advertising influences consumers to buy cars or shirts, and then argue that violence on television or in music has no impact. The idea of media is to influence people's minds, and if you are inciting people to riot, it's very dangerous.

It's also disappointing that they chose to defend themselves. It was a knee-jerk reaction instead of seizing the role to assert moral leadership. They had a great opportunity. Unfortunately, I don't think they will pay for this decision because there is already so much dust in people's eyes.

George Sanborn, then-CEO of Sanborn, Inc., said, "Would you release the album if it said, 'Kill a Jew or bash a fag'? I think we all know what the answer would be. They're doing it to make money."

Marc B. Nathanson, CEO of Falcon Cable Systems Company and a member of the board of directors for the Hollywood Bowl, responded, "If you aren't happy with the product, you don't have to buy it. I might not like what [someone like Ice-T] has to say, but I would vigorously defend his right to express his viewpoint."

Stoney M. Stubbs Jr., chairman of Frozen Food Express Industries, Inc., commented, "The more attention these types of things get, the better the products sell. I don't particularly approve of the way they play on people's emotions, but from a business standpoint [Time Warner is] probably going to make some money off it. They're

protecting the people that make them the money . . . the artists."[243]

Despite the flap over the album, sales were less than spectacular. It reached number 32 on the Billboard Top 200 album chart and sold 300,000 copies.[244]

Levin had defended Time Warner's position:

In the short run, cutting and running would be the surest way to put this controversy behind us. But, in the long run, it would be a destructive precedent. It would signal to all the artists and journalists that if they wish to be heard, then they must tailor their minds and souls to fit reigning orthodoxies.

Time Warner went on to make a pledge to use the controversy to create a forum for discussion of the issues in order to deal with the tensions that Ice-T's song caused to surface. Time Warner also pledged to continue its commitment to truth and free expression for the sake of the country's future.[245]

By August 1992, protests against the song had grown and sales suffered. Ice-T made the decision himself to withdraw "Cop Killer" from the *Body Count* album. Time Warner asked music stores to exchange the *Body Count* CDs for ones without "Cop Killer." Some store owners refused, saying there were much worse records. Former Geto Boys member Willie D said Ice-T's free speech rights were violated. "We're living in a communist country and everyone's afraid to say it."

Following the flap over the song, the Time Warner board met to establish general company policies to bar distribution of music deemed inappropriate. By February 1993, Time Warner and Ice-T agreed that the rapper would leave the Time Warner label because of "creative differences." The split came after Time Warner executives objected to Ice-T's proposed cover for his new album, which showed black men attacking whites. In an ironic twist, Ice-T became a co-star on the NBC television series *Law and Order: Special Victims*

(continued)

[243]"Time Warner's Ice-T Defense Is Assailed," *Wall Street Journal*, July 23, 1992, pp. B1, B8.
[244]Mark Landler, "Time Warner Seeks a Delicate Balance in Rap Music Furor," *New York Times*, June 5, 1995, p. 1B.
[245]Wall Street Journal, Eastern ed. (Staff-Produced Copy Only) by Holman W. Jenkins, Jr. Copyright 1996 by Dow Jones & Co. Inc. Reproduced with permission of Dow Jones & Co. Inc. in the format textbook via Copyright Clearance Center.

Case 3.14

(continued)

Unit as Detective Odafin "Fin" Tutuola, partner of Richard Belzer's character, Detective John Munch.[246]

In 2004, Ice-T introduced his own line of clothing, a trend among rap music stars. He had been on a six-year hiatus from music because of the death of two of his group members. The drummer, Beatmaster V, died of leukemia, and Mooseman, the bass player, was killed in South Central Los Angeles. Ice-T commented that Mooseman's death was the kind of thing "I rap about every day."[247] The album that followed *Body Count—Violent Demise, Last Days*—was barely heard and rarely sold. Living in New Jersey, the man credited with founding gangsta rap prepared for a *Body Count II* album, and has offered the following perspective on the first *Body Count* album and where the country is now:

> I wasn't trying to start all that drama with that *[Body Count]* album. On the song "Cop Killer" I was just being honest. I never really reached for controversy. I just said what was on my mind, like I'm saying now.[248] With Clinton in the White House, everybody became very complacent, everybody kicked back. He had sex in the White House, what's there to worry about? But now we got Bush—or son of a Bush—in there, and he's out to control the world. He's trying to be Julius Caesar and so it's time for more music about things. It's time for *Body Count II*.

Ice-T eventually moved into the mainstream. He has appeared in an ad for Geico insurance, sitting on a lawn with children who are running a lemonade stand. Fans who recognize him shout out, "Ice-T!" And he responds, "No, man! Lemonade!" The ad was well received and effective.

The Time Warner Shift

Following the Ice-T issue, Time Warner's board undertook a strategy of steering the company into more family-oriented entertainment. It began its transition with the 1993 release of such movies as *Dennis the Menace, Free Willy*, and *The Secret Garden*.

However, Time Warner's reputation would continue to be a social and political lightning rod. In June 1995, presidential candidate Senator Robert Dole pointed to Time Warner's rap albums and movies as societal problems. Public outcry against Time Warner resulted.

In June 1995, C. DeLores Tucker, then 67 years old and head of the National Political Congress of Black Women, handed Time Warner Chairman Michael J. Fuchs some explicit lyrics about rape and murder from a Time Warner label recording of "Mind of a Lunatic" by Geto Boys. Tucker told Mr. Fuchs, "Read this out loud. I'll give you $100 to read it." Fuchs declined.

Mrs. Tucker was joined by William Bennett, a GOP activist and former secretary of education. Mrs. Tucker believes Time Warner is "pimping pornography to children for the almighty dollar. Corporations need to understand: What does it profit a corporation to gain the world but lose its soul? That's the real bottom line."

In June 1995, following Mrs. Tucker's national campaign, Time Warner fired Doug Morris, the chairman of domestic music operations. By July, Morris and Time Warner were in litigation. Morris had been a defender of gangsta rap music and had acquired the Interscope label that produced albums for the late Tupac Shakur and Snoop Doggy Dogg. Mr. Fuchs said the termination had nothing to do with the rap controversy.

Rap music grew in popularity for about 12 years, but from 2005 to 2006 dropped 21% in sales. In 2006, no rap album made it into the top 10 albums for the year. Rap is back to its level of a decade ago, which is about 10% of total sales in the record industry. About 50% of Americans believe that rap/hip-hop is a negative influence in society. Some retail chains, including Walmart, have refused even during the upswing in popularity of rap/hip-hop to carry gangsta rap albums, and some radio stations have declined to play the songs. The songs cited included the following:

> I'd rather use my gun 'cause I get the money quicker . . . got them in the frame—Bang! Bang! . . . blowing [expletive] to the moon.[249]
>
> **—Tupac Shakur, "Strugglin'"**

These lyrics contain slang expressions for using an AK-47 machine gun to murder a police officer:

> It's 1-8-7 on a [expletive] cop . . . so what the [expletive] does a nigger like you gotta say? Got to take trip to the MIA and serve your ass with a [expletive] AK.[250]
>
> **—Snoop Doggy Dogg, "Tha' Shiznit"**

(continued)

---

[246]http://www.nbc.com/lawandorder. (accessed July 12, 2010).
[247]http://www.vh1.com/artists/news/1459713/01272003/ice_t.jhtml.
[248]*Id.*

[249]http://www.azlyrics.com/lyrics/2pac/strugglin.html.
[250]http://rapgenius.com/Snoop-dogg-tha-shiznit-lyrics#note-234016.

Case 3.14

(continued)

Discussion Questions

1. Was Ice-T's song an exercise of artistic freedom or sensationalism for profit?

2. Would you have taken Levin's position?

3. Evaluate the First Amendment argument.

4. Would shareholder objections influence your response to such a controversy?

5. What was Time Warner's purpose in firing Morris? By November 1995, Time Warner's Levin had fired Michael Fuchs. What message is there for executives in controversial products?

6. Offer your thoughts on Ice-T's role on television as a police officer and his acceptance by the public.

Case 3.15

Cancel Culture

The Ice-T story, Case 3.14, took place over a quarter of a century ago but was the beginning of behaviors and responses that would become known as "cancel culture." With the power of social media, those who object to music, art, films, artists, actors, comedians, individuals, political beliefs, statues, monuments, and television shows can make their views widely known. The result is that jobs are lost and films, writing, photos, and television shows are censored through the power of a media mob. Censorship is accomplished not by government mandate but through the voices of protest heard through social media. Following are examples of how cancel culture has evolved and become a powerful and often destructive means of censorship.

Lil Wayne and the Rolling Stones

Rapper Lil Wayne used lyrics from the Rolling Stones' 1965 song "Play with Fire" in his "Playing with Fire" song that was part of his *The Carter III* CD. Abkco Music filed an infringement suit against Lil Wayne for using the lyrics after it had denied him permission. Abkco was going to grant permission to Lil Wayne until it read all the song's lyrics, described as "explicit, sexist, and offensive." The suit was settled in an interesting manner. Abkco, under the terms of the settlement, required Lil Wayne to remove the song from the CD and from iTunes. The Rolling Stones didn't want the money—they didn't want to be associated with Lil Wayne.

Are the Rolling Stones controlling artistic expression? Is this the same right exercised by Time Warner, but the other way? Is it artists stopping other artists? Is it artists stopping companies?[251] Is this cancel culture or just the Rolling Stones controlling the use of their intellectual property?

Reebok and Rick Ross, a Celebrity Endorser

Reebok had contracted with Rick Ross, Swizz Beatz, and Tyga to make marketing inroads into the urban and hip-hop fan markets. The marketing strategy can be effective unless the star who is endorsing the product has a misstep that causes public outcry.

Mr. Ross released a new song and video called "U.O.E.N.O," a song that includes the following lyrics:

> Put Molly all in her Champagne, she ain't even know it
>
> I took her home and I enjoyed that, she ain't even know it.[252]

After the song was released, a new women's rights group, UltraViolet, began a Twitter, YouTube, and phone campaign to Reebok headquarters in Massachusetts to have Mr. Ross removed as a Reebok spokesperson because of his insensitivity to women and the issue of rape following the use of drugs or alcohol.

Mr. Ross gave several interviews and issued apologies on Twitter, but Reebok terminated his endorsement contract because, as the company explained in a statement, "While we do not believe that Rick Ross condones sexual assault, we are very disappointed he has yet to display an understanding of the seriousness of this issue or an appropriate level of remorse. At this time it is in everybody's best interest for Reebok to end its partnership with Mr. Ross."[253]

(continued)

---

[251]For more information, see Ethan Smith, "Rapper to Pull Song in Copyright Fight," *Wall Street Journal*, January 30, 2009, p. B8.
[252]http://rapgenius.com/Rocko-uoeno-lyrics.
[253]Tanzina Vega and James C. McKinley Jr., "Social Media, Pushing Reebok to Drop a Rapper," *New York Times*, April 13, 2013, p. C1.

Case 3.15

(continued)

The endorsement contract, like others involving celebrities who become embroiled in public controversies or questionable conduct (Kate Moss, Michael Phelps, Tiger Woods, Lance Armstrong), contains a "morals clause." These types of clauses vary significantly but provide the company with the opportunity to end the contract (without damages being paid) if the celebrity's conduct results in public backlash. The conduct could be a crime (indictment, charges, investigation, and/or conviction), a controversial statement, or, as in this case, the nature or content of a celebrity's performance.

Experts note that one of the distinctions of this particular termination of a celebrity contract is its speed. UltraViolet was very effective in using social media to gain traction for its concerns. The Tweets and YouTube video resulted in physical petitions that were delivered to the company. Another result of the intense and active social media campaign was demonstrations outside Reebok headquarters, which then resulted in national and international coverage and the company's rapid decision to end its relationship with the rapper. Mr. Ross had issued an apology, "I don't condone rape. Apologies for the #lyric interpreted as rape." Based on negative feedback, Mr. Ross followed up with yet another Tweet: "Apologies to my many business partners, who would never promote violence against women." That note specifically mentioned Reebok and UltraViolet, but the words chosen were not enough to reflect an understanding of the issue to those who were protesting.

In 2017, Disney Company's Maker Studio, a network of online video creators, and Google's YouTube had to cut their business ties with Felix Kjellberg, aka PewDiePie— who had 53 million subscribers—because of crude anti-Semitic jokes and references to Hitler in his videos. Nissan, who had paid PewDiePie for a promotional video, announced that it would not work with him again.

Celebrity endorsements do garner customer attention but are not without risk. Carefully drafted contracts, however, provide companies with the legal protection they need when the conduct of celebrity sponsors harms the brand.

What kinds of conduct would you cover in a morals clause if you were hiring a celebrity to endorse your product? Would you have guidelines on the types of celebrities you would use for your product endorsements? Who are the stakeholders in product endorsement contracts? Does the use of social media influence a company's decision to end a relationship with a celebrity?

Dave Chappelle and "The Closer"

Dave Chappelle, a cutting-edge and controversial comedian, filmed a comedy special for Netflix. Two Netflix employees were offended by some of the content of Mr. Chappelle's act that focused on the "trans community" and the "very validity of transness." They asked that Netflix place a disclaimer on transphobic content on the Chappelle program. They did not ask that the Chappelle special be pulled from the Netflix platform.

Ted Sarandos, the CEO of Netflix, has stood by the program and noted that he supported Mr. Chappelle's "artistic freedom." He said that what Mr. Chappelle discusses in the video is not hate speech, which he defines as "something that would intentionally call for physically harming other people or even remove protections. For me, intent to cause physical harm cross[es] the line, for sure."[254]

The two Netflix employees filed a complaint with the National Labor Relations Board that alleged Netflix quelled employees from speaking up.[255] One was suspended for attending an online meeting of senior Netflix executives without authorization. She was reinstated quickly after the suspension. The other was fired for leaking Netflix financial information, including details on the cost of production of "The Closer." However, the suspended employee left Netflix after she and the other employee resolved the issues raised in their labor complaint. Their lawyer described the resolution as one that included discussion of their concerns in "a thoughtful and meaningful way."[256]

Discussion Questions

1. What is different about this situation from the others?
2. What is the same? What lessons could managers learn from how this situation was handled?
3. Evaluate the employee's decision to release confidential Netflix documents. Which ethical category does that action fall under?
4. Is it acceptable to commit an ethical breach to accomplish a social goal?
5. Would Time Warner have made the same decision in this case as it did with Ice-T? Why or why not?

(continued)

---

[254]Helena Andrews Dyer, "Dave Chappelle's Controversial Comedy Special Is a Catalyst for Change as Netflix Walkout Leads to Calls for Reform," *Washington Post*, October 20, 2021, https://www.adn.com/arts/film-tv/2021/10/20/dave-chappelles-controversial-comedy-special-is-a-catalyst-for-change-as-netflix-walkout-leads-to-calls-for-reform/.
[255]Omar Ardel-Baque, "Chappelle Critic Leaves Netflix," *Wall Street Journal*, November 24, 2021, p. B5.
[256]Id.

Case 3.15

(continued)

Nancy Pelosi in the Beauty Salon Without a Mask

The speaker of the U.S. House of Representatives, Nancy Pelosi, was captured on video in a San Francisco beauty salon having her hair done at a time when beauty salons were on lockdown and had not been open in nearly a year. Masks were also required both indoors and outdoors in California at the time.

Video of the speaker's visit was captured on the salon's camera and went viral. Mrs. Pelosi said that she was the victim of a "setup." Erica Kious, the salon owner, denied the "setup" claim and said that she was traveling at the time. She did not know about the appointment because she rents chairs to stylists and they book their own appointments. She later reviewed security camera footage from her shop and discovered the images of Mrs. Pelosi and disclosed them publicly.

Ms. Kious said at that time that she began receiving threats.[257] "I started to just get a ton of phone calls, text messages, emails, all my Yelp reviews . . . saying that they hope I go under and that I fail."[258] A year after the incident, Ms. Kious said that she had lost her business: "I thought if I ever lost my business, I would have lost it in an earthquake. Never did I ever think that I would have lost everything I worked for [because of] . . . leftist politics. Gone."[259]

6. Explain the distinction between this situation and the artistic freedom cases. Should someone lose their business for sharing footage of a customer?

7. Were there ethical lapses in this situation? By whom? What were those lapses?

8. Explain the risk of cancelling businesses because of political views.

9. Explain the risks of business owners being involved in political issues.

---

[257]Caitlin O'Kane, "Salon Owner Responds to Nancy Pelosi's 'Setup' Claim After Video of Her Salon Visit Surfaces," *CBS News*, September 4, 2020, https://www.cbsnews.com/news/nancy-pelosi-salon-setup-video-owner-responds/.

[258]David Aaro, "San Francisco Salon Owner Who Exposed Pelosi Talks About Losing Her Business a Year Later," *Fox News*, https://www.foxnews.com/politics/san-francisco-salon-owner-exposed-pelosi-losing-business-year.
[259]Id.

Case 3.16

Ashley Madison: The Affair Website

Ashleymadison.com is known as an "infidelity website" with a motto, "When monogamy becomes monotony." The site, owned by Avid Dating Life, Inc., now Ruby Corporation, once had as its motto, "Life is short. Have an affair." Its mottos, past and present, give a clear insight into its purpose: to allow people who want to have an affair to meet and proceed with that affair. However, the site has its issues and stakeholders.

For example, on July 15, 2015, Ashley Madison suffered a data breach that resulted in the leak of personal information about site users, including government officials (1,405 in the United States), employees (311 from IBM) celebrities, college students (Cornell had the top number at 273), clergymen, military (6,700 from the army and 1,600 from the navy), and quite a few fake female clients.[260] The site was hacked by the Impact Group, a vigilante group that seeks to shut certain sites down because "they profit off the pain of others."[261] The hackers initially released a few names obtained from the site with a demand that the site be shut down. When that demand was not met, the hackers released the names of 32 million more site users. After the breach, Ashley Madison's CEO, Noel Biderman, stepped down.

A class-action lawsuit by Ashley Madison users who had had their identities revealed or private information

(continued)

---

[260]Nicole Perlroth, "Ashley Madison Chief Steps Down after Data Breach," *New York Times*, August 28, 2015, p. B1. About 34% of the accounts on Ashley Madison are fake.

[261]Eric Basu, "Cybersecurity Lessons Learned from the Ashley Madison Hack," *Forbes*, October 26, 2015, http://www.forbes.com/sites/ericbasu/2015/10/26/cybersecurity-lessons-learned-from-the-ashley-madison-hack/#29026540ed99. Accessed April 20, 2016.

Case 3.16

(continued)

compromised was settled for $11.2 million, distributed among the 37 million users.[262]

The settlement seems small, given the magnitude of harm to the lives of so many. But one of the obstacles that the suit faced was that the plaintiffs bringing the suit did not want to disclose their true identities. The court held that they would be required to reveal their identities in order to file suit.

Apart from the data breach issues are the connections made via the site. Robert Schindler filed suit against the site and its parent company for alienation of affection because his wife, Teresa Moore, found Eleazar "Chay" Montemayor, a married professor of civil engineering, on the site and the two had an affair. The affair resulted in the breakup of Schindler and Moore's 13-year marriage. (Moore and Montemayor are now married.[263])

The suit was brought in North Carolina, one of the few remaining states that permit recovery for alienation of affection. The twist in the case is that the suit asks for third-party liability for the alienation of affection. That is, Schindler does not seek recovery from Montemayor; he seeks recovery from the company that he says facilitated the affair. Noel Biderman, the attorney and sports agent turned CEO of Ashley Madison who created the site, says that what he set up through his company is no different from what telephone companies and hotels do, which is facilitate affairs. However, Schindler's lawyer has argued that hotels and telephones have different purposes in society. Ashley Madison has only one *raison d'etre*, which is to facilitate affairs. It serves no other purpose.

The concept of vicarious liability has been applied in Internet cases, such as when YouTube had to take down videos that infringed copyrights once it became aware of the ownership and the damage that would result. In an earlier technological era (2001), Napster was shut down because its sole purpose was to enable users to download copyrighted music from the Internet for free. However, the Ashley Madison case is unique in that the site facilitated the contact but not the affair itself.

In July 2016, the FTC announced an investigation into Ashley Madison's business practices, alleging that the site was misrepresenting the backgrounds and file information on individuals listed on the site. The FTC did fine a similar British site, JDI Dating, after its investigation found that the company was creating fake profiles. The FTC also investigated JDI for its use of "fembots," or fake female profiles. JDI settled with the FTC by agreeing to stop using fembots and pay refunds of $616,165 to JDI users who had been deceived. In December 2016, Ashley Madison settled with the FTC for the data breach, agreeing to pay a fine of $17.5 million and implement a data-security program that is reviewed by third parties for adequate protection.[264]

Discussion Questions

1. The Ashley Madison website does not violate the law, so why do we worry about the site?

2. List the stakeholders affected by the business that Ashley Madison is running.

3. What other consequences do you see from the site's operations and for whom?

[262]*In re Ashley Madison Customer Data Security Breach Litigation,* 2016 WL 1366616 (E.D. Missouri 2016); Jonathan Stempel, "Ashley Madison Parent in $11.2 Million Settlement over Data Breach," *Reuters,* July 14, 2017, https://www.reuters.com/article/us -ashleymadison-settlement/ashley-madison-parent-in-11 -2-million-settlement-over-data-breach-idUSKBN19Z2F0.
[263]Snejana Farberov, "Jilted Husband Sues Online Infidelity Service Ashley Madison for Breaking Up His Marriage After His Wife's Affair," *The Globe,* December 13, 2013.

[264]"Operators of AshleyMadison.com Settle FTC, State Charges Resulting from 2015 Data Breach That Exposed 36 Million Users' Profile Information," December 14, 2016, https://www.ftc.gov /news-events/press-releases/2016/12/operators -ashleymadisoncom-settle-ftc-state-charges-resulting.

Why Didn't They Say Something? 3.3

When a Friend Is Using Ashley Madison

What if you knew that a married friend was using the Ashley Madison website to meet women? Suppose that your friend's wife is also your friend. Would you say something? Should you say something? Is there an ethical category that applies to this situation?

Section

C

Social Responsibility and Sustainability

Case 3.17

Biofuels and Food Shortages in Guatemala

Biofuels were developed as an alternative to the use of oil and the dangers of its carbon footprint. Biofuels are made from corn, and the production of cars that run on biofuels has been mandated in Europe and the United States. However, there has been an unanticipated effect. The demand for corn has driven corn prices higher, particularly in poorer nations. For example, in Guatemala, the price of eight tortillas was one quetzal (about 15 cents USD) in 2010. Today, one quetzal will buy just three tortillas. The price of eggs has tripled because chickens feed on corn, and the cost of the feed is passed along in the price of eggs.

More than prices are affected. Individual farmers are unable to grow crops because large farmers have taken over the land. Individual farmers can be found planting crops on medians in the highways because, as they explain, "There is no other land, and I have to feed my family."[265] The same farmer's children, ages four and six, appear to be victims of chronic malnutrition. *Scientific American* has documented the problem in their slide presentation, "Biofuels Land Grab: Guatemala's Farmers Lose Plots and Prosperity to 'Energy Independence.'"[266] Protestors in Guatemala carry banners that read, "Don't gamble with our food."[267]

The same shortages of land and spike in food prices can be found in Asia, Africa, and Latin America. Guatemala's experience is worse because, as one expert notes, the small Central American country has been hit from demands for biofuels from both sides of the Atlantic—the United States and Europe.

Meanwhile, the renewable fuel standard in the United States requires increasing volumes of biofuel per year; Europe has met its 2020 mandate of using 10% biofuels.[268] Scientists have been raising questions about the sustainability of the continued use of certain countries as their resource for biofuels. With increasing goals on the percentage use of ethanol and other biofuels, the demand for the plant bases used for those biofuels is increasing. The corn demand in Guatemala has resulted in 60,000 jobs, but the large number of poor are not beneficiaries of the jobs, and the result is increasing poverty. Even before the biofuel demands on corn crops, the poor were spending two-thirds of their income on food. With the spike in prices, their food budgets are now consuming all of their income. Pantaleon Sugar Holdings, Guatemala's largest sugar producer, has experienced annual sales growth of 30%. Labor unions in Guatemala have been appealing to European politicians regarding their biofuel standards because of the resulting increase in world hunger.

One of the great ironies of the biofuel movement and its impact on Guatemala's food supply is that as of 2021, Guatemala has no ethanol and gasoline blends available for sale or distribution within its own borders.[269] Guatemala has no biofuel market. Guatemala is an exporter of ethanol

(continued)

[265]Elisabeth Rosenthal, "As Biofuel Demand Grows, So Do Guatemala's Hunger Pangs," *New York Times*, January 6, 2013, p. A6.
[266]http://www.scientificamerican.com/slideshow/biofuels-land -grab-guatemala/ (accessed April 20, 2016).
[267]Id.

[268]Julia Tomei, "The European Biofuels Juggernaut: Sustainable and Secure?" *UCL Energy Institute*, White Paper (2021), https: //www.exeter.ac.uk/energysecurity/documents/ese_resources _May2012/Julia_Tomei_presentation.pdf.
[269]Luis Cutz, Julia Tomei, and Luis Augusto Horta Nogueira, "Understanding the Failures in Developing Domestic Ethanol Markets: Unpacking the Ethanol Paradox in Guatemala," 1 *Energy Policy* 45 (2020).

Case 3.17

(continued)

and an importer of oil. The price that biofuel exporters receive is so high that there is no incentive for Guatemala to develop its own biofuel program.[270] As other countries transition from fossil fuels, Guatemala's economy has become increasingly dependent on foreign oil, both for energy purposes and for fueling, as it were, its biofuel exports.

Discussion Questions

1. Discuss the meaning of this statement within the context of the biofuel movement and the impact on countries such as Guatemala: "Good intentions don't always produce good results."

2. Explain the stakeholders in the biofuels movement. Does sustainability increase poverty? Is sustainability to the benefit of some countries at the expense of other countries?

3. Discuss the disincentives that countries such as Guatemala have for developing their own biofuels markets.

[270]Id.

Case 3.18

Herman Miller and Its Rain Forest Chairs

> A business is rightly judged by its products and services, but it must also face scrutiny as to its humanity.
>
> —D. J. De Pree, founder, Herman Miller, Inc.

Early Dedication to the Environment

In March 1990, Bill Foley, research manager for Herman Miller, Inc., began a routine evaluation of new types of wood to use in the firm's signature piece—the $2,277 (the 1990 cost) Eames chair. The Eames chair is a distinctive office chair with a rosewood exterior finish and a leather seat and was sold in Sharper Image's stores and catalogue.

At that time, the chair was made of two species of trees: rosewood and Honduran mahogany. Foley realized that Miller's use of tropical hardwoods was helping destroy rain forests. Foley banned the use of those woods in the chairs once existing supplies were exhausted. The Eames chair would no longer have its traditional rosewood finish. Foley's decision prompted former CEO Richard H. Ruch to react: "That's going to kill that [chair]."[271] Effects on sales could not be quantified at the time.

Herman Miller, based in Zeeland, Michigan, and founded in 1923 by D. J. De Pree, a devout Baptist, manufactures office furniture and partitions. The corporation follows a participatory-management tradition and takes environmentally friendly actions. In 1991, the vice president of the Michigan Audubon Society noted that Miller had cut the amount of trash it hauls to landfills by 90% since 1982: "Herman Miller has been doing a super job."[272]

During this same time period, Herman Miller built an $11 million waste-to-energy heating and cooling plant. The plant saved $750,000 per year in fuel and landfill costs. The company also found a buyer for the 800,000 pounds of scrap fabric it had been dumping in landfills. A North Carolina firm shreds the fabric for use as insulation in automobile roof linings and dashboards. Selling the scrap fabric also saves Miller $50,000 per year in dumping fees.

Herman Miller employees once used 800,000 Styrofoam cups a year. But in 1991, the company passed out 5,000 mugs to its employees and banished Styrofoam. The mugs carried the following admonition: "On spaceship earth there are no passengers . . . only crew." Styrofoam in packaging was also reduced 70% for a cost savings of $1.4 million.

(continued)

[271]David Woodruff, "Herman Miller: How Green Is My Factory?" *BusinessWeek*, September 16, 1991, pp. 54–55.

[272]Id.

Case 3.18

(continued)

Herman Miller also spent $800,000 for two incinerators to burn 98% of the toxic solvents that escape from booths where wood is stained and varnished. These furnaces exceeded the 1990 Clean Air Act requirements. It was likely that the incinerators would be obsolete within three years, when nontoxic products became available for staining and finishing wood, but having the furnaces was "ethically correct," former CEO Ruch said in response to questions from the board of directors.[273]

The Business Impact of Voluntary Sustainability Efforts

Herman Miller continued to pursue environmentally safe processes during this period, including finding a use for its sawdust by-product. However, for the fiscal year ended May 31, 1991, its net profit had fallen 70% from 1990 to $14 million on total sales of $878 million. In 1992, Herman Miller's board hired J. Kermit Campbell as CEO. Mr. Campbell continued in the Ruch tradition and wrote essays for employees on risk taking and for managers on "staying out of the way." From 1992 to 1995, sales growth at Herman Miller was explosive, but as one analyst described it, "Expenses exploded." Despite sales growth during this time, profits dropped 89% to a mere $4.3 million.

Management Changes and Strategy Shifts

Miller's board, concerned about Campbell's lack of expedience, announced Campbell's resignation and began an aggressive program of downsizing. Between May and July 1995, 130 jobs were eliminated. Also in 1995, sales dropped from $879 to $804 million. The board promoted Michael Volkema, then 39 and head of Miller's file cabinet division, to CEO.[274] Volkema refocused Herman Miller's name with a line of well-made, lower-priced office furniture, using a strategy and division called SQA (simple, quick, and affordable). The dealers for SQA work with customers to configure office furniture plans, and Miller shipped all the pieces ordered in less than two weeks.

Revenues in 1997 were $200 million, with record earnings of $78 million. In 1998, Miller acquired dealerships around the country and downsized from its then 1,500 employees.[275]

Volkema Noyrf that staying too long with an "outdated strategy and marketing" nearly cost the company. By 1999, Herman Miller was giving Steelcase, the country's number one office furniture manufacturer, stiff competition, as it were, with its Aeron chair. The Aeron chair, which comes in hundreds of versions, has lumbar adjustments, varying types of arms, different upholstery colors, and a mesh back. Its price is $765 to $1,190, and capitalized on its "Austin Powers-like" look. The chair has 35 patents and is the result of $35 million in R&D expenditures and cooperation with researchers at Michigan State, the University of Vermont, and Cornell who specialize in ergonomics. The seat features a sort of spine imprimatur. That is, the chair almost conforms to its user's spine.[276]

Herman Miller's market performance since the Volkema realignment has been remarkable, with its spike in share price in 1997 as it achieved recognition for both its products and sustainability efforts. If you had purchased 38 shares of Herman Miller stock in 1980 at a price of $25.87 per share and held on to them, your investment in 1997 would be worth $36,196.83, a return of 3,581.38%.[277] Herman Miller's share price reached an all-time high of $41 in 2017 and settled in at $38 in 2021. However, the company has continued to pay dividends throughout this time of growth. Herman Miller's earnings declined during the 2008–2012 period, but the company still paid dividends (albeit smaller) and was able to maintain its promises to shareholders. Since the 2012 dip, the dividend per share has more than doubled.

Herman Miller's Accolades

Tributes to Herman Miller's sustainability initiatives and socially responsible operations are too lengthy to list. Since 2002, the company has been named one of the "Sustainable Business 20," which is a list of the top 20 stocks of companies with strong environmental initiatives and

(continued)

[273]*Id.*

[274]Susan Chandler, "An Empty Chair at Herman Miller," *BusinessWeek*, July 24, 1996, p. 44.

[275]Bruce Upjohn, "A Touch of Schizophrenia," *Forbes*, July 7, 1997, pp. 57–59.

[276]Terril Yue Jones, "Sit on It," *Forbes*, July 5, 1999, p. 53–54.

[277]http://investor.shareholder.com/mlhr/calculator.cfm.

Case 3.18

(continued)

financial performance. The list is compiled by *Progressive Investor*, a publication of SustainableBusiness.com. In announcing the list, SustainableBusiness.com said, "Our goal is to create a list that showcases public companies that, over the past year, have made substantial progress in either greening their internal operations or growing a business based on an important green technology."[278] For 11 years, Herman Miller was named to the Dow Jones Sustainability World Index of 100 companies. However, as of 2020, Herman Miller is no longer on the list. Interestingly, Steelcase, its competitor, made it onto the list as #100.

For 14 years, since 2007, Herman Miller has received a perfect score on the Human Rights Index, a measure of the treatment of employees in factories located in other countries. Its accolades in the area of human capital are too numerous to list but include the following:

- Consistently appearing in *CRO* magazine's "100 Best Corporate Citizens"

- Named 24 times by *Fortune* magazine as one of the "Most Admired" companies in the United States

- One of *Fortune*'s "Top 100 Companies to Work For" for a decade[279]

- In 2008, began consistent ranking as one of the top 20 safest companies in the United States because of its low employee workplace injury rate

Beyond the sustainability and social responsibility awards, Herman Miller has been recognized nationally and internationally with design awards for its products. Its website lists 13 design awards won from 2019–2021. In 2021, *Fast Company* named Herman Miller one of the most innovative companies in the United States.

Herman Miller's Ongoing Product Strategies

Herman Miller has developed a strong international sales presence. Experts attribute this to its reputation for sustainable products and operations. Herman Miller has changed significantly since its 1968 invention of the office cubicle, a design that has now fallen out of favor. Its evolution into new fields, new products, and sustainability

has resulted in increasing sales and profits. Herman Miller has been working to expand its product base to include home furnishings.

Despite the earnings setback during the 2008–2012 period, Herman Miller continued its focus on sustainability.[280] Announced in 2004 and known as its "Perfect Vision" strategy, the company had pledged also to have zero emissions, zero hazardous waste, zero landfill, zero process water use, and 100% green energy use. These goals were modified in 2020 to 50% by 2023. Currently, the company is using 100% renewable energy for its electricity.[281]

Herman Miller has creative sustainability tools. Its solutions to factory problems are unique. For example, it has a mantra, "We Design with—Not Against—Nature." As an example, their annual report included the following problem resolution.

Two hundred seagulls nesting on the roof of our new Herman Miller facility in PortalMill in the UK were literally making a mess of things and interfering with the rooftop rainwater collection system needed for flushing toilets. So we brought in some muscle (and feathers)—Willow.

A trained Harris hawk who patrolled the Olympic Stadium in London during the 2012 Games, Willow came to our facility with a handler every day for a month, which was long enough to convince the seagulls to relocate. The birds "aren't as dumb as you think they are," says Willow's handler. "They say, 'I'm not nesting here' after getting a few good looks at Willow." Even so, Willow still comes once a month just to make sure they don't change their minds.[282]

Herman Miller's Values

Herman Miller's recruiting page includes the following:[283]

You can make a salary making furniture. Or you can make a difference. Or you can work at Herman Miller and make

(continued)

---

[280]Herman Miller's annual report on its "Better World Program" can be found at http://www.hermanmiller.com/content/dam/hermanmiller/documents/a_better_world/Better_World_Report.pdf (accessed April 20, 2016).
[281]Herman Miller: Our Vision and Policy, https://www.hermanmiller.com/better-world/sustainability/our-vision-and-policy/.
[282]"Herman Miller: Sustainability Snapshot," *Why Magazine,* as reproduced on the Herman Miller website, https://www.hermanmiller.com/stories/why-magazine/sustainability-snapshot/.
[283]www.hermanmiller.com. Look under employment opportunities.

---

[278]"Sustainable Business 20," *Progressive Investor*, July 17, 2007, http://www.sustainablebusiness.com. The website for *Progressive Investor* is difficult to access and use and the data on its rankings could not be located.
[279]As of 2021, Herman Miller is no longer on the *Fortune* list.

Case 3.18

(continued)

both. Speak up, solve problems, lead others, and be an owner. All while giving back to the community and caring for a better world. Join us and make your mark.

Speak Up

People who speak up and share ideas make for a strong business. Embracing good ideas and sharing the rewards with everyone is one way we stand apart.

Solve Problems

We use design to do that. You don't have to be a "designer" to make things better—for customers, for the communities we do business in, and for a better world.

Lead

Envision the future and help others reach their potential. Sometimes you'll lead and other times follow. We believe everyone does both, depending on the problem to be solved.

Own

At Herman Miller everyone can be a shareholder. But more so, you'll be a stakeholder, because we're all challenged to design solutions and make decisions that improve our community, our business, and our world.

Discussion Questions

1. Evaluate Foley's decision on changing the Eames chair woods. Consider the moral standards at issue for various stakeholders.

2. Is it troublesome that Herman Miller's profits were off when Foley made the decision?

3. Is Herman Miller bluffing with "green marketing"? Would Albert Carr (Reading 2.4) support Herman Miller's actions for different reasons?

4. Herman Miller's founder also offered this insight, quoted at the beginning of this case, into his views on business: "In the long run, businesses and business leaders will be judged not by their profits or their products, but by their impact on humanity."[284] With which writers on ethics and social responsibility and philosophers that you have studied in Units 1, 2, and 3 does his view on the role of business most closely fit?

5. Why would Herman Miller decide to buy equipment that exceeded the 1990 Clean Air Act standards when it would not be needed in three years?

6. During 2008–2012, Herman Miller went through a slump in sales and earnings but retained its sustainability focus. Despite advice from shareholders and experts, the company refused to cut costs by eliminating some of its green programs. Did the sustainability focus help the company with its sales and profits?

7. Place the seagull problem and its resolution under the either/or conundrum and ethical analysis. What was Herman Miller doing as it found conflicting values of keeping the factory running, keeping conditions in the factory sanitary, and keeping the seagulls alive?

---

[284]"Herman Miller: Sustainability Snapshot," *Why Magazine*, as reproduced on the Herman Miller website, https://www.hermanmiller.com/stories/why-magazine/sustainability-snapshot/.

Case 3.19

The Nonsustainability of the EV/Alt-Fuel and Troubled Truck Industry:

Nikola Tesla

Nikola Tesla was a masterful engineer and showman. An Italian immigrant, he wowed celebrities, the rich, and the famous with his clever inventions. After becoming a naturalized citizen, he made progress with wireless communication but, alas, ran out of funding before that invention could make it to public use. Many engineers in the EV-alt-fuel truck industry follow in his footsteps.

Nikola

Nikola, a start-up hydrogen power truck company, began its quest to conquer the alternative-fuel truck market in 2015. It went public in June 2020. It had a charming founder and CEO, Trevor Milton, who was able to bring underwriters, investors, and GM along for the ride, as it were, although who knew it might never be.[285] At one point, Nikola's value was greater than that of Ford.[286] And all without a single running vehicle. With two analyst reports questioning the legitimacy of the company, a U.S. Securities and Exchange Commission (SEC) fraud investigation,[287] a stock price drop of 50%,[288] and a market cap drop from $30 billion to $11 billion, Milton stepped down and disappeared (from social media, too). A GM executive was tapped to step in as Nikola CEO.

No one knows if or when the trucks will roll. No one from GM has taken a ride in one because they could not—not a single truck existed, just a video. All the trucks can do is roll. A report by Nathan Anderson, founder and CEO of Hindenburg Research, concluded that the 2016 video

of a Nikola truck was deceptive because the truck was in motion only because it was rolled down a hill. Nikola has acknowledged that the truck shown in the video was not moving on its own electric power.[289] Engineers at Nikola had warned then-CEO Trevor Milton not to call the company's hydrogen-powered truck "functioning" and "fully built."[290] Still, Milton went ahead and held an event at which a Nikola prototype was pushed down a hill while making a video that made it look like the truck was really clipping along on flat road. The video was posted to YouTube, and Mr. Milton called the truck "functioning" and "fully built."[291] Laws of gravity being what they are, it sure looked like the truck was humming away. However, the truck had no fuel cell or even hydrogen gas storage tanks. A company turned into a multi-billion-dollar operation on the basis of a video and the promise of a truck that, after five years, still did not exist even as a prototype.

In fairness to GM, when the thirtysomething Nikola CEO disappeared, GM scaled back its dollar investment in Nikola and will no longer be making a hydrogen truck. Nikola's stock dropped 27% ($7.52) per share to $20.41 upon GM's announcement. Nikola's value has dropped to $8 billion, which is one-fourth of its value when it had its market debut.[292]

In addition to the video that duped the market and GM, there was another slightly misleading statement about Nikola's potential. Mr. Milton had said publicly that the company had "billions of billions of dollars in orders." Reality check: Nikola had only one binding order.

New management at the company has disclosed that it will pay a $125 million fine to the SEC for making false claims.[293] The company also offered a "Not to worry," because it will seek reimbursement from Mr. Milton. Mr. Milton, through his lawyer, said that he would

(continued)

[285]Claire Bushey, "General Motors Takes 11% Stake in Electric Vehicle Maker Nikola," *Financial Times*, September 8, 2020, https://on.ft.com/2IalitZ.

[286]Pippa Stevens, "Meet Nikola, the Speculative Electric Vehicle Stock That Traders Believe Is as Valuable as Ford," *CNBC*, updated June 17, 2020, https://cnb.cx/2IbAisl.

[287]Edward Ludlow, "Nikola Founder Exaggerated the Capability of His Debut Truck," *Bloomberg*, June 17, 2020, https://www.bloomberg.com/news/articles/2020-06-17/nikola-s-founder-exaggerated-the-capability-of-his-debut-truck; "Nikola: How to Parlay an Ocean of Lies into a Partnership with the Largest Mark Vaughn, "Justice Dept., SEC Probe Fraud at Nikola," *Autoweek*, September 16, 2020, https://bit.ly/3eG8fx8; "Auto OEM in America," *Hindenburg Research*, September 10, 2020, https://hindenburgresearch.com/nikola/.

[288]Gregory Zuckerman, "How Nikola Stock Got Torched by a Short Seller," *The Wall Street Journal*, September 23, 2020, https://on.wsj.com/36ntDnd.

[289]Neal E. Boudette and Jack Ewing, "Head of Nikola, a G.M. Electric Truck Partner, Quits Amid Fraud Claims," *New York Times*, September 21, 2020, https://nyti.ms/3pcoZ3P.

[290]Neal E. Boudette, "G.M. Scales Back Alliance with Electric Truck Firm," *New York Times*, December 1, 2020, p. B1.

[291]Dave Michaels, "Nikola Expects $125 Million Penalty over Its Claims," *Wall Street Journal*, November 5, 2021, p. B5.

[292]Neal E. Boudette, "G.M. Scales Back Alliance with Electric Truck Firm," *New York Times*, December 1, 2020, p. B1.

[293]Dave Michaels, "Nikola Expects $125 Million Penalty Over Its Claims," *Wall Street Journal*, November 5, 2021, p. B5.

Case 3.19

(continued)

defend against "false allegations leveled against me by outside detractors." An internal report and now an SEC investigation have concluded that Mr. Milton made nine false statements and did not have a truck that was operational. Those darn detractors. An outside review by the law firm of Kirkland & Ellis, LLP, concluded that nine statements made by Trevor Milton, founder of the electric truck company Nikola, were inaccurate. Amazingly, when the SEC settlement was announced, Nikola's stock rose 11% to $14. Its high point was $28.77. At the end of 2021, it was down to $9.87.

The federal government has indicted Mr. Milton on charges of securities and wire fraud.[294] The indictment focuses on the fact that Mr. Milton targeted "retail investors," or investors with little to no investment experience. The indictment alleges that he targeted those investors through social media and television, print, and podcast interviews. The false statements alleged include the following:

(a) false and misleading statements that Nikola had early success in creating a "fully functioning" semi-truck prototype known as the "Nikola One," when Mr. Milton knew the prototype was inoperable;

(b) false and misleading statements that Nikola had engineered and built an electric- and hydrogen-powered pickup truck known as "the Badger" from the "ground up" using Nikola's parts and technology, when Mr. Milton knew that was not true;

(c) false and misleading statements that Nikola was producing hydrogen and was doing so at a reduced cost, when Mr. Milton knew that in fact no hydrogen was being produced at all by Nikola, at any cost;

d) false and misleading statements that Nikola had developed batteries and other important components in-house, when Mr. Milton knew that Nikola was acquiring those parts from third parties; and

(e) false and misleading claims that reservations made for the future delivery of Nikola's semi-trucks were binding orders representing billions in revenue, when the

majority of those orders could be canceled at any time or were for a truck Nikola had no intent to produce in the near-term.

Mr. Milton was convicted at the trial of one count of securities fraud and two counts of wire fraud. The crimes carry a 25-year prison term.

Lordstown

Lordstown Motors, an electric pickup truck company, was touted as an example of bringing back lost American jobs. The company took over a closed GM plant in Lordstown, Ohio: it was a company doing the right thing by providing jobs to an economically challenged area by building an alt-fuel truck. It got its start not by going public but just by merging with a special purpose acquisition company (SPAC), an investment tool that permits small companies to go public without all that IPO scrutiny. The value of Lordstown rose to $4 billion after that merger.

After the SPAC merger, Lordstown filed an SEC disclosure revealing that it might not have enough money to even start production.[295] Before that announcement was made, five executives sold their Lordstown stock over a three-day period, raising questions from accountants and lawyers for the firm about the adequacy of its internal controls.[296] The Department of Justice has subpoenaed the company records and is looking into the merger.[297] The issue of the advance stock sales has not yet been targeted.

Hindenberg also uncovered the iffy nature of Lordstown's Endurance trucks. Lordstown's much-touted pre-orders were not even commitments to buy trucks. First, there were no trucks in production. One prototype had burst into flames in Detroit (no criminal activity involved, just spontaneous combustion). Another prototype dropped out of a 280-off-road race in Baja, California, after driving just 40 miles.

(continued)

[294]https://www.justice.gov/usao-sdny/pr/former-nikola-corporation-ceo-trevor-milton-charged-securities-fraud-scheme.

[295]Neal E. Boudette and Matthew Goldstein, "Lordstown Motors Offers Test Rides of Prototypes to Ease Concerns," *New York Times*, June 22, 2021, p. B5.
[296]Ben Foldy, "Lordstown Officials Sold Shares Ahead of Financial Returns," *Wall Street Journal*, June 22, 2021, p. A1.
[297]Ben Foldy, "Lordstown Discloses DOJ Probe of Business," *Wall Street Journal*, July 17–18. 2021, p. B1.

Case 3.19

(continued)

Now the chairman of the board of Lordstown is offering test rides in the company parking lot and promised 1,000 trucks by the end of 2021, a statement that contradicted its going-concern filing with the SEC on its lack of capital for starting production.[298] The chair of the board is handling parking lot test rides because the company's founder and CEO and his executives resigned shortly after the questions about the validity of the orders arose; some are busy with those stock sales questions. In September 2022, Lordstown announced that it will finish 50 trucks by the end of 2022 and 450 in 2023.

Lordstown began touting pre-orders for its vehicles of the future to lure investors. But one really can't count a nonbinding "kinda, maybe, if" deal as an order. Those accountants get testy about "mirages," as a short-seller called Lordstown orders, being counted as sales. Lordstown has admitted that its claimed orders were nonbinding.[299] Two executives departed after that shortcoming in definitions was discovered by the law firm of Sullivan & Cromwell, a law firm hired by the board to examine the statements about orders.

Lordstown has now sold its factory to Foxconn and will work jointly with the contract assembler to build its Endurance trucks.[300] Foxconn is also under contract to build vehicles for a competitor, Fisker.

Rivian Motors

Rivian Motors, an electric truck company, was started in 2019. It has sold 5,694 vehicles.[301] Its stock went public in November 2021, and the company is now worth $120.5 billion. That value dropped to $33 billion in 2022. For comparison, General Motors is worth $89 billion and sold 6.8 million vehicles in 2020. So, Rivian is now the fifth largest vehicle company in the world with most sales to employees and shareholders.

One of the important things to understand in the case of these alt-fuel trucks is that the market excitement comes from the government support available for their production and purchase. Companies that purchase electric vehicles get a 30% tax credit. In 2021, the federal government mandated that all federal agencies use all zero-emissions vehicles by 2035.[302] The U.S. Post Office alone could keep Rivian in business if it threw business their way. Consumers can get a $7,500 tax credit for vans, trucks, and SUVs with zero emissions.[303] And you can spend up to $80,000 and still get the credit. Rivian has 55,400 orders; customers will have to wait until 2023 to take delivery.[304]

Rivian does have a very cautious disclaimer in its SEC filings, a warning that its business is dependent upon government policies on gas-powered vehicles and government tax credits for purchasers. Rivian is benefiting from government policy that is directing investors to companies that are building what the government wants built. And Rivian also has Amazon as an investor and customer. Amazon has purchased 100,000 Rivian vehicles.

Rivian has no dealers and will be following the Tesla model of selling in shopping malls. Charging stations represent a challenge to consumers. Charging electric SUVs doing their off-roading may be problematic. The Rivian mantra of "Keep the world adventurous forever" takes on new meaning as you look for a charging station in the Klondike.

Rivian's risk disclosures in its initial primary offering materials are long and detailed, but if we summed it all up in lay language, the risks would be as follows:

1. We have never done this before.
2. We are not sure if we can do this.
3. We have limited parts suppliers.
4. We have only one customer presently—Amazon—and they're a shareholder.
5. Pre-orders are fully refundable and cancellable.
6. Charging stations could be a problem.
7. If the government changes its mind on EVs or its policies, we may not be able to sell the vehicles.

(continued)

[298]Neal E. Boudette and Matthew Goldstein, "Lordstown Motors Offers Test Rides of Prototypes to Ease Concerns," *New York Times*, June 22, 2021, p. B5.
[299]Dave Sebastian, "Lordstown Clarifies Nonbinding Orders," *Wall Street Journal*, June 18, 2021, p. B3.
[300]Christina Rogers and Ben Foldy, "Lordstown Motors to Sell Factory to Foxconn," *Wall Street Journal*, October 1, 2021, p. B1.
[301]Peter Eavis and Neil E. Boudette, "Is Rivian Worth $86 Billion?" *New York Times*, November 11, 2021, p. B1.

[302]"Biden Wants an All-Electric Fleet," *Washington Post*, January 28, 2021, https://www.washingtonpost.com/climate-solutions/2021/01/28/biden-federal-fleet-electric/.
[303]"Rivian, the Government Unicorn," *Wall Street Journal*, November 12, 2021, p. A16.
[304]Peter Eavis and Neil E. Boudette, "Is Rivian Worth $86 Billion?" *New York Times*, November 11, 2021, p. B1.

Case 3.19

(continued)

8. We have no structure for repairs. We also have no experience in repairs.

9. It isn't clear whether consumers want electric vehicles.

10. Our lithium batteries could catch fire.

11. It takes a lot of time to build these cars.

12. The chip shortage is a problem.

13. We have no idea how much this all is going to cost.[305]

The good news is that Rivian has laid it all out on the table. The bad news is that those who have invested $89 billion are going to wait sometime for a return on investment (ROI). In 2022, Rivian announced that it was struggling to get parts because of the post pandemic supply chain issues as well as the war in Ukraine.[306] That announcement was followed by another disclosing that Rivian's output for 2022 from 40,000 vehicles to 25,000.[307] By the end of the 2022 quarter, Rivian had produced 7,363 trucks. Rivian is also facing a lawsuit by a shareholder seeking class-action status for its sudden price increases of $10,000 to $20,000 per vehicle for all customers who pre-ordered the trucks.[308] CEO RJ Scaringe explained the price increase, "Building anything complex is going to be filled with mistakes. We made mistakes. We're going to do better."[309]

Discussion Questions

1. List the ethical lapses that you see in the stories of Nikola, Lordstown, and Rivian. Does the fact that they

were pursuing a socially responsible product excuse those lapses?

2. List the decision points these companies faced and why they continued a "fake it until you make it" approach to luring investors.

3. Read the following excerpt from Marianne M. Jennings, "The Social Responsibility of Business Is Not Social Responsibility: Assume That There Are No Angels and Allow the Free Market's Touch of Heaven," 16 *Berkeley Business Law Journal* 2 (2019), pp. 325–462.

> Scrutiny is the stuff of common sense. Oh, the hype in the field of alt-fuel vehicles. Why, the investor enthusiasm, particularly by large corporations, is positively, well, electric.
>
> Electric and then shocking.
>
> A company that pursues a subsidized product area is not refined by the buffetings of the free market nor is it pushed to excellence. A business that is forgiven for missteps in the form of CSR investment funds despite shortcomings or permitted to continue operating with subsidies is deprived of the opportunity to reach excellence and success. As in the cases of Solyndra, Solar Tech, and SolarCity, all the CSR rankings and subsidies could not keep them from bankruptcy and/or acquisition. If solar power makes economic sense, the market will beat a path to the door of any companies pioneering this technology. However, all the subsidies, imprimaturs, screens, and social media chatter that the CSR movement can muster have not been able to keep these Humpty Dumptys from falling to failure.

Is the CSR/ESG imprimatur a cover for companies that may not be forthright with their R&D and products? Is it possible that the seal of social responsibility shields hucksters?

4. Is there anything different about Rivian's behavior from the other alt-fuel companies?

---

[305]https://www.sec.gov/Archives/edgar/data/1874178/000119312521289903/d157488ds1.htm#toc157488_2.

[306]Stephen Wilmor, "Heard on the Street, Rivian, Lucid Drive off Course," *Wall Street Journal*, March 7, 2022, p. B10.

[307]Mike Colla, "Rivian Cuts Its 2022 Output," *Wall Street Journal*, March 11, 2022, p. B4.

[308]Christina Rogers, "Rivian Sued Over Pricing Practices," *Wall Street Journal*, March 9, 2022, p. B11.

[309]Id.

Government as a Stakeholder

The Government Mattresses at the Border

Wayfair employees staged a walkout to protest Wayfair's sale of $200,000 of bedroom furniture to a southern border facility for migrant children. The walkout involved hundreds of people carrying signs such as one that read, "A prison with a bed is still a prison."[310] An employee said, "I needed to hit the street to make sure I was proud of my company." The employees were expressing their disapproval of then Trump administration's policies on immigration and resulting overcrowding at border detention facilities from ICE enforcement of those policies.

The employees were missing an important piece of information. Wayfair was not selling mattresses to ICE, as some stories reported, or the federal government, as most of the stories reported. Wayfair was selling mattresses to Baptist Children's Family Services, a nonprofit government contractor running detention centers. Baptist Children's Family Services works at the border to try to make conditions better in that humanitarian crisis. A spokesperson for BCFS said, in response to the Wayfair walkout, "We believe youth should sleep in beds with mattresses."[311]

There are countless nonprofit organizations that serve food, provide shelter, and offer basic hygiene products to the migrants. In short, hundreds of companies provide food, hygiene products, bedding, and other needs to care for the immigrants. If employee walkouts are staged to protest government policies, then companies that make toothpaste, potato chips, milk, and lettuce should be boycotted as well.

At the time of the walkout, Wayfair was struggling financially. Turning down customers because of their activities or how their products will be used does introduce risk for a company. Businesses do not have to support a customer's views or actions to do business with them. Ironically, employees' vocal positions on these safe issues will produce the same negative consequences for their employers that their reticence and silence on the legal and safety issues do: you destroy the business (not even taking into account the customer backlash that could follow). Neutrality is a form of balancing interests.

Wayfair did agree to make a donation to the Red Cross (a donation greater than the profit Wayfair will make on the mattress sales). The Red Cross stays away from all things border, so the donation cannot help the immigrants' conditions there. However, employees settled for that inaction.

Discussion Questions

1. Is the workplace the best place for sorting through political hot-button issues?

2. Is not selling your products to a religious nonprofit organization that is giving teens a mattress antithetical to the goals of social responsibility? Is this a bar that is set too high?

3. Is the government a stakeholder in Wayfair's decision to sell mattresses and furniture?

4. Is it better to make your objections to immigration policy known by withholding basic comforts from immigrants?

5. Is there a company that sells products to entities, agencies, governments, other companies, and human beings that no one finds objectionable?

6. Who is actually being targeted by the walkout? Is harming third parties an effective way to bring about change?

[310]Charlie McGee and Jennifer Levitz, "Employees Push Activism at Wayfair," *Wall Street Journal*, June 27, 2019, p. A3.
[311]Jennifer Levitz, "Wayfair Workers Stage Walkout Over Sales to Border," *Wall Street Journal*, June 26, 2019, https://www.wsj.com/articles/wayfair-workers-stage-walkout-over-sales-to-border-camps-11561575827?mod=Searchresults_pos3&page=1.

Why Didn't They Say Something? 3.4

The Brave Employee Political Protests

The purpose of the Wayfair walkout was to require that their employer adopt their political views on immigration policies. It is interesting to note that employees find it difficult to raise issues about defective products, shoddy production, money laundering, or insider trading. They remain sullen and mute on legal and safety violations because that factor of "I don't want to lose my job" comes up often when employees are asked why they did not say something about those types of issues. Why are issues such as the one with Wayfair the ones to emerge when it comes to employees voicing concerns about their employers? What makes it easier for employees to raise political issues but not product safety or fraud issues?

Famous Lines from Art and Literature

A nation's greatness is measured by how it treats its most vulnerable.

—**Mahatma Gandhi**

Case 3.21

Public Policy and COVID-19 in Nursing Homes

Letitia James, the attorney general for the state of New York, released a preliminary report on nursing homes and COVID.[312] The report is deeply troubling on many levels. There are the usual nursing home issues with cleanliness, staffing, and lack of equipment. However, the pandemic exacerbated those deficiencies. The report includes two additional disturbing behaviors:

- A larger number of nursing home residents died from COVID-19 than the New York Department of Health (DOH) data reflected.[313]

- The nursing homes did not report COVID-19-related deaths for their infected residents who were sent to hospitals and died there—an understatement estimated at about 50%. The data that nursing homes furnished to the Office of the Attorney General investigators were different from the data reported to the DOH.

Investigators were unable to find explanations for all the discrepancies.

The data for the state of New York showed that at least 12,743 long-term care residents died of the virus as of January 19, 2021; however, the official tally as reported by the governor's office was 8,505. New York's death rate was still one of the highest in the nation.[314]

Government guidance requiring the admission of COVID-19 patients in nursing homes may have put residents at increased risk of harm in some facilities and may have obscured the data available to assess that risk. The relevant order from the New York Department of Health, dated March 25, 2020, provided:

"[N]o resident shall be denied re-admission or admission to the nursing home solely based on a confirmed or suspected diagnosis of COVID-19.

(continued)

[312]"Nursing Home Response to COVID-19 Pandemic," New York State Office of the Attorney General Letitia James, January 30, 2021.

[313]Jesse McKinley, Danny Hakim, and Alexandria Alter, "Celebratory Memoir by Cuomo Undercut by Covid Data Report," *New York Times*, April 1, 2021, p. A1.

[314]Marina Villeneuve, Bernard Condon, and Matt Sedensky, "NY Data Show Nursing Home Deaths Undercounted by Thousands," *AP News*, https://apnews.com/article/new-york-nursing-home-coronavirus-deaths-a6c214f4467976efdfca9ba75f8adaef.

Case 3.21

(continued)

Nursing homes are prohibited from requiring a hospitalized resident who is determined medically stable to be tested for COVID-19 prior to admission or re-admission." DOH, Advisory: Hospital Discharges and Admissions to Nursing Homes, March 25, 2020.

The March 25 order put those with COVID-19 into homes occupied by those most vulnerable to the disease. The most vulnerable were placed in the most dangerous place and led to an increased risk for residents.[315]

The governor of New York at the time, Andrew Cuomo, who issued the order, said that he had no other place for the nursing home patients to go. However, at that time, the federal government had a Navy hospital ship in New York Harbor and had set up the Javitz Center as a portable hospital for the treatment of COVID-19 patients. In addition, the nonprofit organization Samaritan's Purse had set up one of its portable hospitals that they use around the world for treating patients when local hospitals are overwhelmed by a pandemic or highly infectious diseases spreading in an area. All of those facilities were empty at the time and staffed to take COVID-19-positive patients.

The New York State Bar Association concluded in a 242-page report of its investigation that Governor Cuomo's directive increased the death toll in nursing home and that his failure to lift the unreasonable mandate sooner than it needed to be in effect resulted in more deaths.[316] The report was adopted by the New York State Assembly.

Following Governor Cuomo's resignation, new governor Kathy Hochul apologized to the families of those who had lost their relatives in nursing homes to COVID-19: "I apologize for the pain that those families had to endure."[317]

Discussion Questions

1. Who were the stakeholders in the decision to issue the order to the nursing homes?

2. Was there information missing before the order was issued?

3. Did government intervention help or exacerbate the pandemic crisis?

4. What analysis tools would you recommend to government officials and public health officials?

5. What ethical lapses do you see in the underreporting of deaths?

---

[315]"Nursing Home Response to COVID-19 Pandemic," New York State Office of the Attorney General Letitia James, January 30, 2021, p. 36.

[316]"Cuomo Nursing Home Order Did Cause More Deaths, Should Have Been Reversed Sooner: Task Force," *New York Post*, June 15, 2021, https://nypost.com/2021/06/15/cuomo-nursing-home-order-caused-more-deaths-task-force/.

[317]Mary Murphy, "Gov. Hochul Apologizes to Nursing Home Families for 15,000-Plus COVID Deaths," *CBS News 10*, October 21, 2021, https://www.news10.com/news/ny-capitol-news/kathy-hochul/new-york-apologizes-over-covid-deaths-at-nursing-homes-after-19-months-of-waiting/.

Unit 3 Key Terms

Corporate social responsibility (CSR)   p. 153
Environmental, social, and governance (ESG)   p. 176
Regulatory cycle   p. 156
Milton Friedman   p. 159
Latency stage   p. 162

Public awareness stage   p. 162
Activism stage   p. 201
Regulation/litigation stage   p. 162
Conscious capitalism   p. 186
"You didn't build that" theorem   p. 172

Unit 4

Ethics and Company Culture

The conscience that is dark with shame for his own deeds or for another's, may well, indeed, feel harshness in your words; Nevertheless, do not resort to lies, let what you write reveal all you have seen, and let those men who itch scratch where it hurts. Though when your words are taken in at first they may taste bitter, but once well-digested they will become a vital nutrient.

—Dante, *Paradiso* Canto XVII, 124–132

I have no idea what I was thinking. . . . I don't know why there was a lapse of judgment, but there was. I won't be practicing before the SEC, but it'll be something. I'll wait tables.[1]

—Scott London, CPA and former KPMG partner, after being charged with securities fraud for passing along client information to a friend

Learning Objectives

- List and give examples of the categories of ethical development of individuals.

- Explain what organizational factors can influence the ethical culture in an organization and how they can be used to provide employees with support for ethical decisions.

- Describe the layers of ethical issues that exist and who is responsible for addressing the challenges in each area.

- Give examples of how leaders' behaviors influence the ethical choices of employees throughout the organization.

- Discuss the factors that create fear and silence in organizations and what can be done to encourage employees to report ethical concerns.

- Explain how and why a belief in the goodness of the organization can skew ethical choices.

At times, individuals who have become part of a larger organization feel that their personal values conflict with those of the organization. The types of ethical dilemmas that arise between individuals and their organizations include conflicts of interests and issues of honesty, fairness, and loyalty. Rogue employees do happen, but it is possible that good apples turn rogue (rotten) in a bad barrel. Sometimes employees make poor ethical choices because their personal temptations are too great, and they cross those lines established in personal and individual ethics in Units 1 and 2. Other ethical lapses happen because of organizational practices. Bonus and incentive plans will get results from employees, but those results may be achieved by crossing a few ethical lines and violating the credo here and there. Then there are the industry practices. When your entire industry is engaged in subprime lending, are you not hurting your customers if you also do not write subprime loans despite the impact of those loans on the markets and the economy? This unit looks at all three of these sources of pressure that contribute to ethical missteps: personal, company, and industry.

---

[1]Stuart Pfeifer, "Former KPMG Partner Sentenced for Insider Trading," April 24, 2014, *Los Angeles Times*, https://www.latimes.com/business/la-fi-kpmg-london-20140425-story.html.

Temptation at Work for Individual Gain and That Credo

No one wakes up one day and thinks, "You know what would be good? A gigantic fraud! I believe I will create a gigantic fraud and make money that way." We ease ourselves into fraud. No one wakes up one day and says, "I believe I will go to work and embezzle $100,000." We begin by using the postage meter or copier for personal reasons and work up to the $100,000, perhaps even taking it in small increments to adjust the comfort level experienced with such conduct. One of the tasks we have in studying, understanding, and living ethics in business is drawing lines for ourselves on what we will not do and then honoring the lines we have chosen. At those decision points (discussed in Unit 2) what we are doing doesn't seem so bad. Just a little thing, right? If we start moving the lines, we can find ourselves in complete violation of the standards and absolutes we have set for ourselves, and how we got there incrementally. The following concise and insightful reading provides pithy insight into this process of moving the line.

Reading 4.1

The Moving Line

George Lefcoe, a renowned USC law professor and expert in real property, zoning, and development and, for a time, a commissioner of the Los Angeles County Regional Planning Commission, offered the following thoughts on his retirement and the seduction of public office:[2]

> I really missed the cards from engineers I never met, the wine and cheese from development companies I never heard of and the honey baked ham from, of all places, Forest Lawn Cemetery, even though the company was never an applicant before the commission when I was there.

> My first Christmas as a commissioner—when I received the ham—I tried to return it, though for the record, I did not, since no one at Forest Lawn seemed authorized to accept the ham, apparently not even for burial. My guess is that not one of the many public servants who received the ham had ever tried to return it.

> When I received another ham the next Christmas, I gave it to a worthy charity. The next year, some worthy friends were having a party so I gave it to them. The next year I had a party and we enjoyed the ham.

> In the fifth year, about the tenth of December, I began wondering, where is my ham?

---

[2]From George Lefcoe, quoted in "Notable, Quotable," *Wall Street Journal*, December 18, 1998, p. A14.

Discussion Questions

1. What was Professor Lefcoe's absolute line?

2. How did he cross it? As you review his gradual slippage, be sure to think about your credo and personal lines that Unit 1 encouraged you to develop. Think about this question: How did he go from an absolute standard of accepting nothing—indeed, returning the gifts—to expecting the gifts?

3. As you think about Professor Lefcoe, rely on this metaphor. When you buy a new car, think about your initial feelings on food and beverages in the car—perhaps only bottled water at first. Then you move into the brown beverages. Then food enters the new car and then red punch, sundaes, and ketchup. How did we evolve to a position that is the exact opposite of our original absolute line? In answering this question about the line, consider the following reading.

Reading 4.2

Not All Employees Are Equal When It Comes to Ethical Development[3]

When it comes to ethical or moral development, not all employees are created equal. Ethics training may be enough for one type. Ethics training for others may be water off a duck's back. The need to begin a process of evaluating employees for their moral development came to mind in the final days of October 2009. Galleon, [at that time] one of the country's largest hedge funds, was a longstanding beneficiary of inside information from employees, traders, brokers, and others. This inside information was then used to create the legendary and unusually consistent returns for which Galleon was famous. Identified in the Galleon-related indictments is the notorious "Tipper A." The tipper is the one providing the inside information, i.e., stock tips, to the tippees, the outsiders who use the inside information to position themselves for market gains in advance of the information's public disclosure.

Who is Tipper A? Roomy Khan. Yes, right out of a Grisham novel comes a character named Roomy Khan, a former Intel employee who, ironically, was under house arrest for six months in 2002 for passing along proprietary inside information about Intel to those who then profited by using that information to dabble in the stock market before the market had that information. Mind you, Roomy Khan does not pass along inside info out of the goodness of her heart or a profound belief in the market's need for asymmetrical information. Roomy Khan had to pay back her own gains made alongside her tippees.

One cannot help but wonder: Why would someone who has already experienced legal difficulties return to the same behaviors? More relevantly for ethics and compliance officers, why would a publicly traded company hire someone who has a history of passing along inside information? Most importantly, why would any company that hired Roomy Khan not keep a close watch on her activities? And keeping an eye on any stock trades that seem to occur in advance of public announcements would also be a good idea. Ethics training will not have much effect on our Roomy Khans because there is a different psychology at work in her behavior. Understanding that different employees require different compliance techniques is a concept in its infancy stages of development and application. But there is a framework to consider.

[3]Marianne M. Jennings, "Not All Employees Are Equal When It Comes to Moral Development," *New Perspectives: Journal of the Association of Healthcare Auditors*, March 2010, p. 19.

Years of study and interaction with organizations and their employees have yielded the following categories of employees when it comes to ethical development. Herewith is a list with a brief explanation and an example. Understanding the categories helps organizations to decide what can and should be done about our merry moral categories.

- **Ethically clueless.** These folks do not seem to be aware of rules. They function in their own world and have little or no sensitivity to the impact of their conduct on others or even the impropriety of that conduct. The character George Costanza in the *Seinfeld* series was a classic example. In one episode, Mr. Costanza was caught in the act of having an affair with a member of the janitorial staff on the desk of a colleague. When caught, his response was, "What? Is there something wrong with this? Who knew?"

- **Ethically superior/ethical egotist.** The ethical egotist believes that the rules are for others who are less gifted. Rules were developed for the plodders, not the stars. During the era of the dot-com boom, we had many morally superior characters. For example, Sanjay Kumar, the former CEO of Computer Associates often explained his creative accounting on his company's results as follows, "Standard accounting rules [are] not the best way to measure [CA's] results because it had changed to a new business model offering its clients more flexibility."[4] Dullards follow rules. Ethical egotists soar. At least until they run into the SEC. Mr. Kumar was sentenced to 12 years for securities fraud. He was released from prison in 2017, after serving 10 years. Computer Associates became known as the company whose earnings were reported on a new calendar innovation: the 35-day month. With super-star docs and researchers, we often see the ethical egotist syndrome. They cannot be bothered with all the regulation and the concerns about conflicts of interest. Ethical egotists believe it is impossible for them to experience a conflict of interest because they can process influences better than others who must follow such rules.

- **Inherently ethical.** Ah, the ethics officer's dream. These are the folks who, if you put them in a room and said, "Don't move from this chair," would not move from the chair, with or without a surveillance camera observing them. They will always do the right thing because they have a strong moral code that they live. Mother Teresa comes to mind. In the secular world there is the following example from cinema.

---

[4]Alex Berenson, "Computer Associates Officials Stand by Their Accounting Methods," *New York Times*, May 1, 2001, pp. C1, C7.

Famous Lines from Art and Literature

Absence of Malice

The late Wilford Brimley played James Wells, an assistant U.S. attorney general attempting to clean up a prosecutorial mess in Miami, including prosecutors leaking information about investigations. He cautions the group he is questioning, "We can't have people go around leaking stuff for their own reasons. It ain't legal. And worse than that, by God, it ain't right."[5]

---

[5]*Absence of Malice* (1981).

- **Amoral technician.** This character makes no determinations about right or wrong. The amoral technician does not violate rules. The amoral technician simply finds out what the rules are, what the law is, and then functions within those parameters, right down to the line/wire. They work, and often game, the system with personal feelings and ethics being irrelevant. Andrew Fastow, the once CFO of the now defunct Enron, was an amoral technician, brilliant in his use of FASB and accounting loopholes and absolutely unaffected by the impact this loophole approach had on those who had invested in his company.

- **Ethical schizophrenic.** This type of ethical development means that the employee has one set of ethics at work and another in personal life, and vice versa, one set of ethics in personal life and another at work. The NBA referee Tim Donaghy, who was betting on NBA games even as he called them, was known in his personal life for a phenomenal summer basketball camp for children with developmental disabilities and issues. The ethical schizophrenic is capable of saying, "Okay, so I threw a few NBA games for gambling. But look what I did with the money!" Donaghy entered a guilty plea and did 15 months.

- **Ethical procrastinator/postponer.** This category of employee is fully aware of ethical issues and the rules and laws but has made a conscious decision to worry about the "ethics stuff" and morality at some time in the future. That time in the future is after they have made enough money. Andrew Carnegie is the classic example. Mr. Carnegie made a fortune as an industrialist, an industrialist with some moments in labor management that saw fatalities. Mr. Carnegie gave his fortune away. If you have been in a public library in the United States, you were a beneficiary of his *noblesse oblige*. But it was an oblige born of postponing ethics until a time when the income was not in jeopardy.

- **Ethical compartmentalizer or rationalizer.** You hear rationalizations (see Reading 1.5) from the ethical compartmentalizer: "Everybody does this." "That's the way we have always done things." "I only do this in certain situations." "I would never allow my kids to do this." This is the Willy Loman syndrome: a man has to sell, sell, sell, no matter what. Ethics apply sometimes, but when you are involved in sales, those lines do have to bend just a bit.

- **Ethically desensitized.** These are the souls who should provide the motivation for working on ethical culture. These employees were once keenly aware of ethical lines and issues but have been beaten down in their objections and have given up raising those concerns. They cope with the cognitive dissonance in their value system by no longer being affected by them. Indeed, they may just join in on the unethical festivities. During the Watergate scandal in the Nixon administration, Charles Colson was a classic example of an ethically desensitized soul. He was an experienced and respected lawyer, but because no one was making any headway in stopping the cascading consequences of the Watergate burglary, he just joined in with the group and found himself in prison. Until the time of his death, Mr. Colson took the lessons of his experience and used them to help businesspeople. He founded a program that focuses on teaching inmates about ethics and faith.

- **Ethically detached.** Herein is another group that should find us striving to improve organizational culture. The ethically detached are still acutely aware of ethical issues, but the rules of the sandbox have worn them down so that they simply go along in a depressed manner. They will not join in, but they do stop objecting. These folks are sometimes called the ethically disengaged or the ethically disillusioned. The former ethics officer and associate counsel at Hewlett-Packard at the time of the board's great pretexting plan (i.e., the company using private investigators to spy on board members) fell into this category. He was worried about the pretexting, asked security about the pretexting, and inquired as to whether they were crossing legal lines. However, he was unable to make any headway because the directive was coming from the very top of the company. He simply distanced himself from the activities. He did not participate, but he also did not leave nor report the conduct.

Famous Lines from Art and Literature

Casablanca

Scene in a bustling and illegal casino operation:
Captain Renault, the chief enforcement officer for the Vichy government: "I'm shocked, shocked to find that gambling is going on here!"
The croupier: "*Your winnings, sir.*"
Captain Renault: "Oh, thank you very much!"
Casablanca (1942)

- **Ethical chameleon.** These frightening characters adapt to the ethics of those with whom they work. One's ethics depend. Those ethics can change depending upon which industry you are in and which company has hired you. They adapt as high schoolers do with their cliques. If one group is making fun of the math club and they are in that group, they join in on the math ridicule. For example, in the Marsh McLennan bid collusion case, one broker was worried about the issue of price fixing. He prefaced his note expressing his concerns with, "I'm not some goody two-shoes. . . ." He wanted his colleagues to know he was one of them even though he was worried about their practices. A Ford truck ad was an ethical chameleon's dream, if they are part of the pick-up driving group. The ad boasted about the trucks, "Made by the guys we used to cheat off in high school."

- **Ethical sycophant.** Present far too often in organizations, this character adopts the ethics of those who are in charge. They will be whatever kind of sycophant the leaders want them to be. In October 2009, the *New York Times* ran a lengthy story about the former employees in Lehman and their involvement in the largely worthless mortgage instrument markets. "I was just following orders," was the common explanation. One brave broker also added, "I have blood on my hands."[6] But, as all sycophants explain, and ethical issues aside, he too was just following orders.

Discussion Questions

1. Are you able to place yourself in any of these categories? Why? Give the circumstances that led to your response and behavior.

2. Think of the individuals involved in the cases you have studied so far and develop a chart that categorizes their behavior according to these categories of ethical development.

---

[6]Louise Story and Landon Thomas Jr., "Tales from Lehman's Crypt," *New York Times*, September 9, 2009, SB, p. 1.

Famous Lines from Art and Literature

101 Dalmatians

In the film *101 Dalmatians*, Glenn Close plays the autocratic and evil Cruella de Vil. She has an assistant who hops to, agrees with whatever she says, and is a classic sycophant. At one point, he voices a different opinion. Following dead silence and a deadlier stare, Cruella asks him, "What kind of a sycophant are you?" The assistant's response is, "What kind would you like me to be?" The sycophant follows orders, always.

Ethics in Action 4.1

The Shuttle Free-Rider

I was staying at a Marriott Residence Inn in Washington, D.C. There were two more Marriott hotels in that same area, a Courtyard and the Marriott Marquis (the most expensive of the three). Marriott runs an airport shuttle to all three hotels. After boarding the shuttle with others at the Residence Inn, we made the rounds to the Courtyard and then picked up one gentleman at the Marquis.

Arriving at the airport, the Marquis gentleman and I got off the shuttle bus last, and he walked alongside me and confessed, "I really was not staying at the Marquis. I just walked there from my meeting to catch the shuttle. I am just too cheap to take a cab."

Classify the Marquis gentleman under the categories of ethical development.

Case 4.3

Bob Baffert: The Winningest Horse Trainer in History

Bob Baffert is a purebred horse trainer who has won six Kentucky Derbys (seven if you count a controversial one—see below), seven Preaknesses, three Belmonts, and two Triple Crowns. However, there are some resolved and unresolved questions about how his horses win. Like Lance Armstrong and his incredible record for winning races, questions about illegal substance use have swirled around Mr. Baffert.

In his autobiography *Baffert: The Dirt Road to the Derby*, Mr. Baffert confessed that in 1976 he let "a guy" give something to his horse that would make his horse win. He explained that he was a college student who did it partly out of ignorance and partly because of the pressure to win.[7] The horse with "something," in fact,

did not win, but the horse was spot-checked and tested positive for a pain killer.

Mr. Baffert's father drove him to Hollywood Park to the California Horse Racing Board offices for what they thought was his hearing on the matter. While they were driving his father was "trying to think of a story."[8]

The office staff there had no resolution and offered only that they would get back to him. Mr. Baffert later received a letter indicating he had missed his hearing (he was supposed to go to the Sacramento board offices, not Hollywood Park). A new hearing was scheduled for six months later. While the resolution was pending, Mr. Baffert was unable to take the horses he trained to races for those six months. When the hearing finally

(continued)

---

[7]Bob Baffert and Steve Haskin, *Dirt Road to the Derby* (1999), pp. 83–86.

[8]Baffert and Haskin, p. 84.

Case 4.3

(continued)

came, Mr. Baffert went and told his "story, which was that security was "lax" and "suspicious characters" were lurking about. He testified that he fell victim to one of those suspicious characters.

The Board concluded that he "seemed like a nice kid" so only suspended him for a year and made it retroactive. Mr. Baffert's take was, "I had already done six months and didn't care."[9]

During the remaining six months of his suspension, Mr. Baffert and his dad continued to train horses at their ranch in Tucson. Mr. Baffert explained that he also went to races with those horses, "[W]henever we'd haul a horse to the track, my dad would hide me in the trailer when we came to the gate. After we got to the barn, I'd get out and get the horse ready, and stayed in the barn. After we cooled the horse out, I'd get back in the trailer and leave. That's the way it went for the next six months."[10]

Evaluate the categories that applied to Mr. Baffert early in his career. Discuss what lines he crossed.

Now, consider Mr. Baffert's history during his career in pursuit of wins and Triple Crowns. Mr. Baffert has had 29 failed drug tests by his horses over the course of his career, and the issues and resolution of those cases appear below.

The Thyroid Hormones

Mr. Baffert was investigated in 2013, when seven horses he was training died within a 16-month period. The horses had been given a thyroid hormone without a diagnosis of any underlying thyroid problems. Mr. Baffert said that he gave the horses the drug to build them up. The drug can cause weight loss. No action was taken against Mr. Baffert.

Scopolamine, or Jimsonweed, and the 2018 Triple Crown

In 2018, Justify, Mr. Baffert's horse that went on to win the triple crown, had tested positive for scopolamine following his win in the Santa Anita Derby, a race just prior to the Kentucky Derby. Scopolamine is also a banned substance that can clear the airways and optimize the heart rate,

thus enabling horses to run faster. Mr. Baffert's defense was that scopolamine can be found in jimsonweed, which can grow in the wild where dung is found. That dung-ridden soil is where hay and straw are produced, thereby introducing jimsonweed into feed, which then goes straight into the horse's mouth. This defense, based on naturally occurring substances finding their way into horses, is known as "environmental contamination" and is a recognized defense when horses test positive. Whether there is an illegal level is dependent on the amounts found in the urine and blood of the horse.

At that time, the rules required that Justify be disqualified from the Kentucky Derby pending the outcome of the tests and a hearing, but Mr. Baffert and Justify were permitted to move along to the Derby. Mr. Baffert had worked for the chair of the California Horse Racing Board, the body charged with enforcement of the rules and hearings at that time. In fact, seven of the Board members had employed Mr. Baffert as their trainer.

The Board investigated for four months, allowing Justify to enter in the Preakness and Belmont Stakes, thereby winning the Triple Crown.

In August 2018, a month after Justify had secured the Triple Crown and his breeding rights had been sold for $60 million, the California Racing Commission Board found that Justify's failed test was the result of "environmental contamination." The charges against Mr. Baffert were dismissed.

The 2020 Racing Season

The 2020 racing season was a tough one for Baffert horses. Two Baffert-trained horses, Gamine and Charlatan, tested positive for lidocaine. Mr. Baffert and others argued that the horses had been accidentally exposed to lidocaine (or betamethasone, a corticosteroid injected into joints to reduce pain and swelling) by an assistant trainer who had applied a medicinal patch to his own back, i.e., he used Salonpas. Mr. Baffert alleged that small amounts of lidocaine on the trainer's hands then made it into the horses when assistant trainers applied their tongue ties. The tongue tie keeps horses from getting their tongues over the bit—it is elastic wrapped around a horse's tongue and then tied along the lower jaw. Following a hearing, Mr. Baffert was suspended for

---

[9]Baffert and Haskin, p. 86.

[10]Baffert and Haskin, p. 86.

(continued)

Case 4.3

(continued)

15 days and the first-place wins for the horses were taken back, along with the cash prizes.

Gamine had already tested positive for betamethasone, which Mr. Baffert says was not illegal but was administered outside of the permitted 14-day window for administration under racing rules.[11]

Also in 2020, Mr. Baffert's horse Merneith tested positive for dextromethorphan, an ingredient found in cough syrups. Mr. Baffert explained that a staff member was taking the drug for COVID-19 but offered no explanation as to how the drug got into the horse.[12]

Mr. Baffert did win the Kentucky Derby in 2020 with Authentic, bringing his number of Derby wins to six, a tie with Ben Jones for the most victories in horse racing.[13]

Federal Prosecutions and New Regulations

In 2020, the federal government issued indictments against 27 people on various charges that alleged a scheme to secretly dope horses as a means of deceiving those who bet on horse races. Included among those charged was Jason Servis, who had trained Maximum Security, the 2019 first finisher of the Kentucky Derby. That first place was taken away when the Kentucky Racing Commission disqualified the horse for nearly tumbling a rival horse in one of the turns, something that slowed the momentum of other horses as well.[14]

At the end of 2020, Congress passed the federal Horseracing Integrity and Safety Act.[15] The federal act was passed and signed into law because of a significant number of horse collapses on tracks as well as the ongoing medication scandals. One of the problems with the act is that the Federal Trade Commission (FTC) will be responsible for its enforcement. However, the FTC has a significant caseload in handling consumer fraud and other cases. In addition, the FTC has no animal expertise

on staff, something that perhaps was available through the Department of Agriculture, which also has a significantly smaller caseload. The act took effect in 2022, and the FTC has proceeded with developing the processes for testing and regulating training and racing.

2021, Medina Spirit, and the Kentucky Derby

In 2021, Medina Spirit, the Baffert horse with 12–1 odds, won the Kentucky Derby by a nose. Following the race, Medina Spirit tested positive for betamethasone. There was a twist to the story this time. Mr. Baffert said that the accusations were a result of "cancel culture."[16] That initial story changed to Mr. Baffert's claim that he would never give his horses betamethasone. That story quickly fell apart because we know, however, from Gamine testing, that he did not deny giving the horse betamethasone. Rather, he confessed to giving the horse betamethasone outside the window permitted.[17]

The story then changed and went back to the Baffert original formula: Medina Spirit had dermatitis on his bottom and the vet recommended Otomax, a cream that contains betamethasone, as the treatment. Mr. Baffert says that he did not know about that treatment, but the vet says that he informed Mr. Baffert. The question became one of determining whether the 21 picograms of betamethasone in Medina Spirit's drug test could be explained by the cream. Medina Spirit finished third in the Preakness, but the New York Racing Association prohibited Mr. Baffert from entering any of his horses in the Belmont or at any of New York's other tracks. Churchill Downs has prohibited Mr. Baffert from entering horses in the next two Kentucky Derbys. Mr. Baffert said in response to the actions taken against him, "I am the most scrutinized trainer. And I am okay with that. The last thing I want to do is jeopardize the greatest sport. This is a pretty serious accusation. We're going to get to the bottom of it (as it were.) We didn't do it."[18]

(continued)

---

[11]Merneith, Another Baffert Charge Tests Positive for Banned Substance, *Online Gambling*, October 22, 2020, https://www. onlinegambling.com/news/merneith-another-baffert-charge-tests-positive-for-banned-substance/.

[12]Joe Drape, "Baffert Enters Breeder's Cup Trailed by Suspicion, *New York Times*, November 6, 2020, p. B9.

[13]*Id.*

[14]Joe Drape, "Failed Drug Test Puts Derby Win at Risk and a Trainer Under Fire," *New York Times*, May 10, 2021, p. A1.

[15]15 U.S.C. §§3501 *et seq.*

[16]Jared Diamond, "Derby-Winning Colt Dies After Workout," *Wall Street Journal*, December 7, 2021, p. A6.

[17]Joe Drape, "Baffert Enters Breeder's Cup Trailed by Suspicion, *New York Times*, November 6, 2020, p. B9.

[18]Joe Drape, "Failed Drug Test Puts Derby Win at Risk and a Trainer Under Fire," *New York Times*, May 10, 2021, p. A1.

Case 4.3

(continued)

The fate of Medina Spirit's 2021 victory in the Kentucky Derby has yet to be determined. A New York lab has confirmed that the topical ointment the vet gave to Medina Spirit did contain betamethasone. However, the determination of whether its presence was at levels high enough to improve Medina Spirit's performance will be made posthumously. Medina Spirit collapsed and died after a workout at Santa Anita in December 2021.[19] Mr. Baffert said of the colt's death, "I will always cherish the proud and personal memories of Medina Spirit and his tremendous spirit."[20]

---

[19]Id.

[20]Id.

Discussion Questions

1. Under which category does the Baffert explanation strategy in responding to drug tests fit?

2. What do you learn about stories and the power of inconsistencies from tracing the positive drug tests in Mr. Baffert's horses?

3. Is there an industry issue that needs to be addressed before individual trainers' ethical standards can improve? Why was the Horseracing Integrity and Safety Act necessary? Is there a regulatory cycle evident in the issue of winning horses testing positive so many times?

The Organizational Behavior Factors

Reading 4.4

The Preparation for a Defining Ethical Moment

Marianne M. Jennings[21]

When we face those life-defining, career-defining, and organization-defining ethical dilemmas, are we sufficiently prepared through the ethics training our organizations offer? There are things that organizations can do to better prepare employees for those tough ethical choices they may face.

Preparation: The Formal Ethical Infrastructure

Organizations have their codes of ethics, handbooks, and training. Organizations that lack these formal ethical infrastructures are not giving their employees a critical aspect of preparation. The presence of these tools is some way of assuring that at least everybody has access to the same information.

One of the components missing in too many of the codes, manuals, and training is instructions on how to raise questions and report issues and the language to use when confronted by a supervisor asking them to cross an ethical line. Or, what to do when no one seems interested in addressing an ethical issue they are raising. Where do I go? What do I say? What happens if no one responds? Employees need a chart, a sort of checklist, on how to proceed, especially when they hit a blockade in that orderly chart. Alternatives when nothing is working is what most employees find they need when facing an ethical issue. When everyone has been exposed to the same training, repeated regularly, crises situations find them relying on what has been drilled into them and made a part of the culture.

Preparation: Studying the Missteps

Unless and until we study the situations in which people make mistakes, we continue along the cheery path of believing that nothing could possibly go wrong in our organization, because we have the formal ethical infrastructure of training and a good code.

Unless employees understand what it feels and looks like for ethics to go south, they will not make good decisions in averting an ethical crisis. There are common factors that precede ethical crises. For example, in Enron, HealthSouth,

---

[21]Adapted from "The Preparation for a Defining Ethical Moment," 35 *New Perspectives* 11 (2016), with permission.

Madoff, Finova, Fannie Mae, and other companies, unprecedented performance preceded the ethical collapse. Volkswagen's ethical and legal issue of the installation of software to shut off emissions controls except during emissions testing is historical precedent for ethical issues. Years prior to the revelation of the falsified emissions, many within Volkswagen were raising questions about how Volkswagen was achieving such low emissions with diesel engines. In fact, California regulators raised questions about the phenomenal emissions performance of the cars two years before Volkswagen made its announcement of the deception. Studying what ethical lapses look and feel like and the precursor warnings help employees to spot the signs and raise questions or take actions to avert damage.

Preparation: Look around the Industry—No One Is Immune

Too many times, we turn a blind eye to what is happening in our industry with the assumption of, "Not at our company." Volkswagen leaders should have been asking questions because the auto industry has a longstanding history of evading emissions regulations.[22] Volkswagen, Ford, and Chrysler were all fined for various forms of cheating on auto emissions, starting as early as 1972. In fact, there was a term in the industry for engineering around emissions requirements: "defeat devices." Perhaps the better approach in our preparation would be to look around the industry and explore this question, "Why would we be immune from what everybody else seems to be doing?" Once we explore the immunity question, we can start looking at organizational actions and see if we might be doing exactly the same thing.

Preparation: Simulations

In ethics training, we use hypotheticals and, on occasion, real examples that have happened in our own organizations. However, we seem to be missing the depth of simulation training. We can sit in training classrooms or at our computers and determine the correct answer to the ethical dilemma, but we are not doing so under the reality of pressure. Pressure comes from a supervisor, peers, goals, looming performance evaluations, or bonuses hanging in the balance. We solve the ethical dilemmas in a sterile environment with no time, earnings, or other clocks ticking as they are in flight and other mechanical simulators.

Ethics simulation training is available; we just fail to recognize it. All of us tromp through ethical dilemmas each day but fail to recognize them as training. Learning to see that the day-to-day dilemmas, no matter how small, are the training for the defining ethical dilemmas at work is critical to preparation. Ethical dilemmas are the same in terms of underlying issues. Only the fact patterns change. We need to see the blockades employees faced in raising issues in hypotheticals. We need to see what rationalization looks like as employees grapple with ethical dilemmas. It is not just a matter of studying the issue itself. We have to study what responses occurred, why, and how they could have been addressed to get to the heart of the ethical issue.

A student offered the following example of an ethical dilemma that she had faced. "When working at a fast-food place, I saw my co-workers giving out free food to their friends. We are not supposed to do that." The students all groaned with observations, "That's no big deal!" "Who doesn't do that?" "No one is really hurt by that!" A follow-up example was different in fact pattern and earned different reactions, "I worked as a waiter and a big table of people I had served walked out without paying. I have to make up for that. The restaurant makes me pay." The

---

[22]Danny Hakim and Hiroko Tabuchi, "An Industry with an Outlaw Streak against Regulation," *New York Times*, September 24, 2015, p. B1.

students were outraged, "That's awful!" "Who does that?" The same issue of free food was involved, but it was all a question of who did what to whom. When they experience the loss, the ethical analysis is different from when free food is the restaurant's loss. The analysis is the same. Somehow when our ox is gored, we do not see the issue in the same way as when someone else feels the pain.

The reactions? "Well, there is pressure because you want a job from the internship." "That's what people do to get things funded." "Everybody does it." "It gets you in the door and then you can change the proposal later." This simulation brought in the pressures students feel about getting a job, wanting to fit in, and, perhaps, not having the knowledge or understanding about how, when, and to whom to raise ethical issues.

Ironically, the hypotheticals are identical. Both involve taking something that does not belong to you. Both involve losses for someone. Both involve one person taking advantage of another. However, the perceptions changed because of the pressures in the simulation were different. Training for that life-defining ethical dilemma at work requires the practice of making ethical decisions in the day-to-day situations so that we begin to see the patterns and understand the issues. When we learn to categorize ethical issues simply—is this true? is this fair? is this how I would want to be treated?—we train for the ethical dilemmas of financial reporting, billing codes, certifications, audit sampling, depreciation formulas, reserves, and other seemingly complex events of work.

We need to explore missteps by employees that show we are tempted to conceal, and even wild behavior by employees who skirt regulations in the name of expediency, a misguided good cause, or (fill in your own experience here). At that moment, the training, the infrastructure, the case studies, and the hypotheticals come together to provide the decision tree that produces a good decision despite the unexpected. But, the preparation must have been constant, varied, and applied daily for "that day" when we really need it all.

Discussion Questions

1. Explain the components of good preparation for seeing and resolving ethical dilemmas.

2. Why do we differ in our responses to some hypotheticals when the underlying ethical category and issue are the same?

Case 4.5

Swiping Oreos at Work: Is It a Big Deal?

Penny Winters was a 63-year-old maintenance worker at the Portage, Indiana, Walmart store. The surveillance cameras caught Ms. Winters eating Oreos that she had not paid for during her evening shift at the store. When asked why she did it, Ms. Winters explained that she did not have the money to buy the cookies. She earned $11.40 per hour (the usual Walmart pay was then $8.87 per hour), but her son had been in a motorcycle accident and was unable to work, thus making her the sole wage earner in her home.

Ms. Winters also confessed that she had been taking Oreos, gum, deli sandwiches, chocolate, and potato chips for more than eight years, with four of the years being at a Walmart in Tucson, Arizona, where Ms. Winters originally lived.[23] She confessed to taking one to two items per week during her shift. She indicated that she began eating Oreos that were open and near cash registers because

(continued)

---

[23]The information was taken from the Portage Police Department report, found at http://www.thesmokinggun.com/file/oreo-cookie-bust.

Case 4.5

(continued)

she assumed that they could not be sold and would just be thrown away. However, when the opened packages were not available, she would simply remove the food from the shelves and then take it into the break room, where she would eat it. The result was, because junk food costs add up over eight years, that Ms. Winters was charged with felony theft. She has come to be known as the "Oreo Grandma."

Discussion Questions

1. Explain the gradual drift of Ms. Winters and discuss her justification for the drift.

2. Some have suggested that Walmart should not prosecute Ms. Winters because of her circumstances. Walmart loses $3 billion per year to employee theft of merchandise. Are there stakeholders involved in this decision?

3. The police report indicates that Ms. Winters has never had any legal charges filed against her. Police could not locate any parking tickets or moving violations in Indiana or Arizona. Given her lifetime of obeying the law, explain what happened that would cause Ms. Winters to take the food.

4. A security manager for a major retail store explained what she called the 80% factor. Her store's experience was that 10% of the people they hire are absolutely honest; they would never steal anything from the store no matter how easy it might be or what opportunities they had to do so. She also added that another 10% would always steal from the store. In fact, she noted that some people seek jobs from their store just to steal. She explained that they do not have to worry about the "absolutely honest 10%." She also said that there is not much they can do with the stealing 10% group except get them out of there when they catch them. She finished by saying that they spend their time and effort in trying to prevent the 80% from being in situations where it is tempting and easy for them to steal. In other words, she worked on preventing the "not so bad" yet "not so good" from falling into bad behavior. What does the retail experience say about ethical infrastructure? What does it say about character? What does it say about the costs of unethical behavior by employees?

Reading 4.6

The Effects of Compensation Systems: Incentives, Bonuses, Pay, and Ethics[24]

How are the mighty fallen![25] As we watched the financial firms and businesses fold in near domino fashion following the 2008 financial crisis, we found ourselves wondering what we did or could now do differently that has or will serve to distinguish us from the fallen. By July 2010, the **Dodd–Frank Wall Street Reform and Consumer Protection Act** took effect. Companies regulated under the 1934 Securities Exchange Act had to comply with new requirements for setting executive pay, including independent compensation committees and a requirement of outside compensation consultants to review compensation packages and compare them with peer companies' compensation systems. By 2011, companies had to comply with the so-called **"say on pay" provisions** adopted pursuant to Dodd–Frank, which required shareholders to vote on the frequency of their approvals on the compensation packages for executives. The shareholder vote is advisory only but the company's compensation discussion must include disclosures

---

[24]Adapted from an article by Marianne M. Jennings in *Corporate Finance Review* 13(4): 37–40 (2009).

[25]2 Samuel 1:27. The reference is to King Saul who, along with his three sons, died during a battle with the Philistines. Saul died by the now infamous fate of falling on his sword because the Philistines had defeated Israel, his kingdom.

of whether the compensation committee and board have taken the shareholder advisory vote in establishing compensation. The disclosures are mandatory for all 1934 Act companies and each proxy season finds refinement in disclosures and more shareholder attention to the issue of executive compensation. Proxy materials must include the following information:

- The median of the annual total compensation of all its employees, except the CEO;
- The annual total compensation of the top five executives in the company (including the CEO and CFO);
- The ratio of those two amounts (employee median compensation and executive median compensation); and
- A summary compensation table with other tables that show stock options, long-term incentive awards, pension plans, employment contracts, and any related compensation arrangements.

Beyond the regulatory disclosure requirements, the issue of compensation is critical in creating and sustaining an ethical culture. Compensation and incentive plans motivate employees. When board compensation committees and boards are establishing compensation and incentive plans, they need to study the effects of both components on behaviors, culture, and the ability of leaders and employees to see and address ethical issues that arise as employees try to meet goals for their compensation, incentive, and bonus plans.

Suspend Your Compensation Plans, and Revisit Your Incentive and Compensation Formulas and Processes

Since the time the first pay disclosure requirements went into effect, we have seen increasing attention and more proposals for more disclosure and even stepping into that final frontier of compensation regulation, that of actually curbing executive pay. Companies have two choices on compensation packages: (1) They can opt to self-regulate; or (2) they can wait for new regulation to place limitations that could produce further unintended consequences as they add additional compliance costs. Shareholders are also driving controls. For the 2021 proxy season, there were 49 proposals by shareholders of 1934 Act companies on executive compensation, with the largest number of those proposals focusing on including environmental, social, and cybersecurity factors as a part of executive compensation. There is one additional issue that has been addressed by about half of the S&P companies. That issue is disclosure of the full relationship between the company and the company's pay consultants. Many of the consulting firms providing companies opinions on the structure and soundness of the companies' executive pay structure are retained by those same companies to provide the frameworks for and elements of that pay structure. During one of many congressional hearings on the topic of executive compensation, the evidence showed that 113 of the top *Fortune* 250 firms had pay consultants that played dual roles for those companies. The evidence also showed that two-thirds of the companies with these extensive relationships with their pay consultants did not disclose the extent of those relationships.

In other words, pay consulting firms are doing what audit firms were doing pre-Enron. The same firms who are offering their imprimatur for the soundness of the companies' practices are the ones that designed those practices. Here, however, the disparity between the consulting services and the certification services is more along the lines of 10:1 as opposed to the audit firms, which were about split evenly between consulting and audit fees. We realized post-Enron that it takes a fairly strong-willed firm that designed a company's internal controls to turn around and say that those internal controls are no good. So it is with pay structure design and pay structure soundness. Those functions must now be performed by separate firms. Presently, the compensation conflicts are where the audit conflicts were pre-Enron. The law requires that companies disclose only the identity of the firm that provides the opinion on the soundness of the companies' compensation packages and formulas. The companies need not disclose the extent of their additional consulting relationships with the certifying firm.

Tackling the Testy Issues in Compensation, Bonus, and Incentive Plans

There are some steps companies can take to make their compensation, bonus, and incentive plans more transparent and less likely to face shareholder challenges and regulatory mandates.

1. Establish better relationships with shareholder groups that have reform proposals:[26] Disclose the extent of the company's relationships with pay consultants. Questions arise as to whether the companies that do not disclose these consulting arrangements are in compliance with SEC rules on executive compensation consultant disclosures. The SEC rule provides that there must be disclosure of "any role of compensation consultants in determining or recommending the amount or form of executive and director compensation."[27] The SEC has also offered interpretive guidance that requires companies to disclose all consultants that played a role in determining pay.[28] The Conference Board offers the following suggestion:

   > When the compensation committee uses information and services from outside consultants, it must ensure that consultants are independent of management and provide objective, neutral advice to the committee. . . . The economics of the consultants' engagement for services is very important as an insight into independence. Any imbalance in fees generated by management versus fees generated on behalf of the committee should receive intense scrutiny;[29]

2. Consider bifurcation of the design and certification functions of pay consultants;

3. Check with compensation consulting firms to see what checks and balances they have implemented internally to guard against potential conflicts and independence;[30] and

---

[26]Two activist groups that have an open forum in Congress are the Institute for Policy Studies and United for a Fair Economy. Also see faireconomy.com. These groups have been successful in gaining mandatory shareholder approval votes in some companies and, as noted earlier, have been successful in obtaining symbolic, but required, shareholder votes on compensation packages.

[27]SEC, Final Rules on Executive Compensation and Related Party Disclosures, Items 402 (b) and 407 (e) of Regulation S-K (2020).

[28]SEC, Staff Interpretation: Item 407 of Regulation S-K — Corporate Governance (March 13, 2007).

[29]The Conference Board, "US Top Executive Compensation Report: 2014 Edition," and "The Five Most Important Things Companies Need to Know and Do about the SEC's Proposed Pay Ratio Rules," 2013, www.conferenceboard.org. Accessed April 22, 2016.

[30]Some of the executive compensation consulting firms have voluntarily implemented internal rotation and independence policies akin to those audit firms use, that is, senior consultants must rotate out from account after five years and/or another senior consultant must review the work of the consultant that works with the company. On the other hand, some of the executive compensation firms have internal documents that reflect the desire of the firm to "cross-sell" companies on a wide variety of services the firms provide. Their goal is more business.

4. Consider bold reforms in compensation packages, looking at issues such as upper limitations, pay relationship limitations (limits on pay of executives as compared to employee salaries),[31] kill clauses (events in which no bonuses will be paid), and limits on or elimination of perks (see following).

5. Revisit the metrics. Behaviors do not change when you measure output. If one measure of bonuses is a goal of no safety breaches (or a minimum amount), employees and managers will meet the goal, but the numbers may not be real. Managers redefine what a safety issue is by reclassifying events or asking employees to hold off on getting treatment. The number of safety breaches is the output. Behavior-based compensation such as the number of safety hazards addressed will reduce the output figure and really make the company safer.

Plenty of goodwill is out there for companies that undertake bold reforms in executive compensation.

Check Your Perks

An insurance company clearly needs to reward those agents who sold, sold, sold. But now is the time for all good managers to come to the aid of their companies by issuing general edicts on perks. Once again, there is goodwill for the taking for companies that voluntarily cut back on perks during this era of angst, job losses, and poor earnings results. The following suggestions would be a way to accomplish these self-restraints with full cooperation of employees who might be affected.

- Bring employees into the loop and ask for their ideas on how to cut costs without cutting jobs.
- Ask for ideas from all areas of the company and all employees. In one company, employees suggested that in lieu of the company holiday party, all employees simply participate in a Saturday community cleanup event that was sponsored by a group that has been a part of one employee's life for nearly 20 years.
- Set the tone by cutting expenses at the top. Private jet travel, auto allowances, and private car services are a few of the executive expenses being voluntarily cut as a way of setting an example for employees.

There are many free marketers and Friedman disciples among us who are able to make the intellectually sound argument that the market will remedy excesses and that pay decisions are best left to the companies with the oversight of shareholders who are free to participate through their votes or vote through their departure from the companies that are not performing but are rewarding managers nonetheless. In theory, they are correct. However, economic theory must operate within the reality of human emotion. Human emotion is controlling the markets these days. Perception is everything. Taking control of those negative perceptions, even when logic supplies an explanation, creates goodwill and results in trust. These voluntary actions must be simple and symbolic, along the lines of those provided here. With trust restored, we may be able to find our way out of the teetering economy so susceptible to perceptions of breach.

---

[31]Dramatic increases in executive compensation have widened the gulf between CEO pay and the pay of the average worker. In 1980, CEOs in the United States were paid 40 times the average worker. In 2020, the average CEO pay was 351 times the average worker. Lawrence Mishel and Jori Kandra, "CEO Pay Has Skyrocketed 1,322% since 1978," *Economic Policy Institute*, August 10, 2021, https://www.epi.org/publication/ceo-pay-in-2020/.

Discussion Questions

1. Develop a chart that shows the distinctions between prevalent compensation packages and the new approaches suggested.

2. *USA Today* had an article that listed several CEOs who made $9,000 per hour.[32] The CEOs included Starbucks' Howard Schultz, CVS's Larry Merlo, and L Brands' (the parent company of Victoria's Secret) Leslie Wexner (now former CEO). The article ran during a time when the $15 minimum wage debates were erupting all over the United States. What does this type of coverage and article tell you about the importance of executive compensation inside companies as well as in their external relationships?

3. Apply the issues of social responsibility and the regulatory cycle (Unit 3) to issues in executive compensation.

Reading 4.7

Measures, Metrics, and Gaming — Part A

The human mind knows no limits when it comes to figuring out ways to meet goals, even if it means gaming the system an organization has created for measuring performance and awarding compensation, bonuses, and incentives. The BP (2.8), Penn State (2.10), and Fannie Mae (3.8) cases illustrate the concepts in those units but also show the effects of incentives on employee behaviors and decisions. The structures the organization puts into place influence employee behaviors. We are human and we respond to avoiding the pain that confronts us immediately as opposed to avoiding pain in the future.

Ethics in Action 4.2

The Way to Meet Fitness Goals

Sam's company was offering every employee a fitness tracker. If employees met their fitness goals (included standing, steps, and minutes exercising) they received a reduction in their health insurance premiums for every week of meeting their goals. His company's health insurer was giving the company a corresponding cost reduction for a healthier workforce.

Sam was sitting with his mother, talking. As they chatted, Sam would occasionally raise his arm over his head. After several of these random motions, Sam's mother asked if anything was wrong. Sam explained, "No. It's just that I have not met my standing goal for today and I know that if I just raise my hand above my head it counts and I can meet my goal. Sam's mother was confused, "But you didn't stand up!" Sam replied, "But they don't know that and they put the program in place."

1. Describe what ethical categories are involved in Sam's behavior in "meeting" his goals.

2. Into what ethical development category would you put Sam?

3. Who are the stakeholders in this dilemma?

4. What would happen if all employees at his company did what Sam was doing?

---

[32]Matt Krantz, "$15 an Hour? Try $9,000 or More for These CEOs," *USA Today*, April 18, 2016, p. 1B.

There are 1,000 mantras about goals, incentives, and compensation. Jim Collins offered his advice in *Built to Last* to set **"Big, Hairy, Audacious Goals" or BHAGs.** Set the goals high and watch employees stretch to meet them. Boldness, bravado, braggadocio.

The history of business ethics teaches and these pages will recount examples aplenty debunking the assumption that the numbers employees produce that are tied to their compensation, incentives, and bonuses are real. What if the numbers are inflated? Employees will reach those BHAGs, but the numbers they post could have everything from footnote qualifications to fraud. These manipulations have gone on for so long that we keep passing laws to try and stop them. Following a string of accounting frauds in the 2001–2002 period (think multibillion-dollar restatements of income), new federal legislation required officers of corporations to repay any bonuses they earned during periods when their bonuses were based on falsified numbers that they created. In addition, Congress added a new crime for certification of false financial statements. Anyone in a corporation who, by signature, certifies false financial statements could be sentenced to up to 20 years. That's how real "gaming" compensation systems is.

The design of rewards, incentives, and bonuses needs reforms (what and when we measure) and organizations need controls for catching gaming strategies that employees develop to make their numbers. The following cases illustrate the kinds of creative gaming employees can use to meet their numbers. Following these cases is Part B (Reading 4.11 Measures, Metrics, and Gaming—Part B) of this reading to summarize what you will learn from studying the cases that involved poorly designed, poorly monitored, and misaligned incentives.

Case 4.8

VA: The Patient Queues

The Veterans Administration (VA), the country's largest health care system with 9 million Veteran patients and 1,200 facilities, had a plan. It was a program begun with the best of intentions: reward and evaluate employees and managers on getting the waiting times down for veterans seeking treatment at the VA's clinics and hospitals. It was a plan with good intentions, but bad results. A program begun in 2009 became the focus of a Government Accountability report, the subject of congressional and inspector general (OIG) reports, and a target for the public's outrage.

The Program

In 2011, the VA's goal was to have no patient wait longer than 30 days for treatment. In 2011, that number was changed to 14 days, and meeting that goal was nearly the singular criterion for performance awards and salary increases. However, because of staffing and facility limitations, the 14 days was as unattainable as the 30 days. Interestingly, the undersecretary of health who

changed the goal from 30 days to 14 days told veterans groups that the target was unrealistic. Just days after that disclosure, he resigned from his position before the program was implemented.

As a result, the schedulers in the VA system were under tremendous pressure and were told by supervisors and others to take steps that would make the wait times "appear more favorable."[33] The strategies used by the schedulers were entering incorrect data into the software about the patient's treatment and timing for tests and consultations (13% of employees). In some cases, the schedulers created "secret" wait lists that were unauthorized and resulted in patient records of treatment and contact being lost (done by 8% of employees).[34] Patients who were lost in the system were never called

(continued)

---

[33]Ben Kesling, "Internal VA Audit Confirms Tampering with Patient Wait Times," *Wall Street Journal*, May 30, 2014, http://www.wsj.com/articles/internal-va-audit-confirms-tampering-with-patient-wait-times-1401481139. Accessed October 24, 2016.

[34]*Id.*

Case 4.8

(continued)

back for follow-up tests or treatment. Following the delivery of the audit report to then-president Obama, the then-VA secretary Eric Shinseki submitted his resignation, which Mr. Obama accepted. Mr. Shinseki said that the VA had a "systemic, totally unacceptable lack of integrity" that he was unable to explain.[35] Mr. Obama said, "When I hear allegations of misconduct—any misconduct—whether it's allegations of VA staff covering up long wait times or cooking the books, I will not stand for it. Not as commander in chief, but also not as an American."[36]

The Office of the Medical Inspector (OMI) audit report recommended removing the 14-day target and suspending the program for performance awards and salary increases that were tied to getting the queue times down.

What Went Wrong

The VA employees developed these methods to meet a goal that simply was not attainable. Because queue data were manipulated, the VA was able to cover up a problem that was inevitable because of the new waves of veterans returning from Iraq and Afghanistan as well as the increasing needs of Vietnam era veterans who were experiencing the increasing medical care demands of aging. The problem was systemic, with no solution possible without additional providers and facilities. The 2014 data indicated that the VA failed to treat three of every five veterans within its 14-day goal.[37] The Office of Special Counsel (OSC) sent a letter to the president that described the scheduling problems and issues:

- A shortage of providers caused the facility to frequently cancel appointments for veterans. After cancellations, providers did not conduct required follow-up, resulting in situations where "routine primary care needs were not addressed."

- The facility "blind scheduled" veterans whose appointments were canceled, meaning veterans

were not consulted when rescheduling the appointment. If a veteran subsequently called to change the blind-scheduled appointment date, schedulers were instructed to record the appointment as canceled at the patient's request. This practice had the effect of deleting the initial "desired date" for the appointment, so records would no longer indicate that the initial appointment was canceled by the facility.

- At the time of the OMI report, nearly 3,000 veterans were unable to reschedule canceled appointments, and one nurse practitioner alone had a total of 975 patients who were unable to reschedule appointments.

- Staff were instructed to alter wait times to make the waiting periods look shorter.

- Schedulers were placed on a "bad boy" list if their scheduled appointments were greater than 14 days from the recorded "desired dates" for veterans.

In addition, OSC investigated reprisal allegations by schedulers including two who were reportedly removed from their positions at Fort Collins and reassigned to Cheyenne, WY, for not complying with the instructions to "zero out" wait times. After these employees were replaced, the officially recorded wait times for appointments drastically "improved," even though the wait times were actually much longer than the officially recorded data.

Despite these detailed findings, the OMI report concluded, "Due to the lack of specific cases for evaluation, OMI could not substantiate that the failure to properly train staff resulted in a danger to public health and safety."[38]

Most of the complaints filed with the OIG for the VA were dismissed as "harmless errors."[39] The chairman of the Veterans Affairs Committee in the House of

(continued)

[35]Richard A. Oppel Jr., "Investigator Issues Sharp Criticism of VA Response to Allegations about Care," *New York Times*, June 24, 2014, p. A15.

[36]Gregg Zoroya and Aamer Madhani, "Obama Vows to Get Tough on VA," *USA Today*, May 22, 2014, p. 1A.

[37]Meghan Hoyer and Gregg Zoroya, "Fraud Masks VA Wait Times," *USA Today*, June 3, 2014, p. 1A.

[38]U.S. Office of Special Counsel, "Continued Deficiencies at Department of Veterans' Affairs' Facilities," June 23, 2014, http://i2.cdn.turner.com/cnn/2014/images/06/23/osc.va.letter.pdf. Last visited October 25, 2016.

[39]Richard A. Oppel Jr., "Investigator Issues Sharp Criticism of VA Response to Allegations about Care," *New York Times*, June 24, 2014, p. A15.

Case 4.8

(continued)

Representatives said, in response to the findings, "In the fantasy land inhabited by the VA's Office of Medical Inspector, serious patient safety issues apparently have no impact on patient safety."[40]

The VA went 849 days without a permanent IG heading up the VA Office of the Inspector General.[41] The presence of an interim official made it difficult to follow up on reports, ongoing investigations, and tracking of responses and changes.

There were a number of whistleblowers who came forward, but whatever evidence they offered was often ignored or they were driven out of the VA system. A U.S. Senate Report called the office of the VA inspector general a "failure" to vets: "This investigation found the problems at the VA are far deeper than just scheduling. Over the past decade, more than 1,000 veterans may have died as a result of VA's misconduct and the VA has paid out nearly $1 billion to veterans and their families for its medical malpractice."[42]

The Problem Continues

After investigating allegations from a whistleblower at the Phoenix Veterans Administration Health Care System (PVAHCS), the OIG (Office of Healthcare Inspections division, or OHI) issued the following summary:

> Of the 215 individual patients' records reviewed, OHI determined that untimely care from PVAHCS may have contributed to the death of 1 patient. OHI found that this patient never received an appointment for a cardiology exam that could have prompted further definitive testing and interventions that could have forestalled his death. OHI determined that the remaining patients' records

reviewed did not die because they did not receive the requested consult in a timely fashion before they died. We did not substantiate that the facility was having non-clinical staff discontinue consults for vascular patients to hide the fact that a patient died while waiting for care. In regard to the consults reviewed of patients who died while they had open consults, we found that PVAHCS closed these consults because VHA and PVAHCS business rules and policy both required that a consult be discontinued if the patient is deceased. However, facility staff did not consistently comply with this policy and some consults remained open long after patients' deaths.[43]

That finding on a lack of links between delays and deaths was later reversed, as VA officials acknowledged that there was a link between delays and patient deaths. VA officials indicated that the OIG could not "conclusively assert" was "completely misleading" and that the report "played down" the concerns.[44]

In its audit of care discontinuation at the PVAHCS, the OIG determined that 74 of the 309 consults they examined were discontinued inappropriately. For example, some were discontinued because the patient did not show up for treatment but were discontinued without any follow-up with the patients to determine the reason for the no-show. In some cases, no reason was documented for discontinuing care. Non-clinicians discontinued care in 11 cases despite the system's requirement that a clinician (a physician or certain types of health care professionals) is required to make that determination.

Audit reports obtained by *USA Today* as part of a Freedom of Information Act request indicated the problem with wait times continued. Employees at 40 VA medical centers in 19 states and Puerto Rico had regularly "zeroed out" wait times.[45]

(continued)

[40]*Id.*

[41]The Honorable Michael J. Missal was nominated by President Barack H. Obama to serve as the inspector general of the Department of Veterans Affairs (VA) on October 2, 2015, and confirmed by the Senate on April 19, 2016. He assumed responsibility as Inspector General on May 2, 2016. The interim OIG served for 2.5 years prior to the assumption of duties of Mr. Missal, so from 2013 to 2016, the OIG did not have a permanent appointee in charge of the OIG.

[42]Mark Flatten, "New Tom Coburn Report Describes Veterans Affairs Department Wracked by Incompetence, Corruption, Coverups," *Washington Examiner*, June 24, 2014, http://www.washingtonexaminer.com/new-report-describes-veterans-affairs-dept.-wracked-by-corruption-cover-ups/article/2550079. Accessed October 25, 2016.

[43]Veterans Health Administration, "Review of Alleged Consult Mismanagement at the Phoenix VA Health Care System," October 4, 2016, http://www.va.gov/oig/pubs/VAOIG-15-04672-342.pdf. Accessed October 24, 2016.

[44]Richard A Oppel, Jr., "V.A. Officials Acknowledge Link Between Delays and Patient Deaths," *New York Times*, September 18, 2014, p. A17.

[45]Donovan Slack, "VA Bosses Falsified Veterans' Wait Times," *USA Today*, May 31, 2016, p. 1A.

Case 4.8

(continued)

Oversight and Management

One of the problems with the VA and 14 other federal agencies in terms of addressing employee misconduct is that terminations are rare. The Office of Personnel Management has disclosed that only 0.47% of the federal labor force is fired for cause (as compared to 3% terminations for cause in the private sector).[46] Only three senior VA executives were terminated following the ongoing reports from the 2014 period.[47] As a result, Congress passed civil service reform that gives the VA greater flexibility in terminations. However, the legislative reform applies only to the top 360 executives in the VA and not its 360,000 employees. The legislation does not appear to be working. The former head of the Phoenix VA was fired after six months of paid leave but has appealed that decision on the grounds that it is unconstitutional for a non-appointed employee to preside over a case involving an appeal by a senior executive. Then–attorney general Loretta Lynch conceded in the lawsuit that the former director was correct.[48]

Ironically, one of the congressional fixes for the problems was to give the VA more money, funds that now allow it to refer veterans out for private care at no cost when the VA system is oversubscribed.[49] The result is that the underlying problem of additional staffing and facilities will not be solved because the private sector will receive the patients the VA cannot handle and the VA will not be able to handle unless and until the system is expanded and improved.

The former CEO of Procter & Gamble, Robert McDonald, was confirmed by the Senate by a 97–0 vote as the new head of the VA. A graduate of West Point and a retired army captain, Mr. McDonald worked for P&G for 33 years,

with his last 4 years as CEO. Mr. McDonald seemed to be an ideal fit. However, within months of his appointment, he apologized publicly for lying about serving with the special operations forces. In his apology released by the VA, he said, "While I was in Los Angeles, engaging a homeless individual to determine his veteran status, I asked the man where he had served in the military. He responded that he had served in special forces. I incorrectly stated that I had been in special forces. That was inaccurate and I apologize to anyone that was offended by my misstatement."[50] Mr. McDonald had to later apologize for a remark he made about waiting times: "When you go to Disney, do they measure the number of hours you wait in line? What's important is, what's your satisfaction with the experience?"[51] Mr. McDonald said he does and will continue to take the VA mission seriously.

In July 2016, the VA stopped sending quality of care data to the national data base for consumers despite a 2014 law that required the VA to submit such data.[52] When it was initially tested in 2021, the VA's new health record system actually slowed down the delivery of health care. The formal rollout began in March 2022 at one facility and will expand to others. The VA has estimated that it will take 10 years and more than $15 billion to update the system across all facilities and get it working efficiently.[53]

The Phoenix VA, one of the epicenters of the system's problems, has a new director, RimaAnn Nelson, the seventh director in three years. The new director came from a small VA facility in the Philippines where she was sent following a series of incidents that occurred while she served as director for the St. Louis VA. The incidents involved patient infection exposure from breaches in the cleaning and sterilization of medical equipment. There were concerns about 1,769 veterans being exposed to

(continued)

[46]Office of Personnel Management, Report on Terminations Other Than Retirement, https://www.opm.gov/policy-data-oversight/data-analysis-documentation/personnel-documentation/processing-personnel-actions/gppa31.pdf.

[47]Mark Hemingway, "The Real VA Problem," *The Weekly Standard*, June 9, 2014, p. 10.

[48]"Firing Federal Workers Is Hard to Do," *USA Today*, September 22, 2016, p. 7A.

[49]"Scandal Pays Off for the VA," *Wall Street Journal*, August 4, 2014, p. A12. The VA received $17 billion for the interim expenses and $5 billion for hiring more staff and $1.5 billion for new leases of facilities.

[50]Office of Public and Intergovernmental Affairs, Transcript of Secretary McDonald Press Conference, February 25, 2015, http://www.stripes.com/news/veterans/va-secretary-apologizes-for-false-claim-reactions-mixed-1.331346.

[51]Daniel Henninger, "We're All in Disney World," *Wall Street Journal*, May 26, 2016, p. A11.

[52]Donovan Slack, "VA Quit Sending Info to Database for Comparisons," *USA Today*, September 12, 2016, p. 1A.

[53]Dave Philipps, "V.A.'s Big Software Upgrade Is Plagued By Hidden Costs and Flawed Training," *New York Times*, July 10, 2021, p. A 11.

Case 4.8

(continued)

hepatitis and HIV infections.[54] Some concluded that she showed leadership and took immediate remedial action. Others concluded that her transfer to the smallest VA facility in the world speaks for itself. Amid expressed concerns from Arizona's congressional delegation, Mr. McDonald scheduled meetings to allow concerns to be aired. Ms. Nelson was promoted to a national VA position in 2019 and subsequently was appointed as VA Assistant Undersecretary for Health for Operations in January 2022. The Phoenix VA is now headed by a director who has been with that unit since 2010.

The VA Today

Dr. Shulkin's Departure

Following the 2016 presidential election, President Trump nominated Dr. David Shulkin to head the VA. Dr. Shulkin was unanimously confirmed by the Senate in early 2017. As celebrated as his appointment was and despite his credentials, Dr. Shulkin's tenure as VA director was short-lived. There was great controversy about Dr. Shulkin's travel for what appeared to be personal reasons just after his confirmation. By early 2018, Dr. Shulkin had resigned. The inspector general issued a report on Dr. Shulkin's July 2018 trip to Europe.[55] Herewith, some highlights:

1. Less than two weeks before the 11-day trip in July 2017 began, the VA secretary sent out a memo to VA employees titled "Essential Employee Travel." The memorandum instructed staff that before approving any employee travel, managers must determine whether the travel is "essential." The goal was to decrease "employee travel and generate savings" within VA.

2. The trip included 3.5 days of conference and meetings in Denmark to study their veteran's programs and facilities. Given the vast Danish army, one understands the need for that detour.

3. The VA paid for Dr. Shulkin's wife's travel because Dr. Shulkin's chief of staff represented to the VA that Dr. Bari (aka Mrs. Shulkin) was an "invited guest" for an award ceremony. There was no award or ceremony. The IG made a criminal referral to the Justice Department for possible prosecution for the fraudulent statements about the award. The DOJ declined prosecution at that time.

4. Dr. Shulkin and his wife received tickets to the women's finals at Wimbledon from someone they called a friend of Dr. Bari (Mrs. Shulkin). When the IG's office interviewed the "friend," after 19 attempts to contact her, the "friend" could not recall or did not know Dr. Bari's first name. The VA ethics officer had approved the gift of the tickets under the "relationship" exception to federal officials accepting gifts.

5. The total cost of the trip for Dr. Shulkin and his wife was $122,334, not counting the time a staff member spent arranging the leisure travel for the secretary and his wife. The OIG concluded that this VA staff member became the secretary's travel concierge.

   The substantive conclusions of the report were:

   a. VA's Chief of Staff Made False Representations to a VA Ethics Official and Altered an Official Record, Resulting in VA Improperly Paying for Dr. Bari's [aka Mrs. Shulkin] Air Travel

   b. Secretary Shulkin Improperly Accepted Wimbledon Tickets

   c. Secretary Shulkin Directed the Misuse of a Subordinate's Official Time

   d. Inadequate Documentation to Assess the Accuracy and Appropriateness of the Costs of the Trip

   e. Misleading Statements to the Media

Discussion Questions

1. Explain what VA employees were doing and why. Discuss the issues underlying the falsification of the wait times.

2. Why were the whistleblower complaints ignored or minimized? What more could the whistleblowers have done?

(continued)

---

[54]Dennis Wagner, "New VA Boss, Old Problems?" *Arizona Republic*, September 30, 2016, p. A1.

[55]"Administrative Investigation: VA Secretary and Delegation Travel to Europe," VA Office of the Inspector General, Report # 17-05909-106, February 14, 2018, https://www.va.gov/oig/pubs/vaoig-17-05909-106.pdf.

Case 4.8

(continued)

3. How do the VA operations and employee behaviors compare to the operations and behaviors of the for-profit companies that you have studied in this unit?

4. Offer Dr. Shulkin some advice on making personal ethical choices based on what you learned in Units 1 and 2. What tests could he have applied in making his decisions about his travel? What rationalizations did

he not recognize as part of his thinking processes? What are the categories of ethical dilemmas that apply to him?

5. Given what happened with incentives and performance goals at the VA and the ultimate solution of private care, apply the models you studied in Unit 3 for social responsibility and explain what happened with the VA.

Case 4.9

The Atlanta Public School System: High Test Scores, Low Knowledge Levels

An Introduction and Overview

For nearly a decade, the Atlanta Public School (APS) system and its test scores were touted as remarkable. APS was winning awards as teachers, principals, and the system superintendent and her staff all got bonuses because the test scores of the students were on a continual upward climb. APS was studied, rewarded, bragged about, and lionized as a model for running schools and school systems. With Beverly Hall leading the way, and principals following along, APS was studied and emulated. During this period from 1999 until 2010, Beverly Hall was named National Superintendent of the Year and APS was on the list of the best run school districts.[56]

But all this turned out to be a façade. APS drives home this adage: outlier performance generally involves some type of gaming, if not outright cheating. If performance seems too good to be true, there is gaming going on somewhere. Time will cause the gaming to percolate and the numbers to crash.

What the media, too busy covering APS as a success story, failed to pick up was a bizarre culture and cheating that defied even the aforementioned boundless human capacity for gaming incentive systems. The cheating

began in 2001, whistleblower reports began during 2005, and the *Atlanta Journal Constitution* did a 2008 statistical analysis of APS's Criterion-Referenced Competency Tests (CRCT) that questioned the probability of the system's test scores. For example, between 2002 and 2009, the scores for eighth-graders' reading capacity jumped 14 points, the highest jump in any urban district in the United States. In 2009, a state investigation revealed an unusually high number of erasures on the tests. Allegations of racism reached fever pitch in response to the questions being raised about the test scores. The school board was thrown into political turmoil. By 2011, the Georgia Bureau of Investigation (GBI) released the results of its investigation, which found that 44 of the 56 schools in the APS had cheated on CRCT scores.

The APS Incentive Program

The final investigative reports (from both the GBI and the governor's office) outlined the incentive programs at APS. The district set unrealistic test-score goals, or "targets."[57] For example, the target each year was always higher for each grade even if the students entering that grade had lower test scores from the previous years. The compensation for meeting test scores was not bad. Ms. Hall earned $383,000 in bonuses over a decade for the scores achieved through the manipulations. Teachers who achieved their test scores were given

(continued)

[56]Kim Severson, "Systematic Cheating Is Found in Atlanta's School System," *New York Times*, June 5, 2011. https://www.nytimes.com/2011/07/06/education/06atlanta.html. Governor's Report, CRCT (Criterion Referenced Competency Test) Investigation (hereinafter CRCT Report), April 2011, vol. 1, http://www.atlanta.k12.ga.us/Page/410.

[57]*Id.*

Case 4.9

(continued)

bonuses between $750 and $2,600. Twenty-five percent of principals' performance evaluations was based on test scores. Principals whose schools did not achieve targets within three years were terminated.

Once the scores were inflated by the cheating, it became impossible to attain the new target scores without cheating. The governor's investigation concluded: "Cheating one year created a need for more cheating the next," and "Once cheating started, it became a house of cards that collapsed on itself."[58] The report also concluded that APS became a "data-driven" system, with unreasonable and excessive pressure to meet targets.[59] Like businesses that fool around with their reported numbers, once you start you cannot stop because the decline would be too difficult to explain. There are only two options: keep cheating or come clean. The pain of the latter makes the former appear to be the best option.

How the Cheating Began and How Far It Went

There are three types of teacher cheating outlined in the academic literature. Yes, there is research that explains how teachers cheat. The APS crowd must have studied up because they managed to dabble in all three forms. There is cheating *ex ante*, otherwise known as test score manipulation, or cooking the books on reporting the scores—sort of the accounting form of cheating. There is also a form of this type of cheating that controls the reporting pool for test scores. Some principals placed strategic calls prior to test days to parents of low-performing students to explain that their children need not come to school on testing days because they had already been tested and met their grade levels. In other words, principals kept the low performers from taking the tests.

The second type of cheating is known as contemporaneous cheating that occurs when teachers guide students to the correct answer during the exam or give students the correct answers during the exam. In this form of cheating, teachers stand over the desks of students and watch them fill in their answers. When they spot a wrong answer they point to students' papers and exclaim, "Oh, you might want to change that one."

Finally, teachers use cheating *ex post,* which involves correcting wrong answers after students turn in their exams.[60] An example of *ex post* cheating came near the end of the decade when the teachers met for what they called "test cleanup" parties on the weekends, some of which were held at principals' homes. The teachers donned gloves (fingerprint prevention) and changed answers on the Scantron sheets.[61]

The forms and amount of APS teacher cheating increased with each passing year of the lost decade because the targets were impossible to begin with and only got more difficult as the cheating reflected improvement. Some examples of the creativity documented in the governor's investigative report are listed below. Notice how the more subtle cheating strategies changed to blatant actions over the years.

- Teachers looked ahead to the questions for the next day and discussed them with the students before they took the next day's test.

- Teachers arranged classroom seating so that struggling students were better able to "cheat off" the brighter students.

- First- and second-grade teachers used voice inflection when reading the questions and answers to their students (the tests are administered orally in those grades because not all students can read at that point) to give away the correct answers.

- Teachers pointed to correct answers while standing next to students' desks as they took the test.

- Some teachers just gave the answers aloud to their students.

- Some teachers allowed students to go back and change answers on their tests that they had taken the day before.

(continued)

---

[58]CRCT Report.

[59]Tim R. Sass, Jarod Apperson, and Carycruz Bueno, "The Long-Run Effects of Teacher Cheating on Student Outcomes," A Report for the Atlanta Public Schools, May 5, 2015, https://www.atlantapublicschools.us/crctreport.

[60]Id.

[61]CRCT Report, p. 3.

Case 4.9

(continued)

- Teachers and students erased incorrect answers and put in correct answers after the testing was complete.

- Changing answers became so sophisticated that plastic transparency answer sheets were created to make changing more efficient.

- One child who had sat under his desk on testing days and refused to take the test still had a test turned in with a passing score.

What Incentives Did to the APS Culture

Beyond the luring of teachers into dishonesty, the incentives and fear combined produced a bizarre culture of pressure, silence, and humiliation. When a teacher/whistleblower filed a report on the cheating problems, an area superintendent in the district had him alter what he said in his report and then put a reprimand in his file.[62] No one took any action to address the cheating reported by the reprimanded teacher. Another teacher who witnessed tampering with test answers sheets was told that if she did not "keep her mouth shut," she would "be gone."[63] In several cases, the whistleblowers were given poor performance evaluations as a means of terminating them so that the scandal did not become public knowledge.

The investigative report includes pages of examples of retaliation against principals and teachers who raised objections to changing answers and questioned the validity of the test scores. In situations where those who raised questions were terminated, their claims against the school district were settled if they claimed retaliation so that the matters were kept from the public eye. Ms. Hall emphasized test results and doled out public praise for those who achieved those results "at the expense of ethics."

At district meetings, principals who attained the target level of test scores were permitted to sit up front near Ms. Hall. Those principals who resisted the cheating and did not attain the target scores were forced to sit in the bleachers along the side.[64] Teachers with low test scores

were forced to sit under tables in meetings. At the annual convocation ceremony, only the faculty of those schools that met at least 70% of their targets for test scores would be seated on the floor of the convocation venue. The faculty of the schools with the highest percentages of targets met sat closest to the stage. The faculty of schools that did not meet 70% of their targets were seated in the bleachers or other remote seating.[65] The honor of a seat on the floor was referred to casually among the schools as "making the floor" when discussing their goals for testing.[66]

The Criminal Investigations, Charges, Trials, and Effects

Ms. Hall and other employees of the school system were indicted by the Fulton County District Attorney on a variety of white-collar crimes, including falsifying records, conspiracy, racketeering, false swearing, and obtaining money or property through false pretenses. The last charge related to the bonuses Ms. Hall and others were paid for reaching certain goals on the test scores. In addition to district administrators who were indicted (including the director of human resources), the indictment charged teachers and principals at elementary, middle, and high schools with similar counts of criminal activity.

Because all the documents involved, including the tests themselves, are considered to be state records, most of those indicted were charged with falsification or alteration of public documents, a felony.

The 21-month investigation by the district attorney's office included information obtained when whistleblowers wore wires and gathered recordings of those indicted that reflect their alteration of exam answer sheets. The disclosures in the recorded conversations are particularly damning from a criminal perspective, even as they are heart wrenching as those involved realized the consequences for their behaviors. The following is one of the recorded conversations reflected in the indictments between Clarietta Davis, a principal

(continued)

[62]CRCT Report, p. 18.
[63]CRCT Report, p. 138.
[64]Michael Winerip, "A New Leader Helps Heal Atlanta Schools, Scarred by Scandal," *New York Times*, February 21, 2012, p. A12.

[65]CRCT Report, p. 159.
[66]CRCT Report, p. 159.

Case 4.9

(continued)

at one of the schools, and Milagros Moner, the testing coordinator at the school:

Ms. Moner: I can't eat. I can't sleep, my kids want to talk to me, I ignore them. . . . I don't have the mental energy.

Ms. Davis: You wouldn't believe how people just look at you. People you know.

Ms. Moner: You feel isolated.

Ms. Davis: There's no one to talk to. . . . See how red my eyes are? And I'm not a drinking woman.

Ms. Moner: It has taken over my life. I don't want to go to work. I pray day and night. I pray at work.

Ms. Davis: You just have to pray for everybody.[67]

Ms. Davis invoked the Fifth Amendment when investigators came to talk to her after the tape was recovered from Ms. Moner.[68]

By the time prosecutors, auditors, and special commissions were done, 35 teachers and administrators, including Ms. Hall, were indicted. All but 12 entered into plea agreements. Of the 12 who remained, two died awaiting trial (including the superintendent, whose lawyer maintained that she was unaware of test-score cheating in APS) and one was acquitted following an eight-month trial in 2015. Their appeals failed. The prison sentences ranged from a few months to 20 years. The level of cheating was so extensive that, apart from the criminal charges, 178 teachers and principals were terminated for cause for changing test answers. Termination of any teacher is no small feat in public educational systems. Only three teachers had their licenses revoked. Many had two-year suspensions, but some had no suspensions. A prison sentence may be the only guaranteed way to get bad teachers out.

The Final Fall-Out: Repairs and Impacts on the Students

APS was placed on probation by the accrediting bodies for public education systems. Erroll C. Davis

was appointed as APS's superintendent and the school system slogged through the long pathway for correcting the problems that resulted from the falsified scores, including the realities that some students were five grade levels behind in their reading scores despite excellent test scores for the past five years. There were significant difficulties with special ed students because they had been unable to get the help that they needed with their work during the cheating era because their test scores were too high to qualify them for assistance.

The worst befell the innocent student victims. There were 11,553 students in the APS systems whose test scores had been altered who found themselves in remedial classes after school and on the weekends to make up for the decade of lost learning. Because the teachers did not change the test scores of those who did well on the tests, the students most affected were those who were already struggling. Thousands who had already graduated from APS schools found themselves taking remedial courses in their first year or two at the state colleges and universities because they could not pass the screening exams that permitted them to enroll in regular classes. Imagine being in college and just learning multiplication whilst your peers are enrolled in the required Calculus 1 class. APS graduates' college degrees cost them one to two years of extra tuition so they could take remedial courses just to qualify for their freshmen-level requirements.

Discussion Questions

1. Why did the cheating culture exist?
2. What made the cheating culture continue?
3. Explain how those who raised questions were treated.
4. Make a list of all who were affected by the cheating and the consequences.
5. Explain why teachers, principals, and administrators continued to participate in the cheating.
6. What effect did the incentives have on the APS culture?

---

[67]The indictment can be found at http://www.ajc.com/documents/2013/mar/29/read-indictment/.

[68]Michael Winerip, "35 Indicated in Test Scandal at Atlanta Schools," *New York Times*, March 30, 2013, p. A1.

Case 4.10

The Wells Way

For a time, Wells Fargo was the bank those in finance looked to as one that understood how to grow, profit, and even run ethics and compliance programs. But beneath those numbers that seemed to scream "Success!" was a dark culture hiding a secret that would stun the world when it eventually percolated to the surface.

Wells and the Origins of Cross-Selling

What produced the Wells growth, real though it was not, as we shall see, was a strategy of cross-selling. That cross-selling strategy came from the 1998 merger of Wells with Norwest Bank. Norwest had a decentralized matrix structure that gave managers great leeway and absolute authority. Leadership at Wells assumed ethics. One must never assume ethics when incentives are in play. The Norwest mantra was "Run it like you own it." Translation: Beginning with the merger, Wells allowed each division to run its own staff and control functions. Even risk and HR were not centralized. As a result, no one was looking over the shoulder of Carrie Tolstedt as she began running the Community Bank at Wells in 2002. The more successful Ms. Tolstedt was, the more independent her operations became. If her success continued, no one was asking questions.

Ms. Tolstedt embraced cross-selling with a vengeance, integrating the Norwest philosophy into the Community Bank. Cross-selling was the sum total of all management at Wells. If there were mortgage or CD holders, employees offered those customers home-equity credit lines, credit cards, or checking account services to increase the number of services and accounts each customer had. Once you had the consumers on checking accounts and credit cards, retirement accounts awaited only the sales push. The Norwest/Wells motivational mantra was, "Go for Gr-EIGHT!" There were no analytics underlying the goal number. The banking industry average was 2.7 products per customer. Wells made it to 6.3 products (in theory) per customer before the fake products were uncovered.[69] Wells settled on having employees shoot for eight products per customer because eight allowed for the clever mantra.

Wells, Goals, and Incentives

The Community Bank had a sales goal model of "consistent year-over-year sales growth."[70] Sales had to increase every year. Once the making-stuff-up-cheating began, it only increased because there was no way to obtain growth unless you made more stuff up to gain over last year's made-up numbers. The sales goals were so unrealistic that many of the regions did not meet their goals in a particular year. The central and regional leaders in the Community Bank referred to their sales goals as "50/50 plans."[71] About half of the regions would meet their goals and the other half would not.

Employees at bank branches were paid hourly wages but also given quarterly bonuses for all new accounts and new account services that they managed to rope in whilst laboring in the trenches of consumer banking. The Wells CEO at the height of cross-selling was John Stumpf, a Norwester who lived and breathed multiple product sales. In 2014, he told a *Forbes* reporter, "I will not be satisfied until every creditworthy customer who calls us their bank caries our credit card."[72]

The Pressure at Wells: Fear, Retaliation, and Sackings

Meeting Numbers

As was the case with APS, not only were there carrots for success in the cross-selling/new-account program, but there were also sticks, the cultural pressures to meet those numbers. Wells had its so-called "Motivator Reports."[73] These were monthly, quarterly, and year-to-date sales goals and rankings for the retail bank districts. The reports, according to employees interviewed as part of the investigation, put tremendous pressure on managers. Those managers were receiving emails from regional

(continued)

---

[69]Aaron Back, "Wells Fargo Isn't Sorry Enough," *Wall Street Journal*, September 14, 2016, p. C12.

[70]"Independent Directors of the Board of Wells Fargo & Company Sales Practices Investigation Report," April 10, 2017, https://www08.wellsfargomedia.com/assets/pdf/about/investor-relations/presentations/2017/board-report.pdf, p. 19 (hereinafter referred to as "*Board Report*").

[71]*Id.*

[72]Lauren Debter, "Why It Could Pay to Get a Credit Card from Your Regular Bank," *Forbes*, January 23, 2014, https://www.forbes.com/sites/laurengensler/2014/01/23/why-it-could-pay-to-get-a-credit-card-from-your-regular-bank/?sh=107dc46c33af.

[73]*Board Report*, at p. 20.

Case 4.10

(continued)

managers about the results: "[T]his morning we are #15 on the motivator L and we are at 99% of solutions [products], 93% of profit and 105% of checking. I hate numbers that start with 9! I like ones that have three digits and start with a 1, as in 105 or 110."[74] In the Los Angeles region, the regional managers had district managers dress in costumes and run a gauntlet to write the number of sales they had achieved in their districts on a white board.

The Motivator Reports continued until a meeting in 2014 when regional leaders complained that the reports were creating a culture of pressure and shaming. That meeting, following an investigation by the *Los Angeles Times* in 2013 about the sales pressure culture at Wells, led to an investigation into Wells' sales practices by the Los Angeles County District Attorney. Still, the program continued.

Employees were measured by their "scorecards." The scorecards showed how the employees were doing in comparison to their individual goals. The cards were updated daily, and meeting their scorecard goals became the sole objective of employees. Every January, employees were encouraged to participate in the "Jump in January," a program to up their goals for the year and place a special focus on a big start in January. As a result, employees would develop lists of potential contacts in December and "sandbag" those prospects to save them for January so that they could meet the higher goals in that month's special focus.

Some employees reported that they were meeting with their managers two to three times per day to discuss their cross-selling goals and progress. Employees were creating accounts without customers' signatures. Some were forging their customers' signatures.[75] A widespread practice was to use an email address of noname@wellsfargo.com to set up fake customer accounts. One would think that internal audit or risk might have picked up on this "noname" character and all his new accounts and new-account services.

Overdraft protection cost $35 per month. The goal was to sign up 80% of all account holders for this opt-in feature.

The branches that were hovering at 5 to 38% sign-ups were humiliated by district managers.[76]

Wells was known externally as *the* place to work and the bank with the most branches and assets. Internally, however, the bank was a pressure cooker environment. In some branches, if employees did not meet their quotas for the day, they had to stay at work getting enough family and friends to sign up for new accounts or new-account services that they would meet their quotas.[77] A Wells employee described his branch manager's order, "He would say, 'I don't care how you do it—but do it, or else you're not going home.'"[78]

The rewards were great for those who achieved, but those employees who did not meet their goals were shown to the door. Those who questioned the incentive/new services boat were also shown the door.

Whistleblowers and Retaliation

Employees who reported other employees for practices such as signing customers' names without their customers' knowledge to create new accounts and banking products were also given the boot. One employee, Yesenia Guitron, reported the customer signature issues she was seeing to her manager. With no action taken at that level, she called the ethics hotline. With no response from that part of the bank, she eventually went to HR. Not only was there no investigation, Ms. Guitron was fired for insubordination.[79] Those HR folks have backbones of steel.

The examples of fear and retaliation at Wells rank right up there with the antics at APS. Christopher Johnson, as a new employee, noted that his fellow Wells employees were creating accounts and account services for customers who were elderly or did not speak English well. He did what he had been instructed to do in his ethics training prior to beginning his job: He called the ethics hotline.

(continued)

---

[74]*Board Report*, at p. 23.

[75]James B. Stewart, "Wells Fargo Case Tests a Get-Tough Approach," *New York Times*, September 23, 2016, p. B1.

[76]E. Scott Reckard, "Wells Fargo's Pressure-Cooker Sales Culture Comes at a Cost," *Los Angeles Times*, December 21, 2013, https://www.latimes.com/business/la-fi-wells-fargo-sale-pressure-20131222-story.html.

[77]*Id.*

[78]*Id.*

[79]Stacy Cowley, "Wells Fargo Workers Claim Retaliation for Playing by the Rules," *New York Times*, September 27, 2016, p. B1.

Case 4.10

(continued)

Within days, Mr. Johnson was fired "for not meeting expectations." He had worked only two weeks.

Ricky M. Hansen, Jr., a branch manager in Arizona, was filling in for another manager at a branch and discovered that employees in the branch were inventing fake businesses and then opening accounts for them.[80] He called HR and was told to call the ethics hotline because the failure to report fraud was grounds for termination. When he called the ethics hotline, he was asked for specifics, including account numbers. He pulled up the accounts and shared that information with the ethics investigators. One month later, he was fired with the ethics investigator explaining that the reason for his termination was improperly looking up customer account information, an ethics violation.[81]

The Gaming at Wells

Wells had a definition of gaming in its code of ethics: "the manipulation and/or misrepresentation of sales or referrals . . . in an attempt to receive compensation or to meet sales goals."[82] And game they did. The most common strategy was taking funds from existing accounts and placing those funds in new accounts to meet new-account goals. In 2011, Rasheeda Kamar, a branch manager in New Jersey, sent an email directly to Mr. Stumpf explaining this strategy: "Funds are moved to new accounts to 'show' growth when in actuality there is no net gain to the company's deposit base."[83] Her email became part of the Senate record for the hearings on Wells' ethical collapse.

Employees opened accounts for existing customers, making up their license numbers and date of issuance on the account forms. Another employee caught one fake account when he noticed a license number for customer Bill Moore as "MOOREWFooooo," and an issue date on a Saturday, when the DMV was closed.[84]

In California, bankers would set customers up with premium bank accounts because one of their needs was to wire money to family in Mexico and premium accounts provided that service. A premium account could be opened with just a $50 deposit. However, there was a slight glitch. At the end of three months, if the customer had not deposited at least $25,000, the fee for the account was $30 per month. So, employees closed each premium account just days before the $25,000 requirement kicked in and then opened a new premium account to keep the customer going through a process of closing and creating every month.[85] This strategy still provided a new-account credit for employees every three months.

Some employees opened new lines of credit for their customers, without telling the customers. The employees put their own addresses on the lines of credit so the customers would not know. However, those credit reporting companies did them in with many customers. Once the large credit lines showed up on their credit reports, the customers hotfooted it to the branch to complain.

"Friends and family" accounts were those opened by employees to meet sales goals. One branch manager had a teenage daughter with 24 accounts, an adult daughter with 18 accounts, a husband with 21 accounts, a brother with 14 accounts, and a father with 4 accounts.[86] Employees opened accounts for existing customers and funded them with their own money, only to close them after the quarterly results were tabulated.[87]

Employees also had strategies for avoiding detection of their gaming, a sort of gaming to protect the gaming. One strategy was to put incorrect telephone numbers on the account information so that no one from the bank could contact the customers for verification of the account or any additional services or cards. At a higher level, the board Risk Committee was not given the correct number for employee terminations related to gaming because the Community Bank leaders had argued against disclosure of the 1% termination figure as well as giving the board the

(continued)

[80]*Id.*

[81]*Id.* at B3.

[82]Bethany McLean, "How Wells Cutthroat Culture Allegedly Drove Bankers to Fraud," *Varity Fair*, Summer, 2017, https://www.vanityfair.com/news/2017/05/wells-fargo-corporate-culture-fraud.

[83]Stacy Cowley, "Fake Accounts at Wells Fargo Raised Alarms Starting in 2005," *New York Times*, October 12, 2016, p. B1, at B3.

[84]Bethany McLean, *Varity Fair*, Summer, 2017, https://www.vanity-fair.com/news/2017/05/wells-fargo-corporate-culture-fraud.

[85]Reckard, *Los Angeles Times*, https://www.latimes.com/business/la-fi-wells-fargo-sale-pressure-20131222-story.html.

[86]Board report, p. 36, footnote 16.

[87]Board report, p. 36.

Case 4.10

(continued)

actual numbers of terminations. The board was told the terminations for 2013 and 2014 for gaming totaled 230. The number was really 1,293.[88]

In addition, management slow-walked the information to the board. The unfolding of the crisis in Community Banking took place over several board meetings and required the board to demand additional information, outside expertise, and transparency. As the board's frustrations were playing out, leaders' emails and discussions reflected a strategy of presenting just general information to the board, not specifics. The board's report reflects an embarrassing scenario of back-and-forth demands met with a lack of responsiveness by management. Eventually, the board restructured itself and terminated Carrie Tolstedt following a disagreement about her promising in writing not to exercise any of her stock options until the board's investigation was complete, with the investigation to determine whether those options would be forfeited.[89] It was not until that termination that the real scope of the gaming could be known because of the managerial information blockades.

The Timeline on Wells and the Fake Accounts: Management Living in Denial: The Initial Percolations

It was just after Wells began its new account/new-account services incentive program that the first reports of employees gaming the system began to flow into ethics and compliance, HR, audit, and risk. In 2000, just two years after the merged Norwest "Gr-eight!" mantra took hold, there were 63 reports received of employees gaming the system. By 2004, the number rose to 680. By 2007, one quarter found 288 allegations of gaming. By 2013, the year of the *Los Angeles Times* article, there were 1,469 reports in the fourth quarter.[90]

During this time, Mr. Stumpf remained convinced that all was well in Wells land. He relied on the 1% figure: "Do you know only around 1% of our people lose their jobs [for] gaming the system, i.e., changing phone numbers, etc.

Nothing could be further from the truth on forcing products on customers. In any case, right will win and we are right. Did some things go wrong – you bet and that is called life. This is not systemic."[91]

In 2002, Internal Investigations at Wells found that nearly an entire branch in Colorado had engaged in gaming, including issuing debit cards without client consent. Wells' fidelity bond company required that employees committing such offenses be terminated. Rather than do so, Wells negotiated an exception with its bonding company to allow the employees to stay.[92] Wells did form a task force to develop recommendations on sales integrity and "clarification of roles" when breaches occur. The result was that employees received sales integrity training.

In 2004, Wells' Internal Investigations issued a report with the following: "[I]t is the conclusion by Corporate Security Internal Investigations" [that] whether real or perceived, team members on the current Corporate Sales Incentive Plan feel they cannot make sales goals without gaming the system. The incentive to cheat is based on the fear of losing their jobs for not meeting performance expectations."[93] That report was sent to the Wells chief auditor, an employment lawyer, Community Bank HR, and the head of sales and service development at Community Bank. The 2004 report "recommended that Wells Fargo consider similarly reducing or eliminating sales goals for employees and removing the threat of employee termination if goals were not met."[94] There was no evidence of any response to the report.

Percolations in Other Areas of the Bank
The C-Suite Contacts

As early as 2005 (2007 was the year Mr. Stumpf became CEO), an employee had notified HR about what she was witnessing: "[E]mployees opening sham accounts, forging customer signatures, and sending out unsolicited credit cards."[95] In 2007, Mr. Stumpf received two similar

(continued)

---

[88]Board report, pp. 105–106.

[89]Board report, p. 110, footnote 33.

[90]Geoff Colvin, "Can Wells Fargo Get Well?" *Fortune*, June 15, 2017, p. 138, at p. 144.

[91]*Id.*, at p. 146.

[92]Board report, pp. 73–74.

[93]Board report, p. 89.

[94]*Id.*

[95]Stacy Cowley, "Fake Accounts at Wells Fargo Raised Alarms Starting in 2005," *New York Times*, October 12, 2016, p. B1.

Case 4.10

(continued)

letters from employees. In 2010, the chairman of the Wells board received a similar letter. Mr. Stumpf had the sales quality manual updated to remind employees to get the customer's signature before opening an account. One of the employees who wrote to corporate was fired, but her supervisors remained with Wells. Congressional hearings and whistleblower lawsuits documented these percolating events.

Litigation Activities in Legal

By 2011, lawyers in the Wells Employment Law Section were seeing an increase in litigation by terminated employees who were raising the defenses of "everybody does it" and that what they had done had been condoned by their managers. Their claims of unjust termination struck a nerve with the lawyers (or they at least saw a mounting risk), so the lawyers were made part of another task force that examined "reputational risk" associated with both the sales practices as well as the terminations. Nonetheless, the issue of risk with the gaming and the terminations did not make it to the board level until 2014.[96] In 2013, Wells' head of Enterprise Services briefed general counsel and the chief risk officer on the lawyer-motivated task force's conclusions and expressed concerns that the issue of gaming and resulting terminations and litigation had not been escalated. The issue was still not escalated, but Wells created a "Core Team" to determine what was now motivating the investigation by the Los Angeles City Attorney's office into Wells sales practices (an investigation begun following publication of the *Los Angeles Times* article).

The Auditors

From 2011 to 2016, Wells Fargo Audit Services rated Community Bank's processes and controls as "effective" in detecting, investigating, and remediating sales practice violations. In 2011, Audit did learn about a potential sales practice issue related to debit cards from Internal Investigations and rated Community Bank's controls in that area as "Moderate."[97] Audit did rely on Community Bank's quality assurance group for its reviews until it discovered in 2012 that issues were not

being remediated. It issued a "Needs improvement" rating for Community Bank's quality assurance group and stopped using the group as a resource thereafter.[98] In evaluating Wells' culture, Audit found Community Bank's compensation plan balanced and that the Community Bank's culture was "focused on the customer." Audit did not issue a "Needs improvement" on Community Bank's culture until its 2016 report.[99]

The HR Component

Threaded throughout all these other parts of Wells were Hope Hardison and Patricia Callahan. Ms. Hardison joined Wells in 1993 and became corporate HR director in 2010. Ms. Hardison reported to Patricia Callahan, the chief administrative officer at Wells, until 2014, when Ms. Callahan retired. Ms. Hardison then reported to Mr. Stumpf.

Ms. Callahan had a long history of grappling with gaming in the Community Bank division. In 2002, as the then head of HR, Ms. Callahan had helped to deal with the 2002 Colorado branch gaming by employees, the disciplinary actions taken, and the need for negotiating an exemption with Wells' bonding company. In her numerous roles in HR and eventually as Wells' HR director, Ms. Hardison received regular reports on the sales integrity violations. By 2013, both women had urged the involvement of enterprise representatives in finding the root cause of the high termination rates and the reports of gaming in the Community Bank. Both also raised the issue of reputational risk in not reining in the gaming behaviors.[100]

Both women ran into Ms. Tolstedt's resistance and dressings-down in their attempts to reform Community Bank compensation.[101] Ms. Callahan did not raise her concerns to the HR or Corporate Responsibility Committees of the board until late 2014 and early 2015. Ms. Hardison raised her concerns about sales practices to the board's HR committee in 2014. The board report describes Ms. Tolstedt as the barrier to implementing change in the Community Bank. Ms. Tolstedt did not participate in the

(continued)

---

[96]Board report, pp. 75–76.
[97]Board report, p. 91.

[98]Board report, pp. 92–93.
[99]Board report, pp. 93–96.
[100]Board report, pp. 83–86.
[101]Board report, pp. 83–86.

Case 4.10

(continued)

board's investigation on advice of counsel. No changes were made to compensation formulas for the Community Bank until 2016, initiated by CEO Stumpf and finalized by the board for January 2017.

A glance back through the timeline shows that the issues with cross-selling and compensation emerged across the bank in different areas and for different reasons. However, the lack of checks and balances over Ms. Tolstedt's leadership of the Community Bank as well as the failures of the silos of legal, HR, compliance, audit, and risk to share data and concerns and raise both produced a cauldron that was ever-percolating and rapidly approaching full boil. In September 2016, the boiling pot overflowed. The reputational risk, that many within the bank had seen coming, would prove far more costly and run for five years after the initial settlement in the case for $185 million.

The Culture of Wells: The Nefarious Nature of Cross-Selling Crossed into Other Revenue Areas

Wells tried to paint a picture in its public statements and congressional hearings that consumer cross-selling in the Community Bank was its only bad-behavior cultural issue. However, Wells' behavior in other areas of banking puts the lie to that attempt to isolate causation. Consumer overdraft protection was an evolving issue in the banking industry from 2000 to 2010.[102] The overdraft business was a cash cow for banks because of bank processing mechanisms. Banks could charge their $35 overdraft fees on individual transactions if they processed customer checks, withdrawals, and payments by order of size. If a customer had $400 in his account and had debits of $200, $150, $75, $15, an $10, banks would take out the largest amounts first, thus bringing in three overdraft fees. Taking out the smallest amounts would only bring in two overdraft fees. Wells was in with the industry gang on maximizing returns from overdraft fees.

The Federal Reserve (at that time in charge of consumer banking) had issued regulations prohibiting surprise overdraft protections and the need for advance disclosure of the overdraft process. The Fed would continue to battle Wells and other banks on their meaning of the requirements for "disclosure" on their overdraft processes and costs.

Ever so clever, Wells opted for a different approach when the Fed got sticky about disclosure. Wells trained its employees to sell overdraft protection. Those employees learned to use just the right words to make it seem as if the overdraft protection was either required or "came with the account."[103] It was just enough disclosure to satisfy the Fed and get customers hooked for overdraft protection, for a fee. Wells had a sort of side incentive program for overdraft sales. The branch employees with the most overdraft protections for the day were rewarded with a $15 Subway card.[104] The branch employee with the most overdraft sign-ups for the quarter received a $100 gift card. The human mind, when free Subway is involved, knows no bounds on sales tactics.

But overdraft issues were, again, but one issue among many. The following lists cover most of the other types of regulatory violations that were going on at Wells as all the new-account and account services scurrying was in full swing. These activities carry that common thread of revenue maximization. The following activities came up as questions for Mr. Stumpf during the congressional hearings. In fact, congressional staff members were kind enough to turn the list into a PowerPoint slide on display during Mr. Stumpf's testimony.

- Subprime loan abuses
- Discrimination in lending against African Americans
- Foreclosure violations
- Violations of the rate cap on interest that can be charged members of the military
- Improper seizure of vehicles owned by members of the military who had fallen behind on their payments (The federal Soldiers and Sailors Relief Act prohibits mortgage foreclosure and vehicle repossession while members of the military are on active duty.)[105]

(continued)

---

[102]AnnaMaria Andriotis and Emily Glazer, "Wells Pushed Overdraft Services," *Wall Street Journal*, October 11, 2016, p. C1.

[103]*Id.*

[104]*Id.*, at p. C2.

[105]Stacy Cowley, Wells Fargo's Reaction to Scandal Fails to Satisfy Lawmakers," *New York Times*, September 30, 2016, p. B1.

Case 4.10

(continued)

There were other violations that members of congressional staffers missed. This was not Wells' first rodeo when it came to shenanigans and gaming:

- Wells was part of a group that overcharged merchants for their Visa and Mastercard interchange fees. The group paid $6.6 billion to settle the claims of the merchants.

- Wells agreed to pay $10 billion in fines for issuing FHA mortgages that it knew did not qualify for FHA insurance.

- Wells also paid a $1.2 billion fine for receiving FHA funds for mortgage defaults that did not qualify for payment.

- Wells paid $203 million to customers who were victims of Wells operational processes that allowed customer payments to make it to the ledger before deposits did, thus causing the customers to have to pay overdraft fees.[106]

- In 2013, a federal judge in Massachusetts granted Wells a victory on a case brought by a mortgagor against the bank for its actions during the foreclosure process. The grounds for the decision for Wells was federal preemption of state consumer protection laws. Nonetheless, the judge also found that Wells' conduct in dealing with the mortgagor was outrageous and called on Wells to do the right thing and waive its defense of preemption. The order in the case also required Wells' lawyers to provide the court with a corporate resolution signed by a majority of the board of directors and the president indicating that they supported the lawyers' litigation tactics of winning on a technicality despite the unfairness and cost to the mortgagor.[107]

- Wells paid $2 billion for selling toxic mortgage-backed securities prior to the 2008 financial crisis despite its own internal testing concluding that there was significant variance between borrower-reported income and income reported on tax returns of those borrowers.[108]

It would be fun to see the resolution of that suit, but, alas, it could not be located. The case was dismissed, however, so the board resolution must have been forthcoming and provided the judge with the affirmation needed.

Wells ran a bank that was like a used car lot. There is always something missing in customer disclosure, the product you are getting is less than it seems, and the commission rates for the salespeople wreak havoc with honesty. By the end of November 2016, monthly new account openings at Wells were down 44% from the previous year.[109]

The Fallout for Wells: Lessons in the Unforeseen Costs of Risk

As noted, there were those in the belly of Wells who were raising the red flag of "reputational risk." However, by the time the cross-selling/rewards, incentives, and performances programs were shut down, Community Banking was responsible for 57% of Wells' earnings, as well its fake earnings. Risk assessment falls by the wayside when earnings are clicking along.

The Regulatory Sanctions

The issues with cross-selling became public on September 8, 2016, with the settlement of charges by the Los Angeles County attorney. However, that $185 million fine was only the beginning and a drop in the bucket of fines Wells would eventually pay. The factors that are often unclear as companies assess reputational risk are the extent of the regulatory arm. The regulatory arm grows once there is a regulatory event. In fact, to mix metaphors, regulators descend with a microscope on a company already in regulatory difficulty to further examine operations. Because of the initial fine and findings, the microscope has a critical lens and what may have been ordinary industry practices in the past look diabolical with the hindsight of any regulatory misstep, even in areas unrelated to the area involved in the wrongdoing, albeit not admitted, that resulted in the fine.

(continued)

---

[106]Matt Krantz, "Yet Again, Penalties Pile Up at Wells Fargo," *USA Today*, September 12, 2016, p. 1B.

[107]*Henning v. Wachovia Mortgage, FSB, n/k/a Wells Fargo Bank*, 969 F. Supp. 2d 135 (D. Mass. 2013).

[108]Emily Glazer, "Wells Settles Mortgage Case for $2 Billion," *Wall Street Journal*, August 2, 2018, p. B1.

[109]Emily Glazer, "Fewer Customers Stop at Wells Fargo," *Wall Street Journal*, November 18, 2016, p. B6.

Case 4.10

(continued)

In 2018, the Federal Reserve prohibited Wells from growing beyond its 2017 asset base of $1.95 trillion. On her last day as chair of the Fed, Janet Yellen imposed that constraint and issued a statement explaining the board's reasoning: "We cannot tolerate pervasive and persistent misconduct at any bank and the consumers harmed by Wells Fargo expect that robust and comprehensive reforms will be put in place to make certain that the abuses do not occur again."[110] Wells would struggle for years to fully grasp the seriousness and scope of their cultural problems.

It would not be until 2020 that the federal government finally settled with Wells for all its issues. In February 2020, Wells signed a deferred prosecution agreement (DPA) and paid a $3 billion fine to settle all criminal and civil investigations. Under the terms of the DPA, the Justice Department reserved its right to bring criminal prosecutions in the future if Wells does not honor the terms of the agreement, which include full cooperation with the federal government as well as staying clean (no more violations) and working on its ethical culture.[111] In addition, Wells had to set up a $500 million fund to compensate shareholders for its failure to inform them that its account growth was not quite as robust as it seemed on paper. During the final five years of the cross-selling goal system, the bank did not disclose that it had fired thousands of employees for falsifying banks records and disciplined tens of thousands more as part of a process of sort of cleansing without coming clean.[112]

The Market Impact

The market effects on Wells shares provide an idea of the scope of damage that follows a reputational hit. By 2018, Wells stock had risen just 8%. In comparison, the NASDAQ bank index had arisen 53%.[113] Wells missed the impact of the Trump tax cuts and the economic boom that followed. The asset cap was a big handicap for Wells—it simply could not grow.

The Impact on Customer Loyalty

Despite the valiant efforts of Wells to isolate its problems, its customers found working with Wells to be problematic, even when they were not consumer customers. The Fire and Police Pension Fund of Chattanooga began looking into the activities of the fund's trustee, Wells Fargo. The board of the fund discovered that Wells had been improperly retaining rebates from the mutual funds in the $215-million fund. Wells had collected a total of $47,000 in rebates that should have gone into the client's fund.[114] The board then terminated its relationship with Wells: "The Board has lost confidence that the answers provided by Wells to date are complete."[115] The board then brought in the Securities Exchange Commission by filing a whistleblower complaint and bringing in the Commodities Futures Trading Commission with the same allegations.

Illinois State Treasurer Michael Frerichs suspended its $30-billion investment activity with Wells for one year, noting, "I hope to send the message that their unscrupulous practices are not welcomed and will not be tolerated."[116] You know you have crossed an ethical line or two when the state that has sent four of its past five governors to prison for corruption will no longer do business with you. But Wells was ready, taking an arrogant sniff and swatting the issue away, "Today, the Illinois Treasurer was quoted at a press conference concerning Wells Fargo that the bank would lose 'millions' of dollars in lost revenue by at least temporarily stopping business between his office and the bank. Respectfully, the actual amount in lost revenue for the company

(continued)

[110]Jen Wieczner, "Janet Yellen's Last Act at the Federal Reserve: Punishing Wells Fargo," *Fortune*, February 2, 2018, https://fortune.com/2018/02/02/wells-fargo-janet-yellen-fed/#:~:text=Upbraiding%20Wells%20Fargo%20(WFC)%20for,in%20the%20competitive%20financial%20industry.

[111]Ben Eisen, "Wells Fargo Settles U.S. Probes," *Wall Street Journal*, February 22–23, 2020, p. A1.

[112]Emily Flitter, "To Settle Fraud Actions, Wells Fargo to Pay $3 Billion," *New York Times*, February 22, 2020, p. B1.

[113]Aaron Back, "It's Too Soon to Bet on Wells Fargo," *Wall Street Journal*, May 11, 2018, p. B12.

[114]Gretchen Morgenson and Emily Glazer, "Wells Kept Client's Fund Fee Rebates," *Wall Street Journal*, May 10, 2018, p. B1.

[115]*Id.*, at p. B2.

[116]Mike Snider, "Illinois Suspends Business Dealings with Wells Fargo," *USA Today*, October 4, 2016, p. 1B.

Case 4.10

(continued)

from business conducted with the Illinois Treasurer's office is approximately $50,000 per year."[117] The incident was representative of Wells' tin ear when it came to understanding the scope of its problems and what was and was not an appropriate response.

After the fake accounts came to light, Stumpf made his first mistake by trying to issue a press release that used the accounting standard of materiality to swat the issue away. By October 9, 2016, Wells was running full-page ads in major newspapers around the country listing the following:

1. Putting customer interests first. Wells eliminated its sales goals numbers in Retail Banking.

2. Providing customers with a summary of actions taken when the customers visited a retail bank.

3. Listing account actions taken online on customer accounts so that customers could see any changes at any time by going online (referred to as "Full transparency").

4. Working on refunds for customers who had been paying for services and accounts that they did not agree to open.

5. Promising, "The trust you place in us means everything and we will work hard every day to earn it back."[118]

John Stumpf, following his disastrous testimony before Congress as well as the bank's tepid and often bizarre responses in a crisis, abruptly resigned on October 12, 2016, as CEO and chairman. He was not given a severance package, but he walked away with $134 million in Wells stock. That number reflected the $41 million clawed back from his compensation following his congressional testimony on bonuses and incentives awarded based on the Retail Banking unit performance.[119] Stumpf had been CEO for 10 years and with Wells for 35 years.[120] The board elected an external director to fill the chairman of the board slot and permanently split the role of CEO and chairman.[121] One day later, in a King Saul–like moment, Stumpf also resigned from his board seats at Chevron and Target.[122]

Yet in another tin-eared move, the Wells board appointed president and COO, and Stumpf's heir apparent, Timothy Sloan, as CEO. Yes, to clean up an internal mess at the bank, the board turned to a 29-year veteran to run the show and get the bank out of its reputational hole. Oh, but there was this rationalization—Mr. Sloan was not in retail banking. Ah, but the other stuff listed above was in his area. And shouldn't the man in charge of operations have some clues about all operations? An understanding and oversight of processes, especially those for establishing accounts with suspicious emails listed for employees setting them up, should have perhaps caught his eye. In 2013, when the *Los Angeles Times* was investigating Wells for its cross-selling tactics and pressure on its sales force, Sloan issued the following statement, "I'm not aware of any overbearing sales culture."[123] Wells did, however, apologize to its customers, and note at that time that it was creating an Ethics Program Office.[124] Wells was also in the process of settling some claims by employees (without admitting wrongdoing). Nearly three years would pass between the *Los Angeles Times* article and the settlement with the federal government. In those years, Wells slow walked looking into the sales tactics issue.

The Wells Fallout

The effect on Wells has been stunning. Within one month after Wells announced the discovery of the first phase of the fake accounts, Wells reported a return on

(continued)

---

[117]*Id.*

[118]From a full-page ad appearing in the *New York Times*, October 9, 2016, p. A13. The same ad appeared in the *Wall Street Journal* on October 13, 2016, on p. A5 and again in the *New York Times* on October 16, 2016, at p. A7.

[119]Matt Krantz, "Wells Fargo CEO Abruptly Departs," *USA Today*, October 13, 2021, p. 1A.

[120]Emily Glazer, "Wells Chief Quits Under Attack," *Wall Street Journal*, October 13, 2016, p. A1.

[121]*Id.*

[122]Matt Krantz, "Another Bad Day for Former Wells Fargo CEO John Stumpf," *USA Today*, October 14, 2016, p. 2B.

[123]Maggie McGrath, "Wells Fargo Fined $185 Million for Opening Accounts Without Customers' Knowledge," *Forbes*, September 8, 2016, https://www.forbes.com/sites/maggiemcgrath/2016/09/08/wells-fargo-fined-185-million-for-opening-accounts-without-customers-knowledge/?sh=7735f44951fc.

[124]Reckard, *Los Angeles Times*, https://www.latimes.com/business/la-fi-wells-fargo-sale-pressure-20131222-story.html.

Case 4.10

(continued)

equity (ROE) that was down 11.2%.[125] Checking account applications were down 25%, credit card applications were down 20%, and community bank profits were down 9.4%. By the time of the pandemic, Wells had still not fixed its internal issues in retail banking and its stock price was down to $21 a share. At this writing, Wells stock is at $42, almost back to its $44 a share, the price at the time the fake accounts were disclosed. Five years of drag following poor management does take its toll."

Senator Elizabeth Warren has asked the Federal Reserve to break up Wells into two banks (consumer-retail and commercial-investor) because it still has not fixed the internal problems that resulted in the fake accounts.

Changing a culture is difficult. Changing culture whilst trying to use the same people who were at the helm as the culture was created and rewarded is just shy of impossible.

An example of how clueless the Wells culture remained following the exposure of 3.5 million in fake accounts, a Wells spokesperson offered the following rationalization:

> The vast majority of the accounts reviewed did not generate fees or result in net income for the company. In fact, it costs Wells Fargo more than $10 million to open and service those accounts, which generated the $2.6 million in fees that was returned to the customers."[126]

The analysis is classic rationalization through the use of numbers to illustrate this point: just because we were creating fake accounts does not mean we made money from them. Going right over the heads of both the executives and their spokesperson was this point: the bank's strategy was so flawed that its own incentive programs were driving employees to dishonestly create fake accounts and fake account services that ended up costing the bank money instead of making money. 'Tis a heck of an incentive program that gets you results that actually produce losses for your company. Why wasn't someone doing the analysis on what the new accounts and new-account services were actually doing for the bottom line? Even without the cheating, revisiting the cross-selling strategy's efficacy and contribution to earnings might have been a good idea. However, the spokesperson still seemed to think that this was a legitimate response to decades of cheating and duping customers, to wit, "We may have done all that but we really did not make any money. And don't forget! We ended up having to pay the customers back." It is difficult to know which is worse—that folks at the bank went through and did this analysis or that the spokesperson actually chose to say it in an interview with a major newspaper.

Discussion Questions

1. Explain cross-selling.
2. Make a list of the signals that Wells received in the years when its new-account achievements were increasing.
3. Give examples of what happened when those within Wells raised issues, concerns, and questions about cross-selling efforts within the bank.
4. What categories of ethical dilemmas do you find throughout the case study?
5. Discuss why Wells has struggled so much to reform its culture after the fake accounts became public. Be sure to highlight any errors they made in handling the situation.
6. List the resulting harms and costs to Wells.
7. What should have been done during the years of cross-selling to prevent employee gaming of the compensation system for new accounts?

[125]Emily Glazer, "Wells Details Branch Fallout," *Wall Street Journal*, October 15–16, 2021, p. B2.

[126]Gretchen Morgenson, "Wells Fargo Must Make Clean Break," *New York Times*, October 16, 2016, p. SB1.

Reading 4.11

Measures, Metrics, and Gaming—Part B

From the three cases—the VA, APS, and Wells—there are a multitude of lessons about incentive plans. The following sections walk through those lessons and how they can be applied, as the remainder of this unit covers different cultural issues that all involve incentives of some type.

What Is It That You Want? Focus on Behaviors, Not Metrics

APS really wanted educated students. What they measured and incentivized were test scores. The result was an achievement that was the exact opposite of the goal: the students were less educated. Instead of focusing on test scores, APS should have been focusing on understanding what teaching techniques work for learning and measuring teacher performance by their use of those techniques. If you do the hard work of determining how students learn, then the students learn and the test scores follow because of the learning. There are other behaviors to incentivize that will get the scores up. For example, parental involvement is a critical factor in learning because teachers and students need their help in providing reinforcement of learning at home. Teachers who reach goals of parental involvement are rewarded for those efforts because the test scores improve as a function of those measured goals. More difficult to achieve, time-consuming to measure, and delayed results are the unavoidable characteristics of behavior measures. However, they do last and are almost impossible to game.

Another example for most organizations involves safety. The classic metrics for safety are measuring lost work-days, reportables, and all-injury rates. However, those are lagging indicators. What organizations need are behaviors that ensure safety. When Paul O'Neill took over at Alcoa, an international industrial firm, he saw that they were meeting their goals on those metrics. However, tragically, many Alcoa employees were injured at work. At the annual shareholder meeting, Mr. O'Neill announced, "Every year, numerous Alcoa workers are injured so badly that they miss a day of work. I intend to make Alcoa the safest company in America. I intend to go for zero injuries."[127] Mr. O'Neill eliminated the numbers goal and began a program whereby managers reported all injuries with recommendations for changes to prevent accidents in the future. Those recommended changes were then implemented company-wide. Before that change, Mr. O'Neill did not learn about a major accident at a plant until a Benedictine nun whose order had purchased shares raised it at a shareholder meeting. Mr. O'Neill switched the focus from tracking injuries to tracking the causes of injuries and fixing them. The numbers went to zero. Harder to do. More difficult to measure. Even more difficult to game.

Checks and Balances for Gaming

A *Fortune* writer put it this way, "Every managerial program has a life span. Employees figure out how to game the program."[128] With incentives, there must be an accompanying analytics program to catch what employees develop to game the system. At Wells, the VA, and APS, employees had developed additional tactics for meeting goals without real achievement. Wells employees encouraged customers to open new accounts with *de minimis* deposits that they could then close after the date when the sales goals were measured. While the January Jump resulted in a big month for new accounts, it was the lowest month for the amount in actual funds deposited. By February, both the accounts and their funds were long gone. No one was effectively tracking the time the new accounts lasted. No one was really checking to see how deposits clicked along (or didn't) in those accounts.

At APS, no one was measuring the erasure rate or checking attendance records to see who was at school on the days of testing. No one was checking chain of custody on the exams and they ended up in teachers' homes on the weekends for test clean-up parties. A statistical analysis of the score improvement, as the *Atlanta Journal Constitution* did, would have put the big kibosh on the myths of the APS wonder district.

---

[127]David Burkus, "How Paul O'Neill Fought for Safety at Alcoa," April 28, 2020, https://david-burkus.com/2020/04/how-paul-oneill-fought-for-safety-at-alcoa/.

[128]Geoff Colvin, "Can Wells Fargo Get Well?" *Fortune*, June 15, 2017, p. 138, at p. 143.

At the VA, no one was calling patients randomly to check on their status. At Wells, no one was checking to see if customers really had opened new accounts. Another analytic that Wells missed was tracking sales violations. The Los Angeles region led the country for meeting sales goals, but it also led the country in reports of sales tactics that violated bank rules. Wells was even providing training on how to create accounts without funding with topics such as, "Not all new accounts must be funded to count. Shoot for 87.5% funded."[129]

The data showed that as the sales goals increased, the quality of the accounts decreased. The bank and the board were just waiting to come up with some metric to factor in quality of accounts into the sales goals. It would take Wells years just to remove secondary checking accounts as eligible new accounts for the incentive program. It was not until the story in the *Los Angeles Times* appeared that there was even a reduction in the sales goals.[130]

Sometimes, looking at the wrong analytics means that you miss the gaming. Mr. Stumpf relied on the firing of just 1% of employees for gaming. Naively, one Wells senior leader noted, "Mind boggling to me it's so low—I think it shows our [employees] are significantly more ethical than the general population (no data to back that up, just impressionistic comment!)."[131] Mr. Stumpf added, "The 1% that did it wrong, who we fired, terminated, in no way reflects our culture nor reflects the great work the other vast majority of people do. That's a false narrative."[132] Actually, Cato (to quote Cher in the movie *Clueless*), that is exactly what it means. If it happens on your watch and involved 5,300 employees, it is your culture and it is your fault. That 1% was the focus, but the executives were not looking at the 30–40% turnover rate at the branches. No one connected the high turnover to the sales results. There was a direct line, not a dotted one.

Do Not Live in Denial

Despite all of Wells' problematic tactics, Mr. Stumpf told the *Wall Street Journal* editorial board, "There was no incentive to do bad things."[133] As Senator Patrick Toomey put it during the Senate hearings on Wells and the testimony of Mr. Stumpf that the bank was merely cross-selling, "This isn't cross-selling, it's fraud."[134] The incentive plans were established to reward employees for providing customers with products that helped them with their needs and do so within their means. But the unrealistic sales goals, the way employees were treated if they fell short, the terminations for not meeting goals, and the gray-area messages of managers turned a customer service program into a Machiavellian game of intrigue that evolved into just making stuff up. In short, the application of the incentive plan, its surrounding pressures, and the continual repetition of goals and mantras created a poisonous culture.

"Misaligned incentives" is a misleading term—the correct term is *misapplied incentives*. In the Wells case, at the VA, and at APS, the incentives were used as a hammer over employees, a hammer that controlled compensation, rewards, bonuses, promotions, and even the ability to retain a job.

---

[129]Board Report, at p. 26.

[130]*Id.*, at p. 44.

[131]Board report, at p. 33.

[132]*Id.*, at p. A2.

[133]Emily Glazer and Christina Rexrode, "Wells Boss Says Staff at Fault for Scams," *Wall Street Journal*, September 14, 2016, p. A1.

[134]James B. Stewart, "Wells Fargo Case Tests a Get-Tough Approach," *New York Times*, September 23, 2016, p. B1 at B5.

Other members of the management team joined in on the justifications/rationalizations and issued qualifiers—that it was not really an incentive program but rather a program in which employees had to meet minimum goals to keep their jobs and they created fake accounts to do so.[135] Note to leaders everywhere: Goals and metrics that are part of performance evaluations and not necessarily an incentive and bonus plan still produce the same bad behaviors. Indeed, employees feel more justified in gaming the system because they are doing so for survival reasons, not bonuses. When *Forbes* ran its article on the initial Wells exposure in 2016, it received an email from a Wells employee who opened accounts for family and friends with small balances to meet quotas and goals shared this thought, "What I want people to understand, it was more survival. To say we were under pressure is an understatement."[136]

Assume That Employees Who Report Wrongdoing Are Correct

If an employee reports wrongdoing, just assume that what they are saying needs to be investigated. If they are correct, you have a problem. If they are incorrect, you also have a problem. Either way, things need to be investigated and addressed. Employees do not tell executives what is going on in the trenches.

Reliance on surveys on engagement and ethical culture is foolhardy. If management and consultants keep those beloved demographics in the questions, fear keeps employees quiet. Even without the demographics, employees fear detection. In some cases, supervisors talk to employees about their responses (and "warn" would be the better verb) because the supervisors were being measured by the survey results.

Letters from employees or outsiders or even customers could be complaints from a crank, or they could be evidence of culture issues. Assume the latter. My eldest son was one of the Wells letter writers. He had a part-time job at a Wells branch during his senior year in college. When he began work, he was quite proud of his hourly wage as well as the potential for the quarterly bonuses based on new accounts and services. In the early days of his employment, he often reported on how many new accounts and services he had set up and how his check for the quarter would be fabulous.

However, a few months into his job, he stopped by to talk with me about his work. His branch was located in a retirement area, and not a wealthy retirement area. He said that the customers were coming back in, concerned about charges and extra services they did not need. Some even closed their accounts. My son said, "I am the one who did this to them."

We talked about how he should discuss his concerns with his supervisor. Understanding how anyone in banking could believe that what was going one would bring continuing growth to the bank was a tall order. When my son talked with his supervisor, he was told that he would be measured by the accounts he landed and the services he added to existing customer accounts. If he expected to get ahead, he needed to accept these measures of success. His supervisor also told my son that if he did not meet his goals that he would be assigned to the drive-thru all the time. No one wants to set up accounts via the drive-thru, so my son saw the writing on the wall. We talked again, and my son, in a proud parenting moment, decided to resign. He resigned with notice and gave a letter to his supervisor explaining why he was quitting. The supervisor laughed and crumpled the letter. My son sent the letter to Wells Fargo headquarters in San Francisco. He never received a response.

---

[135]*Id.*, at p. A2.

[136]McGrath, *Forbes*, https://www.forbes.com/sites/maggiemcgrath/2016/09/08/wells-fargo-fined-185-million-for-opening-accounts-without-customers-knowledge/?sh=7735f44951fc.

Eight years later, when the news of Wells Fargo and the fake accounts broke, I texted my son. He responded, "I already posted it on Facebook, along with the letter I had kept on my computer. I feel so vindicated." He had tried to offer leaders front-line insights into their culture.

News from the trenches does not come in marching-band format, "Your culture is a problem!!!" There is a slow drumbeat, and without attention, even when the bands draw a crowd, the culture can make employees believe that whatever they are doing to meet their numbers, it is good. The Wells story that the problems were limited to consumer/retail banking turned out to be false. During the year following the revelations about the fake consumer accounts, Wells fired at least 24 employees in Wells Fargo Merchant Services who were inflating the sales numbers of small merchant customers so that those customers could qualify for debit- and credit-card services. These employees inflated the customer sales numbers so that the customers would qualify for services they really could not afford so that the employees could earn sales commissions and meet their sale numbers.[137] Sound familiar?

The problems at Wells were neither isolated nor limited to singular areas. Nor was this approach to small-merchant sales unique. American Express had the same problem with its small merchant sales staff.[138] And American Express issued the same kind of statement in response, "We are cooperating with all of these inquiries and have continued to enhance our controls related to our sales practices. We do not believe this matter will have a material adverse impact on our business or results of operations."[139] There's that issue again. So, the question arises once again: If what was being done was not helping your financial performance, why were the employees doing it? Because our incentive plans created the impression that results, whether real or fake, whether based on real or falsified customer financials, are what employees needed to survive.

Discussion Questions

1. If you were setting up an incentive plan for a fast-food franchise, what would you incentivize and why? What would you not incentivize and why?

2. Explain why it is important to respond to unsolicited feedback from employees or other sources?

3. What are examples of lagging indicator measurements in incentive plans?

Ethics in Action 4.3

If You Quit, Do You Need to DO More?

Like the young man who worked at a Wells branch—should he have done more about the situation at Wells? Many of his coworkers said to him, "I wish I could quit, but I need the job."

1. Is it impossible in some circumstances to effect a change?
2. Was the top leadership a blockade at Wells for any possible change?

---

[137]Emily Glazer and Ruth Simon, "Wells Uncovers More Abuses," *Wall Street Journal*, April 6, 2017, p. B6.

[138]AnnaMaria Andriotis, "DOJ, Others Reviewing Card Sales," *Wall Street Journal*, February 13–14, 2021, p. B1.

[139]*Id.*, at B2.

Accounting and Governance Factors

The Psychological and Behavior Factors

Sometimes individuals make poor ethical choices; for example, when a public official accepts a bribe. However, sometimes the organization enables and drives individuals to make certain decisions. For example, if an employee of a hedge fund is rewarded because he brings in inside information, he will keep seeking inside information despite the fact that it is illegal. This section of the unit covers the layers of ethical issues—sometimes individuals make decisions not because of misguided personal ethical compasses but because of signals, rewards, and perhaps fear, given by the organization.

Famous Lines from Art and Literature

"The numbers don't lie, but we can fix that."
Wall Street Journal, "Pepper . . . and Salt," October 2–3, 2021, p. A12.

Reading 4.12

A Primer on Accounting Issues and Ethics and Earnings Management[140]

When Arthur Levitt was the chairman of the Securities Exchange Commission (SEC), he gave a speech at New York University (NYU) that became known as the "Numbers Game" speech. He spoke presciently about companies and their efforts to use earnings management, a process in which they use accounting rules and financial manipulations to meet goals or make their earnings seem smooth. Mr. Levitt said, "Too many corporate managers, auditors, and analysts are participants in the game of nods and winks. In the zeal to satisfy consensus earnings estimates and project a smooth earnings path, wishful thinking may be winning the day over faithful representation. . . . Managing may be giving way to manipulation; integrity may be losing out to illusion."[141]

Earnings management has been business practice for so long, so often, and by so many that many businesspeople no longer see it as an ethical issue but an accepted business practice. *Fortune* magazine has even offered a feature piece on

---

[140]Adapted from an article by Marianne M. Jennings in *Corporate Finance Review* 3(5): 39–41 (March/April 1999). Reprinted from *Corporate Finance Review* by RIA, 395 Hudson Street, New York, NY 10014.

[141]Arthur Levitt, Chairman, Securities and Exchange Commission, "The Numbers Game," speech, NYU Center for Law and Business, New York, September 28, 1998.

the how-to's and the importance of doing it. It remains an unassailable proposition, based on the financial research, that a firm's stock price attains a quality of stability through earnings management. However, the financial issues in the decision to manage earnings are but one block in the decision tree. In focusing on that one block, firms are losing sight of the impact such activities have on employees, employees' conduct, and eventually on the company and its shareholders.

Issues on financial reporting and earnings management are at the heart of market transparency and trust. Understanding the issue of earnings management is important as you begin to study the cases involving companies that used this process, perhaps to an extreme. What is earnings management? How is it done? How effective is it? How do accountants and managers perceive it from an ethical perspective?

The Tactics in Earnings Management

Earnings management consists of actions by managers to increase or decrease current reported earnings to create a favorable picture for either short- or long-term economic profitability. Sometimes managers want to make earnings as low as possible so that the next quarter, particularly if they are new managers, the numbers look terrific, and it seems as if it is all due to their new management decisions. Earnings management allows managers to meet or exceed earnings projections to increase the company's stock value.

You can pick up just about any company's annual report and see how important consistent and increasing earnings are. Tenneco's 1994 annual report provides this explanation in the management discussion section: "All of our strategic actions are guided by and measured against this goal of delivering consistently high increases in earnings over the long term." Eli Lilly noted it had 33 years of earnings without a break. Bank of America's annual report noted, "Increasing earnings per share was our most important objective for the year."[142]

The methods for managing earnings are varied and limited only by manager creativity within the fluid accounting rules. The common physical techniques that have been around since commerce began are as follows:

- Write down inventory.
- Write up inventory product development for profit target.
- Record supplies or next year's expenses ahead of schedule.
- Delay invoices.
- Sell excess assets.
- Defer expenditures.

However, in his NYU speech, Chairman Levitt noted five more transactional and sophisticated methods for earnings management.

1. Large-charge restructuring
2. Creative acquisition accounting
3. Cookie jar reserves
4. Materiality
5. Revenue recognition

---

[142]Bank of America's woes, post-2008, with its ill-fated acquisition of Merrill Lynch, have resulted in a new CEO, a struggle for earnings, and a number of multibillion dollar settlements with the federal government.

Yet another accounting issue, not noted by Mr. Levitt, percolates throughout the financial collapses and misstatements of companies.

6. EBITDA (earnings before interest taxes, depreciation, and amortization) and non-**GAAP (generally accepted accounting principles)** financial reporting.[143]

In the following sections, you can find an explanation of each of these accounting issues that present both ethical and legal questions and provide the squishy areas too many companies have used to ultimately mislead investors, creditors, and the markets about their true financial status.

Large-Charge Restructuring

This type of earnings management helps clean up the balance sheet (often referred to as the **"big bath"**). A company acquiring another company takes large expenses for the acquisition because, during the next quarter, its new and effective management and control, without those added expenses, makes things look so much better. Often referred to as **spring-loading,** this technique was part of Tyco's acquisition accounting. The strategy here is to toss in as many expenses as possible in the quarter of the acquisition. Even bills not due and charges not accrued are plowed in, with the idea of showing a real dog of a performer at the time of the acquisition. Management looks positively brilliant by the next quarter when the expenses are minimal. Indeed, the next quarter, with its low expenses, may afford the opportunity for some cookie jar reserves (see following) to be set aside for future dry periods of revenues or increased expenses.

Creative Acquisition Accounting

This method, also employed by WorldCom and Tyco and other companies that went on buying binges in the 1990s, is an acceleration of expenses as well. In 2015, Valeant, with its acquisition strategy, was able to report earnings that were deceptively high because of its accounting strategies for the companies it purchased. One acquisition strategy is to designate the acquisition price as "in-process" research. The tendency for managers is to overstate the restructuring charges and toss the extra charges, over and above actual charges, into reserves, sometimes referred to as the *cookie jar*.[144] For example, a company makes an acquisition and books $2 billion for restructuring charges. Its earnings picture for that year is painted to look quite awful.[145] However, the actual costs of the restructuring are spread out over the time it takes for the company to restructure, which is actually two to three years, and some of the charges booked may not ever be incurred.[146] The charges taken are often called *soft charges* or *anticipated costs* and can include items such as training, new hires, computer consulting, and so forth. It is possible that those services may be necessary, but it is literally a guess as to whether they will be needed and an even bigger guess as to how much they will cost. However, the hit to earnings has already been taken all at once, with the resulting rosier picture of earnings growth

---

[143]A seventh issue was the tactic of shipping debt off the books to decrease the leverage ratios. Lehman Brothers did so by shipping off its debt equity just before quarterly earnings and then buying it back at a loss. The appearance of low leverage enabled Lehman to take on more debt, something that eventually resulted in its bankruptcy. See Case 4.20 for more information on the Lehman tactic.

[144]Geoffrey Colvin, "Scandal Outrage, Part 3," *Fortune*, October 28, 2002, p. 56.

[145]"Firms' Stress on 'Operating Earnings' Muddies Efforts to Value Stocks," *Wall Street Journal*, August 21, 2001, pp. A1, A8.

[146]Carol J. Loomis, "Lies, Damned Lies and Managed Earnings: The Crackdown Is Here," *Fortune*, August 2, 1999, pp. 75, 84.

in subsequent years. Also, although not entirely properly so, managers have been known to use these in a future year of not-so-great earnings to create a smoother pattern of earnings and earnings growth for investors.[147] Indeed, the reserves have been used to simply meet previously announced earnings targets.[148] So, taking the example further, if the actual charges are $1.5 billion, then the company has $500 million in reserves to feed into earnings in order to demonstrate growth in earnings where there may not be actual growth or to create the appearance of a smooth and upward trend.

For example, in an acquisition, there will be costs associated with merging computer systems. When one airline buys another, the two reservations systems must be merged. Some mergers of computer systems have been done with relative ease and little in the way of either labor costs or consulting fees. However, the acquiring airline has taken a charge, anticipating a large cost of this merger. Its numbers look low for the quarter and year of the charge. The next quarter and year, however, those numbers look dramatically improved. The acquiring airline gains value because of this performance and likely double-digit growth in earnings. The market responds with increased share value. That increased value is not grounded in real performance; changing markets; or superior skill, foresight, and industry on the part of the airline. Rather, the simple manipulation of the timing on reporting expenses yields results. The hit to earnings in one fell swoop means the financial reports do not reflect the airline's expenses and evolving challenges. The hit to earnings may not be real, and certainly we cannot know whether the anticipated costs and expenses actually occur. Again, future earnings look better, and the door is open again for cookie jar reserves.

Cookie Jar Reserves

This technique uses unrealistic assumptions to estimate sales returns, loan losses, or warranty costs. These losses are stashed away, because, as the argument goes, this is an expense that cannot be tied to one specific quarter or year (and there has been much in the way of interpretation as to what types of expenses fit into this category). Companies then allocate these reserves as they deem appropriate for purposes of smoothing out earnings. They dip into the reserves when earnings are good to take the hit and then also use the reserves when earnings are low, to explain away performance issues. The discretionary dip is the key element of the cookie jar. You dip in as needed.

Materiality

Companies avoid recording certain items because, they reason, they are too small to worry about. They are, as the accounting profession calls them, *immaterial*. The problem is that hundreds of immaterial items can and do add up to make material amounts on a single financial statement. Also, these decisions on whether items are material versus immaterial, and to report or not to report certain things, seem to create a psychology in managers that finds them always avoiding reporting bad news or trying to find ways around disclosure. An example comes from Sunbeam, Inc., a maker of home appliances, such as electric blankets, the Oster line of blenders, mixers, can openers, and electric skillets. Sunbeam carried a rather large inventory of parts it needed for the repair of these appliances when they came back while under warranty. Sunbeam used a warehouse owned by EPI Printers to store

---

[147]Id., pp. 74, 84.

[148]Louis Uchitelle, "Corporate Profits Are Tasty, but Artificially Flavored," *New York Times*, March 28, 1999, p. BU4.

the parts, which were then shipped out as needed. Sunbeam proposed selling the parts to EPI for $11 million and then booking an $8 million profit. However, EPI was not game for the transaction, because its appraisal of the parts came in at only $2 million. To overcome the EPI objection, Sunbeam let EPI enter into an agreement to agree at the end of 1997. The "agreement to agree" would have EPI buy the parts for $11 million, which Sunbeam would then book as a sale with the resulting profit. However, the agreement to agree allowed EPI to back out of the deal in January 1998. The deal was booked, the revenue recognized, Sunbeam's share price went up, and all was well—and all without EPI ever spending a dime.

Arthur Andersen served as the outside auditor for Sunbeam during this time, and its managing partner, Phillip E. Harlow, did raise some questions about the EPI deal and didn't particularly care for the Sunbeam executives' responses. Mr. Harlow asked the executives to restate earnings reflecting changes he deemed necessary. Management refused, but Mr. Harlow and Arthur Andersen certified the Sunbeam financials anyway.

Mr. Harlow reasoned that he did not see the change as "material," something that Sunbeam executives were required to restate prior to his certification. For example, under accounting rules, the "agreement to agree" with EPI, although nothing more than a sham transaction, was not "material" with regard to its amount in relation to Sunbeam's level of income. However, Mr. Harlow had defined *materiality* only in the sense of percentage of income. Although the amount was immaterial, the transaction itself spoke volumes about management integrity as well as the struggle within Sunbeam to meet earnings projections. Both of those pieces of information are material to investors and creditors. The nondisclosure of the sham transaction meant that the true financial, strategic, and ethical situation in Sunbeam was not revealed through the financial statements intended to give a full and accurate picture of where a company stands.

Further, if one added together the total number of items that were deemed immaterial individually in the Sunbeam situation, the amount of those items (items that the SEC eventually challenged as improper accounting) totaled 16% of Sunbeam's profits for 1997.

There is no question that Sunbeam, Mr. Harlow, and Andersen were correct in their handling of the Sunbeam issues, if we measure from a strict application of accounting rules. As the certification reads, Sunbeam's financial statements "present fairly, in all material respects, the financial position of, in conformity with generally accepted accounting principles."

In fact, Mr. Harlow hired PricewaterhouseCoopers to go over Sunbeam's books and his (Harlow's) judgment calls, and those auditors from another firm agreed independently that Mr. Harlow certified "materially accurate financial statements."[149] However, the real issues in materiality are not the technical application of accounting rules. Rather, the issues surround the question of intent in using the materiality trump card.

The amounts involved in many of the noted Sunbeam improprieties were not "material" in a percentage-of-income sense. The problem is that an individual auditor's definition of *materiality* is the cornerstone of a certified audit. All an auditor does is certify that the financial statements "present fairly, in all material respects, the financial position of the Company."

There is no definition of *materiality* for the accounting profession. Research shows that most auditors use a rule of thumb of 5% to 10% as a threshold level of

---

[149]Andersen has settled the suit brought against it by shareholders for $110 million. Floyd Norris, "S.E.C. Accuses Former Sunbeam Official of Fraud," *New York Times*, May 16, 2001, pp. A1, C2.

disclosure, such as 5% of net income or 10% of assets or vice versa.[150] They may also use a fixed dollar amount or an index of time and trouble in relation to the amount in question.[151]

However, it is clear just from the amount of regulatory action, shareholder litigation, and judicial definitions that the standard for materiality employed by auditors is not the same as the standard other groups would use in deciding which information should be disclosed. Called the *expectations gap*, this phenomenon means that auditor certification and executive disclosure are at odds with the expectations of investors and creditors. They expect more disclosure even as the technical application of accounting rules allows for less disclosure. The U.S. Supreme Court standard for materiality in securities fraud cases is "a substantial likelihood that the disclosure of the omitted fact would have been viewed by the reasonable investor as having significantly altered the 'total mix' of information made available."[152]

As a company establishes its ethical standards for materiality and disclosure, it should adopt the following questions as a framework for resolution:

- What historically has happened in cases in which these types of items are not disclosed? In our company? In other companies?
- What are the financial implications if this item is not disclosed now?
- What are our motivations for not disclosing this item?[153]
- What are our motivations for booking this item in this way?
- What are our motivations for not booking this item?
- How do we expect this issue to be resolved?
- Are our expectations consistent with the actions we are taking vis-à-vis disclosure?
- If I were a shareholder on the outside, would this be the kind of information I would want to know?

Revenue Recognition

These are the operational tools of earnings management. These tools allow timing to be used to overstate revenue and/or understate expenses. Some examples include **channel stuffing**, or shipping inventory before orders are placed. Sales are recognized as final and booked as revenue before delivery or final acceptance, sometimes without the buyer even knowing. The financial reporting issues at Krispy Kreme Doughnuts resulted from this ploy of reflecting sales of franchise items to franchises without those franchises actually having ordered those items.

Hewlett-Packard hit an embarrassing snag after it paid $11.1 billion for the software firm Autonomy. Shortly after the acquisition, the accounting and earnings spool of Autonomy began to unwind. Autonomy pushed the envelope on earnings reports and booking revenue, even under the more liberal British standards. For example, Autonomy made a $9 million software sale to VMS

---

[150]Marianne M. Jennings, Philip M. Reckers, and Daniel C. Kneer, "A Source of Insecurity: A Discussion and an Empirical Examination of Standards of Disclosure and Levels of Materiality in Financial Statements," 10 *The Journal of Corporation Law* 639 (1985).

[151]K. R. Jeffries, "Materiality as Defined by the Courts," 51 *CPA Journal* 13 (1981).

[152]*Basic, Inc. v. Levinson*, 485 U.S. 224 (1988).

[153]In thinking about this question, the words of outgoing SEC Chairman Arthur Levitt are instructive: "In markets where missing an earnings projection by a penny can result in a loss of millions of dollars in market capitalization, I have a hard time accepting that some of these so-called nonevents simply don't matter." *Id.*

Information but agreed to buy $13 million in licenses for data from VMS as part of the deal. The $9 million was booked as revenue, but the $13 million was booked as a marketing expense, making the deal look like a lucrative sale.[154] A more diabolical HP discovery is that Autonomy used the old Global Crossing "round trip" accounting trick in which buyer and seller buy and sell something from each other at an inflated price. Sales numbers look great, but no cash or other form of payment actually ever takes place.

The following chart summarizes the companies that have been involved in inflation of revenues and reduction of costs to manipulate earnings using creative tools from timing to early shipment to cost deferrals.

Tesco[155]	Overstatement of profits by early booking of income and delayed booking of costs	$400 million
Healthcare Services Group[156]	Failure to accrue losses on private litigation; resulted in higher EPS	Overstated EPS by two times over the course of a decade
Kraft Heinz[157]	Recognizing unearned discounts from suppliers (improperly reported costs)	$208 million
Under Armour[158]	Shifting sales from quarter to quarter to manage earnings	$600 million
Uber[159]	Treated discounts and cash incentives to customers as marketing expenses instead of reductions in sales	$1.4 billion
Lyft[160]	Treated discounts and cash incentives to customers as marketing expenses instead of reductions in sales	$388.4 million
Baxter[161]	Foreign currency exchange gains	$272 million

The other tools related to revenue recognition can be broken down into categories. Operations earnings management would involve delaying or accelerating research and development expenses (R&D), maintenance costs, or the booking of sales (channel stuffing). Finance earnings management is the early retirement of debt. Investment earnings management consists of sales of securities or fixed assets. Accountings earnings management could include the selection of accounting methods (straight-line versus accelerated depreciation), inventory valuation (last in, first out [LIFO] or first in, first out [FIFO]), and the use of reserves (the cookie jar).

---

[154]Ironically, VMS declared bankruptcy, owing over $6 million to Autonomy. Ben Worthen, Paul Sonne, and Justice Scheck, "Long Before H-P Deal, Autonomy's Red Flags," *Wall Street Journal*, November 27, 2012, p. A1.

[155]Peter Evans and Lisa Fleisher, "Tesco PLC Uncovers Problems in Its Books," *Wall Street Journal*, September 23, 2014, p. B1.

[156]Cydney Posner, "SEC Charges Healthcare Services Company Engaged in Earnings Management," *Cooley PubCo*, August 25, 2021.

[157]SEC Press Release, "SEC Charges The Kraft Heinz Company and Two Former Executives for Engaging in Years-Long Accounting Scheme," September 3, 2021, https://www.sec.gov/news/press-release/2021-174.

[158]Micah Maidenberg, "Under Armour Posts Big Drop in Revenue, Outlines Steep Cost Cuts," *Wall Street Journal*, May 12, 2020, p. B2; Khadeeja Safdar, "SEC Readies Under Armor Case," *Wall Street Journal*, July 28, 2020, p. B1.

[159]Howard Schilit, "Do Ride-Sharing Customers Sit in Front?" *Wall Street Journal*, April 29, 2019, p. A13.

[160]Id.

[161]Micah Maidenberg, "Baxter Probes Accounting Errors in Statements," *Wall Street Journal*, October 25, 2019, p. B4.

EBITDA and Non-GAAP Financial Reporting

Earnings management does hit those roadblocks of the application of accounting rules and their interpretation. So, rather than risk the wrath of the SEC and the litigation of shareholders and creditors, managers began using a different sort of financial statement. Sanjay Kumar, the former CEO of Computer Associates, once said that "standard accounting rules [are] not the best way to measure Computer Associate's results because it had changed to a new business model offering its clients more flexibility."[162]

The "pro forma" financial statement, with all the assumptions and favorable earnings management techniques, was born. Also known as **non-GAAP measures or *pro forma* statements,** this is accounting that does not comply with the rules established by the American Institute of Certified Public Accountants (AICPA), developed through its work with the SEC, scholars, and practitioners as they debate that elusive question of "Are these financials fair?"

Non-GAAP measures of financial performance can be enormously helpful and insightful in assessing the true financial condition and performance of a company. However, non-GAAP measures can also be used in a way that obfuscates or even conceals the true financial condition and performance of a company. As of 2003, under the SEC Regulation G, companies may provide non-GAAP financials, but the company must also include GAAP financials, something that shows those using the financial statements the difference between the two approaches to reporting. However, issues remain, and companies are subject to civil and SEC actions for their methodologies in computing their non-GAAP numbers.

The Types of Non-GAAP Measurements and Their Use

EBIT (earnings before interest and taxes) and **EBITDA (earnings before interest taxes, depreciation, and amortization)** are not as much accounting tools as financial analysis tools. They were developed because of concerns on the part of those who evaluated financial performance and worth that the rigidity of GAAP necessarily resulted in the omission of information that was relevant for determining the true value of a company and the richness of its earnings. EBIT and EBITDA were means of factoring out the oranges so that the apples of real earnings growth in a company could be determined.

Although the dot-coms of 1998–2001 and other firms of the gig economy are often viewed as those that popularized EBITDA as the measure of valuation for companies, its origins actually go back to the time of Michael Milken and the junk bond era of the 1980s. The takeovers of the Milken era, with their characteristics of very little cash, were accomplished through the magic of the EBITDA measurement. If an acquirer could reflect an EBITDA of just $100 million per year, that amount was sufficient to attract investors for purposes of acquisition of up to a $1 billion company. Milken, in effect, leveraged EBITDA numbers to structure takeovers.[163] However, the EBITDA figures that Milken used did not include the long-term capital expenditures and principal repayments that were, in effect, assumed to be postponed and postponable, thus allowing a portrayal of a company that could see itself through to a state of profitability. Factoring out expenses such as the cost of equipment replacement meant that earnings growth was reflected at a substantially higher rate. Investors were thus lulled into a sense of exponential earnings growth at the acquired company, not realizing the balloon type of investment that would be required when equipment replacement became inevitable.

---

[162]Alex Berenson, "Computer Associates Officials Stand by Their Accounting Methods," *New York Times*, May 1, 2001, pp. C1, C7.

[163]Herb Greenberg, "Alphabet Dupe: Why EBITDA Falls Short," *Fortune*, July 10, 2000, p. 240.

EBITDA, for some companies, is perhaps the only forthright way to reflect the actual value of a company. A company dependent on equipment, with its resulting replacement costs, has its earnings growth and value distorted through EBITDA, because investors should have the cost of replacement reflected in the numbers. Depreciation is the means whereby that cost is reflected in GAAP measurements. If an equipment-heavy company, such as a manufacturer, has the same EBITDA as a service company, with only minimal equipment investment because of its focus on human resources, then EBITDA is a misleading measure. For example, Sunbeam, the small appliance manufacturer, clearly a company in which replacement of manufacturing equipment is a significant cost, was a proponent and user of EBITDA. Firms in different industries cannot be compared accurately using only EBITDA numbers, because the nature of their business attaches significance to those numbers. GAAP measures that include depreciation provide a better means for cross-comparison, with the financial statement user able to note the depreciation component and make independent judgments about the quality of earnings.

Providing these non-GAAP measures in creating *pro forma* numbers is also particularly useful to investors and analysts when a company changes an accounting practice. For example, when a company switches its inventory evaluation method from LIFO to FIFO, the ability to present to financial statement users the contrast between what the company's performance would have been under the previous accounting practices versus the new methods shows users the real performance versus performance that includes the new methodology.

The original intent in *pro forma* numbers was a desire on the part of the accounting profession to offer more information and a better view of the financial health of a company. That intent was particularly justified in those cases in which a company has undergone a change in accounting practice that affects income in perhaps a substantial way but would actually have little impact if prior treatments had continued. The booking of options as an expense is an example. The change in the rule is important, but investors and users of financial statements will want to know what income would have looked like under the old methodology so that they are better able to track trends in real performance. However, these original good intentions in the use of *pro forma* reports changed. *Pro forma* became the accepted metric, with the *pro forma* results often manipulated with the idea of meeting earnings expectations or the practice of earnings management.

Warren Buffett described resorting to non-GAAP methods as a means of "manufacturing desired 'earnings.'"[164] Mr. Buffett has been concerned about non-GAAP accounting since writing about the expensing of stock option compensation as an expense in his 1998 letter to Berkshire Hathaway shareholders. In 2016, he once again reiterated his non-GAAP concerns about the failure to record stock-option compensation as well as other non-GAAP issues, "I suggest that you ignore a portion of GAAP amortization costs. But it is with some trepidation that I do that, knowing that it has become common for managers to tell their owners to ignore certain expense items that are all too real. Stock-based compensation is the most egregious example. The very name says it all: 'compensation.' If compensation isn't an expense, what is it? And, if real and recurring expenses don't belong in the calculation of earnings, where in the world do they belong?"[165]

---

[164]Uchitelle, "Corporate Profits Are Tasty, but Artificially Flavored," p. BU4.

[165]Sam Ho, "Warren Buffett Shines a Spotlight on the 'Most Egregious' Example of Financial Deception," *Yahoo Finance*, October 20, 2016, http://finance.yahoo.com/news/warren-buffett -shines-a-spotlight-on-the--most-egregious--example-of-financial-deception-121857624. html#. Last accessed October 20, 2016.

However, among academicians and analysts there was substantial disagreement about whether EBITDA and other non-GAAP measures were meaningful forms of valuation.[166] In 2000, prior to the dot-com bubble bursting, Moody's analyst Pamela Stump created a furor by releasing her 24-page examination of EBITDA in which she concluded that its use was excessive and that it was no substitute for full and complete financial analysis.[167] Former SEC Chief Accountant Lynn Turner was more harsh in his assessment of the pervasive use of EBITDA, calling such usage a means of lulling the "investing public into a trance with imaginary numbers, just as if they had gone to the movies. Little did they know that the theater was burning the entire time."[168] An example of EBITDA in action can be found in the WorldCom case (see Case 4.15).

As early as 1973, the SEC had issued its cautionary advice on the use of *pro forma* financial statements.[169] Nonetheless, the use of non-GAAP measures continued and expanded, and the accounting profession offered its imprimatur and certification for pro forma releases. By 2001, 57% of publicly traded companies used *pro forma* numbers along with GAAP numbers in their financial reports, whereas 43% used only GAAP numbers.[170] For the years 1997 to 1999, Adelphia, the company that collapsed in 2002 and has had two of its officers convicted and sentenced, included on the cover of its annual report charts that reflected its EBITDA growth. Geoffrey Colvin of *Fortune* has said that EBITDA stands for "Earnings Because I Tricked the Dumb Auditor."

Following the passage of **Sarbanes–Oxley,** the SEC defined both EBIT and EBITDA as non-GAAP measures of financial performance.[171] Although both can be offered in financial reports, the SEC requires a joint appearance of the two measures of financial performance.[172] The critical portion of the rules is that the non-GAAP measures must be accompanied by GAAP measures.[173] These regulations and appropriate uses of non-GAAP measures are so complex that the SEC has been forced to post responses to the 33 most frequently asked questions (FAQs) it has received on non-GAAP financial measures.[174]

---

[166]*Id.* In his 2000 annual report to shareholders, Mr. Buffett wrote, "References to EBITDA make us shudder." Elizabeth MacDonald, "The EBITDA Folly," *Forbes*, March 17, 2003, http://www.forbes.com.

[167]Greenberg, "Alphabet Dupe," p. 240.

[168]MacDonald, "The EBITDA Folly," *supra* note 43, at p. 3.

[169]Securities and Exchange Commission, Accounting Series Release No. 142, Release No. 33–5337, March 15 (Washington, DC: Securities and Exchange Commission, 1973); and Securities and Exchange Commission, Cautionary Advice regarding the Use of "Pro Forma" Financial Information, Release No. 33–8039 (Washington, DC: Securities and Exchange Commission, n.d.).

[170]Thomas J. Phillips Jr., Michael S. Luehlfing, and Cynthia Waller Vallario, "Hazy Reporting," *Journal of Accountancy*, August 2002, http://www.aicpa.org/pubs/jofa/aug2002/phillips (original publication URL).

[171]15 C.F.R. § 244.1101(a)(1). The rule provides, "A non-GAAP financial measure is a numerical measure of a registrant's historical or future financial performance, financial position or cash flows that: (i) excludes amounts, or is subject to adjustments that have the effect of excluding amounts, that are included in the most directly comparable measure calculated and presented in accordance with GAAP in the statement of income, balance sheet or statement of cash flows (or equivalent statements) of the issuer or (ii) Includes amounts, or is subject to adjustments that have the effect of including amounts, that are excluded from the most directly comparable measure so calculated and presented." Non-GAAP measures do not include ratios.

[172]SEC Release No. 34–47226, "Conditions for Use of Non-GAAP Financial Measures," 17 C.F.R. §§ 228, 229, 244, and 259 (Washington, DC: Securities and Exchange Commission, n.d.).

[173]Running parallel to the SEC changes is a project by the Financial Accounting Standards Board (FASB) called *Financial Reporting by Business Enterprises*. The purpose of the project is to focus on how key performance measures are presented and the calculation of those measures. The project will also address the general issues of whether current accounting standards and their rigidity prevent the release of full and accurate portrayals of the financial health of a company.

[174]The FAQs on non-GAAP measures can be found at the Securities and Exchange Commission website, http://www.sec.gov/divisions/corpfin/faqs/nongaapfag.

Some of those FAQs have produced the following clear rule interpretations from the SEC:

- Companies should never use a non-GAAP financial measure in an attempt to smooth earnings.

- All public disclosures are covered by Regulation G (the rule that requires the presentation of GAAP and non-GAAP measures together).

- The fact that analysts find the non-GAAP measures useful is not sufficient justification for their presentation.

Non-GAAP measures make sense in certain circumstances, when their use is, in fact, necessary to provide the financial statement user with a full and fair picture of the company's financial health.

A Follow-Up to Levitt: Ethical Issues in Financial Reporting, Earnings Management, and Accounting

How Effective Is Earnings Management?

Earnings management is effective in increasing shareholder value. A consistent pattern of earnings increases results in higher price-to-earnings ratios. That ratio is larger the longer the series of consistent earnings. Firms that break patterns of consistent earnings experience an average 14% decline in stock returns for the year in which the earnings pattern is broken. However, the discovery of earnings manipulation at a company results in a stock price drop of 9%. In short, there appears to be a net upside for engaging in earnings management.

In addition to the shareholder value argument, there are other drivers that make earnings management such a treacherous area for managers and employees. Executive and even employee compensation contracts may provide dramatic incentives for managing earnings. Incentives for earnings management can also come from sources other than compensation incentives for executives. Covenants in debt contracts, pending proxy contests, pending union negotiations, pending external financing proposals, and pending matters in political or regulatory processes can all be motivational factors for earnings management. Many managers use earnings management as a strategic tool to have an impact on pending matters.

The Ethics of Earnings Management

The question that fails to arise in the context of management decisions on managing earnings is whether the practices are ethical. Managers and accountants comply with the technical rules, but technical compliance may not result in financial statements that are a full and fair picture of how the company is doing financially. In a system dependent upon reliable (known as *transparent*) financial information, the practice of earnings management conceals relevant information. Research shows that firms that engage in earnings management are more likely to have boards with no independence and eventually higher costs of capital.

The new approach to accounting rules and earnings management focuses on the ethical notion of balance: If you were the investor instead of the manager, what information about earnings management would you want disclosed? If you were on the outside looking in, how would you feel about the decision to book extra expenses this year to even out earnings in a year not so stellar? In short, when all the complications of LIFO, FIFO, EBITDA, and spring-loading are discussed, we are left with the simple notions of ethical analysis provided in Unit 1, from the categorical imperative to the Blanchard–Peale and Nash questions of "How would I feel if I were on the other side?" When involved in complex situations, reducing the complexities to their simplest terms gives you the common denominator of those basic tests and analysis methods for all ethical issues.

For example, in evaluating the use of non-GAAP measures, the following questions prove helpful: Why is this measure important for the company? Why do we choose to rely on it? What insight does this measure give that is not afforded by traditional GAAP methods? Does this method of reporting mislead users of financial statements? How reliable is this measure? Is it based on models, or is it simply theory?

In addition to the examination of intent, these questions require those who prepare and audit financial statements should also consider the amount of discussion and analysis that is necessary in order for them to offer a fair explanation on their decisions to use alternative reporting metrics.

An example provides a look at the wide-swath interpretations that these alternative metrics can cut as financial reports are prepared. A company has the following financials:

- Operating revenues: $1 million
- Nonrecurring, nonoperating gain: $300,000
- Nonrecurring, nonoperating loss: $800,000
- Operating expenses: $600,000

The questions are as follows: What are the company's earnings? What earnings number should be released to the press? The GAAP answer is that the company has experienced a $100,000 loss. The EBITDA answer is that the company has $400,000 profit because $400,000 does indeed reflect the operating profit. However, some EBITDA proponents would conclude that there was $700,000 in profit, because they would eliminate the nonrecurring loss but recognize the nonrecurring gain.[175]

The ultimate ethical question in all financial reporting and accounting practices is "Do these numbers provide fair insight into the true financial health and performance of the company?" Further, the example given illustrates that numbers alone, even if concluded to be fair, may not be sufficient because only MD&A can provide a full and complete picture of what the non-GAAP measures mean, why they were used, and how they should be interpreted. The juxtaposition of GAAP and non-GAAP measures, now mandated by law, has also been a critical component to the effective use of both sets of numbers. The presentation of both provides checks and balances for the excesses in financial reporting during the 1990s as the non-GAAP measures became the standard for financial reports.

Discussion Questions

1. Describe the risks in earnings management.

2. What are the motivations for moving around expenses and revenues in quarters and years?

3. Don't shareholders benefit by earnings management? Who is really harmed by earnings management?

4. Put earnings management into one of the ethical categories you have learned.

5. Make up a headline description of earnings management.

6. How do you respond to a CFO who says the following? "Everybody does earnings management. If I don't do it, I am at a disadvantage."

---

[175]Modified from an example given in Phillips, Luehlfing, and Vallario, "Hazy Reporting."

Sources

David Burgstanler and Ilia Dichev, "Earnings Management to Avoid Earnings Decreases and Losses," 24 *Journal of Accounting and Economics* 99 (1997).

Patricia M. Dechow, Richard G. Sloan, and Amy P. Sweeney, "Causes and Consequences of Earnings Manipulation: An Analysis of Firms Subject to Enforcement Actions by the SEC," 13 *Contemporary Accounting Research* 1 (1996).

James Jiabalbo, "Discussion of 'Causes and Consequences,'" 13 *Contemporary Accounting Research* 37 (1999).

Arthur Levitt, "The Numbers Game," September 28, 1998, New York University, http://www.sec.gov/news/speech/speecharchive/1998/spch220.txt.

Kenneth A. Merchant and Joanne Rockness, "The Ethics of Managing Earnings: An Empirical Investigation," 13 *Journal of Accounting and Public Policy* 79 (1994).

Kenneth Rosen Zweig and Marilyn Fischer, "Is Managing Earnings Ethically Acceptable?" *Management Accounting,* March 1994, p. 31.

Reading 4.13

Prevention Tools for the Layers of Ethical Issues: Individual, Organization, Industry, and Society[176]

Just as all employees are not created ethically equal, all ethical issues are not created equal when it comes to root cause. When studying causation factors for ethical lapses, the four layers of ethical issues emerge once again (Reading 2.1). Those layers are fueled by organizational culture. Because the root causes for these levels differ, tools for prevention must also be different. The levels of lapses as well as the prevention tools are depicted in Figure 4.1, followed by discussion and examples.

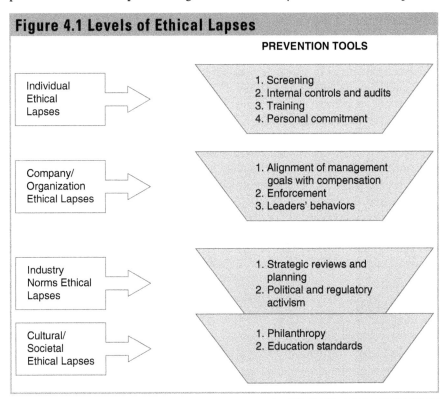

Figure 4.1 Levels of Ethical Lapses

PREVENTION TOOLS

Individual Ethical Lapses
1. Screening
2. Internal controls and audits
3. Training
4. Personal commitment

Company/ Organization Ethical Lapses
1. Alignment of management goals with compensation
2. Enforcement
3. Leaders' behaviors

Industry Norms Ethical Lapses
1. Strategic reviews and planning
2. Political and regulatory activism

Cultural/ Societal Ethical Lapses
1. Philanthropy
2. Education standards

---

[176]Adapted from Marianne M. Jennings, "Grappling with the Four Levels of Ethical Issues," *Corporate Finance Review*, 15(3): 36–44 (2010).

The Individual Ethical Lapses

Individual ethical lapses are the lapses that result from individuals making their own decisions. Some examples include the resignation/termination of former Hewlett-Packard CEO, Mark Hurd. Public reports and company statements indicate that Mr. Hurd had an "inappropriate relationship" with a marketing vendor and misled the company on his expense reimbursement requests to conceal the extent of the relationship.[177]

Adam Neumann, a founder and once CEO of WeWork, had questionable judgment, had three weekend houses all near New York City, walked barefoot around Manhattan, and wanted to solve the problem of "150 million orphans."[178] When the company's initial S-1 registration statement became public, the mission statement indicated that the purpose of WeWork was to "elevate the world's consciousness."[179] That thought was taken from Mr. Neumann's spirituality gurus at the Kabbalah Centre, which was providing spiritual sessions for employees at WeWork. His behavior resulted in the postponement of the company's IPO and the discovery of various issues in its financials that caused underwriters to end their involvement.

Poor judgment is an individual decision. Those individual decisions affect organizations, but nothing the organization is doing is driving individuals to engage in these behaviors. However, enough individual decisions within an organization can affect the culture. For example, Activision's atmosphere of harassment resulted from too many employees going along with or tolerating the behaviors of those employees who were harassing female employees. Externalities such as organizational and industry pressure from the other layers did not cloud the beginning individual's decision processes. They are doing what *they* want to do, regardless of the effect on the organization.

Prevention Tool One for Individual Ethical Lapses: Screening

Screening is one tool for preventing individual missteps. Neither proven nor perfect, this tool employs various psychological and security exams to detect individual tendencies to engage in behavior such as taking things that don't belong to you. Retailers have the most well-developed screens for their potential employees because they are focused on that singular aspect of theft.

However, there are some other more casual methods that other organizations can use in the interview process to offer insights into the ethical character of the applicant. One question that has proven effective in screening is asking applicants to describe an ethical dilemma that they have faced personally or professionally and how they handled the dilemma. If an applicant cannot describe an ethical dilemma, the employer has obtained some great insight. Sometimes applicants provide examples that are not really ethical dilemmas, such as HR types of issues on performance reviews and employee feedback. They feel a situation was not handled correctly, and they are perhaps correct in their assessment. However, those organizational behavior issues are not a matter of ethics but manners.

---

[177]Ben Worthen and Joann S. Lublin, "At Oracle, Hurd Lands In," *Wall Street Journal*, September 9, 2010, p. B1.

[178]Ginia Bellafante, "WeWork Stumbles, and Some Myths Unravel," *New York Times*, October 6, 2019, p. A27.

[179]Shayndi Raice and Konrad Putzier, "WeWork Boss Mixed Spirituality, Business," *Wall Street Journal*, October 17, 2019, p. B1.

Prevention Tool Two for Individual Ethical Lapses: Internal Controls and Audits

As forensic auditors teach us, embezzlement has its origins in opportunity and need. The need is difficult to prevent but the opportunity can be limited. Sarbanes–Oxley (see Reading 4.18) Section 404 has resulted in the continual reevaluation of the adequacy of internal controls. There is some value in what is often viewed as an added expense. Mr. Hurd's conduct was discovered when there was an audit of expense reports of senior officers. With Mr. Neumann, studying the financials revealed the extent of his expenditures.

Prevention Tool Three for Individual Ethical Lapses: Training

There are some employees who need instruction and reminders of the dos and don'ts while at work. At a power plant, two consultants who were not really well known to plant employees watched as a carpenter who earned $90,000 per year stopped at the supply desk and pocketed a package of double-A batteries for home use. An audit revealed that such little "heists" were apparently a way of life. Training serves to provide employees with examples as well as information on consequences. Fear works in organizations as well as it works in parenting. The understanding that "it is not worth my job" is an important training message.

Prevention Tool Four for Individual Ethical Lapses: Personal Commitment

This tool goes beyond the training to ask employees to embrace a set of values that are then used as part of the identity of the organization. The Viad Corporation adopted a commitment principle of "Always honest." The company then used that theme in its communications with vendors, customers, and regulators as part of its identity and brand. The use of the phrase in training and with employees was universal and part of a strategy to have them commit to the culture of a company that was always honest.

The Company or Organization Ethical Lapses

These types of lapses are those that employees may commit individually, but organizational externalities contribute to their poor analysis of the ethical dilemma and their ultimate choices. For example, during the 1990s, Bausch & Lomb settled financial reporting issues with the SEC because it had overstated its revenues. In announcing the settlement, Bausch & Lomb emphasized that the SEC found no evidence that top management knew of the overstatement of profits (the amount was a 54% overstatement) at the time it was made. However, the SEC's associate director of enforcement said, "That's precisely the point. Here is a company where there was tremendous pressure down the line to make the numbers. The commission's view is that senior management has to be especially vigilant where the pressure to make the numbers creates the risk of improper revenue recognition."[180]

The employees of Bausch & Lomb had some "creative" ways of meeting their numbers in terms of sales goals. "Creative" translates to unethical choices that were to the point of illogical. The term coined for these activities is often "loading dock fraud," or the kinds of overstatements of earnings that result from physical transfers

---

[180]Mark Maremont, "Judgment Day at Bausch & Lomb," *BusinessWeek*, December 25, 1995, p. 39; and Floyd Norris, "Bausch & Lomb and SEC Settle Dispute on '93 Profits," *New York Times*, November 18, 1997, p. C2.

of goods. For example, the company's Hong Kong unit was faking sales to real customers but then dumping the glasses at discount prices onto gray markets. The contact lens division shipped products that were never ordered to doctors to boost sales. Some distributors had up to two years of unordered inventories. The U.S., Latin American, and Asian contact lens divisions also dumped lenses on the gray market, forcing Bausch & Lomb to compete with itself.

The mistake that organizations make is in treating these poor choices by employees as individual ethical lapses. They then use the prevention tools for category one lapses when what the company is experiencing is a category two lapse. The root cause rests with the organizational drivers. "Here's your number" was the common direction Bausch & Lomb managers gave to sales personnel and even accountants within the company. When "the number" was not made, they were confronted with this question: "Do you want me to go back to the analysts and tell them we can't make the numbers?"[181] One division manager, expecting a shortfall, said he was told to make the numbers but "don't do anything stupid." The manager said, "I'd walk away saying, 'I'd be stupid not to make the numbers.'" Another manager said that to meet targets, they did 70% of their shipments in the last three days of the month.[182] Managers lived in fear of what they called "red ball day." *Red ball day* was the end of the calendar quarter, so named because a red sticky dot was placed on the calendar. As red ball day approached, credit was extended to customers who shouldn't have had credit; credit terms went beyond what was healthy and normal for receivables; and deep discounts abounded. One employee described panic-stricken managers doing whatever it took to meet the number for red ball day.

Another form of company/organizational lapse is one that begins with an individual lapse but ripens into an organizational one because of the reaction. For example, an employee at a competitor could be applying for a new job. That employee might offer, as was the case with Boeing's troubles related to the hiring of a Lockheed-Martin employee, to bring along proprietary information (see Case 2.12). If Boeing turns down the offer and the employee, the lapse remains an individual one. If, however, Boeing hires the Lockheed-Martin employee and encourages the document bring-along and then uses those documents, the issue becomes a company/organization lapse. The question becomes why would a manager agree to go along with the conduct proposed by an individual? The answer lies in the signals, pressures, and incentives present in the hiring company.

All could be well with the prevention tools on category one lapses, but employees will still engage in these behaviors because the organization rewards those who get results, however achieved, and punishes those who do not. The prevention tools are different and require modification of company policies.

Prevention Tool One for Company/Organization Lapses: Alignment of Management Goals with Compensation

Companies provide all the trappings of an ethical culture in addressing the individual level of ethical lapses. Those types of checklists and dashboard measures are reportable, carry physical evidence, and produce numbers results; that is, 97% of all employees completed the company's online ethics training. But if the compensation system is not properly aligned with both goals and values, the prevention tools for the individual level will not be as effective as when they run in parallel with company/organization prevention tools.

---

[181]Mark Maremont, "Blind Ambition," *BusinessWeek*, October 23, 1995, pp. 78–92.
[182]*Id.*

If employees perceive hypocrisy between the messages to them about ethics and the types of behaviors engaged in by employees who are then rewarded, there are several ill effects. The employees develop resentment, something that affects productivity. In addition, employees' sense of justice and equity is violated and they undertake unilateral actions to align espoused values with rewards. An employee who does not earn a bonus or is passed over for a promotion because he or she did not engage in the behaviors outlined in the "loading dock fraud" scenarios may resort to embezzlement and feel perfectly justified in doing so because the theft is a means of achieving justice. The failure to fix company/organizational ethical lapses undermines efforts to address individual lapses.

Managers need to examine the pay, bonus, and incentive structures in place. It remains an unassailable proposition that incentive plans work to motivate employees and achieve goals. Performance and incentive plans not encased in the company values will result in ethical lapses that might not otherwise occur without the drivers those plans produce. Alignment helps employees understand that results are important but not at the expense of the values exhorted in the individual lapses prevention tools (see Case 4.10 The Wells Way and Reading 4.11 Measures, Metrics, and Gaming for discussion of incentives and alignment).

Prevention Tool Two for Company/Organization Lapses: Enforcement

A company discovered that a top performer in sales had been able to circumvent the firewall and tap into a competitor's website and obtain proprietary information that he was then able to use to obtain new customers, mostly from the competitor. Hence, his top performer status was achieved. He was rewarded for his ill-gotten sales results and the company was prepared to look the other way. There was hesitation on the enforcement action.

Without enforcement, employees ignore the admonitions about behavior and perform according to the standards set by management action. One executive notes, "It does not matter what you said. It is what they heard." Lack of enforcement is what employees hear over all the individual prevention tools of training and values. Lack of enforcement trumps the prevention steps with individual lapses.

Prevention Tool Three for Company/Organization Lapses: Leaders' Behavior

In writing a report when he was serving as inspector general for the Department of Interior, the late Earl Devaney disclosed and recommended the following when he discovered ethical lapses by the leaders of that department: "For many people, it's good to see senior officers are disciplined like others. There is a perception that senior folks have a way around the regulations. Short of a crime, anything goes at the highest level of the Department of Interior. Ethics failures on the part of senior department officials—taking the form of appearances of impropriety, favoritism, and bias—have been routinely dismissed with a promise of not to do it again."[183] Mr. Devaney appeared before Congress to explain his findings because the leaders failed to understand and act upon the serious findings in his report.

---

[183]Testimony of the Honorable Earl E. Devaney, Inspector General for the Department of the Interior before the Committee on Government Reform, U.S. House of Representatives, May 5, 2004, http://www.doioig.gov/images/stories/pdf/050504Testimony%20of%20Earl%20E.%20 Devaney.pdf.

Often referred to as "the tone at the top," the piece that is often missing is the realization by company and organizational leaders that they are indeed the top, and their behavior and decisions constitute the tone. Translating the importance of leaders' examples and conducts is relatively easy to do with some simple pieces of advice: The rules apply to everyone. A leader who stops to self-enforce the company's or organization's rules against himself gains the respect of employees even as he moves them along to ethical choices. A CEO stopped accepting reimbursement for meals when he was on the road. He submitted his expenses for transportation and lodging but explained, "I have to eat anyway." He does not expect employees to not seek reimbursement for their meals on the road, but he is showing that he is careful about travel expenses and appreciates that it is not his money and that he owes a fiduciary duty to those who do provide the money by their investments for the company. Leaders need to be ever vigilant in their conduct, choices, and decisions to curb company and organizational lapses.

Industry Norms Ethical Lapses

In response to the federal court decision on its overdraft fees, a Wells Fargo spokesperson, in explaining the bank's appeal of the decision, offered, "Many banks process customers' transactions in high-to-low order because it gives priority to larger transactions such as mortgage, rent, or car payments."[184] The spokesperson is absolutely correct; Wells was the defendant in a class action suit, but other banks were following the same accounting processes for overdraft fees. In this situation, the company or organization has simply followed the industry policies and achieves a great deal of ethical comfort from the assurance, "Everybody does this." (see Reading 1.5 on rationalizations.) However, such an approach is simply rationalization and not analysis of the ethical issue. The comfort of that rationalization tool deprives the company or organization of analysis of the implications and long-term costs of the practice, however pervasive.

Other examples of accepted industry practices that later proved problematic for industries as well as the general state of the economy included the substantial increase in subprime loans in the 2003–2006 period, the development and sale of mortgage-backed securities without verification of the quality of the mortgage pools, and, pre-Enron, the undertaking of both audit and consulting functions by accounting firms. These behaviors were all widely practiced and generally accepted. In fact, those who did not follow these practices were perceived to be at a competitive disadvantage.

No matter how effective the individual or company ethical lapse prevention tools have been, this level of ethical lapse will, once again, trump the efforts at those other levels. Those in the position to make strategic decisions about the companies' products, services, and directions miss the ethical implications of what everyone is doing, because they have accepted the flawed reasoning of this relativistic ethical standard. Prevention here occurs at higher levels in the company and does require deeper analysis and longer term strategies.

Prevention Tool One for Industry Lapses: Strategic Reviews and Planning

This prevention tool requires managers to look at revenues and ask how the numbers are arrived at and the sources of the revenues. Wells Fargo was absolutely accurate in its assessment that it was not the only bank following the overdraft accounting practice. However, there were other banks in the industry that had taken a strategic look at the

---

[184]Joel Rosenblatt and Karen Guillo, "Wells Fargo Must Pay Consumers $203 Million in Overdraft Case," Bloomberg News, August 11, 2010, http://www.bloomberg.com/news/2010-08-11/wells-fargo-should-pay-203-million-in-overdraftfees-lawsuit-judge-rules.html.

practice and changed course. In March 2010, Bank of America announced that it was changing its overdraft policy so that when customers were going to cause an overdraft in their account, the transaction would be declined until the customer agreed to pay the fee. In response to customers who said don't charge me $40 for a $5 cup of coffee, the bank offered the warning solution, something that resulted in a drop in fees and a resulting hits to revenue estimated at "tens of millions."[185] Federal rules changes requiring such a warning were looming, but Bank of America made a strategic choice to change its behaviors in a way that differentiated it from its competition and allowed it to have the processes in place prior to regulation taking effect.

The "everybody does it" is a lagging strategy that is fraught with ethical risk of accepting the industry standard as an acceptable ethical standard. Preventing a fall into the industry ethical lapses requires strategic review and leadership in strategy changes, not a ride of the "everyone" wave until the regulatory halt.

Prevention Tool Two for Industry Lapses: Political and Self-Regulatory Activism

This prevention tool finds the leader who has made voluntary changes to correct the "everybody does it" on an industry-wide level. For example, the cruise-line industry, the nuclear power industry, the chemical industry, and others have all established self-regulatory bodies that set safety and reporting standards for members that impose higher requirements than the law and serve to distinguish the members because of the trust the affiliation builds. This form of self-regulation also serves to isolate the organizations with questionable practices that could result in government controls that may be expensive, but not effective in solving the problems. Those who know the industry best are equipped to address its ethical issues in an effective and preemptive manner.

Cultural and Societal Ethical Shifts

There is always a little bit of pushback when folks view the latest stats on cheating by our high school and college students. There is a dismissiveness, to wit, "They are not cheating more; they are just more honest about it!" or "Don't you think it's the Internet? We just find out about these things more?" "It was more of a disgrace back then, so we didn't talk about it!" "Every generation thinks the next generation is worse!"

The examples of cheating have been eye-popping. For example, Ernst & Young paid a $100 million fine to settle with the SEC because of its awareness and inaction when it learned its auditors were cheating on their annual ethics certification exams.[186] At Brophy College Preparatory School in Phoenix the principal discovered that students there had devised a system to pay classmates to falsify their identities in a math course's digital assessment system and then complete their online homework and assessments.[187] The Inspector General for the Justice Department issued a report that concluded FBI agents and some supervisors were cheating on their surveillance tests, that is, the tests that determined whether the agents knew the law regarding what they can and cannot do to initiate surveillance and how it is to be conducted. We have uncovered cheating rings on the GMAT exams as well

---

[185]Andrew Martin, "Bank of America to End Debit Overdraft Fees," *New York Times*, March 10, 2010, p. B1.

[186]Dave Michaels, "EY to Pay $100 Million Fine in Ethics-Cheating Scandal," *Wall Street Journal*, June 29, 2022, p. A1.

[187]Marissa Sarbak, "Brophy College Preparatory Students Caught in 'Widespread' Cheating Scandal, Principal Says," FOX 10, May 21, 2022, https://www.fox10phoenix.com/news/brophy-college-preparatory-students-widespread-cheating-scandal-principal.

as the exams for the certification of physicians for internal medicine specialization. The American Board of Internal Medicine (ABIM) has taken some sort of disciplinary action against 140 doctors who cheated on their ABIM certification exams. In a lawsuit that the ABIM had filed previously against Arora Board Review, a company that does exam review courses for certification, the discovery process yielded information that proved to be more damaging for the docs than for Arora. The documents in the settled case included emails and other correspondence from the doctors to Arora, which revealed that the docs knew many of the questions and, indeed, followed up by sending along memorized test questions from their own certification exams to Arora to help those awaiting taking the exam.[188]

The shift is real and troubling, and the prevention tools at the individual, company or organization, and industry levels will not curb these shifts because the controlling perception of individuals, companies, and industries is that their behaviors are now the norm. When the norm has shifted, the steps of training, commitment, alignment, and strategy are of little help because the societal acceptance level has changed.

However, that the acceptance level has changed does not equate to no danger here. Students moving on to college work without adequate high-school education will experience setbacks and possibly failures. Law enforcement left in the hands of those who do not know the boundaries for surveillance opens the door to undermining of the rule of law. Medicine practiced by those who have not attained the knowledge competency levels for diagnosis and treatment carries a self-explanatory risk. Projects undertaken and supervised by engineers who do not have the requisite skills result in structures with flaws and safety issues. In other words, societal shifts in ethical norms are inherently dangerous. They can be addressed with two prevention tools that require business activism at levels beyond the company and industry but can certainly be undertaken with industry cooperation.

Prevention Tool One for Cultural/Societal Ethical Shifts: Philanthropy

This prevention tool finds companies and organizations committed to improvement of the formulation of character in young people. Companies and industries need not reinvent the wheel but can contribute to organizations that are working toward bringing the norm back to original position. For example, the Josephson Institute specializes in the training of teachers who can then use their acquired skills to inculcate the concept that "character counts" in students. At schools where this program is used, data indicate that the campuses are safer; an atmosphere of respect between and among students and teachers takes hold; and there is a better focus on education. The program has decades of achievement behind it and is a means for shifting the societal norm back to its starting point of civility.

Recognizing employees, students, and citizens who "do the right thing" gets their stories out there and reawakens the importance of ethics in personal and professional lives. J. P. Hayes was playing the Q school (pro golf's qualifying school, a series of games in which players compete for the top 25 slots, a position that allows them to enter most PGA tournaments without qualifying). While playing one of the Q school rounds at Houston's Deerwood Country Club in mid-November 2008, Hayes chipped his ball onto the green and placed a marker. After finishing the hole, he realized that he had used a different ball. He called himself on it, and he took a two-stroke penalty. Oh, but there's more. Later Mr. Hayes realized that the ball he had used was not one that was PGA approved. He had some Titleist prototypes

---

[188]*ABIM v. Arora Board Review* (E.D. Pa), January 5, 2010.

in his bag that he had been testing for the company. He had used a newfangled, unapproved ball. To call or not to call PGA officials? Disqualification versus six-figures in earnings several times over? Mr. Hayes notified PGA officials. He said, "I pretty much knew at that point that I was going to be disqualified." It was a mistake, and Mr. Hayes didn't know how the prototypes remained in his bag. Players generally make certain that they eliminate those issues before the round.

Mr. Hayes put a year of his career on the line to be honest. Being in the Top 25, the rank the Q school gives you, means about $1 million in earnings. Being disqualified from the Q means Mr. Hayes, at his rank, looked at fewer tournaments and about $300,000 in earnings. Mr. Hayes took full responsibility and held himself accountable, and all when no one would have known. The PGA, to its credit, made sure the story got out there to remind us that the higher road is a possibility.

Prevention Tool Two for Cultural/Societal Ethical Shifts: Educational Standards

The fact that the cheating scandals seem to always be with us is not a justification for abandoning the goal of upholding educational standards. If those who are hired or who are seeking professional qualification are required to demonstrate mastery of knowledge and skills, then the burden shifts back to them for knowledge acquisition. There is no benefit in dishonesty used to earn grades if effective testing awaits prior to entry into the workforce or the profession. For example, an engineering graduate may be able to find ways to obtain questions, answers, and intelligence on exams. However, a practical exam that requires application of knowledge in the field remains an effective screen for which there is no alternative, easier path. A utility executive bemoans the fact that recent engineering hires do not seem to have the knowledge base necessary for understanding a power plant's functional interaction. A controller worries that a recent finance graduate seems unable to compute something as simple as APR. These skills are easily tested in the workplace, using a simple problem that requires response in real time. The facile reliance on the multiple-choice test has netted the scandals described earlier. A return to the apprenticeship form of examination circumvents the shifted norm on cheating. However, such an approach also serves to tell us what we need to know: Is this individual qualified?

Thoughts in Conclusion

Addressing ethical lapses has been a one-size-fits-all approach that centers on the tools in preventing individual ethical lapses. However, the types of ethical lapses and their root causes are much more complex than those tools. The complexity, however, should not be a barrier to entry into those other layers of prevention tools that can be effective in addressing the root causes even as they shift our norms in a way that changes our behaviors, standards, and strategies.

Discussion Questions

1. Using what you have learned from the Wells case and this reading, describe how overdraft fee practices progressed through layers and became so pervasive in the banking industry.

2. Explain what must be fixed at the company level that is different from the fixes for individual ethical lapses.

3. Provide a list of other examples of peer pressure that result in industry-level choices.

4. Refer back to Unit I to classify the cases there according to their layer type of ethical issue.

Case 4.14

FINOVA and the Loan Write-Off

The FINOVA Group, Inc., was formed as a commercial finance firm in 1992. It was created as a spin-off from the Greyhound Financial Corporation (GFC). GFC underwent a complete restructuring at that time and other spin-offs included the Dial Corporation.

FINOVA, headquartered in Phoenix, Arizona, quickly became a Wall Street darling. Its growth was ferocious. By 1993, its loan portfolio was over $1 billion both through its own loans as well as the acquisition of U.S. Bancorp Financial, Ambassador Factors, and TriCon Capital. In 1994, FINOVA had a successful $226 million stock offering. By 1995, its loan portfolio was $4.3 billion. Standard & Poor's rated the company's senior debt as A, and Duff & Phelps upgraded its rating to *A* in 1995 when FINOVA issued $115 million in convertible preferred shares and its portfolio reached $6 billion. FINOVA's income went from $30.3 million in 1991 to $117 million by 1996 to $13.12 billion in 1999. *Forbes* named FINOVA to its Platinum 400 list of the fastest-growing and most profitable companies in January 2000.

FINOVA was consistently named as one of the top companies to work for in the United States (it debuted as number 12 on the list published by *Fortune* magazine in 1998 and subsequent years). Its benefits included an on-site gym for employee workouts and tuition for the children of FINOVA employees (up to $3,000 per child) who attended any one of the three Arizona state universities under what FINOVA called the "Future Leaders Grant Program."[189] FINOVA also had generous bonus and incentive plans tied to the stock price of the company. *Fortune* magazine described the 500 stock options each employee is given when hired, the free on-site massages every Friday, concierge services, and unlimited time off with pay for volunteer work as a "breathtaking array of benefits."[190]

The name *FINOVA* was chosen as a combination of "financial" and "innovators." However, some with language training assert that FINOVA is a Celtic term that means "pig with lipstick." FINOVA took pride in its strategic distinction from other finance companies. It was able to borrow cheaply and then make loans to businesses at a premium. Its borrowers were those who were too small,

too new, or too much in debt to qualify at banks.[191] Its 1997 annual report included the following language from FINOVA's CEO and chairman of the board, Sam Eichenfield:

> FINOVA is, today, one of America's largest independent commercial finance companies. We concentrate on serving midsize business—companies with annual sales of $10 million to $300 million—with arguably the industry's broadest array of financing products and services. The goals we set forth in our first Annual Report were to:
>
> - grow our income by no less than 10 % per year;
> - provide our shareholders with an overall return greater than that of the S&P 500;
> - preserve and enhance the quality of our loan portfolios; and
> - continue enjoying improved credit ratings.
>
> We have met those goals and, because they remain equally valid today, we intend to continue meeting or surpassing them in the future. Many observers comment on FINOVA's thoughtfulness and discipline and, indeed, FINOVA prides itself on its focus.

FINOVA also had a reputation for its generous giving in the community. Again, from its 1997 annual report:

> FINOVA believes that it has a responsibility to support the communities in which its people live and work. Only by doing so can we help guarantee the future health and vitality of our clients and prospects, and only by doing so can we assure ourselves of our continuing ability to attract the best people.
>
> Over the years, not only have FINOVA and its people contributed monetarily to a broad range of charitable, educational and cultural causes, but FINOVA people have contributed their time and energy to a variety of volunteer efforts.
>
> In 1996, FINOVA contributed more than $1.5 million and thousands of volunteer hours to educate and develop

(continued)

---

[189]Dawn Gilbertson, "Finova's Perks Winning Notice," *Arizona Republic*, December 22, 1998, pp. E1, E9.

[190]"The 100 Best Companies to Work For," *Fortune*, January 11, 1999, p. 122.

[191]Riva D. Atlas, "Caught in a Credit Squeeze," *New York Times*, November 2, 2000, pp. C1, C21.

Case 4.14

(continued)

youth, house the homeless, feed the hungry, elevate the arts, and support many other deserving causes around the country.

FINOVA's ascent continued in the years following the 1997 report. Its stock price climbed above $50 per share, and management continued to emphasize reaching the income goals and the goals for portfolio growth. Throughout the company, many spoke of the unwritten goal of reaching a stock price of $60 per share. That climb in stock price was rewarded. The stock traded in the $50 range for most of 1998 and 1999, reaching a high of $54.50 in July 1999.

At the end of 1998, FINOVA reported that Mr. Eichenfield's compensation for the year was $6.5 million, the highest for any CEO of firms headquartered in Phoenix. More than half of the compensation consisted of bonuses. Mr. Eichenfield and his wife purchased a $3 million home in nearby Paradise Valley shortly after the year-end announcement in 1998 of his compensation.[192] Mr. Eichenfield was named the 1999 Fabulous Phoenician by *Phoenix Magazine*, which included the following description:

> A true mensch in every sense of the word, Sam casually says, "I do what I can," referring to the community for which he has done so much. While he maintains a modest air on the outside, Sam admits, "I take a lot of pride in having created a lot of opportunity for a lot of people." As long as Sam is head of FINOVA and lives in this community, we're sure there will be many more people who will benefit from his kindness and his generosity.[193]

It was sometime during the period from 1996 through 1998 that issues regarding financial reporting arose within the company. FINOVA had a decentralized management structure that created autonomous units. There were at least 16 different finance divisions, such as Commercial Equipment Finance, Commercial Real Estate Finance, Corporate Finance, Factoring Services, Franchise Finance, Government Finance, Health-Care Finance, Inventory Finance, Transportation Finance, and Rediscount Finance. Each of these units had its own manager, credit manager,

and financial manager. In many cases, the failure of one unit to meet prescribed goals resulted in another unit making up for that shortcoming through some changes in that unit's numbers that they would report for the consolidated financial statements of FINOVA.

The Resort Finance division was a particularly high-risk segment of the company. Resort Finance was the term used to describe what were time-share interests that FINOVA was financing.[194] Time-share financing is a particularly risky form of financing because lenders are loaning money to borrowers who live in France for property located in the Bahamas that has been built by a company from the Netherlands and is managed by a firm with its headquarters in Britain. The confluence of laws, jurisdiction, and rights makes it nearly impossible to collect should the borrowers default. And the default rate is high because time-sharing interests are a luxury item that are the first payments to be dropped when households experience a drop in income because of illness or the loss of a job.

Resort Finance would prove to be a particularly weak spot in the company and an area in which questions about FINOVA's financial reporting would arise. For example, FINOVA had a time-share property loan for a recreational vehicle (RV) park in Arkansas that had a golf course and restaurant. The idea, when first acted on in 1992, was that folks could pay for a place to park their RV in beautiful Arkansas for a week or two in a time-share RV resort. When the loan was made in 1992, the property had a book value of $800,000. At the time of the default in 1995, the property was worth $500,000. FINOVA took back the property but did not write down the loan. It did, however, continue to report the loan as an earning asset even as it capitalized the expenses it incurred to maintain the golf course and restaurant. By 1997, FINOVA was carrying the Arkansas time-share resort on its books as a $5.5 million earning asset. One manager remarked, "You couldn't sell all of Arkansas and get $5.5 million and we were carrying a bad loan at that amount."[195]

Because of its lending strategies, FINOVA had higher risk in virtually all of its lending divisions. For example,

(continued)

---

[192]"Finova Chief Splurges on $3 Million Mansion," *Arizona Republic*, January 23, 1998, pp. E1, E7.

[193]*Phoenix Magazine*, 1999.

[194]Interviews with Jeff Dangremond, former finance/portfolio manager, FINOVA, 1996–2000.

[195]*Id.*

Case 4.14

(continued)

it was highly invested in high-tech companies because they fit the category of too new and too risky for banks.

However, FINOVA edged into the Fortune 1000 and built new company headquarters in Scottsdale, Arizona, as part of a revitalization project there. Its headquarters housed 380 employees, cost $50 million to construct, and was located just north of the tony Scottsdale Fashion Square shopping mall. FINOVA had about 1,000 other employees at offices around the world.

In the first quarter of 1999, FINOVA again caught national attention for the cover of its annual report that would soon be released. The cover featured a robot, but the head of the robot had an underlying wheel that readers could rotate. There were six heads to the robot, all photos of FINOVA employees. The torso of the robot was a safe, and the arms and legs were made of symbols of the various industries in which FINOVA had lending interests. "When you have innovators in your name, you can't do a generic annual report," was the description from a FINOVA PR spokesman.[196]

However, the buzz over the annual report cover was small compared to what happened when the cover, printed 10 weeks in advance of the content, was to be coupled with the numbers inside the report. FINOVA announced that its annual report would be delayed. It was unclear what was happening until its long-standing auditors, Deloitte and Touche, were fired. Mr. Eichenfield explained that FINOVA fired its auditors because they had waited so long to discuss their concerns and issues with management. He indicated that he felt they should have raised the issues much earlier than on the eve of the release of the numbers.[197]

FINOVA then hired Ernst & Young, but when the annual report was finally released, the company also announced that it would be restating earnings for the year. The price of the company's stock began to decline. FINOVA worked diligently to restore credibility, with its officers noting that the auditors' disagreements with management's numbers were often because the company was too conservative

in its accounting and that there were counterbalances for decisions on aggressive versus conservative accounting practices.[198] However, with a shift in economic conditions and the end of the high-tech market run, the asset quality of FINOVA's portfolio was deteriorating. FINOVA's acquisition of the Fremont Financial Group of California for $765 million only increased investors' concerns about the direction of the company and the quality of its management. By the end of 1999, its stock price had dipped to $34 per share.

In early 2000, when it was again time for the release of the annual report, there was to be another announcement about FINOVA's financial position. FINOVA announced that it was writing down a $70 million loan to a California computer manufacturer. Ernst & Young refused to certify the financial statements until the write-off was taken and a resulting shake-up followed.[199] At the same time as the announcement of the write-off, the FINOVA board announced Sam Eichenfield's retirement with a compensation package of $10 million.[200]

FINOVA had to take an $80 million hit, or $0.74 per share, in one day to cover the loan write-off of $70 million plus the compensation package. FINOVA's stock, which had dipped to $32 per share when the 1998 issues on the annual report delay first surfaced, dropped to $19.88 in one day of heavy trading. The 38% dip in stock value was the largest for any stock that day on the New York Stock Exchange, March 27, 2000.[201] As analysts noted, there was a downward spiral because the trust had been breached in 1998; confidence was not regained, and this latest write-off and its delay served to shake investor confidence. Two rating agencies immediately lowered FINOVA's credit ratings, and the costs of its funds jumped dramatically.[202]

Shareholder lawsuits began in May 2000, with several alleging that the $70 million loan had been in default

(continued)

[196]"Cover of Finova's '98 Report Turns Heads," *Arizona Republic*, April 9, 1999, p. E1.

[197]Dawn Gilbertson, "Finova Record Smudged," *Arizona Republic*, April 18, 1999, pp. D1, D2.

[198]Max Jarman, "Finova Group's Stock Sinks," *Arizona Republic*, December 10, 1999, pp. E1, E2.

[199]Anne Brady, "Shareholders Sue Finova Executives," *Mesa Tribune*, May 20, 2000, p. B1.

[200]Dawn Gilbertson, "Surprises at Finova," *Arizona Republic*, March 28, 2000, pp. B1, B9.

[201]*Id.*

[202]Rhonda L. Rundle, "Finova Retains Credit Suisse Unit to Assess Operations," *Wall Street Journal*, May 10, 2000, p. A12.

Case 4.14

(continued)

eight months earlier but that, because of bonus and compensation packages tied to the share price, the officers and managers opted not to write the loan off to maximize their compensation packages, which were computed at the end of December before the write-off was taken.

Also during May 2000, Credit Suisse First Boston, hired to aid the company strategically, announced that FINOVA had lost a $500 million line of credit from banks. Such a loss was seen as mandating the sale of the company because commercial loan companies must have $1 in a credit line as backup for every $1 in commercial paper. FINOVA's stock fell to $12.62 on May 9, 2000.[203] Analysts noted that FINOVA's aggressive growth strategy placed it in a particularly vulnerable situation because, as credit lines dried up, it had more exposure on its large loan portfolios. Further, the nature of those portfolios was such that its default rate was higher than other commercial lenders. Analysts valued its loan portfolio at $0.58 on the dollar.[204]

By early 2001, FINOVA was reporting that it had lost $1 billion for the year.[205] It declared Chapter 11 bankruptcy on March 7, 2001. Finova's default on its bond debt was, at that time, the largest since the Great Depression. Its bankruptcy was, at that time, the eighth largest in history, with Enron displacing it in fall 2001 (Case 4.23) and WorldCom then displacing Enron (see Case 4.20) (now number 3). Lehman Brothers displaced them all in 2008. By April 2001, Finova's stock price was down to $1.64 per share. But the fall was not complete. Finova stock would drop to $0.88 per share until Warren Buffett's Berkshire Hathaway Company and Leucadia National Corporation made a buyout proposal for FINOVA, which caused the stock to jump to $2.13 in later 2001.[206] Berkshire Hathaway owned $1.4 billion of FINOVA's debt, including $300 million in bank debt and $1.1 billion in public bonds.

GE Capital and Goldman Sachs then countered the Buffett offer, but the bankruptcy court approved the Buffett offer.[207] However, pursuant to its rights under the agreement, the Buffett team backed out of the purchase. Berkshire Hathaway did purchase 25% of FINOVA's shares, and FINOVA was able to restructure itself in Chapter 11 bankruptcy. FINOVA emerged from Chapter 11 in 2001, but in November 2006, the company's board of directors voted to liquidate the company. The business was officially closed on December 4, 2006. The company's 10-K report for 2006 indicated that it would not be able to repay its note holders and that its limited assets had been pledged to existing creditors. All the company offices, except one located in Scottsdale, Arizona, have been closed, with the resulting reduction in force of nearly all employees. The offices in Scottsdale have been moved from the opulent headquarters on Scottsdale Road, and the building FINOVA built is now occupied by a number of companies and professional offices. Its stock reached a high price of $0.12 per share during 2006, with a low price of $0.06. Its bankruptcy ended in December 2009.[208]

Discussion Questions

1. Why do you think the officers and managers waited until the auditors required it to write off the $70 million loan? Review Reading 4.12. What kinds of accounting tools were they using to make their earnings and share price better? Given FINOVA's fate and its free-fall in stock price to a final price of $0.12, what issues did the executives miss in analyzing the decision to write down or not write down the loan? Whose interests were served by the decision?

2. Do you think the incentive plans had any effect on the reported earnings? Why or why not?

3. Was FINOVA so generous with its perks for employees that there was a resulting loyalty that was blinding the employees to the real financial condition of the company

(continued)

[203]Donna Hogan, "Finova Finances May Force Sale," *Mesa Tribune*, May 9, 2000, pp. B1, B2.

[204]Riva D. Atlas, "Caught in a Credit Squeeze," *New York Times*, November 2, 2000, pp. C1, C21.

[205]Max Jarman, "Finova Posts $1 Billion Loss," *Arizona Republic*, April 3, 2001, p. D1.

[206]Paul M. Sherer and Devon Spurgeon, "Finova Agrees to a Bailout by Berkshire and Leucadia," *Wall Street Journal*, February 28, 2001, pp. C1, C18.

[207]Edward Gately, "Bankruptcy Court OKs Finova Plan," *Mesa Tribune*, August 11, 2001, p. B1.

[208]However, there is a Finova Capital Corporation located in Phoenix, with a securities offering issued in 2009 for $250,000,000; the supplemental prospectus lists some of the same officers as those in the original FINOVA. https://www.sec.gov/Archives/edgar/data/43960/000095014799001034/0000950147-99-001034-d1.html.

Case 4.14

(continued)

and the financial reporting issues? Would these perks have had an effect on you if you worked for FINOVA?

4. Was FINOVA forthcoming about the level of risk in its business?

5. Discuss the actions of the audit firms in refusing to issue financials or in requiring restatements. Construct a decision process for those audit firms as they dealt with FINOVA in its last days. Should the objections to the failure to write down the loans have been raised earlier?

Compare & Contrast

The FINOVA employees are gone or have been laid off. What impression do you think their time at FINOVA makes as prospective employers read their résumés? Do you see any lines for your credo in the experience of these young businesspeople at a young company?

Case 4.15

Organizational Pressures in the Academy: Those Rankings

Rankings in academic programs are critical to enrollments and, in many cases, to the jobs and compensation of those who are directing those programs. The following examples show how the same factors that influence conduct in companies also influence those in nonprofit organizations.

Claremont McKenna and Its *U.S. News & World Report Rankings*

From 2005 to 2011, Claremont McKenna, ranked number nine on *U.S. News & World Report*'s best liberal arts colleges in the country, had been slathering on a few points here and there to its entering students' average SAT score before reporting those numbers to *U.S. News & World* report and rating organizations such as the Princeton Review. For example, in 2010, its combined median score was reported as 1,410, rather than its actual 1,400. And its 75th percentile was reported at 1,510, when it was, in reality, 1,480.

Claremont McKenna's vice president and dean of admissions was removed from the college website. President Pamela B. Gann explained the problem and concluded, "As an institution of higher education with a deep and consistent commitment to the integrity of our academic activities, and particularly, our reporting of institutional data, we take this situation very seriously."[209]

The rankings and ratings organizations did not reflect as much outrage. Robert Franek of the Princeton Review noted, "That is a pretty mild difference in a point score. That said, 10 points, 20 points to a student that isn't getting that score on the SAT could be an important distinction," and "I feel like so many schools have a very clear obligation to college-bound students to report this information honestly."[210] Although the points added seemed immaterial, the manipulations veiled the reality that the critical reading scores for the 2011 class were the lowest since 2007, and the mean math score had been boosted by 28 points.

Discussion Questions

1. What is troubling about Mr. Franek's reflections on adding points to test scores?

2. Why do you think the dean of admissions added on the points?

3. Explain how the role of rankings would influence behaviors among employees at colleges and universities.

4. Is this similar to earnings management by companies? Are they adding to their numbers?

(continued)

---

[209]Daniel E. Slotnik and Richard Pérez-Peña, "College Says It Exaggerated SAT Figures for Ratings," *New York Times*, January 31, 2012, p. A12.
[210]*Id.*

Case 4.15

(continued)

Temple University and Its MBA Program Rankings

Temple University hired law firm Jones Day to conduct an investigation of its Fox Business School. The investigation concluded that under the leadership of the dean of Fox, false information had been sent to at least one of the rankings organizations for the years 2014–2018. Temple climbed from a position of 53 in 2014 to 17 in 2017. Temple's Fox had held the number one slot in the *U.S. News & World Report* rankings for its online MBA programs. Temple self-reported the problems to the rankings services and fired Dean Moshe Porat.

Pennsylvania's state attorney general announced its own investigation into whether Temple broke any laws in its advertisements, which touted the rankings. *U.S. News & World Report* revised its published rankings to list Temple as "unranked" and has asked Temple for additional information to determine whether information for other colleges at Temple and for Temple itself to determine whether rankings beyond the Fox Business School are accurate. Temple took steps to have the numbers vetted internally in the future before they were submitted to the ranking services.

The U.S. Department of Education brought a complaint against Temple for using false data to buoy its rankings in various MBA public ranking services. In settling the charges by the DOE, Temple did not admit any wrongdoing or liability, but the settlement agreement did disclose that Temple submitted false information in the following categories:

1. the number of Fox School entrants providing GMAT scores as part of the application process,

2. the mean undergraduate GPAs of students admitted to certain programs offered by the Fox School,

3. the number of offers of admission extended by the Fox School to applicants,

4. the debt levels of Fox School students who borrowed loans to pay tuition, and

5. the ratio of full-time technology support personnel to supported faculty members at the Fox School.[211]

Temple agreed to pay a $700,000 fine. Temple had already settled a lawsuit brought by current and former business students over the false data for $5.5 million. The Jones Day investigation commissioned by the University found that there were similar data reporting issues in six other university programs.

Temple administrators said that they had taken steps to ensure data verification prior to its submission for external use. Temple now has a data-verification unit. Temple also settled a suit brought by the Pennsylvania attorney general, a settlement that also required certain internal changes to ensure data accuracy.

Dean Porat was terminated but filed suit against the university for defamation. He advanced an "under the bus" defense, calling himself a "scapegoat" for the university.[212] Dr. Porat was charged by the U.S. attorney for the Eastern District of Pennsylvania with wire fraud and conspiracy to commit wire fraud and was convicted on November 28, 2021.[213]

Columbia: From #2 to Unranked

Columbia University was unranked by *U.S. News & World Report*'s college and university ranking system in July 2022.[214] Columbia had been ranked as #2 on the magazine's top universities. However, when *U.S. News & World Report* learned of questions about Columbia's data in March 2022, it requested that Columbia provide the data to substantiate what it had submitted for ranking purposes. By July, with no "satisfactory responses" to its requests forthcoming, *U.S. News & World Report* unranked the school. Columbia went from #2 to "appearing nowhere on this list." Harvard and MIT have one less competitor in the #2 slot they shared with the now deranked Columbia. Yale stands alone at #1.

(continued)

[211]"Findings and Recommendations from Jones Day Investigation into Rankings Information Provided by Fox School to U.S. News," July 2018, https://news.temple.edu/sites/news/files/images/findings_and_recommendations.pdf.

[212]Patrick Thomas, "Temple to Pay Penalty over M.B.A.-Rankings Scandal," *Wall Street Journal*, December 5–6, 2020, p. B14.

[213]Alyssa Lukpat, "Former Temple U. Dean Found Guilty of Faking Data for National Rankings," *New York Times*, November 29, 2021, https://www.nytimes.com/2021/11/29/us/temple-university-moshe-porat-fraud.html.

[214]Anemona Hartocollis, "With Data in Doubt, Columbia Falls From No. 2 to 'Unranked,'" *New York Times*, July 9, 2022, p. A1.

Case 4.15

(continued)

Columbia Professor of Mathematics, Michael Thaddeus, explained why he believed the numbers submitted were not accurate in an analysis he conducted. Professor Thaddeus began his inquiry because he felt that Columbia had moved to the top of the *U.S. News & World Report* too quickly. In an executive summary of his analysis of Columbia's submitted data,[215] Professor Thaddeus described gaming in many areas, including defining the size of classes as well as the number of full-time faculty and the number of faculty with doctoral degrees. In addition, Professor Thaddeus found that Columbia had two budgets—one that goes to the Department of Education and one that goes to *U.S. News & World Report.* The

difference between the two was the amount of the budget spent on instruction expenses.

In 2021, the Wharton School, Columbia, Stanford, and Harvard announced that they would not be submitting numbers to the rankings because of COVID effects.

Discussion Questions

1. What category of ethical dilemma is involved when deans engage in numbers manipulation with ranking services?

2. What would be the organizational factors that influence their decisions to submit incorrect information? List factors that could influence their conduct.

3. What did they miss in their analysis of their decision to submit incorrect information? Could there be industry factors at play?

4. Was this an example of how ratings can be gamed?

[215]Michael Thaddeus, "An Investigation of the Facts Behind Columbia's U.S. News Ranking," March 2022, http://www.math.columbia.edu/~thaddeus/ranking/investigation.html.

Ethics in Action 4.4

Submitting the Data on Job Placement of Graduates

Carol Forrester is the placement director at the University of Transylvania (creative name to avoid identification). Her compensation is based on percentage levels of placement of the graduates in their MBA program. The ranking services have a cut-off date of July 31 of each year for computing the percentage of graduates placed.

Due to an economic downturn, the companies that recruited at Transylvania were slow in making offers to graduates. By the end of July, placements were down 15 percentage points from the prior year. When their new fiscal years started on August 1, several companies came through with offers for Transylvania graduates. Ms. Forrester is thinking that because some of the offers came from companies located in different time zones, it would be easy to submit them as having been sent before the cut-off date of July 31—even though they missed the deadline in Transylvania's time zone. Help Carol decide whether to include the August 1 data in her submissions for the placement data for the year. Use your tools of ethical analysis from Units 1 and 2.

Case 4.16

Organizational Pressures in the Academy and Parental Pressure Outside: Operation Varsity Blues

It all began with a hedge-fund trader. The federal investigation into college admissions cheating (labeled Operation Varsity Blues [OVB]) actually started when the Justice Department pulled Morrie Tobin over in April 2018 (and served a warrant on his Los Angeles home) for suspected securities fraud. Mr. Tobin was allegedly part of a pump-and-dump scheme. Pump-and-dump occurs when a trader buys stock in a company, and then, through the large purchase (which sends signals to the market) and a great deal of public discussion by the buyer, the result is a pumped-up value (artificially) for the stock. When others, not in on the scheme, take the bait and buy the pumped-up stock, the pumper then sells his shares, at its peak value. Those who took the bait are left holding the bag on the artificially overvalued stock.

In the course of talking with prosecutors in Boston for a plea deal on the securities fraud, Mr. Tobin tipped them off to the payments he had made to get his children into Yale, Mr. Tobin's alma mater. Mr. Tobin had been a participant in a fraudulent admissions scheme. In exchange for leniency on his pump-and-dump charges, Mr. Tobin agreed to be part of a set-up for the Yale women's soccer coach, Rudy Meredith (a facilitator in OVB). Mr. Tobin said he had previously paid bribes to Coach Rudy to get his children into Yale as special admit student-athletes. His children were not student-athletes, but Coach Rudy was willing to say that they were and get them into Yale in exchange for the payments.

A meeting between Mr. Tobin and Mr. Meredith in a Boston hotel room was recorded. Mr. Meredith, in the recorded meeting, offered to name one of Mr. Tobin's daughters as a soccer recruit in exchange for $450,000. Once the Boston office had Mr. Meredith on tape with the bribery offer, Mr. Meredith offered the tip that William "Rick" Singer was the mastermind behind these connections, payments, and special admissions. Federal authorities went to Mr. Singer, who then confessed to authorities that he was indeed the mastermind behind a network of contacts for getting unqualified kids into college for fees ranging from $15,000 to $16,000,000.

Mr. Singer cooperated fully with the federal government by allowing agents access to his phone calls, emails, and other forms of electronic communications with parents seeking to have their children get into top colleges and universities. The result was, after a year of tracking Mr. Singer's interactions, indictments of 57 people, including 33 parents, on charges of wire fraud, money laundering, and conspiracy. Some also faced charges related to income tax evasion.

This case offers much in instruction on ethical issues that arise at the personal, industry, and societal layers.

What Mr. Singer Was Doing

Mr. Singer had been a coach who was good at advising young people on the admissions process. He then created a company called Edge College and Career Network (called "The Key") that had a nonprofit subsidiary, Key Worldwide Foundation, which was based in Newport Beach.[216] Through Key, Mr. Singer set up a network of coaches who could be paid to allow the children of wealthy parents to be tagged as special admit student-athletes. Once they were admitted, they might hang around the athletic department for a year as if they were an athlete, but none ever participated in college athletics.

Mr. Singer also set up additional parts of his network that included test proctors and site administrators (who could be used to give more time on standardized tests or change answers); a test taker (who could take standardized tests for the applicants); guidance counselors, psychologists, psychiatrists (who could certify disabilities in order to give the applicants more time on the standardized tests); and some academic administrators (who were willing to grant special admissions in exchange for donations). Many of the children were not aware of what their parents were doing. During testing, they were told to write their answers on a plain piece of paper and turn those into the proctor, who would then mark the bubble sheet, correcting any of the wrong answers enough to raise their scores.[217]

(continued)

---

[216]Jennifer Medina, Katie Benner, and Kate Taylor, "U.S. Accuses Rich Parents of College Entry Fraud," *New York Times*, March 13, 2019, p. A1.

[217]Douglas Belkin and Jennifer Levitt, "The Man Behind the Cheating Scandal," *Wall Street Journal*, March 13, 2019, p. A4.

Case 4.16

(continued)

Parents not only paid the money but staged photographs with their children to make it seem as if they were athletes. In some cases, Mr. Singer added fraudulent photographs with images blurred to make it seem as if the applicant were participating in team sports in high school.[218] Between 2011 and 2019, $25 million went through the Key Foundation. With that being a 501(c)(3) organization, the parents paid bribes that were deductible, at least until the scam blew up thanks to a hedge-fund trader.

Who Was Using Mr. Singer for Their Children

Mr. Singer roped in the rich, the famous, the rich and famous, and the rich but not famous. They included Hallmark Channel actress Lori Loughlin and her husband, fashion designer Mossimo Giannulli; actress Felicity Huffman; lawyers; businesspeople; entrepreneurs; a USC associate professor of dentistry; *American Lawyer*'s "Dealmaker of the Year"; a vineyard owner; and even the heiress to the Hot Pockets fortune.

Mr. Singer said that what he delivered was a different way to secure college admission, albeit a very expensive way. Mr. Singer explained,

> "If I can make the comparison, there is a front door of getting in where a student just does it on their own, and then there's a back door where people go to institutional advancement and make large donations, but they're not guaranteed in. And then I created a side door that guaranteed families to get in. So that was what made it very attractive to so many families, is I created a guarantee."[219]

The Lessons of OVB

The fate of those involved in OVB is summarized in the PowerPoint supplement for this edition. But there were so many lessons learned for the parents, their children, the colleges and universities, and that layer of society and its shift in ethical standards.

Lesson One from OVB: Never trust the people you cheat with. They will throw you under the bus.

Once two people, a dyad in management speak, have engaged in questionable behavior with each other, two things happen. One is that it is easier to cheat in a dyad.[220] In offices and at school or, apparently in trying to get into school, if we have fellow travelers in the road to hell, what we are doing does not seem so hellish. One side gives the other side reassurance about their suspect conduct. For example, one of the recorded conversations is between Mr. Singer, and the father of a young woman with an ACT test score of 22. The father, Gordon Caplan, then the co-chairman of Wilkie, Farr, & Gallagher, LLP, and *American Lawyer*'s dealmaker of the year, had negotiated with Mr. Singer to increase that test score to a 32 (Mr. Singer had proposed an increase to 33, but Dad felt that was a bit too high) and had the following exchange with Mr. Singer:

Father: "To be honest, I'm not worried about the moral issue here. I'm worried about the, if she's caught doing that, you know, she's finished. . . . Let me put this differently: If somebody catches this, what happens?"

Singer: "The only one who can catch it is if you guys tell somebody."

Father: "I am not going to tell anybody."[221]

The two were parties to a transaction that they would not want disclosed to anyone, and they became prisoners of each other. Each side has something worrisome, unethical, or illegal on the other side, and they cannot cross each other because of the inside information each holds on the other.

(continued)

---

[218]*Id.*

[219]Jennifer Medina, Katie Benner, and Kate Taylor, "U.S. Accuses Rich Parents of College Entry Fraud," *New York Times*, March 13, 2019, p. A1, at A17.

[220]Christina Nikolova, Cait Lamberton, and Nicole Verrochi Coleman, "Stranger Danger: When and Why Consumer Dyads Behave Less Ethically Than Individuals," 45 *Journal of Consumer Research* 90 (2017).

[221]"Prosecutors Charge 33 Parents," *Wall Street Journal*, March 13, 2019, p. A5.

Case 4.16

(continued)

Lesson Two of OVB: Watch that first step when a fellow employee asks for help in a situation that crosses an ethical or legal line, however small.

Prisoner relationships are formed on the smallest of fellow-employee transactions. From clocking in for someone who is caught in traffic to allowing a physician to tell an off-color joke, we have those moments when we are complicit in conduct. By saying nothing, we become part of the problem because the issues will continue to grow. There will be future requests for clocking in, requests that easily turn into a habit. Neither the tardy employee nor the helpful friend in the dyad can speak up because they both have violated organizational ethical standards. By not curbing the physician's bad taste, we send a signal on our standards or at least our tolerance for such conduct.

Lesson Three of OVB: Ethical lapses can happen to anyone.

Mr. Caplan, the lawyer in the Singer exchange, is an intelligent man and respected professional. Yet, he fell for a rather risky and silly scheme to get his daughter a higher test score on her ACT score. Mr. Caplan had to have a psychologist certify his daughter as having a learning disability so that his daughter could take the ACT exam at one of the locations where Mr. Singer had bribable test administrators. Mr. Caplan and his daughter flew out to California; Ms. Caplan took the ACT; and, thanks to the administrator (another facilitator) who changed her answers, her previous score jumped from a low 22 to 32 (thanks also to the $75,000 Mr. Caplan paid for Mr. Singer's efforts).

Exploring the reasons for this phenomenal departure from ethical, professional, and legal standards is a critical part of post-lapse analysis. Mr. Caplan, in entering his guilty plea to paying Mr. Singer $75,000 for the improved ACT test score, said all the right things, "[t]he remorse and shame that I feel is more than I can convey. I apologize not only to my family, friends, colleagues and the legal bar, but also to students everywhere who have been accepted to college through their own hard work."[222]

Lesson 4 of OVB: Pressure Clouds Judgment

So why did all of this reality escape Mr. Singer as he was setting up the scam? Like most ethical and legal scandals, those involved were under significant pressure. Pressure causes us to minimize risk and provides us with cover for our actions because we are attempting to do something important: help our children, save a company, salvage a stock offering, sell a house, and the list goes on. Parenting pressure is real. Some of the parents believed that they were giving their children the very best chance of success through an Ivy League education, a belief that is well grounded.[223] Other parents enjoyed having the bragging rights that come with a child placed in a prestigious college.

For all of us, the pressure to meet goals, make numbers, keep our jobs, get a promotion, or pay our bills can cloud our judgment. Recently, in Brazil, an inspector said that he was pressured to conclude that the bridges he was inspecting met engineering standards. The pressure that he felt was that he needed his job. It is dangerous to certify dilapidated bridges, and human life was at stake. But the pursuit of a valid goal can seem to be the right thing to do, even when, in hindsight, the decision was wrong.

To prevent misguided, pressure-induced decisions, we need guardrails. Those guardrails include clear lines that no one in the organization should cross in doing their jobs. We all know not to forge documents, but where are the lines on signing for someone else with permission? Or in asking someone else to sign for us? Allowing someone else to use our password because of timing or convenience issues?

Lesson 5 of OVB: The Small Steps That Slowly Corrupt

In finding those guardrails and lines, we have to look at the smaller things we might have done or are doing to meet our goals. In the pursuit of college admission, parents everywhere are crossing little lines. That essay we intended only to proof but ended up editing so that the child's original work is non-recognizable in the final product. Writing the admissions statement for your

(continued)

---

[222]"Lawyer to Plead Guilty to Admissions Scandal," *New York Times*, April 6, 2019, p. B2.

[223]Zlati Meyer, "Prestige Schools Can Provide Connection," *USA Today*, March 18, 2019, p. 1B.

Case 4.16

(continued)

child seems helpful, not an ethical issue. Hiring college counseling firms who may be crossing lines in their assistance is not that far of a step from the pay-to-admit scam. Some parents have their children take on more than they can handle to build up the service and humanitarian components of their admissions files. As one psychologist noted, some parents are so involved in the educational profile and efforts of their children that the child never has a chance to develop a unique identity.[224]

The internalized lessons here for parents are the need for stepping back and thinking critically about the goals and their intentions. Parents may have to stop comparing their children, their grades, and their scores to others. Parents may need to draw some lines: Never write, rewrite, or pay someone to write an essay, for college admission or otherwise. Those are the guardrails and provide the parameters for being more reflective on what we are doing that may be edging us closer and closer to the guardrails.

Lesson Six of OVB: It Takes an Interconnected Web to Execute an Ethical/Legal Lapse, So Keep an Eye on the Weak Points in Your Web

Mr. Singer, the perpetrator, had a staff of ringers stationed at test centers around the country for college admissions exams. These grad students (also facilitators) would proctor exams and perform the additional services of changing exam answers or taking the exams for the not-so-gifted children of the rich and/or famous participants. But Mr. Singer also had a ring of coaches (facilitators). In what is often referred to so flatteringly as the "non-revenue sports," there were coaches who were willing to take cash (or in one case, let you buy their homes for twice their value) in exchange for designating your children as a student-athlete they desired for the team.

The Education Industry

There was a large web of interconnected facilitators. We cannot always curb the perpetrators, but we can put checks and balances in place for the facilitators to prevent unilateral authority in decisions, something that limits participants. There was a large educational system where we did not create the checks and balances to inhibit human intervention or manipulation. There was an industry of colleges and universities using the admissions process as a means of raising money.

The Expansion of Admissions Under a Unilateral Process

College admissions created a weak spot in the late 1980s, when special admissions slots were opened wider than they had ever been. Special admissions slots had been generally reserved for applicants who were musically and artistically talented but did not have the academic credentials for the pursuit of a degree other than in their area of exceptional talent. A committee made those decisions based on the documented talent of the candidate, professorial evaluation, and some proof that the candidates would be able to complete a course of study in their fields.

Those special admissions categories were expanded, and the expanded slots went to student-athletes. The result was two distinct problems. The first was that many student-athletes who were admitted simply lacked the skills and abilities to pass college-level courses. Because of unilateral coaching authority to admit, the candidates did not have the screening or evaluation that was originally part of the special admissions process. As a result, the University of North Carolina and many other schools experienced system-wide cheating scandals, from fake courses to papers being written for the athletes by academic counselors.

The second problem was that control of student-athlete special admits was turned over to single individual. Their designation of a recruit for their team under special admissions was, for the most part, a unilateral act. Few questions asked, even less skepticism, and, in short, no checks and balances. The number of these athletic special-admit slots opened that admissions side door. Rick Singer found that side door with no security and exploited it. The coaches were a human weakness (facilitators) in a system that needed COSO guardrails, and the bribes flowed.

(continued)

---

[224]Sue Shellenbarger, "It's Their College Years, Not Yours," *Wall Street Journal*, March 18, 2019, p. A13.

Case 4.16

(continued)

The Testing Processes

In the testing component of admissions, the integrity of the exam process was only as good as the integrity of the test administrators. That they had the latitude to take exams for students and the time and place to make changes on answer sheets after Rick Singer recruits completed their exams exposes a weakness in admissions exams and their security. Again, unsupervised human participants need COSO controls. Reining in facilitators is what breaks down the web. Facilitators with appropriate controls cannot further the perpetrators' work.

Lesson Seven of OVB: Learn to incorporate the ethical implications of strategic and organizational decisions before changes are made.

In understanding the need for controlling the web of perpetrators and the enabling facilitators, we find yet another lesson. Sometimes leaders make strategic decisions without realizing the impact that the proposed action, program, compensation, or incentives will have on their ethical culture. They have not evolved to the layer in ethical development in which all decisions are considered in light of their effect on the ethical culture of the organization. If we allow these special admissions, what could this do to the quality of candidates? What could happen with financial pressures we face in raising funds? Who will have control over these special admissions? Should they be reviewed? Decisions made, in isolation, without input from auditors, ethics and compliance officers, and risk officers can result in unintended consequences of decisions that may have been made with all the best intentions. For example, the Americans with Disabilities Act (ADA) requires that those students who have been certified as being learning disabled or having ADD are entitled to extra time and other accommodations during tests. Many in OVB gamed that requirement in order to take their tests at sites that allowed more time and facilitated the help the Springer ringers were being paid to give to the children of those who were paying for higher scores. Compliance and ethics and risk officers have the insight and training to provide the implications of decisions and possible weaknesses that permit gaming.

That seat at the table for these professionals when these policy decisions are made is critical because they can provide the controls and oversight that others cannot envision. For example, the importance of tagging and investigating numbers that spike, as when there are 10-point jumps in ACT test scores, would be an obvious and common control that compliance, ethics, and risk officers would recommend. They know the weaknesses because they have rich experience with perpetrators, facilitators, and participants.

Final Words

OVB resulted in tragic events in the lives of 57 people and their families, including the children they thought they were helping. However, those of us who were not involved should take the time and think through what lessons we can learn from such a scandal. In fact, when something goes wrong in our own organizations, it is a helpful exercise for all employees to step back and walk through what the perpetrators, facilitators, and participants did, why they did it, and what needs to change in the system to put up those helpful guardrails and the ethical versions of COSO protections that curb the web of deceit.

Discussion Questions

1. Do all organizations have side doors? Are side doors just gaming the system or are they really crimes?

2. List all the stakeholders in admissions processes' front, back, and side doors.

3. Because a Stanford coach was involved in OVB, Stanford convened a special committee to study special admissions. Their report resulted in the following recommendations:

   a. Admission of any applicant, student-athlete or not, cannot be bought, and no donor should ever be under the impression that it can. We are currently codifying this practice into a formal written policy to ensure clarity and transparency.[225]

(continued)

[225]External Review of Athletic Admissions Reaches Conclusions, Recommends Reforms, December 3, 2019, https://news.stanford.edu/2019/12/03/external-review-athletic-admissions-reaches-conclusions-recommends-reforms/.

Case 4.16

(continued)

   b. Fundraising efforts are no longer part of coaches' performance evaluations.

   c. Verification of source of donations by development officers.

   d. Coaches must flag applicants who have come to them from a third party.

   e. Coaches should elevate concerns about unethical behavior by third parties such as donors and admissions counselors.

Are these recommendations similar to what a business could do to curb unethical behavior?

4. Go back to Unit 1 and compare Ethics in Practice 1.1 with what the parents in OVB did. A mother misrepresented her address to get her children into a better public school district and was charged with a felony and convicted. Are they the same or different?

5. Vince Cuseo, an admissions official at Occidental College, got a call from Rick Singer in 2012. Mr. Singer asked that Mr. Cuseo reconsider the denied application of an academically challenged daughter of a wealthy family. Mr. Singer suggested that the parents could give money to Occidental above and beyond the cost of tuition. Mr. Cuseo refused her admission. Mr. Singer said, "Are you kidding? We can create a win–win for both of us."[226] Mr. Cuseo explained that Occidental made a decision in the 1980s to not "chase wealthy students" and instead focus on poorer minority students.[227] He said that a development officer suggested he take a look at the application of a child of a very wealthy family. However, she did not meet Occidental standards and was denied admission. Mr. Cuseo says he has never felt pressure to do otherwise. What was different about Occidental and the schools and coaches of OBV?

---

[226]Jennifer Levitz and Douglas Belkin, "L.A. College Rebuffed Admissions Scammer," *Wall Street Journal*, November 7, 2019, p.A1.
[227]*Id.*

The Structural Factors: Governance, Example, and Leadership

This section deals with those who are in charge—company and organizational leadership and their boards. In many situations, these individuals, however, unwittingly directed or motivated the conduct or prevented employees from raising concerns that would have ended the legal and ethical violations.

Reading 4.17

The Things Leaders Do, Unwittingly, and Otherwise, That Harm Ethical Culture

Organizations spend money, time, and effort on ethics messaging. From videos to sites to desk trinkets to booklets to pens to pads, the goal is to get out that message, "Be ethical." However, the repetition and expense of these physical and tech efforts is too often countermanded by leaders' behaviors. Experience in working with organizations struggling to recover from or hoping to prevent ethical lapses has been an eye-opener. Even the savviest of managers do things, however unwittingly, that harm their ethical cultures. Herewith, a look at some of the leader behaviors that affect their organizations' ethical cultures.

The Big Message: Whom They Hire, Whom They Fire, Whom They Discipline, and When That Discipline Arrives

Often, the most powerful messages about an organization's ethics come from leaders' HR decisions. Whom we hire, fire, and discipline and how that discipline proceeds (if it does at all) serves to reveal the values and priorities of leadership. At one organization, two of the officers who appeared in the video introduction for the company's ethics training emphasizing the importance of ethics at their company ended up involved in serious ethical lapses. The longer the two officers stayed at the company, the sillier the ethics training looked. Even with the officers' introductions removed from the video, employees remembered, and the irony of their continuing presence in the company was impossible to reconcile with the messages in that training. Employee cynicism about ethics had taken hold.

In another experience, a senior executive misrepresented to management the readiness of a new billing system. When the system crashed at the moment of its live run, those relying on his word of full readiness saw their misplaced trust. The organization struggled far too long with the officer's conduct because he had been with the company for years and was close to retirement. Incompetence and/or his lack of candor were not the issues; friendship and likability were. The messages conveyed throughout the culture? Telling the truth is not really necessary. It may be best to just not offer up bad news. Let it go, and you can survive, even when you know about the problems.

The University of Southern California (USC) had a bad run with its inaction on several of its leaders. Dr. Carmen Puliafito, former dean of USC medical school, was a respected ophthalmologist and a miraculous fund raiser for the school. As hundreds of millions flowed into the medical school, its rank improved. However, there was a dark side to Mr. Puliafito. He was a well know partier, and there were photos of him (some on social media) lighting a pipe for a female companion smoking heroin and one of him sharing ecstasy with two female companions before a charity function. There was also the incident that involved the Pasadena police arriving at a hotel room to find Mr. Puliafito there with a woman who had overdosed. No police report was filed for months.[228] Throughout the medical school, the campus, and even the community was this theme: The behaviors were tolerated and, indeed, covered up for a very long time.[229] The message: Raise enough money and there is a certain immunity that protects you.

Only after the *Los Angeles Times* ran a full exposé on Puliafito's activities did USC take action. Then-Dr. Puliafito stepped down as dean for personal reasons but continued as a tenured faculty member as USC struggled with how to handle the situation.[230] USC then appointed an interim dean who had a history of sexual harassment, something known to administrators.[231] At a medical school forum with the provost because of student concerns about their leadership, one medical school student commented, "I really want to talk about the culture that's being propagated at the highest levels of USC leadership, and it is a culture that values money above all else, especially ethics."[232]

Then in 2018, over 200 USC professors signed a letter calling for USC's president's resignation because he had "lost the moral authority to lead the university."[233] The incident that brought the faculty rebellion involved allegations of sexual abuse against gynecologist George Tyndall, who worked at the USC student health center. Despite complaints dating back to 2000, Dr. Tyndall was not placed on leave until 2016 and only left USC in 2017 after reaching a settlement with the university.

The chair of the USC board of trustees expressed confidence in the president and satisfaction with his plan to create a separate office of professionalism and ethics to handle such matters. Shortly after, the trustees appointed an interim president, and after the admissions bribery scandal emerged in March 2019, moved up the announcement of a new president.[234]

---

[228]Paul Pringle, Harriett Ryan, Adam Elmahrek, Matt Hamilton, and Sarah Parvani, "An Overdose, a Young Companion, Drug-Fueled Parties: The Secret Life of a USC Med School Dean," *Los Angeles Times*, July 17, 2017, https://www.latimes.com/local/california/la-me-usc-doctor-20170717-htmlstory.html.

[229]Adam Nagourney and Jennifer Medina, "Scandal Sinks Dean at U.S.C., Shocking a City," *New York Times*, July 26, 2017, p. A1.

[230]Mr. Puliafito lost his medical license because he had not made sufficient progress in his rehabilitation. Matt Hamilton and Harriett Ryan, "State Strips Ex-USC Medical Dean of License, Citing "An Appalling Lack of Judgment," *Los Angeles Times*, July 20, 2018, https://www.latimes.com/local/lanow/la-me-ln-usc-dean-medical-license-20180720-story.html.

[231]Sarah Parvino, Harriett Ryan, and Paul Pringle, "USC Medical School Dean Out Amid Revelations of Sexual Harassment Claim, $135,000 Settlement with Researcher," *Los Angeles Times*, October 5, 2017, https://www.latimes.com/local/lanow/la-me-usc-dean-harassment-20171005-story.html.

[232]Sarah Parvino, Paul Pringle, and Harriett Ryan, "Anger, Questions, At USC After Second Medical School Dean Departs Over Inappropriate Behavior," *Los Angeles Times*, October 6, 2017, http://www.latimes.com/local/lanow/la-me-usc-varma-20171006-story.html.

[233]Melissa Korn, "Calls Grow for USC Head's Ouster," *Wall Street Journal*, May 23, 2018, p. A3.

[234]Melissa Korn, "Hit by Scandal, USC Names New President," *Wall Street Journal*, March 21, 2019, p. A3.

The concerns of the student body and the faculty at USC centered on ethics and morality. There were many afraid to discuss what they knew but did not say until the newspaper reports emerged. The result was a culture of fear and silence. Given what they had witnessed with hiring and firing, there was no certainty that anyone at USC would take timely and appropriate steps.

These tales of various organizations' events illustrate the damage that inaction and delayed HR action can do to a culture. The possible and powerful communication sent by this series of HR issues are:

- Those who perform well are not subject to close scrutiny or required to comply with legal and ethical standards
- Standard procedures on investigations and resulting actions for leaders are not always followed or are set aside until there is external pressure
- Timely action is postponed as long as possible
- Those who are hired do not have adequate background checks done

No ethics training, slogans, or reminders can countermand action and inaction on employee misconduct. If an organization is serious about its values and ethical culture, those values must be consistent with HR actions and decisions.

When Leaders Interfere with Ethics and Compliance

Barclays was a struggling bank because of its LIBOR rate-fixing scandal and other issues when it brought in former JPMorgan Chase executive, James E. (Jes) Staley as its CEO. However, Mr. Staley chose to bring in Tim Main from his days at Chase for his Barclays team, and the facts regarding his actions in protecting Mr. Main at Chase remain a mystery, elusive in verification, deleted from even regulatory body sites.[235] Nonetheless, when Mr. Staley hired Mr. Main at Chase, Barclays' compliance program received a letter from a whistleblower that discussed personal issues involving Mr. Main and how Mr. Staley handled the situation with Mr. Main at Chase. Mr. Staley asked to have the whistleblower unmasked because he believed that the whistleblower was an outsider.[236] He asked a second time to have the identity unmasked, and a request was submitted to the U.S. Postal Inspector under the guise that Barclays was dealing with an issue of insider trading.[237]

When the unmasking attempts were uncovered, Mr. Staley said that he did not know that it was wrong to reveal the identity of a whistleblower. Both Mr. Staley and Barclays were fined by British and U.S. regulators, but Mr. Staley was permitted to remain as CEO.[238] Unmasking a whistleblower or even just the identity of someone who raises an issue informally is serious business. As British regulators phrased it, Mr. Staley's actions, "created an atmosphere in which employees might doubt that it was safe to escalate issues of concern to the bank."[239] Nonetheless, the regulators did

---

[235]Stefania Spezzati and Harry Wilson, "Details of Staley Allegations Are Revealed, Then Deleted, by DFS," *Bloomberg*, December 19, 2018, https://www.bloomberg.com/news/articles/2018-12-19/dfs-reveals-then-removes-detail-on-staley-whistle-blower-case.

[236]Max Colchester, "Barclays CEO Hit with Penalties of $1.5 Million," *Wall Street Journal*, May 12, 2018, p. B1.

[237]Caroline Binham, "Postal Official Was Misled in Barclays Whistleblower Hunt," *Financial Times*, April 12, 2018, https://www.ft.com/content/19dfd0c2-3e64-11e8-b7e0-52972418fec4.

[238]Max Colchester, "Barclays CEO Hit with Penalties of $1.5 Million," *Wall Street Journal*, May 12, 2018, p. B1.

[239]Anthony Noto, "Barclays Fined Millions for CEO's Attempts to Unmask Whistleblower," *New York Business Journal*, December 18, 2018, https://www.bizjournals.com/newyork/news/2018/12/18/barlcays-fined-millions-in-whistleblower-case.html.

not require the board to terminate Mr. Staley because he said that he did not know it was wrong to seek the identity of a whistleblower.

The heart of ethics and compliance is confidential reporting, and Barclays had a CEO who claimed to not know that. By retaining Mr. Staley, Barclays allowed the CEO to contradict one of the most critical aspects of ethics training: if you report anonymously, we will protect you. There was a reason that Barclays paid the highest fine British regulators had ever imposed on a bank: the protection of whistleblowers is a key to having employees come forward.[240] Yet, making the same mistake discussed earlier, the board opted to leave its CEO in place. A CEO who tried to unmask a whistleblower was permitted to "remain in a regulated post."[241] The inevitable result is a chilled environment for reporting. What employee could trust ethics and compliance when the CEO is comfortable seeking to identify whistleblowers?

The Inability to See and Speak Truth

There is perhaps some sort of sociological or anthropological study that should be done on the wide gap between frontline employees' view of truth and that of their senior managements. Perhaps there is an evolving tolerance, perhaps it is the influence of public relations experience, or perhaps it is increasing pressure that is used to justify statements made that are not actually the truth. Whatever the reason, this disparity undermines respect and trust in senior leaders.

In a recent conversation with a respected senior leader with oversight over operations at his company, he shared that he had just gone through a 360-degree evaluation and the feedback was clear from many employees, "He is a liar."

Dismayed, the executive went home that night and counseled with his wife because he did not believe that he was a liar. His wife assured him that the employees had a point. Ah, marital bliss. She asked him why he thought the company had him do so many presentations. He responded that he thought he was a good presenter. His wife said, "No, it's because if there is a fire going on, you will say it is a controlled burn. If the ship is sinking, you will say that it is taking on water." Over the next few weeks as he monitored his own responses in meetings, he realized his tendency to paint a far better picture on issues than reality demanded. In discussing high employee turnover, he suggested that it was due to natural attrition, dismissing HR concerns that resulted from combining high turnover with increasing employee assistance requests, high absenteeism, and higher levels of leave requests. In other words, he was minimizing the need for exploring what might be happening with employees at the company.

When executives decline to see the reality and are less than precise in their facts, employees develop a cynicism that makes ethics training seem hypocritical. In one company, the IT system, in a company that had 24-hour shift work, went down, and there was no back-up. What employees learned during the downtime (it lasted 36 hours) was that only the graveyard shift had been given training on how to handle recordkeeping and reporting when there was an IT shutdown. The other two shifts did not have the training. The company had not conducted the training during the day shift because it was more costly to take employees away from their work in the day. Nonetheless, the CEO issued a press statement that assured the public that operations were normal and "we train for things like this all

---

[240]Samuel Rubenfeld and Oliver Griffin, "Barclays Is Fined Over Whistleblower Pursuit," *Wall Street Journal*, December 19, 20–18, p. B17.

[241]Mac Colchester, "U.K. Will Fine Barclays Chief," *Wall Street Journal*, April 21–22, 2018, p. B10. Mr. Staley left Barclays in 2021 after British regulators provided Barclays' board with information on Mr. Staley's contacts with convicted sex offender, Jeffrey Epstein. Michael J. De la Merced and Matthew Goldstein, "C.E.O. Out At Barclays Over Ties to Epstein," *New York Times*, November 2, 2021, p. B1.

the time." The employees, who had coped with the lack of skills and training and graveyard employees who had been working round the clock to help those on the day shift because they had no training, were outraged. The statement by the CEO was deceptive. The CEO had not told the truth.

One understands the need to keep the public informed and not foment fear. However, the employees knew the real truth and felt that the press release was misleading. The leaders in the company had compromised their moral authority to lead and opened the door to employees using similar types of deception when they were concerned about making disclosures.

Leadership Examples: They Watch Everything Leaders Do

We have seen Robert Kraft, the owner of the New England Patriots, charged with the crime of solicitation. Elon Musk, the founder and CEO of Tesla, continues to taunt the Securities Exchange Commission with his tweets, something for which the company is already under a settlement agreement. Musk, Twitter, and his social media forays, including the video of Musk enjoying marijuana, have been a sore spot for some time. Such exploits are not the kind of thing the head of a federal contractor wants to explain. Indeed, an employee at SpaceX using marijuana would be terminated if he/she failed a drug test because federal contractors must meet federal standards and state legality does not control federal employee standards for work in federal facilities or those of their contractors.

In working at a plant, a picture caught my eye, and I asked a supervisor to explain it. There was another supervisor in the plant who was a stickler for safety culture—compliance with rules, regulations, and procedures—calling anyone and everyone out for the slightest violation. The factory was located in a small town and all the leaders and employees were neighbors and fellow citizens. One Saturday, two employees drove by the stickler supervisor's home and saw that he was standing on a ladder positioned in the bed of his pickup truck that was pulled next to the house so that he could work on his roof. The employees snapped a cell phone picture, blew it up to an 8 × 10 photo with the caption, "Mr. Safety," and posted it in the plant. To his credit, Mr. Stickler/Safety allowed the photo to remain as a reminder to himself to meet the standards he set.

Employees watch everything leaders do. If a leader tells an assistant, "Tell him I'm not here," there is an example. If a leader says, "Just between you me, and the wall, and no one can know this . . . ," there is an example.

Leader Inability to Understand and Manage Conflicts

Like the truth, something happens as folks climb the leadership ladder: the ability to sense and manage conflicts becomes muddled. Muddled management of conflicts gives employees license for their own muddling. In a stunning revelation in an interview with the *New York Times*, Indra Nooyi, the outgoing CEO of Pepsi, shared a story of how she landed at Pepsi:

> Wayne Calloway, who was then CEO of Pepsi, . . . called me at the last minute, just before I was going to join G.E., and made an amazing pitch. He was on the board of G.E., and he said: "I hear you're going to join G.E. It's a great company and Jack Welch is a great C.E.O. But my need at Pepsi is greater than Jack's. We don't have somebody like you here, and you'll make a bigger difference at PepsiCo."[242]

A board member from one company undertook a poaching project with a committed hire from that board's company to recruit for his own company. No

---

[242]David Gelles, "A Onetime Nerd with a Long-Term Outlook," *New York Times*, March 24, 2019, p. BU4.

one apparently saw the conflict at the time, and currently a CEO feels comfortable sharing the story in a recorded interview.

Conflicts are a regular focus in the business press.

- The consulting firm McKinsey failed to disclose its conflict in working as a consultant with companies in bankruptcy.[243] In several cases, McKinsey's retirement plan held stock in the companies in bankruptcy, and the plans McKinsey proposed for restructuring or payments would have benefited stockholders. McKinsey maintained that its pension plan was separate; that there was no conflict and no required disclosure. Oh, but those working for McKinsey on the bankruptcy cases were covered by the retirement plan. A federal judge told the company that he expected "transparency" and "honesty" in the court room upon learning of the conflict.[244]

- Elon Musk's brother was running Solar City, a company that Tesla went on to acquire.[245] The boards of the two companies were intertwined.

- If you run through the SEC filings of companies you will find more often than not that in smaller publicly traded companies, the CEOs own the companies that lease private jets for their use in running the publicly traded companies.

- The chief medical officer at the Memorial Sloan Kettering Cancer Center in New York City, Dr. José Baselga, forgot to disclose the millions of dollars that he received from Roche and Bristol-Myers Squibb and other pharmaceuticals for his work on cancer therapies and breakthrough drugs, a disclosure requirement of the American Association for Cancer Research. In addition, the compensation and relationships with the drug companies were not disclosed in his research articles published in *Cancer Discovery*. Dr. Baselga did not make the disclosures when he served as editor in chief of *Cancer Discovery*.[246]

The undisclosed conflicts came to light when Dr. Baselga put positive spins on Roche-sponsored clinical trials without disclosing his Roche ties and compensation. However, many physicians did not see the trials the same way and questioned the spin on the results. Dr. Baselga responded, "While I have been inconsistent with disclosures and acknowledge that fact, that is a far cry from compromising my responsibilities as a physician, as a scientist and as a clinical leader." That last sentence is indicative of the issue with leaders and conflicts: their personal views of the situation control disclosure, not the basic rules of conflicts, which are (1) Don't; or (2) Disclose.

Sloan Kettering had to revamp its conflicts policy because the issue of conflicts disclosure had become muddled in the organization. In other words, the behaviors of the leaders affected the ethical culture.

Leaders and Expenses

The stories of CEOs ousted or shamed because of their tendency to spend organizational money for personal expenses range from William Aramony at the United Way to Carlos Ghosn at Nissan.[247] Mr. Ghosn at Nissan repeated the

[243]Gretchen Morgenson and Tom Corrigan, "McKinsey Had Dual Roles in GenOn," *Wall Street Journal*, December 27, 2018, p. B10.
[244]*Ibid.*
[245]SolarCity proxy, Apr. 23, 2014. https://www.sec.gov/Archives/edgar/data/1318605/000119312517130746/d318894ddef14a.htm#toc318894.
[246]Charles Ornstein and Katie Thomas, "A Top Doctor Didn't Disclose Corporate Ties," *New York Times*, September 9, 2018, p. A1.
[247]Felicity Barringer, "United Way Head Is Forced Out in a Furor over His Lavish Style," *New York Times*, February 28, 1992, p. A1.

expenditures of Dennis Kozlowski with birthday parties for their wives. Ghosn had a Marie Antoinette costume party in Versailles, and Kozlowski went with a toga theme in Sardinia.[248] Former GE CEO Jeffrey Immelt not only flew in a private jet, he took a second one along in case the first one had mechanical difficulties. An interesting (and expensive) precaution, especially given that GE makes jet engines. WPP is still battling with Martin Sorrell, trying to collect for personal expenses WPP paid for, including travel for his wife and child, ski trips, and items purchased for his apartment.[249]

Top leaders in companies are beneficiaries of a great many perks, and those perks seem to foster a license for expansion.[250] Leader comfort comes from the belief that they are working night and day for the company, so the personal and business are joined as one. There is no line of demarcation between personal and business. However, frontline employees only know that if they used company funds for personal expenses, they would be terminated. The information about leaders' expenses spreads through the organization in an unparalleled system of communication.

One of the reasons perks abuse occurs is that boards do not take the time to review what top leaders are spending and how. A CEO once said to me that the best check on his power would be if someone went through his expenses each month. This cultural influence can be controlled through board oversight, audits, and perhaps even considering a reduction in perks or their structure. That leaders are subject to oversight on their expenses is an ethical culture builder.

Leaders Who Malign Regulators

In my experience, I have never worked in any organization that did not feel its regulators were being unfair, unreasonable, or were just plain ignorant of the real world. These types of organizational assessments of regulators may or may not be true. But the maligning of regulators by leaders creates a culture of noncompliance. In one organization, an officer of the company signed a regulatory report as the chair of the board's audit committee because, as she explained, "I could not reach the audit chair, and the regulators will never know." That tone of defiance grants license and permeates the actions of employees. In this organization, everyone, from the board members to the head of internal audit to frontline employees, had negative things to say about the organization's regulators, and they behaved accordingly.

In many organizations that are under consent decrees or corporate integrity agreements, leaders will say that what happened to them was no different from others in their industry. Or, there is the classic, "The problem is that the regulations are so complex that you cannot help but get into trouble," or, "They have made things so oppressive that we have no leeway." Leaders dedicated to having and maintaining an ethical culture solve problems of interpretation and seek regulator input. Leaders who malign regulators give their cultures license for variance.

When organizations finish their CIAs and deferred prosecution agreements, the language of leaders is critical. If they say, "We can never repeat these mistakes," then the culture takes hold. But if leaders are breathing sighs of relief and talking of "getting back to normal" or "getting down to running the business again," then the culture responds accordingly, and, chances are, the mistakes will take hold again.

---

[248]Liz Alderman, "Renault: Ex-Chief Used Company Funds for Party," *New York Times*, February 8, 2019, p. B1. Don Halasy, "Why Tyco Boss Fell," *New York Post*, June 9, 2002, http://www.nypost.com.

[249]Nick Kostov and Suzanne Vranica, "WPP Asked Ex-CEO to Repay Expenses," *Wall Street Journal*, January 26–27, 2019, p. B1.

[250]Chip Cutter, "Lure of Expense Accounts Can Undo Careers," *Wall Street Journal*, November 24–25, 2018, p. B10.

Final Thoughts

Those are just seven behaviors that leaders engage in that then mold the ethical culture, despite all the resources and efforts devoted to ethics and compliance. There are more, but leaders should remember that what they say, what they do, and how they define the basics of ethics, such as honesty and conflicts, really do matter. In fact, when it comes to culture, these factors may well be controlling.

Discussion Questions

1. List the seven areas in which leaders make ethical missteps and give an example from Units 1–4 of leaders who have made such missteps.

2. Why is the oversight of leaders and their expenses so critical in culture?

3. Explain how hires and terminations affect culture.

4. In companies under consent decrees, corporate integrity agreements, or deferred prosecution agreements, explain how leaders undermine their own successful completion of these civil forms of plea bargains.

Reading 4.18

Re: A Primer on Sarbanes–Oxley and Dodd–Frank[251]

The introduction to Sarbanes–Oxley, SOX, as it has come to be known, gives the following purpose: "An Act to protect investors by improving the accuracy and reliability of corporate disclosures made pursuant to the securities laws, and for other purposes."

The new portions of the law appear at 15 U.S.C. § 7201. However, because many of the provisions amend the Securities Exchange Act of 1934, which begins at 78 U.S.C. § 1 *et seq.*, many of the provisions can be found there.

Title I: The Creation of the Public Company Accounting Oversight Board

This section of SOX established a quasi-governmental entity called the Public Company Accounting Oversight Board (PCAOB, but called "Peek-a-Boo") under the direction of the SEC to (1) oversee the audit of public companies covered by the federal securities laws (the 1933 and 1934 Acts); (2) establish audit report standards and rules; and (3) investigate, inspect, and enforce compliance through both the registration and regulation of public accounting firms.

Under this section of SOX, companies that conduct audits of companies covered under federal securities laws must register with PCAOB. With this registration control, PCAOB is given the power to discipline public accounting firms, including the ability to impose sanctions such as prohibitions on conducting future audits. PCAOB's powers relate to intentional conduct or repeated negligent conduct by audit firms when they are doing company audits and financial certifications. PCAOB's power to regulate was upheld in *Free Enterprise Fund v. Public Company Accounting Oversight Board*, 561 U.S. 477 (2010). Under the Dodd–Frank changes, PCAOB will also have authority to regulate the auditors of broker/dealer firms.

---

[251]Adapted from the House and Senate summary of the Sarbanes–Oxley Act of 2002 that appeared on the Senate website in August 2002.

The SEC is now responsible for determining what are or are not "generally accepted" accounting principles for purposes of complying with securities laws. SOX also directs the SEC to study and adopt a system of principles-based accountings.

Title II: Auditor Independence

This portion of SOX is a bit of a statutory code of ethics for public accounting firms. Accounting firms that audit publicly traded companies cannot also perform the following consulting services for the companies for which they conduct audits:

1. Bookkeeping and other services related to the accounting records or financial statements of the audit client

2. Design and implementation of financial information systems

3. Appraisal and valuation services, fairness opinions, and contribution-in-kind reports

4. Actuarial services

5. Internal audit outsourcing services

6. Management functions and human resources

7. Broker or dealer, investment adviser, and investment banking services

8. Legal services and expert services unrelated to the audit

Another conflicts prohibition is that the audit firm cannot audit, for one year, a company that has one of its former employees as a member of senior management. For example, if a partner from PwC is hired by Xena Corporation as its controller or CFO, PwC cannot be the auditor (for SEC purposes) for Xena for one year. At least one year must elapse between the hire date of the former partner and the start of the audit if PwC is to conduct the audit.

Procedural requirements in this section include rotating the audit partner for the accounting firm every five years. Also, the auditor must report directly to the audit committee of the company.

Title III: Corporate Responsibility

This section of SOX deals with the audit committees of publicly traded companies and makes these committees responsible for the hiring, compensation, and oversight of the public accounting firm responsible for conducting the company's audits and certifying its financial statements. All the members of the audit committee must be members of the company's board of directors and must be independent. *Independent* is defined by the SEC to require that the director be an outside board member (not an officer), not have been an officer for a period of time (if retired from the company), not have close relatives working in management in the company, and not have contractual or consulting ties to the company. The SEC and companies have developed complex checklists to help directors determine whether they meet the standards for independence for purposes of qualifying audit committee membership.

In addition to these structural changes in audit committees, this portion of SOX is also the officer certification section. The company's CEO and CFO are required to certify the financial statements the company files with the SEC as being fair in their representation of the company's financial condition and accurate "in all material respects." CFOs and CEOs forfeit any bonuses and compensation that were received based on financial reports that subsequently had to be restated because they were not materially accurate or fair in their disclosures.

The SEC is given the authority to ban those who violate securities laws from serving as an officer or director of a publicly traded company if the SEC can prove that they are unfit to serve. The standard under the statute is "substantial unfitness." For example, Al Dunlap, the former CEO of Sunbeam, settled SEC charges that he oversaw an accounting fraud on its barbecue sales program, by a fine and agreeing to never serve as an officer or director of a publicly traded company. One final section in Part 3 was passed in response to activity at Enron in the months leading up to its collapse. At Enron, the officers were busily selling off their shares during a time when employees were prohibited from selling shares in their pension plans. Officers, such as Jeffrey Skilling and Clifford Baxter, walked away with the cash from selling at the stock's high point, whereas employees, because of the blackout period, were left to simply watch as Enron's stock lost virtually all of its value.

During the so-called "blackout periods" on pension plans, those times when owners of the plans cannot trade in the company stock, officers of the company are also subject to the blackout periods. The penalty for violating this prohibition on stock dealing is that the officers must return any profits from blackout period trading to the company. This requirement to return the profits exists even when the trading was not intentional.

Title IV: Enhanced Financial Disclosures

This section of SOX is the accounting section. Congress directed the SEC to do something about accounting practices for off-balance sheet transactions, including special purpose entities and relationships that while immaterial in amount may have a material effect upon the financial status of the company. For example, a spin-off company that concealed $2 million in company debt is not a material amount. But if the spin-off company is involved in leveraged transactions (as was the case with Enron) and the company has agreed to serve as a guarantor to investors in the spin-off for those leveraged amounts, then the spin-off can have a material effect. The SEC changed the rules for off–balance sheet transactions quite substantially to require companies to show the economics of such off–balance sheet transactions in a transparent fashion. Lehman Brothers' bankruptcy revealed another debt spin-off strategy that company used to hide its obligations and those types of spin-offs must also be disclosed.

A second portion of Part 4 gets right to the heart of pro forma and EBITDA. Companies must use generally accepted accounting principles (GAAP) and non-GAAP, side by side.

A third segment of Part 4 deals again with officers. Corporations can no longer make personal loans to corporate executives. The only exception is when the company is in the business of making loans, that is, GE executives are permitted to use GE Capital as long as they have the same types of loans that are available to the general public. Another officer requirement shortens the time for them to disclose transactions in the company's shares. Prior to SOX, executives simply had to disclose transactions within 10 days from the end of the month in which the transactions occurred. The disclosure period now is within two business days of the transaction.

As a result of the activities that led to these statutory revisions, SOX also requires companies to develop a separate code of ethics for senior financial officers, one that applies to the principal financial officer, comptroller, and/or principal accounting officer. Interestingly, Enron had just such a separate code of ethics. However, the board waived its provisions to allow former CFO Andrew Fastow to have the off-the-book transactions.

Internal Controls Certification: SOX 404

Referred to fondly now as just "404," a final portion of SOX requires companies to include an internal control report and assessment as part of the 10-K annual reports. A public accounting firm that issues the audit report must also certify and report on the state of the company's internal controls.

Although the audit committee provisions are covered in a different section, Part 4 does mandate that every audit committee have at least one member who is a financial expert. The SEC has already established rules for who qualifies as a financial expert and companies' annual reports identify the financial expert and give the background.

Title V: Analyst Conflicts of Interest

The issue of analysts and their conflicts was one that contributed to the failure of the markets to heed the warning signals at Enron, WorldCom, and also contributed to the 2008 market collapse. The SEC now regulates

1. prepublication clearance or approval of research reports by investment bankers;

2. supervision, compensation, and evaluation of securities analysts by investment bankers;

3. retaliation against a securities analyst by an investment banker because of an unfavorable research report that may adversely affect an investment banker's relationship or a broker's or dealer's relationship with the company that is discussed in the report;

4. separating securities analysts from pressure or oversight by investment bankers in a way that might potentially create bias; and

5. developing rules on disclosure by securities analysts and broker/dealers of specified conflicts of interest.

Under Dodd–Frank, the SEC has been directed to further study analysts' relationships and roles in financial markets and is authorized to promulgate additional rules on conflicts.

Title VIII: Corporate and Criminal Fraud Accountability

This section of SOX expanded and clarified the criminal law portions of securities law by creating new crimes, increasing penalties on existing crimes, and elaborating on the elements required to prove already existing crimes. Also known as the Corporate and Criminal Fraud Accountability Act of 2002, this section theoretically made proving corporate financial crimes a bit easier.

This section amended federal bankruptcy law to make fines, profits, and penalties that result from violation of federal securities laws a nondischargeable debt in bankruptcy. Also, if common-law fraud is involved in the sale of securities, any judgment owed as a result of the fraud is also a nondischargeable bankruptcy debt.

This section also extended the time for bringing a civil lawsuit for securities fraud to not later than the earlier of (1) five years after the date of the alleged violation or (2) two years after its discovery.

Finally, this section prohibits retaliation against employees in publicly traded companies who assist in an investigation of possible federal violations or file or participate in a shareholder suit for fraud against the company. The protections for whistleblowers are expanded under Dodd–Frank to provide for their recovery of 10% to 30% of any fines the company must pay.

Title IX: White-Collar Criminal Penalty Enhancements

This section gives the SEC the authority to freeze bonus, incentive, and other payoffs to corporate officers during an ongoing investigation. The SEC has the authority to banish violating officers and directors from the securities markets as well as from working at a publicly traded company in the future. Auditors must keep their work papers for five years, and the penalties for destruction of documents was increased.

Discussion Questions

1. Many convicted executives allowed pressure (financial, for goals, for recognition) to be the sole factor in processing their decisions and actions, which actually defeated the very purposes of their jobs and their companies. What have you learned in Units 1, 2, 3, and this unit that could help you avoid some of the mistakes you have seen professionals and businesspeople make? Explain why what they did seemed acceptable at the time. Why did so many go along?

2. As you proceed through the cases in this Section, try to connect the provisions of SOX and Dodd–Frank that were passed as a result of the conduct of executives and companies in the case studies.

Case 4.19

Accountants and PCAOB: How Are They Doing?

Many thought that PCAOB was the solution to the problems with accounting firms and their work in auditing public traded companies. Now that we are almost two decades out, we have new information and new behaviors to indicate that was an incorrect assumption.

Enforcement and the Quality of Audit Work

The last time the SEC fined an audit firm $50 million was when Deloitte Touche settled with the agency for its audit work for Adelphia, the cable company run by the Rigas family in Pennsylvania. Deloitte neither admitted nor denied problems with its Adelphia audit work, which meant that the world was unaware that the Rigas family had perpetrated a $2.3 billion fraud on investors by hiding off-the-book liabilities as well as conducting a classic piggy-bank raid of company assets.

However, there has been misconduct, some of it criminal, by the auditors in the Big Four accounting firms, and PCAOB has not been swift with punishments.

Audit Collusion

There is a criminal investigation into the process that Sealed Air followed in selecting Ernst & Young (EY) as its external auditor. Senior executives at Sealed Air allegedly favored EY by leaking details of competitor KPMG's bid. The same two executives worked together at Carlisle Companies 10 years earlier, when EY got that audit contract. Sealed Air has fired one of the senior executives as well as EY. There seems to be a new way of gaming the independent auditor business—set things up through advance communication to make sure the auditors who support management are chosen.

The bidding process issues arose as the SEC was looking into Sealed Air's accounting practices. The agency's questions focus on write-offs related to asbestos claims. In investigating the accounting issue, the SEC ran across the emails that piqued its interest in the bidding process.

Years ago, post-Enron, the audit selection process was placed in the hands of the board's independent audit committee. Management "collusion" (air quotes here in a tip of the hat to the word of our times) was headed off at the pass, we thought. Bid-rigging in one of those old leftovers of corruption that we thought was a thing of the past. A number of professional organizations have codes of ethics that prohibit even the slightest communication between purchasers and vendors during the bid process. Purchasing professionals frown upon saying to vendors something as generic as, "You are going to have to get your price down." In fact, the foundation for these rules is no *ex parte* contact during the bidding process. If there are questions, distribute the question and answer to everyone. If there is confusion, clarify for everyone. What a stunning series of events! What a sad commentary on yet another of the Big Four accounting firms.

(continued)

Case 4.19

(continued)

Audit Deficiencies

Deloitte and KPMG were both auditors on the HP acquisition of Autonomy, which turned out to be an $8.8 billion fraud. PwC was the auditor for AIG, Tyco, Yukos, and Satyam ($1.5 billion fraud). PwC also messed up the Academy Awards best picture award in 2017 (*La La Land* was announced incorrectly as the winner because the PwC partners gave the presenters the wrong envelope). KPMG was fined for the $1.5 billion earnings fraud at Xerox over a four-year period and had a partner plead guilty to charges of insider trading by feeding a friend client information. The so-called Big Four have one heck of a track record when it comes to following the money, or the fake money.

The record for these audit firms, which audit 98% of publicly traded companies, is not stellar.

Getting a Mole at PCAOB

Under SOX, accountants and auditors became highly regulated. Now, 20 years later, we have an opportunity for reflection. Some opportunities for improvement are still there. The oversight and regulations may not have halted conflicts and issues of quality audits.

Several KPMG executives decided on a strategy for audit quality improvement. Their plan was to recruit PCAOB employees to let KPMG folks know which of the KPMG client audits would be subject to PCAOB reviews so that the firm could do a crackerjack job on those audits. KPMG got the advance disclosure information on which KPMG clients PCAOB would be targeting from PCAOB employees for two years.

Those involved in the heist of that information were using prepaid burner phones, codes over Instagram, and a great deal of deletion of phone messages. The intrigue of it all was right up there with *noire* alley films. The head of the SEC enforcement division referred to what was done by KPMG executives in no uncertain terms: "The breadth and seriousness of the misconduct at issue here is, frankly, astonishing,"[252]

KPMG admitted this strategy in a settlement, paid a $50 million fine, and also agreed to have an independent consultant for one year to assess its "remedial measures" and "compliance with ethics and integrity requirements."[253] KPMG reported the conduct of its partners in 2017, immediately upon learning of the scheme to obtain advance information about the focus of PCAOB reviews of its audit work.[254]

David Middendorf, the former national managing partner for audit quality at KPMG, was convicted of four of five counts of conspiracy and wire fraud for his role in the PCAOB heist of information.[255] Mr. Middendorf's strategy for pursuing audit qualify was an interesting one: Obtain information from employees of the federal PCAOB as to which companies that KPMG audited would be on the agency's list for governmental review of audits. KPMG would then pull out the big audit guns when conducting its audits of those companies. Quality is much easier when you get a heads-up on where the regulators are headed.

At his sentencing hearing Mr. Middendorf said that "never in my wildest imagination" did he think that obtaining the names of those KPMG clients that PCAOB was targeting for audit-quality review was criminal.[256] Mr. Middendorf added that what had already happened to him (being taken away in shackles at 5:45 A.M., etc.) was sufficient deterrent for any auditors out there thinking up such scams.

Notice, Mr. Middendorf did not say he did not think it was cheating. The government referred to what KPMG folks did as a "steal the exam" scheme.[257] The goal here was to do a better job on those company audits than the

(continued)

---

[252]Press Release, "KPMG Paying $50 Million Penalty for Illicit Use of PCAOB Data and Cheating on Training Exams," June 17, 2019, https://www.sec.gov/news/press-release/2019-95.

[253]Id.

[254]Matthew Goldstein, "U.S. Says 6 Tried to Help KPMG Shirk Audits," *New York Times*, January 23, 2018, p. B4.

[255]Michael Rapoport, "KPMG Ex-Partner Convicted in Scheme to Steal Information," *Wall Street Journal*, March 12, 2019, p. B3.

[256]Jean Eaglesham, "Ex-KPMG Partner Sentenced to a Year and a Day in 'Steal the Exam' Scandal," *Wall Street Journal*, September 11, 2018, p. B1.

[257]Michael Rapoport, "Trial Begins for Former KPMG Partner," *Wall Street Journal*, February 12, 2019, p. B4.

Case 4.19

(continued)

ones that PCAOB was not going to review. KPMG has also assured that it has invested in new software to improve audit quality.

On the PCAOB side, Jeffrey Sweet, who worked for PCAOB and did reviews of KPMG audits, eventually joined KPMG as an entry partner. He entered a guilty plea to conspiracy and cooperated with the government in the prosecution of Mr. Middendorf as well as Thomas Whittle and David Britt, two other partners at KPMG who were indicted for conspiracy and wire fraud. According to the indictment, Mr. Sweet provided the SEC with the full backdrop for the actions of the partners. At his welcome luncheon when he first joined KPMG, Mr. Middendorf told Mr. Sweet "to remember where his paycheck comes from" and be loyal to KPMG.[258] That welcome was followed by a request for the PCAOB list of audit clients that would be the target of PCAOB reviews.

Jeffrey Wada, another PCAOB employee, was indicted along with Cynthia Holder, who had also inspected KPMG audits for PCAOB before joining KPMG in 2015.[259] Mr. Wada was convicted of three of four counts of conspiracy and wire fraud for passing along audit review targets to KPMG.[260] All the others who did not go to trial entered guilty pleas.[261]

KPMG fired all the employees indicted for their activities. Mr. Middendorf's attorney indicated that he will appeal his conviction because "what happened was not wire fraud."[262]

When PCAOB went back and did a *really* thorough check of KPMG's audits, it found "serious deficiencies" in half of them. When KPMG did not know the PCAOB

folks were coming, the audits were even worse.[263] In other words, PCAOB was able to establish that there really was a "get the exam strategy," for without that advance information, KPMG did not pass its test. "Audit quality" in Mr. Middendorf's title was a bit of a misnomer.

One More Instance of Exam Cheating

To add to the evolving ethical culture at KPMG at the time of the great PCAOB heist, certain employees who had passed the PCAOB training exams (required by PCAOB for all audit firms under its jurisdiction) shared their answers with fellow KPMG employees so that they could be assured of passing the PCAOB exams.

The SEC found the following about the partners and employees of KPMG about the exams:

> They sent images of their answers by email or printed answers and gave them to colleagues. This included lead audit engagement partners who not only sent exam answers to other partners, but also solicited answers from and sent answers to their subordinates.

> Furthermore, the SEC . . . . finds that certain KPMG audit professionals manipulated an internal server hosting training exams to lower the score required for passing. By changing a number embedded in a hyperlink, they manually selected the minimum passing scores required for exams. At times, audit professionals achieved passing scores while answering less than 25 percent of the questions correctly.[264]

The subject of the exams was integrity and other professional topics. It speaks volumes when an accounting firm is cheating on the integrity exam.

Discussion Questions

1. Discuss the issues in audit firms' culture that would contribute to the ongoing problems with cheating.

2. Explain why so many in the audit firms were willing to go along with the cheating schemes.

[258]*U.S. v. Middendorf et al.*, 18 CRIM 036, https://www.justice.gov/usao-sdny/press-release/file/1027801/download. Rebecca Davis O'Brien, Dave Michaels, and Michael Rapoport, "Former KPMG Executives Charged," *Wall Street Journal*, January 20, 2018, p. B1.

[259]Rebecca Davis O'Brien, Dave Michaels, and Michael Rapoport, "Former KPMG Executives Charged," *Wall Street Journal*, January 20, 2018, p. B1.

[260]Michael Rapoport, "KPMG Ex-Partner Convicted in Scheme to Steal Information," *Wall Street Journal*, March 12, 2019, p. B3.

[261]Id.

[262]Id.

[263]Michael Rapoport, "Trial Begins for Former KPMG Partner," *Wall Street Journal*, February 12, 2019, p. B4.

[264]Press Release, "KPMG Paying $50 Million Penalty for Illicit Use of PCAOB Data and Cheating on Training Exams," June 17, 2019, https://www.sec.gov/news/press-release/2019-95.

Ethics in Action 4.5

What Are My Options When My Paycheck Is Threatened?

Put yourself in the position of Mr. Sweet at his welcome luncheon at KPMG, when Mr. Mittendorf offers him advice on loyalty and reminds him about the source of his paychecks.

1. Discuss what options he had. What pressures was he feeling?
2. What information would have helped him in that situation?
3. Just because we cannot find a crime to fit the activity does not mean the activity was ethical. Into what ethical categories did the conduct of the PCAOB employees and KPMG partners fall?
4. What information in the case allows you to conclude that they all knew that what they were doing was wrong?
5. Is this gaming the PCAOB system?

History Repeats

Ethical Lessons Not Learned: Auditors and Accountants Cheating on Ethics and Professionalism Exams

Following the KPMG cheating scandal, the SEC checked with other accounting firms. The question was straightforward: Any cheating going on in your shop? Ernst & Young (EY) responded that there had been incidents reported in the past, but "nothing to see here." Turns out that cheating had been reported and management knew, but no action was taken. There was a whistleblower as well. That's how the SEC got in on the action.

The best part is that the EY employees were cheating on the ethics exams that they must take for their CPA license renewals. Cheating on an ethics exam does cross a few lines.

Under a settlement agreement, and just three years after the KPMG cheating scandal, EY paid a fine of $100 million for the same ethical lapse.[265] EY must also have two external compliance reviews. One will be for determining whether EY is promoting ethics and integrity. The other will find out why EY did not make the disclosures when asked by the SEC as part of its investigation of cheating amongst accountants.

If you cheat, you get caught. If you get caught, big fines result. History repeats.

---

[265]Dave Michaels, "EY to Pay $100 Million Fine in Ethics-Cheating Scandal," *Wall Street Journal*, June 29, 2022, p. A1.

Case 4.20

WorldCom: The Little Company That Couldn't After All[266]

For a time it seemed as if the little long-distance telephone company headquartered in Hattiesburg, Mississippi, would show the world how to run a telecommunications giant. But dreams turned to dust and credits turned to debits, and WorldCom would be limited to showing the world that you cannot stretch accounting rules and hope to survive.

---

[266]Adapted with permission from Marianne M. Jennings, "The Yeehaw Factor," 3 *Wyoming Law Review* 387 (2003).

(continued)

Case 4.20

(continued)

WorldCom: From Coffee Shop Founding to Merger Giant

It was 1983 when Bernard J. (aka "Bernie") Ebbers founded Long Distance Discount Service (LDDS), a discount long-distance telephone company.[267] Local legend has it that Mr. Ebbers, a former junior high school basketball coach from Edmonton, Alberta, launched the plan for what would become a multibillion-dollar, international company in a diner at a Days Inn in Hattiesburg, Mississippi.[268]

The telephone industry in the United States was about to be deregulated, and a new industry, telecommunications, would be born. Because competitors to the once-formidable Ma Bell, long the nation's dominant phone company, would now be welcome, Mr. Ebbers and a group of small investors saw an opportunity. They followed a basic economic model in developing their company: buy wholesale and sell retail, but cheaper than the other retailers. Their strategy was to buy long-distance phone network access wholesale from AT&T and other long-distance giants and then resell it to consumers at a discount. They were about to undercut long-distance carriers in their own markets, using their own lines. There was enough money even in the planned lower margins to make money for LDDS.[269]

By 1985, Mr. Ebbers was growing weary of the new telephone venture because LDDS was in constant need of cash infusions, and the 13-unit budget motel chain Mr. Ebbers owned was the source of the cash. Following another coffee shop meeting, Mr. Ebbers agreed to take over the management of the company.[270] Mr. Ebbers's strategy upon his ascent to management was different from and bolder than just running a Mississippi phone company. Mr. Ebbers envisioned an international phone company and undertook to grow the company through acquisition. One business writer has described the next phase of LDDS as a 15-year juggernaut of mergers.[271] LDDS began regionally, and Ebbers acquired phone companies in four neighboring states. Ebbers also expanded the core business of LDDS from cheaper long distance by expanding into local service and data interchange.

By the time LDDS went public in 1989, it was offering telephone services throughout 11 Southern states and had taken on a new name, WorldCom.[272] By 1998, WorldCom had merged 64 times, including mergers with MFS Communications, Metromedia, and Resurgens Communications Group.[273] WorldCom's 65th merger was its biggest acquisition. WorldCom made a $37 billion offer to purchase MCI in a bidding war with British Telecommunications and GTE.[274] British Telecom had begun the bidding in 1997 with $19 billion, and in a bidding process that enjoyed daily international coverage, the bidding just kept going until Mr. Ebbers offered Bert C. Roberts Jr., the CEO of MCI, the additional perk of making him chair of the newly merged WorldCom-MCI, to be known as WorldCom. WorldCom won the bidding and completed what was at that time the largest merger in history.[275]

WorldCom was on a Wall Street roll, a darling of investors and investment banking firms. It was able to acquire CompuServe and ANS Communications before its merger feast ended in 2000. The ending came abruptly when the Justice Department nixed WorldCom's proposed merger with Sprint, citing a resulting lack of competition in long-distance telecommunications if the $129 billion merger were approved.[276]

Despite the Justice Department's rejection of this merger proposal, WorldCom had grown to 61,800

(continued)

---

[267]Seth Schiesel and Simon Romero, "WorldCom: Out of Obscurity to under Inquiry," *New York Times*, March 13, 2002, pp. C1, C4; and Susan Pulliam, Jared Sandberg, and Dan Morse, "Prosecutors Gain Key Witness in Criminal Probe of WorldCom," *Wall Street Journal*, July 3, 2002, pp. A1, A6.

[268]Kurt Eichenwald, "For WorldCom, Acquisitions Were behind Its Rise and Fall," *New York Times*, August 8, 2002, p. A1; and Schiesel and Romero, "WorldCom."

[269]Barnaby J. Feder, "An Abrupt Departure Is Seen as a Harbinger," *New York Times*, May 1, 2002, p. C1.

[270]Id.

[271]Kurt Eichenwald and Simon Romero, "Inquiry Finds Effort at Delay at WorldCom," *New York Times*, July 4, 2002, p. C1.

[272]Feder, "An Abrupt Departure Is Seen as a Harbinger," p. C1. The company went public on NASDAQ.

[273]Eichenwald, "For WorldCom, Acquisitions Were Behind Its Rise and Fall," p. B1. The MFS merger alone carried a $12 billion price tag; Eichenwald, p. B4.

[274]Feder, "An Abrupt Departure Is Seen as a Harbinger," p. C1.

[275]Schiesel and Romero, "WorldCom," pp. C1, C4.

[276]Rebecca Blumenstein and Jared Sandberg, "WorldCom CEO Quits amid Probe of Firm's Finances," *Wall Street Journal*, April 30, 2002, pp. A1, A9.

Case 4.20

(continued)

employees, with revenues of $35.18 billion. The bulk of its revenues came from commercial telecommunications services, including data, voice, Internet, and international services, with the second largest source of revenue being the consumer services division.[277]

Mr. Ebbers was a Wall Street favorite. One analyst described Mr. Ebbers's meetings with Wall Street analysts as "prayer meetings" in which no one asked any questions or challenged any numbers.[278] Few analysts ever questioned Mr. Ebbers or WorldCom's nearly impossible financial performance.[279] Mr. Ebbers made it clear to Wall Street as well as WorldCom's employees that his goals rested in the financial end of the business, not in its fundamentals. He reiterated his lack of interest in operations, billing, and customer service and his obsession with not just being the number-one telecommunications company but also being the best on Wall Street. Mr. Ebbers described his business strategy succinctly in 1997: "Our goal is not to capture market share or be global. Our goal is to be the No. 1 stock on Wall Street."[280] In a report commissioned by the bankruptcy court on the company's downfall, former U.S. Attorney General Dick Thornburgh referred to WorldCom as a "culture of greed."[281]

WorldCom's revenues went from $950 million in 1992 to $4.5 billion by 1996.[282] Mr. Ebbers always promised more and better in each annual report.[283]

The WorldCom era on Wall Street has been likened by those who were competing with the company to being in a race with an athlete who is later discovered to be using steroids. In fact, at AT&T, Michael Keith, the head of the business services division, was replaced after just nine months on the job because he could not match World Corn's profit margins. When Mr. Keith told C. Michael Armstrong, CEO of AT&T, that those margins were just not possible, he was removed from his position.[284] William T. Esrey, the CEO of Sprint, said, "Our performance did not quite compare and we were blaming ourselves. We didn't understand what we were doing wrong. We were like, 'What are we missing here?'"[285]

Bernie and His Empire

WorldCom's rollicking Wall Street ride was at least partially enabled by Mr. Ebbers's personality and charisma. He was flamboyant, a 6-foot, 4-inch man who tended toward cowboy boots and blue jeans. Mr. Ebbers's charm worked as well in Jackson, Mississippi, as it did with investment bankers and analysts.[286] He was a "native boy" who was making good. Mr. Ebbers was a 1957 graduate of Mississippi College, located in Clinton, Mississippi, about 30 minutes away from Jackson, Mississippi, where Mr. Ebbers built the headquarters for WorldCom.[287] Even as the company stock was falling, few who lived in Mississippi who had invested in WorldCom would let go of their stock because of an abiding faith in Mr. Ebbers.[288] Mr. Ebbers's story was a rags-to-riches one of a Canadian high school basketball player winning a scholarship to a small Mississippi college and then growing an international megabusiness.[289]

Mr. Ebbers's personal life did take some twists and turns. He divorced his wife of 27 years while WorldCom was at its peak and married, in 1998, an executive from WorldCom's Clinton, Mississippi, headquarters who was nearly 30 years his junior. Jack Grubman, the cheerleader

(continued)

---

[277]Feder, "An Abrupt Departure Is Seen as a Harbinger," pp. C1, C2. The annual reports for 2000 and 2001 could be found at http://www.worldcom.com. Presently, go to http://www.sec.gov and look up "WorldCom" in the Edgar database. The financial statements in those reports have been restated many times, with a resulting impact of about $9 billion less in revenue than originally reported.

[278]Feder, "An Abrupt Departure Is Seen as a Harbinger," pp. C1, C2.

[279]*Id.*

[280]*Id.*

[281]Andrew Backover, "Report Slams Culture at WorldCom," *USA Today*, November 5, 2002, p. 1B.

[282]These numbers were all computed using the company's annual reports, found under "Investor Relations" at http://www.worldcom.com. Go to http://www.sec.gov and the Edgar database and plug in "WorldCom" under "Company Name." The numbers were computed using "Selected Financial Data," as called out in each of the annual reports.

[283]In 1998, Mr. Ebbers said that if WorldCom just grew with the market, it would meet its earnings targets.

[284]Seth Schiesel, "Trying to Catch WorldCom's Mirage," *New York Times*, June 30, 2002, p. BU1.

[285]*Id.* Sprint has had its own financial difficulties.

[286]Chris Woodyard, "Pressure to Perform Felt as Problems Hit," *USA Today*, July 1, 2002, p. 3A.

[287]*Id.*

[288]*Id.*

[289]Daniel Henninger, "Bye-Bye Bernie Drops the Curtain on the 1990s," *Wall Street Journal*, May 3, 2002, p. A10.

Case 4.20

(continued)

analyst for WorldCom who worked at Salomon Brothers, attended the wedding and expensed the trip to Salomon Brothers.[290]

Mr. Ebbers's business acumen with his personal investments presented some problems. He was very good at buying businesses but not so good at managing them. Most outsiders believed he overpaid for his investments, and he was so distant in day-to-day management that employees referred to him as "the bank," meaning that they could simply turn to him for cash for those things they desired or when they did not operate at a profit or were just plain short of cash.[291] Still, with the value of his WorldCom holdings alone, by 1999 Mr. Ebbers had a net worth of $1.4 billion, earning him the rank of 174 among the richest Americans. Mr. Ebbers owned a minor-league hockey team (the Mississippi Indoor Bandits), a trucking company, Canada's largest ranch (500,000 acres, 20,000 head of Hereford cattle, a fly-fishing resort, and a general store), an all-terrain cycle ATC dealership, a lumberyard, one plantation, two farms, and forest properties equivalent in acreage to half of Rhode Island.[292]

Mr. Ebbers found himself heavily in debt with his personal investments, and in need of cash, he used his infallible charm in one more venue, that of his board of directors.[293] Mr. Ebbers was able to persuade the board to allow WorldCom to extend loans in excess of $415 million to him, with the money supposedly to be used to rescue his failing businesses.[294] The problem with the loans, among many others, was that the stock Mr. Ebbers used as security was also the stock he had pledged to WorldCom's creditors in order to

obtain financing for the company.[295] The result was that WorldCom's directors were taking a subordinated security interest in stock that had already been pledged, placing it well at the end of the line in terms of creditors, and both the creditors and the board were assuming that the value of the WorldCom stock would remain at an equal or higher level.[296] Although the board's loans to Mr. Ebbers put WorldCom at risk of losing $415 million, the control of the company was actually at greater risk because Mr. Ebbers had pledged about $1 billion in WorldCom stock in total to his creditors as security for loans.[297] Further, if the price of the stock declined and Mr. Ebbers did not meet margin calls, his creditors would be forced to sell the shares. Mr. Ebbers owned 27 million shares of WorldCom stock, and the sale of such large blocks of shares would have had a devastating impact on the price of WorldCom's stock.[298]

Despite all the loans and issues with his personal investments, Mr. Ebbers was a generous philanthropist with his own money as well as with WorldCom's. Clinton Mayor Rosemary Aultman called WorldCom "a wonderful corporate citizen."[299] Ebbers served on the Board of Trustees for Mississippi College and raised $500 million for a fund drive there, more money than had ever been raised by the small college. Interns and graduates from the college worked at WorldCom.

The Burst Bubble and Accounting Myths

Once the Justice Department refused to approve the final proposed merger with Sprint, WorldCom came unraveled. The unraveling had many contributing factors, one of which was the burst in the dot-com bubble and the resulting decline in the need for broadband, Internet access, and all the growth associated with

(continued)

---

[290]Jayne O'Donnell, "Ebbers Acts as if Nothing Is Amiss," *USA Today*, September 18, 2002, pp. 1B, 2B; and Jessica Sommar, "Here Comes the Bribe: Grubman Expensed Trip to Ebbers' Wedding," *New York Post*, August 30, 2002, p. 39.

[291]Jayne O'Donnell and Andrew Backover, "Ebbers High-Risk Act Came Crashing Down on Him," *USA Today*, December 12, 2002, p. 1B.

[292]Susan Pulliam, Deborah Solomon, and Carrick Mollenkamp, "Former WorldCom CEO Built an Empire on Mountain of Debt," *Wall Street Journal*, December 31, 2002, p. A1.

[293]Jared Sandberg and Susan Pulliam, "Report by WorldCom Examiner Finds New Fraudulent Activities," *Wall Street Journal*, November 5, 2002, pp. A1, A11.

[294]Deborah Solomon and Jared Sandberg, "WorldCom's False Profits Climb," *Wall Street Journal*, November 6, 2002, p. A3.

[295]Jared Sandberg, Deborah Solomon, and Nicole Harris, "WorldCom Investigations Shift Focus to Ousted CEO Ebbers," *Wall Street Journal*, July 1, 2002, pp. A1, A8.

[296]Kurt Eichenwald, "Corporate Loans Used Personally, Report Discloses," *New York Times*, November 5, 2002, p. C1.

[297]Sandberg and Pulliam, "Report by WorldCom Examiner Finds New Fraudulent Activities," p. A1.

[298]Id.

[299]Chris Woodyard, "Pressure to Perform Felt as Problems Hit," *USA Today*, July 1, 2002, p. 3A.

Case 4.20

(continued)

the telecommunications industry.[300] The cuts in the telecom industry began in 2000 and were industry-wide. Between 2000 and 2001, Lucent reduced its employment from 106,000 to 77,000; Verizon went from 263,000 to 247,000; and there was a 52.8% decline in employment overall in the telecom industry from 2000 to 2002, cuts that exceeded those in any other industry.[301] When the economy took a general downturn in 2002, WorldCom could no longer sustain what had been phenomenal revenue growth. However, WorldCom's phenomenal revenue growth had not been a function of business acumen. The burst bubble would bring collapses in other industries and regulatory scrutiny of revenues and accounting practices in all industries.

When Enron collapsed, the SEC, under pressure from Congress, state regulators, and investors, announced, in March 2002, investigations into the financial statements of many companies. WorldCom and Qwest, two of the country's telecommunications giants, were among the SEC's targets.[302] The SEC listed the areas to be examined at WorldCom: charges against earnings, sales commissions, accounting policies for goodwill, loans to officers or directors, integration of computer systems between WorldCom and MCI, and the company's earnings estimates.[303] The SEC inquiry was referred to as a "cloud of uncertainty" over WorldCom.[304] The announcement of the SEC investigation caused a drop of $8.39 in WorldCom's share price, a 7% drop.[305] WorldCom had done so well for so long that many analysts expressed doubt that the SEC would find any improprieties. One noted, "I don't think they are going to find anything that they can prosecute. But you may have people try to rewrite the accounting rules so they are not so loose."[306]

At the time that the SEC announced its investigation, Cynthia Cooper, head of WorldCom's internal audit group, was just beginning her internal investigation of the rampant allegations and rumors of creative and not-so-creative accounting practices within the company.[307] With the pressure of the external regulatory investigation and WorldCom's voluntary disclosure that it had loaned Mr. Ebbers the $415 million, WorldCom came to be called "Worldron" by its own employees.[308]

The Acquisitions, Expenses, and Reserves

WorldCom's acquisition strategy required that there always be a bigger and better merger if the company's numbers were going to continue their double-digit growth.[309] If the mergers stopped, so also did the benefits of the accounting rules WorldCom was using to its advantage in booking the mergers.[310]

The pace of the mergers was so frenetic, and the accounting and financials so different because of interim mergers, that even the most sophisticated analysts had trouble keeping up with the books.[311] WorldCom also benefited from the market bubble of the dot-com era, one in which investors suspended intellectual inquiry about these phenomenal performers.[312]

Accounting professor Mike Willenborg commented on this lax attitude about the confusion and inexplicable numbers during this market era: "You wonder where some of the skepticism was."[313] As late as February 2002,

(continued)

[300]Louis Uchitelle, "Job Cuts Take Heavy Toll on Telecom Industry," *New York Times*, June 29, 2002, p. B1.

[301]*Id.*

[302]Andrew Backover, "WorldCom, Qwest Face SEC Scrutiny," *USA Today*, March 12, 2002, p. 1B; and Andrew Backover, "'Cloud of Uncertainty' Rains on WorldCom," *USA Today*, March 13, 2002, p. 3B.

[303]Backover, "'Cloud of Uncertainty' Rains on WorldCom."

[304]*Id.*

[305]*Id.*

[306]*Id.*

[307]Susan Pulliam and Deborah Solomon, "How Three Unlikely Sleuths Discovered Fraud at WorldCom," *Wall Street Journal*, October 30, 2002, p. A1.

[308]Andrew Backover, "Questions on Ebbers Loans May Aid Probes," *USA Today*, November 6, 2002, p. 3B.

[309]Andy Kessler, "Bernie Bites the Dust," *Wall Street Journal*, May 1, 2002, p. A18.

[310]Shawn Tully, "Don't Get Burned," *Fortune*, February 18, 2002, pp. 89, 90.

[311]David Rynecki, "Articles of Faith: How Investors Got Taken In by the False Profits," *Fortune*, April 2, 2001, p. 76.

[312]*Id.* Securities Exchange Commissioner Cynthia Glassman described the market phenomenon in a speech she gave to the American Society of Corporate Secretaries on September 27, 2002; see http://www.sec.gov/news/speech. Accessed June 30, 2010.

[313]"'Going Concerns': Did Accountants Fail to Flag Problems at Dot-Com Casualties?" *Wall Street Journal*, February 8, 2001, pp. C1, C2.

Case 4.20

(continued)

analysts were reassuring themselves that all would be well with WorldCom, and one analyst was on the record as telling clients that the rumor swirls surrounding WorldCom would die down.[314] Indeed, the more confusing, the higher the rate of return and even greater the stock price.[315] WorldCom's stock reached $64.50 per share in June 1999 but was at $0.83 on June 26, 2002, following the announcement of the company's accounting reversals.[316]

Scott Sullivan, the CFO of WorldCom, was able to employ reserves to keep WorldCom going for two years after the merger with Sprint failed in 2000.[317] Because there were no further mergers, the company's phenomenal earnings record would have ended in 2000 had it not been for WorldCom's rather sizeable reserves.[318] One expert estimates the WorldCom's reserves could have been as high as $10 billion.[319]

The Capitalization of Ordinary Expenses

As WorldCom's executive team grappled with what it believed to be strategic issues that needed attention, Ms. Cooper and her team were working nights and weekends to determine how extensive the accounting issues were. By early June 2002, Ms. Cooper went to WorldCom's CFO, Scott Sullivan, with questions about the booking of operating expenses as capital expenses. When Mr. Sullivan was not as forthcoming as she expected, Ms. Cooper became more concerned. Mr. Sullivan was the most respected person in the company, but Ms. Cooper felt that he seemed hostile, and "when someone is hostile, my instinct is to find

out."[320] Mr. Sullivan told Ms. Cooper that he was planning a "write down" in the second quarter if she could just hold off on the investigation.[321]

Ms. Cooper did not feel she could hold off any further on the investigation. She and her internal audit team uncovered layers of accounting issues. With the merger reserves quickly eaten away, Mr. Sullivan had to find a means for maintaining earnings levels, including the expected growth. Although the precise timing for the new accounting strategy remains unclear,[322] most experts agree that at least by the first quarter of 2001, Mr. Sullivan and staff embarked on an accounting strategy that would keep WorldCom afloat but was not in compliance with GAAP.[323] According to his guilty plea and those filed by others working in WorldCom's financial areas, Mr. Sullivan and colleagues were taking ordinary expenses and booking them as capital expenditures to boost earnings.[324]

For example, in 2001, WorldCom had $3.1 billion in long-distance charges.[325] Long-distance wholesale charges are the expenses of a long-distance phone service retailer. The $3.1 billion should have been booked as an operating expense. However, $3.1 billion booked as an expense would have ended the earnings streak of WorldCom with a loss for 2001. So, Mr. Sullivan and his staff charged the $3.1 billion as a capital expense and planned to amortize this amount over 10 years, a far lesser hit to earnings. The difference was that WorldCom, by capitalizing the operating expenses, showed net income of $1.38 billion for 2001, its previously announced target.[326]

However, ordinary and capital expenses require receipts and invoices for the property. The accounting

(continued)

---

[314]E. S. Browning, "Burst Bubbles Often Expose Cooked Books and Trigger SEC Probes, Bankruptcy Filings," *Wall Street Journal*, February 11, 2002, pp. C1, C4.

[315]Matt Krantz, "There's Just No Accounting for Teaching Earnings," *USA Today*, June 20, 2001, p. 1B.

[316]Robin Sidel, "Some Untimely Analyst Advice on WorldCom Raises Eyebrows," *Wall Street Journal*, June 27, 2002, p. A12.

[317]Geoffrey Colvin, "Scandal Outrage, Part III," *Fortune*, October 28, 2002, p. 56.

[318]The reserves and some other creative accounting were often done without the executives in charge knowing that their division's accounting figures were being changed because the changes were made from headquarters.

[319]Henny Sender, "Call Up the Reserves: WorldCom's Disclosure Is Warning for Investors," *Wall Street Journal*, July 3, 2002, pp. C1, C3.

[320]Amanda Ripley, "The Night Detective," *Time*, December 30, 2002-January 6, 2003, pp. 45, 47.

[321]Kurt Eichenwald and Simon Romero, "Inquiry Finds Effort at Delay at WorldCom," *New York Times*, July 4, 2002, p. C1.

[322]Disclosures near the end of 2002 put the date at 1999. Stephanie N. Meta, "WorldCom's Latest Headache," *Fortune*, November 25, 2002, pp. 34, 35.

[323]"Big Lapse in Auditing Is Puzzling Some Accountants and Other Experts," *New York Times*, June 28, 2002, p. C4.

[324]Jared Sandberg, Deborah Solomon, and Rebecca Blumenstein, "Inside WorldCom's Unearthing of a Vast Accounting Scandal," *Wall Street Journal*, June 27, 2002, p. A1.

[325]Id.

[326]Id., p. A8.

Case 4.20

(continued)

lapses began unwinding when Gene Morse, a member of WorldCom's internal audit group, found $500 million in computer expenses but could not find any documentation or invoices.[327] Mr. Sullivan had demanded that employees keep line costs at 42%; anything beyond that was just shifted to capital expenditures.[328] The result was that staff members spun numbers out of whole cloth, but costs were kept down even as profits were pumped artificially high. The initial disclosure of the $3.85 billion sent shock waves through the business world,[329] but before the year was out, that number would rise to $9 billion.[330]

Other Accounting Issues

An investigation and report commissioned by the WorldCom board and completed by former Attorney General Richard Thornburgh indicates that accounting issues extended into the reporting of revenues, not just expenses.[331] Mr. Thornburgh's report, partially excised at the time of its release in deference to the Justice Department investigation, reveals that there were eventually two sets of books prepared for David Myers and Mr. Sullivan by Buford Yates. Mr. Myers was the controller of WorldCom, and Mr. Yates was the head of general accounting. Mr. Myers also held a senior vice president's position at WorldCom and was well liked by the other officers and the staff. Described as a WorldCom "cheerleader" by coworkers, Mr. Myers was referred to around the company as "Mr. GQ" because he dressed so fashionably.[332] Mr. Yates prepared two charts for Mr. Myers and Mr. Sullivan, with one chart offering the real revenues and the other chart showing the revenue numbers WorldCom needed to post to make

the numbers the company had given to Wall Street analysts.[333]

Because of WorldCom's international organization and worldwide offices, those at the corporate level were able to use computer access to these offices' financial records and thereby change the company's final financial statements. For example, Steven Brabbs, a WorldCom executive who was based in London and who was the director of international finance and control, raised the question of the accounting changes, which had affected his division, to David Myers. Mr. Brabbs discovered, after his division's books had been closed, that $33.6 million in line costs had been dropped from his books through a journal entry.[334] Unable to find support or explanation for the entry, Mr. Brabbs raised the question of documentation to Mr. Myers. When he had no response, he suggested that perhaps Arthur Andersen should be consulted to determine the propriety of the changes.[335] Mr. Brabbs also raised his concerns in a meeting with other internal financial executives at WorldCom. Following the meeting, Mr. Myers expressed anger at him for so doing.[336]

When the next quarter financials were due, Mr. Brabbs received instructions to make these transfers at his level rather than having them done by journal entry at the corporate level. Because he was still uncomfortable with the process but could get no response from headquarters, he established an entity and placed the costs in there. He felt his solution at least kept his books for the international division clean.[337] He continued to raise the question about the accounting propriety, but the only response he ever received was that it was being done as a "Scott Sullivan directive."[338]

Congressional documents verify that many within the company who were concerned about the accounting changes approached Mr. Myers from as far back as July 2000, but he apparently disregarded them and

(continued)

---

[327]Pulliam and Solomon, "How Three Unlikely Sleuths Discovered Fraud at WorldCom," p. A1.

[328]Sandberg, Solomon, and Harris, "WorldCom Investigations Shift Focus to Ousted CEO Ebbers," pp. A1, A8.

[329]WorldCom's initial $3.8 billion was six times the Enron restatement of earnings. Sandberg, Solomon, and Blumenstein, "WorldCom Investigations Shift Focus to Ousted CEO Ebbers," p. A1.

[330]Kurt Eichenwald and Seth Schiesel, "SEC Files New Charges on WorldCom," *New York Times*, November 6, 2002, pp. C1, C2.

[331]Sandberg and Pulliam, "Report by WorldCom Examiner Finds New Fraudulent Activities," p. A1.

[332]Jim Hopkins, "CFOs Join Their Bosses on the Hot Seat," *USA Today*, July 16, 2002, p. 3B.

[333]Andrew Backover, "Trouble May Have Started in November 2000," *USA Today*, July 1, 2002, p. 3A.

[334]Kurt Eichenwald, "Auditing Woes at WorldCom Were Noted Two Years Ago," *New York Times*, July 15, 2002, pp. C1, C9.

[335]*Id.*, p. C9.

[336]*Id.*

[337]*Id.*

[338]*Id.*

Case 4.20

(continued)

went forward with the accounting changes anyway.[339] Rep. Billy Tauzin described the congressional findings related to the culture of fear and pressure as follows: "The bottom line is people inside this company were trying to tell its leaders you can't do what you want to do, and these leaders were telling them they had to."[340] When Steven Brabbs continued to raise his concerns about the accounting practices at WorldCom, and even with Arthur Andersen, he received an email from David Myers ordering him to "not have any more meetings with AA for any reason."[341] Although the accounting issues continued to concern employees, it would be some time before they would percolate to the board level.

It was clear that those involved were aware that they were violating accounting principles.[342] An email sent on July 25, 2000, from Buford Yates to David Myers, controller, reflected his doubts about changing the operating expense of purchased wire capacity to a capital expense, "I might be narrow-minded, but I can't see a logical path for capitalizing excess capacity."[343] Mr. Yates sent an email to Scott Sullivan that read, "David and I have reviewed and discussed your logic of capitalizing excess capacity and can find no support within the current accounting guidelines that would allow for this accounting treatment."[344] Mr. Myers admitted to investigators that "this approach had no basis in accounting principles."[345] Nonetheless, the change from operating expenses to capitalization went forward, with Betty Vinson and Troy Normand, employees in accounting, making the

adjustments in the books per orders from Mr. Myers.[346] Ms. Vinson and Mr. Normand were both fired, and Mr. Yates resigned shortly after he was indicted.

Before making the decision on the accounting changes, neither Mr. Myers nor Mr. Sullivan consulted with WorldCom's outside auditor, Arthur Andersen.[347] The criminal complaint in Mr. Myers's case, and the one to which he entered a guilty plea, included the following description of the role of financial pressures in their decisions and accounting practices: "Sullivan and Myers decided to work backward, picking the earnings numbers that they knew the analysts expected to see, and then forcing WorldCom's financials to match those numbers."[348]

Mr. Sullivan had assumed the helm of WorldCom's finances as CFO in 1994, at age 32.[349] The joke around the WorldCom offices when Mr. Sullivan assumed the CFO slot was that he was "barely shaving."[350] Arriving at WorldCom in 1992 through its merger with Advanced Telecommunications, where he had been since 1987, Mr. Sullivan and Mr. Ebbers became inseparable in the mergers and deals they put together over the next eight years.[351] He earned the nickname *whiz kid*, and whereas Mr. Ebbers was the showman for WorldCom, Mr. Sullivan was the detail person. Mr. Ebbers frequently answered questions from analysts and others with "We'll have to ask Scott."[352]

(continued)

[339]*Id.*

[340]Jayne O'Donnell and Andrew Backover, "WorldCom's Bad Math May Date Back to 1999," *USA Today*, July 16, 2002, p. 1B.

[341]Jessica Sommar, "E-Mail Blackmail: WorldCom Memo Threatened Conscience-Stricken Exec," *New York Post*, August 27, 2002, p. 27.

[342]A 2001 survey of CFOs indicated that 17% of CFOs at public corporations feel pressure from their CEOs to misrepresent financial results. Hopkins, "CFOs Join Their Bosses on the Hot Seat," p. 3B.

[343]Kevin Maney, Andrew Backover, and Paul Davidson, "Prosecutors Target WorldCom's Ex-CFO," *USA Today*, August 29, 2002, pp. 1B, 2B.

[344]*Id.*, p. 2B.

[345]Kurt Eichenwald, "2 Ex-Officials at WorldCom Are Charged in Huge Fraud," *New York Times*, August 2, 2002, pp. A1, C5.

[346]Kevin Maney, Andrew Backover, and Paul Davidson, "Prosecutors Target WorldCom's Ex-CFO," *USA Today*, August 29, 2002, pp. 1B, 2B. See also Simon Romero and Jonathan D. Glater, "Wider WorldCom Case Is Called Likely," *New York Times*, September 5, 2002, p. C9, for background given on titles of employees noted.

[347]Eichenwald, "2 Ex-Officials at WorldCom Are Charged in Huge Fraud," *New York Times*, August 2, 2002, pp. A1, C5.

[348]*Id.* Yochi J. Dreazen, Shawn Young, and Carrick Mollenkamp, "WorldCom Probers Say Sullivan Implicates Ebbers," *Wall Street Journal*, July 12, 2002, p. A3; and Andrew Backover and Paul Davidson, "WorldCom Grilling Turns Up No Definitive Answers," *USA Today*, July 9, 2002, pp. 1B, 2B.

[349]Shawn Young and Evan Perez, "Wall Street Thought Highly of WorldCom's Finance Chief," *Wall Street Journal*, June 27, 2002, pp. B1, B3.

[350]*Id.*

[351]Barnaby J. Feder and David Leonhardt, "From Low Profile to No Profile," *New York Times*, June 27, 2002, p. C1.

[352]*Id.*

Case 4.20

(continued)

Mr. Ebbers praised Mr. Sullivan publicly and saw to it that he was well compensated for his efforts.[353] Mr. Ebbers rewarded Mr. Sullivan with both compensation and titles. In addition to his role as CFO, he served as the secretary for the board.[354] When Mr. Sullivan was appointed to the WorldCom board at age 34, in 1996, the company press release included this quote from Mr. Ebbers: "Over the years WorldCom, Inc., has benefited immensely from the outstanding array of talent and business acumen of our Board of Directors, and Scott Sullivan will be an excellent addition to that group. He brings to the table a proven background of expertise and dedication to the Company."[355]

According to WorldCom proxy statements, Mr. Sullivan's compensation was as follows: 1997, $500,000 salary and $3.5 million bonus; 1998, $500,000 salary and $2 million bonus; 1999, $600,000 salary and $2.76 million bonus; 2000, $700,000 salary and $10 million bonus; and for 2001, Mr. Sullivan earned a salary of $700,000 and a bonus of $10 million. These figures do not include the stock options, which for the years from 1997 to 2001 totaled $1.5 million, $900,000, $900,000, $619,140, and $928,710, respectively.[356]

Congressional documents indicate that both Mr. Myers and Mr. Sullivan met with other executives, indicating the need to "do whatever necessary to get Telco/Margins back in line."[357] Mr. Myers has subsequently indicated that once they started down the road, it was tough to stop.[358]

Later discussions between Mr. Myers and Cynthia Cooper reflect that he understood "there were no specific accounting pronouncements" that would justify the changes.[359] When Ms. Cooper raised the question to Mr. Myers about how the changes could be explained to the SEC, Mr. Myers, reflecting the view that it was a temporary change to see the company through until the financial picture changed, said that "he had hoped it would not have to be explained."[360]

Corporate Governance at WorldCom

The board at WorldCom was often referred to as "Bernie's Board."[361] Carl Aycock had been a member of the board since 1983, when the original company was founded.[362] Max Bobbitt and Francesco Galesi, who were friends of Mr. Ebbers, joined the board in 1992.[363] And one board member, Stiles A. Kellett Jr., an original board member and friend of Mr. Ebbers from the early motel-meeting days, resigned in October 2002 after revelations about his extensive use of the company jet.[364] All of the directors became millionaires after the days of their humble beginnings, when the board meetings were held at the Western Sizzlin' Steakhouse in Hattiesburg, Mississippi.[365] A former board member, Mike Lewis, said few board members would disagree with Mr. Ebbers: "Rule No. 1: Don't bet against Bernie. Rule No. 2: See Rule No. 1."[366]

Although board members were entitled to WorldCom or MCI stock in lieu of fees and were awarded options each year, their annual retainer was $35,000 per year, with $750 for committee meetings attended on the same day as the board meetings and $1,000 for other committee

(continued)

---

[353]*Id.*, p. C6. Following his release from prison in 2009, Sullivan returned to live in a home in Florida that is valued at $178,000. At the time of his indictment, Mr. Sullivan and his wife were in the process of constructing a home in the Boca Raton, Florida, area at a cost estimated to be $10 million, with the lot costing $2.45 million. The 24,000-square feet house was sold for $9.7 million. Mr. Sullivan surrendered the proceeds from the sale to WorldCom investors.

[354]WorldCom, WorldCom Proxy Statement, April 22, 2002, http://www.sec.gov. Accessed June 30, 2010.

[355]"WorldCom, Inc. Appoints New Board Member," press release, March 12, 1996, http://www.worldcom.com. Accessed January 22, 2003.

[356]See proxy statements, 14-A, at http://www.sec.gov under WorldCom for 1997–2001.

[357]Donnell and Backover, "WorldCom's Bad Math May Date Back to 1999," p. 1B.

[358]*Id.*

[359]Yochi J. Dreazen and Deborah Solomon, "WorldCom Aide Conceded Flaws," *Wall Street Journal*, July 16, 2002, p. A3.

[360]*Id.*

[361]Jared Sandberg and Joann S. Lublin, "An Already Tarnished Board Also Faces Tough Questions over Accounting Fiasco," *Wall Street Journal*, June 28, 2002, p. A3.

[362]Seth Schiebel, "Most of Board at WorldCom Resign Post," *New York Times*, December 18, 2002, p. C7.

[363]*Id.*

[364]Susan Pulliam, Jared Sandberg, and Deborah Solomon, "World-Com Board Will Consider Rescinding Ebbers's Severance," *Wall Street Journal*, September 10, 2002, p. A1.

[365]Jared Sandberg, "Six Directors Quit as WorldCom Breaks with Past," *Wall Street Journal*, December 18, 2002, p. A3.

[366]Sandberg and Lublin, "An Already Tarnished Board Also Faces Tough Questions over Accounting Fiasco," p. A3.

Case 4.20

(continued)

meetings.[367] But this was a generous board when it came to Mr. Ebbers. Even upon Mr. Ebbers's departure, with significant loans due and owing, the board gave Mr. Ebbers a severance package that included $1.5 million per year for the rest of his life, 30 hours of use of the company jet, full medical and life insurance coverage, and the possibility of consulting fees beyond a minimum amount required under the terms of the package.[368]

The WorldCom board was not an active or curious one. Despite experiencing a lawsuit in which employees with specific knowledge about the company's accounting practices filed affidavits, the board made no further inquiries. In fact, the company dismissed the employees and ignored their affidavits when a judge dismissed the class action suit.[369] The board was not aware of $75 million in loans to Mr. Ebbers or a $100 million loan guarantee for Mr. Ebbers's personal loans until two months after the loans and guarantees had been signed for him. Two board meetings went by after the loan approvals before the board was informed and approval given. Further, the board's approval came without any request for advice from WorldCom's general counsel.[370]

What Went Wrong: Management and Operations

The creative and not-so-creative accounting at WorldCom may have been a symptom, and not the problem. Mr. Ebbers made no secret of the fact that he was often bored by business details, operations, and fundamentals. He far preferred the art of the deal.[371] When Mr. Ebbers did get involved in operations, his involvement was more like that of an entrepreneur or small businessperson trying to micromanage details.

For example, when Mr. Ebbers visited his dealerships in Mississippi, he usually went in with the idea of cutting costs and would do so by focusing on things such as allotting cell phones to sales personnel, eliminating the water cooler, and even requiring that the heating bills be reduced.[372] As a result, WorldCom could hardly be said to have a crackerjack management team.[373] It had an abysmal record on receivables, being lax in bringing in cash from regular billings.[374] One analyst described the operations side of WorldCom as follows: "WorldCom wasn't operated at all, it was just on auto pilot, using bubble gum and Band-Aids as solutions to its problems."[375]

The constant mergers threw the billing system for WorldCom customers into turmoil.[376] WorldCom had 55 different billing systems and the litigation from customers to show that the billing systems were not studies in accuracy.[377] MCI customers would find their service disconnected for nonpayment because the WorldCom side, which did the billing, never got the payments, which went to the MCI side.[378] Even when the customer's account was located, there was a great deal of foot-dragging by WorldCom in terms of both bill payment and acknowledgment of customer corrections.[379] Cherry Communications, a large customer of WorldCom, filed suit against WorldCom for $100 million in "false and

(continued)

---

[372]Jayne O'Donnell and Andrew Backover, "Ebbers' High-Risk Act Came Crashing Down on Him," *USA Today*, December 12, 2002, pp. 1B, 2B.

[373]Feder, "An Abrupt Departure Is Seen as a Harbinger," pp. C1, C2.

[374]Marcy Gordon, "WorldCom CEO Blames Former Execs for Woes," *The Tribune*, from the Associated Press, July 2, 2002, p. B1.

[375]Eichenwald, "For WorldCom, Acquisitions Were behind Its Rise and Fall," p. A1.

[376]One analyst noted that Mr. Ebbers may not have even seen the importance of operations: "Bernie viewed this as a series of financial-engineering maneuvers and never truly understood the business that he was in." Eichenwald, "For WorldCom, Acquisitions Were behind Its Rise and Fall," p. C2.

[377]The CEO of one WorldCom customer said, "They can't even tell you what they're owed." Scott Woolley, "Bernie at Bay," *Fortune*, April 15, 2002, p. 63.

[378]Eichenwald, "For WorldCom, Acquisitions Were behind Its Rise and Fall," p. A1.

[379]Kevin Maney, "WorldCom Unraveled as Top Execs' Unity Crumbled," *USA Today*, June 28, 2002, pp. 1B, 2B.

---

[367]http://www.sec.gov; and WorldCom proxy for 2001, p. 6. Accessed June 30, 2010.

[368]*Id.*

[369]Neil Weinberg, "WorldCom's Board Alerted to Fraud in 2001," *Forbes*, August 12, 2002, p. 56. See also Kurt Eichenwald, "Auditing Woes at WorldCom Were Noted Two Years Ago," *New York Times*, July 15, 2002, p. C1.

[370]Andrew Backover, "Questions on Ebbers Loans May Aid Probes," *USA Today*, November 6, 2002, p. 3B.

[371]Feder, "An Abrupt Departure Is Seen as a Harbinger," pp. C1, C2; and Eichenwald, "For WorldCom, Acquisitions Were behind Its Rise and Fall," p. A1.

Case 4.20

(continued)

questionable" bills from 1992 to 1996.[380] Cherry went into Chapter 11 bankruptcy owing WorldCom $200 million in uncollectable revenues, less the $100 million in disputes spread across the 55 billing systems. WorldCom did get stock in a reorganized Cherry Communications—a typical result, because WorldCom extended credit to small companies that were high credit risks. On average, two to three of WorldCom's commercial customers filed for bankruptcy during any given quarter.[381]

One part of the SEC investigation of WorldCom focused on whether WorldCom capitalized on the chaotic billing system to boost revenues. One technique investigated was whether services sold to one customer were then booked twice as revenues in different divisions, all at different rates and under multiple billing systems.[382] In fact, three stellar performers at WorldCom were fired because they had used the fact that revenues could often be booked twice in the confusing systems to pump up the commission figures for their sales teams. The three simply listed sales from other divisions for their employees and were able to boost commissions substantially.[383] In September 2000, WorldCom did take a write-down of $685 million for uncollectable revenues.[384]

The merger problems were never solved because of one additional management issue, and that was the constant merger of executives from other companies with WorldCom managers.[385] One former WorldCom employee summarized the company atmosphere: "Nobody had time to adjust. There was a [reorganization] every couple of months, so people didn't know who they were supposed to be reporting to or what they were supposed to be working on."[386] MCI had the experience, but WorldCom had control. No one took the lead in an integration effort, and the result was that WorldCom was saddled with excess and expensive capacity from improperly integrated dual systems. Power

struggles apparently contributed to a type of nepotism in which Mississippi-based executives were awarded the vice president positions in charge of operations and billing, and they lacked the experience and expertise that was necessary to fix the problems created by the mergers and create an effective billing system and integrated technology.

WorldCom Bubble Bursts

While the operations in the company became more and more fractured, the internal auditors' work continued. However, they were forced to work secretly.[387] The internal auditors worked at night to avoid detection and, at one point, concerned that their work might be sabotaged, purchased a CD-ROM burner privately and began recording the data they were gathering, and storing the CDs elsewhere.[388] Indeed, so chilly was their reception when they met with Mr. Sullivan that Ms. Cooper arranged to meet with Max Bobbitt, the head of the board's audit committee, in secret fashion at a local Hampton Inn so that there would be no repercussions for her or her staff as they completed their work.[389] Ms. Cooper was forced to go to the board and the audit committee because she was unable to secure an adequate explanation from Mr. Sullivan, who, as noted earlier, had even asked her to delay her audit.

At one point, while Ms. Cooper's internal audit team was conducting its investigation, Mr. Sullivan confronted one of her auditors, Gene Morse, in the cafeteria. During his five years at WorldCom, he had only spoken to Mr. Sullivan twice. Mr. Sullivan asked what he was working on, and Mr. Morse responded with information about another project, "International capital expenditures," which seemed to satisfy Mr. Sullivan.[390]

Mr. Sullivan was given an opportunity to respond at that board meeting but could offer no explanation other than his belief that the expenses were correctly booked. He refused to resign and defended his accounting

(continued)

---

[380]*Id.*

[381]Scott Woolley, "Bernie at Bay," *Fortune*, April 15, 2002, p. 64.

[382]*Id.*

[383]Yochi J. Dreazen, "WorldCom Suspends Executives in Scandal over Order Booking," *Wall Street Journal*, February 15, 2002, p. A3.

[384]Eichenwald, "For WorldCom, Acquisitions Were behind Its Rise and Fall," p. A1.

[385]Maney, "WorldCom Unraveled as Top Execs' Unity Unraveled," pp. 1B, 2B.

[386]Eichenwald, "For WorldCom, Acquisitions Were behind Its Rise and Fall," p. A1.

[387]Pulliam and Solomon, "How Three Unlikely Sleuths Discovered Fraud at WorldCom," pp. A1, A6.

[388]Ripley, "The Night Detective," pp. 45, 47.

[389]There is a certain irony here. WorldCom was hatched in a low-priced motel, and its unraveling began at a similar location.

[390]Pulliam and Solomon, "How Three Unlikely Sleuths Discovered Fraud at WorldCom," pp. A1, A6.

Case 4.20

(continued)

practices until that final meeting, when he was fired that day by the board.[391] David Myers, the controller for the company, resigned the following day.[392] Following sufficient review by Ms. Cooper and the company's new auditor, KPMG, WorldCom announced on June 25, 2002, that it had overstated cash flow by $3.9 billion for 2001 and the first quarter of 2002 by booking ordinary expenses as capital expenditures.[393] WorldCom's shares dropped 76%, to 20 cents per share.[394] Trading was halted for three sessions, and when it was reopened, more than 1.5 billion shares of WorldCom were dumped on the market, sending the share price down from 20 cents to 6 cents in what was then the highest-volume selling frenzy in the history of the market. It was the first time in the history of the market that more than 1 billion shares had ever been traded in one day. The pace exceeded the previous record of 671 million shares sold in one day, a record WorldCom held only for a few days until this trading reopened. WorldCom was delisted from the NASDAQ on July 5, 2002.[395]

WorldCom's bonds dropped from 79 cents just before the announcement of the accounting irregularities to 13 cents just following the announcement.[396] There was a flurry of subpoenas from Congress for the officers of the company.[397] The officers all took the Fifth Amendment, and $2 billion in federal contracts held by WorldCom were under review by the General Services Administration

because federal regulations prohibit federal agencies from doing business with companies under investigation for financial improprieties.[398]

The SEC filed fraud charges within three days and asked for an explanation from WorldCom about exactly what had been done in its accounting.[399] On August 8, 2002, WorldCom announced that it had found an additional $3.3 billion in earnings misstatements, from 2000, with portions from 1999.[400] WorldCom declared bankruptcy on July 22, 2002, the largest bankruptcy, at that time, in the history of the United States.[401]

Shortly after WorldCom filed for bankruptcy, the federal government indicted Scott Sullivan, David Myers, Betty Vinson, Buford Yates, Troy Normand, and a host of other characters involved in developing the company's financial reports.[402] Mr. Ebbers was not indicted until after Mr. Sullivan entered a guilty plea.[403]

Mr. Sullivan was indicted on federal charges of fraud and conspiracy on August 1, 2002.[404] Mr. Myers entered a guilty plea to three felony counts of fraud on September 26, 2002.[405] Mr. Yates initially entered a not guilty plea.[406] However, just one month later,

(continued)

---

[391]Ripley, "The Night Detective," p. 49.

[392]Id.

[393]Andrew Backover, Thor Valdmanis, and Matt Krantz, "WorldCom Finds Accounting Fraud," *USA Today*, June 26, 2002, p. 1B.

[394]Id. This restatement remained the largest in history, more than doubling the previous record set by Rite-Aid of $1.6 billion, until Parmalat and Lehman collapsed. See http://www.bankruptcy-data.com.

[395]Matt Krantz, "Investors Dump WorldCom Stock at Record Pace," *USA Today*, July 3, 2002, p. 3B; and WorldCom, "Press Releases, 2001," July 29, 2002, http://www.worldcom.com. These press releases may or may not be available at http://www.mci.com. However, they were researched when the WorldCom site was functioning.

[396]Henny Sender and Carrick Mollenkamp, "WorldCom Bondholders Study Plan," *Wall Street Journal*, July 5, 2002, p. A6.

[397]Andrew Backover and Thor Valdmanis, "WorldCom Scandal Brings Subpoenas, Condemnation," *USA Today*, June 28, 2002, p. 1A; and Michael Schroder, Jerry Markon, Tom Hamburger, and Greg Hitt, "Congress Begins WorldCom Investigation," *Wall Street Journal*, June 28, 2002, p. A3.

[398]Yochi J. Dreazen, "WorldCom's Federal Contracts May Be Vital," *Wall Street Journal*, July 10, 2002, p. C4. For information on the Fifth Amendment, see Andrew Backover and Paul Davidson, "WorldCom Grilling Turns Up No Definitive Answers," *USA Today*, July 9, 2002, p. 1B.

[399]Andrew Backover and Thor Valdmanis, "WorldCom Report Will Face Scrutiny," *USA Today*, July 1, 2002, p. 1B.

[400]Kevin Maney and Thor Valdmanis, "WorldCom Reveals $3.3B More in Discrepancies," *USA Today*, August 9, 2002, p. 1B.

[401]Simon Romero and Riva D. Atlas, "WorldCom Files for Bankruptcy; Largest U.S. Case," *New York Times*, July 22, 2002, p. A1; and Kevin Maney and Andrew Backover, "WorldCom's Bomb," *USA Today*, July 22, 2002, pp. 1B, 2B.

[402]Kurt Eichenwald, "2 Ex-Officials at WorldCom Are Charged in Huge Fraud," *New York Times*, August 2, 2002, p. A1. See also Deborah Solomon and Susan Pulliam, "U.S., Pushing WorldCom Case, Indicts Ex-CFO and His Aide," *Wall Street Journal*, August 29, 2002, p. A1.

[403]Simon Romero and Jonathan D. Glater, "Wider WorldCom Case Is Called Likely," *New York Times*, September 5, 2002, p. C9.

[404]Eichenwald, "2 Ex-Officials at WorldCom Are Charged in Huge Fraud," p. A1.

[405]Deborah Solomon, "WorldCom's Ex-Controller Pleads Guilty to Fraud," *Wall Street Journal*, September 27, 2002, p. A3.

[406]Jerry Markon, "WorldCom's Yates Pleads Guilty," *Wall Street Journal*, October 8, 2002, p. A3.

Case 4.20

(continued)

Mr. Yates entered a guilty plea to securities fraud and conspiracy and agreed to cooperate with the Justice Department.[407] Ms. Vinson and Mr. Normand also entered guilty pleas to fraud and conspiracy just three days after Mr. Yates's plea.[408] When Ms. Vinson testified she was asked why she made the accounting entries that she knew were wrong, she said she considered quitting, but, as the primary breadwinner in her household, she succumbed: "I felt like if I didn't make the entries, I wouldn't be working there."[409] Ms. Vinson and Troy Normand raised their concerns to Mr. Sullivan, but he was able to convince them to go along.[410] His colorful analogy was that WorldCom was akin to an aircraft carrier. He had some planes out there that he needed to land on deck before they came clean on the creative interpretations.[411] When Betty Vinson was asked how she decided which accounts she would change, her response in court was dramatic and sadly illegal: "I just really pulled some out of the air. I used the spreadsheets."[412] Troy Normand got three years of probation. Betty Vinson was sentenced to five months in jail, and Yates and Myers received one-year-and-a-day sentences.[413] Mr. Sullivan was sentenced to five years.

Before the year ended, most of the WorldCom board had resigned, Michael D. Capellas, the former CEO of Compaq Computers, replaced John Sidgmore (who died of acute pancreatitis at the age of 52 in 2003), and there was another revision of WorldCom revenues, bringing the total revisions to $9 billion.[414] However, WorldCom did reach a settlement with the SEC on the $9 billion accounting problems. The civil fraud suit settlement did not admit any wrongdoing and required the payment of fines totaling $500 million.[415] The consent decree required WorldCom, now MCI, to submit to oversight by a type of probation officer over the company's activities and gave the SEC discretion in terms of the amount of fines that could be assessed in the future.[416] On December 9, 2002, WorldCom ran full-page ads in the country's major newspapers with the following message: "We're changing management. We're changing business practices. We're changing WorldCom."[417]

In what was an unprecedented move, 10 of WorldCom's former directors agreed to personally pay restitution to shareholders as part of the settlement of the lawsuit. The 10 directors paid a total of $18 million to the shareholders to be released from liability in the suit.[418] The funds had to be paid from their own assets; they were not permitted to use insurance funds to pay the settlement. Mr. Ebbers was tried and convicted on multiple counts of conspiracy and fraud in March 2005. In exchange for his sentence of five years, Scott Sullivan testified against his former boss. Mr. Ebbers testified on his own behalf as part of the defense. There was uniform agreement among trial lawyers, experts, and, apparently, the jury, that he did not help his case. Mr. Ebbers appealed his case to the federal court of appeals, but the verdict was affirmed.[419] Mr. Sullivan was released from prison in 2009.

In July 2005, Mr. Ebbers was sentenced to 25 years

(continued)

[407]Id.

[408]"2 Ex-Officials of WorldCom Plead Guilty," *New York Times*, October 11, 2002, p. C10.

[409]Susan Pulliam, "A Staffer Ordered to Commit Fraud Balked, Then Caved," *Wall Street Journal*, June 23, 2003, pp. A1, A6; and "Ex-WorldCom Accountant Gets Prison Term," *New York Times*, August 6, 2005, p. B13.

[410]See Simon Romero and Jonathan D. Glater, "Wider WorldCom Case Is Called Likely," *New York Times*, September 5, 2002, p. C9, for background and titles of employees.

[411]Pulliam, "A Staffer Ordered to Commit Fraud Balked," pp. A1, at A6.

[412]"Ex-WorldCom Accountant Gets Prison Term," p. B13.

[413]Greg Farrell, "Final WorldCom Sentence Due Today," *USA Today*, August 11, 2005, p. 1B.

[414]Seth Schiesel, "WorldCom Sees More Revisions of Its Figures," *New York Times*, November 11, 2002, p. C1; Jared Sandberg, "Six Directors Quit as WorldCom Breaks with Past," *New York Times*, December 18, 2002, p. A3; Andrew Backover and Kevin Maney, "WorldCom to Replace Sidgmore," *USA Today*, September 11, 2002, p. 1B; and Stephanie N. Mehta, "Can Mike Save WorldCom?" *Fortune*, December 9, 2002, p. 163.

[415]Seth Schiesel and Simon Romero, "WorldCom Strikes a Deal with S.E.C.," *New York Times*, November 27, 2002, p. C1.

[416]Jon Swartz, "WorldCom Settles Big Issues with SEC," *USA Today*, November 27, 2002, p. 1B; and *SEC v. WorldCom, Inc.*, 2002 WL 31760246 (S.D.N.Y. 2002).

[417]*New York Times*, December 9, 2002, p. C3; and *USA Today*, December 11, 2002, p. 4A.

[418]Gretchen Morgenson, "10 Ex-Directors from WorldCom to Pay Millions," *New York Times*, January 6, 2005, p. A1.

[419]*Ebbers v. U.S.*, 453 F.3d 110 (2nd Cir. 2006). *cert. den.* 549 U.S. 1274 (2007).

Case 4.20

(continued)

in prison. In addition, Mr. Ebbers had to turn over all of his assets as part of his fine. A federal marshal who was responsible for collecting the property indicated that the government took between $35 and $40 million in assets and left Mr. and Mrs. Ebbers with the furniture in their home and their silverware. They sold their home and all of Mr. Ebbers's personal investments. Mrs. Ebbers was allowed to retain $50,000 as a means for transitioning to self-support. She divorced Mr. Ebbers in 2008.

The judge, in sentencing Ebbers, said,

Mr. Ebbers was the instigator in this fraud. Mr. Ebbers's statements deprived investors of their money. They might have made different decisions had they known the truth.[420] I recognize that this sentence is likely to be a life sentence. But I find a sentence of anything less would not reflect the seriousness of this crime.[421]

Mr. Ebbers did not speak on his own behalf at the hearing, but he had submitted evidence of a heart condition as well as 169 letters from friends and colleagues. Interestingly, Mr. Ebbers is the one executive among all those indicted who was not selling his stock as the market and company collapsed. He retained all his stock and saw his $1 billion in WorldCom holdings all but disappear as the stock dropped from a high of $64 to about $0.10. However, the judge found that neither the letters nor his stock retention was compelling and that Ebbers's heart condition was not serious. She did agree to let Ebbers serve his time in a prison near his home in Mississippi. He drove himself to prison in his Mercedes.[422]

Mr. Ebbers's sentence was the longest of any for the so-called bubble crimes. Jeffrey Skilling received 24.4 years (later reduced). Timothy Rigas of Adelphia was sentenced to 20 years and his father, John, to 15. Mr. Ebbers was released from prison in December 2019, after having served 13 years, because of his deteriorating health.[423] He died February 2, 2020, at the age of 78.

---

[420]Ken Belson, "WorldCom Head Is Given 25 years for Huge Fraud," *New York Times*, July 14, 2005, p. A1.

[421]Dionne Searcey, Shawn Young, and Kara Scannell, "Ebbers Is Sentenced to 25 Years for $11 Billion WorldCom Fraud," *Wall Street Journal*, July 14, 2005, pp. A1, A8.

[422]Sarah Klouse and James R. Hagerty, "Fall of WorldCom CEO Spurred Legal Changes," *Wall Street Journal*, February 8–9, 2020, p. A10.

[423]*Id.*

Discussion Questions

1. Consider the following statement by a government official. Securities Exchange Commissioner Cynthia Classman included the following in a speech she gave to the American Society of Corporate Secretaries on September 27, 2002:

    [T]he distribution of securities by companies that had not made a previous public offering reached the highest level in history. This activity in new issues took place in a climate of general optimism and speculative interest. The public eagerly sought stocks of companies in certain "glamour" industries, especially the electronics industry, in the expectation that they would rise to a substantial premium—an expectation that was often fulfilled. Within a few days or even hours after the initial distribution, these so-called hot issues would be traded at premiums of as much as 300 percent above the original offering price. In many cases the price of a "hot" issue later fell to a fraction of its original offering price.

    What impact do you think the psychology of the market had on allowing WorldCom, Mr. Ebbers, and others to engage in creative accounting? Is this a case of "everyone does it"? What layers of ethical issues were involved? Individual? Company? Industry?

2. Consider the following:

    This phenomenon of confusion ruling in a bullish market is not unique to the 1990s stock market. Following the 1929 stock market crash, one of the biggest collapses, and a shocker to the investment world, was the bankruptcy of Middle West Utilities. The company was run by Samuel Insull according to the prevailing, and confusing, structure of the time, "elaborate webs of holding companies, each helping hide the others' financial weaknesses, an artifice strangely similar to what Enron did with its partnerships."[424] Following the bubble burst in the early 1970s, accounting firm Peat Marwick, Mitchell was censured for its failure to conduct proper audits of five companies that crashed after PMM had given the firms clean and ongoing entity opinions. After the October 1987 crash, Drexel, Burnham & Lambert, Michael Milken's junk bond

    (continued)

---

[424]E. S. Browning, "Burst Bubbles Often Expose Cooked Books and Trigger SEC Probes, Bankruptcy Filings," *Wall Street Journal*, February 11, 2002, pp. C1, C4.

Case 4.20

(continued)

firm, collapsed along with a host of other companies and the savings and loan industry.[425]

What does this market history tell you about
WorldCom? How could the employees in WorldCom
who went along benefit from this information? What
fears did these employees have?

3. Bill Parish, investment manager for Parish & Co.,
explained the collapse of Enron, World Com, and
others with this insight: "There's massive corruption
of the system. Earnings are grossly overstated."[426]
Accounting Professor Brent Trueman at the University
of California, Berkeley, added, "Reported numbers
may not reflect the true income from operations." The
phenomenon accompanies bubbles. "It is absolutely
what almost invariably happens after every bubble.
You should expect them [bankruptcies, scandals, and
accounting disclosures], but that doesn't mean that
people who haven't been through it before aren't going
to be surprised. The bigger the binge, the longer and
more severe the hangover."[427]

Is he right? Is fraud inevitable in a fast-paced market? Are these just natural market corrections? Is this
"everyone does it"?

4. WorldCom was eerily meeting its earnings targets precisely. One analyst did, however, notice that WorldCom
was making its targets for several quarters in a row
within fractions of cents.

"When you see that they're making it by one one-
hundredth of a penny you know the odds of that happening twice in a row are very slim. It indicates they're
willing to stretch to make the quarter."[428] Are investors
to blame for relying on the precise numbers and predic-
tions? Shouldn't they have acted with greater skepticism?

5. Mr. Ebbers's conduct before and after the trial showed
that he still believed he had done nothing wrong. At
church services in Mississippi immediately following
the revelation of the WorldCom accounting impropriety, Mr. Ebbers arrived as usual to teach his Sunday

school class and attend services. He addressed the congregation, saying, "I just want you to know you aren't
going to church with a crook. This has been a strange
week at best. . . . On Tuesday I received a call telling
me what was happening at World-Com. I don't know
what the situation is with all that has been reported.
I don't know what all is going to happen or what mistakes have been made. . . . No one will find me to have
knowingly committed fraud. More than anything
else, I hope that my witness for Jesus Christ [will not
be jeopardized]." The congregation gave Mr. Ebbers
a standing ovation.[429] Mr. Ebbers continued to teach
Sunday school each Sunday at 9:15 A.M. and stay for
the 90-minute service held afterward until he reported to prison.[430] What relationship do religious views
and affiliations play in business ethics? Refer back to
Albert Carr's thoughts on bluffing in Reading 2.4.

6. What did Scott Sullivan miss in making his analysis
to capitalize ordinary expenses? What skills that you
learned in Units 1 and 2 might have helped him see
the decision and the impact of his decision differently? Why did he not listen to employees and block
questions?

7. Even when the first multibillion-dollar restatement
came, many near Clinton, Mississippi, appeared to be
more in mourning than angry. One employee, sharing
the shock with bar patrons at Bravo Italian Restaurant &
Bar, said, "People are taking it with exceptional grace. In
my experience with MCI, I have never worked for a better company."[431] Others, such as Bernie's minister, give
him the benefit of the doubt, concluding that he might
not have known about the distortion of the numbers:
"We've kind of held judgment until we know the entire
story and whether he had knowledge."[432]

Evaluate the effect of these companies on the home-
towns in which they operate. What roles do hubris and
the fear of letting the locals down play in situations
such as WorldCom's?

8. "If it sounds too good to be true, it is too good to be
true." Apply this to WorldCom and the other cases you
have studied. Does this old adage still apply?

---

[425]*Id.*

[426]Matt Krantz, "There's Just No Accounting for Teaching
Earnings," *USA Today*, June 20, 2001, p. 1B.

[427]E. S. Browning, "Burst Bubbles Often Expose Cooked Books
and Trigger SEC Probes, Bankruptcy Filings," *Wall Street Journal*,
February 11, 2002, pp. C1, C4.

[428]Jared Sandberg, Deborah Solomon, and Nicole Harris,
"WorldCom Investigations Shift Focus to Ousted CEO Ebbers,"
Wall Street Journal, July 1, 2002, pp. A1, A8.

[429]*Id.*, p. A1.

[430]Jayne O'Donnell, "Ebbers Acts as if Nothing Is Amiss," *USA
Today*, September 19, 2002, pp. 1B, 2B.

[431]Kelly Greene and Rick Brooks, "WorldCom Staff Now Are
Saying 'Just Like Enron,'" *Wall Street Journal*, June 27, 2002, p. A9.

[432]O'Donnell, "Ebbers Acts as if Nothing Is Amiss," pp. 1B, 2B.

Compare & Contrast

1. At his sentencing, Scott Sullivan told the federal judge of his diabetic wife's need for care and of their 4-year-old daughter and said, "Every day I regret what happened at WorldCom. I am sorry for the hurt caused by my cowardly decisions."[433] Mr. Sullivan stated at his sentencing hearing, "I chose the wrong road, and in the face of intense pressure I turned away from the truth."[434] He added, "It was a misguided attempt to save the company."[435]

   What is the difference between Sullivan at the sentencing hearing and Sullivan at WorldCom making the accounting decisions? What does Mr. Sullivan teach us about what we should be thinking of as we make ethical choices? What elements for your credo can you find in this tale?

2. One analyst noted, "You always had this question about whether WorldCom was a house of cards. Everything was pro-forma. It drove us nuts."[436] Yet another analyst described the WorldCom phenomenon as "a game of chicken, where you get as close as possible to the end before getting out. We all knew World-Com couldn't go on forever."[437] Competitors were flummoxed by the company's performance. Recall the observations of William T. Esrey, the CEO of Sprint, and the replacement of Michael G. Keith, the head of AT&T's business service division, for his failure to reach WorldCom heights. During this time, Sprint and AT&T were considered "dogs," whereas WorldCom was the darling of Wall Street. Howard Anderson of the Yankee Group, a research firm in Boston, said, "Wall Street was more than captivated by these new guys; they were eating the lotus leaves and it made companies like AT&T and Sprint look stodgy in comparison. There was never any question that in terms of the strength and reliability of the network, none of these new guys compared to AT&T. AT&T made a lot of legitimate moves and the stock market did not reward them."[438]

   Another analyst observed about WorldCom upon its collapse, "The real issue isn't accounting. It is the incentive people had to use questionable accounting. The truth is that this never was an industry [that] made phenomenal returns. People forget this was foremost a

---

[433]Greg Farrell, "Sullivan Gets a 5-Year Prison Sentence," *USA Today*, August 12, 2005, p. 1B.

[434]Jennifer Bayot and Roben Farzad, "WorldCom Executive Sentenced," *New York Times*, August 12, 2005, pp. C1, C14.

[435]*Id.*

[436]Rebecca Blumenstein and Jared Sandberg, "WorldCom CEO Quits amid Probe of Firm's Finances," *Wall Street Journal*, April 30, 2002, pp. A1, at A9.

[437]Kurt Eichenwald, "Corporate Loans Used Personally, Report Discloses," *New York Times*, November 5, 2002, p. C1.

[438]*Id.*

utility business."[439] WorldCom's numbers, like Enron's, defied market possibilities:

- WorldCom's revenues went from $950 million in 1992 to $4.5 billion by 1996.[440]

- Operating income rose 132% from 1997 to 1998.

- Sales increased to $800 million, and the price of WorldCom's stock rose 137%.[441]

- In 1999, WorldCom's increase in net income was 217%.[442]

What lessons can competitors and analysts learn from these insights they had at the time of WorldCom's pinnacle?

3. Compare and contrast the WorldCom case with the others you have studied and develop a list of common threads and "takeaways" you would have to incorporate into a company as prevention tools. Be sure to consider elements for your credo in the process.

---

[439]Henny Sender, "WorldCom Discovers It Has Few Friends," *Wall Street Journal*, June 28, 2002, pp. C1, C3.

[440]These numbers were all computed using the company's annual reports found under WorldCom, "Investor Relations," http://www.worldcom.com. The numbers were computed using "Selected Financial Data" as called out in each of the annual reports.

[441]WorldCom, *Annual Report*, 1998, http://www.worldcom.com. No longer available on the web. Go to www.sec.gov and use the EDGAR database to access annual reports.

[442]Bernard Ebbers's letter to shareholders, in WorldCom's *Annual Report*, 1999, http://www.worldcom.com. No longer available on the web. Go to www.sec.gov and use the EDGAR database to access annual reports.

Case 4.21

The Upper West Branch Mining Disaster, the CEO, and the Faxed Production Reports

Massey Energy was once the sixth largest coal company in the United States. By revenue, it was the fourth largest. However, the April 5, 2010, explosion at the company's Upper Big Branch coal mine in West Virginia that resulted in the deaths of 29 miners was the beginning of the company's demise. The explosion was the worst mining disaster in the United States in 40 years. By 2011, the company had been purchased by Alpha Natural Resources. The story of Massey and the deadly explosion is a story of pressure, production, and pushing the line on compliance.

Massey and Production and the Influence of the CEO

Under the leadership of CEO Don Blankenship, Massey went from a family-operated company to a corporation with 150 mines with revenues of $2.6 billion. That growth came in response to Mr. Blankenship's demands and leadership style. He required hourly faxes of production reports from the coal mines.[443] Mr. Blankenship was demanding, often reacting with anger. In a deposition in a lawsuit involving unemployment benefits, Mr. Blankenship's

(continued)

---

[443]David Segal, "The People v. the Coal Baron," *New York Times*, June 21, 2015, p. SB1.

(continued)

maid, Deborah May, testified that Mr. Blankenship grabbed her by the wrist and gave her a lecture because she had purchased the wrong meat in his McDonald's breakfast. One court of appeals justice referred to him as someone whose presence seemed to say, "Bully."[444] He was also described as "arrogant," "micromanaging," and "rude and insulting."[445] He earned $17.8 million in 2009, the year before the mine explosion, by doing what he called getting miners to mine coal the Massey way. Also, as he was known for his staff reductions as he came up through the ranks, employees were fearful that if they did not produce that they would lose their jobs. And Mr. Blankenship made it clear that there were plenty of laborers who could be used to replace those employees who pushed back on production or safety issues.

Mr. Blankenship was also politically powerful in West Virginia. Some even theorize that he packed the West Virginia Supreme Court of Appeals through political clout in order to influence the court's review of a case by a competitor, a case in which the competitor won a $50 million verdict. The West Virginia Supreme Court reversed the decision on the grounds that the forum selection clause should have been honored and the case heard in Virginia, not West Virginia.[446] However, the case ended up in the U.S. Supreme Court, where the reversal was based on the grounds that the judge Mr. Blankenship had helped to elect should have recused himself on the appeal.[447] When the case was remanded to the West Virginia court, the decision was reversed again and the forum selection clause enforced. With the requirement that the case be heard in Virginia, the plaintiff would not be entitled to a large punitive damage award because of Virginia limitations on such awards in contract actions.[448]

Because of his political power, production demands, and tendency toward angry outbursts, few would question management practices. Mr. Blankenship would make on-site visits and hand out cans of Dad's root beer to employees with this admonition, "D-A-D-S stands for 'Do as Don Says.'"[449] Employees said that when Don's helicopter landed at a mine, employees were "terrified."[450] In addition, those employed at the mine knew that their $60,000 to $80,000 salaries could not be replaced with any other jobs in the area. The miners were also keenly aware that other coal companies were failing as Massey was succeeding. Even those who disliked Mr. Blankenship acknowledge that he ran mines differently from all the other companies, and they attributed their jobs to those management efficiencies.

Safety: Incentives and Inspections

Safety was handled in a seemingly contradictory way. Mr. Blankenship said that he demanded mid-day safety reports from all mines so that any necessary action could be taken to fix developing situations.

The mine's safety record was publicly known prior to the explosion. The federal government had issued 61 withdrawal orders at the mine in both 2009 and 2010, which was a rate 19 times the national average for coal mines. A withdrawal occurs when federal inspectors inspect a mine and find it unsafe for occupancy and force an evacuation of all miners.

There were also concerns that were found in an internal memo from a safety official. The memo discussed poor ventilation in the company's mines and that Massey was "plainly cheating" in its samples of coal dust (coal dust is a health hazard for miners and a fire accelerant).[451] Mr. Blankenship kept audio recordings of conversations in his office. In response to the memo, Mr. Blankenship vocally expressed his concern that the safety official who wrote the memo was too focused on the "social aspects of her job." He also concluded, "You've got to have someone who actually understands that this game is about money."[452]

(continued)

---

[444]*Id.* at BU4.

[445]Sheryl Gay Stolberg, "Tapes Portray a Coal Baron Lax on Safety," *New York Times*, October 17, 2015, p. A1.

[446]*Caperton v. A.T. Massey Coal Co.*, 679 S.E.2d 223 (W. Va. 2008).

[447]*Caperton v. A.T. Massey Coal Co.*, 556 U.S. 868 (2009).

[448]*Caperton v. A.T. Massey Coal Co.*, 690 S.E.2d 322 (2009).

[449]Kris Maher, "Ex-Massey CEO Set for Worker-Safety Trial," *Wall Street Journal*, October 1, 2015, p. B1.

[450]Trip Gabriel, "Mine Blast Sent Him to Prison. Miners May Send Him to Senate," *New York Times*, February 26, 2018, p. A1, at A14.

[451]Stolberg, *supra* note 326.

[452]*Id.*, at A3.

Case 4.21

(continued)

Gary Young, a graveyard shift worker who testified at trial against managers and executives, was responsible for spreading limestone, a procedure that keeps down coal dust. He indicated that his equipment was often broken and that he kept a journal to document his frustrations in not being able to do his job. His last journal entry made two weeks before the April 5 explosion included, "I'm set up to fail."[453]

In the third quarter of 2009, Massey had set a goal of 59 safety violations. The actual safety violations for that quarter were 168. No action was taken against managers for failure to meet the goal. In that same quarter, records indicate that Massey had failed to meet the requirements of its hazard elimination program. Despite the problems with ventilation, Mr. Blankenship denied a request to spend $1.8 million on a shaft that would have ventilated sections of the mine that were experiencing the ventilation issues.

There was also a problem that emerged in the charges and trials of other managers at the mine, which was the issue of alerting miners when federal regulators had arrived to make surprise safety inspections.[454] Hughie Stover, the head of security at the mine, had his security officers announce over the radio when mine inspectors arrived at the front gate of the mine. This announcement was not only heard by other guards and management but by miners underground. Mr. Stover was aware that such an announcement was a violation of federal law but maintained that he had received the instruction from management to require the guards to announce whenever mine inspectors appeared at the front gate. Despite the illegality of advance warnings, these incidents were routinely logged by security officers, and those records were then stored in "the barracks," an onsite storage facility.[455]

During the investigation following the explosion, Mr. Stover was deposed by federal non-law enforcement agents in November 2010. During the deposition, during which Mr. Stover had legal counsel present, the federal agents posed their questions in a number of ways to make sure Stover understood. Mr. Stover consistently testified that mine security did not announce the arrival of mine inspectors.

In January 2011, Mr. Stover ordered another guard to dispose of the security records that were stored in the barracks by taking them to a trash compactor/dumpster at the mine. However, after the guard had placed the records in a dumpster but before they were destroyed, the guard was called to testify before the grand jury. The guard testified that Stover had ordered him to dispose of the documents and told the grand jury that he had placed those documents in the dumpster. FBI agents inspected the dumpster and found the documents, because the dumpster had not yet been emptied.[456] The issue of advance notification of inspectors was established and used in other trials. Mr. Stover was convicted of lying to federal investigators and sentenced to three years in prison. Although he appealed his conviction, maintaining his innocence, the court of appeals upheld his conviction.

The Massey Board

The Massey board had been a target of investor and community concerns. In the months prior to the explosion, one of the directors had stepped down because of criticism that she held too many director positions to be able to focus effectively on the Massey issues.[457] In addition, following the explosion, there was some criticism that the company's lead independent director, Bobby R. Inman, had defended Mr. Blankenship and had been resistant to investor demands for greater attention to safety at the company. The investor demands for actions on safety preceded the explosion and were directed to Richard Gabry, the head of the board's committee on shareholder concerns. The board did not take action on the investor safety concerns until after the explosion at the mine.

(continued)

---

[453]*Id.*, at A3.

[454]Alan Blinder, "Ex-Company Man Key to Mine Death Prosecution," *New York Times*, October 22, 2016, p. A23.

[455]*U.S. v. Stover*, 499 Fed.Appx. 267, 2012 WL 6217610 (C.A.4 (W.Va.)).

[456]*Id.*

[457]Joann S. Lubin and Kris Maher, "Massey Board Sets Safety Probe," *Wall Street Journal*, May 5, 2010, p. B1.

Case 4.21

(continued)

The Consequences: Investigations and Criminal Charges

By May 5, just one month after the explosion, the board of directors of Massey had agreed to conduct its own safety investigation at the company. Members of the special board committee to conduct the investigation included Mr. Inman and Mr. Gabry.[458] Mr. Gabry, who had been in charge of investor relationships, including the safety complaints of those investors, was chosen to head the special board safety committee. The U.S. Mine Safety and Health Administration (MSHA) also announced that it had assembled a team to conduct an investigation based on an anonymous tip that it had received on April 5, following the explosion. Additionally, the U.S. Labor Department announced that it had assembled a team to evaluate the actions of the MSHA prior to the April 5 explosion.[459] These announcements followed the commencement of investigations into the explosion by the FBI and West Virginia authorities. By this time, suits by the families of the fallen miners had also begun.

In addition to the convictions discussed in the safety section, Gary May, a former mine superintendent at the Upper Big Branch mine, was sentenced to 21 months in federal prison after entering a guilty plea. Mr. May, an underground operations supervisor, said that he had warned miners about the presence of federal safety inspectors. Mr. May cooperated with the government and was given a lighter sentence because of his cooperation and that he followed orders but did not participate in the decision to provide the warnings.

David Hughart, a former top executive at Massey was indicted, entered a guilty plea, and served a 42-month prison term. In testifying at Mr. Blankenship's trial, he said that he had approved safety shortcuts because of "pressure to run, produce coal."[460]

Mr. Blankenship's Criminal Case

Mr. Blankenship was indicted for a number of charges, including conspiracy to willfully violate mandatory mine,

health, and safety standards. The charges represented the first time in the United States that a CEO was charged criminally with conspiracy to commit workplace-safety rules. He was found guilty of one count of conspiracy to willfully violate mine safety standards.[461]

The trial went from October to December 4, 2015, and included testimony from Christopher L. Blanchard, the executive who was the manager of the Upper Big Branch Mine. In exchange for immunity, Mr. Blanchard testified that the safety initiatives planned for the mine that were documented really did not deal with the operations of the $2-billion revenue mine.[462] However, he also testified that he and Mr. Blankenship never agreed to willfully commit a violation of mine safety regulations. Mr. Blanchard testified that Mr. Blankenship told him, "Be reminded your core job is to make money."[463] Mr. Blanchard's assistant testified that Mr. Blanchard often seemed "defeated" or "whipped" after talking or meeting with Mr. Blankenship.[464]

The jury received the case on November 17, 2015, and struggled to reach a verdict. On November 19, 2015, the jury sent a note to the judge indicating that they could not reach an agreement and inquiring how long they had to deliberate.[465] The judge urged the jury to keep trying. On December 4, 2015, Mr. Blankenship was convicted on only one of the lesser charges (conspiracy to violate federal mine-safety laws), a misdemeanor that carries a maximum sentence of one year. The judge denied the claims for restitution.[466] Mr. Blankenship was defiant at his sentencing: "It's important to me that everyone knows that I am not guilty of a crime."[467]

On April 6, 2016, five years and one day following the mine's explosion, Mr. Blankenship was sentenced to one year in prison and a fine of $250,000 (an amount that exceeds the amount provided under the federal sentencing

(continued)

[458]Id.

[459]Id.

[460]Sheryl Gay Stolberg, "Tapes Portray a Coal Baron Lax on Safety," *New York Times*, October 17, 2015, p. A1.

[461]*U.S. v. Blankenship*, 2016 WL 1623243 (S.D. W.Va. 2016).

[462]Alan Blinder, "Ex-Executive Denies Flouting Rules in a Deadly Coal Mine Blast," *New York Times*, October 24, 2015, p. A12.

[463]Id., at p. A14.

[464]Blinder, at A14.

[465]Kris Maher, "Coal Boss's Trial to Continue as Jury Fails to Reach Verdict," *Wall Street Journal*, November 20, 2015, p. B3.

[466]Alan Blinder, "Mine Chief Is Sentenced in Conspiracy over Safety," *New York Times*, April 7, 2016, p. A12.

[467]Id., at p. A12.

Case 4.21

(continued)

guidelines). He reported to a California prison on May 11, 2016, was released in early 2017, and finished a year of supervised release in 2018. Mr. Blankenship then ran for a U.S. Senate seat in West Virginia in 2018, claiming that he was "a political prisoner."[468]

The federal judge who read the guilty verdict in his case and imposed his sentence is the daughter of a coal miner. The conviction is viewed by experts as a template for other prosecutors to use in holding executives criminally accountable for the actions that they influence but that are carried out by others. Though the sentence was short, one of the prosecutors in the case noted, "You can't always measure justice by the length of a prison sentence" because, ultimately, a CEO was held accountable.[469]

Discussion Questions

1. Discuss the issue of following orders at a company when those orders violate the law.

2. Explain why the conviction of the CEO is said to be an important step in corporate accountability. Why do you think the jury struggled with the case?

3. Describe the culture at Massey and the mine.

4. What would have made the board stronger?

5. Make a list of additional actions that Mr. May and Mr. Blanchard could have taken in their jobs that might have prevented the explosion.

6. In Mr. Blankenship's run for the U.S. Senate, he ran ads on mine safety and how he would work to improve it for the miners. A couple, caring for their grandchild, whose father had been killed in the Upper Big Branch disaster, said, "We're sitting here in our living room with our grandson, and there he sets up on TV—that's sickening. Don can say what he wants about safety and doing all this and that for miners—there was no safety in Massey coal. None whatever."[470] What types of questions should come to mind as companies make decisions about safety and regulatory shortcuts? What do they miss in the drives for productions and keeping costs low? What parallels do you see between this case and that of BP (Case 2.8)? Are there patterns that you see along with similar outcomes?

[468]Trip Gabriel, "Mine Blast Sent Him to Prison. Miners May Send Him to Senate," *New York Times*, February 26, 2018, p. A1.

[469]Kris Maher, "Former Coal CEO Blankenship Is Convicted," *Wall Street Journal*, December 4, 2015, p. B1.

[470]Trip Gabriel, "Mine Blast Sent Him to Prison, Miners May Send Him to Senate," *New York Times*, February 26, 2018, p. A1, at A14.

The Industry Practices and Legal Factors

At this level, companies look around at industry practices and decide that they must make the same decisions as others in their industry or they will be at a competitive disadvantage. They make decisions that they might not otherwise make because they feel there is no choice.

Reading 4.22

The Subprime Saga: Bear Stearns, Lehman, Merrill, and CDOs[471]

"What were they smoking?" The *Fortune* cover story featured those words in a 3.5-inch headline, as well as photos of Chuck Prince, Citigroup ($9.8 billion loss), Jimmy Cayne, Bear Stearns ($450 million loss),[472] John Mack, Morgan Stanley ($3.7 billion loss), and Stan O'Neal, Merrill Lynch ($7.9 billion).[473] Their photos and losses were followed by the subtitle, "How the Best Minds on Wall Street Lost Millions."[474] We had just managed to get our minds around the options backdating problem, with the comfort that came from knowing that such bad habits by executive and too complicit board compensation committees could no longer occur, because Sarbanes–Oxley had more timely reporting requirements. Sure, we were at $5.3 billion in total restatements for options, had one CEO convicted, and 3 out of 10 indicted general counsel pleading guilty, but we had caught the problem, installed statutory prevention tools, and were ready to gloss over this tempest-from-a-past-era teapot.

Like a water torture program, however, the subprime mess trickled forth. Beazer Homes admitted that it broke federal laws in helping buyers qualify for mortgages, but that was just one builder.[475] Countrywide Financial had its problems, but what would you expect in their subprime market? So, by August 2007, we had cut its stock value in half.[476] And we witnessed the default rate on home mortgages

---

[471]Adapted from "The Lessons of the Subprime Lending Market," by Marianne M. Jennings in 12 *Corporate Finance Review*: 44 (2007).

[472]Bear Stearns has since announced a $1.2 billion write-down and a resulting loss, the first loss in the firm's 84-year history. Jennifer Levitz and Kate Kelly, "Bear Faces First Loss, Fraud Complaint," *Wall Street Journal*, November 15, 2007, pp. C1, C2.

[473]The losses for the others changed daily, monthly, and yearly. The author surrenders in terms of how high the figures actually were. One thing is certain—there were multibillion losses.

[474]*Fortune*, November 26, 2007 (cover).

[475]Floyd Norris, "Builder Said It Broke Federal Rules; Will Restate Earnings," *New York Times*, October 12, 2007, p. C3.

[476]James R. Hagerty and Karen Richardson, "Why Is Countrywide Sliding? It's Unclear, That's the Issue," *Wall Street Journal*, August 29, 2005, pp. C1, C4; and Gretchen Morgenson, "Inside the Countrywide Lending Spree," *New York Times*, August 26, 2007, pp. SB-1, 8.

climbing, but attributing that problem to a downturn in the economy, which was due to oil prices, which was due to war, which was due to . . . , gave us comfort.[477] Unmistakably, the mortgage market was melting down, but a shoulder shrug and "so what if a few deadbeats lose their homes" were the responses. However, with collateralized debt obligations (CDOs), a mortgage market runs wider and deeper than even the best of the best on Wall Street contemplated. The banks were heavily invested in that subprime market, and the subprime mortgages had gone south. Once again, we found the classic scenario of companies, operating in a regulatory no-man's land, staying at the party a little too long, and drinking too much. A few had even arrived late and still partook.

Not to pour too much salt on fresh wounds of 35% and 36% share price drops for Citigroup and Merrill, respectively, but we have been down this road of high risk, overly optimistic bets, initial phenomenal returns, and collapses. Junk bonds, savings and loans and their property appraisals, and the high-tech/dot-com boom were of the same pattern from other eras. Different investment vehicles; same crash and burn. A look back at some other *Fortune* covers is an eerie reminder of lessons not learned. The cover of *Fortune* for May 14, 2001, just after that era's bubble burst, featured analyst Mary Meeker and the caption "Can We Ever Trust Again?" How did they miss that one? How could the analysts have been so wrong? Still, one year later the cover of *Fortune* featured Sallie Krawcheck and the caption "In Search of the Last Honest Analyst."[478] We were not confident the problem had been solved. Here we are today, with slightly more plebian phraseology, asking the same question Judge Stanley Sporkin asked in 1990 when we had the S&L losses: "Where were these professionals . . . when these clearly improper transactions were being consummated? Why didn't any of them speak up or disassociate themselves from the transactions?"[479] Once again, we are stunned by the failure of financial wizards to catch these multibillion dollar overvaluations.

However, there is something quite troublingly different about this meltdown from those of the junk bond, S&L, and dot-com eras: we have not managed to make it 10 years without a breach of trust. We were living with the assumption that these types of financial and ethical debacles would only arise once a decade as those new to the businesses affected by the last issue forgot the historical underpinnings of the market and their own institutional histories. Five years out from the promised transparency of Sarbanes–Oxley finds investors asking the same question: Can we trust these people? As the *Fortune* piece noted in its introduction,

> Two things stand out about the credit crisis cascading through Wall Street: It is both totally shocking and utterly predictable. Shocking, because a pack of the highest-paid executives on the planet, lauded as the best minds in business and backed by cadres of math whizzes and computer geeks, managed to lose tens of billions of dollars on exotic instruments built on the shaky foundation of subprime mortgages?[480]

The shocking part is incorrect. The utterly predictable part is indeed correct. Herewith some thoughts on those two thoughts through a discussion of the governance and ethics issues the best of the best missed, once again.

---

[477]Richard Beales, Alex Barker, and Saskia Scholtes, "Fraud Inquiry Goes to Roots of Debt Chaos," *Financial Times*, March 29, 2007, p. 21.

[478]*Fortune*, June 10, 2002, and beneath the caption was the stinging phrase, "Her analysts are paid for research, not deals."

[479]*Lincoln Sav. & Loan Ass'n v. Wall*, 743 F. Supp. 901, at 920 (D.C.Cir.1990). Judge Sporkin referred to both lawyers and accountants/auditors in his question.

[480]Shawn Tully, "Wall Street's Money Machine Breaks Down," *Fortune*, November 26, 2007, pp. 65, 66.

Why We're Not "Shocked, Shocked" at the Losses[481]

Many of us, although unable to quantify the extent of the losses, had been expressing concerns about subprime loans in general, including the use of subprime loans as a foundation for financial instruments. We were, as in the dot-com and Enron eras, pooh-poohed as being overly cautious and, again, overly focused on ethical issues. Yet, the ethical issues in the subprime lending market were compelling. The subprime market saw loans for 100% of purchase price, loans based on false information (the Beazer issue), and loans to those ill-equipped to handle credit generally and certainly incapable of managing ARM mortgages that would find their payments doubling when market rates kicked in on their loans.

Opening up mortgages to the ill-equipped with poor track records resulted in more mortgages, and the low-hanging fruit of high credit risks found the mortgage brokers calling with creative packages. Even with a skill set for applying *caveat emptor*, these credit risks were no match for brokers who had tasted double-digit returns and driven Ferraris, whether leased or owned. Neither business models nor markets can have "taking advantage of those with lesser information or bargaining power" as a foundation. Whether the path is one of pyramid scheme, false advertising, or inherent bargaining disparity, all such roads lead to negative firm and market impact, with perhaps the greatest casually being market trust as we cope with, "Not again!"

Perhaps a contra example of how the subprime market should have been handled makes a compelling case against the companies' argument that they are "shocked, shocked" by their numbers. North Carolina largely escaped the wrath of the subprime foreclosures and resulting market downturn because of tougher lending laws it enacted in 1999. Its so-called predatory lending law, passed in a state with some of the United States' largest financial institutions headquartered there, is one that has become the model for other states as well as for proposed reforms wending their way through Congress. The legislation, which helped consumers, lenders, and the North Carolina economy, is perhaps a case study in how staying ahead of evolving issues and placing restraints on nefarious activities can benefit business. That regulatory cycle emerges again: deal with the abuses in the regulatory no-man's land before they become a financial, regulatory, or litigation crisis.

North Carolina's predatory lending law includes the following protections, protections that surely would have been wise self-restraints by lenders during the real estate boom and certainly would have helped preserve the value and lower the risk in the CDO portfolios of the banks now forced to take the write-downs:[482]

- Limitations on the amount of interest that can be charged on residential mortgage loans in the amount of $300,000 or less, as well as any additional fees lenders add on to the loans

- Limits on fees that may be charged in connection with a modification, renewal, extension, or amendment of any of the terms of a home loan, other than a high-cost home loan. The permitted fees are essentially the same as those allowed for the making of a new loan, with the exception of a loan application, origination, or commitment fee.

- Limits on fees to third parties involved with the processing of the loan

- Elimination of penalties for consumers who pay off their debts early

---

[481]*Casablanca* (Warner Brothers 1942); *see also*, Marianne M. Jennings, "Fraud Is the Moving Target, Not Corporate Securities Attorneys: The Market Relevance of Firing before Being Fired Upon and Not Being 'Shocked, Shocked' That Fraud Is Going On," 46 *Washburn L. Rev.* 27 (2007).

[482]N.C.G.S.A. § 24–8.

- Requirement for lenders to verify income of debtors
- Limitations on fees brokers can collect for arranging mortgages

Martin Eakes, one of the businesspeople (and a trained lawyer) who worked to get North Carolina's law in place, said, "Subprime mortgages can be productive and fruitful. We just have to put boundaries in place."[483] Ah, there it is. There is nothing inherently evil about the subprime market, but those boundaries are important. North Carolina also provided the data for what harms can befall an economy when subprime loans go south.

Studies by then–attorney general Mike Easely (North Carolina's governor from 2001 to 2009) showed what foreclosures did in poorer neighborhoods. The impact on the general area as well as the real estate market was a bit of a foreshadowing of the much larger nationwide economic impact we have witnessed. The systemic effects of subprime loans were documented clearly in this state's reforms even before the real estate market experienced its boom. The impact of the foreclosed loans was the risk inherent in instruments tied to such loans.

The very basic notions of consumer law, fairness, disclosure, and risk were ignored or minimized in the sophisticated models used for structuring and evaluating the portfolios of companies such as Citigroup and Merrill Lynch. A model based on a flawed assumption about something as simple as the quality of the mortgages is still a flawed model. The question underpinning all the CDOs and related derivative investments should have been "How high is the risk on the mortgages?" or "What's the credit quality of the borrower?" That basic question was either not evaluated or not answered realistically for both the investment decisions and the ongoing evaluations of value for purposes of financial reports.

"Utterly Predictable"

If the underlying question on the subprime/mortgage investment vehicles was such a basic finance question, how come so few with so much experience and so many tools at their disposal got it so wrong for so long? The answer to this question rests in the culture of the companies. These companies had many of the same traits that existed in other giants fallen through a lack of financial transparency and the eventual disclosure of a less than pretty picture. Think Enron with its off-the-books debt and mark-to-market accounting, WorldCom with its capitalization of ordinary expenses, Adelphia with its executive loans, and so on. We have a different set of companies in a different industry, but the traits that contribute to the lack of transparency and eventual losses are the same. High risk, little transparency, and iffy evaluation lead to what insiders claim to be surprise losses. However, as dissimilar as the companies are in industry and tactics, there are similarities in culture. There are seven cultural traits that characterize companies that have ethical lapses, such as a lack of transparency in financial statements, with the resulting financial meltdowns. The companies with the largest write-downs had at least four of those traits.

Iconic CEOs

These companies had Wall Street legends at their helms. Chuck Prince was handpicked by Sandy Weill to head up Citigroup. Weill had steered the ship during the rowdiness of Jack Grubman and the WorldCom unwavering support, and Prince was his protégé. Who would question Prince? In fact, even when there were bizarre

---

[483]Nanette Byrnes, "These Tough Lending Laws Could Travel," *BusinessWeek*, November 5, 2007, pp. 70–71.

rumblings, we did not bat an eye. In early 2007, Prince had a mess on his hands as he terminated Todd S. Thomson, the head of global investment, with stories circulating about Thomson's relationship with Maria S. Bartiromo, private jets, and the conflict regarding her role as a CNBC anchor.[484] Known as the "money-honey mess," some outside the company predicted that the ouster, on what were called meager grounds, meant there was more Citigroup bad news on the horizon as Prince found scapegoats.[485] Thomson was a known dissenter when it came to Prince.

Stan O'Neal was an indefatigable "numbers guy" who was brought in to streamline Merrill Lynch. Mr. O'Neal initiated the relationship with Long-Term Capital Management, a hedge fund. O'Neal took Merrill from a safe trading house to a leveraged player. Merrill weathered the storm from the infamous Enron barge deal with a judicial opinion that, although reversing the convictions of the Merrill employers, was not flattering. In a nutshell, the court held that the Merrill employees could not be held criminally liable when the company itself (Enron) made the Enron executives do it, and the Merrill folks were outsiders who could not be considered part of a fraud when the very officers of Enron were presenting the deal as good for Enron (if that makes any sense):

> Here, the private and personal benefit, i.e. increased personal bonuses, that allegedly diverged from the corporate interest was itself a promise of the corporation. According to the Government, Enron itself created an incentive structure tying employee compensation to the attainment of corporate earnings targets. In other words, this case presents a situation in which the employer itself created among its employees an understanding of its interest that, however benighted that understanding, was thought to be furthered by a scheme involving a fiduciary breach; in essence, all were driven by the concern that Enron would suffer absent the scheme. Given that the only personal benefit or incentive originated with Enron itself—not from a third party as in the case of bribery or kickbacks, nor from one's own business affairs outside the fiduciary relationship as in the case of self-dealing—Enron's legitimate interests were not so clearly distinguishable from the corporate goals communicated to the Defendants (via their compensation incentives) that the Defendants should have recognized, based on the nature of our past case law, that the "employee services" taken to achieve those corporate goals constituted a criminal breach of duty to Enron. We therefore conclude that the scheme as alleged falls outside the scope of honest-services fraud.[486]

On the mortgage instrument front, O'Neal stated, just three months prior to the announcement of the multibillion-dollar write-downs, that Merrill's hit was not bad and all was under control. When he announced $5 billion in early October, the market concluded that the extent of the write-down meant the models were flawed.[487] Just three weeks later, the upping of the figure to $8 billion meant his resignation.

John Mack was brought back to Morgan Stanley after Phil Purcell retired under unrelenting pressure from both internal and external sources. Mack had retired in 2001 after Purcell refused to yield in a power struggle. Such a triumphant return is bound to set an iconic tone, to wit, "Mack is back!"[488]

---

[484]Bill Carter, "As Citigroup Chief Totters, CNBC Reporter Is Having a Great Year," *New York Times*, November 5, 2007, pp. C1, C5.

[485]Barney Gimbel, "Deconstructing the Money-Honey Mess," *Fortune*, March 5, 2007, p. 14.

[486]*U.S. v. Brown*, 495 F.3d 509 (5th Cir.2006).

[487]Randall Smith, "A Five Billion Bath at Merrill Bares Deeper Divisions," *Wall Street Journal*, October 6, 2007, p. A1.

[488]Ann Davis, "Morgan Stanley's Change in Focus," *Wall Street Journal*, June 27, 2005, pp. C1, C5.

Jimmy Cayne's status and leadership approach emerged when the Bear Sterns losses did. He spent a good deal of time in recreational activities, something that made for derisive reports, but only from outsiders.[489] No one inside the company would question Cayne.

And there are others in the high-risk fold that were not highlighted on the cover. UBS, Wachovia, Bank of America, and Lehman have all had losses creeping up with trickle releases.

In the three companies with the surprising losses (either by scope or reputation), stars were at the helm and had been brought in to clean up some messiness. For a time, they were all very successful, providing returns to shareholders and premium yields on bonds. But their star quality, coupled with results, meant that few in their companies would either challenge them or be willing to be the bearers of bad news (see below). The write-down "surprises" are easily explained and do not reflect well on either their business models or the willingness of employees to talk with these leaders about emerging issues.

In simplest terms, the problem was the mortgages backing the bonds had been assigned risk levels based on default rates in a primo market, not a declining one. In short, the default rates were faulty (and the risk levels incorrect) because of a failure to take full account of the subprime market and its inherent and higher risk. As noted earlier, this higher risk was not unknown information about subprimes, but no one seemed willing to discuss that issue with their leaders.

Pressure to Meet Numbers

It was not that bright people in the companies did not see the problems or risk. The structure, the incentives, and the returns and rewards all contributed to a silence that belied common sense. One cannot, after all, wish his or her way into value.

One postmortem analysis noted that at Merrill, "They lost more than others. Merrill tended to focus its efforts in the highest risk areas because that's where the rate of return was greatest."[490] An executive commented after the $5 billion loss was announced, "We've seen this before."[491] O'Neal was, ironically, a numbers man who grilled his executives on results. One of his frequent tactics was making comparisons between Merrill and Goldman, such as why Goldman had higher growth in bond profits, with one Merrill executive noting, "It got to the point where you didn't want to be in the office on Goldman earnings days."[492] Employees called operations meetings "staged" and always found O'Neal aloof. And there were a series of terminations in the last year that found three high-ranking Merrill executives summoned for 5- to 15-minute sessions in which they were shown the door for not reaching numbers goals. Those terminations were scuttlebutt throughout the company. Those interested in staying knew that results, not bad news, were the key to remaining employed. When you have forgotten the basic notion that higher returns mean higher risk, that pertinent information needs to percolate to the top and did not in the case of Merrill, because it was afflicted with the same type of culture that allowed the Enron-era companies to go on for so long with so much wrong that was not factored into financials.

---

[489]Cayne was golfing and on a bridge tournament trip during the critical time of the crisis. Kate Kelly, "Bear CEO's Handling of Crisis Raises Issues," *Wall Street Journal*, November 1, 2007, pp. A1, A16. Mr. Cayne spent 10 of July's 21 working days golfing or at the tournament.

[490]Jenny Anderson, "A Big Loss at Merrill Stirs Worries about Risk Control," *New York Times*, October 6, 2007, pp. B1, B2.

[491]*Id.*

[492]Randall Smith, "O'Neal Out as Merrill Reels from Loss," *Wall Street Journal*, October 29, 2007, pp. A1, A16.

Prince had the Thomson termination, something that had a similar chilling effect as the Merrill terminations. Cayne's aloofness created a similar reticence on the parts of employees and executives who probably understood their exposure on CDOs.

The latest research shows that uncovering financial issues and fraud has its best shot in employees.[493] Neither regulators nor auditors are as likely to have information about financial report missteps as employees. The key is creating a culture in which the employees, who now tell us they were aware of the subprime issues and the need for write-downs, have the avenues and motivation for disclosure to those who will respond. Those companies now experiencing the lightest hits from the subprimes had cultures in which the numbers were questioned, from the top. Jamie Dimon at JPMorgan is known for his extensive involvement in operations there and his ability to hone in on numbers and ask the tough questions of employees. His approach is one that signals to employees not that the company wants only results but that the results must be accurate and legitimate.[494] Compare the JPMorgan write-down of $339 million with the other firms' billions. Small write-downs come in comparison because of the hands-on operational experience and drilling techniques of officers who ask where the numbers came from and don't just accept numbers presented.

Innovation Like No Other

"The banks were in denial. They thought they were smarter than the market."[495] Somehow the companies examined here were able to convince themselves that showing phenomenal earnings for such a long stretch meant invincibility and an immunity from the basics of market risk, returns, and exposure. Fancying yourself above the fray means that the rules, whether of the market or accounting, do not apply to your business model. Ignoring those basic principles simply postpones the inevitable subjugation to those principles, and the longer the postponement, the greater the losses.

Weak Boards

All of the boards, including Citigroup, have credentialed members. Robert Rubin, the former treasury secretary, has stepped up as chairman at Citi, but how did he miss the problem? By Rubin's own admission, he did not know what a liquidity put was until the summer of 2007. And in what should be a shocking interview for governance gurus everywhere (and a big help on shareholder litigation), Rubin noted, "I tried to help people as they thought their way through this. Myself, at that point, I had no familiarity at all with CDOs."[496] Those on the board of a bank have an obligation to understand the instruments that are a foundation of the bank's portfolio. Yet Rubin insists it was not his job to know: "The answer is simple. It did not go on under my nose. I am not senior management. I have this side role."[497]

That former AT&T CEO Michael Armstrong missed the signals is even more extraordinary because Armstrong was a survivor of the overvaluation era that characterized the telecoms. Yet, as chair of Citi's audit committee, he did not see the similar strains or was unwilling to raise the flag.

---

[493]Alexander Dyck, Adair Morse, and Luigi Zingales, "Who Blows the Whistle on Corporate Fraud?" *Financial Economics*, February 2007. The authors find that employees are the best source for detecting fraud and support financial incentives for gaining more information from them, for example, more *qui tam* recovery.

[494]Randall Smith and Aaron Lucchetti, "Merrill Taps Thain as CEO," *Wall Street Journal*, November 15, 2007, pp. A1, A21.

[495]Shawn Tully, "Wall Street's Money Machine Breaks Down," *Fortune*, November 26, 2007, pp. 65, 78.

[496]Carol J. Loomis, "Robert Rubin on the Job He Never Wanted," *Fortune*, November 26, 2007, pp. 68–69.

[497]Id.

There is an ugly history with Armstrong, Weill, and Jack Grubman. Weill leaned on Grubman for a favorable AT&T rating in exchange for Weill's influence in getting Grubman's twins into preschool.[498] And Armstrong then sided with Weill in the battle for control of Citi against his co-CEO, John Reed. Credentials do not make for a strong board, and Prince's departure alone cannot fix the lax supervision of numbers at Citi. A board shakeup could have benefited the company back in the Weill days and is necessary now as it moves forward and sheds the Weill and Prince shadows and styles. Indeed, all the boards may want to revisit the notion of expertise: Why did no one on the boards question the risk, the numbers, the operations, or even, just three months prior to the announcements of the write-downs, whether the subprime meltdown would affect their companies' financials? An even more basic question is why did the board members not take the time to understand the definitions and risks of the instruments that were the cornerstone of the companies' portfolios?

"The Sage Advice Lost in the Computer Models"

Even without the common traits analysis, we have some simpler principles that would have helped the boards, the media, the analysts, and even the investors in these banks. That old adage applies: "If it sounds too good to be true, it is too good to be true." The kinds of returns that the banks and their investors were enjoying on investments based on subprime loans were too high to not have high risk associated with them. They simply had not been transparent about that risk.

There is another simple lesson, which is that there is no substitute for learning not just what the numbers are, but how staff got to those numbers. In looking at the companies that have had the least impact we find that, as noted earlier, there was a culture of "How exactly did you get these numbers?"—a natural and ongoing skepticism that signaled to employees that the numbers had to be supportable, not just within range. The value of dissent in companies had been vastly underestimated and underutilized.

One final lesson was noted in the introduction. A sustainable competitive business model cannot be based on taking advantage of those with less information. A market works, not because of asymmetrical information but because of transparency. That transparency was not there at the point of the subprime loan negotiations and the fog carried through to the risk evaluation as well as the valuations of the collateralized mortgage bonds themselves. Throughout the chain, the terms, the value, and the risk were not clear to the players. Such failure to disclose is neither the stuff of ethics nor of thriving markets. The subprime mess, when all is said and done, comes down to the basic ethical standard of forthrightness at all levels of companies and throughout the market.

Discussion Questions

1. What was not clear to investors in subprime mortgages?

2. Was this an industry pressure issue? Why did some succumb to "what everyone else was doing" and others did not?

3. How could the adage "If it sounds too good to be true . . . "influence the structure of an investment portfolio?

4. What is the role of boards in curbing unethical behavior at companies?

5. What cultural factors allowed the companies to keep going despite risks?

---

[498]Mara Der Hovanesian, "Can Citi Regroup?" *BusinessWeek*, November 19, 2007, pp. 31, 32. The history is found at Charles Gasparino, "Ghosts of E-Mails Continue to Haunt Wall Street," *Wall Street Journal*, November 18, 2002, pp. C1, C13; and Charles Gasparino, Anita Raghavan, and Rebecca Blumenstein, "Citigroup Now Has New Worry: What Grubman Will Say," *Wall Street Journal*, October 10, 2002, p. A1.

Case 4.23

Enron: The CFO, Conflicts, and Cooking the Books with Natural Gas and Electricity[499]

Introduction

Enron Corp. was an energy company that was incorporated in Oregon in 1985, with its principal executive offices located in Houston, Texas. By the end of 2001, Enron Corp. was the world's largest energy company, holding 25% of all of the world's energy trading contracts.[500] Enron's own public relations materials described it as "one of the world's leading electricity, natural gas, and communications companies" that "markets electricity and natural gas, delivers physical commodities and financial and risk management services to companies around the world, and has developed an intelligent network platform to facilitate online business."[501] Enron was also one of the world's most admired corporations, holding a consistent place in *Fortune* magazine's 100 best companies to work for. The sign in the lobby of Enron's headquarters read, "WORLD'S LEADING COMPANY."[502]

On the wall in Enron's lobby at its Houston headquarters were the company's values: Integrity, Communication, Respect, Excellence. Employees at Enron's headquarters had access to an on-site health club, subsidized Starbucks coffee, concierge service that included massages, and car washes, all for free.[503] Those employees with Enron Broadband received free Palm Pilots, free cell phones, and free wireless laptops (unique at that time).[504]

In November 2001, a week following credit agencies' downgrading of its debt to "junk" grade, Enron filed for bankruptcy. Until WorldCom the following year, it was the largest bankruptcy ($62 billion) in the history of the United States.[505] Since then, it has dropped and is now just one among the 10 largest bankruptcies in the history of the United States.

Background on Enron

Enron began as the merger of two gas pipelines, Houston Natural Gas and Internorth, orchestrated by Kenneth Lay, emerged as an energy trading company. Poised to ride the wave of deregulation of electricity, Enron would be a power supplier to utilities. It would trade in energy and offer electricity for sale around the country by locking in supply contracts at fixed prices and then hedging on those contracts in other markets.

There are few who dispute that its strategic plan at the beginning showed great foresight and that its timing for market entry was impeccable. It was the first mover in this market and enjoyed phenomenal growth. It became the largest energy trader in the world, with $40 billion in revenue in 1998, $60 billion in 1999, and $101 billion in 2000. Its internal strategy was to grow revenue by 15% per year.[506]

When Enron rolled out its online trading of energy as a commodity, it was as if there had been a Wall Street created for energy contracts. Enron itself had 1,800 contracts in that online market. It had really created a market for weather futures so that utilities could be insulated by swings in the weather and the resulting impact on the prices of power. It virtually controlled the energy market in the United States. By December 2000, Enron's shares were selling for $85 each. Its employees had their 401(k)s heavily invested in Enron stock, and the company had a matching program in which it contributed additional shares of stock to savings and retirement plans when employees chose to fund them with Enron stock.

When competition began to heat up in energy trading, Enron began some diversification activities that proved to be disasters in terms of producing earnings. It acquired a water business that collapsed nearly instantaneously. It also had some international investments that had gone south, particularly power plants in Brazil and India.

(continued)

---

[499]Adapted from Marianne M. Jennings, "A Primer on ENRON: Lessons from a Perfect Storm of Financial Reporting, Corporate Governance and Ethical Culture Failures," 39 *California Western Law Review* 163 (2003).

[500]Noelle Knox, "Enron to Fire 4,000 from Headquarters," *USA Today*, December 4, 2001, p. 1B.

[501]From the class action complaint filed in the Southern District of Texas, *Kaufman v. Enron*, 761 F. Supp.2d 504 (S.D. Tex. 2011).

[502]Bethany McClean, "Why Enron Went Bust," *Fortune*, December 24, 2001, pp. 59–72.

[503]Alexei Barrionuevo, "Jobless in a Flash, Enron's Ex-Employees Are Stunned, Bitter, Ashamed," *Wall Street Journal*, December 11, 2001, pp. B1, B12.

[504]*Id.*

[505]Richard A. Oppel Jr. and Riva D. Atlas, "Hobbled Enron Tries to Stay on Its Feet," *New York Times*, December 4, 2001, pp. C1, C8.

[506]"Why John Olson Wasn't Bullish on Enron," http://knowledge.Wharton.upenn.edu/013002_ss3. Accessed July 28, 2010.

Case 4.23

(continued)

Its $1 billion investment in a 2,184-megawatt power plant in India was in ongoing disputes as its political and regulatory relations in that country had deteriorated, and the state utility stopped paying its bills for the power.[507]

In 1999, Enron announced its foray into fiber optics and the broadband market. Enron over-anticipated the market in this area and experienced substantial losses related to the expansion of its broadband market. Like Corning and other companies that overbuilt, Enron began bleeding quickly from losses related to this diversification.[508]

The Financial Reporting Issues

Mark-to-Market Accounting

Enron followed FASB's rules for energy traders, which permit such companies to include in current earnings those profits they expect to earn on energy contracts and related derivative estimates.[509] The result is that many energy companies had been posting earnings, quite substantial, for noncash gains that they expected to realize some time in the future. Known as *mark-to-market accounting*, energy companies and other industries utilize a financial reporting tool intended to provide insight into the true value of the company through a matching of contracts to market price in commodities with price fluctuations. However, those mark-to-market earnings are based on assumptions. An example helps to illustrate the wild differences that might occur when values are placed on these energy contracts that are marked to the market price. Suppose that an energy company has a contract to sell gas for $2.00 per gallon, with the contract to begin in 2004 and run through 2014. If the price of gas in 2007 is $1.80 per gallon, then the value of that contract can be booked accordingly and handsomely, with a showing of a 20% profit margin. However, suppose that the price of gasoline then climbs to $2.20 per gallon during 2008. What is the manager's resolution and reconciliation in the financial statement of this change in price? The company has a 10-year commitment to sell gas at a price that will

produce losses. Likewise, suppose that the price of gas declines further to $0.50 per gallon in 2008. How is this change reflected in the financial statements, or does the company leave the value as it was originally booked in 2007? And how much of the contract is booked into the present year? And what is its value presently?

The difficulty with mark-to-market accounting is that the numbers that the energy companies carry for earnings on these future contracts are subjective. The numbers they carry depend upon assumptions about market factors. Those assumptions used in computing future earnings booked in the present are not revealed in the financial reports, and investors have no way of knowing the validity of those assumptions or even whether they are conservative or aggressive assumptions about energy market expectations. It becomes difficult for investors to cross-compare financial statements of energy companies because they are unable to compare what are apples and oranges in terms of earnings because of the futuristic nature of the income and the possibility that those figures may never come to fruition.

For example, the unrealized gains portion of Enron's pretax profit for 2000 was about 50% of the total $1.41 billion profit originally reported. That amount was one-third in 1999.

This practice of mark-to-market accounting proved to be particularly hazardous for Enron management because their bonuses and performance ratings were tied to meeting earnings goals. The result was that their judgment on the fair value of these energy contracts, some as long as 20 years into the future, was greatly biased in favor of present recognition of substantial value.[510] The value of these contracts is dependent upon assumptions and variables that are not discussed in the financial statements, are not readily available to investors and shareholders, and include wild cards such as the weather, the price of natural gas, and market conditions in general. One analyst has noted, "Whenever there's a considerable amount of discretion that companies have in reporting their earnings, one gets concerned that some companies may overstate those earnings in certain situations where

(continued)

[507]Saritha Rai, "New Doubts on Enron's India Investment," *New York Times*, November 21, 2001, p. W1.

[508]Complaint, class action litigation, November 2001, *In re Enron Corp. Securities, Derivatives, & ERISA Litigation*, 761 F. Supp. 2d 504 (S.D. Tex. 2011).

[509]Jonathan Weil, "After Enron, 'Mark to Market' Accounting Gets Scrutiny," *Wall Street Journal*, December 4, 2001, pp. C1, C2.

[510]Susan Lee, "Enron's Success Story," *Wall Street Journal*, December 26, 2001, p. A11.

Case 4.23

(continued)

they feel pressure to make earnings goals."[511] A FASB study showed that when a hypothetical example on energy contracts was given at a conference, the valuations by managers for the contracts ranged from $40 million to $153 million.[512]

Some analysts were concerned about this method of accounting because these are noncash earnings. Some noted that Enron's noncash earnings were over 50% of its revenues. Others discovered the same issues when they noted that Enron's margins and cash flow did not match up with its phenomenal earnings records.[513] For example, Jim Chanos, of Kynikos Associates, commented that no one was sure how Enron made money and that its operating margins were very low for the reported revenue. Mr. Chanos concluded that Enron was a "giant hedge fund sitting on top of a pipeline."[514] Mr. Chanos noted that Wall Street loved Enron because it consistently met targets, but he was skeptical because of off-the-balance sheet transactions (see below for more information).[515] Mr. Chanos and others who brought questions to Enron were readily dismissed. For example, *Fortune* reporter Bethany McClean experienced pressure in 2000 when she began asking questions about the revenues and margins. Then-chairman and now the late Ken Lay, called her editor to request that she be removed from the story. Enron's CEO at the time, Jeffrey Skilling, refused to answer her questions and labeled her line of inquiry as "unethical."[516] During an analysts' telephonic

conference with Mr. Skilling in which Mr. Chanos asked why Enron had not provided a balance sheet, Mr. Skilling called Mr. Chanos an "a—h ___."[517] Mr. Chanos opted for selling Enron shares short and declined to disclose the amount of money he made as a result of his position.

John Olson, presently an analyst with a Houston company, reflected that most analysts were unwilling to ask questions. When Mr. Olson asked Mr. Skilling questions about how Enron was making money, Mr. Skilling responded that Enron was part of the new economy and that Olson "didn't get it."[518] Mr. Olson advised his company's clients not to invest in Enron because, as he explained to them, "Never invest in something you can't understand."[519] Mr. Olson was fired by Merrill Lynch following the publication of his skeptical analysis about Enron. Merrill Lynch continues to deny that it fired Mr. Olson for that reason. Enron was a critical client for Merrill Lynch. In fact, Merrill would become known for its role in Andrew Fastow's infamous "Wanna buy a barge?" deal, in which Merrill purchased a barge temporarily from Enron. The purchase permitted Enron to meet its numbers goals, and even the general counsel at Merrill had expressed concern that Merrill might be participating in Enron's earnings management. Four former Merrill investment bankers were indicted and convicted for their roles in the "Wanna buy a barge?" Enron transaction.[520]

All but one of the convictions were reversed on appeal because the investment bankers could not have known the extent of Fastow's frauds or the full scope and meaning of the transaction. The court held that the investment bankers were allowed to rely on the representations of a company's officer and could not be convicted of participating in fraud when an agent of the company arranged the transaction (U.S. v. Brown, 459 F.3d 509 (5th Cir. 2006)). That is, in language that would later become important in reducing Jeffrey Skilling's sentence, they could not be convicted on the basis of honest services fraud. However, there

(continued)

---

[511]*Id.*

[512]Weil, "After Enron, 'Mark to Market' Accounting Gets Scrutiny," p. C2.

[513]McClean, "Why Enron Went Bust," pp. 62–63. Ms. McLean had written a story in the summer of 2001 entitled, "Is Enron Overpriced?" for *Fortune*. The lead line to the story was "How exactly does Enron make its money?" The story was buried. It enjoyed little coverage or attention until November 2001. Ms. McClean quickly became an analyst on the Enron case for NBC and was featured on numerous news shows. Felicity Barringer, "10 Months Ago, Questions on Enron Came and Went with Little Notice," *New York Times*, January 28, 2002, p. A11. Ms. McClean wrote a book with Peter Elkind, *The Smartest Guys in the Room* (2003), which was later made into a successful documentary film.

[514]*Id.*

[515]Cassell Bryan-Low and Suzanne McGee, "Enron Short Seller Detected Red Flags in Regulatory Filings," *Wall Street Journal*, November 5, 2001, pp. C1, C2.

[516]McClean, "Why Enron Went Bust," p. 60.

[517]Bryan-Low and McGee, "Enron Short Seller Detected Red Flags in Regulatory Filings," p. C2.

[518]"Why John Olson Wasn't Bullish on Enron," http://knowledge. Wharton.upenn.edu/013002_ss3. Accessed July 28, 2010.

[519]*Id.*

[520]Kurt Eichenwald, "Jury Convicts 5 Involved in Enron Deal with Merrill," *New York Times*, November 4, 2004, pp. C1, C4.

Case 4.23

(continued)

was a conviction for perjury that was upheld and the four defendants in the case were indicted again with the courts holding that there was no double jeopardy. The back and forth on the verdicts, appeals, and *certiorari* petitions boggles the mind in terms of trying to fathom where the case is and how much the defendants have had to spend on attorney fees,[521] Suffice it to say that the tap-dancing close to the line of legality in this case was costly for all involved, including 19 years of their lives in litigation.

When *U.S. News & World Report* published Mr. Olson's analysis and advice, Kenneth Lay sent Mr. Olson's boss a handwritten note with the following:

> John Olson has been wrong about Enron for over 10 years and is still wrong. But he is consistant [sic].

Upon reading the note sent to his boss, Mr. Olson responded, "You know that I'm old and I'm worthless, but at least I can spell *consistent*."[522]

Off-the-Books Entities

Not only did Enron's books suffer from the problem of mark-to-market accounting but also the company made minimal disclosures about its off-the-balance-sheet liabilities that it was carrying.[523] These problems, coupled with the mark-to-market value of the energy contracts, permitted Enron's financial statements to paint a picture that did not adequately reflect the risk investors had.

Enron had created, by the time it collapsed, about 3,000 off-the-books entities, partnerships, limited partnerships, and limited liability companies (called *special purposes entities*, or SPEs, in the accounting profession) that carried Enron debt and obligations that had been spun off but did not have to be disclosed in Enron's financial reports because, under an accounting rule known as FASB 125, the debt and obligations in off-the-books entities did not have to be disclosed so long as Enron's ownership interests in the entities never exceeded 49%. Disclosure requirements

under GAAP and FASB kicked in at 50% ownership at that time. Under the old rules, when a company owned 50% or more of a company, it had to disclose transactions with that company in the financials as *related party transactions*.

Enron created a complex network of these entities, and some of the officers of the company even served as principals in these companies and began earning commissions for the sale of Enron assets to them. Andrew Fastow, Enron's CFO, was a principal in many of these off-the-book entities. His wife, Lea, also a senior officer at Enron, was also involved in handling many of the SPEs. In some of the SPEs, the two discussed the possibility of having some of the payments come to their two small children.

In 1999, Enron described one of these relationships in its 10K (an annual report companies must file with the SEC) as follows:

> In June 1999, Enron entered into a series of transactions involving a third party and LJM Cayman, L.P. (LJM). LJM is a private investment company, which engages in acquiring or investing in primarily energy-related investments. A senior officer of Enron is the managing member of LJM's general partner.[524]

The effect of these partnerships was to allow Enron to transfer an asset from its books, along with the accompanying debt, to the partnership. An outside investor would fund as little as 3% of the partnership, with Enron occasionally providing even the front money for the investor. Enron would then guarantee the bank loan to the partnership for the purchase of the asset. Enron would pledge shares as collateral for these loans it guaranteed in cases where the bank felt the asset transferred to the partnership was insufficient collateral for the loan amount.[525] By the time it collapsed, Enron had $38 billion in debt among all the various SPEs but carried only $13 billion on its balance sheet.[526]

(continued)

[521]*U.S. v. Brown, et al.*, 459 F.3d 509 (5th Cir. 2006), *cert.* denied, 550 U.S. 933 (2007); 571 F.3d 492 (5th Cir. 2009); *cert.* denied, 558 U.S. 1051 (2009); rehearing denied, 559 U.S. 571 (2010); 650 F.3d 581 (5th Cir. 2011), *cert.* denied, 566 U.S. 970 (2012).

[522]"Why John Olson Wasn't Bullish on Enron."

[523]Richard A. Oppel Jr. and Andrew Ross Sorkin, "Enron Corp. Files Largest U.S. Claim for Bankruptcy," *New York Times*, December 3, 2001, pp. A1, A16.

[524]Enron Corp. 10K, Filed December 31, 1999, p. 16.

[525]John R. Emshwiller and Rebecca Smith, "Murky Waters: A Primer on Enron Partnerships," *Wall Street Journal*, January 21, 2002, pp. C1, C14.

[526]Bethany McLean and Peter Elkind, "Partners in Crime," *Fortune*, October 27, 2003, p. 79.

Case 4.23

(continued)

To add to the complexity of these off-the-books loans and the transfer of Enron debt, many of the entities formed to take the asset and debt were corporations in the Cayman Islands. Enron had 881 such corporations, with 700 formed in the Cayman Islands, and, in addition to transferring the debt off its balance sheet, it enjoyed a substantial number of tax benefits because corporations operate tax-free there. The result is that Enron paid little or no federal income taxes between 1997 and 2000.[527] Comedian Robin Williams referred to Enron executives as "the Investment Pirates of the Caribbean."

Relatives and Doing Business with Enron

In addition to these limited liability company and limited partnership asset transfers, there were apparently a series of transactions authorized by Mr. Lay in which Enron did business with companies owned by Mr. Lay's son, Mark, and his sister, Sharon Lay. Jeffrey Skilling had hired Mark Lay in 1989 when Mark graduated with a degree in economics from UCLA. However, Mr. Lay left Enron feeling that he needed to "stand on his own and work outside of Enron."[528] Enron eventually ended up acquiring Mr. Lay's son's company and hired him as an Enron executive with a guaranteed pay package of $1 million over three years as well as 20,000 stock options for Enron shares.[529] There was a criminal investigation into the activities of one of the companies founded by Mark Lay, but he was not charged with wrongdoing. He did pay $315,000 to settle a civil complaint in the matter but admitted no wrongdoing. Mark Lay entered a Baptist seminary in Houston to become a minister.[530]

Sharon Lay owned a Houston travel agency and received over $10 million in revenue from Enron during the period from 1998 through 2001 years, one-half of her company's revenue during that period.[531] Both Ms. Lay and the late Mr. Lay say that they made all the necessary disclosures to the board and regulators about their business with Enron.

Enron's Demise

Enron's slow and steady decline began in the November–December 2000 time frame, when its share price was at $85. By the time Jeffrey Skilling announced his departure as CEO on August 14, 2001, with no explanation, the share price was at about $43. Mr. Skilling says that he left the company simply to spend more time with his family, but his departure raised questions among analysts even as Kenneth Lay returned as CEO.[532]

The *Wall Street Journal* raised questions about Enron's disclosures on August 28, 2001, as Enron was beginning an aggressive movement for selling off assets.[533] By October, Enron disclosed that it was reporting a third-quarter loss and it took a $1.2 billion reduction in shareholder equity. Within days of those announcements, CFO Andrew Fastow was terminated, and in less than two weeks, Enron restated its earnings dating back to 1997, a $586 million, or 20%, reduction.

Following these disclosures and the announcement of Enron's liability on a previously undisclosed $690 million loan, CEO Kenneth Lay left the company as CEO, but remained as chairman of the board.[534] Mr. Lay waived any rights to his parachute, reportedly worth $60 million, and also agreed to repay a $2 million loan from the company.[535] Mr. Lay's wife, Linda, appeared on NBC with correspondent Lisa Meyer on January 28, 2002, and indicated that she and Mr. Lay were "fighting for liquidity."[536] She indicated that all their property was for sale, but a follow-up check by Ms. Meyer found only one of a dozen homes owned by the Lays was for sale. Mr. Lay

(continued)

[527]David Gonzalez, "Enron Footprints Revive Old Image of Caymans," *New York Times*, January 28, 2002, p. A10.

[528]David Barboza and Kurt Eichenwald, "Son and Sister of Enron Chief Secured Deals," *New York Times*, February 2, 2002, pp. A1, B5.

[529]*Id.*

[530]*Id.*

[531]*Id.*

[532]John E. Emshwiller and Rebecca Smith, "Behind Enron's Fall, a Culture of Operating outside Public View," *Wall Street Journal*, December 5, 2001, pp. A1, A10.

[533]John E. Emshwiller, Rebecca Smith, Robin Sidel, and Jonathan Weil, "Enron Cuts Profit Data of 4 Years by 20%," *Wall Street Journal*, November 9, 2001, p. A3.

[534]*Id.*

[535]Richard A. Oppel Jr. and Floyd Norris, "Enron Chief Will Give Up Severance," *New York Times*, November 14, 2001, pp. C1, C10.

[536]Alessandra Stanley and Jim Yardley, "Lay's Family Is Financially Ruined, His Wife Says," *New York Times*, January 29, 2002, pp. C1, C6.

(continued)

consulted privately with the Reverend Jesse Jackson for spiritual advice, according to Mrs. Lay.[537]

The Enron Culture

Enron was a company with a swagger. It had an aggressive culture in which a rating system required that 20% of all employees be rated at below performance and encouraged to leave the company. As a result of this policy, no employee wanted to be the bearer of bad news.

Margaret Ceconi, an employee with Enron Energy Services, wrote a five-page memo to Kenneth Lay on August 28, 2001, stating that losses from Enron Energy Services were being moved to another sector in Enron in order to make the Energy Service arm look profitable. One line from her memo read, "Some would say the house of cards are falling."[538] Mr. Lay did not meet with Ms. Ceconi, but she was contacted by Enron Human Resources and counseled on employee morale. When she raised the accounting issues in her meeting with HR managers, she was told they would be investigated and taken very seriously, but she was never contacted by anyone about her memo. Her memo remained dormant until January 2002, when she sent it to the U.S. House of Representatives' Committee on Energy and Commerce, the body conducting a series of hearings on the Enron collapse.

Ms. Ceconi's memo followed two weeks after Sherron Watkins, a former executive, wrote of her concerns about "accounting scandals" at Enron. Ms. Watkins was a former Andersen employee who had been hired into the executive ranks by Enron. Ms. Watkins wrote a letter to Kenneth Lay on August 15, 2001, that included the following:

> I am incredibly nervous that we will implode in a wave of accounting scandals. I have heard from one manager-level employee from the principal investments group say, 'I know it would be devastating to all of us, but I wish we would get caught. We're such a crooked company.'[539]

She also warned that Mr. Skilling's swift departure would raise questions about accounting improprieties and

stated, "It sure looks to the layman on the street that we are hiding losses in a related company."[540]

In her memo, she listed J. Clifford Baxter as someone Mr. Lay could talk to in order to verify her facts and affirmed that her concerns about the company were legitimate. Ms. Watkins wrote the memo anonymously on August 15, 2001, but by August 22, and after discussing the memo with former colleagues at Andersen, she told her bosses that she was the one who had written the memo.

In the months prior to Enron's collapse, employees became suspicious about what was called "aggressive accounting" and voiced their concerns in online chat rooms.[541] Clayton Verdon was fired in November 2001 for his comments about "overstating profits," made in an employee chat room. A second employee was fired when he revealed in the chat room that the company had paid $55 million in bonuses to executives on the eve of its bankruptcy.[542] Enron indicated that the terminations were necessary because the employees had breached company security.

In his testimony at the trial of his former bosses, Ken Lay and Jeffrey Skilling, former CFO Andrew Fastow offered some insights into the culture at Enron and the tone he set as a senior executive. Andrew Fastow, when confronted by Daniel Petrocelli, lawyer for Jeffrey Skilling, about his clear wrongdoing, offered the following: "Within the culture of corruption that Enron had, that valued financial reporting rather than economic value, I believed I was being a hero."[543] He went on to add, "I thought I was being a hero for Enron. At the time, I thought I was helping myself and helping Enron to make its numbers."[544] He explained further, "At Enron, the culture was and the business practice was to do transactions that maximized the financial reporting earnings as opposed to maximizing the true economic value of the transactions."[545] However, Mr. Fastow said he did see the writing on the wall near

(continued)

[537]Id.

[538]Julie Mason, "Concerned Ex-Worker Was Sent to Human Resources," *Houston Chronicle*, January 30, 2002, www.chron.com.

[539]Michael Duffy, "What Did They Know and When Did They Know It?" *Time*, January 28, 2002, pp. 16–27.

[540]Id.

[541]Alex Berenson, "Enron Fired Workers for Complaining Online," *New York Times*, January 21, 2002, pp. C1, C8.

[542]Id.

[543]March 8, 2006, trial testimony of Andrew Fastow, in Greg Farrell, "Fastow 'Juiced' Books," *USA Today*, March 8, 2006, p. 1A.

[544]Id.

[545]Farrell, "Fastow 'Juiced' Books," p. 1A.

Case 4.23

(continued)

the end and encouraged others to reveal the true financial picture at Enron: "We have to open up the kimono and show them the skeletons in the closet, what our assets are really worth."[546]

The Enron Board

Some institutional investors have raised questions about conflicts and the lack of independence in Enron's board.[547] Members of Enron's board were well compensated with a total of $380,619 paid to each director in cash and stock for 2001. One member of the board was Dr. Wendy L. Gramm, the former chairwoman of the Commodity Futures Trading Commission and wife of Senator Phil Gramm, the senior U.S. senator from Texas, who has received campaign donations from Enron employees and its PAC. Dr. Gramm opted to own no Enron stock and accepted payment for her board service only in a deferred compensation account.

Dr. John Mendelsohn, the president of the University of Texas M. D. Anderson Cancer Center in Houston, also served on the Enron board, including its audit committee. Dr. Mendelsohn's center received $92,508 from Enron and $240,250 from Linda and Ken Lay after Dr. Mendelsohn joined the Enron board in 1999.[548]

After the Fall

Enron had fired 5,100 of its 7,500 employees by December 3, 2001. Each employee received a $4,500 severance package. However, many of the employees were looking forward to a comfortable retirement, basing that assumption on the value of their Enron stock. Many held Enron stock and were compensated with Enron stock options. The stock was trading at $0.40 per share on December 3, 2001, following a high of $90 at its peak. Employee pension funds lost $2 billion. Enron employees' 401(k) plans, funded with Enron stock, lost $1.2 billion in 2001.

"Almost everyone is gone. Upper management is not talking. No managing directors are around, and police are on every floor. It's so unreal," said one departing employee.[549] One employee, George Kemper, a maintenance foreman, who is part of a suit filed against Enron related to the employees' 401(k) plans, whose plan was once worth $225,000 and is now worth less than $10,000, said, "How am I going to retire now? Everything I worked for the past 25 years has been wiped out."[550] The auditors have admitted that they simply cannot make sense of the company's books for 2001 but have concluded that the cash flow of $3 billion claimed for 2000 was actually a negative $153 million and that the profits of $1 billion reported in 2000 did not exist.[551]

Just prior to declaring bankruptcy, Enron paid $55 million in bonuses to executives described as "retention executives," or those the company needs to stay on board in order to continue operations.[552]

Tragically, J. Clifford Baxter, a former Enron vice chairman, and the one officer Ms. Watkins suggested Mr. Lay talk with, took his own life in his 2002 Mercedes Benz about a mile from his $700,000 home in Sugar Land, Texas, a suburb 25 miles from Houston. Mr. Baxter, who earned his MBA at Columbia, had left Enron in May 2001, following what some employees say was his voicing of concerns over the accounting practices of Enron and its disclosures.[553] SEC records disclose that Mr. Baxter sold 577,000 shares of Enron stock for $35.2 million between October 1998 and early 2001.[554]

He had been asked to appear before Congress to testify, was a defendant in all the pending litigation, and was last seen in public at his yacht club, where he took his yacht

(continued)

---

[546]Alexei Barrionuevo, "Ex-Enron Official Insists Chief Knew He Was Lying," *New York Times*, March 2, 2006, p. C3. (Mixed metaphors aside.)

[547]Reed Abelson, "Enron Board Comes under a Storm of Criticism," *New York Times*, December 16, 2001, p. BU4.

[548]Jo Thomas and Reed Abelson, "How a Top Medical Researcher Became Entangled with Enron," *New York Times*, January 28, 2002, pp. C1, C2.

[549]Richard A. Oppel Jr. and Riva D. Atlas, "Hobbled Enron Tries to Stay on Its Feet," *New York Times*, December 4, 2001, pp. C1, C8.

[550]Christine Dugas, "Enron Workers Sue over Retirement Plan," *USA Today*, November 27, 2001, p. 5B.

[551]Cathy Booth Thomas, "The Enron Effect," *Time*, June 5, 2006, pp. 34–36.

[552]Richard A. Oppel Jr. and Kurt Eichenwald, "Enron Paid $55 Million for Bonuses," *New York Times*, December 4, 2001, pp. C1, C4.

[553]Elissa Gootman, "Hometown Remembers Man Who Wore Success Quietly," *New York Times*, January 30, 2002, p. C7.

[554]Mark Babineck, "Deceased Enron Executive Earned Respect in the Ranks," *Houston Chronicle*, January 26, 2002, http://www.chron.com.

Case 4.23

(continued)

out for a sail. Those who saw him indicated that his hair had become substantially grayer since October, when the public disclosures about Enron's condition began. Mr. Baxter was depicted as a philanthropist in the Houston area, having raised money for charities such as Junior Achievement and other organizations to benefit children. He had created the Baxter Foundation with $200,000 from Enron and $20,000 of his own money to assist charities such as Junior Achievement, the American Cancer Society, and the American Diabetes Association.[555]

As noted, Enron had a matching plan for its employees on the 401(k). However, 60% of their plan was invested in Enron stock. Between October 17 and November 19, 2001, when the issues surrounding Enron's accounting practices and related transactions began to surface, the company put a lockdown on the plan so that employees could not sell their shares.[556] Prior to the lockdown, most of the executives had sold off large blocks of Enron stock. For example, Jeffrey Skilling, who left the company in August 2001, sold off 500,000 shares on September 17, 2001.[557] He had sold 240,000 shares in early 2001 and at the time of Enron's bankruptcy owned 600,000 shares and an undisclosed number of options.[558] Mr. Lay also sold a substantial amount of stock in August 2001, but his lawyer had indicated the sale of the stock was necessary in order to repay loans.[559]

In addition to the impact on Enron, its employees, and Houston, there was a worldwide ripple effect. Enron had large stakes in natural gas pipelines in the United States and around the world as well as interests in power plants everywhere from Latin America to Venezuela. Enron was also a partial owner of utilities, including telecommunications networks. Congressional hearings were held as the House Energy and Commerce Committee investigated the company's collapse. Representative Billy Tauzin of Louisiana scheduled the investigations and noted, "How a company can sink

so far, so fast, is very troubling. We need to find out if the company's accounting practices masked severe underlying financial problems."[560] Senator Jeff Bingham, then-chairman of the Senate Energy Committee, said, "I believe that our committee is keenly aware of the need for enhanced oversight and market monitoring."[561]

Enron's bankruptcy filing included a list of creditors 54 pages long. Although the bankruptcy filing showed $24.76 billion in assets and $13.15 billion in debt, these figures did not include those off-the-balance sheet obligations, estimated to be about $27 billion.[562]

Enron energy customers, which included PepsiCo, the California State university system, JCPenney, Owens-Illinois, and Starwood Hotels & Resorts, also felt the effects of the company's collapse. Enron had contracts with 28,500 customers. These customers had to revise their contracts and scramble to put energy contingency plans in place. California's state universities were in negotiations for renewal of their 1998 contract with Enron, but those talks went into a stalemate, and the university system found another provider.[563]

Trammell Crow halted the groundbreaking ceremony for its planned construction of new Enron headquarters, a building that would have been 50 stories high and included offices, apartments, and stores.[564]

The ripple effect stretched into unrelated investments. Five major Japanese money market funds with heavy Enron investments had fallen below their face value by December 3, 2001.[565] These losses had additional consumer-level effects because these funds were held by retirees because they were seen as "safe haven" funds for investors.

(continued)

---

[555]*Id.*

[556]*Id.*

[557]Richard A. Oppel Jr., "Former Head of Enron Denies Wrongdoing," *New York Times*, December 22, 2001, pp. C1, C2.

[558]*Id.*

[559]Richard A. Oppel Jr., "Enron Chief Says His Sale of Stock Was to Pay Loans," *New York Times*, January 21, 2002, pp. A1, A13.

[560]Richard A. Oppel Jr. and Andrew Ross Sorkin, "Ripples Spreading from Enron's Expected Bankruptcy," *New York Times*, November 30, 2001, pp. C1, C6, C7.

[561]"Financial Threat from Enron Failure Continues to Widen," *Financial Times*, December 1, 2001, p. 1.

[562]Rebecca Smith and Mitchell Pacelle, "Enron Files for Chapter 11 Bankruptcy, Sues Dynegy," *Wall Street Journal*, December 3, 2001, p. A2.

[563]Rhonda L. Rundle, "Enron Customers Seek Backup Suppliers," *Wall Street Journal*, December 3, 2001, p. A10.

[564]Allen R. Myerson, "With Enron's Fall, Many Dominoes Tremble," *New York Times*, December 2, 2001, pp. 3–1, MB1.

[565]Ken Belson, "Enron Causes 5 Major Japanese Money Market Funds to Plunge," *New York Times*, December 4, 2001, p. C9.

Case 4.23

(continued)

Person	Title	Charges	Disposition
Ken Lay	Chairman, CEO	Securities fraud	Convicted; conviction reversed following Mr. Lay's untimely death on July 5, 2006, one month after his conviction.
		Wire fraud	Same as above.
Jeffrey Skilling	CEO	Securities fraud	Convicted on all but two counts; sentenced to 24.4 years, but a 2010 U.S. Supreme Court decision (*U.S. v. Skilling* 561 U.S. 358) on honest services fraud remanded the case after reversing his conviction for honest services fraud because he had not engaged in bribery (required for proof of honest services fraud). Mr. Skilling's sentence was reduced to 14 years and he was released from prison after 12 years in 2019.
		Wire fraud	Same as above.
Andrew Fastow	CFO	Securities fraud	Guilty plea; six years (released in four because of his extensive cooperation in the criminal trials of Skilling and Lay as well as the civil suits). Provides litigation support to a law firm and consults with companies
		Wire fraud	Guilty plea.
		Tax evasion	Guilty plea.
Lea Fastow	Senior Officer	Tax evasion	Guilty plea; one year; served (ended with last month in halfway house in July 2005) her term first so that Andrew Fastow could be at home with their two young children before he began his term in 2006.
David Delainey	CEO, Enron North America	Insider trading	Guilty plea; served slightly over one year.
Ben Glisan	Treasurer	Conspiracy	Guilty plea; five years.
Richard Causey	Chief Accounting Officer	Insider trading	Guilty plea to one count of securities fraud in exchange for seven-year sentence recommendation and cooperation with federal prosecutors on Skilling and Lay case.[566] He was sentenced to 5.5 years.
Michael J. Kopper	Officer who worked directly with Fastow	Fraud	Guilty plea to money laundering and conspiracy to commit wire fraud; sentenced to three years and one month.
Kenneth D. Rice	CEO, Enron Broadband		Guilty plea to one count. 27 months in prison; $15 million forfeiture.
Mark Koenig	Vice president of investor relations		Guilty plea to one count of aiding and abetting securities fraud; 18 months.

Note: Thirty-two Enron executives were indicted in total, with guilty pleas or convictions for all. Mr. Lay was the last Enron official indicted, in July 2004.

(continued)

[566]John Emshwiller, "Enron Prosecutors, After Plea Bargain, Can Reduce Technical Jargon at Trial," *Wall Street Journal*, January 4, 2006, pp. C1, C2.

Case 4.23

(continued)

The Enron board hired Stephen F. Cooper as CEO to replace Mr. Lay. Mr. Cooper is a specialist in leading companies through bankruptcy, including TWA and Federated Department Stores.[567]

Enron's collapse ended the movement toward the deregulation of electricity. Following Enron's collapse, federal and state regulators saw the impact on consumers of allowing energy companies to operate in a regulatory no-man's land, and the states moved back to the model of price regulation of the sale of energy to consumers.[568]

The SEC, a national team of lawyers, and the Justice Department began a six-year investigation of the company, its conduct, and it officers.[569] The civil shareholder suit ended with a $72 billion settlement, and the employees received $85 million. The suits by shareholders against various banks were dismissed. In the bankruptcy, Enron's creditors received 18.3 cents on the dollar, an amount far below the normal payout in a bankruptcy.[570]

Many noted at the time of Enron's collapse that "evidence of fraud may well be elusive" as the SEC and prosecutors investigate.[571] Professor Douglas Carmichael, a professor of accounting at Baruch College, is one who agrees: "It's conceivable that they complied with the rules. Absent a smoking-gun e-mail or something similar, it is an issue of trying to attack the reasonableness of their assumptions."[572] One auditor said that it never occurred to him that anyone would "use models to try and forecast energy prices for 10 years, and then use those models to report profits, but that the rule had not placed a limit

on such trades."[573] When asked about the accounting practices of Enron, Mr. Skilling said, "We are doing God's work. We are on the side of angels."[574]

Mr. Skilling and Mr. Lay were tried in a case that ran from February to June 2006. They were both convicted following six days of deliberations by the jurors. Mr. Fastow was the government's key witness against the two men. Both men took the stand as part of their defense, and both men got angry on the stand when faced with cross-examination. Mr. Lay was convicted on all counts. Mr. Skilling was convicted on 18 of 27 counts, Mr. Lay died of a massive heart attack on July 5, 2006, while at his Colorado vacation home.[575] His conviction was set aside because he had not had the opportunity to appeal the verdict. One comment on his passing was "His death was a cop-out."[576] A former Enron employee told the *Houston Chronicle*, "Glad he's dead. May he burn in hell. I'll dance on his grave."[577]

Mr. Skilling was resentenced following a U.S. Supreme Court reversal of his "honest services" fraud conviction.[578] He was resentenced to 168 months or 14 years as part of a negotiation with the Justice Department that also settled civil suits against Mr. Skilling with his agreement to forfeit $42 million in assets to compensate plaintiffs in their civil suits against Enron and its officers. Mr. Skilling was released from prison in 2019 after serving 12 years, the longest of the 21 defendants charged in Enron's collapse. Mr. Petrocelli was paid $23 million from a trust fund Mr. Skilling had set aside for his defense, and Enron's insurer paid $17 million to Mr. Petrocelli's firm of O'Melveny and Myers, for a total of $40 million. However, the firm and Mr. Petrocelli are still owed $30 million for their defense work, an amount Mr. Skilling is unable to pay.[579]

(continued)

[567]Shaila K. Dewan and Jennifer Lee, "Enron Names an Interim Chief to Oversee Its Bankruptcy," *New York Times*, January 30, 2002, p. C7.

[568]Rebecca Smith, "Enron Continues to Haunt the Energy Industry," *Wall Street Journal*, March 16, 2006, p. C1; and Joseph Kahn and Jeff Gerth, "Collapse May Reshape the Battlefield of Deregulation," *New York Times*, December 4, 2001, pp. C1, C8.

[569]Jo Thomas, "A Specialist in Tough Cases Steps into the Legal Tangle," *New York Times*, January 21, 2002, p. C8.

[570]Mitchell Pacelle, "Enron's Creditors to Get Peanuts," *Wall Street Journal*, July 11, 2003, pp. C1, C7.

[571]Floyd Norris and Kurt Eichenwald, "Fuzzy Rules of Accounting and Enron," *New York Times*, January 30, 2002, pp. C1, C6.

[572]Id.

[573]Id.

[574]Neil Weinberg and Daniel Fisher, "Power Player," *Forbes*, December 24, 2001, pp. 53–58.

[575]Bethany McClean and Peter Elkind, "Death of a Disgraced Energy Salesman," *Fortune*, July 30, 2006, pp. 3–32.

[576]Id.

[577]Id.

[578]*Skilling v. U.S.*, 561 U.S. 358 (2010). Conviction affirmed, *U.S. v. Skilling*, 638 F.3d 480 (5th Cir. 2011).

[579]Carrie Johnson, "After Enron Trial, Defense Firm Is Stuck with the Tab," *Washington Post*, June 16, 2006, pp. D1, D3.

Case 4.23

(continued)

Discussion Questions

1. Can you see that Enron broke any laws? Andrew Fastow testified at the Lay and Skilling trial as follows: "A significant number of senior management participated in this activity to misrepresent our company. And we all benefited financially from this at the expense of others. And I have come to grips with this. That, in my mind, was stealing."[580] Is Mr. Fastow correct? Was it stealing? How should Fastow's' relationships with Enron's partially owned subsidiaries have been handled in terms of disclosure.

2. Do you think that Enron's financial reports gave a false impression? Does it matter that most investors in Enron were relatively sophisticated financial institutions? What about the employees' ownership of stock and their 401(k) plans?

3. What questions could the officers of Enron have used to evaluate the wisdom and ethics of their decisions on the off-the-book entities and mark-to-market accounting? Be sure to apply the various models you have learned.

4. Did Mr. Fastow have a conflict of interest?

5. What elements for your personal credo can you take away from the following testimony from David Delainey and Andrew Fastow? As you think about this question, consider the following from their testimony at the Skilling and Lay trial.

   When asked why he did not raise the issue or simply walk away, Mr. Delainey responded, "I wish on my kids' lives I would have stepped up and walked away from the table that day."[581] Mr. Fastow had the following exchange with Daniel Petrocelli, Mr. Skilling's lawyer (Mr. Petrocelli represented the Brown and Goldman families in their civil suit against O. J. Simpson):

   | Petrocelli: | To do those things, you must be consumed with insatiable greed. Is that fair to say? |
   | Fastow: | I believe I was very greedy and that I lost my moral compass.[582] |

   Fastow also testified as follows: "My actions caused my wife to go to prison."[583] Defense attorneys, being the capable souls that they are, extracted even more: "I feel like I've taken a lot of blame for Enron these past few days. It's not relevant to me whether Mr. Skilling's or Mr. Lay's names are on that page. . . . I'm ashamed of the past. What they write about the past I can't affect. I want to focus on the future. Even after being caught, it took me awhile to come to grips with what I'd done. . . . I've destroyed my life. All I can do is ask for forgiveness and be the best person I can be."[584] Mr. Fastow also said, "I have asked my family, my friends, and my community for forgiveness. I've agreed to pay a terrible penalty for it. It's an awful thing that I did, and it's shameful. But I wasn't thinking that at the time."[585]

   Mr. Fastow has quoted Herman Melville's *Moby Dick* as to why Ishmael let himself be dragged into the doomed ship by Captain Ahab as a way of explaining what he did and for so long. "Ishmael said, 'But when a man suspects any wrong, it sometimes happens that if he be already involved in the matter, he insensibly strives to cover up his suspicions even from himself. And much this way it was with me. I said nothing, and tried to think nothing.'" What does he mean by this quote? Apply one of the categories of ethical personalities to his behavior. Amoral technician? Were there industry issues in accounting at that time that were driving behaviors?

6. Was Ms. Watkins a whistleblower? Discuss the timing of her disclosures. Compare and contrast her behavior with Paula Reiker's. Paula H. Reiker, the former manager of investor relations for Enron, was paid $5 million between 2000 and 2001. She testified that she was aware during teleconferences that the numbers being reported were inaccurate. Upon cross-examination she was asked why she didn't speak up, as Mr. Petrocelli queried, "Why didn't you just quit?" Her response: "I considered it on a number of occasions. I was very well compensated. I didn't have the nerve to quit."[586] Did she make the right decision?

[580]Alexei Barrionuevo, "Fastow Testifies Lay Knew of Enron's Problems," *New York Times*, March 9, 2006, pp. C1, C4.

[581]*Id.*

[582]John Emshwiller and Gary McWilliams, "Fastow Is Grilled at Enron Trial," *Wall Street Journal*, March 9, 2006, pp. C1, C4.

[583]*Id.*

[584]Greg Farrell, "Defense Goes after Fastow's 'Greed' with a Vengeance," *USA Today*, March 9, 2006, p. 1; and Alexei Barrionuevo, "Fastow Testifies Lay Knew of Enron's Problems," *New York Times*, March 9, 2006, pp. C1, C4.

[585]Alexei Barrionuevo, "The Courtroom Showdown, Played as Greek Tragedy," *New York Times*, March 12, 2006, pp. 1, 3.

[586]Alexei Barrionuevo, "Enron Defense Chips Away at Witness's Motives," *New York Times*, February 24, 2006, p. C3.

Compare & Contrast

1. Consider the revelations from the testimony of David W. Delainey at the Skilling and Lay criminal trial. Mr. Delainey, the former head of Enron Energy Services retail unit, testified that he saw the legal and ethical issues unfolding as he worked for Enron. When he was asked to transfer $200 million in losses from his unit to another division in order to then show a profit, he testified, "That was the worst conduct I had ever been a part of and everybody knew exactly what was going on at that meeting."[587]
Now compare and contrast his decisions and actions with those of Mr. Olson and Merrill Lynch.

2. Experts have commented that one of the reasons for the success of the Enron task force is that it worked its way up through employees in the company. That is, it got plea agreements and information from lower-level employees and then used the information to go after higher-ranking officers in the company. For example, Mr. Fastow was facing over 180 years in prison if convicted of all the charges in his indictment. He agreed to turn state's evidence in exchange for a recommendation of a prison sentence of 11 years. He did such a good job in testifying against Mr. Skilling and Mr. Lay that the judge sentenced him to only four years. He was released from prison in 2011, served supervised probation until December 2013, and was then released, having served his complete sentence. Mr. Skilling, on the other hand, was sentenced to 24.4 years (later reduced, as discussed above). What is the moral of this story? What can we learn about our role as employees? As officers? When asked to comment about the reduction in Mr. Skilling's sentence, Mr. Fastow noted that 14 years (Mr. Skilling's original sentence) is still a very long time.

3. At a speech to the Association of Certified Fraud Examiners in June 2013, Mr. Fastow said, "I'm here because I'm guilty, and this is a much different place than I thought I would be when I was named CFO of the year in 2000."[588] He then added, "I did not embezzle, avoid taxes or do any sort of insider trading. What I am guilty of is creating financial structures that made Enron look better to the public than it actually was. Accounting rules can be vague and we at Enron viewed that vagueness as an opportunity."[589] Was he operating in gray areas? Was Merrill Lynch operating in gray areas? Are there any inconsistencies in the two statements?

---

[587]Alexei Barrionuevo, "Ex-Enron Official Insists Chief Knew He Was Lying," *New York Times*, March 2, 2006, p. C3.

[588]Walter Pavlo, "Former Enron CFO Andrew Fastow Speaks at ACFE Annual Conference," *Forbes*, June 26, 2013, http://www.forbes.com/sites/walterpavlo/2013/06/26/fmr-enron-cfo-andrew-fastow-speaks-at-acfe-annual-conference/. Accessed August 31, 2013.

[589]Id.

Case 4.24

Arthur Andersen: A Fallen Giant[590]

Arthur Andersen, once known as the "gold standard of auditing," was founded in Chicago in 1913 on a legend of integrity as Andersen, Delaney & Co. In those early years, when the business was struggling, Arthur Andersen was approached by a well-known railway company about audit work. When the audit was complete, the company CEO was outraged over the results and asked Andersen to change the numbers or lose his only major client. A 28-year-old Andersen responded, "There's not enough money in the city of Chicago to induce me to change that report!" Months later, the railway filed for bankruptcy.[591]

Over the years Andersen evolved into a multiservice company of management consultants, audit services, information systems, and virtually all aspects of operations and financial reporting. Ultimately, Andersen would serve as auditor for Enron, WorldCom, Waste Management, Sunbeam, and the Baptist Foundation, several of the largest bankruptcies of the century as well as poster companies for the corporate governance and audit reforms of the Sarbanes–Oxley. However, it would be Andersen's relationship with Enron that would be its downfall.

Andersen served as Enron's outside auditor, and the following information regarding various conflicts of interest became public both through journalistic investigations and via the Senate hearings held upon Enron's declaration of bankruptcy:[592]

- Andersen earned over one-half ($27 million) of its $52 million in annual fees from consulting services furnished to Enron.[593]

- There was a fluid atmosphere of transfers back and forth between those working for Andersen doing Enron consulting or audit work and those working for Enron who went with Andersen.[594]

David Duncan, the audit partner in the Houston offices of Andersen who was in charge of the Enron account, was a close personal friend of Richard Causey, Enron's chief accounting officer, who had the ultimate responsibility for signing off on all of CFO Andrew Fastow's off-the-books entities.[595] The two men traveled, golfed, and fished together.[596] Employees of both Andersen and Enron have indicated since the time of their companies' collapses that the two firms were so closely connected that they were often not sure who worked for which firm. Many Andersen employees had permanent offices at Enron, including Mr. Duncan. Office decorum thus found Enron employees arranging in-office birthday celebrations for Andersen auditors so as to be certain not to offend anyone. In addition, there was a fluid line between Andersen employment and Enron employment, with auditors joining Enron on a regular basis. For example, in 2000, seven Andersen auditors joined Enron.[597]

Andersen's Imprimatur for Enron Accounting

Enron's executives and internal accountants and the Andersen auditors resorted to two discretionary accounting areas, special purposes entities (SPEs) and mark-to-market accounting, for booking the revenues from its substantial energy contracts, approximately 25% of all the existing energy contracts in the United States by 2001.[598] Their use

(continued)

---

[590]Adapted with permission from Marianne M. Jennings, "A Primer on Enron: Lessons from a Perfect Storm of Financial Reporting, Corporate Governance, and Ethical Culture Failures," 39 *California Western Law Review* 161 (2003).

[591]Barbara Ley Toffler, *Final Accounting: Ambition, Greed, and the Fall of Arthur Andersen* (2003), p. 12.

[592]"The Role of the Board of Directors in Enron's Collapse," report of the Permanent Subcommittee on Investigations of the Senate Government Affairs Committee, 107th Congress, Report 107–70, July 8, 2002, 39–41 (hereinafter, "PSI Report").

[593]Deborah Solomon, "After Enron, a Push to Limit Accountants to... Accounting," *Wall Street Journal*, January 25, 2002, p. C1.

[594]Seven Andersen audit employees became Enron employees in the year 2000 alone. John Schwartz and Reed Abelson, "Auditor Struck Many as Smart and Upright," *New York Times*, January 17, 2002, p. C11.

[595]Anita Raghavan, "How a Bright Star at Andersen Fell along with Enron," *Wall Street Journal*, May 15, 2002, pp. A1, A8. See also Cathy Booth Thomas and Deborah Fowler, "Will Enron's Auditor Sing?" *Time*, February 11, 2002, p. 44.

[596]Id.

[597]John Schwartz and Reed Abelson, "Auditor Struck Many as Smart and Upright," *New York Times*, January 17, 2002, p. C11.

[598]Noelle Knox, "Enron to Fire 4,000 from Headquarters," *USA Today*, December 4, 2001, p. 1B.

Case 4.24

(continued)

of these discretionary areas allowed them to maintain the appearance of sustained financial performance through 2001. One observer who watched the rise and fall of Enron noted, in reference to Enron but clearly applicable to all of the companies examined here, "If they had been going [at] a slower speed, their results would not have been disastrous. It's a lot harder to keep it on the track at 200 miles per hour. You hit a bump and you're off the track."[599] The earnings from 1997 to 2001 were ultimately restated, with a resulting reduction of $568 million, or 20% of Enron's earnings for those four years.[600]

Sherron Watkins, who became one of *Time*'s persons of the year for her role in bringing the financial situation of Enron to public light, was the vice president for corporate development at Enron when she first expressed concerns about the company's financial health in August 2001. A former Andersen employee, she was fairly savvy about accounting rules, and with access to the financial records for purposes of her new job, she quickly realized that the large off-the-books structure that had absorbed the company's debt load was problematic.[601] Labeling the SPEs "fuzzy" accounting, she began looking for another job as she prepared her memo detailing the accounting issues, because she understood that raising those issues meant that she would lose her Enron job.[602] Ms. Watkins did write her memo, anonymously, to Kenneth Lay, then-chair of Enron's board and former CEO, but she never discussed her concerns or discussed writing the memo with Jeffrey Skilling, then Enron's CEO, or Andrew Fastow, its CFO, because "it would have been a job-terminating move."[603] She did eventually confess to writing the memo when word of its existence permeated the executive suite. Mr. Fastow

reacted by noting that Ms. Watkins wrote the memo because she was seeking his job.[604]

Andersen had evaluated its exposure in continuing to have Enron as a client. What follows is an excerpt from a 2000 memo that David Duncan and four other Andersen partners prepared as they evaluated what they called the "risk drivers" at Enron. Following a discussion of "Management Pressures" and "Accounting and Financial Management Reporting Risks," the following drivers were listed:

- Enron has aggressive earnings targets and enters into numerous complex transactions to achieve those targets.
- The company's personnel are very sophisticated and enter into numerous complex transactions and are often aggressive in restructuring transactions to achieve derived financial reporting objectives.
- Form-over-substance transactions.[605]

Mr. Duncan presented the board with a one-page summary of Enron's accounting practices.[606] The summary, called "Selected Observations 1998 Financial Reporting," highlighted Mr. Duncan's areas of concern, and was presented to the board in 1999, a full two years before Enron's collapse. Called "key accounting issues" by Mr. Duncan, the areas of concern included "Highly Structured Transactions," "Commodity and Equity Portfolio," "Purchase Accounting," and "Balance Sheet Issues." Mr. Duncan had assigned three categories of risk for these accounting areas, which included "Accounting Judgments," "Disclosure Judgements [sic]," and "Rule Changes," and he then assigned letters to each of these three categories: *H* for high risk, *M* for medium risk, and *L* for low risk.[607] Each accounting issue had at least two *H* grades in the three risk categories.

Andersen's Concerns about Conflicts

Enron's Code of Ethics had both a general and a specific policy on conflicts of interest, both of which had to be waived in order to allow its officers to function as officers

(continued)

---

[599]Bob McNair, a Houston entrepreneur who sold his company to Enron in 1998, quoted in John Schwartz and Richard A. Oppel Jr., "Risk Maker Awaits Fall of Company Built on Risk," *New York Times*, November 29, 2001, p. C1.

[600]John R. Emshwiller, Rebecca Smith, Robin Sidel, and Jonathan Weil, "Enron Cuts Profit Data of 4 Years by 20 percent," *Wall Street Journal*, November 9, 2001, p. A3.

[601]Jodie Morse and Amanda Bower, "The Party Crasher," *Time*, January 6, 2003, pp. 53–55.

[602]*Id.*

[603]Rebecca Smith, "Fastow Memo Defends Enron Partnerships and Sees Criticism as Ploy to Get His Job," *Wall Street Journal*, February 20, 2002, p. A3.

[604]*Id.*

[605]"PSI Report," Hearing Exhibit 2b, Audit Committee Minutes of 2/7/99, p. 18.

[606]*Id.*, p. 16.

[607]*Id.*

Case 4.24

(continued)

of the many off-the-books entities that it was creating. The general ethical principle on conflicts is as follows:

> Employees of Enron Corp., its subsidiaries, and its affiliated companies (collectively the "Company") are charged with conducting their business affairs in accordance with the highest ethical standards. An employee shall not conduct himself or herself in a manner which directly or indirectly would be detrimental to the best interests of the Company or in a manner which would bring to the employee financial gain separately derived as a direct consequence of his or her employment with the company.[608]

Enron's code also had a specific provision on conflicts related to ownership of businesses that do business with Enron, which provides,

> The employer is entitled to expect of such person complete loyalty to the best interests of the Company.... Therefore, it follows that no full-time officer or employee should: ... (c) Own an interest in or participate, directly or indirectly, in the profits of another entity which does business with or is a competitor of the Company, unless such ownership or participation has been previously disclosed in writing to the Chairman of the Board and Chief Executive Officer of Enron Corp., and such officer has determined that such interest or participation does not adversely affect the best interests of the Company.[609]

The board's minutes show that it waived this policy for Andrew Fastow on at least three different occasions.[610] In post-collapse interviews, members of the board have insisted that they were not waiving Enron's code of ethics for Mr. Fastow. In its defense in shareholder lawsuits, the board members and company have argued that in granting a waiver they were simply following the code's policies and procedures.[611] Granting the waiver was a red flag. Even the conflicted Enron board saw the issue and engaged, at least once, in what was called in the minutes "vigorous discussion."[612]

David Duncan was concerned about this conflict of interest, and when Mr. Fastow first proposed his role in the first off-the-books entity, Mr. Duncan, on May 28, 1999, emailed a message of inquiry about the Fastow proposal to Benjamin Neuhausen, a member of Andersen's Professional Standards Group in Chicago. Mr. Neuhausen responded, with some of the response in uppercase letters for emphasis: "Setting aside the accounting, idea of a venture entity managed by CFO is terrible from a business point of view. Conflicts galore. Why would any director in his or her right mind ever approve such a scheme?" Mr. Duncan wrote back to Mr. Neuhausen on June 1, 1999, "[O]n your point 1 (i.e., the whole thing is a bad idea), I really couldn't agree more. Rest assured that I have already communicated and it has been agreed to by Andy that CEO, General [Counsel], and Board discussion and approval will be a requirement, on our part, for acceptance of a venture similar to what we have been discussing."[613] Mr. Duncan, the Andersen audit partner responsible for the Enron account, had expressed concern about the aggressive accounting practices Enron sought to use. Attorney Rusty Hardin, who served as Andersen's lead defense lawyer in the obstruction of justice case against the company for document shredding, noted that "no question David Duncan was a client pleaser."[614] Mr. Duncan also experienced pressure from his client and even consulted his pastor about how to resolve the dilemmas he faced in terms of approval of the financial statements: "He basically said it was unrelenting. It was a constant fight. Wherever he drew that line, Enron pushed that line—he was under constant pressure from year to year to push that line."[615]

Enron and Andersen Fall

The special report commissioned by the Enron board following its collapse described Enron's culture as "a flawed idea, self-enrichment by employees, inadequately designed controls, poor implementation, inattentive oversight, simple (and not so simple)

(continued)

---

[608]Enron Corporation, "Code of Ethics, Executive and Management," (July 2000), p. 12.

[609]*Id.*, p. 57.

[610]"PSI Report," p. 26.

[611]*Id.*, p. 25.

[612]*Id.*, p. 28, citing the Hearing Record, p. 157.

[613]*Id.*, p. 26.

[614]Raghavan, "How a Bright Star at Andersen Fell along with Enron," pp. A1, A8.

[615]*Id.*, p. A8.

Case 4.24

(continued)

accounting mistakes, and overreaching in a culture that appears to have encouraged pushing the limits."[616] In an interview with *CFO Magazine* in 1999, when he was named CFO of the year, Mr. Fastow explained that he was able to keep Enron's share price high because he spun debt off its books into SPEs.[617]

As the problems at Enron began to go from percolating to parboil, there was a cloud of nervousness that hung over Andersen. Based on an increasing number of questions that were coming into the Chicago office as Enron stories continued to appear in the news, Andersen's in-house counsel, Nancy Temple, sent around a memo that included the following advice on the firm's document destruction policy: "It will be helpful to make sure that we have complied with the policy."[618] Andersen's policy allowed for destruction of records when those records "are no longer useful for an audit.[619] There ensued a bit of a fine-line scramble on the Enron papers and documents that Andersen held.

When Enron announced, on October 16, 2001, its third quarter results, the $1.01 billion charge to earnings was not an easy thing for the market to absorb. The release characterized the charge to earnings as "non-recurring." Andersen officials had spoken with Enron executives to express their doubts about this characterization of the charge, but Enron refused to alter the release. Ms. Temple wrote an e-mail to Duncan that "suggested deleting some language that might suggest we have concluded the release is misleading."[620] The following day, the SEC notified Enron by letter that it had opened an investigation in August and requested certain information and documents. On October 19, 2001, Enron forwarded a copy of that letter to Andersen.

Also on October 19, 2001, Ms. Temple sent an internal team of accounting experts a memo on document destruction and attached a copy of the document policy. On October 20, 2001, the Enron crisis-response team held a

conference call, during which Temple instructed everyone to "[m]ake sure to follow the [document] policy." On October 23, 2001, then–Enron CEO Lay declined to answer questions during a call with analysts because of "potential lawsuits, as well as the SEC inquiry." After the call, Duncan met with other Andersen partners on the Enron engagement team and told them that they should ensure team members were complying with the document policy. Another meeting for all team members followed, during which Duncan distributed the policy and told everyone to comply. These and other smaller meetings were followed by substantial destruction of paper and electronic documents.

On October 26, 2001, one of Andersen's senior partners circulated a *New York Times* article discussing the SEC's response to Enron. His email commented that "the problems are just beginning and we will be in the cross hairs. The marketplace is going to keep the pressure on this and is going to force the SEC to be tough."[621] On October 30, 2001, the SEC opened a formal investigation and sent Enron a letter that requested accounting documents. Throughout this time, the document destruction continued, despite reservations by some of Andersen's managers. On November 8, 2001, Enron announced that it would issue a comprehensive restatement of its earnings and assets. Also on November 8, the SEC served Enron and Andersen with subpoenas for records. On November 9, Duncan's secretary sent an email that stated, "Per Dave—No more shredding.... We have been officially served for our documents."[622]

Andersen maintained that the shredding was routine, but the federal government indicted the company and Mr. Duncan. Mr. Duncan entered a guilty plea to obstruction of justice and ultimately testified against Andersen in court. Andersen was convicted of obstruction of justice. Its felony conviction meant that it could no longer conduct audits, and those clients that remained were now required to hire other auditors. Within a period of two years, Andersen went from an international firm of 36,000 employees to nonexistence.

(continued)

---

[616]Kurt Eichenwald, "Enron Panel Finds Inflated Profits and Few Controls," *New York Times*, February 3, 2002, p. A1.

[617]David Barboza and John Schwartz, "The Finance Wizard behind Enron's Deals," *New York Times*, February 6, 2002, pp. A1, C9.

[618]Tony Mauro, "One Little E-Mail, One Big Legal Issue," *National Law Journal*, April 25, 2005, p. 7.

[619]*Id.*

[620]544 U.S. at 700.

[621]544 U.S. at 701.

[622]544 U.S. at 702.

Case 4.24

(continued)

However, Andersen did take the case to the U.S. Supreme Court, which ruled in its favor on the conviction for obstruction of justice.[623] The court found that although there may have been intent on the part of the individuals involved in the shredding, the jury was not properly instructed on the proof and intent required to convict the accounting firm itself. Following the Supreme Court's reversal of the decision, Mr. Duncan withdrew his guilty plea. The government had the option of prosecuting Mr. Duncan but declined to do so in 2005. Mr. Duncan settled charges with the SEC in 2008 without admitting or denying any of the allegations. He is forever barred from serving in the capacity of a CFO or a chief accounting officer who must sign financial statements for submission to the SEC. [624] There were no fines or other sanctions imposed. Mr. Duncan is currently a CFO and managing director at an energy firm in Houston.[625]

Discussion Questions

1. With regard to the destruction of the documents, was there a difference between what was legally obstruction of justice and what was ethical in terms of understanding what was happening at Enron? When the U.S. Supreme Court reversed the Andersen decision, the *Wall Street Journal* noted that the Andersen case was a bad legal case and a poor prosecutorial decision on the part of the Bush administration.[626] Why do you think the prosecutors took the case forward? What changes under SOX would make the case easier to pursue today?

2. David Duncan was active in his church, a father of three young daughters, and a respected alumnus of Texas A&M. Mr. Duncan's pastor talked with the *New York Times* following Enron's collapse and Duncan's indictment and discussed with the reporter what a truly decent human being Duncan was.[627] What can we learn

about the nature of those who commit these missteps? What can you add to your credo because of Duncan's experience? Was the multimillion-dollar compensation he received a factor in his decision-making processes? Can you develop a decision tree on Duncan's thought processes from the time of the first SPE until the shredding? Using the models you learned in Units 1 and 2, what can you see that he missed in his analysis?

3. When a law firm reviewed who knew what and when in the lead-up to the Enron collapse and bankruptcy, the firm concluded that Andersen was aware of all of the off-the-book partnerships that had been created, noting that it appeared that the documents had been reviewed by Andersen. What factors contributed to Andersen's failure to do more regarding the off-the-book entities and other accounting issues at Enron? Based on what you have learned in Units 1 and 2, discuss what reasoning processes and rationalizations those at Andersen may have been using.

   Now, think about the Penn State case (Case 2.10) and how leaders there framed the issue. Then determine how the Andersen partners were framing the Enron issue. Is it difficult to envision bad outcomes or is judgment clouded when you are under pressure or are concerned about your job? How would a credo help when you are evaluating an issue with serious personal and business consequences?

4. One of the tragic ironies to emerge from the collapse of Arthur Andersen, following its audit work for Sunbeam, WorldCom, and Enron, was that it had survived the 1980s savings-and-loan scandals unscathed. In *Final Accounting: Ambition, Greed and the Fall of Arthur Andersen*, the following poignant description appears: "The savings-and-loan crisis, when it came, ensnared almost every one of the Big 8. But Arthur Andersen skated away virtually clean, because it had made the decision, years earlier[,] to resign all of its clients in the industry. S&Ls for years had taken advantage of a loophole that allowed them to boost earnings by recording the value of deferred taxes. Arthur Andersen accountants thought the rule was misleading and tried to convince their clients to change their accounting. When they refused, Andersen did what it felt it had to: It resigned all of its accounts rather than stand behind accounting that it felt to be wrong."[628] What takes a company from the gold standard to indictment and conviction?

[623]*Arthur Andersen LLP v. U.S.*, 544 U.S. 696 (2005).

[624]Kristen Hays, "Andersen Partner Who Audited Enron Settles with the SEC," *Chron*, January 28, 2008, https://www.chron.com/business/energy/article/Andersen-partner-who-audited-Enron-settles-with-1610488.php

[625]*In the Matter of David Duncan*, January 30, 2008, https://www.sec.gov/litigation/admin/2008/34-57234.pdf.

[626]The editorial is "Arthur Andersen's 'Victory,'" *Wall Street Journal*, June 1, 2005, p. A20. The court decision is *Arthur Andersen LLP v. U.S.*, 544 U.S. 696 (2005).

[627]Raghavan, "How a Bright Star at Andersen Fell Along with Enron," pp. A1, A8.

[628]Toffler, *Final Accounting*, p. 19.

Compare & Contrast

Following its declaration of bankruptcy, Lehman Brothers' trustee released a report that indicated it was able to spin off its risky debt instruments to SPEs under what was known as Repo 105. Lehman controlled 25% of the boards of these SPEs, although its relationship with the SPEs was depicted as arms-length.[629] As a result of these layers of transfer, Lehman was able to look financially sound right up until the collapse of the market in 2008 when the CDO market collapsed.

The bankruptcy trustee gave this summary of the Lehman practices:

Lehman employed off-balance sheet devices, known within Lehman as "Repo 105" and "Repo 108" transactions, to temporarily remove securities inventory from its balance sheet, usually for a period of seven to ten days, and to create a materially misleading picture of the firm's financial condition in late 2007 and 2008. Repo 105 transactions were nearly identical to standard repurchase and resale ("repo") transactions that Lehman (and other investment banks) used to secure short-term financing, with a critical difference: Lehman accounted for Repo 105 transactions as "sales" as opposed to financing transactions based upon the overcollateralization or higher than normal haircut in a Repo 105 transaction. By recharacterizing the Repo 105 transaction as a "sale," Lehman removed the inventory from its balance sheet.

The bankruptcy trustee does not address whether the transactions complied with accounting rules because he concludes that the failure to disclose their escalating debt and increasingly worthless securities was material. What does the bankruptcy trustee mean that compliance with the accounting rules is not the issue? Analyze why the lessons of other collapsed companies are not internalized by businesses that use the same strategies.

---

[629]Louise Story and Eric Dash, "Lehman Channeled Risks through 'Alter Ego' Firm," *New York Times*, April 13, 2010, p. A1.

Sometimes those within the organization see critical ethical issues but remain silent, because the culture keeps them silent due to fear, rewards, or just an attitude of "we will survive this."

Case 4.25

HealthSouth: The Scrushy Way

HealthSouth, a chain of hospitals and rehabilitation centers, used its celebrity and sports figure patients as a means of marketing and distinction. Press releases touted sports figures' use of HealthSouth facilities, such as the press release when Lucio, the Brazilian World Cup soccer star, had surgery at a HealthSouth facility.[630]

HealthSouth touted its new hospitals as something others would emulate.[631] The language in their annual reports and brochures was the "hospital model for the future of health care."

HealthSouth's website listed celebrities who have "used HealthSouth facilities: Michael Jordan, Kobe Bryant, Tara Lipinski, Troy Aikman, Bo Jackson, Scottie Pippen, Shaq O'Neal, Terry Bradshaw and Roger Clemens."[632] Its service model, the four steps from diagnosis through surgery, through inpatient rehabilitation, and finally to outpatient rehabilitation, was also its mark of distinction from other health care providers. The four steps were featured in a logo on the website as well as in its annual reports.

HealthSouth called its new hospitals "the hospitals of the future," and competitors began to copy those models.[633] From 1987 through 1997, HealthSouth's stock rose at a rate of 31% per year.[634] The stock had gone from $1 per share at the time of its initial public offering (IPO) in 1986 to $31 per share in 1998. In April 1998, CEO Richard Scrushy told analysts that HealthSouth had matched or beat earnings estimates for 47 quarters in a row.[635] It became a billion-dollar company through acquisitions. HealthSouth profits were restated in 2002 and 2003 to reflect $2.5 billion less in earnings, for periods dating back to 1994, with $1.1 billion less occurring in 1997 and 1998. Revenues were overstated by 2500% more than actual revenues from 1997 through 2001.[636] The stock was trading on pink sheets at $0.165 per share in mid-April 2003, from a $31 high in 1998.[637]

The Corporate Culture

CEO Richard Scrushy held Monday morning meetings with his executives. When the company was not meeting the numbers and analysts' expectations, Mr. Scrushy's instructions to the officers were "Go figure it out."[638]

(continued)

[630]HealthSouth press release, December 12, 2002, http://www.healthsouth.com. Accessed June 23, 2003.

[631]Reed Abelson and Milt Freudenheim, "The Scrushy Mix: Strict and So Lenient," New York Times, April 20, 2003, pp. BU1, 12.

[632]HealthSouth, http://www.healthsouth.com/investor. Accessed June 23, 2003.

[633]Abelson and Freudenheim, "The Scrushy Mix," pp. BU1, 12.

[634]John Helyar, "Insatiable King Richard," Fortune, July 7, 2002, pp. 76, 82.

[635]Abelson and Freudenheim, "The Scrushy Mix," pp. BU1, 12.

[636]Helyar, p. 84.

[637]Id., pp. BU1, 12.

[638]Helyar, p. 84.

Case 4.25

(continued)

At one meeting he announced, "I want each one of the [divisional] presidents to e-mail all of their people who miss their budget. I don't care whether it's by a dollar."[639]

One officer noted, "The corporate culture created the fraud, and the fraud created the corporate culture."[640] In an interview in the fall of 2002, Mr. Scrushy explained his management technique: "Shine a light on someone—it's funny how numbers improve."[641]

Monday morning management meetings with HealthSouth's then-CEO Richard Scrushy and his executive team in which they covered "the numbers" were referred to internally as the "Monday-morning beatings." Mr. Scrushy confronted employees not only with strategic issues, such as hospital performance, but also with the sizes of their cellular telephone bills: "Interviews with associates of Mr. Scrushy, government officials, and former employees, as well as a review of the litigation history of HealthSouth, paint a picture of an executive who ruled by top-down fear, threatened critics with reprisals, and paid his loyal subordinates well."[642]

One of the CFOs recorded conversations he had with Scrushy. For example, Richard Scrushy declared in a recorded conversation with William Owens, one of HealthSouth's CFOs,

> [If you] fixed [financial statements] immediately, you'll get killed. But if you fix it over time, if you go quarter to quarter, you can fix it. Engineer your way out of what you engineered your way into. I don't know what to say. You need to do what you need to do.[643] We just need to get those numbers where we want them to be. You're my guy. You've got the technology and the know-how.[644]

In 1998, employees began posting notices on a Yahoo! message board, using pseudonyms, about HealthSouth along with derogatory comments about Mr. Scrushy. Mr. Scrushy hired security to determine who was

responsible for the postings and eventually shut down employee computer access to the message boards.

Mr. Scrushy was known to place calls to his facility administrators from parking lots of HealthSouth facilities at 1 A.M. to notify them that he was standing in their parking lots and that he had found litter there. They were then forced to come to the facility immediately to fix the problem. He began arriving at work with security guards and kept them outside his door at all times.[645]

HealthSouth had a young officer team. For example, the position of vice president of reimbursements for the company, a critical position because of the importance of compliance in terms of submission sunder Medicare rules as well as the associated financial reporting issues regarding the revenues associated with reimbursement, was given to a 27-year old.[646] HealthSouth had five CFOs from 1998 through 2003, and the final CFO prior to the collapse was just 28 years old when Mr. Scrushy chose him for the ascent to that second-in-command position.[647] Mr. Scrushy did not favor hiring MBAs. He had none in his direct reports, but he did hire what he called "advance-them-up-from-nowhere Alabamians."[648]

Diana Henze, a HealthSouth employee, provided the following testimony at the congressional hearings on the company's collapse:

> My name is Diana Henze, and I began working in HealthSouth's accounting department. In 1995 and 1996, I helped install a standardized accounting software package for the accounting department. In 1997, I was promoted to Assistant Vice President of Finance, and in 1998, I was promoted to Vice President of Finance. My responsibilities were somewhat ad hoc, but included running the accounting computer system, preparing quarterly consolidations and assisting in the SEC filings.

(continued)

---

[639]Helyar, p. 86.

[640]Helyar, p. 84.

[641]Abelson and Freudenheim, "The Scrushy Mix," pp. BU1, 12.

[642]Id., pp. BU1, 12.

[643]"Secret Recording Is Played at a HealthSouth Hearing," *New York Times*, April 11, 2003, p. C2.

[644]Helyar, "Insatiable King Richard," pp. 76, at 82.

[645]Id.

[646]This information was gleaned from a review of HealthSouth's 10-Ks from 1994 through 2002. See Securities and Exchange Commission website, http://www.sec.gov/edgar, for these documents.

[647]Id.

[648]Helyar, "Insatiable King Richard," pp. 76, 84.

Case 4.25

(continued)

Sometime in 1998, after re-running several consolidation processes for one quarter end, I noticed that earnings and earnings per share jumped up. The amount and timing of those changes seemed odd to me so I approached my supervisor, Ken Livesay, who was the Assistant Controller. Ken told me that the increase in earnings was the result of the reversal of some over-reserves and over-accruals. At the time, Ken's explanation appeared to be reasonable and I did not pursue the matter further.

In March, I assisted in preparing the first quarter consolidation and 10Q preparation for 1999. During that process, I noticed the numbers changing again, and I approached Ken Livesay a second time. I told him, "You can't tell me that we have enough reserves to reverse that would justify this type of swing in the numbers." When he told me that I was right, I informed him that I did not understand what was going on, but would have no part in any wrong-doing.

Ken apparently went to Bill Owens, the Controller, with my suspicions because Bill called me in an attempt to justify what they were doing. Bill said that HealthSouth had to make its numbers or innocent people would lose their jobs and the company would suffer. I told Bill that I believed that whatever was going on to be fraudulent, and I would not participate in it and wanted no part of it.

The numbers continued to change in the second and third quarter of 1999. After the third quarter, I went to Ken and said "enough is enough," because the numbers still appeared to be moving with irregularities. I told him I was to going to report these suspicions to our Compliance Department because I suspected that fraud was being committed within the accounting department.

In October or November of 1999, I went to our Corporate Compliance Department and made an official complaint to Kelly Cullison, who was Vice President of Corporate Compliance.

Shortly after I filed the complaint, Ken Livesay was moved to the position of Chief Information Officer

(CIO), and two others were promoted to his previous position of Assistant Controller."[649]

The type of changes and turnover described here were typical for the executive team, particularly among those executives age 50 and older. These executives disappeared rapidly from the slate of officers, and that age group was no longer represented after 1998. Those officers who were experienced were replaced by younger officers who were brought in by Mr. Scrushy. Their bonuses and salaries grew at exponential rates, particularly the longer they stayed.[650] HealthSouth had an extensive loan program for executives in order "to enhance equity ownership." The key executives owed significant amounts of money to the company that they borrowed in order to exercise their stock options.[651]

HealthSouth's former head of internal audit offered the following testimony before Congress on the HealthSouth hearings:

My name is Teresa Sanders, and I was hired by Health-South as the Internal Auditor. During my employment I received three promotions, and when I left my title became Group Vice President and Chief Auditing Officer. My immediate supervisor was Richard Scrushy, and I reported directly to him for over nine years. I left HealthSouth in November of 1999.

I was hired by HealthSouth to audit our field operations. When I started at Health-South, the company had thirty-five (35) field facilities, and by the time I left the number had grown to approximately two thousand (2000). I had complete access to the financial books of the field operations in order to do my audits. However, I did not have access to the corporate financial books. I did not need access to the corporate books to perform field audits. Ernst & Young

(continued)

---

[649]"The Financial Collapse of HealthSouth," Subcommittee on Oversight and Investigations of the House Energy and Commerce Committee, http://archives.energycommerce. house.gov/reparchives/108/Hearings/10162003hearing1110/Cohen1747.htm. Accessed September 17, 2010.

[650]*Id.*

[651]Securities and Exchange Commission, http://www.sec.gov/edgar: see disclosures in proxy statements for 1995–2002.

Case 4.25

(continued)

performed the audit on the corporate books and any reports to the SEC.

As part of my duties as the Chief Auditing Officer, I had to make reports to the audit committee of the Board of Directors. All the meetings that I had with the audit committee were before the full Board except one time in either 1997 or 1998, when I met separately with the audit committee.

In 1996, Richard Scrushy approached me about establishing a fifty (50) point checklist which became known as the "Pristine Audit." Mr. Scrushy informed me the Pristine Audit was to be handled by Ernst & Young.

I developed the fifty (50) point checklist which Mr. Scrushy approved. [t]he Pristine Checklist has nothing to do with auditing the financial books of a field facility. The Pristine Audit was nothing more than a cosmetic, white glove, walk through of a facility. It was in the nature of quality control and had nothing to do with the financial viability of a particular facility.

By the time I left HealthSouth, I was having problems with Mike Martin. He turned off my computer access to the general ledgers of the field operations. I needed access to those ledgers to do my audits. I had to manually retrieve hard copies of those ledgers, if needed, which was very time consuming. Although I heard rumors that "they were playing with the books," I had no knowledge that anyone at HealthSouth was committing fraud. I ultimately left HealthSouth because I received a better job offer.[652]

Scrushy: CEO

Mr. Scrushy was a flamboyant CEO who had Bo Jackson and Jason Hervey, the teenager from the TV series *The Wonder Years*, paid to accompany him to HealthSouth events. Mr. Scrushy had a weekly Birmingham radio show with Mr. Hervey that was sponsored by HealthSouth.

Mr. Scrushy doled out the use of the company jet to politicians and athletes on a regular basis. But he also used the company jet himself for transporting his own rock band to various locations for concerts and company events. Mr. Scrushy was in the process of promoting a female rock trio when HealthSouth collapsed.[653]

Mr. Scrushy's personal assets included a mansion in Birmingham, a $3 million, 14,000-square-foot lakefront home in Lake Martin, Alabama; a 92-foot yacht; and 34 cars, including two Rolls-Royces and one Lamborghini.[654] He owned 11 businesses that he controlled through one operating company that also owned his wife's clothing company, Upseedaisies.[655] On his payroll were four housekeepers, two nannies, a ship captain, boat crew, and security personnel.[656]

Mr. Scrushy's companies did extensive business with HealthSouth. G.G. Enterprises, a company named for Mr. Scrushy's parents, sold computers to HealthSouth, a contract that eventually resulted in an investigation by the federal government for overcharging. Scrushy's personal accountant committed suicide in September 2002, and Scrushy filed a police report after the death accusing the deceased accountant of embezzling $500,000.

From the Junior Miss Pageant of Alabama to scholarships for his community college alma mater, Richard Scrushy, like Bernie Ebbers (see Reading 4.20), was unusually generous with the organizations and people in the small-town atmosphere in which he had experienced his stunning rise to success. The Vestavia Hills Public Library was renamed the Richard M. Scrushy Public Library because of his generous donations.[657] There

(continued)

[652]"The Financial Collapse of HealthSouth," Subcommittee on Oversight and Investigations of the House Energy and Commerce Committee, http://archives.energycommerce. house.gov/reparchives/108/Hearings/10162003hearing1110/ Cohen1747.htm. Accessed September 17, 2010.

[653]Helyar, "Insatiable King Richard," pp. 76, 84.

[654]Abelson and Freudenheim, "The Scrushy Mix," p. C1. During the hearing in which he was asking the federal court to release some of his assets (the judge had awarded him $15,000 per week living expenses previously), Mr. Scrushy could not remember what he owned and didn't own and took the Fifth Amendment against self-incrimination 30 times. "Ousted Chief of HealthSouth Resists Questions on His Assets," *New York Times*, April 10, 2003, p. C4. "I can't recall" and "I can't speak to the accuracy of this" were other responses.

[655]Greg Farrell, "Scrushy 'Was Set Up,' Says Lawyer," *USA Today*, April 15, 2003, p. 3B.

[656]Helyar, "Insatiable King Richard," pp. 76, 84.

[657]Id., pp. 76, 80.

Case 4.25

(continued)

was the Richard M. Scrushy campus of Jefferson State Community College, from which he graduated, and the Richard M. Scrushy Parkway that ran through the center of town. The Scrushy charity activity was weekly, and he used his celebrity sports clients to draw attention to the events.[658]

The HealthSouth Board

Following the $2.5 billion in earnings restatements by HealthSouth, one of its directors, Joel C. Gordon, observed, "We [directors] really don't know a lot about what has been occurring at the company."[659] However, there were the following revelations about the structure and activities of board members:

- One director had earned $250,000 per year on a consulting contract with HealthSouth for a seven-year period.

- Another director had a joint investment venture with Mr. Scrushy on a $395,000 investment property.

- Another director was awarded a $5.6 million contract for his company to install glass at a hospital being built by HealthSouth.

- Med Center Direct, a hospital supply company that operated online and did business with Health-South, was owned by Mr. Scrushy, six directors, and one of those director's wives.

- The audit committee and the compensation committee had consisted of the same three directors since 1986.

- Two of the directors had served on the board for 18 years.

- One director received a $425,000 donation to his charity from HealthSouth just prior to his going on the board.[660]

A corporate governance expert has said the conduct of the HealthSouth board amounted to "gross negligence."[661] One Delaware judge has issued an opinion on one aspect

of litigation against the board and noted, "The company, under Scrushy's managerial leadership, has been quite generous with a cause very important to Hanson (the director who accepted the donation to his College Football Hall of Fame).... compromising ties to the key officials who are suspected of malfeasance."[662]

Dr. Philip Watkins, a cardiologist, testified at congressional hearings on the Health-South collapse and stated the following:

> I became involved with HealthSouth, a brand new company then known as Amcare, in 1983, after I first met Mr. Scrushy. Mr. Scrushy proposed a merger of my practice's cardiac rehabilitation facility with Amcare to form what is known as a "CORF"— Comprehensive Outpatient Rehabilitation Facility. The unique concept of a CORF was to combine outpatient surgery and rehabilitation facilities into one stand-alone medical complex in order to ease patient burden and expense, and ultimately provide for more successful patient recoveries.
>
> In 1984, I was asked by Mr. Scrushy to join the Company's Board of Directors, two years before HealthSouth became a publicly traded company in 1986.
>
> Early on, I was appointed Chairman of the Board's Audit & Compensation Committee. At that time the Company was a startup with such a small board that these two functions were combined to form one committee. At that time, many companies followed this practice. Later, the committees were separated into two distinct committees.
>
> As Chairman of the Audit & Compensation committee, I worked with and relied upon the outside experts hired by our Board. Mercer [Human Resource Consulting] analyzed the compensation trends of similar firms in the healthcare industry and, along with other experts, advised the Compensation Committee. It was based upon this information and advice that we determined the compensation packages of HealthSouth's management team.

---

[658] Id.

[659] Joann S. Lublin and Ann Carrns, "Directors Had Lucrative Links at HealthSouth," *Wall Street Journal*, April 11, 2003, pp. B1, B3.

[660] Id.

[661] Id.

[662] Id.

(continued)

Case 4.25

(continued)

By all accounts, HealthSouth was growing at an exciting pace, and was singled out by numerous industry publications, including *Forbes* and *Fortune*, as an up and coming star in the field of outpatient surgery and rehabilitation. Since I joined the Health-South Board in 1984, I have seen HealthSouth grow from a company with two rehabilitation facilities—one in Little Rock and one in Birmingham—to become the largest outpatient surgery company, rehabilitation company and diagnostic services company in the world with over 48,000 employees throughout the country. The compensation for HealthSouth senior executives, including Mr. Scrushy, was based upon this apparent outstanding performance, and the Committee was always assured by the independent analyses of experts such as Mercer that the Board's compensation philosophy was entirely in keeping with the best practices at the time.

We now know the numbers we relied on and were certified by our outside accountants to calculate senior management compensation were fraudulent. If the Compensation Committee had known of the fraud, Mr. Scrushy and others would have been terminated immediately and would never have received these salaries, bonuses, and stock options.

I was as shocked and angry as the rest of the public when I learned that senior members of HealthSouth's management team had been perpetrating a fraud on Health-South's stockholders. The Board of Directors was similarly deceived. These criminal conspirators were able to fraudulently conceal or otherwise alter information and documents such that all of the experts including the accounting firm of Ernst & Young did not detect the fraud. As a corporate director, I relied on the accuracy of information provided to me by management and by outside experts such as Ernst & Young. It is now evident that because the truth had been so thoroughly concealed by certain former members of management, the probing questions and activism of this Board could not have discovered the existence of this accounting fraud.

It is incomprehensible to me how designated compliance personnel could have received such apparently clear information and could not have told Ernst & Young, the Audit Committee or the Board.

The Audit Committee did meet on a regular basis with Ms. Sanders and Mr. Smith and received their reports and questioned both of them. In fact, I had more internal auditors added to the internal audit staff after talking to Ms. Sanders. They never told us they had any suspicion of impropriety.

Had I known of the hidden fraud being perpetrated on us all, I would have acted quickly and decisively, just as the current Board has in removing those responsible. HealthSouth is one of the great healthcare companies in America and I am confident that it will continue to be under the guidance of the new management team. I look forward to answering any questions you or any other members of the Subcommittee may have.[663]

In 1996, eight of the fourteen board members were also company officers. The ratio of insiders did decrease after 1996.

Trials, Pleas, and Convictions

Fifteen of HealthSouth's executives entered guilty pleas to various federal charges. HealthSouth's former CFOs testified against Mr. Scrushy at his criminal trial and for the government. Only one CFO had no culpability. He left the company because of his concerns about the financial reporting. Scrushy had his going-away cake made for him. The cake read, "Eat ___." The other CFOs entered guilty pleas. The following chart provides a summary of the guilty pleas of the CFOs and other officers.

(continued)

---

[663]"The Financial Collapse of HealthSouth," Subcommittee on Oversight and Investigations of the House Energy and Commerce Committee, http://archives.energycommerce. house.gov/reparchives/108/Hearings/10162003hearing1110/ Cohen1747.htm. Accessed September 17, 2010.

Case 4.25

(continued)

William Owens	CFO	Wire and securities fraud; falsifying financials; filing false certification on financial statements with the SEC
Weston Smith	CFO	Wire and securities fraud; falsifying financials; filing false certification on financial statements with the SEC
Michael Martin	CFO	Conspiracy to commit wire and securities fraud; falsifying financials
Malcolm McVay	CFO	Conspiracy to commit wire and securities fraud; falsifying financials
Aaron Beam	CFO	Wire fraud
Angela Ayers	VP, finance and accounting	Conspiracy to commit securities fraud
Cathy Edwards	VP, asset management	Conspiracy to commit securities fraud
Rebecca Kay Morgan	VP, accounting	Conspiracy to commit securities fraud
Virginia Valentine	Assistant VP	Conspiracy to commit securities fraud
Emery Harris	VP/assistant controller	Conspiracy to commit wire and securities fraud
Kenneth Livesay	Assistant controller/CIO	Conspiracy to commit wire and securities fraud
Richard Botts	Senior VP, tax	Conspiracy to commit securities fraud; falsifying financials; mail fraud[664]

The Scrushy Trial

Mr. Scrushy joined a church in his hometown just prior to the trial and made substantial contributions. The pastors of the church attended the Scrushy trial each day. Leslie Scrushy, Mr. Scrushy's second wife, attended the church regularly and often spoke in tongues from the pulpit. Mr. Scrushy's son had a daily television show on one of the local television stations that Mr. Scrushy owned. He provided daily coverage of the trial, complete with interviews of the pastors and others attending the trial. The show enjoyed very high ratings.

Mr. Scrushy was acquitted of all 36 federal felony charges related to the HealthSouth collapse in June 2005, following long (21 days) and intense deliberations by a jury that seemed to have doubts even after that verdict was returned. One sign held by a former HealthSouth employee who stood outside the courtroom read, "Still guilty in God's eyes."[665] In a post-verdict interview, Scrushy said, "The truth has come to the surface."[666]

Mr. Scrushy was subsequently convicted of bribery of an Alabama official in federal district court. He was sentenced to six years and ten months in federal prison.[667] Because of a U.S. Supreme Court decision on the requirements for proof of "honest services fraud," Mr. Scrushy's conviction was reversed, and the U.S. Supreme Court required that his case be reviewed by a federal district court judge because of that court's 2010 clarification of what constituted "honest services fraud."[668] The federal judge held that Mr. Scrushy's convictions for fraud were supported by the evidence and should stand. In July 2012, he was released from federal prison, following a period in a halfway house, having served almost the full

(continued)

[664]"HealthSouth Guilty Pleas," *USA Today*, May 20, 2005, p. 1B.

[665]Reed Abelson and Jonathan Glater, "A Style That Connects with Hometown Jurors," *New York Times*, June 29, 2005, pp. C1, C4.

[666]Greg Farrell, "Scrushy Acquitted of All 36 Charges," *USA Today*, June 29, 2005, p. 1A.

[667]Bob Johnson, "Scrushy Gets Nearly 7 Years in Prison," *USA Today*, June 29, 2007, p. 2B.

[668]The same decision resulted in a reduction of Jeffrey Skilling's sentence (Enron) to 10 years from 24. *Skilling v. U.S.*, 561 U.S. 358 (2010). (See Case 4.20.)

Case 4.25

(continued)

six years and 10 months. There are a total of $2.28 billion in civil judgments against him. Both of his multimillion-dollar homes have been taken over by the judgment creditors.

Discussion Questions

1. What in the culture of HealthSouth made it difficult for employees to raise concerns about the company's practices and financial reporting?

2. Find the common factors in the other companies in this Unit and HealthSouth. Develop a chart that shows characteristics that the companies had in common.

Compare & Contrast

What is the difference between the CFOs who left the company and officers who stayed, many of whom were promoted? Consider the congressional testimony of the various officers and others associated with HealthSouth. What made them suspicious of the company? Why were others not suspicious?

Case 4.26

Dennis Kozlowski: Tyco and the $6,000 Shower Curtain[669]

Tyco International began as a research laboratory, founded in 1960 by Arthur Rosenburg, with the idea of doing contract research work for the government. By 1962, Rosenburg began doing work for companies in the areas of high-tech materials and energy conversion, and eventually became Tyco Semiconductor and Materials Research Laboratory. By 1964, the company had gone public and expanded to manufacture products for commercial use. By 1990, Tyco had become a conglomerate with a presence in over 100 countries and over 250,000 employees. Between 1991 and 2001, CEO Dennis Kozlowski took Tyco from $3 billion in annual sales to $36 billion in 2001 by paying $60 billion for more than 200 acquisitions.[670] Tyco's performance was phenomenal.

- From 1992 through 1999, Tyco's stock price grew fifteenfold.[671]

- Tyco's earnings grew by 25% each year during Kozlowski's era.[672]

- During 1999, Tyco's stock price rose 65%.[673]

- Tyco spent $50 billion on acquisitions in nine years.[674]

- The company's debt-to-equity ratio nearly doubled from 25% to 47% in one year (2001).[675]

In a move to reduce its U.S. tax bills, Tyco was based out of Bermuda, despite having its headquarters in Exeter,

(continued)

---

[669]Adapted from Marianne M. Jennings, "The Yeehaw Factor," 3 *Wyoming Law Review* 387 (2003).

[670]Daniel Eisenberg, "Dennis the Menace," *Time*, June 17, 2002, p. 47; and Mark Maremont, John Hechinger, Jerry Markon, and Gregory Zuckerman, "Kozlowski Quits under a Cloud, Worsening Worries about Tyco," *Wall Street Journal*, June 4, 2002, pp. A1, A10.

[671]Alex Berenson, "Ex-Tyco Chief, a Big Risk Taker, Now Confronts the Legal System," *New York Times*, June 10, 2002, p. B1.

[672]*BusinessWeek Online*, January 14, 2002, http://www.business-week.com.

[673]*BusinessWeek Online*, January 11, 1999, http://www.business-week.com.

[674]*BusinessWeek Online*, January 14, 2002, http://www.business-week.com.

[675]*Id.*

Case 4.26

(continued)

New Hampshire.[676] Tyco is the parent company to Grinnell Security Systems, health care products companies, and many other acquired firms, which has been its strategy for growth.[677]

Shortly after Enron's bankruptcy, Tyco began to experience a decline in its share price. From December 2001 through the middle of January 2002, Tyco's shares lost 20% of their value.[678] In fact, following a conference in which then-CEO Dennis Kozlowski tried to reassure the public and analysts that Tyco's accounting was sound, the shares were the most heavily traded of the day (68 million on January 15, 2002), and the price dropped $4.45 to $47.95 per share.[679] However, at the same time as the loss of investor confidence in the accounting of public corporations came Tyco's announcement that its earnings had dropped 24% for fiscal year 2001.[680] By February, the share price had tumbled to $29.90, a drop of 50% from January 1, 2002.[681] Tyco was forced to borrow funds as it experienced what one analyst called a "crisis in confidence," noting, "The lack of confidence in the company by the capital markets to a degree becomes a self-fulfilling prophecy."[682]

Another problem emerged on January 28, 2002. Tyco announced that it had paid $20 million to one of its outside directors, Frank E. Walsh, and a charity of which he was the head, for him to broker a deal for one of Tyco's acquisitions.[683] The acquisition was CIT

Group Finance, and Tyco acquired it for $9.5 billion.[684] Mr. Walsh, who would later plead guilty to a violation of a New York statute as well as a violation of federal securities laws, withheld information about the brokerage fee from the Tyco board and did not disclose the information as required in the company's SEC filings.[685] Once the SEC moved in to investigate, the company's stock continued its decline.[686] From January 2002 to August 2002, Tyco's stock price declined 80%.[687]

What Went Wrong: The Accounting Issues

There were some Tyco accounting issues that centered on its acquisitions and its accounting for those acquisitions.[688] What caused investors to seize upon Tyco's financials was that it seemed to be heavily in debt despite the fact that it was reporting oodles of cash flow.[689] This disparity resulted because of Tyco's accounting for its "goodwill."[690] When one company acquires another company, it must include the assets acquired in its balance sheet. The acquirer establishes the value for the assets acquired. From 1998 to 2001, Tyco spent $30 billion on acquisitions and attributed $30 billion to goodwill.

(continued)

---

[676]Information from Tyco, http://www.tyco.com; see "Investor Relations, Tyco History." See also Alex Berenson, "Tyco Shares Fall as Investors Show Concern on Accounting," *New York Times*, January 16, 2002, p. C1.

[677]*Id.* Tyco bought Grinnell, the security system and fire alarm company; Ludlow, the packaging company; and a host of others during its especially aggressive expansion period from 1973 to 1982.

[678]Alex Berenson, "Tyco Shares Fall as Investors Show Concern on Accounting," *New York Times*, January 16, 2002, p. C1.

[679]*Id.*

[680]John Hechinger, "Tyco to Lay Off 44% of Its Workers at Telecom Unit," *Wall Street Journal*, February 8, 2002, p. A5.

[681]Alex Berenson and Andrew Ross Sorkin, "Tyco Shares Tumble on Growing Worries of a Cash Squeeze," *New York Times*, February 5, 2002, p. C1.

[682]*Id.*

[683]Kate Kelly and Gregory Zuckerman, "Tyco Worries Send Stock Prices Lower Again," *Wall Street Journal*, February 5, 2002, p. C1.

[684]Laurie P. Cohen and Mark Maremont, "Tyco Ex-Director Pleads Guilty," *Wall Street Journal*, December 18, 2002, p. C1.

[685]Andrew Ross Sorkin, "Tyco Figure Pays $22.5 Million in Guilty Plea," *New York Times*, December 18, 2002, pp. C1, C2; and E. S. Browning, "Stocks Slump in Late-Day Selloff on Round of Ugly Corporate News," *Wall Street Journal*, June 4, 2002, pp. A3, A8.

[686]Michael Schroeder and John Hechinger, "SEC Reopens Tyco Investigation," *Wall Street Journal*, June 13, 2002, p. A2.

[687]Kevin McCoy, "Authorities Widen Tyco Case, Look at Other Officials' Actions," *USA Today*, August 13, 2003, p. 1A.

[688]Floyd Norris, "Now Will Come the Sorting Out of the Chief Executive's Legacy," *New York Times*, June 4, 2002, pp. C1, C10.

[689]Mark Maremont, "Tyco Made $8 Billion of Acquisitions over 3 Years but Didn't Disclose Them," *Wall Street Journal*, February 4, 2002, p. A3.

[690]"Goodwill" is an asset under accounting rules that takes into account the sort of customer value a business has. For example, if you buy a dry-cleaning business, you are paying not only for the hangers and the pressers and racks but also for that dry cleaner's reputation in the community, the tendency of customers to return, and their willingness to bring their dry cleaning to this establishment—goodwill.

Case 4.26

(continued)

The problem lies in the fact that the assets that were acquired were not carried on Tyco's books with any significant value. Assets, under accounting rules, lose their value over time. Goodwill stays the same in perpetuity. However, if Tyco turns around and sells the assets it has acquired and booked at virtually zero value, the profit that it makes is reflected in the income of the company. The only way an investor in Tyco would be able to tell what really happened in the accounting for an acquisition would be for the investor to have access to the balance sheets of the acquired companies, so that he or she could see the value of the assets as they were carried on the books of the acquired company. The bump to earnings from the sale of the assets is lovely, but the bump to profits, with no offsetting costs, is tremendous.

There were additional accounting issues related to the Tyco acquisitions. One big one was that despite having made 700 acquisitions between 1998 and 2001 for about $8 billion, Tyco never disclosed the acquisitions to the public.[691] The eventual disclosure of the phenomenal number of acquisitions not only explained the lack of cash but resulted in investor realization that they had been deprived of the chance to determine how much of Tyco's growth was due to acquisitions versus running existing businesses.

The nondisclosure of the acquisitions also helped with another accounting strategy. When Tyco made acquisitions, its goal was always to make the company acquired look as much like a "dog" as possible. Tyco was a spring-loader extraordinaire. (See Reading 4.12 for a full explanation of spring-loading.) Spring-loading at Tyco involved having the company being acquired pay everything for which it has a bill, whether that bill was due or not. When Tyco acquired Raychem, its treasurer sent out the following email:

> At Tyco's request, all major Raychem sites will pay all pending payables, whether they are due or not.... I understand from Ray [Raychem's CFO] that we have agreed to do this, even though we will be spending

the money for no tangible benefit either to Raychem or Tyco.[692]

Tyco employees, when working with a company to be acquired, would also pump up the reserves, with one employee of Tyco asking an employee of an acquired firm, "How high can we get these things? How can we justify getting this higher?"[693] The final report of a team led by attorney David Boies (the lawyer who represented the U.S. government in its case antitrust against Microsoft,), retained by the Tyco board to determine what was going on with the company, indicated that Tyco executives used both incentives and pressure on executives in order to get them to push the envelope on accounting rules to maximize results.[694] Mr. Boies referred to the accounting practices of the executives as "financial engineering."

It was not, however, a case in which the accounting issues went unnoticed. The warnings, from the company's outside legal counsel, went unheeded. A May 25, 2000, email from William McLucas of Wilmer Cutler to Mr. Mark Belnick, then–general counsel for Tyco, contains clear warnings about the questionable accounting treatments as well as the pressure those preparing the financial reports were experiencing, "We have found issues that will likely interest the SEC ... creativeness is employed in hitting the forecasts.... There is also a bad letter from the Sigma people just before the acquisition confirming that they were asked to hold product shipment just before the closing."[695] The lawyer concluded that Tyco's financial reports smelled of "something funny which is likely apparent if any decent accountant looks at this."[696]

(continued)

[692]Herb Greenberg, "Does Tyco Play Accounting Games?" *Fortune*, April 1, 2002, pp. 83, 86.

[693]*Id.*

[694]Kurt Eichenwald, "Pushing Accounting Rules to the Edge of the Envelope," *New York Times*, December 31, 2002, pp. C1, C2.

[695]Laurie P. Cohen and Mark Maremont, "E-Mails Show Tyco's Lawyers Had Concerns," *Wall Street Journal*, December 27, 2002, p. C1.

[696]Mark Maremont and Laurie P. Cohen, "Tyco Probe Expands to Include Auditor PricewaterhouseCoopers," *Wall Street Journal*, September 30, 2002, p. A1.

[691]Maremont, "Tyco Made $8 Billion of Acquisitions over 3 Years but Didn't Disclose Them," p. A3.

Case 4.26

(continued)

What Went Wrong: A Profligate Spender as CEO

Tyco was graced with a CEO whose profligate spending cost the company dearly, in dollars and reputation, and whose tight fist with his own money got him indicted. Dennis Kozlowski was a scary CEO whose philosophy was "Money is the only way to keep score."[697] Mr. Kozlowski was one of the country's highest-paid CEOs. In 2001, his compensation package of $411.8 million put him at number two among the CEOs of the Fortune 500 companies."[698] Mr. Kozlowski was featured on the cover of *BusinessWeek* and called "the most aggressive dealmaker in Corporate America."[699] He was included in the magazine's top 25 managers of the year. Indeed, when Tyco's problems and accounting issues emerged, many of Wall Street's "superstar" money managers were stunned.[700]

Mixing Extended Family and Business

In addition to his salary, Mr. Kozlowski was a spender. There were extensive personal expenses documented that began to percolate before problems at Tyco emerged. Tyco's outside legal counsel raised concerns about payments Tyco was making to Mr. Kozlowski's then-mistress (eventually Kozlowski's second ex-wife), Karen Mayo, and advised that they be disclosed in SEC documents. Employees in Tyco refused to make the disclosures and continued making the payments.[701] The email from partner Lewis Liman at Wilmer Cutler, sent March 23, 2000, to Tyco's general counsel, Mark Belnick, read, "There are payments to a woman whom the folks in finance describe as Dennis's girlfriend. I do not know Dennis's situation, but this is an embarrassing fact."[702]

Hedonist Spending

Before Tyco took its dive, Mr. Kozlowski had accumulated three Harleys; a 130-foot sailing yacht; a private plane; and homes in New York City (including a 13-room Fifth Avenue apartment),[703] New Hampshire, Nantucket, and Boca Raton (15,000 square feet); and he was a part owner of the New Jersey Nets and the New Jersey Devils.[704] His Fifth Avenue apartment cost $16.8 million to buy and $3 million in renovations, and he spent $11 million on furnishings.[705] The items were delineated in the press, and the following purchases for the apartment were charged to Tyco: $6,000 for a shower curtain; $15,000 for a dog umbrella stand; $6,300 for a sewing basket; $17,100 for a traveling toilette box; $2,200 for a gilt metal wastebasket; $2,900 for coat hangers; $5,960 for two sets of sheets; $1,650 for a notebook; and $445 for a pincushion.[706]

Tyco also paid Mr. Kozlowski's American Express bill, which was $80,000 for one month. A later report uncovered a $110,000 bill Tyco paid for a 13-day stay by Mr. Kozlowski at a London hotel.[707] Ironically, Mr. Kozlowski told a *BusinessWeek* reporter in 2001, on a tour of Tyco's humble Exeter, New Hampshire, offices, "We don't believe in perks, not even executive parking spots."[708]

(continued)

---

[697]Eisenberg, "Dennis the Menace," 47.

[698]Jonathan D. Glater, "A Star Lawyer Finds Himself the Target of a Peer," *New York Times*, September 24, 2002, pp. C1, C8.

[699]*BusinessWeek Online*, January 14, 2002, http://www.business-week.com.

[700]Gregory Zuckerman, "Heralded Investors Suffer Huge Losses with Tyco Meltdown," *Wall Street Journal*, June 10, 2002, p. C1.

[701]Cohen and Maremont, "E-Mails Show Tyco's Lawyers Had Concerns," p. C1.

[702]*Id.*

[703]Theresa Howard, "Tyco Puts Kozlowski's $16.8M NYC Digs on Market," *USA Today*, September 19, 2002, p. 3B.

[704]Laurie P. Cohen and Mark Maremont, "Tyco Relocations to Florida Are Probed," *Wall Street Journal*, June 10, 2002, p. A3; Alex Berenson and William K. Rashbaum, "Tyco Ex-Chief Is Said to Face Wider Inquiry into Finances," *New York Times*, June 7, 2002, p. C1; and Kris Maher, "Scandal and Excess Make It Hard to Sell Mr. Kozlowski's Boat," *New York Times*, September 23, 2002, p. A1.

[705]Andrew Ross Sorkin, "Tyco Details Lavish Lives of Executives," *New York Times*, September 19, 2002, p. C1. The New York City apartment was sold for $21.8 million in October 2004. William Neuman, "Tyco to Sell Ex-Chief's Apartment for $21 Million," *New York Times*, October 9, 2004, pp. B1, B4.

[706]Kevin McCoy, "Directors' Firms on Payroll at Tyco," *USA Today*, September 18, 2002, p. 1B. These items are also listed in the 8-K for September 17, 2002.

[707]Mark Maremont and Laurie P. Cohen, "Tyco's Internal Inquiry Concludes Questionable Accounting Was Used," *Wall Street Journal*, December 31, 2002, pp. A1, A4; and Alex Berenson, "Changing the Definition of Cash Flow Helped Tyco," *New York Times*, December 31, 2002, pp. C1, C2.

[708]Anthony Bianco, William Symonds, Nanette Byrnes, and David Polek, "The Rise and Fall of Dennis Kozlowski," *BusinessWeek Online*, December 23, 2002, http://www.businessweek.com.

Case 4.26

(continued)

The Toga Birthday Party at Tyco Expense

For his then–new wife Karen Mayo's fortieth birthday, Kozlowski flew Jimmy Buffett and dozens of Karen's friends to a villa outside Sardinia for a multiday birthday celebration.[709] A memo on the party was attached as an exhibit to Tyco's 8-K, filed on September 17, 2002. The process for receiving the guests and the party schedule are described in detail, right down to what type of music was playing and at what level. The waiters were dressed in Roman togas, and there was an ice sculpture of David through which the vodka flowed. The memo includes a guest list and space for the crew of the yacht that the Kozlowskis sailed to Sardinia.[710] The total cost for the party was $2.1 million.[711]

Generosity and Philanthropy, Sometimes with His Own Money

Mr. Kozlowski was on the board of the Whitney Museum of Art and had Tyco donate $4.5 million to the traveling museum shows that the Whitney sponsored.[712] He was an avid fundraiser for various philanthropic endeavors. In fact, he was at a fundraiser for the New York Botanical Garden when the news of his possible indictment (see details following) first spread.[713] Tyco donated $1.7 million for the construction of the Kozlowski Athletic Complex at the private school, Berwick Academy, which one of his daughters attended and where he served as trustee, and $5 million to Seton Hall, his alma mater, for a building that was called the Koz Plex.[714]

Mr. Kozlowski also donated personally, particularly to charities in the Boca Raton area, where he had retained a public relations executive and where he had been given a fair amount of coverage in the *Palm Beach Post* for his contributions to local charities.[715] There is even some confusion about who was donating how much and from which tills. Kozlowski had pledged $106 million in Tyco funds to charity, but $43 million of that was given in his own name.[716] He had donated $1.3 million to the Nantucket Conservation Foundation in his own name with the express desire that the land next to his property there not be developed.[717] Tyco gave $3 million to a hospital in Boca Raton and $500,000 to an arts center there. United Way of America gave Mr. Kozlowski its "million-dollar giver" award.[718]

Hiring and Paying Friends for Personal Expenses

Mr. Kozlowski saw to it that friends were awarded contracts that Tyco paid. For example, Wendy Valliere was a personal friend of the Kozlowskis and was hired to decorate the New York City apartment. Her firm's bill was $7.5 million.[719] However, Ms. Valliere was not alone as a personal employee.[720] In 1996, Mr. Kozlowski also hired Michael Castania, a consultant who had helped him with his yacht, as an executive who was housed at Boca Raton. He was an Australian yachting expert who went on to lead Team Tyco, a corporate yachting racing team, to fourth place in the Volvo Challenge Race in June 2002.[721] Tyco

(continued)

[709]Don Halasy, "Why Tyco Boss Fell," *New York Post*, June 9, 2002, http://www.nypost.com; and Laurie P. Cohen, "Ex-Tyco CEO's Ex to Post $10 Million for His Bail Bond," *Wall Street Journal*, September 20, 2002, p. A5.

[710]Tyco 8-K filing, September 17, 2002, http://www.sec.gov/edgar.

[711]Mark Maremont and Laurie P. Cohen, "How Tyco's CEO Enriched Himself," *Wall Street Journal*, August 7, 2002, p. A1.

[712]Don Halasy, "Why Tyco Boss Fell," June 9, 2002, http://www.nypost.com.

[713]*Id.*; and Carol Vogel, "Kozlowski's Quest for Entrée into the Art World," *New York Times*, June 6, 2002, pp. C1, C5.

[714]Maremont and Cohen, "How Tyco's CEO Enriched Himself," p. A1; and John Byrne, "Seton Hall of Shame," *BusinessWeek Online*, September 20, 2002, http://www.businessweek.com.

[715]*Id.*, p. A6. Barry Epstein, a Palm Beach PR executive, said, "I represented Dennis personally. I reported to him and guided him on community involvement." Mr. Epstein has conceded that most of the money was Tyco's, not Mr. Kozlowski's.

[716]Kevin McCoy and Gary Strauss, "Kozlowski, Others Accused of Using Tyco as 'Piggy Bank,'" *USA Today*, September 13, 2002, pp. 1B, 2B.

[717]Maremont and Cohen, "How Tyco's CEO Enriched Himself," pp. A1, A6.

[718]*Id.*

[719]*Id.*

[720]Mark Maremont and Laurie P. Cohen, "Interior Design on a Budget: The Tyco Way," *Wall Street Journal*, September 18, 2002, pp. B1-B5.

[721]Maremont and Cohen, "How Tyco's CEO Enriched Himself," pp. A1, A6.

Case 4.26

(continued)

also hired Ms. Mayo's personal trainer from the days when she was still married to her ex-husband and Mr. Kozlowski was still married to his ex-wife, but Mr. Kozlowski was supporting Ms. Mayo in a beach condo in Nantucket.[722]

Art Collection

Mr. Kozlowski was also an active player in Manhattan's art market. In June 2002, the *New York Times* reported that Mr. Kozlowski was being investigated by the district attorney's office in Manhattan for evasion of $1 million in sales tax on $13 million in art sales over a 10-month period.[723] Mr. Kozlowski resigned from Tyco immediately following the emergence of the report and before an indictment was handed down. A market that was already reeling from Enron and WorldCom dropped 215 points in one day, and Tyco's stock fell 27% that same day.[724] In fact, the indictment was handed down the following day.[725]

Tyco's Culture

Mr. Kozlowski had a strategy for getting the type of people he needed to succumb to the pressure for numbers achievement. He told *BusinessWeek* that he chooses managers from the "same model as himself. Smart, poor, and wants to be rich."[726] Meeting numbers meant bonuses; exceeding those numbers meant "the sky was the limit." The CEO of one of Tyco's subsidiaries had a salary of $625,000, but when he boosted sales by 62%, his bonus was $13 million.[727]

Mr. Kozlowski was known for being autocratic and prone to temper flare-ups.[728] When he was CEO of Tyco's Grinnell Fire Protection Systems Co., Mr. Kozlowski had an annual awards banquet where he presented awards to the best warehouse manager as well as the worst warehouse manager. The worst manager would have to walk to the front of the room in what other managers described as a "death sentence."[729]

The Loans

Tyco's Key Employee Corporate Loan Program (the "KELP") was established to encourage employees to own Tyco shares by offering dedicated loans to pay the taxes due when shares granted under Tyco's restricted share ownership plan became vested. There was no way to pay the taxes except to sell some of the shares for cash, and the loan program permitted the officers to pledge their shares in exchange for cash that was then used to pay the income tax that was due on this employee benefit.[730] Mr. Kozlowski made it clear that the loan program was available to all of his new hires, including Mark Swartz, the CFO, and Mark

(continued)

[722]Anthony Bianco, William Symonds, Nanette Byrnes, and David Polek, "The Rise and Fall of Dennis Kozlowski," *BusinessWeek Online*, December 23, 2002, http://www.businessweek.com.

[723]Alex Berenson, "Investigation Is Said to Focus on Tyco Chief over Sales Tax," *New York Times*, June 3, 2002, p. C1; Laurie P. Cohen and Mark Maremont, "Expanding Tyco Inquiry Focuses on Firm's Spending on Executives," *Wall Street Journal*, June 7, 2002, pp. A1, A5; and Nanette Byrnes, "Online Extra: The Hunch That Led to Tyco's Tumble," *BusinessWeek Online*, December 23, 2002, http://www.businessweek.com.

[724]Mark Maremont, John Hechinger, Jerry Markon, and Gregory Zuckerman, "Kozlowski Quits under a Cloud, Worsening Worries about Tyco," *Wall Street Journal*, June 4, 2002, p. A1; and Adam Shell, "Markets Fall as Tyco CEO's Resignation Adds to Woes," *USA Today*, June 4, 2002, p. 1B.

[725]Thor Valdmanis, "Art Purchases Put Ex-Tyco Chief in Hot Water," *USA Today*, June 5, 2002, p. 1B; Mark Maremont and Jerry Markon, "Former Tyco Chief Is Indicted for Avoiding Sales Tax on Art," *Wall Street Journal*, June 5, 2002, p. A1; Alex Berenson and Carol Vogel, "Ex-Tyco Chief Is Indicted in Tax Case," *New York Times*, June 5, 2002, p. C1; David Cay Johnston, "A Tax That's Often Ignored Suddenly Attracts Attention," *New York Times*, June 5, 2002, p. C1; Brooks Barnes and Alexandra Peers, "Sales-Tax Probe Puts Art World in Harsh Light," *Wall Street Journal*, June 5, 2002, pp. B1, B3; Susan Saulny, "Tyco's Ex-Chief to Seek Dismissal of Indictments," August 15, 2002, p. C3; Mark Maremont and Laurie P. Cohen, "Former Tyco CEO Is Charged with Two New Felony Counts," *Wall Street Journal*, June 27, 2002, p. A3; and Andrew Ross Sorkin and Susan Saulny, "Former Tyco Chief Faces New Charges," *New York Times*, June 27, 2002, p. C1.

[726]William C. Symonds and Pamela L. Moore, "The Most Aggressive CEO," *BusinessWeek Online*, May 28, 2001, http://www.businessweek.com.

[727]Id.

[728]Bianco, Symonds, Byrnes, and Poleck, "The Rise and Fall of Dennis Kozlowski," http://www.businessweek.com.

[729]Id.

[730]This information was obtained from the press release that the SEC issued when it filed suit against Mark Swartz, Dennis Kozlowski, and Mark Belnick for the return of the loan amounts. http://www.sec.gov/releases/litigation.

Case 4.26

(continued)

Belnick, Tyco's general counsel and executive vice president.[731]

Mr. Kozlowski appeared to be financing his lifestyle through the KELP and relocation loan programs. According to SEC documents, Mr. Kozlowski borrowed more than $270 million from the KELP "but us[ed] only about $29 million to cover intended uses for the loans. He used the remaining $242 million of supposed KELP loans for personal expenses, including yachts, fine art, estate jewelry, luxury apartments and vacation estates, personal business ventures, and investments, all unrelated to Tyco."[732]

The second loan program was a relocation program, which was established to help employees who had to move from New Hampshire to New York. The idea was to provide low-interest loans for employees who had to relocate from one set of company offices to another to lessen the impact of moving to a much costlier housing market.[733] One of the requirements of the relocation program was the employee's certification that they were indeed moving from New Hampshire to New York, or, in some cases, to Boca Raton.

Mr. Belnick has explained through his lawyer that he was entitled to the loans from the "relocation program" because he had such in writing from Mr. Kozlowski. Mr. Kozlowski offered this perk to Mr. Belnick despite the fact that Mr. Belnick was a partner in a New York City law firm and would be working in New York City for Tyco. He received the relocation fee for a difference of 25 miles between his home and Tyco's New York offices, and despite the fact that he had never lived

in New Hampshire as the relocation loan program required. Although he actually didn't need to move, Mr. Belnick borrowed $4 million anyway and used it to buy and renovate an apartment in New York City. Later, he borrowed another $10 million to construct a home in Park City, Utah, because he was moving his family there and would divide his time between the two locations and the extensive international travel his job required.[734] Mr. Belnick got Mr. Kozlowski's approval for both loans, but he didn't do the corporate paperwork for relocation.

Mr. Belnick told friends from the time that he began his work with Tyco that he was uncomfortable because he was not in the loop with information from either Mr. Kozlowski or the board. However, Mr. Kozlowski offered him more lucrative contracts and additional loans, and Mr. Belnick remained on board.[735] There are emails from Tyco's outside counsel, the Wilmer Cutler firm, that indicate some information was seeping through to Mr. Belnick, and that outside counsel had concerns that were kept silent once transmitted to Mr. Belnick.

During the same period, CFO Swartz availed himself of $85 million of KELP loans. However, he used only $13 million for payment of taxes and spent the remaining $72 million for personal investments, business ventures, real estate holdings, and trusts.[736] Mr. Swartz used more than $32 million of interest-free relocation loans and, according to SEC documents, used almost $9 million of those relocation loans for purposes not authorized under

(continued)

---

[731]In an 8-K filed with the SEC on September 17, 2002, Tyco outlined the loans, the spending, and its plans for the future. The 8-K is available at http://www.sec.gov/edgar. A synopsis of the information filed in the 8-K is available at http://www.tyco.com under "Press Releases."

[732]Securities and Exchange Commission, http://www.sec.gov/releases/litigation; and Kevin McCoy, "Directors' Firms on Payroll at Tyco," USA Today, September 18, 2002, p. 1B. These items are also listed in Tyco's 8-K filed on September 17, 2002; see http://www.sec.gov/edgar. See also Theresa Howard, "Tyco Puts Kozlowski's $16.8M NYC Digs on Market," USA Today, September 19, 2002, p. 3B; and Andrew Ross Sorkin, "Tyco Details Lavish Lives of Executives," New York Times, September 18, 2002, p. C1. And see Tyco's 8-K filed on September 17, 2002.

[733]The rate as disclosed in the 2002 proxy was 6.24%.

[734]Nicholas Varchaver, "Fall from Grace," Fortune, October 28, 2002, 112, 115; Amy Borrus, Mike McNamee, Williams Symonds, Nanette Byrnes, and Andrew Park, "Reform: Business Gets Religion," BusinessWeek Online, February 3, 2003, http://www.businessweek.com; and Jonathan D. Glater, "A Star Lawyer Finds Himself the Target of a Peer," New York Times, September 24, 2002, p. C1.

[735]Glater, "A Star Lawyer Finds Himself the Target of a Peer," pp. C1, C8.

[736]Securities and Exchange Commission, http://ww.sec.gov/releases/litigation. The SEC filed suit against Mr. Swartz, seeking the return of these funds. Mr. Swartz was also indicted by the State of New York and spent some time in jail as his family scrambled to post his bail.

Case 4.26

(continued)

the program, including purchasing a yacht and investing in real estate.[737]

Patricia Prue, the vice president for HR at Tyco and responsible for processing the paperwork for the forgiveness of the officers' loans, had benefited from the loan forgiveness program herself. She approached Mr. Kozlowski in September 2000 and asked for documentation that the board had indeed approved all the loan forgiveness for which she was doing the paperwork. Mr. Kozlowski, without ever producing board minutes, wrote a memo to Ms. Prue, "A decision has been made to forgive the relocation loans for those individuals whose efforts were instrumental to successfully completing the TyCom I.P.O."[738] Ms. Prue had received a loan of $748,309, had the loan forgiven, and then was given $521,087 to pay the taxes on the loan forgiveness.[739] Ms. Prue's bonuses totaled $13,534,523, and she was given $9,424,815 to pay the taxes on the bonuses.[740]

The issue of board approval on the loans remains a question, but compensation committee minutes from February 21, 2002, show that the committee was given a list of loans to officers for approval and also approved Mr. Belnick's new compensation package. There was no public disclosure of these developments or the committee's review.[741] In grand jury testimony, Patricia Prue, who testified in exchange for immunity from prosecution, indicated that board member Joshua

Berman pressured her in June 2002 to change the minutes from that February compensation committee meeting.[742] Mr. Berman denies the allegation. However, Ms. Prue did send a memo on June 7, 2002, to John Fort, Mr. Swartz, and the board's governance committee, with the following included: "As a result of the fact that I was recently pressured by Josh Berman to engage in conduct which I regarded as dishonest—and which I have refused to do—I will decline to have any personal contact with him in the future. In addition, I ask that Josh not go to my staff with any requests for information or directions."[743]

Mr. Kozlowski paid $56 million in bonuses to executives eligible for the KELP program, then gave them $39 million to pay the taxes on the bonuses, and then forgave the KELP loans given to pay taxes on the shares awarded in addition to the bonuses. A report commissioned by the Tyco board following the Kozlowski departure refers to the Tyco culture as one of greed and deception designed to ensure personal enrichment.[744]

The Inner Circle of Executives

Mr. Kozlowski's officer team was small and obedient.[745] Tyco had only 400 employees at its central offices, and Kozlowski only interacted with a few, a means of keeping information close to the vest.[746] Mark Swartz, Tyco's former CFO, was 40 years old at the time of Tyco's fall and his indictment on 38 counts of grand larceny, conspiracy, and falsifying business records.[747] Tyco hired him in

(continued)

---

[737]Securities and Exchange Commission, http://www.sec.gov/releases/litigation. These exhibits and lists are found in the 8-K for September 17, 2002, at http://www.sec.gov/edgar. Andrew Ross Sorkin and Jonathan D. Glater, "Tyco Planning to Disclose Making Loans to Employees," *New York Times*, September 16, 2002, p. C1; and "Ex-Chief of Tyco Posts $10 Million in Bail," *New York Times*, September 21, 2002, p. B14.

[738]*Id.*; and Kevin McCoy, "Kozlowski's Statement in Question," *USA Today*, January 9, 2002, p. 1B.

[739]Andrew Ross Sorkin, "Tyco Details Lavish Lives of Executives," *New York Times*, September 18, 2002, pp. C1, C6.

[740]"Helping Fatcats Dodge the Taxman," *BusinessWeek Online*, June 20, 2002, http://www.businessweek.com.

[741]Andrew Ross Sorkin and Jonathan D. Glater, "Some Tyco Board Members Knew of Pay Packages, Records Show," *New York Times*, September 23, 2002, p. A1. Mr. Belnick was fired before he was indicted on felony charges. Laurie P. Cohen, "Tyco Ex-Counsel Claims Auditors Knew of Loans," *Wall Street Journal*, October 22, 2002, p. A6.

[742]*Id.*, p. A22.

[743]*Id.*, p. A22. Both sides acknowledge the authenticity of the memo from Ms. Prue.

[744]Andrew Ross Sorkin, "Tyco Details Lavish Lives of Executives," *New York Times*, September 18, 2002, p. C1. These bonuses are from the year 2000. Kevin McCoy, "Tyco Spent Millions on Exec Perks, Records Say," *USA Today*, September 17, 2002, p. 1B.

[745]Alex Berenson, "Ex-Tyco Chief, a Big Risk Taker, Now Confronts the Legal System," *New York Times*, June 10, 2002, p. B1.

[746]Anthony Bianco, William Symonds, Nanette Byrnes, and David Polek, "The Rise and Fall of Dennis Kozlowski," *BusinessWeek Online*, December 23, 2002, http://www.businessweek.com.

[747]Nicholas Varchaver, "Fall from Grace," *Fortune*, October 28, 2002, pp. 112, 114; and Andrew Ross Sorkin, "2 Top Tyco Executives Charged with $600 Million Fraud Scheme," *New York Times*, September 13, 2002, pp. A1, C3.

Case 4.26

(continued)

1991, away from Deloitte & Touche's due diligence team. By 1993, he was head of Tyco's acquisitions team, and by 1995, he was Tyco's CFO, at age 33. Mr. Kozlowski nominated Mr. Swartz for a CFO award that year, and *CFO Magazine* honored Mr. Swartz with its 2000 Excellence Award.[748] Indeed, Mr. Kozlowski and Mr. Swartz were inextricably intertwined, with Mr. Swartz even serving as trustee for one of Mr. Kozlowski's trusts for holding title to real property.[749] Both men also used a loophole in securities law to sell millions of shares of Tyco stock even as they declared publicly that they were not selling their shares in the company.[750]

Tyco's Fall and the Trials

Mr. Kozlowski and Mr. Swartz were indicted under New York State laws for stealing $170 million from the company and for profiting $430 million by selling off their shares while withholding information from the public about the true financial condition of Tyco.[751] The charges against the two were based on a state law that prohibits a criminal enterprise, a type of crime generally associated with organized crime. Their joint trial began in October 2003 and ran until April 2004, when the case ended in a bizarre mistrial. When the jury began deliberations, one juror, Ruth Jordan, was labeled by some of her fellow jurors as a holdout who refused to deliberate the case. Some courtroom observers felt that Ms. Jordan had flashed an "okay" hand signal to the defendants and their counsel.[752] The judge urged the jurors to continue deliberating despite obvious rancor. Ms. Jordan came to be labeled "holdout granny" and "batty blueblood" in the media.[753] However, several media outlets published her name (one with a photo),

and when she reported to the judge that she had received a threat, the judge declared a mistrial.[754] The thrust of the defense was that everything Mr. Kozlowski and Mr. Swartz did was in the open, with board approval, and therefore did not fit the requirements for a criminal enterprise.[755]

Mr. Belnick was also indicted and tried and was acquitted of all charges.[756]

Mr. Kozlowski and Mr. Swartz were retried. Mr. Kozlowski took the stand to testify, and the jurors indicated that he was simply not a credible witness. When asked why he did not report $25 million in income, he responded that he just wasn't thinking when he signed his tax return. Jurors found an oversight of $25 million difficult to believe.

One portion of the case focused on the use of Tyco funds to buy and redecorate Mr. Kozlowski's New York City apartment (at a cost of $18 million). He acknowledged that he did not oversee it as he should have and that some of the decorations purchased were expensive and "godawful." He told jurors that he later stuffed many of the items "into a closet."[757]

The two were convicted on 22 of the 23 counts of larceny in their indictments. The total amount the prosecution proved was looted from the company was $150 million.

Mr. Kozlowski paid $21.2 million to settle charges related to sales tax evasion on his purchases and sales of his personal art collection. Mr. Kozlowski also settled federal income tax evasion charges. Mr. Swartz faced tax evasion charges related to the underreporting of the income gleaned from the larceny for which they were convicted.

(continued)

---

[748]*Id.*

[749]Alex Berenson, "From Dream Team at Tyco to a Refrain of Dennis Who?" *New York Times*, June 6, 2002, p. C1.

[750]*Id.*, pp. C1, C5.

[751]Andrew Ross Sorkin, "Ex-Tyco Chief, Free Spender, Going to Court," *New York Times*, September 29, 2003, pp. A1, A15.

[752]David Carr and Adam Liptak, "In Tyco Trial, an Apparent Gesture Has Many Meanings," *New York Times*, March 29, 2004, pp. C1, C6.

[753]*Id.*

[754]Andrew Ross Sorkin, "Judge Ends Trial When Tyco Juror Reports Threat," *New York Times*, April 3, 2004, pp. A1, B4; and "Mistrials and Tribulations," *Fortune*, April 19, 2004, 42.

[755]Jonathan D. Glater, "Tyco Case Shows Difficulty of Deciding Criminal Intent," *New York Times*, April 8, 2004, pp. C1, C4.

[756]"Ex-Tyco Official Says Actions Were Proper," *New York Times*, June 26, 2004, p. B14.

[757]Andrew Ross Sorkin, "Ex-Chief and Aide Guilty of Looting Millions at Tyco," *New York Times*, June 18, 2005, pp. A1, B4.

Case 4.26

(continued)

Kozlowski and Swartz were both sentenced on the larceny convictions to between 8⅓ and 25 years in New York State prison. Mr. Kozlowski was also ordered to pay $167 million in restitution and fines. Mr. Swartz was ordered to pay $72 million in fines and restitution. Both were handcuffed and immediately remanded to state prison following their sentences being imposed. The judge did not grant their motion to remain free while their appeals were pending.[758] The two men have been granted parole. In 2016, Mr. Swartz lost an appeal of his IRS assessment for $12.5 million in income from the loan forgiveness.

Tyco agreed to pay $3 billion to settle class action suits brought by its shareholders for fraud committed by Kozlowski and Swartz, the fourth largest shareholder settlement of the Enron era.[759] Tyco's share price dropped from $240 per share in 2002 to less than $25 by 2003. Since 2007, the share price has remained at below $50.

Discussion Questions

1. Recall your readings from Unit 2 on the relationship between ethics and economics. Evaluate this comment from a market observer: "When a CEO steps down for (alleged) tax evasion, it sends the message that all of Corporate America is crooked."[760] "It makes you think, 'Why did he do it? Is there another shoe to drop?'"[761]

2. Warren Rudman, former U.S. senator and a member of the board at Raytheon, who knew and worked with Mark Belnick, was astonished at Mr. Belnick's indictment when it was issued. Mr. Rudman said, when told of Mr. Belnick's fall from grace: "I don't understand. Ethical, straight, cross the t's, dot the i's—that's my experience with Mark Belnick."[762] Mr. Belnick was acquitted of all charges after a jury trial in the summer of 2004. Does his acquittal mean that he acted ethically? What ethical breaches can you find in his behavior at Tyco? What provisions in a credo might have helped Mr. Belnick see the issues more clearly?

3. What do you think of the ethics of Ms. Prue?

4. How do you think the spending and the loans were able to go on for so long?

5. What questions could Mr. Kozlowski and Mr. Swartz have asked themselves to better evaluate their conduct?

6. Evaluate the emails from Wilmer Cutler to general counsel and others in the company. Why were these warnings signs unheeded?

7. Make a list of the lines Mr. Kozlowski crossed in his tenure as CEO. Can any of those items help you in developing your credo? Mr. Kozlowski said, when he was named CEO of the Year by BusinessWeek,

> Most of us made it to the chief executive position because of a particularly high degree [of] responsibility.... We are offended most by the perception that we would waste the resources of a company that is a major part of our life and livelihood, and that we would be happy with directors who would permit waste .... So as a CEO I want a strong, competent board.[763]

What was he not seeing in his conduct? Had he grown complacent? Is it difficult for us to see ethical breaches that we commit?

[758]Andrew Ross Sorkin, "Ex-Tyco Officers Get 8 to 25 Years," *New York Times*, September 20, 2005, pp. A1, C8; Kevin McCoy, "Ex-Tyco Chiefs Whisked Off to Prison," *USA Today*, September 20, 2005, p. 1B; and Mark Maremont, "Tyco Ex-Officials Get Jail Terms, Big Fines," *Wall Street Journal*, September 20, 2005, pp. C1, C4.

[759]Floyd Norris, "Tyco to Pay $3 Billion in Settlement," *New York Times*, May 16, 2007, pp. C1, C14.

[760]Id.

[761]Adam Shell, "Markets Fall as Tyco CEO's Resignation Adds to Woes," *USA Today*, June 4, 2002, p. 1B.

[762]Glater, "A Star Lawyer Finds Himself the Target of a Peer," pp. C1, C8.

[763]"Match Game," *Fortune*, November 18, 2002, p. 34.

Reading 4.27

A Primer on Speaking Up and Whistleblowing

> In the course of performing my duties for the Firm, I have reason to believe that certain conduct on the part of senior management of the Firm may be in violation of the Code. The following is a summary of the conduct I believe may violate the Code and which I feel compelled, by the terms of the Code, to bring to your attention.[764]

So wrote Matthew Lee, on May 18, 2008, to the CFO and chief risk officer of Lehman Brothers, a firm that had employed him as an analyst since 1994. Mr. Lee, who headed global balance-sheet and legal-entity accounting, then went on to describe "tens of billions of dollars" on the firm's balance sheet that could not be substantiated. Mr. Lee also highlighted Lehman's use of Repo 105 (see Reading 4.22).

The response to Mr. Lee was astonishing but typical: (1) Ernst & Young, the firm's auditor, referred to Mr. Lee's memo as "pretty ugly," but concluded the issues that he raised were immaterial and his allegations unfounded and (2) Mr. Lee was fired.

Lehman declared bankruptcy on September 15, 2008. Mr. Lee was correct, and the bankruptcy report is a scathing one that demonstrates the top executives at Lehman were aware of both the level of risk exposure as well as the accounting practices used to conceal that exposure.

As you glance through the cases and examples in Units 1, 2, and 3 and in this unit and seek common threads, there are two they all share with Mr. Lee's experience at Lehman Brothers.

The two powerful common threads are: (1) those involved were aware of their ethical and legal lapses and (2) the warnings of employees and others were not heeded. Fannie Mae, Atlanta Public School System, the Houston Astros, BP, Boeing, Enron, WorldCom, HealthSouth, Under Armour, and all the problem companies that emerged in our turn-of-the-century scandals have those threads.

The key to stopping these schemes and poor ethical choices is getting the information from those in the organization who have it to those who can and will do something about it. Reviewing the tools organizations need that help employees speak up and get information to the right responders is critical in understanding organizational cultures. Those who do take action to resolve an issue are not always the first responders who receive the information. Organizations do fall into the trap of ignoring the employee's warnings. Indeed, too often the bearer of bad news (the messenger) often ends up being killed, which provides the firm with a temporary means of coping. There is a saying an employee gave to me years ago on why he did not disclose a serious problem in his company that he saw unfold before him: "The first whale to the surface always gets harpooned." The tools employees need and companies must have prevent that first whale from being harpooned. Instead, we learn to welcome the whale and all that he has to spout.

Have Your Reporting Systems in Place

Some means of anonymous reporting, either through a hotline or a computer third-party reporting system, is a bare minimum. This company-wide mechanism allows those employees who are uncomfortable in their own environments or, worse, may

---

[764]Letter of Matthew Lee, dated May 18, 2008, as included and discussed in the report of the examiner for the bankruptcy trustee in the Lehman bankruptcy.

be working under the folks involved in the unethical or illegal actions, the chance to raise issues. However, these systems do bring out the cranks and, as a result, do give us the reports that may report anything from a squeaky wheel on a chair to vending machine issues.

However, those reports may come from repeating pockets in the company. Even if the individual report contains no relevant allegations, the employee who submitted may simply not be able to articulate what is happening. However, the pockets of consistent reports indicate something more is afoot than just a manager who irritates employees. Follow sources and patterns to determine whether there may be areas in the company that require more analysis of the complaints to determine the root cause, a cause that may well involve financial reporting issues.

On Dissent and Discussion: The Humble Firm

In a conversation with an executive at a company at the top of its industry and one that is studied by others for its management practices, I asked for a one-line descriptor of the secret to his company's longstanding success. He paused and then gave this pithy response, "We go to work each day and say, 'We suck, now let's get better.'" His point is, however, one worth exploring. In these healthy companies, the arrogance of results and top performance is kept at bay. That humility permits a more open environment to take hold. An open environment is one in which a manager with 14 years of experience would not be fired for raising concerns about possible violations of the code of ethics. Rather, that manager would be given the opportunity to explain his concerns and the issues. Indeed, in a firm of humility, a 14-year manager would not need to write a memo of concern—the issues would come up in discussions.

Meetings in the humble firm have lively discussions, not tense ones. In firms that crash and burn ethically and legally, and usually as a result, financially, managers and employees remained sullen and mute in discussions and meetings. However, they certainly did let loose with their concerns only in their emails, as we witnessed with Boeing (Case 2.12) to colleagues, thus providing the documentation that is the stuff of civil litigation and, on occasion, criminal liability. In the humble firm, the email thoughts are the ones stated publicly, discussed, and evaluated.

Develop Your Own Sensing Mechanisms

Even in the humblest of firms, issues still may not emerge. Follow this advice: Get out of your office. That is, what an employee might never utter in a meeting or put in an anonymous report may come out in the cafeteria, the hallways, or at one of the coffee room birthday celebrations. Often spontaneity comes at employee volunteer projects or unannounced visits to plants, divisions, stores, or offices. This egalitarian access has an effect on employees and their willingness to speak up and raise questions. Once leaders take on a new identity as an approachable individual as opposed to an iconic and feared figure, there is new communication. Daily interaction breaks down the barriers of fear and silence that prevent information from getting from that place in the company where it is common knowledge to those in the company who can and will take appropriate steps and make changes.

Quarterly or annual meetings with the CEO or CFO in small groups of employees are some form of sensing mechanisms. But they are scheduled meetings. Those are formal meetings. Spontaneous "blurts" of concern require spontaneous settings. This sensing tool is really an update of the 1970s organizational behavior

(OB) theory, management by walking around (MBWA). This theory is akin to that employed when parents of teens come home early and unannounced: one never knows what one will find. Some companies are now requiring both executives and boards to have a certain number of "visits" to company sites, plants, offices, and divisions so that they understand what the company does and how it works. Further, those visits cannot be "gaggle" visits, those group visits that are little more than a tour group swoop. Rather, the visits are individual ones with the same goal as the executives' egalitarian interactions.

A television reality show, *Undercover Boss*, finds CEOs, COOs, and CFOs working side by side with employees. They have come away with new insights in what worries employees, what their jobs require, and even when the employees are cheating a bit on their time clocks. The greater the isolation an executive has, the less information flows from the frontlines. The realignment of thinking from meetings to spontaneity as the priority results in fewer meetings, greater productivity, and, most importantly, information about the culture and what is really going on in an organization.

Whistleblowers: In Defense of Tattling

We switch now to the responsibility of employees to report issues. As early as our toddler days, we are told, "Don't be a tattletale." No matter that we were being roughed up by the sandbox bully or had our bucket and shovel taken right out from under our sun bonnets. Don't tattle. As we grew, we learned and even developed new euphemisms for those who report wrongdoing: rats, finks, ratfinks, stool pigeons, stoolies, tattletales, whistleblowers, snitches, and narcs. Clever, albeit ominous, sayings remind us of the consequences of "tattling," "Snitches get stitches and end up in ditches."

We would rather stand by, sullen and mute, watching others, who through their dishonesty, dismantle a church, a nonprofit, a hospital, a corporation, a school, or even a financial market. The rationalizations flow easily: "Not my problem." "I don't want to get involved." "Someone else will do something." "I have to work with these people after I report. Will that work? Will I be able to work?"

Increasingly, current events reflect a callousness that is disturbing. Not only is no one stepping in to help or even just say something, we have cell phone videographers who can hardly wait to post their record that captures harm to others. We have viewed, perhaps too many times, cell-phone videos of police officers watching a fellow officer use excessive force even as they stand sullen and mute. We have cell-phone videographers who document looting and film the looters running away only to say later, "I know nothing."

There are some insights and guidelines for changing this demonization of tattling and lionization of the silent bystander.

Lesson #1 If You See Something, Say Something

Human nature being what it is, where there is opportunity to cut corners or take advantage, humans do seize the moment. "Who's to know?" "How could they find out?" One thing to emphasize in any organization is that there is really nothing that is secret when people are working together each day. Truth is a powerful force and it does want to percolate to the surface. An organization can help to open the door to reporting by training employees to assume that whatever it is they are writing, saying, planning, or putting on social media will become public and that their thoughts, expressed in a private e-mail, will someday see the harsh light of day and expose whatever underlying conduct spawned the emails.

In an organization there is no privacy and no isolation. Any assumption that no one is watching is flawed and has been established in Units 1–4 as case after case illustrated the extensive knowledge many employees had of their organization's missteps. Switching to a mindset that you are being observed curbs behaviors and makes it easier for employees who see something to say something beyond just putting some venting in an e-mail that will later emerge in congressional hearings on their companies' misdeeds.

Lesson # 2 Enforcement Is to Honor What Integrity Cannot Muster

Employees are more likely to report issues when they have seen employers take action to curb behaviors they have reported. Enforcement is perhaps the most clear and precise form of communication an organization can have with its employees. Enforcement is a reflection of values and their importance. For an employee to report a concern, they must believe that their action in coming forward will not be a futile exercise. Part of the reason they report is so that unsafe, fraudulent, or abusive behavior does not continue. If there are no sanctions or consequences for reported behavior or if those sanctions and consequences take too long, employees return to sullen and mute.

Lesson #3 Tattling Is a Tall Order

Tattling is a tall order. At West Point, both self-reporting and reporting on classmates is a requirement under the academy's honor code. As a graduate put it, "You're asking an awful lot of these young people to turn somebody else in." Those who report are rarely revered. So, we leave students and employees to cope with pressure as they wrestle conscience and the potential damage to some peers as well as their relationship with other peers who said nothing.

What we are left with is reliance on Lessons # 1 and #2. To foster a culture of reporting, leaders must establish clear and definitive lines on conduct. Fuzzy rationalizations and slow-walked investigations dissipate clarity and discourage reporting. The very essence of character and leadership was summed up by the great C. S. Lewis, "Integrity is doing the right thing even when no one is watching." But in organizations we need to establish that someone always *is* watching—the employees. And they are the eyes, ears, and mouthpieces necessary for watch duty and reporting. The cases have shown their eyes and eyes are working just fine—they see the ethical issues. Leaders must encourage them to be the mouthpieces.

Discussion Questions

1. What are sensing mechanisms, and why are they important?

2. What is the humble firm, and how does it encourage ethical behavior?

3. Describe what leads to the types of behaviors at Lehman and other companies that eventually collapse.

4. Why can't managers simply rely on their ethics hotlines?

5. What role does enforcement play in the willingness of employees to speak up?

6. Why is "tattling" treated so negatively by others?

Case 4.28

NASA and the Space Shuttle Booster Rockets

Morton Thiokol, Inc., an aerospace company, manufactures the solid-propellant rocket motors for the Peacekeeper missile and the missiles on Trident nuclear submarines. Thiokol also worked closely with the National Aeronautics and Space Administration (NASA) in developing the *Challenger*, one of NASA's reusable space shuttles.

Morton Thiokol served as the manufacturer for the booster rockets used to launch the *Challenger*. NASA had scheduled a special launch of the *Challenger* for January 1986. The launch was highly publicized, because NASA had conducted a nationwide search for a teacher to send on the flight. For NASA's 25th shuttle mission, teacher Christa McAuliffe would be on board.

On the scheduled launch day, January 28, 1986, the weather was cloudy and cold at the John F. Kennedy Space Center in Cape Canaveral, Florida. The launch had already been delayed several times, but NASA officials still contacted Thiokol engineers in Utah to discuss whether the shuttle should be launched in such cold weather. The temperature range for the boosters, as specified in Thiokol's contract with NASA, was between 40°F and 90°F.

The temperature at Cape Canaveral that January morning was below 30°F. The launch of the *Challenger* proceeded nevertheless. A presidential commission later concluded, "Thiokol management reversed its position and recommended the launch of [the *Challenger*] at the urging of [NASA] and contrary to the views of its engineers in order to accommodate a major customer."[765]

Two of the Thiokol engineers involved in the launch, Allan McDonald and Roger Boisjoly, later testified that they had opposed the launch. Boisjoly had done work on the shuttle's booster rockets at the Marshall Space Flight Center in Utah in February 1985, at which time he noted that at low temperatures an O-ring assembly in the rockets eroded and, consequently, failed to seal properly. Though Boisjoly gave a presentation on the issue, little action was taken over the course of the year. Boisjoly conveyed his frustration in his activity reports. Finally, in July 1985, Boisjoly wrote a confidential memo to R. K. (Bob) Lund, Thiokol's vice president for engineering. An excerpt follows:

This letter is written to insure [sic] that management is fully aware of the seriousness of the current O-ring erosion problem.... The mistakenly accepted position on the joint problem was to fly without fear of failure.... [This position] is now drastically changed as a result of the SRM [shuttle recovery mission] 16A nozzle joint erosion which eroded a secondary O-ring with the primary O-ring never sealing. If the same scenario should occur in a field joint (and it could), then it is a jump ball as to the success or failure of the joint.... The result would be a catastrophe of the highest order—loss of human life....

It is my honest and real fear that if we do not take immediate action to dedicate a team to solve the problem, with the field joint having the number one priority, then we stand in jeopardy of losing a flight along with all the launch pad facilities.[766]

In October 1985, Boisjoly presented the O-ring issue at a conference of the Society of Automotive Engineers and requested suggestions for resolution.[767]

On January 27, 1986, the day before the launch, Boisjoly attempted to halt the launch. Mr. McDonald also offered his insights to a group of NASA and Thiokol engineers. However, four Thiokol managers, including Lund, voted unanimously to recommend the launch. One manager had urged Lund to "take off his engineering hat and put on his management hat."[768] The managers then developed the following revised recommendations. Engineers were excluded from the final decision and the development of these findings.[769]

- Calculations show that SRM-25 [the designation for the *Challenger*'s January 28 flight] O-rings will be 20°F colder than SRM-15 O-rings.

(continued)

[765]Judith Dobrzynski, "Morton Thiokol: Reflections on the Shuttle Disaster," *BusinessWeek*, March 14, 1988, p. 82.

[766]Russel Boisjoly et al., "Roger Boisjoly and the *Challenger* Disaster: The Ethical Dimensions," *Journal of Business Ethics* 8 (1989), pp. 2178–2130.

[767]"No. 2 Official Is Appointed at Thiokol," *New York Times*, June 12, 1992, p. C3; and "Whistle-Blowing: Not Always a Losing Game," *EE Spectrum*, December 1990, 49–52.

[768]Boisjoly et al., "Roger Boisjoly and the *Challenger* Disaster," pp. 217–230.

[769]Paul Hoversten, "Engineers Waver, Then Decide to Launch," *USA Today*, January 22, 1996, p. 2A.

Case 4.28

(continued)

- Temperature data not conclusive on predicting primary O-ring blow-by.
- Engineering assessment is as follows:
  - Colder O-rings will have increased effective durometer [that is, they will be harder].
  - "Harder" O-rings will take longer to seat.
  - More gas may pass primary [SRM-25] O-ring before the primary seal seats (relative to SRM-15).
  - Demonstrated sealing threshold [on SRM-25 O-ring] is three times greater than 0.038" erosion experienced on SRM-15.
  - If the primary seal does not seat, the secondary seal will seat.
  - Pressure will get to secondary seal before the metal parts rotate.
  - O-ring pressure leak check places secondary seal in outboard position which minimizes sealing time.
- MTI recommends STS-51L launch proceed on 28 January 1986.
- SRM-25 will not be significantly different from SRM-15.[770]

After the decision was made, Boisjoly returned to his office and wrote in his journal,

> I sincerely hope this launch does not result in a catastrophe. I personally do not agree with some of the statements made in Joe Kilminster's [Kilminster was one of the four Thiokol managers who voted to recommend the launch] written summary stating that SRM-25 is okay to fly.[771]

Seventy-four seconds into the *Challenger* launch, the low temperature caused the seals at the booster rocket joints to fail. The *Challenger* exploded, killing Christa McAuliffe and the six astronauts on board.[772]

The subsequent investigation by the presidential commission placed the blame for the faulty O-rings squarely with Thiokol. Charles S. Locke, Thiokol's CEO, maintained, "I take the position that we never agreed to the launch at the temperature at the time of the launch. The *Challenger* incident resulted more from human error than mechanical error. The decision to launch should have been referred to headquarters. If we'd been consulted here, we'd never have given clearance, because the temperature was not within the contracted specs."[773]

Both Boisjoly and McDonald testified before the presidential panel regarding their opposition to the launch and the decision of their managers (who were also engineers) to override their recommendation. Both Boisjoly and McDonald also testified that following their expressed opposition to the launch and their willingness to come forward, they had been isolated from NASA and subsequently demoted. Since testifying, McDonald has been assigned to "special projects." Boisjoly took medical leave for post-traumatic stress disorder, left Thiokol, but received disability pay from the company. For a time, he operated a consulting firm in Mesa, Arizona and spoke frequently about business ethics until his death in 2012.[774]

In May 1986, then-CEO Locke stated, in an interview with the *Wall Street Journal*, "This shuttle thing will cost us this year 10¢ a share."[775] Locke later protested that his statement had been taken out of context.[776]

In 1989, Morton Norwich separated from Thiokol Chemical Corporation. The two companies had previously merged to become Morton Thiokol. Following the separation, Thiokol Chemical became Thiokol Corporation. Morton returned to the salt business, and Thiokol, remaining under contract with NASA through 1999, redesigned its space shuttle rocket motor to correct the deficiencies. No one at Thiokol was fired following the *Challenger* accident. Because of this incident and defense contractor indictments, the Government Accountability

(continued)

---

[770]Boisjoly et al., "Roger Boisjoly and the *Challenger* Disaster," pp. 217–230.

[771]Interview with Roger Boisjoly, June 28, 1993, M. M. Jennings.

[772]Paul Hoversten, Patricia Edmonds, and Haya El Nasser, "Debate Raged Night before Doomed Launch," *USA Today*, January 22, 1996, pp. A1, A2.

[773]Dobrzynski, "Morton Thiokol," p. 82.

[774]Interview with Roger Boisjoly.

[775]Dobrzynski, "Morton Thiokol," p. 82.

[776]"No. 2 Official Is Appointed at Thiokol," p. C3; and "Whistle-Blowing," pp. 49–52.

Case 4.28

(continued)

Project was established in Washington, DC. The office provides a staff, legal assistance, and pamphlets to help whistleblowers working on government projects.

Discussion Questions

1. Who is responsible for the deaths that resulted from the Challenger explosion?

2. If you had been in Allan McDonald's or Roger Boisjoly's position on January 28, 1986, what would you have done?

3. Evaluate Locke's comment on the loss of 10 cents per share.

4. Should the possibility that the booster rockets might not perform below 30°F have been a factor in the decision to allow the launch to proceed?

5. Roger Boisjoly offered the following advice on whistleblowing:

   - You owe your organization an opportunity to respond. Speak to them first verbally. Memos are not appropriate for the first step.

   - Gather collegial support for your position. If you cannot get the support, then make sure you are correct.

   - Spell out the problem in a letter.[777]

Mr. Boisjoly acknowledges he did not gather collegial support. How can such support be obtained? Where would you start? What would you use to persuade others?

6. Scientist William Lowrance has written that "a thing is safe if its attendant risks are judged to be acceptable."[778] Had everyone, including the astronauts, accepted the risks attendant to the Challenger's launch?

7. Groupthink is defined as

   a mode of thinking that people engage in when they are deeply involved in a cohesive in-group, when the members' strivings for unanimity override their motivation to realistically appraise alternative courses of action.... Groupthink refers to the deterioration of mental efficiency, reality testing, and moral judgment that results from in-group pressures.[779]

   In another NASA accident, a launch pad fire took the lives of Apollo I astronauts Gus Grissom, Ed White, and Roger Chaffee on January 30, 1967. Gene Krantz, the Mission Control Flight Director, addressed his staff by saying, "We were too gungho about the schedule and we locked out all of the problems we saw each day in our work.... Not one of us stood up and said, "Damn it, STOP!"[780]

   Is this what happened when Thiokol's management group took off its "engineering hats"?

---

[777]From an interview with Roger Boisjoly conducted I Mesa, Arizona by Arizona State University MBA students studying the NASA Challenger case.

[778]Joseph R. Herkert, "Management's Hat Trick: Misuse of 'Engineering Judgment' in the Challenger Incident," 10 *Journal of Business Ethics* 617 (1991).

[779]Irving L. Janis, *Victims of Groupthink* (1972).

[780]http://history.nasa.gov/Apollo204. Accessed May 19, 2010.

Section

G

The Culture of Goodness

Sometimes a culture turns to fraud because of its self-perception of goodness. Because they are doing so much good in terms of contributions, sponsorships, and scholarships, the fact that there is fraud afoot is not problematic because the view of this type of culture is, "Look how much good I was able to accomplish with the money that I made!"

Case 4.29

New Era: If It Sounds Too Good to Be True, It Is Too Good to Be True

The Foundation for New Era Philanthropy was founded in 1989 by Mr. John G. Bennett Jr. New Era took in over $200 million between 1989 and May 1995, from 180 nonprofit organizations, before the Securities and Exchange Commission (SEC) brought suit against New Era and the foundation went into bankruptcy.

Mr. Bennett was, at that time, a charismatic individual who was able to bring in many individual and institutional investors (most of them nonprofit organizations that included many colleges and universities) with the promise of a double-your-money return.[781] The foundation began as a matching-gift program. Mr. Bennett would take the funds from the nonprofit, deposit them in a Prudential Insurance account that would earn interest at Treasury rates, and then work to find a matching donor. The intentions were good, and initially the funds were small. Mr. Bennett would later admit that there never were any matching donors. As word of his success spread, the size of the funds the nonprofits deposited increased, and the greater the challenge became for finding a matching donor. And the pressure was growing. Mr. Bennett was receiving attention and accolades for

his efforts. Former Philadelphia mayor (then governor) Ed Rendell felt that Mr. Bennett's efforts had the potential for changing how people perceived Philadelphia both because of his success and also because the funds were helping nonprofits in their educational and community improvement efforts.[782]

Mr. Bennett often met personally with investors or their representatives and opened and closed his sessions with them with prayer. Among the individual investors in New Era were Laurance Rockefeller; singer Pat Boone; then-President of Procter & Gamble John Pepper; John Whitehead, the former cohead of Goldman Sachs; and former Treasury Secretary William Simon. The institutional investors included Harvard, Princeton, University of Pennsylvania, the Nature Conservancy, and the National Museum of American Jewish History.[783]

In 1991, Melenie and Albert Meyer moved from their native South Africa to Michigan, where Mr. Meyer took a tenure-track position as an accounting professor at Spring Arbor College. Because there were only three accounting majors at the time he was hired, Mr. Meyer

(continued)

---

[781]Robert Allen and Marshall Romney, "Lessons from New Era," *Internal Auditor*, October 1998, http://findarticles.com/. Accessed July 1, 2010.

[782]Steve Wulf, "Too Good to Be True," *Time*, May 29, 1995, p. 34.
[783]Steve Secklow, "A New Era Consultant Lured Rich Donors over Pancakes, Prayer," *Wall Street Journal*, June 2, 1995, pp. A1, A4.

Case 4.29

(continued)

was also required to work part-time in the business office.[784]

During his first month in the business office, Mr. Meyer found that the college had transferred $294,000 to Heritage of Values Foundation, Inc. He connected the term *Heritage* with Reverend Jim Bakker and went to the library to research Heritage of Values Foundation, Inc. Although he found no connection to Jim Bakker, he could find no other information on the foundation. Mr. Meyer asked his supervisor, the vice president for business affairs, Ms. Janet M. Tjepkema, about Heritage of Values and the nature of the transfer. She explained that Heritage was the consultant that had found the New Era Foundation and had advised the college to invest in this "double your investment" fund.

Mr. Meyer attempted to research New Era but could find no registration for it in Pennsylvania, its headquarters location. He could not obtain information from New Era (there was no registration in Pennsylvania ever filed, and no tax returns were filed until 1993). Mr. Meyer continued to approach administrators of the college, but they seemed annoyed. He continued to collect information about New Era for the next two years. He gathered income tax returns and even spoke directly with Mr. Bennett. Mr. Meyer remained silent during the time that he gathered information because he was untenured and on a temporary work visa.[785] He also had a family to support, with three children. He was convinced that his concerns were justified when he discovered that New Era had reported only $34,000 in interest income for one year. With the portfolio it purported to hold, the interest income should have been about $1 million.

After he had collected files of information on New Era, which he labeled "Ponzi File," Mr. Meyer wrote a letter to the president of Spring Arbor as well as the chairman of the board of trustees for the college, warning them about his concerns regarding New Era. Mr. Meyer had also tried to talk with his colleagues about the information he

had uncovered. He felt shunned by administrators and his colleagues, and by April 1994, he and his wife were no longer attending any social functions held by the college. He was told by administrators that raising funds was tough enough without his meddling. He repeatedly tried to convince administrators not to place any additional funds with New Era. His advice was ignored, and Spring Arbor invested an additional $1.5 million in New Era in 1994. At that time, Spring Arbor College's total endowment was $6 million. The $1.5 million would later be lost as part of the New Era bankruptcy.

In March 1995, Mr. Meyer received tenure and began to try to help others by warning them about his concerns about New Era. He wrote to the SEC and detailed his information and concerns. The SEC then notified Prudential Securities, which was holding $73 million in New Era stock. Prudential began its own investigation and found resistance from New Era officers in releasing information. New Era began to unravel, and by June 1995 it was in bankruptcy. There were 300 creditors named, and net losses were $107 million. New Era was nothing but a Ponzi scheme. It was able to pay out double the investment, but only so long as it could recruit new participants. When it could no longer recruit participants, it was unable to pay on demands for withdrawal.

Mr. Bennett was indicted on 82 counts of fraud, money laundering, and tax code violations in March 1997.[786] Following his arraignment, he was released after posting his daughter's $115,000 house to cover his bond.[787] Mr. Bennett entered a no-contest plea in 1997 and was sentenced to 12 years in prison, following six days of testimony during his sentencing hearing, including emotional pleas from Mr. Bennett. In ordering a reduced sentence, the judge departed from the 24.5 years dictated by the federal sentencing guidelines because Mr. Bennett had been "extraordinarily cooperative" in the investigation and because he had voluntarily turned over $1.5 million

(continued)

---

[784]Barbara Carton, "Unlikely Hero: A Persistent Accountant Brought New Era's Problems to Light," *Wall Street Journal*, May 19, 1995, pp. B1, B10.
[785]*Id.*

[786]Steve Secklow, "Retired Judge Will Sort Out New Era Mess," *Wall Street Journal*, June 29, 1995, pp. B1, B16.
[787]Steve Secklow, "How New Era's Boss Led Rich and Gullible into a Web of Deceit," *Wall Street Journal*, May 19, 1995, pp. A1, A5.

Case 4.29

(continued)

in assets to the bankruptcy court to be distributed to New Era participants.[788] The judge also noted what he felt was Mr. Bennett's diminished capacity.[789] The judge, in particularly harsh language, lectured Mr. Bennett on the egregious nature of his conduct: "It is possible for an ostensibly good and reverent person who is a true believer to engage in egregiously reprehensible and societally disruptive behavior."[790]

The nonprofit organizations that had invested in New Era recovered two-thirds of their investments and filed suit against Prudential Securities for recoupment of the remainder. That suit was settled without disclosure of its terms in 1996. The basis of the suit was that their funds were held in a single account at Prudential and that the funds were being used to repay New Era loans from Prudential instead of being invested as promised.

Mr. Meyer was still not embraced at his school for his efforts. Some still say that if Mr. Meyer had remained quiet, Mr. Bennett could have worked out the problems of New Era. Meyer was named a Michiganian of the Year for 1995.

Discussion Questions

1. Why did Mr. Meyer have so much difficulty convincing his college administrators that there was a problem with New Era?

2. Did Mr. Meyer follow the right steps in trying to bring New Era to the attention of the college officials?

3. What impact did Mr. Meyer's personal situation (visa and tenure issues) have on his desire to carry through with his concerns?

4. Why were administrators so reluctant to hear Mr. Meyer out? Mr. Bennett notified Spring Arbor College officials when Mr. Meyer called him and asked administrators to keep Mr. Meyer quiet. How would you read this kind of request? What would you do if you were an administrator?

5. About 40 of the nonprofit organizations that had invested in New Era and withdrawn their funds and earnings prior to its collapse voluntarily agreed to return their money to the bankruptcy pool.[791] An administrator from Lancaster Bible College, in explaining the return of his college's funds to the trustee, quoted St. Paul's letter to the Philippians: "Let each of you look not only to his own interest but also to the interests of others" (Philippians 2:4). Hans Finzel, head of CB International, a missionary fund, said his organization would not be returning the money: "It's true that it's tainted money, but it's also true that we received it in good faith."[792] Compare and contrast the positions of the parties. Would you return the money?

6. Is this case an indication that nonprofits operate as businesses and are susceptible to the same business ethics issues? Should nonprofits have ethics programs and training for their staff and volunteers?

7. What are the characteristics of Mr. Bennett that are similar to leaders in the other cases you have studied?

Sources

Bloom, Michael A., "Key in New Era Settlement," *National Law Journal*, July 15, 1996, p. A4.

Davis, Ann, "Charity's Troubles Put Dechert in Bind," *National Law Journal*, May 29, 1995, p. A6.

Lambert, Wade, "Trustee in New Era Bankruptcy May Pursue 'Donations,'" *Wall Street Journal*, May 22, 1995, p. B3.

Secklow, Steve, "A New Era Consultant Lured Rich Donors over Pancakes, Prayers," *Wall Street Journal*, June 2, 1995, pp. A1.

Secklow, Steve, "New Era's Bennett Gets 12-Year Sentence," *Wall Street Journal*, September 23, 1997, p. B13.

Secklow, Steve, "Prudential Securities Agrees to Settle New Era Suits by Paying $18 Million," *Wall Street Journal*, November 18, 1996, p. A4.

Secklow, Steve, and Joseph Rebello, "IRS Is Studying Whether New Era's Donors Committed Fraud on Deductions," *Wall Street Journal*, May 24, 1995, p. A3.

Slobodzian, Joseph, "New Era Founder Says: God Made Him Do It," *National Law Journal*, March 17, 1997, p. A9.

---

[788]Dinah Wisenberg Brin, "Philanthropy Scam Nets 12 Years," *USA Today*, September 23, 1997, p. 2A.

[789]By the time of his sentencing, the issue of his mental competency was raised. In 2005, his lawyer requested an early release from prison for Mr. Bennett because of health reasons.

[790]Joseph Slobodzian, "Bennett Gets 12 for New Era Scam," *National Law Journal*, October 6, 1997, p. A8.

---

[791]Andrea Gerlin, "Among the Few Given Money by New Era, Many See Blessings in Giving It Back," *Wall Street Journal*, June 20, 1995, pp. B1, B10.

[792]Michael A. Bloom, "Key in New Era Settlement," *National Law Journal*, July 15, 1996, p. A4.

Case 4.30

Giving and Spending the United Way

The United Way, which evolved from the local community chests of the 1920s, is a national organization that funnels funding to charities through a payroll deduction system.

Ninety percent of all charitable payroll deductions in 1991 were for the United Way. This system, however, has been criticized as coercive. Bonuses, for example, were offered for achieving 100% employee participation. Betty Beene, president of United Way of Tristate (New York, New Jersey, and Connecticut), commented, "If participation is 100 percent, it means someone has been coerced."[793] Tristate discontinued the bonuses and arm-twisting.

United Way's system of spending also came under fire through the actions of William Aramony, president of the United Way from 1970 to 1992. During his tenure, United Way receipts grew from $787 million in 1970 to $3 billion in 1990. But some of Aramony's effects on the organization were less positive.

In early 1992, the *Washington Post* reported that Aramony

- was paid $463,000 per year;
- flew first class on commercial airlines;
- spent $20,000 in one year for limousines; and
- used the Concorde for transatlantic flights.[794]

The article also revealed that one of the taxable spin-off companies Aramony had created to provide travel and bulk purchasing for United Way chapters had bought a $430,000 condominium in Manhattan and a $125,000 apartment in Coral Gables, Florida, for his use. Another spin-off had hired Aramony's son, Robert Aramony, as its president.

When Aramony's expenses and salary became public, Stanley C. Gault, chairman of Goodyear Tire & Rubber Company, asked, "Where was the board? The outside auditors?"[795] Aramony resigned after 15 chapters of the United Way threatened to withhold their annual dues to the national office.

Said Robert O. Bothwell, executive director of the National Committee for Responsive Philanthropy, "I think it is obscene that he is making that kind of salary and asking people who are making $10,000 a year to give 5 percent of their income."[796]

In August 1992, the United Way board of directors hired Elaine Chao, the Peace Corps director, to replace William Aramony at a salary of $195,000, with no perks.[797] She reduced staff from 275 to 185 and borrowed $1.5 million to compensate for a decline in donations. By 1995, United Way donations had still not returned to their 1991 level of $3.2 billion. Ms. Chao has since left the United Way and served as director of the Peace Corps, secretary of labor for the Bush administration from 2001–2009, and secretary of transportation in the Trump administration. Ms. Chao is married to Republican U.S. Senator Mitch McConnell of Kentucky.

In September 1994, William Aramony and two other United Way officers, including the chief financial officer, were indicted by a federal grand jury for conspiracy, mail fraud, and tax fraud. The indictment alleged the three officers diverted more than $2.74 million of United Way funds to purchase an apartment in New York City for $383,000, interior decorating for $72,000, a condominium, vacations, and a lifetime pass on American Airlines. In addition, $80,000 of United Way funds were paid to Aramony's girlfriend, a 1986 high school graduate, for consulting, even though she did no work.

On April 3, 1995, Aramony was found guilty of 25 counts of fraud, conspiracy, and money laundering. Two other United Way executives were also convicted. Mr. Aramony was sentenced to 84 months in prison (and fined $300,000) and was released in 2004. United Way executives continue to refer to his tenure and all the problems associated with it as "the great unpleasantness."

(continued)

---

[793]Susan Garland, "Keeping a Sharper Eye on Those Who Pass the Hat," *BusinessWeek*, March 16, 1992, p. 39.

[794]As reported in "Ex-Executives of United Way Indicted," *(Phoenix) Arizona Republic*, September 14, 1994, p. A6.

[795]Garland, "Keeping a Sharper Eye on Those Who Pass the Hat," p. 39.

[796]Felicity Barringer, "United Way Head Is Forced Out in a Furor over His Lavish Style," *New York Times*, February 28, 1992, p. A1.

[797]Desda Moss, "Peace Corps Director to Head United Way," *USA Today*, August 27, 1992, p. 6A; and Sabra Chartrand, "Head of Peace Corps Named United Way President," *New York Times*, August 27, 1992, p. A8.

Case 4.30

(continued)

By April 1998, donation levels were still not completely reinstated but did increase (up 4.7%) for the first time since the 1992 Aramony crisis. Relationships between local chapters and the national organization were often strained, and the Boy Scouts of America boycott created additional tension. United Way's donations fell 11% since 1991, while overall charitable giving was up 9%.

In January 2000, a federal district court judge awarded Mr. Aramony the full value of his deferred compensation plan, or $4.2 million. Judge Shira Scheindlin ruled in favor of Mr. Aramony because she said there was no clause for forfeiting the money if Mr. Aramony committed a felony. Such a so-called bad boy clause had been discussed by the board when it was in the process of approving the deferred compensation plan for Mr. Aramony and other United Way executives. However, the bad boy clause never made it into the final agreement.[798]

Judge Scheindlin also ruled that United Way could withhold $2.02 million of the amount due under the deferred compensation plan to cover salary, investigation costs, and interest on those amounts. She did not award Mr. Aramony attorneys' fees for having to bring the suit against United Way to collect his deferred compensation.

Many in the nonprofit field say that the shadow of William Aramony looms over the nonprofit world. However, when he was released from prison in 2002, the warden, guards, and inmates, who all called him "Mr. Aramony," spoke of him with fondness because of his work in prison in trying to provide educational opportunities for his fellow inmates. They described him as being tireless in his efforts to teach everything from reading to math to, ironically,

business operations. Mr. Aramony passed away in November 2011.

Discussion Questions

1. Was there anything unethical about Aramony's expenditures?
2. Was the board responsible for the expenditures?
3. Is the perception as important as the acts themselves?
4. If Aramony were a CEO of a for-profit firm, would your answers change?
5. What obstacles did Chao face as she assumed the United Way helm?
6. Do you think Aramony should have asked for his deferred compensation funds? Why would the board pay him those funds? What could boards do to limit compensation paid to CEOs who resign following misconduct at the company?

Sources

Allen, Frank E., and Susan Pulliam, "United Way's Rivals Take Aim at Its Practices," *Wall Street Journal*, March 6, 1992, pp. B1, B6.

Barringer, Felicity, "Ex-Chief of United Way Vows to Fight Accusations," *New York Times*, April 10, 1992, p. A13.

Duffy, Michael, "Charity Begins at Home," *Time*, March 9, 1992, p. 48.

"Ex-Executives of United Way Indicted," *Arizona Republic*, September 14, 1994, p. A6.

Kinsley, Michael, "Charity Begins with Government," *Time*, April 6, 1992, p. 74.

Moss, Desda, "Change Is Focus of United Way Meeting," *USA Today*, August 19, 1992, p. 7A.

Moss, Desda, "Former United Way Chief Charged with Looting Funds," *USA Today*, September 14, 1994, p. 1A

Moss, Desda, "United Way's Ex-Chief Guilty of Using Funds," *USA Today*, April 14, 1995, p. 1A.

[798]David Cay Johnston, "Ex-United Way Chief Owed $4.2 Million," *New York Times*, January 5, 2000, p. C4.

Case 4.31

The Baptist Foundation: Funds of the Faithful

Although founded in 1948, the Baptist Foundation of Arizona (BFA) took a dramatic strategic step in 1984 with a shift away from raising funds for starting up churches to a real estate investment nonprofit corporation. In its early days of the new strategy, the BFA did quite well because with a real estate boom, property values were increasing. In addition to a profitable real estate market, the BFA had a psychology going with its fund and with recruiting investors. Each year, at its annual convention, the BFA distributed its "Book of Reports," a financial compilation given to the convention attendees. However, the "Book of Reports" could be given to others as a means of recruiting new investors. The BFA used the term *stewardship investment* to describe the sort of higher calling that those who invested in BFA had. And for a good many years it looked as if Providence had had some hand in the BFA, for it was offering higher than market returns.[799]

However, by 1988 both the Arizona economy and its real estate market were sinking fast. Rather than disclose that the downturn had affected its holdings (as it had for all other real estate firms, for-profit and nonprofit alike), BFA opted not to write down its properties. The management team's compensation was tied to the performance of the fund. Arthur Andersen, the auditor for BFA, noted the presence of specific revenue targets set by management for each quarter, with compensation packages tied to those targets.

The nondisclosure was accomplished through the use of complex layers of transactions with related parties, accounts receivable, and a host of other accounting sleights of hand that allowed BFA to look as if it still had both the assets and income it had before the market downturn. BFA carried the properties at their full original values on its books, not at their true market values, figures that would have been significantly less and were driving many other real estate investment firms into bankruptcy.

---

[799]This information can be found in the criminal information, cease and desist order, and bankruptcy filings all located at the Arizona Corporation Commission website, http://www.ccsd.cc.state.az.us.

BFA's income doubled between 1996 and 1997 and had climbed from $350,000 in 1988 to $2.5 million in 1997. The numbers seemed quite nearly inexplicable given the downturn and the performance of all other real estate funds. BFA was selling its properties to board members and companies of board members at their book value or slightly higher in an effort to show gains, income, and cash flow for the BFA.

Funds never really changed hands in these related parties' transactions. The transfers of funds and properties were like a large shell game among and between various nonprofit entities. Some of the 21 individuals on the BFA board who decided against writing down the properties were also parties to the pseudo sales transactions of the properties to ALO and New Church Ventures. According to forensic auditors, a former director of BFA created ALO, Inc., and New Church Ventures, Inc., also nonprofit organizations. These corporations were shell corporations with no employees. However, significant amounts of BFA income were transferred to these two nonprofits as management fees, accounting fees, and marketing and administrative services fees. ALO purchased BFA's overvalued real estate holdings in exchange for promissory notes. Arizona Corporation Commission records show that for 1997, ALO reported that it owed BFA $70.3 million and New Church ventures $173.6 million.

BFA also created a web of other subsidiaries, including Christian Financial Partners, EVIG, and Select Trading Group. This tangled web made it difficult for potential investors to understand what BFA was doing or how it was earning its funds.

Because BFA's financial statements looked phenomenal, more investors joined, and the fraud lasted until 1999. In 1999, state officials issued a cease and desist order to stop BFA from soliciting and bringing in new investors. In 1998, Andersen identified "earnings management" as a significant problem at BFA. However, Andersen did not see the earnings management as enough of a problem to halt its certification of BFA's financial statements. Andersen did question the significant transfers of fees to ALO and New Church Ventures. However, BFA officials never responded

(continued)

Case 4.31

(continued)

to auditors' requests for these two entities' records. Interestingly, the Arizona Corporation Commission records that showed the negative net worth of these two companies would have been available to anyone as a public record.

By the time the Baptist Foundation of Arizona collapsed in 1999, about 11,000 investors would lose $590 million.[800] The Arizona Attorney General's Office, which issued indictments and tried the fraud cases, called BFA the largest "affinity fraud" in U.S. history. Pastors and ministers had encouraged their parishioners to invest in BFA for their retirement even as the BFA used the funds to "do the Lord's work,"[801] including using the funds to build nursing homes for the aging and infirm, pay the salaries of pastors, and provide funding for Baptist ministries and missionary work. The fund was not a difficult sell because of the pledged noble efforts. The BFA's stated purpose was included in its literature: "*In response to the love God expressed in Jesus Christ, the Baptist Foundation of Arizona is a ministry which is committed to providing asset management services to Christians who desire to benefit worthy ministries while earning a market return on their investments.*"

Andersen was charged with violations of Arizona securities laws for its failure to issue a qualified opinion on BFA when it became aware of the failure to write down properties as well as the earnings management strategies. Andersen settled with Arizona officials and agreed to pay $217 million in losses to investors, but by the time of the settlement, Andersen was embroiled in the Enron and WorldCom settlements, and the ability to collect on the agreement was limited. Eight former BFA employees were indicted. Six entered guilty pleas and agreed to testify against Thomas

Grabinski, the BFA's former general counsel, and William Crotts, the former BFA president. Following a trial that lasted 10 months, Crotts was sentenced to six years and Grabinski to eight years for convictions on fraud and racketeering.[802]

The two men were also required to pay $159 million in restitution. Interestingly, the jury acquitted the two men of theft, and the trial judge reversed several of the convictions following a motion for post-judgment relief. The sentences were not imposed until September 2006, and the appeal on their cases was decided in 2009, with the appellate court affirming their convictions.[803] The appeal centered on an evidentiary question about a former officer who had entered into a plea agreement in exchange for his testimony. During the course of the trial, the former officer told prosecutors that he had lied in his earlier testimony. However, the appellate court concluded that defense lawyers were given additional time to recall witnesses and clear up the record and that there was no reversible error.

Discussion Questions

1. What similarities do you see between this nonprofit case and the cases of Enron, WorldCom, and Tyco? Compare Andersen's conduct in Enron with Andersen's conduct in this case.

2. List the conflicts of interest you can see from the case.

3. Why do you think the board members thought they were immune from the economic cycle Arizona was experiencing?

Source: Criminal information, the cease and desist order, and bankruptcy filings are all located at the Arizona Corporation Commission website: http://www.azcc.gov.

---

[800]*Arizona v. Crotts*, Az. App. June 2, 2009 (unpublished opinion), http://www.cofad1.state.az.us/memod/cr/cr060818.pdf. Accessed July 1, 2010.

[801]Michael Kiefer, "2 Given Prison for Fraud Involving Baptist Group," *Arizona Republic*, September 30, 2006, pp. B1, B2.

[802]*Id.*

[803]*Arizona v. Crotts*, 2009 WL 1531024 (Az. App. 2009). (unpublished opinion), http://www.cofad1.state.az.us/memod/cr/cr060818.pdf. Accessed July 1, 2010.

Unit 4 Key Terms

Amoral technician   234

Big Bath   273

Big Hairy Audacious Goals
   (BHAGs)   248

Channel stuffing   276

Cookie jar reserves   274

Defining ethical moment   240

Dodd–Frank Wall Street Reform and
   Consumer Protection Act   243

earnings before interest taxes
   depreciation and amortization
   (EBITDA)   278

Earnings before interest and taxes
   (EBIT)   278

Earnings management   272

Ethical chameleon   235

Ethical compartmentalizer   234

Ethical egotist   233

Ethical procrastinator   234

Ethical postponer   234

Ethical rationalizer   234

Ethical sycophant   235

Ethically clueless   233

Ethically superior   233

Ethically schizophrenic   234

Ethically detached   234

Ethically desensitized   234

Gaming   266

Generally accepted accounting
   principles (GAAP)   273

Inherently ethical   233

Materiality   274

Measures   266

Metrics   266

Misaligned incentives   268

Pro forma   278

Sarbanes–Oxley   280

Sarbanes–Oxley and Dodd–Frank   312

Say-on-pay provisions   243

Spring-loading   273

The moving line   231

Unit 5 Ethics and Contracts

> I'd like to emphasize that no contract has been signed yet.
>
> **—Elon Musk, CEO Tesla Motors, tweet on Hertz press release that it had ordered 100,000 Tesla A3 models from Tesla**

> As we announced last week, Hertz has made an initial order of 100,000 Tesla electric vehicles. . . .
>
> **—Hertz's response to the Musk tweet[1]**

> An insured should not have to consult a long line of case law or law review articles and treatises to determine the coverage he or she is purchasing under an insurance policy.
>
> *—Kovach v. Zurich Am. Ins. Co.,* **587 F.3d 323 (6th Cir. 2009)**

Learning Objectives

- Explain the differences between legal and ethical standards for forming, performing, and interpreting contracts.

- Apply the ethical categories involved in forming, performing, and interpreting contracts.

- Describe the non-signatory stakeholders in contract formation, performance, and interpretation and the effects they experience from ethical dilemmas the signing parties face.

- Discuss the effects of corruption on government contracting.

Contracts are a tricky business, and the role of ethics in contracting, drafting, and performing contracts is at the heart of successful business relationships. Without ethical bearings, the parties end up in expensive litigation. When Paul Ceglia made his claim that he had a contract with Mark Zuckerberg for 50% ownership in Facebook (seven years after the alleged contract was signed and only after the success of a Hollywood film on the formation of Facebook that included a storyline about Zuckerberg defrauding others), the two ended up in litigation. There were 137 filings in the litigation and 32 judicial decisions over an 11-year period. Before any of the appeals of what eventually became two lawsuits could be completed, Mr. Ceglia was arrested on charges of mail and wire fraud in connection with the expert witness report on the authenticity of the alleged contract between the two.

The heart of the case was a two-page agreement that Mr. Zuckerberg said had his signature on page two. However, Mr. Zuckerberg testified that the first page contained things that he had not agreed to. Handwriting and documents experts examined the first page and concluded that Mr. Ceglia had baked the first page in the sun to make the ink look aged. Another effect of the baking would be the expert's inability to test the ink. The expert reports found markings on that first page—clip marks where the document had been hung in the sun. One expert said that the clip markings were like the tan lines caused by a swimsuit. The suit was eventually dismissed; shortly after, Mr. Ceglia strapped his ankle electronic GPS monitor to a moving contraption in his house and absconded to parts unknown with his wife, two children, and the family dog.[2]

There is contract law. There are standards of proof for contract agreements. And then there are the ethical issues, such as baking a piece of paper in the sun to establish that you have proof of an authentic contract. This section examines the ethical issues in contracts: from advertising to obtain contracts, to the failure to keep the promises in a contract once you have it.

---

[1]Omar Abdel-Baqui, Alexander Gladstone, and Nora Naughton, "A Musk Tweet Muddies Tesla's Big Hertz Deal," *Wall Street Journal,* November 3, 2021, p. A1.

[2]*Ceglia v. Zuckerberg,* 600 Fed, Appx. 34 (2nd Cir. 2015).

Contract Negotiations: All Is Fair and Conflicting Interests

Case 5.1

Johnny Depp and His Lawyer's $30 Million in Percentage Earnings

Hollywood agents and lawyers typically receive 5% of their client's earnings for the film, endorsement, and appearance contracts that they negotiate. Despite the large amounts involved, the agreements tend to be oral agreements that then grow into personal relationships that run for years. One agent noted, "Napkin deals are actually when we're getting formal."

Johnny Depp, star of the *Pirates of the Caribbean* film franchise, learned that his lawyer/agent had received $30 million in earnings from Mr. Depp's films and other projects. Arguing that there was only an oral agreement, Mr. Depp filed suit to have the oral agreement and payments to his lawyer/agent set aside. The court agreed with Mr. Depp, holding that California's statute of frauds requires that contingency fee contracts (compensation for one party is a percentage of the total amount paid by a third party to the client) must be in writing to be enforceable.[3]

Without that writing, Mr. Depp's lawyer would have to use other grounds for recovery because the oral agreement was not enforceable.[4]

Discussion Questions

1. Legally, did Mr. Depp owe an obligation to pay his lawyer/agent? Ethically, did Mr. Depp owe an obligation to pay his lawyer/agent?

2. What ethical category (or categories) is involved in this relationship of client and lawyer/agent?

3. Where does the analysis of "could" vs. "should" fit in this situation?

4. At the time of this litigation and subsequent litigation against the agent and law firm, Mr. Depp was experiencing financial strain. Are those financial problems justifications for having his oral agreement set aside?

[3]California Business and Professional Code, § 6147. (a) An attorney who contracts to represent a client on a contingency fee basis shall, at the time the contract is entered into, provide a duplicate copy of the contract, signed by both the attorney and the client, or the client's guardian or representative, to the plaintiff, or to the client's guardian or representative. The contract shall be in writing and shall include, but is not limited to, all of the following:
(1) A statement of the contingency fee rate that the client and attorney have agreed upon.

(2) A statement as to how disbursements and costs incurred in connection with the prosecution or settlement of the claim will affect the contingency fee and the client's recovery.
(3) A statement as to what extent, if any, the client could be required to pay any compensation to the attorney for related matters that arise out of their relationship not covered by their contingency fee contract. This may include any amounts collected for the plaintiff by the attorney.
[4]*Depp, et al. v. Bloom Hergott Diemer Rosenthal la Viollette Feldman Schenkman & Goldman, LLP, et al.*, 2018 WL 4344241 (Cal.Super.)

Famous Lines from Art and Literature

"I'm so sick of it. Your niceness and your decency." Muriel Lang (Rosie Perez), married to Charlie Lang (Nicholas Cage), an NYPD officer. Lang had orally pledged to give a waitress (Yvonne Biasi [Bridget Fonda]) one-half of his lottery ticket winnings as a tip if he won. The next day, he and his wife won $4 million. Lang made good on his oral promise, much to his wife's dismay.
It Could Happen to You (1994)

Case 5.2

The Governor and His Wife: Product Endorsement and a Rolex

On November 3, 2009, Robert McDonnell was elected the 71st governor of Virginia. When Mr. McDonnell took office, in January 2010, he was struggling financially. A real estate LLC (Mobo) that he owned with his sister was losing more than $40,000 each year. By 2011, they owed more than $11,000 per month in loan payments. Each year, their loan balance increased, and by 2012, the outstanding balance was nearing $2.5 million. Mr. McDonnell and his wife also had a combined credit card balance exceeding $74,000, which, by September 2010, had grown to $90,000.

Shortly after the election, the McDonnells met Jonnie Williams, the founder and CEO of Virginia-based Star Scientific Inc. Star was close to launching a new product: Anatabloc. For years, Star had been evaluating the curative potential of anatabine, an alkaloid found in the tobacco plant, focusing on whether it could be used to treat chronic inflammation. Anatabloc was one of the anatabine-based dietary supplements Star developed following years of evaluation.

The McDonnells had used Williams's plane during the gubernatorial campaign, and the McDonnells wanted to thank Mr. Williams over dinner in New York. During dinner, Mr. Williams ordered a $5,000 bottle of cognac, and the conversation turned to the gown Mrs. McDonnell would wear to the inauguration. Mr. Williams mentioned that he knew Oscar de la Renta and offered to purchase Mrs. McDonnell an expensive custom dress. Following this dinner, the McDonnells and Mr. Williams began a symbiotic relationship illustrated by the following chart.

(continued)

Case 5.2

(continued)

Date	Gift/Meeting	Conversation	Action
October 2010	Mr. McDonnell traveled on Williams's plane, from California to Virginia.	Mr. Williams asked for help in promoting Anatabloc; both agreed to "independent testing in Virginia."	Mr. McDonnell agreed to introduce Mr. Williams to Dr. William Hazel, Virginia's secretary of health and human services.
April 2011	Williams took Mrs. McDonnell on a shopping spree; they lunched and shopped at Bergdorf Goodman and visited Oscar de la Renta and Louis Vuitton stores on Fifth Avenue. Mr. Williams bought Mrs. McDonnell dresses and a white leather coat from Oscar de la Renta; shoes, a purse, and a raincoat from Louis Vuitton; and a dress from Bergdorf Goodman. Mr. Williams spent approximately $20,000 on Mrs. McDonnell during this shopping spree.	Mr. Williams sat with the McDonnells at a political rally in New York City that evening.	
April 29, 2011	Mr. Williams joined the McDonnells for a private dinner at the Governor's Mansion.	The discussion centered on Anatabloc. Mr. McDonnell was "intrigued that [Star] was a Virginia company with an idea," and he wanted to have Anatabloc studies conducted within Virginia.	Two days after this private dinner, Mrs. McDonnell received an email from Mr. Williams that included a link to an article titled "Star Scientific Has Home Run Potential," which discussed Star's research and stock. Mrs. McDonnell forwarded this email to her husband.
May 2, 2011	Mrs. McDonnell and Mr. Williams met at the Governor's Mansion to discuss Anatabloc.	Mrs. McDonnell began explaining her family's financial woes—thoughts about filing for bankruptcy, high-interest loans, the decline in the real estate market, and credit card debt. Mrs. McDonnell then offered, "I have a background in nutritional supplements and I can be helpful to you with this project, with your company. The governor says it's okay for me to help you and—but I need you to help me. I need you to help me with this financial situation." Mr. Williams agreed to loan money to the McDonnells. When Mrs. McDonnell also mentioned that she and her husband owed $15,000 for their daughter's wedding reception, Mr. Williams agreed to provide the money.	Mr. Williams called Mr. McDonnell to "make sure [he] knew about it" and then cut the checks requested by Mrs. McDonnell.

(continued)

Case 5.2

(continued)

Date	Gift/Meeting	Conversation	Action
May 5, 2011	Mr. McDonnell met with Secretary Hazel and Chief of Staff Martin Kent to discuss the strategic plan for the state's health and human resources office.		Mr. McDonnell directed his assistant to forward to Hazel the article about Star that Mrs. McDonnell had earlier brought to his attention.
May 23, 2011	Williams delivered two checks: a $50,000 check made out to Mrs. McDonnell and a $15,000 check that was not made out to anyone but was going to the wedding caterers.		
May 28, 2011			Mr. McDonnell expressed his gratitude in a May 28 email to Mr. Williams: "Johnnie [sic]. Thanks so much for all your help with my family. Your very generous gift to Cailin was most appreciated as well as the golf round tomorrow for the boys. Maureen is excited about the trip to fla [Florida]to learn more about the products…."
May 29, 2011	Mr. McDonnell, his two sons, and his soon-to-be son-in-law spent the day at Kinloch Golf Club in Manakin–Sabot, Virginia. During this outing, they spent more than seven hours playing golf, eating, and shopping.		
June 1, 2011			Mrs. McDonnell traveled to Florida at the start of June to attend a Star-sponsored event at the Roskamp Institute. She addressed the audience, expressing her support for Star and its research. She also invited the audience to the launch of Anatabloc, which would be held at the Governor's Mansion.
June 1, 2011	Mrs. McDonnell purchased 6,000 shares of Star stock at $5.1799 per share, for a total of $31,079.40.		

(continued)

Case 5.2

(continued)

Date	Gift/Meeting	Conversation	Action
June 2011	Mr. Williams made a "$100,000 in-kind contributor to the McDonnell campaign and the PAC" and flew the McDonnell children to the resort for a PAC retreat. Messrs. McDonnell and Williams played golf together at the retreat. A few days later, Mr. Williams sent golf bags with brand-new clubs and golf shoes to Mr. McDonnell and one of his sons.		
July 2011	Mr. McDonnell and his family vacationed at Mr. Williams's multimillion-dollar home at Smith Mountain Lake in Virginia. Mr. Williams allowed the McDonnells to stay there free of charge. He also paid $2,268 for the McDonnells to rent a boat. Mr. Williams provided transportation for the family: the McDonnell children used Mr. Williams's Range Rover for the trip, and Mr. Williams paid more than $600 to have his Ferrari delivered to the home for Mr. McDonnell to use.		
July 31, 2011	Mr. McDonnell drove the Ferrari back to Richmond at the end of the vacation. During the three-hour drive, Mrs. McDonnell snapped several pictures of them driving with the Ferrari's top down.		Mrs. McDonnell emailed one of the photographs to Williams at 7:47 p.m.
July 31, 2011			At 11:29 p.m., after returning from the Smith Mountain Lake vacation, Mr. McDonnell directed Secretary Hazel to have his deputy attend a meeting about Anatabloc with Mrs. McDonnell at the Governor's Mansion the next day.

(continued)

Case 5.2

(continued)

Date	Gift/Meeting	Conversation	Action
August 1, 2011	Hazel sent staffer Molly Huffstetler to the meeting, which Mr. Williams also attended.	Mr. Williams—with Mrs. McDonnell at his side—told Dr. Clore that clinical testing of Anatabloc in Virginia was important to McDonnell. Mr. Williams discussed clinical trials at the University of Virginia ("UVA") and Virginia Commonwealth University ("VCU"), home of the Medical College of Virginia ("MCV"). Then Mr. Williams and Mrs. McDonnell met with Dr. John Clore from VCU, who Mr. Williams said was "important, and he could cause studies to happen at VCU's medical school."	After the meeting ended, Mrs. McDonnell noticed Mr. Williams's Rolex watch. She mentioned that she wanted to get a Rolex for Mr. McDonnell. When Mr. Williams asked if she wanted him to purchase one for Mr. McDonnell, she responded affirmatively.
August 2, 2011	Mrs. McDonnell purchased another 522 shares of Star stock at $3.82 per share, for a total of $1,994.04.		
August 13, 2011	Mr. McDonnell and one of his sons returned to Kinloch Golf Club. The bill for this golf outing was $1,309.17, which Mr. Williams paid.		
August 14, 2011	Mr. Williams purchased a Rolex from Malibu Jewelers in Malibu, California. The Rolex cost between $6,000 and $7,000 and featured a custom engraving: "Robert F. McDonnell, 71st Governor of Virginia."		Mrs. McDonnell later took several pictures of Mr. McDonnell showing off his new Rolex—pictures that were later sent to Williams via text message.
August 30, 2011	Luncheon at Governor's Mansion. Invitations bore the Governor's seal and read, "Governor and Mrs. Robert F. McDonnell Request the Pleasure of your Company at a Luncheon." Invitees included Dr. Clore and Dr. John Lazo from UVA.	Mr. McDonnell thanked the attendees for their presence and "talked about his interest in a Virginia company doing this, and his interest in the product."	Each place setting featured samples of Anatabloc, and Mr. Williams handed out checks for grant applications—each for $25,000—to doctors from various medical institutions.

(continued)

Case 5.2

(continued)

Date	Gift/Meeting	Conversation	Action
Fall 2011		Star's president, Paul L. Perito, began to worry that Star had lost the support of UVA and VCU. In the fall of 2011, Mr. Perito was working with those universities to file grant applications. During a particular call with UVA officials, Mr. Perito felt the officials were unprepared. When Mr. Williams learned about the lack of preparation, "[h]e was furious and said, 'I can't understand it. Mr. McDonnell and his wife are so supportive of this and suddenly the administration has no interest.'"	
December 2011	Mrs. McDonnell sold all of her 6,522 shares of Star stock for $15,279.45, resulting in a loss of more than $17,000.		The sale allowed Mr. McDonnell to omit disclosure of the stock purchases on a required financial disclosure form known as a Statement of Economic Interest (filed on January 16, 2012).
January 7, 2012	Mr. McDonnell made another golf visit to Kinloch Golf Club, running up a $1,368.91 bill, which Williams paid.		The outing was not disclosed, and other golf outings were not disclosed on other 2011 golf trips.
January 20, 2012	Mrs. McDonnell purchased 6,672 shares of Star stock at $2.29 per share, for a total of $15,276.88.		
January 2012	Williams discussed the Mobo properties with Mrs. McDonnell, who wanted additional loans.		Williams agreed to loan more money. Mrs. McDonnell was "furious when [Williams] told her that [they were] bogged down in the administration." Later, Mrs. McDonnell called Mr. Williams to advise him that she had relayed this information to Mr. McDonnell, who "want[ed] the contact information of the people that [Star] [was] dealing with at [UVA]."
February 3, 2012	Mrs. McDonnell requested another $50,000 loan.		

(continued)

Case 5.2

(continued)

Date	Gift/Meeting	Conversation	Action
February 6, 2012	Mr. Williams wrote a check to Mobo on $50,000.		Mrs. McDonnell received an email containing the names of the UVA officials with whom Star had been working. She forwarded this list to Mr. McDonnell and his chief counsel, Jacob Jasen Eige, on February 9.
February 10, 2012			While riding with Mr. McDonnell, Mrs. McDonnell followed up with Eige: "Pls call Jonnie today [and] get him to fill u in on where this is at. Gov wants to know why nothing has developed w studies after Jonnie gave $200,000. I'm just trying to talk w Jonnie. Gov wants to get this going w VCU MCV. Pls let us know what u find out after we return....."
February 16, 2012		Mr. McDonnell emailed Williams to check on the status of certificates and documents relating to loans Mr. Williams was providing for Mobo.	Six minutes after Mr. McDonnell sent this email, he emailed Eige: "Pls see me about anatabloc issues at VCU and UVA. Thx."
February 2012	Governor's Mansion reception for the doctors and Star officials. Mr. McDonnell, Mrs. McDonnell, Mr. Williams, and two doctors went out for a $1,400 dinner on Williams's dime.	During dinner, the diners discussed Anatabloc. Mrs. McDonnell talked about her use of Anatabloc, and Mr. McDonnell asked one of the doctors—a Star consultant—"How big of a discovery is this?"	Mrs. McDonnell invited the two doctors to stay at the Governor's Mansion for the evening—the doctors accepted.
May 18, 2012		Mr. McDonnell sent Mr. Williams a text message concerning yet another loan: "Johnnie. Per voicemail would like to see if you could extend another 20k loan for this year. Call if possible and I'll ask mike to send instructions. Thx bob."	Twelve minutes later, Mr. Williams responded, "Done, tell me who to make it out to and address. Will FedEx. Jonnie."
May 18–26, 2012	Mr. McDonnell and his family vacationed at Kiawah Island in South Carolina. The $23,000 vacation was a gift from William H. Goodwin Jr., characterized as a personal friend of the McDonnells.		Vacation was not disclosed on Mr. McDonnell's 2012 Statement of Economic Interest.

(continued)

Case 5.2

(continued)

Date	Gift/Meeting	Conversation	Action
April–July 2012		Mr. McDonnell emailed and texted Mr. Williams about Star stock on four occasions, each coinciding with a rise in the stock price.	
July 3, 2012		Mr. Williams texted Mr. McDonnell: "Johns Hopkins human clinical trials report on Aug. 8. If you need cash let me know. Let's go golfing and sailing Chatham Bars inn Chatham mass labor day weekend if you can. Business about to break out strong. Jonnie."	
Labor Day weekend 2012	Mr. Williams spent more than $7,300 on Chatham vacation for the McDonnells. Williams paid the McDonnells' share of a $5,823.79 bill for a private clambake.	Also joining the Chatham excursion was one of the doctors who attended the February health care leaders' reception, whom Mr. Williams invited "to try to help get the Governor more involved."	
December 12, 2012		Mr. McDonnell learned of his wife's repurchase of Star shares: "[I]t was her money that she had used for this. But I told her, you know, 'Listen. If you have this stock, you know, this is—again, triggers a reporting requirement for me. I really don't appreciate you doing things that really—that affect me without—without me knowing about it.'"	
December 25, 2012	Mrs. McDonnell transferred her Star stock to her children as a gift. Williams gave the McDonnells' daughter, Jeanine, a $10,000 wedding gift.		The stock was not required to be disclosed for the 2012 Statement of Economic Interest.

(continued)

Case 5.2

(continued)

Mr. McDonnell was convicted of conspiracy to commit honest-services wire fraud, three counts of honest-services wire fraud, conspiracy to obtain property under color of official right, and six counts of obtaining property under color of official right.[5] He appealed. The Court of Appeals affirmed the decision.[6] Mr. McDonnell appealed to the U.S. Supreme Court, and the court reversed his conviction on the grounds that there was no official government action taken in exchange for all the Williams' favors. The case against both Mr. and Mrs. McDonnell was then dismissed.[7]

Discussion Questions

1. Give a summary of what was going back and forth between the McDonnells and Mr. Williams.

2. What was Mr. Williams looking to obtain from the governor and Mrs. McDonnell?

3. The following is an excerpt from the U.S. Supreme Court decision:

[T]he Government's expansive interpretation of "official act" would raise significant constitutional concerns. Section 201 prohibits **quid pro quo** corruption—the exchange of a thing of value for an "official act." In the Government's view, nearly anything a public official accepts—from a campaign contribution to lunch—counts as a *quid*; and nearly anything a public official does—from arranging a meeting to inviting a guest to an event—counts as a *quo*.

But conscientious public officials arrange meetings for constituents, contact other officials on their behalf, and include them in events all the time. The basic compact underlying representative government *assumes* that public officials will hear from their constituents and act appropriately on their concerns—whether it is the union official worried about a plant closing or the homeowners who wonder why it took five days to restore power to

their neighborhood after a storm. The Government's position could cast a pall of potential prosecution over these relationships if the union had given a campaign contribution in the past or the homeowners invited the official to join them on their annual outing to the ballgame. Officials might wonder whether they could respond to even the most commonplace requests for assistance, and citizens with legitimate concerns might shrink from participating in democratic discourse.

This concern is substantial. White House counsel who worked in every administration from that of President Reagan to President Obama warn that the Government's "breathtaking expansion of public-corruption law would likely chill federal officials' interactions with the people they serve and thus damage their ability effectively to perform their duties." Six former Virginia attorneys general—four Democrats and two Republicans—also filed an *amicus* brief in this Court echoing those concerns, as did 77 former state attorneys general from States other than Virginia—41 Democrats, 35 Republicans, and 1 independent.

None of this, of course, is to suggest that the facts of this case typify normal political interaction between public officials and their constituents. Far from it. But the Government's legal interpretation is not confined to cases involving extravagant gifts or large sums of money, and we cannot construe a criminal statute on the assumption that the Government will "use it responsibly."

There is no doubt that this case is distasteful; it may be worse than that. But our concern is not with tawdry tales of Ferraris, Rolexes, and ball gowns. It is instead with the broader legal implications of the Government's boundless interpretation of the federal bribery statute. A more limited interpretation of the term "official act" leaves ample room for prosecuting corruption, while comporting with the text of the statute and the precedent of this Court.

Why is the term official act important on appeal? Was there a *quid pro quo*? Is there a conflict of interest? How does the court feel about the interaction between Mr. Williams and the McDonnells?

(continued)

---

[5]Mrs. McDonnell was also convicted, but their appeals were handled separately. Mrs. McDonnell's appeal to the Fourth Circuit was put on hold after the U.S. Supreme Court decision. Federal prosecutors moved to drop the case in September 2016.

[6]*U.S. v. McDonnell*, 792 F.3d 478 (4th Cir. 2015).

[7]*McDonnell v. U.S.*, 579 U.S. 550 (2016).

Case 5.2

(continued)

4. Despite what the court concluded in *McDonnell v. U.S.*, evaluate the ethics of the McDonnells and Williams's conduct.

5. Why do we worry about public officials taking gifts and money in exchange for advancing the business opportunities and contracts of constituents?

6. List the stakeholders in public corruption cases. What are the risks in *quid pro quo* government contracts? Be sure to refer back to the Boeing case (Case 2.12) and the actions of Darlene Druyon.

Ethics in Action 5.1

"Just Trying to Make You Think"

Tamela Lee was a member of the Summit County Council representing District 5 in Akron, Ohio. Omar Abdelqader owned a business in District 5. Mrs. Lee knew Abdelqader through her husband, and Abdelqader helped support Mrs. Lee when her husband unexpectedly left the country for long stretches of time. Mrs. Lee had substantial financial difficulties because of her husband's departure, and Abdelqader supported her by allowing her to take items from his convenience store, paying for services for her, and giving her money.

On June 1, 2014, Abdelqader's nephews, Sharif Hamed and Samir Abdelqader, were arrested for felonious assault after an altercation in Akron. The two hit an uninvolved pedestrian with their car. Abdelqader phoned and asked Mrs. Lee for help with his nephews' case. Mrs. Lee and Abdelqader discussed her financial problems, and Abdelqader promised her that they would "work it out." She received $300 from Abdelqader after talking with the judge in the case and then the prosecutor saying, "I'm not trying to influence you, you can't say I'm trying to influence you. I'm trying to make you think. That's all I'm trying to do; just trying to make you think."[8]

1. Is this a *quid pro quo*?
2. Does it make a difference that what Abdelqader was asking for did not involve a contract or his business?

[8]*U.S. v. Lee*, 919 F.3d 340 (6th Cir. 2019).

Ethics in Action 5.2

Lightning Round of Corruption Cases

a. Senators Pat Toomey and Cynthia Loomis sit on the Senate Banking Committee, have been advocates for light government regulation of the growing cryptocurrency market, and hold investments in various cryptocurrency investments. Is this a conflict? Is it corruption? Senator

(continued)

Toomey, when questioned about his holdings responded, "Tell me what part of the economy we don't get involved in? Following the logic, then I guess no one in the Senate can invest in anything. That would be ridiculous."[9]

b. Jovanda R. Peterson, an official at the Federal Emergency Management Agency (FEMA), was charged with taking bribes from Donald Ellison, the president of Cobra, a power company in Puerto Rico. The indictment for bribery and federal corruption alleged that in exchange for first-class air trips and the use of Mr. Ellison's credit card, Ms. Peterson used her influence in FEMA to insist that Cobra be awarded the clean-up and repair contracts for the electrical systems following the devastation of Hurricane Maria in 2017.[10] Is this a *quid pro quo*?

[9]Chad Day, Julie Bykowicz, and Paul Kiernan, "Senators on Banking Panel Own Cryptocurrency Assets," *Wall Street Journal*, December 21, 2021, p. A4.

[10]Patricia Mazzei and Frances Robels, "Former FEMA Official Accused of Taking Bribes in Hurricane Maria Recovery," *New York Times*, September 10, 2019, https://www.nytimes.com/2019/09/10/us/puerto-rico-fema-arrests-corruption.html

Compare & Contrast

Refer back to Unit 1 and Reading 1.1 You, That First Step, the Slippery Slope, and the Credo. How did corruption begin in the case of the McDonnells? How did it begin in the other examples? How can elected officials having lunch with business owners ripen into bribery?

Case 5.3

Descriptive Honesty and Social Media Hype: An 11-Inch Subway vs. a Footlong Subway and Tuna vs. Tuna

A *New York Post* reporter took a ruler and discovered something interesting: the Subway Footlong he had purchased was only 11 inches long. The *Post* was running anecdotal data following a Subway customer from Perth, Australia, displaying his Subway Footlong Turkey next to a tape measure, with the Footlong coming up one inch short.

The *Post*'s discovery started further investigations that revealed that Subway was not alone. The *Post* then uncovered other sub shops with similar length issues. Four of every seven sandwiches came up short on length, measuring 11 to 11.5 inches.

Subway's initial response was that "Footlong" is just the name for the sandwich and is not intended to represent the length of the sandwich. Following the posting of 100,000

likes on the Perth customer's Facebook photo, Subway Australia posted on its Facebook page that FOOTLONG was a registered trademark of Subway and not intended to be a description. Indeed, in many countries, the metric system is followed, where the "Footlong" is still used, as a trademarked name for the sandwich.

A group of sandwich lovers filed a class action suit against Subway, seeking compensation for the one-half inch to one inch in sandwich that they were missing when they purchased their "Footlongs."[11] One of the plaintiffs in the case said, "They advertise in all these commercials,

(continued)

[11]Nadia Arumugam, "Why Lawsuits over Subway's Short Footlong Sandwiches Are Baloney," *Forbes*, January 27, 2013.

Case 5.3

(continued)

'Footlong, Footlong, Footlong,' and now I feel like an idiot." He told *The Post,* "I can't believe I fell for that trick. The sandwiches are anywhere between a half-inch to an inch shorter ... I feel cheated."[12]

Subway Australia indicated that sandwiches do vary in length because of their construction process.[13] Subway issued the following statement:

We regret any instance where we did not fully deliver on our promise to our customers. We freshly bake our bread throughout the day in our more than 38,000 restaurants in 100 countries worldwide, and we have redoubled our efforts to ensure consistency and correct length in every sandwich we serve. Our commitment remains steadfast to ensure that every Subway Footlong sandwich is 12 inches at each location worldwide.[14]

The basis for the suits was deceptive advertising. The damage claim was $5 million. In early discovery in the case, the evidence established that Subway's claim was accurate:

- Subway's raw dough sticks weigh exactly the same, so the rare sandwich roll that fails to bake to a full 12 inches actually contains no less bread than any other.

- The minor variations that do occur are wholly attributable to the natural variability in the baking process and cannot be prevented.

- No customer is shorted any food *even if* a sandwich roll fails to bake to a full 12 inches. Subway sandwiches are made to order in front of the customer; meat and cheese ingredients are standardized, and "sandwich artists" add toppings in whatever quantity the customer desires.

- The length of the bread has no effect on the quantity of food each customer receives.

Nonetheless, Subway settled the suit by paying $520,000 in attorney fees to the plaintiffs' lawyers and a $500

incentive award for each class representative (translation: the plaintiffs would get a coupon for a discount on a Subway sandwich).

Subway also agreed to the following changes in its operations:

1. franchisees would "use a tool" for measuring sandwich rolls;

2. corporate quality-control inspectors would measure a sampling of baked bread during each regularly scheduled compliance inspection;

3. the inspectors would check bread ovens during each compliance inspection "to ensure that they are in proper working order and within operating specifications"; and

4. Subway's website and each restaurant would post a notice explaining the natural variability in the bread-baking process will sometimes result in sandwich rolls that are shorter than the advertised length.[15]

However, one of the plaintiffs challenged the settlement on the grounds that the plaintiffs got nothing. The Seventh Circuit Court of Appeals rejected the settlement and dismissed the case noting that, "Because the settlement yields fees for class counsel and 'zero benefits for the class,' the class should not have been certified and the settlement should not have been approved. Because these consolidated class actions 'seek] only worthless benefits for the class,' they should have been 'dismissed out of hand.'"[16]

The Late-Great-Mistaken Tuna Scandal

Subway continues to be a target for scrutiny of its products and operations. In January 2021, Subway became a defendant in a class-action suit that alleges Subway's tuna was not top-grade tuna. The complaint alleged that Subway tuna sandwiches were not made from sustainably caught "skipjack or "yellowtail tuna" or from healthy tuna stock such as Albacore or Tongol. The plaintiffs sought

(continued)

---

[12]*Id.*

[13]That post has since been deleted. You can find it reproduced at http://www.huffingtonpost.com/2013/01/19/subway-response-footlong-controversy-measurment_n_2511316.html.

[14]Tiffany Hsu, "Subway Pledges to Make All Its Footlong Sandwiches 12 Inches," *Los Angeles Times,* January 25, 2013, http://articles.latimes.com/2013/jan/25/business/la-fi-mo-subway-footlong-20130125.

[15]*In re Subway Footlong Sandwich Marketing and Sales Practice Litigation,* 869 F.3d 551, 554 (7th Cir. 2017).

[16]*In re Subway Footlong Sandwich Marketing and Sales Practice Litigation,* 869 F.3d 551, 557.

Case 5.3

(continued)

damages for the premium prices they paid for premium tuna but did not get that in their sandwiches. They also alleged that Subway should have known that its supply chain was not offering the best quality of tuna.[17]

However, a federal district court in the Northern District of California dismissed the suit. Judge Jon S. Tigar said that he "struggled" to find any "reliance" on the parts of the plaintiffs in Subway's description of its sandwich as "tuna" and their claims.[18] The plaintiffs then amended their complaint to allege that Subway tuna is actually made up of pork and chicken, with the DNA of cattle also detected.[19]

A *New York Times* investigation found that a lab could not detect tuna DNA in the tuna the *Times* purchased from the Subway supplier. However, the lab did offer its explanation: "There are two conclusions. One, it's so heavily processed that whatever we could pull out we couldn't make an identification. Or we got some and there's just nothing there that's tuna."[20] However, when the *Times*

sent tuna from Subway shops in for testing, the labs found that there was indeed tuna in the tuna being used in the sandwich shops. Another expert noted that the issue is more with suppliers and their labeling and processing and not at Subway's level.[21]

Discussion Questions

1. The Menu Labeling Act, a federal law, requires restaurant chains (with 20 or more outlets) to disclose calorie and nutrition information for food sold in the stores. There are also state laws, known as Truth in Menu laws, that require accurate descriptions—the label cannot say "Made in Vermont," if the syrup was not made in Vermont. And jelly jars cannot say, "Made with real fruit" if there is no real fruit in the jelly. Did Subway violate any of these laws with its alleged less-than-a-foot-long Footlong?

2. What ethical categories are involved in these examples?

3. Apply the ethical categories to the actions of those who filed and settled the footlong suit and those bringing the tuna suit. Is there a "could vs. should" issue in their conduct?

4. On the tuna lawsuit, which is still pending, is this a supply chain issue and should Subway be held responsible for using the labels its suppliers use for their products?

5. What ethical issues exist in social media stories flourishing and tainting companies and their products? Is there an ethical responsibility for follow-up postings that provide the final outcome?

[17]Alex Ledsom, "Is a Subway Tuna Sandwich Made of Bread and Tuna? It Depends on the Lawsuit," *Forbes*, August 10, 2021, https://www.forbes.com/sites/alexledsom/2021/08/10/is-a-subway-tuna-sandwich-made-of-bread-and-tuna-it-depends-on-the-law-suit/?sh=6e14479014c4.

[18]Ron Ruggless, "Federal Judge Dismisses Subway Tuna Lawsuit," *Nation's Restaurant News*, October 11, 2021, https://www.nrn.com/quick-service/federal-judge-dismisses-subway-tuna-lawsuit.

[19]Reuters, "Lawsuit over Subway Tuna Now Claims Chicken, Pork, cattle DNA Detected," November 11, 2021, https://www.nbcnews.com/news/us-news/lawsuit-subway-tuna-now-claims-chicken-pork-cattle-dna-detected-rcna5387.

[20]Julia Carmel, "What's in This Tuna Sandwich?" *New York Times*, October 20, 2021, p. SS1 at SS 10.

[21]Id.

Case 5.4

Sears, High-Cost Auto Repairs, and Its Ethical and Financial Collapse

In 1991, the California Department of Consumer Affairs began investigating Sears Auto Repair Centers. Sears' automotive unit, with 850 repair shops nationwide, generated 9% of the merchandise group's $19.4 billion in revenues. It was one of the fastest growing and most profitable divisions of Sears over the previous two years.

In the California investigation, agents posed as customers at 33 of the 72 Sears automotive repair shops located from Los Angeles to Sacramento. They found that they were overcharged 90% of the time by an average of $223. In the first phase of the investigation, the agents took 38 cars with worn-out brakes but no other mechanical problems to 27 Sears shops between December 1990

(continued)

Case 5.4

(continued)

and December 1991. In 34 of the cases, the agents were told that their cars needed additional work. At the Sears shop in Concord, a San Francisco suburb, the agent was overcharged $585 to replace the front brake pads, front and rear springs, and control-arm bushings. Sears advertised brake jobs at prices of $48 and $58.[22]

In the second phase of the investigation, Sears was notified of the investigation, and 10 shops were targeted. In seven of those cases, the agents were overcharged. No springs and shocks were sold in these cases, but the average overcharge was $100 per agent.

Up until 1990, Sears had paid its repair center service advisors by the hour rather than by the amount of work.[23] But in February 1990, Sears instituted an incentive compensation policy under which employees were paid based on the amount of repairs customers authorized.[24] Service advisors also had to meet sales quotas on specific auto parts; those who did not meet the quotas often had their hours reduced or were assigned to work in other departments in the Sears stores. California regulators said the number of consumer complaints they received about Sears shops increased dramatically after the commission structure was implemented.

The California Department of Consumer Affairs charged all 72 Sears automotive shops in the state with fraud, false advertising, and failure to clearly state parts and labor on invoices.

Jim Conran, the director of the consumer affairs department, stated:

> This is a flagrant breach of the trust and confidence the people of California have placed in Sears for generations. Sears has used trust as a marketing tool, and we don't believe they've lived up to that trust. The violation of the faith that was placed in Sears cannot be allowed to continue, and for past violations of law, a penalty must be paid.[25]

Dick Schenkkan, a San Francisco lawyer representing Sears, charged that Conran issued the complaint in response to bipartisan legislative efforts to cut his agency's funding because of a state budget crunch and claimed, "He is garnering as much publicity as he can as quickly as he can. If you wanted to embark on a massive publicity campaign to demonstrate how aggressive you are and how much need there is for your services in the state, what better target than a big, respected business that would guarantee massive press coverage?"[26]

Richard Kessel, the executive director of the New York State Consumer Protection Board, stated that he also had "some real problems" with Sears' policy of paying people by commission. "If that's the policy," Kessel said, "that in my mind could certainly lead to abuses in car repairs."[27]

Immediately following the issuing of the California complaint, Sears said that the state's investigation was "very seriously flawed and simply does not support the allegations. The service we recommend and the work we perform are in accordance with the hig hest industry standards."[28]

Sears then ran the following ad:

> With over two million automotive customers serviced last year in California alone, mistakes may have occurred. However, Sears wants you to know that we would never intentionally violate the trust customers have shown in our company for 105 years.

Ten days after the complaint was announced, the chairman of Sears, Edward A. Brennan, announced that Sears was eliminating the commission-based pay structure for employees who propose auto repairs.[29] He conceded that the pay structure may have created an environment in which mistakes were made because of rigid attention to goals. Brennan announced the compensation system would be replaced with one in which customer satisfaction would now be the primary factor in determining service personnel rewards, shifting the emphasis away from quantity to quality. An outside firm would be hired to conduct

(continued)

---

[22]James R. Healey, "Shops under Pressure to Boost Profits," *USA Today*, July 14, 1992, p. 1A.

[23]Gregory A. Patterson, "Distressed Shoppers, Disaffected Workers Prompt Stores to Alter Sales Commissions," *Wall Street Journal*, July 1, 1992, pp. B1, B4.

[24]James R. Healey, "Sears Auto Cuts Commissions," *USA Today*, June 23, 1992, p. 2B.

[25]Lawrence M. Fisher, "Sears' Auto Centers to Halt Commissions," *New York Times*, June 23, 1992, p. C1.

[26]Id.

[27]Id.

[28]Tung Yin, "Sears Is Accused of Billing Fraud at Auto Centers," *Wall Street Journal*, June 12, 1992, p. B1.

[29]Lawrence M. Fisher, "Accusation of Fraud at Sears," *New York Times*, June 12, 1992, pp. C2, C12.

Case 5.4

(continued)

unannounced shopping audits of Sears Auto Centers to be certain the hard sells were eliminated. Further, Brennan said, the sales quotas on parts would be discontinued. Although he did not admit to any scheme to recommend unnecessary repairs, he emphasized that the system encouraged mistakes, and he accepted full responsibility for the policies. "The buck stops with me," he said.[30]

Sears auto repair customers filed class action lawsuits in California, and a New Jersey undercover investigation produced similar findings of overcharging. New Jersey officials found that 100% of the Sears stores in its investigation recommended unneeded work compared to 16% of stores not owned by Sears.[31] On June 25, 1992, Sears ran a full-page ad in all major newspapers throughout the country. The ad, a letter signed by Brennan, had the following text:

An Open Letter to Sears Customers

You may have heard recent allegations that some Sears Auto Centers in California and New Jersey have sold customers parts and services they didn't need. We take such charges very seriously, because they strike at the core of our company—our reputation for trust and integrity.

We are confident that our Auto Center customers' satisfaction rate is among the highest in the industry. But after an extensive review, we have concluded that our incentive compensation and goal-setting program inadvertently created an environment in which mistakes have occurred. We are moving quickly and aggressively to eliminate that environment.

To guard against such things happening in the future, we're taking significant action:

We have eliminated incentive compensation and goal-setting systems for automotive service advisors—the folks who diagnose problems and recommend repairs to you. We have replaced these practices with a new non-commission program designed to achieve even higher levels of customer satisfaction. Rewards will now be based on customer satisfaction.

We're augmenting our own quality control efforts by retaining an independent organization to conduct ongoing, unannounced "shopping audits" of our automotive services to ensure that company policies are being met.

We have written to all state attorneys general, inviting them to compare our auto repair standards and practices with those of their states in order to determine whether differences exist.

And we are helping to organize and fund a joint industry-consumer-government effort to review current auto repair practices and recommend uniform industry standards.

We're taking these actions so you'll continue to come to Sears with complete confidence. However, one thing we will never change is our commitment to customer safety. Our policy of preventive maintenance— recommending replacement of worn parts before they fail—has been criticized by the California Bureau of Automotive Repair as constituting unneeded repairs. We don't see it that way. We recommend preventive maintenance because that's what our customers want, and because it makes for safer cars on the road. In fact, 75 percent of the consumers we talked to in a nationwide survey last weekend told us that auto repair centers should recommend replacement parts for preventive maintenance. As always, no work will ever be performed without your approval.

We understand that when your car needs service, you look for, above all, someone you can trust. And when trust is at stake, you can't merely react, we must overreact.

We at Sears are totally committed to maintaining your confidence. You have my word on it.

Ed Brennan
Chairman and Chief Executive Officer
Sears, Roebuck and Co.[32]

On September 2, 1992, Sears agreed to pay $8 million to resolve the consumer affairs agency claims on overcharging in California. The $8 million included reimbursement costs, new employee training, and coupons for discounts at the service center. Another

(continued)

---

[30]Gregory A. Patterson, "Sears' Brennan Accepts Blame for Auto Flap," *Wall Street Journal*, June 23, 1992, p. B1.

[31]Jennifer Steinhauer, "Time to Call a Sears Repairman," *New York Times*, January 15, 1998, pp. B1, B2.

[32]"Open Letter," *Arizona Republic*, June 25, 1992, p. A9.

Case 5.4

(continued)

$15 million in fines was paid in 41 other states to settle class action suits.[33]

In December 1992, Sears fired John T. Lundegard, the director of its automotive operations. Sears indicated that Lundegard's termination was not related to the controversy surrounding the auto centers.

Sears recorded a net loss of $3.9 billion despite $52.3 billion in sales in 1992—the worst performance ever by the retailer in its 108-year history and its first loss since 1933. Its Allstate Insurance division was reeling from damage claims for Hurricane Andrew in the Gulf Coast and Hurricane Iniki in Hawaii ($1.25 billion). Auto center revenue dropped $80 million in the last quarter of 1992, and Sears paid out a total of $27 million to settle state overcharging claims. Moody's downgraded Sears debt following the loss announcement.

In 1994, Sears partially reinstated its sales incentive practices in its auto centers. Service advisors were required to earn at least 40% of their total pay in commissions on the sale and installation of tires, batteries, shock absorbers, and struts. Not included on commission scales are brakes and front-end alignments (the core of the 1992 problems). Earnings in auto centers never returned to pre-1992 levels. Many of the auto centers were closed and then, in 1994, Sears limited the services offered in its auto centers.

Despite the claims of innocence in its auto centers, the ethical culture at Sears had been and continued to be one of ethical lapses. Although incentive systems may have created the auto center fraud problems, the following dilemmas involving Sears arose after the time of its auto center fraud cases:

- Montgomery Ward obtained an order from a federal court prohibiting Sears from hiring employees away from Ward as it worked its way through Chapter 11 bankruptcy. The order was based on an email sent from Sears' regional vice president, Mary Conway, in which Sears managers were instructed to "be predatory" about hiring away Montgomery Ward managers.
- A class action civil suit filed in Atlanta against Sears by consumers alleged that Sears sold them used batteries as new. One of the plaintiffs in the suit alleged that an

investigator purchased 100 "new" batteries from Sears in 1995 (in 32 states) and that 78 of them showed signs of previous usage.[34] A Sears internal auto center document explains that the high allowances the centers must give customers on returns of batteries cut into profits and induced the sale of used batteries to compensate. Sears initially denied the allegations and attributed it to disgruntled former employees and not understanding that a nick does not necessarily mean a battery is used.)[35] By 2001, Sears had settled the suits and an action by the federal government for $63 million.[36] Sears then sued its battery manufacturer, Exide.

- Sears admitted to "flawed legal judgment" when it made repayment agreements with its credit card customers who were already in bankruptcy, a practice in violation of creditors' rights and priorities. Sears agreed to refund the amounts collected from the 2,700 customers who were put into the program. Sears warned the refunds could have a "material effect" on earnings. The announcement caused a drop in Sears' stock price of $37.00. Sears included the following notice to its credit card customers:

> NOTICE: If you previously filed for personal bankruptcy under Chapter 7 and entered into a reaffirmation agreement with Sears, you may be a member of a Settlement Class in a proposed class action settlement. For information, please call 1-800-529-4500. There are deadlines as early as October 8, 1997 applicable to the settlement.

Sears entered a guilty plea to criminal fraud charges in connection with the bankruptcy issues and agreed to pay a $60 million fine, the largest in the history of bankruptcy

(continued)

---

[33]Barnaby J. Feder, "Sears Post First Loss since 1933," *New York Times*, October 23, 1992, p. C1; and "Sears Gets Handed a Huge Repair Bill," *BusinessWeek*, September 14, 1992, p. 38.

[34]"Lawsuit Claims Sears Is Selling Used Die Hard Batteries As New," *Wall Street Journal*, April 1, 1997, https://www.wsj.com/articles/SB859848762336466000.

[35]There were questions and investigations surrounding Exide Corporation, Sears' battery supplier. The questions related to the quality of the batteries, and Exide at one point announced that it expected to face criminal indictment for certain of its business practices. Keith Bradsher, "Exide Says Indictment Is Likely over Its Car Battery Sales to Sears," *New York Times*, January 11, 2001, pp. B1, B7.

[36]Sears, U.S. Reach Civil Settlement Over 1994–1995 Automotive Battery Advertising," *Transform Co.*, December 21, 2001, https://transformco.com/press-releases/pr/1601.

Case 5.4

(continued)

fraud cases.[37] The company also settled with the 50 state attorneys general, which included $40 million in state fines, $12 million for state shareholder suits, and a write-off of the $126 million owed by the cardholders involved, which was forgiven as part of the settlement.[38]

Sears also settled the class action suit on the bankruptcy issue by agreeing to pay $36 million in cash and issuing $118 million in coupons to those cardholders affected by its conduct toward bankruptcy customers. Sears did not admit any wrongdoing as part of the settlement but indicated the action was taken "to avoid the litigation."[39] Sears spent $56 million in legal and administrative costs in handling the bankruptcy cases.

These legal battles were evidence that Sears was rounding corners as a means of survival. However, it was not addressing its business issues, such as the competition of Best Buy in selling appliances or the changing ways customers were shopping. In the 1990s, Sears closed its catalog operations and continued to struggle to find its market niche. In 2001, it was forced to close 89 stores as it watched its competitor, Montgomery Ward, close its doors for good.[40] In 2004, Kmart purchased Sears, and despite efforts to make the power of combining companies, continued to close stores through 2017.

Sears, as one of its CEOs noted, was once the Amazon of its time.[41] It sold everything anyone needed from farm implements to shoes to appliances. However, it missed the shift to online shopping and was stuck with stores that were in malls while shoppers flocked to the stand-alone Walmarts and Targets.

Sears declared Chapter 11 bankruptcy in 2019 and began liquidation in 2020.

Discussion Questions

1. What temptations did the employee compensation system present?

---

[37]Joseph B. Cahill, "Sears Agrees to Plead Guilty to Charges of Criminal Fraud in Credit-Card Case," *Wall Street Journal*, February 10, 1999, p. B2.

[38]*Id.*

[39]Leslie Kaufman, "Sears Settles Suit on Raising of Its Credit Card Rates," *New York Times*, March 11, 1999, p. C2.

[40]Amy Merrick, "Sears to Shut 89 Stores and Report Big Changes," *Wall Street Journal*, January 5, 2001, p. A4.

[41]"How Sears Lost the American Shopper," *Wall Street Journal*, March 16–17, 2019, B6, at B7.

2. If you had been a service advisor, would you have felt comfortable recommending repairs that were not immediately necessary but would be eventually?

3. A public relations expert has said of the Sears debacle: "Don't make the Sears mistake. When responding to a crisis, tell the public what happened and why. Apologize with no crossed fingers. Then say what you're going to do to make sure it doesn't happen again."[42] What are the ethical standards in this public relations formula?

4. What do you believe created Sears' auto center culture?

5. List all of the ethical categories you see in the conduct in the auto centers as well as in other areas of Sears.

6. What pressures were Sears employees feeling in the auto centers as well as in the other areas that had ethical issues?

7. Are ongoing ethical issues a signal of impending financial difficulties at a company?

8. Are there principles for a credo for, as an example, the mechanics at the auto centers? What about the lawyers who worked for Sears on the bankruptcy issues? Is there a fine line between fraud and salesmanship or is there a chasm between the two?

Sources

Berner, Robert, "Sears Faces Controversy over Car Batteries," *Wall Street Journal*, August 26, 1997, p. B2.

Berner, Robert, and JoAnn S. Lublin, "Sears Is Told It Can't Shop for Ward Brass," *Wall Street Journal*, August 13, 1997, pp. B1, B6.

Conlin, Michelle, "Sears: The Turnaround Is for Real," *Forbes*, December 15, 1997.

Flynn, Julia, Christina Del Valle, and Russell Mitchell, "Did Sears Take Other Customers for a Ride?" *BusinessWeek*, August 3, 1992, p. 24.

Fuchsberg, Gilbert, "Sears Reinstates Sales Incentives in Some Centers," *Wall Street Journal*, March 7, 1994, p. B1.

Miller, James, "Sears Roebuck Expects Loss in Third Period," *Wall Street Journal*, September 8, 1992, p. A3.

Patterson, Gregory A., "Sears Debt of $11 Billion Is Downgraded," *Wall Street Journal*, December 11, 1992, p. A3.

"Sears Roebuck Fires Head of Its Auto Unit," *Wall Street Journal*, December 21, 1992, p. B6.

Stevenson, Richard W., "Sears' Crisis: How Did It Do?" *New York Times*, June 17, 1992, p. C1.

Woodyard, Chris, "Sears to Refund Millions to Bankrupt Customers," *USA Today*, April 11–13, 1997, p. 1A.

---

[42]Nat B. Read, "Sears PR Debacle Shows How Not to Handle a Crisis," *Wall Street Journal*, January 11, 1993, p. A14.

The Mechanics at Sears Auto Centers

Why did the mechanics remain quiet for so long? When the investigations were announced in advance, why didn't they say anything about the conduct they were engaged in for compensation? Why do those in an organization remain silent even when they can see the self-destruction coming?

Case 5.5

Kardashian Tweets: Regulated Ads or Fun?

It began in typical Kardashian fashion. Just an Instagram post showing Ms. Kardashian West holding up a bottle of Diclegis, an anti-nausea drug manufactured by Duchesnay, Inc., with the following post:

> OMG. Have you heard about this? As you guys know my morning sickness has been pretty bad. I tried changing things about my lifestyle, like my diet, and nothing helped, so I talked to my doctor. He prescribed Diclegis. I felt a lot better and most importantly, it's been studied and there was no increased risk to the baby. I'm so excited and happy with my results that I'm partnering with Duchesnay USA to raise awareness about treating morning sickness, [sic] be safe and sure to ask your doctor about the pill with the pregnant woman on it and find out more. www.diclegis.com.[43]

The Food and Drug Administration (FDA) sent a warning letter to Duchesnay with the following concern:

> The social media post was also submitted as a complaint to the OPDP Bad Ad Program. The social media post is false or misleading in that it presents efficacy claims for DICLEGIS but fails to communicate any risk information associated with its use and it omits material facts.[44]

The FDA ordered the company to "cease misbranding."[45] Ms. Kardashian issued a corrective post the day after

the FDA letter was received explaining the limitations of Diclegis and providing a link to obtain information about this prescription drug.[46]

The FDA has had a rough battle with trying to rein in the use of social media in advertising prescription drugs. The FDA's concern is that the posts do not adequately disclose the risks of prescription drugs. The problem it faces is the rapidity with which the information flows due to social media.

The FDA does have celebrity endorsement guidelines, which include, among other things, that the celebrity must actually use the product being advertised. The celebrities must also indicate their relationship with the company. Ms. Kardashian West's statement indicated that she was "partnering" with Duchesnay. And, as in the Kardashian West ad, the celebrity cannot overstate the product's qualities or performance.

If the statements are made independently by the celebrity, then the FDA has no control because the company is not participating. When a celebrity just posts that he or she uses a product and that it is a great product, the self-generated announcement is not FDA regulated. If there is, however, a connection with the company, whether through compensation or through the company providing the language for the celebrity endorsement, then the FDA can control the social media use.

The FDA believes that celebrity endorsements serve to create consumer demand and patients pressuring doctors to prescribe certain drugs. The FDA worries that

(continued)

---

[43]http://www.fda.gov/downloads/Drugs/GuidanceCompli-anceRegulatoryInformation/EnforcementActivitiesbyFDA/WarningLettersandNoticeofViolationLetterstoPharmaceutical-Companies/UCM457961.pdf.

[44]http://www.fda.gov/downloads/Drugs/GuidanceCompli-anceRegulatoryInformation/EnforcementActivitiesbyFDA/WarningLettersandNoticeofViolationLetterstoPharmaceutical-Companies/UCM457961.pdf. Last visited October 25, 2016.

[45]Christine Hauser, "Kardashian Promotes a Pill, and the F.D.A. strikes," *New York Times*, August 13, 2015, p. B1.

[46]https://consumerist.com/2015/08/31/after-fda-warning-kim-kardashian-posts-corrected-endorsement-of-morning-sickness-pill/.

Case 5.5

(continued)

these prescriptions may not be in the best interests of the patient but are fueled through celebrity examples and endorsements.

In the past, the FDA has halted celebrity social media endorsements for Adderall XR. For example, Ty Pennington's endorsement of that drug had to be changed because his endorsement focused only on the positive effects of the drug and did not disclose the risks and downside of using the prescription drug.

Discussion Questions

1. List the requirements for celebrity endorsements of prescription drugs to be allowed by the FDA.

2. What additional information does the FDA want in celebrity endorsements of prescription drugs?

3. What are the risks of product tweets? Do celebrities have an ethical responsibility related to their tweets about products?

Case 5.6

Political Misrepresentation: When Is It a Lie?

In May 2010, Richard Blumenthal, the then-attorney general for the state of Connecticut made the following statements:

Date/Place	Statement	True or False?
June 2008 Veterans Ceremony	"We have learned something since the days I served in Vietnam."	
2003 (speech to troops and their families upon their return from overseas)	"When we returned, we saw nothing like this. Let us do better by this generation of men and women."	
2008 (speech at Veterans War Memorial)	"I served during the Vietnam era. I remember the taunts, the insults, sometimes even physical abuse."	
When questioned about correcting newspapers calling him a Vietnam veteran	"I don't know if we tried to do so or not. I can't possibly know what is reported in all [the articles written about him].[47]	

Here is a summary of Mr. Blumenthal's military record:

1965–1970   Took five military deferments to avoid the draft for Vietnam

1970   Last deferment expired; he was #152 in the draft lottery and those up to #195 were being drafted, so he joined the Marine Reserves

Conducted toy drives and cleaned up parks in the Washington DC area

He never served in Vietnam or in combat. He never left Washington, DC.

Discussion Questions

1. Evaluate Mr. Blumenthal's statements about his military service. Are they true or false?

2. What are the remedies for false or misleading statements in contract negotiations?

3. Is puffing (making the product look as good as possible) an ethical issue? Is it bluffing?

4. Compare what Senator Blumenthal said (he won the Senate seat) with the discussions of résumés in Unit 1. What are the penalties for puffing on a résumé? For lying? And what are the differences?

---

[47]Raymond Hernandez, "Richard Blumenthal's Words on Vietnam Service Differ from History," *New York Times*, May 17, 2010, https://www.nytimes.com/2010/05/18/nyregion/18blumenthal.html.

Promises, Performance, and Reality

Did you really perform what was required under the contract terms? There are issues about what constitutes "close enough" and questions about authority under contract terms that offer ethical dilemmas on both sides of the contract. There are also the issues that affect third parties, the non-signing parties to a contract that it not performed. For example, government entities contract for the management of government employee pension plans. If those managers breach their agreement with their government entity, those affected include those who are under the pension plan. Ethical analysis on not performing under a contract looks at the third-party and societal effects of not doing what you promised to do in a contractual agreement.

Case 5.7

The Ethics of Walking Away and No Eviction During Pandemics

Leaving the Mortgage Behind But Taking the Plumbing with You

Facing foreclosure, mortgagors who have loans that exceed their property value often have a sense of hopelessness and "nothing to lose." These mortgagors simply leave the property, something that is likely in an underwater mortgage because they have so little to lose. Their credit rating is affected, but they no longer have the payments or the worries of maintenance. In some cities, mortgagors who have abandoned their homes have stripped the property of everything from the stove to the copper plumbing. The federal government has set up special task forces to try to stop the stripping of properties by mortgagors.

Most mortgage agreements require the mortgagor to maintain the property in livable condition, but again desperate times bring desperate actions. Also, taking items from the mortgaged property is not theft unless and until title has been taken back through the foreclosure process. Stripped and abandoned properties bring down the value of neighborhoods and result in increased crime levels. Areas with high levels of abandoned properties now unoccupied and held by lenders that are unable to sell them have been labeled "foreclosure ghettos." In cities with high foreclosure rates, "walk-aways" and stripping resulted in urban blight in certain areas. Cities are passing ordinances that require lenders to maintain the abandoned properties or taking back the properties through eminent domain so that the abandoned homes do not become drug houses or residences for the homeless.

Discussion Questions

1. Does the fact that many are walking away or selling their properties through "short sales" (a sale of the property below the mortgage amount that is approved by the original lender) make it ethical for all owners to do the same?

2. List who is affected by a decision to walk away and explain how they are affected.

(continued)

Case 5.7

(continued)

No Rent Due and No Eviction[48]

Shortly after the COVID-19 cases emerged in the United States in February and March 2020, the Coronavirus Aid, Relief, and Economic Security Act (CARES Act) was passed.[49] The CARES Act included a 120-day prohibition on eviction proceedings of those living in "covered properties." "Covered properties" included those properties that were part of a federal program or financed by federally backed loans. The CARES Act was not renewed, and the eviction prohibition lapsed on July 27, 2020.

In some cases, state and local governments then stepped in to pass prohibitions on evictions because of the effect on public health of increasing the homeless population. In September 2020, the CDC issued its regulation, "Temporary Halt in Residential Evictions to Prevent the Further Spread of COVID-19."[50]

On December 21, 2020, Congress passed the Consolidated Appropriations Act.[51] The Act included specific relief to aid residential tenants and landlords by providing for $25 billion in emergency rental assistance and extending the Centers for Disease Control and Prevention (CDC) moratorium on residential evictions.

As of April 2021, there were 46 appellate court cases involving challenges to the COVID-19 moratorium on evictions. Beyond the issue of the law being eventually declared unconstitutional, there were many tenants taking advantage of the law while it was in place despite not qualifying for protection against eviction under the law.

In the case *Meade Communities LLC v. Walker*, the landlord brought a unlawful detainer action (eviction proceeding) against a tenant who owed $5,000 in back rent.[52] However, the tenant had never asserted that he qualified for protection under the CDC order for non-eviction. Still, even without the tenant invoking the CDC protections, the court, citing the health risk of evicting a tenant during a pandemic, held that the landlord could not exercise the right of eviction. The tenant was given the CDC protection despite having made no effort to comply with the requirements for invoking CDC protections.[53] The requirements included loss of income, loss of a job, lost work hours, extraordinary medical expenses, and a good-faith effort to pay the rent.

The judge expanded the CDC non-eviction protections to any defaulting tenant, not just tenants who could establish the requirements under the CDC order and now the federal statute. So, at least under Maryland's state laws, under general pandemic statewide orders, those tenants in default must stay put even if they do not meet the economic conditions of the CDC order for their protection.

Discussion Questions

1. Discuss the applicable ethical categories in this situation.

2. List who is affected when tenants are permitted to live rent-free and landlords have no remedy.

3. Refer back to the discussion in Unit 1 and the models for asking questions as you resolve ethical dilemmas. What happens to housing availability and paying tenants when there are these types of statutory protections?

4. During the Spanish flu pandemic at the turn of the 20th century, the Great Depression, and World War II, there were no rent protections. Why were the protections implemented in this pandemic? Why did so many take advantage of rent-free housing when it was not clear they met the statutory requirements?

---

[48]Adapted with permission from Marianne M. Jennings, "Tiger Lily, the CDC, and Eviction for Nonpayment of Rent," 50 *Real Estate Law Journal* 426 (2021).

[49]Pub. L. No. 116-136, 134 Stat. 281 (2020).

[50]85 Fed. Reg. 55,292 (September 4, 2020).

[51]Pub. L. No. 116-260 (2020)."

[52]*Meade Communities LLC v. Walker*, 2020 WL 5759762 (D. Md. 2020).

[53]*Id.*

Case 5.8

Pension Promises, Payments, and Bankruptcy: Companies, Cities, Towns, and States

In 2011, the city of Detroit was paying out almost $200 million per year in pension benefits to its retired workers. The city's annual contributions to its pension plan at that time were less than half of that sum.[54] As payments out have increased, payments in have decreased. How is it possible to have a fully funded pension plan with these numbers? Professionals, including auditors, fiduciaries, and actuaries, have certified that the aggressive investment policies for the fund should make up the difference.[55] Still, those who one day expect to be beneficiaries and receive their payouts soon recognized the harsh reality that would soon play out with pension funds throughout the United States.[56] The city of Detroit filed for bankruptcy in 2013. Five years later those on the pension plan were still facing the burden imposed by the bankruptcy trustee that required pensioners to pay for their health care and cut pension payments 4.5%.[57]

When Detroit declared bankruptcy, pensioners had few rights. The issue of pension obligations continues to arise when funding falls short, when there is a bankruptcy, or, because of a pandemic, more employees retire at an earlier age, increasing the number of pensioners suddenly. Despite all the imprimaturs from professionals, pension benefits elsewhere have been cut, plans changed, and, in some cases, payments to retirees stopped altogether. All accomplished with plenty of litigation.

The ability to change terms is difficult for state pension plans but there has been some success and a great deal of pushback. One expert noted:

> Workers in government pensions around the world can count on politicians and taxpayers running to legislatures and courts to cut benefits workers have been "promised" when these already struggling government pensions start to run out of money. For example, after Croatia's parliament recently approved a government proposal to raise the retirement age from 65 to 67 and trim pensions for people who retire early, three top trade unions revolted and the government backed down—for now. [58]

Business Pensions and Bankruptcy: A Regulatory History

When United Airlines declared bankruptcy in 2002, its pension liabilities were discharged. The ability of a company to renege on pension benefits when so many protections were built into the law under the Employee Retirement Income Security Act (ERISA) has been an ongoing concern. Congressional hearings following the losses in the United case uncovered loopholes in the accounting processes for pension fund reporting that permitted United, and many others, to report pension numbers that made the health of the fund look better than it was. The loopholes were Enronesque in nature, allowing obligations to be spun off the books so that the existing levels of obligations of the plan looked small and the assets very rich.

Federal Regulation of Pensions

Because of United's pension bailout, Congress changed the accounting for pension plans to avoid the problem of the rosy picture when pension funds actually

(continued)

---

[54]Michael Cooper and Mary Williams Walsh, "Public Pensions, Once Off Limits, Face Budget Cuts," *New York Times*, April 26, 2011, p. A1. For more background information on pensions, actuaries, and fund losses, see Marianne M. Jennings and Sally Gunz, "A Proactive Proposal for Self-Regulation of the Actuarial Profession," 48 *American Business Law Journal* 641 (2011).

[55]*Id.*

[56]Simon Baribeau and David Mildenberg, "State Workers Run for the Exits," *Bloomberg Businessweek*, April 25–May 1, 2011, p. 32. See also Steven Greenhouse, "States Want More in Pension Contributions," *New York Times*, June 16, 2011, p. B1; and Jeanette Neumann and Michael Korkery, "Public Pension Fund Squeeze," *Wall Street Journal*, March 23, 2011, p. C1.

[57]Susan Tompar, "Even 5 Years Later, Retirees Feel the Effects of Detroit's Bankruptcy," *Detroit Free Press*, July 18, 2018, https://www.freep.com/story/money/personal-finance/susan-tompor/2018/07/18/detroit-bankruptcy-retirees-pension/759446002/.

[58]Edward Siedle, "Kiss Your State Pension Goodbye," *Forbes*, April 23, 2020, https://www.forbes.com/sites/edwardsiedle/2020/04/23/kiss-your-state-pension-goodbye/?sh=1d34fdc561f9

Case 5.8

(continued)

need funding. The Pension Protection Act closed the accounting loopholes. The effect of the changes is to require companies to fund their pension plans according to the numbers they have reported to the SEC in their financials. Apparently, the numbers reported to the SEC vis-à-vis pensions are accurate, whereas the numbers reported for ERISA purposes are inflated. If United had funded its plans when its SEC numbers indicated it needed to (e.g., 1998 would have been the year when funding was first needed), the plan would have been sufficiently funded at the time of the United bankruptcy. However, under ERISA guidelines, it was not required to kick in funds until 2002, when it was grossly underfunded.

The Pension Benefit Guarantee Corporation (PBGC) was created under ERISA and provides insurance for employees for underfunded pensions.[59] The presence of this protection results in a moral hazard. With the presence of the PBGC as a stopgap measure for pension plans that fail or end, there is lax responsible funding and management of pension plans. The pension plan no longer represents a source of exposure. Funding decisions, especially in relation to promised benefits, are often made with inflated expectations or little regard for reality. As one commentator noted,

> Nevertheless, union leaders, who negotiate most pension agreements, often seek pension promises that even they know are excessive, in large part because the PBGC insures these promises. In addition, unions and their constituents rarely ensure that their pensions are fully funded: "As a result of federal pension insurance, employees lack the proper incentives to monitor their employers' funding levels because the employees will not bear the full costs of their inattention." In an effort to resolve this tension, the PBGC does not insure any and all pension promises, instead it resolves nonpayment issues by companies by limiting yearly payouts to beneficiaries. Ironically, the PBGC does this to give employees incentives to make sure their employer funds their plans adequately.

Nevertheless, many pension promises are not as insured as most employees would believe.[60]

A conflicts issue that arises in the funding and management of pension plans is that employers who hire actuaries often signal their concerns about the impact of increased funding on earnings. Simultaneously, beneficiaries signal their desire for continuing present funding levels that still provide promised benefits. That tension affects the role of the actuary who determines funding levels and can result in the use of overly optimistic actuarial assumptions.

When markets decline and retirement rates increase, more plans fail.[61] By 2021, the PGC had a deficit of $48.3 billion because of the payouts it was making to claimants due to underfunding as well as the bankruptcies of major companies such as United.[62]

Reductions in Force and Buyouts to Relieve Pension Tension

There have been significant reductions in force (RIF) since the 1980s, with post-2008 being a period of significant RIFs. Because of the extensive benefits employees at these companies have, like GM, retirement benefits as their largest expense. One analyst quipped that GM is running a pension plan and building cars as a hobby. To reduce expenses, GM periodically buys out employees at a cheaper cost than it can continue to pay them and have them accrue retirement benefits. One GM worker, who received a $140,000 payment, has a small dealership in Doraville, Georgia, where the GM plant is located, at which he sells used pickup trucks. He is not married and has no children, rents out six homes that he owns, and co-owns

(continued)

---

[59]29 U.S.C. § 1302 (2000).

[60]Joshua Gad-Harf, "The Decline of Traditional Pensions, the Impact of the Pension Protection Act of 2006, and the Future of America's Defined-Benefit Pension System," 83 *Chicago-Kent Law Review* 1409, 1417 (2008).

[61]*Id.*

[62]Marcy Gordon, "Pension Safety Net in a Jam," *Arizona Republic*, November 16, 2005, p. B1. See also Nicholas Varchaver, "Pitchman for the Gray Revolution," *Fortune*, July 11, 2005, p. 63 (noting that the FPGC assumed responsibility for the obligation to United Airlines plan members).

Case 5.8

(continued)

a beauty parlor. He will retire comfortably from his own investments.

Despite pension buyouts, GM was still in dire financial condition. In 2008, the U.S. government provided General Motors with $5.8 billion in funds to facilitate emergence from Chapter 11 bankruptcy. As security for the loan and for the advancement of additional billions in bailout funds to the company, the U.S. government held a 10% ownership stake in the auto company. GM also had to agree to certain management changes and promise to repay the funds. GM also had to agree to provide 39% share ownership of the company to employees of the company. GM promised to cut 40% of its car dealers and eliminate 7,000 jobs. Following its emergence from bankruptcy, GM did cut its car dealers by 40%, but public outcry on the termination of longstanding dealers found GM reinstating terminated dealers. GM consolidated plants and closed its Saturn division for a 7,000-job cutback. A government official said that the loss of jobs if the automaker failed was too great to risk and thus required government intervention. The pensions were saved through government payments and RIFs. Pension plans in business are underfunded, not particularly enforceable, and have become dependent on the federal government when businesses have setbacks or bankruptcy.

Other Strategies for Coping with Pension Issues

As the problems of declining returns and increasing payouts increase, companies have begun taking additional steps to make ends meet on their pension plans. With so many employees leaving the workforce following the pandemic, the pool of pensioners is now increasing at a rate neither the companies nor the actuaries anticipated. AT&T has been making cuts to the benefits its retirees have been receiving.[63] AT&T noted, "We are working hard to responsibly balance the needs of the business and our taking care of our 200,000 employees and 500,000 retirees and their dependents."[64] Over the years, AT&T has cut spousal benefits, eliminated life insurance policies for new employees, cut some

health benefits, and halved many other benefits. The life insurance cuts were a function of economics. The company owed $12.75 billion in those benefits and was only funded for $3.8 billion. After December 31, 2021, an employee with a $63,000 life insurance policy will receive $15,000.

AT&T is not alone. When retailer Barneys declared bankruptcy, it only had about half the money it needed to pay its employees promised severance pay.[65] There have been 20 lawsuits filed against employers for their management of retirement plans. Employees are taking matters into their own hands and using a handful of lawyers experienced in retirement funds to demand accountability and responsibility in the management of these funds by businesses.[66] Even when the employees lose the suits, the exercise of reexamining management of the funds has helped both the businesses and the employees.

Conflicts Emerge in Government Pension Plans: Actuaries and Pension Experts

Beyond the issues in business retirement plans is a monster problem with public pensions and their fund managers and actuaries. For example, the New York State Pension fund relied on actuarial numbers that, when made public in 2008, made little economic sense. Even under broad standards of interpretation, there was no method for reconciling the actuary firm's findings with actual funding levels. As the details of the questionable numbers that were used for continual expansion of public pension benefits emerged, so also did details about the relationships of the actuary with those affiliated with the pension plan. For example, the actuarial firm providing the professional opinion for New York on the adequacy of the fund to meet current liabilities was paid at least in part for its opinions by the existing members of the plan who had an inherent interest in the fund being deemed sufficient, something that would not trigger political budget battles.[67]

(continued)

---

[63]Theo Francis and Drew Fitzgerald, "AT&T Cuts Hit Retiree Benefits," *Wall Street Journal*, December 27, 2021, p. A1.
[64]Id.

[65]Sapna Maheshwari, "Barneys's Slow Death March Leaves Workers in the Lurch," *New York Times*, January 17, 2020, p. B1.
[66]Tara Siegel Bernard, "N.Y.U. Prevails in Retirement Plan Suit," *New York Times*, August 2, 2018, p. A2.
[67]Id.

Case 5.8

(continued)

When actuaries certify a pension plan as sufficiently funded when it is not, due to their poor assumptions, the resolution of the deficit is like kicking a can down the road. Accountability is inevitable and the longer the reality check is postponed, the greater the pain.

California's Public Employee Retirement System (CalPERS), the nation's largest public retirement plan, announced in late 2021 that it would have to borrow money and take on riskier investments and would still only earn a 6.2% rate of return, far below the conservative 6.8% return it established in 2021.

Public pension plans are left with the choices of reducing benefits, something courts have been reluctant to approve when pensioners litigate, or taking on the political battles to put more funds into the plans. Both options have serious political implications. Increasing funding means raising taxes and carries with it the wrath of taxpayers.[68]

In 2011, there was a legislative standoff in the state of Wisconsin because of a reality check: the public employees' pension plans were underfunded, the state budget exceeded revenues, and the state was unable to fund the plan sufficiently for promised benefits.[69] Act 10, as it was called, required members to increase the amount they paid into their pension plan. As of 2021 the bitterness remains because of those costs to pensioners.[70]

As of 2016, the funding gap for state pension plans was $1 trillion.[71] In some states, funding increased over 300%. However, government pension plans also found

a third option for dealing with the funding gaps. New employees do not get the same level of benefits under earlier plans. As a result and due to unique 25% returns during the volatile market of the pandemic, the Pew Trust places the adequate funding rate for state government pensions at 80%.[72] However, that increase in adequate funding carries a caveat—many of the states are still paying down debt that they took on to see them through their underfunded days. There is one additional caveat— the Pew funding study does not cover local government pensions, which includes most emergency personnel, teachers, city, county, and town officials unless they are brought under their state plans.

The Role and Liability of Actuaries

There were a number of lawsuits against actuaries in Alaska; Texas; San Diego, California; Milwaukee, Wisconsin; Evanston, Illinois; and Fort Worth, Texas.[73] The theory underlying these lawsuits was that pension benefits were widely given and expanded because the actuarial methods used undervalued the benefits. The plaintiffs in these suits sought recovery from the professionals who provided their certification that the numbers supported a sufficient investment pool and returns to meet cash distributions at the times provided for in the plan to the full range of plan beneficiaries.[74] However, the suits have not been slam dunks for the government pension plans unless the actuaries committed malpractice, such as by using outdated actuarial tables on age and death. Optimistic return rates are not necessarily malpractice and the courts have held the line on recovery by the cities, towns, and states. Further, actuaries are the expert witnesses in

(continued)

---

[68]One actuary noted the conflict and the outdated models caused "[f]inancial burdens [to be] hidden." Cooper and Walsh, *supra* note 36, p. C1. Similar standoffs loom in New York and New Jersey.

[69]Lisa Colangelo, "As Ground Zero in Bargaining Debate, Wisconsin Union Battle Has Repercussions," *New York Daily News*, February 22, 2011, http://articles.nydailynews.com/ 2011-02-22/local/28639649_1_pension-reform-unionleaders-and-lawmakers-ground-zero.

[70]WXOW, "'Scars Are Still There: Act 10 Left Its Impact on Wisconsin," February 12, 2021, https://www.wxow.com/news/ politics/scars-are-still-there-act-10-left-its-impact-on-wisconsin/ article_13530e2a-c16e-59f0-b27c-ba9e9b242992.html.

[71]Timothy W. Martin, "Pension Returns To Hit New Lows," *Wall Street Journal*, July 26, 2016, p. A1.

[72]Pew Trust Issue Brief: "The States Pension Funding Gap: Plans Stabilized in Wake of Pandemic," September 14, 2021, https://www.pewtrusts.org/en/research-and-analysis/issue-briefs/2021/09/the-state-pension-funding-gap-plans-have-stabilized-in-wake-of-pandemic.

[73]See Cooper and Walsh, *supra* note 36, p. C7 (noting that San Diego's pension numbers were so off base that the SEC took action against the city for securities fraud).

[74]Id.

Case 5.8

(continued)

these cases and are not likely to turn on their fellow professionals. Government pension funds are finding that actuarial firms are requesting liability limitation clauses before they will undertake government pension work.[75]

Public Pensions and Corruption

In addition to the questionable actuarial opinions and the conflict created by beneficiaries paying for those favorable opinions, there are pending charges of corruption regarding the retention of investment advisers, actuaries, and other professionals for pension plan management.[76] In 2009, four actuary firms entered guilty pleas in connection with their retention of fund management contracts for New York's public pension fund.[77] California filed a suit against several private equity firms for their relationships with CalPERS executives that included perks and that, the suit concludes, resulted in "improper relationships" between the firms and the public pension fund.[78] That would not be the only time CalPERS experienced legal and ethical difficulties with the management of the nation's largest pension fund. CalPERS' chief investment officer (CIO) left after only two years in the position because he was making personal investments in securities that were eventually affected by his investment decisions on the $415 billion fund he was managing. In short, the CIO had the power to move markets and was investing personally to take advantage of those movements. In addition, he was not forthright

and complete in disclosing his holdings as required under California statute.

States have been addressing the relationships between and among fund managers, consultants, and pension boards. For instance, Illinois now prohibits pension trustees, employees, and consultants from benefiting from investment transactions.[79] Several states introduced more competitive processes for procuring consulting and investment services.[80] Other states now require their pension systems to conduct performance reviews of consultants and managers, including a comparison of costs of services. The reforms brought a breather in the litigation and funding concerns as government pension plans enjoy a respite from underfunding.

Discussion Questions

1. Describe the regulatory cycles on pension fund accounting and pension funding.

2. Explain the conflicts issue in the management of pension plans.

3. Give a list of the economic and ethical issues in pension funding, employee wages, and RIFs.

4. Explain the ethical obligations of elected officials regarding underfunding of pension plans.

5. Are there social responsibility issues in eminent domain cases for corporate benefits?

Sources

Maynard, Micheline, "G.M. Will Offer Buyouts to All Its Union Workers," *New York Times*, March 23, 2006, pp. A1, C4.
Maynard, Micheline, "G.M. Will Offer Buyouts to All Its Union Workers," *New York Times*, March 23, 2006, pp. A1, C4.

Williams Walsh, Mary, "Pension Law Loopholes Helped United Hide Its Troubles," *New York Times*, June 7, 2005, p. C1.
Williams Walsh, Mary, "Pension Law Loopholes Helped United Hide Its Troubles," *New York Times*, June 7, 2005, p. C1.

---

[75]Edward Siedle, "Actuarial Limitations of Liability? (LOL) Laugh Out Loud!" *Forbes*, September 9, 2010, http://www.forbes.com/sites/edwardsiedle/2010/09/09/actuarial-limitations-of-liability-lol-laugh-out-loud-december-1-2002/#4bd68f5e676a.

[76]Michael J. de la Merced, "4 Firms Agree to Settlement in New York Pension Fund Inquiry," *New York Times*, August 19, 2009, p. B1.

[77]Id.

[78]Gina Chona, "Brown Targets Pension Middleman," *Wall Street Journal*, May 7, 2010, p. C5b (noting that the suit alleges executives were offered standing employment opportunities and trips to New York and Florida that resulted in $63,000 in expenses being reimbursed by the company that was awarded $700 million in a CalPERS fund investment).

---

[79]Mary Williams Walsh, "Illinois Plan for Pensions Questioned," *New York Times*, January 26, 2011, p. B1.

[80]Id.

Case 5.9

"I Only Used It Once": Returning Goods

Even the well-seasoned Dillard's manager was taken aback by this one. A customer brought in a pair of moderately expensive dress shoes, expressing a desire to return them because they just weren't quite right. As the manager processed the order, she checked inside the box to be sure that the shoes in the box were the shoes that matched the box—past experience dictated such follow-up on returns. The shoes were the correct ones for the box, but the customer had another issue. The shoes had masking tape on the bottom—masking tape that was dirty. Returning to the customer, the manager said, "You forgot to remove the masking tape from your shoes." The customer responded, "I only wore them once. That's all I needed them for."

From Neiman Marcus to Saks to Dillard's and back, managers have to stay one step ahead of customers—or rather, lessees—who buy—or rather, lease for free—dresses and now shoes for one use with premeditated intent to return the merchandise. Stores now place tags strategically so that the dresses cannot be worn without cutting them off and there are no returns if the tags are cut off on formal wear.

Lest you think that the problem is limited to women and formal wear, talk to your Ace Hardware or Home Depot manager about the folks who "buy" a special tool, use it once, and then try to return it. The hardware/home improvement stores are left with opened packaging and used goods by buy-it-temporarily customers.

Amazon led the way down a new path on returns policies with its return whatever, at Amazon's expense, and Amazon will take it back. Other online retailers as well as the brick-and-mortar stores have had to adjust. As a result, stores such as Macy's have adopted very liberal return policies. Macy's advertises that it will take anything back, anytime. The horror stories abound. Macy's employees in the luggage department call their area "the rental luggage department," because customers buy the luggage, use it on a trip, and then return it. If the customer says he will be leaving in the morning and returning in a week, the clerks note that so they can time the return of that luggage: they will also be back to return their newly purchased luggage in a week.[81]

An unanticipated consequence of the liberal returns policies is the effect on employee pay. There are employees who are on commission plan for a certain amount of income in a week or believe that they have earned a certain amount of income. However, with these types of return policies, they can lose their commissions on any returns within six months after purchase. The policies on commission were created to stop employees from having friends and family come in and purchase goods, allowing the employee to earn the commission but then returning the goods. Without the hit to the employee on commission loss for returned goods, there would be gaming of the system. However, customers seem to be gaming the system. In 2020, according to the National Retail Federation, customers in the United States returned $428 billion in goods, a 53% increase in seven years.[82] The amount returned was 16% of total sales. By 2021, those numbers had climbed to $761 billion,[83] an increase of 78%. E-Commerce rates of return are 30%.

Union leaders are pressing the major department stores to change their return policies to 150 or 120 days instead of 180 days so that employees can better budget and plan on incomes, and possible reductions in income due to returns. A 2008 university study found that sales employees believe that returns have become too lax. The impact on earnings for retailers from so many returns has resulted in reductions in the number of sales employees, with many who remain being reduced to part-time schedules.

On the customer side, and from the legal perspective of contracts, if the store advertises a 180-day-no-questions-asked return policy, the store must honor what has been advertised. And, after 180 days, the customer could have done a great deal of walking on those shoes and taken quite a few trips with the luggage, along with appearances at proms and formals.

Discussion Questions

1. What is the ethical category here?

2. Who is affected by the returners and their conduct?

3. Explain the impact of return policies.

---

[81] Rachel Abrams, "The Sting of a Liberal Retail Returns Policy," *New York Times*, June 14, 2016, p. B1.

[82] "428 Billion in Merchandise Returned in 2020," *National Retail Federation*, January 11, 2021, https://nrf.com/media-center/press-releases/428-billion-merchandise-returned-2020.

[83] Melissa Ripko, "A More Than $761 Billion Dilemma: Retailers' Returns Jump as Online Sales Grow," *CNBC*, January 25, 2022, https://www.cnbc.com/2022/01/25/retailers-average-return-rate-jumps-to-16point6percent-as-online-sales-grow-.html

Famous Lines from Art and Literature

Paper Moon (1973)

Grifter/Con artist Moses Pray (Ryan O'Neal) to Addie Loggins (Tatum O'Neal) (a 10-year-old orphan):

"I got scruples too, you know. You know what that is? Scruples?"

Addie:

"No, I don't know what it is, but if you got 'em, it's a sure bet they belong to somebody else!"

Case 5.10

When Corporations Pull Promises Made to Government

The interrelationships of corporations with government entities have become a critical part of community development and economic redevelopment. However, sometimes there are benefits but reneged promises. The following scenarios illustrate the types of problems that result from these interrelationships.

Susette Kelo, Little Pink Houses, and Pfizer

When the U.S. Supreme Court decided *Kelo v. City of New London*, 545 U.S. 469 (2005), a constitutional and legislative shock wave rumbled across the country. States changed their statutes and constitutions on when and how local government could take private property for redevelopment purposes, and property owners began resisting local redevelopment plans.

The *Kelo* case began in 1978, when the city of New London, Connecticut, undertook a redevelopment plan for the area in and around the existing park at Fort Trumbull. The plan had the goal of a lovely state park, including the absence of existing pink cottages and other architecturally eclectic homes that had long been part of the area, one of which was owned by Susette Kelo. The central focus of the plan was getting the Pfizer pharmaceutical company to bring its new research facility to the Fort Trumbull area with a hoped-for economic boost from a major corporate employer.

Under the plan, Kelo's and others' homes would be razed to make room for Pfizer and its facilities. The homeowners filed suit, challenging New London's legal authority to take their homes. The trial court issued an injunction preventing New London from taking certain of the properties, but allowed others to be taken. The appellate court found for New London on all the claims; the Connecticut Supreme Court affirmed (in a 4–3 decision); and the landowners appealed to the U.S. Supreme Court, which affirmed the Connecticut Supreme Court decision by a 5–4 vote.

Ms. Kelo's home and 15 others were razed. Pfizer merged with Wyeth in 2009 and closed all company operations in New London. The Fort Trumball area has no houses, no research park, no businesses, and is now an undeveloped land. However, following Hurricane Irene, officials from the city of New London announced that the citizens of their fair city could dump their branches and fallen trees at the site where Ms. Kelo's home once sat. Her house was saved; Fort Trumball lies vacant and undeveloped.

Journalist Jeff Benedict, whose book *Little Pink Houses* documents the story of Ms. Kelo and her neighbors and the failed project, spoke at a dinner honoring the members of the Connecticut Supreme Court. Ms. Kelo was in the audience, along with the justices who had decided her case. Mr. Benedict told the story of the failed city project and the impact on Ms. Kelo and others. Afterward, Justice Richard Palmer thanked

(continued)

Case 5.10

(continued)

Mr. Benedict for telling the story and then apologized to Ms. Kelo for what happened to her. Ms. Kelo cried because she said it was the first time in the 12-year-battle that anyone had offered an apology. Her home has been moved to a site now protected by the New London Historical Society.

The Power to Control Taxes and Exercise Influence: Amazon the Giant

Local officials want Amazon desperately. If Amazon pays a reduced rate, oh the tax revenue they bring. Amazon brings jobs, jobs, jobs. Amazon makes political donations. But Amazon can change its mind. When political waters get rough or taxes too high, it relocates. When Amazon announces that it is looking to place warehouses, offices, or other facilities, it negotiates:

- Tax breaks and what state and local governments are willing to give Amazon

- Development hurdles, including help with any zoning issues

- Assistance in dealing with unions

Even after Amazon arrives, it uses its economic clout to influence proposed tax increases. Amazon's growth in Seattle created a housing crisis. The city council proposed a $500 per employee tax on large employers to provide funds for housing the homeless in Seattle's high-priced housing market. Amazon opposed the measure at a time when its decision on locating its second headquarters (HQ2) was in process. The tax passed, although it was only $275 per employee.[84] Still, Amazon

shifted its Seattle presence: its new HQ2 would not be in Washington, a loss of 50,000 jobs and $5 billion in tax revenue.[85]

Amazon explored placing its HQ2 in Long Island City, Queens, New York. Then-governor Andrew Cuomo and then-mayor Bill DeBlasio courted Amazon heavily, despite opposition from city council members, members of Congress, and progressives.[86] Amazon's HQ2 became a political hot potato, driving the narrative in elections.[87] Amazon pulled out from Long Island City and chose Northern Virginia for its HQ2 location.

Discussion Questions

1. What do the government incentives do, and how are they accomplished?

2. Apart from legal rights here, are there any "ethical qualms" about accepting and/or promising benefits for corporations in exchange for government benefits?

3. List the stakeholders and discuss the impact on them when a corporation controls the development promise as well as the time it stays.

4. Are there social responsibility issues in eminent domain cases for corporate benefits?

---

[84]Elizabeth Weiss, "Amazon's Aggressive Side Shows in Seattle Tax Fight," *USA Today*, May 17, 2018, p. 1B.

[85]*Id.*

[86]J. David Goodman and Karen Weise, "A Brash City Was Too Much. Amazon Fled," *New York Times*, February 16, 2019, p. A1 at A19.

[87]Corey Kilgannon, "A City Debates the Death of the Headquarters," *New York Times*, February 16, 2019, p. A19.

Case 5.11

Intel and the Chips: When You Have Made a Mistake

Intel introduced the powerful Pentium chip in 1993. Intel had spent $1 billion developing the chip, and the cost of producing it was estimated to be between $50 and $150

each. When the Pentium chip was finally rolled out, Intel shipped 4 million of the chips to computer manufacturers, including IBM.

(continued)

Case 5.11

(continued)

In July 1994, Intel discovered a flaw in the "floating-point unit" of the chip, which is the section that completes complex calculations quickly.[88]

The flaw caused errors in division calculations involving numbers with more than eight digits to the right of the decimal, such as in this type of equation:[89]

$$\frac{4,195,835}{3,145,727} \times 3,145,727 = 4,195,835$$

Pentium-equipped computers computed the answer, in error, as 4,195,579. Before introducing the Pentium chip, Intel had run 1 trillion tests. Those tests showed that the Pentium chip would produce an error once every 27,000 years, making the chance of an average user getting an error one in 9 billion.

In November, Thomas Nicely, a mathematician at Lynchburg College in Virginia, discovered the Pentium calculations flaw described above. On Thanksgiving Day 1994, Intel publicly acknowledged the flaw in the Pentium chip, and the next day its stock fell from 651/8 to 637/8. Intel explained that the problem had been corrected, but flawed chips were still being shipped because a three-month production schedule was just ending. Intel initially offered to replace the chips, but only for users who ran complicated calculations as part of their jobs. The replacement offer carried numerous conditions.[90]

On December 12, 1994, IBM announced that it would stop all shipments of its personal computers because its own tests indicated that the Pentium flaw was far more frequent than Intel had indicated.[91] IBM's tests concluded that computer users working on spreadsheets for as little as 15 minutes per day could produce a mistake every 24 days. Intel's then-CEO Andrew Grove called IBM's reaction "unwarranted." No other computer manufacturer adopted IBM's position. IBM's chief of its personal computing division, G. Richard Thoman,

emphasized that IBM had little choice: "It is absolutely critical for this industry to grow, that people trust that our products work right."[92] Following the IBM announcement, Intel's stock price dropped 6.5%, and trading had to be halted temporarily.

On December 20, 1994, CEO Grove announced that Intel would replace all Pentium chips:

> We were dealing with a consumer community that was upset with us. That they were upset with us—it has finally dawned on us—is because we were telling them what's good for them ... I think we insulted them.[93]

Replacing the chips could have cost up to $360 million. Intel offered to send owners a new chip that they could install or to have service firms replace chips for customers who were uncomfortable doing it themselves.

Robert Sombric, the data-processing manager for the city of Portsmouth, New Hampshire, found Intel's decision to continue selling flawed chips for months inexcusable: "I treat the city's money just as if it were my own. And I'm telling you: I wouldn't buy one of these things right now until we really know the truth about it."[94]

Following the replacement announcement, Intel's stock rose $3.44 to $61.25. One market strategist praised the replacement program: "It's about time. It's very clear they were fighting a losing battle, both in public relations as well as user confidence."[95]

Grove responded that Intel's delay in offering replacements was based on concerns about precedent.

(continued)

[88]Evan Ramstad, "Pentium: A Cautionary Tale," *Arizona Republic*, December 21, 1994, p. C1.

[89]Janice Castro, "When the Chips Are Down," *Time*, December 26, 1994, p. 126.

[90]James Overstreet, "Pentium Jokes Fly, but Sales Stay Strong," *USA Today*, December 7, 1994, p. 1B.

[91]Ira Sager and Robert D. Hof, "Bare Knuckles at Big Blue," *BusinessWeek*, December 26, 1994, pp. 60–62.

[92]Bart Ziegler and Don Clark, "Computer Giants' War over Flaw in Pentium Jolts the PC Industry," *Wall Street Journal*, December 13, 1994, pp. A1–A11.

[93]Jim Carlton and Stephen Kreider Yoder, "Humble Pie: Intel to Replace Its Pentium Chips," *Wall Street Journal*, December 21, 1994, pp. B1–B9.

[94]Jim Carlton and Scott McCartney, "Corporations Await More Information: Will Consumers Balk?" *Wall Street Journal*, December 14, 1994, pp. B1–B5; and Stephen Kreider Yoder, "The Pentium Proposition: To Buy or Not to Buy," *Wall Street Journal*, December 14, 1994, p. B1.

[95]Carlton and Kreider Yoder, "Humble Pie," pp. B1–B9; "Intel Eats Crow, Replaces Pentiums," *Mesa Tribune*, December 21, 1994, p. F1; and Catalina Ortiz, "Intel to Replace Flawed Pentium Chips," *Arizona Republic*, December 21, 1994, pp. A1–A8.

Case 5.11

(continued)

"If we live by an uncompromising standard that demands perfection, it will be bad for everybody," he said.[96] He also acknowledged that Intel had agreed to sell the flawed Pentium chips to a jewelry manufacturer.[97]

By December 16, 1994, 10 lawsuits in three states involving 18 law firms had been filed against Intel for the faulty chips. Chip replacement demands by customers, however, were minimal.

Intel's internal employee newsletter had an April 1, 1995, edition that spoofed the infamous chip.[98] A spoof form provided in the newsletter required customers with Pentium chips to submit a 5,000-word essay on "Why My Pentium Should Be Replaced."

In 1997, Intel launched two new products: Pentium Pro and Pentium II. A new potential bug, again affecting only intensive engineering and scientific mathematical operations, was uncovered. Intel, however, published the list of bugs, with technical information and remedies. One analyst commented on the new approach, "They have learned a lot since then. You can't approach the consumer market with an engineering mindset."[99]

In 2021, Intel was facing shortages in key supplies and would fall behind on shipping its chips. Combined with decreasing demand in sales of personal computers, Intel announced that its gross margins would decline, that it was working to develop its own supplies, and that it would continue to miss sales projections.[100] Intel stock dropped 10% to $49.46. Intel said that it was looking to the future by announcing bad news early.

Discussion Questions

1. Should Intel have disclosed the flaw in the Pentium chip when it first discovered it in July 1994? Did Intel learn from its experience with the chip? When?

2. Should Intel have issued an immediate recall? Why do you think the company didn't do that? Discuss what issues their executives missed by applying the models you learned in Units 1 and 2.

3. What ethical categories apply to Intel's series of actions on the chips?

4. A joke about Intel's Pentium chip (source unknown) circulated on the Internet: Top Ten Reasons to Buy a Pentium-Equipped Computer:

   10. Your current computer is too accurate.

   9. You want to get into the Guinness Book of World Records as "owner of most expensive paperweight."

   8. Math errors add zest to life.

   7. You need an alibi for the IRS.

   6. You want to see what all the fuss is about.

   5. You've always wondered what it would be like to be a plaintiff.

   4. The "Intel Inside" logo matches your decor perfectly.

   3. You no longer have to worry about the CPU overheating.

   2. You got a great deal from the Jet Propulsion Laboratory.

   1. And the number one reason to buy a Pentium-equipped computer: It'll probably work.[101]

   Based on this circulating joke, discuss the long-term impact on Intel of Intel's decisions on handling the chip.

---

[96]Ziegler and Clark, "Computer Giants' War over Flaw in Pentium Jolts the PC Industry," pp. A1–A11.

[97]Otis Port, "A Chip on Your Shoulder—Or Your Cuffs," *BusinessWeek*, January 23, 1995, p. 8.

[98]Richard B. Schmitt, "Flurry of Lawsuits Filed against Intel over Pentium Flaw," *Wall Street Journal*, December 16, 1994, p. B3.

[99]James Kim, "Intel Proactive with Potential Buy," *USA Today*, May 6, 1997, p. 1B.

[100]Dan Gallagher, "Intel Looks to the Future By Delivering the Bad News Now," *Wall Street Journal*, October 23–24, 2021, p. B13.

---

[101]From a memo furnished to the author by Intel employee at the time of the Intel chip problems.

Ethics in Action 5.3

Speaking Up in a Meeting

Assume that you are an Intel manager invited to the 1994 post-Thanksgiving meeting on how to respond to the public revelation of the flawed chips. You believe the failure to offer replacements will damage the company over the long term. Further, you feel strongly that providing a replacement is a balanced and ethical thing to do. However, CEO Grove disagrees. How would you persuade him to offer replacements to all purchasers?

If you could not persuade Grove to replace the chips, would you stay at Intel?

Compare & Contrast

Consider the following analysis (from "Intel Eats Crow, Replaces Pentium," *Mesa Tribune*, December 21, 1994, p. Fl):

> Regarding your article "Bare Knuckles at Big Blue" (News: Analysis & Commentary, Dec. 26), future generations of business school students will study Intel Corp.'s response to the problems with the Pentium chip as a classic case study in how to transform a technical problem into a public-relations nightmare. Intel's five-point plan consisted of the following:
>
> 1. Initially deny that the problem exists.
> 2. When irrefutable evidence is presented that the problem exists, downplay its significance.
> 3. Agree to only replace items for people who can demonstrate extreme hardship.
> 4. Continue running your current ad campaign, extolling the virtues of the product as if nothing has happened.
> 5. Count the short-term profits.[102]

List other companies discussed in this book or in other readings that followed this same five-point pattern.

(continued)

---

[102]"Intel Eats Crow, Replaces Pentiums," p. F1.

Compare & Contrast

In 2003, the math department at the University of Texas at Austin complained to Dell Computers that its computers were failing. Dell examined the computers for the university, one of its major customers and a major tie-in to the student body there. Dell concluded that the computers were failing because those using them in the math department were performing too many complex math calculations that overtaxed the computers.

However, internal emails that surfaced in the discovery process of a class action lawsuit indicate that the computers sent to UT–Austin had faulty electrical components that were leaking chemicals into the computer, thus resulting in the failures. Ironically, the cause was so clear and so common that all the computers shipped with these faulty parts failed at the same time.

Despite this knowledge, Dell employees were instructed to tell customers that the problems were not a big issue. There were also emails and instructions to employees about downplaying the problem, telling them, "Don't bring this to the attention of the customer proactively. Emphasize uncertainty."[103] In fact, there were safety issues because of the risk of fire from the failed computers with leaking components.

Discussion Questions

1. Was Dell's response similar to or different from Intel's?

2. Dell has settled the litigation that resulted from the failed computers. Is this a difference from Intel's response?

3. Dell has been a Harvard Business School case since its initial success for its unique strategy, supply chain, production, and distribution. What conclusions can you draw about business acumen and praise and ethical lapses?

4. Why do you think Dell employees participated in the cover-up of the underlying problems with the computers?

---

[103]Ashlee Vance, "Suit over Faulty Computers Highlights Dell's Decline," *New York Times*, June 29, 2010, pp. B1, B2.

Case 5.12

GoFundME!!!

Today, the use of online sites has made raising funds easy and successful. GoFundMe projects raise about $4 million each day. Through 2018, those using the site had raised $5 billion for medical bills.

The Internet as a resource for fundraising is new, but the problem of charities and individuals not using funds in a manner consistent with the purposes depicted in their fundraising campaigns is quite old. The grifter/flim-flam artist raising money for a noble cause and then spending the funds for different purposes has been with us as long as fundraising has existed. Professor Harold Hill purportedly raised money for a River City marching band. But Professor Hill was not a professor and the

(continued)

Case 5.12

(continued)

money was for him, not a marching band.[104] Following the September 11, 2001, attacks on the World Trade Center and Washington, D.C., the outpouring of support from the American public was overwhelming. The public donated $543 million for the September 11 disaster relief fund.[105] However, the Red Cross used the funds the public donated for its own "infrastructure support," and not all of the funds would go to victims and their families.

The American public was outraged and demanded the promised use of the funds. The Red Cross eventually relented; admitted an error in judgment; and agreed to the limited, stated, and intended use of the funds.

Brandi Weaver-Gates, once Miss Pennsylvania, Miss USA Pageant, raised $30,000 for her leukemia treatments. She did not have leukemia. She had shaved her head and had her sister take her to two different hospitals for alleged chemotherapy. Her sister waited downstairs at the hospitals as Brandi wandered throughout the hospital for the six to eight hours of her alleged treatment. Locals even held a Bingo-for-Brandi fundraiser. She kept the fundraisers going through her online posts about occasional remissions.

She was sentenced for two to four years in state prison for felony theft by deception and stripped of her title. She was also ordered to repay the money. She explained that she did it all "to get more attention from her family."[106]

Others raise money for their pets but spend it on themselves. Some raise money for their illnesses but then spend the money on "Clash of Clans" video game "stuff."[107]

These are just a few examples, but the problem is so widespread that there is a site, GoFraudMe, that tracks fraudulent fundraising efforts across the United States. There are sites that provide tips to avoid being duped by online fraudsters raising money for "good causes."

Discussion Questions

1. Did the Red Cross commit an ethical violation in its initial decision to use the money for expenses other than 9/11 victims?

2. Is there a difference between the Red Cross' use of funds and Brandi Weaver-Gates's fundraising efforts?

3. Who are the stakeholders in misrepresented or fake charitable fundraisers?

4. Could there be a regulatory cycle (See Reading 3.3) developing with online personal fundraising?

5. What policies should nonprofits and online fundraising sites adopt to protect donors from fraud?

---

[104]*The Music Man* (1962).

[105]Marvin Olasky, "Charity Doesn't Have to Mean Bureaucracy," *Wall Street Journal*, November 21, 2001, p. A15.

[106]Max Gelman, "Ex-Pennsylvania Beauty Queen Brandi-Weaver-Gates Going to Prison After Faking Cancer to Raise Money," *New York Daily News*, July 27, 2016, https://www.nydailynews.com/news/crime/ex-beauty-queen-sentenced-prison-faking-cancer-money-article-1.2728769.

[107]Martin Morse Wooster, "Giving to Individuals Rather Than Organizations," *Philanthropy Daily*, March 15, 2018, https://www.philanthropydaily.com/giving-to-individuals-instead-of-organizations/

Case 5.13

Scarlett Johansson and Disney: Payments for *Black Widow*

Disney+ may not be the happiest place on earth. Disney+ offered its subscribers access to *Black Widow*, actress Scarlett Johansson's contribution to the Marvel Comic Books series of movies that do well at the box office.

In this era, having a film on a subscriber service is not unusual. What is unusual is that Disney placed the film on Disney+ simultaneously with its big-screen release. What

(continued)

Case 5.13

(continued)

that means for Ms. Johansson, whose compensation for the film is largely tied to the film's ticket sales, is much less money. The chart below depicts the differences in her compensation.

Movie	Wide-screen release first 3 days	Disney+Total	Total compensation
Black Widow first 3 days	$158,000,000	$60,000,000	$20,000,000 – Ms. Johansson; Disney gets 60% of theatre tickets and 100% of Disney+ sales
Black Widow total	$379,000,000	Figures not released	$20,000,000 – Ms. Johansson; Disney gets 60% of theatre tickets and 100% of Disney+ sales
Captain Marvel total	$1,000,000,000	No Disney+ for 90–120 days	
Black Panther total	$1,000,000,000	No Disney+ for 90–120 days	

By contrast, Ms. Johansson made $56 million on her previous Marvel release.

Ms. Johansson maintained that Disney promised that it would not make *Black Widow* available on Disney+ for 90–120 days after its big-screen release. By that time in a film's run, 60% of the tickets will have been sold. Ms. Johansson had also contacted Disney for clarification on its dual-release strategy when she read that others stars of the Marvel franchise of films had renegotiated their contracts with Disney to permit dual release but were paid $200 million for that change. Ms. Johansson was assured that her film would have only a wide-screen release. An attorney for Marvel wrote, "[I]t is 100% our plan to do a typical wide release of 'Black Widow.' Should that change we would need to discuss this with you and come to an understanding as the deal is based on a series of (very large) box office bonuses."[108]

In response to the suit, a Disney spokesperson said that Ms. Johansson's lawsuit was "especially sad and distressing in its callous disregard for the horrific and prolonged global effects of the Covid-19 pandemic."[109] After some stinging press coverage, Disney and Ms. Johansson settled their suit for a purported $40 million.[110] She had asked for $80 million.[111]

Discussion Questions

1. What are the consequences when contract terms are not honored? Who are the stakeholders affected?

(continued)

---

[108]Erick Schwartzel and Joe Flint, "Scarlett Johansson Storms the Magic Kingdom," *Wall Street Journal*, September 4–5, 2021, B1 at B4.

[109]Joe Walsh, "Scarlett Johansson Sues Disney for Releasing 'Black Widow' on Streaming Service," *Forbes*, July 29, 2021, https://www.forbes.com/sites/joewalsh/2021/07/29/scarlett-johansson-sues-disney-for-releasing-black-widow-on-streaming-service/?sh=16fe528b6b65.

[110]Kimberlee Speakman, "Scarlett Johansson Settles 'Black Widow' Lawsuit with Disney," *Forbes*, October 1, 2021, https://www.forbes.com/sites/kimberleespeakman/2021/09/30/scarlett-johansson-settles-black-widow-lawsuit-with-disney/?sh=74b828f543aa.

[111]*Id.*

Case 5.13

(continued)

2. Was there a possible ambiguity in the contract? What are the ethical obligations then? Did Disney's renegotiation with other stars affected by the dual-release strategy show intent to deceive?

3. Did the executives have a conflict in making this decision on dual-release when their compensation is tied to Disney earnings?

Key Terms

Quid pro quo   408

Ethics in International Business

The world is your oyster.

—William Shakespeare,
The Merry Wives of Windsor

To take down all products from a region without a valid reason hides an ulterior motive, reveals stupidity and short-sightedness, and will surely have its own bad consequences.[1]

—Chinese Central Commission for Discipline Inspection on Walmart's decision to comply with a new U.S. law that bans the import and sale of goods produced in Xinjiang because of Uyghur labor camps in that region

Learning Objectives

- Explain the effects of ethical differences among and between countries for multinational businesses.

- Discuss the origins and purposes of the FCPA and resulting cultural conflicts for U.S. companies.

- List the risks in U.S. companies operating with an international supply chain.

- Describe the impact of bribery and corruption on a country's economic system.

- Analyze the risks of country differences on product and workplace safety standards.

Although we have a global market, we do not have global safety laws, ethical standards, or cultural customs. Businesses face many dilemmas as they decide whether to conform to the varying standards of their host nations or to attempt to operate with universal (global) standards. What we would call a bribe and illegal activity in the United States may be culturally acceptable and necessary in another country. Could you participate in such a practice?

---

[1]Brendan Case, "China Accuses Walmart of 'Stupidity' Over Missing Xinjiang Goods," *Bloomberg*, December 31, 2021, https://www.bloomberg.com/news/articles/2021-12-31/china-warns-walmart-on-missing-xinjiang-goods-as-tensions-rise.

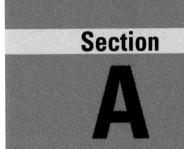
Conflicts Between the Corporation's Ethics and Business Practices in Foreign Countries

Reading 6.1

Why an International Code of Ethics Would Be Good for Business[2]

The global market presents firms with more complex ethical issues than they would experience if operations were limited to one country and one culture. Ethical standards vary across cultures. In some cases, cultures change and evolve to accept conduct that was not previously acceptable. For example, in some countries, it is permissible for donors to sell body organs for transplantation. Residents of other countries have sold their kidneys to buy televisions or just to improve their standard of living. In the United States, the buying and selling of organs by individuals is not permitted, but recently experts have called for such a system as a means of resolving the supply-and-demand dilemma that exists because of limited availability of donors and a relative excess of needy recipients.

In many executive training seminars for international business, executives are taught to honor customs in other countries and to "do as the Romans do." Employees are often confused by this direction. A manager for a U.S. title insurer provides a typical example. He complained that if he tipped employees in the U.S. public-recording agencies for expediting property filings, the manager would not only be violating the company's code of ethics but could also be charged with violations of the Real Estate Settlement Procedures Act and state and federal antibribery provisions. Yet, that same type of practice is permitted, recognized, and encouraged in other countries as a cost of doing business. Paying a regulatory agency in the United States to expedite a licensing process would be considered bribery of a public official. Yet, many businesses maintain that they cannot obtain such authorizations to do business in other countries unless such payments are made. So-called "**grease**," or **facilitation**, **payments** are permitted under the Foreign Corrupt Practices Act, but legality does not necessarily make such payments ethical.

An inevitable question arises when custom and culture clash with ethical standards and are adopted by a firm. Should the national culture or the company code of ethics be the controlling factor?

Typical business responses to the question of whether cultural norms or company codes of ethics should take precedence in international business operations are the following: Who am I to question the culture of another country? Who am I to impose U.S. standards on all the other nations of the world? Isn't legality the equivalent of ethical behavior? The attitude of businesses is one that permits ethical

---

[2]Adapted and updated from Larry Smeltzer and Marianne M. Jennings, "Why an International Code of Business Ethics Would Be Good for Business," *Journal of Business Ethics* 17, 1998, pp. 57–66.

deviations in the name of cultural sensitivity. Many businesses fear that the risk of offending is far too high to impose U.S. ethical standards on the conduct of business in other countries. As the opening chapter quotes indicate, doing business in China involves some inevitable conflicts and a high risk of offending the Chinese.

Ethics in Action 6.1

The Retailers Who Surrendered to Pressure from China

Company	Nature of Statement	China Response	Company Action
Walmart	Announced that it was no longer stocking goods from Xinjiang in the Chinese equivalent of Walmarts and Sam's Clubs to comply with U.S. law that prohibits U.S. companies from selling goods produced in Xinjiang area	Criticism on social media and cancellations of Sam's Club memberships. "[Walmart] is eating China's rice, yet slapping our face."[3] Walmart has been targeted by the Chinese government on its "lax" cyber-security processes, something that can result in denial of Internet access	
H&M	Expressed concerns on its website about labor conditions in Xinjiang	H&M banned from Internet in China; landlords closed 20 of H&M's 500 stores in China	Pulled statement from its site; H&M has returned to its online platform in China
Inditex (Zara, Massimo Dutti)	Expressed concern about social and labor "malpractice" in Xinjiang		Removed its statement after the H&M shutdown
L Brands (Bath & Body Works) (spinning off Victoria's Secret)	Statement on website that it was "committed" to eliminating forced labor, including in Xinjiang		
PVH (Calvin Klein, Tommy Hilfiger, Van Heusen, and Izod)	Originally expressed concerns about Xinjiang		Removed "concerns" and posted a notice that it follows all U.S. government regulations on imports

[3]Liza Lin, "Walmart Draws Anger in China Over Xinjiang," *Wall Street Journal*, December 28, 2021, p. A1.

VF Corporation	In a post on its website, raised concerns about forced labor conditions in Xinjiang (in 2019) and that it would not source goods from Xinjiang		Initially shortened the Xinjiang post after H&M was blocked by the Chinese government and later removed it (7% of its sales are in China); VF then put the post back within 24 hours, emphasizing its longstanding policy that predated the U.S. prohibition
The North Face Jackets	Expressed concerns on its website about labor conditions in Xinjiang March 2021, quietly pulled a statement on forced labor in China		Under VF parent company, has legal compliance statements on labor under UK and California compliance
Vans	March 2021, quietly pulled a statement on forced labor in China		Under VF parent company, has legal compliance statements on labor under UK and California compliance
Intel	Sent out a letter to its global suppliers telling them that products sourced from the Xinjiang region of China were problematic	Chinese social media exploded	"We deeply apologize for the confusion caused to our respected Chinese customers, partners and the public."[4]

In December 2021, the United States passed its Uyghur Forced Labor Prevention Act unanimously in both houses of Congress, and it was signed into law by President Biden. The law bans all imports from Xinjiang. However, there is an exception. If U.S. companies can certify "No forced Uyghur labor was used in the making of these goods," then they can import from the region. The companies now face having to comply with U.S. law, something that results in boycotts because of Chinese social media reactions. If the companies do something as limited as notifying their suppliers or announcing on their websites that they will follow the new U.S. law, they have been targeted by both social media and the Chinese government.

---

[4]Liza Lin, "Intel Regrets Causing Furor in China," *Wall Street Journal*, December 24, 2021, p. B1.

The companies are all members of the Better Cotton Initiative (BCI), an industry trade group that has raised concerns about labor conditions around the world, including those in Xinjiang.[5] Xinjiang produces 80% of China's cotton and 20% of the world supply. Nearly all clothing retailers and manufacturers will use some cotton from Xinjiang in the clothing they produce and sell. BCI operates an assurance program that examines factory conditions around the world so that manufacturers and retailers have full information about their current or potential cotton sources and conditions. BCI's website lists 2,000 manufacturer and retail members and 1.5 million cotton farmer members. BCI's annual report for 2020 indicates that it suspended all inspections and activities in the Xinjiang Uyghur area in March 2020 and no longer offers BCI certification for farmers or manufacturers in that region.[6] The BCI website has no discussion of the labor conditions in Xinjiang or members' difficulties with the Chinese government after members took individual positions on the Uyghur labor camps.

The Chinese government denies the allegations about the labor camps. However, in addition to the clothing manufacturers and retailers, other companies use technology-related suppliers located in Xinjiang, including Huawei, Lenovo, Dell, Acer, LG, Microsoft, Samsung, Sony, Cisco, and Electrolux. Auto companies with ties to Uyghur labor include BMW, General Motors, Jaguar, Land Rover, Tesla, and Volkswagen. Retailers include Kohl's, Nordstrom, Target, Tesco, TJ Maxx, Marshalls, and Walt Disney.

Discussion Questions

1. A fashion industry analyst said, "Younger customers are more interested than ever in buying brands that reflect their values and represent a mission and purpose. On the flip side, Western brands are searching for growth, and they don't want to be locked out of the Chinese market."[7] Is this an either/or argument? Is it possible to do business in China and remain in compliance with U.S. laws?

2. What decision points did the companies miss that resulted in the standoff with boycotts and regulatory oversight?

3. Is there a place for a company credo in resolving this business dilemma? An editorial in the Chinese government propaganda newspaper the *Global Times* called for Beijing to make it "increasingly expensive for companies to offend China."[8] Are companies going to have to compromise ethical principles in order to do business internationally?

[5]You can see the list of retail members, cotton producers, supply chain companies, and others at https://bettercotton.org/membership/find-members.

[6]BCI Annual Report (2020), at pp. 7 and 14, https://bettercotton.org/wp-content/uploads/2021/09/BCI-2020AnnualReport.pdf.

[7]Stu Woo, Suzanne Kapner, and Brian Whitton, "Apparel Maker Pulled, Restored China Rebuke," *Wall Street Journal*, June 21, 2022.

[8]Liza Lin, "Intel Regrets Causing Furor in China," *Wall Street Journal*, December 24, 2021, p. B1.

One of the misunderstandings of U.S.-based businesses is that ethical standards in the United States vary significantly from the ethical standards in other countries. Operating under this misconception can create a great deal of ethical confusion among employees. What is known as the "Golden Rule" in the United States has existed for some time in other religions and cultures and among philosophers. Following is a list of how this simple rule is phrased in different writings. The principle is the same even if the words vary slightly (as noted in Reading 1.8). Strategically, businesses and their employees are more comfortable when they operate under uniform standards. This simple rule may provide them with that standard.

Categorical Imperative: How Would You Want to Be Treated?

Would you be comfortable with a world in which your standards were followed?

Christian Principle: "The Golden Rule":

And as ye would that men should do to you, do ye also to them likewise.

—Luke 6:31

Thou shalt love … thy neighbor as thyself.

—Luke 10:27

Confucius:

What you do not want done to yourself, do not do to others.

Aristotle:

We should behave to our friends as we wish our friends to behave to us.

Judaism:

What you hate, do not do to anyone.

Buddhism:

Hurt not others with that which pains thyself.

Islam:

No one of you is a believer until he loves for his brother what he loves for himself.

Hinduism:

Do nothing to thy neighbor which thou wouldst not have him do to thee.

Sikhism:

Treat others as you would be treated yourself.

Plato:

May I do to others as I would that they should do unto me.

The successful operation of commerce is dependent on an ethical business foundation. A look at the three major parties in business explains this point. These parties are the risk takers, the employees, and the customers. Risk takers—those furnishing the capital necessary for production—are willing to take risks on the assumption that their products will be judged by customers' assessment of their value. Employees are willing to offer production input, skills, and ideas in exchange for wages, rewards, and other incentives. Consumers and customers are willing to purchase products and services so long as they receive value in exchange for their furnishing, through payment, income, and profits to the risk takers and employers. To the extent that the interdependency of the parties in the system is affected by factors outside of their perceived roles and control, the intended business system does not function on its underlying assumptions.

The business system is, in short, an economic system endorsed by society that allows risk takers, employees, and customers to allocate scarce resources to competing ends. Although the roots of business have been described as primarily economic, this economic system cannot survive without recognition of some fundamental values. Some of the inherent—indeed, universal—values built into our capitalistic economic system, as described here, are as follows: (1) The consumer is given value in exchange for the funds expended; (2) employees are rewarded according to their contribution to production; and (3) the risk takers are rewarded for their investment in the form of a return on that investment. This relationship is depicted in Figure 6.1.

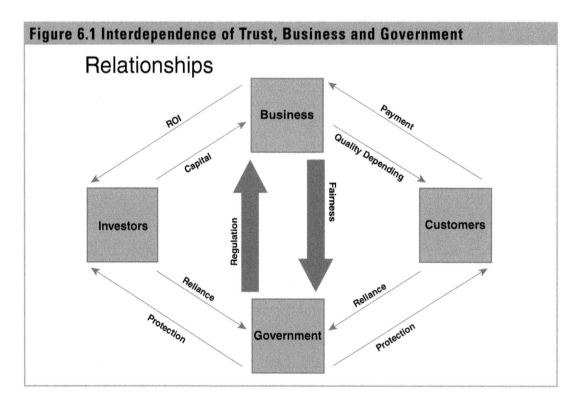

Figure 6.1 Interdependence of Trust, Business and Government

Everyone in the system must be ethical. An economic system can be thought of as a four-legged stool. If corruption seeps into one leg, the economic system becomes unbalanced. In international business, very often the government slips into corruption, with bribes controlling which businesses are permitted to enter the country and who is awarded contracts in that country.

To a large extent, all business is based on trust. The tenets for doing business are dissolved as an economy moves toward a system in which one individual can control the market to maximize personal income.

Suppose, for example, that the sale of a firm's product is determined not by perceived consumer value, but rather by access to consumers, which is controlled by government officials. That is, your company's product cannot be sold to consumers in a particular country unless and until you are licensed within that country. Suppose further that the licensing procedures are controlled by government officials and that those officials demand personal payment in exchange for your company's right to even apply for a business license. Payment size may be arbitrarily determined by officials who withhold portions for themselves. The basic values of the system have been changed. Consumers no longer directly determine the demand.

Beyond just the impact on the basic economic system, ethical breaches involving grease payments introduce an element beyond a now recognized component in economic performance: consumer confidence in long-term economic performance. Economist Douglas Brown has described the differences between the United States and other countries in explaining why capitalism works here and not in all nations. His theory is that capitalism is dependent on an interdependent system of production. For economic growth to be possible, consumers, risk takers, and employees must all feel confident about the future, about the concept of a level playing field, and about the absence of corruption. To the extent that consumers, risk takers, and employees feel comfortable about a market driven by the basic assumptions, the investment and commitments necessary for economic growth via capitalism will be made. Significant monetary costs are incurred by business systems based on factors other than customer value, as discussed earlier.

In developing countries where there are "speed," or grease, payments and resulting corruption by government officials, the actual money involved may not be significant in terms of the nation's culture. Such activities and payments introduce an element of demoralization and cynicism that thwart entrepreneurial activity when these nations most need risk takers to step forward.

Bribes and *guanxi* (gifts) in China given to establish connections with the Chinese government are estimated at 3% to 5% of operating costs for companies. Perhaps Italy and Brazil provide the best examples of the long-term impact of foreign business corruption. Although the United States, Japan, and Great Britain have scandals such as the subprime mortgage market collapse, political corruption, and college admissions bribery, these forms of misconduct are not indicative of corruption that pervades entire economic systems. The same cannot be said about Italy. Elaborate connections between government officials, the Mafia, and business executives have been unearthed. It has been estimated that the interconnections of these three groups have cost the Italian government $200 billion, as well as compromising the completion of government projects.

In Brazil, the level of corruption has led to a climate of murder and espionage. The *Wall Street Journal* offered an example of how Brazil's corruption has damaged the country's economy despite growth and opportunity in surrounding nations. The governor of the northeastern state of Paraiba in Brazil, Ronaldo Cunha Lima, was angry because his predecessor, Tarcisio Burity, had accused Lima's son of corruption. Lima shot Burity twice in the chest while Burity was having lunch at a restaurant. The speaker of Brazil's Senate praised Lima for his courage in doing the shooting himself as opposed to sending someone else. Lima was given a medal by the local city council and granted immunity from prosecution by Paraiba's state legislature. No one spoke for the victim, and the lack of support was reflective of a culture controlled by self-interest that benefits those in control.

A São Paulo businessman observed, "The fundamental reason we can't get our act together is we're an amoral society."[9] A private business sector really does not exist in Brazil. In 2016, the *Wall Street Journal* concluded that the problem is that most of Brazil's 27 political parties see growth of the state, the Leviathan, as the only way for progress to take hold.[10] The state oil company, Petróleo Brasileiro, is a classic study in Brazilian corruption. For almost 10 years, politicians, oil executives, and businesspeople hired and paid each other, siphoning money off for themselves or political party accounts in Switzerland. By the time the investigation was complete, 6 of every 10 members of Brazil's Congress were undergoing some type of criminal investigation. Yet those involved in these corruption cases are still reelected despite convictions as long as their appeals are pending.

Despite being a country of fertile land, rich natural resources, and a diverse population, Brazil has been unable to sustain economic growth. Many political scientists believe it is because it lacks the political leadership to make ethical reforms that foster competition, stop government officials from awarding contracts based on donations, and halt the expansion of its debt, which is often increasing exponentially. As a result, there have been cycles of four-digit level inflation. A nation of 200 million with a rich foundation for success spends 41% of its economy on government bureaucracy, a bureaucracy that spends money on "grease" payments and not on what is in Brazil's best interests. Corruption undermines economic growth, the rule of law, and even attempts for its reform. Corruption stifles competition and impedes safety and progress. The economic engine is stalled, leaving hungry and impoverished stakeholders.

Discussion Questions

1. What did you learn about universal values and ethics from the **categorical imperative** list?

2. What happens when a society does not have ethical standards? Be sure to discuss the example of the situation in Brazil.

3. Who are the victims of corruption and graft?

4. Do you think following U.S. ethical standards in other countries is wise? Would it be unethical not to follow those standards? Explain your answer.

---

[9]Thomas Kamm, "Why Does Brazil Face Such Woes? Some See a Basic Ethical Lapse," *Wall Street Journal,* February 4, 1994, p. A1.

[10]John Lyons and David Luhnow, "Brazil's Giant Problem," *Wall Street Journal,* April 22, 2016, https://www.wsj.com/articles/brazils-giant-problem-1461359723.

Case 6.2

The Tennis Player with COVID Visa Problems

Novak Djokovic, a Serbian tennis player, has won 20 Grand Slam tournaments. He is known for his eccentricity when it comes to his health. His egg-shaped pod is always with him at his tournaments. Mr. Djokovic believes that the pressurized pod improves circulation, raises his red-blood cell production, and removes lactic acid from his muscles.[11]

Mr. Djokovic tested positive for COVID-19 in June 2020. Following that bout with COVID, he tested positive on December 16, 2021. Mr. Djokovic attended a charity event with children on December 17. On December 18, he participated in an interview and photoshoot for the French

(continued)

---

[11]Matthew Futterman, "Modern Grudge Match Pits the Individualist Vs. the Greater Good," *New York Times,* January 7, 2022, p. B6.

Case 6.2

(continued)

sports newspaper, *L'Equipe*.[12] He then traveled to Belgrade, Serbia, on December 25 and Madrid on December 31, as his social media photos showed.

He applied for and received a medical exemption by Victorian province officials in Melbourne to allow him to enter Australia and play in the Australian Open without proof of vaccination. He flew to Melbourne, Australia, on January 5 from UAE. When he entered Australia, he was detained because border officials declared his exemption invalid and held him to the country's standard of "no vaccine, no entry." His medical exemption was not valid according to immigration officials. Australia's prime minister, Scott Morrison, tweeted, "Rules are rules, especially when it comes to our borders. No one is above these rules."[13] Mr. Djokovic was detained in a hotel room until January 10, 2022, when a judge permitted him to enter the country.

Border officials then discovered that Mr. Djokovic had declared on his visa documentation that he had not traveled anywhere for 14 days before his flight into Australia (although he maintains that his agent simply "ticked" the wrong box). Mr. Djokovic has admitted that his travel documents were incorrect and that he had traveled, but that the omissions were "not deliberate."[14] He also added that he attended the event on December 17 because he had not yet received the results of the December 16 COVID test.[15] He also admits that the photoshoot for *L'Equipe* was a mistake but that he felt obligated to keep what was a longstanding commitment.

Back home in Serbia, they are rooting for their native son, even those who believe that what he did was wrong, "They thought they had God-given powers, that this world is their world, and it is impossible that a young man from a small, poor country can be the best in their sport."[16]

Once Australian officials were able to verify that Mr. Djokovic had not self-quarantined as required and that he had misrepresented his travel record on his application, they revoked his visa again.[17] One day before the Australian Open was scheduled to begin, an Australian appeals court canceled his visa for his "reckless disregard" in traveling and meeting with journalists after he had tested positive for COVID-19. Mr. Djokovic left the country on January 16, 2022.[18]

After a period of self-banishment from the sport in February 2022, Mr. Djokovic returned to play in a match in Monte Carlo in April 2022 and lost 6–3, 6–7 (5), 6–1 in a three-hour match. Mr. Djokovic said his vaccine-refusal absence "has been difficult, mentally and emotionally" but he is "moving on."[19]

Discussion Questions

1. What was Mr. Djokovic missing in his analysis to keep his commitment to *L'Equipe*?

2. Name the stakeholders in his decision to continue traveling following his positive COVID test in December.

3. Are the representation issues on his visa paperwork separate from or part of the battle between government agencies on Mr. Djokovic's admission to play?

4. Does the fact that other countries permit medical exemptions for athletes relevant in analyzing the Djokovic situation?

5. What ethical categories apply to Mr. Djokovic's conduct?

6. A social psychology professor explained the Australian actions as follows, "At this point, it's about social norms and enforcing those norms to continue to get people to move in the same direction to overcome this pandemic. In this culture, in this country, a sense of suddenly upending norms has a great cost politically and socially."[20] Explain from what you have learned in Units 1 and 2 what theories and principles of ethics the professor is using.

[12]Joshua Robinson and Stuart Condie, "Djokovic Hits Court Amid Covid Tensions," *Wall Street Journal*, January 12, 2022, p. A10.

[13]Damien Cave, "An Accidental Symbol of Australia's Fraught Immigration Policies," *New York Times*, January 12, 2022, p. A5.

[14]Yan Zhuang, "Djokovic Admits Australia Travel Document Contained False Information," *New York Times*, January 13, 2022, p. A6.

[15]*Id.*

[16]Marc Santora, "A Divisive Figure Around the World, Djokovic Is a Hero in Serbia," *New York Times*, January 14, 2022, p. A11.

[17]Damien Cave, "In the Djokovic Drama, a Lesson in the Rules of the Covid Era," *New York Times*, January 15, 2022, pp. A1 and A9.

[18]Christopher Clarey, "Is Adversity Finally Set to Defeat Djokovic?" *New York Times*, January 17, 2022, p. D1.

[19]AP News, "Former World No. 1 Labels Novak Djokovic 'King of Stupidity' Ahead of Tennis Return," *Fox Sports*, April 11, 2022, https://www.foxsports.com.au/tennis/former-world-no-1-labels-novak-djokovic-king-of-stupidity-ahead-of-tennis-return/news-story/4c53629a682b1eb91c6fbbe5f6420a59.

[20]Damien Cave, "An Unstoppable Force in Tennis Meets an Immovable Object," *New York Times*, July 17, 2022, p. A11.

Case 6.3

The Former Soviet Union: A Study of Three Companies and Values in Conflict

PwC and the Russian Tax Authorities[21]

PricewaterhouseCoopers (PwC), one of the United States' "Big 4" accounting firms, has had a tax practice in Russia since the time that country changed from Communist rule. One of PwC's clients in Russia was Yukos, a major Russian oil company that is now bankrupt.

Russia's Federal Tax Service, an agency similar to the United States' IRS, filed suit against PwC, alleging that it concealed tax evasion by Yukos for the years 2002 to 2004. The Tax Service also announced a criminal probe of PwC's conduct for its tax services for Yukos. Twenty agents with the Federal Tax Service searched PwC's offices in Moscow and questioned PwC employees about the Yukos account. PwC withdrew its audit reports for Yukos for 1995–2004, and the Tax Service cleared PwC of any wrongdoing in its audit work. Yukos lost its tax case with a finding that it owed $3.4 billion in taxes and $9.4 million in penalties. Yukos defaulted on $1 billion in loans, and the Russian government seized its assets.

Many saw the battle between PwC and the Tax Service as part of the Russian government's ongoing battle to sell off the assets of Yukos and avoid the surrender of the company's assets to investors and creditors who have filed claims. Some analysts believe that the Russian government pressed PwC into revealing information that enabled it take back the Yukos assets.

In a situation such as this, if PwC is found to have engaged in evasion, it loses its license to do business in Russia, but if it turns over information, it is likely to lose its clients in Russia for breach of the client confidence.

Discussion Questions

1. How did PwC get into this situation in the first place? What issues should a company consider before doing business in an economically developing country? What are the risks? Did this ethical dilemma begin long before the Russian government's demands of PwC?

2. When countries are open to capitalism and economic freedom, there is much cream for rapid taking—that

---

[21]Neil Buckley and Catherine Belton, "Moscow Raids PwC Ahead of Yukos Case," *Financial Times*, March 11, 2007, p. 1.

is, businesses can move in easily and capture markets with little effort. However, what are the issues that accompany this ease of initial business capture?

3. What two PwC values would be in conflict if the Russian government demanded disclosure by PwC?

Ikea and the Generators

When Ikea was poised to open a flagship store outside Moscow in 2001, its executives were approached by employees of a local utility. If Ikea wanted electricity for its planned grand opening, some bribes were needed. Ikea is known for its stringent policy of not paying bribes. However, Ikea was, on the eve of a grand opening, complete with creditors and employees who needed payments. Ikea's solution was to rent diesel generators.

But corruption does have its ways in other countries, even when foreign companies are trying to follow the anti-bribery laws of their own countries. Ikea discovered that one of its managers was accepting kickbacks from the rental company that furnishes Ikea with the generators for operating its stores. Ikea ended the manager's Ikea career, as well as the contract with the rental company, and went to court in Russia to seek damages.

Ah, but who runs the courts? Judges who are, apparently, quite fond of utility workers who demand bribes. Ikea ended up owing damages to the rental company for its breach of contract. As one Ikea board member noted, "This is unlike anything" the international company has encountered in any of its operations. Ikea is still running stores in Russia, but not expanding. Its disclosure of the details of its electricity/generator experience was done by design: the company hopes that the public can sway corrupt officials into adopting a more transparent way of doing business.

Discussion Questions

1. By not succumbing to the prevailing attitude, "Well, you either bribe or you don't do business there," Ikea found an end-run, a creative solution to international

(continued)

Case 6.3

(continued)

business's ubiquitous either/or conundrum: to bribe or not to bribe. However, what issues did Ikea miss in its analysis of the situation?

2. What issues do the PwC/Yukos situation and the Ikea situation have in common?

3. What are the decision points in doing business internationally and when do they occur?

AES and the Power Plant

AES, the U.S.-based energy company, provides power in developing countries. Because it does business in Colombia and Brazil, the problems of regimes, corruption, and expropriation are not unusual ones for the company. However, its operation of the Maikuben coal mine in northern Kazakhstan was new and different even for the seasoned international player AES had come to be.

When AES opened the mine in the former Soviet republic in 1996, it had a management experience about which most companies will only dream. The residents who were miners there dug coal in freezing temperatures and took only tea breaks every other hour to warm up before going right back to digging. As AES expanded its operations to include power plants and transmission lines, it found a workforce with high technical abilities. Further, the work ethic of the Kazakhs was remarkable. It took only five to seven AES managers to supervise 6,500 Kazakhs.

If the employees were great, the customers were terrific. Electric utility customers, grateful for the consistency of electric service, paid on time, even with 20% rate increases in some years.

However, the company's relations with the Kazakhstan government were also a unique experience. At one point, in 2005, 24-foot soldiers armed with AK-47s entered the office of the Maikuben mine and demanded documents for a tax case the government had brought against AES. AES officials were able to negotiate a pullback of the forces after two days of phone conversations with regional government officials. The soldiers left, AES paid a fine, and the tax case continued. By 2008,

with continuing tense relationships and demands, AES, despite a $200 million investment in a power plant in the country, walked away. AES sold its assets there at fire-sale prices.

The tax rate for companies in Kazakhstan is 30%, plus the country's value-added tax. In addition, the regional tax officials do come calling on the companies for collection of additional revenues. Kazakhstan is a country that is rich not only in resources but also abundant in corruption. Parker Drilling, a company with $655 million in revenue and $104 million in net profits in 2008, paid $51 million that same year in taxes for its drilling rights to Kazakhstan. ExxonMobil paid a $5 billion fine for project delays.

AES managers were grilled about their political affiliations and placed under investigation because, as local officials explained, they worked for "Americans who steal from us."[22] Many managers left the country once AES was charged with antitrust violations, because of a fear that they would be arrested. One manager explained that what was once at least considered taboo, that is, the jailing of business managers, became the norm in the country. AES's arbitration case for the return of $1.29 billion in assets was dismissed by the arbitration body, the London International Center for Settlement of Investment Disputes. AES was required to pay the costs of the arbitration.

Discussion Questions

1. What is the underlying cause of AES's difficulty in doing business in Kazakhstan?

2. Use the three cases in this segment to develop a list of questions and concerns for companies considering expansion into countries with rich resources but rugged due process and governance.

3. What factor must be evaluated in doing the numbers related to operations or drilling in other countries?

---

[22]Nathan Vardi, "Power Putsch," *Forbes*, June 2, 2008, pp. 84, 90.

Reading 6.4

International Production: Risks, Benefits, and That Supply Chain

The majority of U.S. businesses during the period from 1998–2012 subcontracted productions of their products to factories around the world. There were economic reasons for the shift to production outside the United States. There were tax issues as well as the draw of inexpensive labor. Events changed those benefits. In addition, because of the COVID-19 pandemic, supply chains around the world were snarled. Many of the factories in the countries that were unable to handle the care and treatment of those with COVID-19 had to slow or halt their production. In some cases, national lockdowns in those countries resulted in a halt to shipments of existing inventory and months-long interruptions in production.

The decision to pursue international production did not adequately analyze either the extent of stakeholders or their harms or the possibility of unanticipated risks and costs. Worldwide shortages did not seem possible in the decade from 2000–2012 as the international economy expanded. Today, international expansions receive different scrutiny.

Famous Lines from Art and Literature

If a foreign country can supply us with a commodity cheaper than we ourselves can make it, better buy it of them with some part of our own industry, employed in a way in which we have some advantage.

—Adam Smith, *The Wealth of Nations*

The Labor Issues in Fabric and Clothing Production

One must always assume strict scrutiny when creating production sources in other countries. The issue of factory conditions in the production of fabric and clothing is an emotional one that has been with us for decades. Mahatma Gandhi said, "There is no beauty in the finest cloth if it makes hunger and unhappiness."[23] Since Mr. Gandhi's passing in 1948, the focus on the conditions for employees in fabric and clothing production has only increased.

The list of nonprofit groups that provide oversight on factory conditions in countries outside the United States has grown exponentially. Some examples include Human Rights Watch, Women in Informal Employment Globalizing and Organizing (WIEGO), Fair Labor Association, Verité, Sustain Your Style International Labor Organization, and Worker Rights Consortium. The National Labor Committee (NLC) was the nonprofit organization that policed production facilities from 1998 to about 2012 and was one of the pioneers in certification of factories for meeting established employee rights and conditions. In addition, the NLC issued several reports on international labor conditions during that time, which resulted in worldwide attention, particularly on college campuses, and boycotts of certain brands in college bookstores and in sports team apparel.

---

[23]https://quotefancy.com/mahatma-gandhi-quotes.

However, while still active, its website data is limited to that era. The International Labour Organization (ILOSTAT) now provides data on production facilities and wages. The highest minimum wages by month are $3,800 in Switzerland; the lowest are $2.00 in Uganda. In between are Ireland at $1,854, the United States at $1,257, Hungary at $518, Iran at $311, China at $217, Cambodia at $182, Vietnam at $181, Afghanistan at $71, and India at $51.

The Shifting Attention and Attitudes

Over the decades, attention to labor conditions has shifted from country to country and brand to brand. For example, in 1996, celebrity Kathie Lee Gifford was shocked to learn that her clothing line was produced through child labor.[24] She became an activist for reform, and, for a time, other brands and the retailers that carried those brands made pledges to change conditions. Nike and Vietnam were the center of attention during the 1998–2002 period. Presently, as noted in Ethics in Action 6.1, China is a focus because of forced labor among the Uyghurs and the companies using production facilities or buying products from that region.

Some companies have tried to withdraw from using international production facilities because of conditions and their inability to monitor plants or implement changes. For example, Levi Strauss was one company that pulled its manufacturing and sales operations out of China in 1993 because of human rights violations. However, five years later, in 1998, Levi announced that it would expand its manufacturing in China and begin selling clothing there. Peter Jacobi, then-president of Levi Strauss, indicated that the company had the assurance of local contractors that they would adhere to Levi's guides on labor conditions. Jacobi stated, "Levi Strauss is not in the human rights business. But to the degree that human rights affect our business, we care about it."[25]

Benefits and Risks of International Production and Suppliers

U.S. companies' investments in foreign manufacturing in major developing nations like China, Indonesia, and Mexico have produced some positive effects. In Hong Kong, Singapore, South Korea, and Taiwan, where plants make apparel, toys, shoes, and wigs, national incomes have risen from 10% to 40%. In Indonesia, since the introduction of U.S. plants and subcontractors, the proportion of malnourished children in the country has gone from one-half to one-third.[26] However, as the economics of international production have changed and wages have increased in foreign production, the issue of safety of the factories has risen to the forefront. The factories are housed in facilities that were not designed to hold heavy production equipment or even the number of workers required for production of clothing and fabric. The May 2013 collapse of a clothing factory in Bangladesh resulted in the deaths of 617 workers there, and another 112 workers were killed in a fire in another factory there. In the case of the building collapse, there were five factories operating in a single building that had not been approved for industrial use.

---

[24]Accessed from http://www.youtube.com/watch?v=zCszZ5lwAgA. 5. American Apparel and Footwear Association, ApparelStats 2012 Report, https://www.aafaglobal.org/AAFA /Priorities/Supply_Chain/AAFA/Priority/Supply_Chain.aspx?hkey=10497d02-a393-4112 -95cf-4e1d3f680c01.

[25]Mark Landler, "Reversing Course, Levi Strauss Will Expand Its Output in China," *New York Times*, April 9, 1998, p. C1; and G. Pascal Zachary, "Levi Tries to Make Sure Contract Plants in Asia Treat Workers Well," *Wall Street Journal*, July 28, 1994, pp. A1, A5.

[26]Allen R. Myerson, "In Principle, a Case for More 'Sweatshops,'" *New York Times*, June 22, 1997, p. E5.

Eighty percent of Bangladesh's exports are to the United States and Europe and are comprised of textiles. These exports are 10% of the country's GDP. The collapsed factory produced clothing for JCPenney, Walmart, and Benetton.

Both the companies involved and U.S. officials have been concerned about the safety of the factories in Bangladesh. The United States had been considering revoking the country's most favored nation trade status, but did not do so just prior to the building collapse, based on assurances that government officials would increase both standards and inspections. In 2011, a group of companies that used production facilities in Bangladesh had considered joint sponsorship of independent inspections in Bangladesh but did not reach agreement because of the cost of $500,000 for the paid inspections. Clothing is still most likely to be produced in China, where Zengcheng is known as the "Blue Jeans Capital of the World."[27]

Audits and Transparency

Apple dealt with a safety issue that made international headlines because workers at its China Foxconn production factory were committing suicide.[28] As a result, Apple obtained an audit done by the Fair Labor Association, which was revealing and troubling.[29] Apple also followed the examples of Hewlett-Packard, Intel, and Nike and released a list of its suppliers to introduce transparency in its overseas vendors.[30] In addition, Apple has continued to add components to its oversight of supplier working conditions and has created systems for audits, compliance, investigations, and probationary programs for violations. Apple's 2021 disclosure of its suppliers indicates that nearly all of their suppliers have production facilities or offices in mainland China.[31] Apple's ESG report for 2022 indicates that it has trained 23.6 million of its suppliers' employees on human rights and conducts 1,777 audits of its suppliers, compared with 663 audits in 2011.[32] Apple has begun direct surveys of supplier employees and surveyed 352,589 employees in 191 factories during 2021. For those cited for violations of the Apple Code of Conduct for Suppliers, Apple implements a 30- to 90-day corrective action plan. If the suppliers do not meet the conditions and requirements of the plan within the time limit assigned, they are terminated as an Apple supplier.

Nike and New Solutions

Nike has long been a target of labor activists and continues to be, with a unique twist of campus protests and boycotts for its overseas plant conditions. Students protest against their colleges and universities signing licensing agreements with Nike. For example, Nike ended negotiations with the University of Michigan for a six-year, multimillion-dollar licensing agreement because Michigan joined the student consortium to boycott Nike. Nike founder and then-CEO Phil Knight withdrew a pledge to make a $30 million donation to the University of Oregon because the university had joined the consortium. Nonetheless, Knight acknowledged a brand

[27]Gordon G. Chang, "China's 'Conflict Handbags,'" *Forbes*, June 26, 2011, http://www.forbes.com/sites/gordonchang/2011/06/26/chinas-conflict-handbags/.

[28]You can read Apple's initial Supplier Responsibility report here: https://www.apple.com/supplierresponsibility/.

[29]FOXCONN Technology Group Workforce Perception and Satisfaction Report, 2012, https://archive.ilr.cornell.edu/sites/default/files/independent-investigation-of-apple-supplier.pdf.

[30]People and Environment in Our Supply Chain: 2021 Annual Progress Report, https://www.apple.com/supplier-responsibility/pdf/Apple_SR_2021_Progress_Report.pdf.

[31]You can find Apple's supply list here: https://www.apple.com/supplier-responsibility/pdf/Apple-Supplier-List.pdf.

[32]Apple's ESG Report 2022, https://s2.q4cdn.com/470004039/files/doc_downloads/2022/08/2022_Apple_ESG_Report.pdf.

image problem: "Nike product has become synonymous with slave wages, forced overtime, and arbitrary abuse."[33]

Since the time of the campus boycotts, Nike has been looking for systematic change that improves conditions across the supply chain, not solutions once problems are exposed."[34] As a result, Nike has introduced "lean manufacturing" into the supply chain. This form of production shifts from low-skill assembly lines to organizing workers into multitask teams. The team members require more training, something that requires factory owners to invest in their workers. With that investment, the worker abuse is reduced or stopped because the factory owners want to hang on to the trained employees in order to enjoy returns on the skills training they have given.

Another change Nike has made focuses on its decision processes for shoe design and production. The teams in Beaverton, Oregon, learned that their last-minute changes placed unnecessary stress on the factories and, as a result, the workers. Reducing the production crunch has also reduced the hours, stress, and likelihood of abuse. Beaverton has now developed a sensitivity that its design changes, schedule, and final decisions do impact the supply chain, including the labor conditions.

Nike is also working with suppliers to solve the strains rather than pushing all the responsibility onto them for compliance with company standards. The adoption of this quasi-partnership means of solving labor issues is also a result of Nike's realization that just terminating contracts is problematic. When Nike simply ended a contract with a company that produced its soccer balls in Pakistan because of labor issues there, Nike experienced backlash from that country for the loss of jobs. Nike and other retailers have learned that international production provides not only cost savings but also requires a tough balancing act that is sensitive to workers, the nature of the country and its economy, and the needs and practices of their suppliers.

Child Labor

Another troubling issue that clothing companies continue to face is that it is widely accepted in other countries for children, ages 10 to 14, to work in factories for 50 or more hours per week. Their wages enable their families to survive. School is a luxury, and children attend only until they are able to work in a factory. The Gap and Levi Strauss have been listed in social responsibility literature as exploiting their workers.[35] Foxconn Technology Group has admitted that it has employed interns as young as age 14 for work in its Yantai facility, a facility that puts together Nintendo hardware. The young workers were sent to the facility as part of a program the company had with local vocational schools. Foxconn did not check identification for the young workers, and, as a result, the young students were working in an area of the factory that produced accessories. They were paid $244 per month but had to work overtime if they did not complete their assigned projects. The internships usually lasted 3.5 months. Foxconn's labor force of 1.2 million had 2.7% interns in the 14- to 16-year-old age group.

Nintendo quickly denounced the use of child labor and explained that it was a violation of its company policy on social responsibility as well as the provisions it has in its contracts with all suppliers. Foxconn issued a statement indicating that no

---

[33]Eugenia Levenson, "Citizen Nike," *Fortune*, November 24, 2008, p. 165.

[34]*Id.*

[35]Dana Canedy, "Peering into the Shadows of Corporate Dealings," *New York Times*, March 25, 1997, pp. C1, C6.

Apple products were assembled at its Yantai facility and that it had moved quickly to return the students to their vocational schools.

China Labor Watch indicated that the schools were primarily responsible for sending the underage workers to the plants, but that Foxconn was responsible for confirming their ages.

Industry and Regulatory Efforts

The American Apparel and Footwear Association (AAFA) (formerly the American Apparel Manufacturers Association [AAMA]) and the Footwear Industries of America (FIA), which merged into the AAFA, has 425 U.S. garment makers and shoemakers, representing 1,000 brands, in its membership, and has a database for its members to check labor compliance by contractors.[36] Seventy-five percent of clothing retailers in the United States are members of AAFA. The National Retail Federation has established its Principles on Supplier Legal Compliance (now signed by 250 retailers):

1. We are committed to ensuring that sewn products are produced under lawful, humane and ethical conditions. As such, AAFA members make every effort to eliminate the use of forced and child labor from their supply chain.

2. AAFA strongly supports the concept behind the ILO/IFC Better Work program—taking a comprehensive approach to improving compliance with international labor standards within a country.

3. In our purchase contracts, we require our suppliers to comply with all applicable laws and regulations.

4. If it is found that a factory used by a supplier for the production of our merchandise has committed legal violations, we will take appropriate action, which may include canceling the affected purchase contracts, terminating our relationship with the supplier, commencing legal actions against the supplier, or other actions.

5. We support law enforcement and cooperate with law enforcement authorities in the proper execution of their responsibilities.

6. We support educational efforts designed to enhance legal compliance on the part of the U.S. apparel manufacturing industry.[37]

The U.S. Department of Labor made the following recommendations to companies to improve the international labor situation:

1. All sectors of the apparel industry, including manufacturers, retailers, buying agents and merchandisers, should consider the adoption of a code of conduct.

2. All parties should consider whether there would be any additional benefits to adopting more standardized codes of conduct.

3. U.S. apparel importers should do more to monitor subcontractors and homeworkers [the areas where child labor violations occur].

4. U.S. garment importers—particularly retailers—should consider taking a more active and direct role in the monitoring and implementation of their codes of conduct.

5. All parties, particularly workers, should be adequately informed about codes of conduct so that the codes can fully serve their purpose.[38]

---

[36]https://www.aafaglobal.org/AAFA/Solutions/Tools_Resources_Nav/AAFA/Solutions_Pages/Tools_Research.aspx?hkey=15779e99-86fe-435f-b154-a6723544e8e9

[37]Martha Nichols, "Third-World Families at Work: Child Labor or Child Care?" *Harvard Business Review* (January–February 1993), pp. 12–23.

[38]Daniela Deane, "Senators to Hear of Slave Labor on U.S. Soil," *USA Today*, March 31, 1998, p. 9A.

Some states, such as California, have passed transparency laws that require companies doing business in California to disclose whether the company does the following:[39]

1. Engages in verification of product supply chains to evaluate and address risks of human trafficking and slavery;

2. Conducts audits of suppliers to evaluate supplier compliance with company standards for trafficking and slavery in supply chains;

3. Requires direct suppliers to certify that materials incorporated into the product comply with the laws regarding slavery and human trafficking of the country or countries in which they are doing business;

4. Maintains internal accountability standards and procedures for employees or contractors failing to meet company standards regarding slavery and trafficking; and

5. Provides company employees and management, who have direct responsibility for supply chain management, training on human trafficking and slavery, particularly with respect to mitigating risks within the supply chains of products.[40]

The Surprise Supply Chain Crisis and Rethinking Globalization

While companies were working feverishly developing codes of conduct for suppliers, auditing suppliers, training employees on rights, and conducting audits, the supply chain, due to COVID restrictions economic setbacks, became clogged late in 2021. Retailers, manufacturers, and even grocery stores viewed photos of the cargo ships coming into the United States with foreign goods sitting, unloaded, in a pile-up off the coast of California. As a result, CEOs have begun rethinking globalization, moving workers and production facilities closer, and rejecting the global economy for the homefront even if the cost is higher.[41] Ellen Cullman, the CEO of Carbon Inc., and the former CEO of Dupont, noted, "It's about control. I want to have more control in an uncertain world."[42]

The strategy for the past 20 years has been to minimize manufacturing expenses, send low-skill jobs offshore, and cut costs with JIT (just-in-time deliveries of supplies from vendors and product). However, those cheaper costs and not having to carry inventory came with risk. The supply chain is inflexible when it comes to external events, such as weather issues, wars, and a worldwide pandemic. Online ordering has been plagued with "Out of Stock" responses to customers trying to place orders. Every website notes that there may be delays in delivery. Benetton, one of the companies that was hit with labor issues in its overseas production, had an awakening when its CEO tried to order a navy-blue coat. It was "out of stock" because its factories simply could not get raw materials for clothing production.

One appliance dealer had virtually all his appliances on backorder. To keep a customer from going elsewhere to buy, he allowed one customer to come to his home to do his laundry.[43] Over the months-long wait for the appliances for his new home,

---

[39]California Transparency in Supply Chains Act of 2010. (S.B. 657) codified at Cal. Civ. Code.

[40]Cal. Civ. Code §1714.43 (2013).

[41]Thomas Gryta and Chip Cutter, "CEOs Rethink Global Production Playbook," *Wall Street Journal*, November 2, 2021, p. A1.

[42]*Id.*

[43]Austen Hufford, "Kitchen Appliance Delays Force Buyers to Cook Up Alternatives," *Wall Street Journal*, October 8, 2021, p. A1.

the customer said that he felt like a college student again, hauling his laundry out to wash it. The only difference was that no quarters were required. Some appliance stores loaned their wait-listed customers mini-refrigerators to see them through until their new full-size appliances arrived. Customers waiting for dishwashers and sinks were hauling their dishes from their dining rooms to the bathroom basins and tubs.

Outsourcing company needs to contractors was yet another because of the difficulties contractors were having in hiring employees. Generous government benefits found many leaving the workforce and businesses having to raise pay rates to compete with those government benefits if they were going to obtain and retain employees. Outsourced functions are now coming back inside the company, with new hires receiving higher wages than they were earning formerly by working for contractors. Builders are constructing their own manufacturing plants for windows and doors because they cannot get those critical components to complete housing developments. The CEOs are learning that control over production is not just limited to factory conditions. They are learning that moving the factories back home eliminates the international ethical issues of wages, working conditions, and hours.

Benetton had 58% of its production in Asia before the pandemic. Within one year, Benetton plans to cut that in half and bring production back to Italy and other Mediterranean countries.[44] The cost savings on monitoring, certification, and transportation cover the higher labor costs for domestic production and bring an accompanying certainty of delivery as well as higher quality of finished goods. And there were also significant costs of keeping waiting customers satisfied.

Discussion Questions

1. One executive noted, "We're damned if we do because we exploit. We're damned if we don't because these foreign economies don't develop. Who's to know what's right?" Is this phrasing the issue, as an either/or conundrum? How do Apple's policies respond to this observation?

2. Would you employ a 12-year-old in one of your factories if it were legal to do so?

3. Would you limit hours and require a minimum wage even if it were not legally mandated?

4. Would you work to provide educational opportunities for child laborers?

5. What does the case reveal about the costs of production? What factors were CEOs not considering as they dealt with all the labor issues? Did they define the problem as "we can't compete unless we outsource production overseas"? Was their assessment accurate? Were they missing critical numbers factors in their analyses? Was the ethical issue addressed without understanding the real costs? Did they miss risks and impact on stakeholders?

---

[44]*Id.*

Compare & Contrast

Levi Strauss & Company, discovering that youngsters under the age of 14 were routinely employed in its Bangladesh factories, could either fire 40 underage youngsters and impoverish their families or allow them to continue working. Levi compromised and provided the children both access to education and full adult wages.

(continued)

Nike had shoe factories in Indonesia, and the women who worked in those factories netted $37.46 per month. However, as Nike pointed out, their wages far exceeded those of other factory workers. Nike's Dusty Kidd notes, "Americans focus on wages paid, not what standard of living those wages relate to."

Economist Jeffrey D. Sachs of Harvard has served as a consultant to developing nations such as Bolivia, Russia, Poland, and Malawi. He observes that the conditions in sweatshops are horrible, but they are an essential first step toward modern prosperity. "My concern is not that there are too many sweatshops, but that there are too few. These are precisely the jobs that were the steppingstone for Singapore and Hong Kong, and those are the jobs that have to come to Africa to get them out of their backbreaking rural poverty."[45]

Business executives responded as follows:

If someone is willing to work for 31 cents an hour, so be it—that's capitalism. But throw in long hours, abusive working conditions, poor safety conditions, and no benefits, and that's slavery. It was exactly those same conditions that spawned the union movement here in the U.S.

—John Waldron

If the wages of 31 cents per hour were actually fair wages, adults would gladly do the work instead of children.

—Wesley M. Johnson

Just when you think the vile remnants of those who would build empires on the blood and bones of those less fortunate than ourselves have slithered off into the history books, you come across this kind of tripe. For shame for rationalizing throwing crumbs to your fellow human beings so that you and your ilk can benefit at their expense.

—Jose Guardiola

Discussion Questions

1. Discuss the views presented and why they are so different.

2. There was child labor in the United States until the federal labor legislation addressed it fully during the 1930s. Economists maintain that wages increase as skills do, and the initial wages are just a first step in economic development for the country.[46] Discuss the economic, social, and ethical issues of plants and wages in developing countries.

3. Discuss the merits in the various positions on child labor and sweatshops in a company's supply chain and in light of the recent issues that have emerged in the supply chain.

Sources
Gibbs, Nancy, "Suffer the Little Children," *Time,* March 26, 1990, p. 18.
Mitchell, Russell, and Michael O'Neal, "Managing by Values," *Business Week,* August 1, 1994, p. 40.
"Nike's Workers in Third World Abused, Report Says," *Arizona Republic,* March 28, 1997, p. A10.
"Susie Tompkins," *Business Ethics,* January/February, 1995, pp. 21–23.

---

[45]Allen R. Myerson, "In Principle, a Case For More Sweatshops," *New York Times,* June 22, 1997, Section 4, p. 5, https://www.nytimes.com/1997/06/22/weekinreview/in-principle-a-case-for-more-sweatshops.html.
[46]For additional perspective on these issues, see "Invasion of the Job Snatchers," *The Economist,* November 2, 1996, p. 18. © 1996 The Economist Newspaper Group Inc.

Bhopal: When Safety Standards Differ[47]

Bhopal is a city in central India with a population, in 1984, of 800,000. Because it was, at that time, home to the largest mosque in India, Bhopal was a major railway junction. Its main industries consisted of manufacturing heavy electrical equipment, weaving and printing cotton cloth, and milling flour.

In 1969, American Union Carbide Corporation, a company headquartered in Danbury, Connecticut, reached an agreement with the Indian government for the construction of a Union Carbide plant in Bhopal. Union Carbide would hold a 51% interest in the plant through its share of ownership of an Indian subsidiary of American Union Carbide. The agreement was seen as a win–win situation. India would have the plant and its jobs as well as the production of produce pesticides, a product needed badly by Indian farmers to increase agricultural productivity. In addition, Union Carbide also agreed that it would use local managers, who would be provided with the necessary skills and management training so that the plant would be truly locally operated.

The plant used methyl isocyanate (MIC) gas as part of the production process for the pesticides. MIC is highly toxic and reacts strongly with other agents, including water. Operation of a plant with MIC processes requires detailed monitoring as well as security processes to prevent sabotage.

Although the plant began operations with high hopes, by 1980 the relationships were strained because the plant was not profitable. Union Carbide had asked the Indian government for permission to close the plant, but the government felt the products from the plant, as well as the jobs, were needed for the Indian economy.

Sometime in the early morning hours of December 3, 1984, MIC stored in a tank at the Bhopal plant came in contact with water, and the result was a boiling effect in the tank. The backup safety systems at the plant, including cooling components for the tanks, did not work. The result was the toxic mixture began to leak, and workers at the plant felt a burning sensation in their eyes. The boiling of the water and MIC caused the safety valves on the tank to explode. Following the explosion, the white smoke from the lethal mixture escaped through a smokestack and began to spread across the area to the city of Bhopal.

As the gas spread, it wove its way through the shantytowns that were located near the plant. Over 600,000 people were exposed to the poisonous gases.

The occupants of these shantytowns were Bhopal's poorest. As the gas floated through these makeshift neighborhoods, 3,500 lives were lost and 200,000 were injured. Thousands of animals were killed by the gas. The injuries included blindness, burns, and lesions in the respiratory system. In 2014, the Indian government put the death toll at 15,000 after it was able to track the long-term illnesses and resulting deaths caused by the gas leak.[48]

Of the women who were pregnant and exposed to the MIC, one-fourth either miscarried or had babies with birth defects. Many of the women who were pregnant at the time of the leak had physically and mentally disabled children. Children developed chronic respiratory problems. Smaller children who survived the toxic gas were sick for months and, weak from a lack of nutrition and ongoing illnesses, also died. MIC also produced strange boils on the bodies of many residents, boils that could not be healed. The problem of tuberculosis in the area was exacerbated by the lung injuries caused by the leaking MIC.

In the year following the accident, the Indian government spent $40 million on food and health care for the Bhopal victims. Warren M. Anderson, Union Carbide's chairman of the board at the time of the accident, pledged that he would devote the remainder of his career to solving the problems that resulted from the accident. However, by the end of the first year, Mr. Anderson told *Business Week*, "I overreacted. Maybe they, early on, thought we'd give the store away. [Now] we're in litigation mode. I'm not going to roll over and play dead."[49]

Following the accident, Union Carbide's stock fell sixteen points and it became, in the go-go 1980s, a takeover target. When GAF Corporation made an offer, Union Carbide incurred $3.3 billion in debt to buy 56% of its own stock to avert a takeover. Through 1992, Union Carbide remained in a defensive mode as it coped with litigation, takeover attempts, and the actions of the Indian government in seeking to charge officers, including Anderson, with crimes.[50]

(continued)

---

[47]Adapted from Marianne M. Jennings, *Case Studies in Business Ethics*, 2nd ed.

[48]Alan Taylor, "Bhopal: The World's Worst Industrial Disaster, 30 Years Later," *The Atlantic*, December 2, 2014, https://www .theatlantic.com/photo/2014/12/bhopal-the-worlds-worst -industrial-disaster-30-years-later/100864/.

[49]Leslie Helm et al., "Bhopal, a Year Later: Union Carbide Takes a Tougher Line," *BusinessWeek*, November 25, 1985, p. 96.

[50]Scott McMurray, "Union Carbide Offers Some Sober Lessons in Crisis Management," *Wall Street Journal*, January 28, 1992, p. A1.

Case 6.5

(continued)

U.S. lawyers brought suit in the United States against Union Carbide on behalf of hundreds of Bhopal victims, but the case was dismissed because the court lacked jurisdiction over the victims as well as the plant.[51] Union Carbide did settle the case with the Indian government for a payment of $470 million. There were 592,635 claims filed by Bhopal victims. The victims received, on average, about $1,000 each. The ordinary payment from the Indian government, as when a government bus harms an individual, is $130 to $700, depending upon the level of the injury. Individual awards were based on earning capacity, so, for example, widows of the Bhopal accident received $7,000.

The Indian government also pursued criminal charges, including against Mr. Anderson. Lawyers for the company and Mr. Anderson continued to fight the charges, largely on the basis that the court had no jurisdiction over Mr. Anderson. However, to be on the safe side, Mr. Anderson did not return to India because of his fear of an arrest.

In May 1992, the Indian government seized the plant and its assets and announced the sale of its 50% interest in the plant. When the sale occurred and Union Carbide received its share of the proceeds, it contributed $17 million to the Indian government for purposes of constructing a hospital near Bhopal. The plant now makes dry-cell batteries.

Following the accident, Union Carbide reduced its workforce by 90%. Because of the share purchase, Union Carbide had a debt-to-equity ratio of 80%. In addition, the Union Carbide brand was affected by the accident, and the

company could not seem to gain traction. Dow Chemical would acquire the company in 1999 for $11.6 billion.

In 2008, a study revealed that pesticide residues in the water supply for the area surrounding the plant were at levels above permissible ones. There are about 425 tons of waste buried near the former plant. There have been no studies of the effects of the contamination on the residents there. Advocates continue to appear at Dow shareholder meetings to demand cleanup. Dow's response is, "As there was never any ownership, there is no responsibility and no liability—for the Bhopal tragedy or its aftermath."[52]

Discussion Questions

1. Should the Bhopal plant have been operated using U.S. safety and environmental standards? What would the U.S. policy be on the shantytowns?

2. Should the case have been moved to the United States for recovery?

3. List all the costs of the accident to Union Carbide.

4. Evaluate Dow's position on the cleanup.

5. Later studies seem to indicate that the lack of adequate training for the local workforce operating the plant may have been a cause of the accident. Some have theorized that the cause of the accident was sabotage. Although the plant met all standards of the Indian government for operation, it would not have met U.S. requirements for the operation of such a chemical plant. How does this additional information affect your analysis?

---

[51]In re *Union Carbide Corp. Gas Plant Disaster at Bhopal*, 634 F. Supp. 842 (S.D.N.Y. 1986), In re *Union Carbide Corp. Gas Plant Disaster at Bhopal*, 809 F.2d 195 (2nd Cir. 1987). *cert.* denied, 484 U.S. 871 (1987).

[52]Somini Sengupta, "Decades Later, Toxic Sludge Torments Bhopal," *New York Times*, July 7, 2008, p. A1.

Case 6.6

Product Dumping

Once the Consumer Product Safety Commission prohibits the sale of a particular product in the United States, a manufacturer can no longer sell the product to U.S. wholesalers or retailers. However, the product can be sold in other countries that have not prohibited its sale.

The same is true of other countries' sales to the United States. For example, Great Britain outlawed the sale of the prescription sleeping pill Halcion, but sales of the drug continue in the United States.[53] The British medical

(continued)

---

[53]"The Price of a Good Night's Sleep," *New York Times*, January 26, 1992, p. E9.

Case 6.6

(continued)

community reached conclusions regarding the pill's safety that differed from the conclusions reached by the medical community and the Food and Drug Administration here. Some researchers who conducted studies on the drug in the United States simply concluded that stronger warning labels were needed.

The Consumer Product Safety Commission outlawed the sale of three-wheel all-terrain cycles in the United States in 1988.[54] Although some manufacturers had already turned to four-wheel models, other manufacturers still had inventories of three-wheel cycles. Testimony on the cycles ranged from contentions that although the vehicles themselves were safe, the drivers were too young, too inexperienced, and more inclined to take risks (e.g., to "hot dog"). However, even after the three-wheel product was banned here, outlawed vehicles could still be sold outside the United States.

For many companies, chaos follows a product recall because inventory of the recalled product may be high. Often, firms must decide whether to "dump" the product in other countries or to take a write-off that could damage earnings, stock prices, and employment stability.

---

[54]"Outlawing a Three-Wheeler," *Time*, January 11, 1988, p. 59.

Discussion Questions

1. If you were a manufacturer holding a substantial inventory of a product that had been outlawed in the United States, would you have any ethical concerns about selling the product in countries that do not prohibit its sale?

2. Suppose the inventory write-down that you will be forced to take because of the regulatory obsolescence is material—nearly a 20% reduction in income will result. If you can sell the inventory in a foreign market, legally, there will be no write-down and no income reduction. A reduction of that magnitude would substantially lower market share price, which in turn would lead your large, institutional shareholders to demand explanations and possibly seek changes in your company's board of directors. In short, the write-down would set off a wave of events that would change the structure and stability of your firm. Do you now feel justified in selling the product legally in another country?

3. Is selling the product in another country simply a matter of believing one aspect of the evidence—that the product is safe? Is this decision a matter of the credo as well?

4. Would you include any warnings with the product?

Case 6.7

Nestlé: Products That Don't Fit Cultures

The Cultural Differences and Sales Tactics

Although the merits and problems of breastfeeding versus using infant formula are debated in the United States and other developed countries, the issue is not so balanced in third-world nations. Studies have demonstrated the difficulties and risks of bottle-feeding babies in such places.

First, refrigeration is not generally available, so the formula, once it is mixed or opened (in the case of premixed types), cannot be stored properly. Second, the lack of purified water for mixing with the formula powder results in diarrhea or other diseases in formula-fed infants. Third, inadequate education and income, along with cultural differences, often lead to the dilution of formula and thus greatly reduced nutrition.

Medical studies also suggest that regardless of the mother's nourishment, sanitation, and income level, an infant can be adequately nourished through breastfeeding. In spite of medical concerns about using their products in these countries, some infant formula manufacturers heavily promoted bottle-feeding.

These promotions, which went largely unchecked through 1970, included billboards, radio jingles, and posters of healthy, happy infants, as well as baby books and formula samples distributed through the health care systems of various countries.

Also, some firms used "milk nurses" as part of their promotions. Dressed in nurse uniforms, "milk nurses"

(continued)

Case 6.7

(continued)

were assigned to maternity wards by their companies and paid commissions to get new mothers to feed their babies formula. Mothers who did so soon discovered that lactation was undermined and could not be achieved, so the commitment to bottle-feeding was irreversible.

Awareness of the Impact of International Formula Sales

In the early 1970s, physicians working in nations where milk nurses were used began vocalizing their concerns. For example, Dr. Derrick Jelliffe, then the director of the Caribbean Food and Nutrition Institute, had the Protein-Calorie Advisory Group of the United Nations place infant formula promotion methods on its agenda for several of its meetings.

Journalist Mike Muller first brought the issue to public awareness with a series of articles in the *New Internationalist* in the 1970s. He also wrote a pamphlet on the promotion of infant formulas called "The Baby Killer," which was published by a British charity, War on Want. The same pamphlet was published in Switzerland, the headquarters of Nestlé, a major formula maker, under the title "Nestlé Kills Babies." Nestlé sued in 1975, which resulted in extensive media coverage.

In response to the bad publicity, manufacturers of infant formula representing about 75% of the market formed the International Council of Infant Food Industries to establish standards for infant formula marketing. The new code banned the milk nurse commissions and required the milk nurses to have identification that would eliminate confusion about their "nurse" status.

The code failed to curb advertising of formulas. In fact, distribution of samples increased. By 1977, groups in the United States began a boycott against formula makers over what Jelliffe called "comerciogenic malnutrition."

One U.S. group, Infant Formula Action Coalition (INFACT), worked with the staff of U.S. Senator Edward Kennedy of Massachusetts to have hearings on the issue by the Senate Subcommittee on Health and Human Resources, which Kennedy chaired. The hearings produced evidence that 40% of the worldwide market for infant formula, which totaled $1.5 billion at the time, was in Third World countries. No regulations resulted, but Congress did tie certain forms of foreign aid to the development by recipient countries of programs to encourage breastfeeding.

The Impact on Nestlé

Boycotts against Nestlé products began in Switzerland in 1975 and in the United States in 1977. The boycotts and Senator Kennedy's involvement heightened media interest in the issue and led to the World Health Organization (WHO) debating the issue of infant formula marketing in 1979 and agreeing to draft a code to govern it.

After four drafts and two U.S. presidential administrations (Jimmy Carter and Ronald Reagan), the 118 member nations of WHO finally voted on a code for infant formula marketing. The United States was the only nation to vote against it; the Reagan administration opposed the code being mandatory. In the end, WHO made the code a recommendation only, but the United States still refused to support it.

The publicity on the vote fueled the boycott of Nestlé, which continued until the formula maker announced it would meet the WHO standards for infant formula marketing. Nestlé created the Nestlé Infant Formula Audit Commission (NIFAC) to demonstrate its commitment to and ensure its implementation of the WHO code.

In 1988, Nestlé introduced a new infant formula, Good Start, through its subsidiary, Carnation. The industry leader, Abbott Laboratories, which held 54% of the market with its Similac brand, revealed Carnation's affiliation: "They are Nestlé," said Robert A. Schoellhorn, Abbott's chairman and CEO.[55] Schoellhorn also disclosed that Nestlé was the owner of Beech-Nut Nutrition Corporation, officers of which had been indicted and convicted (later reversed) for selling adulterated apple juice for babies.[56]

Carnation advertised Good Start in magazines and on television. The American Academy of Pediatrics (AAP) objected to this direct advertising, and grocers feared boycotts.

The letters "H.A." came after the name "Good Start," indicating the formula was hypoallergenic. Touted as a medical breakthrough by Carnation, the formula was made from whey and advertised as ideal for babies who were colicky or could not tolerate milk-based formulas.

Within four months of Good Start's introduction in November 1988, the FDA was investigating the formula

(continued)

---

[55]Rick Reiff, "Baby Bottle Battle," *Forbes*, November 28, 1988, pp. 222–224.
[56]For details of the Beech-Nut apple juice case, see Case 8.16.

Case 6.7

(continued)

because of six reported cases of vomiting due to the formula. Carnation then agreed not to label the formula hypoallergenic and to include a warning that milk-allergic babies should be given Good Start only with a doctor's approval and supervision.

Continuing Debate over Infant Formula

In 1990, with its infant formula market share at 2.8%, Carnation's president, Timm F. Crull, called on the AAP to "examine all marketing practices that might hinder breast-feeding."[57] Crull specifically cited manufacturers' practices of giving hospitals education and research grants, as well as free bottles, in exchange for having exclusive rights to supply the hospital with formula and to give free samples to mothers. He also called for scrutiny of the practice of paying pediatricians' expenses to attend conferences on infant formulas.

The AAP looked into prohibiting direct marketing of formula to mothers and physicians' accepting cash awards for research from formula manufacturers.

The distribution of samples in Third World countries continued during this time. Studies by the United Nations Children's Fund found that a million infants were dying every year because they were not breastfed adequately. In many cases, the infant starved because the mother used free formula samples and could not buy more, while her own milk had dried up. In 1991, the International Association of Infant Food Manufacturers agreed to stop distributing infant formula samples by the end of 1992.

In the United States in 1980, the surgeon general established a goal that the nation's breastfeeding rate be 75% by 1990. The rate remains below 60%, however, despite overwhelming evidence that breast milk reduces susceptibility to illness, especially ear infections and gastrointestinal illnesses. The AAP took a strong position that infant formula makers should not advertise to the public, but, as a result, new entrants into the market (such as Nestlé with its Carnation Good Start) were disadvantaged because the long-time formula makers Abbott and Mead Johnson were well established through physicians. In 1993, both the state of Florida and Nestlé filed an antitrust suit alleging a conspiracy among the AAP,

Abbott, and Mead Johnson. Florida settled the case with the formula manufacturers.[58] Nestlé lost its case against Abbott with a jury concluding that Abbott and others did not conspire to block competitors from entering the infant formula market.[59]

In 2006, the Centers for Disease Control and Prevention (CDC) conducted a study that reviewed 11 studies on the effects of distributing discharge packets with formula samples on new mothers and their decisions to stop or continue breastfeeding. Seven of the 11 studies concluded that there was lower breastfeeding continuation among those who received sample packets vs. those who did not and that receiving the sample packets reduced the amount of time the new mothers continued to breastfeed.[60]

As a result, the CDC adopted the World Health Organization's International Code of Marketing of Breast-Milk Substitutes. The code contains the following provisions:

- No advertising of breast-milk substitutes directly to the public.

- No free samples to mothers.

- No promotion of products in health care facilities.

- No commercial product representatives to advise mothers.

- No gifts or personal samples to health workers.

- No words or pictures idealizing artificial feeding, including pictures of infants on the products.

- Information to health workers should be scientific and factual.

- All information on artificial feeding, including product labels, should explain the benefits of breastfeeding and the costs and hazards associated with artificial feeding.

- Unsuitable products, such as condensed milk, should not be promoted for babies.

(continued)

---

[57]Julia F. Siler and D. Woodruff, "The Furor over Formula Is Coming to a Boil," *BusinessWeek*, April 9, 1990, pp. 52–53.

[58]*Florida v. Abbott Laboratories*, No. 91-40002, In re *Infant Formula Antitrust Litigation*, MDL 878 (N.D. Fal. 191); 1993-1 Trade Cas (CCH) ¶70,241 (N.D. Fla. 1993) (Settlement Agreement).
[59]Bloomberg, "Jurors Reject Antitrust Case Against Maker of Baby Formula: Consumer Products: Nestlé Brought Suit to Challenge Abbott Lab's Market Dominance," *Los Angeles Times*, June 21, 1995, https://www.latimes.com/archives/la -xpm-1995-06-21-fi-15552-story.html.
[60]Strategy 9. Addressing the Marketing of Infant Formula, https:// www.cdc.gov/breastfeeding/pdf/strategy9-addressing-marketing -infant-formula.pdf.

Case 6.7

(continued)

- All products should be of high quality and take into account the climatic and storage conditions of the country where they will be used.[61]

The code remains a voluntary set of rules in the United States. Some 200 U.S. hospitals have voluntarily stopped distributing discharge packs from formula makers to their maternity patients because they felt it "important not to appear to be endorsing any products or acting as commercial agents."[62] UNICEF and WHO offer "Baby Friendly" certification to maternity wards that take steps to eliminate discharge packs and formula samples.

Discussion Questions

1. If you had been an executive with Nestlé, would you have changed your marketing approach after the boycotts began?

2. Did Nestlé suffer long-term damage because of its third-world marketing techniques?

3. Does the CDC code address the concerns of the AAP and WHO?

4. Is anyone who worked in the infant formula companies responsible for the deaths of infants described in

the United Nations study? Is there a line that companies could draw that emerges in this case?

5. Analyze whether a company should comply voluntarily with the CDC Code.

6. If you were a hospital administrator, what policy would you adopt on discharge packs?

7. What if formula makers' ads had a conspicuous notation or warning, "Remember, breast is best"? Would that address the issue with influencing new mothers' decisions on breastfeeding?

Sources

"Breast Milk for the World's Babies," *New York Times*, March 12, 1992, p. A18.

Burton, Thomas B., "Methods of Marketing Infant Formula Land Abbott in Hot Water," *Wall Street Journal*, May 25, 1993, pp. A1, A6.

Freedman, Alix M., "Nestlé's Bid to Crash Baby-Formula Market in the U.S. Stirs a Row," *Wall Street Journal*, February 6, 1989, pp. A1, A10.

Freedman, Alix M., "Nestlé's Bid to Crash Baby-Formula Market in the U.S. Stirs a Row," *Wall Street Journal*, February 6, 1989, pp. A1, A10.

Garland, Susan B., "Are Formula Makers Putting the Squeeze on the States?" *BusinessWeek*, June 18, 1990, p. 31.

Meier, Barry, "Battle over the Market for Baby Formula," *New York Times*, June 15, 1993, pp. C1, C15.

Post, James E., "Assessing the Nestlé Boycott: Corporate Accountability and Human Rights," *California Management Review* 27 (1985): 113–131.

Star, Marlene C., "Breast Is Best," *Vegetarian Times*, June (1991): 25–26; "What's in a Name?" *Time*, March 29, 1989, p. 58.

---

[61]Id.

[62]Andrea Gerlin, "Hospitals Wean from Formula Makers' Freebies," *Wall Street Journal*, December 29, 1994, p. A1.

Case 6.8

Doing Business in China: The NBA and Ethical Minefields

The National Basketball Association (NBA) has a good relationship with the Chinese government. The market potential in China for games as well as the sale of sports paraphernalia by the teams is the NBA's greatest source of newfound revenue. There are 1.2 billion potential fans in China. However, between the Chinese takeover of Hong Kong and the treatment of the Uyghurs, those involved in the NBA in the states cannot resist tweets, interviews, and chiming in whenever possible on China.

The Morey Tweet Heard Round the World, Especially in China

Houston Rockets General Manager Daryl Morey tweeted the following on Friday, October 4, 2019: "Fight for freedom, stand with Hong Kong."[63] The Chinese consulate in Houston was offended, the owner of the Houston

(continued)

---

[63]Jordan Greer, "The Daryl Morey Controversy Explained: How a Tweet Created a Costly Rift Between the NBA and China," *Sporting News*, October 23, 2019, https://www.sportingnews.com/us/nba/news/daryl-morey-tweet-controversy-nba-china-explained/togzszxh37fi1mpw177p9bqwi.

Case 6.8

(continued)

Rockets contemplated termination of Morey, and there was considerable upheaval. Mr. Morey walked things back a bit with another tweet, "I did not intend my tweet to cause any offense to Rockets fans and friends of mine in China. I was merely voicing one thought, based on one interpretation, of a complicated event. I have had a lot of opportunity since that tweet to hear and consider other perspectives."[64] Mr. Morey then added some groveling, "I have always appreciated the significant support our Chinese fans and sponsors have provided and I would hope that those who are upset will know that offending or misunderstanding them was not my intention. My tweets are my own and in no way represent the Rockets or the NBA."[65] Enter the NBA on Sunday, October 6, with this statement released in English in the United States:

> "We recognize that the views expressed by Houston Rockets General Manager Daryl Morey have deeply offended many of our friends and fans in China, which is regrettable. While Daryl has made it clear that his tweet does not represent the Rockets or the NBA, the values of the league support individuals' educating themselves and sharing their views on matters important to them. We have great respect for the history and culture of China and hope that sports and the NBA can be used as a unifying force to bridge cultural divides and bring people together."

And then there was the version in Chinese that appeared in that country:

> "We are extremely disappointed with the inappropriate comments made by Houston Rockets general manager Daryl Morey, who has undoubtedly seriously hurt the feelings of Chinese fans. Morey has clarified that his remarks do not represent the position of the Rockets and the NBA. Under the values of the NBA, people can learn more about what they are interested in and share their opinions. We respect China's history and culture with great respect. We hope that sports and the NBA, as a positive energy of unity, will continue to

build bridges for international cultural exchanges and bring people together."

The NBA maintains that the translation was not correct in the Chinese statement and that the English version is the NBA's position. "Views expressed" and "inappropriate comments" do not translate the same way in any language.

Then we had the clarifying remarks from Adam Silver, NBA commissioner,

> "I recognize our initial statement left people angered, confused or unclear on who we are or what the NBA stands for. Let me be more clear. Over the last three decades, the NBA has developed a great affinity for the people of China. We have seen how basketball can be an important form of people-to-people exchange that deepens ties between the United States and China. At the same time, we recognize that our two countries have different political systems and beliefs. And like many global brands, we bring our business to places with different political systems around the world. But for those who question our motivation, this is about far more than growing our business. Values of equality, respect and freedom of expression have long defined the NBA—and will continue to do so. As an American-based basketball league operating globally, among our greatest contributions are these values of the game. In fact, one of the enduring strengths of the NBA is our diversity—of views, backgrounds, ethnicities, genders and religions. Twenty-five percent of NBA players were born outside of the United States and our colleagues work in league offices around the world, including in Beijing, Hong Kong, Shanghai and Taipei. With that diversity comes the belief that whatever our differences, we respect and value each other; and, what we have in common, including a belief in the power of sports to make a difference, remains our bedrock principle. It is inevitable that people around the world—including from America and China—will have different viewpoints over different issues. It is not the role of the NBA to adjudicate those differences. However, the NBA will not put itself in a position of regulating what players, employees and team owners say or will not say on these issues. We simply could not operate that way. Basketball runs deep in the hearts and minds of our two

[64]Jordan Greer, "The Daryl Morey Controversy Explained: How a Tweet Created a Costly Rift Between the NBA and China," *Sporting News*, October 23, 2019, https://www.sportingnews.com/us/nba/news/daryl-morey-tweet-controversy-nba-china-explained/togzszxh37fi1mpw177p9bqwi.

[65]Id.

(continued)

Case 6.8

(continued)

peoples. At a time when divides between nations grow deeper and wider, we believe sports can be a unifying force that focuses on what we have in common as human beings rather than our differences."

There was an editorial in China about the NBA kerfuffle with this sentence, "Sports loses out when politics enters play." The CCP asked that the NBA fire Morey, but the NBA pushed back, noting that "these American values—we are an American business—travel with us wherever we go. And one of those values is free expression."[66] Mr. Silver added, "No chance we'll even discipline him."[67] Still, the Chinese government is one-party rule and there is no freedom of speech. The Gap was selling T-shirts in China with a Chinese map that did not include Taiwan. China objected, and the Gap destroyed the T-shirts, apologizing for not using the "correct map" of China.[68] The Rockets did not escape unscathed for their manager's tweet. The team has been banished from China since 2019, and CCTV has not resumed its regular streaming of NBA games.

While Mr. Morey and the NBA were busily tweeting and issuing statements, LeBron James and his Lakers teammates were in Shanghai playing. Mr. James tweeted, "My team and this league just went through a difficult week. I think people need to understand what a tweet or statement can do to others. And I believe nobody stopped and considered what would happen. Could have waited to send it."[69] Mr. James is very outspoken on U.S. political issues, and he incurred the wrath of U.S. fans with his tweet, so he went back to Twitter and offered the following, "Let me clear up the confusion. I do not believe there was any consideration for the consequences and ramifications of the tweet. I'm not discussing the substance. Others can talk about that."[70]

Enes Kanter Freedom, His Shoes, and the NBA

He is a 6' 10" immigrant from Turkey and a basketball player who has played with the Portland Trail Blazers and the Boston Celtics. When he denounced the dictatorship in Turkey in 2017, his passport was revoked and his father was imprisoned. He was disciplined by the NBA for wearing shoes on the court that were custom painted in the colors of Tibet and imprinted with "Free Tibet." In response to the shoes being worn at the Celtics opening-night game, Tencent Holdings, a streaming service that had resumed carrying NBA games, abruptly cut its coverage of the game.[71] Shortly after, Mr. Kanter posted a video of himself wearing a T-shirt with an image of the Dalai Lama and called CCP leader Xi Jinping a "brutal dictator" and called for him to "free Tibet."[72] Chinese citizens are equally active in censorship. One blogger in China, with 1.4 million followers, wrote, "My identity as Chinese is more important than my identity as a basketball fan. I won't post any more NBA-related videos."[73]

However, when a parent at a summer basketball camp challenged him for being a human rights activist but not standing with the Uyghurs in China, Mr. Kanter had an awakening. At that point, he decided to do all that he could to bring awareness of the plight of the Uyghurs.[74] Mr. Kanter was an effective advocate. He put so much pressure on the Turkish government that his father was released from prison in 2020.

On October 20, 2021, the Chinese pulled all Celtics games from their streaming services. On November 19, 2021, the Celtics played the Los Angeles Lakers. Mr. Kanter wore shoes that were painted to show bags of money; one shoe also showed LeBron James bowing down before President Xi Jinping, while Mr. James' comments about

(continued)

---

[66]Sopan Deb, "China Asked N.B.A. to Fire Morey, Commissioner Says," *New York Times,* October 18, 2019, p. B1 at B10.

[67]*Id.,* at B1.

[68]Brent Schrotenboer, "Are LeBron, NBA Right to Bow to China?" October 16, 2019, p. 2C.

[69]Dan Wolken, "James Undermines Values He's Espoused for So Long," *USA Today,* October 16, 2019, p. 1C.

[70]Ben Cohen, "LeBron Caught in NBA-China Storm," *Wall Street Journal,* October 16, 2019, p. A16.

[71]Eva Xiao, "NBA Player Calls for Free Tibet, Drawing Backlash from China," *Wall Street Journal,* October 22, 2021, p. A11.

[72]*Id.*

[73]Nathan Vanderklippe, "NBA Faces Wrath of China, and Its People," *Globe and Mail,* October 10, 2019, p. B1.

[74]Thuan Le Elston, "Meet the NBA Player Who Is Taking on China and LeBron James in the Name of Human Rights," *USA Today,* December 15, 2021, https://www.usatoday.com/story/opinion/voices/2021/12/15/boston-celtics-enes-freedom-protests-china/6433177001/.

Case 6.8

(continued)

Mr. Morey's tweet were on the other shoe. Mr. Kanter has invited LeBron to travel with him to China to learn about the plight of the Uyghurs.

Mr. Kanter became a U.S. citizen on November 29, 2021, and changed his last name to "Freedom" at the same time. He has challenged Mr. James to meet with him to learn about the Uyghurs and to join with him in boycotting China. In February 2022, Mr. Freedom was traded by the Celtics to the Houston Rockets. In July 2022, Mr. Freedom was released by the Rockets but remains optimistic about his future even as he stays vocal and active in bringing attention to the Uyghurs.

The Warriors and the Venture Capitalist

On the podcast *All In,* Silicon Valley billionaire and part owner of the Golden State Warriors Chamath Palihapitiya weighed in on the Uyghurs, "Nobody cares about what's happening to the Uyghurs. I'm telling you a very hard, ugly truth. Of all of the things that I care about, I'd say it is below my line."[75]

The Warriors organization attempted to distance itself from Mr. Palihapitiya by tweeting, "Mr. Palihapitiya does not speak on behalf of our franchise, and his views certainly don't reflect those of our organization."[76]

Mr. Palihapitiya then reviewed his podcast and took to Twitter with the following, "In re-listening to this week's podcast, I recognize that I come across as lacking empathy. To be clear, my belief is that human rights matter, whether in China, the United States or elsewhere."[77]

Discussion Questions

1. An advisor with a strategic advisory firm notes that Beijing officials prefer that those who operate within their borders keep their opinions to themselves: "So companies have to make that decision. If they want to be in China, they have to understand the rules of the game in China."[78] What issues will companies need to address and explain to employees before doing business in China?

2. There were calls by many in the United States as well as by Enes Freedom for the United States to boycott the 2022 Winter Olympics in China. The United States decided to have only a diplomatic boycott. In 1936, the United States did not boycott the Olympics in Germany. However, the United States was not permitted to send any of its Jewish athletes, and Jessie Owens, who had won several gold medals in track and field events, was not permitted to receive those medals because of Hitler's racist views. In 1980, the United States did boycott the Olympics when they were held in the USSR (Russia/Soviet Union) because of that country's invasion of Afghanistan. Sixty-five countries joined the United States in the boycott.[79] The Soviet Union won the most medals, but there was little coverage of the games in the United States. Many of the 450 athletes who had qualified for participation in those Olympics were never able to compete again. Who are the stakeholders in the issue of boycotting the Olympics? What is accomplished by a boycott? What is accomplished through participation? What ethical categories are involved?

3. Are there ethical issues in individual tweets that affect organizations? What ethical categories apply to individual actions that harm organizations?

4. Is the NBA/Uyghur issue one that cannot be addressed without harm to some stakeholders?

---

[75]Gareth Vipers, "Warriors Investor Chamath Palihapitiya Responds to Criticism Over Comments on China's Uyghurs," *Wall Street Journal,* January 18, 2022, https://www.wsj.com/articles/warriors-investor-chamath-palihapitiya-says-nobody-cares-about-chinas-uyghurs-11642505637.

[76]Id.

[77]Id.

[78]Nathan Vanderklippe. "NBA Faces Wrath of China, and Its People," *Globe and Mail,* October 10, 2019, p. B1.

[79]Rick Maese, "Invisible Olympians," *Washington Post,* July 16, 2020, https://www.washingtonpost.com/graphics/2020/sports/1980-usa-olympic-boycott-team-carter/.

Bribes, Grease Payments, and "When in Rome. . . ."

Reading 6.9

A Primer on the FCPA[80]

The **Foreign Corrupt Practices Act (FCPA)** (15 U.S.C. §§ 78dd-1) applies to organizations that have their principal offices in the United States. The FCPA has antibribery provisions as well as accounting controls and was passed to curb the use of bribery in foreign operations of these companies.

History, Purpose, and Application of the FCPA

First passed in 1977, the FCPA is the result of an investigation by the Securities and Exchange Commission (SEC) that uncovered questionable foreign payments by U.S. firms in their international operations.

The FCPA prohibits making, authorizing, or promising payments or gifts of money or anything of value to government and NGO officials with the intent to corrupt for the purpose of *obtaining* or *retaining business* for or with or *directing business.*

What Constitutes a Payment under the FCPA?

The decisions in cases and Justice Department guidelines have given us the following examples of what constitutes a payment under the FCPA: cash, country club memberships, excessive comped travel (travel that does not include seminars or presentations and consists of, for example, shopping trips to Paris for government officials or their spouses), cash donations to political parties, loans, paying for medical equipment and treatments, sports equipment, payment of cell phone or utility bills for government officials, and giving luxury gifts such as sports cars and furs to government officials or their spouses.

In 2020, the Justice Department published the second edition of its Resource Guide for the Foreign Corrupt Practices Act (FCPA). The 133-page guide, which is available online, is updated by the Justice Department website on the FCPA (https://www.justice.gov/criminal-fraud/foreign-corrupt-practices-act) and includes permitted and prohibited actions under the FCPA. For example, the following are not violations of FCPA according to the guide:

1. Small gifts of expressions of gratitude, provided there is transparency in the giving

2. Small gifts to local charities, provided the gift is consistent with the company's general philanthropic goals and is not "large"

---

[80]Adapted from Marianne M. Jennings, *Business: Its Legal, Ethical, and Global Environment,* 12th ed.

3. Wedding gift to a government official (if not too large)

4. Hats, T-shirts, pins, and pens that companies offer at trade show booths that government officials take

5. Payment of the bar tab for drinks for government officials at a group meeting

6. Payment for travel (even including cab fare, but not chauffeur driven limos) and reasonable meals to the United States for training at a company's facility (foreign dignitaries can even take in a baseball game at company expense during such training without the company risking an FCPA violation)

Payments to foreign officials for "facilitation," often referred to as grease payments, are not prohibited under FCPA so long as these payments are made only to get the officials to do jobs that they might not do ordinarily or would do slowly without some payment. More detail on facilitation payments follows.

What Is "Obtaining, Retaining, or Directing Business"?

The types of activities included under "obtaining, retaining, or directing business" are the following: winning contracts, influencing a procurement process, circumventing rules in order to get products imported, gaining access to non–public bid information, evading taxes or penalties, influencing the outcome of lawsuits or regulatory actions, obtaining exceptions to regulations, avoiding contract termination, asking regulators or officials to exclude your competitors from their country, evading customs duties, and extending drilling contracts.

For example, if an American company trying to win a bid on a contract for the construction of highways in a foreign country paid a government official there who was responsible for awarding such construction contracts a "consulting fee" of $25,000, the American company would be in violation of the FCPA. The payment was of money, it was made to a foreign official, and it was made for the purpose of obtaining business within that country. Titan Corporation violated the FCPA when the money it paid to an agent in Benin was passed along to the reelection campaign of the president of Benin. The result was an increased management fee for Titan's operation of the telecommunications system in Benin. The payments were uncovered as Lockheed Martin was conducting due diligence for purposes of a merger with Titan. Titan voluntarily disclosed the payment and paid a total fine of $28.5 million.

Who Is Covered under FCPA?

The types of officials covered under the FCPA (to whom gifts may not be directed) include foreign officials, political parties, party officials, candidates for office, and any NGO personnel. Using any person (intermediary) to transmit the gift or money to one of the other types of people also is prohibited. NGOs include officials with the United Nations, the Olympics, or the IMF. The bribery involved in awarding the 2002 Olympics held in Salt Lake City resulted in this expansion of the statute's coverage. The international 2015 FIFA investigation that resulted in FCPA charges is another example of an NGO (The International Federation of Association Football) being subjected to the antibribery laws.

Use of Agents and the FCPA

When the FCPA was passed initially, many companies tried to find ways around the bribery prohibitions. Companies would hire foreign agents or consultants to help them gain business in countries and allowed these "third parties" to act independently. However, many of these consultants paid others who then paid bribes to officials. Under the FCPA, even these types of arrangements can constitute a violation if the consulting fees are high, odd payment arrangements occur, or the company has reason to know of a potential or actual violation. Companies must be able to establish that they have performed "due diligence" in investigating those hired as their agents and consultants in foreign countries. For example, if a U.S. company hired a consultant who charged the company $25,000 in fees and $25,000 in expenses, the U.S. company would be, under Justice Department guidelines, on notice for excessive expenses that could signal potential bribes being paid. These types of expenses are known as *red flags* for U.S. companies. The Justice Department uses this information as a means of establishing intent, even when the company may not know precisely what was done with the funds and what was paid to whom.

The use of agents, risky as it is under the FCPA, is still common practice. A Stanford Law School study found that between 1977 and 2017, 91% of all the cases handled by the Justice Department involved the use of agents or consultants.[81]

The FCPA and "Grease" or Facilitation Payments

Payments to foreign officials for "facilitation," often referred to as **grease payments**, are not prohibited under FCPA so long as these payments are made only to get the officials to do jobs that they might not do ordinarily or would do slowly without some payment. These grease payments can be made for obtaining permits, licenses, or other official documents; processing governmental papers, such as visas and work orders; providing police protection and mail pickup and delivery; providing phone service, power, and water supply; loading and unloading cargo or protecting perishable products; and scheduling inspections associated with contract performance or transit of goods across the country.

Penalties for Violation of the FCPA

Penalties for individuals who have violated the FCPA can run up to $250,000 per violation and five years' imprisonment. Corporate fines can be up to $2 million per violation. Also, under the Alternative Fines Act, the Justice Department can seek to obtain two times the benefit of the bribe attempted to gain, known as **disgorgement**. For example, if a company paid a bribe to obtain a $100 million contract for computer services for a foreign government, the potential fine could be twice the profit on that contract, or $20 million if the profit on the contract was $10 million.

The Justice Department and the SEC continue a steady stream of FCPA charges. During 2010, FCPA charges peaked at 74. In 2011, there were 48 charges and in 2012 only 23. From 2013 to 2015, there were 25 FCPA cases brought. In 2021, there were 24 cases in total. The charges have involved many large companies, including Bristol-Meyers Squibb, Avon, Hitachi, Mead-Johnson, Goodyear, and Ralph Lauren. Ralph Lauren Corporation reported that the Lauren Argentina subsidiary had been paying the customs agents in that country what was called "Loading and Delivery Expenses," ranging between $750 and $3,847 per payment, for a total of $593,000 over a five-year period to get Lauren goods into the country. In addition, the customs agents were given purses and other high-dollar items to secure their favor for goods entry.[82] Lauren paid a $1.6 million fine to settle the case and closed the Argentina subsidiary.

---

[81]"Third-Party Intermediaries," available at http://fcpa.stanford.edu/chart-inter mediary.html.
[82]Peter Lattman, "Ralph Lauren Corp. Agrees to Pay Fine in Bribery Case," *New York Times*, April 23, 2013.

The U.S. Justice Department believes that, "U.S. companies that are paying bribes to foreign officials are undermining government institutions around the world. It is a hugely destabilizing force."[83] The Department prosecutes accordingly. Former Halliburton executive Albert J. Stanley (aka Jack Stanley) received a seven-year sentence—the longest one ever imposed since the FCPA was passed in 1977.[84] In 2008, Siemens agreed to pay an $800-million fine, the largest since the FCPA passage.

When the Justice Department Declines Prosecution

The Justice Department does have a process it follows in making a decision to prosecute a company under the FCPA. For example, in 2020, the Justice Department declined to prosecute World Acceptance Corporation despite the fact that its employees in its Mexican subsidiary had funneled $4,000,000 through intermediaries to government officials in order to obtain contracts with Mexican unions in order to make loans to union members. The Department gave the following reasons for its decision:

1. World promptly made full disclosure of the conduct once it was discovered

2. World disclosed all information to the Justice Department and cooperated fully in the investigation

3. The nature and seriousness of the offense

4. World adding additional FCPA training to its compliance program

5. Termination of the executives involved in setting up the intermediaries and payments

6. Termination of all relationships with the intermediaries and third parties who made the payment

7. World's repayment to the Justice Department its "ill-gotten gains" from the loan programs with the unions.[85]

When the Justice Department Throws the Book at Companies for Bribery

When companies do not meet the standards discussed above for lenient treatment, the Justice Department is able to assess large fines. For example, Glencore, an international mining and commodities trading company, entered a guilty plea and agreed to pay $1.1 billion to settle charges that it had violated the FCPA.[86] Among the findings by the Justice Department were the following factors that resulted in the large fine:

1. The illegal payments had begun in 2007.

2. The payments were made in countries around the world.

3. Glencore had weak internal controls that permitted the distribution of cash without checks and balances on its purposes.

4. In 2011, Glencore closed its four cash desks that permitted the bribery to occur but did not conduct further investigations or adopt stronger internal controls.

---

[83]Russell Gold and David Crawford, "U.S., Other Nations Step Up Bribery Battle," *Wall Street Journal*, September 12, 2008, pp. B1, B6.

[84]Because of Mr. Stanley's plea deal, more indictments are expected as he shares information.

[85]Declination of Prosecution of World Acceptance Corporation letter, August 5, 2020, https://www.justice.gov/criminal-fraud/file/1301826/download.

[86]*U. S. v. Glencore International*, https://www.justice.gov/usao-sdny/pr/glencore-entered-guilty-pleas-foreign-bribery-and-market-manipulation-conspiracies.

5. Glencore did not open an investigation into the possible abuses by the cash desks.

6. Glencore did not notify the Justice Department of the issues with the cash desks.

7. Glencore had paid out over $100 million in bribes to government officials.

8. Glencore had a company-wide practice of using agents for purposes of influencing government officials without using the necessary steps to verify the backgrounds of those agents.

The FCPA and U.S. Competitiveness

One of the long-standing concerns about the FCPA is whether it has placed U.S. businesses at a competitive disadvantage in those countries in which bribery is generally accepted for winning contracts and government benefits. However, a survey by the U.S. Government Accounting Office of the companies affected by the FCPA found that the ability of companies from other countries to bribe officials did not give them a competitive advantage. The survey found that U.S. trade increased in 51 of 56 foreign countries after the FCPA went into effect. The increase was attributed to the position adopted by U.S. companies with respect to their competitors—if they could not bribe government officials, they would disclose publicly information about bribes made by any of the companies from other nations.

Discussion Questions

1. Explain the difference between a bribe and a facilitation payment.

2. Discuss the responsibilities of companies in preventing FCPA violations.

Case 6.10

FIFA: The Kick of Bribery

The Fédération Internationale de Football Association (FIFA) is the world's foremost soccer (or fútbol/football) governing body. FIFA's purpose is to regulate and promote soccer around the world. FIFA consists of six constituent continental confederations—the Confederation of North, Central American and Caribbean Association Football (CONCACAF), the Confederación Sudamericana de Fútbol (CONMEBOL), the Union des Associations Européennes de Football (UEFA), the Confederation Africaine de Football (CAF), the Asian Football Confederation (AFC), and the Oceania Football Confederation (OFC) and affiliated regional federations, national member associations, and sports marketing companies.[87] There

are 209 various level associations affiliated with FIFA and all are required to pay annual dues to both their regional associations and FIFA. Headquartered in Zurich, Switzerland, FIFA has ties to the United States through soccer affiliates and banking and a development office begun in the United States in 2011.

What began as a tiny operation run from a house in Switzerland has evolved into the FIFA multibillion dollar franchise with an international web of soccer organizations, marketing companies, and commercial rights. FIFA held several types of world championship events, but its men's teams' championship, the World Cup, is the most watched television event in the world. That

(continued)

---

[87]The background information on FIFA was obtained from the FBI indictment, https://www.justice.gov/opa/pr/nine-fifa-officials-and-five-corporate-executives-indicted-racketeering-conspiracy-and. Last visited October 22, 2022.

Case 6.10

(continued)

draw brings FIFA corporate sponsorships, ad dollars, and a steady flow of countries and cities seeking the event as a boost for their countries. According to FIFA's published income statement for 2011–2014, it had total revenues of $5.718 billion, 70% of which ($4.008 billion) was from the sale of television and marketing rights to the 2014 World Cup. FIFA's profits during this period were $338 million. The television rights for 2015–2022 brought in $1.5 billion from the United States rights, consisting of Fox Sports (United States) and Telemundo (Spanish). FIFA funds are given as development funds to members for the promotion of soccer. Through this funds distribution, FIFA president, Sepp Blatter, was able to develop strong voting ties with countries around the world. The FIFA development program dispensed $1.5 billion for the 2011–2014 period. Mr. Blatter is an enormously popular figure, particularly among the African member nations.

However, in May 2015, the U.S. Federal Bureau of Investigation (FBI), along with law enforcement officials from other countries, conducted a pre-dawn raid at a luxury hotel in Zurich where members of FIFA's governing body (the Executive Committee, or ExCo, of its congress), which consists of representatives from the associations and federations listed above, were staying as part of one of their international meetings. As a result of the raid, 14 current and former FIFA officials and members of its congress were indicted on corruption charges by the FBI. Despite these events, Mr. Blatter retained his position, with a vote by the congress just a few months following the arrests. In December 2015, there was another raid at the same hotel in Zurich and another 16 officials were indicted.

FIFA Ethics, Activities, and Suspicions

FIFA has long been suspected of corruption and, in fact, in 2012 hired former U.S. attorney Michael Garcia to conduct its own internal investigation to determine whether there was indeed corruption within the organization. Mr. Garcia delivered a 350-page report in 2014. However, FIFA refused to release the report and instead issued its own executive summary in which it stated that the Garcia report was "materially incomplete," with "erroneous representations of the facts and conclusions."[88] *Sports Illustrated*'s introduction to its article on the FIFA arrests read, "For any of us who've followed soccer over the years, for any of us who love the World Cup but reject the men who run it, we've been waiting for the day of reckoning for FIFA."[89] That day of reckoning was coming through criminal charges, not reports.

FIFA's code of ethics was first adopted in 2004 and revised in 2006, 2009, 2012, and 2019. The code provides that FIFA officials were prohibited from accepting bribes or cash gifts and from otherwise abusing their positions for personal gain. The code also established that FIFA and its confederations and member associations owed a duty of absolute loyalty to FIFA. By 2009, the code was changed to spell out that all FIFA officials have a fiduciary duty to FIFA and all its constituent confederations, member associations, leagues, and clubs. Personal gain by FIFA officials from confederations, member associations, leagues, and clubs was prohibited. The 2019 code added a provision on zero tolerance for human rights violations by member countries.

FIFA really began to attract attention (and investigators) when it made the decision to award the 2022 World Cup to the teeny, tiny nation of Qatar. Qatar had neither the weather (120 degrees in the summer) for the Cup nor the manpower to build the necessary facilities. There have been deaths of migrant workers due to heat exhaustion they experienced during construction of facilities for the event. The Qatar decision was a puzzler for many. The FBI three-year investigation of FIFA began shortly after the Qatar decision and culminated in the Zurich raid.

The Process for the World Cup Country Selection

The ExCo typically followed a process for awarding the World Cup that allowed bid committees for the competing nations to campaign for votes among the members of the executive committee. At least six years prior to each World Cup, the ExCo typically held a vote in which its

(continued)

---

[88]"The Ugly Game," *Wall Street Journal*, June 6–7, 2015, p. A10.
[89]Grant Wahl, "World Corrupt," *Sports Illustrated*, June 6, 2015, p. 13.

Case 6.10

(continued)

members cast their votes via secret ballot. For example, for the 2022 World Cup, the campaigning and voting occurred in 2010 with the United States, Australia, South Korea, Japan, and Qatar competing. Qatar was awarded the World Cup by the secret ballot. Every confederation member has one vote. So, for example, Qatar has an equal vote with France, Italy, or Brazil.

It was the voting structure that allowed what is described in the indictment to occur. The goal for attaining the World Cup for your country was to line up as many votes as you could. This part of the process is where money entered the picture. With development grants doled out to various confederations, their votes were secured. However, a portion of the FIFA money doled out was then kicked back to members of the FIFA ExCo. Likewise, the marketing companies could enter the picture by using their funds to influence votes to maximize their commercial rights. Money flowed up and down the hierarchy of confederations as the vote approached.

Sports Marketing

FIFA and its affiliates had contractual relationships with sports marketing companies. These companies would pay FIFA for the rights to license, market FIFA, and negotiate television contracts. During the 24-year period covered by the indictment, a network of these marketing companies developed to capitalize on the expanding media market for soccer, particularly in the United States. Over time, the marketing companies became increasingly intertwined as they spread throughout the world, including the United States.

Those who owned the marketing companies or were associated with them were also members of the FIFA ExCo and were able to generate "unprecedented profits through the sale of media rights to soccer." Because of the fiduciary duty provisions of the FIFA code of ethics, these transactions that benefited FIFA officials, but not FIFA, had to be concealed. To conceal the transactions, the marketing companies and their owners established shell companies, various bank accounts, and other structures to conceal the flow of money to those who were not permitted to retain funds that rightfully belonged to FIFA.

Once the use of marketing companies became so lucrative, competition sprung up among the marketing companies and the officials were able to obtain payments in exchange for awarding marketing contracts.

In addition to these activities, those operating the marketing companies became officials of the various confederations for soccer and then rose to positions at FIFA or on FIFA's ExCo. As members of the ExCo, they began to solicit bribes from representatives of countries that were seeking to hold the World Cup in exchange for their votes. Because many of the marketing companies and confederation offices were in the United States and many of those involved were either U.S. citizens or doing business in the United States, they were subject to U.S. laws, including the FCPA. Because FIFA was an NGO, payment of bribes to FIFA officials was a violation of the FCPA. The indictment describes a 24-year scheme of bribery among and between FIFA executives, businesses, and governments that required money laundering, fraud, and conspiracies to accomplish.

Some of the specific allegations in the 47-count indictment include:

- Members of the executive committee of FIFA accepted bribes from Morocco for it to hold the 1998 World Cup. Apparently, Morocco was low on its bid because France eventually got the 1998 World Cup.

- Chuck Blazer, a U.S. citizen, and once the general secretary of CONCACAF, FIFA's umbrella organization for North and Central America and the Caribbean, was charged with and has entered a guilty plea to accepting a $10 million bribe to award the World Cup to South Africa. Mr. Blazer served on FIFA's ExCo from 1997 to 2013. Mr. Blazer was indicted previously in 2013 and his guilty plea settled the criminal charges, but the record of his case was sealed until the 2015 indictments. Mr. Blazer cooperated with federal authorities in building their case.

- The general secretary of FIFA, who worked for Mr. Blatter, is alleged to have transferred $10 million from FIFA accounts in Switzerland to a Caribbean soccer

(continued)

Case 6.10

(continued)

organization as a bribe to secure votes for South Africa's bid to win the World Cup.

- Members of the executive committee accepted bribes for the award of broadcast rights for the CONCACAF Gold Cup in 1996, 1998, 2000, 2002, and 2003.

- Overall, the indictment alleged a total of $150 million in bribes.

The FIFA Third Parties

One of the issues that has been raised is the obligation of those who were doing business with FIFA to further explore the widespread allegations of corruption or the problematic transfers of money around the world in chain bank transactions. For example, Adidas, Coca-Cola, Visa, and Nike are all sponsors of the World Cup and other soccer events run by FIFA. Despite percolating criminal charges, reports, and other issues, none of the companies withdrew their sponsorships or raised questions or objections. However, all have indicated cooperation with federal authorities on the pending cases.

The indictment mentioned "a multinational sportswear company headquartered in the United States" and is called "Sportswear Company A," which is described as having signed a sponsorship with the Brazilian national soccer federation in 1996. Nike's website describes the same thing, but Nike is not named in the indictment. Nike has pledged cooperation noting, "Nike believes in ethical and fair play in both business and sport and strongly opposes any form of manipulation or bribery."[90]

Adidas has been an official sponsor of FIFA for over 40 years and in 2014, it made $2.29 billion in revenue from its soccer products, up 20% from the previous year. Adidas has also noted that it demands "the highest standards of ethics and compliance" from its partners and is cooperating.[91]

KPMG was FIFA's auditor but issued clean opinions for the organization for 16 years.[92] During that time, KPMG did raise questions about several payments, but did not raise objections. In 2002, FIFA's general secretary wrote a letter to the ExCo accusing Mr. Blatter and others of fraud. While the letter made its way into the media, KPMG only noted the matter and did not pursue the allegations in the letter. Also, a member of the audit committee for FIFA left the committee because he had been charged with fraud and money laundering in connection with a card-swiping system for public hospitals in his native Cayman Islands. The only disclosure made by FIFA was that the member had temporarily left the audit committee. KPMG did not note or disclose the criminal charges.[93] KPMG severed its relationship with FIFA in June 2016. KPMG has its own internal investigation into its audit work for FIFA. PwC was appointed by FIFA as its replacement.

FIFA Follow-Up

Despite the vote of confidence in Mr. Blatter in the days following the raid in Zurich, he agreed to step down as FIFA's chief executive on June 2, 2015, saying, "What counts most to me is the institution."[94] His presidency, which began in 1998, ended abruptly and surprisingly as authorities in the United States were continuing their investigation. It was not until 2020 that Switzerland's attorney general indicted Mr. Blatter and his ally at FIFA, Michael Platini, for fraud, forgery, and criminal mismanagement.[95] Mr. Blatter was banned from soccer by the committee for eight years. There had been a recommendation of a lifetime ban, but Mr. Blatter appealed the decision and his suspension was cut to six years.[96]

The United States charged 27 soccer officials, including the former president of Honduras, Rafael Callejas, who entered a guilty plea. Mr. Blatter was not charged in the

(continued)

[90]Sara Germano, "Nike Is Cooperating with Investigations," *Wall Street Journal*, May 28, 2015, p. A11.

[91]*Id.*

[92]Lynnley Browning, "Corruption in FIFA? Its Auditor Saw None," *New York Times*, June 6, 2015, p. B9.

[93]*Id.*

[94]Matthew Futterman and Joshua Robinson, "Soccer Boss Quits amid U.S. Probe," *Wall Street Journal*, June 3, 2015, p. A1.

[95]Tariq Panja, "Former FIFA Officials Indicted on Fraud Charges Over Secret Payment," *New York Times*, November 3, 2020, p. B10.

[96]ESPN Staff, "Sepp Blatter, Michael Platini Bans Reduced to 6 years by FIFA," *ESPNFC*, February 26, 2016, https://www.espn.com/soccer/blog-fifa/story/2814374/fifa-cuts-sepp-blatter-and-michel-platini-bans-to-6-years. Last visited October 22, 2022.

Case 6.10

(continued)

U.S. cases but there are still investigations of his activities, including loans to The Trinidad Federation that were made and then almost immediately written off by Mr. Blatter. There is a payment of $2 million to Mr. Platini that Mr. Blatter says was for work done in 1984 when Mr. Platini was the captain of France's champion team. However, the payment was made when Mr. Blatter was facing a challenger for his FIFA presidency. Mr. Blatter says it was a "late wage payment" and that he will be able to "clear his name."[97]

Two officials have been found guilty of conspiracy and racketeering, and most of the 40 total defendants charged entered guilty pleas. The president of Guatemala's soccer association entered a guilty plea to wire fraud conspiracy and was the first to be sentenced, receiving eight months in prison.[98] The indictments in the case indicated that more than $150 million in bribes had been paid to FIFA officials for marketing and licensing rights for the World Cup and related soccer activities. However, after a seven-year investigation, both Mr. Blatter and Mr. Platini were found not guilty by a Swiss court.[99] Both men testified

that they had an "employment arrangement" and that Mr. Blatter had agreed to pay Mr. Platini his demanded compensation of $1 million for playing the role of an adviser to Mr. Blattner. Mr. Blattner referred to their arrangement as a "gentlemen's agreement."[100] The Swiss government was required to pay $20,000 each to the two men for the "moral injury" that had experienced because of the charges. Both men have, however, been banned by FIFA from participating in the game of soccer and FIFA until 2028.

Discussion Questions

1. What does the decision about Qatar teach us about the impact of bribery?

2. Explain why third parties did not raise issues, questions, or concerns about FIFA operations.

3. Why did other nations not raise questions about the Qatar vote?

4. How do you think the payments for votes began?

5. Are there additional risks with nonprofits and NGOs for corruption? What was FIFA missing in its internal operations?

[97]Tariq Panja, "Former FIFA Officials Indicted on Fraud Charges Over Secret Payment," *New York Times*, November 3, 2020, p. B10.

[98]Rebecca R. Ruiz, "Top Soccer Officials Found Guilty in FIFA Case," *New York Times*, December 23, 2017, p. B5.

[99]Tariq Panja, "Acquittals in $2 Million FIFA Fraud Trial," *New York Times*, July 9, 2022, p. B9.

[100]*Id.*

Case 6.11

Siemens and Bribery, Everywhere

Siemens is a German conglomerate that has been in business since 1847 with its three divisions of energy, health care, and industry. Siemens has 293,000 employees producing wind turbines and high-speed trains and providing engineering services on all types of construction

projects. A large portion of Siemens's revenues has always come from projects with governments and their agencies. As a result of a multi-country investigation, authorities uncovered a four-year pattern of bribery by Siemens that is shown in the chart below.

(continued)

Case 6.11

(continued)

Country	Product	Bribes Paid	Period
Russia	Medical devices	$55 million	2000–2007
Argentina	Identity cards project	$40 million	1998–2004
China	High-voltage transmission lines	$25 million	2002–2003
China	Metro trains	$22 million	2002–2007
Israel	Power plants	$20 million	2002–2005
Bangladesh	Mobile tele-phone works	$5.3 million	2004–2006
Venezuela	High-speed trains	$16.7 million	2001–2007
Russia	Traffic-control systems	$0.75 million	2004–2006
Vietnam	Medical devices	$0.5 million	2005
China	Medical devices	$14.4 million	2003–2007
Nigeria	Telecom-munications projects	€4.2 million	2003
Iraq	Power station	$1.7 million	2000
Italy	Power station	€6.0 million	2003
Greece	Telecommuni-cations	€37 million	2006

Both the SEC and the Justice Department agencies concluded that Siemens had paid more than 4,283 bribes totaling $1.4 billion to government officials to secure contracts. The SEC maintained that the bribes resulted in the company obtaining $1.1 billion in profits. Siemens did follow what is known as "the four-eyes principle" of internal control for the FCPA, which is that all payments required two signatures. However, the company had made so many exceptions to the four-eyes principle that, operationally, it was not in effect. The SEC complaint noted how many red flags the board ignored in the years during which the bribery was occurring.

For example, when Germany signed on to the antibribery provisions of the OECD, Siemens's executives expressed concerns about all the companies involved in bribery around the world. Siemen's CEO at the time of the OECD adoption also voiced concern to the board about the number of Siemens executives who were under investigation by the German government for bribery activities. He asked the board to take protective measures because its members could be held responsible for inaction. Despite his plea, the bribes continued with support from some board members.

In 2001, general counsel for the board notified the members that for the company to meet U.S. standards for its new New York Stock Exchange (NYSE) listing, it needed to end its practices of having off-the-books accounts for the payment of the bribes. The company took no steps to investigate or end its practices. The SEC noted there was a stunning lack of internal controls at Siemens as well as a tone at the top that did not take the FCPA seriously. The bribes involved employees at all levels of the company and revealed a culture that had long been at odds with the FCPA.[101]

The company's cooperation with the U.S. government since 2006, as well as its efforts to correct the violations, resulted in a reduction of Siemens's fine from $2.7 billion to $800 million. Siemens's efforts to correct its culture included cooperating with the government, turning over all documents it found, and replacing all but one officer and the board. Two of the company's former managers were convicted of bribery charges for their role in the ongoing bribery web. Siemens has paid a total of $1.3 billion in fines in other countries for the violations.

(continued)

---

[101]www.sec.gov/litigation. Accessed May 19, 2010.

Case 6.11

(continued)

Discussion Questions

1. Add together all the fines and compare with the profits made from the bribes to determine whether Siemens made a good business decision with its approach to winning contracts.

2. Peter Loscher, the CEO who was hired to take over following the settlement of the FCPA charges, indicated that the company was a great innovator but no longer had marketing skills because it had relied on the facile approach of bribery for so long.[102] Thinking about his statement, offer a risk associated with using bribes as a business model.

3. Reinhard Siekaczek, the former Siemens employee, largely responsible for Siemens's accounting system that hid bribes for five years, and who was charged with breach of trust under German law, made the following statements about his activities, the bribes, and the consequences:

"People will only say about Siemens that they were unlucky and that they broke the 11th Commandment. The 11th Commandment is: 'Don't get caught.'"[103]

"It was about keeping the business unit alive and not jeopardizing thousands of jobs overnight."

"I was not the man responsible for the bribery. I organized the cash."

"I would have never thought I'd go to jail for my company. Sure, we joked about it, but we thought if our actions ever came to light, we'd get together and there would be enough people to play a game of cards."

Can you describe what level of ethical development is involved here? What did he miss in his evaluation of his conduct and the risks? What lines did Siemens cross in getting to this level of bribery payments? What rationalizations do you see in his comments?

---

[102]Anita Raghavan, "No More Excuses," *Forbes*, April 27, 2009, p. 121.

[103]*U.S. v. Siemens*, SEC Complaint, 1 :08-cv-02167 (December 12, 2008).

Case 6.12

Walmart in Mexico

At the time of its expansion into Mexico, one of every five new Walmart stores around the world was located there. Growing to 209,000 employees in Mexico, Walmart became the largest private employer in the country. The expansion of the giant retailer in Mexico was remarkable. It was not clear how Walmart was able to accomplish its expansion when other retailers struggled with permits, zoning, and inspections. As a result, Walmart began an internal investigation that ran nearly in tandem with one by the U.S. Justice Department for violations of the FCPA.

The internal investigation began in 2005 when a senior U.S. Walmart executive received an email from a former Walmart executive in Mexico, who revealed that Walmart had paid bribes all over the country to obtain permits to build the new stores rapidly and ubiquitously. Following

the resulting internal investigation, Walmart uncovered $24 million in payments to government officials in exchange for permits for building the stores. The subsequent follow-up and training were delegated to Walmart's general counsel in Mexico City, the man who was identified as having authorized the payments.

However, despite the discovery, Walmart made no public disclosure about the payments or its investigation. Then-chairman of Walmart, H. Lee Scott, told internal investigators that they were being "too aggressive" in handling their work. The payments and evidence were not disclosed to the U.S. Justice Department until December 2011. That disclosure was made after U.S. executives learned that the *New York Times* was investigating and had both documents

(continued)

Case 6.12

(continued)

and statements from those involved in paying the bribes. The *Times* was the first news organization to break the story.[104] Walmart issued a response to the story that explained the steps that it had taken and ones it would be taking to eliminate the problems.[105]

One of the critical issues in the outcome was whether the payments were facilitation payments, a means of getting the company's voice heard on obtaining permits, or whether they really were bribes to government officials. The Walmart internal report describes the payments as follows: "They targeted mayors and city council members, obscure urban planners, low-level bureaucrats who issued permits—anyone with the power to thwart Walmart's growth. The bribes bought zoning approvals, reductions in environmental impact fees and the allegiance of neighborhood leaders."[106] How the funds were used and to whom they were paid and in exchange for what are critical in determining whether there was a violation of the FCPA.[107]

An Example of the Bribery

One example illustrates the efforts the company made for expansion in Mexico. Walmart wanted to build a new store in Elda Pineda's alfalfa field, located just one mile from the Mayan ruins that draw tourists from around the world. The estimated activity of the store was 250 customers per hour, if the location in the alfalfa field could be approved by the city council in San Juan Teotihuacán, Mexico. However, the city council members wanted to limit commercial development near the ruins to preserve the area. As a result, the city's zoning map that was approved by the city council prohibited commercial development in the alfalfa field. The zoning map would take effect once it was published

in the newspaper. Walmart officials in Mexico City paid $52,000 to a city official to redraw the zoning area on the map prior to publication. The map that was published included the alfalfa field as part of the area zoned for commercial development. The store's construction began a few months later and opened for business in time for Christmas 2004.[108]

Walmart's general counsel had been pushing for a policy of "no payments to government officials," regardless of the reason. However, Walmart executives in Mexico had a business strategy using *gestores*, a type of unofficial lobbyist who is able to get through to local government officials and who takes a 6% commission for winning an expedited permit for the company's new stores. That practice continued even as red flags about the payments arose and general counsel continued to express concerns.

The Final Resolution

Following the findings in Mexico, the Justice Department continued its investigation into Walmart and its business model for its expansion in India, Brazil, Argentina, Chile, Japan, China, and South Africa. In Brazil, Walmart used a woman they called the "sorceress" because she was able to obtain permits for building the stores so quickly.[109] The investigation found that Walmart was making payments in countries around the world from 2000 through 2011.

Walmart has spent $900 million on legal fees, investigation costs, and in improvements in its ethics and compliance area.[110] Both the SEC and the Justice Department noted that Walmart was sloppy in its bookkeeping, carrying the fees paid for the bribes on their books as "professional services" or "incidentals."

Walmart struggled to settle its case with the Justice Department. The settlement talks, which involved a reported $600 million fine, were stalled during the Obama administration's waning days because of the

---

[104]David Barstow, "Vast Mexico Bribery Case Hushed Up by Wal-Mart After Top-Level Struggle," *New York Times*, April 21, 2012.

[105]You can read the company statement here: https://corporate .walmart.com/newsroom/2012/12/17/walmart-statement-in -response-to-december-17-new-york-times-article-about -allegations-of-corruption-in-mexico.

[106]David Barstow, "Vast Mexico Bribery Case Hushed Up by Wal-Mart After Top-Level Struggle," *New York Times*, April 21, 2012.

[107]Details from the interviews in the investigations give an idea of the amount and nature of the payments, https://www.nytimes .com/2012/04/22/business/at-wal-mart-in-mexico-a-bribe-inquiry -silenced.html.

[108]David Barstow and Alexandra Xanix von Bertrab, "The Bribery Aisle: How Wal-Mart Used Payoffs to Get Its Way in Mexico," *New York Times*, December 18, 2012, p. A1.

[109]Michael Corkery, "Graft Met by a Walmart 'Wink': Company Is Fined $282 Million," *New York Times*, June 22, 2019, p. A1.

[110]*Id.*

Case 6.12

(continued)

government's desire to have Walmart banned from accepting food stamps. A provision such as that causes companies to lose federal contractor status and is a common part of settlements with corporations. For Walmart, the inability to accept food stamps would be a loss of $13 billion annually in sales.[111] The other sticking point in the negotiations was the demand that Walmart have an independent monitor for a specified time to observe company behavior.

Walmart eventually settled the case in 2019, agreeing to return $144 million in gains that came from its expanded international operations to the SEC and paid a $138 million penalty to the Justice Department.[112] Walmart was not banned from accepting food stamps but was required to have a monitor for two years to oversee reforms in its accounting practices for classifying payments and requiring closer supervision of work with government officials in other countries. The SEC's chief for the FCPA unit said, "Walmart valued international growth and cost-cutting over compliance. Walmart repeatedly failed to take red flags seriously."[113]

---

[111]Joann S. Lublin, Aruna Viswanatha, and Sarah Nassauer, "Obstacles Remain in Talks to Settle Wal-Mart Bribery Probe," *Wall Street Journal*, January 27, 2017, https://www.wsj.com/articles/obstacles-remain-in-talks-to-settlewal-mart-bribery-probe-1485546521.

[112]Dave Michaels and Sarah Nassauer, "Walmart to Pay $282 Million in Settlement of Bribery Probe," *Wall Street Journal*, June 21, 2019, p. B3.

[113]*Id.*

Discussion Questions

1. Why do we worry about these types of payments if the result is more jobs for those in Mexico, Brazil, and the other countries?

2. Why does it make a difference whether the payments were bribe or "grease"/facilitation payments?

3. Why was general counsel pushing for a "no payments to government officials" policy?

4. Why did Walmart keep its findings from the federal government? Describe the benefits of self-reporting.

5. Subsequent to the discovery of the payments in Mexico, issues about Walmart behaviors in India emerged. A business consultant there said that the payments result because it is so difficult to open businesses in India and that "All of these conditions have only made India a poorer country."[114] Eventually Walmart pulled out of India because of the difficulty in opening businesses there.[115] However, it returned and, through payments similar to those made in Mexico and Brazil, was able to grow the business there. Do the restrictions or the bribery hurt the country's economy more?

---

[114]Vikas Bajaj, "India Unit of Wal-Mart Suspends Employees," *New York Times*, November 24, 2012, p. B1.

[115]Garinder Harris, "Wal-Mart Drops Ambitious Expansion Plan for India," *New York Times*, October 10, 2013, p. B3.

Why Didn't They Say Something? 6.1

The situation at Walmart presents an interesting dilemma. There were those within the company who were speaking up but were ignored or told "to relax." What materials from Units 1 and 2 would provide those employees with some suggestions on how to address the seriousness of the issues they were seeing?

Case 6.13

GlaxoSmithKline in China

It all began with a raid by Chinese officials on a small travel agency in Shanghai. What the investigators found were fake contracts and travel invoices that were used to cover payments to doctors, hospitals, foundations, government officials, and anyone else who had connections to China's health care industry.[116] The investigation and raid resulted from Chinese government concerns about a widespread market for fake receipts. The fake receipts are used as a front by pharmaceutical companies to funnel money and perks to individuals in the health care system. The purpose of these types of gifts, cash and otherwise, is to influence decision makers in the system to recommend the use of a particular pharmaceutical company's drugs.

Travel agencies were an ideal source for the receipts because pharmaceutical companies do indeed arrange for travel for physicians to medical conferences, a type of perk that is permitted under both the FCPA and U.S. laws and regulations. However, providing escorts, shopping sprees, and cash go well beyond permitted conference benefits. The travel agency was, however, a way to accomplish those secondary and illegal perks under the guise of the protected perks. For example, the *Wall Street Journal* obtained an itinerary from a three-day trip that GSK arranged for 30 doctors to get them to begin using Botox. The trip was to Guilin, a city where you can take in Elephant Trunk Hill and Seven Stars Park.[117] One doctor said she learned a great deal on the trip even though there was no space on the itinerary for Botox training. The doctors also received a lecture fee for attending.

Following the Chinese government investigation, the July 2013 conclusion was that use of the small Shanghai travel agency was part of a conspiracy that involved tens of millions of dollars and had gone on for years and involved senior executives at GlaxoSmithKline (GSK).[118] As Chinese officials outlined their case at a news conference, the following allegations emerged:

- GSK had organized fictitious conferences to cover the payments.

- GSK then used the fictitious receipts generated by the travel agency to obtain reimbursement from their companies for payments made to the health care officials, hospitals, doctors, and foundations.

- Bribery was part of the strategy of the company.

- GSK used cash, luxury travel, and young women to engage in sexual activities.[119]

One of the investigators said, "It's like a criminal organization—there's always a boss. And in this case, GSK is the boss." The police announced just before the press conference that several GSK executives had confessed to bribery and tax fraud.[120] The four GSK executives were Chinese nationals taken into custody and included GSK's head of the legal department, head of business development, and two vice presidents. Mark Reilly, GSK's head of Chinese operations, a British national, left China shortly after the raid of the Shanghai travel agency.[121] The Chinese prohibited GSK's finance chief, Steve Nechelput, from leaving the country.[122]

The U.K.'s Serious Fraud office had already begun an investigation into GSK activities in China based on an anonymous tip that it received in January 2013. The tipster also sent the information to GSK, something that was reported in the *Wall Street Journal* at the time. GSK conducted a four-month investigation but concluded that it found no evidence of wrongdoing.[123] Two months later the Chinese government found the wrongdoing for them. Finally, on July 23, 2013, GSK issued a statement that it had found that several of its senior executives in China accused of engaging in bribery had violated Chinese law.[124]

GSK explained that the executives, who knew the company systems well, "have acted outside of our

(continued)

---

[116]David Barboza, "A Graft Case in China May Expand," *New York Times*, July 22, 2013, p. B1.

[117]*Id.*

[118]David Barboza, "Glaxo Used Travel Firms for Bribery, China Says," *New York Times*, July 16, 2013, p. B1.

[119]*Id.*

[120]*Id.*

[121]Jeanne Whalen, Christopher M. Matthews, and Laurie Burkitt, "Amid Bribery Probe, China Bars Glaxo Official from Leaving," *Wall Street Journal*, July 18, 2013, p. B3.

[122]*Id.*

[123]Christopher M. Matthews and Jeanne Whalen, "Two Accusers Get Differing Responses from Glaxo," *Wall Street Journal*, July 25, 2013, p. B1.

[124]Laurie Burkitt and Jeanne Whalen, "Glaxo Cites Possible China Violations," *Wall Street Journal*, July 23, 2013, p. B3.

Case 6.13

(continued)

processes and controls."[125] GSK apologized, pledged cooperation with Chinese authorities, and reduced prices of its drugs in China in response to what it believed may have been prices set through illegal control of the market.

In June 2014, one year after the bribery charges became public, a "sex tape" emerged that had been shot of Mr. Reilly and a partner (Mr. Reilly was separated from his wife at the time). The tape was sent to GSK anonymously while GSK was in the four-month period of investigating the bribery allegations that had come in from another whistleblower.[126]

In September 2014, a Chinese court found GSK guilty of bribery and the company paid a $500 million fine.[127] Five managers were given suspended prison sentences. The trial lasted one day and the fine was, at that time, the largest corporate fine that had ever been imposed in China.

The United States concluded its investigation into the GSK conduct in China in 2016 and GSK paid a $20 million fine to the SEC.[128] GSK fired 110 employees in China following its internal investigation after the Chinese charges.[129]

Discussion Questions

1. Why do you think GSK found nothing based on its whistleblower complaint?

2. What factors would have influenced these behaviors by the GSK staff and executives?

3. What is the impact of bribery on the pharmaceutical market in China?

4. How would you respond if GSK said that it was doing what everyone does in China?

---

[125] Id.

[126]Laurie Burkitt, "Sex Video Sheds Light in Glaxo Case," *Wall Street Journal*, June 30, 2014, p. B3.

[127]Hester Plumridge and Laurie Burkitt, "Glaxo Fined $500 Million by China," *Wall Street Journal*, September 20–21, 2014, p. B1.

[128]Matt Robinson, "Glaxo to Pay $20 Million SEC Fine over Bribery in China," *Bloomberg News*, September 30, 2016, http://www.bloomberg.com/news/articles/2016-09-30/glaxo-to-pay-20-million-sec-fine-over-bribing-chinese-officials. Last visited October 28, 2016.

[129]Andrew Ward, "GSK Fires 110 Staff in China after Corruption Scandal," *Financial Times*, March 6, 2015, https://www.ft.com/content/9a72fa68-c44e-11e4-a949-00144feab7de. Last visited October 28, 2016.

History Repeats

The Lessons of Bribery Not Learned

As you review the four cases in Section B on bribery, you should see patterns in behaviors and business strategies. List those patterns and discuss what you would watch for in a company that was conducting international business.

Key terms

Categorical imperative   p. 444
Disgorgement   p. 467

Foreign Corrupt Practices Act (FCPA)   p. 465
Grease or facilitation payments   p. 437, 467

Ethics, Business Operations, and Rights

> Whenever there is fear, you will get wrong figures.
>
> —**W. Edwards Deming**

Learning Objectives

- Discuss the risks in having two sets of books for reporting purposes and actual internal results.

- Explain how compensation systems affect safety and operations.

- Develop a list of the types of workplace conflicts and how they affect results and operations.

- Analyze the effects the ethics of leaders have on the organization's culture.

- Provide the processes for confrontation of coworkers and leaders on ethical concerns and issues.

- List the areas of concern in workplace diversity.

This unit deals with the interrelationships of companies, managers, and employees and the rights of all those employees. From safety risks to questions of employee privacy and on through to the obligations of employees to throw down the flag when they are concerned about issues and practices in the workplace, this section grapples with the delicate balances required for preserving a safe work environment with open communication.

Workplace Safety

Reading 7.1

Using Two Sets of Books for One Set of Data

Following a 12-day trial in 2012, Walter Cardin, a safety manager for the Shaw Group, was convicted of eight counts of fraud against the United States for falsifying injury reports for his company's work at the TVA's Brown's Ferry Nuclear Station. Based on the false reports, the Shaw Group was able to collect safety bonuses worth over $2.5 million from TVA. The jury heard evidence of over 80 injuries, including broken bones; torn ligaments; hernias; lacerations; and shoulder, back, and knee injuries that were not properly recorded by Mr. Cardin. The Shaw Group has paid back twice the amount of the ill-gotten safety bonuses as well as a $1.6 million fine in the Brown's Ferry project.[1]

Workers Comp vs. OSHA Reportables

The problem of interpretation of what is and is not an injury has been growing and seems to be pervasive. OSHA 2020 reportable figures (as found in the Bureau of Labor Statistics), or those injury statistics reported by employers, are 25% lower than the number of injuries the study found in worker compensation claims. Injuries have declined since 2000, as have fatalities, particularly during the COVID lockdown periods.

Workers' comp numbers are the real thing. Employees don't care what employers report to OSHA—they want coverage for work-related injuries. Why the disparity? Some believe that because incentive plans include safety goals related to the injury rate, managers are motivated to put pressure on workers to not report injuries. Some managers even pressure doctors into characterizing an injury as non-work related. Other managers ask doctors to write a different diagnosis to avoid a reportable injury. Employees often share stories about their managers going with them to the hospital or doctor to get the injury characterized in the "right" way.

There is always the wiggle room of technical compliance with the lost workday reporting requirements. Without question, federal regulations on reportable injuries are confusing, and reasonable minds could differ on some close calls. However, interpretations seem to cut a wide swath. For example, if an employee can return to work, the injury is not classified as a lost workday. Dr. Robert McClellan, formerly the president of the American College of Occupational and Environmental Medicine, often cites an example of a worker being wheeled onto a construction site with his

---

[1]OSHA Quick Takes, July 2, 2012, http://passregion2.typepad.com/pass/osha-quick-takes/.

broken leg to avoid a lost workday report. So, an employee reported for beam work with a cast and in a wheelchair, and there was no OSHA reportable injury.

Nursing Home Staffing Levels

Beyond the OSHA and Bureau of Labor Statistics numbers, there are also the nursing home numbers on staff levels. Appropriate staff levels are necessary for Medicare approval for care facilities. To avoid the costs of Medicare-level staffing but still meet those levels for purposes of being rated, nursing homes have **two sets of books**. One set is for Medicare reporting and the second set has the actual number of employees and their hours for purposes of payroll taxes. The second set contains fewer numbers of employees. More than one-half of the facilities met Medicare staffing levels less than 20% of the time when actual wage-and-hour records are compared with the self-reporting Medicare staffing levels.[2]

In 2018, Medicare began requiring the submission of the tax records for review of staffing levels. Even with this change that now brings both sets of books to Medicare, there is a loophole. Medicare may have an actual employee count but will not be able to tell if those listed as having worked are qualified to give nursing care. That would require going through each report and obtaining staff qualifications.

Medicare also provides a rating system for nursing homes, but the nursing homes self-report the data for the ratings, including staffing levels and infection rates. In addition, the homes were notified in advance of the ratings inspections. Those homes with a five-star rating are permitted to charge more for the care that they provide.

Discussion Questions

1. What are the parallels between this part of business reporting and financial reports?

2. What risks do you see in keeping two sets of books?

3. What happens to safety and patient care as a result of these approaches to reporting?

4. What lessons about self-reporting are important for regulators to learn from these examples?

---

[2]Alex Kacik, "Nursing Home Staffing Levels Often Fall Below CMS Expectations," *Modern Healthcare*, July 1, 2019, https://www.modernhealthcare.com/providers/nursing-home-staffing-levels-often-fall-below-cms-expectations.

Ethics in Action 7.1

COVID Nursing Home Deaths and Two Sets of Death Numbers

In the state of New York, 15,000 residents in nursing homes died of COVID, a number that comprises one-third of all COVID deaths in the state.[3] One of the reasons for the high death rate was an executive order issued on March 25, 2020, that required that "[n]o resident [of a nursing home] shall be denied

---

[3]Jimmy Vielkind, "Cuomo Rebuked over Data," *New York Times*, February 13–14, 2021, p. A7.

re-admission or admission to the nursing home solely based on a confirmed or suspected diagnosis of COVID-19. Nursing homes are prohibited from requiring a hospitalized resident who is determined medically stable to be tested for COVID-19 prior to admission or re-admission."[4] This guidance was eventually rescinded on May 10, 2020.

An investigation by the New York Attorney General (NYOAG) found that the number of deaths in nursing home due to COVID was understated by 55.74%.[5] The reason for the understatement was that the nursing homes did not count the deaths of their residents if they died after being transferred to a hospital. For the state of New York, then-governor Andrew Cuomo held off releasing the true number of nursing home deaths to state legislators because of political reasons.

In recordings of a meeting between the legislators and a senior Cuomo aide, the aide explained:

"We froze. We were in a position where we weren't sure if what we were going to give to the Department of Justice or what we give to you guys and what we start saying was going to be used against us and we weren't sure if there was going to be an investigation."[6]

At the time of the meeting with the legislators, the *New York Times* had already uncovered the underreporting of nursing home deaths and Mr. Cuomo's book, *American Crisis: Leadership Lessons from the COVID-19 Pandemic* was just being released. Also, at the time of the hearing, the nursing homes had changed their methods for reporting nursing home deaths following the report by the NYOAG report.

Discussion Questions

1. What were the risks and benefits to stakeholders of higher vs. lower numbers?

2. What do you see as the motivation behind two sets of numbers in any industry or situation?

3. What does the adage, "Figures don't lie but liars do figure" mean?

4. Also part of the NYOAG report was a finding of a correlation between Medicare's adequate staffing rating for the nursing homes and the death rate. 1 was the lowest rating for staffing, and 5 was the highest. The lower the staff rating, the higher the death rate. Also, the lower the staff rating, the less the nursing home can charge its occupants. Explain what motivation the rating systems played in the reporting of deaths.

---

[4]New York State Office of the Attorney General Letitia James (NYOAG), "Nursing Home Response to COVID-19 Pandemic," January 30, 2020, p. 11, https://ag.ny.gov/press-release/2021/attorney-general-james-releases-report-nursing-homes-response-covid-19.
[5]NYOAG, p. 36. DOH, Advisory: Hospital Discharges and Admissions to Nursing Homes, March 25, 2020.
[6]Jesse McKinley, Danny Hakim, and Alexandra Alter, "Celebratory Memoir by Cuomo Undercut by Covid Data Report," *New York Times*, April 1, 2021, p. A1.

Why Didn't They Say Something? 7.1

We All Knew

Nursing home medical directors, staff, and the families of the patients were aware of the problems with COVID in the nursing homes as well as the high death numbers. Yet it was not until the August legislative hearing, months after the March order on requiring nursing homes to accept COVID patients, that the issues emerged. Many of the families said that they were unable to break through the government bureaucracies. Others said they were ignored. Others said that media outlets were not interested in their concerns. Janice Dean, who lost both her mother-in-law and father-in-law (both in nursing homes) to COVID, wrote in *USA Today:*

> At first, we didn't blame anyone for their deaths. This is a pandemic, and the virus is particularly dangerous for the elderly. Then we learned about the Cuomo administration's March 25 order that recovering coronavirus patients be placed into nursing homes. The mandate also barred nursing homes from requiring incoming patients "to be tested for COVID-19 prior to admission or readmission."
>
> That order stayed in effect for 46 days during which time over 6,000 patients with the virus were placed into these facilities housing our most vulnerable. To date, at least 6,500 of our most helpless seniors have been killed by the virus. Even the governor himself said the virus could sweep though nursing homes "like fire though dry grass."[7]

1. Who can help with issues that fail to gain the attention of those in charge of the issue?

2. What do you learn about the limits of speaking up?

[7]Janice Dean, "COVID-19 Killed My In-Laws After Cuomo's Reckless New York Nursing Home Policy," *USA Today,* July 22, 2020, https://www.usatoday.com/story/opinion /voices/2020/07/22/andrew-cuomo-nursing-homes-coronavirus-janice-dean-new-york -column/5472713002/.

Case 7.2

Cintas and the Production Line

In 2007, Eleazar Torres-Gomez fell into an industrial dryer at the Cintas plant where he worked. He was trapped for 20 minutes in the dryer at a temperature of 300°.[8] He was killed before anyone noticed that he had fallen into the dryer from the moving conveyor belt where he was picking up loose clothes. The manufacturer of the equipment provides warnings about not having people on the conveyor belt while it is moving. Warnings on the belt caution Cintas employees not to get on the belt while it is moving. All Cintas employees received training that warned them against getting onto the moving belts at any time. However, surveillance tapes show that at the Tulsa plant where Mr. Torres-Gomez worked and at other Cintas plants the practice was routine. The tapes show employees jumping on the moving belts to clear jams of clothing

(continued)

[8]Steven Greenhouse, "U.S. Proposes $2.78 Million Fine in Worker's Death," *New York Times,* August 18, 2007, https://www .nytimes.com/2007/08/18/washington/18cintas.html.

Case 7.2

(continued)

as they headed into the dryer chutes. Some tapes even showed employees sticking their knees into the chutes as a means of unclogging the clumps of wet laundry making their way into the dryer from the moving belts.

Cintas had an internal memo from its director of safety in 2004 that cautioned the plants about the problem and required plant managers to implement several safety procedures before trying to dislodge laundry. The procedures were not followed at the Tulsa plant.

In interviews with OSHA officials, employees said that they were under a great deal of pressure to keep the laundry moving and not shut down the belt. Cintas has per-piece goals for employees to meet, but Cintas officials say that the goals established for employees are reasonable.

Cintas has had 70 OSHA investigations since 2002, more than any other laundry company, and OSHA has found violations in 40 of the investigations. Forty-two of the violations found were "willful." Cintas felt that it had more inspections because a union organizing effort was ongoing, and employees were reporting violations even when there are no violations. Nonetheless, Cintas settled the case with OSHA, agreeing to pay a $2.8 million fine, a penalty four times larger than any previous OSHA penalty.[9] Cintas also agreed, as part of the settlement, to implement new protections and enhanced safety programs.

By 2011, Cintas had changed its safety vision and practices. Cintas became the first industrial laundry (located in Chandler, Arizona) to achieve OSHA "Star"

status in OSHA's Voluntary Protection Programs (VPP). The program is, as it is aptly named, voluntary, but requires the implementation of management systems to reduce injury rates below industry averages and requires the involvement of company executives and employees at all levels as they work together for what Cintas calls its every-facility-injury-free program. The manager at the Chandler plant said that they work together to be sure that every employee "gets home every day injury free."[10] Productivity has also improved, with the facility processing 210,000 pounds of uniforms, towels, mats, and linens per week. By 2015, 10% of Cintas's plants had achieved VPP status.[11]

Discussion Questions

1. Based on what you learned in Reading 4.6 on compensation and the accompanying cases, discuss what happens to employees who are given goals to meet. What happens to the culture and compliance with rules?

2. What were the values in conflict at Cintas that resulted in the accident and death?

3. What has Cintas changed since the time of the death of an employee? What have been the results?

Source: Bandler, James, and Kris Maher, "House Panel to Examine Cintas Plants' Safety Record," *Wall Street Journal*, April 23, 2008, pp. B1, B2.

[9]Bruce Beggs, "Cintas Faces $2.78 Million in OSHA Fines," *American Laundry News*, August 17, 2007, https://americanlaundrynews.com /articles/cintas-faces-278-million-osha-fines.

[10]"OSHA 'Star' Plant: Cintas' First," *TRSA100+*, January 25, 2011, https://www.trsa.org/news/osha-star-plant-cintas-first/.

[11]"Cintas' Portland Plant Gains OSHA Safety Star," *Laundry and Cleaning News International*, October 26, 2015, https://www .laundryandcleaningnews.com/news/newscintas-portland-plant -gains-osha-safety-star-4701892.

Case 7.3

Theranos: The Lab That Wasn't Safe or Real and Fake the Numbers Until You Make It

In 2003, Elizabeth Holmes, founder and CEO and sophomore dropout of Stanford, established Theranos. Theranos was a health care technology company that Holmes envisioned would change the way patients

had blood screens, for the better. Her vision was that by using just a few drops of blood from a finger prick, she would be able to provide lab results quickly and inexpensively.

(continued)

Case 7.3

(continued)

The Fast and Impressive Start

As the company raised $9 billion in capital, Ms. Holmes became the first female billionaire in the Silicon Valley.[12] The board was an impressive and credentialed group, including former U.S. senators Sam Nunn and Bill Frist, former secretary of defense William Perry, former five-star general James Mattis (who resigned in 2016 when he became secretary of defense in the Trump administration), former secretaries of state George Shultz and Henry Kissinger, as well as former U.S. Navy admiral Gary Roughead.

In 2013, Tyler Shultz, the grandson of George Shultz, was hired by Theranos. However, eight months into his work there, he realized that those in the company were doctoring the results of the tests being run by Edison, the name of the Theranos blood screening device.[13] He asked to speak with Ms. Holmes but was rebuffed and received a letter from Ramesh "Sunny" Balwani, the former chief operating officer of Theranos and boyfriend of Ms. Holmes, that indicated he was responding only because of his grandfather's position on the Theranos board. Tyler Shultz quit his job and notified his grandfather. George Shultz then resigned from the board and notified the state of New York about Theranos and its manipulation of test results. That report was the first report made to regulators, but it would not be the last regulatory body to begin investigations of Theranos.

The CME Investigation and Lab Difficulties

By 2016, the company was struggling with meeting federal government standards in its labs. The Centers for Medicare and Medicaid Services (CME) found five violations at the company's lab that posed "immediate jeopardy to patient health and safety" and would be likely to cause, at any time, serious injury or harm, or death, to individuals served by the laboratory or to the health and safety of the general public."[14] Ms. Holmes explained that the CME inspections and letter did not reflect current conditions at the lab.[15]

At that time, the only test for which Theranos had been given outside approval was for herpes. Just before the CME complaint letter, Theranos hired a new lab director, a certified pathologist, Dr. Kingshuk Das.[16]

Walgreens Pulls Out

Because of the CME findings, Walgreens, Theranos's main retail partner, began raising questions but was not receiving satisfactory answers. Walgreens had already invested $50 million in Theranos and was debating whether to close the 41 wellness centers it had set up for Theranos lab screening. There was no revenue being generated, and Theranos was not providing any financial information. Walgreens was able to confirm that Theranos was outsourcing testing to labs at the University of California San Francisco (UCSF) and ARUP Labs, affiliated with the University of Utah. Theranos was charging patients $7.19 for a comprehensive blood screen. UCSF was charging Theranos $300 to run the screen.[17] In 2016, a *Wall Street Journal* report emerged that found that the majority of tests that Theranos was offering were being run on traditional lab machines and not its Edison machine with its alleged breakthrough technology.[18] Theranos refused to disclose how many of its tests were being run on commercial machines and refused to disclose the results from its Edison machines.[19] Slowly but surely, Theranos was looking more and more like a fraudulent operation.

In 2016, Walgreens filed suit against Theranos, alleging breach of contract for its failure to develop the blood-testing machines it had promised for 40 stores. Theranos shut down its blood-testing operations and said that it would focus on selling products to outside labs. The decision was fueled in part by federal regulators

(continued)

---

[12]Sara Ashley O'Brien, "Elizabeth Holmes Trial: Journalist Who Helped 'Raise to Prominence' Theranos CEO Takes Witness Stand," *CNN Business,* November 18, 2021, https://edition.cnn.com/2021/11/18/tech/elizabeth-holmes-trial-roger-parloff/index.html.

[13]Marco della Cava, "Theranos' Dramatic Rise, Fall," *USA Today,* March 16, 2018, p. 1B.

[14]John Carreyrou, "'Deficient Practices' A Found at Theranos," *Wall Street Journal,* January 28, 2016, p. A1.

[15]Id.

[16]John Carreyrou, Christopher Weaver, and Michael Siconolfi, "Problems Found at Theranos Lab," *Wall Street Journal,* January 26, 2016, p. B1.

[17]Id. at B10.

[18]Mason Wilder, "Theranos' Appeal Not Enough to Cover Up Massive Alleged Fraud" *ACFE Insights,* https://www.acfeinsights.com/acfe-insights/theranos-elizabeth-holmes-massive-alleged-fraud.

[19]John Carreyrou, "Theranos Executive to Exit Amid Probes," *Wall Street Journal,* May 12, 2016, p. B1.

Case 7.3

(continued)

banishing founder Elizabeth Holmes from the blood-testing industry for two years.[20]

Reshuffling the Board and Exiting Sunny

Also in 2016, Mr. Balwani left Theranos and Ms. Holmes brought Fabrizio J. Bonanni, a retired Amgen vice president, Dr. William H. Foege, the former director of the Centers for Disease Control and Prevention, and Richard M. Kovacevich, a former CEO of Wells Fargo, onto its board.[21] Those changes were made as the U.S. Securities and Exchange Commission (SEC) continued its investigation into the company.

When a Theranos employee raised concerns about the company's research and test results, he also requested a meeting with Ms. Holmes. When rebuffed, the employee contacted the *Wall Street Journal*. The *Wall Street Journal* then published a critical report on Theranos, alleging rampant management incompetence based on interviews with ex-employees.[22] The report concluded that Theranos had inflated the capabilities of its proprietary technology. Just prior to publication of that article, Ms. Holmes was still working to raise another $200 million in capital for the company. Ms. Holmes approached Rupert Murdoch seeking his help in quashing the story because his News Corporation owns the *Wall Street Journal*, but Mr. Murdoch refused to intervene.

The SEC Steps In

In 2018, the SEC charged Ms. Holmes and Mr. Balwani with securities fraud. By that time, Theranos had raised nearly $1 billion from investors through an elaborate, years-long fraud in which they made false statements about the company's technology, business, and financial performance.[23] The $1 billion was gone.[24] Among those who lost all of their investment in Theranos were Betsy DeVos (former secretary of education) and her family, Larry Ellison (CEO of Oracle), the Walmart family heirs, Rupert Murdoch, the Cox family, Robert Kraft, Riley Bechtel (former chairman of Bechtel Construction), and Carlos Slim.[25] Mr. Murdoch had invested $125 million in Theranos but sold his shares back to the company in 2015 for $1 per share. Although the company was a fraud, the richest of the rich had invested in it.[26]

The Trial of Holmes

Testimony at the trial revealed that Theranos secretly ran its blood tests on commercial devices because its technology only did 12 blood screens and the results on those tests were implausible. The technology never worked.[27] Ms. Holmes, who testified at her trial, said that she relied on Mr. Balwani for information about how the product development was going and that he was the source of her information that she shared with investors. However, one of the key pieces of evidence was that Ms. Holmes affixed the logos of pharmaceuticals such as Pfizer on documents to show investors when Pfizer had not validated the Theranos technology.[28] She also misrepresented to investors that Theranos had contracts with the military for handling its field testing when it did not.

Also at the trial, Dr. Adam Rosendorff, once the lab director at Theranos, testified that nine days before the product launch for patients (August 31, 2013), Ms. Holmes asked in an email how many tests for their product had completed federal regulatory guidelines. The completion of this testing is required by the federal government before it can be used for patients. A staff member responded that the answer

(continued)

---

[20]Christopher Weaver, John Carreyrou, and Michael Siconolfi, "Walgreens Takes Theranos to Court," *Wall Street Journal*, November 9, 2016, p. B1.

[21]Reed Abelson, "Blood-Testing Firm Takes Steps to Regain Confidence," *New York Times*, May 12, 2016, p. B3.

[22]John Carreyrou, *Bad Blood: Secrets and Lies in a Silicon Valley Startup* (2018).

[23]John Carreyrou and Christopher Weaver, "Theranos Retreats from Blood Tests," *Wall Street Journal*, October 6, 2016, p. A1.

[24]Heather Sommerville, "Intent Is at Heart of Case Against Holmes," *Wall Street Journal*, November 22, 2021, p. B4.

[25]John Carreyrou, "Theranos Hurt Big-Name Investors," *Wall Street Journal*, May 4, 2018, p. B1.

[26]Carreyrou, "Theranos Hurt Big-Name Investors." at B2.

[27]Reed Abelson, "U.S. Regulator Finds a Theranos Lab Violated Some Blood Test Standards," *New York Times*, January 28, 2016, p. B3; Laura Kusisto and Sara Randazzo, "Intent Key to Holmes Prosecution," *Wall Street Journal*, September 8, 2021, p. B3.

[28]"The Theranos Fraud," *Wall Street Journal*, January 5, 2022, p. A14.

Case 7.3

(continued)

was none.[29] The tests continued to produce inaccurate and implausible results. Dr. Rosendorff left Theranos in 2014. By 2017, the Centers for Medicare and Medicaid Services and other regulators were suspending Theranos labs for their flaws in operations that put patients at risk.[30]

Ms. Holmes was convicted on 4 of the 11 charges of fraud.[31] Mr. Balwani's trial followed Ms. Holmes's conviction. Mr. Balwani was convicted on 12 of 12 counts of fraud.[32] His fraud counts related to patient fraud whereas Ms. Holmes was convicted of securities fraud charges.

Discussion Questions

1. One of the issues in the case is related to proving intent to deceive (defraud) investors. The defense argued that everyone knows start-ups fail. The issue was whether Ms. Holmes knew that the technology was not working and that the results were not accurate. What information in the case points to intentional deceit?

2. What two sets of numbers patterns existed at Theranos?

3. How was Ms. Holmes able to convince so many impressive people about her company and its plan?

4. What conflicts of interest do you see in the case?

5. Evaluate the actions of Tyler and George Shultz.

[29]Heather Somerville, "Lab Director Raised Alarm About Theranos Tests," *Wall Street Journal*, September 25–26, 2021, p. B1.

[30]Christopher Weaver, "Theranos Hit with Sanctions Over Lab," *Wall Street Journal*, February 23, 2017, p. B5.

[31]Erin Griffith and Erin Woo, "Holmes Guilty on Four Charges in Fraud Case," *New York Times*, January 4, 2022, p. A1.

[32]Heather Somerville and Meghan Bobrowsky, "Second Top Theranos Leader Convicted in Federal Fraud Case," *Wall Street Journal*, July 8, 2022, p. A1.

Case 7.4

Aaron Feuerstein and Malden Mills[33]

The late Aaron Feuerstein was the third generation chief executive officer and chairman of the board of Malden Mills, a privately held company started in Massachusetts that produced fabric and evolved to manufacture Polartec, an advanced fleece fabric that became a favorite of outdoor clothiers. Located in Methuen, Massachusetts, its success from Polartec came not only from the fabric's functionality but also that it is a fabric made from recycled plastic that stays dry and provides warmth. Polartec was used in everything from ski parkas to blankets by companies such as L.L. Bean, Patagonia, Lands' End, and Eddie Bauer. Malden employed 2,400 locals, and Mr. Feuerstein and his family steadfastly refused to move production overseas as other fabric producers were making that transition. Malden's labor costs were the highest in the industry—then an average of $12.50 per hour. Malden Mills was also the largest employer in what was, and remains, one of Massachusetts's poorest towns.

On December 11, 1995, a boiler explosion at Malden Mills resulted in a fire that injured 27 people and destroyed three of the buildings at Malden Mills's factory site. With only one building left in functioning order, many employees assumed they would be laid off temporarily. Other employees worried that Mr. Feuerstein, then 70 years old, would simply take the insurance money and retire. Mr. Feuerstein could have retired with about $300 million in insurance proceeds from the fire.

Instead, Mr. Feuerstein announced on December 14, 1995, that he would pay the employees their salaries for at least 30 days. He continued that promise for six months, when 90% of the employees were back to work. The cost to the company of covering the wages was approximately $25 million. During that time, Malden ran its Polartec through its one working facility as it began and completed the reconstruction of the plant, at a cost of $430 million. Only $300 million of that amount was covered by the insurance on the plant; the remainder was borrowed so that Malden Mills would be a state-of-the-art, environmentally friendly plant. Interestingly, production output during this time was nine times what it had been before the fire. One worker noted, "I owe him everything. I'm paying him back."[34] After the fire and Feuerstein's announcement, customers pledged their support, with one customer, Dakotah, sending in $30,000 to help. Within the first month following the fire, Malden Mills received $1 million in donations.[35]

Malden Mills was rededicated in September 1997 with new buildings and technology. About 10% of the 2,400 employees were displaced by the upgraded facilities and equipment, but Feuerstein created a job training and placement center on site to ease these employees' transition to other types of jobs.

By the end of 2001, six years after the fire, Malden Mills had debts of $140 million and was teetering near

(continued)

---

[33]Adapted from Marianne M. Jennings, "Aaron Feuerstein—an Odd CEO," in *Business: Its Legal, Ethical, and Global Environment*, 9th ed. (2017), pp. 634–635.

[34]"Maiden Mills," *Dateline NBC*, August 9, 1996.

[35]Steve Wulf, "The Glow from a Fire," *Time*, January 8, 1996, p. 49.

Case 7.4

(continued)

bankruptcy. However, Malden Mills had been through bankruptcy before, in the 1980s, and emerged very strongly with its then new product, Polartec, developed through the company's R&D program.

Some have suggested that Mr. Feuerstein's generosity during that time after the fire was responsible for the resulting financial crisis. However, the fire destroyed the company's furniture upholstery division, and customers became impatient. They were not inclined to wait for production to ramp up, and Malden Mills lost most of those customers. It closed the upholstery division in 1996.

Also, the threat of inexpensive fleece from the Asian markets was ignored largely because of the plant rebuilding and the efforts focused there. Finally, in 2000, the company had a shakeup in its marketing team just as it was launching its electric fabrics—fabrics with heatable wires that are powered by batteries embedded in the fleece.

Once again, however, the goodwill from 1995 remained. Residents of the town sent in checks to help the company, some as small as $10, and began an Internet campaign to "Buy Fleece." The campaign enjoyed some success as Patagonia, Lands' End, and L.L. Bean reported increased demand. In addition, the U.S. military placed large orders for fleece jackets for soldiers fighting in Operation Enduring Freedom in Afghanistan.

Then-senators Ted Kennedy and John Kerry lobbied GE not to involuntarily petition Malden Mills into bankruptcy. GE Capital held one-fourth of Malden Mills' debts. Its other creditors included Finova Capital, SAI Investment, Pilgrim Investment, LaSalle Bank, and PNC Bank. The lobbying was to no avail. By 2002, Malden Mills was in bankruptcy. Feuerstein labored to raise the money to pay off creditors and buy his company back, but he was unable to meet the bankruptcy deadline. Malden Mills emerged from bankruptcy on September 30, 2003, but under management other than Mr. Feuerstein. He still hoped to buy the company back, but the price, originally $93 million, had increased to $120 million. Feuerstein served as the president of Malden Mills and on its board, for a salary of $425,000 per year, but he was no longer in charge of day-to-day operations or decisions and could not be unless and until the creditors were repaid.

In January 2004, members of the U.S. House and Senate lobbied to convince the Export-Import Bank to loan Mr. Feuerstein the money he needed to buy back his company. The EXIM Bank, swayed by Mr. Feuerstein's commitment to keep Malden's production in the United States, increased the loan amount from the $20 million it had originally pledged to the $35 million Mr. Feuerstein needed.

By the end of January 2004, the new Malden Mills had three changed strategies: Mr. Feuerstein was selling Polarfleece blankets on QVC; the company would be in partnership in China with Shanghai Mills; and the company announced it would expand its military contracts. Mr. Feuerstein remained as president and chairman of the board.

The patience of the company's union was wearing thin. During the 2002–2003 time frame of the bankruptcy, the union leader said, "We're ready to make sacrifices for a little while. Whatever he asks us to do to keep the place going."[36] However, a threatened strike in December 2004 resulted in negotiations and a new union three-year contract, a more expensive one for the company.

As for Mr. Feuerstein, his view is simple: "There are times in business when you don't think of the financial consequences, but of the human consequences. There is no doubt this company will survive."[37] In 2006, Malden Mills landed a $16 million contract with the U.S. Department of Defense to be a supplier of the lightweight Polartec blankets for the U.S. military branches. By February 2007, private equity investors took over the company, now known as Polartec LLC, owned by Chrysalis Partners. By July 2007, the company announced its last shipment from the factory, and the factory has been closed. The Pension Benefit Guaranty Corporation (PBGC) had to take over the underfunded pension (it was underfunded by 49%) for the 1,500 Malden employees who were trying to start their own fabric-making enterprise. However, the assets of the company were sold, and the missed pension plan payments allowed the PBGC to end its commitment. The employees lost one-half of their pensions.

(continued)

---

[36]Lynnley Browning, "Fire Could Not Stop a Mill, but Debts May," *New York Times*, November 28, 2001, pp. C1, C5.
[37]Id., p. C1

Case 7.4

(continued)

Four of the five buildings of Malden Mills were purchased by a developer and turned into a mixed-income community.[38] Mr. Feuerstein passed away on November 4, 2021, at the age of 95.

Discussion Questions

1. Mr. Feuerstein once stated, "I don't deserve credit. Corporate America has made it so that when you behave the way I did, it's abnormal." Given the final outcome, did Mr. Feuerstein end up in the same position as the CEOs of failed companies?

2. Mr. Feuerstein is a Talmudic scholar who often quotes the following proverbs:

   "In a situation where there is no righteous person, try to be a righteous person."

   "Not all who increase their wealth are wise."[39]

   Did he live by the proverbs? What wisdom for your credo comes from these two insights?

3. Did the fact that Malden Mills is privately held make a difference in Mr. Feuerstein's flexibility?

4. Did Mr. Feuerstein focus too much on benevolence and not enough on business? Did he rely only on goodwill to survive, and did he neglect the basics of strategy, marketing, and addressing the competition? At the time of his 90th birthday in 2015, he said, "[I]n our business schools we're taught the object of business is 100 percent profitability to the shareholder. The people who own the place are the ones who have to get 100 percent profitability, not 99 percent, not 98 percent. They have to have it all. That is most unfortunate." Is he correct or is a balance necessary?

---

[38]Joan Vennochi, "'The Mensch of Malden Mills' at 90," *Boston Globe*, November 29, 2015, https://www.bostonglobe.com /opinion/editorials/2015/11/29/the-mensch-malden-mills /0BvhlVZgPxveuD9s9eAY1O/story.html.

[39]Rabbi Avi Shafran, "Bankruptcy and Wealthy," *Society Today*, July 29, 2007, https://aish.com/48881397/

Case 7.5

JCPenney and Its Wealthy Buyer

Purchasing agent Jim G. Locklear began his career as a retail buyer with Federated Department Stores in Dallas, where he became known for his eye for fashion and ability to negotiate low prices. After 10 years with Federated, he went to work for Jordan Marsh in Boston in 1987 with an annual salary of $96,000. But three months later, Locklear quit that job to take a position as a housewares buyer with JCPenney, so he could return to Dallas. His salary was $56,000 per year; he was 38 years old; he owed support payments totaling $900 per month for four children from four marriages; and the bank was threatening to foreclose on his $500,000 mortgage.[40]

Locklear was a good performer for Penney. His products sold well, and he was responsible for the very successful JCPenney Home Collection, a color-coordinated line of dinnerware, flatware, and glasses that was eventually copied by most other tabletop retailers. Locklear took sales of Penney's tabletop line from $25 million to $45 million per year and was named the company's "Buyer of the Year" several times.

However, Locklear was taking payments from Penney's vendors directly and through front companies. Some paid him to get information about bids or to obtain contracts, whereas others paid what they believed to be advertising fees to various companies that were fronts owned by Locklear. Between 1987 and 1992, Locklear took in $1.5 million in "fees" from Penney's vendors.

(continued)

---

[40]Andrea Gerlin, "How a Penney Buyer Made Up to $1.5 Million on Vendors' Kickbacks," *Wall Street Journal*, February 7, 1995, pp. A1, A18.

Case 7.5

(continued)

Penney hired an investigator in 1989 to look into Locklear's activities, but the investigator uncovered only Mr. Locklear's personal financial difficulties.

During his time as a buyer, Locklear was able to afford a country club membership, resort vacations, luxury vehicles, and large securities accounts. Although his lifestyle was known to those who worked with him, no questions were asked again until 1992, when Penney received an anonymous letter about Locklear and his relationship with a Dallas manufacturer's representative. Penney investigated, uncovered sufficient evidence of payments to file a civil suit to recover those payments, and referred the case to the U.S. attorney in Dallas for criminal prosecution.

Mr. Locklear was charged by the U.S. attorney with mail and wire fraud. Mr. Locklear entered a guilty plea and provided information to the U.S. attorney on suppliers, agents, and manufacturers' reps who had paid him "fees." Mr. Locklear was sentenced to 18 months in prison and fined $50,000. Penney won a $789,000 judgment against him, and Mr. Locklear's assets were attached for collection purposes.[41]

Discussion Questions

1. Given Locklear's lifestyle, why did it take so long for Penney to take action? Do you see any red flags in the facts given?

---

[41]Andrea Gerlin, "J. C. Penney Ex-Employee Sentenced to Jail," *Wall Street Journal*, August 28, 1995, p. A9.

2. A vendor who paid Locklear $25,000 in exchange for a Penney order stated, "It was either pay it or go out of business." Evaluate the ethics of this seller. What rationalizations was he using?

3. Do you agree that both the buyer and the seller are guilty in commercial bribery cases? Is the purchasing agent "more" wrong?

4. Many companies provide guidelines for their purchasing agents on accepting gifts, samples, and favors. For example, under Walmart's "no coffee" policy, its buyers cannot accept even a cup of coffee from a vendor. Any samples or models must be returned to vendors once a sales demonstration is complete. Other companies allow buyers to accept items of minimal value. Still others place a specific dollar limit on the value, such as $25. What problems do you see with any of these policies? What advantages do you see?

5. Describe the problems that can result when buyers accept gifts from vendors and manufacturer's representatives.

6. Mr. Locklear said at his sentencing, "I became captive to greed. Once it was discovered, I felt tremendous relief." Mr. Locklear's pastor said Locklear coached Little League and added, "Our country needs more role models like Jim Locklear."[42] Evaluate these two quotes from an ethical perspective. Are there any lessons for your credo in Mr. Locklear's experience?

---

[42]Id.

Case 7.6

The Trading Desk, Perks, and "Dwarf Tossing"

Wall Street firms dream of acquiring the trading business of a mutual fund like Fidelity Investments. Wooing those Fidelity traders during 2006 resulted in at least one Wall Street firm, Jeffries & Co., going well over the $100 limit that the National Association of Securities Dealers (NASD) places as the upper edge for "stuff" that can be

given by investment firms to traders. The traders were wooed with, among other things:

- A bachelor party in Miami for Fidelity Boston traders, complete with bikini-clad women, free charter flights from Boston to Miami that cost Jeffries $31,000,

(continued)

Case 7.6

(continued)

and hotel suites with a party that included "dwarf tossing"

- Trips to the Super Bowl, all free

- $19,000 for Wimbledon tickets

- $7,000 for U.S. Open tickets

- $2,600 for six bottles of 1998 Opus One wine

- $47,000 in chartered flights from Boston to the Caicos Islands

- $1,200 for Justin Timberlake and Christina Aguilera tickets

- $1,000 for a portable DVD player

- $500 for golf clubs

Jeffries spent a total of $1.6 million on 14 Fidelity traders.[43]

The SEC and the National Association of Securities Dealers (NASD) (now FINRA—Financial Industry Regulatory Authority) brought civil charges against Jeffries and required the firm to pay $5.5 million in fines and $4.2 million to disgorge profits made because of the gifts to the Fidelity traders. The SEC was able to tie the bestowing of the gifts to the timing of trades made by the Fidelity traders.[44]

Fidelity disciplined the brokers when news of the bachelor party trickled back to Boston and the company began looking beneath the tip-of-the-iceberg party.[45]

Following the Fidelity settlement for the employees, Peter Lynch, one of the firm's principals, was investigated, and the SEC discovered that Mr. Lynch was getting tickets to events such as the Ryder Golf Classic and U2 and Santana concerts. Lynch's eclectic tastes aside, he was earning between $3 million and $10 million per year when he solicited through Fidelity employees the $15,948 in tickets. Mr. Lynch agreed to repay the value of the tickets plus interest of $4,183 and also expressed regret: "In asking the Fidelity equity trading desk for occasional help locating tickets, I never intended to do anything inappropriate and I regret having made those requests."

Through his use of the Fidelity traders for tickets, Lynch placed his imprimatur on a system of getting and giving "stuff" for Fidelity's trades. In addition to Mr. Lynch, other Fidelity traders and officers racked up $1.6 million in goodies from brokers who were wooing Fidelity trades. One Fidelity trader commented, "Word is out that the order flow is for sale."

The various reports Fidelity had prepared on the trader goodies and stuff from brokers concluded that the conduct resulted in "adverse publicity, loss of credibility with principal regulators, and a loss of Fund shareholders." The SEC noted, "The tone is set at the top. If higher-ups request tickets from a trading desk, it may send a message that such misconduct is tolerated and could contribute to the breakdown of compliance on the desk."[46] It seems the leap from U2 concert tickets to bachelor parties with "dwarf tossing" as entertainment is relatively shorter than most of those at the top realize.

Discussion Questions

1. Why should we worry about gifts now and then to traders? Aren't all investment firms about the same, offering the same levels of service?

2. Why do NASD, now FINRA, and the SEC worry about traders receiving stuff?

3. Can you draw a definitive line for your credo from this case?

4. What level of discipline would be appropriate for the Fidelity brokers? Was the discipline for Mr. Lynch sufficient?

5. What signals did Mr. Lynch's conduct send to the traders?

---

[43]Greg Farrell, "Jeffries to Pay $9.7 Million to Settle Fidelity Gift Case," *USA Today*, December 5, 2006, p. 9B.

[44]See http://www.sec.gov/news/press/2008/2008-291.htm for press releases. Accessed September 2, 2013.

[45]https://www.marketwatch.com/story/fidelity-brokers-traders -found-by-nasd-in-violation.

[46]Kara Scannell, Susanne Craig, and Jennifer Levitz, "Gifts' Case Nabs a Star," *Wall Street Journal*, March 6, 2008, p. C1.

Case 7.7

The Analyst Who Needed a Preschool

The stock market of the late 1990s and early 2000s represented a period of irrational exuberance. Investors invested as they never had, egged on by analysts who could say no evil of the companies they were to evaluate. For example, Citigroup is the parent company of Salomon Smith Barney, an investment banker and broker whose star telecommunications analyst, Jack Grubman, was perhaps WorldCom's biggest cheerleader.[47] There was a glowing quote from Mr. Grubman included in its 1997 annual report, which was still posted on its website through July 2002, "If one were to find comparables to World-Com ... the list would be very short and would include the likes of Merck, Home Depot, Walmart, Coke, Microsoft, Gillette and Disney."[48] The sycophantism of Mr. Grubman is difficult to describe because it seems almost parody, as the WorldCom ending is now known. Mr. Grubman introduced Mr. Ebbers at analyst meetings as "the smartest guy in the industry."[49] It was not until the stock had lost 90% of its value, and just six weeks before its collapse, that Mr. Grubman issued a negative recommendation on WorldCom.[50] Mr. Grubman was free with his negative recommendations on other telecom companies. And Salomon would earn $21 million in fees if the WorldCom–Sprint merger were approved in 1999. He wrote, "We do not think any other telco will be as fully integrated and growth-oriented as this combination."[51] Mr. Grubman attended WorldCom board meetings and offered advice.[52]

The Loans from Citi

Citicorp was WorldCom's biggest lender as well as a personal lender for Bernie Ebbers, WorldCom's CEO (see Case 4.20). [The personal loans to Mr. Ebbers brought results for the banks in terms of WorldCom

business.[53] However, the loans were secured by Mr. Ebbers' stock and any default on those loans and the sale of those securities would have altered WorldCom's capitalization.

The IPO Allocations

Mr. Grubman's relationship with WorldCom's senior management was a target of investigation at the congressional level and elsewhere for reasons other than the personal loan relationships and the glowing reports from Mr. Grubman.[54] WorldCom gave the bulk of its investment banking business to Salomon Smith Barney, and it gave Mr. Ebbers and others the first shot at hot initial public offering (IPO) stocks.[55] The figures in congressional records indicate that Mr. Ebbers made $11 million in profits from investments in 21 IPOs recommended to him by Salomon Smith Barney and, more particularly, Mr. Grubman.[56] Apparently, complex games were going on in terms of how those shares were allocated initially, and Mr. Ebbers was one of the players let in on the best IPOs by Salomon Smith Barney. One expert described the allocation system as follows:

> Looking back, it looks more and more like a pyramid scheme. The deals explain why people weren't more diligent in making decisions about funding these small

(continued)

---

[53]At least one lawsuit by a shareholder alleged that the loans were made in exchange for business with WorldCom. Andrew Backover, "Suit Links Loans, WorldCom Stock," *USA Today*, October 15, 2002, p. 3B.

[54]Charles Gasparino, Tom Hamburger, and Deborah Solomon, "Salomon Made IPO Allocations Available to Ebbers Others," *Wall Street Journal*, August 28, 2002, p. A1.

[55]Gretchen Morgenson, "Ebbers Made $11 Million on 21 Stock Offerings," *New York Times*, August 31, 2002, p. B1; and Gretchen Morgenson, "Ebbers Got Million Shares in Hot Deals," *New York Times*, August 28, 2002, p. C1; and Gretchen Morgenson, "Deals within Telecom Deals," *New York Times*, August 28, 2002, pp. BU1, BU10.

[56]See Morgenson, "Ebbers Got Million Shares in Hot Deals," for Ebbers information; and Andrew Backover, "World Com, Qwest Face SEC Scrutiny," *USA Today*, March 12, 2002, p. 1B, for information on Qwest inquiry; see also Thor Valdmanis and Andrew Backover, "Lawsuit Targets Telecom Execs' Stock Windfalls," *USA Today*, October 1, 2002, p. 1B.

---

[47]Neil Weinberg, "Walmart Could Sue for Libel," *Forbes*, August 12, 2002, p. 56.

[48]Id.

[49]Randall Smith and Deborah Solomon, "Ebbers's Exit Hurts WorldCom's Biggest Fan," *Wall Street Journal*, May 3, 2002, p. C1.

[50]Id.

[51]Id, p. C3.

[52]Id.

Case 7.7

(continued)

companies. If the money was spread all over the place and everyone who participated early was almost guaranteed a return because of the hype, they had no incentive to try and differentiate the technology. And in the end, all the technology turned out to be identical and commodity-like.[57]

The Glowing Reports

Mr. Grubman continued to issue nothing but positive reports on WorldCom as he became completely intertwined with the company, Mr. Ebbers, and the company's success.[58] In emails uncovered by an investigation of analysts conducted by then–New York attorney general Eliot Spitzer, Mr. Grubman had complained privately that he was forced to continue his "buy" ratings on stocks that he considered "dogs." Mr. Spitzer filed suit against the analysts for "profiteering" in IPOs.[59]

Further, Mr. Ebbers was not the sole beneficiary of the Salomon Smith Barney IPO allocations, although he was the largest beneficiary.[60] Others who benefited from the IPO allocations and who were affiliated with WorldCom included Stiles A. Kellett Jr. (director, 31,500 shares), Scott Sullivan (CFO, 32,300 shares), Francesco Galesi (director), John Sidgmore (officer, director, and CEO after Ebbers's ouster), and James Crowe (former director of WorldCom).[61] Apparently, those who enjoyed the benefits of Salomon's allocations also stuck with Mr. Grubman in terms of his advice once the shares were allocated, often keeping the shares for too long because of Mr. Grubman's overly optimistic views on telecommunications-related companies' stock. However, Citigroup and Salomon both

denied that any *quid pro quo* existed among Ebbers, WorldCom, and the companies for WorldCom's investment banking business.[62]

The Pre-School Deal

No charges were ever brought against Mr. Grubman. He operates his own firm today. However, one additional story related to Mr. Grubman's role as an analyst illustrates that financial analysis may not be as math oriented as we believed. Through a series of emails, we learned that Mr. Grubman used his position for some help on the home front. Mr. Grubman was the father of twins whom he wanted to see admitted to one of Manhattan's most prestigious preschools—the 92nd Street Y.

Mr. Grubman wrote a memo to Sanford Weill, the then-chairman of Citigroup, with the following language:

On another matter, as I alluded to you the other day, we are going through the ridiculous but necessary process of preschool applications in Manhattan. For someone who grew up in a household with a father making $8,000 a year and for someone who attended public school, I do find this process a bit strange, but there are no bounds for what you do for your children.

Anything, anything you could do Sandy would be greatly appreciated. I will keep you posted on the progress with AT&T which I think is going well.

Thank you.

The backdrop for the memo is important. Citigroup pledged $1 million to the school at about the same time Grubman's children were admitted.

Mr. Weill, Mr. Grubman's CEO, asked Mr. Grubman to "take a fresh look" at AT&T, a major corporate client of Citigroup.

Mr. Weill served on the board of AT&T. AT&T's CEO, C. Michael Armstrong, served as a Citigroup director, and Mr. Weill was courting Armstrong's vote for the ouster of his co-chairman at Citigroup, John Reed.

(continued)

[57]Backover, "WorldCom, Qwest Face SEC Scrutiny," p. 1B; and Valdmanis and Backover, "Lawsuit Targets Telecom Execs' Stock Windfalls," p. 1B.

[58]Smith and Solomon, "Ebbers's Exit Hurts WorldCom's Biggest Fan," p. C1; and Andrew Backover and Jayne O'Donnell, "WorldCom Scrutiny Touches on E-mail," *USA Today*, July 8, 2002, p. 1B.

[59]Valdmanis and Backover, "Lawsuit Targets Telecom Execs' Stock Windfalls," p. 1B.

[60]Charles Gasparino, Tom Hamburger, and Deborah Solomon, "Salomon Made IPO Allocations Available to Ebbers Others," *Wall Street Journal*, August 28, 2002, p. A1.

[61]Morgenson, "Deals within Telecom Deals," pp. BU1, BU10.

[62]Gretchen Morgenson, "Ebbers Got Million Shares in Hot Deal," p. C15.

Case 7.7

(continued)

A follow-up email from Mr. Grubman to Carol Cutler, another New York analyst, connected the dots:

> I used Sandy to get my kids in the 92nd Street Y preschool (which is harder than Harvard) and Sandy needed Armstrong's vote on our board to nuke Reed in showdown. Once the coast was clear for both of us (ie Sandy clear victor and my kids confirmed) I went back to my normal self on AT&T.

At the same time as all the other movements, Mr. Grubman upgraded AT&T from a "hold" to a "strong buy." After Mr. Reed was ousted, Mr. Grubman downgraded AT&T again.

Mr. Grubman said that he sent the email "in an effort to inflate my professional importance."

In another email, Mr. Grubman wrote, "I have always viewed [AT&T] as a business deal between me and Sandy."

Discussion Questions

1. Were there conflicts of interest?

2. What personal insights do you gain from Mr. Grubman's emails and conduct? What elements can be added to your credo from this case?

3. All analysts were participating in the same types of favors and *quid pro quo* as Grubman. Does industry practice control ethics?

4. Then–attorney general Eliot Spitzer (now ex-governor of New York) pursued the analysts and the investment houses for their lack of independence. Although they all settled the cases brought against them, what types of criminal conduct could they be charged with?

5. Mr. Spitzer found the bulk of his evidence for his cases in candid emails the analysts sent describing the eventual collapse of these companies even as their face-to-face evaluations of companies were most positive. Does he have the right to view their emails?

Compare & Contrast

Refer to Case 7.3 and compare the actions of Tyler Shultz with those of Jack Grubman. Describe the differences in their approach to ethics. Consider their personal interests and then think about whether their personal credos had an impact on their careers and decisions.

Case 7.8

Nissan and Carlos Ghosn: Corporate Resources vs. Personal Spending

Carlos Ghosn's grandfather moved from Beirut to Brazil when he was just 13 years old, taking only a suitcase. Mr. Ghosn was born in Brazil but was sent to Beirut when he was six years old to live with his grandmother, mother, and other relatives. He was educated in the best schools in Paris. He took a job with Michelin Tire there, working on the factory floor, preparing the rubber. Eventually, he became a Michelin plant manager and then the CEO of Michelin North America, which he successfully turned around.[63] When he realized that he was working for

a family company and could never rise to be Michelin's CEO, he went back to France and joined Renault.[64] Renault was also going through a rough stretch after a failed merger with Volvo. Mr. Ghosn turned that company around, earning the name "Le Cost Killer" because of his skill in cutting expenses.

When Nissan, a Japanese company was on the brink of bankruptcy, Mr. Ghosn pushed through a deal for Renault to buy the company. Renault ended up owning 37% of

(continued)

[63]David Gelles and Motoko Rich, "The Jarring Fall from Grace of Nissan's Highest Achiever," *New York Times*, November 21, 2018, p. B1, at B4.

[64]Sean McLain, Phred Dvorak, Sam Schechner, and Patricia Kowsmann, "Lavish Lifestyle Spelled End for Carlos Ghosn at Nissan," *Wall Street Journal*, December 17, 2018, p. A1, at A12.

Case 7.8

(continued)

Nissan, and Nissan purchased 15% of Renault. Mr. Ghosn then moved to Tokyo in 1999 as the chief operating officer. Employees referred to him as "7–11" for the long hours that he worked, but the work paid off, with Nissan's earnings climbing.

Ghosn Compensation

By 2009, Mr. Ghosn was earning $15,000,000 per year, a figure well above what the other executives in the company were earning. However, in 2010, there was a change in Japanese pay disclosure laws (anything above $880,000 had to be disclosed). Mr. Ghosn asked a close ally (Greg Kelly) in HR to defer a good portion of his compensation, thereby avoiding the disclosure requirement. Mr. Kelly did so and was subsequently arrested and tried for his role in Mr. Ghosn's unauthorized compensation and expense issues. The company's external auditor, Ernst & Young, felt that the Kelly interpretation of nondisclosure of the deferred compensation was a stretch. Japanese board governance being what it was at the time, there were no compensation committees and, as a result, no board controls over compensation. Even with the deferrals, the Ghosn compensation that was reported still got the shareholders riled up at the annual meeting.

The Ghosn Perks

In addition to the compensation and deferred compensation issues, Mr. Ghosn was using Nissan funds for a plethora of perks, largely unbeknownst to the board. Nissan purchased several jets for Mr. Ghosn, jets that were well used: the flight logs show that he was on an airplane 100 days each year. The last jet was a Gulf Stream with a bedroom. The autobiography of Mr. Ghosn that once appeared on the Nissan website included this quote, "This kind of lifestyle can take a toll on you physically and socially. It is not without a price to pay and you have to manage that . . . . It helps that I can sleep well on an airplane."[65] Mr. Ghosn held a party at Versailles to celebrate his second marriage and his new wife's 50th birthday. Nissan asked a French prosecutor to look into how the party was financed. Nissan had made a €2.3 million donation for a Versailles sponsorship.[66] The sponsorship was for renovations at the palace, and in exchange Nissan had the right to use the facilities for up to 25% of the value of the donation. Mr. Ghosn held the party in the Grand Trianon, valued at a cost of €50,000.[67] The investigation focused on whether corporate funds were misused for the private party.

There were also the lesser expenditures for what Nissan has labeled personal expenses. Following Mr. Ghosn's arrest and with full access to the company records, auditors found the following Nissan expenses that were flagged as being personal:

- Cartier watches
- A trip to Brazil for Carnival
- Charges of $30,000 on the corporate credit card for suits at Ermenegildo Zegna[68]

The expenses totaled $12.9 million between 2009 and 2018. Mr. Ghosn's spokesman issued a statement that the audit was "part of a well-orchestrated effort to turn Mr. Ghosn into a caricature and dismantle his reputation for integrity and excellence built over several decades. All of these expenses were both authorized and tied to legitimate business purposes."[69] The audit indicates that the expenses were approved solely by the CEO. Mr. Ghosn noted that he purchased the suit at the behest of the Nissan design team, who felt his dress was not appropriate for his position.

The Web of Companies, Shell Companies, and Purchases

Mr. Ghosn also created a plethora of companies and shell companies separate from Nissan, a structure that permitted him to spend Nissan money for personal expenses. Although he told the board that he was creating a separate entity (Zi-A) for venture capital purposes,

(continued)

[65]*Id.*

[66]Nick Kostov and Stacy Meichtry, "Renault Flags Ghosn's Versailles Gala," *Wall Street Journal,* February 8, 2019, p. B1.

[67]Nick Kostov and Stacy Meichtry, "Renault Flags Ghosn's Versailles Gala," *Wall Street Journal,* February 8, 2019, p. B, at B2.

[68]Nick Kostov and Sean McLain, "Ghosn Ran Up Millions in Suspect Expenses, Audit Finds," *Wall Street Journal,* May 1, 2019, p. B3.

[69]*Id.*

Case 7.8

(continued)

he used the entity to purchase homes for himself. The structure of the entity was complex, with many layers and shell companies, making the discovery of where the money was going very difficult. Those "venture capital" funds purchased a mansion in Beirut, a beach apartment in Rio de Janeiro, and other homes in Amsterdam and Paris.[70] Ernst & Young did raise questions and an internal investigation began without Mr. Ghosn or Mr. Kelly knowing. Eventually, what the internal investigation and auditors discovered was turned over to former Japanese prosecutors, who then turned it all over to current prosecutors. Only in Japan would auditors skip notifying the board and go straight to the prosecutors.

Mr. Ghosn also allegedly transferred Nissan funds to an overseas distributor for the purchase of a yacht as well as the funding for a company run by his son.[71]

In November 2018, Tokyo police boarded Mr. Ghosn's luxurious jet and arrested him. He was charged with understating his pay in government disclosure documents by $44 million. Mr. Kelly, who was meeting Mr. Ghosn, was also taken into custody and charged. Several months after the initial charges, the Japanese government added that Messrs. Kelly and Ghosn had also understated Nissan's income.[72]

Mr. Kelly's wife, Donna "Dee" Kelly, issued a public statement saying that her husband has been "wrongly accused as part of a power grab by several Nissan executives headed up by the current CEO, [Hiroto] Saikawa."[73] Mr. Kelly was found guilty of evading Japanese executive compensation disclosure laws during one year of his work at Nissan but was acquitted of all other charges. He was given a suspended sentence and permitted to return to the United States in March 2022.[74]

Mr. Saikawa took over as CEO upon Mr. Ghosn's arrest. Ironically, in September 2019, Mr. Saikawa was forced to resign as CEO for allegedly falsifying documents to increase his performance pay. The board indicated that, unlike the situation with Mr. Ghosn, it was able to monitor and provide oversight and avoided the rubberstamped management that allowed Mr. Ghosn's free reign.[75] Mr. Saikawa denied that he was improperly paid.[76]

The Ongoing Charges and the Great Escape

Mr. Ghosn would be questioned, granted bail, "rejailed," released, and charged with additional crimes from the time of his original arrest through late December 2019. On December 28, 2019, Mr. Ghosn learned that his trial would be delayed again. At the time, he was at his home but on a monitor. He was permitted to go anywhere in Tokyo but could not leave the country and could not speak to his wife. He had not spoken to his wife for seven months. His bail was set at almost $13 million. Security cameras show him leaving his home in Tokyo at 2:30 P.M. Somehow he managed to get to Osaka. Michael Taylor, a former Green Beret known for his security services, and George Zayek packed Mr. Ghosn into a crate generally used for transporting concert equipment and had it loaded onto a private jet at an airport in Osaka.[77] When it comes to private jet travel, the VIPs sometimes bypass the screening.

From Osaka, Mr. Ghosn flew to Turkey, where he took a smaller private jet to Beirut, Lebanon. Eventually, Mr. Ghosn arrived there at 8:00 A.M. on Monday, December 29. His current and former wife are both from Lebanon, and he owns a vineyard there. He is a citizen of Lebanon, Brazil, and France. There were billboards in Beirut with his picture and the caption, "We are all Carlos Ghosn."

Michael Taylor and Peter Taylor, his son, were arrested on charges of aiding in the Ghosn escape. They

(continued)

---

[70]David Gelles and Motoko Rich, "The Jarring Fall from Grace of Nissan's Highest Achiever," *New York Times*, November 21, 2018, p. B1.

[71]Sean McLain, "Ghosn Indicted on Misappropriation Charge," *Wall Street Journal*, April 23, 2019, p. B3.

[72]Hiroko Tabuchi and Motoko Rich, "Ex-Nissan Chief Faces Fresh Charges in Japan As Legal Battle Escalates," *New York Times*, January 12, 2019, p. B3.

[73]Chester Dawson, "Nissan Director's Wife Calls His Jailing a Plot," *Wall Street Journal*, December 20, 2018, p. B1.

[74]Sean McLain, "Japan Lets Former Ghosn Aide Leave," *Wall Street Journal*, March 8, 2022, p. A3.

[75]Sean McLain, "Nissan Ousts CEO After Probe Finds He Pocketed Extra Pay," *Wall Street Journal*, September 10, 2019, p. A1.

[76]Ben Dooley, "Nissan's Chief Says He Was Improperly Overpaid," *New York Times*, September 6, 2019, p. B6.

[77]David Gauthier-Villars, Mark Maremont, Sean McLain, and Nick Kostov, "Ghosn Left Japan in a Crate," *Wall Street Journal*, January 4–5, 2020, p. A1,

Case 7.8

(continued)

had been paid $860,000 for logistics and $500,000 for attorney fees upfront by Mr. Ghosn. Mr. Ghosn told them that he needed to escape because he did not believe that he could get a fair trial in Japan. They entered a guilty plea in June 2021 after fighting extradition from the United States.[78] They were sentenced to two years (Michael) and one year and eight months (Peter) in prison in July 2021.[79]

---

[78]Sean McLain, "Ghosn's Helpers Plead Guilty," *Wall Street Journal*, June 15, 2021, p. B1.
[79]Sean McClain, "Ghost Escape Planner Michael Taylor Is Sentenced to Two Years in Prison, Wall Street Journal, July 29, 2021, https://www.wsj.com/articles/ghosn-escape-planner-michael-taylor-is-sentenced-to-two-years-in-prison-11626669860.

Discussion Questions

1. How does Mr. Ghosn's alleged behavior as a CEO compare with the CEOs that you studied in Unit 4? What CEO also staged a costly birthday party for his second wife?

2. Who was supervising Mr. Ghosn?

3. Did Mr. Ghosn fall victim to the Bathsheba syndrome? See Reading 2.5 How Leaders Lose Their Way: The Bathsheba Syndrome and What Price Hubris.

4. Where did Mr. Ghosn's loyalties lie?

5. As you go over his expenses and activities in acquiring homes, were there some gray areas?

6. What rationalizations did Mr. Ghosn offer for his decisions?

Case 7.9

Kodak, the Appraiser, and the Assessor: Lots of Backscratching on Valuation

This tale of a sort of sting operation required participation from business, government, and a professional. John Nicolo was a real property appraiser who did appraisal work for Eastman Kodak, Inc. (Kodak) at the request of one of Kodak's now-former employees, Mark Camarata, who served as Kodak's director of state and local taxes. Charles Schwab was the former assessor for the town of Greece, New York, an area that included Kodak headquarters. Kodak was then both the largest employer and the largest property owner in the town of Greece.

According to the indictments in the case, Schwab made reductions in Kodak's real property tax assessment. Those reductions, according to calculations completed by Nicolo and Camarata, saved Kodak $31,527,168 in property taxes over a 15-year period. But Schwab did not make those reductions as a matter of assessor policy, fond feelings for Kodak, or the goodness of his public servant heart. He made those reductions at the behest of the other two in exchange for payment. Nicolo's fee from Kodak, computed

as a percentage of the amount he was able to save Kodak in taxes, was to be $7,881,798 (about 25% of Kodak's projected tax savings). After being paid over $4,000,000 of his fee from Kodak, Nicolo paid Camarata $1,553,300 for his role in hiring him and then paid Schwab $1,052,100. The essence of the arrangement was that the appraiser agreed to split the tax savings fee with the assessor in exchange for the reduction and with the Kodak employee in exchange for hiring him.

The group also managed to involve companies that were buying property from Kodak. For example, in 2004, ITT bought one of Kodak's buildings in its industrial park as Kodak was downsizing. Immediately upon its acquisition of the building, ITT got an assessment from Schwab that quadrupled the value of the building for purposes of tax assessment. Mr. Camarata referred the ITT officers to Mr. Nicolo, who then talked Mr. Schwab into reducing the assessment value. However, unbeknownst to ITT, the

(continued)

Case 7.9

(continued)

whole scenario had been set up by the group, according to trial testimony. Schwab reduced the assessment value, and Nicolo split his fee with Camarata and Schwab.

Camarata entered a guilty plea to various federal fraud charges and agreed to cooperate with federal authorities in their prosecution of the other two in the property tax triumvirate, who were charged with 56 counts of fraud, money laundering, and other federal crimes. Mr. Camarata faced a possible penalty of 20 years, but was sentenced to two years because of what U.S. Federal District Judge David Latimer described, as follows: "Your cooperation with the government was immediate and complete. Without your testimony, I think the verdict might have been much more difficult for the government to accomplish ... your help was the linchpin for the government's case."

Mr. Camarata was ordered to pay $10 million in restitution as part of his federal prosecution, but the total amount he actually owed remains unclear because of federal income taxes owed, civil damages to Kodak and ITT, and taxes owed to the city based on the undervaluations.

Mr. Schwab entered a guilty plea. Following an 11-week trial, Mr. Nicolo was convicted of 51 counts of fraud, tax evasion, money laundering, and conspiracy. Both were sentenced to 12 years in federal prison. Mr. Nicolo requested home confinement due to health issues and alleged threats and beatings by prison officials but was denied the request. Mr. Schwab died in prison at age 66 in 2013.[80] Mr. Nicolo was still serving his sentence in a minimum federal security prison when he died in 2014.[81]

[80]Gary Craig, "Ex-Greek Assessor Charles Schwab Dies," *Democrat & Chronicle*, December 10, 2013, https://www .democratandchronicle.com/story/news/2013/12/10/ex-greece -assessor-charles-schwab-dies/3958999/.

[81]Staff writer, "John Nicolo Has Died in Fort Worth, Texas," *The Chronicle-Express*, June 4, 2014, https://www .democratandchronicle.com/story/news/2014/06/04/john -nicolo-kodak-greece-fraud-prison/9950373/.

When Kodak learned of the schemes, it immediately began discussions with the town of Greece for the reappraisal of its properties. Kodak also filed suit against Camarata and others seeking reimbursement from them for the fees that were paid as part of the scheme.[82] The federal government has been able to sell off most of the property belonging to Mr. Nicolo and others. In 2013, a federal court ordered Mr. Nicolo's lakefront property, estimated to be worth $500,000, to be sold by auction. The federal and local governments have already recovered $10 million from Mr. Nicolo. Kodak received $7.8 million of the amount recovered as its settlement in the case.[83]

Discussion Questions

1. Was anyone really hurt by this? Didn't Kodak benefit?

2. Why do we worry about an agreement by an assessor to reduce the assessed value? Couldn't he have done that anyway, regardless of receiving payment?

3. Does the method for paying appraisers on a contingency basis encourage this type of involvement by government officials?

4. Why do you think the three (possibly five) decided to engage in the scheme? Do any thoughts for your credo come from your observations about what happened?

5. After his guilty plea and agreement to cooperate, Mr. Camarata's fellow defendants referred to him as a "liar and thief." What lessons do you learn from this reaction and interaction?

6. What checks and balances are required for those who hold positions of trust in government and in their professions?

Source: *Indictment, U.S. v. Camarata*, May 5, 2005, http://www.fbi.gov.

[82]*Eastman Kodak Co. v. Camarata, et al.* 23 F.R.D. 372, (W.D.N.Y. 2005).

[83]*U.S. v. Nicolo*, 597 F. Supp. 2d 342 (W.D.N.Y. 2009).

Workplace Diversity and Atmosphere

Case 7.10

English-Only Workplaces

The Equal Employment Opportunity Commission (EEOC) has taken the position that a workplace rule that requires employees to speak only English is nondiscriminatory if it is a business necessity. The EEOC rule (29 C.F.R. § 1606.7(b)) provides that an English-only rule must address only the business necessity. Examples of a business necessity include a rule that applies to communications:

- with customers, coworkers, or supervisors who only speak English

- in emergencies or other situations in which employees must speak a common language to promote safety. Examples include operating rooms, work environments that involve dangerous equipment or substances, and cooperative work environments (employees developing reports or working on litigation)

- that enable a supervisor who only speaks English to monitor the performance of an employee whose job duties require communication in English with coworkers or customers

The business necessity exception does not apply to casual conversations between employees when they are not performing job duties.

Examples of employers that have implemented English-only policies include the Salvation Army, All-Island Transportation (a Long Island taxi company), a geriatric center in New York, and Oglethorpe University in Atlanta.

The current body of case law deals with workplace policies that have what is known as "English-only facilities." Under these types of rules, employees are required to speak English at all times in all parts of the facilities. In *Lopez v. Mountain View Care and*

Rehabilitation Center, LLC, 2022 WL 202955 (M.D. Pa. 2022), the court dealt with the implementation of a new policy at Mountain View that was referred to as a "no Spanish" or "no language other than English" policy. During training on the policy, Maria Fitzgerald, Mountain View's director of education, told employees that they could not speak Spanish in front of the patients or in other areas of the facility or even on the outside grounds of the facility.

Michelle Lopez and Nancy Acosta, two employees at the facility asked Ms. Fitzgerald about the policy and learned that they could not speak Spanish in employee-only areas such as the break room, lunchroom, smoking area, and parking lot. Ms. Lopez and Ms. Acosta then went to talk with Michael Hetzel, the Center's administrator, to discuss with him the policy and how it made them feel uncomfortable and singled out because of their Hispanic origin. Ms. Lopez described the meeting in her deposition:

> Nancy [Acosta] asked me to go with her to see Mr. Hetzel and speak to him about the situation because we felt targeted that it was – that the slide [from the training] only said "Spanish."

> And we went to his office.... Nancy, she told him her concerns and stuff. And I didn't speak much till we got to the part where he was telling Nancy about ... his grandfather that if we would have met him, you know, he would have told us about himself because this is America and, you know, we should be speaking English.

> And I told Mr. Hetzel, My husband does not speak or understand too much English, so if he calls me and Maria just said we're not supposed to even speak Spanish in the break room, what am I supposed to do?

(continued)

Case 7.10

(continued)

Mr. Hetzel said, Well—this was his words and I won't forget it—If I was eating a sandwich and, you know, I don't speak Spanish and you're speaking Spanish next to me, I can't even eat my sandwich in peace because I don't know if you're speaking about, you know, about me in Spanish. It's offensive to the other coworkers. So he said we shouldn't be speaking Spanish in the break room.

And I said, So what am I supposed to do, go to the parking lot? And that's when he also specifically told me, There's family members that walk through that parking lot. Sometimes they take their family—you know, the residents outside to sit out in the parking lot. They can't—you know, you're not supposed to even speak Spanish around them because they're in the parking lot, so you will have to leave the premises to speak to your husband.[84]

Ms. Acosta and Ms. Lopez and others who attended the training session filed suit against Mountain View for

violation of Title VII. Mountain View moved for summary judgment on the grounds that their policy was based in business necessity. The business necessity was that patients suffering from dementia might be confused upon hearing another language and become agitated or unwilling to ask for help. Their family members when visiting might be concerned that the patients could not communicate effectively, be confused, or not know how to ask for help.

The court did not grant the motion for summary judgement, so the case will move forward to trial.

Discussion Questions

1. List the stakeholders affected by these types of policies.
2. Is the "No Spanish"/"English only" policy a business necessity?
3. Why did Mountain View present the concerns about the patients and their families?
4. Does the facility-wide policy of Mountain View meet the business necessity requirement?

---

[84]*Lopez v. Mountain View Care and Rehabilitation Center*, 2022 WL 202955 (M.D. Pa. 2022).

Why Didn't They Say Something? 7.2

When Something Feels Iffy

If you were an employee in the training session with the Hispanic employees, would you have raised questions about the "No Spanish" policy? What could you have asked Ms. Fitzgerald to explain? Could you have helped the facility with understanding the impact, effects, and legality of its policy?

Ethics in Action 7.2

When the English Spoken Is Difficult to Understand

Often, when calling for assistance with software, computers, or cell phones, we have a representative who speaks English but whose accent makes it difficult to understand what is being said. Could an employer impose a rule that required the ability to speak "clear English"? Is that a business necessity? What solutions could you offer to employers?

Case 7. 11

Ban-the-Box and Fair Chance: Do You Have Any Criminal Convictions?

Called the "ban the box" movement, its goal is to stop employers from using criminal convictions as an automatic screening device. Koch Industries, a U.S. corporation employing more than 60,000 people in the United States alone, dropped its application question about prior criminal convictions. Koch's general counsel and senior vice president said that the reasoning behind the company's decision was simple, "Do we want to be judged for the rest of our lives for something that happened on our worst day?"[85] Target and Walmart are two other major companies that have adopted the "Ban the Box" policy internationally.

There are 70 million people in the United States who have some type of criminal record. The number of individuals returned each year to society following their incarceration is 700,000. Men with criminal records account for 34% of all unemployed males between the ages of 25 and 54.

The goal of "Ban the Box" is to find employment for these individuals in jobs where they do not present a liability risk. For example, those who have convictions for violent offenses present security and safety issues for companies and potential liabilities so caution in placement and supervision is required. Those who have been convicted of financial crimes present a risk for bonding and insurance purposes and must be placed in non-access types of positions. Also, there are some licensed positions for which convicted felons cannot be qualified. For example, licensed insurance and securities dealers require special clearance from state and, sometimes, federal agencies to return to their professions following any type of felony conviction.

The goal is to open doors for careful placements as opposed to precluding those who have a criminal record from all job opportunities. Most Koch Industries jobs are in manufacturing, a highly supervised and structured environment where safety and security can be controlled.

The theory is that once the question is banned, applicants are judged solely by their education and experience. The question about convictions comes up only during interviews when the applicants would have the opportunity to explain their past history. Proponents believe that this open process gives ex-felons a better chance of being hired because they are not rejected automatically from the hiring pool.[86] However, many small businesses have expressed their concerns that under ban-the-box they must spend a great deal of time and effort in screening and interviewing applicants only to find out that their convictions are disqualifying for legal or safety reasons.

The EEOC position does not require employers to "ban the box." The EEOC has given the following guidance: Employers cannot discriminate against people with equal criminal backgrounds on the basis of race, gender, national origin, or religion.[87] In addition, employers cannot use employment screens that disproportionately impact by race, gender, national origin, or religion. In other words, the statistical impact issue could arise because of these employer screens. Also, the EEOC makes a distinction between arrest and conviction records because arrest records are not proof that the individual committed a crime and the agency suggests caution in using such screens.

There are 25 states and 150 cities and towns that have "fair chance" or ban-the-box hiring policies. As noted, ban-the-box jurisdictions prohibit questions about criminal convictions on employment applications. These are no-ask laws. In fair-chance jurisdictions, employers cannot use criminal convictions as a screen for applicants but they can make a conditional offer of employment with one condition being no criminal convictions. Once employers have the information about criminal convictions, they can assess whether the applicants' backgrounds would present a risk in the workplace.

One of the concerns about these laws is that they are piecemeal. HR managers struggle to meet the legal requirements when there is, for example, no state law but they may be subject to ordinances in cities and towns. Some employers have asked for a uniform standard so that they can have uniform hiring policies.

(continued)

---

[85]Fredreka Schouten, "Koch Gives Job-Seeking Ex-Cons a Break," *USA Today*, April 28, 2015, p. 1B.

[86]See the National Employment Law Project website for more information.

[87]https://www.eeoc.gov/arrestandconviction.

Case 7.11

(continued)

Discussion Questions

1. Explain the distinction in the hiring process when the "box" is eliminated.

2. Discuss the risks employers face in hiring those who have convictions and the precautions they can take.

3. Discuss the risks employers face if they do not comply with fair-chance and ban-the-box statutes and ordinances.

4. Discuss how the diversity of a company workforce is affected by using criminal records as a preliminary exclusion from consideration.

5. What issues are being addressed and what issues are raised through legislative solutions to employment of those with criminal convictions? How could they be handled using ethical models and questions?

Compare & Contrast

Even when the criminal record is not disclosed, studies show that those who are handling the hiring process simply assume that African American males are more likely to have a criminal record and hire them less often than when they are aware of the criminal record.[88] What issues exist here and how can they be addressed by an employer?

[88]*Sociological Images*, "Race, criminal background, and employment," blog entry by Gwen Sharp, April 3, 2015, thesocietypages.org.

Case 7.12

The NFL and Its Rooney Diversity Rule: Coach Flores and the Mix-Up on Texts

In 2002, two minority coaches had been fired despite good records following an off-season. The result was that there was only one minority coach in the National Football League (NFL). Dan Rooney, the former owner of the Pittsburgh Steelers, led an initiative in 2002 to mandate that NFL teams interview minority candidates for coaching and front-office positions.[89] The rule was successfully put in place and later expanded to apply to general manager positions as well.

Under the rule, NFL clubs must interview at least two minority candidates (as of 2020) from the NFL Career Development Panel List or another minority candidate not currently employed with their club. The rule also contains

certain procedural requirements on maintaining records and who participates in the interviews.

Brian Flores had interviews with the Denver Broncos and the New York Giants in 2019. Mr. Flores said that the interviews were "sham interviews" done solely to comply with the Rooney Rule. He explained that John Elway, the general manager for the Broncos, and CEO Joe Ellis were an hour late for his 2019 interview, disheveled, and not interested in a substantive interview.[90] Mr. Flores had coached the Miami Dolphins from 2019 to 2021. He was fired following the 2021 season despite three successful seasons.

In 2022, Mr. Flores had an interview with the New York Giants for a coaching position. Before his interview even

(continued)

[89]Zac Al-Khateeb, "What Is the Rooney Rule? Explaining NFL Mandate to Interview Minority Candidates, Its Effectiveness and Criticisms," *The Sporting News*, February 2, 2022, https://www.sportingnews.com/us/nfl/news/what-is-rooney-rule-nfl-minority-candidates-effectiveness-criticisms/1k4m7oilxr8nv1xjs9f9bw2k7d.

[90]Zac Al-Khateeb, "Brian Flores Lawsuit, Explained: Former Dolphins Coach Sues NFL, Teams for Discriminatory Hiring Practices," *The Sporting News*, February 2, 2022, https://www.sportingnews.com/us/nfl/news/brian-flores-lawsuit-explained-nfl-dolphins/17pmh4f1j1pmm15u24qvwjvvmv.

Case 7.12

(continued)

took place, Bill Belichick, the coach of the New England Patriots, sent Mr. Flores a text congratulating him on getting the Giants coach job. The text was intended for Brian Daboll, the offensive coordinator for the Buffalo Bills, who had already been given the job. The text exchange is reproduced in the suit Mr. Flores filed against the teams and the NFL for violations of the Title VII Civil Rights Act and for their conspiratorial behavior in seeking to exclude minority coaches.

> Bill Belichick (BB) to Brian Flores: Sounds like you have landed.
>
> Brian Flores (BF) to BB: Did you hear something I didn't hear?
>
> BB to BF: Giants?!?!?!
>
> BB to BF: Got it – I hear from Buffalo and NYG that you are their guy. Hope it works out if you want it to!!
>
> BF to BB: That's definitely what I want! I hope you're right coach. Thank you.
>
> BF to BB: Coach, are you talking to Brian Flores or Brian Daboll. Just making sure.

> BB to BF: Sorry—I "f....." this up. I double-checked & misread the text. I think they are naming Daboll. I'm sorry about that. BB
>
> BF to BB: Thanks.[91]
>
> BF to BB: I interview on Thursday. I think I have a shot.
>
> BB to BF: Got it.

Discussion Questions

1. What is the significance of Coach Belichick's error in sending the congratulatory text to the wrong Brian?

2. Is it discriminatory to simply interview without the intent to hire?

3. Are procedural rules effective means for achieving diversity?

4. If you were the NFL or one of the teams involved, how would you address the issues raised by Mr. Flores?

5. What texting cautions do you carry away from this case?

---

[91]*Flores v. The National Football League* et al., complaint (S.D.N.Y. 2022), https://www.wigdorlaw.com/wp-content /uploads/2022/02/Complaint-against-National-Football -League-et-al-Filed.pdf.

Case 7.13

On-the-Job Fetal Injuries

Johnson Controls, Inc., is a battery manufacturer. In the battery-manufacturing process, the primary ingredient is lead. Exposure to lead endangers health and can harm a fetus carried by a female who is exposed to lead.

Before Congress passed the Civil Rights Act of 1964, Johnson Controls did not employ any women in the battery manufacturing process. In June 1977, Johnson Controls announced its first official policy with regard to women who desired to work in battery manufacturing, which would expose them to lead:

> Protection of the health of the unborn child is the immediate and direct responsibility of the prospective parents. While the medical professional and the company can support them in the exercise of this responsibility, it cannot assume it for them without

simultaneously infringing their rights as persons.

> Since not all women who can become mothers wish to become mothers (or will become mothers), it would appear to be illegal discrimination to treat all who are capable of pregnancy as though they will become pregnant.[92]

The policy stopped short of excluding women capable of bearing children from jobs involving lead exposure but emphasized that a woman who expected to have a child should not choose a job that involved such exposure.

Johnson Controls required women who wished to be considered for employment in the lead exposure jobs to

(continued)

---

[92]*International Union v Johnson Controls, Inc.*, 499 U.S. 187, 191 (1991).

Case 7.13

(continued)

sign statements indicating that they had been told of the risks lead exposure posed to an unborn child: "that women exposed to lead have a higher rate of abortion ... not as clear as the relationship between cigarette smoking and cancer ... but medically speaking, just good sense not to run that risk if you want children and do not want to expose the unborn child to risk, however small."

By 1982, however, the policy of warning had been changed to a policy of exclusion. Johnson Controls was responding to the fact that between 1979 and 1982, eight employees became pregnant while maintaining blood lead levels in excess of 30 micrograms per deciliter, an exposure level that OSHA categorizes as critical. The company's new policy was as follows:

> It is Johnson Controls' policy that women who are pregnant or who are capable of bearing children will not be placed into jobs involving lead exposure or which would expose them to lead through the exercise of job bidding, bumping, transfer or promotion rights.[93]

The policy defined women capable of bearing children as "all women except those whose inability to bear children is medically documented." The policy defined unacceptable lead exposure as the OSHA standard of 30 micrograms per deciliter in the blood or 30 micrograms per cubic centimeter in the air.

In 1984, three Johnson Controls employees filed suit against the company on the grounds that the fetal-protection policy was a form of sex discrimination that violated Title VII of the Civil Rights Act. The three employees included Mary Craig, who had chosen to be sterilized to avoid losing a job that involved lead exposure; Elsie Nason, a 50-year-old divorcee who experienced a wage decrease when she transferred out of a job in which she was exposed to lead; and Donald Penney, a man who was denied a leave of absence so that he could lower his lead level because he intended to become a father. The trial court certified a class action that included all past, present, and future Johnson Controls' employees who had been or would continue to be affected by the fetal-protection policy Johnson Controls implemented in 1982.

At the trial, uncontroverted evidence showed that lead exposure affects the reproductive abilities of men and women and that the effects of exposure on adults are as great as those on a fetus, although the fetus appears to be more vulnerable to exposure. Johnson Controls maintained that its policy was a product of business necessity.

The employees argued in turn that the company allowed fertile men, but not fertile women, to choose whether they wished to risk their reproductive health for a particular job. Johnson Controls responded that it had based its policy not on any intent to discriminate, but rather on its concern for the health of unborn children. Johnson Controls also pointed out that inasmuch as more than 40 states recognize a parent's right to recover for a prenatal injury based on negligence or wrongful death, its policy was designed to prevent its liability for such fetal injury or death. The company maintained that simple compliance with Title VII would not shelter it from state tort liability for injury to a parent or child.

Johnson Controls also maintained that its policy represented a *bona fide* occupational qualification and that it was requiring medical certification of nonchildbearing status to avoid substantial liability for injuries.

Discussion Questions

1. To what extent should a woman have the right to make decisions that will affect not only her health but also the health of her unborn child? To what extent should a woman's consent to or acknowledgment of danger mitigate an employer's liability? What if a child born with lead-induced birth defects sues? Should the mother's consent apply as a defense?

2. The U.S. Supreme Court eventually decided Johnson Controls' policy was discriminatory and a violation of Title VII.[94] The court focused on the issue of men capable of reproduction not being covered by the policy.[95] What steps would you take as director of human resources to deal with the issue?

3. The fallout from the Johnson Controls decision has been that many women have been working in jobs that expose them to toxins. The U.S. Supreme Court did acknowledge in its holding that tort liability might result from its decision, but that such liability was often

(continued)

---

[93]*Id.*

[94]*International Union v. Johnson Controls, Inc.,* 499 U.S. 187 (1991).
[95]*Id.*

Case 7.13

(continued)

used as a guise or cover for gender discrimination. However, 14 years after the decision, women who were held to be entitled to the high-risk jobs are now suing their employers for the birth defects in their children. For example, IBM faced several suits from employees and their children against it for defects allegedly tied to production-line toxins.[96] The position of many of the

---

[96]Stephanie Armour, "Workers Take Employers to Court over Birth Defects," *USA Today*, February 26, 2002, pp. 1 A, 2A. For more information, go to http://www.cdc.gov/niosh.

employers is that even if evidence existed linking the toxins to birth defects, the women took the jobs with knowledge about the risk and agreed to that risk. How can employers, legislators, and public policy specialists reconcile antidiscrimination laws and these risks of exposure?

4. At what times, if any, should discrimination issues be subordinate to other issues, such as the risk of danger to unborn children?

Case 7.14

Political Views in the Workplace

Facebook has a policy on removing hate speech from its site. That policy may have seemed easy to determine and enforce at the time of its creation, but Facebook has grappled with significant challenges in applying the policy.

The 2016 Election

During the 2016 election, some Facebook employees argued that Donald Trump's posts about immigration should have been removed for violating the site's hate speech policy. The argument reached Mr. Zuckerberg's desk. Mr. Zuckerberg decided that it would be "inappropriate to censor the candidate" by removing the Trump comments.[97]

The decision was not well received. Using the company's internal messaging service as well as in-person conversations with Mr. Zuckerberg, managers and employees complained that Facebook was bending the site's rules for Mr. Trump. Some of the employees in the Facebook group that reviews content threatened to quit. In a statement, Facebook indicated that its site could be a valuable one for political discourse and "an important part of the conversation around who the next U.S. president will be."[98]

---

[97]Deepa Seetharaman, "Trump's Posts Fuel Discord in Facebook Ranks," *Wall Street Journal*, October 20, 2016, p. 3A.
[98]Id.

In a town-hall meeting with employees, Mr. Zuckerberg acknowledged that the Trump posts would be considered hate speech under Facebook policies but that the implications of removing the posts were too drastic. One employee commented, "Banning a U.S. presidential candidate is not something you do lightly."[99] Employees continued to object for months after the decision was made, but Facebook stuck with its initial decision.

Peter Thiel, Donations, and Censorship

Mr. Zuckerberg stepped into another hornet's nest when he defended PayPal founder Peter Thiel's $1.25 million donation to Mr. Trump's presidential campaign. Mr. Zuckerberg posted the following message on Facebook's internal messaging system:

We can't create a culture that says it cares about diversity and then excludes almost half the country because they back a political candidate. There are many reasons a person might support Trump that do not involve racism, sexism, xenophobia, or accepting sexual assault.

(continued)

---

[99]Id.

Case 7.14

(continued)

> We care deeply about diversity. That's easy to do when it means standing up for ideas you agree with. It's a lot harder when it means standing up for the rights of people with different viewpoints to say what they care about. That's even more important.[100]

A screenshot of the message made its way onto the site Boing. Once the information became public, the ripple effects continued. Ellen Pao, founder of Project Include, the Silicon Valley diversity initiative, announced it was cutting its ties to Y Combination, in which Mr. Thiel is a partner. Y Combination is known for its efforts to advance diversity and inclusion.

First Amendment and Facebook

Facebook, as a private company, is permitted to make its own policies for its site. Blocking certain posts is within their discretion. The First Amendment applies to government censorship of speech, not private curbs. Likewise, employees cannot force employers to reverse themselves on policy decisions that violate no laws.

Mr. Zuckerberg and Facebook have found themselves in the middle of a debate that has divided the country along political lines. However, Facebook's policy has weighed the impact of Mr. Trump's posts versus the consequences of a business censoring political speech and decided to stay neutral on the ability of candidates to post their views on issues.

Subsequent Issues: The Effect of Calming Things Down with MSI

When Facebook employees scrawled "All lives matter" over "Black lives matter" posts, Mr. Zuckerberg reprimanded the employees, required fixes, and pointed out the need to allow free expression. There was a realization that trying to control issues with decisions on a case-by-case basis was creating inconsistencies. As a result, Facebook developed what is known as its MSI algorithm. MSI stands for "meaningful social interaction."

The goal was to get Facebook users interacting with each other in a more meaningful way.[101]

The algorithm was designed to reward likes, comments, and reshares in Facebook's decisions about what it places in its all-important News Feed. The News Feed is what gets users to go to content. Advertising revenues are based on the ability of Facebook to grab user interest. In 2017, it was clear that Facebook user interest was declining. The intent of employing the algorithm was to get users interacting with each other. The effect was that publishers and political parties were posting professionally made content that was sensational in nature or got users outraged. With a formula that gave a point to likes and five points to reactions and reshares, the Facebook News Feed was loaded with controversial content. In Europe, some political parties told Facebook that they were shifting their positions on issues so that they could engage and resonate with voters.

Within Facebook, there were warnings that the effort to make Facebook a less divisive platform was succeeding in making it worse. However, fixing the algorithm to reduce divisiveness also meant a reduction in user engagement. The Facebook business model suffered when the controversial disappeared. The decline in user engagement became very clear in early 2022 when Facebook's new parent, Meta, announced a decline in earnings as its ad revenues declined.[102]

Also within Facebook were employee political divides over the impact on some online publishers vs. others. The algorithm served to cut off content from conservative news outlets such as Breitbart, losing 46% of its traffic from Facebook, while Buzzfeed lost only 13%. The *Wall Street Journal* ran a five-part series on the internal battles at Facebook with its access through employees to internal emails and documents. Current and former employees had reached out to try and reform the internal screening processes being used.

(continued)

---

[100]Jessica Guynn, "Mark Zuckerberg Defends Thiel's $1.25M Trump Gift," *USA Today*, October 20, 2016, p. 3A.

[101]Keach Hagey and Jeff Horwitz, "Facebook Tried to Make Platform Healthier. It Got Angrier Instead," *Wall Street Journal*, September 16, 2021, p. A1.
[102]Deepa Seetharaman and Salvador Rodriguez, "Facebook Parent's Results Rattle Investors," *Wall Street Journal*, February 3, 2022, p. A1.

Case 7.14

(continued)

Discussion Questions

1. Explain the legal issues in Facebook's decisions on controlling user posts.

2. Discuss the stakeholders in the issue of censoring candidate speech. Be sure to consider all levels of candidates who use Facebook. That is, beyond presidential elections, consider the state and local candidates who rely on internet communications as a means of connecting with the public.

3. What are the implications of employer policies on political speech in the workplace? Is this a Milton Friedman issue—no matter what action or position you take, you lose customers? See Reading 3.1. Is it impossible because of the nature of its business for Facebook to avoid political discussions in the workplace?

Case 7.15

Facebook, YouTube, Instagram, LinkedIn, and Employer Tracking

Employers have been using online resources for doing background searches on their potential employees. These resources are free and easily accessible but sometimes misleading and inaccurate. There are legal issues as well as the ultimate question: Does such screening help employers make better hiring decisions?

Do Employers Use Social Media as a Pre-Employment Screen?

The surveys have slightly different results, but the percentages are all high.

- 98% of all employers do some form of online checking on job candidates

- 90% check candidates' social media activity before making a hiring decision

- 43% use Google to research job applicants

- 79% of HR managers say that they have declined to hire someone because of what they have posted on their social media sites[103]

- 61% of professional service firms, including accounting, consulting, engineering, and law firms, do Google searches on their job candidates and use what they find, including YouTube, TikTok, and MySpace references, in the search to gather background on applicants

- 50% of professional services employers hired to do background checks use Google as well as YouTube, Tik Tok, and MySpace

One employer commented that a Google search is so simple that it would be irresponsible not to conduct such a search. Only about one-third of employers ask permission to examine candidates' social media postings. If the postings are public, they do not need to ask permission.

A 2018 CareerBuilder survey found that 54% of employers have rejected applicants based on what they find on social media.[104] Uncovering information such as a stolen identity is helpful in job screening. Other factors that can result in rejection that are not as clear include social media posts that contain profanity, indicate gambling, or referenced alcohol or drug use.

Is It Legal?

Looking at the reasons for employers rejecting candidates based on their social media, the legal red flags should be clear. In fact, attorneys express concern that screening social media is a way to obtain information the employer could not ask about in an interview such as sexual orientation, disabilities, pregnancy, political views,

(continued)

---

[103]Kelsey McKeon, "5 Personal Branding Tips for Your Social Media," *The Manifest*, April 28, 2020, https://themanifest.com/digital-marketing/5-personal-branding-tips-job-search.

[104]Rose Wong, "Stop Screening Job Candidates' Social Media," *Harvard Business Review*, September–October 2021, https://hbr.org/2021/09/stop-screening-job-candidates-social-media.

Case 7.15

(continued)

age, gender, sexual behavior, and religious affiliation.[105] Finding out that information opens the door to litigation for discrimination in hiring.

In addition, about one-half of the states prohibit employers from asking job candidates to pull up their social media during an interview and from asking for their usernames and passwords.[106] The European Union requires consent from job applicants before an employer can use the social media as part of job screening.

Some sites, such as LinkedIn, are exceptions to the coverage because the purpose is to allow recruiters to see potential applicants' profiles. In addition, those joining LinkedIn have options for controlling user access.

The Federal Trade Commission has taken the position that the use of social media in screening applicants could be covered under the Fair Credit Reporting Act (FCRA) if the information is used to look at the applicant's character, mode of living, general reputation, or personal characteristics. Permission would be required to avoid any questions about this federal law's application to employer screening.[107]

The legal advice is for employers to screen their screening:

- Is using the information on social media a good predictor of job performance?

- Have you screened out all information that you would not be permitted to ask by law?

- Are there any applicable state and federal laws that require permission?

- Does it violate any privacy laws?

- Does it violate any rules on not using criminal records in the hiring process?

- Do you need permission under state law?[108]

Does Using Social Media Help?

In a study of 140 job candidates, 39 recruiters were asked to rate the candidates using social media.[109] The recruiters were influenced by what was on social media, and religious affiliations, profanity, alcohol, drugs, and sexual behavior lowered the recruiters' rating. In another study, two groups of recruiters rated the same job candidates. One group of recruiters used social media after receiving training on focusing only on traditional work screening, such as education and writing skills. The other group just used social media using whatever information they found.

The researchers followed up on the applicants 6 to 12 months after they were hired at their new jobs and found that neither group was very good at predicting either job performance or whether the applicants were likely to stay put with their employers. In short, using social media is not a predictor of a candidate's likelihood of being a long-term employee or a good one.

Screening for Red Flags

In some cases, searching social media can reveal some information that will create problems for the company or the applicant, depending on the job they are seeking. For example, in 2018, Google hired Kamau Bobb as a senior member of its diversity team. Just after Mr. Bobb was hired, a post from 2007 on his blog contained an antisemitic remark. Mr. Bobb had written a blog entry that was called, "If I were a Jew," and one of the entries was, "If I were a Jew, I would be concerned about my insatiable appetite for war and killing in defense of myself."[110] When the post emerged, Google reassigned Mr. Bobb to work on science, technology, engineering, and mathematics work and apologized for the remark, calling it "unquestionably hurtful." The presence of information damaging to employers that has appeared on social media is an important to avoid public relations debacles.

(continued)

[105]*Employers Continue Rejecting Job Seekers Because of Social Media Content*, CBIA (August 16, 2018), https://www.cbia.com/news/hr-safety/employers-continue-rejecting-jobseekers-social-media/. *See also A Complete Understanding of Social Media Background Checks*, CFIRST (June 18, 2019), https://www.cfirstcorp.com/understanding-social-media-background-checks/.

[106]Elana Handelman, "The Expansion of Traditional Background Checks to Social Media Screening: How to Ensure Adequate Privacy Protection in Current Employment Practices," 23 *University of Pennsylvania Journal of Constitutional Law* 661 (2021).

[107]*HR Compliance* ¶80820 (CCH), 2015 WL 8766766 (2021).

[108]*HR Compliance* ¶88730 (CCH), 2015 WL 8764307(2021).

[109]Liwen Zhang, *et al.,* "What's on Job Seekers' Social Media Sites? A Content Analysis and Effects of Structure on Recruiter Judgments and Predictive Validity," 105 *Journal of Applied Psychology* 1530 (2020).

[110]Tripp Mickle, "Google Reassigns Diversity Executive," *Wall Street Journal*, June 4, 2021, p. B3.

Case 7.15

(continued)

From the Employee's Side

Colleges and universities are continuing to work to help students understand that what they post on the web is not private information and can often have unintended consequences. The following examples not only resulted in student disciplinary proceedings but also gave the students involved an eternal presence on social media for their college pranks, threats, and effects of inebriation for the world and potential employers to see:

- Several students at Ohio State boasted on Facebook (a networking/socializing site) that they had stormed the field after Ohio State beat Penn State and taken part in what erupted into a riot. Law enforcement officials were able to trace the students through the university system, and 50 Ohio State students were referred to the Office of Judicial Affairs for disciplinary proceedings.

- Students at the University of Mississippi were disciplined for stating on an open site that they wanted to have sex with a professor.

- A student at Fisher College was expelled for threatening to take steps to silence a campus police officer.

Discussion Questions

1. Discuss privacy rights and whether there is an issue of privacy when information is posted voluntarily on the Internet.

2. Would employers using these sources for background checks involve any sort of discrimination?

3. Professor Harold Abelson has explained rights, privacy, and the Internet as follows: "In today's online world, what your mother told you is true, only more so: people can really judge you by your friends."[111] In which school of ethical thought would you place Professor Abelson in relation to his views on this question of the Internet and privacy?

4. Do employers have a responsibility to adequately screen their applicants before hiring?

5. Describe how an organization can protect the hiring process against the unlawful use of social media information.

Source: Bathija, Sandhya, "Have a Profile on MySpace? Better Keep It Clean," *National Law Journal*, June 4, 2007, p. 10.

---

[111] "Quotation of the Week," *New York Times*, March 21, 2010, p. SB2.

Tough Issues and Confrontation in the Workplace

Reading 7.16

The Ethics of Confrontation

Why We Avoid Confrontation

The "Don't rock the boat" attitude is frequently seen as the virtuous road. **Confrontation** is messy—there are often hurt feelings. There are embarrassing revelations. There are destroyed careers. There are costs. Whether confrontation involves sexual misconduct by a CEO or cooking the books by a manager or bond trader, the impact is the same.

Human nature flees from such situations. Further, there is within human nature that rationalization that avoiding confrontation is being "nice," and nice is associated with ethics.

There are also the harsh realities of confrontation. To confront a CEO with allegations and carry through with a disciplinary process for the loss of a job and contractual compensation obligations are time-consuming efforts and reflect on those who hired the CEO in the first place. There is exposure to liability.

A good employee evaluation means that the employee is happy, and there are no reviews, no messy discussions, and no allegations of discrimination. Not confronting a rogue trader means enjoying the ride of his performance and earnings and worrying about consequences at another time when perhaps something else will come along to counterbalance any of the harmful activities. Not insisting that a loan be written down carries with it the comfort of steady growth and earnings and a hope that future financial performance can make up for the loss when it eventually must be disclosed.

There is a great deal of rationalization that goes into avoiding confrontation. There is a comfort in maintaining *status quo*. There is at least a postponement of legal issues and liabilities. Often, avoiding confrontation is a painless road that carries with it the hope that whatever lies beneath does not break through and reveal its ugliness. Often, confrontation carries with it the hope that a problem will solve itself or become a moot issue.

The Harms of Avoiding Confrontation

Postponing confrontation does not produce a better result when the issue at the heart of the needed confrontation inevitably emerges. Those harms include liability, individual harms, reputational damage, and the loss of income as the issue chugs along without resolution.

The Deceptive Lull of "Being Nice"

One of the faulty assumptions in avoiding confrontation is that the "niceness" benefits the individuals affected. A good performance evaluation is beneficial to the employee. Not taking disciplinary action permits executives and managers to continue their careers and earn a living. Not raising a financial reporting issue means that shareholders can continue to enjoy returns and market value. Not questioning an employee's unusual success means that the earnings figures stand unscathed. Avoiding confrontation is a temporary reprieve for those involved.

The difficulty with the protection argument is that it presumes that the truth will not emerge. When it does, the preservation of a career in light of keeping critical information tamped down introduces greater liability. Termination of an employee for cause may carry with it the difficulties of challenge and even litigation. Not terminating an employee for cause who goes on later to do more harm exposes the company to liability. The difficulty with not disclosing matters that affect earnings is that when those matters do emerge, there is not just the resulting restatement of earnings but also the accompanying lack of investor trust and resulting reduction in market value. What timely confrontation could have minimized is exacerbated by the postponement.

The Ethics of Confrontation

Although not widely accepted as a principle of virtue, there is an ethical duty of confrontation. Edmund Burke was a proponent of such a duty with his admonition of two centuries ago, "All that is necessary for evil to triumph is for good men to do nothing." Modern phraseology holds that if there is a legal or ethical problem in a company and an employee or manager or executive says nothing, they become part of the problem.

However, one of the reasons for the hesitancy in confrontation not yet discussed is a certain degree of ineptness on the part of those who must do the confronting. If confrontation is indeed a virtue, are there guides for its exercise? The following points offer a model for ethical confrontation.

Determine the Facts

An underlying disdain for confrontation arises because too often those who do the confronting are wrong. Prior to confrontation, prepare as if you were working on a budget, a product launch, or a financing. Know what is happening or what has happened and obtain as much background information as possible. Preparation also serves as protection for any fears of liability from acting. Employers need to understand that well-documented personnel actions are not a basis for discrimination suits. And termination of employees who are harming others is not actionable if the harm is clearly established.

If You Don't Know the Facts, or Can't Know the Facts, Present the Issue to Those Involved and Affected

In the case of allegations or when an employee has raised a question about how a particular matter is being carried on the books, you may only be presented with one side. That lack of information need not preclude you from raising the question. In the case of allegations against a school administrator, those involved are often acting based upon an allegation by a student. That is one-sided information. However, those involved in evaluating and dealing with the allegation can go to the other party who stands accused and raise the issue. Or those charged with enforcement or making decisions can proceed with meetings, hearings, or investigations that can perhaps provide corroborating or exonerating information. Meetings, investigations, and hearings are a form of confrontation. There is action being taken.

A financial officer can hear several views from employees on carrying certain items on the books. The very definition of materiality opens the door to that type of disagreement. But a good financial officer knows that an open discussion of the issue, and confrontation of the issue with those who tout various views, is the solution that serves the company best in the long run. Without such confrontation, the failure to listen to an employee's view exacerbates the eventual fallout from a bad decision. The public confrontation of the issue is, in and of itself, insurance against the fallout should that decision prove to be wrong.

Always Give the Opportunity for Self-Remedy

One of the reasons confrontation enjoys such universal disdain is that very often the confrontation is done circuitously. If your attorney has done something questionable, confront the attorney first, and then report the person to the state bar for discipline. If an employee has engaged in misconduct, tell the employee. Don't create a situation where those involved have to hear about allegations you have made from someone else. If earnings are overstated, employees should work within the company for self-remedy before heading to the SEC.

One of the virtue constraints in the ethics of confrontation is having the courage to discuss the issues and concerns with those who are involved in creating them. An end run is not a confrontation. It is an act that postpones the inevitability of facing those who have done something wrong.

Don't Fear the Fallout and Hassle

Among the reasons for the lack of confrontation discussed earlier was the realistic observation that many avoid confrontation because it is too much trouble. However, as also noted earlier, if there is a problem that remains unconfronted, it does not improve with age. Indeed, the failure to make a timely confrontation often proves to result in more costs in the long run. Hassles don't dissipate as confrontation is postponed or avoided.

Conclusion

The ethics of confrontation is, quite simply, that confrontation is a necessary part of managing an honest business. Confrontation openly airs disagreement. Confrontation prevents the damage that comes from concealed truth. Confrontation preserves reputations when it produces the self-remedies that are nearly always cheaper than those imposed from the lack of confrontation. Niceness is rarely the ethical route when issues and facts need to be aired. Confrontation, although not pleasant, is often the resolution of a problem and an opportunity to avoid greater harm.

Discussion Questions

1. What are the consequences of the failure to raise an issue, whether legal or ethical, when it first arises?

2. What factors contribute to the failure to confront an issue?

3. What steps could a business take to encourage confrontation?

4. Is the failure to confront a form of hiding information? Is it giving a false impression? Do any other ethical dilemma categories apply?

Ethics in Action 7.3

The Slacker on the Team

You are part of a five-member team in your strategy class. You have been assigned to work with a local company to help them with the development of a strategic plan. Fifty percent of your grade in the class will come from the report you develop for the company along with a presentation of your plan to the officers of the company and your management professor. The company has made it clear that there is a possibility that it will be hiring as interns or full-time employees the members of any team whose strategic plan is adopted.

Robin, one of your team members, is what your other team members call a "slacker." He has attended only 25% of the team meetings and has not contributed to the writing of the report or compiling the analytics that will be used in the report. The only meetings he has attended are those that involve officers of the company. He is always on time, dressed impeccably, and participates extensively in the discussions with those officers. You and your team members have talked about Robin and his lack of participation but no one has spoken to Robin about your concerns.

Your report is now due, and your professor has required each team member to turn in independently an evaluation of the work and effort of the other team members. That evaluation will count for 50% of that team members' grade for the project. The project is worth 500 points, with 250 going to the professor's evaluation of the report and presentation and 250 points going to team members' evaluations of each other. As a result, if your report earns 235 points from the professor but a team member's evaluation is a "0," then the team member would receive only 235 points, a failing grade. You are going over Robin's evaluation wondering what you should put down for his points and your comments.

Discussion Questions

1. Who are the stakeholders in your ethical dilemma?

2. How did you get into this situation at this point?

3. If you were Robin, how would you want to be treated?

4. If you give Robin a good evaluation, what will be the consequences?

5. What if you learned that Robin has been offered a job by one of the officers of the company because the officer group was impressed with their interactions with him?

6. Why are the ethics of confrontation a critical component in our interactions with others?

Case 7.17

Office Romances and Me Too: McDonald's *et al.*

From Barack and Michelle Obama to Bill Gates and Melinda Gates to Brad Pitt and Angelina Jolie, romance befalls many at work, whether they are working at a law firm or a software company, or making a movie together. Romance is even more prevalent among the less famous. The data indicate that 39% of us have dated a coworker. One question to ask as a follow-up is, "Were your employers aware of the dating?" There are conflicts when supervisors date employees, and sometimes what may seem like an office romance can turn into accusations of harassment. Sometimes, as in the case of Bill and Melinda Gates, dating at the office while still married becomes a problem of harassment as well as divorce.[112]

The number of executives and others involved in office romances, workplace assault or harassment, and inappropriate remarks at work is too great to fit into a single textbook. Because of the "Me Too" movement, where the dating at work was not voluntary, the case studies in this area outnumber the financial reporting case studies. There are three parts to this case:

a. A detailed case study of McDonald's and its termination of its CEO for his conduct as well as the resulting creation of an atmosphere of harassment;

b. A summary of other cases of harassment involving other companies; and

c. A reading on creating policies and codes, understanding the confrontation piece and how to approach investigations, discipline, and preserving a culture free from sexual pressures and harassment.

The McDonald's Drama

In November 2019, the McDonald's corporate board did an abbreviated investigation into the conduct of its then CEO, Steve Easterbrook. Mr. Easterbrook had admitted that he had engaged in a sort of electronic relationship with an employee. McDonald's policy standards prohibited employees who have a direct or indirect reporting relationship from "dating or having a sexual relationship."[113] McDonald's explanation of the policy highlighted the reason, "It is not appropriate to show favoritism or make business decisions based on emotions or friendships rather than the best interests of the company."[114]

Although the investigation verified that there was a type of electronic relationship, the investigation went no further. In addition, Mr. Easterbrook had assured the board that there was no sexual relationship involved. No one collected all of Mr. Easterbrook's emails, a standard practice in investigations, especially those involving CEOs and other executives. Rather, having the desire to put the ugliness of it all behind, the board concluded that it did not have enough evidence to prove that Mr. Easterbrook's behavior (sending sexually explicit text messages and photographs and engaging in FaceTime calls with an employee) involved "dishonesty, fraud, illegality or moral turpitude."[115] Had the board known of the newly discovered emails, those four contractual words in Mr. Easterbrook's contract would have been grounds for termination without the severance package. The board was left initially with policy violations and poor judgment. Upon his termination, Mr. Easterbrook was given $700,000 in cash and $17.4 million in stock grants. The stock grants, depending on when they were exercised, could reach a value over $100 million.

The Post-Settlement Evidence

The board settled with Mr. Easterbrook before finishing the standard elements of such an investigation. The board had not reviewed all of Mr. Easterbrook's emails, including those on the company server. In its haste to resolve the issues and put the ugliness behind it, the board did not do the type of forensic sweep of the company's server for deleted or sent email. The board also did not conduct interviews with employees about Mr. Easterbrook's conduct. As is the case in all organizations, frontline employees have significant information about the conduct of their leaders.

Shortly after Mr. Easterbrook's departure and the board's brief investigation was closed, at least three employees came forward and reported that they had had sexual relationships with Mr. Easterbrook.[116]

(continued)

---

[112]Anupreeta Das, Emily Flitter, and Nicholas Kulish, "Culture of Fear Is Said to Reign At Gate's Firm," *New York Times*, May 27, 2021, p. A1.
[113]David Yaffe-Bellany, "Firing Reflects Rise in Scrutiny of Work Relationships," *New York Times*, November 5, 2019, p. B6.

[114]*Id.*
[115]David Gelles and Julie Creswell, "Chief Repays McDonald's $105 Million After Ouster," *New York Times*, December 17, 2021, p. B1.
[116]David Enrich and Rachel Abrams, "McDonald's Wants Ex-C.E.O.'s, Severance Back," *New York Times*, August 11, 2020, p. A1.

Case 7.17

(continued)

Further review of emails on the company server revealed that Mr. Easterbrook had attempted to remove from the company server his emails that were to women in the company (and others) and were sexual in nature. Those emails had been forwarded to his Hotmail account and deleted from the company server. Mr. Easterbrook apparently did not understand that sending those emails to himself left them in his "Sent" box. Ironically, in investigations, those are the types of emails easily tracked because they appear in chain form and are all sent to another of the sender's email accounts. Those emails corroborated the allegations that had emerged post-settlement. Within the emails were "dozens of nude, partially nude or sexually explicit photographs and videos of various women, including photographs of the reporting company employees that Easterbrook had sent as attachments to messages from his company account to his personal e-mail account."[117]

The board found that Mr. Easterbrook had violated his "dishonesty" and "moral turpitude" contractual clause and filed suit to clawback the severance payment, something Mr. Easterbrook initially challenged.[118] However, after one year, and the discretion to see what evidentiary discovery in the case would do to his reputation, Mr. Easterbrook returned $105 million in compensation, "the largest clawback in corporate history."[119] Mr. Easterbrook issued a statement upon his termination, "During my tenure as C.E.O., I failed at times to uphold McDonald's values and fulfill certain of my responsibilities as a leader of the company. I apologize to my former co-workers, the board and the company's suppliers for doing so."[120]

Board chairman Enrique Hernandez, Jr. issued his own statement about what happened, noting that it was important to hold Mr. Easterbrook "accountable for his lies and misconduct, including the way in which he exploited his position as C.E.O."[121]

---

[117]David Gelles and Julie Creswell, "Chief Repays McDonald's $105 Million After Ouster," *New York Times*, December 17, 2021, p. B1, at B3.
[118]David Enrich and Rachel Abrams, "McDonald's Sues Former C.E.O., Accusing Him of Lying and Fraud," *New York Times*, August 10 2020, https://www.nytimes.com/2020/08/10/business/mcdonalds-ceo-steve-easterbrook.html.
[119]David Gelles and Julie Creswell, "Chief Repays McDonald's $105 Million After Ouster," *New York Times*, December 17, 2021, p. B1, at B3.
[120]*Id.*
[121]*Id.* at B1.

Additional Issues: The Culture

Another aspect of the deeper dive that came about after the initial settlement was the board of directors identifying HR as the root of the apparent party culture that had consumed McDonald's during the Easterbrook tenure. The board concluded that the head of HR, David Fairhurst, who was brought from the United Kingdom with Mr. Easterbrook, made women in the company feel uneasy. The women described his behavior at a holiday party that involved heavy drinking and inappropriate physical contact.[122] In addition, employees were reluctant to raise concerns because of fear of retaliation. While the board initially allowed Mr. Fairhurst to leave with an announcement that he was moving on to other opportunities, the new head of HR announced to employees nine months later that he had been fired for his behavior.[123]

The electronic meeting that the new head of HR held was unusual in the sense of its candor. At the meeting, the changes in policies and direction were clear as the new head of HR, or as McDonald's renamed the position, Global Chief People Officer, told employees not only of the terminations but that the leadership team now in place in the company and in HR was different from those who occupied those positions before. The meeting and candid disclosures were done to set a different cultural tone.

Discussion Questions

1. McDonald's performed very well under Mr. Easterbrook's leadership. He is credited with the turn-around McDonald's experienced, including through his breakfast-all-day initiative. Stock performance was excellent, with shares nearly doubling in value. Does performance level affect whether organizations do investigations and take disciplinary action?

2. What do you learn about the privacy of your emails on your work servers?

3. Referring back to Unit 4, what other factors existed in the culture at McDonald's that prevented the information about the behaviors of Mr. Easterbrook and Mr. Fairhurst from being reported for so long?

4. Make a list of the mistakes the board made in conducting its investigation.

5. Describe the hesitation the board members might have felt in asking Mr. Easterbrook about his conduct.

---

[122]Heather Haddon, "McDonald's Inquiry Turns to HR," *Wall Street Journal*, August 31, 2020, p. B1.
[123]*Id.*

Case 7.18

Examples of Other Organizations with Atmospheres of Harassment

Organization	Individual(s)	Charges	Outcome
Air Force	General John E. Hyten, nominated for vice chairman of Joint Chiefs of Staff[124]	Unwanted touching, kissing of female Air Force colonel	Investigation found insufficient evidence to corroborate; confirmed as vice chairman
Anchorage, Alaska	Ethan Berkowitz, mayor of Anchorage[125]	Inappropriate relationship with local news anchor	Consensual but ended with anchor posting pictures of nude mayor on social media; anchor fired
Apollo Global Management	Leon Black, CEO[126]	Investigation of relationship with Jeffrey Epstein; model accused him of rape and being a sexual predator	Left company for health reasons; sued model who accused him of rape for defamation[127]
CBS	Les Moonves, CEO[128]	Sexual misconduct with employees	Terminated
Sixty Minutes (CBS)	Don Hewitt, creator and executive producer[129]	Sexual assault of employee	Negotiated settlement with employee ($5 million paid out since 1990 on the $450,000 settlement agreement)
Sixty Minutes (CBS)	Jeff Fager, executive producer[130]	Sexual misconduct (groping and kissing) and failure to stop sexual misconduct by others	Terminated
Sixty Minutes (CBS)	Ira Rosen, producer[131]	Inappropriate sexual comments	Resigned after Mr. Fager left; says he made inappropriate sexual comments at an investigative journalism conference but was encouraging reporters to use their sex appeal to secure information[132]
Sixty Minutes (CBS) Morning Show (CBS)	Charlie Rose, correspondent, and anchor	Sexual misconduct	Terminated

(continued)

---

[124]Helene Cooper, "Colonel Accuses Top Military Nominee of Assault," *New York Times*, July 29, 2019, p. A1.

[125]Mike Baker, "Alaska Mayor 'Admits' Inappropriate Messaging with TV Anchor," *New York Times*, October 14, 2020, p. A12.

[126]Miriam Gottfried, "Apollo Reviews CEO's Ties to Epstein," *Wall Street Journal*, October 21, 2020, p. B1.

[127]Andrea Cavallier, "Billionaire Financier and Epstein Pal, Leon Black, 70, Claims His Apollo Co-Founder 'Bankrolled Russian Model Who Accused Him of Rape in Failed Coup to Take Over Investment Firm,'" *The Daily Mail*, January 20, 2022, https://www.dailymail .co.uk/news/article-10422953/Billionaire-financier-Leon-Black-claims-secretly-bankrolled-model-accused-rape.html.

[128]Rachel Abrams and John Koblin, "'60 Minutes' Permitted Bad Conduct,'" *New York Times*, December 7, 2018, p. B1.

[129]*Id.,* at B3.

[130]*Id.,* at B3.

[131]*Id.,* at B3.

[132]Lloyd Grove, "Former '60 Minutes' Producer Airs Dirty Laundry About Mike Wallace, Diane Sawyer, Katie Couric," *The Daily Beast*, February 15, 2021, https://www.thedailybeast.com/former-60-minutes-producer-ira-rosen-airs-dirty-laundry-about-mike-wallace-diane -sawyer-katie-couric; "Egos, Ulcers and Misbehavior," *Washington Post*, February 19, 2021, https://www.washingtonpost.com/outlook /egos-ulcers-and-misbehavior-at-60-minutes/2021/02/19/e71fc4a8-6e3f-11eb-ba56-d7e2c8defa31_story.html. See his book, *Ticking Clock: Behind the Scenes at 60 Minutes* (2021)

Case 7.18

(continued)

Organization	Individual(s)	Charges	Outcome
U.S. Army	General David Petraeus[133], top military commander in the Middle East	Affair with biographer	Guilty plea to charges of mishandling classified material (related to affair) and being forced to resign as CIA director[134]
Intel	Brian Krzanich[135]	Consensual relationship with employee; violated Intel nonfraternization policy	Resigned
Microsoft	Bill Gates[136]	Flirty invitations and emails to employees	Asked by board to stop
NBCUniversal	Ron Meyer, executive vice chairman[137]	Affair with actress that resulted in extortion	Resigned
Warner Brothers	Kevin Tsujihara, chairman[138]	Affair with same actress as Ron Meyer	Resigned
NBC	Matt Lauer,[139] *Today Show* anchor	Multiple accusations of sexual misconduct	Terminated
U.S. Court of Appeals	Judge Alex Kozinski[140]	Allegations of inappropriate cartoons, jokes, emails, and suggestive comments	Retired
Bank of America	Omeed Malik[141], managing director, hedge funds	Harassment, "bro" culture	Departed
Miramax	Harvey Weinstein[142]	30 years of sexual harassment	Settlements with eight women; 23-year prison sentence for rape and sexual assault
Activision	Throughout the company	Sexual misconduct, retaliation, discrimination, "bro" culture	Suit by California Department of Fair Employment and Housing, an investigation, by the SEC, and a complaint by EEOC that sexual harassment was "so pervasive and severe" that it served to "alter the conditions of employment"[143]

(continued)

[133]Sheryl Gay Stolberg, "After Scandal, Petraeus Stays Under the Radar, but Not Out of the Spotlight," *New York Times*, February 28, 2015, p. A12.
[134]Mark Landler and Jennifer Steinhauer, "Secretary of State Petraeus? Supporters Make Their Case," *New York Times*, December 1, 2016, https://www.nytimes.com/2016/12/01/us/politics/david-petraeus-trump-state-department.html.
[135]Don Clark, "Intel C.E.O. Resigns Post Over Affair," *New York Times*, June 22, 2018, p. B1.
[136]Emily Glazer, "Gates Told in 2008 to Stop Emailing a Staffer," *Wall Street Journal*, October 19, 2021, p. A1.
[137]Brooks Barnes and Nicole Sperling, "Media Titan Resigns Post in Scandal," *New York Times*, August 19, 2021, p. B1.
[138]*Id.*
[139]Jim Windolf, John Koblin, and Rachel Abrams, "Primary Accuser of Ex-NBC Anchor Speaks Out in Book," *New York Times*, October 16, 2019, p. B7.
[140]Jacey Fortin, "U.S. Appeals Court Judge in California Is Accused of Sexual Misconduct," *New York Times*, December 11, 2017.
[141]Jessica Silver-Greenberg and Matthew Goldstein, "Executive Out at Bank After Inquiry of Conduct," *New York Times*, January 20, 2018, p. B1.
[142]Andrea Mandell and Jayme Deerwester, "Harvey Weinstein Hit with 30 Years of Sexual Harassment," *USA Today*, October 6, 2017, p. 5D.
[143]Allysia Finley, "How Did Activision Pass the ESG Test?" *Wall Street Journal*, November 26, 2021, p. A15.

Case 7.18

(continued)

Discussion Questions

1. What common threads and lessons do you see in reviewing the companies, the fates, and the issues?

2. Notice the dates of the cases and the severity—are there lessons being incorporated by organizations to prevent sexual harassment?

3. Pick any of the organizations and do in-depth research on what happened. Determine the who, what, and when in that organization and whether signals were missed or complaints ignored.

Reading 7.19

Creating a Culture Free From Sexual Pressures, Harassment, and Favoritism: Codes, Policies, Investigations, and Confrontation

Having Codes and Policies in Place

Some rules can help both employers and their employees. The goal for employers is to prevent issues of favoritism and sexual harassment. Along the way, the employers' rules may save employees from a broken heart. Below are a few sample rules that companies use for purposes of avoiding the pitfalls of office romance.

1. Some companies simply prohibit employees who work together from having a relationship. Such a rule can be problematic because employees have the relationship anyway and simply hide it from the employer as other employees' gossip. Often, companies accompany this policy with a policy on finding one member of the couple a different position outside of the division or office where both met and are currently working.

2. Some companies prohibit relationships between employees when one reports to the other. For example, Michelle Obama was Barack Obama's supervisor at the law firm when he worked as a summer intern at the same law firm. Many companies would require a transfer or that one leave the firm.

3. Some companies follow this rule: disclose to your supervisor that you are having a romantic relationship with a coworker. The purpose of such disclosure is for the supervisor to determine whether conflicts exist or if an adjustment needs to be made because of reporting lines. That is, two employees who are dating should not be in a direct report relationship. Some companies do not permit even indirect reportees to date supervisors. These companies work to find one of the employees a different position in the company outside of the direct or indirect reporting lines.

4. Most companies remind employees that a consensual relationship that goes south can very often turn into allegations of sexual harassment. Employees are cautioned to proceed within company rules for their own protection. Some companies have what is called a "love contract" that the two employees sign upon disclosure of their relationship so that a written record exists of a consensual relationship—a protection for both the employer and the employees against sexual harassment charges.

5. Although most companies do not address the issue directly, an adulterous relationship between two employees is generally a career killer, at least within the company. During the past year, two CEOs of major firms have had to depart following disclosures of their affairs with employees.[144]

Investigations and Discipline

The McDonald's case study illustrates how not to handle an investigation. If you list the mistakes that the board made that are discussed in the case you have a guide for what not to do. However, there were some things that the McDonald's board handled correctly. Once the board found the scope of the problem, it acted by aggressively seeking return of the severance package, something that signaled to employees that the board was serious about changing the culture and would hold leaders accountable. The board also removed a close confidant of the CEO, the head of HR, who was complicit in permitted behaviors and was known to have participated in a culture of harassment at at least one company event. The board then brought in new leaders who were candid with employees about what had happened and that there was now a new approach to culture.

The Peculiar Awkwardness of Top Leadership Being an Issue

In looking through all the companies throughout this case, note the number of high-level leaders who were involved. One of the weak spots in organizations is the failure to regularly review phone records, travel expenses, flights, and other activities of these leaders. Sometimes an audit and review, by staff and the board itself, can pick up on the red flags. For example, Brian Dunn, former CEO of Best Buy, had an extremely close personal relationship with a 29-year-old employee, according to audit committee findings. The report documented the following: "During one four-day and one five-day trip abroad during 2011, the CEO contacted the female employee by cell phone at least 224 times, including 33 phone calls, 149 text messages, and 42 picture or video messages. In one instance, several photographs were discovered on the CEO's personal cell phone that contained messages expressing affection, one of which included the female employee's initials."[145]

And there is the theme of this section: confrontation is necessary. These are difficult conversations for auditors and boards to have with successful leaders, but they are necessary. Sometimes we are motivated by blindness, and, as a result,

---

[144]Susan Adams, "The State of the Office Romance 2013," *Forbes* online, February 13, 2013, http://www.forbes.com/sites/susanadams/2013/02/13/the-state-of-the-office-romance-2013/.
[145]Emily Carlyle, *Forbes*, "Bust Buy CEO Brian Dunn Gets $6.6 Million Severance Package After Friendship with 29-Year-Old Employee," May 14, 2012, https://www.forbes.com/sites/insights-smartsheet/2020/09/08/re-humanizing-marketing-five-teams-of-executives-collaborate-on-a-purpose-driven-approach/#5fa0483611c9.

we remain silent when we feel it is in our best interest to do so.[146] However, the proper ethical analysis is to review whose interests are being affected and whether, over the long term, it is in your best interests to just let it go. Perhaps, most importantly, it is never in the best interests of the leader or the organization to just let it go.

Discussion Questions

1. Explain the concerns employers have about workplace romances.
2. List the types of policies and rules employers have to avoid liability when such romances blossom.
3. How do you factor in the rights of individuals with regard to these employer policies?

Reading 7.20

The Ethics of Performance Evaluations

Many employees believe that a good performance evaluation does not translate into more money or benefits.[147] And many employees are unclear as to what "meets expectations" means.[148] Some employees believe the annual performance evaluations are a means to protect companies from discrimination suits. Still others believe that they are used to rid the company of the slackers. Employees despise "forced ranking" systems in which one-third of employees are rated high; another one-third are rated average; and the bottom one-third knows that they are on their way out the door. As Jared Sandberg of the *Wall Street Journal* puts it, the performance evaluation system in a company reveals more about the company than it does about those being evaluated.

Performance evaluation systems and employee cynicism about them could be a function of ethics. There are some basic ethical values that could improve the evaluation process.

1. Is the evaluation honest?

Employees explain that they just want to know where they stand. One factor that contributes to the perception of dishonesty is that there is too little communication throughout the year about goals, progress, and issues that have developed. For example, a loan officer's volume could be affected by new lending standards at the bank, not because of a lack of hustle on her part. A discussion of those changed standards during the year prevents a "does not meet expectations" at the end of the year.

In some situations, the annual review focuses on issues not really addressed in the original performance plan so that there is a sudden shift from what the employee thought were the goals and the achievement standards. If professionalism and personal metrics are not part of the evaluation process until the end, the employee has had no chance to work on them.

---

[146]Max H. Bazerman and Ann Tenbrunsel, "Blind Spots: Why We Fail to Do What's Right," "Ethical Breakdowns," *Harvard Business Review*, April 2011, https://hbr.org/2011/04/ethical-breakdowns.
[147]"Good Performance Does Not Mean Good Pay," *USA Today*, August 29, 2007, p. 1B.
[148]Jared Sandberg, "Performance Reviews Need Some Work, Don't Meet Potential," *Wall Street Journal*, November 20, 2007, p. B1.

In forced ranking systems, the employees must be grouped, and those groupings may not really reflect the work and effort of employees, but the numbers have to be met. Under these systems, the last-minute scramble to meet assigned rankings finds that the performance may have been good, but the ranking does not reflect that performance. The disconnect is perceived as dishonest.

Finally, the employee deserves honest feedback during the evaluation process. If coworkers are having difficulty working with an employee, that employee deserves to know that and is entitled to concrete examples. "Difficult to work with" does not provide much information. "Will not cover the front office for others when we need help" is the type of information the employee being evaluated needs to have.

2. Are the evaluation standards and terms clear?

The lion's share of the work on performance evaluations should be done in setting up the employee's work plan for the year. Employees need to understand what "You are not doing your job" means. Tardiness, customer complaints, missed deadlines, and mistakes are the kinds of substantive examples that fill in the details for employees. "Meets expectations" requires a list of expectations at the beginning of the year and feedback during the year so that this nebulous standard has measurable metrics. For example, a company had as one measurement for managers, "Emphasizes ethics and ethical culture in the company." The measurable standards were whether the manager had 100% participation by employees in ethics training, whether the manager discussed an ethical issue with employees during the year, whether ethical issues raised by employees were addressed, and whether employees all had a copy of the code of ethics.

3. Is everyone taking responsibility for the effects of performance evaluations?

If a manager tells an employee that there are problems with the employee's performance, then the manager has the responsibility to work with that employee to help with improvement. Part of evaluation is direction: tell the employee how to get better. If the employee has made mistakes, determine why those mistakes occur. Is it a need for more training? Is the employee responsible for too many areas or assignments? Is there a lack of support in the employee's job function?

Perhaps the performance evaluation process could take an ethical turn if those conducting the evaluations would remember the following:

1. Have I told the employee the truth?
2. Is the rating I have assigned consistent with the truth?
3. Are the standards for performance clear, and have I given examples?
4. Have I figured out the whys of performance and offered insights for improvement?

Discussion Questions

1. Why are managers less than truthful in performance evaluations?

2. What are the effects of not being truthful in performance evaluations?

3. Is "being nice" easier than offering candid evaluations?

4. What are some examples of ambiguous evaluation criteria?

Case 7.21

Ann Hopkins and Price Waterhouse

Ann Hopkins was a senior manager in the Management Advisory Services division of the Price Waterhouse (now PwC) Office of Government Services (OGS) in Washington, DC. After earning undergraduate and graduate degrees in mathematics, she taught mathematics at her alma mater, Hollins College, and worked for IBM, NASA, Touche Ross, and American Management Systems before beginning her career with Price Waterhouse in 1977.[149] She became the firm's specialist in large-scale computer system design and operations for the federal government. Although salaries in the accounting profession are not published, estimates put her salary as a senior manager at about $65,000.

At that time, Price Waterhouse was known as one of the "Big 8," or one of the top public accounting firms in the United States.[150] A senior manager became a candidate for partnership when the partners in her office submitted her name for partnership status. In August 1982, at the end of a nomination process that began in June, the partners in Hopkins's office proposed her as a candidate for partner for the 1983 class of partners. Of the 88 candidates who were submitted for consideration, Hopkins was the only woman. At that time, Price Waterhouse had 662 partners, 7 of whom were women.[151] Hopkins was, however, a stellar performer and was often called a "rainmaker." She was responsible for bringing to Price Waterhouse a two-year, $25 million contract with the U.S. Department of State, the largest contract ever obtained by the firm.[152] Being a partner would not only bring Hopkins status, but her earnings would increase substantially. Estimates of the increase in salary were that she would earn almost double, or $125,000 annually, on average (1980 figures).

The partner process was a collaborative one. All the firm's partners were invited to submit written comments regarding each candidate, on either "long" or "short" evaluation forms. Partners chose a form according to their exposure to the candidate. All partners were invited to submit comments, but not every partner did so. Of the 32 partners who submitted comments on Hopkins, one stated that "none of the other partnership candidates at Price Waterhouse that year [has] a comparable record in terms of successfully procuring major contracts for the partnership."[153] In addition, Hopkins' billable hours were impressive, with 2,442 in 1982 and 2,507 in 1981, levels that none of the other partnership candidates' billable hours even approached.

After reviewing the comments, the firm's Admissions Committee made recommendations about the partnership candidates to the Price Waterhouse Policy Board. The recommendations consisted of accepting the candidate, denying the promotion, or putting the application on hold. The Policy Board then decided whether to submit the candidate to a vote, reject the candidate, or hold the candidacy. There were no limits on the number of persons to whom partnership could be awarded and no guidelines for evaluating positive and negative comments about candidates. Price Waterhouse offered 47 partnerships to the 88 candidates in the 1983 round; another 27 were denied partnerships; and 20, including Ms. Hopkins, were put on hold. Ms. Hopkins had received more "no" votes than any other candidate for partnership, with most of those votes coming from members of the partnership committee outside the firm's government services unit.

The comments on Hopkins were extensive and telling. Thirteen of the thirty-two partners who submitted comments on Hopkins supported her, three recommended putting her on hold, eight said they did not have enough information, and eight recommended denial. The partners in Hopkins's office praised her character as well as her accomplishments, describing her in their joint statement as "an outstanding professional" who had a "deft touch," a "strong character,

(continued)

---

[149]Reports conflict in regard to her starting date at Price Waterhouse. Some reports indicate 1977, and some indicate 1978.
[150]Price Waterhouse no longer exists, having merged into PricewaterhouseCoopers, and the "Big 8" is now the "Big 4" due to the collapse of Arthur Andersen and the mergers of most of the other firms.
[151]There are factual disputes over the number. Hopkins maintains that there were only six female partners at the time.
[152]Ann Hopkins, "Price Waterhouse v. Hopkins: A Personal Account of a Sexual Discrimination Plaintiff," 22 *Hofstra Lab. & Emp. L.J.* 357 (2005).

[153]*Price Waterhouse v. Hopkins*, 490 U.S. 228 (1989).

Case 7.21

(continued)

independence, and integrity." Clients appear to have agreed with these assessments. One official from the State Department described her as "extremely competent, intelligent," "strong and forthright, very productive, energetic, and creative." Another high-ranking official praised Hopkins's decisiveness, broad-mindedness, and "intellectual clarity"; she was, in his words, "a stimulating conversationalist."[154] Hopkins "had no difficulty dealing with clients and her clients appear to have been very pleased with her work."[155] She "was generally viewed as a highly competent project leader who worked long hours, pushed vigorously to meet deadlines, and demanded much from the multidisciplinary staffs with which she worked."[156]

On too many occasions, however, Hopkins's aggressiveness apparently spilled over into abrasiveness. Staff members seem to have borne the brunt of Hopkins's brusqueness. Long before her bid for partnership, partners evaluating her work had counseled her to improve her relations with staff members. Although later evaluations indicate an improvement, Hopkins's perceived shortcomings in this important area eventually doomed her bid for partnership. Virtually all of the partners' negative remarks about Hopkins—even those of partners who supported her—concerned her "interpersonal skills." Both "[s]upporters and opponents of her candidacy indicated that she was sometimes overly aggressive, unduly harsh, difficult to work with, and impatient with staff."[157]

Another partner testified at trial that he had questioned her billing records and was left with concern because he found her answers unsatisfying:

I was informed by Ann that the project had been completed on schedule within budget. My subsequent review indicated a significant discrepancy of approximately $35,000 between the proposed fees, billed fees [and] actuals in the WIPS. I discussed this matter with Ann who attempted to try and explain away or play down the discrepancy. She insisted there had not been a discrepancy in the

amount of the underrealization. Unsatisfied with her responses, I continued to question the matter until she admitted there was a problem but I should discuss it with Krulwich [a partner at OGS]. My subsequent discussion with Lew indicated that the discrepancy was a result of 500 additional hours being charged to the job (at the request of Bill Devaney ... agreed to by Krulwich) after it was determined that Linda Pegues, a senior consultant from the Houston office working on the project had been instructed by Ann to work 12–14 hrs per day during the project but only to charge 8 hours per day. The entire incident left me questioning Ann's staff management methods and the honesty of her responses to my questions.[158]

Clear signs indicated, though, that some of the partners reacted negatively to Hopkins's personality because she was a woman. One partner described her as "macho," whereas another suggested that she "overcompensated for being a woman," and a third advised her to take "a course at charm school."[159] One partner wrote that Hopkins was "universally disliked."[160] Several partners criticized her use of profanity. In response, one partner suggested that those partners objected to her swearing only "because it[']s a lady using foul language."[161] Another supporter explained that Hopkins "ha[d] matured from a tough-talking somewhat masculine hardnosed manager to an authoritative, formidable, but much more appealing lady partner candidate."[162] In order for Hopkins to improve her chances for partnership, Thomas Beyer, a partner who supervised Hopkins at OGS, suggested that she "walk more femininely, talk more femininely, dress more femininely, wear make-up, have her hair styled, and wear jewelry."[163] Ms. Hopkins said she could not apply makeup because that would require removing her trifocals and she would not be able to see. Also, her allergy

(continued)

---

[158]Appellant's brief, *Price Waterhouse v. Hopkins*, 490 U.S. 228 (1989).
[159]*Price Waterhouse v. Hopkins*, 490 U.S. 228 (1989), p. 235.
[160]Hopkins, "*Price Waterhouse v. Hopkins.*" See footnote 152, supra.
[161]*Id.*
[162]*Id.*
[163]*Id.*

---

[154]*Id.*, p 234.
[155]*Id.*
[156]*Id.*
[157]*Id.*, p. 235.

Case 7.21

(continued)

to cosmetics made it difficult for her to find appropriate makeup. Mr. Beyer also suggested that she should not carry a briefcase, should stop smoking, and should not drink beer at luncheon meetings.

Dr. Susan Fiske, a social psychologist and associate professor of psychology at Carnegie-Mellon University who would testify for Hopkins in her suit against Price Waterhouse, reviewed the Price Waterhouse selection process and concluded that it was likely influenced by sex stereotyping. Dr. Fiske indicated that some of the partners' comments were gender biased, and even those comments that were gender neutral were intensely critical and made by partners who barely knew Hopkins. Dr. Fiske concluded that the subjectivity of the evaluations and their sharply critical nature were probably the result of sex stereotyping.[164]

However, there were numerous comments such as the following that voiced concerns about nongender issues:

In July/Aug 82 Ann assisted the St. Louis MAS practice in preparing an extensive proposal to the Farmers Home Admin (the proposal inc 2800 pgs for $3.1 mil in fees/expenses & 65,000 hrs of work). The proposal was completed over a 4 wk period with approx 2000 plus staff/ptr hrs required based on my participation in the proposal effort & sub discussions with St. L MAS staff involved. Ann's mgmt style of using "trial & error techniques" (ie, sending staff assigned off to prepare portions of the proposal with little or no guidance from her & then her subsequent rejection of the products developed) caused a complete alienation of the staff towards Ann & a fear that they would have to work with Ann if we won the project. In addition, Ann's manner of dealing with our staff & with the Houston sr consultant on the BIA project, raises questions in my mind about her ability to develop & motivate our staff as a ptr. (No) [indicates partner's vote][165]

I worked with Ann in the early stages of the 1st State Whelan Dept proposal. I found her to be a) singularly

dedicated, b) rather unpleasant. I wonder whether her 4 yrs with us have really demonstrated ptr qualities or whether we have simply taken advantage of "workaholic" tendencies. Note that she has held 6 jobs in the last 15 yrs, all with outstanding companies. I'm also troubled about her being (having been) married to a ptr of a serious competitor.[166] (Insuff—but favor hold, at a minimum)

Ann's exposure to me was on the Farmers Home Admin Blythe proposal. Despite many negative comments from other people involved I think she did a great job and turned out a first class proposal. Great intellectual capacity but very abrasive in her dealings with staff. I suggest we hold, counsel her and if she makes progress with her interpersonal skills, then admit next year. (Hold)[167]

Although Hopkins and 19 others were put on hold for the following year, her future looked dim. Later, two partners withdrew their support for Hopkins, and she was informed that she would not be reconsidered the following year. Hopkins, who maintains that she was told after the second nomination cycle that she would never be a partner, then resigned and filed a discrimination complaint with the Equal Employment Opportunity Commission (EEOC).[168]

The EEOC did not find a violation of Title VII of the Civil Rights Act of 1964 (which prohibits discrimination in employment practices) because of the following: (1) Hopkins had resigned and not been terminated; and (2) at that time, the law was not clear, and the assumption was that Title VII did not apply to partnership decisions in companies. With the EEOC refusing to take action, Hopkins filed suit against Price Waterhouse. She has stated she filed the suit to find out why Price Waterhouse made "such a bad business decision."[169] After a lengthy trial and numerous complex appeals through the federal system, the Supreme Court found that Ms. Hopkins did

(continued)

---

[164]Cynthia Cohen, "Perils of Partnership Reviews: Lessons from Price Waterhouse v. Hopkins," *Labor Law Journal* (October 1991): 677–682.
[165]*Price Waterhouse v. Hopkins*, 490 U.S. 228 (1989).

[166]Ms. Hopkins left Deloitte Touche when her husband was made a partner there and firm policy prohibited partners' spouses from working for the company.
[167]*Price Waterhouse v. Hopkins*, 490 U.S. 228 (1989).
[168]*Id.*, p. 233.
[169]M. Jennings, Interview with Ann Hopkins, June 18, 1993.

Case 7.21

(continued)

indeed have a cause of action for discrimination in the partnership decision.

Hopkins was an important employment discrimination case because the Supreme Court recognized stereotyping as a way of establishing discrimination. However, the case is also known for its clarification of the law in situations in which employers take action against employees for both lawful and unlawful reasons. Known as *mixed-motive cases*, these cases involved forms of discrimination that shift the burden of proof to the employer to establish that it would have made the same decision if using only the lawful considerations and despite unlawful considerations that entered into the process. The "same-decision" defense requires employers to establish sufficient grounds for termination or other actions taken against employees that are independent of the unlawful considerations.

In 1990, on remand, Ms. Hopkins was awarded her partnership[170] and damages. She was awarded back pay plus interest, and although the exact amount of the award is unclear, Hopkins later verified that she paid $300,000 in taxes on her award that year and also paid her attorneys the $500,000 due to them. Ms. Hopkins was also awarded her partnership status and rejoined Price Waterhouse as a partner (principal) in 1991.

In accounting firms today, women are 50% of full-time employees. The number of female principals (partners—see footnote 170) has grown from 1% in 1983 to 23% today.[171] Ms. Hopkins retired from PricewaterhouseCoopers in 2002 and wrote a book about her experience as a litigant, *So Ordered: Making Partner the Hard Way* (1996). You can find it on Amazon for $130.32. She also experienced years' long litigation over the death of her youngest son, who was struck by a drunk driver. She enjoyed gardening and grandchildren before her death in 2018. She remains a pioneer for the rights of professional women.

Discussion Questions

1. What ethical problems do you see with the Price Waterhouse partnership evaluation system?

2. In what ways, if any, do you find the subjectivity of the evaluation troublesome? What aspects of the evaluation would you change?

3. To what extent did the partners' comments reflect mixed motives (i.e., to what extent did their points express legal factors while at the same time expressing illegal ones)?

4. Ms. Hopkins listed three factors to help companies avoid what happened to her: (1) clear direction from the top of the enterprise, (2) diversity in management, and (3) specificity in evaluation criteria. Give examples of how a company could implement these factors.

---

[170]Technically, Ms. Hopkins was made a principal, a title reserved for those reaching partner status who do not hold CPA licenses.

[171]"Women in Accounting (Quick Take)," *Catalyst: Workplaces That Work for Women*, June 29, 2020, https://www.catalyst.org /research/women-in-accounting/.

Why Didn't They Say Something? 7.3

The Silent Women Partners

Suppose that you were a partner and a member of either the admissions committee or the policy board when Ann Hopkins came up for review. What objections, if any, would you have made to any of the comments by the partners? What would have made it difficult for you to object? How might your being a female partner in that position have made objection more difficult?

Compare & Contrast

Ms. Hopkins described her interactions with and reactions to Kay Oberly, the lawyer who argued Price Waterhouse's case before the U.S. Supreme Court:

In the years since she argued the firm's case before the Supreme Court, I have had the pleasure of meeting Kay Oberly on several occasions.

"Nothing personal. Litigation polarizes," she said when we were first introduced. The warmth of her smile and the sincerity that radiated from troubled eyes banished any recollection I had of her at the arguments. I gave her a ride to the airport once. I was driving to work and noticed her unsuccessfully trying to hail a cab. We chatted about being single parents and the trauma of divorce proceedings, matters that we had in common. I like Kay. "Nothing personal. Litigation polarizes." I'm sure it wasn't personal to her, but it was to me. Discrimination cases tend to get very personal, very fast. My life became a matter of public record. Attorneys pored over my tax returns. People testified about expletives I used, people I chewed out, work I reviewed and criticized, and they did so with the most negative spin they could come up with. I'm no angel, but I'm not as totally lacking in interpersonal skills as the firm's attorneys made me out to be.[172]

Offer your thoughts on personal feelings, personal ethics, and litigation. Can we separate out who we are personally from the battles we find ourselves in at work and professionally? Is there a danger in having two different approaches to your personal life and your work life? For example, suppose you felt that Ann Hopkins was dealt with unjustly—could you argue against her position? Suppose that you felt your company was being unfair in not promoting a fellow employee, would you make a case on her behalf?

---

[172]Id., p. 366.

Famous Lines from Art and Literature

You've Got Mail (1998)

Joe Kelly is a chain bookstore owner who is about to put Kathleen Kelly, a small bookshop owner, out of business. They have the following exchange:

Joe Fox: It wasn't . . . personal.

Kathleen Kelly: What is that supposed to mean? I am so sick of that. All that means is that it wasn't personal to you. But it was personal to me. It's *personal* to a lot of people. And what's so wrong with being personal, anyway?

Joe Fox: Uh, nothing.

Kathleen Kelly: Whatever else anything is, it ought to begin by being personal.

Case 7.22

The Glowing Recommendation[173]

Randi W. was a 13-year-old minor who attended the Livingston Middle School, where Robert Gadams served as vice principal. On February 1, 1992, while Randi was in Gadams's office, Gadams sexually molested Randi.

Gadams had previously been employed at the Mendota Unified School District (from 1985 to 1988). During his time of employment there, Gadams had been investigated and reprimanded for improper conduct with female junior high students, including giving them back massages, making sexual remarks to them, and being involved in "sexual situations" with them.

Gilbert Rossette, an official with Mendota, provided a letter of recommendation for Gadams in May 1990. The letter was part of Gadams's placement file at Fresno Pacific College, where he had received his teaching credentials. The recommendation was extensive and referred to Gadams's "genuine concern" for students and his "outstanding rapport" with everyone and concluded, "I wouldn't hesitate to recommend Mr. Gadams for any position."

Gadams had also previously been employed at the Tranquility High School District and Golden Plains Unified District (1987–1990). Richard Cole, an administrator at Golden Plains, also provided a letter of recommendation for the Fresno placement file that listed Gadams's "favorable" qualities and concluded that Cole "would recommend him for almost any administrative position he wishes to pursue." Cole knew at the time he provided the recommendation that Gadams had been the subject of various parents' complaints, including that he "led a panty raid, made sexual overtures to students, [and made] sexual remarks to students." Cole also knew that Gadams had resigned under pressure because of these sexual misconduct charges.

Gadams's last place of employment (1990–1991) before Livingston was Muroc Unified School District, where disciplinary actions were taken against him for sexual harassment. When allegations of "sexual touching" of female students were made, Gadams was forced to resign from Muroc. Nonetheless, Gary Rice and David Malcolm, officials at Muroc, provided a letter of recommendation for Gadams that described him as "an upbeat, enthusiastic administrator who relates well to the students" and who was responsible "in large part" for making Boron Junior High School (located in Muroc) "a safe, orderly and clean environment for students and staff." The letter concluded that they recommended Gadams "for an assistant principalship or equivalent position without reservation."

All the letters provided by previous administrators of Gadams were sent in on forms that included a disclosure that the information provided "will be sent to prospective employers."

Through her guardian, Randi W. filed suit against the districts, alleging that her injuries from Gadams's sexual touching were proximately caused by their failure to provide full and accurate information about Gadams to the placement service.

Discussion Questions

1. If you were a former administrator to whom Gadams reported, what kind of recommendation would you give?

2. Should the previous administrators have done something about Gadams prior to being placed in this dilemma?

3. Do administrators owe their loyalty to employees? To students? To the school district? To the parents? Are they all stakeholders?

4. Is this type of recommendation commonly given to get rid of employees?

5. Should friendship have a higher value than honesty?

6. Why do you think the administrators said nothing?

---

[173]Adapted from *Randi W. v. Muroc Joint Unified School District*, 929 P.2d 582 (Cal. 1997).

Ethics in Action 7.4

Loudon County School Board Silence

On May 28, 2021, a gender-fluid boy, age 15, who was wearing a skirt, raped a 9th grade girl in the women's bathroom at Stone Bridge High School, a Loudoun County school. The assailant was arrested on July 13, 2021, and charged with two counts of forcible sodomy and one count of forcible fellatio.[174]

At the June 2021 meeting of the Loudoun County School Board (LCSB), there was a discussion of the board's transgender policy because parents had raised concerns about sexual assault. The Loudoun County Public Schools (LCPS) superintendent told those in the hearing that their concerns were not justified because the LCSB had no record of any assaults in any school bathrooms. At that point, a woman told Scott Smith, the father of the 9th grader who had been raped, that she did not believe his daughter. A police officer pulled Mr. Smith's arm as he had a heated exchange with the woman. When Mr. Smith pushed the officer away, there was a scuffle. Mr. Smith was handcuffed, pulled across the floor with his pants pulled down, and charged with disorderly conduct.

The assailant was transferred to another LCSD school, where he assaulted another student in a classroom on October 7, 2021. He was found "not innocent" of the charges from May and entered a no contest plea to the charges from October.[175] He was sentenced in January 2022 to supervised probation in a residential facility until he is 18 and must register as a sex offender for life.[176]

The LCSB hired a law firm to investigate the LCPS's handling of the assaults. That report has been completed but has not been released.[177] Mr. Smith was found guilty of disorderly conduct and sentenced to 10 days in jail, suspended, contingent on a year of good behavior.[178]

---

[174]Luke Rosiak, "Loudoun County Schools Tried to Conceal Sexual Assault Against Daughter in Bathroom, Father Says," *Daily Wire.com*, https://www.dailywire.com /news/loudoun-county-schools-tried-to-conceal-sexual-assault-against-daughter -in-bathroom-father-says.
[175]Brittany Bernstein, "Loudoun County Schools Double Down, Won't Release Report on Sexual Assault Allegations," *National Review*, January 14, 2022, https://www.nationalreview.com/news/loudoun-county-schools-double-down -wont-release-report-on-sexual-assault-allegations/.
[176]Hayley Milon Bour, "High School Sexual Assailant to Register as Sex Offender," *LoudounNow*, January 12, 2022, https://www.loudounnow.com/news/education /high-school-sexual-assailant-to-register-as-sex-offender/article_972daaa4-a60d -5a2d-a519-a28d74cfa26d.html.
[177]Hayley Milon Bour, "Loudon School Division Withholding Sexual Assault Report," *LoudounNow*, January 11, 2022, https://loudounnow.com/2022/01/11 /loudoun-school-division-withholding-sexual-assault-report/.
[178]Renss Greene, "Smith Found Guilty in School Board Scuffle," *LoudounNow*, August 17, 2021, https://loudounnow.com/2021/08/17/smith-found-guilty-in -school-board-scuffle/.

Discussion Questions

1. Why did the LCPS superintendent not disclose in the public meeting that an assault had occurred?

2. Was the desire to protect the transgender bathroom policy a factor in how the hearing was handled?

3. What will be the effects of the assaults and the hearing on the LCSB and parents in the LCPS district going forward?

Key Terms

Confrontation   p. 512

Two sets of books   p. 482

Unit **8** Ethics and Products

Learning Objectives

- Discuss the ethical categories that apply in evaluating advertising content.

- Explain the ethical issues and analysis in dealing with product safety issues.

- Apply ethical analysis to the types of sales techniques that businesses use.

- Describe how the culture of a company influences decisions about advertising, product safety, and sales techniques.

Products are points of pressure. There is pressure to get those products out there on the market. There is the pressure to sell, sell, sell those products. Even buyers, on occasion, feel the pressure to buy, buy, buy. And there is even the pressure that comes when problems with a product arise—to recall or not to recall, that is the question. Or is it?

Advertising Content

Ads sell products. But how much can the truth be stretched? Are ads ever irresponsible by encouraging harmful behavior?

Case 8.1

Elon Musk and Puffing

The Initial Tweets

On August 7, 2018, at 12:48 P.M. EDT, Elon Musk, then chairman of Tesla Motors, tweeted to his over 22 million Twitter followers, "Am considering taking Tesla private at $420. Funding secured."[1] Over the next three hours, Mr. Musk made a series of tweets, including:

- "My hope is *all* current investors remain with Tesla even if we're private."

- "Would create special purpose fund enabling anyone to stay with Tesla."

- "Shareholders could either to [sic] sell at 420 or hold shares & go private."

- "Investor support is confirmed. Only reason why this is not certain is that it's contingent on a shareholder vote."[2]

Market and Company Responses

When he sent the tweets out, Mr. Musk had never discussed a going-private transaction at $420 per share with a potential funding source. He had discussed selling shares to a Saudi investment fund but had done nothing to investigate whether it would be possible for all current investors to remain with Tesla as a private company via a "special purpose fund" and had not confirmed support of Tesla's investors for going private.

Mr. Musk later explained that the funding would be through a Saudi investment fund, but there had only been oral discussions with the fund. There was no agreement or even an outline of a potential agreement for funding "going private."[3] Also, no Foreign Investment application had been filed; a government process required before foreign funds can purchase interests in U.S. companies.

Still, depending on how investors viewed the Musk tweets, there was significant market reaction and a great deal of buying and selling of Tesla stock. From the time of Musk's first tweet until the close of trading on August 7, Tesla's stock price increased by more than 6% with significantly increased volume and closed up 10.98% from the previous day. Some market participants invest in the stock with the belief that what has been said will come to pass. But there are other types of market investors—those who look at the same information and believe that the price of a company's stock will fall—the short sellers. They have contracted to sell shares in the future. When stock is shorted, these investors, who do not own shares at the time of the sale, believe the price of the stock will fall and hope to buy the stock at the lower price to cover their short positions and earn a profit. If the price of the stock rises, short sellers

(continued)

---

[1] *SEC v. Musk*, CV No. 1:18-cv-8865, https://www.sec.gov /litigation/complaints/2018/comp-pr2018-219.pdf.

[2] *Id.*

[3] Jessica Silver-Greenberg, Neal E. Boudette, Kate Kelly, and London Thomas Jr., "Tweet on Tesla Going Private Was a Surprise," *New York Times*, August 14, 2018, p. A1.

Case 8.1

(continued)

end their short positions by purchasing the stock at the higher price, with the resulting losses. By August 2018, more than $13 billion worth of Tesla shares were "shorted."

The Chaos

After the announcement, there was great uncertainty in the market. Nasdaq had to halt trading by 2:08 P.M. EDT that day because of uncertainty and confusion. When Tesla's investment relations office and CFO were flooded with questions, Mr. Musk tweeted more:

One Twitter user asked, "Could we still invest once private?" Musk responded, "Yes, but liquidity events would be limited to every 6 months or so (like SpaceX)."[4]

Musk responded to another Twitter user who wrote, "Or if you do take Tesla private, please have a provision for retail investors who have held Tesla shares prior to Dec 31, 2016 that those shares will be converted into private shares in the new private company. . . ." by tweeting, "Absolutely. Am super appreciative of Tesla shareholders. Will ensure their prosperity in any scenario."[5]

The U.S. Regulators Step In

On September 27, 2018, the SEC filed a civil complaint against Mr. Musk alleging that he misled shareholders. The SEC sought in the complaint to have Mr. Musk ousted and was considering a remedy of banning him from serving as an officer or director of a publicly traded company. When the SEC complaint was filed, Tesla shares dropped 9.9%, to $277. The Department of Justice then opened a criminal investigation.[6] The share price dropped 3.4% when that investigation was disclosed.

The complaint listed the following as allegedly false, misleading, or incomplete information not included in the tweets:

- The board had not approved taking Tesla private (the board had not discussed "going private" with Mr. Musk).

- The board was not aware of the "going private" discussions until receiving an email from Mr. Musk

---

[4]*SEC v. Musk*, CV No. 1:18-cv-8865, https://www.sec.gov/litigation/complaints/2018/comp-pr2018-219.pdf.

[5]*SEC v. Musk*, CV No. 1:18-cv-8865, https://www.sec.gov/litigation/complaints/2018/comp-pr2018-219.pdf.

[6]Tim Higgins and Dave Michaels, "Tesla Is Subject of DOJ Probe," *Wall Street Journal*, September 19, 2018, p. B1.

on August 2 explaining why he thought it was a good idea to take Tesla private.

- Mr. Musk did not disclose how the $420 price was determined, which was quite a story and not based on anything strategic or calculated with the help of financial and market advisers. He calculated that price per share based on a 20% premium over that day's closing share price because he thought 20% was a "standard premium" in going-private transactions. This calculation resulted in a price of $419, and Musk stated that he rounded the price up to $420 because he had recently learned about the number's significance in marijuana culture and thought his girlfriend "would find it funny, which admittedly is not a great reason to pick a price."

- The discussions with the investment fund did not include discussions of percentage of ownership or share price.

- Part of the discussions focused on a requirement that Tesla build a factory in the Middle East.

- There was no discussion of whether the investment fund had the liquid capital available for such a purchase.

- Mr. Musk believed that there was only a 50% chance that the going-private deal could go through.

- Mr. Musk had talked with a private equity fund purchaser who told him that what he was proposing to do was unprecedented.

In addition to the SEC concerns, Mr. Musk had not followed a Nasdaq rule that required listed companies to notify Nasdaq at least 10 minutes prior to publicly releasing material information about corporate events like a proposed going-private action.

The Legal Issues

If Mr. Musk were selling goods, the legal analysis could be that he was puffing. **"Puffing"** is salesmanship. "This is the greatest car on the market." "You will search high and low before you find potato chips this good." But when it comes to statements about companies that are

(continued)

Case 8.1

(continued)

publicly traded, there is little room for puffing. There were too many facts and figures in the Musk tweets to fit into the category, "You are going to love the new Tesla model" type of advertising.

In response to the initial tweets, some market analysts and reporters were not convinced that the tweets were real. The confusion continued. A business reporter texted Musk's chief of staff, "Quite a tweet! (Is it a joke?)."[7] Another reporter sent Musk an email with the subject, "Are you just messing around?" and wrote, "Reaching out to see what's going on with your tweets about taking the company private? Is this just a 420 joke gone awry? Are you serious? It seems like you are dancing into some pretty tricky legal territory by messing about with the markets this way. Is there an actual explanation coming?"[8]

The pretty tricky legal territory was an accurate statement. It was not until August 24 that the market got a glimpse of the obstacles going private faced when Mr. Musk posted the following on his blog:

> Given the feedback I've received, it's apparent that most of Tesla's existing shareholders believe we are better off as a public company. Additionally, a number of institutional shareholders have explained that they have internal compliance issues that limit how much they can invest in a private company. There is also no proven path for most retail investors to own shares if we were private. Although the majority of shareholders I spoke to said they would remain with Tesla if we went private, the sentiment, in a nutshell, was "please don't do this."[9]

On the next trading day, August 27, 2018, Tesla stock closed at $319.27, down over 15% from the closing price of $379.57 on August 7, the date of Musk's initial tweets about taking Tesla private.[10]

There were baseless assumptions, missing material facts, uncertainty beyond a shareholder vote, and clear confusion, even among market experts.

The Resolution of the Complaint

Mr. Musk initially fought the SEC complaint, "This unjustified action by the S.E.C. leaves me deeply saddened and disappointed. I have always taken action in the best interests of truth, transparency, and investors. Integrity is the most important value in my life and the facts will show I never compromised this in any way."[11] Mr. Musk rejected an SEC offer of stepping down for two years as chairman and paying a $10 million fine.[12] However, just two days after rejecting the SEC settlement offer, the SEC announced a settlement agreement with Tesla and Mr. Musk with these harsher terms:

- Musk will step down as Tesla's Chairman and be replaced by an independent Chairman. Musk will be ineligible to be re-elected Chairman for three years;

- Tesla will appoint a total of two new independent directors to its board;

- Tesla will establish a new committee of independent directors and put in place additional controls and procedures to oversee Musk's communications;

- Musk and Tesla will each pay a separate $20 million penalty. The $40 million in penalties will be distributed to harmed investors under a court-approved process. [13]

In 2019, the SEC asked a judge to hold Mr. Musk in contempt for his failure to follow the terms of the settlement that required approval for his tweets.[14] The SEC also cited Tesla for its failure to supervise Mr. Musk's tweets. The judge told the parties to "take

(continued)

---

[7]*Id.,* at p. 13.

[8]*SEC v. Musk,* CV No. 1:18-cv-8865, https://www.sec.gov/litigation/complaints/2018/comp-pr2018-219.pdf, p. 2.

[9]*Id.,* at pp. 15–16.

[10]*Id.,* at p. 16.

[11]Matthew Goldstein and Emily Flitter, "Tesla Chief Elon Musk Is Sued by S.E.C. in Move That Could Oust Him," *New York Times,* September 27, 2018, https://www.nytimes.com/2018/09/27/business/elon-musk-sec-lawsuit-tesla.html.

[12]Matthew Goldstein, "Elon Musk Steps Down as Chairman in Deal with S.E.C. Over Tweet About Tesla," *New York Times,* September 29, 2018, https://www.nytimes.com/2018/09/29/business/tesla-musk-sec-settlement.html.

[13]"Elon Musk Settles SEC Fraud Charges; Tesla Charged With and Resolves Securities Law Charge," *SEC Press Release,* September 29, 2018, https://www.sec.gov/news/press-release/2018-226.

[14]Dave Michaels and Tim Higgins, "Musk, SEC Reach Deal to End Court Fight over Tesla CEO's Tweets," *Wall Street Journal,* April 26, 2019, https://www.wsj.com/articles/elon-musk-sec-propose-deal-to-end-latest-court-fight-over-tesla-ceos-tweets-11556314495.

Case 8.1

(continued)

a deep breath, put their reasonable-ness pants on and work it out."[15] They were ordered to develop a list of what Mr. Musk could tweet about without approval from Tesla lawyers.

Discussion Questions

1. One analyst noted about the whole series of events, "There is a fine line between hyperbole and falsehood."[16] Is that statement accurate about what Mr. Musk tweeted?

2. Mr. Musk said that one of the reasons he wanted to go private was to defeat the "shorts," the shortsellers, because of his concerns that they released negative and false information into the news as a means of driving Tesla's stock price down to preserve their positions. Are shortsellers doing their own form

of puffing or misrepresentation? The shortsellers on Tesla lost $5 billion between 2016 and 2018.[17] Tesla's stock climbed 27% during that same time frame. But, thanks to the Musk tweets on going private, the shortsellers made $1 billion in one week. Whom are the shortsellers harming?

3. During an earnings conference call with analysts and investors just prior to his "going private" tweets, Mr. Musk told them that they asked, "boring, bonehead questions."[18] Based on what you have learned about leaders in Units 4 and 7, what warnings, insights, and lessons did Mr. Musk need at the time of the SEC complaint against him?

4. Make a list of the kinds of things that Mr. Musk could tweet with the standard of "reasonableness pants."

---

[15]Edward Helmore, "Tesla CEO Elon Musk in 'Clear Violation' of SEC Restraint," *The Guardian*, April 4, 2019, https://www.theguardian.com/technology/2019/apr/04/elon-musk-tesla-sec-court-new-york.

[16]Charley Grant, "Tesla Gets a Moment of Reckoning," *Wall Street Journal*, September 28, 2016, p. B12.

[17]Stephen Grocer, "$1 Billion Gift to Investors Who Want to Fail," *New York Times*, August 18, 2018, p. B1.

[18]James B. Stewart, "Inside the Mind of a Visionary," *New York Times*, August 16, 2018, p. B1, at B3.

Case 8.2

Burger King and the Impossible Vegan Burger

Burger King introduced a new product called the "Impossible Burger" and advertised it as a "vegetarian patty, topped with tomatoes, lettuce, pickles, onions, ketchup, and mayonnaise" and "100% Whopper, 0% beef."[19]

However, the vegan patties were cooked on the same grill as the beef patties, so vegan customers brought a class-action suit against Burger King accusing the chain of false and misleading ad claims.

There were also some instances in which customers who had ordered the Impossible Burger were given a real beef patty instead. Burger King experienced another suit in 2001 when it described its French fries as vegetarian because they were fried in vegetable oil. However, it failed to disclose that it used beef flavor in its French fries.

Multiple Hindu customers filed suit because cows are considered holy animals in Hinduism. McDonald's faced the same issue and settled the suit by donating $10 million to vegetarian and Hindu groups.

In 2016, a judge dismissed a suit against Buffalo Wild Wings for its failure to disclose that its French fries and mozzarella sticks were cooked in beef tallow. The judge held that the parties failed to show how they were injured.

Discussion Questions

1. Is there a difference between intentional misrepresentation and an oversight in disclosure?

2. Who are the stakeholders in ongoing suits against chains and restaurants for the failure to disclose ingredients?

3. If you are selling food to the public, make a checklist for the questions you should ask about your product and the cooking processes and develop a disclosure statement.

---

[19]Abdi Latif Dahir, "Impossibly Close for Comfort, Suit Says," *New York Times*, November 20, 2019, p. B4.

Case 8.3

About Returning That Rental Car and the Gas Tank: Contract Terms

When you rent a car, you are told to be sure to return the car with the gas tank full or you will be charged for a full tank of gas or, with some of the nicer companies, for the cost of the gas you used given the car's mileage. However, you must be sure to read the fine print. In that fine print are many conditions, such as:

- You must have filled up the car at a gas station within five miles of the rental car return location.

- You must have filled up the car within one-half hour of the time of your return to the rental car location.

- If you have not filled up the tank and the rental company prorates the gas charge by miles driven, the rental car company will compute the cost of gas based on miles driven and mpg. However, the computations always seem to be done using Hummer rather than Nissan mileage—no matter which size car you actually rent, the computation of mpg will involve a gas guzzler. You do not get subcompact gas mileage when they compute what you owe for gas.

- You must have a receipt that has a matching date as well as the time on it.

- You must have a receipt that indicates that it is your receipt—that the credit card information matches your credit card. If you pay cash, good luck with this provision.

- Generally, low-cost rental companies have the most rules on gas tank and refilling and less willingness to give customers a break. What you save in rental fees is lost when the gas bill comes in.

- Not all the rules are on the refueling notice posted on the board that you see as you check out your car. You must read the contract.

Discussion Questions

1. Use one of the ethical questions from Unit 1 to provide an ethical standard that the rental car companies might use to prevent customer dissatisfaction.

2. Is fairness an ethical standard?

3. Why have the rental car companies developed so many rules on the gas tanks and returning them full?

Sources
David Segal, "Bring It Back Full, or Don't. You'll Pay Either Way," *New York Times*, July 3, 2016, p. BU3.
Marianne M. Jennings—21 years of car rental experience

Product Safety

Quality, safety, service, and social responsibility—customers want these elements in a product and a company. Does the profit motive interfere with these traits?

When is a product safe enough for sale? What happens if the product develops problems after it has been sold? What if a product cannot be made safe?

Reading 8.4

A Primer on Product Liability

From Shunning to Anonymity

When someone purchased the butter churner or the wagon wheel from a neighbor in the era of wagons and churning, there was no need for the Restatement of the Law of Torts. If the churner or the wheel was defective, the neighbor simply made good on the product or risked the mighty shunning that the community would dish out for those who dared to be less than virtuous, forthright, and in a relationship of good rapport with one's fellow village dwellers. When neighbor manufactured for neighbor, the rule of law was *caveat vendor*, which, loosely translated, meant, "If you want to continue living here, you had better take care of the problem with the crooked wagon wheel."

The birth of the industrialized society changed the community dynamic so that some communities made wheels, some made churners, and those in other communities purchased those goods even as they sold their specialties that they produced. The result was that buyers knew the merchant who sold them the wheel or the churn but had no idea who really put together either, or, in many cases, were not even sure which community produced either. The one-to-one process of implementing product quality and guarantees disappeared. Even the ads for the wheels and churns were written by some copywriter far, far away who was a subcontractor of an advertising agency working for the manufacturing companies of these products.

The physical and production distance between seller and buyer meant that the one-on-one confrontation and shunning methods were no longer effective. The law shifted from *caveat vendor* to *caveat emptor*, which, translated, means "buyer beware." Now the buyer had to be on guard, ever vigilant in inspecting goods before buying, and had to investigate the company doing the selling so they could at least be sure of the company's reputation. The greater these physical and supply chain distances, the less likely the buyer was to have any information about the company, the product, or the history of either. And it was even less likely that the buyer could count on a seller repairing or replacing defective goods. Anonymity created a marketplace in which there were few or no buyer remedies.

Ralph Nader and Unsafe at Any Speed

During the 1960s, the law began to whittle away at the anonymity protections and immunity that manufacturers and sellers enjoyed when they sold their wares. In 1965, Ralph Nader published *Unsafe at Any Speed: The Designed-In Dangers of the American Automobile*, a book that was directed in its specific analysis at General Motors' Corvair but that urged liability for auto manufacturers for their failure to research and implement product safety standards in their automobiles. Because of the stir the book created, a U.S. Senate subcommittee asked the CEOs of the automakers to testify about their commitment to auto safety research. Then–U.S. Senator Robert Kennedy had the following exchanges with then-CEO James Roche and then-Chairman of the Board of General Motors Frederic Donner:

Kennedy:	What was the profit of General Motors last year?
Roche:	I don't think that has anything to do—
Kennedy:	I would like to have that answer if I may. I think I am entitled to know that figure. I think it has been published. You spend a million and a quarter dollars, as I understand it, on this aspect of safety. I would like to know what the profit is.
Donner:	The aspect we are talking about is safety.
Kennedy:	What was the profit of General Motors last year?
Donner:	I would have to ask one of my associates.
Kennedy:	Could you, please?
Roche:	$1,700,000,000.
Kennedy:	What?
Donner:	About a billion and a half, I think.
Kennedy:	About a billion and a half?
Donner:	Yes.
Kennedy:	Or $1.7 billion, you made $1.7 billion last year?
Donner:	That is correct.
Kennedy:	And you spent $1 million on this?
Donner:	In this particular facet we are talking about....
Kennedy:	If you gave just 1 percent of your profits, that is $17 million.

The drama of the moment was historically significant. From that point forward, the nature of seller and manufacturer liability, in the auto industry and consumer products generally, changed. The message was clear: part of the cost of manufacturing consumer products is ensuring their safety. Within the decade, we would see the first appellate court decision that held Johns-Manville responsible for the damage to workers' lungs from asbestos exposure. Strict liability, or full accountability for one's products akin to the days of one-on-one sales, had returned.

The Legal Basis for Product Liability

Product liability has two foundations in law. The first is in contract found in the Uniform Commercial Code (UCC). The second is under tort law.

Contract/UCC Product Liability

Express Warranties: What You Say, Display, and Picture

An express warranty as provided in the Uniform Commercial Code (UCC) is an express promise (oral or written) by the seller as to the quality, abilities, or performance of a product (UCC § 2-313). The seller need not use the words *promise* or *guarantee* to make an express warranty. A sample, a model, or just a description of the goods is a warranty. Promises of what the goods will do are also express warranties. "22 mpg" is an express warranty, which is why the claim is always followed by "Your mileage may vary." Other examples of express warranties are "These goods are 100 percent wool," "This tire cannot be punctured," and "These jeans will not shrink."

Any statements made by the seller to the buyer before the sale is actually made that are part of the basis of the sale or bargain are express warranties. Also, the information included on the product packaging constitutes an express warranty if those are statements of fact or promises of performance. So, ads count as warranties. Statements by salespeople count as warranties.

The Implied Warranty of Merchantability: At Least Average Goods

The implied warranty of merchantability (UCC § 2-314) is given in every sale of goods by a merchant seller. Merchants are those sellers who are engaged in the business of selling the goods that are the subject of the contract. This warranty requires that goods sold by a merchant "are fit for the ordinary purposes for which goods of that description are used." This warranty means that food items are not contaminated and that cars' steering wheels do not break apart. Basketballs bounce, mobile homes do not leak when it rains, and brakes on cars do not fail.

The Implied Warranty of Fitness for a Particular Purpose

The implied warranty of fitness for a particular purpose (UCC § 2-315) is the salesperson's warranty. If a buyer asks the owner of a nursery what weed killer would work in his garden and the nursery owner makes a recommendation that proves to kill the roses, the nursery owner has breached this warranty and has liability to the rose gardener. An exercise enthusiast who relies on an athletic shoe store owner for advice on which particular shoe is appropriate for aerobics also gets the protection of this warranty.

Product Liability Under Tort Law

The second basis for product liability lies in tort law. Under the Restatement of Torts (Section 402A), anyone who manufactures or sells a product is liable to the buyer if the product is in a defective condition that makes it unreasonably dangerous. A product can be defective by design, the allegation that Mr. Nader made against GM for its Corvair when he stated that the position of the engine in the rear of the car made it dangerous for the occupants of the car. A product can also be dangerous because of shoddy manufacturing, as when there is a forgotten bolt or a failure to attach a part correctly. Finally, a product can be defective because the instructions or warnings are inadequate. "Do not stand on the top of the ladder," "Do not use this hair dryer near water," and "Not suitable for children under the age of three" are all examples of warnings that are given to prevent injuries through use of the product.

Tort liability exists even when the manufacturer or seller is not aware of the problem. For example, a prescription drug may cause a reaction in adults who take aspirin. The manufacturer may not have been aware of this side effect, but the manufacturer is still responsible for the harm caused to those who have the reaction. The idea behind strict liability rests in the Senate hearings exchange: manufacturers need to devote enough resources to product development and research to determine that their products are made safely and that risks are discovered and disclosed before consumers are harmed.

The expansion of product liability from just UCC/contract law to tort law also meant that the traditional notion of "privity of contract" was no longer required. *Privity of contract* is a direct contract relationship between parties. Prior to the restatement standard, a buyer would not have a remedy against a manufacturer for its defective product and certainly could not go back to the bolt supplier or to the manufacturer if the bolt in a product turned out to be defective. The effect of strict tort liability is to hold sellers and manufacturers fully accountable for products up and down the supply chain. The defect may begin with a supplier, but the manufacturer and seller are not excused from liability because "someone else did it." Under strict tort liability standards, all companies associated with the design, production, and sale of defective products have responsibility for damages and injuries caused by that product.

Discussion Questions

1. Who are the stakeholders in the question of who should bear the costs of defective products?

2. Relate the discussion of the development of product liability theories for recovery to the regulatory cycle (see Reading 3.1).

Case 8.5

Peanut Corporation of America: Salmonella and Indicted Leaders

The Peanut Corporation of America was a supplier of processed peanuts to some of the largest food-production companies in the United States, including ConAgra, a major producer of peanut butter. The company was founded by Hugh Parnell Sr. when he was selling ice cream vending machines in the 1960s. When he was restocking a machine, he noticed that the peanuts on the Nutty Buddy ice cream cones came from a plant in the North. He decided to begin a company that processed peanuts in the South, where they were grown. The company grew with plants in Lynchburg, Virginia; Blakely, Georgia; and Plainview, Texas.[20] The company produced peanut paste, which is the base used in the production of peanut butter, cookie filling, and other types of peanut-flavored foods.

Stewart Parnell entered the business in the 1970s, when he complained to his father that those in his major, oceanography, often ended up working on oil rigs. His father offered him a job, and Stewart left college to begin work in the Virginia facilities. The company's sales grew, and in 1995 the Parnells sold the company to Morvan Partners LLP. Stewart worked as a consultant for the new buyer but bought back the company in 2000. By 2008, gross sales were $30,000,000 per year. Michael Parnell, Stewart Parnell's brother, was the vice president of P.P. Sales, a Lynchburg, Virginia, food broker for producers, manufacturers, and producers of food. Michael oversaw the negotiation and execution of contracts for Peanut Corporation's products, including supervision of the biological testing of those products.

Peanut Corporation's base was sold to its customers for use in peanut butter, ice cream, cookies, and crackers. Peanut Corporation was known for its cost

(continued)

---

[20]The information on Peanut Corporation and its history and products was found in the criminal indictment following the salmonella poisonings, https://www.justice.gov/iso/opa/resources/61201322111426350488.pdf. Last visited October 25, 2022. *U.S. v. Parnell*, 1:13-CR-12-WLS.

Case 8.5

(continued)

cutting. When a prospective customer came back with a bid from another peanut product company that was lower, Stewart Parnell, the CEO of Peanut Corporation, would always cut the price by a few cents to win over the potential customer.

The price cuts were possible because of cost-cutting at the plant. Peanut Corporation paid low wages to temporary workers and offered few benefits programs. Emails reflect Parnell's concerns about costs. When a salmonella test was positive, Peanut Corporation was required to hold off shipment for a retest. However, in response, Parnell wrote in an email, "We need to discuss this. Beside the cost, this time lapse is costing us $$$$ and causing us obviously a huge lapse from the time when we pick up the peanuts until the time we can invoice."[21] When he was informed that the test results for salmonella were not complete, he also wrote, "Turn them loose."[22] When Mr. Parnell was notified by a customer that the products the customer had received tested positive for salmonella, Mr. Parnell responded in email, "I am dumbfounded by what you have found. It is the first time in my over 26 years in the peanut business that I have ever seen an instance of this. We run Certificates of Analysis EVERY DAY with tests for Salmonella and have not found any instances of any, even traces, of a Salmonella problem." (Emphasis in original.)[23]

When the FDA made the connection between Peanut Corporation and the salmonella poisonings, Mr. Parnell wrote, "Obviously we are not shipping any peanut butter products affected by the recall but desperately at least need to turn the raw peanuts on the floor into money."[24]

Following the discovery of Peanut Corporation as the source of salmonella in peanut products that were sickening customers in 44 states, Congress held hearings into Peanut Corporation's operations. Stewart Parnell took the Fifth Amendment when members of the Commerce Committee in the House of Representatives asked him questions about his company.

The peanut product caused 700 illnesses in 44 states and resulted in nine deaths because of the salmonella that then made its way into peanut butter, peanut butter crackers, and other products that use a peanut base. The company declared Chapter 7 bankruptcy on February 13, 2009.

In 2013, the Department of Justice filed a 76-page indictment against Mr. Parnell, three former managers, and food broker, Michael Parnell, with charges of criminal fraud. The indictment names Mr. Parnell, the former owner of Peanut Corporation; Samuel Lightsey, a plant operator at the company; and the company's former quality-assurance manager, Mary Wilkerson. The indictment alleges that the four engaged in a conspiracy to hide the fact that tests showed the presence of salmonella in the peanut meal, or peanut base. The indictment was stunning in that it alleged that the group worked together to fabricate test results to show salmonella-free product when salmonella was present.

Experts note that criminal charges in food-poisoning cases are rare because the proof of intent, or *mens rea*, is difficult or impossible to demonstrate when there is a one-time problem. However, as discussed above, Mr. Parnell was being notified by customers that his company's product was testing positive, and yet he still continued production without cleaning up the plant. In addition, Michael Parnell was charged with providing fictitious certifications (COAs) to customers. An email from Michael to Stewart read, "Truthfully if a customer called and needed one (COA) that was for 2 pallets or so [Peanut Corporation of America] would create one. Most of the time smaller people will accept one produced with your company heading on it that looked professionally done. The girl in TX was very good at white-out."[25] The indictment also alleges that the four who were charged misled FDA inspectors in January 2009, conduct that added obstruction of justice to the charges in the indictment.

Mr. Parnell went to trial.[26] However, one portion of the indictment includes an email from an employee about

(continued)

---

[21]Jane Zhang and Julie Jargon, "Peanut Corp. Emails Cast Harsh Light on Executive," *Wall Street Journal*, February 12, 2009, p. A3.
[22]Id.
[23]Indictment, p. 26.
[24]Id.

[25]Indictment, p. 27.
[26]Sabrina Tavernise, "Charges Filed in Peanut Salmonella Case," *New York Times*, February 22, 2013, p. B6.

Case 8.5

(continued)

peanut meal containers at the plant that could be shipped to fill orders, but "[t]hey need to air hose the opt off though because they are covered in dust and rat crap."[27] Mr. Parnell responded to the employee, "Clean 'em all up and ship them."[28]

The jury convicted the defendants, and Mr. Parnell was sentenced to 28 years, which, at his age of 63 at the time, is in effect a life sentence. His brother was sentenced to 20 years. Mr. Parnell filed a motion to have his verdict vacated on the grounds that he did not have adequate legal representation. The judicial decision on that motion is pending.

Discussion Questions

1. Discuss the theories for imposing liability on Peanut Corp.

2. Based on what you have studied in the financial and workplace cases in Units 4, 5, and 7, explain how the group working together was able to justify falsifying tests and risking the presence of salmonella.

3. Mr. Parnell's father, Hugh Parnell Sr. said, "He's being railroaded. Why would anybody send something out that would ruin his own company? It's like an auto dealer sending a car out with no brakes."[29] What defense is he raising for his son? Explain why Mr. Parnell acted as he did. What rationalizations entered into his decisions and emails?

Sources

Schmidt, Julie, "Peanut President Refuses to Testify," *USA Today*, February 12, 2009, p. 2B.

Zhang, Jane, "Peanut Corp. for Bankruptcy," *Wall Street Journal*, February 14–15, 2009, p. A3.

---

[27] From the indictment, https://www.justice.gov/iso/opa/resources/61201322111426350488.pdf, p. 29.

[28] Indictment, pp. 4–6.

[29] Ilan Bray and Julie Jargon, "Career in Peanuts Began as a Detour from Oceanography," *Wall Street Journal*, February 19, 2009, p. A6.

Case 8.6

Tylenol: The Product Safety Issues

The Chicago Capsule Poisonings

In 1982, 23-year-old Diane Elsroth died after taking a Tylenol capsule laced with cyanide. Within five days of her death, seven more people died from taking tainted Tylenol purchased from stores in the Chicago area.

At that time, Tylenol generated $525 million per year for McNeil Consumer Products, Inc., a subsidiary of Johnson & Johnson. The capsule form of the pain reliever represented 30% of Tylenol sales. McNeil's marketing studies indicated that consumers found the capsules easy to swallow and believed, without substantiation, that Tylenol in capsule form worked faster than Tylenol tablets.

The capsule's design, however, meant they could be taken apart, tainted, and then restored to the packaging without evidence of tampering. After the Chicago poisonings, which were never solved, McNeil and Johnson & Johnson executives were told at a meeting that processes for sealing the capsules had been greatly improved, but no one could give the assurance that they were tamperproof.

The executives realized that abandoning the capsule would give their competitors, Bristol-Myers (Excedrin) and American Home Products (Anacin), a market advantage, plus the cost would be $150 million just for 1982. Jim Burke, then-CEO of Johnson & Johnson, told the others that without a tamperproof package for the capsules, they would risk the survival of not only Tylenol but also Johnson & Johnson. The executives decided to abandon the capsule.

Frank Young, a Food and Drug Administration (FDA) commissioner, stated at the time, "This is a matter of Johnson & Johnson's own business judgment,

(continued)

Case 8.6

(continued)

and represents a responsible action under tough circumstances."[30]

Johnson & Johnson quickly developed "caplets"—tablets in the shape of a capsule—and then offered consumers a coupon for a bottle of the new caplets if they turned in their capsules. Within five days of the announcement of the capsule recall and caplets offer, 200,000 consumers had responded. Johnson & Johnson had eliminated a key product in its line—one that customers clearly preferred—in the interest of safety. Otto Lerbinger of Boston University's College of Communication cited Johnson & Johnson as a "model of corporate social responsibility for its actions."[31]

Then-President Ronald Reagan, addressing a group of business executives, said, "Jim Burke, of Johnson & Johnson, you have our deepest admiration. In recent days you have lived up to the very highest ideals of corporate responsibility and grace under pressure."[32]

Within one year of the Tylenol poisonings, Johnson & Johnson regained its 40% market share for Tylenol. Although many attribute the regain of market share to tamperproof packaging, the other companies had moved to that form as well. However, it is interesting to note that McNeil was able to have its new product and packaging on the shelves within weeks of the fatal incidents. There had been some preparation for the change prior to the fatalities, but the tragedy was the motivation for the change to safer packaging and product forms.

McNeil has continued to enjoy the goodwill from its rapid response to the poisonings as well as its willingness to take the financial hit for what experts believed was a very small risk that more cyanide-laced Tylenol was out on the shelves. In fact, the recall was so indelibly etched in the public's mind and in the minds of those in the field of business ethics that McNeil, Johnson & Johnson, and Tylenol itself were often given free passes on conduct that did pose safety risks to customers. As new issues with Tylenol have developed, McNeil seems to be

given the benefit of the doubt because of the goodwill and reputational capital it purchased with the capsule recalls.[33]

Tylenol and Liver Damage

On December 21, 1994, the *Journal of the American Medical Association (JAMA)* published the results of a five-and-a-half-year study showing that moderate overdoses of acetaminophen (known most widely by the brand name Tylenol) led to liver damage in 10 patients.[34] The damage occurred even in patients who did not drink and was most pronounced in those who did drink or had not been eating. Further, the study by Dr. David Whitcomb at the University of Pittsburgh Medical School found that taking one pill of acetaminophen per day for a year may double the risk of kidney failure.[35] By 2001, 450 deaths resulted from liver failure due to Tylenol overdoses.

At that time, the American Association of Poison Control Centers called acetaminophen poisonings the most common of all reported poisonings.[36] The number of pediatric poisonings from overdoses of acetaminophen has more than tripled since 1996. As a result, the FDA adjusted the adult and pediatric doses that were acceptable in 2009. However, adult deaths from overexposure are more likely to be the result of suicidal ingestion.

Tylenol is a stunning source of revenue for McNeil and Johnson & Johnson, with revenue totals growing at double-digit rates as Tylenol expanded market presence into 5,000 convenience stores with new and smaller packaging of its product and its new formulas, such as Tylenol PM.[37]

Tylenol users who claimed they were victims of overdose and liver damage and the lack of effective warnings have not been successful against

(continued)

---

[30]"Drug Firm Pulls All Its Capsules Off the Market," *(Phoenix) Arizona Republic*, February 18, 1986, p. A2.

[31]Pat Guy and Clifford Glickman, "J & J Uses Candor in Crisis," *USA Today*, February 12, 1986, p. 2B.

[32]"The Tylenol Rescue," *Newsweek*, March 3, 1986, p. 52.

[33]"Legacy of Tampering," *Arizona Republic*, September 29, 1992, p. A1.

[34]"Acetaminophen Overdoses Linked to Liver Damage," *Mesa (Arizona) Tribune*, December 21, 1994, p. A12; and Doug Levy, "Acetaminophen Overuse Can Lead to Liver Damage," *USA Today*, December 22, 1994, p. 1D.

[35]"Second Tylenol Study Links Heavy Use to Kidney Risk," *(Phoenix) Arizona Republic*, December 22, 1994, p. A6.

[36]www.aapcc.com. Accessed June 10, 2010.

[37]Thomas Easton and Stephan Herrera, "J&J's Dirty Little Secret," *Forbes*, January 12, 1998, pp. 42–44.

Case 8.6

(continued)

Johnson & Johnson.[38] McNeil has modified the recommended dosages, the ad claims, and language on its labels. The product labels before current modification read, "Gentle on an infant's stomach," and Tylenol's ad slogan was "Nothing's safer." That language has been removed, and McNeil added to its infant Tylenol label: "Taking more than the recommended dose … could cause serious health risks" because of liver damage in children.[39]

McNeil also responded to data that showed patients who combine Tylenol with alcohol have produced 200 cases of liver damage in the past 20 years, with fatality in 20% of those cases. The level of alcohol use by patients among these cases was multiple drinks every day. McNeil modified its labels to include bold warnings about alcohol use and the dangers of combining Tylenol with any drinking.

Despite the extensive coverage of the issues surrounding Infant Tylenol, Tylenol overdoses, and issues with liver damage from combining alcohol and Tylenol, the company did not experience any loss of market share or even extensive negative media coverage. The goodwill from Tylenol's earlier recall appeared to see it through these crises. However, other issues were emerging.

The Tylenol Quality Control Program

Metal Debris in Products

In May 2010, the FDA was considering bringing criminal charges against McNeil for a pattern of violations in its quality control in the production of children's Tylenol. The charges would spring from the April 30, 2010, recall by McNeil of 136 million bottles of liquid pediatric Tylenol, Motrin, Benadryl, and Zyrtec because the medicines contained too much metal debris or too much of the necessary active ingredient in these over-the-counter drugs. Because of the presence of metal debris, the medicine batches failed FDA testing. However, prior to the FDA testing and the recall, there was evidence that McNeil was aware of the developing problem but took no public action.

Silence and the Surreptitious Recall

A purchase order that the company turned over to congressional investigators indicated that McNeil had hired a contractor in 2009 to visit 5,000 stores and buy Motrin from the shelves. The contractor's PowerPoint materials instructed employees to act like any other customer and make "no mention of this being a recall when making a purchase."[40] McNeil told congressional investigators that "The Motrin Purchase Project" was created by a McNeil subcontractor without its knowledge and approval. McNeil said it notified the FDA about two Motrin lots that did not dissolve properly and that it was removing the Motrin from the shelves.

The evidence submitted for the hearings showed that McNeil had received 46 complaints from consumers about black particles in Tylenol and other McNeil products. However, McNeil did not notify the FDA nor did it recall the medicines. The inaction in the face of customer harm represented the straw that broke the FDA's back of tolerance, because the company, at that point, was finishing two years of an ongoing tussle with regulators over quality control. At one plant that manufactured Children's Tylenol, seven batches of product were released after testing revealed problems in three batches. The agency's frustration in dealing with the plants and managers for inaction and ongoing violations led to the review of the company for possible criminal charges.

The surreptitious removal of Motrin from retail stores because McNeil had discovered quality-control problems with that product was referred to by the FDA as, in effect, an unannounced, or "phantom," recall.[41] Also in 2008, McNeil failed to notify the FDA that it had received complaints from customers about a moldy smell in some of the products made in its Puerto Rican production facilities and, at the same time, failed to disclose complaints from customers about stomach problems experienced after they had used the "moldy" products. McNeil tested the products and found no problems, but

(continued)

[38]Deborah Sharp, "Alcohol-Tylenol Death Goes to Trial in Florida," *USA Today*, March 24, 1997, p. 3A.

[39]Richard Cole, "Tylenol Agrees to Warning on Labels of Risk to Children," *Arizona Republic*, October 19, 1997, p. A5.

[40]Natasha Singer, "Johnson & Johnson Seen as Uncooperative on Recall Inquiry," *New York Times*, June 11, 2010, pp. B1, B4.

[41]Natasha Singer, "F.D.A. Weighs More Penalties in Drug Recall," *New York Times*, May 28, 2010, p. A1.

Case 8.6

(continued)

the complaints continued through 2009. Further testing showed that the medicine had been contaminated by a chemical used in the plant for the treatment of wooden shipping pallets. One member of Congress noted that the recall on the "smell" issue took one year and that it should have taken three days.

At another plant, the FDA found that the company "knowingly" used an ingredient that was tainted with *Burkholderia cepacia*, a bacteria that most healthy people can handle, but that can cause serious infections in those with chronic illnesses such as cystic fibrosis.[42] Another member of Congress said of the congressional inquiry, "We are not getting the kind of information and cooperation from Johnson that I would like."[43]

The Fallout on Sales

As consumers purchased generic brands to substitute for the recalled Tylenol products, McNeil's sales of Tylenol dropped 55%, a loss of $1.4 billion in sales. Its market share dropped to number eight after being at number two, behind only Advil prior to the public disclosure of the issues and the lack of a recall.[44] The FDA and Johnson & Johnson entered into a consent decree that required McNeil to correct the problems that had been discovered in several of the company's plants, including revamping the production and testing requirements that would require independent verification. McNeil terminated several executives, including its vice president for OTC drugs, and restructured the management team as well as the supervisory teams at many of its production facilities.

As a result of the Tylenol issues, the FDA began inspections of other OTC manufacturers that resulted in 43 letters being sent to OTC drug factories for their failure to correct "shoddy manufacturing practices that may have exposed patients to health risks."[45] The letters indicated

that FDA inspectors had found insects in equipment and ingredients, improper testing, failure to conduct required tests, and disregard for customer complaints. More than half of the plants inspected had violations, even if those violations did not rise to the level of receiving the agency's letter warning.

In congressional hearings on the issues discovered at McNeil, the House Committee on Oversight and Government Reform chastised McNeil executives: "The information I've seen during the course of our investigation raises questions about the integrity of the company. It paints a picture of a company that is deceptive, dishonest, and has risked the health of many of our children."[46]

In 2012, McNeil suffered another setback when it had to issue a recall for 574,000 bottles of Infant Tylenol due to design defects in the bottles. The recall came shortly after the company had met standards and returned the infant Tylenol to the market. One expert on pharmaceutical marketing noted that restoring consumer confidence is difficult and "now, they have another uphill battle."[47]

Other Products and the Split

Johnson & Johnson is the parent company for over 250 subsidiaries. Between 2021 and 2023, J & J announced that it would be splitting the company into two subsidiaries. All of the recalls, product safety issues, and litigation have taken their toll on the company.

The Baby Powder (Talc) Liability

J & J currently has 34,600 product liability lawsuits pending against it for ovarian cancer, asbestos poisoning, and other illnesses that plaintiffs maintain were caused by their use of J & J baby powder. Because of the presence of asbestos in the powder (something J & J denied), the product was removed from retail stores. J & J now sells a baby powder that has no talc, just corn starch. A Missouri verdict in 2018 resulted in a $4.7 billion verdict for 24 women (that was later reduced to $2.1 billion), and the U.S. Supreme court refused to

(continued)

[42]Alison Young, "Plant in Recall Had Other Violations," *USA Today*, May 27, 2010, p. 3A.

[43]Natasha Singer, "Johnson & Johnson Seen as Uncooperative on Recall Inquiry," *New York Times*, June 11, 2010, p. B1.

[44]Jonathan D. Rockoff, "J & J Recalls Infants' Tylenol," *Wall Street Journal*, February 18–19, 2012, p. B1.

[45]Alison Young, "FDA Warns 43 Drug Manufacturers," *USA Today*, May 27, 2010, p. 3A.

[46]Mina Kimes, "Why J & J's Headache Won't Go Away," *Fortune*, September 6, 2010, p. 100.

[47]Id.

Case 8.6

(continued)

grant *certiorari* in the appeal of that case.[48] With that decision and $4 billion in legal expenses disclosed in its annual 10K report, J & J placed its talc subsidiary that manufactured into bankruptcy in late 2021 "to resolve all claims related to cosmetic talc in a manner that is equitable to all parties."[49]

The *Huffington Post* labeled J & J "America's Most Admired Lawbreaker," a play on the company's consistent presence in *Fortune* magazine's rankings for the most admired companies in the United States. The *Huffington Post* ran a 15-part series on the J & J drugs that resulted in product liability litigation."[50] Nonetheless, the company remains at the top of that *Fortune* list.

Discussion Questions

1. Were the shareholders' interests ignored in the decision to take a $150 million write-off and a possible loss of $525 million in annual sales by abandoning the capsules?

2. Suppose that you were a Tylenol competitor. Would you have continued selling your capsules?

3. Was Mr. Burke's action a long-term decision? Did it consider the interests of all stakeholders? How did Mr. Burke's action help the company with the liver-damage issues? Mr. Burke, who served as Johnson & Johnson's CEO from 1970–1989, died on October 1, 2012. A full-page ad in the *Wall Street Journal* on October 2, 2012, read, "What you taught us will live on, In fond memory of James E. Burke."[51] Have Burke's teachings survived?

4. What can you conclude from the quick development and appearance of the new product line following the poisoning deaths?

5. Following the 2010 misstep, Tylenol's competitors sent out free samples and coupons to Tylenol customers who participated in the Tylenol recall as a way of getting them to try their products. Why would such a campaign at this time result in more sales of their products? What is different about this issue versus the cyanide poisonings? Make a list of the distinctions between the two series of events, including descriptions of company and customer responses.

6. General Robert Wood Johnson, the CEO of Johnson & Johnson from 1932 to 1963, wrote a credo for his company, "We believe our first responsibility is to the doctors, nurses, and patients, to mothers and fathers, and all others who use our products and services." The next layer of responsibility was to the "world community" and finally to its shareholders.[52] List each issue and explain whether Johnson & Johnson followed its credo.

7. Why did the company drag its heels on the later recalls? What was the purpose of the phantom contractor and the resulting unannounced recall?

8. Does the company ride the coattails of its recall recognition from the 1987 poisonings? Does its reputation established in the recall fuel the "Most Admired" rankings?

9. A lawyer who represents clients suing McNeil offered the following observations: "It [McNeil] markets itself as a company that takes children's safety very seriously and that's why they can charge a premium price for the Tylenol. People are willing to pay a premium price because of a reputation for safety. Now they're being deceived."[53] Another lawyer who represents companies before the FDA added, "The value of the brand is such that that's got to be the first thought."[54] What thoughts are the lawyers offering on cost analysis in ethical issues through their experiences and observations?

---

[48]Brent Kendall and Peter Loftus, "Justices Let Stand Verdict Against J & J in Powder Suit," *Wall Street Journal*, June 2, 2021, p. B1. *Ingham v. Johnson*, 608 S.W.2d 663 (Mo. App. 2020), *cert.* denied, 114 S.Ct. 2716 (2021).

[49]Andrew Scurra, "J & J Places Talc Liabilities in Chapter 11," *Wall Street Journal*, October 15, 2021, p. B6.

[50]Steven Brill, "America's Favorite Lawbreaker," *The Huffington Post*, https://highline.huffingtonpost.com/miracleindustry/americas-most-admired-lawbreaker/.

[51]*Wall Street Journal*, October 2, 2012, p. A7.

[52]"Brief History of Johnson & Johnson," company pamphlet, 1992.

[53]Carrie Levine, "Tylenol's Growing Headache," *National Law Journal*, June 7, 2010, p. A1.

[54]*Id.*

Ethics in Action 8.1

Supreme Court Justices and Conflicts Recusals

In the U.S. Supreme Court decision on the J & J verdict in the baby powder case, two justices did not participate in the decision on the case: Justices Samuel Alito and Brett Kavanaugh recused themselves. Justice Alito's family owns J & J stock and Justice Kavanaugh's father was a cosmetics sales lobbyist who had argued against warning labels for talc products.[55] What ethical category was at issue here, and why were their recusals needed?

[55]Brent Kendall and Peter Loftus, "Justices Let Stand Verdict Against J & J in Powder Suit," *Wall Street Journal*, June 2, 2021, p. B1at B2.

Case 8.7

Ford, GM, and Chrysler: The Repeating Design and Sales Issues

The Ford Pinto

In 1968, Ford began designing a subcompact automobile that ultimately became the Pinto. Lee Iacocca, then a Ford vice president (and portrayed in the movie *Ford v. Ferrari* for his role in developing the Shelby Mustang), conceived the idea of a subcompact car and was its moving force. Ford's objective was to build a car weighing 2,000 pounds or less to sell for no more than $2,000. At that time, prices for gasoline were increasing, and the American auto industry was losing competitive ground to the small vehicles of Japanese and German manufacturers.

The Rushed Project

The Pinto was a rush project. Ordinarily, auto manufacturers work to blend the engineering concerns with the style preferences of consumers that they determine from marketing surveys. As a result, the placement of the Pinto fuel tank was dictated by style, not engineering. The preferred practice in Europe and Japan was to locate the gas tank over the rear axle in subcompacts because a small vehicle has less "crush space" between the rear axle and the bumper than larger cars.[56] The Pinto's styling, however, required the tank to be placed behind the rear axle, leaving only 9 to 10 inches of "crush space"—far less than in any other American automobile or Ford overseas subcompact.

In addition, the Pinto's bumper was little more than a chrome strip, less substantial than the bumper of any other American car produced then or later. The Pinto's rear structure also lacked reinforcing longitudinal side members, known as "hat sections," and horizontal cross members running between them, such as those in larger cars produced by Ford. The result of these style-driven changes was that the Pinto was less crush-resistant than other vehicles. An additional problem was that the Pinto's differential housing had an exposed flange and bolt heads. These resulting protrusions meant that a gas tank driven forward against the differential by a rear impact would be punctured.[57]

Ford tested the Pinto prototypes, as well as two production Pintos, to determine the integrity of the fuel system in rear-end accidents. Ford also tested to see whether the Pinto would meet a proposed federal regulation requiring all automobiles manufactured in 1972 to be able to withstand a 20-mile-per-hour fixed-barrier impact and those made after January 1, 1973, to withstand a 30-mile-per-hour fixed-barrier impact without significant fuel spillage.[58]

The crash tests revealed that the Pinto's fuel system as designed could not meet the proposed 20-mile-per-hour standard. When mechanical prototypes were struck from the rear with a moving barrier at 21 miles per hour, the fuel tanks

(continued)

[56]Rachel Dardis and Claudia Zent, "The Economics of the Pinto Recall," *Journal of Consumer Affairs* (Winter 1982), pp. 261–277.

[57]Id.

[58]Id.

Case 8.7

(continued)

were driven forward and punctured, causing fuel leakage exceeding the proposed regulatory standard. A production Pinto crashing at 21 miles per hour into a fixed barrier resulted in the fuel neck being torn from the gas tank and the tank being punctured by a bolt head on the differential housing. In at least one test, spilled fuel entered the driver's compartment through gaps resulting from the separation of the seams joining the rear wheel wells to the floor pan.

Other vehicles Ford tested, including modified or reinforced mechanical Pinto prototypes, proved safe at speeds at which the Pinto failed. Vehicles in which rubber bladders had been installed in the tank and were then crashed into fixed barriers at 21 miles per hour had no leakage from punctures in the gas tank. Vehicles with fuel tanks installed above rather than behind the rear axle passed the fuel system integrity test at 31 miles per hour against a fixed barrier. A Pinto with two longitudinal hat sections added to firm up the rear structure passed a 20-mile-per-hour fixed-barrier test with no fuel leakage.[59]

The vulnerability of the Pinto's fuel tank at speeds of 20 and 30 miles per hour in fixed-barrier tests could have been remedied inexpensively, but Ford produced and sold the Pinto without doing anything to fix the defects. Among the design changes that could have been made were side and cross members at $2.40 and $1.80 per car, respectively; a shock-absorbent "flak suit" to protect the tank at $4; a tank within a tank and placement of the tank over the axle at $5.08 to $5.79; a nylon bladder within the tank at $5.25 to $8; placement of the tank over the axle surrounded with a protective barrier at $9.59 per car; imposition of a protective shield between the differential housing and the tank at $2.35; improvement and reinforcement of the bumper at $2.60; and addition of eight inches of crush space at a cost of $6.40. Equipping the car with a reinforced rear structure, smooth axle, improved bumper, and additional crush space at a total of $15.30 would have made the fuel tank safe when hit from the rear by a vehicle the size of a Ford Galaxy. If, in addition, a bladder or tank within a tank had been used or if the tank had been protected with a shield, the tank would have been safe in a rear-end collision of 40 to 45 miles per hour. If the tank had been located over the rear axle, it would have been safe in a rear impact at 50 miles per hour or more.[60]

Engineering Doubts

As the Pinto approached actual production, the engineers responsible for the components of the project "signed off" to their immediate supervisors, who in turn "signed off" to their superiors, and so on up the chain of command until the entire project was approved for release by the lead engineers, and, ultimately, Mr. Iacocca. These decision-makers knew the Pinto crash test results when they decided to go forward with production.

In 1969, the chief assistant research engineer in charge of cost-weight evaluation of the Pinto and the chief chassis engineer in charge of crash testing the early prototype both expressed concern about the integrity of the Pinto's fuel system and complained about management's unwillingness to deviate from the design if the change would cost money. At an April 1971 product review meeting, a report by Ford engineers on the financial impact of a proposed federal standard on fuel-system integrity and the cost savings that would accrue from deferring even minimal "fixes" of the Pinto was discussed. J. C. Echold, Ford's director of automotive safety, studied the issue of gas-tank design in anticipation of government regulations requiring modification. His study, "Fatalities Associated with Crash Induced Fuel Leakage and Fires," included the following cost-benefit analysis:

> The total benefit is shown to be just under $50 million, while the associated cost is $137 million. Thus, the cost is almost three times the benefits, even using a number of highly favorable benefit assumptions.[61]

Benefits

Savings—180 burn deaths, 180 serious burn injuries, 2,100 burned vehicles. Unit cost—$200,000 per death, $67,000 per injury, $700 per vehicle. Total benefits—(180 × $200,000) + (180 × $67,000) + (2,100 × $700) = $49.15 million Costs

- Sales—11 million cars, 1.5 million light trucks
- Unit cost—$11 per car, $11 per truck
- Total costs—(11,000,000 × $11) + (1,500,000 × $11) = $137 million

(continued)

---

[59]*Grimshaw v. Ford Motor Co.*, 174 Cal. Rptr. 378 (1981).
[60]*Id.*

[61]Ralph Drayton, "One Manufacturer's Approach to Automobile Safety Standards," CTLA News, February 8, 1968, p. 11.

Case 8.7

(continued)

Component	1971 Costs ($)
Future productivity losses	
Direct	132,000
Indirect	41,300
Medical costs	
Hospital	700
Other	425
Property damage	1,500
Insurance administration	4,700
Legal and court	3,000
Employer losses	1,000
Victim's pain and suffering	10,000
Funeral	900
Assets (lost consumption)	5,000
Miscellaneous accident cost	200
Total per family	$200,725

Source: Mark Dowie, "Pinto Madness," *Mother Jones*, September/October 1977, p. 28.

Ford's unit cost of $200,000 for one life was based on a National Highway Traffic Safety Administration (NHTSA) calculation developed as shown in the table above. Despite the concerns of the engineers and the above report, Ford went forward with production of the Pinto without any design change or any of the proposed modifications.

Shortly after the release of the car, significant mechanical issues were recurring, with complaints by vehicle owners, as well as a number of fiery rear-end collisions. One of the most public cases happened in 1971, when the Gray family purchased a 1972 Pinto hatchback (the 1972 models were made available in the fall of 1971). The Grays had trouble with the car from the outset. During the first few months of ownership, they had to return the car to the dealer for repairs several times. The problems included excessive gas and oil consumption, downshifting of the automatic transmission, lack of power, and occasional stalling. A heavy carburetor float was eventually pinpointed as the cause.

The Accidents and Injuries

On May 28, 1972, Mrs. Gray, accompanied by 13-year-old Richard Grimshaw, set out in the Pinto from Anaheim, California, for Barstow to meet Mr. Gray. The Pinto was then six months old and had been driven about 3,000 miles. Mrs. Gray stopped in San Bernardino for gasoline, then got back onto Interstate 15 and proceeded toward Barstow at 60 to 65 miles per hour. As she approached the Route 30 off-ramp where traffic was congested, she moved from the outside fast lane into the middle lane. The Pinto then suddenly stalled and coasted to a halt. The carburetor float had become so saturated with gasoline that it sank, opening the float chamber and causing the engine to flood. The driver of the vehicle immediately behind Mrs. Gray's car was able to swerve and pass it, but the driver of a 1962 Ford Galaxy was unable to avoid hitting the Pinto. The Galaxy had been traveling from 50 to 55 miles per hour but had slowed to between 28 and 37 miles per hour at the time of impact.[62]

The Pinto burst into flames that engulfed its interior. According to one expert, the impact of the Galaxy had driven the Pinto's gas tank forward and caused it to be punctured by the flange or one of the bolts on the differential housing so that fuel sprayed from the punctured tank and entered the passenger compartment through gaps in the floor pan. By the time the Pinto came to rest after the collision, both occupants had been seriously burned. When they emerged from the vehicle, their clothing was almost completely burned off. Mrs. Gray died a few days later of congestive heart failure as a result of the burns. Grimshaw survived only through heroic medical measures. He underwent numerous and extensive surgeries and skin grafts, some occurring over the 10 years following the collision. He lost parts of several fingers on his left hand and his left ear, and his face required many skin grafts.[63]

As Ford continued to litigate Mrs. Gray's lawsuit and thousands of other rear-impact Pinto suits, damages reaching $6 million had been awarded to plaintiffs by 1980. In 1979, Indiana filed criminal charges against Ford for reckless homicide.

(continued)

---

[62]"Who Pays for the Damage?" *Time*, January 21, 1980, p. 61.
[63]Adapted from *Grimshaw v. Ford Motor Co.*, 174 Cal. Rptr. 348 (1981).

Case 8.7

(continued)

Discussion Questions

1. If you had been one of the engineers who were concerned, what would you have done differently?

2. Do you think there was anything that could have changed management thinking on spending money for the proposed fixes?

3. What if the engineers had quit? Should they have quit?

The Chevrolet [GM] Malibu

On July 9, 1999, a Los Angeles jury awarded Patricia Anderson, her four children, and her friend, Jo Tigner, $107 million in actual damages and $4.8 billion in punitive damages from General Motors in a lawsuit the six brought against GM because they were trapped and burned in their Chevrolet Malibu when it exploded on impact following a rear-end collision.[64]

Jury foreman Coleman Thornton, in explaining the large verdict, said, "GM has no regard for the people in their cars, and they should be held responsible for it." Richard Shapiro, an attorney for GM, said, "We're very disappointed. This was a very sympathetic case. The people who were injured were innocent in this matter. They were the victims of a drunk driver."[65]

The accident occurred on Christmas Eve 1993 and was the result of a drunk driver striking the Andersons' Malibu at 70 miles per hour. The driver's blood alcohol level was .20, but the defense lawyers noted they were not permitted to disclose to the jury that the driver of the auto that struck the Malibu was drunk.

The discovery process in the case uncovered a 1973 internal "value analysis" memo on "post-collision fuel-tank fires" written by a low-level GM engineer, Edward C. Ivey, in which he calculated the value of preventing fuel-fed fires. Mr. Ivey used a figure of $200,000 for the cost of a fatality and noted that 500 fatalities occur per year in GM auto-fuel fire accidents. The memo also stated that his analysis must be read in the context of how "it is really impossible to put a value on human life." Mr. Ivey wrote that the cost of these explosions to GM would be $2.40 per car. After an in-house lawyer discovered the memo in 1981, he wrote,

> Obviously Ivey is not an individual whom we would ever, in any conceivable situation, want identified to the plaintiffs in a post-collision fuel-fed fire case, and the documents he generated are undoubtedly some of the potentially most harmful and most damaging were they ever to be produced.[66]

In the initial cases brought against GM, the company's defense was that the engineer's thinking was his own and did not reflect company policy. However, when the 1981 lawyer commentary was found as part of discovery in a Florida case in 1998, GM lost that line of defense. In the Florida case in which a 13-year-old boy was burned to death in a 1983 Oldsmobile Cutlass station wagon (the Cutlass was the Oldsmobile version of the Malibu), the jury awarded his family $33 million.

The two documents from the engineer and the lawyer became the center of each case brought against GM. Judge Ernest G. Williams of Los Angeles Superior Court, who upheld the verdict in the $4.9 billion Los Angeles case but reduced the damages, wrote in his opinion,

> The court finds that clear and convincing evidence demonstrated that defendants' fuel tank was placed behind the axle of the automobiles of the make and model here in order to maximize profits—to the disregard of public safety.[67]

The class action lawsuits were still being resolved around the country through 2006. The suits centered on GM's midsize "A-cars," which include the Malibu, Buick Century, Oldsmobile Cutlass, and Pontiac Grand Prix. Approximately 7.5 million cars were equipped with this gas-tank design. On appeal, the Los Angeles verdict was, as noted above, reduced from $4.9 billion (total) to $1.2 billion.[68]

(continued)

[64]Ann W. O'Neill, Henry Weinstein, and Eric Malnic, "Jury Orders GM to Pay Record Sum," *Arizona Republic*, July 10, 1999, pp. A1, A2.

[65]Id.

[66]Milo Geyelin, "How an Internal Memo Written 26 Years Ago Is Costing GM Dearly," *Wall Street Journal*, September 29, 1999, pp. A1, A6.

[67]Id.

[68]Margaret A. Jacobs, "BMW Decision Used to Whittle Punitive Awards," *Wall Street Journal*, September 13, 1999, p. B2.

Case 8.7

(continued)

Discussion Questions

1. If you had found the 1973 memo, what would you have done with it?

2. What happens over time when memos such as this engineer's discussion are concealed?

3. What did the GM managers miss in ignoring the engineer's concerns? What ethical tests from Unit 2 might have helped the engineers convince management? Why do you think they said he was acting on his own?

4. Offer some general lessons from these two cases for business managers.

GM and the Ignition Switch

In 1999, as GM was developing several new smaller model cars (including the Cobalt), its test drivers reported problems with the ignition on the cars. If the keys were bumped, the cars experienced a sudden shutdown. The shutdown not only resulted in the car stopping from full speed to zero speed, thus making it difficult to control, but it also caused the airbags to fail, thus making any crashes that resulted more likely to be fatal. GM took no action to change the ignition switch, and in 2002 test drivers reported the same problems with the ignition switch.

The First Customer Reports

In 2004, two years before GM would finish its litigation over the Malibu, GM received the first reports from customers about engines shutting down in Chevrolet Cobalts.[69] By 2005, GM received its first reports of an ignition failure and the failure of the airbag to deploy, events that resulted in the death of Amber Marie Rose, age 16. During 2005, a GM engineer proposed redesigning the key head on the ignition, but his proposal was rejected by management. Also in 2005, a GM employee who drove one of the Cobalt-like models sent the following email to several engineers and managers in the company:

> We have a serious safety problem here. I am thinking big recall. I was driving 45 mph when I hit the pothole and the car shut off, and I had a car behind me that swerved around me. I don't like to imagine a customer driving their kids in the back seat, on I75, and hitting a pothole in rush hour traffic.

Raymond DiGiorgio, a senior engineer at GM, began to refer to the ignition switch on the cars as "the switch from hell." At the end of 2005, GM issued a service bulletin to its dealers that alerted them to the ignition problem, but GM did not issue a recall.

Simultaneous Financial Problems

During this time, GM was experiencing financial pressures. In fact, GM has had a history of financial problems. In 1991, GM closed 25 plants and laid off 74,000 workers.[70] In 2006, GM announced that it was shedding 47,600 GM workers through early retirement or buyout offers.[71] The company would ultimately be taken over by the federal government in 2009 as a means of obtaining cash infusion and emerging from bankruptcy.

The Surreptitious Engine Switch

The accidents and notifications related to ignition failures continued through 2006. GM took no further action except to switch out the part for the ignition. The part number was not changed as required by federal regulations. If a part is not changed, there is no requirement that the NHTSA be notified. In a series of emails, GM's supplier, Delphi, pushed back on the failure to change the part number, but proceeded with the change and the resulting sales. One Delphi employee observed in a June 2005 email, "Cobalt is blowing up in their faces."[72] But GM engineers observed at the time, "What we are dealing with here is an issue of 'customer convenience, not safety.'"

The Recalls

By the summer of 2010, GM halted production of the Cobalt, and by December 2013, GM determined that there had been 31 accidents caused by ignition failure and that 13 of those crashes resulted in deaths. NHTSA concluded that the problem crossed models and classified 303 deaths as

(continued)

[69]Christopher Jensen, "In G.M. Recalls, Inaction and a Trail of Fatal Crashes," *New York Times*, March 3, 2014, p. B1.

[70]William McWhirter, "Major Overhaul," *Time*, December 30, 1991, p. 56.

[71]As one analyst phrased it, "This Is a Big, Big Hunk of Ballast over the Side." Nick Bunkley, "47,600 Take Offer of Buyouts at G.M. and Delphi," *New York Times*, July 2, 2006, p. B2.

[72]Bill Vlasic, "A Fatally Flawed Switch, and a Burdened Engineer," *New York Times*, November 14, 2014, p. B1.

Case 8.7

(continued)

related to the ignition switch problem.[73] In February 2014, GM recalled 619,000 vehicles, a recall that would slowly be expanded as problems across models emerged to 16.5 million vehicles, including the 2003–2007 Cobalts, the 2003–2007 Saturn ION, the 2006–2007 Chevrolet HHR, the 2007 Saturn Sky, and the 2007 Pontiac G5.[74] The recall included a warning for owners not to drive with any objects on the keychain because the weight of the keychain seemed to be a factor in causing the switch failure.

Unfortunately, the recall was not done quickly enough to prevent additional deaths. Lara Gass, a third-year law student, received an email from her father that her car, a 2006 Saturn ION, was just issued another recall and that GM would be sending her a letter. Her father signed the email, "FYI Love, Dad." Ms. Gass responded:

> Oh, great, one thing after another with that car. Thanks for the heads up! See you in a couple of days! Love you, Lara. [75]

Unfortunately, her ignition turned off when she was on the way to her internship for a federal judge, and she was killed when the car hit a tractor-trailer in front of her and the airbag did not deploy. She never got to read an additional email from her father that warned her about her keychain and taking all the other keys off of it and using her ignition key separately.

GM, Culture, and Response

When the issues with the ignition made the news because of the recall, GM CEO Mary Barra issued a statement that included, "Something is wrong, and we are going to find out what happened," and "This behavior is unacceptable at GM." In her congressional testimony, Ms. Barra said that GM had been operating under a "cost culture," but that it was now changing to a "customer culture." She testified that, "Today's GM will do the right thing."[76]

Ms. Barra set up a group to conduct a study on how the company failed to issue a recall until 10 years after the first email indicated a problem with the ignition, "I asked our team to redouble efforts on pending product reviews, bring them forward, and resolve them quickly."[77] In a press conference she added, "Clearly this took too long. We will fix our process."[78]

However, 25 years ago, when Ross Perot served on the GM board, he created quite a stir with his observations about GM's slow-to-move culture, "If you see a snake, just kill it—don't appoint a committee on snakes. At GM, if you see a snake, the first thing you do is go hire a consultant on snakes. Then you get a committee on snakes, and then you discuss it for a couple of years. The most likely course of action is—nothing. You figure, the snake hasn't bitten anybody yet, so you just let him crawl around on the factory floor. We need to build an environment where the first guy who sees the snake kills it."[79]

Ms. Barra has been with GM since she was 18 (1979) and climbed the ranks to the CEO position. She has consistently maintained that she knew nothing about the switch problem until December 2013 or January 2014 and took swift action once she was aware of the issue.

Following an internal investigation, Ray DiGiorgio, the engineer who approved the parts switch without changes and notification, was placed on unpaid leave and was fired in June 2014.[80] In post-employment interviews, Mr. DiGiorgio stated, "You stay in your box and you do your job. And you don't let anyone else into your box."[81] Jim Federico, chief engineer for small cars and electric vehicles, retired after 36 years at GM. John Calabrese, head of the product development division, retired after 33 years at the company.[82]

(continued)

---

[73]Danielle Ivory and Hilary Stout, "303 Deaths Seen in G.M. Cars with Failed Air Bags," *New York Times*, March 14, 2014, p. B1.

[74]"Auto Safety Regulator Slow to Respond to Deadly Defects," *New York Times*, September 14, 2014, p. A1.

[75]Hilary Stout, "After a Recall, a Fiery Crash and a Payout," *New York Times*, p. A1.

[76]Jeff Bennett and Siobhan Hughes, "GM's Troubled Legacy Weighs on CEO in Capitol Hill Grilling," *Wall Street Journal*, April 2, 2014, p. A1.

[77]Bill Vlasic and Christopher Jensen, "Something Went 'Very Wrong' at G.M., Chief Says," *New York Times*, March 17, 2014, p. B1.

[78]James R. Healy, "GM CEO Admits Recall Tardy," *USA Today*, March 19, 2014, p. 1B.

[79]Thomas Moore, "The GM System Is Like a Blanket of Fog," *CNN Money*, as reported in *Fortune*, February 15, 1988, http://money.cnn.com/magazines/fortune/fortune_archive/1988/02/15/70199/.

[80]Bill Vlasic, "A Fatally Flawed Switch, and a Burdened Engineer," *New York Times*, November 14, 2014, p. B1.

[81]*Id.*

[82]Jeff Bennett, "GM Executive Involved Early in Recall Leaves," *Wall Street Journal*, May 6, 2014, p. B3.

Case 8.7

(continued)

The internal investigation revealed that the culture of GM was one of keeping bad news and evolving issues from the senior management team. The top executive team has been referred to as "insulated from many of the company's inner workings, including active safety reviews."[83] The report also indicated that this insular atmosphere was possible because of the creation of so many committees within the company. There was a recall committee, a safety committee, a design committee, and a host of other groups that dealt with interdivision issues after divisions had dealt with them. The result was a slow-moving culture caught up in processes. GM's internal report indicated that GM knew enough about the switches 12 years prior to the recall to actually issue a recall.[84] Mr. DiGiorgio recently reflected, "All I can say is that I did my job. I didn't lie, cheat, or steal. I did my job the best I could."[85] Mr. DiGiorgio was deposed in GM litigation on June 18–19, 2015. The deposition contradicted what later document releases confirmed about the part switch.

The Fall Out

The litigation on the ignition switches continued through a winding path. Most of the suits related to the early ignition switch accidents were discharged when GM declared bankruptcy in 2009. However, discharges in bankruptcy can be set aside if the debtor made false statements regarding the claims.[86] A federal judge ruled that GM's withholding of the information about the ignition switches constituted fraud and allowed the plaintiffs to reinstate their claims.[87] There were some cases where the juries concluded that the engine switch issue did not cause the accidents for which the plaintiffs filed suit. However, by September 2016, GM had settled all the engine switch cases brought after the bankruptcy.[88] The pre-bankruptcy cases were reinstated by an appellate decision that was denied review by the U.S. Supreme Court. The potential liability for those cases was estimated at $10 billion.[89]

GM paid a $35 million fine to the NHTSA for its failure to report the parts change in 2006. Following the recall, GM took a $1.2 billion charge to earnings to cover the costs.[90] To settle the criminal charges on the switch issues, shareholder suits for withholding information about the switches, and other fines and penalties, GM paid a total of $2.1 billion.[91]

Ms. Barra terminated 15 employees, including lawyers and engineers. The GM lawyers who handled the litigation prior to the recall were investigated by the federal government as to whether they withheld evidence and made misleading statements to federal regulators.[92] The termination of the lawyers followed an investigation by an outside law firm. Included in the terminations were former North American general counsel, Michael Robinson, who had since been named vice president for environmental, sustainability and regulatory affairs, and Jaclyn Palmer and Ronald Porter, who had settled cases involving Chevrolet Cobalts. Two other lawyers who were involved in a January 2011 meeting were also fired. In that meeting, Ms. Palmer had discussed the issue of whether the airbag nondeployment could be linked to an ignition switch.[93]

(continued)

[83]Bill Vlasic, "Recall at GM Is Early Trial for New Chief," *New York Times*, March 8, 2014, p. A1.

[84]"Mary Barra's (Unexpected) Opportunity," *Fortune*, October 6, 2014, p. 102.

[85]Bill Vlasic, "A Fatally Flawed Switch and a Burdened Engineer," *New York Times*, November 14, 2014, p. A1. Mr. DiGiorgio denied in a 2013 deposition that he authorized the 2006 switch change. Emails contradict that assertion. He had, however, asked the GM safety committee in 2005 to change the switch, but the request was denied. Jeff Bennett, "GM Ordered New Switches Seven Weeks before Recall," *Wall Street Journal*, November 10, 2014, p. A1.

[86]Rebecca R. Ruiz, "Documents Show GM Kept Silent on Fatal Crashes," *New York Times*, July 16, 2014, p. A1.

[87]Danielle Ivory, "GM Loses Bid to Dismiss Switch Suit," *New York Times*, August 10, 2014, p. A19.

[88]Mike Spector, "GM Settles Last Suits on Switches," *Wall Street Journal*, September 6, 2016, p. B2.

[89]Peg Brickley and Mike Spector, "Court Opens Door to GM Ignition Claims," *Wall Street Journal*, July 14, 2016, p. B1. In the Matter of Motors Liquidation Company, 829 F.3d 135 (2nd Cir. 2016).

[90]James R. Healey, "Recall Hits the Brakes on Income," *USA Today*, July 28, 2014, p. 1B.

[91]Paul Ingrassia, "Hail, Mary," *Fortune*, September 15, 2016, p. 85.

[92]Christopher M. Matthews and Joann S. Lublin, "Prosecutors Probe Lawyers at GM," *Wall Street Journal*, August 22, 2014.

[93]Martha Neil, "6 Attorneys Fired by GM After Law Firm Ignition-Switch Probe Are Reportedly Identified," *ABA Journal*, June 10, 2014, http://www.abajournal.com/news/article/attorneys_fired_by_gm_after_law_firm_ignition-switch_probe_are_reporte1/. See also the external GM report: http://www.nytimes.com/interactive/2014/06/05/business/06gm-report-doc.html?_r=0.

Case 8.7

(continued)

The other lawyers fired have been identified only by unconfirmed individual sources. None of the lawyers were disciplined by the Michigan State Bar.

The Justice Department investigated the GM switch issues, including the company's failure to make full disclosures about the 111 deaths that resulted from ignition switch problems. The Department of Justice began using wire fraud charges to hold automakers accountable for slow recalls or the failure to issue recalls as well as the failure to make clear the risks when accidents occur that involve design issues.[94] Toyota settled wire fraud charges in its alleged failure to disclose the scope of its "sudden acceleration" problem. Toyota settled the charges for $1.2 billion. That settlement remains the largest in automotive history. GM wire fraud issues were settled with a guilty plea and a $900 million fine.[95]

GM continues to work at culture change. In her first town hall meeting with employees following the recalls and congressional testimony, Ms. Barra told them, "I never want to put this behind us. I want to put this painful experience permanently in our collective memories."[96] She also emphasized accountability, something that had been brought up in the past when GM executive VP Elmer Johnson said in 1988, "No individual is ever responsible or accountable for the success or failure of a project. We employ the fiction of 'institutionalizing responsibility.'"[97]

Ms. Barra explained that she expected directness, candor, and transparency, and such traits are not a request, but a requirement. "People died in our cars," Ms. Barra said in announcing the guilty plea of the company to criminal charges.[98] Ms. Barra holds an annual meeting of the 300 top leaders at GM each year and the first thing they do is drive GM cars because "That's what we do."[99] And then leaders

are asked to answer this question: If you could change one thing at this company, what would it be? Then, Ms. Barra notes, they begin to work on those changes.

Discussion Questions

1. Explain the issues in the GM culture.
2. Why did Mr. DiGiorgio do what he did?
3. What role did financial pressure play in the events?
4. What role did organizational structure play in the decisions?
5. Is there a common thread in all of these vehicle cases of trying to keep internal information from outsiders? What should managers and engineers be trained to do based on these cases?

Chrysler and the Jeep

In 2010, NHTSA opened an investigation into questions about Chrysler's Jeep products because there had been consumer complaints that the fuel tanks in the cars seemed to be vulnerable to explosions in rear-end collisions.

In 2012, Chrysler had its first lawsuit related to the fuel-tank issues. The suit was brought by the parents of a toddler who died when his parents' Jeep was rear-ended and the gas tank exploded and engulfed the back seat of the car in flames, killing the child in his car seat.

In 2013, NHTSA asked the Chrysler Corporation to recall 2.7 million Jeeps because of the increasing numbers of fuel-tank fires in Jeep rear-end collisions. NHTSA's investigation revealed that the placement of the fuel tank behind the rear axle made the Jeep more susceptible to fires in a rear-end crash. The NHTSA studies indicated that the rate of fatal rear-end collisions involving fires was double the rate for other sports utility vehicles.

Initially, Chrysler refused to do the recall and responded as follows:

These vehicles met and exceeded all applicable requirements of the Federal Motor Vehicle Safety Standards, including FMVSS 301, pertaining to fuel-system integrity. Our analysis shows the incidents, which are the focus of this request, occur less than once for every million years of vehicle operation. This rate is similar to comparable vehicles produced and sold during the time in question. Chrysler Group stands behind the

---

[94]Greg Gardner, "GM May Be Charged with Wire Fraud in Ignition Switch Investigation," *Detroit Free Press*, June 9, 2015, http://www.freep.com/story/money/cars/general-motors/2015/06/09/gm-wire-fraud-ignition-switch/28733367/.

[95]Mike Spector and Christopher M. Matthews, "GM Admits to Criminal Wrongdoing," *Wall Street Journal*, September 18, 2015, p. B1.

[96]*Id.*

[97]*Id.*, p. 106.

[98]Spector and Matthews, *supra* note 81.

[99]Ingrassia, *Fortune*, at p. 88.

(continued)

Case 8.7

(continued)

quality and safety of its vehicles. It conducts voluntary recalls when they are warranted, and in most cases, before any notice or investigation request from NHTSA.[100]

Following a meeting with the NHTSA, Chrysler reversed its position and agreed to a recall of most of the vehicles (1.56 million of the original 2.7 million demanded by NHTSA). Under the agreement, Chrysler did not have to admit that the vehicles were defective. The recall involved installing a towing hitch on the cars, something that puts more metal between the back of the car and the gas tank. The proposed fix is much cheaper than other proposals for fixing the gas-tank issue.

In July 2014, NHTSA contacted Chrysler about the lack of speed in the recalls and Chrysler's installation of the hitch.[101] As of March 2015, NHTSA was still receiving complaints from Jeep owners about their inability to get the hitch repair done on their vehicles. By July 2015, Chrysler agreed to pay a $105 million fine for its slow performance on the recalls.

In early 2015, the trial of the case involving the toddler began. The jury viewed a videotaped deposition of Fiat Chrysler CEO Sergio Marchionne that included the following:

- He did not believe that there was any safety defect in any Jeep vehicles.

- He had no way of knowing whether the change of the fuel tank position in more recent Jeep models was safer.

- He did not know the Chrysler engineer whose testimony discussed the change in design in later years and its benefits.

A NHTSA official has noted that the problem never would have been addressed without pressure being applied by his agency.

Discussion Questions

1. Why the resistance by Chrysler?
2. Should Chrysler have done the recall voluntarily?
3. Why did Chrysler reverse its position on the recall?
4. An oft repeated mantra in Jennings's classes is, "Dying customers is always bad for business." How could this stark statement help internal discussions and debates about product safety?

---

[100]"Chrysler Group LLC Responds to NHTSA Recall Letter," June 4, 2013, https://static.nhtsa.gov/odi/inv/2010/INRL-AQ10001-60750.pdf.

[101]Mike Spector and Christina Rogers, "CEO Testifies in Jeep Trial," *Wall Street Journal*, March 25, 2015, p. B6.

Case 8.8

The Beginning of Liability: Games, Fitness, Fun, and Injuries

In most of the cases in this section, we are studying product liability from hindsight. We are looking at the court cases and resulting liability as well as all the information that we did not know from internal records at the time injuries began. However, we can take the lessons from our hindsight cases and think through issues as they are evolving to address them before we face regulation and litigation. The following discussions focus on evolving areas of product liability.

VR Headsets

Virtual reality (VR) headset sales increased 70% last year. As of February 2022, there were 7.9 million VR headsets in the hands of customers.[102] The injuries are quick in coming. The *Wall Street Journal* covered the story of a 14-year-old who set up his VR headset at 2:00 P.M. on

(continued)

---

[102]Sarah E. Needleman and Salvador Rodriguez, "VR to the ER: Metaverse Early Adopters Prove Accident-Prone," *Wall Street Journal*, February 2, 2022, p. A1.

Case 8.8

(continued)

Christmas day and began playing "Superhot VR." His mother said by 8:00 P.M. Christmas day, they were in the emergency room because her son had fractured his knee cap. He had lost his balance while playing.

The headsets trick the mind into believing it is in vast spaces. In reality, the mind and body are in a bedroom or living room surrounded by furniture, breakable vases, and other people. Documented cases have them hitting all three of those while playing. Some players wanted to enjoy the thrill of jumping off a building and jumped into and onto their TVs.

Facebook's Meta has placed a grid function on its headset to alert users when they are getting close to an object (human or otherwise). Some manufacturers advise using a safety mat to keep the players in a confined area. There are warnings, but the warnings have yet to capture all of the risks because they are different depending on what players might attempt in each game.

Discussion Questions

1. If you manufactured a VR headset, what data would you be collecting to stay ahead of consumer mishaps?

2. How would you use that data and what voluntary actions would you take?

3. In the ad for Meta VR headsets, Facebook founder Mark Zuckerberg was shown using the headsets in front of floor-to-ceiling screens in a room with no furniture or walls. Mr. Zuckerberg moved freely throughout the room and between screens. What issues do you see with the ad in terms of liability?

4. What product warnings would you make voluntarily?

Tesla, Autopilot, and In-Car Video Games

Since 2006, Tesla has acknowledged at least 12 fatal accidents in Teslas while the drivers were using autopilot. The video games that Tesla provides in the A3 can be used with a screen mounted on the dashboard while the car is running. One driver who realized this combination of autopilot and game-playing was possible noted, "[I]t just seems inherently dangerous to me."[103]

---

[103]Neal E. Boudette, "Video Games in Tesla Cars Are Raising Safety Fears," *New York Times*, December 9, 2021, p. B1.

The National Highway Traffic Safety Administration (NHTSA) is talking with Tesla about the video game issue. The chair of NHTSA has said that Tesla has not yet followed its suggestions on driver monitoring systems so that the driver's lack of attention can be detected and warnings can be added. She noted, "It's incredibly frustrating, We're trying to warn the public and tell Tesla, Hey you need to put some safeguards in. But they have not."[104] Fiat Chrysler has installed a mechanism that makes its video screen for games go dark if the car moves out of park.

Discussion Questions

1. Referring back to Unit 3, where is the regulatory cycle on both self-driving cars and on car video games?

2. What should Tesla's response to and role with its regulator, NHTSA, be at this point?

3. What data should Tesla be examining and why?

The Peloton Treadmill

The Peloton +Tread (a treadmill, $4,295) came under a U.S. Consumer Product Safety Commission (CPSC) warning following reports of one death and 38 injuries as a result of the treadmill.[105] The urgent warning advised that those with small children not have the Treadmill+ in their homes. The agency noted injuries such as abrasions, fractures, and death because they can get caught beneath the treadmill. The CPSC was asking Peloton to do a voluntary recall.

Peloton initially pushed back against the warning, noting that the Treadmill+ was not dangerous to small children if owners followed the safety instructions with the product, one of which was to use it in a separate room with a closed and locked door. Under CPSC regulations, companies have the power to resist a voluntary recall, which Peloton did, standing by its warnings. Peloton was very public in resisting the recall.[106]

Four months after the initial CPSC warning, Peloton issued a recall and continued discussions with the CPSC about what requirements and changes were needed in

(continued)

---

[104]Neal E. Boudette, "Video Games in Tesla Cars Are Raising Safety Fears," *New York Times*, December 9, 2021, p. B1 at B4.

[105]Jesus Jimenez, "Peloton Disputes U.S. Agency's Warning on Treadmill Linked to One Death," *New York Times*, April 18, 2021, p. A20.

[106]Sharon Terlep, "Peloton's Safety Standoff," *Wall Street Journal*, August 7, 2021, p. B2.

Case 8.8

(continued)

order to put the Treadmill + back on the market. As of February 2022, Peloton was not selling the Treadmill+ and had only instructed website users to "check back." Also as of February 2022, Peloton's CEO had resigned, and the company had announced layoffs of 2,800 employees.[107]

---

[107]Cara Lombardo, "Peloton CEO to Step Down, Company to Cut 2,800 Jobs," *Wall Street Journal*, February 9, 2022, p. A1.

Discussion Questions

1. Again, referring to Unit 3, where is Peloton in the regulatory cycle on its Treadmill+?

2. Is resistance to regulatory authority helpful to stakeholders? Shareholders?

3. What did the CEO miss in his analysis of the Treadmill+ injuries and death?

History Repeats

Ethical Lessons Not Learned: Fighting Recalls and Dying Customers Are Never Good for Business

In most of the safety issues covered in Case 8.8 The Beginning of Liability: Games, Fitness, Fun, and Injuries, companies did not understand that they were facing the same kind of issue that other companies have faced before. When there is a problem with the product, the initial response is that the customer is somehow at fault and there is a resulting reluctance to seize the moment and voluntarily fix the problem. Resisting a recall means that the company is already too far down the slope of the cycle to change its own fate. Public trust has been dissipated and regulators have taken over. They lose their freedom for self-regulation.

Case 8.9

E. Coli, Jack-in-the-Box, and Cooking Temperatures

On January 11, 1993, young Michael Nole and his family ate dinner at a Jack-in-the-Box restaurant in Tacoma, Washington, where Michael enjoyed his $2.69 "Kid's Meal." The next day, Michael was admitted to Children's Hospital and Medical Center in Seattle with severe stomach cramps and bloody diarrhea. Several days later, Michael died of kidney and heart failure.[108]

At the same time, 300 other people in Idaho, Nevada, and Washington who had eaten at Jack-in-the-Box restaurants were poisoned with *E. coli* bacteria, the cause of Michael's death. By the end of the outbreak, more than 600 people nationwide were affected.[109]

Jack-in-the-Box, based in San Diego, California, was not in the best financial health, having just restructured $501 million in debt. The outbreak of poisonings came at

---

[108]Catherine Yang and Amy Barrett, "In a Stew over Tainted Meat," *BusinessWeek*, April 12, 1993, p. 36.

[109]Fred Bayles, "Meat Safety," *USA Today*, October 8, 1997, p. 1A.

a difficult time for the company. However, the company was also at the beginning of what was proving to be an effective ad campaign with the introduction of "Jack," the executive with a white, spherelike head and clown features. The company was making inroads in the market shares of Burger King and Wendy's.

Federal guidelines require that meat be cooked to an internal temperature of 140 degrees Fahrenheit. Jack-in-the-Box followed those guidelines. In May 1992 and September 1992, the state of Washington notified all restaurants, including Jack-in-the-Box, of new regulations requiring hamburgers to be cooked to 155 degrees Fahrenheit. The change would increase restaurants' costs because cooking to 155 degrees slows delivery of food to customers and increases energy costs.

At a news conference one week after the poisonings, Jack-in-the-Box president Robert J. Nugent criticized state

(continued)

Case 8.9

(continued)

authorities for not notifying the company of the 155-degree rule. A week later, the company found the notifications, which it had misplaced, and issued a statement.

After the Jack-in-the-Box poisonings, the federal government recommended that all states increase their cooking temperature requirements to 155 degrees. Burger King cooks to 160 degrees; Hardee's, Wendy's, and Taco Bell cook to 165 degrees. The U.S. Agriculture Department also changed its meat-inspection standards.[110]

The poisonings cut sales at Jack-in-the-Box by 20%.[111] Three store managers were laid off, and the company's plan to build five new restaurants was put on hold until sales picked up. Jack-in-the-Box scrapped 20,000 pounds of hamburger patties produced at meat plants where the bacteria were suspected to have originated. It also changed meat suppliers and added extra meat inspections of its own at an expected cost of $2 million a year.[112]

Consumer groups advocated a 160-degree internal temperature for cooking and a requirement that the meat no longer be pink or red inside.

A class action lawsuit brought by plaintiffs with minor *E. coli* effects was settled for $12 million. Two other suits, brought on behalf of children who went into comas, were

---

[110]Richard Gibson and Scott Kilman, "Tainted Hamburger Incident Heats Up Debate over U.S. Meat-Inspection System," *Wall Street Journal*, February 12, 1993, pp. B1, B7; and Martin Tolchin, "Clinton Orders Hiring of 160 Meat Inspectors," *New York Times*, February 12, 1993, p. A11.

[111]Ronald Grover, Dori Jones Yang, and Laura Holson, "Boxed In at Jack-in-the-Box," *BusinessWeek*, February 15, 1993, p. 40.

[112]Adam Bryant, "Foodmaker Cancels Expansion," *New York Times*, February 15, 1993, p. C3.

settled for $3 million and $15.6 million, respectively.[113] All of the suits were settled by the end of 1997, with most of the settlements coming from a pool of $100 million established by the company's 10 insurers.[114]

Discussion Questions

1. In 1993, Jack-in-the-Box adopted tougher standards for its meat suppliers than those required by the federal government so that suppliers test more frequently for *E. coli*. The link between cooking to a 155-degree internal temperature and the destruction of *E. coli* bacteria had been publicly known for five years at the time of the outbreak. The Centers for Disease Control and Prevention (CDC) tests showed Jack-in-the-Box hamburgers were cooked to 120 degrees. Referring back to the regulatory cycle discussion in Unit 3, was there a regulatory cycle issue with cooking temperatures? Was taking voluntary action on cooking temperatures debated without using the questions and models of Unit 2? What did the food chains miss in analyzing whether to switch voluntarily to higher temperatures?

2. What does the misplacement of the state health department notices on cooking temperature say about the culture at Jack-in-the Box?

3. A plaintiff's lawyer praised Jack-in-the-Box, saying, "They paid out in a way that made everybody walking away from the settlement table think they had been treated fairly." What do we learn about the company from this statement?

---

[113]Bob Van Voris, "Jack-in-the-Box Ends E-Coli Suits," *National Law Journal*, November 17, 1997, p. A8.

[114]Id.

Case 8.10

PGE: Electricity, Fires, and Liability

In 2018, the Camp Fire swept through the foothills of Sierra Nevada, killing 85 people and leaving nothing to the town of Paradise. Investigators determined that the origin points for the fire were a transmission line snapping near Pulga, California, as well as vegetation stuck on other Pacific Gas & Electric (PG&E) transmission lines.[115]

---

[115]Katherine Blunt, "California Faults PG&E for Camp Fire," *Wall Street Journal*, May 16, 2019, p. A1.

Investigation Findings About PG&E Operations

Subsequent investigations into PG&E operations determined that PG&E had repeatedly delayed maintenance on the snapped line (known as the Caribou–Palermo line) because the cost of line repairs was estimated at over $300 million. The California Public Utility Commissions report on PG&E and the fires found that

(continued)

Case 8.10

(continued)

PG&E had not inspected the transmission tower where the transmission line snapped since 2001.[116] In addition, the investigation concluded that line workers had falsified company records, beginning in 2010, to make it appear as if they were keeping up with their line maintenance and safety work when they were not.[117]

By 2014, midlevel managers were telling executives that an overly ambitious agenda was creating pressure in the company for the workers to falsify on-time maintenance results.[118] PG&E has acknowledged the falsification of records and explained that employees, "fell short of the high standards of integrity and the ethical action to which the company is committed."[119]

Substandard Safety Practices

The company's safety practices have been a central focus of both legislative and regulatory oversight. The result has been a new CEO as well as a new board of directors. PG&E declared bankruptcy in 2019 and agreed to pay penalties of almost $2 billion for the Camp Fire and other smaller fires that resulted from PG&E's "failure to identify and abate dying, diseased or weakened trees and tree parts; improper performance of vegetation management activities, such as pruning, removal, etc.; failing to perform a complete patrol of its system and according to best practices its own procedures; failing to retain documents related to vegetation inspections and a work order; late completion of work orders according to PG&E's own procedures; and for PG&E's records indicating that a work order had been completed when, in fact, the work had not been performed; and for allowing vegetation to contact energized, bare conductors operating at distribution voltages."[120]

Liability

While PG&E had settled its regulatory issues, the civil liability for the damage to property remained an issue. When PG&E entered bankruptcy, it had $71.4 billion in assets and $51.7 billion in liability, making its bankruptcy the sixth largest in history.[121] The judge ruled that the bondholders and victims of the fires should have priority over other stakeholders in developing a plan for PG&E's bankruptcy exit. California Governor Gavin Newsom threatened PG& E with a government takeover if it did not reshape itself in a manner that did not find it "limping" out of bankruptcy.[122] PG&E emerged from bankruptcy in July 2020 by placing $5.4 billion and 22.19% of its stock into a trust for the victims of the Camp Fire.[123] At the end of 2020, PG&E used those set-asides to pay property owners $13.5 billion for their property damage and losses caused by the Camp Fire.[124]

PG&E entered a guilty plea to 84 counts of involuntary manslaughter for the victims of the Camp Fire and still faces criminal charges from other counties and subsequent fires.[125] When there is criminal liability, the shareholders must pay the costs, costs that cannot be passed along to ratepayers through rate increases. With each additional fire since the time of the Camp Fire, PG&E faced more penalties, with $1.15 billion added for the 2021 Dixie Fire for PG&E's continuing failure to fix the transmission line issues.[126] PG&E continues to struggle with its maintenance schedule and recently vowed to place all transmission lines underground, a best practice for most utilities in avoiding the safety and fire issues with above-ground transmission lines.

(continued)

---

[116]Ivan Penn and Peter Eavis, "Utility's Future More Uncertain After Scathing Report on Fire," *New York Times*, December 4, 2019, p. B3.

[117]Rebecca Smith, "PG&E's Wildfire Mistakes Followed Years of Violations," *Wall Street Journal*, September 6, 2019, p. A1.

[118]*Id.*

[119]*Id.*

[120]California Public Utility Commission, "Approval of Joint Settlement Agreement with PG&E," June 27, 2019, https://www.cpuc.ca.gov/-/media/cpuc-website/industries-and-topics/documents/wildfire/staff-investigations/i1906015joint-motion-for-approval-of-settlement-agmt121719pdfa.pdf?sc_lang=en&hash=F41C-897C2EF8D228824BBCEF43AEF1CF.

[121]Russell Gold and Katherine Blunt, "Bankruptcy Sets PG&E Up for Overhaul," *Wall Street Journal*, January 30, 2019, p. B1.

[122]Ivan Penn and Peter Eavis, "Governor Has a Plan B for PG&E: Take It Over," *New York Times*, February 7, 2020, p. B1, at B6.

[123]Ivan Penn, "PG&E, Troubled California Utility, Emerges from Bankruptcy," *New York Times*, July 1, 2020, as updated on July 28, 2020, https://www.nytimes.com/2020/07/01/business/energy-environment/pge-bankruptcy-ends.html.

[124]Ivan Penn, "PG&E Says Wildfire Victims Back Settlement," *New York Times*, May 19, 2020, p. B4.

[125]Ivan Penn, "Dixie Fire Costs PG&E $1.15 Billion Plus Inquiry," *New York Times*, November 2, 2021, p. B3.

[126]*Id.*

Case 8.10

(continued)

Discussion Questions

1. How is this liability case different from the other company products in this unit?

2. Is this a standard of strict liability or negligence being applied?

3. What similarities do you see between how PG&E was being operated and the cases in Unit 4 that involved financial fraud?

4. In 2019, a federal judge who had found that PG&E was not taking the necessary steps to fix its natural gas lines following a 2010 explosion of a gas pipe in San Bruno, California, ordered its board of directors to pay an onsite visit to the former town of Paradise to see the devastation caused by the Camp Fire.[127] The judge said, "There is a very clear-cut pattern here—that PG&E is causing these fires."[128] Mayor Jody Jones of Paradise said, "Seeing it has an effect on people."[129] Link those two statements and explain what the judge and mayor are trying to help PG&E executives understand. Have they developed a new test to be applied as companies make decisions about safety issues and repairs and maintenance schedules and costs?

---

[127]Lauren Hepler, "PG&E Ordered to Visit Ravaged Town," *New York Times*, May 8, 2019, p. B3.

[128]*Id.*

[129]*Id.*

Why Didn't They Say Something? 8.1

The Failing Transmission Lines and Maintenance Programs

Because of the records falsification, the failure to do inspections, and other lapses in maintenance, mid-level managers and frontline workers were aware of the issues with PG&E transmission lines and their risks. They remained quiet from 2001 to 2010 and even after initial reports of the issues remained silent through 2019. What were the forces that were controlling their decisions to remain quiet?

The *way* a company sells is as important as *what* it sells. Good hustle wins sales, but too much hustle can cross ethical and then legal lines.

Case 8.11

Chase: Selling Your Own Products for Higher Commissions

In banks and investment firms, employees who are guiding customers have a variety of mutual funds products available for those customers. Many banks offer their own mutual funds as potential investments for those customers. In some cases, the performance of those mutual funds is only average; other mutual fund vehicles are available for customers that would bring them greater returns. However, employees at the banks and investment firms earn higher commissions on placing customers in their own company's funds as opposed to placing those funds in the mutual funds managed by other banks and firms. In some cases, the bank or investment firm collects double fees when a customer invests. That is, in addition to the cost of investing in the mutual fund, the bank or investment firm also collects a management fee from the customers. However, in some banks, their fees, even with double-charging, could be less than the fees charged by other mutual funds.

For example, in 2015, JPMorgan Chase entered into a settlement with the Securities Exchange Commission for its failure to tell its wealth management customers that it steered them into Chase's own mutual fund offerings or fund offerings that it co-managed with other banks as opposed to offering the clients independently managed

funds that would have generated higher returns.[130] The SEC said the settlement, in which Chase paid a total of $127.5 million in disgorged profits and $40 million in penalties, was evidence of the agencies' desire to pursue undisclosed conflicts of interest. Chase was also required to hire an independent consultant to review its client offerings and to include an annual statement of compliance and disclosure from that consultant. A spokesman for Chase indicated that the disclosure weaknesses were "not intentional."[131]

Discussion Questions

1. Discuss the ethical issues involved in the sales of a salesperson's own company's products versus others available on the market.

2. Explain the role of compensation in this sales issue. Refer back to Unit 4 for discussion of incentives and compensation plans.

3. Explain how the issue could be resolved with customers. Is the Chase monitor, mandated by the SEC, a solution?

---

[130]Aruna Viswanatha, "J.P. Morgan in Settlement," *Wall Street Journal*, December 21, 2015, p. C8.
[131]*Id.*

History Repeats

Ethical Issues Not Learned: Wells Missed the Chase Problem

In 2018, as Wells Fargo was trying to work its way through the problems with 3.5 million fake bank accounts created by employees under pressure to cross-sell (see Case 4.10), an issue emerged with its investment advisers. The advisers had been urging clients to invest in products that generated additional fees, products that generated more revenue for Wells (Wells was a partial owner), products that gave them bigger bonuses, or products in which Wells was the majority owner.[132]

The actions of the advisers became public when four Wells Fargo employees sent a letter in 2017 to the Justice Department SEC detailing the practices. In 2018, two Wells financial advisers filed a formal complaint with the SEC about the Wells practices for selling.

The fake accounts became public in October 2016. By 2017, Wells was pledging changes in its operations and a more transparent environment almost immediately. Yet the employees still did not feel comfortable reporting the issues that they were experiencing that were not different from the Chase issues of 2015. Leaders in the same industry who witness their competitors going through regulatory issues should undertake their own investigations to see if their own organizations needed some changes.

[132]Emily Glazer, "Whistleblowers Detail Wells Fargo Wealth Management," *Wall Street Journal*, July 27, 2018, https://www.wsj.com/articles/whistleblowers-detail-wells-fargo-wealth-management-woes-1532707096.

Case 8.12

The Mess at Marsh McLennan

Background and Structure

Marsh McLennan (MMC) is a multinational insurance broker that, at its peak in 2004, had 43,000 employees at offices around the world.[133] MMC's revenues were $2 billion more than its closest competitor, Aon Corporation.[134] MMC is actually a conglomerate that consists of Marsh, its risk and insurance division; Putnam Investments, a mutual fund and investment management company; and Mercer, Inc., a human resources consulting company.

The Pay-to-Play Ploy

MMC employees, who were generously rewarded for gaining more clients, had developed a "pay-to-play" format for obtaining bids for insurance coverage that was almost

a sure thing. The pay-to-play scheme came into play, as it were, when MMC corporate customers came up for renewal on their policies. MMC, as the world's largest insurance broker, had all its insurers for its corporate customers agree to just roll over their coverage on renewals. MMC's plan was to eliminate all the nastiness of rebidding and competition among insurers for the renewal. Rolling over is, in many ways, both literally and figuratively easier. For example, if Insurer A were up for renewal with Customer Y, Insurers B and C would submit fake and higher bids for Customer Y that MMC would then take to Customer Y. And the no-brainer for executives at Customer Y was to go with the lowest bidder.

Then–New York State Attorney General Eliot Spitzer was able to show that MMC did not even have official bids from the competing insurers in some of these rollover situations. MMC sometimes sent bids forward that had not even been signed by the insurers who were playing along at the higher bid. Of course, those who played along and didn't get the renewal had the others play along when

[133]Monica Langley and Ianthe Jeanne Dugan, "How a Top Marsh Employee Turned the Tables on Insurers," *Wall Street Journal*, October 23, 2004, pp. A1, A9. Some put the number of employees at 60,000. Gretchen Morgenson, "Who Loses the Most at Marsh? Its Workers," *New York Times*, October 24, 2004, pp. B1 (Sunday Business 1), at B9.

[134]Monica Langley and Theo Francis, "Insurers Reel from Bust of a 'Cartel,'" *Wall Street Journal*, October 18, 2004, pp. A1, A14.

(continued)

Case 8.12

(continued)

their turn came for renewal with an existing customer. No competitive bidding took place; only a façade existed.

Once MMC got the pay-to-play system in place, its insurance revenue was 67.1% of its total revenue.[135] Commissions from these rollovers represented one-half of MMC's 2003 income of $1.5 billion.[136] When MMC agreed to drop the system as part of a settlement with Spitzer's office, it reported a 94% drop in its third-quarter profit for 2004 from 2003. MMC's income for 2003 was $357 million, but for 2004, it was just $21 million.[137]

The Communication about Pay-to-Play

Mr. Spitzer, in filing suit against MMC, referred to it as part of a cartel.[138] In the complaint, Mr. Spitzer quoted this email from an ACE assistant vice president to ACE's vice president of underwriting (ACE is a "competitor" of MMC and American International): "Original quote $990,000.... We were more competitive than AIG in price and terms. MMGB (Marsh McLennan Global Broking) requested we increase the premium to SLIM to be less competitive, so AIG does not lose the business."[139]

Emails show that employees understood that they were violating antitrust laws. In one email quoted in the Spitzer suit, an MMC executive (whose name is redacted) even jokes about the practice of sending a fake emissary to a meeting with a customer who was taking bids for insurance renewal. The email read, "This month's recipient of our Coordinator of the Month Award requests a body at the rescheduled April 23 meeting. He just needs a live body. Anyone from New York office would do. Given recent activities, perhaps you can send someone from your janitorial staff—preferably a recent hire from the U.S. Postal Service."[140] The response to this email, in all capital letters, showed some disgust with the process: "WE DON'T HAVE THE STAFF TO ATTEND MEETING JUST FOR THE SAKE OF BEING A 'BODY' WHILE YOU MAY NEED 'A LIVE BODY,' WE NEED A 'LIVE OPPORTUNITY' WE'LL TAKE A PASS."[141]

An executive at Munich RE, an insurer that worked with MMC, indicated some concerns in another email:

> I am not some Goody Two Shoes who believes that truth is absolute, but I do feel I have a pretty strict ethical code about being truthful and honest. This idea of "throwing the quote" by quoting artificially high numbers in some predetermined arrangement for us to lose is repugnant to me, not so much because I hate to lose, but because it is basically dishonest. And I basically agree with the comments of others that it comes awfully close to collusion and price-fixing.[142]

The Pressures on Pay-to-Play

As MMC's profitability increased under the pay-to-play scheme, it became more and more difficult to meet the past numbers and even increase them, as management was demanding. One branch manager explained, "We had to do our very best to hit our numbers. Each year our goals were more aggressive."[143] Jeff Greenberg, the MMC CEO, frightened even his direct report, Roger Egan, the president and chief operating officer of MMC, who stated to his direct reports in a meeting on the goals and achieving them, "Each time I see Jeff [Greenberg] I feel like I have a bull's eye on my forehead."[144]

An accounting employee who was at that meeting provided the information to Mr. Spitzer and agreed to testify if it became necessary. It was never necessary for him to testify because MMC settled the suit, agreeing to pay an $850 million fine.[145] Within two months of the settlement, MMC had cut 5,500 jobs. MMC's share price dropped 28% over the same period. Its revenues dropped 70%.[146]

(continued)

---

[135]Langley and Dugan, "How a Top Marsh Employee Turned the Tables on Insurers," pp. A1, A9.

[136]*Id.*

[137]Thor Valdmanis, "Marsh & McLennan Lops off 3,000 Jobs," *USA Today*, November 10, 2004, p. 1B.

[138]Alex Berenson, "To Survive the Dance, Marsh Must Follow Spitzer's Lead," *New York Times*, October 25, 2004, pp. C1, C8.

[139]Thor Valdmanis, Adam Shell, and Elliot Blair Smith, "Marsh & McLennan Accused of Price Fixing, Collusion," *USA Today*, October 15, 2004, pp. 1B, 2B.

[140]Alex Berenson, "Once Again, Spitzer Follows E-Mail Trail," *New York Times*, October 18, 2004, pp. C1, C2.

[141]*Id.*, p. C1.

[142]*Id.*, p. C2.

[143]*Id.*, p. C2.

[144]Langley and Dugan, "How a Top Marsh Employee Turned the Tables on Insurers," pp. A1, A9.

[145]Ian McDonald, "Marsh & McLennan Posts Loss, Unveils Dividend and Job Cuts," *Wall Street Journal*, March 2, 2005, p. C3.

[146]Ian McDonald, "Marsh Post 70 percent Drop in Earnings," *Wall Street Journal*, May 4, 2005, p. C3.

Case 8.12

(continued)

Discussion Questions

1. What cultural issues do you see that affected decisions at MMC?

2. Whose interests were served by the pay-to-play cartel?

3. What thoughts does this case offer for your credo?

Compare & Contrast

Evaluate the thoughts of the insurer who indicates there is no absolute truth. Why did he react differently from the others who were involved in the pay-to-play scheme?

Case 8.13

The Opioid Pandemic

The Opioid Market and Effects

In 1999, Americans were experiencing a revolution of thought in American medicine. Pain was being undertreated.[147] The Sackler family had the solution, with its new drug, OxyContin, which it introduced in 2000. By 2001, sales had reached $1 billion. Other pharmaceutical companies would follow with their new pain pills, such as Insys, with its fentanyl. Since 1999, 450,000 Americans have died from opioid overdoses. The rate of opioid overdose in 2015 was 2.5 times the rate in 1999.[148] By 2020, there were thousands of lawsuits filed by surviving family members as well as state governments seeking reimbursement for the cost of caring for those who recovered from overdoses. Theft, forgeries, armed robberies, and other crimes involving opioids were on the rise, even in the rural counties of America.

Still, with all the tragic deaths, crimes, and desperation, opioids are prescribed and used because of effective

marketing by pharmaceutical firms at all levels of the supply and distribution chain.

Insys, Fentanyl, and Racketeering Marketing

Insys produced a fentanyl painkiller, Subsys, which is 100 times more powerful than morphine. In addition to the power of the drug, there was the force of Insys's marketing strategies. Insys sales representatives bribed doctors to choose the more expensive drug, Subsys, for their patients by paying those doctors for lectures that were part of boondoggles that included such entertainment as lap dances.

Recorded conversations of employees at the Insys Reimbursement Center were also revealing about the company's sales strategies. The Reimbursement Center was created within the company as a means of obtaining insurance coverage for Subsys prescriptions. Insys employees at the Center posed as doctors' assistants offering insurers false information about patients' needs and health to obtain insurance reimbursement for them.

The culture of the company was evident in both the compensation of their sales representatives as well as what took place at their sales meetings. At one sales meeting, the sales reps were treated to a video with a

(continued)

---

[147]For the complete history of the introduction of and addiction to painkillers in the United States, see Beth Macy, *Dopesick* (2018), pp. 44–47.

[148]"Insys Therapeutics and the Systemic Manipulation of Prior Authorization," U.S. Senate Homeland Security and Governmental Affairs Committee, Minority Report (2017).

Case 8.13

(continued)

rap performer in a Subsys dispenser costume.[149] Insys also had an email program that contacted patients with high doses of pain medication on their refills because, as the sales representatives were instructed, these are the patients who will "refill their monthly prescriptions indefinitely."[150] Sales representatives' compensation was tied to the number of prescriptions of Subsys credited to their efforts, and their compensation was well above what other pharmaceutical company sales representatives were earning. Sales reps repeated mantras such as "Pill mills mean dollar signs" (i.e., target doctors with large numbers of opioid prescriptions). [151]

The founder and four former executives of Insys Therapeutics were convicted of racketeering for their sales methodologies. Insys settled a civil liability suit with the Justice Department for $225 million on June 3, 2019. However, Insys, which had earned 90% of its revenue from opioid sales, filed for bankruptcy on June 10, 2019.[152] The Justice Department was left to stand in line with other creditors to obtain any payment: those creditors are owed $16 billion. Each will get 10 cents on the dollar in payment. The former CEO and president of Insys was sentenced to 5.5 years in prison.[153]

OxyContin, Purdue, and McKinsey

Purdue Pharma LP, the maker of OxyContin owned by the billionaire Sackler family, was guided to higher sales of its opioid drug by McKinsey and Company, the prestigious consulting firm. In 2014, McKinsey advised the Sackler family to aggressively market OxyContin. Following the meeting, Arnab Ghatak, a senior partner at McKinsey, received an email from Martin Elling, McKinsey's leader for North American Pharmaceuticals, that read, "By the end of the meeting, the findings were crystal clear to everyone and they gave a ringing endorsement of moving forward fast."[154]

Documents that later emerged in the Purdue suits revealed PowerPoint presentations that McKinsey gave that described how Purdue could "turbocharge" OxyContin sales.[155] McKinsey's slides included figures that projected that 2,484 CVS customers would either overdose or become addicted in 2019. A rebate of $14,180 per "event" (overdose or addiction) would require Purdue to pay CVS $36.8 million for its 2019 rebate. Anthem would be given the same opportunity for its customers using OxyContin.[156] Both Anthem and CVS released statement indicating that while they may have been used as examples in presentations, they were never paid rebates.

When Purdue could not make headway with the pharmacies, McKinsey recommended visits to doctors directly, especially those doctors who prescribed OxyContin regularly. The sales figures showed that the doctors with the most sales rep visits had the greatest increases in prescription rates. When sales reps could not make headway with the doctors, McKinsey recommended "patient pushback," or getting patients to ask their doctors for OxyContin.[157]

The Sackler and Purdue Fates

Purdue filed for bankruptcy in 2019 and entered a guilty plea to three felonies related to the company's marketing and distribution of OxyContin.[158] The penalties and fines totaled $8.34 billion. Since the Sacklers had moved most of Purdue's profits into various off-shore accounts, it remains unclear if the amount can be paid.[159]

(continued)

[149]Jonathan Saltzman, "In Rap Video, Insys Opioid Salesmen Boasted of Their Prowess," *Boston Globe*, February 13, 2019, https://www.bostonglobe.com/business/2019/02/13/rap-video-opioid-salesmen-boasted-their-prowess/YsPTTbiDYDq1ZlpEtobmXL/story.html.

[150]Marianne M. Jennings, "Insys, Opioids, and Racketeering," *The Ethical Barometer*, May 6, 2019, https://www.mariannejennings.com/insys-opioids-and-racketeering/.

[151]Marianne M. Jennings, "Insys, Opioids, and Racketeering," *The Ethical Barometer*, May 6, 2019, https://www.mariannejennings.com/insys-opioids-and-racketeering/.

[152]Peg Buckley, "Opioid Firm Insys Files for Chapter 11," *Wall Street Journal*, June 11, 2019, p. B1.

[153]Joseph Walker and Jon Kemp, "Founder of Opioid Maker Gets Jail Time," *Wall Street Journal*, January 24, 2020, p. B1.

[154]Peg Buckley, "Opioid Firm Insys Files for Chapter 11," *Wall Street Journal*, June 11, 2019, p. B1.

[155]Walt Bogdanich and Michael Forsythe, "McKinsey Advised Purdue to Pay Rebates to Distributors for OxyContin Overdoses," *New York Times*, November 28, 2020, p. A17, https://beta.documentcloud.org/documents/20421781-mckinsey-docs.

[156]Id.

[157]Id.

[158]U.S. Department of Justice, Plea Agreement with Purdue Pharma L.P., October 20, 2020, https://www.justice.gov/opa/pr/opioid-manufacturer-purdue-pharma-pleads-guilty-fraud-and-kickback-conspiracies.

[159]U.S. Department of Justice, Plea Agreement with Purdue Pharma L.P., October 20, 2020, https://www.justice.gov/opa/press-release/file/1329576/download. p. 26.

Case 8.13

(continued)

To pay the fines and settle the civil suits, the Sackler family proposed turning the company into a corporate trust that would continue to sell OxyContin, with all the proceeds going to the public. The corporate trust would develop drugs for treatment addiction. The solution did not fly. In fact, the Sacklers were banished from the opioid industry for life and agreed to pay a $225 million fine.[160] The Sacklers were not charged criminally because they testified that they had relied, as board members, on the representations of management that what Purdue was doing was legal.

McKinsey's Fate

McKinsey also provided advice to Johnson & Johnson for its fentanyl patch (by Janssen Pharmaceuticals, a subsidiary of J & J) on how to increase sales. The states of Oklahoma, Massachusetts, and New Jersey used McKinsey records to help build their case that Janssen engaged in irresponsible marketing of its fentanyl patch.

Two of the states settled, but Johnson & Johnson went to trial on the state of Oklahoma's case, where the McKinsey name kept emerging.[161] In fact, Johnson & Johnson threw McKinsey under the bus. Twice an executive from Johnson & Johnson said that the marketing plan consisted of "McKinsey's words," not ours.[162] However, the executive, Kimberly Deem-Eshleman, admitted that McKinsey was not fired, and, in fact, is still used by Johnson & Johnson today for "different projects."[163]

Johnson & Johnson lost the case and was initially ordered to pay $572 million to the state of Oklahoma.[164] When the judge determined that he had made a math error, the verdict was reduced to $465 million.[165]

McKinsey announced that it has withdrawn from any opioid advising engagements and issued a *quasi*-apology for its sales advice.[166] Part of it appears below:

As we look back at our client service during the opioid crisis, we recognize that we did not adequately acknowledge the epidemic unfolding in our communities or the terrible impact of opioid abuse and addiction on millions of families across the country.[167]

McKinsey assured that its work supported "the legal prescription and use of our clients' products."[168] While the PowerPoint slides tell a slightly different story, McKinsey said that its work was not intended to boost sales. In 2019, McKinsey halted all opioid consulting and paid a $573 million settlement to the attorneys general of 47 states for the marketing advice it gave to Purdue.[169]

Retail Pharmacies and Oxycodone Sales

CVS

During the height of the opioid pandemic, the Drug Enforcement Administration (DEA) moved to revoke the controlled medication licenses of two CVS pharmacies because the pharmacies were filling prescriptions for oxycodone in excess of their monthly allowances for controlled substances. In addition, the DEA alleged that the pharmacies' corporate entity failed to conduct on-site inspections and failed to notice that 42%–58% of all the sales of the substances were cash sales, something that is considered a red flag in the sale and distribution of controlled substances.

CVS won an injunction against the license revocation in federal district court. License revocation proved to be a tall hurdle in the courts. Yet the rate of cash sales at these pharmacies was eight times the national rate for filling prescriptions with cash. Pharmacists at the drug stores, in interviews with the DEA agents, indicated

(continued)

[160]U.S. Department of Justice, Plea Agreement with Purdue Pharma L.P., October 20, 2020, https://www.justice.gov/opa/press-release/file/1329576/download.

[161]Sara Randazzo and Jonathan Randles, "McKinsey Reaches Settlement for Opioid Work," *Wall Street Journal,* February 4, 2021, p. A1.

[162]Walt Bogdanich, "McKinsey Advised Johnson & Johnson on Increasing Opioid Sales," *New York Times,* July 25, 2019, https://www.nytimes.com/2019/07/25/business/mckinsey-johnson-and-johnson-opioids.html.

[163]*Id.*

[164]Sara Randazzo and Jared S. Hopkins, "Judge Rules Johnson & Johnson Helped Fuel Opioid Epidemic," *Wall Street Journal,* August 27, 2019, p. A1.

[165]Sara Randazzo, "Johnson & Johnson Opioid Verdict Cut," *Wall Street Journal,* November 16–17, 2019, p. A3.

[166]Walt Bogdanich and Michael Forsythe, "Rare Apology by McKinsey for OxyContin Work," *New York Times,* December 9, 2020, p. B9.

[167]Walt Bogdanich and Michael Forsythe, "Rare Apology by McKinsey for OxyContin Work," *New York Times,* December 9, 2020, p. B9.

[168]*Id.*

[169]Sara Randazzo and Jonathan Randles, "McKinsey Reaches Settlement for Opioid Work," *Wall Street Journal,* February 4, 2021, p. A1.

Case 8.13

(continued)

that the customers paying cash for the oxycodone were "shady," and that they suspected that some of the prescriptions were not legitimate. Another red flag was that the levels of shipment of oxycodone to the pharmacies increased five times. In one on-site visit by a DEA agent, the following information was gathered: one of every three cars that came to the drive-thru window had a prescription for oxycodone; many patients living at the same address had the same prescriptions for oxycodone from the same doctor.

CVS indicated in court filings that it had changed its practices and provided training to pharmacy personnel so that pharmacists and technicians could spot these types of illegal prescriptions and report suspicious activity. In addition, CVS terminated customers, meaning that they no longer filled their prescriptions. DEA settled the case with CVS with the internal controls changes, training, and a $8-million fine.

Cardinal Health

Cardinal Health, also operating pharmacies in Florida, agreed to pay $44,000,000 to the federal government following a DEA investigation that revealed its subsidiary distributor's failure to report increases in the volume of shipments of opioids to Cardinal Health pharmacies.[170] The company would pay a total of $63,000,000 in fines from 2016 to 2019 for its failure to report increased levels of sales. Compliance employees at Cardinal Health noted that out of the 40,000 employees, only 2 were assigned to track and report increasing opioid sales. They noted that asking for additional resources to track more effectively was like asking "for a Ferrari."[171]

There was also a bit of gaming going on when pharmacies placed orders. If the pharmacy ordered an amount of opioids that triggered FDA reporting, the companies would reject those orders but then permit them if the pharmacy submitted them in smaller lots that did not trigger reporting.[172]

Walgreens

As these cases evolved, Walgreens also faced investigations and enforcement and agreed to pay a fine of $80 million to settle charges by the DEA that it too did not have sufficient internal controls in place to stop widespread distribution of this narcotic.[173] When Walgreens reached the settlement with the DEA, it agreed to tighten up enforcement on illegal prescriptions.[174] As a result of these changes, Walgreens' orders with Purdue dropped 18%.[175] When McKinsey saw the drop in Walgreens' purchases, it recommended to Purdue executives that they "lobby Walgreens to loosen up."[176]

The city of San Francisco won a case in August 2022 that found that Walgreens had exacerbated the opioid crisis by issuing so many prescriptions without appropriate controls. The court found that Walgreens had created a public nuisance because of the impact on the people of San Francisco. A separate trial to determine liability is pending as is an appeal of the decision.[177] The unique legal theory of public nuisance made the case a first in the opioid liability litigation across the country.

In November 2022, Walgreens and CVS reached a negotiated settlement to pay $10 billion to settle all opioid suits by government entities.[178]

Discussion Questions

1. Why is there responsibility for drug distribution when there is not direct knowledge?

2. Interviews with pharmacy employees indicated that many were aware of a problem and were concerned. Consider the following statements and explain why the

(continued)

[170]U.S. Department of Justice, "Cardinal Health Agrees to $44 Million Settlement for Alleged Violations of Controlled Substances Act," December 23, 2016, https://www.justice.gov/usao-md/pr/cardinal-health-agrees-44-million-settlement-alleged-violations-controlled-substances-act.

[171]Danny Hakim, William K. Rashbaum, and Roni Caryn Rabin, "The Giants at the Heart of the Opioid Crisis," *New York Times*, April 22, 2019, https://www.nytimes.com/2019/04/22/health/opioids-lawsuits-distributors.html.

[172]Id., https://www.nytimes.com/2019/04/22/health/opioids-lawsuits-distributors.html.

[173]Barry Meier, "Chain to Pay $80 Million in Drug Fine," *New York Times*, June 12, 2013, p. B1.

[174]Michael Forsythe and Walt Bogdanich, "Firm played Role in Opioid Crisis," *New York Times*, February 2, 2019, p. B4.

[175]Id.

[176]Id.

[177]Jennifer Calfas, "Walgreens Is Found Liable Over Opioids in San Francisco Suit," *Wall Street Journal*, August 11, 2022, p. A3.

[178]Sharon Terlep, "Walgreens, CVS Reach $10 billion Deal Over Opioids," *Wall Street Journal*, November 3, 2022, p. A1.

Case 8.13

(continued)

employees did not speak up and tell someone at their companies about their concerns.

- "We have goals for revenue."
- "This is a busy pharmacy, and I am oversubscribed for my full shift. Who has time to worry about this?"
- "Who's to know?"
- "Nobody else seems to see it."
- "There are lots of orthopedic patients in this area. It's possible."
- "Not my place. Other people watch for this stuff."

- "If I say something, they'll get someone else, and I'm unemployed."

3. What should the companies have done to encourage the employees to raise their concerns?

4. In an internal email forum, when McKinsey employees learned of McKinsey's efforts with Purdue, one employee wrote, "Then, of course, it's ok to maximize shareholder value, seek profits. But not at all costs, not at the cost of our moral values and our society's well being."[179] Refer back to Chapter 3 and decide which view of social responsibility this employee was advocating.

---

[179]*Id.*

History Repeats

Ethical Issues Not Learned: McKinsey's Awakening

When McKinsey's work with Purdue became a public issue, one of McKinsey's partners noted, "While we can't change the past, we can learn from it." However, McKinsey had been struggling with ethical issues for some time. One of its former employees, Jeffrey Skilling, went on to become CEO of Enron, one of the great business frauds in American history.

Federal bankruptcy rules require that financial consultants and advisors in bankruptcy (generally Chapter 11) proceedings file conflicts disclosures. Yet, McKinsey paid an $11 million fine after it finally revealed that its firm's retirement hedge fund held investments in the companies involved or were affected by the restructurings and debt resolutions in those bankruptcies. For example, McKinsey's fund held interests in two hedge funds that were creditors of GenOn Energy Inc. Yet, McKinsey served as an adviser in the Chapter 11 bankruptcy of that company. *De minimis,* they said, but they paid a fine of $15 million plus damages to companies affected by their conflicted bankruptcy work.

McKinsey's hedge fund was an investor in Valeant, a company that purchased pharmaceutical firms, raised prices 5,000% or more, and eventually collapsed, with one executive sent to prison for fraud. McKinsey was advising the firm on drug pricing and acquisitions.[180]

When doing government work at Rikers, a McKinsey partner told government officials and members of his team to use Wickr, a messaging site that automatically deletes messages in a timetable set by the users for hour or days. Wickr helps avoid public records requests on the project—the records automatically disappear. Not illegal, but an interesting approach to transparency on government work.

McKinsey worked for Boeing by exploring options for obtaining titanium (in short supply in 2006) for its planes. McKinsey came up with the idea of Boeing investing in a titanium mine in India and thereby eliminating the suppliers by obtaining titanium at the source. McKinsey had a PowerPoint slide on a potential investment in a mine in India in cooperation with a Ukrainian oligarch that would require influencing eight government officials; the officials were listed in the slide. The partner encouraged Boeing to "respect traditional bureaucratic processes, including the use of bribes." McKinsey responded by saying that it did not encourage violation of the FCPA but declined to provide the full slide set on the mining opportunity.

---

[180]Michael Forsythe, Walt Bogdanich, and Bridget Hickey, "A Double Role Puts McKinsey Under Scrutiny," *New York Times,* February 19, 2019, p. A1.

The list could go on with the power company in South Africa, and the GSA and contract pricing rules that McKinsey got changed in its favor, something that the GSA's Office of the Inspector General concluded "violated requirements governing ethical conduct."[181]

1. Find and classify the ethical issues you see in McKinsey's history.
2. Does the term *amoral technician* (see Reading 4.2) apply to the firm?
3. What was different about the Purdue situation that caused reflection within the firm?
4. McKinsey's firm history describes itself as similar to the Marines, the Catholic Church, and the Jesuits, and their consultants as "analytically rigorous, deeply principled seekers of knowledge and truth."[182]
5. Is the description accurate?

---

[181]Ian McDougall, "How McKinsey Makes Its Own Rules," *New York Times*, December 15, 2019, SB, p. 2.
[182]Ian McDougall, "How McKinsey Makes Its Own Rules," *New York Times*, December 15, 2019, SB, p. 2.

Famous Lines from Art and Literature

"[I] got caught in the cross hairs between a very politically ambitious prosecutor [and] a judicial system of juries that don't really understand sophisticated financial crimes."
  Rajat K. Gupta, former McKinsey consultant.
  Mr. Gupta tipped off a friend on information he had gained about Goldman Sachs as a Goldman director. The friend made a great deal of money on Goldman stock using that inside scoop. Mr. Gupta breached his fiduciary duty as a director in so doing. That's insider trading, with or without a politically ambitious prosecutor and "stupid" juries. He was sentenced to two years in prison.

Case 8.14

Frozen Coke and Burger King and the Richmond Rigging[183]

Tom Moore, president of Coca-Cola's Foodservice and Hospitality Division, was looking at sales in the fountain division, a division responsible for one-third of all of Coke's revenues. The fountain division sells fountain-dispensed soda to restaurants, convenience marts, and theaters. Sales were stagnant, and he knew from feedback from the salespeople that Pepsi was moving aggressively in the area. In 1999, Pepsi had waged a bidding war to try to seize Coke's customers. Coke held about 66% of the fountain drink business and 44.3% of the soda market overall. Pepsi held 22% of the fountain

market and 31.4% of the overall soda market. The war between the two giants had been reduced to a price war. One might say that Coke's fountain sales were flat.

However, Moore envisioned a potential new product line as he looked at the Frozen Coke products. At that time, Frozen Coke was a convenience store item only. Frozen Coke was still a little-known product, and Moore's team at Coke pitched the idea of having Frozen Coke at Burger King, along with a national advertising push that would push Coke's fountain sales but also increase food sales at Burger King as customers came in to try the newly available product. Their pitch to Burger King was that

---

[183]The author has done consulting work with the Burger King team of Coca-Cola. All information in this case is from public records and/or third-party publications.

(continued)

Case 8.14

(continued)

Frozen Coke would draw customers and that the sales of all menu items would increase as a result. Burger King was not ready for a marketing push because it had just lived through two marketing disasters. The first was the failure of the introduction of its new fries, and another was a costly ad campaign to boost sales of the Whopper, with no impact but a great many angry franchise owners who had been required to help pay for the ads. Before Burger King would invest in another ad campaign, it wanted to see some test marketing results. Burger King asked Coke to do a promotion of Frozen Coke in a test market. Burger King chose the Richmond, Virginia, area as a good test market.

If the Richmond market did not show sales during the marketing test, Moore knew that Coke risked not only no more growth in fountain sales but also loss of Burger King's confidence and perhaps an open door for Pepsi to win Burger King over.

Promotions and the marketing test in Richmond began in February 2000. Initial sales were not good. Burger King executives made what Coke employees called "excoriating" calls to Coke team members about the poor performance. Coke pulled out all the stops and hired mystery shoppers to make sure that Burger King employees were offering the Frozen Coke to customers as had been directed during the promotion. Coke gave T-shirts and other promotional items to Burger King managers to encourage them to promote Coke sales. John Fisher, the Coke executive who had just been given the Burger King account to manage, was getting more nervous the closer Coke got to the end of the Richmond promotion time frame.

The Coke team told its own employees to buy more value meals at Burger King, the menu item that was being promoted with the Frozen Coke. Finally, Robert Bader, the Coke marketing manager who was in charge of the Richmond test, decided to hire a marketing consultant, Ronald Berryman, to get more purchases at Burger King. Mr. Berryman, who had worked with Coke in the past, developed a plan that included working with the Boys & Girls Clubs in the area. Using $9,000 wired to him by Mr. Bader from Mr. Bader's personal Visa card, Berryman gave cash to directors of these clubs and developed a homework reward program: if the kids came to the clubs and did their homework, they could go and buy a value meal at Burger King. The directors at the clubs assumed

that the money for the value meals was a donation from either Burger King or Coke.

The result of the Berryman plan was that the Richmond area Burger Kings had a 6% increase in sales during the Frozen Coke promotion. Other Burger King stores had only 0% to 2% growth during the same period. As a result, Burger King agreed to invest $10 million in an ad program to promote Frozen Coke. Burger King also invested $37 million in equipment, training, and distribution in order to carry the Frozen Coke in its franchises, but sales did not follow the Richmond pattern. Estimates are that Burger King's total investment in the Frozen Coke promotion was $65 million.

Matthew Whitley, who had been with Coke since 1992, was its finance director in 2000. During some routine audit work at Coke, he ran across an expenses claim from Mr. Berryman in the amount of $4,432.01, a claim that was labeled as expenses for the "mystery shop." Mr. Whitley questioned Mr. Bader about this amount and others, what the funds were for, who Mr. Berryman was, and what the "mystery shop" submission label represented. Mr. Bader responded that the methods might be "unconventional," but they were "entrepreneurial." Mr. Fisher wrote in a memo in response:

> I would never have agreed to move forward if I believed I was being asked to commit an ethics code or legal transgression.... We had to deseasonalize the data in order to have an accurate measure. These actions were wrong and inconsistent with values of the Coca-Cola Co. Our relationships with Burger King and all our customers are of the utmost importance to us and should be firmly grounded in only the highest-integrity actions.[184]

Mr. Whitley recommended that Mr. Fisher be fired because of the excessive expense and his authorization for it. Coke did not fire Mr. Fisher, but Mr. Moore took away half of his bonus for the year, saying in his memo of explanation to Mr. Fisher, "These actions exposed the Coca-Cola Co. to a risk of damage to its reputation as well as to the relationship with a major customer."[185]

(continued)

[184]Chad Terhune, "How Coke Officials Beefed up Results of Marketing Test," *Wall Street Journal*, August 20, 2003, pp. A1, A6.
[185]*Id.*

Case 8.14

(continued)

However, Coke did fire Mr. Whitley, who then filed suit for wrongful termination. Coke first told Burger King of the issues the day before Mr. Whitley filed his suit. Mr. Whitley's lawyer had contacted Coke and offered to not file the suit if Coke would pay Mr. Whitley $44.4 million within one week. Coke declined the offer and disclosed the Whitley and Frozen Coke issues to Burger King. The Coca-Cola board hired the law firm of Gibson, Dunn & Crutcher and auditors Deloitte & Touche to investigate Whitley's claim.

Mr. Whitley then filed his suit. The *Wall Street Journal* uncovered the lawsuit in court documents when a reporter was doing some routine checking on Coke and ran a story on August 20, 2003, describing Mr. Whitley's experience and suit.

The reports of the law and audit firms concluded that the employees had acted improperly on the Richmond marketing test. Also, as a result, Coca-Cola issued an earnings restatement of $9 million in its fountain sales.

Burger King's then-CEO, Brad Blum, was informed of the report following the investigation and calling the actions of the Coke employees "unacceptable," he issued the following statement:

We are very disappointed in the actions ... confirmed today by the Coca-Cola audit committee. We expect and demand the highest standards of conduct and integrity in all our vendor relationships, and will not tolerate any deviation from these standards.

Coke's then-president and chief operating officer, Steve Heyer, sent an apology to Mr. Blum:

These actions were wrong and inconsistent with values of the Coca-Cola Co. Our relationships with Burger King and all our customers are of the utmost importance to us and should be firmly grounded in only the highest-integrity actions.[186]

Coke had to scramble to retain Burger King's business because Burger King threatened to withdraw Coca-Cola products from its restaurants. Burger King is Coke's second largest fountain customer (McDonald's is its largest). The settlement requires Coke to pay $10 million to Burger King and up to $21.2 million to franchisees who will still have the right to determine whether they will continue to carry the Frozen Coke products.

Coke continued with its litigation against Mr. Whitley, maintaining that he was "separated" from the company because of a restructuring and that his "separation" had nothing to do with his raising the allegations. However, in October 2003, Coke settled the lawsuit for $540,000: $100,000 in cash, $140,000 in benefits including health insurance, and $300,000 in lawyer's fees. Mr. Whitley said when the settlement was reached, "I have reflected on my relationship with Coca-Cola, a company I still respect and love ... the company has taken seriously the issues I raised. That's all I ever wanted."[187]

Deval Patrick, then–executive vice president and Coke's general counsel, also issued the following statement when the settlement was reached:

Mr. Whitley was a diligent employee with a solid record. It is disappointing that he felt he needed to file a lawsuit in order to be heard. We want everyone in this company to bring their issues to the attention of management through appropriate channels.[188]

Mr. Fisher was promoted to a top marketing position in the fountain division at Coke in 2003. However, In April 2003, Coke's internal auditors raised questions with Mr. Fisher about why he exchanged two Disney theme park tickets that had been purchased by the company for Notre Dame football tickets. Mr. Fisher resigned shortly after, but no one at Coke has offered an explanation. He has since worked at the Linbeck Group and is now employed at The Pantry as a senior vice president running retail and restaurant operations for the company.

Mr. Bader remained as marketing manager in the fountain division, but he no longer worked on the Burger King account. He is now the vice president of marketing

(continued)

---

[186]Chad Terhune, "Coke Employees Acted Improperly in Marketing Test," *Wall Street Journal*, June 18, 2003, pp. A3, A6.

[187]Sherri Day, "Coca-Cola Settles Whistle-Blower Suit for $540,000," *New York Times*, August 26, 2003, pp. C1, C2.
[188]*Id.*

Case 8.14

(continued)

strategy at OSI Restaurant Business Partners, owners of Outback Steakhouse and Carrabba's Italian Grill.

Tom Moore resigned following both the settlements. A spokesperson for Coca-Cola said, "As he reflected on the events, he felt that change was necessary to avoid distractions and move the business forward."[189]

Sales of Frozen Coke at Burger King fell to half of Coke's original estimates. Burger King proposed changing the name to Icee.[190] Coke did sign the Subway chain for its fountain beverages, a contract that gave Coke the three largest fountain drink contracts in the country: McDonald's, Burger King, and Subway.[191] Pepsi had previously held the Subway contract.

As a result of the Whitley lawsuit, the SEC and the FBI began investigating Coke. Coke cooperated fully with the government investigations. In 2005, those investigations were closed, with no action taken against the company or any individuals about the marketing scenario or the response to Mr. Whitley's report on the consultant's conduct in the Richmond test market.[192] As part of the settlement, in which Coke neither admitted nor denied the allegations, Coke agreed to put compliance and internal

control processes in place and work to ensure an ethical culture. Coke was also able to settle private suits on the channel-stuffing issues.[193]

Discussion Questions

1. Why did the executives at Coke decide to go forward with the marketing studies? What questions from the models you have studied could they have asked themselves in order to avoid the problems that resulted?

2. Make a list of everyone who was affected by the decision to fix the numbers in the Richmond test market. Reflect on their career paths following the Burger King issues. Were they able to recover professionally?

3. Make a list of all of the consequences Coke experienced as a result of the Richmond rigging. "The initial decision was flawed, and the rest of the problems resulted from that flawed decision," was an observation of an industry expert on the Richmond marketing test. What did the expert mean with this observation?

4. List the total costs to Coke of the Richmond rigging. Be sure to list any costs that you don't have figures for but that Coke would have to pay. Do you think those costs are done and over?

5. What lessons should companies learn from the Whitley firing and lawsuit? What changes do you think Coke has made in its culture to comply with the SEC settlement requirements? Are there some lessons and elements for a credo in the conduct of individuals in this case?

[189]Sherri Day, "Coke Executive to Leave His Job after Rigged Test at Burger King," *New York Times*, August 26, 2003, pp. C1, C2.

[190]Terhune, "How Coke Officials Beefed Up Results of Marketing Test," pp. A1, A6.

[191]Sherri Day, "Subway Chain Chooses Coke Displacing Pepsi," *New York Times*, November 27, 2003, pp. C1, C2.

[192]"Coke Settles with SEC," April 19, 2005, accessed June 20, 2010, from http://www.BevNet.Com.

[193]Sherri Day, "Coke Employees Are Questioned in Fraud Inquiry," *New York Times*, January 31, 2004, pp. B1, B14.

Case 8.15

Adidas and the Intercollegiate Bribery Problems

A sports agent, an Adidas executive, some assistant coaches, and some parents worked together to come up with a win–win–win–win proposition. Adidas would funnel money to the parents' of the young men who were debating which basketball scholarship to accept. The wins were the young men got their scholarships, the parents got some cash, Adidas had the advertising

franchise at the schools the young men chose, and the sports agents had a client for life.

USC, the University of Arizona, Oklahoma State, Auburn, and Louisville were all part of the win–win–win–win pay-to-have-a-child-play scheme. The one glitch was the FBI was tipped off by a financial adviser from Pittsburgh.

(continued)

Case 8.15

(continued)

The financial adviser came under the FBI's wide net due to embezzlement from his professional athlete clients. In exchange for the FBI telling his sentencing judge about his cooperation on the NCAA matters, Louis Martin Blazer served as the FBI's cooperating witness on the basketball bribery investigation. The U.S. attorney who brought the Adidas bribery charges said that he was exposing the "dark underbelly of college basketball" and that the men circled "blue-chip prospects like coyotes."

The First Trial

All but the basketball-playing young men ended up charged with fraud, conspiracy, money laundering, and most white-collar crimes for the scheme. Brian Bowen Sr., one of the parents, testified in the first trial that he made the arrangements to receive $100,000 in exchange for having his son, Tugs Bowen, a star basketball player, choose Louisville.[194] When asked if his son was involved in the meetings, Mr. Bowen responded, "Of course not, no." When asked why, Mr. Bowen responded, "I mean. I don't want him to be involved in something that's wrong or something like that."[195] Mr. Bowen testified that he also received the following offers through agent Christian Dawkins:

- $50,000 from Arizona via former assistant coach Joe Pasternack

- Ex-Oklahoma State assistant Lamont Evans (who was indicted by the FBI) offered $8,000 for a car, $150,000 in cash and additional money for housing

- Former Texas assistant Mike Morrell said the Longhorns would "help with housing"

- Creighton said it would pay $100,000 and get Bowen Sr. "a good job" through assistant Preston Murphy.[196]

The defense lawyers did not dispute the payments for Tugs to go to Louisville. Defense lawyers used a theory of "There's no criminal behavior here" because there are no victims. The colleges benefited from the Adidas "program" under which assistant coaches worked together with Adidas reps to talk high school players into going to colleges that had Adidas sponsorships. The parents benefited. Adidas benefited. The sports agents benefited. The universities benefitted. Young men got full-ride scholarships to good schools.

The defense arguments failed, and former Adidas executive Jim Gatto was sentenced to nine months in prison following his convictions on wire fraud and conspiracy.[197] Also sentenced to six months for their role in the basketball scheme to sign players were Merl Code (former Adidas consultant) and Christian Dawkins (an aspiring sports agent).

The Fates of the Others

USC's assistant coach Tony Bland hired the New York attorney who had defended John Gotti Jr. and Joaquin "El Chapo" Guzman. USC suspended Bland and said that it was "shocked." Following a guilty plea, Bland got two years of probation.[198]

University of Arizona assistant basketball coach Emanuel "Book" Richardson entered a not guilty plea and hired lawyer Brick Storts. The University of Arizona said it was "appalled" at the charges and suspended Book. He pleaded guilty and was sentenced to three months in prison.[199]

Auburn University suspended assistant coach Chuck Person. Auburn added that it was "saddened, angry, and disappointed." Mr. Person entered a guilty plea to accepting $100,000 to steer players toward agents.[200]

(continued)

[194]Adam Klasfeld, "In NCAA Corruption Trial, 'Tugs' Tale Pulls at Heartstrings," *Courthouse News Service*, October 4, 2018, https://www.courthousenews.com/in-ncaa-corruption-trial-tugs-tale-pulls-at-heartstrings/.

[195]Danielle Lerner and Christian Red, "Brian Bowen, Sr. Testifies About Bribes from Louisville, Arizona, Others," *Louisville Courier-Journal*, October 4, 2018, https://www.courier-journal.com/story/sports/college/louisville/2018/10/04/brian-bowen-sr-testifies-bribes-louisville-basketball-arizona-creighton/1521488002/.

[196]Danielle Lerner and Christian Red, "Brian Bowen, Sr. Testifies About Bribes from Louisville, Arizona, Others," *Louisville Courier-Journal*, October 4, 2018, https://www.courier-journal.com/story/sports/college/louisville/2018/10/04/brian-bowen-sr-testifies-bribes-louisville-basketball-arizona-creighton/1521488002/.

[197]Rebecca Davis O'Brien, "Sports Bribery Case Yields Two Convictions," *Wall Street Journal*, May 9, 2019, p. A5.

[198]Tim Daniels, "Ex-USC Basketball Coach Tony Bland Gets 2 Years' Probation in Bribery Scandal," *Bleacher Report*, June 5, 2019, https://bleacherreport.com/articles/2839573-ex-usc-basketball-coach-tony-bland-to-be-sentenced-in-ncaa-bribery-scandal.

[199]Adam Zagoria, "Book Richardson Sentenced, Says He Has No Knowledge of Sean Miller Paying Players," *Arizona Daily Star*, March 17, 2020, https://tucson.com/sports/arizonawildcats/basketball/book-richardson-sentenced-says-he-has-no-knowledge-of-sean-miller-paying-players/article_db224d3c-8873-11e9-a87d-8f03eed70d2b.htm.

[200]Marc Tracy, "Ex-Auburn Coach Pleads Guilty to Bribery Charges," *New York Times*, March 20, 2019, p. B9.

Case 8.15

(continued)

Oklahoma State said it was "surprised" and suspended assistant coach Lamont Evans, also charged. He entered a guilty plea and served three months in prison.[201]

Former Louisville head coach Rick Pitino said the charges that Adidas had paid one of his recruits came as a "complete shock." He was not charged but was fired for alleged NCAA issues and now coaches at Iona College.

Tugs was banished from NCAA sports. The NCAA found the charges to be "deeply disturbing." Tugs played in Australia for a year and then was drafted by the Indiana Pacers. He is now a free agent. His family received only $25,000 of the promised money because Mr. Gatto was not able to work through the Adidas' bureaucracy for the remaining amount.[202]

[201]Tim Daniels, "Ex-College Basketball Coach Lamont Evans Sentenced to 3 Months for Bribes," *Bleacher Report*, June 7, 2019, https://bleacherreport.com/articles/2839976-ex-college-basketball-coach-lamont-evans-sentenced-to-3-months-for-taking-bribes.

[202]Marc Tracy and Adam Zagoria, "A Prized Recruit's Path to Stardom, Lined with Prosecutors," *New York Times*, October 5, 2017, p. A1.

Discussion Questions

1. One basketball coach said he was not surprised about the behaviors of the assistant coaches participating in the bribery scandal. "You look at some of the assistants who have been hired that are paid a lot of money, and you don't see them on the floor coaching. Well, what is their job then? Their job is to get kids. So if you're not getting kids or kids aren't coming, then maybe there is some pressure."[203] Refer to Unit 4, do those in sales and marketing face the same pressures as executives with financial performance?

2. Was Tugs punished for something he did not do? Was the NCAA wrong to banish him? Why did the NBA not draft him?

3. Do the universities bear any responsibility for the behaviors of the assistant coaches?

4. How is the principle of "truth percolates" evident in this case?

[203]Lindsay Schnell, "Dark Cloud Hangs Over New Season," *USA Today*, October 20–22, 2017, p. 1C, at 6C.

Case 8.16

Beech-Nut and the No-Apple-Juice Apple Juice

Beech-Nut was heavily in debt, had only 15% of the baby food market, and was operating out of a badly maintained 80-year-old plant in Canajoharie, New York. Creditors and debt were growing. Beech-Nut needed to keep its costs down, keep its production up, and increase its market share. In 1977, Beech-Nut made a contract with Interjuice Trading Corporation (the Universal Juice Corporation) to buy its apple juice concentrate. The contract was a lifesaver for Beech-Nut because Interjuice's prices were 20% below market, and apple concentrate was used as a base or sweetener in 30% of Beech-Nut's baby food products.

With this much-lower-cost key ingredient (the savings were estimated to be about $250,000 per year), Beech-Nut had reached a turnaround point. Here was a little company that could take on Gerber Baby Foods, the number-one baby food company in the United States. Nestlé Corporation, the international food producer based in Switzerland,

saw potential in this little company and bought Beech-Nut in 1979. By the early 1980s, Beech-Nut had become the number-two baby food company in the United States. However, because of its substantially increased marketing costs, Beech-Nut's money pressures remained.

LiCari Raises Questions . . . Often

Dr. Jerome J. LiCari was the director of research and development for Beech-Nut Nutrition Corporation. Beech-Nut still had the low-cost Interjuice contract, but LiCari was worried. There were rumors of adulteration (the addition or substituted use of inferior substances in a product) flying about in the apple juice industry. Chemists in LiCari's department were suspicious, but they did not yet have tests that could prove the adulteration.

In October 1978, Dr. LiCari learned from other sources that the concentrate might be made of syrups and edible

(continued)

Case 8.16

(continued)

substances that are much cheaper than apples. LiCari reported what he had learned to John Lavery, Beech-Nut's vice president for operations. Lavery's job included management of the purchasing and processing of apple juice concentrates.

Concerned, Lavery sent two employees to inspect Universal's blending operation. What the employees found was only a warehouse without any blending facility. Lavery did nothing more and did not ask about where Interjuice's blending operation was or whether he could have it inspected. Instead, he had Universal officers sign a "hold harmless" agreement, an addendum to the purchase contract that was intended to protect Beech-Nut if any legal claims or suits related to the juice resulted.

Under federal law, a company can sell a product that tastes like apple juice but is not really apple juice as long as the label discloses that it is made from syrups, sweeteners, and flavors. However, Beech-Nut's labels indicated that there was apple product in its apple juice and apple sweetener in the other products in which the concentrate was used, such as the baby fruits, where it provided a sweeter taste. Selling products labeled as apple juice or as containing apple product when they are in fact made with syrups and flavorings is a federal felony. Lavery wanted the hold-harmless agreement for protection against any claims that might be filed under these laws.

During this time, LiCari and his staff were able to develop some tests that did detect the presence of corn starch and other substances in the apple concentrate that were consistent with the composition of adulterated juice. LiCari continued to tell Lavery that he was concerned about the quality of the concentrate supplied by Universal. LiCari told Lavery that if a supplier were willing to adulterate concentrate in the first place, it would likely have little compunction about continuing to supply adulterated product even after signing a hold-harmless document.

Lavery reminded LiCari that Universal's price to Beech-Nut for the concentrate was 50 cents to a dollar per gallon below the price charged by Beech-Nut's previous supplier. He also reminded LiCari of the tremendous economic pressure under which the company was operating. The revenue from Beech-Nut's apple juice was $60 million between 1977 and 1982. Lavery told LiCari that he would not change suppliers unless LiCari brought him tests that would "prove in a court of law that the concentrate was adulterated." He also told LiCari that any further testing

of the product was to be a low item on his list of work assignments and priorities.

In 1979, LiCari sent the concentrate to an outside laboratory for independent analysis. The test results showed that the concentrate consisted primarily of sugar syrup. LiCari told Lavery of the lab results, but Lavery did nothing. In July 1979, Lavery also received a memorandum from the company's plant manager in San Jose, California, that indicated that approximately 95,000 pounds of concentrate inventory was "funny" and "adulterated," in that it was "almost pure corn syrup." The plant manager suggested that Beech-Nut demand its money back from the supplier. Instead, Lavery told the manager to go ahead and use the tainted concentrate in the company's mixed juices. Beech-Nut continued to purchase its apple juice concentrate from Universal.

LiCari and his staff continued their efforts to communicate to Lavery and other company officials that the Interjuice concentrate was adulterated. In August 1981, LiCari sent a memorandum to Charles Jones, the company's purchasing manager, with a copy to Lavery, stating that although the scientists had not proven that the concentrate was adulterated, there was "a tremendous amount of circumstantial evidence" to that effect, "paint[ing] a grave case against the current supplier." LiCari's memorandum concluded that "[i]t is imperative that Beech-Nut establish the authenticity of the Apple Juice Concentrate used to formulate our products. If the authenticity cannot be established, I feel that we have sufficient reason to look for a new supplier."[204]

Lavery took no action to change suppliers. Rather, he instructed Jones to ignore LiCari's memorandum, criticized LiCari for not being a "team player," and called his scientists "Chicken Little." He threatened to fire LiCari.[205] In his evaluation of LiCari's performance for 1981, Lavery wrote that LiCari had great technical ability but that his judgment was "colored by naiveté and impractical ideals."[206]

In late 1981, the company received, unsolicited, a report from a Swiss laboratory concluding that Beech-Nut's apple juice product was adulterated, stating, "The apple juice

(continued)

---

[204]Chris Welles, "What Led Beech-Nut Down the Road to Disgrace," *BusinessWeek*, February 22, 1988, pp. 124–128.

[205]*U.S. v. Beech-Nut, Inc.*, 871 F.2d 1181 (2nd Cir. 1989), at 1185; 925 F.2d 604 (2nd Cir. 1991); *cert. denied*, 493 U.S. 933 (1989).

[206]Welles, "What Led Beech-Nut Down the Road to Disgrace," p. 128.

(continued)

is false, can not see any apple."[207] Lavery reviewed this report, and one of his aides sent it to Universal. Universal made no response, and Beech-Nut took no action.

New Leadership at Beech-Nut

Niels Hoyvald became the CEO of Beech-Nut in April 1981. Both before and after becoming president of Beech-Nut, Hoyvald was aware, from several sources, about an adulteration problem. In November 1981, Beech-Nut's purchasing manager raised the problem. Hoyvald took no action. Rather, he told Lavery that, for budgetary reasons, he would not approve a change in concentrate suppliers until 1983.[208]

In the spring of 1982, Paul Hillabush, the company's director of quality assurance, advised Hoyvald that there would be some adverse publicity about Beech-Nut's purchases of apple juice concentrate. On June 25, 1982, a detective hired by the Processed Apple Institute visited Lavery at Beech-Nut's Canajoharie, New York, plant, and told him that Beech-Nut was about to be involved in a lawsuit as a result of its use of adulterated juice. The investigator showed Canajoharie plant operators documents from the Interjuice dumpster and new tests indicating that the juice was adulterated. The institute invited Beech-Nut to join its lawsuit against Interjuice (a suit that eventually closed Interjuice). Beech-Nut declined. It did cancel its future contracts with Interjuice but continued to use its on-hand supplies for production because of the tremendous cost pressures and competition it was facing.

LiCari also took his evidence of adulteration to Hoyvald. Hoyvald told LiCari he would look into the supplier issue. Several months later, after no action had been taken, LiCari resigned. After leaving Beech-Nut, LiCari wrote an anonymous letter to the U.S. Food and Drug Administration (FDA) disclosing the juice adulteration at Beech-Nut. He signed the letter, "Johnny Appleseed." The FDA began an investigation of Beech-Nut and its products and supplier, but Beech-Nut was not cooperative. The explanation managers offered was simple. When the FDA first notified the company of the problem, Beech-Nut had 700,000 cases of the spurious juice. By stalling, Beech-Nut was able to sell off some of those cases and ship others overseas

(details follow), leaving it with the destruction of just 200,000 cases of the fake product.

An FDA investigator observed,

> They played a cat-and-mouse game with us. When FDA would identify a specific apple juice lot as tainted, Beech-Nut would quickly destroy it before the FDA could seize it, an act that would have created negative publicity?[209]

The Cat-and-Mouse Chase

When New York State government tests first revealed that a batch of Beech-Nut's juice contained little or no apple juice, Beech-Nut had the juice moved during the night, using nine tanker trucks. CEO Hoyvald realized that not being able to sell the inventory of juice the company had on hand would be financially crippling. So, he began delaying tactics designed to give the company time to sell it.

To avoid seizure of the inventory in New York by state officials in August 1982, Hoyvald had this juice moved out of state during the night. It was transported from the New York plant to a warehouse in Secaucus, New Jersey, and the records of this shipment and others were withheld from FDA investigators until the investigators independently located the carrier Beech-Nut had used. While the FDA was searching for the adulterated products but before it had discovered the Secaucus warehouse, Hoyvald ordered virtually the entire stock in that warehouse shipped to Beech-Nut's distributor in Puerto Rico; the Puerto Rico distributor had not placed an order for the product and had twice refused to buy the product even at great discounts offered personally by Hoyvald.

In September 1982, Hoyvald ordered a rush shipment of the inventory of apple juice products held at Beech-Nut's San Jose plant and took a number of unusual steps to get rid of the entire stock. He authorized price discounts of 50%; the largest discount ever offered before had been 10%. Hoyvald insisted that the product be shipped "fast, fast, fast" and gave a distributor in the Dominican Republic only 2 days, instead of the usual 30, to respond to this product promotion. In order to get the juice out of the warehouse and out of the country as quickly as possible, Beech-Nut shipped it to the Dominican Republic on the first possible sailing date; because it was from an unusually distant port, that raised the freight cost to an amount nearly equal to the value of the goods themselves.

(continued)

[207]*U.S. v. Beech-Nut, Inc.*, 871 F.2d 1181 (2nd Cir. 1989), at 1185; 925 F.2d 604 (2nd Cir. 1991); *cert. denied*, 493 U.S. 933 (1989).
[208]*Id.*
[209]Welles, "What Led Beech-Nut Down the Road to Disgrace," p. 128.

Case 8.16

(continued)

Finally, this stock was shipped before Beech-Nut had received the necessary financial documentation from the distributor, which, as one Beech-Nut employee testified, was "tantamount to giving the stuff away."[210]

Hoyvald also used Beech-Nut's lawyers to help delay the government investigation, thereby giving the company more time to sell its inventory of adulterated juice before the product could be seized or a recall could be ordered. For example, in September 1982, the FDA informed Beech-Nut that it intended to seize all of Beech-Nut's apple juice products made from Universal concentrate; in October, New York State authorities advised the company that they planned to initiate a local recall of these products. Beech-Nut's lawyers, at Hoyvald's direction, successfully negotiated with the authorities for a limited recall, excluding products held by retailers and stocks of mixed-juice products. Beech-Nut eventually agreed to conduct a nationwide recall of its apple juice, but by the time of the recall, Hoyvald had sold more than 97% of the earlier stocks of apple juice. In December 1982, in response to Hoyvald's request, Thomas Ward, a member of a law firm retained by Beech-Nut, sent Hoyvald a letter that summarized the events surrounding the apple juice concentrate problem as follows:

From the start, we had two main objectives:

1. to minimize Beech-Nut's potential economic loss, which we understand has been conservatively estimated at $3.5 million, and

2. to minimize any damage to the company's reputation.

We determined that this could be done by delaying, for as long as possible, any market withdrawal of products produced from the Universal Juice concentrate....

In spite of the recognition that FDA might wish to have Beech-Nut recall some of its products, management decided to continue sales of all such products for the time being.... The decision to continue sales and some production of the products was based upon the recognition of the significant potential financial loss and loss of goodwill, and the fact that apple juice is a critical lead-in item for Beech-Nut.

Since the mixed fruit juices and other products constituted the bulk of the products produced with

Universal concentrate, one of our main goals became to prevent the FDA and state authorities from focusing on these products, and we were in fact successful in limiting the controversy strictly to apple juice.[211]

The Charges and Fates

In November 1986, Beech-Nut, Hoyvald, and Lavery, along with Universal's proprietor, Zeev Kaplansky, and four others ("suppliers"), were indicted on charges relating to the company's sale of adulterated and misbranded apple juice products. Hoyvald and Lavery were charged with (1) one count of conspiring with the suppliers to violate the FDCA, 21 U.S.C. §§331(a), (k), and 333(b) (1982 & Supp. IV 1986), in violation of 18 U.S.C. §371; (2) 20 counts of mail fraud, in violation of 18 U.S.C. §§1341 and 2; and (3) 429 counts of introducing adulterated and misbranded apple juice into interstate commerce, in violation of 21 U.S.C. §§331(a) and 333(b) and 18 U.S.C. §2. The suppliers were also charged with introducing adulterated concentrate into interstate commerce.

Hoyvald and Lavery pleaded not guilty to the charges against them. Eventually, Beech-Nut pleaded guilty to 215 felony violations of §§331(a) and 333(b); it received a $2 million fine and was ordered to pay $140,000 to the FDA for the expenses of its investigation. Kaplansky and the other four supplier-defendants also eventually pleaded guilty to some or all of the charges against them. Hoyvald and Lavery thus went to trial alone. LiCari testified at the trials, "I thought apple juice should be made from apples."[212]

The trial began in November 1987 and continued for three months. The government's evidence included that previously discussed. Hoyvald's principal defense was that all of his acts relating to the problem of adulterated concentrate had been performed on the advice of counsel. For example, there was evidence that the Beech-Nut shipment of adulterated juices from its San Jose plant to the Dominican Republic followed the receipt by Hoyvald of a telex sent by Sheldon Klein, an associate of the law firm representing Beech-Nut, which summarized a telephone conference between Beech-Nut officials and its attorneys as follows:

We understand that approximately 25,000 cases of apple juice manufactured from concentrate purchased from Universal Juice is [sic] currently in San Jose.

(continued)

---

[210]*U.S. v. Beech-Nut, Inc.*, 871 F.2d, at 1186. This segment of the case was adapted from the judicial opinion.

[211]*Id.*, pp. 1186–1187.

[212]Welles, "What Led Beech-Nut Down the Road to Disgrace," p. 128.

Case 8.16

(continued)

It is strongly recommended that such product and all other Universal products in Beech-Nut's possession anywhere in the US be destroyed before a meeting with [the FDA] takes place.[213]

Hoyvald and Klein testified that they had a follow-up conversation in which Klein told Hoyvald that, as an alternative, it would be lawful to export the adulterated apple juice products.

The jury returned a verdict of guilty on all of the counts against Lavery. It returned a verdict of guilty against Hoyvald on 359 counts of adulterating and misbranding apple juice, all of which related to shipments after June 25, 1982. It was unable to reach a verdict on the remaining counts against Hoyvald, which related to events prior to that date.

The federal district court sentenced Hoyvald to a term of imprisonment of a year and a day, fined him $100,000, imposed a $9,000 special assessment, and ordered him to pay the costs of prosecution. In March 1989, the federal court of appeals for the second circuit reversed the conviction on the ground that venue was improperly laid in the Eastern District instead of the Northern District of New York. The case was remanded to the district court for a new trial.[214] In August 1989, Hoyvald was retried before Chief Judge Platt on 19 of the counts on which a mistrial had been declared during his first trial. After four weeks of trial, the jury was unable to agree on a verdict, and a mistrial was declared.

Rather than face a third trial, Hoyvald entered into a plea agreement with the government on November 7, 1989. The government recommended that the court impose a suspended sentence; five years of probation, including 1,000 hours of community service; and a $100,000 fine. On November 13, 1989, the district court accepted the plea and imposed sentence. At that plea proceeding, Judge Platt agreed, at Hoyvald's request, to defer the beginning of his community service to give him three weeks to travel to Denmark to visit his 84-year-old mother.

Six months later, in May 1990, Hoyvald again requested permission from his probation officer to return to Denmark to visit his mother and then to be permitted to visit "East and West Germany, Switzerland, Hungary, Czechoslovakia, and Greece" on business, a journey that would take slightly more than three weeks. The Probation Department expressed no opposition to the trip as long as he "supplies an appropriate itinerary and documentation as to the business portions of his trip." The United States Attorney did not oppose the request. On May 22, 1990, Hoyvald requested permission to travel to the other European countries to "look for a job and to investigate business opportunities" in those countries. The district court ruled that Hoyvald could visit his mother in Denmark but denied the request to travel to other countries.

Discussion Questions

1. No one was ever made ill or harmed by the fake apple juice. Was LiCari overreacting?

2. Did LiCari follow the lines of authority in his efforts? Is this important for a whistleblower? Why?

3. What pressures contributed to Beech-Nut's unwillingness to switch suppliers?

4. Using the various models for analysis of ethical dilemmas that you have learned, point out the things that Lavery, Hoyvald, and others in the company failed to consider as they refused to deal with the Interjuice problem.

5. Why did LiCari feel he had to leave Beech-Nut? Why did LiCari write anonymously to the FDA?

6. Is it troublesome that Hoyvald and Lavery escaped sentences on a technicality? Was the sentence too light?

7. Why do you think Hoyvald and the others thought they could get away with the adulterated juice? Why did they play the "cat-and-mouse" game with the FDA? What principles about ethics have you learned that might have helped them analyze their situation more carefully and clearly? Are there some ideas for your credo from both their decisions and LiCari's actions?

8. Beech-Nut's market share went from 19.1% of the market to 15.8%, where it has hovered ever since. Why? What were the costs of Beech-Nut's fake apple juice and its "cat-and-mouse game"? Do you think consumers still remember this conduct?

---

[213]*U.S. v. Beech-Nut, Inc.*, 871 F.2d 1181, at 1194. Again, this material is adapted from the case.

[214]*U.S. v. Beech-Nut Nutrition Corp.*, 871 F.2d 1181 (2nd Cir.), cert. denied, 493 U.S. 933, 110 S.Ct. 324, 107 L.Ed.2d 314 (1989).

Unit 8 Key Term

Puffing   p. 534

Unit 9 Ethics and Competition

Learning Objectives

- Understand when covenants not to compete are needed and valid.

- Explain the legal and ethical standards of fairness in competition.

- Discuss the extent of intellectual property protections and when rights are infringed.

A business's relations with its competitors can be a sticky wicket. Producing similar products, poaching employees, and pricing all present ethical challenges that are often about as close to the legal line as ethical issues come. The heat of competition often creates dilemmas about what you can take with you to your new job or just how similar your product can be to your competitor's.

Covenants Not to Compete

Reading 9.1
A Primer on Covenants Not to Compete: Are They Valid?[1]

Covenants not to compete take two forms. The first type is found in the sale of a business. To keep the seller of the business from trotting down the street and opening another business to compete, courts enforce covenants not to compete in these business purchase agreements as long as they are reasonable in length and geographic scope. The questions of time and scope are based in economics; that is, how many dry cleaners can be located within this radius and still find a sufficient customer base?

The second type of **covenant not to compete** is a bit testier than those found in the sale of a business. This type of covenant applies to employees. Employers require their new hires, as part of their contractual arrangement, to agree not to compete with their employer should they decide to leave their employ. When owners sell a business, they have income from the sale as a means of a support. When employees leave their employers, a banishment from that area of doing business, in other words, from using their skills, can be tantamount to a ban on employment.

In dealing with these covenants, courts strike a balance between employees' right to work and employers' right to protect the trade secrets, training, and so on, that former employees have and then take with them to another company or use to start a business.

Balance and Noncompete Agreements

Many companies have their employees sign contracts that include covenants not to compete or covenants not to disclose information about their former employers should the employees leave their jobs or be terminated from their employment.

The increase in the number of small businesses and the nature of competition have brought back the issue of noncompete and confidentiality agreements. In dealing with these covenants, courts are striking a balance between the employees' right to work and an employer's right to protect the trade secrets, training, and so forth that the former employee has and then transfers to another company or to himself or herself for purposes of starting a business.

---

[1]Adapted from Marianne M. Jennings, *Business: Its Legal, Ethical, and Global Environment*, 12th ed. (2022).

Requirements for Noncompete Agreements

The Need for Protection

The laws on noncompete agreements vary from state to state, with California and a handful of states being the most protective of employees. However, across all states, courts are clear in their positions that there must first be an underlying need or reason for the noncompete agreement—that is, the employee must have had access to trade secrets or be starting his or her own business in competition with the principal/employer.

Reasonableness in Scope

The covenant must also be reasonable in geographic scope and time. These factors depend on the economic base and the nature of the business. For example, a noncompete in a high-tech employee's contract could be geographically global but must be shorter in duration because technology changes so rapidly. A noncompete for a collection agency could not be global but might be longer in duration because the nature of that business is one of relationships.

Valid Formation

Noncompete agreements are also subject to the basics of contract law. There must be consideration and there cannot be duress. For example, one dot-com company agreed to give its employees stock options if they would sign a noncompete agreement. Amazon.com offered downsized employees an additional 10-week pay plus $500, in addition to the normal severance package, if they would sign a three-page "separation agreement and general release" in which they promised not to sue Amazon over a layoff or disparage it in any way. Amazon, as a longstanding practice, has had employees sign a confidentiality agreement at the beginning of their employment that restricts their use of information and systems knowledge they gained while working at Amazon. Some of these confidentiality agreements are running into difficulties with federal agencies because they are being used by employers to stop employees from reporting or discussing wage, discrimination, and other issues that arose during the course of employment.

Some states provide protection for employees who refuse to sign noncompete agreements, punishing employers with punitive damages for wrongful termination in cases brought by employees terminated following their refusals to sign.

Other Theories for Noncompete Enforcement

Because so many legal issues have arisen with covenants not to compete, new forms of controlling post-employment competition have evolved.

Tortious Interference with Contract

Some employers have begun to use the tort of **tortious interference** with contract as a means of preventing former employees from working for competitors or beginning their own competing businesses. In those states in which noncompete clauses are unenforceable, the tort avenue has been used as a means of enjoining the former employee's business activities. For example, in *TruGreen Companies, LLC v Mower Brothers, Inc.*, 199 P.3d 929 (Utah 2008), the Utah Supreme Court held that a company whose former employer had gone to work for a competing company and recruited other employees to join him was liable for tortious interference and allowed recovery of lost profits.

Confidentiality or Nondisclosure Agreements

Another possible avenue of protection is a confidentiality agreement, one signed by employees, that prohibits them from disclosing confidential and proprietary information they learned of during their employment. For example, the information in a sealed bid is proprietary. An employee who takes that information along when hired by a competitor breaches a confidentiality agreement. This type of agreement does not prohibit employment, but it does control the type of work the employee can do at the new company and what information can be used in doing that new job.

The Doctrine of Inevitable Disclosure

Still another new approach that has developed is the use of the **doctrine of inevitable disclosure**. Employers cannot stop former employees from working for a competitor but can stop them from working in direct competition. For example, a marketing executive for Campbell's soup could not go to work for Heinz's soup division but could work in the Heinz ketchup area. There is an inevitability that the marketing executive would disclose something proprietary about Campbell's in a Heinz soup position but could work in marketing ketchup and not be in direct competition with Campbell's.

Discussion Questions

1. What is the balance in covenants?

2. What alternatives exist to covenants not to compete?

Case 9.2

Sabotaging Your Employer's Information Lists before You Leave to Work for a Competitor

Eagle Gate College hired an admission consultant from Stevens-Henager College (Janna Miller). After she was hired, Ms. Miller hired other employees from Steven-Henager, and some of those employees had access to a confidential database at Steven-Henager that included leads for recruiting students. Before leaving Stevens-Henager, the employees went into the college's database on leads and altered the information on the individuals in the list in such a way that it impeded or prevented Stevens-Henager's ability to contact those leads. One Stevens-Henager official said, "We continue to use any leads that come into the college from time to time, and with the loss of adequate phone numbers ... it became difficult, if not impossible, to use our own leads. ..."[2]

Discussion Questions

1. Evaluate the ethics of Ms. Miller in her recruitment efforts. What category of ethical issue applies to her conduct?

2. What about the conduct of the employees in altering the database so that it could no longer be used? What categories apply there?

3. Are there any prevention tools that might have helped the colleges from becoming involved in the resulting litigation?

4. What advice would you give to employers about the computers of employees who are departing for another job?

Source: *Stevens-Henager College v. Eagle Gate College*, 248 P.3d 1025 (Utah 2011).

---

[2]*Stevens-Henager College v. Eagle Gate College*, 248 P.3d 1025 at 1028 (Utah App. 2011).

Case 9.3

The Hallmark Channel and Countdown to Christmas

Bill Abbott left the Hallmark Channel following a dust-up at the network over a commercial featuring a same-sex couple being aired. Hallmark withdrew the commercial when a conservative group pressured the network. Days later, however, Hallmark began airing the commercial again after a gay-rights advocacy group threatened an advertising boycott of the Hallmark Channel. There was no explanation given when Mr. Abbott left to head GAC Family, a competing network.

Mr. Abbott began making Christmas movies to compete with Hallmark's "Countdown to Christmas" November to December marathon of holiday movies. In fact, Mr. Abbott hired Hallmark actors from Hallmark movies for his GAC productions. Lori Laughlin, was sentenced to prison for payments she made to get her daughter into USC in the college admissions scandal, AKA "Operation Varsity Blues." Mr. Abbott permitted her return to television by casting her in a GAC Christmas movie. GAC made 12 Christmas movies for the 2021 Christmas season, and 96% of the lead actors in those films had appeared in Hallmark Christmas movies.[3]

Mr. Abbott says that he is not poaching from the Hallmark Channel, that most of the contact between him and Hallmark actors is their reaching out to him. Two of Hallmark's

major leading stars have signed two-year contracts with GAC. More than one dozen Hallmark stars have signed to do movies with GAC. A Hallmark series star of *Home and Family,* Debbie Matenopoulos, has left the Hallmark Channel and signed with GAC. Ms. Matenopoulos hosted GAC's Christmas Preview Special. Hallmark responded, "It's talent's prerogative where they want to work, and we are certainly allowing people to work where they want."[4]

The Hallmark Channel has 20 times the number of viewers as GAC for Christmas programming. Mr. Abbott denied that he is "getting back" at Hallmark for his termination. But, GAC has been criticized already for its lack of diversity. Mr. Abbott says what is going on is just competition.

Discussion Questions

1. Could Hallmark have protected its formula for television success?

2. Is it ethical for Mr. Abbott to use the Hallmark formula and recruit the Hallmark talent?

3. Would it be possible for Hallmark to have exclusive contracts with its talent?

4. Is there some other type of restriction Hallmark could place on its talent to stop the poaching?

---

[3]Lillian Rizzo, "Twice as Sweet? Christmas Movie Battle Has Fans Seeing Double," *New York Times*, December 15, 2021, p. A1.

[4]*Id.*

Case 9.4

Bimbo Bakery and the Nooks & Crannies

Botticella's Work at Bimbo

Bimbo, with its principal place of business in Pennsylvania, is one of the four largest bakery companies in the United States. Bimbo distributes baked goods throughout the country, including Thomas Entenmann's, Arnold, Oroweat, Mrs. Baird's, Stroehmann, and Boboli. Chris Botticella began working for Bimbo in 2001 and was, until January 13, 2010, its vice president of operations for California. Mr. Botticella, who earned an annual salary of $250,000 per year, was directly responsible for five production facilities and oversaw a variety of areas,

including product quality and cost, labor issues, and new product development. Mr. Botticella worked closely with Bimbo's sales staff on sales promotion.

Mr. Botticella had access to a broad range of confidential information about Bimbo, its products, and its business strategy. For example, he was one of a select group of individuals with access to the code books containing the formulas and processes for all of Bimbo's products. He also regularly attended high-level meetings with other top Bimbo executives to discuss the company's

(continued)

Case 9.4

(continued)

national business strategy. Mr. Botticella was one of only seven people who knew how to replicate independently Bimbo's popular line of Thomas' English Muffins, including the secret behind the muffins' unique "nooks and crannies" texture. Thomas' English Muffins make up one-half billion dollars' worth of Bimbo's annual sales income.

Mr. Botticella signed a "Confidentiality, Non-Solicitation and Invention Assignment Agreement" with Bimbo in which he agreed not to compete directly with Bimbo during the term of his employment, not to use or disclose any of Bimbo's confidential or proprietary information during or after the term of his employment with Bimbo, and, upon ceasing employment by Bimbo, to return every document he received from Bimbo during the term of his employment. The agreement, however, did not include a covenant restricting where Mr. Botticella could work after terminating his employment at Bimbo.

Mr. Botticella had access to the following Bimbo trade secrets:

- The formulas and designs for Thomas English muffins and Oroweat breads

- Profitability plans for Bimbo, including formula optimizations, process improvements, and new product launches with estimated savings of $75 million in one year

- Knowledge of how Bimbo produces breads from scratch and not from mixes

- Promotional strategies for particular customers

- Customers targeted for bids

Hostess and the Job Offer

Interstates Brand Corporation, later known as Hostess Brands, offered Mr. Botticella a job in Texas as vice president of bakery operations for the eastern region. The salary was $200,000 with both bonuses and stock options. Mr. Botticella accepted the job but did not disclose that to Bimbo for several months. Hostess had Mr. Botticella sign an agreement that he would not disclose any confidential information, trade secrets, or other proprietary information from Bimbo. Bimbo learned of the Botticella plans when Hostess made the announcement on January 12 about his starting with Hostess on January 18. Bimbo ordered Mr. Botticella to vacate his office at Bimbo on January 13.

The Computer Forensics Expert

Bimbo hired a computer forensics expert to review Mr. Botticella's laptop. The expert found that Mr. Botticella had accessed files within a span of 13 seconds on January 13, immediately following his phone conversation with Bimbo executives about his new job with Hostess. The files accessed included the following:

- Cost-reduction strategies

- Product launch dates

- Anticipated plant and line closures

- Labor contract information

- Production strengths and weaknesses at Bimbo facilities

- Cost for individual products by brand

The computer showed that Mr. Botticella had used thumb drives on the computer as well as an external hard drive. The external hard drive was never located, and the expert could not determine what had been placed on the thumb drives. Mr. Botticella admitted that he did copy files from his computer to external devices but that he did so "only to practice his computer skills in preparation for his new job."

Bimbo filed suit to obtain an injunction to stop Mr. Botticella from working for Hostess.

Discussion Questions

1. What needs to be balanced in this case? What are the parties' interests at issue?

2. Apply the ethical categories to Mr. Botticella's actions in which you see an ethical issue and decide which categories apply to those actions.

3. Do you believe the reason Mr. Botticella gave for downloading the files?

4. Is there a compromise solution available to the parties based on what you learned from reading the Primer on Covenants Not to Compete (Reading 9.1)?

5. What lessons should companies and employees leaving companies learn from this case?

Source: *Bimbo Bakeries USA, Inc. v. Botticella,* 613 F.3d 102 (3rd Cir. 2010).

Case 9.5

Starwood, Hilton, and the Suspiciously Similar New Hotel Designs

The Hotel Setup and Background

Starwood and Hilton are direct, head-to-head competitors. In 2007, the Blackstone Group, a private equity firm, acquired Hilton for over $20 billion in a top-of-the-market, highly leveraged buyout. Financial analysts suggested that because Blackstone had paid a super-premium price for Hilton, the hotel chain would be under intense pressure to deliver immediate results. Ross Klein and Amar Lalvani were president and senior vice president, respectively, of Starwood's Luxury Brands Group. Both were intimately involved in and aware of the strategy and planned future development of Starwood's lifestyle and luxury hotel brands: the St. Regis, W Hotels, and The Luxury Collection. Both Messrs. Klein and Lalvani had access to strategic development plans, and both had signed written confidentiality agreements with Starwood.

Hilton Recruits from Starwood

In February 2008, Christopher Nassetta, Hilton's president and chief executive officer, began recruiting Mr. Klein to join Hilton. Mr. Klein then began requesting large volumes of confidential information from Starwood employees, which he took home and loaded onto a personal laptop computer and/or forwarded to a personal email account, before joining Hilton. After Mr. Klein obtained a severance payment of more than $600,000 from Starwood, he joined Hilton and used the information he took from Starwood in the development of a new Hilton high-scale hotel known as Denizen.

In March 2008, Steven Goldman, Hilton's president of global development and real estate, began recruiting Mr. Lalvani to join Hilton. Goldman told Lalvani that Hilton was a "clean slate" and "you're the first guy on my list." Mr. Lalvani provided Mr. Goldman with his ideas for Hilton, including the following from an email: "Other idea is bring over the core W team which has created an enormous amount of value and is very loyal to me to build a new brand for you guys. Not sure your appetite but I know I could make that happen as well."[5] Before joining Mr. Goldman at Hilton, Mr. Lalvani also secretly downloaded large quantities of confidential Starwood documents, which he brought with him and used at Hilton.

By June 2008, Messrs. Klein and Lalvani were both at Hilton as Hilton's global head of Luxury & Lifestyle brands and global head of Luxury & Lifestyle brand development, respectively.

Hilton's press release included the following statement upon the arrival of the two:

> These new hires will help advance Hilton's strategic goal of further developing its presence in the luxury and lifestyle sectors. At Hilton, Mr. Klein will oversee the company's global luxury and lifestyle brand portfolio, including Waldorf-Astoria, the Waldorf-Astoria Collection and Conrad, and will spearhead the company's entry into the lifestyle segment. Mr. Lalvani will lead the global development of Hilton's luxury and lifestyle segments.[6]

The Paper Hiring Bonus

Between the two men, they brought along to Hilton over 100,000 electronic Starwood documents that contained proprietary information that Hilton then used in creating its new Denizen hotel chain. The documents included the following:

- Starwood's Forward-Looking Strategic Development Plans

- Starwood's Principal Term Prioritization Worksheets, containing Starwood's highly confidential and proprietary current and prospective negotiation strategies with owners, ranked by importance to Starwood for numerous deal terms

- Starwood's Property Improvement Plan templates for how to create "the Ultimate W Experience" in conversion properties, providing step-by-step details for how to convert a hotel property to a W-branded hotel

- Starwood's confidential computer files containing the names, addresses, and other nonpublic information for its Luxury Brands Group owners, developers, and designers compiled by Starwood

- Recent presentations to Starwood's executive leadership team, containing current and prospective financial, branding, and marketing information for Starwood's lifestyle and luxury brands

(continued)

---

[5]*Starwood Hotels & Resorts Worldwide, Inc. v. Hilton Hotels Corporation*, Klein & Lalvani, trial pleading, 2009 WL 1025597 (S.D.N.Y.).

[6]*Id.*

Case 9.5

(continued)

- Starwood's site-specific Project Approval Requests, which set out in detail highly sensitive and competitively useful information for Starwood properties and targeted properties around the world
- Confidential and proprietary marketing and demographic studies for which Starwood paid third parties over $1 million
- Starwood's W Residential Guidelines 2008, containing Starwood's strategies and proprietary toolkits for residential development in or at W hotels
- Starwood's W Hotels "Brand in a Box" modules and training materials, containing Starwood's proprietary

training, operational materials, and procedures for opening a new lifestyle hotel

- A board presentation on future strategies for the chain
- Starwood's Luxury Brands Group "Brand Bibles," brand handbooks, brand immersion materials, and brand marketing plans

The Recruiting Raids

Upon their arrival at Hilton, Messrs. Klein and Lalvani also recruited additional Starwood employees to join them at Hilton and to bring with them to Hilton additional confidential, competitively sensitive Starwood information. A list appears below:

Individual	Former Starwood Position	Current Hilton Position
Christopher Kochuba	Vice President, Development Planning & Design Management, Luxury Brands Group	Vice President, Planning and Programming, Global Luxury and Lifestyle Brands
Erin Shaffer	Senior Manager, Brand Marketing, Luxury Brands Group	Senior Director, Communications and Partnerships
Jeff Darnell	General Manager, W Hotel Los Angeles	Vice President, Brand Operations
Stephanie Heer	Marketing Manager, W Hotel Los Angeles	Brand Marketing Manager, Conrad Hotels
Erin Green	Director, W Development, Europe, Africa, and Middle East	Senior Development Director, Luxury and Lifestyle (Europe and Africa)
Elie Younes	Senior Director, Acquisitions & Development, Europe, Africa, and Middle East	Vice President, Development (Middle East)
Leah Corradino	Marketing Manager, W Hotel San Diego	Brand Marketing Manager, Waldorf Astoria and Waldorf Astoria Collection
Susan Manrao	Senior Manager, Interior Style & Design Standards	Senior Director of Design and Brand Experience[7]

The Arbitration and Truth Percolates

Because of the ongoing poaching, Starwood commenced an arbitration action against Mr. Klein in November 2008 to enforce the nonsolicitation provisions in his employment contract and his separation agreement with Starwood.

In February 2009, pursuant to a Starwood discovery request of Hilton, Hilton delivered eight large boxes of computer hard drives, zip drives, thumb drives, and paper records containing the information listed above. Hilton also acknowledged that the former employees had additional Starwood materials "at home." However, Hilton took

no action against Mr. Klein or any of the other former Starwood employees.

Hilton's general counsel said in a cover letter included with the eight boxes of documents that he did not think the information was proprietary or confidential but that he was sending them back as a precaution.

However, Starwood noted that files that had been taken included its development plans for its "zen den" that it was going to put in its upscale W hotels. Hilton's development plans for Denizen referred to it as their "den of zen."

---

[7]Id.

(continued)

Case 9.5

(continued)

Hilton and Starwood settled their suit in 2010, with Hilton agreeing not to create a luxury "lifestyle" hotel until 2012. In addition, Hilton was banned from ever using its Denizen brand and was required to have a court-appointed monitor review its marketing and branding materials to be sure that nothing it was doing resulted from its access to the Starwood documents. Damages were also part of the settlement, with Hilton paying Starwood an unspecified amount of damages.[8] Individuals within the companies disclosed that the payment was $75 million.[9] The settlement mirrored the temporary injunction that the court had put into place prior to trial that placed the same restrictions on Hilton. Messrs. Klein and Lalvani were prohibited under the agreement from working with certain hotel chains for two years.

Following a criminal investigation, the U.S. attorney declined to bring charges against Hilton. The investigations into the conduct of individuals did not result in any criminal charges. Marriott purchased Starwood in 2016.

Discussion Questions

1. In developing a concept for a new chain (Denizen is geared at the high-end market), companies spend years and millions of dollars on studying consumer needs and preferences, social trends, lighting, costs, food choices, and even fabrics and designs. What ethical category does the conduct of the former Starwood executives fall into beyond just the breach of their employment contract covenants?

---

[8]Alexandra Berzon, "Hilton Settles Spy Suit," *Wall Street Journal,* December 23, 2010, p. B1.

[9]Peter Lattman, "2 Big Hotel Chains Settle a Theft Suit," *New York Times,* December 23, 2010, p. B1.

2. The following clause appears in the former Starwood employees' contracts:

> [Employee] acknowledges that during the course of his/her employment with [Starwood], Employee will receive, and will have access to, "Confidential Information" ... of [Starwood] and that such information is a special, valuable and unique asset belonging to [Starwood] ... All [Documents (broadly defined)] which from time to time may be in Employee's possession ... relating, directly or indirectly, to the business of [Starwood] shall be and remain the property of [Starwood] and shall be delivered by Employee to [Starwood] immediately upon request, and in any event promptly upon termination of Employee's employment, and Employee shall not make or keep any copies or extracts of the Documents. ... Employee shall not disclose to any third person any information concerning the business of [Starwood], including, without limitation, any trade secrets, customer lists and details of contracts with or requirements of customers, the identity of any owner of a managed hotel, information relating to any current, past or prospective management agreement or joint venture, information pertaining to business methods, sales plans, design plans and strategies, management organization, computer systems and software, operating policies or manuals ... financial records or other financial, commercial, business or technical information relating to the company.

> Is this an enforceable provision? Do you believe the employees violated this provision by their conduct?

3. What components of a personal credo would have helped in this situation?

4. Where does "fair play" fit into ethics? Competition? Law?

All's Fair, or Is It?

We all look for that angle, that piece of information, that extra effort that gives us a winning moment financially. But ethical issues arise in how we obtain that one piece of information and how we use it.

Reading 9.6
Adam Smith: An Excerpt from the Theory of Moral Sentiments

1.1.28

The man who, by some sudden revolution of fortune, is lifted up all at once into a condition of life, greatly above what he had formerly lived in, may be assured that the congratulations of his best friends are not all of them perfectly sincere. An upstart, though of the greatest merit, is generally disagreeable, and a sentiment of envy commonly prevents us from heartily sympathizing with his joy. If he has any judgement, he is sensible of this, and instead of appearing to be elated with his good fortune, he endeavours, as much as he can, to smother his joy, and keep down that elevation of mind with which his new circumstances naturally inspire him. He affects the same plainness of dress, and the same modesty of behaviour, which became him in his former station. He redoubles his attention to his old friends, and endeavours more than ever to be humble, assiduous, and complaisant. And this is the behaviour which in his situation we most approve of; because we expect, it seems, that he should have more sympathy with our envy and aversion to his happiness, than we have with his happiness. It is seldom that with all this he succeeds. We suspect the sincerity of his humility, and he grows weary of this constraint. In a little time, therefore, he generally leaves all his old friends behind him, some of the meanest of them excepted, who may, perhaps, condescend to become his dependents: nor does he always acquire any new ones; the pride of his new connections is as much affronted at finding him their equal, as that of his old ones had been by his becoming their superior: and it requires the most obstinate and persevering modesty to atone for this mortification to either. He generally grows weary too soon, and is provoked, by the sullen and suspicious pride of the one, and by the saucy contempt of the other, to treat the first with neglect, and the second with petulance, till at last he grows habitually insolent, and forfeits the esteem of all. If the chief part of human happiness arises from the consciousness of being beloved, as I believe it does, those sudden changes of fortune seldom contribute much to happiness. He is happiest who advances more gradually to greatness, whom the public destines to every step of his preferment long before he arrives at it, in whom, upon that account, when it comes, it can excite no extravagant joy, and with regard to whom it cannot reasonably create either any jealousy in those he overtakes, or any envy in those he leaves behind.

Discussion Questions

1. What happens to our relationships with those who enjoy success very quickly?

2. What are the ethical issues in resenting others' success and in turning against them?

3. Is Smith right, that a longer climb to success is better for the individual and his friends? Be sure to return to Units 4–8 to think through the stories of those who did enjoy sudden success and their fates.

Case 9.7

The Battle of the Guardrail Manufacturers

Trinity Industries is the manufacturer of a product you see every day—the guardrails in the middle of highways, freeways, tollways, and byways around the country. There is a back story of intrigue, whistleblowing, and a small competitor in those guardrails.

The Trinity Guardrail System

Early highway guardrail systems helped prevent drivers from running off the road. But there was still a risk with this protection. In a head-on collision with an automobile, the blunt ends of the guardrails could "spear" or penetrate vehicles' passenger compartments. Burying the end of the guardrail stopped the "spearing" but resulted in a different risk. The guardrails became a launch ramp that rolled out-of-control vehicles sometimes back into traffic. Engineers at the Texas A&M Transportation Institute ("TTI") developed a guardrail "end terminal" system known as the ET-2000, which became the ET-Plus.

Trinity was the manufacturer of the ET-Plus guardrail system, the preferred system used in road construction. In a head-on collision, the ET-Plus' head flattens to slide along the rail and push it out of the way of the vehicle. Simultaneously, this effect "gates" the vehicle with the sequential failures of the pre-drilled posts. The result is a slowing of vehicles to safer stops thus lessening the risk of the rail launches.

After successful TTI testing, the ET-Plus system was accepted by the Federal Highway Administration (FHWA) in 2000 for use on the National Highway System. At that time, the ET-Plus was designed for 27-and-3/4-inch-high guardrails. By 2005, the increase of vehicles with higher centers of gravity (SUVs) turned the research to taller guardrails. Trinity and TTI developed a modified ET-Plus system for use with 31-inch guardrails. Trinity had to change

the terminal head on the rails from 5 inches to 4 inches. The changes resulted in a $2 saving for every rail for Trinity.

TTI crash tested the new ET-Plus at the 31-inch height and prepared a report on the tests, which Trinity sent to FHWA. On September 2, 2005, FHWA approved the modified ET-Plus for the 31-inch guardrail height. Trinity did not include the drawing of the terminal head change in its crash-test report on the ET-Plus nor was there an explanation of 5-inch to 4-inch change.

Joshua Harman and SPIG and Selco: Head-to-Head Competition

Joshua Harman had been a customer of Trinity, purchasing their products and installing them in the eastern United States. Harman was also a one-time competitor of Trinity, manufacturing his own end terminal heads through SPIG and Selco, businesses he owned with his brother. SPIG and Selco failed. Harman still hoped to compete with Trinity in the future.

Harman set out on a cross-country trip looking for accidents that involved guardrails. He acquired six to eight terminal heads from the guardrails in the accidents and found the 5-inch to 4-inch change. He determined that the change was the cause of the accidents. Upon searching, he could not find FHWA records of approval for the changes. FHWA requires notification and approval of any design changes in materials, systems, and products used in highway construction.

Harman Seeks Help from the Federal Government

Harman presented the results of his investigation to FHWA in January 2012 using a PowerPoint presentation that included explanations of the 2005 changes and accident scene photographs.

FHWA then met with Trinity in February 2012 to discuss Harman's allegations. Trinity explained that while the change

(continued)

Case 9.7

(continued)

in the guide channel width was inadvertently omitted from the report sent to FHWA, the May 2005 crash tests were done with an ET-Plus system and the modified head. FHWA met twice more with Harman and his counsel. During this time, FHWA was responding to inquiries about the ET-Plus from various state departments of transportation as to whether the ET-Plus was eligible for reimbursement.

The federal government does not build the highways (state and local governments do), but these government agencies are not eligible for federal funds if they do not build roads in compliance with federal standards and requirements. Changes in designs and materials must be approved by the FHWA to receive funds. If a company receives federal funds or reimbursement and has not complied with standards or provided false information, it is liable to the federal government under the False Claims Act.

In March 2012, Harman filed a False Claims Act (FCA) suit in federal court.[10] The federal government is permitted to intervene in such cases but declined to do so. The FHWA released an official memorandum declaring that it had "validated" the ET-Plus and that use of the system was eligible for federal funds reimbursement. The Department of Justice sent an email to the court, with a copy of the FHWA memo, seeking to exclude all testimony from federal government employees related to the issues in the case:

> Please find attached a memorandum issued by FHWA today that addresses all of the issues raised by the parties in their respective requests for information. DOT believes that this should obviate the need for any sworn testimony from any government employees. If the parties disagree, please let me know at your earliest convenience.[11]

Running parallel to the FCA litigation was other litigation between Harman and Trinity. Trinity had sued Harman, once for patent infringement related to SPIG-manufactured heads in 2011 and twice for defamation related to his public statements about his findings on the guardrail heads.

The FCA Trial and Outcome

The case went to trial two times. In the first attempt, the court was forced to declare a mistrial with only two hours of testimony left. The federal district judge declared a mistrial because of "errors, gamesmanship, inappropriate conduct, and matters that should not be part of any trial where a fair and impartial verdict is expected."[12] The conduct the court cited in declaring the mistrial was that Trinity's president, Gregg Mitchell, went to the office of Dr. Dean Sicking, a professor at the University of Alabama who was slated to testify for Harman. Mr. Sicking said that Mr. Mitchell intimidated him by a threat that he would "smear anyone who testified against him." However, Trinity's lawyer, Ethan Shaw, told the judge in chambers that the trial should not go forward because he had been prevented from deposing Dr. Sicking.[13] The judge noted in granting a motion for a mistrial that, "Trinity's memory of this exchange seems to have failed."[14]

In the second trial, Harman presented evidence of five failed tests by TTI that involved the same guardrail heads that were not disclosed to FHWA. Dr. Roger Bligh, a Texas A & M professor and a research engineer at TTI, testified that he met with the FHWA's lead engineer on the ET-Plus investigation but did not disclose that the tests involving the same guardrail head had been done and had failed.[15] Dr. Bligh testified that the information about the change in the design of the guardrail heads was left out of its report to FHWA because "we made a mistake."[16] Dr. Bligh testified in a videotaped deposition, introduced into evidence during trial, that FHWA's representative Nicholas Artimovich, after learning of the 2005 changes, reviewed video footage

(continued)

---

[10]*Harman on behalf of the U.S. v. Trinity Industries Inc.*, 12-cv-00089, U.S. District Court, Eastern District of Texas (2014).

[11]For reasons not clear from the record, the district court excluded this statement from evidence, a ruling consistent with Harman's contention that the opinion of the government does not matter.

[12]"UPDATE: Judge Declares Mistrial in Trinity Guardrail Case," (undated), but date of declaration of mistrial was July 17, 2014, https://bergermontague.com/update-judge-furiously-declares -mistrial-trinity-guardrail-case/.

[13]*Id.*

[14]*United States ex rel. Harman v. Trinity Indus., Inc.* (E.D. Tex. 2014), https://casetext.com/case/united-states-ex-rel-harman-v -trinity-indus-1.

[15]Aaron M. Kessler and Danielle Ivory, "Guardrail Tests Went Unre-ported, Court Hears," *New York Times*, October 15, 2014, p. B3.

[16]*Id.*

Case 9.7

(continued)

from the 2005 testing and concluded that "the tests done in 2005 used a terminal head with [the narrower] feeder channel."[17]

The trial judge excluded from evidence that Harman ran into difficulties with the Commonwealth of Virginia because of issues with the guardrail heads he was installing due to the problems with the Trinity heads. Virginia's state materials engineer removed Selco, Harman's company, from the approved installers list. The judge held that such evidence was "improper" and was being used as "a backdoor way to attack [Harman's] character."[18]

What did come into evidence at the trial through Trinity's cross-examination was that Harman hoped to compete with Trinity and "with the entire industry" again in the future, admitting that he intended to use the proceeds from this litigation to recapitalize his business and begin manufacturing competing heads. Trinity also introduced into evidence a prospectus that an investment manager had prepared to pitch to potential SPIG investors. That prospectus stated that a "[r]ecall of Trinity's modified end terminals would mean removal and replacement of approximately one million units in the [United States], a one-billion-dollar revenue opportunity windfall for SPIG."[19] Also, the prospectus looked to the future with SPIG's "[p]lans to capture 20% of the U.S. end terminal market in 18 to 24 months, then continue rapid growth to take market share from an exposed Trinity."[20]

The jury found for Harman, and the trial court entered a judgment for Harman in July 2014 in the amount of $663,360,750 (the largest FCA damages in history)—consisting of $575,000,000 in trebled damages as allowed under the FCA, and $138,360,750 in civil penalties for 16,771 false claims—plus an additional $19,012,865 in attorney's fees and costs.[21]

Post-Trial Events

Following the trial, states began demanding the test results, and a University of Alabama study concluded that the ET-Plus was three times as likely to cause a fatality as the federally approved standard guardrail.[22] The state of Virginia demanded to see the safety tests. Within months of the public disclosure of the failure to disclose the tests, Virginia began removal of its 11,000 guardrails.[23] More than 30 states banned the ET-Plus guardrails from their roads and began the costly process of replacement, a cost that they intended to bill to Trinity.[24]

Because of the conflicting results and confusion, FHWA ordered independent testing of the guardrails, and Trinity suspended its sales of the ET-Plus units. FHWA announced the results of the independent testing in March 2015:

> A joint task force—consisting of state, federal, and foreign transportation experts—examined over one thousand existing ET-Plus installations across the country between November 2014 and January 2015 and concluded that: (1) "[t]here is no evidence to suggest that there are multiple versions [of the ET-Plus] on our nation's roadways" and (2) the units that were crash tested were "representative of the devices installed across the country."[25]

Following the results, Trinity moved for a judgment as a matter of law, which was denied. The case was appealed, and the Fifth Circuit reversed the case, as a matter of law, because FHWA knew of the omissions by Trinity but,

(continued)

[17]*U.S, ex rel. v. Harman*, 872 F.3d 645, 671 (5th Cir. 2019).

[18]*U.S, ex rel. v. Harman*, 872 F.3d 645, 671 (5th Cir. 2019).

[19]*U.S, ex rel. v. Harman*, 872 F.3d 645, 649 (5th Cir. 2019).

[20]*U.S, ex rel. v. Harman*, 872 F.3d 645, 649 (5th Cir. 2019).

[21]*U.S, ex rel. v. Harman*, 872 F.3d 645 (5th Cir. 2019).

[22]Aaron M. Kessler and Danielle Ivory, "Virginia Threatens to Remove Guardrails Unless Manufacturer Performs New Tests," *New York Times*, October 15, 2014, p. B3.

[23]Aaron M. Kessler and Danielle Ivory, "Virginia Threatens to Remove Guardrails Unless Manufacturer Performs New Tests," *New York Times*, October 15, 2014, p. B3; and Aaron M. Kessler and Danielle Ivory, "Virginia to Remove Suspect Guardrails," *New York Times*, October 28, 2014, p. B3.

[24]Aaron Kessler, "Critical Tests to Begin on Highway Guardrail Banned in Most States," *New York Times*, December 10, 2014, p. B5.

[25]*U.S, ex rel. v. Harman*, 872 F.3d 645, 651 (5th Cir. 2019).

Case 9.7

(continued)

feeling that they were immaterial, paid all the funds due and owing Trinity. The appellate court held that there can be no false claims action if the federal agency itself is not deceived.[26]

Harman appealed to the U.S. Supreme Court and the court did not grant *certiorari*.[27]

Other Legal Actions

There were other suits by the families of those who died claiming that the deaths were a result of the guardrail design. Most of the suits have been settled or were won by Trinity.[28] In August 2016, the U.S. attorney for Massachusetts closed its investigation into the company without filing criminal charges.

The Government Accountability Office issued a report on its investigation of federal oversight on guardrails and concluded that its oversight of the guardrail program needed to be "more robust."[29] Harman's lawyer said after the loss at the Fifth Circuit, "We are disappointed, but believe the true objective of the case has been achieved. Because of Joshua Harman's efforts, there is more federal and state scrutiny than ever before to ensure the safety of our nation's roads and highways."[30]

Discussion Questions

1. Explain the False Claims Act and who gets how much when a contractor makes false statements or fraudulent claims for federal monies.

2. List the ethical categories you see in the conduct of the parties in this case.

3. Describe how Harman and Trinity behaved as competitors and assign ethical categories to each of their actions, on both their products and during their litigation.

4. What lessons about competition and ethics can a business learn from this case?

5. What do you learn about ethics in the litigation process?

6. The judge in the appellate case closed his opinion with these eloquent thoughts:

It is charged that the accused product remains along nigh every highway in America, killing and maiming, but the government will not remove it. We can assume that this and contrary views are debatable, but we must accept that the choice among them lies beyond the reach of seven citizens of Marshall, Texas (the site of the trial), able though they may be. As revered as is the jury in its resolution of historical fact, its determination of materiality cannot defy the contrary decision of the government, here said to be the victim, absent some reason to doubt the government's decision as genuine. For the demands of materiality adjust tensions between singular private interests and those of government and cabin the greed that fuels it. As the interests of the government and relator diverge, this congressionally created enlistment of private enforcement is increasingly ill served. When the government, at appropriate levels, repeatedly concludes that it has not been defrauded, it is not forgiving a found fraud —rather it is concluding that there was no fraud at all.[31]

Is the judge issuing a type of apology for the decision? Why? Did the Government Accountability Office reach the same conclusion?

[26]*U.S,* ex rel. v. *Harman,* 872 F.3d 645 (5th Cir. 2019).

[27]139 S.Ct. 784 (2019).

[28]Mark Curriden, "Exclusive: Trinity Fights for Legal Principle, Dignity & Billions of Dollars," *The Texas Lawbook* (2016), https://texaslawbook.net/z-exclusive-trinity-fights-for-legal-principle-dignity-billions-of-dollars/.

[29]Government Accountability Office, "Highway Safety: More Robust Oversight of Guardrails and Other Roadside Hardware Could Further Enhance Safety," June 2016, GAO-16-575, http://www.gao.gov/assets/680/677735.pdf. Last visited November 8, 2016.

[30]Nate Raymond and Lawrence Hurley, "U.S. Top Court Declines to Take Up Trinity Industries Guardrail Case," *Reuters*, January 7, 2019, https://www.reuters.com/article/us-usa-court-trinity-inds/u-s-top-court-declines-to-take-up-trinity-industries-guardrail-case-idUSKCN1P11JB.

[31]*U.S,* ex rel. v. *Harman,* 872 F.3d 645, 669-670 (5th Cir. 2019).

Case 9.8

Bad-Mouthing the Competition: Where's the Line?

When the competition is stiff, the product, service, and price may not be the deciding factor. What the buyer believes about the competitor may be controlling. The following are statements made by contractors as they were in the process of trying to win a remodeling contract with a homeowner:

- "You could go with them—they do good work, but they use illegal immigrants on their jobs."

- "Be sure to get a time frame from them before you make a decision. Sometimes they can be slow."

- "You need to be careful with X Company because I have heard that they are close to bankruptcy."

- "Check the registrar of contractors at the state level—they have had all kinds of complaints filed against them."

- "The Better Business Bureau has not given them a very good rating."

- "I can give you a list of people they've done work for and I have had to go in and clean up the mess they have made."

- "You can go with low price, but you get what you pay for."

Discussion Questions

1. Evaluate each of the statements from an ethical perspective.

2. What risks do you see in competitors making each of the statements?

3. Which of the statements would you feel comfortable using?

Case 9.9

Online Pricing Differentials and Customer Questions

The *Wall Street Journal* investigated online pricing and discovered that your price may vary indeed.[32] Using your zip code, online retailers determine the price of your stapler, your saw, or even your language program, based on whether that retailer has competition in the area (whether there is a Staples and an OfficeMax near your home) as well as other factors such as the costs of rent, labor, and other economic factors in your area. According to the *Journal*, Staples, Rosetta Stone, and Home Depot consistently adjust prices on items based on information these companies obtain about you, the online buyer. Some of the online retailers even vary the types of items available to you online based on your zip code. The study found the strongest lower price correlation with the distance from where the buyer is to competitors. So, someone 10 miles away from you may pay more for a set of markers because the online seller assumes that it would not be worth the drive for that buyer to go to the competitor's retail store.

Technology allows online retailers to find your location, although you now have the option to click "do not allow."

However, there are some price differences that appear to be unrelated to geographic proximity to competitors but may truly be due to economic factors. For example, you are going to pay more for your office supplies if you order from your zip code in Manhattan or Staten Island and less if your zip code happens to be in Brooklyn or Queens.

The products are the same. For example, prices on a simple Swingline stapler varied by $1.50 in a 10-mile area, even though the staplers shipped to the geographically different customers are the same. Rosetta Stone customers buying multiple levels of language lessons from the United States receive a 20% discount, but buyers from the United Kingdom and Argentina never see the 20% special. Home Depot has six different prices for a 250-foot spool of wiring. And the wire is most expensive in New York and least expensive in Ashtabula, Ohio.

Even credit card offers vary by geographic location. Discover offers special credit card rates to consumers in Denver, Kansas City, and Dallas. But consumers in Scranton,

(continued)

---

[32]Jennifer Valentino-DeVries, Jeremy Singer-Vine, and Ashkan Soltani, "Online Retailers Vary Prices Based on a User's Location," *Wall Street Journal*, December 24, 2012, p. A1.

Case 9.9

(continued)

Pennsylvania and Los Angeles, California will not see those special credit card offers popping up on their screens. Known as part of credit card companies' acquisition strategies, the companies are mum on why they target certain areas and not others in soliciting new users.

There is no violation of the Robinson–Patman Act and its prohibitions on price discrimination if the retailers can show that they are pricing to meet the competition or according to differences in costs (such as labor and rent). The interesting question that the practice presents is that these are online prices so that the differences in cost may not actually exist. That is, the shipping may well be the same regardless of retail store costs in that area. However, the connection between the location of a competitor and the online price then falls into the protected area of price differentials to meet the competition.

Discussion Questions

1. Do pricing differentials help or hinder competition?

2. Should the online retailers disclose the pricing differentials? What ethical category is involved with the pricing differentials?

3. Some online retailers provide pricing information to help customers. For example, Stamps.com provides its customers with a choice between UPS and the post office (USPS). There is a pop-up that tells the customer which way of shipping would be cheaper. Could that be an effective competitive strategy?

Case 9.10

Brighton Collectibles: Terminating Distributors for Discounting Prices

Leegin Creative Leather Products, Inc. (Leegin), designs, manufactures, and distributes leather goods and accessories under the brand name Brighton. The Brighton brand has now expanded into a full line of women's fashion accessories and is sold across the United States in over 5,000 retail stores. PSKS, Inc. (PSKS) runs Kay's Kloset, a Brighton retailer in Lewisville, Texas, that carried about 75 different product lines but was known as the place to go for Brighton products. Kay's ran Brighton ads and had Brighton days in its store.

Leegin's president, Jerry Kohl, who also has an interest in about 70 stores that sell Brighton products, believes that small retailers treat customers better, provide customers with more services, and make their shopping experience more satisfactory than do larger, often impersonal retailers. In 1997, Mr. Kohl released a new strategic refocus for Brighton by explaining: "[W]e want the consumers to get a different experience than they get in Sam's Club or in Wal-Mart. And you can't get that kind of experience or support or customer service from a store like Wal-Mart." As a result, Leegin instituted the "Brighton Retail Pricing and Promotion Policy," which banished retailers that discounted Brighton goods below suggested prices. The policy had an exception for products not selling well that the retailer did not plan on reordering. The established prices gave its retailers sufficient margins to provide customers with the quality service central to Brighton's strategy.

In December 2002, Leegin discovered Kay's Kloset had been marking down Brighton's entire line by 20%. Kay's Kloset said it did so to compete with nearby retailers who also were undercutting Leegin's suggested prices. Leegin, nonetheless, requested that Kay's Kloset cease discounting. Its request refused, Leegin stopped selling to the store. The loss of the Brighton brand had a considerable negative impact on the store's revenue from sales (about 40% to 50% of its profits were from Brighton).

Discussion Questions

1. Is it fair for some stores to carry Brighton products at a discount but not provide the service and ambience that the company is seeking for its products? What is the ethical issue or category in this business strategy?

2. Do deep discounters benefit from the services and information provided at stores that do not do the deep discounting?

3. What is the role of the customer as stakeholder in your ethical analysis?

Source: *Leegin Creative Leather Products, Inc. v. PSKS, Inc.*, 551 U.S. 877 (2007).

Case 9.11

Park City Mountain: When a Competitor Forgets

Powdr Corporation runs Park City Mountain. It owns the parking lots, owns the land at the foot of the mountains, and benefits from the skiers and tourists who visit year-round. It employs 1,200 people and benefited in 2002 when the Winter Olympics were held there. However, there is one interesting aspect of its operations that is creating serious concerns about its survival. Powdr Corporation leases the actual ski slopes of Park City from Talisker Land Holdings. Powdr had a long-term lease at the rock bottom price of $155,000 per year. But through what a local paper has called "one of the most monumental blunders in Utah business history," Powdr forgot to renew its lease in 2011.[33] Powdr claims that it was simply a delay in giving formal notice and that Talisker was aware that there would be a renewal.

There were three years of litigation as a result, but a judge has ruled that the lease required formal written notice and Powdr did not give that notice. The judge concluded that when a lease ends, it ends. And Talisker had begun the process of eviction as it was leasing to a new tenant. That new tenant is Vail Resorts, a company that runs 10 ski resorts around the country.

While the legal battle has been depicted as the battle of small-town owners against a big corporation, Powdr actually has its own national structure, operating or owning ski resorts around the country, including in Vermont and Nevada. And Powdr has two advantages

in the dispute. It owns all the land up to the ski slopes. In other words, anyone who leases the slopes cannot get to those slopes without crossing Park City Mountain's property. In addition, Park City Mountain owns the water rights, something that is necessary for producing the extra snow necessary early in the ski season.

The law had its determination, but land ownership gets in the way of lease rights. In September 2014, Powdr Corporation sold its Park City resort to Vail Resorts for $182.5 million. Powdr's CEO said, "Selling was the last thing we wanted to do, and while we believe the law around this issue should be changed, a protracted legal battle is not in line with our core value to be good stewards of the resort communities in which we operate. A sale was the only way to provide long-term certainty for employees and the Park City community."[34]

Discussion Questions

1. If the judge had ruled in the case, why did the dispute continue?

2. What lessons can businesses learn from this experience?

3. Would you warn a tenant about a lease expiration if you thought you could benefit from it? What is the ethical category?

---

[33]Jack Healy, "Ski Town May Face Winter without Popular Path to Slopes," *New York Times*, August 20, 2014, p. A11.

[34]Jason Blevins, "Powdr Sells Park City Mountain Resort to Vail Resorts," *Denver Post*, September 11, 2014, http://www.denverpost.com/2014/09/11/powdr-sells-park-city-mountain-resort-to-vail-resorts/.

Case 9.12

Electronic Books and the Apple versus Amazon War

The U.S. Department of Justice (DOJ) filed an antitrust suit against Apple and five of the largest publishers in the United States (Simon & Schuster, HarperCollins, Hachette, Penguin, and Macmillan), alleging that Apple conspired with the five to battle Amazon, the market leader on e-book sales, by agreeing ahead of the release of the iPad tablet and iBook to raise prices for e-books. The move by the publishers was undertaken to force Amazon, if it wanted

the books in electronic form, to raise its prices. Amazon has traditionally charged $9.99 for its e-books, a price that other publishers could not compete with. (Simon & Schuster, HarperCollins, and Hachette settled the suit with the DOJ before the suit was even announced.)

The government antitrust case was based on its theory that the agreement caused e-book prices to climb to

(continued)

Case 9.12

(continued)

$2 to $3 per book in early 2010 when the iPad was released. The subsequent trial outlined the communication between and among the CEOs of Apple and the publishing houses. During December 2009 and January 2010, the publisher defendants' U.S. chief executives placed at least 56 phone calls to one another.

Apple went to trial, was found guilty of engaging in price-fixing (a violation of Section 1 of the Sherman Act) in relation to e-book prices. As part of the penalty phase of the case, the Justice Department asked for and the court ordered the presence of a monitor at the company to be sure that Apple did not engage in price-fixing again and that the company was putting the types of tools in place that would prevent price-fixing in the future.[35] Since the time of the appointment of Michael Bromwich as the monitor, there has been significant contention between him and company officials.

Apple took the monitor issue to court for a decision on three issues: (1) getting rid of the monitor until Apple exhausts its appeals on the guilty verdict; (2) limiting the work and access of the monitor because of his demands for interviews with board members as well as CEO Tim Cook and the rest of the executive team; and (3) curbing the billable hours and rate of Mr. Bromwich. Mr. Bromwich bills at a rate of $1,100 per hour and billed Apple $138,432.40 for his first two weeks of work as a monitor.[36] Apple and its monitor have been arguing and posturing since the final decision in the trial court case.

The federal district judge rejected all of Apple's requests. She reconfirmed the need for a monitor and noted that Apple's lawyers earn $1,800 per hour. Based on an affidavit from Mr. Bromwich that noted his access was less than it has been with other companies he monitors, the judge concluded that Apple needed to stop "stonewalling" and cooperate with the monitor. The judge also noted that Apple did not have much negotiating power on the issue of the monitor because of the guilty verdict.[37] Apple had not developed the training programs it was required to develop as part of the penalties in the

case and, in the judge's mind, made very little progress in demonstrating that it was changing its culture and behaviors with regard to antitrust issues.[38]

Amazon vs. the Authors vs. Publishers

However, as the cleanup on the e-book battle proceeded, Amazon had another pricing battle with publishers in the United States and Europe. The heart of the battle is between Amazon and Hachette, the parent company of Little Brown and publisher of authors such as Malcolm Gladwell. Hachette and Amazon are negotiating pricing, and the negotiations have gone so poorly that the private discussions have spilled over into the media. Hachette wants more money for its books, and Amazon wants to sell at lower prices. However, Amazon delayed shipments of Hachette books and raised book prices so that the sales of Hachette titles were affected. Amazon also recommended other books for customers in lieu of the Hachette books. The authors affected the most by the Amazon tactics are new authors who do not have a fan base. Those in the publishing world say that Amazon is controlling market entry in terms of new authors' works being able to compete with established authors.[39]

The interesting aspect of the situation is whether there can be antitrust implications in a situation in which the refusal to deal is the result of Amazon trying to get lower book prices for its customers. The Justice Department is not involved because it cannot see why a drive for lower prices is anticompetitive. However, antitrust experts point to the creation of a monopoly, and not for reasons based on skill, foresight, or industry (hard work). The risk of monopolization is the economic competition concern.

In addition, for Amazon, an evolving issue is whether customers will become irritated by not being able to buy certain books from their favorite "point, click, and buy" site.

A question to contemplate is whether the first publisher to reach a deal with Amazon will leave the other publishers behind and whether there is the risk of a one-publisher world. But an aspect of Amazon's business that prevents

(continued)

---

[35]*United States v. Apple Inc.*, 952 F. Supp. 2d 638 (S.D.N.Y. 2013).

[36]Christopher M. Matthews, "Judge Blasts Apple in E-Book Case," *Wall Street Journal*, January 14, 2014, p. B1.

[37]*U.S. v. Apple*, 992 F. Supp. 2d 263 (S.D.N.Y. 2014).

[38]Matthew Goldstein, "Secretive Apple Squirms in Gaze of U.S. Monitor," *New York Times*, January 14, 2014, p. A1.

[39]Jonathan Mahler, "Toe-to-Toe with a Giant," *New York Times*, June 2, 2014, p. B1.

Case 9.12

(continued)

monopolization there is that Amazon runs a highly successful self-publishing business for authors. Amazon is able to offer more types of books by a wider array of authors.

Jeff Bezos, the CEO of Amazon, purchased the *Washington Post*. The newspaper has covered the Hachette battle but has not been able to get a comment from its owner on his company's tactics. The *Post* stories on Amazon have disclosed who owns the paper—the guy at the center of the story.

Discussion Questions

1. What strikes you about the methods of competition in the publishing world? Any ethical issues and in what categories?

2. In its inception, as a bookseller, Amazon enabled publishers to break through the hold that bookstores had

on the success of their books. When readers could order books online from a store that just took and filled orders, the major bookstores lost control. Publishers were not stuck with book returns, a protection clause that bookstores demanded. Buyers and sellers were matched through one source without the traditional big orders for books that might or might not sell. Has Amazon flipped on competition with its new approach?

3. What are the implications when a company is found guilty of antitrust law violations? What types of penalties are imposed?

4. Is Amazon's failure to sell certain books as a means of controlling pricing ethical?

5. What conflict of interest exists when Mr. Bezos is the owner of a newspaper?

Case 9.13

Martha vs. Macy's and JCPenney

Macy's had what it believed to be an exclusive merchandising agreement with Martha Stewart, with Ms. Stewart agreeing to provide her name and endorsement to certain Macy's household products. Several years later, JCPenney entered into a similar merchandising agreement with Ms. Stewart for her to endorse several of its household products.

In 2013, Macy's filed suit against Penney's and Ms. Stewart alleging that Ms. Stewart had breached her contract of exclusivity with Macy's and that Penney's had interfered with its contractual relationship with Ms. Stewart. The case proceeded to trial, a trial that included Ms. Stewart as a witness. However, by the time the trial arrived, Ms. Stewart and Macy's had settled their portion of the suit, and the battle for tortious interference with contracts continued just between Penney's and Macy's.

The tort of contractual interference requires proof that a third party acted to intentionally cause a party to an existing contract to breach that contract or minimize its value. Penney's did so by soliciting Ms. Stewart. The

trial consisted of evidence that the product lines were different, and there were different products, but there were also several products endorsed by Ms. Stewart that were available at both stores.

A judge issued his ruling in the case, holding that Penney's had unlawfully interfered with Macy's contractual relationship with Ms. Stewart. The judge referred to Penney's conduct as "adolescent behavior in the worst form."[40]

The final phase of the case determined that Penney's was not required to pay punitive damages for its behavior but was liable for Macy's costs and other economic damage throughout the long and winding road to the verdict in the case.[41]

Ironically, the plan to bring on Ms. Stewart was part of a new strategy for Penney's of obtaining exclusive licensing

(continued)

---

[40]Hilary Stout, "Ruling Against Penney in Its Macy's Dispute," *New York Times*, June 17, 2014, p. B3.

[41]*Macy's v. Martha Stewart Living Omnimedia, Inc.*, 127 A.D. 3d 48 (Sup. Ct. 2015).

Case 9.13

(continued)

arrangements to attract shoppers. The plan failed terribly because what Penney's shoppers wanted was not exclusive licensing and products, but a bargain. Penney's returned to its bargain strategy and abandoned the licensing arrangements. However, the strategy proved ineffective– Penney's declared Chapter 11 bankruptcy in 2020. It emerged from Chapter 11 with new owners in 2021 and is now selling Forever 21 jeans but still continues to close more of its stores.

Discussion Questions

1. Why would the judge refer to Penney's behavior as adolescent? What about Ms. Stewart's behavior? What ethical categories would you assign to their actions?

2. Is there a line in competition between competing and self-destruction?

Case 9.14

Mattel and the Bratz Doll

Mattel, Inc., is the world's largest manufacturer and marketer of toys, dolls, games, and stuffed toys and animals. Mattel employed Carter Bryant as a product designer from September 1995 through April 1998 and from January 1999 through October 2000. Upon starting his second term of employment in 1999, Bryant signed an Employee Confidential Information and Inventions Agreement, in which he agreed not to "engage in any employment or business other than for [Mattel], or invest or assist (in any manner) any business competitive with the business or future business plans of [Mattel]." Also, Bryant assigned to Mattel all rights, title, and interest in the "inventions" he conceived of, or reduced to practice, during his employment.

Bryant also completed Mattel's Conflict of Interest Questionnaire and certified that he had not worked for any of Mattel's competitors in the prior 12 months and had not engaged in any business dealings creating a conflict of interest. Bryant agreed to notify Mattel of any future events raising a conflict of interest.[42]

A July 18, 2003, *Wall Street Journal* article suggested Bryant had copied a scrapped Mattel project, known as "Toon Teens," in creating the Bratz doll line. The article reported that MGA said that the Bratz line was designed by Carter Bryant, a former member of Mattel's Barbie team. Bryant hadn't worked on a similar line that

Mattel scrapped in 1998, but most Barbie designers had seen the prototypes. Although the Mattel doll line that was scrapped wasn't exactly like the Bratz, they were remarkably similar, with the Bratz's oversized heads, their pursed lips, cartoonish eyes, and big feet, to the dolls the Barbie team had created. Lily Martinez, a designer still then working at Mattel, came up with the idea for the big doll heads and posted her sketches on her cubicle where anyone could see them.[43]

By 2003, MGA's revenues were about $800 million, with 65% of that coming from the Bratz doll line.

After investigating the situation reported in the *Wall Street Journal*, Mattel discovered in November 2003 that Bryant had secretly entered into an agreement with MGA during the time that he was employed by Mattel, to receive royalties for "works for hire." In an agreement signed September 18, 2000, Bryant agreed to provide product design services for MGA's line of Bratz dolls in exchange for $5,500 per month for the first six months and $5,000 per month for the next three months, as well as a 3% royalty on the Bratz he worked on. Mattel filed its copyright registration for the Toon Teens drawings on November 28, 2003, four years after the drawings were created.

(continued)

---

[42]*Mattel, Inc. v. MGA Entertainment, Inc.*, 782 F. Supp. 2d 911 (C.D. Cal. 2011).

[43]Maureen Tkacik, "Dolled Up: To Lure Older Girls, Mattel Brings in Hip-Hop Crowd; It Sees Stalwart Barbie Lose Market Share, So 'Flavas' Will Take on the 'Bratz,'" *Wall Street Journal*, July 18, 2003, at p. A1.

Case 9.14

(continued)

Bryant's last day of employment at Mattel was October 20, 2000. Bryant went through the usual Mattel checkout. The checkout form used for Bryant misquoted Bryant's Inventions Agreement, which did not expressly assign to Mattel Bryant's interest in his ideas. This error may have resulted from the fact that prior versions of Mattel's Inventions Agreement expressly assigned the contracting employee's interest in his ideas. Bryant's agreement identifies "discoveries, improvements, processes, developments, designs, know-how, data computer programs and formulae, whether patentable or unpatentable," language did not include "ideas."

Mattel filed suit against Bryant for (1) breach of contract, (2) breach of fiduciary duty, (3) breach of duty of loyalty, (4) unjust enrichment, and (5) conversion.[44] MGA intervened in that case. Mattel settled with Bryant but amended its complaint against MGA alleging intentional interference with contract; aiding and abetting breach of fiduciary duty, aiding and abetting breach of duty of loyalty, conversion, unfair competition, and copyright infringement.[45]

However, MGA counterclaimed against Mattel for appropriation of trade secrets. MGA's counterclaim arose out of the activities of Mattel's Market Intelligence Group, a collection of employees dispatched to international toy fairs and directed to gather information from the private showrooms of Mattel's competitors through the use of false pretenses. Allegations in the counterclaim stated that the employees had made copies of identification credentials to gain access to the private showrooms, showrooms that were intended for buyers to be able to see what was available for purchase from MGA in the future.

A jury found for Mattel on all counts, concluding that Bryant conceived the idea for the name Bratz and created the concept drawings and sculpt for the Bratz dolls during his second term of employment with Mattel (January 4, 1999, to October 4, 2000). The federal district court placed the Bratz trademarks in a constructive trust and enjoined MGA from continuing to sell dolls. MGA appealed, and the case was remanded for a new trial. Upon remand, both companies moved for summary judgment on various issues. The court denied summary judgment on some issues but required a trial for others, including MGA's counterclaims on Mattel's market intelligence group.[46]

Following approximately two weeks of deliberations, the jury found that Mattel had misappropriated 26 trade secrets owned by MGA and awarded MGA $3.4 million in damages for each act of misappropriation, reaching a total award of $88.5 million. The jury also found that Mattel's misappropriation had been willful and malicious, thus entitling MGA to exemplary damages under Cal. Civ. Code § 3426.3, for a total verdict of $177.5 million, followed by an award by the court of $2.52 million in attorneys' fees and costs to MGA.[47] However, that decision, including the determination of attorney's fees, was reversed and went back to federal district court. However, the Ninth Circuit Court of Appeals seemed to have a sense of irony after a decade of litigation. The Ninth Circuit wiped out MGA Bratz's $177.5 million verdict but left intact the $137 million award of attorney's fees MGA had expended in defending the suit. So, if you can do the math carefully, nobody won anything through all the suits, trials, appeals, and retrials.[48]

Following the decision, the CEO of MGA vowed to retry the case. MGA filed suit against Mattel for trade secret appropriation in California state court. However, as Mattel pointed out, the statute of limitations on its trade secret claims had expired after three years, and the California court agreed.[49] All are punished.

(continued)

---

[44]The case has a fascinating history of procedural questions, including an issue of diversity of jurisdiction that resulted in an appellate decision. *Mattel, Inc. v. Brandt*, 446 F.3d 1011 (9th Cir. 2006).

[45]*Mattel, Inc. v. Bryant*, 441 F. Supp. 2d 1081 (C.D. Cal. 2005).

[46]*Mattel, Inc. v. MGA Entertainment, Inc.*, 2011 WL 3420571 (C.D. Cal.).

[47]*Mattel, Inc. v. MGA Entertainment, Inc.*, 801 F. Supp. 2d 950 (C.D. Cal. 2011).

[48]*Mattel, Inc. v. MGA Entertainment, Inc.*, 705 F.3d 1108 (9th Cir. 2013).

[49]*MGA Entertainment, Inc. v. Mattel, Inc.*, 41 Cal. App. 5th 554 (2019).

Case 9.14

(continued)

Discussion Questions

1. One expert commented that the litigation "killed" the Bratz line and nearly destroyed MGA as a competitor. Were the competitors killing each other?

2. List each of the ethical issues you see and classify them in categories.

3. Should Mattel have done more to protect its trade secrets? Is an agreement with an employer necessary to keep you from taking trade secrets to your next employer?

4. In law there is the doctrine of unclean hands, which means that you cannot collect for harm from another when you were imposing the same harm on the party against whom you make the claim. Is that what happened with Mattel and MGA? Into which ethical category would you place the doctrine of unclean hands?

Intellectual Property and Ethics

When does an idea belong to someone else? Laws on patents and copyrights afford protection in some cases, but other situations are too close to call—or are they?

Case 9.15

Louis Vuitton and *The Hangover*

As incongruous as it seems, *The Hangover* movie franchise is a hotbed of intellectual property issues. Warner Brothers settled a lawsuit brought by the tattoo artist who did Mike Tyson's facial tattoo that was then replicated on a character in the original *The Hangover*. Now, Louis Vuitton has filed suit in federal court for trademark infringement of its famous bags.

The ne'er-do-well character played by Zach Galifianakis has coined a pop-culture phrase by warning his fellow imbibers when they touch his Louis Vuitton bag, "Careful, that is a Louis Vuitton."

The lawsuit seeks to have the trademark bag excised from the film as well as a share of the movie's profits. The company seems most irritated because it alleges that the bag used in the movie is a knock-off.

Louis Vuitton is very aggressive in enforcing its trademark rights and has sued artists who have used the signature handbags and luggage in their paintings. In one such case, the company did not fare well against the artist because the court held that such use in a work of art was not infringement. The company not only lost the suit against the artist but was required to pay the court costs in the case.

The underlying question is one of artistic license and the use of trademarks in commercial works that constitute art. Stopping trademark usage in films has proven difficult. Wham-O, the makers of Slip 'N Slide, filed suit against Paramount Pictures for its use of the product in *Dickie Roberts: Child Star*. The use depicted in the film did not follow the product's instructions and warnings, so the company was concerned about the possible impact of the film on consumer use of the product. Still, the court refused to have the scene excised and went with the protection of the artistic work and commentary.

A *Wall Street Journal* writer has suggested that Louis Vuitton capitalize on the movie's use of the product by trademarking the phrase "Careful, that's a Louis Vuitton" and use it in its marketing. Then the worry would be whether Warner Brothers would have an action against Louis Vuitton for using a line from its movie.

Discussion Questions

1. How would you react to your product being lionized in a silly film? Is there marketing potential?

2. Why is Louis Vuitton so concerned about the use of its products in a film such as *The Hangover Part II*?

Case 9.16	

Forcing Farmers to the Dealerships: That Right to Repair Goes Public

Farmers are by nature, geography, and seasons, tinkerers. That is, they repair, make do, use baling wire, or do whatever is necessary to keep trucks, tractors, and all their farm equipment running. Today's new farm equipment, however, is loaded with technology and features. Tractors have the software and screens to program planting, tune-ups, and scheduling.

However, when something goes wrong with these highfalutin', high-functioning machines, it's all in the software. Companies that manufacture tractors and other farm equipment will not sell their proprietary software to independent dealers or farmers. The local repair shop cannot fix the farm equipment and farmers cannot even get the necessary software online. Farmers must turn to the dealerships for repairs and that generally translates to monopoly pricing.

During planting and harvest seasons, all farmers are using their equipment. During these heavy-use periods breakdowns are most likely happen. A single dealership in a rural area gets backed up quickly on repairs, and farmers cannot afford to wait because their crops cannot wait when it comes to planting and harvesting. Nature can be brutal when there are delays.[50]

There have been two effects from the proprietary software movement by farm equipment manufacturers. The first is that farmers are holding on to their old equipment because they can fix it. The second effect is legislation, with farmers proposing bills called "right-to-repair" acts. There are auto right-to-repair acts proposed in the U.S. Congress as well as in state legislatures. In 2013, Massachusetts passed the first state statute requiring auto makers to supply documents and information to repair shops and consumers. Farmers are proposing more-specific bills that target manufacturers of farm equipment.

It's Not Just for Farmers

The issue of dealership-only repairs is now in the activism stage of the regulatory cycle (see Reading 3.2). The Federal Trade Commission submitted its study on the effects of requiring dealership-only repairs on consumer goods to Congress in May 2021.[51]

Leading the way on "only we can do repairs" in farming is John Deere; in consumer goods, it is Apple. Apple has reserved the right to not sell parts and tools to anyone who does not work at an Apple store, and having your Apple products repaired at a non-Apple business voids your warranty.

A consumer advocacy group known as The Repair Association is working to obtain a national law along with any progress that can be made in passing state laws.[52] The group raises an interesting legal question: What am I buying when I buy an iPhone? And for farmers: What am I buying when I buy a combine? Is it the good itself and all the rights to tinker, repair, alter, modify, or is it the right to use it with support only from the manufacturer? Is it a purchase or is it a subscription?

Manufacturers enjoy the dealership only position by, as one analyst noted, "doing nothing."[53] By not sending out information or selling parts, the manufacturer creates a monopoly: either repair with them or buy new.

Existing Laws

The Protections of Section 102(c) of the Magnuson–Moss Warranty Act (MMWA)

The anti-tying provision, Section 102(c) of the MMWA, prohibits a manufacturer of a consumer product from conditioning its warranty on the consumer's using any service that is identified by brand name unless the article or service is provided without cost. This provision bars automobile manufacturers from voiding a warranty if a consumer has scheduled maintenance performed by someone other than the dealer, prohibits a printer manufacturer from conditioning its warranty

(continued)

[50]Kevin O'Reilly, "It Shouldn't Cost the Farm to Fix the Tractor," *Wall Street Journal*, March 24, 2021, p. A15.

[51]"Nixing the Fix: An FTC Report to Congress on Repair Restrictions," May 2021, https://www.ftc.gov/system/files/documents /reports/nixing-fix-ftc-report-congress-repair-restrictions/nixing _the_fix_report_final_5521_630pm-508_002.pdf.

[52]Wallace Witkowski, "'Right to Repair' Law May Run into the Changing Definition of Ownership," *Market Watch*, October 2, 2021, https://www.marketwatch.com/story/right-to-repair-law -may-run-into-the-changing-definition-of-ownership-11633108731.

[53]*Id.*

Case 9.16

(continued)

on the purchaser's use of only the manufacturer's ink, and forbids a smartphone manufacturer from voiding a warranty when a consumer has a new battery installed at a kiosk at the mall or any repair shop. Manufacturers cannot tie warranty coverage for waivers to use of repair shops or replacement parts manufactured by third parties.[54] However, farmers are not covered due to their commercial status. The FTC concluded that manufacturers are ignoring Section 102(c).

Antitrust Issues

The antitrust issue is tying. Tying occurs when a seller who has market power requires a buyer to purchase a product or service that the buyer does not want or can find for a better price with a third party. Manufacturers exercise their market power by making parts and diagnostic tools unavailable (manuals and software), claiming patent protection, using designs that make third-party repairs unsafe, disparaging the quality of third-party

repairs, or making it difficult to open up the equipment to do repairs.

Manufacturers cited their reasons for repair restrictions: safety, liability and reputational harm, cybersecurity, and the protection of intellectual property. The Repair Association cited timing, cost, and harm to small businesses.

Recommendations from the FTC Study

The report concludes that self-regulation is not possible because of the diversity of products and industries but that it would be worth the effort and time for the FTC to pursue some form of regulation.

Discussion Questions

1. What ethical categories would you assign to the way manufacturers are handling their customer repairs?

2. As you balance the arguments each side makes, where is the greater protection for those buying the goods?

3. Would advance disclosure be an important part of regulation?

4. With the issue in activism, what disadvantages do the manufacturers now face?

---

[54]"Nixing the Fix: An FTC Report to Congress on Repair Restrictions," May 202, at p. 5, https://www.ftc.gov/system/files/documents/reports/nixing-fix-ftc-report-congress-repair-restrictions/nixing_the_fix_report_final_5521_630pm-508_002.pdf.

Case 9.17

Tiffany vs. Costco

It all began in 2012, when a Tiffany's customer wrote to Tiffany's to complain that the high-end retailer was selling its engagement rings at Costco. That was news to Tiffany's: the company was not aware of the sales and had not authorized them. An investigator went to the Huntington Beach Costco and saw the rings, complete with the Tiffany brand and referred to by the Costco sales personnel as "Tiffany rings." Interestingly, Costco did not offer the rings online, something that Tiffany alleged was done to avoid detection of the infringement.

Tiffany filed suit in 2013.[55] In 2014, the case survived a Costco motion for summary judgment. Costco had argued

that "Tiffany" was a generic term used to describe a certain type of engagement ring setting, that is, a "Tiffany setting." The court held that there was a genuine issue of fact on the question of the generic meaning and/or infringement.[56] In September 2015, a federal judge held that Costco did indeed infringe the Tiffany trademark.[57] The court found that "Tiffany setting" was not a generic term. The damage portion of the trial included evidence that Costco had sold 2,500 "Tiffany" rings, for a total of about $10 million. However, the sale of the Tiffany engagement ring is 30% of Tiffany's total sales each

(continued)

---

[55]*Tiffany & Company and Tiffany (NJ) LLC v. Costco Wholesale Corp, U.S. District Court*, Southern District of New York, 13-1041.

[56]*Tiffany and Company v. Costco Wholesale Corporation*, 994 F. Supp. 2d 474 (S.D.N.Y. 2014).

[57]*Tiffany and Company v. Costco Wholesale Corporation*, 127 F. Supp. 3d 241 (S.D.N.Y. 2015).

Case 9.17

(continued)

year. Tiffany had asked for $2 million in damages, but a federal jury awarded Tiffany $5.5 million in compensatory damages and $8.25 million in punitive damages, along with other damages that totaled $21,010,438.35.[58] Costco appealed the decision.

In 2020, the case was remanded for a new trial because there were factual issues that had not been addressed, such as whether consumers were actually confused and thought that they were buying a real Tiffany ring, whether Costco had acted in bad faith, whether Costco had used "Tiffany" as a mark or a descriptor, and whether using a descriptor was protected by the fair use exception for copyrights and trademarks. [59]

Discussion Questions

1. Explain, apart from the legal issues, what the ethical issue and category is in the case.

2. Is "Tiffany ring setting" a generic term? Why is that issue important?

3. What questions or tests could you apply to reach a conclusion about the ethics of Costco's marketing of the rings?

---

[58] "Costco Now Has to Pay $8.25 Million in Punitive Damages for Selling Fake Tiffany Rings," *Fortune*, October 5, 2016, http://fortune.com/2016/10/05/costco-tiffany-jewelry/. Last visited November 8, 2016.

[59] *Tiffany and Company, LLC v. Costco Wholesale Corporation*, 971 F.3d 74 (2nd Cir. 2020).

Unit 9 Key Terms

Covenant not to compete   p. 581

Confidentiality or nondisclosure agreements   p. 583

Doctrine of inevitable disclosure   p. 583

Tortious interference   p. 582

The Ethical Common Denominator (ECD) Index

The Common Threads of Business Ethics

Overall Theme Areas	Description	Subcategories	Cases	Readings
Philosophical Foundations	Case/reading affords opportunity for exploring ethical theories	Utilitarianism, moral relativism, egoism, divine command, rights, justice, virtue ethics	Case 1.6 Case 3.12 Case 3.13 Case 3.14 Case 3.15 Case 3.20 Case 5.2 Case 5.7 Case 5.10 Case 6.8 Case 8.15	Reading 1.3 Reading 1.7 Reading 2.1 Reading 2.2 Reading 2.3 Reading 3.1 Reading 3.4 Reading 3.5 Reading 3.6 Reading 3.7 Reading 3.8 Reading 3.9 Reading 3.10 Reading 4.22
Ethical analysis	Case/reading provides opportunity for logical walk-through of ethical dilemmas and their resolution	Either/or conundrum; models for decision-making	Case 1.6 Case 1.11 Case 1.13 Case 1.14 Case 1.17 Case 1.18 Case 1.19 Case 1.20 Case 1.21 Case 2.8 Case 2.10 Case 2.12 Case 3.15 Case 4.3 Case 5.2 Case 5.12 Case 6.2 Case 7.11 Case 7.14 Case 9.4 Case 9.7 Case 9.16	Reading 1.4 Reading 1.5 Reading 1.6 Reading 1.7 Reading 1.8 Reading 1.9 Reading 1.10 Reading 2.1 Reading 2.2 Reading 2.3 Reading 2.4

(continued)

Overall Theme Areas	Description	Subcategories	Cases	Readings
Psychology of decision-making	Case/reading provides insight into psychological factors that overpower ethical reasoning	Pressure; financial constraints; hubris; rationalizations; drivers; enablers	Case 1.6 Case 2.8 Case 2.11 Case 3.20 Case 4.9 Case 4.10 Case 4.25 Case 4.29 Case 5.11 Case 6.8 Case 7.2 Case 8.6 Case 8.13 Case 9.4 Case 9.7	Reading 1.5 Reading 2.1 Reading 2.5 Reading 2.7 Reading 4.2 Reading 4.6 Reading 4.7 Reading 4.11
Culture/organizational behavior	Case/reading provides insight into how the organization and culture overpower ethical reasoning; the bad apple vs. bad barrel syndrome	Compensation systems; enforcement; confrontation; raising ethical issues; fear and silence in organizations	Case 1.6 Case 1.20 Case 1.21 Case 2.7 Case 3.15 Case 3.17 Case 3.19 Case 3.21 Case 4.8 Case 4.9 Case 4.10 Case 4.14 Case 4.15 Case 4.16 Case 4.19 Case 4.20 Case 4.23 Case 4.24 Case 4.25 Case 4.26 Case 4.29 Case 5.4 Case 5.11 Case 6.3 Case 6.12 Case 7.8 Case 7.12 Case 8.5 Case 8.13 Case 8.14 Case 8.16 Case 9.2 Case 9.12 Case 9.14	Reading 2.5 Reading 4.2 Reading 4.7 Reading 4.11 Reading 4.13 Reading 4.17 Reading 7.16 Reading 7.20

(continued)

Overall Theme Areas	Description	Subcategories	Cases	Readings
Economic theory	Case/reading provides backdrop for discussion of relationship between ethics and economics	Minimum wage; downsizing; property rights; laissez-faire; moral hazard; nature of markets; effects of demand and supply	Case 1.18 Case 2.10 Case 3.13 Case 3.17 Case 5.7 Case 5.8 Case 5.10 Case 6.5 Case 7.4 Case 9.5 Case 9.9 Case 9.12 Case 9.16	Reading 1.4 Reading 3.1 Reading 3.4 Reading 3.7 Reading 3.9 Reading 3.10 Reading 9.1
Personal introspection; credo	Case/reading provides an opportunity for students to put themselves in the position of those facing the dilemmas; developing tools for resisting pressure	Personal ethics vs. business ethics; the lines you would never cross to get a job, to keep a job, to earn a bonus, to meet goals	Case 1.6 Case 1.17 Case 1.18 Case 1.20 Case 3.12 Case 4.9 Case 4.10 Case 4.21 Case 5.7 Case 6.6 Case 7.7 Case 7.12 Case 8.5 Case 8.7 Case 8.11 Case 9.2	Reading 1.1 Reading 1.2 Reading 1.15 Reading 1.16 Reading 2.4 Reading 2.5 Reading 2.6 Reading 2.9 Reading 3.7 Reading 4.1 Reading 4.4 Reading 4.27
Social responsibility	Case/reading provides opportunity for discussion of the role of business in society	Tension between profits and impact on society; the role of philanthropy by business; tension between short-term gains and long-term impacts; balancing social and public policy issues with business activities	Case 3.2 Case 3.3 Case 3.11 Case 3.12 Case 3.14 Case 3.15 Case 3.17 Case 3.18 Case 3.19 Case 3.20 Case 4.19 Case 4.21 Case 4.31 Case 5.10 Case 6.2 Case 6.3 Case 6.5 Case 6.6 Case 6.7 Case 6.8 Case 7.3 Case 8.10 Case 9.11	Reading 3.1 Reading 3.4 Reading 3.5 Reading 3.6 Reading 3.7 Reading 3.8 Reading 3.9

(continued)

Overall Theme Areas	Description	Subcategories	Cases	Readings
Stakeholder theory	Case/reading provides opportunity for learning how to list stakeholders and examine their perspective on an ethical dilemma	Systemic effects; who is affected by decision and/or action; implications if everyone chose your course of behavior	Case 1.18 Case 2.8 Case 3.11 Case 3.12 Case 3.13 Case 3.14 Case 3.15 Case 3.16 Case 3.17 Case 3.18 Case 4.29 Case 5.7 Case 6.13 Case 7.4 Case 7.11 Case 7.14 Case 8.15	Reading 3.4 Reading 3.8
Leadership	Case/reading provides an opportunity for understanding the role of managers in company culture and decisions	Tone-at-the-top; example; conduct of managers and supervisors; manager's responses to employee concerns	Case 1.21 Case 2.12 Case 3.2 Case 3.3 Case 3.21 Case 4.9 Case 4.14 Case 4.24 Case 4.28 Case 5.4 Case 6.8 Case 7.6 Case 9.5 Case 9.14	Reading 1.2 Reading 2.5 Reading 3.1 Reading 4.6 Reading 4.17 Reading 7.19
Corporate governance	Case/reading provides an opportunity for examining the role of the board and corporate processes in culture and ethical analysis and decision-making	Compensation systems; compliance; internal controls	Case 2.10 Case 2.12 Case 4.14 Case 4.20 Case 4.23 Case 4.25 Case 4.26 Case 5.4 Case 5.13 Case 6.13 Case 7.3 Case 7.8 Case 8.14	Reading 4.13 Reading 4.18 Reading 4.27

(continued)

Overall Theme Areas	Description	Subcategories	Cases	Readings
Whistle-blowing	Case/reading examines individual actions in dealing with ethical issues	Speaking up; approaches to raising issues	Case 1.6 Case 1.11 Case 2.10 Case 3.11 Case 4.10 Case 4.20 Case 4.25 Case 4.28 Case 4.29 Case 6.8 Case 7.12 Case 7.17 Case 9.2	Reading 4.2 Reading 4.13 Reading 4.17 Reading 4.18 Reading 4.27
The Gray Area and Gaming	Case/reading focuses on Law vs. ethics – can vs. should? The loophole; gaming the system	Regulatory cycle; industry behaviors; slippery slope; gray area	Case 1.19 Case 1.20 Case 2.10 Case 3.2 Case 3.12 Case 4.8 Case 4.26 Case 5.9 Case 6.2 Case 7.5 Case 8.6 Case 9.14	Reading 1.5 Reading 1.8 Reading 3.1 Reading 3.6 Reading 4.1 Reading 4.2
Categories of ethical dilemmas	Case/reading helps to illustrate where ethical dilemmas exist	Honesty; false impression; balancing ethical issues; conflicts of interest; taking adv.	Case 1.14 Case 1.18 Case 2.12 Case 3.11 Case 3.12 Case 4.19 Case 4.21 Case 5.5 Case 5.10 Case 5.13 Case 6.7 Case 6.10 Case 7.3 Case 7.9 Case 7.15 Case 8.7 Case 9.4 Case 9.10 Case 9.17	Reading 1.4 Reading 1.9 Reading 1.10

The Business Topic Areas	Description	Subcategories	Cases	Readings
Financial reporting/accounting	Case/reading involves FASB, GAAP issues and interpretation of rules	Red flags; materiality; EBITDA; loading dock behaviors; cookie-jar reserves; spring-loading	Case 4.14 Case 4.20 Case 4.25 Case 4.26 Case 4.29 Case 4.30 Case 4.31 Case 6.13 Case 7.7	Reading 4.12 Reading 4.18 Reading 4.22
Product liability	Case/reading involves decision on product quality/safety	Design defects; recalls; product dumping; risk tolerance; low probability events	Case 2.12 Case 3.14 Case 4.28 Case 5.4 Case 5.5 Case 6.6 Case 6.7 Case 8.5 Case 8.6 Case 8.7 Case 8.8 Case 8.9 Case 8.10 Case 8.11	Reading 8.4
Technology	Case/reading involves ethical dilemmas that arise due to new technologies	Privacy of individuals; privacy of employees; social networking; theft; screening; testing	Case 3.16 Case 5.3 Case 5.11 Case 7.15 Case 9.2 Case 9.9 Case 9.12	Reading 1.16
Supply chain	Case/reading involves issues in contracts, relationships with vendors, purchasing managers	Conflicts of interest; commercial bribery; contracts	Case 3.17 Case 3.20 Case 6.6 Case 6.8 Case 6.5 Case 6.10 Case 6.11 Case 6.12 Case 6.13	Reading 6.4 Reading 6.9

(continued)

The Business Topic Areas	Description	Subcategories	Cases	Readings
Marketing and sales	Case/reading involves ethical issues in advertising, pricing, product distribution	Antitrust issues; PR; framing issues; psychological tools of marketing; services marketing;	Case 1.21 Case 3.14 Case 3.21 Case 5.1 Case 5.3 Case 5.4 Case 5.6 Case 5.10 Case 6.6 Case 6.7 Case 6.8 Case 7.3 Case 8.1 Case 8.2 Case 8.3 Case 8.6 Case 8.7 Case 8.11 Case 8.12 Case 8.13 Case 8.14 Case 8.15 Case 8.16 Case 9.2 Case 9.7 Case 9.8 Case 9.9 Case 9.11 Case 9.12	Reading 1.15 Reading 3.8 Reading 8.4 Reading 9.1
Government activities	Case/reading involves business relationships with and within government	Bribery, conflicts of interest, public issues and debate; PACs; government contracting	Case 2.11 Case 3.14 Case 3.20 Case 3.21 Case 4.8 Case 4.9 Case 4.19 Case 4.28 Case 5.2 Case 5.8 Case 6.10 Case 6.13 Case 7.11	Reading 3.1 Reading 4.12 Reading 6.9

(continued)

The Business Topic Areas	Description	Subcategories	Cases	Readings
Sustainability	Case/reading involves business relationship with environment	Climate issues; pollution; carbon footprints;	Case 1.13 Case 2.8 Case 3.17 Case 3.19 Case 6.5	Reading 3.1 Reading 3.6
Discrimination	Case/reading deals with issues in equal opportunity	Affirmative action; sexual harassment; diversity in the workforce; HR policies	Case 7.10 Case 7.11 Case 7.12 Case 7.13 Case 7.14 Case 7.15 Case 7.17 Case 7.18 Case 7.21 Case 7.22	Reading 7.16 Reading 7.20
Intellectual property	Case/reading deals with ownership of property and competitors' access	Copyrights; trademarks; reverse engineering; anti-compete clauses; downloading; software copies	Case 9.2 Case 9.4 Case 9.5 Case 9.15 Case 9.16 Case 9.17	Reading 9.1
International business	Case/reading covers ethical issues in operating multi-nationally	FCPA; bribery; product dumping, living wage, factory conditions, geopolitical issues; fair trade; human rights violations; mercenary issues	Case 3.20 Case 6.2 Case 6.3 Case 6.5 Case 6.6 Case 6.7 Case 6.8 Case 6.10 Case 6.11 Case 6.12 Case 6.13	Reading 6.1 Reading 6.4 Reading 6.9
Financial markets	Case /reading focuses on issues in the capital markets	Insider trading, short sales, risk; disclosure; hedge funds	Case 3.11 Case 4.14 Case 4.20 Case 5.8 Case 7.7 Case 8.1	Reading 4.12 Reading 4.18 Reading 4.22

(continued)

The Business Topic Areas	Description	Subcategories	Cases	Readings
Employee rights and responsibilities	Case/reading focuses on employee work and employer supervision	Employee privacy; employee productivity; personal activity employer monitoring; employer use of social networks	Case 4.5 Case 5.8 Case 6.3 Case 7.2 Case 7.4 Case 7.6 Case 7.17 Case 7.18 Case 7.21 Case 7.22	Reading 4.6 Reading 4.17 Reading 4.27 Reading 7.1 Reading 7.19 Reading 7.20
Operations	Case/reading focuses on production	Safety; reg compliance; training; work conditions	Case 3.21 Case 4.8 Case 4.21 Case 5.5 Case 6.8 Case 7.2 Case 8.16	Reading 3.1 Reading 4.2 Reading 7.1
Contract obligations and performance	Case/reading focuses on legal and ethical obligations under contracts	Performance; damages; breach; interpretation	Case 1.17 Case 3.15 Case 5.1 Case 5.3 Case 5.10 Case 5.11 Case 5.13 Case 8.3 Case 8.16 Case 9.4 Case 9.5	Reading 1.3
Nonprofit organizations	Unique character of nonprofits	Good intentions vs. good actions	Case 2.10 Case 3.12 Case 4.29 Case 4.30 Case 4.31 Case 5.12	Reading 3.1 Reading 3.5

Alphabetical Index

Business Discipline Index

Compliance Programs

Conflicts of Interest

Corporate Governance

Cyberlaw

Economics

Finance

Government

Health Care

International Operations

Purchasing

Quality Management

Social Responsibility

Strategy

Supply Chain Management

Sustainability

Whistle-Blowing

Product/Company/ Individuals Index

WorldCom

World Health Organization (WHO)

Yates, Buford

Yukos

Zuckerberg, Mark

Topic Index

Conflicts of Interest

Contracts

Contributions

Cookie Jar Reserves

Corporate Governance

Copyright Infringement

Deontology

Discrimination

Downsizing

EBITDA

Egoism

Environment

Equity

Executive Compensation

Finance

Foreign Countries–Differing Business Practices

Government Contracts

Government Employees